Contemporary Literary Criticism

Guide to Gale Literary Criticism Series

When you need to review criticism of literary works, these are the Gale series to use:

If the author's death date is:	You should turn to:
After Dec. 31, 1959 (or author is still living)	***CONTEMPORARY LITERARY CRITICISM*** for example: Jorge Luis Borges, Anthony Burgess, William Faulkner, Mary Gordon, Ernest Hemingway, Iris Murdoch
1900 through 1959	***TWENTIETH-CENTURY LITERARY CRITICISM*** for example: Willa Cather, F. Scott Fitzgerald Henry James, Mark Twain, Virginia Woolf
1800 through 1899	***NINETEENTH-CENTURY LITERATURE CRITICISM*** for example: Fedor Dostoevski, George Sand, Gerard Manley Hopkins, Emily Dickinson
1400 through 1799	***LITERATURE CRITICISM FROM 1400 TO 1800 (excluding Shakespeare)*** for example: Anne Bradstreet, Pierre Corneille, Daniel Defoe, Alexander Pope, Jonathan Swift, Phillis Wheatley
	SHAKESPEAREAN CRITICISM Shakespeare plays and poetry

Gale also publishes related criticism series:

CONTEMPORARY ISSUES CRITICISM

Presents criticism on contemporary authors writing on current issues. Topics covered include the social sciences, philosophy, economics, natural science, law, and related areas.

CHILDREN'S LITERATURE REVIEW

Covers authors of all eras. Presents criticism on authors and author/illustrators who write for the preschool to junior-high audience.

Volume 27

Contemporary Literary Criticism

Excerpts from Criticism of
the Works of Today's Novelists,
Poets, Playwrights, Short Story
Writers, Scriptwriters,
and Other Creative Writers

Jean C. Stine
Editor

Bridget Broderick
Daniel G. Marowski
Associate Editors

Gale Research Company
Book Tower
Detroit, Michigan 48226

STAFF

Jean C. Stine, *Editor*

Bridget Broderick, Daniel G. Marowski, *Associate Editors*

Robyn V. Young, *Senior Assistant Editor*

Lee Ferency, Jeanne A. Gough, Roger Matuz, Jane E. Neidhardt, James E. Person, Jr.,
Lisa Rost, Jane C. Thacker, Marjorie Wachtel, Debra A. Wells, *Assistant Editors*

Emily Wade Barrett, Sharon R. Gunton, Thomas Ligotti,
Phyllis Carmel Mendelson, *Contributing Editors*

Robert J. Elster, Jr., *Production Supervisor*
Lizbeth A. Purdy, *Production Coordinator*
Denise Michlewicz, *Assistant Production Coordinator*
Eric F. Berger, Paula J. DiSante, Maureen Duffy,
Amy T. Marcaccio, Yvonne Robinson, *Editorial Assistants*

Linda M. Pugliese, *Manuscript Coordinator*
Donna Craft, *Assistant Manuscript Coordinator*
Rosetta Irene Simms Carr, Colleen M. Crane, Maureen A. Puhl, *Manuscript Assistants*

Karen Rae Forsyth, *Research Coordinator*
Jeannine Schiffman Davidson, *Assistant Research Coordinator*
Victoria Cariappa, Robert J. Hill, Harry Kronick, James A. MacEachern,
Kyle Schell, Valerie Webster, *Research Assistants*

L. Elizabeth Hardin, *Permissions Supervisor*
Filomena Sgambati, *Permissions Coordinator*
Janice M. Mach, *Assistant Permissions Coordinator*
Patricia A. Seefelt, *Assistant Permissions Coordinator, Illustrations*
Susan D. Nobles, *Senior Permissions Assistant*
Margaret A. Chamberlain, Mary M. Matuz, Joan B. Weber, *Permissions Assistants*
Sandra C. Davis, Dorothy J. Fowler, Virgie T. Leavens, *Permissions Clerks*

Copyright © 1984 by Gale Research Company

Library of Congress Catalog Card Number 76-38938
ISBN 0-8103-4401-7
ISSN 0091-3421

Contents

Preface

Literary criticism is, by definition, "the art of evaluating or analyzing with knowledge and propriety works of literature." The complexity and variety of the themes and forms of contemporary literature make the function of the critic especially important to today's reader. It is the critic who assists the reader in identifying significant new writers, recognizing trends in critical methods, mastering new terminology, and monitoring scholarly and popular sources of critical opinion.

Until the publication of the first volume of *Contemporary Literary Criticism* in 1973, there existed no on-going digest of current literary opinion. *CLC,* therefore, has fulfilled an essential need.

Scope of the Work

CLC presents significant passages from published criticism of work by today's creative writers. Each volume of *CLC* includes excerpted criticism on about 65 authors who are now living or who died after December 31, 1959. Since the series began publication, more than 1,600 authors have been covered. The majority of authors covered by *CLC* are living writers who continue to publish; therefore, an author is frequently covered in more than one volume. There is, of course, no duplication of reprinted criticism.

Authors are selected for inclusion for a variety of reasons, among them: the publication of a critically acclaimed new work, the reception of a major literary award, or the dramatization of a literary work as a movie or television screenplay. For example, the present volume includes Gabriel Garciá Márquez and William Golding, who each won a recent Nobel Prize in literature; Douglas Adams, whose *Hitchhiker's Guide to the Galaxy* became a best-seller on college campuses and also generated a television series; and John Barth, whose recent novel *Sabbatical* received much critical attention. Perhaps most importantly, authors who appear frequently on the syllabuses of high school and college literature classes are heavily represented in *CLC*. Lawrence Durrell, Bernard Malamud, and Lawrence Ferlinghetti are examples of writers of this stature in the present volume. Attention is also given to several other groups of writers—writers of considerable public interest—about whose work criticism is often difficult to locate. These are the contributors to the well-loved but nonscholarly genres of mystery and science fiction, as well as writers who appeal specifically to young adults and writers for the nonprint media, including scriptwriters, lyricists, and cartoonists. Foreign writers and writers who represent particular ethnic groups in the United States are also featured in each volume.

Format of the Work

Altogether there are about 750 individual excerpts in each volume—with an average of about eleven excerpts per author—taken from hundreds of literary reviews, general magazines, scholarly journals, and monographs. Contemporary criticism is loosely defined as that which is relevant to the evaluation of the author under discussion; this includes criticism written at the beginning of an author's career as well as current commentary. Emphasis has been placed on expanding the sources for criticism by including an increasing number of scholarly and specialized periodicals. Students, teachers, librarians, and researchers frequently find that the generous excerpts and supplementary material provided by the editors supply them with all the information that they need to write a term paper, analyze a poem, or lead a book discussion group. However, complete bibliographical citations facilitate the location of the original source as well as provide all of the information necessary for a term paper footnote or bibliography.

A *CLC* entry consists of the following elements:

- The **author heading** contains the author's full name, followed by birth date, and death date when applicable. Pseudonyms and other forms are also listed.

- A **portrait** of the author is included when available.

• A brief **biocritical introduction** to the author and his or her work precedes the excerpted criticism. However, *CLC* is not intended to be a definitive biographical source. Therefore, *cross-references* have been included to direct the user to other useful sources published by the Gale Research Company: the *Contemporary Authors* series now includes detailed biographical and bibliographical sketches of more than 74,000 authors; *Children's Literature Review* presents excerpted criticism on the works of authors of children's books; *Something about the Author* contains heavily illustrated biographical sketches on writers and illustrators who create books for children and young adults; *Contemporary Issues Criticism* presents excerpted commentary on the nonfiction works of authors who influence contemporary thought; and *Dictionary of Literary Biography* provides original evaluations of authors important to literary history. Previous volumes of *CLC* in which the author has been featured are also listed.

• The **excerpted criticism** represents various kinds of critical writing—a particular essay may be normative, descriptive, interpretive, textual, appreciative, comparative, or generic. It may range in form from the brief review to the scholarly monograph. Essays are selected by the editors to reflect the spectrum of opinion about a specific work or about an author's writing in general. The excerpts are presented chronologically, adding a useful perspective to the entry. All titles by the author featured in the entry are printed in boldface, which enables the user to readily ascertain the work being discussed.

• A complete **bibliographical citation** designed to facilitate location of the original essay or book follows each excerpt. An asterisk (*) at the end of a citation indicates the essay is on more than one author.

Other Features

• An **Appendix** lists the sources from which material has been reprinted in a volume. Many other sources have also been consulted during the preparation of the volume.

• A **Cumulative Index to Authors** lists all the authors who have been included in *Contemporary Literary Criticism, Twentieth-Century Literary Criticism,* and *Nineteenth-Century Literature Criticism,* along with cross references to the Gale biographical series described above: *Contemporary Authors, Children's Literature Review, Something about the Author, Contemporary Issues Criticism,* and *Dictionary of Literary Biography.* Users will welcome this cumulated author index as a useful tool for locating an author within the various series. The index, which lists birth and death dates when available, will be particularly valuable for those authors who are identified with a certain period but whose death date causes them to be placed in another, or for those authors whose careers span two periods. For example, F. Scott Fitzgerald is found in *TCLC,* yet a writer often associated with him, Ernest Hemingway, is found in *CLC.*

• A **Cumulative Index to Critics** lists the critics and the author entries in which their work appears.

• A list of **Authors Forthcoming in *CLC*** previews the authors to be researched for future volumes.

Acknowledgments

The editors wish to thank the copyright holders of the excerpted articles included in this volume for permission to use the material and the photographers and individuals who provided photographs for us. We are grateful to the staffs of the following libraries for making their resources available to us: Detroit Public Library and the libraries of Wayne State University, the University of Michigan, and the University of Detroit. We also wish to thank Jeri Yaryan for her assistance with copyright research.

Authors Forthcoming in *CLC*

To Be Included in Volume 28

Juan Benet (Spanish novelist, short story writer, and essayist)—He is a major contributor to the Spanish New Wave literary movement. His recently translated novel, *A Meditation,* has been highly praised both here and abroad.

Walter Van Tilburg Clark (American novelist, short story writer, and poet)—He is known for his western novel about mob violence, *The Oxbow Incident.*

Hilda Doolittle (H.D.) (American poet and novelist)—Her work and life as one of the leading Imagist poets is commanding new attention with the posthumous publication of *End to Torment* and *HERmione.*

Umberto Eco (Italian scholar, editor, and novelist)—Known primarily among scholars for his work in the fields of semiotics and medieval studies, Eco gained wider recognition with the publication of his first novel, *The Name of the Rose.*

Roy Fuller (British novelist and poet)—In a career which spans over forty years, Fuller has produced work well respected by critics. His recent books include two volumes of memoirs, *Souvenirs* and *Vamp Till Ready.*

John Gardner (American novelist, short story writer, and essayist)—An accidental death in 1982 ended the career of this prominent author. Commentary on his last books, *The Art of Living and Other Stories* and *Mickelsson's Ghosts,* will be presented.

William Kennedy (American novelist)—He has succeeded in putting Albany, New York, on America's literary map, having recently completed *Ironweed,* the acclaimed third novel in his Albany cycle.

Norman Mailer (American novelist)—In his long-awaited *Ancient Evenings,* Mailer creates a panoramic portrayal of life in Egypt 3,000 years ago.

Bobbie Ann Mason (American short story writer and critic)—Her first work of fiction, *Shiloh and Other Stories,* was highly praised by critics.

Marsha Norman (American dramatist)—Considered an important new playwright when her first play, *Getting Out,* was produced in 1977, Norman won the 1983 Pulitzer Prize in drama for *'night, Mother.*

Katha Pollitt (American poet)—Her first book, *Antarctic Traveler,* won the 1982 National Book Critics' Circle Award.

Manuel Puig (Argentine novelist)—Puig parodies popular art forms to satirize small town life. His recent *Eternal Curse on the Reader of These Pages* is his first book to be written in English.

Paul Theroux (American novelist and short story writer)—The novels of this expatriate American reflect his passion for travel and exotic settings. His most recent novel, *The Mosquito Coast,* is a potpourri of characters, myths, and adventures.

James Wright (American poet and translator)—The posthumous publication of his last poems in *This Journey* enhances Wright's reputation as one of America's finest contemporary poets.

To Be Included in Volume 29

Van Wyck Brooks (American literary critic and historian)—One of the foremost critics of the early twentieth century, Brooks won the 1937 Pulitzer Prize in history for *The Flowering of New England.*

Noel Coward (English dramatist, short story writer, poet, essayist, and editor)—Recent publication of *The Collected Short Stories of Noel Coward* and *The Noel Coward* *Diaries* has renewed popular and critical interest in this prolific writer.

Leon Edel (American biographer and literary critic)—His five-volume biography of Henry James has been praised by Joseph Epstein as "the single greatest work of biography produced in our century."

Michel Foucault (French literary critic and

philosopher)—Widely regarded as one of the most original thinkers of the twentieth century, Foucault examines in his writings the psychological origins of the human sciences.

John Guare (American dramatist)—He is highly regarded for such theatrically innovative plays as *House of Blue Leaves* and *Lydie Breeze.* Guare has been compared with Edward Albee for his ability to combine farce with poignant social commentary.

David Hare (English dramatist)—A left-wing political playwright whose works focus on post-World War II Britain, Hare has gained popular and critical recognition in the United States for his play *Plenty.*

Jack Kerouac (American novelist and poet)—He was a central figure in the Beat Movement and his life and work have generated a significant amount of new biographical and critical material.

Charles R. Larson (Black American novelist, short story writer, essayist, critic, and editor)—A scholar of African, Indian, and other third world literatures, Larson recently published his third novel, *Arthur Dimmesdale.*

William Least Heat Moon (American travel writer)—Moon's first book, *Blue Highways: A Journey into America,* recounts his travels along the backroads of the United States in search of his Indian and American roots.

Judith Rossner (American novelist)—Her recent best-selling novel, *August,* is a story of the relationship between a middle-aged New York psychoanalyst and her teenaged client.

William Stafford (American poet, editor, and critic)—A prolific writer of calm, understated verse, Stafford continues to create a uniquely American style of contemporary poetry in his recent volume, *A Glass Face in the Rain.*

Richard Tillinghast (American poet and critic)—Tillinghast's recent collection, *The Knife and Other Poems,* reinforces his growing reputation as an important modern poet.

Michel Tremblay (French Canadian dramatist and novelist)—One of Canada's most widely known dramatists writing in French, he has recently written his first novel, *The Fat Lady Next Door Is Pregnant.*

Amos Tutuola (Nigerian novelist)—One of the earliest Nigerian writers to achieve international recognition, he recently published his first book in fourteen years, *The Witch Herbalist of the Remote Town.*

Christa Wolf (East German novelist, short story writer, and essayist)—Her recently translated novel, *A Model Childhood,* reflects Wolf's moral impetus to understand her country's past and how it affects the present. Criticism will also be included on another recent book, *Kein Ort, Nirgends.*

Douglas (Noel) Adams

1952-

English scriptwriter and novelist.

After writing comedy for a number of successful British television shows, Adams wrote *The Hitchhiker's Guide to the Galaxy* and sold it for broadcast on British radio. The program proved immensely popular, spawning a theater production, a television series, albums and cassettes, and a novel trilogy, with a motion picture in preparation. The trilogy has spread Adams's fame abroad, adding to an already large and enthusiastic following, especially on college campuses.

In *The Hitchhiker's Guide to the Galaxy* (1979), along with *The Restaurant at the End of the Universe* (1980), and *Life, the Universe and Everything* (1982), Adams uses the literary devices of science fiction to spoof humanity. The trilogy unfolds the adventures of Englishman Arthur Dent and his alien friend Ford Prefect as they hitch rides across the galaxy after Earth is destroyed to make room for an intergalactic highway. Along the way they meet new life forms that demonstrate Adams's inventiveness. The trilogy is fast-paced and, like the irreverent comedy of Monty Python, mixes deadpan humor, absurdity, satire, and silliness. Most critics have reacted favorably to *Hitchhiker*, viewing it as rollicking farce seldom seen in science fiction.

(See also *Contemporary Authors*, Vol. 106.)

Photograph by Mary Allen from Life, the Universe and Everything by Douglas Adams; copyright © 1982 by Douglas Adams; used by permission of Harmony Books, a division of Crown Publishers, Inc.

KIRKUS REVIEWS

[*The Hitchhiker's Guide to the Galaxy* is science fiction] *Monty Python*-style—as West England villager Arthur Dent becomes the only survivor of Earth, rescued by Ford Prefect of Betelgeuse, a roving researcher for *The Hitchhiker's Guide*. . . . The hideous Vogons torture our heroes by reading poetry to them, but then they're miraculously picked up by the Starship Heart of Gold—which is powered by "the Infinite Improbability Drive," commanded by Galactic President Zaphod Beeblebrox, and staffed by an epically depressed robot named Marvin with a smark-aleck computer that sings "You'll Never Walk Alone." They're all headed for the legendary planet Magrathea, where roaming Arthur discovers Slartibartfast, the guy who originally made Earth ("Norway . . . that was one of mine. Won an award, you know. Lovely crinkly edges") and is now working on Earth Mark Two. . . . Lots of pure silliness, too many English references for U.S. readers, but—like moviegoers who sat through [the *Monty Python* movie] *Life of Brian* for the sake of a few good chuckles—fans of absurd deadpan-parody will happily flip through this likable send-up in order to extract a couple of dozen fine giggles.

A review of "A Hitchhiker's Guide to the Galaxy," in Kirkus Reviews *(copyright © 1980 The Kirkus Service, Inc.), Vol. XLVIII, No. 14, July 15, 1980, p. 941.*

LISA TUTTLE

[*The Hitchhiker's Guide to the Galaxy* is] science fiction and it's extremely funny—a rare and precious conjunction in a field where what usually passes for humor is a bad pun at the end of a dull story.

There's nothing dull about the *Guide,* which is inspired lunacy that leaves hardly a science fictional cliché alive. It relates, in an almost linear fashion, the adventures of an interstellar hitchhiker who calls himself Ford Prefect (when he's visiting that mostly harmless planet called Earth, at any rate) and his dazed companion Arthur Dent, who is fated to see not only his house but his entire world demolished to make way for a new expressway. On their travels they encounter, among other things, aliens, computers, a depressed robot, the third worst poetry in the universe, and even the long sought after answer to the great question of Life, the Universe and Everything. It's all over much too soon. But—don't panic—there's a sequel on the way.

Lisa Tuttle, "As Other Worlds Turn," in Book World—The Washington Post *(© 1980, The Washington Post), November 23, 1980, p. 6.**

PETER KEMP

Douglas Adams's book, *The Hitch-Hiker's Guide to the Galaxy*—a spin-off from his radio series—shot hilariously away from the gravity that so often weighs down modern science fiction, and proved an appropriately astronomical success. Now, he has launched a follow-up, *The Restaurant at the End of the Universe.*

It contains the same central figures: Arthur and Trillian, who escaped just before the Earth was destroyed to make way for a hyperspatial express route; Ford, who 'was in fact from a small planet somewhere in the vicinity of Betelgeuse and not from Guildford as he usually claimed'; Zaphod, rogue President of the Galaxy, 'recently voted the Worst Dressed Sentient Being in the Known Universe'; and Marvin the Paranoid Android, an oppressively depressive robot with 'this terrible pain in all the diodes down my left side'.

In *The Hitch-Hiker's Guide*—a sardonically funny exercise in galactic globe-trotting—they hurtled through space. Here, they also speed through time—finally reaching Milliways, the fabled 'Restaurant at the End of the Universe', an ultra-chic eatery boasting 'lavatory facilities for all of fifty major life-forms' and laying on apocalypse as cabaret, since it is situated at the closing moments of the cosmos (for those who want to go to the opposite extreme, there is the Big Bang Burger Bar).

Not that Adams's characters spend much time eating. As usual, they are propelled through a series of interplanetary adventures. . . .

What makes this book, like its predecessor, almost unputdownable is its surreal, comic creativity. Adams's galaxy blazes with spectacular phenomena like binary sunrises, and swarms with highly coloured worlds—like Golgafrincham, a planet 'rich in legend, red, and occasionally green with the blood of those who sought in days gone by to conquer her'.

To fabricate it, he has taken hints from Lewis Carroll and Edward Lear: there are logical extensions of mad premises, grotesque creatures with crazily evocative names, chattering objects, moments of satiric farce, and picturesquely absurd landscapes. The tone, though—this is often wise-guy sci-fi—owes a lot to Raymond Chandler (one of Arthur's big regrets after the Earth's destruction was that all the Bogart movies had been wiped). In the previous book, the chunky Vogon ships 'hung in the sky in much the same way that bricks don't'. Here, there are snappy bouts of repartee: the droning robot is snubbed with the line, 'Stay out of this, Marvin . . . this is organism talk.'

Finally, the book comes down to earth—or, in any rate, to a replica of it being repopulated by detritus from another planet: ad-men, middle-management consultants and the like. It's not the best of manoeuvres since it means that Adams's weakness—a sporadic tendency to Monty Pythonesque silliness—is given too much scope, while his genially weird inventiveness rather goes into abeyance. But for most of the book, the characters zoom exuberantly through other worlds.

> Peter Kemp, "Wise-Guy-Sci-Fi" (© British Broadcasting Corp. 1980; reprinted by permission of Peter Kemp), in The Listener, Vol. 104, No. 2692, December 18 & 25, 1980, p. 866.

GERALD JONAS

["**The Hitchhiker's Guide to the Galaxy**"] is the book that answers "The Great Question, The Ultimate Question of Life, the Universe, and Everything." The answer, as it happens, is "forty-two." Since the largest computer ever built (known as Deep Thought) takes seven-and-a-half million years to come up with the answer, the disappointment of the original ques-

tioners is perhaps understandable. They are even more disappointed when they learn that the only way to understand the answer is to phrase the question a little more specifically. For this, an even bigger computer and another ten million years are required. It turns out that this computer. . . .

But that is telling the story in chronological order, a narrative trick that Douglas Adams (who once wrote discontinuity for "Monty Python's Flying Circus") is never guilty of. He prefers to tell his stories backward, sideway and even inside out if that will help anyone, which it probably won't. (p. 24)

Humorous science fiction novels have notoriously limited audiences; they tend to be full of "in" jokes understandable only to those who read everything from Jules Verne to Harlan Ellison. The **"Hitchhiker's Guide"** is a delightful exception, being written for anyone who can understand the thrill that might come to a crew of interstellar explorers who discover a mysterious planet, dead for five million years, and then hear on their "sub etha" radio a ghostly voice, hollow, reedy, insubstantial: "Greetings to you. . . . This is a recorded announcement, as I'm afraid we're all out at the moment. . . ." (p. 25)

> Gerald Jonas, in a review of "The Hitchhiker's Guide to the Galaxy," in The New York Times Book Review (© 1981 by The New York Times Company; reprinted by permission), January 25, 1981, pp. 24-5.

PHILIP HOWARD

Hot Black Desiato has made so much money out of ear-shattering plutonium rock music that he is having to spend a year dead for tax reasons. Gargravarr is a man whose mind and body have agreed to live apart on the grounds of incompatibility. And here again, bleep bleep hooray, is Marvin the Paranoid Android robot, who manages to look permanently lugubrious, as far as it is possible for something with a totally metal face to show self-pity.

In short, and indeed in prolixity, chums, [*The Restaurant at the End of the Universe*] is the sequel to *The Hitch Hiker's Guide to the Galaxy,* which has attracted a cult even among those normally impervious to the mechanical charms of science fiction. A summary of the plot would read like case notes of a nervous breakdown. Here be further adventures of Ford Prefect and his companions with odd numbers of heads in the highways and byways of the Universe. It is not *le silence eternel* of these infinite spaces that terrifies, but the incessant smart-aleck chatter of creatures like the nastier plastic things that come out of cornflake packets. Put your analyst on danger money, baby, before you read this. . . .

It is a space *1066 and All That* crossed with [*Alice in Wonderland*] and *Gulliver's Travels,* best read after a Pan Galactic Gargle Blaster slug of the universal hooch, Jynnan Toenick. [Jonathan Swift in *Gulliver's Travels*] satirized contemporary politics. Adams has fun with the trendy manners of our time, from worship of the motor car to jogging, and from the pedantry of committee meetings, Point of Order Madam Chairperson, to religious enthusiasm and, engagingly, Sci-Fi itself. All whimsy is the Beeblebrox; and the ark ship in space is full of deep-frozen middle management men sent to colonize another planet for their own planet's good. . . .

The plot, such as it is, is a sequence of episodic disasters and hilarities. Douglas Adams is a master of the Onomastics and

Paronomasia of Space. Paradox proliferates. Beautiful monsters have to be rescued from ravening princesses. And a simple space song follows the familiar theme of boy-being meets girl-being beneath a silvery moon, which then explodes for no adequately explored reason.

The Man who rules the Universe turns out to be a solipsist linguistic philosopher who believes in nobody else, except, thank heavens, his ginger cat. The travellers come to rest on a primitive planet that turns out to be prehistoric Earth, so becoming their own ancestors. Science fiction I can usually take, or preferably leave. But if this does not make you laugh, gee you guys are so unhip, it's a wonder your bums don't fall off.

Philip Howard, "Bleep Bleep Hooray," in The Times, *London (© Times Newspapers Limited 1981), February 7, 1981, p. 9.*

KIRKUS REVIEWS

[*The Restaurant at the End of the Universe* is the] sequel to *The Hitchhiker's Guide to the Galaxy*—and again the sf parody here is deranged, deadpan, satirical, hyperbolic, wildly erratic . . . but with rather less of a British accent than its predecessor. . . . [The heroes encounter] Milliways, the restaurant at the end of the universe (where dinner walks up to introduce itself, and the entertainment is, literally, doomsday); Hotblack Desiato, leader of the galaxy's loudest rock band (he's spending a year dead for tax purposes); a colony of joggers, hairdressers, and PR men (they'd like to invent the wheel, but can't decide what color it should be); and the man who rules the universe (he's not at all sure that he or the universe really exists). Sometimes lame, limp, or just plain silly—but, at its best, very funny indeed.

A review of "The Restaurant at the End of the Universe," in Kirkus Reviews *(copyright © 1981 The Kirkus Service, Inc.), Vol. XLIX, No. 23, December 1, 1981, p. 1490.*

JOHN CLUTE

I don't think anyone could pretend that Douglas Adams' *The Hitchhiker's Guide to the Galaxy,* which novelizes part of his extraordinarily successful BBC radio series of the same name, ever amounted to much more than a job of media transplant for its author who, having once already told the jokes and the story they engendered, was very likely, at the point he wrote the novel, also preparing to run the whole package through yet another transformation—into a television series, also successful. But whatever form this blatant package comes in, it's a joy.

To begin with, *Hitchhiker* is indeed a novel about how to travel free around the galaxy; somewhere in between it is a cosmological fable about the construction of our Earth as a gigantic living computer designed to solve the riddle of existence (all costs covered by the creatures who had us built and who manifest themselves in the shape of white mice so they can watch us experiment); but it all ends before anything is properly resolved because there is a sequel, *The Restaurant at the End of the Universe*. . . . But no thumb-waving at the actual flow of story can do much more than deflate the underlying jokes which clearly structure the sometimes slightly pixy moves of the tale. If we hear that Earth is about to be demolished to make way for an interstellar turnpike, then sooner or later Earth

will be demolished, and all her citizenry die, with the exception of some white mice, and the heroes, who are hitchhiking. (pp. 34-5)

Given its music-hall premises, the tone of *Hitchhiker* is sometimes damagingly sophomoric, and there is a constant taint of collegiate wit in the naming of silly names and the descriptions of silly alcoholic beverages; and the smooth finger-licking cynicism of the book does sometimes remind one of Kurt Vonnegut's lesser moments. But so it goes. There is enough joy throughout, enough tooth to the zaniness, and enough rude knowingness about media-hype versions of science fiction, to make *Hitchhiker* one of the genre's rare genuinely funny books. (p. 35)

John Clute, in a review of "The Hitchhiker's Guide to the Galaxy," in The Magazine of Fantasy and Science Fiction *(© 1982 by Mercury Press, Inc.; reprinted from* The Magazine of Fantasy and Science Fiction*), Vol. 62, No. 2, February, 1982, pp. 34-5.*

CLAUDIA MORNER

[The hitchhikers in *The Restaurant at the End of the Universe*] are searching for a perfect cup of tea and for a question, the answer of which is 42. They blunder onto one absurd situation after another, such as the Restaurant of the title, which is located in space and time at the very end of the universe. It is a nightclub that offers its guests the opportunity to watch the universe come to an end as floor-show entertainment every evening at the same time. Reminiscent of Stanislaw Lem's writing (without his underlying seriousness) and of Kurt Vonnegut's science fiction, it is both an entertaining, silly story and a successful satire of the worst of S.F. novels. As a sequel to *The Hitchhiker's Guide to the Galaxy* . . . , it maintains the disrespectful, crazy tone and should be popular.

Claudia Morner, in a review of "The Restaurant at the End of the Universe," in School Library Journal *(reprinted from the April 15, 1982 issue of* School Library Journal, *published by R. R. Bowker Co./A Xerox Corporation; copyright © 1982), Vol. 28, No. 8, April 15, 1982, p. 87.*

SALLY EMERSON

Douglas Adams's latest space extravaganza this time starts life as a novel [*Life, the Universe and Everything*]. The first two novels of the series—*The Hitch-hiker's Guide to the Galaxy* and *The Restaurant at the End of the Universe*—were first born as a radio series. . . .

The major characters of the first books return—the vulnerable, bemused Dent; the wise-cracking, know-all Ford Prefect; the cool, half-comatose Zaphod and the manic depressive robot Marvin. Although the plot flags a little here and there much of the writing is dazzling and there are episodes of comic genius, in particular the confrontation between the time-travelling Dent (still in his original dressing gown) and the enraged being whom Dent has inadvertently killed in each of his reincarnations—as a fly, a rabbit, a bowl of petunias, even a human being.

But the early scene at Lord's cricket ground is the finest. Like Hesse and Ballard, it is when the wildness is rooted in reality that Adams is at his best.

Sally Emerson, in a review of "Life, the Universe and Everything" (reprinted by permission of A D Peters & Co Ltd), in The Illustrated London News, *Vol. 270, No. 7010, September, 1982, p. 59.*

KIRKUS REVIEWS

If *The Hitchhiker's Guide to the Galaxy* was a work of genuine lunacy, and its sequel *The Restaurant at the End of the Universe* less inspired and considerably more ragged, [*Life, the Universe and Everything*] is a much busier but practically mirthless offering: the whole notion palls, the dialogue is frequently reduced to the characters telling one another to "zark off," and even the chunks of furious hyperbole have an ominously serious ring. . . . [There] are some amusing spots, including: Wowbagger the Infinitely Prolonged, bored with being immortal, has decided to travel about insulting everybody in the universe—in alphabetical order; and the longest, most destructive party ever held, attended by the winner of the prestigious Rory award for Most Gratuitous Use of the Word "Belgium" in a Serious Screenplay. Overall, however: an effortful enterprise which at best achieves a sort of slow-witted camp pulp—and only for Adams addicts.

A review of "Life, the Universe, and Everything," in Kirkus Reviews *(copyright © 1982 The Kirkus Service, Inc.), Vol. L, No. 17, September 1, 1982, p. 1020.*

TOM HUTCHINSON

Humour is not that rare a quality in science fiction, but Douglas Adams's contribution to future mock must surely be unique: he violates SF taboos while at the same time and quite obviously regarding them with deep affection: you only hurt the genre you love. He is a treasure and science fictioneers should place a preservation order upon him.

Life, The Universe and Everything . . . , his latest guide to such spatial hitch-hikers as everymanic Arthur Dent, the insufferable Ford Prefect, and guru Slartibartfast has them saving the Galaxy from the revived Krikkit robots and their kind. The game of flanneled fools, you will be interested to know, is a racial memory of a previous, horrendous galactic war. And that is the kind of joke—the combining of domestic detail with far-out concepts—that Mr Adams makes with such skill; his anti-climaxes scatter our preconceptions like so many stumps.

There is a serious undertow to all this, of course, a Vonnegut-appreciation of the universe's futility which allows Mr Adams to slip in some moments of sly terror so that the smile freezes on our face like ancient winter. But what with a talking mattress, a spaceship powered by Italian-bistro power and polluted time-streams, we are soon laughing again. Like a stricken Ford Prefect all it needs is "a strong drink and a peer-group" to bring us round.

Tom Hutchinson, "Hitching Another Hike to the Stars," in The London Times, *September 9, 1982, p. 7.**

RICHARD BROWN

Television and radio announcers have a distinctive but necessarily rather limited critical vocabulary. They use up all their superlatives on "gripping sagas", "action-packed crime-busters" and "uproarious, side-splitting" comedies, and have little left with which to package anything more genuinely youthful, imaginative and funny. It reflects rather badly on everyday programming that Douglas Adams's clever science-fiction comedies *The Hitch-Hiker's Guide to the Galaxy* are unfamiliar enough to be introduced into the domestic arena as "zany" and "madcap", and it is a comment on the mass audience that the enjoyment of such unexceptional pleasures should be thought of as some kind of cult.

[British programmes] such as *I'm Sorry I'll Read That Again, Monty Python's Flying Circus* and *Not the Nine O'Clock News* manage to thrive on this special status—on the fact that they are held at a distance from the rest of the evening's offerings. They build up a semi-private language of stock situations, favourite satirical targets and recurring comic triggers, and have established an anarchic, facetious, though also teasingly symbiotic relationship with the fully domesticated mainstream. The good-humour of that relationship shows up clearly in the characteristic play they make with the manners and language of news-readers and announcers themselves.

There is a rich vein of satire here into which Adams's writings fall, suggesting, in general, that some science-fiction takes itself just as appallingly seriously as, and can be exposed as no more imaginative than the reading of the news. . . .

The mini-genre is one which seems to have evolved within the electronic media. *The Hitch-Hiker's Guide,* with its clipped, up-to-date, joke-a-minute style, bristling with gimmickry and microtechnological blobs and bleeps, seemed ideally suited to radio and even more so to television, where its diagrams and print-outs have an appeal somewhere between watching *Ceefax* and playing Space-Invaders.

As followers will know, the formula has been transferred with some success to the printed page. This latest volume, *Life, the Universe and Everything,* is the third, following on from *The Hitch-Hiker's Guide to the Galaxy* and *The Restaurant at the End of the Universe.* This gives the publishers the opportunity to talk of a "trilogy".

The constant element in Adams's plot is the helpless, semi-clad character of Arthur Dent, last remaining inhabitant of the Earth, which has been demolished to make way for an interstellar by-pass. [In *Life, the Universe, and Everything*], Arthur and his know-all space friend Ford Prefect find themselves caught up in the malevolent plan of the rulers of the planet Krikkit to destroy everything that isn't cricket and to seize the Golden Bail that will give them great power. Meanwhile Arthur hopes to discover the Ultimate Question of Life, knowing already that the Ultimate Answer to the Question is forty-two. The pair come across a number of extra-terrestrial phenomena, such as the planet of Squornshellous Zeta, whose swamps are inhabited by mattresses, and the Campaign for Real Time. This, though, is only the plot. Much of the comedy arises from a variety of pseudo-high-tech mis-information. . . .

The Hitch-Hiker's Guide retains its life on the page because much of this humour is primarily verbal, using mild parody, making the everyday absurd by giving it a strange name or simply by giving it a capital letter. It has an imaginative energy which derives as much from its consistent play with a cosy, familiar world—the suburban English world of cricket, dressing-gowns and by-passes—as from the extravagance of its characters and settings.

Adams's writing has a likeable, posh-school, wide-eyed, naive manner related, perhaps, to the primitive manner currently in vogue in high-brow poetic circles. It would be wrong, though, to claim too much for the books. Print shows up also the extent to which the humour depends on a limited repertoire of gimmicks, and this third volume, though by no means lacking in enthusiastic drive, does little to suggest that the idea could or should be taken much further from here.

Richard Brown, "Posh-School SF," in The Times Literary Supplement *(© Times Newspapers Ltd. (London) 1982; reproduced from* The Times Literary Supplement *by permission), No. 4147, September 24, 1982, p. 1032.*

PETER STOLER

Whimsy is currently in short supply, a deficiency that makes Douglas Adams' new book all the more welcome. *Life, the Universe and Everything* . . . is like nothing ever published before except, perhaps, *The Hitchhiker's Guide to the Galaxy,* also written by Douglas Adams. Once again the protagonist is a reluctant wanderer named Arthur Dent; once again his intergalactic guide is an extraterrestrial named Ford Prefect. Vooming around the void accompanied by a two-headed, three-armed creature who once controlled the universe and a sexy space cadet, Dent manages to avert Armageddon and save the world for life as we never knew it. Adams delights in cosmic pratfalls, and if he sometimes loses track of his narrative, he more than makes up for it by confirming what many have suspected all along: "He learned to communicate with birds and discovered that their conversation was fantastically boring. It was all to do with wind speed, wingspans, power-to-weight ratios and a fair bit about berries." Adams fails, however, to resolve the discrepancy between the Ultimate Question and the Ultimate Answer. The answer, provided in Adams' first book, is 42. The question, postulated in his second book, *The Restaurant at the End of the Universe,* is: What is six times nine? The third book says that *Q.* and *A.* cancel each other out—and take the universe with them. (pp. 93, 95)

Peter Stoler, "Five Novels Revive a Genre," in Time *(copyright 1982 Time Inc.; all rights reserved; reprinted by permission from* Time*), Vol. 120, No. 20, November 15, 1982, pp. 92-3, 95.**

BRIAN STABLEFORD

It is probable that no one will enjoy *Life, the Universe and Everything* as much as its predecessors. Once you expect the unexpected, it is no longer unexpected, and that which is startling and amusing only as long as it remains surprising cannot endure being spun out into trilogies. The books, in any case, cannot be as funny as the radio show: the dialogue of Marvin the paranoid android, for instance, is pretty dull in print but a real scream when rendered in . . . [a] magnificently morose (and electronically distorted) voice. Then again, this third volume gives way more than the second (and much more than the first) to the inherent gloominess of Adams' temperament. His irony was always bitter, underlaid—and, indeed, fuelled—by the supposition that things can and must not only go wrong, but go wrong in the most grotesque possible fashion, that being what you'd expect of our kind of universe. The answer to the riddle of life, the universe, and everything is 42, largely because by the time you get to that age (because you're as young as you feel, some people reach it much earlier than others, including Douglas Adams, who is only thirty) you know perfectly well that it doesn't matter a damn whether the riddle has an answer or not, or whether there's a riddle at all. Personally, I appreciate Adams' work, but can't really get all that enthusiastic about it because I've been ninety-two since I was fifteen and there's nothing he can tell me about the awful ways of the infinitely silly universe. (pp. 19-20)

Brian Stableford, in a review of "Life, the Universe and Everything," in Science Fiction & Fantasy Book Review *(copyright © 1983 by Science Fiction Research Association), No. 12, March, 1983, pp. 19-20.*

William (Christopher) Barrett

1913-

American literary critic, philosopher, and editor.

Barrett, an expert on existentialism and other philosophies and an astute literary critic, is widely known for his affiliations with *Partisan Review*, the most influential journal of leftist and modernist ideas published in the United States in the 1940s and 1950s. Begun during the 1930s by William Phillips, Philip Rahv, and other anti-Stalinist Marxists, this journal was considered the voice of post-World War II New York intellectuals. Written and edited by such prominent figures as Hannah Arendt, Mary McCarthy, Delmore Schwartz, and Lionel Trilling, *Partisan Review* has been described as the first evidence of "an independent and literate left" in the United States. Its initial program called for Marxism in politics and modernism in the visual arts and literature. Barrett, who served there as an associate editor between the years 1945-1953, was valued especially for his ability to translate the then new and "abstract Continental philosophy into lucid prose." His "What Is Existentialism?," an essay which appeared in *Partisan Review* in 1947, is among the clearest explanations of that philosophy. Tired of the intense intellectual atmosphere at *Partisan Review* and increasingly disaffected with the political positions of the magazine's staff, Barrett, who became increasingly conservative as his career progressed, left the publication in the 1950s. He went on to serve as a professor of philosophy at New York University from 1950-1979 and acted as the literary reviewer for the *Atlantic Monthly* in the 1960s.

Barrett's philosophical views are expressed most clearly in his books *Irrational Man* (1958), now considered a classic introduction to existential philosophy, and *The Illusion of Technique: A Search for Meaning in a Technological Civilisation* (1978). In both of these works, Barrett's main thesis is that the greatest threat to modern civilisation and the cause of "the modern malaise of nihilism" is that which he calls "deranged rationality." The source of the phenomenon, in Barrett's view, may be found in the philosophy of Plato and Aristotle and the evolution of Greek rationalism. Greek philosophers, who depended on abstract models to explain the world, detached reason from "the mythic, religious, and poetic impulses from which it had formerly been mixed." In doing so, in Barrett's opinion, they began a movement which led toward modern nihilism. Barrett calls for a return to the belief that life, in its mystical and mysterious grandeur, cannot be "enclosed in a completely rational system." He advocates a "new conception of thinking," one that recognizes the limitations of reason in the determination of truth and one that takes into account the "anxieties and dilemmas of ordinary men."

Barrett's philosophical views inform and shape his literary criticism and aesthetic theory. In *Time of Need: Forms of Imagination in the Twentieth Century* (1972), for example, he examines how the work of twentieth-century literary and visual artists reflect nihilistic tendencies and a burgeoning sense of alienation. An informal survey of works by such artists as Albert Camus, Samuel Beckett, and Ernest Hemingway, *Time of Need* shows Barrett to be sympathetic with those authors whose work gropes beyond the limits of rationalism. Renowned primarily as a philosopher, Barrett's literary criticism is also

© Thomas Victor 1983

considered important and relevant to the contemporary reader because of the broad associations it makes between literature, philosophy, and the problems of the modern age.

Barrett's recent work, *The Truants: Adventures among the Intellectuals* (1982), is both a memoir of his personal and professional relationships with writers at *Partisan Review* and an examination of New York's intellectual life. Described by some critics as an important contribution to the intellectual history of the twentieth century, *The Truants* contains portraits of Philip Rahv, Delmore Schwartz, Mary McCarthy, and others.

(See also *Contemporary Authors*, Vols. 13-16, rev. ed.)

JOHN WILD

In this suggestive book ["**Irrational Man: A Study in Existential Philosophy**"] William Barrett shows that Greek rationalism was much more than just a set of abstract theories. It established a structure of consciousness, an attitude towards life, which persisted throughout our subsequent history, and still plays a dominant role in contemporary life and thought. This attitude turned away from the individual subject and the concrete world in which he exists. Instead of trying to understand the human person from the inside as he lives, this rationalistic attitude was content to regard him from the outside as a thing before the mind, and to fit him into a universe of objects. . . .

Mr. Barrett points out that the romantic poets were already rebelling against the abstract intellect which, if universalized, means the death of man. Developing certain suggestions of Whitehead, he shows how many existential insights can be found in Wordsworth. This poet knew that man exists not as an isolated substance but rather as always open to a world in essential relation to him. . . . The author has a genuine understanding of modern art and literature, and he indicates with a wealth of example and insight how they have already gone far beyond romanticism in challenging the rationalist conceptions of cosmic symmetry, and in revealing the absence of man, as he is in his dark inner depths, from such artificial constructions. There is no doubt that art and philosophy are at last moving in parallel directions. Can it be that the ancient quarrel between the philosophers and the poets which began with the writing of Plato's "Republic," and which has raged ever since at the heart of our culture is now at an end?

Indeed we sense this as we read Mr. Barrett's lucid account of those modern philosophers who were able to transcend provincial limitations, to break with academic technicalities, and to become, as they now are, a living force in the Western world as a whole. We think of this new philosophy of existence as a French, or at the widest, a European phenomenon. This is a serious error. Russian thinkers like Soloviev, Shestov, and Berdiaev must be included, and certainly the American philosopher William James, though this is not commonly recognized. . . . Mr. Barrett is certainly right in identifying basic existential themes in his writings. This insight should be noted and developed further by historians of American thought.

The existential thinkers interpreted by Mr. Barrett diverge on many points. Nevertheless they all see the dangerous partiality of that objective rationalism which is so deeply ingrained in our tradition, and seek for new ways of shedding light on those obscure regions of being-in-the-world which it has disregarded. (p. 19)

Mr. Barrett lays a heavy emphasis on the narrative side of this development, and in his last chapter interprets it as a revealing of the dark irrational "furies" in man which are at last being recognized and respected. This is an anticlimax, for, as his own discussions show, the new philosophy is much more than this. As a matter of fact, it is neither rational nor irrational: it has penetrated to a deeper ground beneath them both from which it is able to understand man and his world in a new and more revealing light. Mr. Barrett does not thoroughly explore the new conception of a relative human truth and its implications for philosophy. Nevertheless, he has written a brilliant and penetrating book of deep concern not only to the professional philosopher but to the layman as well—to all men, in fact, who are interested in the living thought of our time. It portends a near future when philosophy in this country may stop trying to produce second-rate imitations of science and by returning to its own field, the human life-world, may once again become an inquiry that matters to living men. (p. 38)

John Wild, "Recovery of the Sense of Being," in The Saturday Review, *New York (© 1958 Saturday Review Co.; reprinted by permission), Vol. XLI, No. 36, September 6, 1958, pp. 19, 38.*

CHARLES FRANKEL

[In **"Irrational Man: A Study in Existential Philosophy"**] William Barrett has presented the most thorough account yet writ-

ten for the American layman of the philosophy that has attracted so much attention in Europe since World War II—Existentialism. This philosophy is a protest against the submersion of the individual in a mass society, and Mr. Barrett . . . shares in this protest. A man with a taste for both poetry and politics, an independently minded philosopher and a writer of vigor and passion, he believes that the intellect in the modern world has become an inhuman gadget and that organized reason has given our civilization unprecedented powers, which it uses without taste or moral insight.

The author, however, does not think that our troubles come from having failed to take reason seriously enough. They come, he believes, from having taken reason too seriously. For the belief in reason, to his mind, has accelerated the drift toward a cold and collectivized world instead of combating it. Western culture, he asserts, has been in the grip of a myth—a fantasy that there is such a thing as the rational intellect, detached, pure, objective, and master of all it surveys. This is the main cause of the "divorce of mind from life" that plagues us. And he believes that Existentialism, more than any other philosophy on the current scene, is aware of this problem and has significant things to say about how to deal with it.

Mr. Barrett places his exposition of four leading Existentialists—Kierkegaard, Nietzsche, Heidegger and Sartre—in a broad context. A good deal of his book is devoted to a detailed study of such varied products of modern culture as the painting of Cézanne and the cubists, the writing of men like Joyce and Faulkner, and the Principle of Uncertainty in modern physics. All of these developments, in his view, reveal the growth of a new conception of human experience and a common conviction that the traditional categories and ideas of abstract reason are insufficient to place men in touch with reality.

Existentialism, Mr. Barrett argues, has captured this central theme. It expresses the realization that there are "subterranean forces of life" with which pure reason cannot deal and that reason itself has its roots in these irrational forces. Existentialism wants a new conception of human thinking, which recognizes that existence is primary and logic only secondary. It asks, in short, for an intellectual revolution, for a new set of standards by which the works of the mind can be judged.

On the whole, Mr. Barrett summarizes rather than analyzes the arguments of the Existentialists, but his account nevertheless does much to illuminate this philosophy about which much has been said but relatively little known. Despite the sweeping character of some of the author's generalizations about art, science and culture, **"Irrational Man"** makes it plain that Existentialism is not just a fad and that it reflects developments in our society profoundly challenging the ideal of the life of reason.

The book is all the more useful because Mr. Barrett is himself "engaged" and "committed," and has offered his own Existialist interpretation of modern Western history and culture. Whatever we may think of his position, it is good to read a philosopher who thinks that philosophy should have something to say about the anxieties and dilemmas of ordinary men.

Nevertheless, the position for which Mr. Barrett has chosen to argue is much less than persuasive. Because the "subterranean forces of life" are unaware of the laws of logic, he argues that we too should keep logic in its place. Because human reason is fallible, he believes that we ought to supplement it with irrational methods when we form our basic beliefs. These are astonishing inferences to draw from rather ordinary platitudes.

Despite the anguished tones with which the existentialists announce their discovery, it is, after all, rather stale news that human reason is fallible. (p. 6)

It is not hard to understand why contemporary pressures should encourage a resurgent hostility toward rationality and its works. But it is hard to understand why a professional intellectual, who emphasizes that reasonable ideals are always precariously situated, should propose to strengthen reason by granting the right of "subterranean forces" to be recognized as sources of truth. These forces are not, after all, inherently orderly and harmonious, and some principle is necessary to choose among them. If it is not to be reason, all that is left is impulse, desire and sheer brute force.

Mr. Barrett believes that there is a kind of knowledge which "is not the kind . . . that man can have through reason alone, or perhaps through reason at all; he has it rather through body and blood, bones and bowels. . . . Yet it is knowledge all the same." Everyone will grant that we come to our beliefs in all sorts of ways. But to misuse the word "knowledge" as Mr. Barrett does is to make it impossible to distinguish between just having beliefs and having beliefs that are true. Though it may not be his intention, it is equivalent to a request that we drop all standards from the governance of human affairs. Logic alone, as Mr. Barrett says, is surely not enough. Unhappily, illogic, whether alone or in company is even worse. (pp. 6, 18)

Charles Frankel, "Reason and Reality," in The New York Times Book Review *(© 1958 by The New York Times Company; reprinted by permission), September 7, 1958, pp. 6, 18.*

LESLIE DEWART

The title of [*What Is Existentialism?*] would lead one to expect a pedestrian but systematic introduction to the subject of the sort usually addressed in the preface "to the general reader" or to "the educated public"—but which normally mystifies and rarely educates. Happily, the title is deceptive. This volume is neither a systematic treatment nor one which deals with existentialism in general. It offers instead two essays, related and partly overlapping, on the thought of one philosopher, Martin Heidegger. Moreover, these two essays, the composition of which was separated by "more than a dozen years," represent the author's attempt, not to popularize, but to divine the significance of Heidegger's thought as an event in the history of philosophy.

But in the end Mr. Barrett's accomplishment of this task does constitute, in a way, a highly successful introduction to existentialism; indeed, this is one of the best secondary sources yet available in English on the subject. The reason is that Mr. Barrett is one of the relatively few English-speaking philosophers who has attempted to view the contemporaneity of existentialism not as a novel or bizarre phenomenon, but as a historically present reality. The author, therefore, is far removed from that legion who, with the unquestionable but lifeless expertise of a Thomas Langan, dissect existentialism as if it were an unidentified body washed up to our domestic shores. . . . Mr. Barrett conveys the more important truth that existentialism is not simply an interesting episode in the annals of recent academic fads, but the conceptualization and intellectualization of a culture-wide phenomenon, deeply rooted in the history of the Western mind, and sufficiently pervasive and

powerful to warrant recognition as the philosophical type which manifests the thermonuclear age.

Understandably, Mr. Barrett achieves this less aptly in the earlier of his two essays than in the second. For apparently it was only gradually, as the author studied "the later Heidegger," that he discovered what is perhaps one of the central points of Heidegger's philosophical contribution to the development of the human mind: "the history of philosophy, for Heidegger, is not isolated from the rest of human history. On the contrary, it is human history brought to its fullest revelation, so that what happens in philosophy is prophetic of what is to happen later in the rest of man's social and political life. Heidegger's interpretation of the history of philosophy thus entails a very definite interpretation of the whole history of Western civilization . . . ".

The same "positioning" of Heidegger's thought as a philosophy of history which is itself a historical, cultural event, enables Mr. Barrett to explain more satisfactorily than most critics do the relation of Heidegger to modern literature and art, and his profound interest in poetry at a certain stage of his development as well as his life-long preoccupation with language. (p. 23)

More important, Barrett shows that "the theme of history is central to the later Heidegger, and whatever he attempts to interpret—whether it be poetry, the meaning of technology, or a pre-Socratic philosopher—is understood within his own bold and simple scheme for Western history as a whole." However, it must be remarked that "all, or nearly all, the details" in Heidegger's interpretation of contemporary times in philosophical terms "are commonplace matters." . . . But, if so, in what consists Heidegger's originality? It consists "in the way he sees this fact as embedded within the whole history of Western philosophy. This historical vision is granted him because he takes philosophy itself as a central and decisive fact within Western history. The great philosophers are not merely idle speculators whose ideas may happen, in some passive way or other, to reflect the changes that are going on in the substratum of history; on the contrary, these philosophers project the future by laying down certain schemata of thought within the framework of which subsequent history plays out the details." This original interpretation, lucidly and convincingly defended, is Mr. Barrett's notable contribution to the literature on the subject. (pp. 23-4)

Leslie Dewart, "Historical Vision," in The Canadian Forum, *Vol. XLV, April, 1965, pp. 23-4.*

JOHN V. McDONNELL

Convinced that modern academic philosophy has largely given up on its responsibility to pursue the meaning of human life or even to ask the questions most vital to man, philosopher William Barrett [in *Time of Need: Forms of Imagination in the Twentieth Century*] turns to the testimony of modern art for a schema of the human condition. His choice of artists is wide and varied, ranging from Camus and Hemingway to sculptor Henry Moore and director Stanley Kubrick. The prevalent theme is, of course, nihilism and the struggle of major artists to express the plight of man alone in a universe bereft of meaning and value. The author's approach is leisurely and informal, more the result of his "haphazard reading and looking" than an attempt at formal literary or artistic explication. In short, we are here in the company of a highly intelligent guide as he searches among his favorite writers, painters and sculptors for ''a truth valid for all of us.''

Obviously this truth is hard-won and elusive, and much of the author's concern is to detail the ''negative'' vision of modern literature. Tracing the evolution of nihilism in literature from the 19th-century Russian novelists who, he says, were fascinated by lonely ''abnormal figures'' acting out their rebellion within an acceptable universe, to the heroes of Camus, Beckett and Hemingway who find themselves in a world no longer rational or acceptable, Barrett finds the dominant mood to be unflinching pessimism. (pp. 156-57)

This sounds familiar, of course, and if the author were content simply to rework the analyses of other critics his book would remain redundant and unnecessary. But there is another ''positive'' dimension of modern literature, he reminds us, and it is in exploring this ''reaction to the ominous drift of our time'' that the author is most challenging. This dimension is difficult to define explicitly, but one might say that it is an occasional awareness of ''the presence of mystery'' in the universe, a feeling on the part of characters that somehow they ''belong to something cosmic that is not of man and not of men, . . . but toward which in the deepest part of themselves they can never feel alien.'' . . .

Clearly the author is in sympathy with those writers who would go beyond the limits of rationalism and despair toward faith in the vital primal forces of life itself. To some readers his vision may appear to be another type of romantic and optimistic irrationalism. And yet it is founded on a just assessment of the most negative writers of the century. ''In the end,'' he says, ''the answer to nihilism is not intellectual but vital.'' Here is an excellent sourcebook for those rare intimations of harmony and meaning that have surfaced in twentieth-century art and literature. (p. 157)

> *John V. McDonnell, in a review of ''Time of Need: Forms of Imagination in the Twentieth Century,'' in* America *(reprinted with permission of America Press, Inc.; © 1972; all rights reserved), Vol. 127, No. 6, September 9, 1972, pp. 156-57.*

ANATOLE BROYARD

In **''Time of Need,''** the author is saying, like a teacher to a lazy student, ''I'm afraid that's a very superficial reading.'' And he goes on to prove it. Examining Camus, Hemingway, Faulkner, Kafka, Joyce, Hesse and even E. M. Forster—as well as Giacometti, Henry Moore, Picasso and others in the visual arts—he shows them moving beyond rational meaning, which is not the business of art, toward myth, mysteries and perspectives even deeper than those in de Chirico's paintings.

For all the pages that have been written about them, his interpretations of these artists are startlingly fresh and provocative. . . .

With Beckett, [Barrett] has outdone himself—and perhaps the reader as well. Beckett is seen as a ''post-neurosis'' writer, one whose art may have developed to such a point that it becomes almost self-defeating. He has passed through so many stages of renunciation that we cannot believe that this journey to the end of the void is without issue. Surely, there must be some sort of trash-can beatitude at the bottom of this descent. Perhaps it was not necessary to go all the way back to the primeval ooze, but then Mr. Beckett is not one for half-measures.

Mr. Barrett's reading of ''Finnegans Wake'' is at once more simple and more complex than most. Camus, according to Mr. Barrett, is rescued from the ''nausea'' of existentialism by his stubborn provincialism, his refusal to set abstractions above the processes of life itself. He will not be satisfied with Levi-Strauss's remark that ''We have put art on a reservation.'' Although he is known primarily as a literary critic and philosopher, Mr. Barrett is a formidable ''reader'' of the visual arts as well. He remarks of Giacometti's thin men that the head has sucked up the body's vitality until it is on the point of vanishing. This is the root of the problem. Man, he says, is the being whose being is always open to the menace of nonbeing. Once upon a time, Christianity erected a magnificent myth to protect us against this menace: now, with the waning of that myth, art has taken over the job of humanizing the void for us.

> *Anatole Broyard, ''Between Body and Spirit,'' in* The New York Times *(© 1972 by The New York Times Company; reprinted by permission), September 27, 1972, p. 45.*

JOHN WAIN

[*Time of Need*] is written out of a belief that Western man has exhausted his dynamo, that the time of need is now. The pride which once drove us to place the human alongside the divine—even if in the process the divine must give way and crumble to dust—has turned into sickness and self-doubt. Man's journey away from the primitive began with the Enlightenment, which promised to rid him of superstition and fear. At the same time the scientific revolution began to put into his hands the keys of the physical world. He has, so far, used those keys only for robbery and blasphemy. It was all right as long as man could see himself as being in cahoots with God, but when in the 19th century this partnership dissolved, man looked round and found himself alone. The shock was a profound one, and with the passage of years the situation has grown no easier. Hence the phenomenon of nihilism, of which Mr. Barrett offers no formal definition but to which he reverts continually.

Nihilism is that state of intellectual and spiritual heebie-jeebies in which the human spirit defines itself against the void and realizes that there is nothing to stop the void from swallowing it. . . . [Modern] man carries at the back of his mind the suspicion that all his feverish activity is either random competitiveness (''a blind man battering blind men'') or an empty exercise of the unanchored will, urging itself on toward dissolution against a background of eternal night. . . . The characteristic modern artist either rubs our noses in the futility of human constructions (Beckett) or strives to set up some counter-principle that will hold us steady in the face of the fathomless threat. And on the whole Mr. Barrett is satisfied that he has identified this counter-principle. It is the ''primal, primordial, primitive.'' (pp. 99, 102)

[Style] is not the only positive which Mr. Barrett discerns. There is another and more fundamental positive, which he defines at one point by invoking the myth of Deucalion and Pyrrha. These two survivors of the Flood were commanded to throw their mother's bones over their shoulders. They interpreted this, correctly, as referring to the stones that were lying on the ground; they threw them; they sprang up as men and women. The Earth as mother, the Earth as provider of life and source of the generations—here, Mr. Barrett sites the main argument of his book. He sees in the imaginative utterance of the past fifty years a hunger to be reunited with the "primal, primordial, primitive." In the Greek myth, stones came up as men and women; in Henry Moore's "Reclining Figure," the human form seems to be settling back into the loam, its features only faintly discernible, its contours worn into smoothness in the way that Nature works on stone.

Mr. Barrett follows this *leitmotif* through many books and authors. He sees it in Hemingway's preoccupation with the concrete, in the revolt of Camus from the abstractions of urban intellectual life and his kinship with "the world of the sea and the stars," in the blood-and-kinship rituals of Faulkner, in the mythopoeic imagination of Joyce. The display of examples is cumulative. It ends with a clear warning. We, as a species, are making for the first time a determined effort to cut free of Nature, to enclose ourselves in an envelope of technology from which we exclude the remnants of primitive consciousness within us. (p. 102)

Beneath his reasonableness and the moderate tone of his voice (very welcome in this bawling epoch), Mr. Barrett is uttering a strong warning. He wants to arrest the lemming-rush of modern man by the most effective means in his power, namely, by calling into testimony the collective voice of the imagination, man's own wise heart speaking against his foolish head.

On these terms, I find *Time of Need* true and moving. In matters of detail—sometimes quite large detail—I think it can be faulted. The choice of examples is, as Mr. Barrett himself says, necessarily random. But I think it should have included one or two, at least, of those writers whose defense against Nihilism is stated in the terms of this world whose answer has not been transcendental but rooted in the nature of man as a social being. Pasternak in *Dr. Zhivago*, for instance, comes close to stating a satisfying doctrine of immortality in terms of the flowing river of the human race; . . . [he] interprets history as something living rather than as the blind power-appetite of the party. An even more serious omission is the absence of any but the most tangential mention of D. H. Lawrence, who after all made one of the first complete and overt statements of the thesis that man must be true to the "primordial" in himself. . . . Mr. Barrett's account of the quarrel between Sartre and Camus does not really succeed in clarifying the differences between them, as we might expect a philosopher to be able to do. But no book on a large scale is without some "looped and windowed raggedness." As a whole, *Time of Need* is thoroughly valuable. It is written with passion, lucidity, wisdom. (pp. 102-03)

John Wain, "Art and Nature," in Commentary (reprinted by permission; all rights reserved), Vol. 54, No. 6, December, 1972, pp. 98, 102-03.

ALLEN LACY

In a series of articles published in *Commentary* between 1967 and 1976, Barrett presented his interpretation of such modern philosophers as William James, Martin Heidegger, and Ludwig Wittgenstein. Readers of these provocative and lively essays could have easily predicted their eventual publication in a single volume.

The Illusion of Technique is that volume. Rather surprisingly, Barrett has chosen to embed his reflections on major figures in 20th-century philosophy in an examination of "the nature of technique—its scope and limits." . . .

Barrett's thesis about "technique" provides him with both villains and heroes. His villains are sometimes the technicians who design detention camps to exorcise such quirky souls as Alexander Solzhenitsyn, sometimes the computer people who would love to reduce all human activity to a simple formula, sometimes social scientists of a behaviorist bent.

For the "bland summer hotel" that B. F. Skinner presented as a Utopian ideal in *Walden II*, Barrett has utter contempt. He mocks especially Skinner's assertion that his Waldenites will have a high appreciation for all the arts. What would a person conditioned to live without tension make of Oedipus or Hamlet? "Two cases of very badly bungled conditioning," suggests Barrett.

Barrett's heroes are people like Solzhenitsyn and all other dissidents; eccentric monomaniacs like Bobby Fischer (whose passion for excellence and for chess would disturb the placid waters of a Walden II); and workers whose random and erratic bathroom trips are sufficient to drive computer people to desperate frenzy.

As a book about technique, Barrett's new book fails. He shows a fine indifference to the work of Lewis Mumford, Jacques Ellul, and others who have tried to present technique as a social and philosophical problem for our time. Occasionally he has to distort his material, wrenching it into place to make it serve his rather vague overall thesis. Often in reading *The Illusion of Technique*, I wasn't sure what he meant by his central term. Furthermore, I'm not at all sure that it is technique that is the sole enemy. "Informing visions" (such as a 1,000-year Reich) have worked much mischief in the world. Nevertheless, *The Illusion of Technique* is a very engaging book, one in which the parts are somehow greater than the whole.

Like *Irrational Man, The Illusion of Technique* is no scholarly monograph addressed to Barrett's fellow philosophers. Some of them will probably find it too sermonic, too high-flown in its rhetoric and its ambitions, for their tastes. Nevertheless, the philosophical commentary and interpretation Barrett gives of James, Heidegger, and Wittgenstein is lucid. He communicates a good sense of the questions each thinker wrestled with—and those they failed to pursue. He considers the development of their thought, and he pursues the degree to which their work, admittedly very different in style, is deeply interconnected.

Although Barrett gives his major attention to the three thinkers he considers to be the undisputed philosophical eminences of this century—and of these James satisfies him most—he also discusses Husserl, Russell, Nietzsche, Hegel, Kant, and Descartes. To read *The Illusion of Technique* is thus to travel, really very pleasantly, through the territory Western philosophy has explored ever since Descartes embarked on his expedition of radical doubting of all that he thought he knew.

Barrett's own philosophical style is rather paradoxical. He writes lucidly about the need for mystery. He describes, beautifully and elegantly, the need to recognize the claims of the silent and the wordless over our being. He argues rationally for the preservation of our freedom, for the maintenance of sufficient disorder in human existence that it will always be a bit unpredictable.

Finally, it is not William Barrett's concern for the demonic possibilities of "technique" that unifies his book, nor is it his clear presentation of the dominant figures of recent philosophical history. It is Barrett himself. Unlike *Irrational Man, The Illusion of Technique* gives the reader a view of the author, of how he lives, of what he thinks important. (p. R13)

One senses, by the time one has finished the book, that even the great philosophers whose thought Barrett analyzes and dissects are like familiar objects in his life, that he has moved toward age in the company of William James's *Varieties of Religious Experience* much as some people do who have come to look on an old Oriental carpet or a treasured vase as a deeply personal friend.

The Illusion of Technique is finally a very powerful and moving testament to the values for which it argues. (p. R14)

Allen Lacy, "Rational Arguments for Human Disorder," in The Chronicle Review (copyright © 1978 by The Chronicle of Higher Education, Inc.), November 13, 1978, pp. R13-R14.

ANTHONY QUINTON

[*The Illusion of Technique*] is room service philosophy, presented with the utmost consideration for the presumed limitations of its readers. . . .

The Illusion of Technique is, mainly, a meditation on the condition of man in the modern world that shows an increasing tendency to turn into an account, with modestly exemplary intentions, of a personal return to a strongly felt, if very nebulous, next best thing to religious faith. The project is carried out in a curious way as a more or less critical exposition of themes in the philosophies of Wittgenstein, Heidegger and William James. At times this seems an odd choice, as if a work of Vaughan Williams had been arranged for an orchestra of surgical instruments. (p. 460)

Wittgenstein is an odd choice as representative of the kind of science-oriented philosophy Barrett sees as the main enemy. The bulk of his written work falls within the rather circumscribedly cognitive domain of interest of analytic philosophers in this century, but in both its forms it is exceptionally cryptic. What is more it is associated with, and sometimes accompanied by, a lot of self-denigrating matter of a very different kind. Barrett quotes the letter to Engelmann in which Wittgenstein says that what is important is precisely what he has *not* written, that whereof we must remain silent. And he returns several times to the formulation of Heidegger's fundamental problem: 'it is not *how* things are in the world that is mystical, but *that* it exists.'

Analytical philosophers are simply not in the business that interests Barrett, that of articulating a 'philosophy of life', a system of attitudes to the world and man's place in it. Vague and indirect intimations of such a thing can be identified by a kind of recreational hermeneutics, but it will not be simple Comtean optimism. Barrett has to do a fair amount of interpreting of Heidegger to get from his etymological abstractions about Being and about truth as openness to the programme of unreflective nature-mysticism he arrives at, but he has the warrant of Heidegger's later style of life in woodland seclusion and at least it gives some content to the strangely elusive utterances involved.

Hovering around the edges of this book is a confessional autobiography and it would certainly have been fresher and more interesting. Barrett is a pleasant writer, for all his anxiety to be accessible, with a wide range of knowledge and interests inside and outside philosophy. But there is something rather listless and unconvincing about the way in which he tries to put all his cultural bits and pieces to the service of a largely conventional message of spiritual consolation. (pp. 460, 462)

Anthony Quinton, "At Home in the World," in New Statesman (© 1979 The Statesman & Nation Publishing Co. Ltd.), Vol. 98, No. 2532, September 28, 1979, pp. 460, 462.*

JOSEPH J. FAHEY

"It is easy to let the age have its head; the difficulty is to keep one's own." While this quotation from G. K. Chesterton does not appear in [*The Illusion of Technique*], it nevertheless is the substance of its message. We live in an age fascinated with a "technology of behavior," and the consequence is that person is treated as object rather than subject. William Barrett's purpose here is to seek the meaning of person in relationship to being in technological civilization.

He posits that freedom is *the* philosophical question today which must be addressed if we are to avoid both a Marxist and Skinnerian conditioning of behavior, which understand person only in a technical or functional sense. It is Professor Barrett's conviction that we can avoid both nihilism and determinism only through understanding person on a far deeper level than mere "technique," a level which verges on the "poetic" and "mystical." Person is, in short, more than technique. There cannot even be technique without freedom since "technique presupposes freedom for its own being." (pp. 129-30)

Professor Barrett concludes from a lengthy discussion of [Ludwig Wittgenstein, Martin Heidegger, William James, and many other] philosophers that an attempt to program or condition human nature logically is futile because nature, while logical and capable of being systematized, is also poetic, mystical, and thus at heart quite *in*determinate. It is precisely the latter side of human nature which makes human beings "free"— free to create, free to dream, and free to commune with "being." These freedoms can never be understood in a purely logical, technical, or political sense. Thus the individual can never be the object of science or the state but must ever be their subject, or that which freely creates logic or politics. (p. 130)

There is a sense in which this book is timeless. Human beings have always struggled to understand the relationship between freedom and determinism. By including the mystical and poetic in human nature, Barrett persuasively argues for freedom. But the book also very much relates to our time in which behaviorists pursue the illusion that human beings can be neatly quantified, codified, and computerized. No, we are more than that and it is in seeking "more" that sometimes we defy the rules of logic and technique, and so discover our freedom.

The book does have two drawbacks. One, it is too long and at times too technical. Better editing would have avoided some rambling in spots. Second, despite Professor Barrett's disclaimer, the book should have dealt explicitly with concrete social issues of our time. Our future is threatened not only by a technical understanding of human nature but also by nuclear weapons and war. Issues like these may even challenge professor Barrett's thesis that *the* fundamental issue which faces us is not freedom or even meaning, but simple survival. Also, perhaps more explicit treatment of "homo religiosus" would strengthen Professor Barrett's argument.

This book is quite useful for professors of philosophy and religion. . . . Pastors and church persons with a philosophical orientation may want to read this book because of its excellent discussion of humankind's search for meaning and freedom in a technological age which, somewhere along the line, has replaced religion as the "new priesthood." It is a difficult but rewarding book and for those who believe that philosophy is still a partner with theology in understanding the human predicament and promise, it is a *sine qua non.* (pp. 130-31)

> *Joseph J. Fahey, in a review of "The Illusion of Technique: A Search for Meaning in a Technological Civilization," in* Theology Today *(© 1980 Theology Today), Vol. XXXVII, No. 1, April, 1980, pp. 129-31.*

HILTON KRAMER

The great interest of William Barrett's new book ["**The Truants**"] is that it takes us inside the lives and the minds of one of [the] pivotal intellectual coteries—the Partisan Review circle as it emerged in the years immediately before and after World War II—and reexamines both its leading personalities and its governing ideas with an unusual degree of intimacy, intelligence and candor. "**The Truants**" is, first of all, an insider's vivid and poignant memoir. It closes, indeed, with its author in tears, and it contains many other pages that, without ever becoming mawkish or self-indulgent, stir the emotions.

The book is exceptionally well written, and it abounds in brilliant portraiture. Particularly stunning are the accounts of Philip Rahv and Delmore Schwartz. Rahv, the critic and editor who was the leading spirit of Partisan Review until his ouster in the 1960's, remains for Mr. Barrett the quintessential example of that now mythical figure—the New York intellectual. Schwartz, the ill-fated poet, short-story writer and critic who introduced Mr. Barrett to the group in the winter of 1937-38, was for many years the author's closest friend. These, certainly, are the dominant characters in the story that is told here, and it is to their memory that "**The Truants**" is dedicated. But the book contains sharp glimpses, too, of Hannah Arendt, William Phillips, Clement Greenberg, Mary McCarthy, Edmund Wilson, Lionel Trilling, Sidney Hook, Paul Goodman and other eminences of the early Partisan Review circle. (pp. 1, 32)

This book is something more than an exercise in personal reminiscence, however. It is also a penetrating analysis of the intellectual life of its period. And because our culture is still beset by so many of the illusions that were spawned and codified in the milieu that Mr. Barrett has set out to describe in this book, "**The Truants**" is very much a text for *our* time as well. The arguments it recounts, the positions it defines, the careers it retraces, the whole literary, artistic and political ethos that is so cogently evoked in its pages—all of this turns out to contain a good deal of the intellectual debris that continues to litter the cultural scene today.

Foremost among the articles of belief upheld by Partisan Review in its heyday was the conviction that it was somehow possible for intellectuals to hold in tandem a steadfast commitment to what Mr. Barrett describes as "the two M's . . . Marxism in politics and Modernism in art," and to do so, moreover, without any sense of contradiction or any fear of their ultimate incompatibility. The immense appeal exerted by Partisan Review—for Mr. Barrett and subsequently for others—lay precisely in this independent and large-minded embrace of both radicalism and the avant-garde, a position that required courage as well as independence in the political climate of the 30's. . . .

[The magazine] foundered when its principal editors—Philip Rahv and William Phillips among them—could no longer ac-

commodate themselves to the Moscow-dominated party line in either politics or culture. It was thus as a dissident Marxist journal that Rahv and Phillips, now joined by Dwight Macdonald, Mary McCarthy, F. W. Dupee and the painter George L. K. Morris, revived Partisan Review in 1937, and made it the leading intellectual magazine of the anti-Stalinist left. . . . [The] founders of the new Partisan Review, as Mr. Barrett writes, "were attacking Stalin and the Soviet Union from the point of view of a purer Marxism, and it was above all the purity of their radicalism that lured me on."

At the same time, he writes, "this radical and avant-garde attitude was not to be confined only to politics; it was to embrace literature and the arts as well." This enlightened cultural program was initiated at a time when the Communist Party and its large liberal following—the so-called fellow travelers then very powerful in the press, in publishing and in certain university circles—were continually upbraiding the avant-garde, often in vicious terms, for its failure to serve the interests of the masses, while the reactionary academic world still looked upon the modern movement in literature and art as little more than a distasteful hoax. "In this situation," Mr. Barrett writes, "it was a bracing challenge to be on the side of the difficult and the rare, and to defend the artist's freedom to be as complex as he wishes within the boundaries of his talent and his medium."

Such, in any case, were the intellectual ideals that launched this coterie of writers and critics, and won them an important following in the years to come.

About the cold-war period Mr. Barrett has much to tell us—much, indeed, that casts an illuminating light on more recent efforts by the intellectual left to ascribe all blame for the cold war to the evil designs of American foreign policy, and to acquit the Soviet Union of all malevolent intent. It is positively chilling, for example, to read the essay called "The 'Liberal' Fifth Column," which Mr. Barrett wrote for the Summer 1946 issue of Partisan Review and which he has now reprinted as an appendix to "**The Truants**," and be made to realize how little has actually changed in the thinking of the American left in the last 36 years.

It was, then, one of the principal missions of Partisan Review in this immediate postwar period to take a strong stand against this widespread misperception of Soviet policy—a policy, after all, that had already sent millions to their deaths and enslaved many millions more—and the magazine upheld this position with a steadfastness that was unusual at the time. Yet there was, all the same, a great flaw in the position that Partisan Review adopted toward Communism and the Soviet Union, and this, too, is one of the central themes explored in Mr. Barrett's book, and the theme that is alluded to in the very title of "**The Truants**." . . .

[In] attempting to speak for a "purer Marxism" than Stalin's, Partisan Review remained theoretically hostile to the values of bourgeois democracy and categorically opposed to the very ethos of American capitalism. The magazine's own concept of an ideal Marxist revolution may have been confused, and indeed something of a chimera. Its commitment in that direction was certainly muted during the early years of the cold war, when the magazine was seeking—and finding—a wider and less ideological readership. But for Rahv, at least, this intellectual strategy turned out to be more a matter of discretion than of hope or belief. Marxism remained for him an unquestioned faith, and the revolutionary ideal—however quiescent at times—was never abandoned. The death of Stalin in 1953 gave it a new luster and impetus, and the radical movement of the 60's a new sense of opportunity and purpose.

There thus occurred what Mr. Barrett speaks of as "a drastic reversal" in Rahv's political stance—his "conversion away from anti-Communism," and his open and increasingly shrill avowal of radical causes. This was truancy indeed, for his re-emergence as a Marxist firebrand came, as it happened, at a time when Rahv's personal fortunes were prospering as they never had in the past. He was appointed to a professorship at Brandeis University and occupied a huge townhouse on Beacon Street in Boston. He took up cooking as a hobby and prided himself on living well. Yet the more he prospered, the more violently did he denounce the system that had brought his success. (p. 32)

The portrait of Philip Rahv strikes me as quite the best thing in Mr. Barrett's book. Written with delicacy, precision and even at times a grim humor, it is not only an important contribution to intellectual history but a literary feat of no small distinction. Rahv was indeed a formidable personality of considerable influence, and Mr. Barrett has now succeeded in making his unusual story a permanent part of our literature.

If the portrait of Delmore Schwartz, fine as it certainly is, does not achieve quite the same distinction, it is only because this story of a shattered talent and a shattered life has already been told by Saul Bellow (in "Humboldt's Gift") and James Atlas (in his biography of the poet) at even greater length. What Mr. Barrett adds, however, is important in two respects. He gives us a very moving account of the vicissitudes of a high-spirited, intellectual friendship that, for him, ended in the scene of madness and tears that closes the book. And he recalls for us the sharp and divisive controversy between Schwartz and Lionel Trilling that defined not only the differences separating two of the most gifted writers to be associated with Partisan Review, but the deeper division that put into question the magazine's abiding role as a champion of modern literature and avant-garde culture.

It was Trilling's belief that the classics of modern literature so beloved by the radicals of Partisan Review could not, in the end, truly be reconciled with their political outlook. (Rahv's late reversal in repudiating the work of Henry James after his early and very persuasive defense of it would certainly bear this out.) Trilling's was not a position that Partisan Review wanted to hear, however, and it earned him the enmity not only of Delmore Schwartz and Philip Rahv but of the whole community of literary and artistic modernists, and the issues raised by this dispute have continued to haunt Trilling's posthumous reputation as a critic to the present day.

Mr. Barrett gives us a marvelous account of these issues in the chapter of **"The Truants"** called **"Beginnings of Conservative Thought"**—a discussion that also contains one of the most intelligent analyses of Trilling's criticism anyone has given us. Trilling, writes Mr. Barrett, was "calling attention to the value of class distinctions for the writer, speaking sympathetically, even when critically, of the middle class, and bringing forward a less audacious and experimental canon of authors to be admired. Where the intellectuals had been preoccupied with figures like Joyce and Proust, or Dostoevski and Kafka, Trilling urged the case of more conventional novelists like E. M. Forster and Jane Austen. . . . All of this was disquieting to the more austerely modernist tastes of the magazine." . . .

It might be true that such writers could not be reconciled to the magazine's politics, but neither, in Mr. Barrett's view,

could Trilling's own critical outlook—despite the value it placed on complexity and flexibility—really come to terms with the depths of their vision. For Mr. Barrett, Trilling remained at heart—despite the fact that he was "ahead of his time" in preparing the way for a more conservative criticism of modern culture—"a thoroughgoing liberal to the end: the cast of his mind was the rational, secular, and non-religious one of classical liberalism." And it is from this perspective that Mr. Barrett accomplishes something very remarkable in his analysis of Trilling's thought. He takes up the critique of the liberal mind that Trilling launched in "The Liberal Imagination" and extends it to Trilling's own writings in that book. In the end, though he parts company with Schwartz's radical views, he nonetheless defends the modern vision, and his own criticism of Trilling's position is, as a result, even more profound than anything Schwartz had attempted.

In this section of **"The Truants,"** the author reminds us that he is not only an invaluable witness to the events and personalities he has memorialized in these memoirs, but one of our best critics as well. . . .

"Follow the zigs and zags of any given intellectual," Mr. Barrett observes at one point in his narrative, "and you may turn out to be reading the fever chart of the next generation." In **"The Truants"** certainly, William Barrett has written a book that not only illuminates the "zigs and zags" of the Partisan Review intellectuals, but a "fever chart" that is essential reading for anyone attempting to understand the art and culture and politics of the present age. (p. 33)

Hilton Kramer, "Partisan Culture, Partisan Politics," in The New York Times Book Review (© *1982 by The New York Times Company; reprinted by permission), February 7, 1982, pp. 1, 32-3.*

SEYMOUR KRIM

[In a sense, *The Truants*] reads like a thoughtful novel—[Barrett] cannot separate *Partisan Review* and its sometimes overbearing contributors from the cultural and historical pressures of the period. As evidence, just when we are thoroughly hooked by his first-rate personality portraits, we see that Barrett is really after a lot bigger game than we had originally expected. . . .

William Barrett now looks back upon [the] bold effort to link together the values of high art and revolution as by and large a self-willed illusion. Although he himself was a Marxist during his days on *Partisan Review,* he finds that he and his fellow editors never once questioned the inherent loss of liberty that would occur in art and thought if their beloved "socialism" ever came into being. They were self-hypnotized utopians "escaping for a while from the harshness of . . . practical reality," hence the title of his book, *The Truants*. . . . More, by searching for "original and sweeping ideas," the *Partisan Review* intellectuals conveniently forgot the number one condition for their own existences: the survival of the United States as "a free nation in a world going increasingly totalitarian."

Thus does William Barrett's loving memoir of the New York radical/intellectual life ultimately turn into a finger-pointing lecture before it is wrapped up. One could never really fault a man as decent and serious as Professor Barrett for coming out of the ideological closet and declaring himself, even though the sternness of his chastising moral tone is sometimes at odds with the warm tolerance that flavors the rest of his book. It is obvious that like other New York thinkers and polemicists of the day who have been through the mill of radicalism, he has come to embrace fundamental American values as a crucial bulwark against a darker future than the intellectual adventurers of the *Partisan Review* era could imagine. Certainly he has earned the right to his pulpit.

But the simple truth is that most readers will be much more enthralled by Barrett's authentic sketches of people and scenes than in his grave, schoolmasterish warnings. History will very likely cross us up again as unexpectedly as it has in the author's own lifetime, and some of his topical rhetoric may soon be left high and dry. What will remain unchanged is his honest, witty, compassionate record of a time and place that can never come again. And for that indelible picture we are all enormously indebted to William Barrett, scrupulous reporter, even more than to William Barrett, critic of failed hopes.

Seymour Krim, "Partisan Review: Legends of the Old Left," in Book World—The Washington Post *(© 1982, The Washington Post), February 28, 1982, p. 5.*

PEARL BELL

[One] cannot help suspecting that *The Truants* was originally conceived on a more modest scale—a memoir in the form of portraits—than what it finally became: a tantalizingly suggestive, but thinly realized attempt to draw, from the exhaustion of Marxism and modernism as they played themselves out in the story of *Partisan Review,* a far-reaching polemical lesson about the imperative need for a new moral and religious consciousness in our time. The issues he raises are indisputably important, but in this anecdotal context of recollection Barrett fails to do them justice.

There remains a nagging question: what can these memories of the *Partisan Review* intellectuals mean to those who were never part of that passionate, noisy, incestuous little world? It was, Barrett remembers, "as closed and inbred as a conventicle of monks," and elsewhere, in an ethnically more exact image, he speaks of the ghetto-like mentality of Rahv & Co., who rarely ventured above 14th Street and regarded midtown Manhattan as "an alien territory, the haunt of the middlebrows and philistines of the cultural world." Certainly the political and literary issues that obsessed these nonstop talkers and schemers, while they undoubtedly have some relevance to the present day, are no longer so clear-cut as they seemed thirty years ago. Neither of *PR*'s incompatible fealties—to Marxism in politics and to modernism in art—has the same holy authority for intellectuals today, though neither doctrine has by any means withered away. Among those survivors of the monkish conventicle like Barrett himself, the will to believe has for excellent reasons moved in a very different direction from the Marxist-modernist certainties, taking a conservative and vaguely religious form that is anathema to those radical pieties still lingering in American culture. Those young intellectuals who have any curiosity about the political battles of the mid-century will most likely be repelled by the conservative conclusions Barrett reaches, and it hardly needs saying that the modernist

exhilarations of an earlier era have long since subsided, the daring experiments of, say, *Ulysses* and *The Waste Land* being now thoroughly absorbed into the classical canon. . . .

The plot is gripping, for Barrett tells the story with great vividness, but what about the actors—what interest do they hold for those who could never have known them? Neither Philip Rahv nor Delmore Schwartz left behind a large and significant body of work, and though Barrett loyally—and rightly—singles out those few poems and stories such as "In Dreams Begin Responsibilities," that will, he thinks, perdure, he must finally acknowledge that, given such extraordinary gifts, Delmore Schwartz's literary career must be judged "a human failure." Though a considerable number of Rahv's critical essays are by no means negligible, as a whole his work, too, is disappointingly fragmentary, the major book on Dostoevsky still unfinished when he died. It is possible to foresee a time when the stubbornly elusive personality of Philip Rahv, hunted like a fox in countless memoirs, will overwhelm whatever interest remains in his achievement as a critic. . . .

To those readers too young to have known the *PR* circle personally, the appeal of *The Truants* may well be that of a period piece exceptionally rich in lively gossip and wisecracks. As we know from all the Bloomsbury volumes, the literary memoir can provide the writer with too *blanche* a *carte* for settling scores best left buried in the dust of the past. Unfortunately William Barrett has not resisted this temptation strongly enough, though he disingenuously claims at one point that he sought to protect the living, "who are still struggling to cope with things, and who are easily upset by any disobliging remark." Having forgotten absolutely nothing, Barrett is not above using the rattlesnake wit of, among others, the young Mary McCarthy to denigrate a few living monuments along with the dead. Philip Rahv rationalized his loose and malicious tongue as "analytic exuberance," which Delmore Schwartz translated as "Philip's euphemism for sticking a knife in your back," and some of that "exuberance" clings to Barrett's memoir. With all the admiration he expresses for Lionel Trilling, he cannot suppress a gratuitous flick of malice in equating Trilling with Walter Lippmann as a Jew "who eschewed religious attachment lest it exclude him from the American mainstream." Barrett is too intelligent not to realize that this comparison is unjust and far from the truth.

The world of the New York Jewish intelligentsia was, as Barrett has skillfully demonstrated, manically complex and as manically diverse as the different personalities that composed it. There is the risk, which all generalizations run, of overriding those idiosyncratic differences that make any intellectual milieu distinctive. Only occasionally does Barrett sound like Lady Jean Campbell, an ex-wife of Norman Mailer, who in a moment of exquisite delirium once told the Catholic novelist Wilfrid Sheed, "All you Jewish intellectuals are alike." But then, Barrett also knows, and better than most, that some are less alike than others. (p. 35)

Pearl Bell, "The Meaning of PR," in The New Republic *(reprinted by permission of* The New Republic; © 1982 The New Republic, Inc.), Vol. 186, No. 11, March 17, 1982, pp. 32-5.*

John (Simmons) Barth

1930-

American novelist, short story writer, and essayist.

Barth is a major practitioner of the postmodern literary movement known as metafiction. Many of his works may be seen as studies of how fiction is created and how the reader and the text interact. Barth's approach to writing derives from his belief that the traditional novel is unsatisfactory. In his essay "The Literature of Exhaustion" (1967), published in *The Atlantic Monthly*, he describes the new writer as one who "confronts an intellectual dead end and employs it against itself to accomplish new work."

In his search for new fictional modes, Barth utilizes and parodies traditional forms such as the epic and the epistolary novel. Although the structure of his work varies, there are several common elements: the "protean fictionalizers" or narrators with whom Barth identifies; the black humor, often bawdily overstated; the negative diagnosis of the plight of modern man; the blurring of past and present; and the use of sex as a symbol of human vitality. The settings of Barth's novels range from seventeenth-century Maryland in *The Sot-Weed Factor* (1960), to a modern-day university in *Giles Goat Boy or, the Revised New Syllabus* (1966). His main consideration always is how individuals can learn to deal with reality.

Experimentation characterizes all of Barth's work, including his collections of short fiction. Only three of the stories in *Lost in the Funhouse* (1968) are traditional in form; in the others Barth seeks alternatives to conventional writing and the stories become fantastic creations continually changing shape. In the three novellas of *Chimera* (1972), Barth makes new use of Arabic, Greek, and Roman mythology to show that myth permeates everyday life.

In his recent novels, *Letters* (1979) and *Sabbatical* (1982), Barth again utilizes imaginative techniques. *Letters* incorporates the main characters from his previous works, adding only one new one who becomes the point where the narrative threads meet. In *Sabbatical* Barth gives his two main characters more attention and illumination than he has since his early works. Here the metafictional qualities of his work are most apparent, for his two main characters are in the process of writing the book which the reader is reading.

Throughout his career, critics have been divided in their estimations of Barth. While some feel he is pretentious, others praise his verbal agility and his courage to experiment with new forms.

(See also *CLC*, Vols. 1, 2, 3, 5, 7, 9, 10, 14; *Contemporary Authors*, Vols. 1-4, rev. ed.; *Contemporary Authors New Revision Series*, Vol. 5; and *Dictionary of Literary Biography*, Vol. 2.)

CHARLES TRUEHEART

Whether or not we are ever so rewarded, most of us believe we deserve a sabbatical, a time outside the scheme of our lives to rest and ruminate, to reckon how far we have come and, if we're lucky, to recognize where we must go. That's the theory,

© Helen Marcus 1981

anyway. It is also the earnest hope of Fenwick Scott Key Turner, 50, and Susan Rachel Allan Seckler, 35, in their seventh year of marriage and in John Barth's seventh work of fiction [*Sabbatical*], as they cut loose on a year's cruise from their native Chesapeake Bay to the Yucatan and the West Indies and home again.

These two are no idle dreamers, for whom forced indolence would be unnecessary. Fenn, as he's called, is a career CIA officer some years lapsed; in the time since his retirement from active duty he has tried to make peace with himself, if not with the agency, by publishing a devastating exposé of its clandestine services division, one of several such tell-alls to appear in the 1970s. Now he is contemplating his next move. A novel? A professorship? An eternity of sailing?

So too is Susan contemplating her future. She teaches English at Washington College in Chestertown, Maryland, and carries with her an offer to join the faculty of Swarthmore at sabbatical's end. She also carries a disconcerting urge to bear children before her biological clock runs out. Such are the competing possibilities Fenn and Susan entertain at sea. . . .

Sabbatical purports to be their running notes, recorded during the last weeks of spring, 1980, as their 33-foot sailboat *Pokey* tacks and reaches its way from the mouth of the Chesapeake Bay, island by island, toward home. The exact location and

25

nature of "home," to be sure, is one of those vexing uncertainties the narrative entertains.

Although the novel is no retrogression, stylistically or thematically, for Barth, it does respect those rudiments of storytelling Barth has been willing to sacrifice of late. He attends to characters and the illumination of their drama more scrupulously and straightforwardly than in anything he has written since his first pair of novels, *The Floating Opera* and *The End of the Road.* As a consequence, *Sabbatical* lodges itself firmly in our imaginations and memories—and it is a pleasure to read besides.

A significant pleasure is the one the lovers share. Life aboard *Pokey* is heaven on . . . well, not even on earth. . . .

Morning swims in secluded coves and evening constitutionals on forgotten islets; lunches of grilled lamb chops, cheese, grapes, and cold Saint-Estèphe followed by languid lovemaking and the separate pleasures of *The New York Review of Books* (for her) and *The Tempest* (for him, for the hundredth time). It is a wonder their predicament has any urgency at all; it is a delicate accomplishment of Barth's fine novel that it does. (p. 4)

Those who have come to know Barth through his most recent novels should rest assured. Time has not healed his tic of overweening cleverness or his predilection for authorly commentaries on the story at hand. Because this is a record of the couple's sea journey, it is also a record of its own composition. Fenn and Susan argue incessantly about the proper way to tell the story, dispute the timing or pertinence of flashbacks, and remind one another of the literary traditions into which their narrative falls. The novel is littered with footnotes. Reality and illusion, of course, are forever at issue.

Yet the self-consciousness of the sabbatical exercise somehow is congenial to this sort of playfulness. Fenn and Susan have a curious but utterly convincing respect for the story they are making together, as if they had given it a life and will of its own. Indeed, they seem to look to its independent momentum for guidance in the great decisions they must make.

Fenn's career in intelligence is not merely a curiosity of his background. The specter of espionage lurks at every turn in their cruise. Fenn's twin brother Manfred was also an agency operative until he drowned in the Chesapeake Bay from a fall— or a push—from the selfsame *Pokey.* The resemblance to the real-life death of the CIA's John Paisley under circumstances of like mystery is not merely oblique here; the Paisley saga is laid out in nearly 20 pages of news accounts drawn verbatim from back issues of *The Sun* in Baltimore.

Barth's fascination with this sort of thing is logical enough. Author and agency share a fondness for elaborate deceptions, and like to muddle conspiracy and coincidence. Such intellectual sport may be said to represent the Washington component of this tale of two cities; the Baltimore component, as you might guess, is straight from the heart—and more knowing and affecting by far.

Susan's mother Carmen is an eccentric restaurateur in the Fells Point section of that city, and the mistress of a household circus. (pp. 4, 12)

Sabbatical, come to think of it, is a long meditation on family, from Carmen's delightful theories about sperms and eggs (that they are our real children, and the fruits of *their* union actually our grandchildren) to Fenwick's brainstorms about creation and

procreation to Susan's outbursts about affairs and abortions— and motherhood. . . .

Has Barth gone all soft and gooey on us after all this time? I think not. Like his characters, he is coming home to primordial things, and understanding them in new ways. Sixteen years ago he published an extraordinary story called **"Night-Sea Journey."** It is narrated by a sperm—"tale-bearer of a generation"—as it thrashes its way to an inexorable and holy union with an egg, from which will come "some unimaginable embodiment of myself." *Sabbatical* is a full-length reprise of that story, an examination of mortality and human purpose in the face of humble and ambiguous choices. It wonders aloud whether one's pride and joy in life need be one's flesh and blood, whether being a bearer of tales isn't embodiment enough. (p. 12)

> *Charles Trueheart, "John Barth: Sailing Inner Waters," in* Book World—The Washington Post *(© 1982, The Washington Post), May 23, 1982, pp. 4, 12.*

JAMES WOLCOTT

After the slow-grinding, interlocking minutiae of *Letters,* John Barth may have thought that his readers deserved a breather, and he's given them one: *Sabbatical.* Set largely on a sailboat nosing along the chops of the Chesapeake Bay, *Sabbatical* is a chummily facetious scribble about a former CIA officer and his sweetie and all the weird, wacky things that happen to them "twixt stern and starboard." Like other Barth novels, this one ladles on the Maryland lore: the tweeting couple is named Fenwick Scott Key Turner and Susan Seckler (nicknamed "Black-Eyed Susan," after the Maryland state flower), and their sailboat is dubbed *Pokey,* in honor of those two Baltimore legends Francis Scott Key and Edgar Allan Poe. A comical twosome, Fenwick and Susie trade teasing wisecracks like a nautical Sonny and Cher, announcing flashbacks and flashforwards, unfurling digressive reminiscences, bringing chapters to a close as if cutting to a commercial. (p. 16)

As their voices crisscross on the page, the novel seems to be broadcasting in stereo, with static crackling from each speaker. The static is set off by the noisy busyness of Barth's language: the clever-boots names (Eastwood Ho, Edgar Allan Ho), the sudden bursts of alliteration ("bald, brown, bearded, barrelchested" is how Barth describes Fenwick, while Susan is "sunburnt, sharp, and shapely"), the clickety-clack interior rhymes of—well, this: "Fenwick steadies the tiller in the crack of his ass and trims the starboard genoa sheet for the new tack." Barth also busies up his text with footnotes, mock headlines, and clippings about the CIA scissored from the Baltimore *Sun.*

For all its snappy patter and kissy-poo antics, however, *Sabbatical* soon proves to be a chirruping ode to nothingness. . . . As in the story **"Night-Sea Journey,"** . . . the ruling conceit of this novel of the upward swim of sperm toward ovum, a teeming migration beset with strife. . . . So the thinning-out of sperm becomes a metaphor for the absurd random chanciness and epic waste of life itself, with an added peril tossed in: abortion. . . . "Stories can abort, too," Susan tells Fenn. "Plenty are stillborn; most that aren't die young. And of the few that survive, most do just barely." Slain fetuses, decimated sperm— creation in *Sabbatical* is one long trail of casualties and squelched possibilities.

Sex continues to exact a punishing toll long after all that prepartum turmoil. Pages of squirming detail are devoted to the mutilations of Susan's twin sister Miriam, who one Sunday afternoon in 1968 is gang-raped by a pack of motorcyclists. . . . [Only] to be tortured again by a "rescuer" who peppers her body with cigarette burns and eventually leaves her kneeling in the dirt, a beer bottle sticking out of her assaulted bottom. Staggering out of the woods, reeking of sweat, blood, and dried urine, Miriam is raped *again* by a burly dude in a pickup trick.

When Fenwick makes unconvincing clucking noises of concern and tries to subdue Susan's too-graphic account, saying, "The details are just dreadfulness . . . ," she disagrees: "Rape and Torture and Terror are just words; the details are what's real." But the details too are mere words, and the accumulation of sadistic flourishes only serves to distance us from the experience, to turn it into a virtuoso literary exhibition—a novelistic form of knife-juggling. Whether it's a horse being subjected to squealing anguish in *Virginie* or a woman running a rapist gauntlet in *Sabbatical,* the horror seems to derive less from life than from the author's desire to furnish his novel with showy scenes of blood and humiliation. The horror is so clumsily and shamelessly stage-managed that you end up feeling not so much pity or terror for the victims (who are simply used as straw dogs), as a mild lurch of disgust at the authors for misapplying their talent so. They give in to sadism dutifully, like apprentice floggers. Perhaps it's fussily old-fashioned of me, but I prefer humming sensations to deadened nerves, pleasure and play to defilement, firm footing to these drifting, sealed-off islands of nothingness. Sade is a master only for those intellectualized out of their wits.

But it would be a mistake to leave the impression that what's wrong with these novels is that they defame the dignity of life (whatever that is) or violate John Gardner's notions of what constitutes moral fiction. Reviewing *The Auroras of Autumn* by Wallace Stevens, Randall Jarrell praised Stevens's intelligence and cool mastery but lamented that "it would take more than these to bring to life so abstract, so monotonous, so overwhelmingly *characteristic* a book." What's sapping about these books is that they too are so *characteristic*. Once again John Hawkes has given us a novel loaded with soiled sex, acres of a damp rot, and bird and flower imagery. . . . Once again John Barth has tricked up a novel which mimics the stratagems that go into the tricking-up of a novel. (pp. 16-17)

James Wolcott, "Straw Dogs," in The New York Review of Books *(reprinted with permission from* The New York Review of Books; *copyright © 1982 Nyrev, Inc.),* Vol. XXIX, No. 10, June 10, 1982, pp. 14, 16-17.*

MICHAEL WOOD

"We'll have to stick to the channel," John Barth wrote in his first novel, **"The Floating Opera,"** and let the creeks and coves go by." His new work [**"Sabbatical"**] explores all the creeks and coves it can, both literally and figuratively. It drifts with what one of its characters calls the narrative tide, it goes back, goes forward, stands still. It begins with a storm at sea, describes an uncanny island not to be found on any chart and records the surfacing of a hefty sea monster in Chesapeake Bay. "Have we sailed out of James Michener," the narrator wonders, "into Jules Verne?"

The metaphors, as Barth said of his earlier use of them, are not gratuitous, and that's putting it mildly. "If life is like a voyage," we read in **"Sabbatical,"** "a voyage may be like

life." "Not the least of sailing's pleasures, in our opinion, is that it refreshes, by literalizing them, many common figures of speech: one is forever and in fact making things shipshape from stem to stern, casting off, getting under way. . . ." Barth's list lumbers on ("making headway, giving oneself leeway"), tilting a promising thought toward pedantry. The implication is that symbol and reality, unlike broken Humpty Dumpty, can be put together again. In practice, reality comes off handsomely—the boat, the bay, the weather, clothes, flesh, language, the looks and gestures of people—while the symbols clank like loosely stowed gear.

"Sabbatical" recounts the end of a voyage made by Susan Seckler, a literary academic who is wondering whether to return to teaching and/or have a child, and Fenwick Turner, her husband, a former C.I.A. man who has written, in the manner of Philip Agee, a scathing book about the Agency—his heart divided, as he says, between patriotism and dismay. (pp. 1, 24)

[The] story fills up with the rough contemporary world. The West sinks into the sun, as Susan puts it. Does the Company have a new drug that can induce utterly convincing heart attacks? Fenwick has had two episodes; his friend and former colleague dies of one in the course of the book. Calm conversations hide secrets; it becomes increasingly difficult to tell a promise from a threat. Susan and Fenwick know their sabbatical is over, yet are grateful for the breathing space. They are conscious of their luck, their privilege: "We are reasonably healthy, reasonably successful, reasonably well off . . . unpersecuted, unoppressed, and still in love after seven years of marriage: the favored of the earth."

Is this enough? Perhaps nothing is enough—the suggestion runs through Barth's fiction from its beginnings. But Susan and Fenwick survive—she an abortion and he his fear of losing her—and make their anxious homecoming into a story, and their story into a shelter. It is this story we read, with Susan and Fenwick telling it and talking to us about it—about the story and about making the story. The author, far from being the demiurge of this world, is *their* puppet. . . . Mostly Susan and Fenwick speak as *we* ("My hat is off to us. Well done, us").

This sounds elaborate (it is elaborate), but it reads easily enough and persuasively makes the story seem to belong to its inhabitants. Fenwick's and Susan's energetic worrying about each other and the significance of things is attractive, and the book obviously represents the sort of spilling over of personal fact into fiction that Barth spoke of in **"Letters":** "What's involved here strikes me less as autobiography than as a muddling of the distinction between art and life."

But there is a flatness in the book that these likable characters cannot redeem. Partly this is the result of the heavy-handedness that is felt everywhere. "That storm blew up like a sawed-off simile," Fenwick says. Mock solemnity keeps turning into the real thing: "To Susan's mind, it is appropriate that, in a manner of speaking, we are involved in a nighttime voyage, one common feature of wandering-hero myths." . . . [The] book's gravest pretension . . . is to surround the literal voyage with homilies about the stream of life and the sea of the womb ("Sperm swim up; ova float down"), about forks in the river and shoals in a charted course ("To go forward, we must go back"). "The road is better than the inn," Fenwick thinks, switching his imagery to land; Susan says to her mother, "Life is too strange, Ma!" Platitude upon platitude. The problem is not that Barth fails to deliver grander meanings but that he looks so hard for them, so restlessly tries to convert a modest and engaging trip into a wind-filled portent. (pp. 24-5)

Michael Wood, "A Metaphoric Novel of the Sea,"
in The New York Times Book Review (© *1982 by*
The New York Times Company; reprinted by per-
mission), June 20, 1982, pp. 1, 24-5.

LORNA SAGE

With *Sabbatical* John Barth confirms that he has joined the ranks of the Old Poops. A useful category this, invented by Kurt Vonnegut for purposes of self-description. OPs are writers who once upon a time were prodigally talented, funny and full of bright and savage ideas, but have now "mellowed" into premature anecdotage; cuddly, avuncular, sermonizing old buffers, whose main text is how, once upon a time . . . etc, since of course OPs are nothing if not self-aware. Self-aware-ness was one of the tricks that made their writing so exciting in the 1960s, and now it provides them with a kind of narrative afterlife, "on in death like hair and fingernails" as Barth wrote less than ten years ago in *Chimera,* his last book before the onset of OP-hood. OPs have not become conservative exactly, but they're into conservation; in fact their central preoccupation is survival, simply going on (and on).

The cold war ethos OPs helped to dissipate in their early, euphoric period of fictive gamesmanship now once again dominates the mental weather. Our hero in *Sabbatical,* one Fenwick Scott Key Turner, is an ex-CIA man turned aspiring writer, resignedly aware that the Company's account of so-called reality, which had seemed shattered into a thousand and one quite different stories, is well on the way to reassembling itself. . . . Writing becomes a variety of salvage operation—not, this time, as in Barth's last tome, *Letters,* a matter of resurrecting all one's old characters and themes and lining them up to be counted, but a smaller scale enterprise, a case of cordoning off a modest corner where the minimal imaginative properties (a Muse, a Mythical Monster) can live.

The official story, as it were, belongs to the CIA. You fit your narrative in the gaps and interstices, and round the edges. So middle-aged Fenn and his newish second wife Susan are discovered, when the book opens, returning from a nine month sabbatical cruise in their sailing yacht Pokey to home waters in the Chesapeake Bay, and looking around for ways of avoiding mainland America, staying metaphorically afloat and offshore.

The sea voyage motif, as Fenn and Susan (who is a professor of Am Lit), are very well aware, is the oldest one in the book, and that is its point. At times of stress it's best, goes the argument, to retreat to the fundamental formulae and reenact the mythic commonplaces. If the metaphors creak a bit and the story line seems a little slack, so much the better; there's something reassuring about being at the mercy of the old pattern, the narrative winds and tides. Why not return to innocence? . . .

Innocence is hard to come by. All very well for Fenn to anti-theorize the life of the imagination—"realism is your keel and ballast of your effing Ship of Story and a good plot is your mast and sails. But magic is your wind"; however, it's not possible to remain out of sight of land. And as soon as you disembark the old Companyspeak starts doing very unrefreshing things to your figures of speech.

Take "cruise", for a start. Or much more sinister, "episode". This artless narratological ploy takes on a whole range of tangled, threatening meanings: for example, the cardiac "episode" or mini heart attack that sent Fenn off on his sabbatical in the first place, and that may, just may, reflect "the Company's rumoured new cardiac arrest capability", since they were naturally not too pleased with Fenn's first venture into the world of letters, a book exposing a small part of their grubby and multifarious dealings. All this we gather by way of "episode". And as the novel gets under way and starts to tack back and forth, more and more terrible and tacky and paranoid possibilities materialize. "Aspiration", as Susan will demonstrate, is a brisk technique for abortion.

The plot thickens alarmingly as we enter "the world of information, disinformation, even superdisinformed supercoded disinformation". Both Susan and Fenn turn out to be twins. . . . In short (in long, in truth, it's much more complicated) Fenn and Susan are intimately twinned with Right and Left America.

Indeed, since Fenn claims to be descended from the man who wrote "The Star Spangled Banner" (F. S. Key) and Susan, despite or because of being Jewish, inherits a family tradition that she is distantly related to Edgar Allan Poe (hence their boat's name, Pokey) they are obviously doomed to take on board (ho ho) the American Experience. And although all the twins business may sound reminiscent of the pre-OP John Barth, the epic-mocker of *The Sot-Weed Factor,* in fact it is presented in an unmagical fashion as a tired conundrum, a device for mooring our hero and heroine, against their will, to a past and threatening them with a future.

The more we learn about their family and Company connections the more we realize why they are so anxious to stay at sea or, as Fenn likes to put it, "in medias fucking res". . . . A trip through a maze of supercoded disinformation only serves to establish that in the world scripted by the Company no "story" is ever happily resolved, or even resolved at all. To survive imaginatively, creatively, it is necessary to refuse their rotten intrigues: "Reality is wonderful . . . Dreadful . . . What it is. But realism is a fucking bore." Thus Fenn will accept his cardiac "episode" as a foretaste of death, but not, for now, part of his story. And Susan will abort the child she has conceived on their cruise because the fiction she and Fenn exist in and on is too marginal to support three-D offspring. . . .

So Fenn becomes a Writer, Susan his Muse/Reader. This way they will cheat time for a while longer—"There will be sex and supper, storms and sleep; with luck there will be some years of loving work and play—and then the end, the end unspeakable." Voluntary sterility, stories about stories about, is *it:* "The doing and the telling, our writing and our loving—they're twins. That's our story."

Procreation (look at Plato) is the literal-minded version of the marriage of true minds. When Susan aborts her foetus she fertilizes Fenn, who promptly conjures up in the waters of the bay a bona fide mythical monster to stand in for the children of the flesh. Not, it has to be said, a very convincing monster . . . but that, we are meant to understand, is hardly the point. For the creative life Barth has in mind is not—he's frank about it—particularly vivid, or inventive, or magical; more a matter of talking about writing and writing about talking, a kind of continuous Creative Writing seminar (Muse and Prof), in which all you do is play with your possibilities.

It is this tone that makes *Sabbatical* a quintessentially Old Poop product. Prof Susan, who succumbs surely too readily to the suggestion that she's somehow creating Literature by reading it nicely and screwing a would-be writer, is allowed to point out that "stories can abort too. Plenty are stillborn; most die young." But this spooky thought drowns in the narrative sea with barely a plop. So insistent is the propaganda about not rocking the boat that we seem blackmailed into accepting any hint of fictional activity as involving the whole corpus of Literature. Whereas most of the time we are responding to something less grand—vague echoes of earlier Barthian motifs, for example. One is prompted, indeed (if one can contrive to slip out from under the insidious authorial ''we'') to the thought that his early black comedies (**The Floating Opera, The End of the Road**) were much more inspiriting and much better written than this post-OP, valetudinarian, chatty stuff. Also, to the realization that the more reverently he talks about the pleasures of the text, the more trivial they seem. Is the Ship of Story really such a fragile vessel? Surely not. It is characteristic of Poopedness to insinuate (cheerfully, in the manner of a good old boy who's faced up to the worst) that tiredness is universal, and that coming clean about it is all there's left to do. Which is not to say that **Sabbatical** is merely dull or depressing. OPs may be shadows of their former selves, but then their former selves were quite something. Which in its turn is of course one of the most infuriating things about them.

Lorna Sage, ''Getting Pooped Aboard the Ship of Story,'' in The Times Literary Supplement (© *Times Newspapers Ltd. (London) 1982; reproduced from* The Times Literary Supplement *by permission), No. 4138, July 23, 1982, p. 781.*

CHARLOTTE RENNER

Asked by the editors of the *New York Times Book Review* . . . to explain how he became a writer, John Barth gave a surprising answer. "It is my fate and equally my sister's to have been born opposite-sex twins, between whom everything went without saying." But "after circumstances and physical maturation" separated him from his sister, Barth was forced to sail belatedly into society on the changeable winds of language, "talking to the Others, talking to oneself."

Coming from a student or critic, that sort of analysis would undoubtedly seem far-fetched, yet it works as the key to Barth's latest novel, *Sabbatical: A Romance*. There, Fenwick Turner, the 50-year-old narrator, himself a twin, preaches to his 32-year-old wife, Susan, another narrator, also a twin, that "we literal twins . . . are each of us the fallen moiety of a once-seamless whole . . . and our habit of wholeness ought to make us ideal partners, especially for another twin . . . particularly if our original half falls by the way."

Barth's novel seems deliberately—perhaps too deliberately—built on this psycho-philosophical foundation. As if to prove Fenn's theory, Barth obligingly ensures that Susan's twin sister and Fenn's twin brother do "fall by the way"; the former into drugs and decadence, the latter, fatally, into Chesapeake Bay. This leaves a motley cast of relatives who make brief comic entrances and exits as [Fenwick and Susan] . . . slowly return to Maryland from a nine-month sabbatical cruise around the Caribbean. . . .

Barth's principal sub-plot is an informal inquiry by the two narrators into the art of novel-writing. As narrators whose conversations are transcribed, Susie and Fenn do not claim to make literary news; they are sailing in the wake of Boccaccio, Chaucer, Conrad, Faulkner. What does distinguish Barth's

technique from the strategies of earlier authors is that, unlike most narrators who talk or write to each other, Susie and Fenn normally share a single point of view on a single set of events. Why, then, need their voices be plural at all? Moreover, since they recognize without much debate their literary limitations, those limitations sometimes weaken the novel itself. Temporarily losing his nautical and narrative way at one point, ''Fenn is able to shrug and declare that we set our story's ideal course and then sail the best one we can, correcting and improving from occasional fixes in our actual position.''

Life, in other words, can throw art off course. But we know that Barth is doing the steering anyway. Despite all the double talk about doubles talking, isn't this book finally and exclusively Fenwick's attempt to write ''for the Others'' a fictional autobiography that will stand in place of the child Susan considers having, and thereby immortalize their romance? If so, then Susan and the reader may feel, in the end, doubly duped.

Charlotte Renner, in a review of ''Sabbatical: A Romance,'' in Boston Review (*copyright © 1982 by Boston Critic, Inc.), Vol. VII, No. 4, August, 1982, p. 28.*

ROBERT TAUBMAN

'There was a story that began—' begins *Sabbatical,* and the story is then interrupted for two nights and a day by a storm at sea, itself interrupted by a dialogue on Aristotle's distinction between *lexis* and *melos*. Like most Post-Modernist fantasies, *Sabbatical* takes a lot of unpacking. But this is John Barth in a holiday mood, and a virtuoso display of techniques brought together from different kinds of novel is here frankly offered for enjoyment. One of its methods is purely realistic: it is full of information, for instance, about sailing in the Chesapeake Bay. . . . *Sabbatical* is as devotedly a novel about sailing as *The Riddle of the Sands;* and like that rather staid classic it uses a sailing trip to get its crew involved in a real-life mystery story. Where Erskine Childers was writing about the Kaiser's invasion plans, Barth is writing about the CIA. An island not on the charts, a shot in the morning mist, deaths and disappearances occur, to a running commentary of texts and footnotes documenting CIA practices. And then there's realism of a more sociological cast, in a trip ashore to Susan's family at Fells Point, Baltimore. The period is almost exactly that of John Updike's last Rabbit novel, and one recognises the same obsession with the placing of America at a moment in time—the stuff in the shops, the news items, the current stresses of family life, the curious national mood of confidence combined with irony, shame and foreboding.

But this novel is capacious. A legendary sea-monster appears, looking no more out of place than the one in *Phèdre*. Fenwick and Susan—he an aspiring writer, she a professor of classic American literature—have literary imaginations; and symbolism out of Poe and erudition about *luc-bát* couplets in Vietnamese oral poetry help to feed the fantasy. . . . When not fully employed in sailing the boat, they have weird dreams in common, which include flashbacks and flashes forward. Or again, at the same healthy level as the sailing, this is also a love story: a shipboard romance after seven years of marriage. . . . Realism does its job, so that when they conclude that their story has their love in it, this is convincing. A happy love story is a rare event in the Post-Modernist novel.

Playing like this with mixed modes of fiction tends to foreground, as they say, the author. Barth sidesteps by engaging

Fenwick and Susan as supposed authors, as if to divert suspicion of too much authorial cleverness. Even so, the technical aplomb, the stylishness of the cutting between one mode and another, do have the effect of focusing the attention on a game of skill, and of distancing the reader from what isn't altogether play in the book. How truthful is it, for instance, about the United States. The sociological observation and the documentary evidence about the CIA make use of plenty of real facts: but all they can tell us, in their context here, is that the ostensibly real world is even more fantastic than sea-monsters and the novel's other mysteries. Susan and Fenwick themselves have a broad suspicion that 'we have been, in the main, indulging ourselves, amusing ourselves,' and even that 'our years together, precious as they've been to both of us, are themselves a kind of playing: not finally serious . . .' It shows in the kind of playing which is the story they make of their lives. And this becomes a moral question when the novel touches directly on real horror, as it does in the episode of Susan's sister's rape—which the subtitle calls 'The Story of Miriam's *Other* Rapes' ('Mim's *other* rapes! Jesus, Susan!'). This is as full and particular as realism demands, and it sickens Susan, telling it. But for the reader it is horror distanced into fantasy, even into a kind of black comedy. So was the horror of the Dresden bombing in *Slaughterhouse Five;* perhaps there is no other way of dealing with maximum horror. But here, in a mainly sunny and engaging book, one comes up against a limitation. The note of fantasy looks like an evasion. If the scene belongs perfectly to the tone of the book, that is because the book guards itself against being taken too seriously.

> *Robert Taubman, "Playing" (appears here by permission of the* London Review of Books *and the author), in* London Review of Books, *August 5 to August 18, 1982, p. 19.**

DOUG BOLLING

In the no man's land of contemporary fiction, Barth has always been a willing occupier of the trenches, a writer concerned both to advance and defend, and this posture has given us works both of great interest and unevenness. His newest, *Sabbatical,* continues the pattern of engagement and stands as a worthy effort, if a flawed one. As with the earlier novels so with this one: the false starts and rough edges in *Sabbatical* derive not at all from a lack of skill but rather from the difficulties inherent in juggling diverse rhythms and mixed modes. Some of the features of the new novel remind one of other postmodern writing and also of the asymmetries and unresolved tensions in mannerist art as it sought to move out of the high Renaissance. *Sabbatical* explores anew Barth's long-standing interest in the way in which writer, text and reader interact, in how these swirling, buzzing energies achieve a momentary stability in a work of fiction. And not unexpectedly, the new novel probes certain genre considerations as well. It is said to be a "Romance" and part of the intellectual game of the work lies in the reader's recognition of how it modifies, negates and parodies this genre. *Sabbatical* is about a number of matters, and one of these is John Barth on Northrop Frye. Peace.

At plot level the work narrates the adventures of its principals, Fenwick Scott Key Turner and wife Susan Rachel Allan Seckler, as they return from a nine month cruise to the Caribbean aboard their motorized sailboat. The two took their voyage in order to take stock of themselves and life, but they return home to find that some important questions remain unanswered. Reality, Barth pleasantly reminds us, eludes definition just as

"real" fictional characters escape the constraints and abstractions of literary typology. In their journey up Chesapeake Bay to Baltimore and home port aboard the *Pokey,* Fenn and Susan gradually realize that "homecoming" is more a beginning than an ending. Enroute they encounter an uncharted island, a "sea monster," and—more crucially—themselves in their desolation, dreams and love. In the process the reader learns a good deal about the respective families—the mysteries, aspirations and tragedies in the lives of figures such as Manfred, Miriam, Carmen, Dumitru and others—and also about the ravaged, brutal, sterile nature of contemporary America. CIA intrigues (Fenn is a former member), gang rapes, mysterious disappearances and the moral complexities of abortion (Susan's) emerge as manifestations of our waste land, reminders that leviathan swims inscrutably onward. Clearly the "fresh, green breast of the new world" remains as elusive in *Sabbatical* as it was in *Gatsby,* but there is a compensation in Barth's novel. Unlike Daisy Buchanan and Jay Gatsby, Fenn and Susan manage to sustain a loving, sexually satisfying and intellectually vibrant relationship. Their "romance" (perhaps the real meaning of the subtitle) endures because of the pair's sense of humor, mutual forbearance and maturity—and of course because John Barth adds to these virtues the *mana* of art. Susan and Fenwick shape their story as they sail the waters of Chesapeake Bay and Americana; a significant part of their virtu flows from the fact that they are "makers" as well as sufferers.

Sabbatical is a "Romance," then, in the sense that it is an imitation of Romance, mythic and archetypal flights and perchings complete with a hero and heroine embarked on the necessary quest. At this level—perhaps loosely seen as the "allegorical" one—Susan and Fenn are tokens or types acting out their teleological imperatives. But there is more. For *Sabbatical* is also a novel in which "novelistic" energies assert themselves against the enervation and abstraction of the high mimetic. Fenn and Susan become "real" folk struggling with the unpredictability, messiness and absurdity of a culture deeply out of touch with itself—but still worth redemption. Ironically, it is at this level that the novel begins to lose the vigor it deserves but doesn't quite earn. For all their admirable qualities and the skillful orchestration of their eminently credible navigation of the "real" waters of the Bay, the two main characters tell us more about themselves than we finally want to know and the result is cloying. The heavy foregrounding of Susan and Fenwick is deliberate, a central strategy in the work's aesthetic, but it too often leads to a surfeit rather than to a vital accommodation. *Sabbatical* simply bogs down at times in cumbersome commentary and flat, somewhat coy, somewhat breezy characterization.

Not surprisingly to readers of Barth's earlier fictions, *Sabbatical* offers yet a further twist. As suggested above, Fenn and Susan are more than participants in a fictional structure; they also "compose" their own "story" and share their thoughts about this activity with the "reader." "John Barth," the putative author, fades into irrelevance as Fenn and Susan seemingly expropriate more and more of their creator's traditionally granted omniscience. The principals claim their freedom both from the allegorical and the authorial. In effect they become the fabricators of their own life story and thus stand outside both the mythic/Romance dimension of *Sabbatical* and the novelistic dimension. Real people twice removed from an imaginary voyage, so to speak. With John Barth put out to pasture and the fictive enterprise put on hold, at least temporarily, Fenn and Susan affirm their own being and freedom and immediacy: "The doing and the telling, our writing and our loving

. . . That's our story.'' As the novel nears its end, the two figures also come to understand that the actual voyaging—not the goal—is what matters. (p. 19)

Critics such as Gerald Graff to the contrary, there *is* a postmodern movement alive in the world today; and John Barth's newest novel provides evidence of it. Not that Barth is on the frontier of experimentalism but rather that he substantiates and reflects the reality of certain fundamental—if albeit not yet adequately defined—changes, gestures, attitudes. This reviewer for one regrets that Barth didn't succeed better in his newest effort. A novel lives or dies on its ability to immerse the reader in a sustained *experience*—whether illusional or mimetic or antirealist and refractive—and *Sabbatical* too often lets its internal dynamic get in the way of this. (p. 20)

Doug Bolling, ''Minors from Majors: 'Sabbatical','' in The American Book Review *(© 1983 by* The American Book Review*), Vol. 5, No. 4, May-June, 1983, pp. 19-20.*

Wendell (Erdman) Berry

1934-

American poet, novelist, and essayist.

Whatever genre Berry chooses, his message is consistent: we must seek to live in harmony with nature. Like Thoreau, with whom he is often compared, Berry is a writer of place. He uses his life on his Kentucky farm as an example of how the ordering and healing qualities of nature should be allowed to function in one's life. In all of Berry's work, and especially in his ecological essays, he speaks of the danger inherent in disrupting the natural cycle of life. Berry particularly emphasizes the importance of physical exercise to mental well-being and the dangers of what he calls "agribusiness," the capitalist treatment of the land. Critics consider *Recollected Essays 1965-1980* (1982) to be the finest volume of Berry's expository prose.

Berry's early novels, *Nathan Coulter* (1960) and *A Place on Earth* (1967), received a moderate amount of positive critical attention. It is nevertheless as a poet and an essayist that Berry has earned his literary reputation. Although no single volume of Berry's verse stands out, critics have appraised his poetry as being consistently good. Both Berry's poetry and prose are noted for the very direct use of language. His recent collections of verse, *A Part* (1981) and *The Wheel* (1982), are characteristically pastoral.

(See also *CLC*, Vols. 4, 6, 8; *Contemporary Authors*, Vols. 73-76; and *Dictionary of Literary Biography*, Vol. 6.)

ROBERTS W. FRENCH

They attached me to the earth. It is the experience of such attachment that Wendell Berry writes about in *Farming: A Handbook.* Indeed, the book has little to say about anything else; as much as any I can recall in recent years, it is a book of a single theme, played without significant variation. Berry has something he very badly wants to tell us. He said it in *The Long-Legged House,* a book of essays published in 1969, he said it again in *The Hidden Wound* (1970), an essay centered upon the author's experience of racism, and he says it yet once more in his new poems. The insistent didacticism becomes tiring; one soon gets the message. . . .

What men have done, however, must be compared with what men *could* do; and here again Berry is explicit. He comes to us with a cure for our ills. (p. 472)

Essentially, Berry's poems are pastorals of withdrawal, advising us to retreat to the earth, where salvation may be found. . . . The image of sowing is central and recurrent. What can a man do in times of crisis? He can enrich the earth. Berry appears to be quite serious about this. . . . Faced with the monstrous creations of our technological age, one can well understand this longing for a primitive Golden Age; but one may also ask whether such longing is anything more than an escape into pastoral idealization. . . .

Speaking as one who has admired much of Berry's previous work, I must conclude, reluctantly, that this book is a mistake. It comes too soon after the last one (*Openings,* 1968), and it contains too many poems that might better have been kept back for further revision and further tightening. . . . Much of the writing in the book is diffuse and slack; the memorable lines are few. The book preaches incessantly at us, urging us to marriage with the earth. Whatever the attractions of the idea, one soon has enough of it. (p. 473)

Roberts W. French, "From Maine to Kentucky," in The Nation (copyright 1970 The Nation magazine, The Nation Associates, Inc.), Vol. 211, No. 15, November 9, 1970, pp. 472-74.*

JOHN W. HATTMAN

[*The Hidden Wound*] is one of the finest documents on the racial question that has been published in recent years. It is a sincere, moving and inspirational account of one man's attempt to comprehend the ways in which racism has influenced him. Berry's central thesis is: "If white people have suffered less obviously from racism than black people, they have nevertheless suffered greatly; the cost has been greater perhaps than we can yet know. If the white man has inflicted the wound of racism upon black men, the cost has been that he would receive the mirror image of that wound into himself." . . . (pp. 374-75)

The book is devoted to the author's attempt to discover the depth and nature of his wound and find a way to cure it. The most striking point of the volume is that this is a man who realizes the sickness of racism and is determined to avoid passing it on to his own children. In his effort to understand what has happened to him, the author reflects on his childhood and his relations with the black people on his grandfather's farm. . . .

One passage that is particularly striking, I believe, serves as a devastating refutation to those who argue that slavery was not a totally damnable institution. "My great-grandfather, John Johnson Berry, once owned a slave who was a 'mean nigger,' too defiant and rebellious to do anything with. And writing that down, I sense as I never have before the innate violence of the slave system, and the innate flaw of the slavery myth. For if there was any kindness in slavery it was dependent on the docility of the slaves; any slave who was *unwilling* to be a slave broke through the myth of paternalism and benevolence, and brought down on himself the violence inherent in the system."

This, then, is a sensitive and convincing study of the terrible harm the white man does to himself by the evil of his racism. It is compassionate and understanding in its approach, but it insists that white America must cease to exist as a racist society or it will destroy itself. This is a work that I highly recommend to all who are concerned with the tragic division in our society. (p. 375)

> *John W. Hattman, in a review of "The Hidden Wound," in* Best Sellers *(copyright 1970, by the University of Scranton), Vol. 30, No. 17, December 1, 1970, pp. 374-75.*

PATRICK CALLAHAN

The Hidden Wound is an autobiographical meditation which also serves as an *apologia*. Berry attempts to justify his recent retreat to a Kentucky farm, where, having fled the life of an urban nomad, he has attempted to come to grips with both his and the nation's past. The "hidden wound" of the book's title is racism, and Berry's study of it is refreshingly free from the sloganeering which surrounds that issue today.

Berry grew up on a farm in Kentucky, and his childhood memories are rich with his friendship to two blacks, the hired man Nick, only one generation removed from the overseer's lash, and his wife, "Aunt Georgie," only one generation removed from "massa's" nocturnal lusts. Only with the awakening reflection brought on by his manhood has Berry come to understand how fully his family covertly exploited the poor blacks, whose bondage of poverty differed only in degree from the outright, contractual ownership of slavery. Berry exorcises the guilt of his heritage by revisiting his past, by returning home to become a farmer after his father, and by researching in depth the history of his immediate locale. His depth-exploration of one slice of Middle America reminds me of Williams' *Paterson*, the more so since Berry's beautifully sonorous prose at times approaches the poetic, textured by a poet's ear and imagery.

Farming: A Hand Book is in many respects a poetic counterpoint to the prose of *The Hidden Wound*. The domain of these poems is demarcated by the boundary fences of Berry's farm. He explores not outward, but downward toward the roots. These are poems with the smell of soil on them, a rich addition to the current nature poetry being written by William Stafford,

Gary Snyder, James Wright, and others. Berry . . . writes (as did Wordsworth) of discoveries in nature that are deep revelations into himself. . . . (pp. 273-74)

Among the most interesting pieces in *Farming: A Hand Book* are the poems of the "mad farmer," who is the only sane man, one suspects, in a world of the mad. The **"Prayers and Sayings of the Mad Farmer"** are couched in the blunt language of real Midwestern farmers, but always turned toward the values of rain, growth, life, and love that any but the blind can learn from a farm. . . .

As Berry stresses in ["**The Mad Farmer in the City**"] the organic simplicities, when seen with vision, pale all our steel and neon to insignificance. (p. 274)

> *Patrick Callahan, "Roots," in* Prairie Schooner *(reprinted from* Prairie Schooner *by permission of University of Nebraska Press; © 1971 by University of Nebraska Press), Vol. XLV, No. 3, Fall, 1971, pp. 273-74.*

SPEER MORGAN

Since 1960 Wendell Berry has published five books of poetry, three volumes of essays and three novels. With the recent publication of two books of poetry, *Farming: A Handbook* and *The Country of Marriage,* and a volume of essays, *A Continuous Harmony,* Berry has come to fruition as a major voice in America. By far his best work is his most recent, and so to read him chronologically is to observe steady growth in depth, refinement, and certainty. . . . Wendell Berry's transformation . . . has been a steady clarification and improvement of essentially the same stuff, his poetry growing more obviously and naturally out of itself, his own life, and death.

Death is the primary fact to Wendell Berry. It *is,* and he cannot forget it; he derives from his death and the death of all that he loves, not from new fashions in poetry or sociology, but the fact that he will be a rotting carcass in the foreseeable future. To him, carcasses are in one sense as dead an end as in Sartre; they are real and final. In another, equally important sense, they are like the carcasses in the fourth book of Virgil's *Georgics,* eight sacrificed cattle out of whose decay emerges a swarm of golden bees, creators of wholesome sweetness. Berry's sweetness, like Virgil's, is accompanied by stinging political and philosophical convictions, manifested both in simple didacticism and in implied contrast to the ideal agricultural life. This is clear from the first: Berry is a moralist; he constructs an ideal according to the life he is trying to live, and he develops an extended critique of America's abuse of power and wealth—the voraciousness, arrogance, and inhumanity of her mad scramble to deny the balancing points in nature, the intersections of life and death, light and dark, freedom and necessity that are essential to all being. In an age when literary didacticism has become a dangerous business, Berry's voice has grown equal to the task.

Unlike most contemporary poets who are fearful of being considered too tendentious or "simple-minded," Berry is not evasive about his principles. He lives in Kentucky, where the land has been literally scraped raw by money seeking more money. . . . Although by no means a pious ecologist, Berry speaks out against the "disease of our material economy" as teacher, lobbyist, writer, and farmer. To him, as to Thoreau, the cancer in our economy spreads to other realms of life. (pp. 868-70)

Unlike Thoreau, Berry searches for an etiology of the disease and arrives at a view of both cause and solution: "Because death is inescapable, a biological and ecological necessity, its acceptance becomes a spiritual obligation, the only means of making life whole . . .". Ceasing to deny the darkness, gaining life through relinquishment, is the core of Berry's task as farmer and idealist, and in his poetic development of this "simple" idea may be seen his growing excellence as a new kind of agrarian.

Berry's existential simplemindedness is getting more perfect in his maturity. As his ethic, passions, writing style, and whole life become more integral, his thought acquires the status of a practical metaphysic, a way of acting according to his understanding of the ground of being. In his poetry especially, Berry's maturity is defined by increasingly elegant simplicity. His style is that of a farmer who plants and tends straight rows, not a Romantic who wanders temporarily in the luxuriance of a wild or infinite nature. (p. 870)

Despite his avoidance of the exotic in theme or style, of flaunting nature's lore, enumerating his spots of time or ninth-month midnights, Berry achieves a mysteriously uplifting resonance. (p. 871)

Berry's poetic maturation may be traced through his handling of death. In *The Broken Ground,* his first volume, he announces the theme which will run throughout his poetry.

> I am derived from my death,
> Marked by the black river.
> With this knowledge I will enter morning. . . .

Death is the power to be reckoned with; it is the primary fact for the man who has submitted himself to living on the earth, with it, according to its terms. By dealing with death the man achieves—if he is to achieve them at all—wholeness and light: "With this knowledge I will enter morning." In these lines as in the early poems generally, Berry calls death by name and deals with it overtly, as an abstraction. (p. 872)

Openings, Berry's second book of poetry, is marked by an increasing concern with public issues, particularly war and ecology, and consequently an expansion of the death theme into the public realm. **"A Discipline"** evokes the possibility of massive death, a holocaust by the engines of civilization—death by bomb, fallout or pollution. (p. 873)

The balance of life and death is the mainspring of Berry's more particular themes: the burden and inescapability of history; the gift of renewal; the necessity for active love, work, and usefulness; the importance of means over ends in achieving hope and a sense of meaning; submission to nature; and the practicality of discipline and morals. Consistently, his work as a farmer and writer has been motivated by the urge to learn the patience, humility, and discipline necessary to discern the primary laws of natural existence, the simplest and most enduring facts of life, and then to implement this understanding in his own life. The final purpose is to make his life and work at one with this understanding. (pp. 873-74)

The Country of Marriage . . . evolves from Berry's struggle to conform his life, here the life of his marriage in particular, to the unity of all life. The book marks a culmination in the life-death metaphysic, for here the contrariety becomes most believably complementary and most skillfully subsumed in the poet's other concerns. **"An Anniversary,"** which ends the book, is another instance of Berry's passion to find and make a higher integration of the essential. . . . It is a love poem concerning the marriage between a man and woman and between them and the land. Here, and throughout the book, marriage symbolizes the larger intention of discerning and enacting harmony. . . . The marriage of man and wife is one ring in a widening pattern of rings that reaches out to the land, like the waves of a rock dropped in water rather than a relationship in a void. . . . Their history, transient as it may be, leaves its mark upon the country. Responsibility is as incumbent upon the resident as upon the spouse. The relationship is intimate and capable of great fertility or great devastation. (pp. 874-76)

Discovering and saying yes to what he has been given—life that lives in the shadow of death—is the theme that Berry sometimes proclaims, sometimes struggles with, but here celebrates. It is his old theme, in this poem subsumed magnificently in the specific. A few lines treat an entire year, conveying the celerity with which his marriage, here memorialized, moves toward darkness. From the first line on, time's inexorability is evoked and reevoked in a patterned movement, weaving in and out of its opposites—healing, renewal, harvest. Knowledge of the intricate dependency of the light and dark emerges in a joyfulness which is ardent, deep, and yet tinged with anguish. . . . In the context of the poem and of Berry's work generally, death as sexual metaphor is profoundly meaningful, because to him it is not merely a paradox or an apt description of a feeling, but most deeply what he, as poet and farmer, is concerned with.

The theme of the poem—and what Berry has been working toward for several years—is contained in these lines:

> Lovers live by the moon
> Whose dark and light are one,
> Changing without rest.

The simple elements are typical of Berry. But also typical is the extraordinary design he constructs with them. The statement "Lovers live by the moon" implies the conjunction of both the woman's cycle and the farmer's labor with that of the moon; more importantly the moon symbolizes the dark and light continually at work in one perfect circle: its essence is the "changing without rest," which suggests the joy of lovemaking itself as well as the pang of sorrow that the lovers, capable of imagining static perfection, may feel in the face of transience. For the lovers, "dark and light are one" because they are together in the dark and their fulfillment comes through "death" in each other's arms; they are made "one" by the light which is immediately dark.

Unlike Thoreau, to whom "The sun is but a morning star" in the face of a potential light within, Berry's lovers are dependent upon the moon. They must live "by" it. It proclaims their blessings and their limits. Whereas the Romantic monk wanders in the temple of nature, cultivating his own infinite soul, the husbandman lives in light and darkness, cultivating the ground of his marriage. And for this farmer the sun is light enough. To increase it would make it too hot. The great paradox is that although Wendell Berry is dying, he tries to live in one place, with one family, in such a way that he could live there forever. He has no ultimate reason for this, no irrefutable justification: what he serves, finally, is a mystery. (pp. 876-77)

Speer Morgan, "Wendell Berry: A Fatal Singing"
(copyright, 1974, by Speer Morgan), in The Southern
Review, *Vol. X, No. 4, October, 1974, pp. 865-77.*

D. E. RICHARDSON

Sayings & Doings is for the most part an anthology of short epigrams heard in conversation in the country. In a short prefatory note Berry likens these poems to the "found objects" of the sculptors but insists that the verse form in which these epigrams appear is necessary because "it makes clear that memorable speech is *measured* speech." . . .

Some, if not all, of these epigrams come close to the jokes of the "Hee-Haw" television program: the comparison is cruel and wrong but often hard to fend off. For example,

> We have to eat
> early at our house.
> Ain't got enough to eat
> to feed a *hungry* man.

Our great southern prose writers—Faulkner, O'Connor, Welty—have worked such phrases into moments of great beauty and they have not sacrificed "*measured* speech." But standing by themselves such phrases remind us of the vulgar exploitation of the popular southern idiom in the world of "country music." . . . Berry's book forces us to feel that the old rural popular world of the South is somehow inaccessible to a mature poetic imagination today. (p. 883)

> D. E. Richardson, "Southern Poetry Today" (copyright, 1976, by D. E. Richardson), in The Southern Review, *Vol. XII, No. 4, October, 1976, pp. 879-90.*

PETER STITT

[In] *Clearing,* Wendell Berry tells the story of how he rescued a piece of Kentucky land, which had been neglected and abused by generations of past owners, and, through his own labors and the help of a few horses, brought it back to life. . . .

Berry's self-imposed task is indeed a noble and an arduous one—just reading his descriptions of the work makes one's shoulders ache. The artistic goal is equally noble; in **"Work Song,"** Berry states his wish to make "Memory, / native to this valley, . . . grow / into legend, legend into song, song / into sacrament." Unfortunately, something has gotten in the way of artistic fulfillment; is it, as the poet seems to suspect, the labor itself? (p. 955)

Whatever the cause, Berry's sense of his own failure is all too accurate. He venerates memory, but has taken his history not from his own recollections or those of area old-timers, but from the county records. Here is an example of how he presents the past owners of the land: "Asa Batts kept it / for only six years / and in 1871 sold it / —Sullinger's Landing had now / become Lanes Landing— / to A. J. & Matilda Jones, / who divided it . . ." Is it not possible that there is a good story or two behind this property? . . . And shouldn't a poet, the owner and venerator of that land, have done more to seek out and present such stories?

As for legends, I could find only a single attempt at one. In the best poem here (best because it comes the closest to being a poem), **"The Bed,"** Berry speaks of coming across an unreal "party of hunters by a low fire, / two men and a boy: / a third man, wounded, lies still." The third man eventually dies and is quickly buried by the others, before they rush on in fear of their pursuers. But who are they, and who are the pursuers? Berry never tells us. I assume he is trying either to tell or create

a legend, but the attempt remains unrealized, another dimension unreached. (pp. 955-56)

Berry's lines in this book only masquerade as poetry—in truth they are a flat and uninteresting kind of prose. I have no inherent prejudice against a poet's writing prose and presenting it as poetry—many of the prose poems of Robert Bly, James Wright, and others are quite good poetry. The reason is not far to seek—these writers have paid careful attention both to their images and to their cadences. But I cannot feel that Wendell Berry has paid attention here to any matter of artistry, save the purely mechanical task of writing down on paper the first words that sprang to his mind. And that is very far from being enough. (pp. 956-57)

> Peter Stitt, in a review of "Clearing," in The Georgia Review (copyright, 1977, by the University of Georgia), *Vol. XXXI, No. 4, Winter, 1977, pp. 955-57.*

DAVID IGNATOW

No one could deny the nobility of Wendell Berry's dream of the sanctity of the soil. I will not comment on his techniques in *Clearing,* . . . they are all that we have read before by writers of equal talent in the free forms of William Carlos Williams. Occasionally he works skillfully at the traditional rhymed and metered verse, but Berry should be singled out for his vision. He is a poet who is a farmer, who is a professor of English, who cannot write an evil word about the work of living but must make his farm the podium from which to write eloquently of our relationship to the earth. He suffers his tasks in the field and in the barn gladly. . . . [He] celebrates the small, ordinary farmer who has no pretension to wealth but asks only that the earth return to him in kind the love and care he brings to it. Berry's own devotion to the earth is quite the same, if not more so, in that one gets the feel in his poems of a lover and his beloved in mystical union. He is fervently dedicated to reform of the treatment of the earth as it has been treated by greed and shortsightedness, and his poetry often glows with the spirit of his pursuit.

> David Ignatow, in a review of "Clearing," in Partisan Review (copyright © 1977 by Partisan Review), *Vol. XLIV, No. 2, 1977, p. 317.*

VERNON YOUNG

Clearing is familiar history; ecology; memoir: a poem about the making of a poem—the making of two poems, the one we read and the other: a farm and forty acres. . . . Berry is the most subtle of American naturists. The vocabulary of his emotion is even-tempered; far from unpoetic, he deprecates the more showy forensics that have commonly underlined his subject: despoliation and the way back. *Clearing* is a ruminating lyrical monologue in seven principal sections, delivered by a man who has chosen at great cost—in the worldly meaning, beside the expense of spirit entailed—to *do* as well as to *be* or to talk: actively to conserve, not be content with polemics on conservation. And the consequence—never *achieved,* always in process of achievement—is far from satisfying the poet who thinks, as it does satisfy the man who toils. **"Work Song,"** the most troubled, and the most musical, sequence of the narrative, discloses the anxiety at the heart of Berry's expenditure—anxious not only for the future, which will not be in his hands; anxious over the present in which he is being devoured by his own commitment. . . . There lies the poet's fear, as dark as dark. He has cut the brush, fenced and sown the fields, brought crops back to the bottom land, and he asks if his labors might not, eventually, absorb him, lead him quite away from the life of books, from reading them, from making them. . . . No fate more mocking than to be halved between one's vocations; to be torn asunder by equally compelling duties; no worse despair than a writer's when not writing what he feels he ought. *Clearing* is thereby more than a lyric of ecological resurrection, though it is beautifully that; it is the expressive chronicle of a man who sought unity, stricken by division. (pp. 579-81)

Vernon Young, "The Death, the Lullaby, the Glory," in The Hudson Review *(copyright © 1977 by The Hudson Review, Inc.; reprinted by permission), Vol. XXV, No. 4, Winter, 1977-78, pp. 579-81.**

MICHAEL HAMBURGER

Clearing includes history quite as specific, localized and personal, yet runs no comparable risk. All his work in verse and prose is sustained by a pervasive vision, as much ethical as aesthetic, that gives weight and substance and depth to any thing or any figure named in it. The old-fashioned word for this was dedication; and it is consistent with Berry's freedom from trendy sophistication that his opening poem, **"History,"** should include an invocation to the Muse. His historical preoccupations become critical in the next poem, **"Where,"** with its accounts of the antecedents of the place he celebrates throughout the collection, his Kentucky farm. Here documentary faithfulness stretches the "objective correlative"—or rather the "subjective correlative," since his material is facts—to its limit, yet he gets away with it because the setting down of these facts of ownership, exploitation or "nurture" of land, are crucial to his theme; and there was no way of making them more poetic than they are without faking. To Berry his theme is everything; all his art and all his life are at its service.

Except for the six poems that make up **"Work Song,"** this whole collection consists of longer poems more meditative, or even didactic, than purely lyrical, as compared with the short poems in Berry's preceding book *The Country of Marriage* or those published in limited editions only in recent years. Yet all the different strands in Berry's work—even the prose of his novels, to one of which Part I of **"Work Song"** alludes, or the essays in *A Continuous Harmony* and in his recent tract on culture and agriculture *The Unsettling of America*—are drawn together by a unifying vision, by his urgent concern with energies that flow through individuals fulfilling them in life and death, and flow out again into the world, provided there is a world left that can generate and receive such energies. To say that Berry's theme is "ecology" or "environmentalism" is to vulgarize and falsify it. As a poet, he begins not with a cause or program, but with a commitment to what he loves and cares about. . . . In *The Unsettling of America* he expresses his disagreement with the very institution, the Sierra Club, that published his book, on the grounds that its conservation policies put too much stress on "recreational" wilderness, not enough on the use of land, on small farms and those who have been, or are still being, driven out of them. That the same organization published the book is a proof both of its integrity and of Wendell Berry's.

It seems likely that at some point Berry's dedication to his theme and cause will involve him in an acute conflict between the demands on him as a campaigner and the requirements of poetry. . . . In *Clearing,* the didacticism and the lyricism support each other, just as the physical labor of farming flows into the rhythm and muscle of the verse, thanks to the interchange that becomes explicit in the poem **"Reverdure."** . . . Wendell Berry's poetry has such strength and rightness that one wishes him many more moments when "the world / lives in the death of speech / and sings there," . . . while understanding that they have to be paid for constantly, and fought for constantly as long as "life's history" is threatened by "the coming of numbers." Fortunately, Berry is not quite alone in his struggle. More and more writers throughout the world are on his side, whatever reason they may have to doubt that they can make any impression on the private or corporate destroyers. (pp. 70-1)

Michael Hamburger, "Substantial Poetry," in The Boston University Journal *(copyright © 1978 by the Trustees of Boston University), Vol. XXV, No. 3, 1978, pp. 69-72.**

STEVEN WEILAND

[*The Unsettling of America*] continues the exploration of Berry's central themes: agriculture considered historically and in its present state, and marriage and domesticity. Much of what he says is in response to the question he posed in a poem in *Farming: A Handbook* . . . : "What must a man do to be at home in the world?" He must, this latest book suggests, discover personal solutions for what are identified as the three crises we face: of character, agriculture and culture. All three are the result, Berry claims, of "the abstract values of an industrial economy preying upon the native productivity of the land and its people." . . .

One strength of *The Unsettling of America* is the compelling case it makes against recent agricultural policy and its treatment of related issues like the negative effects of the land-grant colleges and schools of agriculture on American farming. Berry identifies "specialization" and "expertise" as the expressions of a misguided policy and educational philosophy, ignorant of the interrelation of culture and agriculture. (p. 99)

In the long chapter at the center of *The Unsettling of America,* "The Body and The Earth," Berry finds that our several cultural crises are all based on the "isolation of the body from the many specialized activities which dominate everyday life and from all other living things." In his view modern work is too abstract and our relation to the land plainly exploitative. Our bodies, he says, are too weak and joyless. "Contempt for the body is unavoidably manifested in contempt for other bodies—the bodies of slaves, laborers, women, plants and the earth itself. Relationships with all other creatures become competitive and exploitative rather than collaborative and convivial." We are now divided within ourselves and from each other and the land. These divisions are identified as first "sexual" and then "ecological"—the most important divisions because the most fundamental.

The divisions can be bridged and critical connections reestablished through "fidelity" considered as a cultural discipline. Berry's interest in this most traditional of virtues is based on his belief in its social practicality and its relation to the conservation of energy. . . . One expression of fidelity . . . is in marriage, which Berry sees as the central cultural bond on which many others depend. He blends a realistic view of its rhythms with an insistence on its symbolic force. "What marriage offers—and what fidelity is meant to protect—is the possibility of moments when what we have chosen and what we desire are the same. Such a convergence obviously cannot be continuous. No relationship can continue very long at its highest emotional pitch. But fidelity prepares us for the *return* of these moments, which give us the highest joy we know.''

Many supporters of Berry's timely views on ecology will no doubt find his conviction on certain necessities of domesticity less congenial. From his point of view, however, they are inseparable. Private and public life, love and work are bound historically and practically by the household. The failure of marriage and abuse of the land constitute for him the "two estrangements" most responsible for our sense of cultural loss. (pp. 100-01)

Culture is a term Berry has often used in his essays to identify the particular set of traditions and qualities he admires. He is, of course, only one of many who now make "culture" the subject of critical comment and study. The number of books and articles in the humanities and social sciences with "culture" in the title is, however, more a suggestion of the ambitions of the authors than proof of agreement about what the term actually means. . . . Berry very wisely shows no interest in this essentially academic debate over the definition of "culture" and the most appropriate methods for its study. His understanding of culture is based essentially on his experience as an observer and participant. (p. 102)

Berry has no general theory of cultural analysis, only the particular instruments of its practice: a commitment to high ideals of human behavior, analytical interest in the arts and learning including attention to literature and history, and daily attention to the traditions and routines of everyday life, especially of agriculture.

Though he admires the personal or domestic values of "fidelity" rather than the political values of "solidarity" Berry also believes in the need for a common culture. He stresses the development in individuals of the disciplines necessary to healthy family and community life: fidelity in one's relations with other people and with the land. These constitute, in a productive culture, recognition of the essentially cyclical nature of human life. "It is only in the processes of the natural world," he wrote in 1972, "and in analogous and related processes of human culture, that the new may grow usefully old and the old be made new." For these reasons culture is never progressive but neither is it simply the cumulative display of art and learning. It is the network of disciplines, as Berry defines them, applied to the facts of everyday life and the possibilities for the future. . . . His methods of cultural analysis are decidedly less elaborate than . . . contemporary anthropologists' but his findings are equally pointed and certainly, because of his prescriptive posture, more practical. Solidarity, finally, suggests the primacy of social answers to questions of value facing individuals. Fidelity is preeminently a trait of healthy individuals and citizens. Berry stresses settlement as the goal of private and family life and the source, therefore, of a society firmly rooted in its own home-made culture. (p. 104)

> *Steven Weiland, "Wendell Berry: Culture and Fidelity," in* The Iowa Review *(copyright © 1979, by The University of Iowa), Vol. 10, No. 1 (Winter, 1979), pp. 99-104.*

PETER DOLLARD

Berry's direct and easily understood verse [in *A Part*] is worlds removed from the self-indulgent and often contrived obscurity so common in contemporary poetry. "Clear" poetry can be amateurish, trite, and maudlin, but Berry's is the very opposite—intelligent, sensitive, and a pleasure to read. For the most part, the poems are nature poems that deal with such subjects as river ice, snow, trees, lilies, and the Kentucky scene. Two very nicely handled translations from Ronsard are also included. Good poetry that is easily accessible is a rarity, but Berry's work meets that description well.

> *Peter Dollard, in a review of "A Part," in* Library Journal *(reprinted from* Library Journal, *September 15, 1980; published by R. R. Bowker Co. (a Xerox company); copyright © 1980 by Xerox Corporation), Vol. 105, No. 16, September 15, 1980, p. 1864.*

LARRY WOIWODE

One of the rewards of being a fairly faithful reader arrives when you open a new book and realize it's the one you've been reading toward for years. That has been this reader's experience with both of these books by Wendell Berry, *Recollected Essays 1965-1980* and *The Gift of Good Land*. . . .

These books are the kind that you spend months with, hate to give up, and plan to return to soon and often. There is that much pure pleasure in them, both in the spare and crafted elegance of their prose, and in the breadth and depth of their content. They're reference works of the body and soul, and books of practical reference for anybody who cares about the earth and the quality of his life upon it, which should include us all. Certain pages and even paragraphs have the power to lift you off into hour-long stretches of contemplation and personal reassessment—those periods when a reader seems to be staring out a window but is really watching his interior reform. Both are that extraordinary; both keep revealing new riches.

Berry's focus is on the land, or agriculture, with equal emphasis on both halves of that word, for he writes not only of land and animal husbandry, but of industrialization and "agribusiness," the youth movement and the family, contemporary education and the lack of it, politics and government, and on into ever-widening realms, which is as it should be. Without the land none of these structures would exist, as Berry makes clear. None of us would. This is an unalterable truth that seems to have got lost in most urban areas, and thus in much of America today. Berry makes us wonder how we imagine we eat, for example, when all consciousness of our dependence on farmers for our existence seems to have been wiped out. This is at the heart of his many concerns.

His approach is the opposite of shrill and slapdash, as anyone who enters the tempered prose of *Recollected Essays* will soon discover. . . .

If one were to distill the thrust of his thought, it might be, All land is a gift, and all of it is good, if we only had the eyes to see that. Again, making no claims for himself, which brings the reader along, Berry functions not only as our eyes but as an entire body and intelligence responding to the land. It's a response one can hardly return from unmoved. . . .

Of these two books, *Recollected Essays* unfolds with the most poetic density, as is natural, since a person of Berry's convictions can make the commitment and move that he's made only once, and keeps thrusting up bright nuggets: "A political speech on television has to be first and last a show, simply because it has no chance to become anything else. The great sin of the medium is not that it presents fiction as truth, as undoubtedly it sometimes does, but that it cannot help presenting the truth as fiction." . . .

The pieces collected in *The Gift of Good Land,* most of which were first written for magazine publication, are somewhat thinner but in the best pragmatic sense more useful, since they represent accounts of the actual working out of Berry's ideas in specific application to life on the land. . . . It is life as it was meant to be lived, and was and is lived, still, in spite of experts who say it won't work and are ready with other "advice." Though Berry details, especially in this second book, the different kinds of death and destruction this advice has caused across our land (and which will continue out of its own momentum more than common sense), one comes away from his books with hope, because of his stand, and through becoming acquainted with others who are taking it, or have always so stood; and hope, too, in a larger sense, for this stripped and dammed and befouled planet that in the face of our insults to it continues to sustain the equipoise of life among immeasurable galaxies stretching off from it in different degrees of burning or frigid sterility.

Larry Woiwode, "Wendell Berry: Cultivating the Essay," in Book World—The Washington Post *(© 1982, The Washington Post), January 31, 1982, p. 5.*

CHARLES HUDSON

Like E. B. White and Noel Perrin, Wendell Berry writes in the country, and he writes mainly about country life, but he owes nothing to either of these writers. His spiritual ancestor is Henry David Thoreau, and his *Recollected Essays,* though looser in structure than *Walden,* resembles it in several respects. Like Thoreau, his prose style is clear and utterly free of affectation. He read Thoreau as a young man, and was clearly influenced by him, but his prose style may have come to him as much from his upbringing as from reading *Walden.* . . .

Like Thoreau, one of Berry's fundamental concerns is working out a basis for living a principled life. And like Thoreau, in his quest for principles Berry has chosen to simplify his life, and much of what he writes about is what has attended this simplification, as well as a criticism of modern society from the standpoint of this simplicity. (Perhaps I should say "apparent" simplicity, because Berry argues that it may be easier to prepare a person to be an astronaut than to be a small farmer.) (p. 220)

[Berry left New York and] bought a small house and twelve acres of land near Port Royal, on the Kentucky River. . . . This was to have been a writer's retreat and a summer place, but . . . as he became more and more immersed in the place, he resigned his job at the University of Kentucky to live the life of a writer and small farmer.

The essays he has selected for this volume show that if Port Royal is a grain of sand, a world exists within it, and this world is connected to the entire universe. The first essay, "The Rise," is altogether admirable. . . . It is about a brief canoe ride with a friend on the Kentucky River in high water, but it is also retrospective, exploring the meaning of high water for him when he was a boy, as well as a lyrical evocation of the experience of high water. (pp. 220-21)

In "The Long-Legged House" and "A Native Hill," Berry settles into Port Royal, extending his knowledge and under-

standing of the place beyond what he knew and understood as a boy. He set out to see the country as never before, to experience it afresh, and to ponder about the meaning of it. Here his writing is suffused with excitement, discovery, and hope. He began to understand a feeling within himself that few Americans have; namely, that in some sense he *belonged* to the place where he lived. (p. 221)

The later essays are not so much *about* Port Royal as they are *from* Port Royal. More specifically, they are written from the point of view of a small farmer, and they ask more difficult questions. "Discipline and Hope" . . . asks why are we "in a state of cultural disorder"? Berry's answer is that we suffer a failure of "discipline," though the sense he attaches to this word is not immediately clear. Berry's "discipline" seems to be a social value, an ideal fraught with potential for organizing human effort, standing as a viable alternative to "efficiency," the social value that now prevails in our increasingly specialized society. (pp. 221-22)

In the end, the view from Port Royal is much like the view from Walden Pond. It is appealing for its critique of modern society, and yet it does not offer an adequate explanation . . . for how things have gotten to be the way they are. And in the absence of explanation, it cannot prescribe a cure. (pp. 222-23)

Even more than Thoreau, Wendell Berry has chosen to live an exemplary life. In an age when many writers have committed themselves to their "specialty"—even though doing so can lead to commercialism, preciousness, self-indulgence, social irresponsibility, or even nihilism—Berry has refused to specialize. He is a novelist, a poet, an essayist, a naturalist, *and* a small farmer. He has embraced the commonplace and has ennobled it. And he will leave a few acres of Henry County soil healthier and more fertile than he found them. (p. 223)

Charles Hudson, in a review of "Recollected Essays, 1965-1980," in The Georgia Review *(copyright, 1982, by the University of Georgia), Vol. XXXVI, No. 1, Spring, 1982, pp. 220-23.*

RICHARD PEVEAR

In their differences, Wendell Berry's *Recollected Essays* and *The Gift of Good Land* balance each other nicely. The first, a selection of descriptive and reflective essays drawn from five previously published books, presents the major themes of his thought as it has developed over the years (1965-1980). It is essentially a personal book . . . though the reflective pieces go far beyond the personal. The second is a collection of articles written since the publication of *The Unsettling of America* in 1977. These are more directly concerned with farming, and take us outside of Mr. Berry's native Kentucky to Pennsylvania, the Midwest, the Southwest, and as far as Peru, studying a variety of techniques, tools, and crops, their propriety or impropriety in relation to the land and the people who live on it. (p. 341)

The value of Mr. Berry's work, and the basis of his polemic with the dominant mentality and methodology of "technological civilization," lies in his insistence on making these connections, or rather, on revealing the connections between culture and agriculture, in his detailing of a wide and subtle network of relations between human activity and the surrounding natural world, a network that leads finally to "mystery" because it vastly exceeds our knowledge and control. Within that network man has a place, determined as much by his ignorance as by his knowledge, and past cultures have over long periods of time worked out delicate systems of self-control, moral and religious "disciplines" as well as agricultural ones, to keep themselves in that place, in a fruitful balance with the life of the earth. . . . The loss of these connections, on the other hand, or the willful breaking of them, brings serious consequences, some of which might be foreseeable but others of which will appear unexpectedly, perhaps disastrously, in time. A disruption of the network at one point will disrupt it at all points; the relations exist and are not of our making; the humility of enquiring into them is proper to man. Thus ecological thinking acquires an almost religious tone, markedly so in Mr. Berry's writing. He points out that with present day methods of industrialized agriculture . . . six bushels of Iowa topsoil are lost for each bushel of corn harvested, at which rate there will be no topsoil left in Iowa by the year 2050. The cultural causes and cultural effects of such an agricultural and natural disaster should be obvious. The "spirit" in which this kind of farming is done would be difficult to defend on any grounds, yet it is the ruling spirit of our economy. To change it also means a change of "spirit."

This brings me to a second point of agreement with Mr. Berry. He is quite unabashedly an opponent of industrialization, technological "problem solving," and the "economy of scale." It is a hard position to maintain in the face of facts. One is inevitably accused of various lapses—romantic utopianism, nostalgia for the past, reactionary agrarianism—all of which come down to a refusal to face facts. But Mr. Berry has arrived at his position precisely by facing facts. He says, in "Discipline and Hope":

> Though I can see no way to defend the economy, I recognize the need to be concerned for the suffering that would be produced by its failure. But I ask if it is necessary for it to fail in order to change; I am assuming that if it does not change it must sooner or later fail, and that a great deal that is more valuable will fail with it.
>
> (pp. 341-42)

The most concise statement of Mr. Berry's analysis appears in his essay "Agricultural Solutions for Agricultural Problems," from *The Gift of Good Land*. Much of what he says there, and elsewhere, about the plight of the farmer in "agribusiness" has been said before about industrial workers. . . . But these problems appear most acutely in relation to farming, which is the most elementary human activity and rests on the most fundamental relations to the earth, relations which are not a matter of choice, taste, "life style," or of ideological persuasion. That, having come down to that realization, we may also work back up from it, is Mr. Berry's hope. (p. 343)

One can act on one's own, and one can encourage others to act, for instance by writing books. But here we come to another problem, that of clear perception, and to "discipline" of another sort. (p. 344)

Mr. Berry, as the sequence of his *Recollected Essays* makes clear, has always been a "religious" thinker, though the emphasis in his work has shifted more and more to practical problems and solutions. The change he calls for is not only one of method or economy, it is a change of mind and heart, a change of "values," and he recognizes that such a change can come about only by "inspiration," not by imposition. He

sees it as a *re-ligio* in the most literal sense, a "binding back" to relations that once existed and have been broken, to the "sacred ties" of man and earth, man and woman, household and community. Precisely because we have so much power to do harm, we must choose "the good." But to do so we must know what "the good" is, or at least where to turn our attention in search of it. The point at which religious vision defines itself against ideology is in the question of true inspiration. Inspiration *comes to* us; it is not an idea or "value" that we create. But where does it come *from*?

In search of a source of value and of a humbling power that might correct the arrogance of our civilization, a source of persuasive authority beyond human limits, Mr. Berry arrives at the order of nature—that great, integral system which does not depend on us but upon which we depend for our existence, and to which we must submit if we wish that existence to continue. From the order of nature he derives the various relations and disciplines of human culture, which take their propriety from their practicality, that is, from necessity. He arrives, in other words, at a Stoic deification of Nature. Which is not without dignity. But, though there appears to be a compelling unity in his vision, I believe that it is, in truth, deeply inconsistent, contradictory, and argued with a certain amount of intellectual "bad faith." That it closes the openings through which a true inspiration might come, and that it finally does not serve his own cause very well.

I do not have room to trace in detail the development of this religious view of nature in Mr. Berry's work. . . . Various aspects of this vision appear in different places in his work, but they can be brought together under one particular statement from the end of "Discipline and Hope":

> What I have been preparing at such length to say is that there is only one value: the life and health of the world.
>
> (pp. 344-45)

Certain conclusions follow from it, which I will list here: (1) The Creation creates itself and is complete in itself (denial of God, of "spirit," of transcendence, of incarnation). (2) Man is the zoological species "man" (denial of the "person" in the Christian sense). (3) History, cultural tradition, community have no meaning except as they affect the life and health of the world and, subordinate to that, the survival of the human species (in the West these effects have been increasingly harmful, whence a marked contempt for "humanity"). (4) Time is cyclical in motion, "cosmic" time. (5) Means are the only real ends (there are no ends). (6) Death is part of the process and should be accepted. (7) The necessary is "the good."

Each of these points could be illustrated by a number of quotations from Mr. Berry's writings. Together they make up a consistent view of life, though he never brings them together in one place. It is a view that dispenses with the entire Judaeo-Christian tradition, not only its "teachings" but its deepest motives. It also dispenses with a good deal of Greek tradition. Mr. Berry may mean to dispense with these things. But he does not always keep his own conclusions in mind, and often ignores their implications. For instance, he frequently speaks of "mystery" and "transcendence," of sacraments and rituals, of community and spirituality, though none of these words can have any meaning for him. And his language tends constantly towards paraphrases and quotations from the Bible, particularly the Gospels, though he denies the very basis of their vision. . . . (p. 345)

Hatred of our civilization has as its worst fruit ignorance of its meaning and spirit. That meaning and spirit have been oppressed for some time; they are as eroded as Iowa's topsoil—a connection Mr. Berry does not make. On the contrary, the marks of that erosion show rather clearly in his work. As examples I would cite his defense of a cyclical as opposed to a linear view of time; his definition of "freedom" ("Men are free precisely to the extent that they are equal to their own needs"); his criticism, repeated in several places, of the "separation of body and soul" in Christianity—all of which he undertakes rather lightheartedly, as if these were not the central issues of our culture, as if his only opponents were a few mindless capitalists. (p. 346)

While [Berry] denounces man's oppression of nature, he accepts as necessary, and therefore good, nature's oppression of man. Which leads to the deepest contradiction in his thought.

Nature idolatry is finally a worship of power. It was for her grandeur and power that the Stoics worshipped nature. It is this power that Mr. Berry worships, the "Native Hill" that eats its owners, the power that will turn him into humus—an event he anticipates with peculiar enthusiasm. It is this power and grandeur that he wants to protect from the petty attacks of humanity. That is what he means when he says that "the life and health of the world" is the only value. In terms of geological time, he need not worry; the wilderness will win. But does nature care what sort of wilderness she is? A barren desert is also a wilderness. If mankind should succeed in turning the world into a barren desert, nature will not object, any more than she objects to the planet Mercury or the planet Pluto or the empty surface of the moon. She will not notice the disappearance of mankind, whose "history in the world, their brief clearing of the ground," as Mr. Berry says rather coolly, "will seem no more than the opening and shutting of an eye." By harming nature, we only harm ourselves. We cannot live

in a barren desert. The entire ecological system of the earth is the "value" only for human life. But what is human life worth, if it is only to be plowed back into the topsoil? Job, whose humility Mr. Berry praises, would not accept that "spiritual obligation". . . . (p. 347)

Richard Pevear, "On the Prose of Wendell Berry," in The Hudson Review *(copyright © 1982 by The Hudson Review, Inc.; reprinted by permission), Vol. XXXV, No. 2, Summer, 1982, pp. 341-47.*

PUBLISHERS WEEKLY

The color and shadings of the work of poets come out of the life they choose to support their art, financially and spiritually. There are city poets and country poets, academic hacks and bohemians, politicians and recluses. Wendell Berry happens to be a farmer from Kentucky. His poetry, not unexpectedly, often returns to the study of the earth, the fields, the hills. His eighth collection [*The Wheel*] has a particular theme, however: the cycle called the Wheel of Life. Ordered in six sections, Berry's Wheel begins at the end, with two poems about the death of old friends, and graduates to the promise of new life in the marriages of his children. This drama takes place partly in the mind of the poet and is partly set in the landscape of his home. There is a great deal of intelligent feeling in Berry's work, with the same undercurrent of doubt we feel in similar affirmations of faith in the mature works of Eliot and Yeats. Like those masters, Berry is concerned as a poet with the pursuit of wisdom.

A review of "The Wheel," in Publishers Weekly *(reprinted from the September 10, 1982 issue of* Publishers Weekly, *published by R. R. Bowker Company, a Xerox company; copyright © 1982 by Xerox Corporation), Vol. 222, No. 11, September 10, 1982, p. 73.*

Mongo Beti

1932-

(Pseudonym of Alexandre Biyidi; also wrote under the pseudonym Eza Boto) Cameroon francophone novelist, short story writer, and nonfiction writer.

Beti has been called among the most perceptive of the French-African writers in his presentations of African life from an African perspective. His first novel, *Ville cruelle* (1954; *Cruel Town*), appeared under the name Eza Boto. Although Beti eventually rejected both novel and pen name, the book foreshadowed the subjects of his later work, especially the confusions experienced by rural villagers trying to adjust to cultural changes in an emerging Africa. Beti's theme is the destructive influence of colonialism, particularly in education and religion, which results in the loss of African identity and tradition. His principal method of conveying his ideas is satire, often presented in colloquial dialect or language inappropriate to the situation, from the viewpoint of a young, naive narrator.

The focus of both *Le pauvre Christ de Bomba* (1956; *The Poor Christ of Bomba*) and *Le roi miraculé* (1958; *King Lazarus*) is on the attempts of European missionaries to Christianize the Africans. Part of the failure of these attempts stems from the paternalistic assumptions by the priests that the people have no valuable culture of their own and must therefore be enlightened by the West. *Mission terminée* (1957; *Mission to Kala*) satirizes the shortcomings of the colonial educational system. Though the book has no European characters, their ideology is embodied in the protagonist, a lycée-educated African student. The pretensions of the student, as of the priests before him, are exposed by the very villagers whom both had discounted as inferior. Recently, after a sixteen-year hiatus from fiction writing, Beti published *Remember Ruben* (1974), a documentary-styled account of colonial politics. It was followed by *Perpetué* (1974), a sympathetic treatment of the plight of the modern African woman in a traditional, male-dominated society.

Critics praise Beti for his humanistic presentations of characters from different, even conflicting, viewpoints. While he satirizes misguided missionaries or self-important students, he also sympathizes with them as human beings. In this way, Beti relates specifically African matters to the larger context of humanity in general.

A. C. BRENCH

[In *Mission terminée*] Jean-Marie Medza returns home having failed his second baccalauréat. He discovers, to his horror, that he is the advocate-designate whose responsibility it is to bring back the wayward wife of his distant cousin, Niam.

He sets off towards the unknown mounted on the chief's bicycle. Horror is now replaced by pride and self-satisfaction—until he reaches Kala, the backwood village to which the woman fled. Here, he meets his cousin Zambo and Mama, his cousin's father. They introduce him to the many, varied characters and aspects of their village. (p. 63)

Courtesy of Mongo Beti

His classical education earns him—and Mama—a fine flock of animals and birds; his new-discovered physical prowess—tutored by Zambo—brings him the distinction of marriage to Edima, young daughter of the chief.

At last Niam's wife returns; she is summarily condemned and fined. Jean Marie and Edima are immediately dispatched on the path of matrimonial bliss and he then decides to return home to face his father, absent at the beginning of the holiday.

On his return, he discovers that his father's anger is untempered by the delay. Jean-Marie decides to leave Edima, home, flock, everything to go in search of ideal happiness with Zambo, his faithful shadow, always at his side.

While [Ferdinand] Oyono and [Mongo] Beti demonstrate basically the same attitude towards colonial Africa and its inhabitants in their novels, their treatment, style and presentation are different in many ways. Oyono takes the classical situations, an almost stylized representation of colonial life among Europeans and Africans. Beti is an experimenter, creating various situations and examining their evolution and the results. All the various side issues have equally to be analysed and occasionally—as with Kris in *Le roi miraculé*—a foreign element is added to give a little more spice to the brew. His novels are much more rambling than Oyono's. Many more aspects of colonial life among Africans are dealt with and the novels' effect, from the point of view of social criticism, is less direct, less forceful than those of Oyono. On the other hand, Beti's Europeans are not only the colonial 'type' but also, and more especially, the kind who want to do good for the Africans but, unfortunately for them, start from the premise that all Africans are unable to organize their lives unless helped by Europeans. His favourite butts are, for this reason, missionaries and dedicated colonial administrators.

These innocents, the Reverend Father Le Guen in *Le roi miraculé* for example, are put among a backwoods people, given an opportunity to do good, according to their lights, and then left to fend for themselves. Their failure and disillusionment are not wholly due to the Africans' positive social qualities but to their more powerful instinctive urge to survive: self-interest is clearly the motivating force behind his characters, Africans and missionaries alike. This primitive and not very creditable reaction is, in the context of Beti's novels, not natural but the result of pressure put upon people by the colonial situation.

Mission terminée is different in some respects from [*Le pauvre Christ de Bomba* and *Le roi miraculé*]. . . . In this novel Europeans are absent. However, Jean-Marie, with his French education, his feeling of superiority and general self-confidence, is an adequate substitute. Initially, he looks upon this mission as a means of parading his superior knowledge. Only later does he realize how inadequate his education and understanding of life really are. (pp. 63-5)

The contrast between Jean-Marie's simple self-confidence and faith in the universal truths taught by the Europeans and the villagers' direct, materialistic approach to life is the foundation of Beti's comedy. It is enhanced by the contrast between Jean-Marie's narrative style and language and the carefully weighed words of the Kalaians. . . . Jean-Marie, like a three-headed man in a circus, is paraded from compound to compound. He gives his version of world affairs, answers questions and, the following morning new sheep, fowl or sacks of grain add to his wealth. These evening sessions, during which the villagers probe deeper into his learning than any school examiners, make Jean-Marie question the infallibility of his knowledge for the first time. (p. 65)

The situations which the juxtaposition of such contrasting personalities create are a succession of riotous, slap-stick circuses. They are, for the most part, entirely unrelated and are made to appear the result of fortuitous conjunctions of events. Jean-Marie is never able to know for sure what surprise the village and its inhabitants have next in store for him. His stay is a perpetual battle of wits. He wants to maintain his reputation as a cultured man-about-town; they are determined to assimilate everything into their unbending view of life. Jean-Marie appreciates more and more, as his stay lengthens, the positive qualities they have and which he has never been able to acquire. But this is hidden behind the Rabelaisian humour which subjects everything to its influence.

This humour is the expression of a fundamentally brutal attitude to traditional ways and prejudices. Nothing is sacred: prejudices, passions, ideals, purity are all corrupted by Beti's unrelenting laughter and insistence on the physical nature of things. Jean-Marie's first meeting with Edima, his first, tender calf-love is described in terms of his carnal appetites. His attempts to tell the villagers what they want to know are turned into inquisitions during which they force him to question his solidarity with them. Yet, behind all this there is this inexpressible sadness, as if a great deception had made life bitter and cynical humour was the only relief.

Beti's language is as riotous as his humour. It is rich in French idiom; images are taken from any source available and as many clichés as he could discover are thrust into the narrative. . . . This language gives vitality and humour to the story but, in fact, seems to be somewhat inappropriate. This strangeness is a deliberate device which emphasizes the peculiar position of the narrator. (pp. 66-7)

The development of Jean-Marie's character at the critical stage of the change from adolescence to manhood is, sometimes despite and sometimes helped by the comedy, made to appear natural and unforced. It is a continuous sequence which leads from stage to stage without any one of them having more significance than the other. There is no climax but an inevitable progression . . . which is imperceptible to everyone in the novel. . . .

There are, then, many threads running through *Mission terminée*. There are so many and so often they lead nowhere or are still between our hands at the end of the novel that it is impossible to say what this mission accomplished. The overwhelming aspect of the novel is its humour, good-natured but uncompromising, which distorts but, finally, does not destroy. It is a farce but, at the same time, there is bitterness and sorrow. It is the story of a young man's first encounter with the life his ancestors and elders lived when he has reached an age at which he has been completely alienated from this traditional life and at the most impressionable time of his adolescence. He is both very assured but self-conscious, blasé and sensitive, critical but unsure of his foundations. The result is ribald but nostalgic.

In [*Le roi miraculé*] Beti uses much the same themes, setting and techniques as in *Mission terminée* and *Le pauvre Christ de Bomba*. He contrasts the naïve goodness of the missionary, Le Guen in this case, with the cunning of the villagers in their struggle over the fate of twenty-two of the chief's wives after the chief has, somewhat ambiguously, been converted to Roman Catholicism. He shows how superficial Catholic influence is and how, if tribal customs and Catholicism exert conflicting pressures on the Africans in the backwoods, the former is the stronger. This theme is a parallel to that in *Le pauvre Christ de Bomba* where Father Drumont discovers that his Christian teaching is being interpreted in terms of local beliefs, with disastrous consequences. (p. 68)

In all three novels, the action is set in the backwoods where traditional ways, although without their former social significance, are still strong. They are, in fact, strong enough to withstand and reject any attempt to change or destroy them. The village . . . [is the centre] of tight, inward-looking societies whose members look upon the outside world as an extension of their own. In this way, Beti emphasizes the futility of their resistance to change while, at the same time, showing that the alternative being offered in the cases he gives has nothing to commend it either.

Beti's comedy is essentially boisterous and depends on the development of incongruous situations based on complete misunderstanding or incomprehension. The outsiders, Jean-Marie or the missionaries, find themselves faced with a society which is totally incomprehensible and uncomprehending. Their imagination and reason are stretched to the limit in their attempts to come to terms with the problems caused by this lack of contact. However, to the outside observer, these efforts appear grotesquely absurd because, in the central character's terms of reference, there is obviously no satisfactory conclusion which could possibly be found. Events are, therefore, entirely outside their control.

In *Mission terminée* and *Le pauvre Christ de Bomba,* the story is told by an intermediary who plays an important part in the novel. Jean-Marie tells his own story while Denis, Drumont's general steward, records his master's misfortunes in his diary. Their style, racy in the first case, naïve in the second, gives the comedy its outrageous flavour and, at the same time, makes the events seem plausible. In *Le roi miraculé* Beti replaces Denis by Gustave, Le Guen's steward, and Jean-Marie by Kris. Neither recount the story but their attitudes, Kris's cynicism and Gustave's mixture of naïvety, sharp wits and intuitive understanding, influence the reader's interpretation of events, emphasizing certain aspects and implications, which bring out the less obvious and, sometimes discreditable, motivations behind a character's actions. Kris's presence at the great battle which is the climax of the struggle for power between the various factions in the tribe makes it appear a rather primitive and childish squabble while Gustave's reactions to the scene between the chief's first wife, Makrita, and Le Guen in the church show just how far out of his depth the good missionary has ventured, and how absurd he now appears. The personal note in the narrative is supplied by Le Guen's letters to his mother with their naïve appreciation of the situation as it appears to him. Extracts are put into the narrative at moments when the events he describes have obviously an entirely different significance for everyone else to that which he gives them. (pp. 69-70)

Beti's language and style are similar in all three novels. In *Le roi miraculé,* however, although the language is colloquial, he does not use slang and outrageous imagery as in *Mission terminée.* Nor is it totally naïve as Denis's presentation of events in *Le pauvre Christ de Bomba.* The effect is one of objective cynicism while he also attempts to present actions and events as seen through the eyes of the various protagonists, giving each individual's peculiar inflexion to the scene he is witnessing. For this novel expands on a theme suggested by Mama in *Mission terminée* and by the attitude Beti finds among the elders of Jean-Marie's village on the 'grande route': self-interest motivating every person's acts and thoughts. This is the source of the basic comedy in the novel and Beti delves into his characters' personalities, presenting them through their own words and actions which, in the actual situation, are ridiculously pompous or foolish. (pp. 70-1)

There are a multitude of side-issues surrounding [the central plot of *Le roi miraculé*]. Some of them exert an influence, obvious or implicit on the developments, others are simply extraneous but link up, imperceptibly, with similar minor events. The whole story makes a composite description of a certain period in Essazam's history, with the complex interplay of events making it impossible for the motivating forces behind them to be discerned. What are given as cause and effect by the protagonists and by the administration's apparently impartial findings, tell, as Beti makes quite obvious, only half the story. The villagers are much better politicians than God's servant, Le Guen, and eternal values have to give way to traditional concerns and the needs of colonial policy. (p. 72)

The characters of this novel have in fact much more importance in the novel and greater independence of action than those in the other two. Here, instead of being presented through the descriptions of a narrator, they are developed through their own words and acts, without a third person to interpret them. They are important because it is the interaction of their desires

and interests which forms the basis of the comedy and satire of the novel. Because their motivations are an important factor in the novel Beti makes these characters much more definite as individuals. Their own personal interests are shown influencing every gesture and, in one case at least, the result is tragically grotesque rather than farcical. (p. 73)

This novel is the last published by Beti. Like his others and those of Oyono it is, behind the humour, totally negative. The satirical attack on colonial Africa is totally destructive. This novel, with its emphasis on self-interest is, in this respect, Beti's most pessimistic. Altogether, these novels by Beti and Oyono represent the watershed . . . in the Africans' attitude to Europeans. (p. 74)

A. C. Brench, "Two Pamphleteers from Came-roon," in his The Novelists' Inheritance in French Africa: Writers from Senegal to Cameroon *(© Oxford University Press 1967; reprinted by permission of Oxford University Press), Oxford University Press, London, 1967, pp. 47-74.**

THOMAS CASSIRER

All three [of Mongo Beti's novels, *Le Pauvre Christ de Bomba, Mission terminée,* and *Le Roi miraculé,*] comment, in a mixture of light-hearted farce and bitter satire, on the problems encountered in the quest for an "intellectual direction," and present us with a critical portrayal of the man of ideas, the potential guide of the disoriented African.

Mongo Beti has not been generally considered in this light. Critics have usually spoken of him as one of Africa's foremost authors, "a formidable satirist and one of the most percipient critics of European colonialism," or, like Wole Soyinka and Robert Pageard, they have stressed his realistic portrayal of African life and praised his work. . . . In a sense Mongo Beti himself is responsible for this one-sided appreciation of his work, for he has chosen to set his portrayal of the man of ideas in the incongruous locale of the bush village, rather than in the modern city that might have seemed more appropriate. Yet this incongruity is not introduced merely as an effective comic device. It also serves to present the universal problem of disorientation in specifically African terms.

Mongo Beti's African village is situated at the meeting point between traditional communal life and a new awareness of imminent change. Within this context he raises the problem of "intellectual direction" by introducing into the village protagonists who are bearers of Western ideas as well as actual or potential guides for the villagers in their prospective odyssey into the modern world. The novels form a loose trilogy that describes the encounter between the village and the protagonists during the last three decades of European colonial rule: *Le Pauvre Christ de Bomba* takes place in the late nineteen thirties, at a time when European colonialism is still in complete control of Africa. *Le Roi miraculé* is set in the late nineteen forties and touches on the liberalization of the colonial regime brought about by the war. In *Mission terminée,* set in the nineteen fifties, the colonial authorities no longer appear and the action takes place in an entirely African community.

This time-span of some twenty years brings only one essential change to the village. The two novels set in the post-war world highlight a situation of conflict between the generations that is not mentioned in the pre-war world of *Le Pauvre Christ de Bomba.* Apart from this development, . . . there is little to distinguish the earthy peasant society of one novel from that of another. It is an essentially pagan society, but pagan in the popular sense of the word, with none of the animist religious tradition that we find in Camara Laye's Kouroussa or Achebe's Umuofia. Mongo Beti's peasants are fun-loving materialists, possessed of an earthy good sense and considerable physical vitality. They live in what is still a stable, at times even stagnant, village society that is tightly ruled by the conventions of African social tradition.

Into this stable peasant world Mongo Beti introduces two types of protagonists: European missionaries and African students. Both of these, as one would expect, bring with them Western ideas, but in the context of Mongo Beti's conception of a materialist and socially conservative African society they also represent a new kind of man whose life is guided by ideas and learning, and not solely by convention or self-interest. These two protagonists follow each other in the chronological sequence of the novel trilogy's epic time. The first novel is dominated by the figure of the "Christ" of the mission of Bomba, the Reverend Father Drumont. In the novel set in the late nineteen forties, *Le Roi miraculé*, Father Drumont's former assistant, Father Le Guen, shares the spotlight with two African students, Kris and Bitama. In *Mission terminée* an African student, Jean Medza, is the sole protagonist.

The missionaries are fully rounded figures whose characterization is drawn with a mixture of empathy and critical verve. Mongo Beti avoids the facile anticlericalism that turns the missionary figures of his fellow Camerounian Ferdinand Oyono into caricatures of the most unchristian type of priest, selfish, materialist, and scornful of the black man. Mongo Beti's missionaries have come to Africa inspired by what one might call a "primitivist" Christian faith, a belief in the childlike virtues of the African which should allow him to enter the Kingdom of Heaven far more easily than the white man once he has accepted the Christian message. The missionaries are the only figures in the novels whose life is guided by single-minded devotion to a faith, and they are also the only ones who explicitly believe in a universal humanity that transcends barriers of race and culture. . . . Yet the missionaries' faith in universal humanity remains purely abstract because their primitivist view of the African leads them to treat him as a pure child of nature with no cultural identity of his own. They cannot even conceive of adapting Christianity to African customs, an inflexibility that seems particularly striking in the representatives of a Church that has always been known for its ability to incorporate indigenous pre-Christian beliefs and practices into its structure.

It comes then as no surprise that the Africans in *Le Pauvre Christ de Bomba* repeatedly explain the missionary's failure with the statement that "Christ was not a Black man." From the time of the novel's publication, when it provoked considerable protest in Catholic and colonial circles, this has also generally been considered to be the essence of Mongo Beti's thesis. Yet the missionaries in his novels are too complex to be merely typed as the butt of an anticolonialist and anti-Christian satire. The predicament of Father Drumont in particular does not result merely from his disregard of the vitality of African customs. He finds himself defeated as well by the pervasive influence of Western materialist civilization even in the African bush. It was his opposition to this materialism that originally brought him to Africa filled with the hope of converting the natives to the Christian faith and thus protecting them from the forces which had corrupted the Europeans. He discovers, however, that his apparent success during the early years of his mission stemmed from a complete misunderstand-

ing between him and his African converts, who flocked to him precisely in search of the secret of European material success. . . . This mutual misunderstanding between the missionary and his African parishioners comes to a head at the climactic ending to the novel when Father Drumont discovers that over the years his African assistants had turned his mission from a center of Christian piety into a hotbed of corruption. Like other Catholic missions in Cameroun the mission at Bomba included a *sixa,* a house where African girls spent some months before their marriage to be instructed in the duties of a Christian wife. Father Drumont belatedly becomes aware that his assistant, his cook, and his other acolytes have exploited the *sixa* as a ready source of labor, money, and sexual pleasure. In fact the *sixa* is revealed to be spreading not so much Christian morals as venereal disease throughout the region. Faced with this horrendous proof that he has unknowingly served as an agent for the very corruption from which he tried to protect the Africans, Father Drumont returns to Europe in despair.

There is a certain ambivalence in Mongo Beti's treatment of the missionary. While on the one hand both *Le Pauvre Christ de Bomba* and *Le Roi miraculé* are thesis novels that refute the missionary's claim to leadership in modern Africa, these same novels also present the missionary protagonist sympathetically as the man of ideals and ideas who strives heroically to overcome conservatism and materialism. Mongo Beti treats the missionary as a comic figure yet also brings the reader into sympathy with him through such devices as having the narrative of *Le Pauvre Christ de Bomba* told by Denis, the young mission boy who is the only sincere Christian among the Africans and in a sense Father Drumont's spiritual son, or by introducing into *Le Roi miraculé* pages from Father Le Guen's letters to his mother that reveal his idealism and spirituality.

The missionaries are also the only figures in Mongo Beti's novels whose action the author characterizes as revolutionary. They are unsuccessful, wrongheaded revolutionaries, to be sure, but in both *Le Pauvre Christ de Bomba* and *Le Roi miraculé* the author introduces an analogy between missionary and revolutionary activity that seems designed to highlight the missionary's role as a catalyst of change. (pp. 223-27)

Thus Mongo Beti gives us a double perspective of his protagonist. Seen from the point of view of the uncomprehending African villagers his prestige dissolves into comedy and his downfall brings proof of the power of resistance of the African bush to an alien European way of life. The point of view of the author himself, however, goes beyond this narrow perspective. He discerns the heroic as well as the comic qualities of his protagonist. He respects and even admires the missionary's dedication to an idea even as he rejects the validity of that idea for Africa. The missionary emerges in Mongo Beti's novels as the outsider per se, the man of ideas and ideals who finds himself in conflict with the structure of society. His elimination at the conclusion of the novel is tragic as well as comic, since it signifies that the forces of inertia, represented both by the village and by the colonial administration, have forced out the troublesome agent of change. From the perspective of the village this might be a welcome development, but from the author's point of view it still leaves the village defenseless before the encroaching influence of European civilization.

Mongo Beti's other type of protagonist, the African student, is most fully delineated in *Mission terminée.* . . . Jean Medza, a student at the *lycée* in a nearby city, who is about eighteen, relates his experiences in the course of a summer vacation spent in a village located deep in the bush. It is again the humorous account of the adventures of a protagonist who proves inadequate to the situation in which he finds himself. In the course of this narrative Mongo Beti provides us with a half-comic, half-serious analysis of the situation of the African intellectual in Africa, and voices as well his criticism of the inadequacy of the Western-educated student. (pp. 228-29)

[The] mock-heroic tone, which is sustained throughout the book, gives a light touch and perspective to the hero's philosophical quest for paradise. Like the missionaries Medza views the village in the African bush through the illusions of primitivism. He tends to think of Kala as a happy Eden peopled by ignorant natives who have been spared the torments of a troubled intellectuality. He is very careful, for instance, in what he tells them about his studies because, as he remarks repeatedly, he wants to avoid giving them complexes. He also feels a boundless admiration for the four illiterate village youths who are his constant companions, and bemoans the fact that his education prevents him from joining fully in what he conceives to be their uncomplicated instinctual existence. . . . (pp. 229-30)

By the end of the novel Medza has gained a more realistic understanding of African village society and his position within it. But his development is the exact opposite of Father Drumont's experience. While the missionary arrives in the bush country of the Tala tribe convinced of the importance of his role and finds himself rejected by the African village, Medza arrives in Kala convinced that he is an insignificant failure and discovers that he is a man of great importance in the village. The inhabitants regard him as a man of learning who can initiate them into the mysteries of the modern world. His efforts to satisfy their demands keep him so busy that he scarcely has time to enjoy his summer vacation. . . . Medza himself is so wrapped up in the psychological problem of reconciling his position as an educated man with his sense of failure that he seems scarcely aware of the potential material benefits of his position, but they are considerable, in wealth, in social standing, and even in sexual attractiveness.

This humorous tale of the rewards that education can bring in a backwoods village is interwoven with a more serious analysis of the social structure of village society: Mongo Beti's village is divided by tradition into two mutually antagonistic groups, the old and the young, who are kept from open strife only because the older generation is the sole possessor of power, wealth, and prestige. Medza's entrance brings a new factor into this stratified society of which he himself becomes aware only after some time. Although he belongs to the younger generation his position as an educated man permits him to rise to a position of wealth and influence that is characteristic of the older generation. But there is a price to be paid for this rapid rise. Wealth and success come to Medza because he has allowed the older generation to exploit him for its own purposes. The knowledge he has brought to the village serves to buttress the status quo and in fact to reinforce the advantage which the elders hold over the youth in the village. Thus, for example, his uncle Mama profits greatly from his nephew's stay since he accumulates a large herd of goats as his share of the presents Medza receives from the villagers. The local chief also strengthens his position as he enters into an alliance with the new educated class by trapping Medza into marriage with one of his daughters, in one of the most amusing scenes in the novel.

Medza, however, refuses to pay the price of his success and decides to remain loyal to the only real friends he has made in Kala, the four young men whose carefree existence he shared whenever he could escape from his duties in the village. He can only do this through a negative act, by refusing the position, the wealth, and the wife which he has acquired thanks to his education, and setting out on a wandering quest that takes him far from the village of Kala, to other countries and other continents.

Thus Mongo Beti's student protagonist ends up in exile from Africa, as did the missionaries. Yet this is not an entirely negative ending since Medza's exile is voluntary. His mission to Kala has given him a certain awareness of the predicament of modern Africa and of his role as an educated man. For the first time in his life he is able to make a choice and does not let himself be carried along by circumstances. Although he is not capable of pursuing a positive goal, he at least refuses to compromise on material success and chooses instead the uncertainty of the quest. (pp. 230-31)

Mongo Beti's fiction is a record of failure, the failure to discern either the "intellectual direction" of the new Africa or the type of leader who can initiate the African into the mysteries of the modern world. But it is a successful record of failure. The author's ability to assume a multiplicity of frequently contradictory points of view, his capacity to bring out the humor in the contradictions and incongruities of modern Africa, as well as his realistic appraisal of African village society, indicate a critical detachment, an intellectual stance, which are rare in contemporary African literature. (p. 233)

Thomas Cassirer, "The Dilemma of Leadership as Tragi-Comedy in the Novels of Mongo Beti," in L'Esprit Créateur *(copyright © 1970 by L'Esprit Créateur), Vol. X, No. 3, Fall, 1970, pp. 223-33.*

O. R. DATHORNE

[In *Ville cruelle*] Beti is not yet doing his thing. He is bending over backward in an effort to write a certain European recipe. The ingredients are there: the wicked colonialist, the virtuous blacks, the need to please the stereotyped dying mother. There are inexplicable events that result from an unsureness of artistic control: the convenient loss and recovery of the suitcase, the brother, Koumé, who slips on a log and falls into the river, the happy marriage at the end of the book. Often some of this builds up into sheer melodrama or fairy tale solutions. However, the novel did not exist as a genre in traditional Africa, so the African writer could choose to create his own form of the novel.

[With *King Lazarus*] Beti moved away from imitating European modes to a style and manner more his own. The setting is again in a remote area, but the stock figures are absent. The chief of Essazam has resisted Christian interference. It seems likely, however, that he will die; and as Le Guen, the missionary, is absent, his Aunt Yosifa [a Christian convert] decides that she has to undertake [his baptism]. . . . (pp. 8-9)

[Yosifa's baptizing of the chief] is the high point of the novel, and the rest of the action demonstrates that the imposition of one set of practices upon another is bound to lead to misunderstanding. In *King Lazarus* the author distances himself from the material of recall: he is no spokesman for a given occasion as in the context of African oral-traditional performances; nor is he the detached perverter of values as in *Ville cruelle,* forcing the plot into a happy ending. Throughout *King Lazarus* there are gateway manifestations which make us perceive and examine the wholeness in life which conventional novel-patterns deny us.

Between the two works, *Ville cruelle* and *King Lazarus,* two novels spelled out the direction in which *King Lazarus* would go: *Le Pauvre Christ de Bomba* . . . , which first mentions Le Guen, and *Mission to Kala* . . . , which first deals with the town-educated gadabout who is confronted with the culture of the bush which he cannot understand. In *King Lazarus,* Le Guen plays a minor role as does Kris, for by the time of the writing of *King Lazarus,* Beti saw his own role more properly as that of an outsider, to distill in cryptic and enigmatic form the truth of the African experience. *Ville cruelle* juxtaposes victim and agent. *Le Pauvre Christ de Bomba* presents the conflict between Christian and pagan power. *Mission to Kala* demonstrates with a great deal of satire how European culture is no match for the indigenous civilization, that indeed the *évolué* falters when confronted with his own background. The themes combine in *King Lazarus* as a tussle for power; both the chief of Essazam and the missionary Le Guen are civilizing agents. The novel seeks to explore the nature of power, and this is really the serious purpose that underlies the humor. In this way it speaks more positively about the nature of the African experience than Beti's earlier books. (pp. 9-10)

At the center of the tension of a Beti novel there is [an] . . . outer manifestation and inner need. Jean-Marie Medza in *Mission to Kala* is a failure in the European world in the sense that he has not succeeded in passing his baccalaureate examination. He returns to his village and is surprised to find himself a hero to the villagers who all think of him as educated. Because of this, he is chosen to retrieve a runaway wife, and in Kala the *évolué* schoolboy comes up against the deeper, instinctive longings that are really part of himself. To the villagers he seems like a European, yet he himself knows he does not have their strength. His tragedy is the tragedy of Africa, "that of man left to his own devices in a world which does not belong to him, which he has not made and does not understand," as Beti states.

In *Le Pauvre Christ de Bomba* and in *Mission to Kala* both of the chief characters grow up to a new understanding of self. The crisis of growth which had been hinted at in *Ville cruelle* manifests itself more fully in these two novels and is more fully documented. (p. 12)

And in the final analysis, for Beti, personal growth is a movement toward a newer and deeper understanding of the tribe—the very tribe that had been rejected by the *évolué* values. From outside, the new man, initiated into tribal norms and confirmed into Christian values, can look at it all with wonder. No longer is the problem one of belonging . . . it is now the motif of choice. (p. 13)

[*King Lazarus* is], in a way, a savage piece of writing. Under the guise of laughter—that is, within the tradition of the masquerade—Mongo Beti exposes the romanticized Africa of tradition and the modernized Africa of the city. The chief is a rogue, as is the missionary; the novel opens with a truce between thieves. . . . All matters become a question of politics and policies, and winning souls is as much a business as ruling bodies. Behind the facade of proclaimed ideals lurks the very heart of villainy. At all stages *King Lazarus* reveals the sour contradictions in the human psyche.

There are no artificial agents of execution in the novel. The satire, if a commitment to exposure can be thus termed, is used to emphasize the plight of priest and pagan. They both seek to restore the crumbling, decaying walls of their ideologies; they both barely manage to prop up the decaying foundations. It is for his own glorification that Father Le Guen seeks to bring about the chief's conversion; this much is evident in his letters to his mother and in his desire not to fail as a previous priest had failed. The chief resists for reasons that are purely selfish. He is conservative, selfish, avaricious, but also cunning and politically expedient. (pp. 13-14)

In *King Lazarus* Beti refuses to take sides; basically the world is corrupt. All actions mask a play for power. The African past was not one in which wicked Europeans fought innocent Africans, but one in which the underdog was trodden upon by both the indigenous aristocracy and the expatriate overlord. In all of Beti's novels, beyond the wall of the laughter of dissent lie human concern and pathos for the undying ones who have waited for centuries. Beti's alienation makes him castigate a system that would seek to establish enclaves. By emancipating himself from group loyalty, he is freer to impale both the foe without and those who speak the language of the kinsmen within. (p. 14)

> O. R. Dathorne, "Introduction" (reprinted with permission of Macmillan Publishing Company; copyright © 1971 by Macmillan Publishing Co., Inc.), in King Lazarus: A Novel by Mongo Beti, Macmillan/Collier, 1971, pp. 7-14.

ROBERT P. SMITH, JR.

The fact that Mongo Beti, a brilliant and praiseworthy [novelist] . . . , has broken his silence with another important novel, should not be a news item which provokes great surprise. That the main theme of this author's most recent literary offering, *Perpétue,* treats of the victimization of the modern African woman in today's independent Africa, is a noteworthy event which should arouse the interest and curiosity of most scholars of African literature. In short, Mongo Beti is taking a critical look at well-known and accepted African traditions, in his homeland as well as in greater Black Africa. (p. 301)

In painting such a depressing picture of a new Africa which has emerged from decades of foreign misrule, Mongo Beti seems to have taken up the protest begun by another internationally known West African of French expression and author of the explosive novel *Dramouss,* Camara Laye from Guinea. Allusions to a new attitude on the part of West African writers have been made by several literary critics. . . . The conclusion is that the West African novel finds itself on the threshold of a new realism and a new objectivity. . . . Thus the so-called African literature which might well be called anti-colonial literature . . . must now look to its writers for that genuine artistic effort which may bring about the particular type of awakening necessary for each one in his turn to create his own national literature.

In the middle of the dismal political atmosphere exposed in *Perpétue,* where the Black is persecuted by his Black brother and where independence is a travesty, Mongo Beti has introduced a new dimension: the slave-like condition of the African woman. The story of Perpétue, the heroine of the novel by the same name, is narrated with great energy and realism. (pp. 303-04)

[*Perpétue* is] a dramatic indictment of the ill-fated independence in [Beti's] native land dominated by corrupt dictatorial power, as well as a forceful denunciation of the disgraceful status of African women in such regimes. With this novel

Mongo Beti proves once again that he is one of the best of the contemporary Black African novelists, who seek to promote true liberty in Africa and to insure a lasting dignity for her. With **Perpétue** the author's outstanding literary talent is again confirmed. The picturesque art of the story-teller is still there. Because of the seriousness of purpose and manner which the themes of politics and status of women demand of the author, one does not find an abundance of Mongo Beti's usual humor here and laughter does not dominate completely the various situations presented. Except for the doomed but sincere affection exchanged between Perpétue and [her lover] Zeyang, tender love has no chance of survival in this novel. True friendship and camaraderie, as portrayed in the relationship between Perpétue and Anna-Marie her trusted and faithful companion, occupy great space in the book. The jealousy and treachery which [her husband] Edouard unbridles against Perpétue never seem to be justified, but serve the author's purpose in dramatizing the status of African women.

In the study of the main characters of the novel one sees how intense Mongo Beti's censure is against oppressed Blacks who seek refuge in alcohol or the famous "karakara" which poisons all ambition to seek a better world; against the mediocre and corrupt African officials, who were placed in their positions by the departed colonizers; against African dictators who have personal airplanes, helicopters, palaces, property on the French Riviera, ultra-modern automobiles, etc., while African citizens are dying from lack of food and medicines; and finally against African parents who still sell their daughters into situations comparable to slavery.

Mongo Beti has broken his silence, not to criticize the colonial past as was his custom, but to accuse the present period of independence and self-government, and to attempt to pave the way to a better future for Africa and Africans. (p. 311)

> *Robert P. Smith, Jr., "Mongo Beti: The Novelist Looks at Independence and the Status of the African Woman," in CLA Journal (copyright, 1976 by the College Language Association; used by permission of The College Language Association), Vol. XIX, No. 3, March, 1976, pp. 301-11.*

CHARLES E. NNOLIM

Someone has suggested [that Beti's **Mission to Kala**] is a picaresque novel and that the protagonist, Jean-Marie, is a picaresque hero. The statement is misleading because the plot of the classic picaresque novel is mainly episodic, and character growth is almost nil. Beyond this, the classic picaro normally comes from the lowest stratum of society, has little breeding, lives on his wits, and only a very thin line separates his rascality from actual criminality. A picaro is always a prankster and a rascal who begins and ends as one with little or no character development.

But the plot of **Mission to Kala** is not strung together haphazardly. The story line has causality, and events are ordered and arranged organically. There is a marked growth, change, and development at the end in the character of Jean-Marie. The characters themselves are convincingly motivated, and there is a dynamic interaction among them. (p. 181)

Another critical misjudgment is that **Mission to Kala** is a satire pure and simple. Now, a satire squarely in its genre, is one in which the protagonist suffers disillusionments by trying to apply systems to a world that is far from systematized (Candide, for example, sets out with incredible naivete, believing that

"all is for the best in the best of all possible worlds"). In such works—Voltaire's *Candide*, Rabelais' *Gargantua*, and the like—characters are usually presented as mouthpieces of the ideas they represent so that the ultimate result would be caricatures due to the stylized nature of character delineation. Emphasis on ideas and a free play of intellectual fancy are the hallmarks of satire. Of course, one must admit that **Mission to Kala** makes satiric jabs at the self-deceptions and facile assumptions of superiority which Jean-Marie (a laughable example of the colonized mind), with his half-digested bits of Western education, clothes himself; but the work is squarely in the novel tradition. (p. 182)

Mission to Kala is a novel in which the journey motif (physical and metaphorical) shapes the novelistic form. It traces the physical journey of Jean-Marie Medza . . . from his village to Kala, to retrieve his uncle's runaway wife and bring her back. He succeeds in his mission. . . . But in the process, he gains an insight into himself and achieves maturity. An undercurrent of irony pervades the action and enriches it. (p. 183)

At the end of the physical journey, the mission is successful—Niam's wife is brought back. . . .

But it is the temporal or metaphorical journey which assumes greater importance in the book, for the journey motif provides Medza with opportunities for growth, maturity, and self-discovery. In the process, he goes through a series of "admissions," "discoveries," and "initiations" which constitute the movement and rhythm of the novel. In the manner of Don Quixote and Sancho Panza, Jean-Marie is the *alazon* or self-deceiver, posturing with an inflated self-image of himself—this "scholar," this "prodigy," as he likes to think of himself—while Duckfoot Johnny and Zambo play the part of the *eiron* or self-depreciators who, in fact, possess sophistication.

At the beginning of his journey, Jean-Marie regards himself not just as a mere boy sent on a delicate family mission, but as "a brigand chief, a pirate, a true Conquistador" on a "splendid machine" (his borrowed bicycle, mind!) going to conquer a foreign land. He imagines himself "the star in the ascendant, the coming man of the tribe." He refers to the "primitive savagery" he witnessed in Kala on his arrival. He took time out to ask "by what miraculous process this man could be related to me in any way?" on seeing Zambo, his cousin, to whom he refers as "a great hulking devil." . . . Duckfoot Johnny, who pretends ignorance, leads him into further self-deception. . . . (p. 184)

The self-deception continues in social drinking where Jean-Marie found out, to his dismay, that he could not handle alcohol like any of his friends in Kala. In one scene, he recruits Zambo to help him deceive his friends by surreptitiously consuming his share of the liquor for him, misleading Duckfoot Johnny into the belief that Jean-Marie is a guzzler like himself. . . . Even in the intellectual sphere which is the source of his snobbery of Kala villagers, Jean-Marie found on close questions from the ignorant villagers, "vast gaps in the frontiers of my kingdom." It was a very sobering admission—the beginning of Jean-Marie's admission of his other weaknesses. . . . (p. 185)

After his stay in Kala, Jean-Marie felt grown-up enough to rebel against his father and to confront him as a man. . . . In Freudian terms, his rebellion against his father—a rejection of paternal authority—becomes part of the inevitable road he must traverse in his journey to adulthood. In this journey, events have forced Jean-Marie to see himself as he really is and even to regret part of his past, especially, his education from which his inflated self-image stems. He came to discover, to his chagrin, that his education had been a veneer all along. . . . (pp. 186-87)

What gives aesthetic shape to **Mission to Kala** is the change of place which occurs between Jean-Marie and the Kala villagers in the end: Jean-Marie who sets out on a mission to conquer and educate the Kala rustics with his superior education, remains in Kala, not to educate but to be educated by them and to be initiated into every phase of adult village life. It is this reversal which shapes the novel like an hourglass and gives it its architectonic structure. This is one of the major reasons I contend that **Mission to Kala** is not a picaresque novel, for the plot of the picaresque is episodic and not organic. And organic structure is the hallmark of **Mission to Kala**. It is one of the few novels coming from Francophone Africa with a recognizable structure and pattern. The movement of the novel has a rhythm provided by a series of admissions, discoveries, and initiations by the protagonist in his journey to adulthood and maturity. It is a novel which has, in Aristotelian terms, both discovery and *peripeteia* or "reversal." . . . In **Mission to Kala** the snobbish and arrogant conquistador, Jean-Marie Medza, who went to educate the barbarous savages in Kala remains, not to educate them but to learn a thing or two from them, to imbibe the wisdom of life from them, to be initiated into manhood by them. (pp. 188-89)

I mentioned earlier that the ironic mode is at the base of the comic enjoyment we derive from **Mission to Kala**. Comedy in this novel stems from the ironic posture of the author who laughs up his sleeves at the self-deceptions indulged in by his "prodigy"—Jean-Marie Medza, who tries to cover up more and more potentially embarrassing situations with more and more self-deceptions. He suffers minor discomfitures but the reader and the author love him too much to want to see him suffer any serious distress. It is comedy also that helps define the shape of **Mission to Kala**. The comic pleasure we derive from the novel stems from the concave shape of the plot . . . , as opposed to the convex shape of tragedy . . . , because in spite of everything, the mission is a "success." Niam's wife is brought back to him. The source of the comic pleasure, too, is positive rather than negative. Negative comic pleasure is usually the type we derive from comedy of the classical tradition in which a thoroughly despicable character like Volpone, or Shylock, is made, by reason of his own folly, to lapse from cleverness to suffer a humiliating reversal of fortune, caught, as it were, in his own trap, while trying to overreach himself. Rather, Jean-Marie is, as I mentioned above, a protagonist with whom the reader identifies because of the general goodness of his character. (pp. 189-90)

[However, one] must not close one's eyes to the artistic defects of **Mission to Kala**. The perceptive reader who is interested in the aesthetic quality of the novel will not help noticing that the ending of **Mission to Kala** is an artistic flop. An offending passage (to the aesthetic sense) stems, I think, from Mongo Beti's attempt at the very end, to extend the frontiers of his novel into the picaresque. It reads (after Jean-Marie leaves his father's house for good, joined by Zambo):

> It turned out to be a life of endless wandering: different people, changing ideas, from country to country, and place to place. During these peregrinations my cousin Zambo and I stuck together, like two lambs attached to the same body.

This passage spoils everything. It blemishes an otherwise well-chiselled piece of work. If meaning accretes from the expectations for which the story-line has prepared the reader, it is cheating the reader out of his expectations to suddenly transform Jean-Marie in the end from a mature adult with a wife of his own, into a wandering hobo who, with Zambo, "were imprisoned and tortured together, experienced the same miseries and disillusionments, shared the same joys." As I see it, it is not only artistically crude but offensive to our aesthetic sense to allow Jean-Marie to go through ignorance to experience, maturity, and adulthood with that recognized ticket of admission to adult society and respectability—a wife—and then deface him by presenting to us at the end a depraved and debased image of him. And when the ending also debases Zambo from a hero among his peers in Kala to a wandering picaro in order to make him share the equally abased and reduced stature of Jean-Marie, the reader feels not only disappointed, frustrated, and cheated out of his expectations, but also feels in the sudden turn of events a distortion of the facts. The ending, such as it is, seems to have ignored the simple truth which the novel tells: Medza's successful mission to bring back Niam's wife in the process of which he also grows and matures, gets married, and returns with other admirers from Kala in tow. Medza arriving back in his village gives every impression of a successful man. By allowing Medza's father to chase him out of his household and deny him the enhanced stature of an adult which his own marriage has stanched, is the beginning of a bad ending.

It is possible that Mongo Beti was consciously adhering to modern conceptions and theories of the novel—theories that champion writing an open rather than a closed novel and adopting the technique of *inflationary* and *deflationary* characterization. If this is the case, he unconsciously defaced the rounded edges of his work which he so painstakingly put together. By so doing he has deprived **Mission to Kala** of that beauty which glows from within a finely chiselled piece of work thus depriving the perceptive reader the source of his keenest enjoyment. If I were to end the novel on a note fitting to the structure and meaning of **Mission to Kala**, I would have Jean-Marie's father welcome him and his wife like a man. I would not send him out on further peregrinations after his major mission was so successfully accomplished. (pp. 192-93)

> *Charles E. Nnolim, "The Journey Motif: Vehicle of Form, Structure, and Meaning in Mongo Beti's 'Mission to Kala'," in* Journal of Black Studies *(copyright © 1976 by Sage Publications, Inc.; reprinted with permission of Sage Publications, Inc.), Vol. 7, No. 2, December, 1976, pp. 181-94.*

WOLE SOYINKA

A certain Lothrop Stoddard prophesied as follows (the year was 1920):

> Certainly, all white men, whether professing christians or not, should welcome the success of missionary efforts in Africa. The degrading fetishism and demonology which sum up the native pagan cults cannot stand, and all Negroes will some day be either christians or moslems. . . .

Mongo Beti is perhaps the most assiduous writer to have taken up the challenge of Mr Stoddard dealing expertly and authentically with the claims of Christianity as a filler of spiritual holes.

His weapon is a deceptive generosity which disguises, until the last moment, a destructive logic, incontestible in its consistent exposition of cause and effect. His priests are never complete villains but are revealed to be complete fools. Even where he has presented the representative of the Christian Church as a figure of inner doubts on the way to eventual enlightenment, it is only a refinement of Mongo Beti's delectable hypocrisy—his exactions will be doubly cruel and thorough. Thus, in *King Lazarus* the Rev. Father le Guen, stiff-necked to the last, merely loses his position and is left with the consolation of commiserating with himself as a victim of colonial administrative intrigues. The only reprisal from the victims of his spiritual assault is to witness the reversion of his prize convert to the joys of polygamy. The poor Christ of Bomba is an equally stubborn prelate. He is even more manic in his encounters with 'heathen' practices but by contrast, is revealed as a man tortured by increasing doubts. His inner reflections promise a conversion, some hope for the salvation of the man is awakened in the breast of the reader. But Mongo Beti is not about to redeem his gull. The ramifications of a venereal denouement cover the Father Superior with the stench of failure. Beti's thesis reads: the Church is, by its very nature (doctrine and practice), a contagion; Mongo Beti's expositions are masterly erosions of the Christian myth. (pp. 97-8)

Wole Soyinka, "Ideology and the Social Vision (2): The Secular Ideal," in his Myth, Literature and the African World *(© Cambridge University Press 1976), Cambridge University Press, 1976, pp. 97-139.**

EUSTACE PALMER

Mongo Beti's work falls within the context of [the] reaction against the imposition of western culture on African society. Taken as a whole it probably gives the most thoroughgoing exposure of the stupidity of the imperialist attempt to devalue traditional education and religion and replace them by an inadequate western educational system and a hypocritical Christian religion. One of the most elegant and sophisticated of African writers, Mongo Beti's urbanity of tone should not lull the reader into a feeling that he is complacent about the issues he raises. His intelligence and wide-ranging wit correlate with a determination to face the uglier realities and expose them.

Beti's first novel *The Poor Christ of Bomba* was so effective in its exposure of French imperialist attitudes that it provoked a storm on its publication in 1956. This largely underrated novel deserves more attention, if only because of the adroit manipulation of the rather naive narrator through whose eyes we see the events of the story. The focus is on the Rev. Father Drumont and his unavailing attempts to impose a rather austere and authoritarian version of Roman Catholicism on a proud people. The Father emerges as a harsh, obstinate, unfeeling, and conceited authoritarian in spite of, or perhaps partly because of, the unconcealed admiration he elicits from the naive narrator. (pp. 126-27)

The impulses of this cruel, dehumanized Father are essentially antilife. We also see his inhumanity, which is no different from that of the civil authorities, in extorting forced labour from the people in order to build his church. Particularly disgraceful is his exploitation of the Sixa girls whom he compulsorily houses within the mission, ostensibly to prepare them for the duties of a Christian wife, but in reality to provide cheap manual labour. Such cold inhumanity, such religious bankruptcy and dishonesty, are astonishing. So too is the Father's inflexibility

on matters of church rules. It is an inflexibility which will not allow a penniless old woman to take the sacrament because her church dues have not been paid, even though everyone, including the uncritical narrator, is moved by the old woman's tale of woe and faith and expects the Father to relent. In spite of his zeal, however, the Father's brand of religion exposes him as being basically un-Christian. It consists in reminding his parishioners of their sins, even on those occasions when he finds an exemplary young man or woman. The concepts of love and mercy are completely absent from the Father's creed. In his view, being a good Christian consists in paying one's church dues and if one's relatives happen to be polygamous, then all connections with them should be severed. Prompted by the belief that only the miserable can have faith in God, the Father virtually encourages poverty and prays for the people's unhappiness. His religion is a life-denying force which fails to come to terms with indigenous law and custom. He fails to see that it is both unnecessary and undesirable to attempt to smother beneath the superficial trappings of Roman Catholicism the age-old culture of the people from which they derive their vitality and their sense of identity, and his most high-handed actions are concerned with his attempts to suppress some aspect or other of traditional life. (p. 128)

Mongo Beti's intention is to expose, not just the Father, but the Roman Catholic Church as a whole, emphasizing its lack of appeal for the people. He underlines the fact that, in spite of the Father's zeal, Christianity is a minority religion here, deeply distrusted by the majority of the people, even by those who espouse it. (p. 130)

Christianity turns out in Tala to be an extremely expensive and commercialized religion demanding much from its adherents and imposing several unreasonable tasks and obligations. It is also a religion that imposes its will by means of terror. . . . Christianity here is an extremely naive religion that depends on a simple-minded and uncritical acceptance of its doctrines, thus suggesting its underestimation of the native intelligence of the African peoples. The identification of Christianity with a white civilization is another obstacle to its acceptance in these parts. Since the white priests are always in association with the white administrators, the people quite rightly regard the church as the ally of an oppressive imperialist administration, and the fact that Jesus Christ is always represented as white further intensifies the feeling that Christianity is a white man's religion which is completely unsuited to African conditions. The people are far from being deluded about the church's real nature. They are perfectly aware of its double standards; they know that the Father who rages against polygamy and immorality among Africans fraternizes with whites who live in concubinage with loose women and sees nothing wrong in supposed white Christians associating with 'pagan' women, although he preaches that after baptism the Africans should stop visiting their 'pagan' relations. Finally, they are aware that the church is a disruptive force that threatens to break up their once-stable way of life.

The central action of the novel is the Father's tour through the Tala country accompanied by [his cook] Zacharia and the narrator, Dennis. Like Beti's second novel, *Mission to Kala, The Poor Christ of Bomba* takes the form of a picaresque tale whose significance lies, not so much in the events, as in the moral development of the participants. The journey is necessitated by one of the Father's most misguided policies. He discovers to his chagrin that, far from arousing in the people a stronger desire for the Christian faith . . . , spiritual deprivation has caused them to forget Christianity and return to their traditional ways. . . . [The] people of Tala have found a new independence and prosperity deriving largely from their success as cocoa farmers, and this prosperity is reflected in an obviously high standard of living. Against the Father's restrictive life-denying morality the happy people of Tala posit their vigorous affirmation of life. The naive narrator's condemnation of them as living careless lives alerts us to Beti's real viewpoint at this stage. Since they live away from the towns and main roads, the Talans are not only rural people but also traditionalists who have not allowed their lives to be influenced by the values of western imperialism; and although the narrator dismisses them as backward, it is obvious that they are very alert and in their own way progressive. (pp. 131-32)

Throughout the journey it is the same tale of dilapidated churches, polygamous husbands, unmarried mothers and non-payment of church dues. The message for the Father is clear; after nearly twenty years, Christianity has not really taken hold among these people. And it is significant that during the tour the once-feared Father attracts not only hostility but blatant disrespect.

Zacharia, whose irresponsibility should not blind us to his remarkable sanity and realism, plays a crucial role in the story. He is used by Mongo Beti as a kind of permanent check to the narrator's naivety and the Father's illusions about his mission. The author needs Zacharia on this journey to act as a useful corrective and to be the spokesman for the radical African point of view, and he is able to play this role effectively, not just because he is intelligent, but also because he is a perceptive man of the world who knows his people and is proud of them. He knows that these smart people have realized the importance of money in modern life and are going to chase it no less eagerly than the priests themselves. . . . Because of his peculiar association with the Father, Zacharia can tell the former truths which no one else can, and, what is more he is about the only person to whom the Father listens. On one occasion he bluntly tells the Father that the African did not first hear of God from the white man; if he agreed to embrace the religion of the latter it was because he hoped that such an association would give him the secret of the white man's power and knowledge. Zacharia can see right through the Father and the other whites; he knows their secrets, their illusions and their real desires and he is sensitive enough to be aware of the effect the Father is producing on the people. If the Father changes somewhat during the course of the journey, it is largely owing to Zacharia's influence.

The change that takes place in the Father is one of the most interesting features of the novel. The first signs of it appear shortly after that conversation with Zacharia and the catechist in which the former had tried to enlighten the Father about the real reasons why some of the people have turned to Christianity. In the ensuing conversation with the self-satisfied M. Vidal, the Father begins to express doubts for the first time about the purpose of his mission: and he mentions the point that Zacharia has made—that the people did not first hear about religion from the white man. The Father seems to be gradually groping his way towards a realization of the validity of traditional life and culture. When the bigoted Vidal asserts that the civilization they are trying to impart to the Bantu race involves much more than materialism and technological advancement, that it involves the Christian religion in fact, the Father suggests, following Zacharia, that any religion 'even if it hadn't inspired a policy of conquest, can be none the less real for its adherents'. This is a liberalism which we have never been led to expect

from the Father. Vidal's callousness in proposing to build his road by forced labour also shocks the Father into a realization of his responsibility. Where he once expressed the wish that the people would be unhappy in order that they might return to him, he now sees it as his duty to protect them against the cruelty and depredations of Vidal. The Father cannot yet make a great point about this, however; for one thing, as Vidal sarcastically reminds him, there is the uncomfortable realization that he himself had once used forced labour in the construction of his religious buildings. Nevertheless, his conscience has been stirred and he has moved a very long way from both Vidal and the uncritical narrator who in his naivety rejoices at the people's forthcoming calamity. (pp. 133-34)

Finally there is the realization in conversation with Vidal that he has been a failure and ought to return to Europe. This conversation is central to the novel's themes. It shows the Father's genuine concern now about the imposition of western culture on Bomba: 'These good people worshipped God without our help. What matter if they worshipped after their own fashion—by eating one another, or by dancing in the moonlight, or by wearing bark charms around their necks? Why do we insist on imposing our customs upon them?' . . . At the end of the conversation the Father arrives at a clear perception of what has been going on in Africa: the connivance between the missionaries and the administrators to keep the people in a perpetual state of subjection. The Father then launches on a touching analysis of the motives which had prompted him to come to Africa as a missionary: revolted by Europe's arrogance and technological preoccupation he had decided to extend the kingdom of Christ to people considered disinherited and simple. Arriving in Africa he felt flattered by the deference paid to him and failed to acknowledge the real worth of the people until jolted to reality by the Talans' spirit of independence and the failure of his stratagem. The real measure of the change that has come over the Father is indicated in his acceptance of the stupidity of his opposition to polygamy and his readiness now to be flexible about the question of unmarried mothers. (p. 135)

[Although] the Father had come to a clear realization during the tour of the futility of colonization and the attempt to impose alien customs on the people, he had retained his initial view of Africans as technologically, intellectually and morally backward. And it is what he now sees as the African's incorrigible immorality that administers the final blow and forces him to leave Bomba in a harsher frame of mind than seemed conceivable.

Zacharia's wife's revelation, after a dreadful fight with Catherine, that the latter is from the Sixa, prompts investigations which suggest to the reader, if not to the Father, that it is the latter's policies which are responsible for the descent of Catherine and the other Sixa girls into depravity. By putting a young man like Raphael in charge of a female institution like the Sixa with a lot of other young men around, the Father was merely presenting them with a ready-made brothel. The Sixa turns out to be a den of corruption, largely through the Father's negligence, as Marguerite, one of the girls, tells him. The most startling revelation of all is that the Father's policy has created the perfect conditions for a venereal disease epidemic which now rages through the Sixa.

But the Father now irresponsibly blinds himself to the fact that he is largely the cause of the catastrophic turn of events at Bomba, unleashing his venom instead, not on the men, but on the girls who are the unfortunate victims of his own negligence and the men's incontinence. In a very real sense he has destroyed the lives of almost all these girls, not simply because they are infected with venereal disease, but because their fiancés, fed up with waiting and disgusted by the corrupt activities at the Sixa, have abandoned them. But this completely fails to register on the mind of the racialist Father who now sees the activities at the Sixa as the expression of the unbridled libido of the black race. 'They are all eaten up with lust; Ah, what a race!' . . . We now see some nasty aspects of the Father's character that the relationship with Zacharia may only faintly have suggested. He now turns out to be a voyeur deriving a perverted pleasure from the girls' sordid revelations, vicariously enjoying the delights of sex at second hand. Under the pretence of conducting the investigations he calls up all the girls, one after the other, and forces them to give all the details of their sexual activities with the men, the more modest ones being encouraged with the aid of the cane. The Father also clearly becomes a sadist, for when each girl arrives for her confession she is first given several strokes of the cane on the Father's orders. This contempt for the dignity of the African race is repulsive in a man who is simultaneously demonstrating that he harbours the basest instincts himself. (pp. 139-40)

The Doctor's report on the syphilis epidemic [in the Sixa] is a thorough condemnation of the Father's administration. It speaks of bad sanitation, bad housing, bad cooking arrangements, bad maintenance, low morale and exploitation. One would have expected that this would at last alert the Father to a full realization of his responsibility and moral obligation to the girls, but although he finally admits that he is 'the guilty party in the whole affair', it is an intellectual admission which is not deeply felt and is certainly not followed by repentant action. The height of his irresponsibility and impenitence are revealed when, instead of taking steps to cure the girls, as the Doctor has advised, he decides to pack them off to their homes, presumably to spread venereal disease throughout the country, asserting that they have brought dishonour to his mission. The Father shows at the end that he is even harsher than the opening pages have suggested. (p. 141)

The thorough exploration of this novel's themes might lead one to overlook its artistry or to suppose that it is merely a string of episodes. It is, in fact, a very well constructed novel with a compact, unified plot. The fact that it is the same tale of woe that the Father meets at every station might seem repetitive, but it is necessary in order to demonstrate the Church's universal failure in the Bomba area. Most important, the reader is held spellbound by the gradual revelation of the various aspects of the Father's slow growth into awareness. It is quite obvious that in spite of the wealth of detail Mongo Beti had probably planned almost every aspect of this novel even before he started to write it. Particularly worthy of commendation is the brilliant exposure of the narrator's naivety and the consistency and effectiveness with which the author penetrates the depths of an adolescent mind in convincing language. This gives us splendid passages of introspection resulting in a very full picture, not only of the boy, but of the Father himself. Even more minor characters like Zacharia, Catherine and Vidal are realistically and convincingly presented.

No doubt there will be readers, particularly French ones, who will call the accuracy of Beti's presentation of the French colonial situation into question. It is quite possible that Beti has exaggerated, but exaggeration is a perfectly legitimate literary weapon. In order to assess the literary quality of the book, we must look within it, to the effectiveness of the methods used

by the author, not outside to its historical truth. There is little doubt that, literarily speaking, Beti has produced a most effective denunciation of an unsuitable political and cultural system.

Mongo Beti's next novel, *Mission to Kala,* continues his denunciation of the French colonial exercise, turning the focus this time on the colonial educational system. His thesis, apparently, is that the formal classical education to which young francophones were exposed was ultimately valueless, since it alienated them from their roots in traditional society, taught them to consider the values of that society inferior to French ones and gave them little preparation for the life they were to lead. Beti's manipulation of his persona in this novel is a much more complex exercise. . . . Jean-Marie is often ironically treated in order to reveal his conceit, delusion and stupidity; at other times he himself looks back with disgust at his past follies, and on other occasions he is used straightforwardly as a mouthpiece to deliver Mongo Beti's satire against the French system. The exercise calls for a very deft manipulation of tone and language and suggests, not that Beti does not know what to do with his narrator, but that he is aware that he has a slightly more mature persona than [the narrator of the earlier novel] to deal with this time.

Apart from the more complex manipulation of the persona the other major stylistic development in *Mission to Kala* lies in its richer comedy. One is immediately struck by the narrator's scintillating wit and flippant, ironic and sarcastic tone, even, at times, at his own expense. The comedy also resides in the great number of hilarious scenes, some of them bordering on farce and slapstick. . . . The novel's picaresque nature is announced right at the start by the Fielding-like authorial chapter headings. As with most picaresques it takes the form of a quest during which the hero grows morally and spiritually and returns home a changed man. (pp. 141-43)

[The novel starts] with a boy returning home from school mortally terrified of his father's reaction to his failure in his examinations; it ends with the same boy returning home once more after an adventure of which the father will almost certainly disapprove, but which has taught him invaluable lessons about life, particularly about traditional life. The boy has lost his fear as a result of his experiences and returns to challenge the father. . . . Then follows the most vitriolic denunciation of his father's influence and a scathing exposure of the latter's capitalist tricks. The father emerges as a thoroughly unscrupulous character who has no hesitation in exploiting relations and enemies alike where his financial interests are concerned. (p. 153)

Jean-Marie returns to Kala a rebel, not so much against an educational system, as against his father's tyranny. Indeed, he goes back to school and passes his exams, but the revolt against his father is complete. Leaving his home he becomes something of a delinquent and a wanderer. This is true to form, as a number of psychologists and social workers will testify. A home like Jean-Marie's is bound to produce juvenile delinquents in the end, and it is not surprising that this is what eventually happens to both Medza boys. But Jean-Marie would probably have gone on living in fear if his eyes had not been opened by other vistas of experience during the Kala adventure.

What then should we make of *Mission to Kala*? Is it that the work started as a denunciation of the French educational system and then changed direction to become an exposure of a tyrannical father? The two concerns are, in fact, interrelated. In order to demonstrate the father's tyranny the educational system must be denounced, first in order to show the rigours to which this father subjects the poor boy in his bid to make him successful, and secondly, and perhaps more important, because this rather westernized father uncritically accepts a defective and alien educational system for his child. The denunciation of an unsuitable system of education is therefore quite in place. If it is taken to extremes it is not because Mongo Beti is against education *per se,* but because the father's tyranny has bred in the young boy a temporary pathological hatred for all educational systems.

Mongo Beti's third novel, *King Lazarus,* is a sad disappointment after the brilliance of the first two. Thematically, however, it is similar to the earlier novels since it is also concerned with the exposure of the pretentiousness of an alien cultural and imperialist system which shows little respect for the traditional life and dignity of the people. The attack this time is on the follies of both the Roman Catholic Church and the civil administration. *King Lazarus* differs in narrative technique from the other novels in being written in the third-person omniscient form. The change is for the worse. Gone is the brilliant manipulation of the naive narrator in *The Poor Christ of Bomba;* gone too is the brilliant wit and the captivating tone of voice of Jean-Marie Medza in *Mission to Kala.* Instead we have the rather garrulous omniscient narrator.

The novel is about the turbulent consequences of the conversion of the Chief of the Essazam to Christianity. The chief's new way of life clashes strongly with traditional beliefs and practices and disrupts the life of the community. Le Guen, the faceless assistant to Father Drumont in *The Poor Christ of Bomba,* is the representative of Roman Catholicism here. While lacking Father Drumont's intellect and capacity for rigorous self-analysis, he is more obstinate and insensitive than the latter, and is ultimately more disruptive of traditional ways. His simple, naive teaching illustrates the intellectual bankruptcy of the church and its contempt for the intelligence of the people it seeks to win to its fold. . . . Le Guen completely fails to consider the effects of his advice and decisions on the lives of the people. When he advises the chief to put away all his wives but one, he is apparently unmoved by the fact that such a step cuts right across a tradition which the chief as traditional ruler is supposed to safeguard. Nor is he particularly concerned about the human aspects of the problem—about the fact, for instance, that some of the wives have been married to the chief for years and know no other home, that they are forced to leave without their children who are now deprived of parental love and care, since they are unceremoniously bundled on to 'respectable housewives' around the village with instructions to feed and bring them up. The fact is that Le Guen's ruse to enforce monogamy on the chief completely disrupts the kingdom, setting husband against wife, wife against wife, clan against clan, uncle against nephew, and plunging the tribe into civil war. The misery that his policy precipitates is very touchingly evoked, but he remains insensitive to all this. His zeal might have been partly excused if the conversion to Christianity had made the chief a better man. On the contrary, it seems to liberate the most repulsive impulses in him.

Inevitably, Le Guen comes into confrontation with the civil administration who do not welcome the prospect of an inter-clan warfare. This conflict between the religious and political arm recalls that between Father Drumont and M. Vidal in *The Poor Christ of Bomba,* but in this case it is the man of God who is obstinate while the administrator seems to be the embodiment of sound sense. He reminds the Father that the whole

clan is against him and pleads with him to abandon his crazy policy of converting the chief. . . . [And yet] Beti is far from endorsing the patronizing administrator. If he counsels moderation it is not because of any regard for traditional culture. He merely counsels political expediency to ensure the continuation of the French presence in Africa. Beti's irony throughout this scene is a doubled-edged weapon which simultaneously exposes the insensitivity and obstinacy of Le Guen as well as the chauvinism of Lequeux. Towards the end Lequeux is forced to bare his teeth and reveal in the crudest and most violent kind of language that his entire career has been shaped by his almost pathological hatred of communists. . . . In the end the administrator has the last word in contriving Le Guen's transfer to another post. And the chief, though retaining the [baptismal] name 'Lazarus', soon rediscovers the joys of polygamy and strict obedience to tribal ethics.

Inevitably the French administration is denounced in the most scathing terms. The officials demonstrate a certain measure of efficiency, but it is in the interest of perpetuating a corrupt and unjust system. (pp. 153-56)

It must not be supposed, however, that Beti idealizes traditional society in this novel. This is a significant departure from his usual practice of showing tremendous responsiveness to the dignity and beauty of traditional life. *King Lazarus* presents a very unflattering picture of indigenous African society. The historical background with which the novel starts shows that owing to the impact of world forces on the Essazam they have become increasingly decadent. In this they are quite different from the magnificent people of Kala. They have been racked in internal feuds and vendettas; VD, alcoholism and other 'scourges' of modern civilization have made progressive inroads into their society. The chief is callous and pleasure loving; the young men and women are tireless fornicators; the elders are seen as 'pathetic orang-outangs who have reduced public debate to futility'; the diviners and priests are filthy, greedy old men more concerned with their own importance than with the efficient discharge of their duties; the warriors are even stupid in their fighting. Beti spares no pains to make the tribe as a whole look as ridiculous as possible. (p. 157)

Beti's *forte* in *King Lazarus* is his power of description and ability to bring a scene to life which has by no means deserted him. The account of the onset of the chief's fever is brilliant and the later deathbed scenes are very effectively done. Brilliant too are the series of scenes which, with a maximum of economy, portray the relations between Mama and her children. So are the various battle scenes. Although the rich comedy of *The Poor Christ of Bomba* and *Mission to Kala* is absent here, Beti has still been able to contrive some very funny scenes. . . . Quite often, however, the comedy is of a grotesque sort. Indeed, it is evident that Beti demonstrates a predilection in this work for the grotesque; this comes out in both his comic scenes and his descriptions, and is generally in line with his cynical mood. Be that as it may, the description of people's personal appearance shows superb artistry. (p. 158)

Characterization in *King Lazarus* is by no means as compelling as in the earlier two novels. The main reason for this seems to be that none of the characters' thoughts and actions are presented in such detail that he or she becomes memorable. There are hardly any passages of introspection. Both Le Guen and the chief, the two major characters, have a habit of disappearing from the scene for considerable periods, and in the case of the latter Beti fails to show the process whereby he changes once more from Christianity and monogamy to traditional ways and polygamy. The author's garrulousness is also partly responsible, for instead of allowing us to see and hear the characters wrestling with their dilemmas, he always stands between us and them.

This, then, is a novel marred by a number of flaws. Its prevailing cynicism suggests the bitterness of a man who is probably fed up with most things. It remains to be seen whether it really marks the decline of Mongo Beti. (pp. 158-59)

Eustace Palmer, "Mongo Beti," in his The Growth of the African Novel *(© Eustace Palmer 1979), Heinemann, 1979, pp. 124-59.*

BEN OKRI

[*Remember Ruben*] treats of the relationship between individuals and a complex, clouded situation of emerging national politics. When a solitary, young boy arrives at the village of Ekoumdoum, a new dimension enters village life. The youth, renamed Mor-Zamba, lost, coldly reticent and taunted by the villagers, attracts to himself another youth, Abena, a future revolutionary. Abena's sole ambition, symbolically, is to 'get a gun'. Morzamba's ambition to have the daughter of a prominent villager for wife stirs up forces of hostility which lead to his being taken off to a labour camp. Abena goes to look for him, and from then on their actions become larger than their characters. . . .

Behind everything lurks Ruben, trade union leader, relentless critic of national politics, and later guerrilla leader, whose personality links together the forces of protest. He is a mythical figure, never confronted in the narrative. After his death the phrase 'Remember Ruben' becomes a rallying call and reminder of the need for continuous vigilance.

Beti's depiction of a colony's traumas, confusions and corruptions is vivid and masterly. His treatment of the forces of history and the determination of ordinary individuals recalls Ngugi at his best. But *Remember Ruben* frequently gets bogged down, characters and story line lost, in its documentary portrayal of the patterns and details of colonial politics. The language is elevated, the author using the inclusive 'our' as though the novel were written as a general testament of the village of Ekoumdoum. The style is sometimes grand, sometimes tiresome, but always its energy rolls. . . . (p. 20)

In the end Abena returns, a hero with the new name of Ouragenviet, in time to save Kola-kola, the huge black suburb, from destruction. After 18 years there is a reunion with Mor-zamba, and the contrived revelation of Mor-zamba's true origins. . . . [The] end disappoints, but this does not altogether detract from the novel's importance. (p. 21)

Ben Okri, "Arms & the Man," in New Statesman *(©1981 The Statesman & Nation Publishing Co. Ltd.), Vol. 101, No. 2602, January 30, 1981, pp. 20-1.**

ROBERT P. SMITH, JR.

[In *La ruine presque cocasse d'un polichinelle*] Mongo Béti again evokes admiration for the patriot Ruben Um Nyobé, leader of the opposition in Cameroun, whose memory has been preserved in at least two of the author's previous novels (*Perpétue* and [*Remember Ruben*] . . .), and he also continues an account of life under the regime of the insensitive tyrant Baba Toura, a mysterious President of the Republic whose evil shadow hovered over the events in the two previous novels. Toura's administration, which fosters famine, misery, persecution and corruption in the wake of African independence, is perpetuated by evil characters in the novels against whom heroic protagonists struggle constantly so that justice may prevail.

The present novel recounts the adventures of Mor-Zamba, who leaves the capital of the republic accompanied by two other faithful Rubenists, Mor-Kinda and Evariste, charged with the task of organizing the resistance. . . . The novel takes on a "Robin Hood" atmosphere when the three resolute Rubenists set out on their long journey, robbing the rich and giving to the poor, outwitting the oppressors and conveying courage to the oppressed. Justice triumphs at the end of this lengthy novel after many intricate, thought-provoking, serious and picaresque adventures.

The novel, which Béti has labeled "Remember Ruben 2," is divided into three parts and an epilogue. The author is still a master of French prose when it is a question of portraying major and minor African characters and when he is criticizing Catholic missionaries. The portrayal of the patronizing, hypocritical and finally demented Father Van Den Reitter in the extended part two will certainly remain one of the best in Béti's gallery of portraits. The book is not without its flaws, for sometimes the author burdens his narrative with excessive detail and repetition; however, his storytelling technique remains vibrant and captivating. Of particular interest is the author's sympathetic treatment of African women, especially the character of the militant and proud Ngwane-Eligui la Jeune. Except for the three colorful Rubenists, it is the women in this novel who take it upon themselves to raise the standard of dignity, because fear and lack of self-respect have killed courage in the hearts of the African men.

Robert P. Smith, Jr., "Cameroun," in World Literature Today *(copyright 1982 by the University of Oklahoma Press), Vol. 56, No. 1, Winter, 1982, p. 162.*

Heinrich (Theodor) Böll

1917-

(Also transliterated as Boell) West German novelist, short story writer, dramatist, translator, and essayist.

Böll, the 1972 Nobel laureate, is one of the most prolific and widely read writers of post-World War II Germany. His work, which does not excuse Germany's actions in the war, is primarily about how ordinary people were affected by the reign of the Nazis. Böll's obvious anger at the events of the war years is not directed exclusively at the Third Reich; he also condemns the Catholic church's tolerance of the Nazi regime and the governing powers before and after Hitler. Wilhelm Johannes Schwartz has written that Böll's "predominant attitude to the war is disgust and vexation. . . . He tells only of its boredom, of filth and vermin, senselessness, and futile waste of time."

Born in Cologne and raised by devout but liberal Catholic parents, Böll's humanism was formed early in life. While in his teens, he avoided peer pressure and refused to join the Hilter Youth. In 1939, Böll was drafted into the German infantry and served during the entire war. He was wounded four times in noncombat incidents. As the German army became decimated Böll masqueraded as an Allied soldier. When his true identity was discovered, he was sent to a prisoner-of-war camp. After the war, Böll returned to Cologne and published his first short story in 1947.

Böll's early work reflects his experiences as a soldier. In *Der Zug war pünktlich* (1949; *The Train Was on Time*) and *Wo warst du, Adam?* (1951; *Adam, Where Art Thou?*), Böll focuses on the horror and absurdity of war. *The Train Was on Time* is a haunting story of a soldier who foresees his own death while waiting to be transported to the eastern front. Most critics consider this novel Böll's finest work. Postwar Germany is the setting of Böll's novels of the 1950s. *Und sagte kein einziges Work* (1953; *Acquainted with the Night*) is a tragic story of a family man's difficulty in adjusting to civilian life. This novel received much critical attention and established Böll as a master storyteller. *Haus ohne Hüter* (1954; *Tommorrow and Yesterday*) is the story of daily survival in a war torn city as seen through the eyes of two fatherless boys.

Böll's novels written during the 1960s and 1970s examine Germany's problems in constructing a new identity out of its Nazi past. As with his earlier work, Böll presents this theme on an individual level. In *Ansichten eines Clowns* (1963; *The Clown*), an alienated entertainer exposes the hypocrisy of affluent Germans, including his own family and the Church, who altered their political and moral stance for opportunistic reasons. *Gruppenbild mit Dame* (1971; *Group Portrait with Lady*) is structured as an evaluation of a woman through a series of monologues with people she encounters throughout her life. His recent novel, *Fursorgliche Belagerung* (1982; *The Safety Net*), is about political unrest and terrorism in the present-day.

Critics praise Böll for his ability to convey realistically the terror and effects of war in simple, concise prose. Some critics consider Böll's work a conscious protest against the stylistic complexity of classical German literature and compare his

© Lütfi Özkök

work to that of Ernest Hemingway, whom Böll himself has cited as an influence. His portrayal of the absurdity of life and the struggle for survival, and his skillful use of satire are best exemplified in his two short story collections, *Wanderer, kommst du nach spa* (1950; *Traveller, If You Come to the Spa*) and *18 Stories* (1966).

(See also *CLC*, Vols. 2, 3, 6, 9, 11, 15 and *Contemporary Authors*, Vols. 21-24, rev. ed.)

PAUL PICKREL

Heinrich Böll's **"Acquainted with the Night"** is the first non-political German novel I have seen since the war, and a fine book it is. Brief, unpretentious, technically conventional, it is worth reading because it is written out of the part of life that matters. American fiction more and more retreats into the suburbs. Geographically that may be all right, but spiritually it is slow death. Böll, on the other hand, has the courage and the talent to tackle his subject where it is most living.

A man and a woman who are no longer young and who already have more children than they can afford find that they are going to have yet another child. They live in a single room in a bombed-out German city; for some time the husband has come home only occasionally because he cannot abide being penned up in so little space with the children. Sometimes he beats them. He sees the problem of their lives together as poverty, but his wife knows better. She realizes that, though more money would certainly be a help, her husband is not the kind of man who is ever going to solve their problems economically; indeed, she sees that their problem is not primarily economic. What her husband needs is acceptance—acceptance of himself as a man who has wasted such opportunities as have come his way and as a man who is going to find no sudden magic solution to his problems; acceptance of their love and the children it has brought forth as the best thing they are going to have in this world; acceptance of responsibility for his own actions and for the family.

The book is an account of how a man is recalled to life. (p. 315)

The German background is arresting in at least two ways. For one thing, the scene is a Catholic city and the characters are Catholics, the wife devout, the husband (though he makes his living by operating a switchboard in an ecclesiastical establishment) anti-clerical but by no means outside the Church. Yet a feeling of religious insufficiency pervades the book; though the Church still has a connection with the people, it is faulty and not very much comes through to help them. For another thing, it would be easy for Böll to find the cause of the difficulties of his characters in the war and its aftermath, but he carefully distinguishes between those of their troubles that result from the war and those that result from their own mistakes. A fine sense of responsibility, a real moral awareness, underlies the book. If Heinrich Böll speaks for any considerable part of the new Germany, here is news more encouraging than any account of Bonn prosperity. (pp. 315-16)

> *Paul Pickrel, in a review of "Acquainted with the Night," in* The Yale Review *(© 1954 by Yale University; reprinted by permission of the editors), Vol. XLIV, No. 2, Winter, 1955, pp. 315-16.*

EDWIN KENNEBECK

With some of Ernest Hemingway's simplicity and clarity, Heinrich Böll writes several vignettes about a segment of the German army as it disintegrates in World War II under the Russian advance into Hungary. His stories at times separate into dry and toneless fragments, but often they come together magnetized in some fierce, ironic little catastrophe. A young, frightened corporal at a partially evacuated German hospital goes out into the garden with a Red Cross flag to meet the Russian tanks; he trips on a buried dud bomb, which explodes, kills him, and alarms the Russians into demolishing the defenseless hospital. An efficient engineering officer, by encouraging his men with friendship rather than with fear, gets a bridge rebuilt two days ahead of schedule, just in time to blow it up as the Russians arrive.

Such ironic catastrophes have been the substance of many war stories; they are preserved from staleness here by Mr. Böll's pure honesty and his wry casualness. . . .

[In *Adam, Where Art Thou?*] Mr. Böll's effectiveness is uneven because he does not share Mr. Hemingway's brilliant singleness of tone or attack. A later novel, not about the war, was published here . . . as *Acquainted with the Night*—an unusual, compassionate story about a man and a woman with worlds of misery on their shoulders—a story which was firmly unified by an implicit religious point of view. Its English title suggests the suffering of Christ, and in German its title was an equivalent

of "And He never said a mumbling word." This later work tells of a kind of dumb mortal *patience* that could renew the face of the earth.

Adam, Where Art Thou? does not probe so deeply. Mr. Böll at best attempts to unify its scenes with a vision of senselessness; but that is a vision of nothing. Pieces at the edge of a crumbling mosaic, these sketches do not offer an intuition of a total pattern, because the author keeps his several characterizations and flashbacks rigidly personal and local. His characters here are ordinary, most of them mediocre. They do not think about any large meanings, and they represent no national conscience—thus is Mr. Böll true to his craft. One character is a Catholic Jewish girl who says, "We must pray in order to console God." But the Heinrich Böll of this earlier group of stories gives no further intimations of a positive vision.

> *Edwin Kennebeck, "Ironic Sketches," in* Commonweal *(copyright © 1956 Commonweal Publishing Co., Inc.; reprinted by permission of Commonweal Publishing Co., Inc.), Vol. 63, No. 14, January 6, 1956, p. 360.*

ANTHONY WEST

Heinrich Böll's **"The Train Was on Time"** may be a little disappointing to those who have read his fine novels **"Acquainted with the Night"** and **"Adam, Where Art Thou?,"** but the apparent technical regression in this book represents no falling off in his considerable powers. He has suffered what so often happens in this country to foreign authors; the success (in his case largely critical) of his later books has led to the publication of an earlier one. Like many inexperienced writers, Böll resorted to allegory in **"The Train Was on Time"** and tied his gift for realistic writing to a highly generalized picture. His hero is not only a man going to the Eastern Front; he is *the* Eastern Front fighter. His journey back from a home leave is a journey into the night, away from love and hope toward what he knows is an empty void of despair. Böll expresses this by giving his man a premonition that he is going to be killed; with the clairvoyance of an exhausted man, he even knows the time and the place. The mechanics of this tryst do not convince the reader, but the sentiment does. Böll's soldier is afraid of the East, its spaces, and its confusions, as a poor swimmer is afraid of the sea, knowing that if he gets far enough from the shore he will quite certainly drown. As the eastbound train rolls on—the story is simply an account of the soldier's journey and of incidents during it—he clings to every association, every little thing that will continue to give life meaning. But the void engulfs him, and he at last goes under into absolute meaninglessness. There are some beautifully written passages, such as the one in which men in a sidetracked train watch the endless trains of S.S. troops being rushed past to be thrown into the already lost battle at Cherkassy, and another in which the soldier tries to give a casual encounter with a prostitute some emotional reality. Yet the reviewer finds himself in the awkward position of recommending a book for its brilliant promise when that promise has already been fulfilled; as it is, it is an extremely interesting but unsure exploration. (pp. 113-14)

> *Anthony West, "Paths of Glory," in* The New Yorker *(© 1956 by The New Yorker Magazine, Inc.), Vol. XXXII, No. 17, June 16, 1956, pp. 113-16.**

EDWIN KENNEBECK

[*The Train was on Time*] is not about a man's "whole life" passing before his eyes in his last hours. A person in genuine danger is more likely to be aware of immediate sensations and needs than of general recollections, and though the soldier Andreas does think back into his past, he does so mainly in terms of simple pleasures that he does not expect to enjoy again, or in terms of the irony of his situation—"'life goes on'" even though he is probably going to die. To some degree he shares the feeling of the man in Myshkin's story in *The Idiot*, whose worst thought is that, though he is to be executed, the thousands looking at him are to stay alive; and he shares the perplexity of anyone who, thinking he might not see the end of a certain day, stares with puzzlement and outrage if he sees somebody playing a game, or laughing, or buying food for the next day. . . .

Heinrich Böll cannot be said to "write as a German," unlike, for instance, Hans Werner Richter in *They Fell from God's Hands* or Albrecht Goes in *The Burnt Offering*, who give the impression of writing "on behalf of"—something, somebody. Böll writes about Germans suffering because of the war, but, in this novel as in his *Adam, Where Art Thou?* and *Acquainted with the Night*, he does not have to be judged by such unsuitable and disturbing criteria as threaten to interfere with one's judgment of those other writers. Although *The Train was on Time* appeared in Germany earlier (1949) than the other two novels of Böll that have been published in this country, it is at least as good. Like the other two, it is a work of fiction that is not apology or excuse or explanation; it is only art. By the paradox of art, it makes the best testimonial.

Edwin Kennebeck, "The Premonition," in Commonweal *(copyright © 1956 Commonweal Publishing Co., Inc.; reprinted by permission of Commonweal Publishing Co., Inc.), Vol. LXIII, No. 14, June 29, 1956, p. 329.*

H. M. WAIDSON

Heinrich Böll writes about people living in the present. The last twenty years in European history have been prodigal with raw material for the realistic novelist. Many an author has been under the inward compulsion of writing it all out of his system; often compellingly, though at other times one has the impression that the process of creation may have been more useful to the writer than to the reader. For Böll the war was an experience of horror and waste on an immense scale. What came before 1939 belongs to a past before the deluge, and plays only a small part in his imaginative world. After the war comes the peace; Böll recalls the chaos and starvation amid the ruined towns, the advent of the currency-reform, bringing neon lights and shop-windows for all, and hot sausages and coffee too, if one can spare a mark or so, and the new generation which is growing up with no conscious memory of the war and takes for granted the ubiquitousness of cream cakes and *Volkswagen*. But for Böll the present has been conditioned by the trauma of the years 1939-45.

The first two novels deal directly with war experiences. *Der Zug war pünktlich* (1949) is set in the year 1943, and recounts the brief days in a soldier's life from the time when he boards a special train in the Ruhr in order to be transported back to the Eastern front. The crowded train, the tediousness of the slow but inexorable journey over the north German plain into Poland, the men playing cards and sharing their bread, sausage and schnaps, while their faces grow grey with grime and rough with stubble, are recorded with a realism which is already impressive. But once the train has been left, this short novel falls to pieces. There is an encounter with a young prostitute

in a town near the front, where the hero's sensuality is arrested and sublimated into chaste love, and a few hours later in the early morning he meets a violent end. These latter incidents are less convincing than what has gone before. In the longer second novel, *Wo warst du, Adam* (1950), the experience of war and death is again central. The title is taken from a phrase of Theodor Haecker to the effect that involvement in the war is no alibi before God. Antoine de Saint-Exupéry is quoted: 'La guerre est une maladie, Comme le typhus.' ['War is a disease like typhoid.'] The fate of a group of officers and men who are retreating to Germany from Rumania is narrated in a series of nine pictures. There is more substance and variety of incident and character here than in *Der Zug war pünktlich*. This novel is effective because of its realistic detail and the sense of pity for suffering humanity, though its formal structure is perhaps too episodic. By comparison with Böll's subsequent writing, the characters and situations are perhaps too black and white; but the stark sincerity is impressive.

Wanderer, kommst du nach Spa . . . (1950) is a volume of short stories which depict war and its aftermath, for the most part with a grim pathos and indignation. In these tales, which are companion pieces to the two war books, Böll's sympathies are, as always, with the underdog: the black marketeer who is wanted by the police, the schoolboy whose hopelessness at mathematics brings down upon him the continuous nagging of his teacher, or the man who fails to laugh under a dictatorship which compels everyone to be happy. The effects of war and deprivation, especially on children, arouse Böll to grim satire. . . . In most of these stories, as in the two war novels, it seems as if the author is grappling primarily with the immensity of immediate experiences, where the sheer force of the material moulds the manner of its expression. It is a type of writing which may owe something to Hemingway and has something in common with the sketches and stories of Wolfgang Borchert. But Böll, in contrast to Borchert, has survived to discipline his power and to stand at a further distance from his emotions. Already in a tale like *Über die Brücke* this development is taking place. A clerk has to make the same train journey every Monday, Wednesday and Saturday. Each day, at the first house beyond the bridge over the river, there is a thin, unfriendly looking housewife cleaning her windows. It is always the same sequence of windows. But there are other windows, and these she presumably cleans on Tuesdays, Thursdays and Fridays. So obsessed does he become with this observation that the clerk has a day off on compassionate grouds in order to confirm his hypothesis about the woman's window-cleaning habits. Ten years later the war is over, the town is in ruins, the railway bridge is almost collapsing—but there is still a woman cleaning at the first house beyond the bridge. It is no longer the same woman, though: her daughter, who in the old days played with her dolls on the doorstep, is now wielding the window-leather; she too has a face like stale salad. The jumping-off ground for this story is not a unique, tragic experience, but a trivial, everyday domestic chore. Böll's sharp eye has picked upon the operation of window-cleaning, observed it with alarming accuracy, and with exuberant fertility of imagination has built his story around it. Wars may come and go, but windows continue to be cleaned in the same ceremonious way. The monotony of external routine is a mask to conceal the chaotic emotional reality below, which struggles with the sheer emptiness of a meaningless existence.

The clerk's obsession with window-cleaning in *Über die Brücke* is fairly easily overcome; not so the craving of Tante Milla in *Nicht nur zur Weihnachtszeit* (1952). . . . The narrator of this tale reluctantly recounts deplorable incidents from his family life in an urbane, non-committal manner that might be a parody of Thomas Mann's *Der Erwählte* or *Die Betrogene,* if this were chronologically possible. For Tante Milla the chief hardship caused by the war years was the impossibility of keeping up the traditional Christmas celebrations. Her devoted husband, 'dieser herzensgute Mensch', a prosperous fruit-importer and wholesale greengrocer, was in a position to spare her all contact with uglier reality. But with the return of the full paraphernalia of family Christmas in 1946, complete with an angel that says 'peace' as a doll says 'Mama', Tante Milla's obsession breaks out in an uncontrollable manner. Every day has to be Christmas Day, in February and June as well as in winter; the family must be assembled for half an hour every evening to sing carols and perform the rest of the ritual. The masquerade is kept up, though it turns one son into a Communist and the other into a monk, and causes the daughter, after she has developed a passion for 'existentialist dancing', to emigrate. Böll's satire is directed against the spirit of 'Restauration' as he sees it in post-war Western Germany, the desire to return to the good old days and to evade commitment to memories of the 1930s and 1940s. The narrator's affectation of disengagement from all that is going on around him heightens the irony; middle-class appearances have to be kept up, come what may. The virtuosity of the tale is seen in the repetition of the pantomime of Christmas; the variations indicate the increasing tempo of the degeneration taking place behind the mask, and as in Ravel's *Bolero* the obsessive tune knows no end. Few people, after reading this tale, I suggest, will be able to sing *O Tannenbaum, O Tannenbaum* with the same gusto as before. (pp. 264-67)

The jump from reality to fantasy is illustrated clearly in *Nicht nur zur Weihnachtszeit,* where the more complex obsession with Christmas replaces the window-cleaning operation of *Über die Brücke.* For Böll external realism is not enough, fantasy serves the purpose of penetrating beyond the family portrait to the depths beneath. In *Nicht nur zur Weihnachtszeit,* as indeed elsewhere, he approaches the surrealist manner; here he merges the photograph on the sitting-room mantelpiece with the clinical X-ray. This sense of the instability of the outside world is reflected in a considerable amount of post-war German writing; apart from Elisabeth Langgässer's writing, one might mention the war novels of two contemporaries of Heinrich Böll: Gerd Gaiser's *Eine Stimme hebt au* and *Die sterbende Jagd,* and Werner Warsinsky's *Kimmerische Fahrt.* It is a manner already adumbrated in Kafka's early *Beschreibung eines Kampfes.* . . . That reality merges into fantasy is a statement with psychological and aesthetic implications. The conception of reality as a task or duty leads to a consideration of the novelist as moralist. Böll's two novels of family life illustrate this aspect of his writing: *Und sagte kein einziges Wort* (1953) and *Haus ohne Hüter* (1954). All his fiction is firmly fixed in its social background, and different works satirize or expose various evils of contemporary society, with something of the programmatic approach of Diderot in the *drame bourgeois* or Brecht in his epic theatre; a comparison with Dickens might also be made. Böll's early novels and short stories show the isolation of the little man who is exposed to the sufferings and evils brought about by war and the post-war situation. *Nicht nur zur Weihnachtszeit* is the first delineation of the family as a unity; after this satirical sketch follow the two substantial novels of family life which indicate a further maturing of his art and the exploration of fresh fields of experience, together with a firmer fixing of moral responsibility in the individual. The specific social problem of *Und sagte kein einziges Wort* is the threat to family life of unsatisfactory living conditions; a man and his wife have

been living with their three children for eight years in a single room, exposed to the petty persecution of unfriendly and selfish, respectable and church-going landlords and to the constant noise of the city centre (one thinks of the quarter around Cologne main station, as it was a few years ago). It is the wife who suffers in silence, contends with the grim chores (the bomb-damaged walls shower dust and dirt continuously), struggles to bring up the children and to manage the neuroses of her husband. He is a telephone operator who drinks too much and finds conditions in the one-room home so depressing that he prefers to sleep elsewhere and leave his wife to cope as best she can. . . . The husband has never made any serious attempt to conform with conventional respectability. Behind the bustling efficiency and commercial ambitiousness of German economic recovery he sees emptiness and horror. The bruise of war still preys on his mind, and further back than that, his mother's death when he was seven; it is from this that his neurotic interest in funerals and death dates. This preoccupation with physical aspects of death is paralleled by comparable obsessions in Ernst Kreuder's *Die Unauffindbaren* or Hans Henny Jahnn's *Fluss ohne Ufer.* For the husband in Böll's novel life can have no meaning unless the sting of death is removed. 'Do you believe in the resurrection of the dead?' he asks a priest.

Haus ohne Hüter is less clear-cut than *Und sagte kein einziges Wort,* and as a novel is more interesting for its detail and its individual scenes than as a continuous whole. Much of this novel is seen from the point of view of a couple of eleven-year-old boys who have never known their fathers. Each child recognizes that there is something lacking about his mother; Martin has wealth around him (the family have an interest in a jam factory), but his mother's emotional life has become arrested in a Hollywood daydream, while his grandmother's overriding trait is greed for rich food. Martin is, however, more fortunate than his school friend Heinrich, whose mother, a pathetic figure, is dependent on a succession of 'uncles' to support her and her two children. In this novel Böll ingeniously varies the scenes from urban life which he describes, from the synthetic glitter of prosperity to the shabbiness of the lives of ordinary people. . . . The main purpose of the novel, to describe the problems confronting two boys approaching puberty, is a difficult and delicate undertaking, and the author has made his task more complicated by introducing a large cast of subsidiary figures with their own spheres of interest in the action. *Haus ohne Hüter* is a complex work, containing many fistfulls of reality, but it is less unified and coherent as a whole than Böll's other novels.

Heinrich Böll attacks smugness and hypocrisy in whatever form he finds it. Although a Catholic, he exposes place-seeking in the hierarchy in *Und sagte kein einziges Wort* and prefers to send his characters to the priest who is a failure in his office; there may well be echoes of Graham Greene or Bruce Marshall here. His sympathies are with the oppressed, and the short story, *Die Waage der Baleks* (from the volume *So ward Abend und Morgen,* 1955), makes his attitude to the old-time feudal aristocracy abundantly clear. . . . Intellectual pretentiousness is seen as another aspect of philistine smugness, an escape from immediate social duty. (pp. 267-70)

Das Brot der frühen Jahre (1955) [*The Bread of Our Early Years*], an 'Erzählung', is Böll's first extended love-story. Walter, a twenty-three-year-old mechanic who specializes in repairs to washing machines, falls in love with a young woman whom he has been asked to meet at the station on her arrival at the city. His actions during this fateful Monday are interspersed flashbacks which explain his present mood in terms of earlier deprivations. As a schoolboy and in the early days of his apprenticeship he was constantly hungry, with an obsession for bread which embittered him and caused him to steal. Since then his life has been centred upon work for the sake of money and what money can buy. Falling in love is shown as having a purifying effect, enabling him to make a new moral valuation of himself and others. There is some use of colour symbolism: Iphigenie's lips and Scharnhorst's collar, on two pictures remembered from schooldays, corned beef or the wrong girl's raincoat are red; Hedwig wears a green raincoat, and when Walter wants to buy her flowers, he would like to have green roses, not red ones. The author's attempt to show the hero's love as a unique experience is perhaps less successful than his vivid portrayal of the adolescent's craving for food. The story is, however, undoubtedly original and powerful. (p. 271)

Within less than ten years Heinrich Böll has produced a body of writing which can already be assessed as an achievement, not merely as something that holds out promise. His imagination is fertile and wide in scope. It seems as if almost any aspect of contemporary urban civilization which he encounters is capable of starting off an inventive sequence of fictional situations. He can make his reader see and feel the detail and background of his stories, and can create strong conflicts and tender human situations. Sharp satire with social and moral criticism shades off into light, sparkling comedy. His style is colloquial, assured in its familiarity with the language of mechanized living. There is no doubt about the strength and originality of his writing. (p. 272)

> *H. M. Waidson, "The Novels and Stories of Heinrich Böll," in* German Life & Letters, *n.s. Vol. XII, No. 4, July, 1959, pp. 264-72.*

RICHARD PLANT

Even a cursory glance at a West-German literary magazine will reveal a bewildering number of new writers, most of them unknown to the American public. Among the few who have found an international audience is Heinrich Böll. . . . [He] was a member of the *Group 47,* together with Hans Werner Richter, Paul Schallück, Günther Eich and Alfred Andersch. In the United States, four of Böll's novels have been published so far, and there also exist several college textbooks, containing something like ten of his short stories in German.

The critics have been often bewildered by this new voice. Estimates of Böll as an artist tend to be contradictory. A few commentators classified him as a new representative of that old school of the Twenties and Thirties, "Die neue Sachlichkeit." Some attacked him for being devoid of philosophical depth, for being hypnotized by the gloom of post-war Germany or for being anti-religious, while others were convinced he was a German Hemingway. Since all of this is far off the mark, let us have a short look at the world of Böll.

Perhaps it is typical that Böll called his first published work: *Der Zug war pünklich.* . . . Over three quarters of the action take place on a train. And the reader leafing through Böll's best-known collection of short stories, *Wanderer, kommst du nach Spa* . . . , will discover quite a number of stories which either begin and end at the railroad station, or contain scenes taking place there and on the train itself. We can follow this through to his last works dealing with post-war Germany. In *Und sagte kein einziges Wort* . . . , Bogner, the hero, wastes

much of his time at the desolate station. In both *Haus ohne Hüter* . . .—the author's most brilliant achievement so far—and in the monologuish novella *Das Brot der frühen Jahre* . . . , Boll returns to this locale which might be called the atmosphere and symbol of his universe.

In the dusty, overcrowded waiting rooms of these stations, the characters sit and wait, condemned to inactivity yet never relaxed because timetables know no pity. A railroad station stands outside ordinary life; it forms a world of its own: a world of waiting, of frustrated meetings, of hasty good-byes—played against a background of busy loneliness and noisy melancholy. We meet people by accident, exchange meaningless words, spend a few hours with them and leave, without involvement.

If I wanted to press the point, I could rephrase this description in theological terms but I do not think it will be necessary. Trains take us away just as destiny sometimes leads us into another country, another profession, another relationship. (pp. 125-26)

In Böll's very special world certain places, originally endowed with a character of their own, have been transformed into vestibules of doom or salvation. Hospitals, offices, schoolrooms reveal the same alienation as railroad stations, and the title story of *Wanderer* probably furnishes the best example. It unfolds in an emergency hospital, away from the front proper. War, as rendered by Böll, is the war of muddy ditches where time hangs heavy like the wintry sky of Russia; of forsaken hospitals in Hungary; of isolated patrols killed by stray bullets in a war that was senseless, criminal and lost from the start. Or we enter bombed towns where an untouched icebox still holds guard over the collapsed fourth floor of an apartment house. Böll has caught the poetry of the backwash of the war, of the wasteland that was Germany after 1945.

He possesses a special gift for extracting the essence of that slightly surrealist post-war landscape in which neon-lit ice cream parlors have sprouted on the ground floors of half-ruined Victorian mansions, and where children speculate whether that strange, unfinished structure is a genuine ruin or the beginning of a new house. Böll also seems to feel at home with the people living in the wastelands. . . . The philosophy of indifferent despair, as expressed by the protagonist of "**Geschäft ist Geschäft,**" would fit many leading characters of his fiction. . . . (pp. 126-27)

With this, we hold the key to Böll's heroes. They are unheroic heroes. They are taken along through life as if by a train. The protagonist of Böll's first novella, *Der Zug,* knows that the train will deposit him at a forgotten Polish village where he is going to die. It also becomes apparent, that here, as in nearly all his later fiction, the war-experience has forever conditioned Böll's characters. Thin-skinned, intelligent Cpl. Feinhals of *Wo warst du, Adam,* . . . , animalistic Stobski in "**Abenteuer eines Brotbeutels,**" the mutilated, the demented soldiers of *Wanderer,* rootless Bogner in *Und sagte,* Albert and Nella in *Haus:* less heroic heroes have rarely been made the protagonists of fiction. Just as an aside: Böll's later works usually take place after World War II, in the new miraculous prosperity. Yet the heroes remain victims. They still battle for their lives, trying to obliterate the memory of someone killed for a cause they hated, struggling to get a hold on themselves after years of blood, filth, boredom and false patriotism; they fight for their daily bread by repairing washing machines, supervised by a boss whom they despise as much as Böll's soldiers despise the lieutenants who forever quote Hitler.

What about the female characters? Let us look at Käte Bogner in *Und sagte,* battling against vermin, dirt and a separation from her beloved husband; or at the Polish girl in *Der Zug* who cannot hate the German Feinhals. The women, too, are always victims, and even more so are the children. I can not mention them all, the ethereal Russian girl selling "Chuchen" to our crippled hero; the eleven-year old boy in **"Lohengrin's Tod,"** stealing coal so the younger ones will not starve; the two boys in *Haus,* a novel centered around children used to "Onkel-Ehen," and many others.

Throughout Böll's fiction, we also meet The Others: those who rule, possess, dictate. They show up in many guises—Böll is endowed with enough imagination to give variety to his fictional creatures. They appear as the exact counterpoint to our victimized heroes. Yet in constructing scenes of confrontation between the two, or, rather, in conjuring up these encounters in a stream of consciousness, Böll often ends the following way: the anger, the long-withheld fury of our protagonists suddenly evaporates; its place is taken by a "bleierne Gleich-gültigkeit" ["leaden indifference"]. . . . And thus Bogner, Feinhals, Nella, Albert and others have a different battle on their hands—that against boredom. (pp. 127-28)

Ennui as a vital problem—we may have encountered this in Jean-Paul Sartre, in Graham Greene, in numerous Anglo-Saxon writers, but as far as I could ascertain it sounds a new note in twentieth-century German fiction. Railroads, of course, are breeding stations of boredom; likewise, the war in which Böll's protagonists were involved against their will, has conditioned them to live in boredom, a state of mind in which the real self is not "engagé." In *Und sagte,* the ennui and its accompanying dilemma are the core of Fred Bogner's dilemma. Only on the last pages of the novel, when Bogner is able to face a return to Käte, to the narrow one-room apartment, Bogner's life—and with it Böll's prose—takes on a new freshness, a new vitality.

That the tone of the narrative should change when its protagonists experience what could be called a conversion, is logical: after all, we have watched them continuously from very close. In all his narratives, Böll has moved his camera from close-up to close-up. He conveys his main incidents through inner monologues. A close intimacy between reader and character is established. It almost appears as though we had acquired a real friend. One could say: Böll gives us close-ups of compassion. And here enters a marvellous duplication. Just as we seem to have become a friend of Käte Bogner while participating in her daily struggle against loneliness and dirt, so Böll's protagonists sometimes meet strangers and, imperceptibly, there is born between them understanding and sympathy. In the world of Heinrich Böll it is only this compassion, this consoling alliance of two desolate souls which makes existence bearable. Occasionally, the birth of this sympathy is not gradual but sudden, almost like a revelation, and it may be tied to those unearthly figures which wander through Böll's universe like messengers from another world.

For the French critic Henri Plard, these figures are really angels; he has traced them with considerable care throughout Böll's work. However this may be, it leads into another center of the author's world: his reverent yet ambiguous treatment of religion. Numerous attacks on Böll have concentrated on his alleged cynicism; his defenders, on the other hand, have tended to gloss over his satirical passages. A large number of Böll's protagonists accept the Catholic faith as a matter of course. But they also are angered by the clandestine pettiness of ec-clesiastical organization and administration. With more amused anger than devotion, Fred Bogner watches the traditional church procession marching through the ruins of Köln. The irony reaches a high point when the banners, displaying the first lines of famous hymns, are exchanged for those featuring the slogans of the Association of German Druggists which convenes at the same moment.

Undoubtedly, those three chapters of *Und sagte,* in which the religious and the aggressively commercial are interwoven, contain that spirit of macabre raillery which is apt to antagonize the orthodox. Yet the very same novel also reveals the opposite. . . . Like many a believer before him, Böll lashes out against the tyranny of domineering busybodies like Frau Franke, who hides an indecent worship of money behind her activities on behalf of churchly causes. We must also keep in mind that quite a few of Böll's heroes have hardly survived the war and the lean, chaotic years afterwards. Even though they may have been devout at the beginning, the war experience has shaken them to their depth, particularly since they realized that faith alone does not always furnish protection against despair, loneliness and alcoholism. Böll's ambivalence of acceptance and rejection emerges perhaps most clearly in his first extended work of nonfiction, the *Irisches Tagebuch . . . ,* in which he proclaims—this time not through fictional characters—his love for the faithful in heart, for the honestly devout and meek, as well as his disdain of vainglorious churchly affectation.

The truth is, Böll denounces affectation, hypocrisy, meddlesomeness and over-efficiency in every field of life. His collection, entitled **Dr. Murkes Gesammeltes Schweigen** [*Dr. Murke's Collected Silences*], in which he continues the satirical tradition of such earlier writers as Meyrink, Sternheim, Erich Kästner, is the best proof. But before turning to this aspect, I should like to emphasize the increasing assurance with which Böll uses his narrative tools, especially the "inner monologue," a technique which Schnitzler before him handled with such mastery. But to mention this, is to lay bare the difference: Böll's figures seem determined to make friends with us, while Schnitzler manages the difficult exploit of simultaneously illuminating his characters from within, and keeping us at a distance. . . . Furthermore, the direction of incidents, the musings of the characters necessitate the intimate method, so that what is called content and what is called style have become interlaced in such a way as to be the cause and the effect of one another.

And now to the coda, the unexpected satyr play: side by side with Böll's wasteland, there exist his grotesque stories, his satirical phantasies. (pp. 128-30)

We called the satyr play "unexpected": this is only true if we are content with a surface examination. What Böll ridicules is the "Betriebsamkeit," the universe of the successful from which his hero-victims are forever excluded. It is against these overbearing, extroverts that his outsiders have to fight their battles. . . . Yet just as we know from the old cliché that clowns are really depressives, so the opposite is true, and the clown, or, rather the satirist Böll, could be spotted in **"Mein trauriges Gesicht"** (Wanderer), an early work. Böll's satires, despite their bite and their sparkle, are built on a substructure of pathos. Where they fail is in their basic attitude. In his dislike of the new prosperity with its "nouveau riches," of the pseudo-intellectual bureaucrats in the radio organizations, Böll seems to hint that they are typical only of post-war West Germany. He seems blind to the achievements of that segment of West-Germany which has read and honored him. His caricatures seem to aim not in the wrong direction but too much in *one* direction. Whatever he abhors, so it could be shown easily, grows just as abundantly on Madison Avenue and in Hollywood. It is, however, too early to come to a definite appraisal of Böll's satirical—as well as other—prose works, and it appears to me that his *Irisches Tagebuch* [*Irish Journal*] marks a definite change and a definite breaking away from his earlier pattern. (p. 131)

Richard Plant, "The World of Heinrich Böll," in The German Quarterly *(copyright © 1960 by the American Association of Teachers of German), Vol. XXXIII, No. 2, March, 1960, pp. 125-31.*

MATTHEW HODGART

The background to Heinrich Böll's fine novel [*Billiards at Half Past Nine*] is one of the most mysterious places in the world, the Catholic Rhineland. He writes with piercing clarity of the chemical smoke blowing over willows and black barges, *autobahnen* through the beet fields, Romanesque churches, Roman tombs. (p. 887)

Robert Faehmel, a successful quantity surveyor, had been involved in resistance in 1935 when he was a schoolboy. Through his friend Schrella he joined a strange pacifist sect, known as the Lambs, whose oath was 'never to taste the Buffalo Sacrament'. With Schrella he was beaten up, fled into exile, but returned to join the army and to marry Schrella's sister. A captain in the Engineers in 1945, he blew up the Abbey which his father Heinrich had built; in 1958 his son, Joseph, also an architect, is restoring the Abbey. The action takes place during one day, on which Heinrich is celebrating his 80th birthday, and on which Schrella returns from exile to find out which of his contemporaries have or have not 'tasted the Buffalo Sacrament', that is, have been living out the ancient German dream of war and power. It is significant that Böll does not present the issue as between Nazism and anti-Nazism; the Kaiser and Hindenburg are as much the demons of history as Hitler (who is never mentioned by name) and the Nazis were simply a special case, partaking of the Sacrament more thoroughly than their predecessors. Böll sees modern politics as repeating the ancient patterns, and salvation as lying only in a few, like the Faehmels and the Schrellas, who have remained pure in heart.

I find this quietist solution repellent, but his diagnosis is imaginatively impressive and his technique magnificent. There is a continuous narrative of the day's events, interspersed with flashbacks; the past is recreated in the interior monologue of each character in turn. The structure is thematic: a number of motifs—Holy Lamb, wild boar, Roman children's graves, ballgames, Uhlans, Hölderlin, the river—are woven through the monologues, and the story is given dramatic force and a tight and satisfying musical shape. In these respects Böll seems to owe a good deal to Joyce, and to have made brilliant use of what he has learned. But in his descriptive passages, which are the best things in the book, he is a worthy successor to Thomas Mann. There is a particularly rich and solid set-piece, where Heinrich hears that he has won the architectural competition. On a second reading I found the ending rather falsely contrived, both as a narrative and as structure. Schrella's homecoming and confrontation of his persecutor is beautifully presented, but his last conversation with Robert about politics does not convince: Böll seems to be sliding here into journalism.

I haven't read enough of Böll's work to be able to say how great a writer he is, but I am sure that [*Billiards at Half Past*

Nine] is one of the most exciting and masterly novels to appear since Camus' *La Peste*. (pp. 887-88)

Matthew Hodgart, "Ancient Dreams," in New Statesman *(© 1961 The Statesman & Nation Publishing Co. Ltd.), Vol. LXI, No. 1577, June 2, 1961, pp. 887-88.**

BERNARD BERGONZI

Heinrich Böll's novel [*Billiards at Half Past Nine*] left me feeling that either he is too clever by half or I am not clever enough: either way, I had the utmost difficulty in understanding it. The place is a small Rhineland town, the time a single day in September, 1958, and the main character is Robert Faehmal, a quantity surveyor, who had briefly engaged in anti-Nazi activities in boyhood and then been forced to conform. In the background is a large and inevitably symbolic Benedictine abbey, which Robert's architect father had designed before the 1914 war and which he himself as an army officer had been responsible for destroying in 1945; it is now being rebuilt by the youngest generation. There is more to the novel than this, but Herr Böll's devotion to the most dated techniques of experimental fiction means that much of the story is lost in obscurity. His use of flashbacks is so overdone that any sense of coherent chronology vanishes, while the multiple interior monologues produce a dense confusion of their own. There are more obscure novels in the world, certainly—*Finnegans Wake* for one—but most of them, I suspect, have rather more to offer.

Bernard Bergonzi, "Wessex Gothic," in The Spectator *(© 1961 by* The Spectator; *reprinted by permission of* The Spectator), *No. 6937, June 9, 1961, p. 846.*

JOSEPH P. BAUKE

While there are more sophisticated writers at work in Germany, some of whom are of great promise, Heinrich Böll has no peer as a storyteller. Equally free from the chilly academism of his younger colleagues and the blindness to historical reality so obvious in the novels of the older generation, his is straightforward and unsparingly honest in his scrutiny of character and situation. He is a disciple of Hemingway rather than of Mann or Kafka, and it is not surprising that his sturdy realism occasionally earns him a laurel twig on the other side of the Iron Curtain. . . .

["**Billiards at Half Past Nine**"] differs in scope and setting from his previous works, and should win over readers to whom the typical Böll milieu, with its slightly proletarian aura, does not readily appeal. With an ambition few critics would have credited to him, Böll writes about three generations of an upper-middle-class family and the fate of Germany as experienced by them. The result is not a sequel to "Buddenbrooks," to be sure; but it is an excellent book, and certainly the author's best.

Böll's virtues are all here, though served up with an artistry that calls into question the seeming simplicity of his previous work. He describes the events of a single day in 1958, and by a skilful technique of omission and concentration he manages to cram into it, with an almost showy ease, Germany's victories and defeats since 1907. Some of the *leitmotifs* sag a little under the symbolic weight they are made to bear, and it takes an alert reader to catch all the allusions and the significance that invests even the minor details. But the outline of the plot is clear enough, and once it is established in the reader's mind, all the episodes find their place. (p. 39)

[One] does not know what most to admire: Böll's sure touch at characterization or his handling of epic materials in a novel of ordinary length. The Kaiser's Germany, the great wars, the lean and fat years—he shows how the Germans lived them. It is a harsh and candid picture, full of guilt, brutality, and suffering. Evil shadows from the past loom over the present, while vicious Nazis turn pious democrats.

Yet in this chronicle of false hopes, real frustrations, and unresolved bitterness there are redemptive acts of great moral power, like the shot Robert's mad mother aims at a Nazi. No matter that she only scratches him, or that the few good people are feckless and a bit silly. Heinrich Böll knows how suspect successful saints are, and he communicates his conviction in this memorable new novel. (p. 40)

Joseph P. Bauke, "Obeisance to Empty Forms," in Saturday Review (© 1962 Saturday Review Magazine Co.; reprinted by permission), Vol. XLV, No. 29, July 28, 1962, pp. 39-40.

FRANK J. WARNKE

It is wrong-headed to read *The Clown* as a simple condemnation of German national character, or to find in its wistful hero that mythical figure so dear to our own uneasy sense of virtue—the Good German Intellectual castigating his vicious and hypocritical countrymen. Vice and hypocrisy are the subjects of the book, satiric castigation is its mode, and the twilight of the Nazi era sounds a sinister ground-bass in the memory of the narrator-protagonist, but neither ex-Nazis nor neo-Nazis are conspicuous in the contemporary Rhineland of the clown Hans Schnier. Drinking excessively and in a decline because his Catholic mistress has left him to marry a prominent Catholic layman, he telephones the entire range of his acquaintance in Bonn—ostensibly to borrow money and to locate Marie, but actually to operate as a kind of scourge of villainy, to force his interlocutors to come to an awareness of their true selves and thus to measure those selves against the clear moral imperatives which, the novel implies, only a clown can fully perceive.

A clean record in the bad old days is no guarantee of moral purity, although two of the least savory figures in Böll's gallery were passionate followers of the Führer. The execrable Herbert Kalick, one-time Hitler Youth leader who had menaced the child Hans in the closing days of the war, has become a sentimental democrat, fond of talking about "Jewish spirituality," but the truly appalling thing is that his conversion is perfectly sincere: he is, as Schnier observes, "a born conformist." And Schnier's unspeakable mother, a fervent *Blut und Boden* patriot in the old days, is now active in the "Executive Committee of the Societies for the Reconciliation of Racial Differences." But other characters, with less compromised political pasts, come under as severe attack from the clown, to whom the facile doctrine of collective guilt is quite meaningless. . . . Individual guilt, his experience with the virtuous pillars of society would suggest, is quite sufficient to make recourse to abstractions unnecessary.

Catholics, along with capitalists, come in for a major share of abuse, but the book is, paradoxically, profoundly Catholic in its values. . . . And if Böll's anti-capitalism remains unequivocal, a few succinct anecdotes show that he has even less

faith in Communist society. In 1795 Schiller observed that the "modern" writer, with his self-conscious awareness of the gulf between the ideal and the actual, inevitably would tend to embrace one of three literary modes—the satiric, the elegiac, or the idyllic. His formulation has proved a prophetic one, at least in German letters, and *The Clown* may best be approached, it seems to me, as a traditional satire, a work in which man's aspiration toward a prosperous and generous society is placed against the reality of human meanness, in which the spirit of Christianity is contrasted with the murderous letter evoked by its official representatives, such as the men who have persuaded Marie to leave him.

Many features of this work identify it as belonging to the satiric mode. The most obvious feature is the protagonist's fondness for epigrammatic aperçus—"An artist always carries death with him, like a good priest his breviary," or "Rich people have far more given to them than poor people, and what they do have to buy they generally get cheaper." But other, more profoundly central traits of the satirist's art are also present (one might note the discussion of some of these traits in such studies as Northrop Frye's *Anatomy of Criticism* or Alvin Kernan's *The Cankered Muse*). There is, to begin with, the very range and inclusiveness of the protagonist's attack—wherever he looks he sees venality and hypocrisy; society offers no compensatory vision at all. There is, further, the motif of the violation of the earth: Schnier's capitalist family has made its fortune in connection with the mining interests of the Ruhr. There is also that reflexive movement which might be labeled "the infection of the satirist," in which the scourge of villainy himself ends by partaking of something of the lunacy and corruption of the world he exposes. And Böll, in choosing a clown as his hero, has taken up yet once more our century's distinctive satiric persons (we need only think of Chaplin, or Picasso, or Stravinsky). (pp. 17-18)

At times [Böll's] protagonist displays an innocence, a soft-headedness, and a sweetness rather suggestive of Holden Caulfield. And the novel betrays a certain confusion between the manner of realistic fiction and the non-realistic, extravagantly hyperbolic manner of traditional satire. In these respects it fails to sustain its tone as consistently as some of Böll's shorter satires—the brilliant and biting **"Christmas Every Day,"** for example, or a few of the other stories . . . collected in *Doktor Murkes Gesammeltes Schweigen*. But these are mild reservations about a book which is as impressive in its intensity of feeling as in its smooth mastery of tone. (p. 18)

If one is determined to place this admirable book in a narrowly contemporary context, it seems to me that critical head-shakings about the spiritual condition of modern Germany are scarcely indicated. A vigorous culture produces its own criticism of itself, and the nature of that criticism is inevitably instructive. Böll's astringent satire in *The Clown*, so different from the tragic and nihilistic satire of Brecht's 1930 *Mahagonny*, reflects a society once more in full contact with its historical traditions—traditions which have included, at least since Horace and Juvenal, the capacity for delivering healthy blasts against the ubiquitous vices of mankind. (pp. 18-19)

Frank J. Warnke, "Saeva Indignatio on the Rhine," in The New Republic (reprinted by permission of The New Republic; © 1965 The New Republic, Inc.), Vol. 152, No. 12, March 20, 1965, pp. 17-19).

KURT VONNEGUT, JR.

Disturbing, queer things these—two unconnected novellas in one thin volume [**"Absent Without Leave"**]—tales told in the first person by German males who, like the author, were of military age during World War II. The reader must bring to each his own understanding of Germans and the war, for the principal materials used by Heinrich Böll are blanks and holes.

He uses the qualities of nothingness as a modern sculptor does, which sounds like a rotten idea, but he makes it work like a dream. Take the second of the tales. **"Enter and Exit."** It begins with the first day of the war, and ends with the day of the narrator's return to peace. There is not one word about what happened between those two days. Hey presto! Do what you will with the missing six years.

"Enter and Exit" is easy reading. The two days are odd but natural. The other novella, which has the same title as the whole book, is a royal pain, a mannered, pretentious, patronizing, junky sort of "Notes From the Underground." It seemed a sophomoric piece of work to me. I couldn't imagine the narrator, even though he did his best to tell me wry, funny, warm stories about himself in the war. He was apparently a yardbird, a foul-up, a Schweik, a coward and a fool in the Nazi scheme of things, but he didn't amuse me much.

What burned me up especially was his explicit refusal to tell me this or that, things that would be interesting to know. "The pastor's words at her graveside were so embarrassing," he said of his mother's funeral, "that I prefer not to repeat them." He refused to say what she looked like, too. On his relationship with his wife he said, "It is neither my purpose nor within the scope of my capabilities even to try and describe, let alone explain, the power of love," and so much for that.

The suspicion might be too easily aroused that his work is anti-militarist or even pro-disarmament or anti-armament. "Oh no," he said a little farther on, "I am concerned with something much more exalted, . . . with love and innocence." I thanked heaven that he had at last told me something mildly useful, but then he booted *that* by asking, "Who can describe innocence? Not me. Who can describe the happiness and ecstasies of love? Not me." He refused to try.

So I threw the book across the room. And then I understood: The narrator was being so absurd and evasive, his story was so full of holes because there were so many things he dared not let himself remember. What were they? Who knows? Each reader has to guess. (pp. 4, 54)

I approve. Does anybody really need to go over the nauseatingly familiar details of World War II yet again? Why not call the era "X," or do what Böll has done, which is to leave a blank, and then go on to the more profound business, as Böll does, of what the effects of "X" or blank were on various human souls? . . .

He recommends desertion to the young of today, with this warning: "But watch out when they start shooting! There are some idiots who aim to hit!" In other words, the alternative to dishonor is frequently death. And, from the way the narrator fails to tell his story, the young of today can also learn that the results of service in a bad cause, voluntary or involuntary, can be holes in the memory and a half-dead soul.

> *Kurt Vonnegut, Jr., "The Unsaid Says Much," in*
> The New York Times Book Review (© *1965 by The*
> *New York Times Company; reprinted by permission),*
> *September 12, 1965, pp. 4, 54.*

VICTOR LANGE

Böll is remarkably popular among older German readers: his fiction combines a sharply localized, vivid sort of reporting with that mixture of involvement and spectatorial reserve with which the experiences of the past twenty-five years are viewed by many Germans who have remained emotionally entangled in their aftermath. He is himself—now at 48—not quite one of the "younger" Germans, who view the Nazi decade with far less immediate concern than their elders, and who are anxious to judge the present from a detached, cosmopolitan point of view. To these more independent younger readers Böll has sometimes seemed provincial in attitude and old-fashioned in his technique; they have not, of course, been indifferent to the integrity and seriousness of Böll's moral position, but they have been troubled by his reluctance—or perhaps his inability—to bring the radical resources of modern fiction to bear upon intellectual and emotional issues that cannot be fully explored in the conventional designs of his novels. (p. 37)

Absent Without Leave and *Enter and Exit* . . . are once again characteristic variations on Böll's central theme of isolation and moral indifference. The first relates the experiences of a student—half Jewish, half Christian—in the Nazi labor service and later the German army: his detachment (in order "to make a man of him") to latrine duty, his marriage to the sister of a fellow soldier, his arrest for going AWOL, and the return to his unit. He scarcely sees his wife again, she is killed in an air attack. All of this is twenty-seven years later recalled by the disillusioned survivor of the war, a man still, so to speak, absent without leave, the bitter citizen of a prosperous Germany, whose "aim in life has been to become unfit for duty."

These deliberately sparse and banal events are little more than convenient occasions for Böll's attempt at illuminating the interplay of past and present; confused days are remembered by a narrator who is radical in his cynicism, intensely in doubt as to the intellectual perspectives of the reader whom he specifically addresses, and above all, curiously mocking of his own narrative method. Böll here transcends the straightforward realism of his earlier fiction in favor of a deliberate effort at structural complexity. He adds, in any case, a dimension of rather obvious satire on literary fashions to his customary savage social criticism: he offers the story in the bare outlines of a coloring book, which the reader himself may complete or vary. "Like a miserly uncle or a thrifty aunt, I take for granted the possession of a paintbox or a set of crayons. Those who have nothing but a pencil, a ballpoint, or the remains of some ink, are free to try it in monochrome."

Miscellaneous excerpts from the newspapers of the 22nd of September, 1938—the day on which Neville Chamberlain arrived in Bad Godesberg to settle the Sudeten crisis—are interpolated for whatever use the reader may want to make of them. . . . The narrator is willing to satisfy the reader's expectations of literary gamesmanship. "I hope these flashes back and forth will not upset the reader. By grade 7, if not before, the nearest child knows that this is called changing the narrational level. It is the same thing as change of shift in a factory, except that in my case these changes mark the places where I have to sharpen my pencil before supplying more strokes and dots."

The effect of these elaborate eccentricities is sometimes galvanizing but more often heavy-handed; instead of intensifying the impact of a bizarre history, instead of clarifying the puzzling interconnections between memory and actuality, Böll's self-conscious technique may merely irritate and deflate. If he attempts to provide a sort of musical coherence—gestures, movements, images, quotations, scraps of popular songs and the like echo throughout the story—these elements of continuity remain obvious rhetorical devices and seldom come to life. Böll's passionate desire to illuminate an obscure and pretentious world and to clarify our perception is unmistakable; yet there is a quality of abstraction in his story-telling, a mechanical and pseudo-highbrow allusiveness, and a stubborn recourse to inane stereotypes of speech and behavior. (pp. 37-8)

The second of these stories, **Enter and Exit,** describes, again in almost a monotone, remembered events in the career of a young German soldier, first at the outbreak of the Second World War and then after its end. It is a series of sharply and ironically focussed scenes that evoke the absurdity and inhumanity of life in the army, and in the physical and moral rubble of his native Cologne. What Böll calls forth in both of these topical and allegorical tales is not so much our compassion for the victims of a system, nor our dismay at the prevalence of evil; as a pragmatic moralist he attacks greed, stupidity, pretentiousness and arrogance—the traditional targets of satire—and insofar as they are curable, reminds us of the rational resources that might, with varying degrees of success, be marshalled against them.

The strength and weakness of Böll's art are, even in these minor works, obvious enough: the senselessness of war and the corruptibility of man are its moving themes; the gap between moral pretensions and the pursuit of a pointless existence is hauntingly explored with the fervor of a born storyteller who may at times seem in danger of being swayed by his own compassion into melodrama and sentimentality.

Böll has been compared to Camus: they have a moving emotional integrity in common, and a profound awareness of the need of individual moral commitment in a society of increasingly abstract relationships. Camus is altogether the more impressive analyst of the private dilemma, Böll perhaps the more specific (and satirical) recorder of public attitudes and of a collective experience desperately determined by an inheritance that is probably easier for the younger Germans totally to disavow, than for their parents to transcend. (p. 38)

> Victor Lange, ''Worlds of Desolation,'' in The New Republic *(reprinted by permission of* The New Republic; © 1965 The New Republic, Inc.), Vol. 153, No. 22, November 27, 1965, pp. 36-8.

TAMAS ACZEL

Heinrich Böll belongs to a generation of German writers whose lives are inextricably linked with the historical, social, moral and spiritual collapse of their country. Their individual destinies fused with her political fate. Whether older or younger, they have all grown up in the turmoil of Nazidom, becoming conscious of the world and of themselves either during the war, under the steaming political pressures of a war machine running wild, or in the depressurized aridity during the post-war years, surrounded by a landscape of total defeat, of ruined cities, ruined lives and guilt-complexes. Romantics they may have been; realists they all had to become. This is, perhaps, the main reason why, regardless of form and substance, their primary interests lay from the outset in politics, or rather in the consequences of the political act as reflected in the lives and minds of human beings, however far they may have been from the political center. Thus it would be safe to assume that, excluding their Eastern European counterparts, theirs is the most politically-minded generation in Europe today. Here, however, the similarities end. For while, for instance, Günther Grass or Uwe Johnson, experimenting with style, form, and

subject matter are, willy-nilly, forced to struggle not only with the complexities of their age but also with their respective experiments, Böll developed an artistic approach that is nearer in style, tone, and mood to a Fontane or a Thomas Mann than to his own contemporaries. I am tempted to add, although I am aware of the dangers of oversimplification, that the main difference between Böll and Grass lies in the fact that while Grass sees politics as affected by life, Böll sees life as affected by politics. He proceeds, without fireworks yet with an imposing self-assurance rooted in his philosophy and craftsmanship, to show us the whole sometimes amusing, sometimes frightening panorama of contemporary German society; we are at the very source of his powers. (p. 572)

Yet the past—the war and Nazism—concerns Böll only to the extent that it is, inevitably, the background of the present. Unlike Grass, he is not, in [*18 Stories*] at any rate, preoccupied with the responsibilities and guilt-complexes of the nation and the individuals. In his frame of reference, the immediate past of the country does not signify the point of absolute zero, but rather one of the *coincidentia oppositorum,* where in the blinding light of the Stalin-candles, phenomena, social as well as moral and psychological, showed their very essence with utmost clarity. Thus, in the proper perspective of historical continuity, the present becomes suddenly and stunningly alive, teeming with the people of the *Wirtschaftswunder*. It is, then, against the twilight world of the economic miracle, where there are no great tensions and what is at stake is not life itself but perhaps only a new Mercedes 220, that Böll's irony and satire is directed. For it is ''like a bad dream'' but nevertheless it is true that a man, despite his initial reluctance, may and can be induced by his wife to bribe ''the chairman of a committee which places contracts for large housing projects'' so as to earn an additional ''20,000 marks''; it is like a bad dream, but nevertheless it is also true that the chairman of the committee is perfectly willing, in fact expects, to be bribed for as little as 2,600 marks not only with the connivance but with the active help of his wife. What makes Böll's story so menacingly real is, of course, not its theme—it is as ancient as literature itself—but its atmosphere; the well-furnished comfortable apartment, the French *cognac* and the eighteenth-century crucifix, the pleasantries exchanged during, and the cigars after, dinner, the tacit acceptance of complicity, the self-evident naturalness of a late-night telephone conversation that results in an even better deal and, consequently, in a small rise in the sum of the bribe. In short, the smoothness of the operation reflects its everyday character. And yet, by the end, it becomes suddenly clear that the moment of a common transaction is, in fact, a turning point in the life of the narrator. His uneasy reluctance to go along with the instructions of his efficient wife (which, incidentally, did not prevent him from learning quickly the ''rules of the game'') turns into a disquieting foreboding: the deal is on but his marriage may not survive it. . . . Without fire and brimstone, without moralizing or passing judgment, Böll introduces a new equilibrium between the crass immorality of society and the yet unborn but already stirring awareness of a human being. Man perhaps can be saved, if he is willing to save himself or, rather, to understand what is beyond understanding. It all depends on our choice.

Some of Böll's characters seem to be perfectly aware of the dilemma; they react to it in a variety of ways. The man whose job is ''to throw away'' spends his mornings separating ''the circulars from the letters'' in ''the basement of a respected establishment'' which is ''entirely devoted to destruction,'' to the *throwing away*, that is, of an immense amount of wasted human effort; and although it took him "years to invent my profession, to endow it with mathematical plausibility," he is bound to realize that "the mere throwing away of mail as such has almost ceased to interest me," and instead he now devotes his energies "to calculations concerning wrapping paper and the process of wrapping," for "this is virgin territory where nothing has been done, here one can strive to spare humanity those unprofitable efforts under the burden of which it is groaning," only to arrive at the conclusion that "the wrapping is worth more than the content." What is it that the hero of that delightful satire, who decided "to keep away from morality altogether" because his "field of speculation is one of pure economics," is struggling with? The wastes of society or the frustrations of the individual? Undoubtedly both. Yet, deemed not only a "mental case" but, what is worse, "anti-social" on his "punch-card," he has solved the dilemma, at least for himself. Hiding behind the mask "of an educated business-man" he is now able to defend himself and his world from being "thrown away," thus symbolizing the futility of the society—any society—where morality and economics are kept apart.

From the indirect solution to the direct one; from the man who "throws away" to the man who "collects" tape-recorded silences in order to defend his integrity and dignity, Böll's probing into the depths of our contemporary triumphs and humiliations continues uninterrupted. For Murke, the young, intelligent, though perhaps a bit arrogant, hero of that devastating, bitter and clever satiric *tour de force,* **"Murke's Collected Silences,"** it is glaringly obvious that the impact of his particular "vegeance" on hypocrisy and on the sham-values of society is limited and, in a way, ineffectual; yet it is, nonetheless, completely satisfying. From morning to evening, in the building of the radio station where Murke is working as a member of the cultural department, friendships are born, pomposity is deflated, the name of God is replaced by the more neutral-sounding 'Higher Being' twenty-seven times on a tape-recorded lecture and, as if only by chance, Murke gets his revenge together with some newly-acquired silences. He can now go home, sit back and listen to them. But is the coincidence between his triumph and the world's humiliation wholly coincidental?

Hardly. A Catholic whose belief is anchored not so much in the tenets of the faith as in what C. S. Lewis calls "a dogmatic belief in objective values," Böll views the trials and tribulations of his characters with love, understanding and compassion yet without sentimentality and illusion. Accordingly, his understanding of human motives does not necessarily mean their acceptance or justification, but is invariably based on the metaphysical reality of fundamental value-categories. Primarily, his interests lie in the emergence and evolution of a human consciousness that will eventually include in itself a greater and more encompassing reality; a reality permeated with truth. Unlike Graham Greene's "heroic" Catholicism that perennially struggles with the bonds of faith only to prove their boundlessness, Böll's religion is a quiet and warm-hearted affair, transcending his politics and transforming his bitterness. It enables him to see beyond the relativity of the human condition.

Maybe the time has come when we can—without being called fossilized reactionaries—recognize the merits of writers who are not committed, unflinchingly, to experimenting but only to conveying the landscape and meaning of everyday life, as they perceive it. Heinrich Böll belongs to them—with commendable success, one must add without hesitation. (pp. 573-75)

Tamas Aczel, in a review of "Eighteen Stories," in The Massachusetts Review *(reprinted from* The Massachusetts Review, *The Massachusetts Review, Inc.;* © 1967), Vol. VII, No. 3, Summer, 1967, pp. 571-75.

V. S. PRITCHETT

The novel as interrogation has turned out to be more than experiment; it is as natural a product of war, the fixed trial, as it is of personal guilt and self-defence. Psychoanalysis, sociology, case-histories and the huge bureaucracy of files and records train the novelist for the techniques of inquisition and tempt him away from the private graces on which we contrive, as best we can, to live. Not only are we now watched by Big Brother in what Heinrich Böll (in his new novel for which he will get the Nobel Prize this year) calls 'the achievement-oriented society': this society has produced innumerable Little Brothers who have us taped as well. This is awkward news for novelists who cling to their old omniscience: but Böll has seen a satirical and romantic compromise in interrogating the interrogators. [*Group Portrait with Lady*] is an exhaustive series of plain interviews with the groups of people who knew Leni, his 'heroine' or, rather, 'subject' at discernible stages of her life—which still goes on. With a half-bow to the computing of social, medical and other sciences he poses as a fact-fetishist and calls himself the Au (rather than Author) throughout; and to the objection that emotional states are not easily computed he reduces them to those that produce T and W, L and B (tears and weeping, laughter and bliss). Suffering and pain will also occur to Leni and others, but the encyclopaedia settles that neatly: 'S or P is felt by a person with a severity proportionate to his quality of life and to the sensitivity of his nature.' (p. 694)

But *Group Portrait with Lady* is not straight satire. Herr Böll's interrogation enables him to cut deeply where he chooses into German lives of many kinds from the Thirties, the rise of Nazism, the war, the devastation and the boom, without lecturing us on history. And he has done this as a revaluer. We see all kinds of Germans shifting their ground and their fates as success or disaster catches them. The interrogation method, carried on with tact, irony, impartiality touched by indulgence, stirs each man and woman to a self-justifying account of the desperate moments of their lives. One gets an intimate picture of the war as it demoralises everyday life. It is brilliant that we see Leni's wartime life as a worker in a place, close to a cemetery, where she is making wreaths for the growing population of the killed; and that the daylight raids in the last year give her a chance to get away from supervision into the fields with her lover for an hour or two. Herr Böll's sharp eye for everything that is human in folly, chicanery or the tragic anarchy of defeat that followed, enables him to escape the lumbering quality of panoramic writing. That eye is always on the accident of being human. He is never stuck in set descriptions, but is following his own mind. The Au is not a tape-recorder; he disarmingly elicits the detail he wants to know; if he is inclined to enjoy his own dilatory manner and to lose us in some of his family histories, he does show us people confronting or dodging the awkward facts. His virtue lies in his silences and his humanity; his only serious fault is occasional jauntiness.

Herr Böll's method succeeds completely with the groups and particularly with the women who have been close to Leni; but the portrait of Leni herself suffers from a vital defect. The more we hear about her, the less we see of her. A little more is lost with every new piece of hearsay. She is so thoroughly known factually that she is static. And she is romanticised, if not sentimentalised. It is astonishing to know so much about her and yet not to *see* her except now and then. (One reason for this is that we do not hear her speak: the omniscient novelist would have given her a voice or would have made her silences expressive. Indeed, he would have obeyed his rule of self-effacement, whereas Herr Böll who adores her, overwhelms her with every kind of tentative speculation.) We are also under the strain of seeing her as both symbol and a woman with her own oddities. She has a strong sensual appetite for food, a scatological curiosity—she has picked up near-mystical notions about excrement from a half-Jewish nun hidden in her convent. She has shy but determined notions about sex in the heather; she thinks of love as 'the laying on of hands'; is a bit of a pianist; has a passion for enlarged scientific drawings of all organs of the human body. These convince neighbours that she must be a prostitute. She has given years to a large and still uncompleted drawing of the cross-section of one layer of the retina, to be called 'Part of the Retina of the Left Eye of the Virgin Mary alias Rahel'. Rahel was the Jewish-Celtic nun for whom Leni had had a probably erotic passion as a girl.

Yet at school the robust Leni was voted 'the most German girl of the year'. . . . In the end we see her living with a Turkish worker who is a Mohammedan and already has a wife and children, and vilified by her neighbours, who have the local German hatred of imported foreign labour. She is perfectly happy even though her son is a drop-out who refuses to be anything but a dedicated garbage-collector. According to the psychiatrist's report the youth is suffering from a state called d.u.a. (deliberate under-achievement), though he can speak and write Russian and has read widely. From the achievement society's point of view he is one more victim of 'moral anti-process'; he has been in prison for forging cheques, but that was a personal aggression against his cousins who had adroitly got hold of the property of his mother's family. Not that she cared at all. She is the shadow of Herr Böll's message. Herr Böll's strong convictions are not concealed by his mocking and hearty Rhenish manner. This sometimes runs to a coarse morbidity which is dangerously close to hospital jokeyness. I would do without Klementina, the wavering intellectual nun who at the end of the novel abandons the habit and goes to live with Au and consoles him, after he had corrupted her with a packet of Virginia cigarettes and a kiss. And the episode in which roses are made to bloom miraculously in the wrong season in a convent garden and allegedly from the ashes of Rahel—an unsuspected hot water spring is the cause—is like one of those naughty miracle jokes so often spun out by knowing Irish priests. But these incidents are the errors of a grave writer who is usually sound in farce and comedy. . . . Böll's comedy depends on a gift for turning points of accurate observation into critical fantasy. And he has one quality indispensable to the interrogatory novelist; the ear for the clichés in which ordinary people hide their secrets and the rulers and moneymakers their policies. He is listening to people turning excuses into articles of faith. No doubt Leni is the heroine because she says so little. The Au makes a list of her few known phrases. What did she say to her son when he forged the cheque? What to her young, absurdly formal Turkish lover? How did she escape the unmeaning phrase? Not quite the Virgin Mary, not remorseful enough to be a Magdalene, brighter than Martha—what is she? We shall never be quite sure. (pp. 694-95)

V. S. Pritchett, "Grand Inquisitor," in New Statesman *(© 1973 The Statesman & Nation Publishing Co. Ltd.), Vol. 85, No. 2199, May 11, 1973, pp. 694-95.*

ROBERT C. CONARD

When the war ended in 1945 and the writers returned from the POW camps to the bombed-out cities, they found their homes unfit for habitation and their language not ready for literary use. The corrupting idiom of the Nazi propagandists and the bureaucratic jargon of the government had poisoned the German vocabulary with the taint of death. (p. 28)

Böll's single sentence seems to sum up the problem fairly well: "It was a difficult and hard beginning to write in 1945, considering the depravity and untruthfulness of the German language at that time." . . . Böll and his contemporaries had to overcome these problems and restore the literary quality of their mother tongue. (p. 29)

The linguistic problems were further complicated by the death of German literary tradition. The new writers knew that the image of man which the older generation and its predecessors had inherited could not be revived. They knew that the tradition extending from Goethe to Expressionism was destroyed. Nineteen forty-five was their *Stunde Null*, the point from which the marking of time was started anew. The war had produced a leveling of the cities and the Nazi spirit produced a *Kahlschlag*, a clearing across the terrain of German literature. (pp. 29-30)

Two ways seemed open to authors in the late 1940s: a return to the ABCs of vocabulary and syntax, to the power of primitive expression or a conscious playing on the perverted meaning of words. One of the finest examples of the first method is Günter Eich's poem "Inventory," written about life in a POW camp. In the poem the simplicity of language is used to parallel the elemental human conditions in the camp and to reduce language to a rudimentary level to avoid unwanted connotations. . . .

The opening paragraph of Böll's satirical story **"Mein teures Bein"** [My Expensive Leg] exemplifies his use of this method. . . . (p. 30)

The elemental, repetitive vocabulary and syntax are effectively appropriate for the narrator protesting the unimaginative, one-dimensional, indifferent attitude of a bureaucrat to the problems of a war amputee in a reviving postwar economy. This exchange of dialogue is also paradigmatic of the beginning of many of Böll's early stories contained in the collection **Wanderer kommst du Nach Spa**. . . .

The second method of playing on the perverted meaning of words left behind by the Nazis . . . is also employed by Böll in the years 1947-1950 to create some of the contemporary classics of short German fiction. His **"Wanderer kommst du nach Spa . . ."** . . . effectively debunks the humanistic standards of value furthered by the classical *Gymnasium*. The wounded narrator, as he is carried, mutilated, back to his high school—now a field hospital—evaluates the school's representations of Western tradition—reproductions of Medea; The Boy With the Thorn in His Foot; the Parthenon frieze; statues of Zeus and Hermes; a Greek hoplite; busts of Caesar, Cicero, Marcus Aurelius; pictures of the Great Elector and Frederick the Great—by juxtaposing them to the war memorial with the great gilded Iron cross and the stone laurel wreath. Böll demonstrates by this comparison how the weight of educational tradition, because of its latent martial content, has led to war, not humanism. The semidelirious narrator, not yet aware of his loss of both arms and right leg, remains unconvinced that he is in his old school; to him the familiar motifs are "no proof" for "it is the same in all schools." (p. 31)

As important as the concept of *Stunde Null* is for understanding postwar German literature, it is not a perfectly accurate description of the postwar literary situation; for it is psychologically impossible for a generation of writers to forget the literature they had read in their youth and studied in school. Despite the desire on the part of younger West German writers to remove their work from the continuum of prewar literature, they were not able to do so. In East Germany, writers were not affected by this phenomenon, but consciously adhered to the traditions of prewar Socialist literature and Socialist Realism. In the West the attempt to start a national literature from scratch, to ignore literary tradition, naturally failed; Böll, in fact, did not always try to write as if there were no literary antecedents.

There are several examples of Böll's use of literary tradition, especially in his later work, but even in 1950 an example can be found. The story **"Stranger, Bear Word to the Spartans We . . ."** follows the structure of Schiller's elegiac poem "Der Spaziergang." In mock irony of Schiller's narrator strolling leisurely up a mountain and contemplating the state of civilization, Böll's narrator is carried up a series of stairs as he dwells on the horror of his personal situation. Where Schiller manifests a classical optimism, averring faith in Western man, Böll calls into question a mechanized modern society, expressing fear and suspicion of the state of the world. (pp. 32-3)

Among the foreign influences which Böll absorbed after the war was the traditional form of the American short story developed by Bret Harte and O'Henry and made familiar again in the Germany of the 1940s in Hemingway's terse style. This form—characterized by a quick tempo, a plunge *in medias res*, a lack of denouement (of the twenty-five stories in *Wanderer*, nineteen conclude with an unfinished sentence), use of contemporary subject matter, little consciousness of events anterior to the present time of the story, no anticipation of the future, concentration on a single event which becomes the focal point of the story, a lack of moralism, and a design appropriate for a public with little time to read—penetrated German literature quickly after 1945 due to the catastrophe of the war, the powerful American influence in Europe, the prevailing uncertainty of the times, the changing circumstances inherent in the construction of a new nation (a factor which also contributed to its popularity in the United States), and the twelve years of cultural isolation and deprivation which gave Germans a taste for things new and a desire to leap headlong into the mainstream of modern literature. Although foreign influences of all kinds imploded in West Germany after the war, the borrowed form of the story rapidly became a completely German genre by its concentration entirely on German subject matter in a distinctly German idiom.

Prior to Böll, Wolfgang Borchert had experimented with the new form, using it with traces of Expressionism to relate the horror of war and its attendant suffering. It was with conscious effort that Böll continued Borchert's experiment with colloquial dialogue and emulated Hemingway's device of expressing inner reality through external objects. One of the most important stories in *Wanderer*, **"Der Mann mit den Messern"** [**The Man with the Knives**, 1948], clearly illustrates this technique. . . . The narrator of the story is a day laborer who cleans bricks at the rate of three-fourths of a loaf of bread for every seventy-five bricks, and who, in the course of the story, exchanges a deadly way of life for a merely dangerous job. The final sen-

tence sums up the narrator's position: "But I only understood it an hour later that I now had a real profession, a profession, where I only had to stand for a while and dream. Twelve to twenty seconds. I was the man at whom knives are thrown. . . ." His inner fear, despair, and indifference are conquered. Life has a new meaning for him. It is true the change does not alter the nature of fear in his life; he does not live in perfect safety and security, but he does live with meaning: fear has become incorporated into his work; he is now paid for it, and it becomes at least the means of exchange for goods. The forty marks a night he now shares with his partner means he no longer has to labor most of the day for a part of a loaf of bread. He even has a sense of security in the skill of his friend, a feeling he did not know while at the mercy of an indifferent world. He also experiences hope and trust as they are expressed in the smile of his knife-throwing comrade. To be sure, there is still danger in his existence, but it now has a purpose.

In addition to their indebtedness to Borchert and Hemingway, Böll's stories in *Wanderer* show a marked affinity with the works of Albert Camus. His tales parallel Camus's existential concern for human suffering and have, as often as do the Frenchman's, an outsider as hero, i.e., a protagonist who is not reconciled with the world, who is a metaphysical rebel (though often nonintellectual by nature), who does not accept the unjust order of things. (pp. 33-5)

But there is one major point in regard to which their existential concerns differ. Whereas Camus's contemplation of the human condition leads him to reject the existence of God and to see meaning only in the heroic acceptance of man's absurd situation in the universe, Böll discovers the divine reaffirmed in the waywardness of life. Whereas Camus reasons from the suffering of man that if God existed He would be responsible for man's plight, and that since an unjust God contradicts the meaning of God, God cannot exist, Böll never seriously considers the question of God's responsibility. (p. 36)

In the stories written after 1950 the occupations of Böll's heroes become even more unusual than those of the protagonists of the collection *Children Are Civilians Too*. One character earns his living as an interviewer for a research institute gathering statistics on such questions as "How do you imagine God?": **"Der Zwerg und die Puppe"** [**The Dwarf and the Doll**, 1951]. A professional laugher finds life so serious that a natural laugh never escapes his lips: **"Der Lacher"** [**The Laugher**, 1952]. A linguist spends his life mastering an esoteric island language which the natives themselves no longer speak and which has produced no literature: **"Im Lande der Rujuks"** [**In the Land of the Rujuks**, 1953]. . . . Another hero specializes in the scientific sorting and throwing away of junk mail: **"Der Wegwerfer"** [**The Thrower-away**, 1957].

All of these eccentric occupations occur in the satires written in the 1950s, Böll's most productive period for the short story. . . . In the satires, Böll replaces the outrage and indignation of the early works with bitter laughter and warns through humor of even more threatening dangers to the human spirit—dangers which have become less tangible, less obvious than the war, and now lurk behind the facade of a prosperous society. Böll's satires mock social pretentiousness, religious and artistic snobbishness, self-satisfied smugness, and criticize greed, social waste, perversion of culture for profit, and the pathological urge of the Germans to forget the Nazi past. They also reveal a society without conscience, obsessed with senseless productivity, whose only gods are money and success. The popularity of these satires is due in part to their applicability to the whole of Western culture.

Besides the characters who expose the contradictions of their milieu and those persons who, like the thrower-away, cleverly exploit the irrationalities of society for their own interest and financial advantage, Böll has created another type of character, who by his very existence condemns Western society even more completely—the dropout who refuses to work at all. These characters are usually men who have never recovered from the war, who are not physically injured, but who are, nevertheless, dead to the postwar spirit of competition and progress. They are sometimes lazy but always lethargic; they lack energy and ambition, exude an aura of malaise and indifference. They are "those who," as Böll says, "came back from the war . . . not angry, not sad, just tired and hungry." . . . They are passive and quiet people, beyond indignation and rage. (pp. 45-6)

These lethargic heroes also form the nucleus of a prototypical character who, in varying guises, manifests himself in most of Böll's work. This person, whom Klaus Jeziorkowski calls (taking the phrase from Böll's **"The Thrower-away"**) the "happy asocial individual," is independent of the social system, its pressures and associations, and totally free to develop according to his or her own inner nature. The passivity of these characters, however, seldom demonstrates outright laziness, but often signifies a protest against the nonhumanist values of a profit society. (p. 47)

Although some of Böll's short stories after 1960 go over material treated in the collection *Wanderer kommst du nach Spa . . .* as do the 1961 and 1962 stories **"Als der Kreig ausbrach"** [**When the War Started**] and **"Als der Kreig zu Ende war"** [**When the War Ended**], still the 1960s represent in Böll's work a period of postmodernist, formal experimentation. In his search for new literary forms, Böll was part of a worldwide movement to find new literary ways to express old realities. Böll experimented with mythological themes, tried the epilogue as a story form, and in the work **"Warum ich kurze Prosa wie Jakob Maria Hermes and Heinrich Knecht schreibe"** [**The Seventh Trunk**, 1965] attempted to explain in narrative style the craft of writing fiction, i.e., chose a theme more appropriate for an essay to handle in the guise of a story. (p. 80)

"The Seventh Trunk" can be read as a model of Böll's artistic theory which tenders that every work of art will contain some element defying explanation, analysis, and understanding. The essence of art is, then, as Böll maintains in the essay **"Kunst und Religion,"** a "secret." . . .

The story, however, reveals more of Böll's art by symbolic implication than by prescriptive theory. Hermes, the name of the first author, is also the name of the god of invention, imagination, and fantasy. He is the proper god of Böll's work, more so than Apollo, the god of beauty and the sublime. Furthermore, the full name Jakob Maria Hermes evokes the name of the author Johann Peter Hebel, a writer whose calendar stories Böll much admires and whose work reveals an economy of means and a tolerant love of humanity parallel to Böll's. The pseudonym Heinrich Knecht indicates the other side of Böll's artistic ideal. A *Knecht* is someone who serves, i.e., the name Heinrich Knecht indicates the social function of literature, suggests that literature must relate to society, must be *engagé* and corresponds to Böll's statement: "For me commitment (*Engagement*) is a prerequisite; it is the foundation, and what I build on this foundation is that which I understand

as art." The name Heinrich Knecht also evokes the writer Heinrich von Kleist who, along with Hebel, represents the other major influence on his work. In the reference to Hermes and Knecht, Böll acknowledges in his cryptic fashion that art must have the fantasy and invention of a Hermes, the craftsmanship of a Hebel and a Kleist, and the commitment of a *Knecht*. (p. 81)

As an artist Böll has never received universal critical acceptance, not even from those who find his stories some of the best written in the middle decades of this century. That sentimentalism and idealism dominate his work and that he cannot always adequately execute his intentions are the charges most often heard. Minor weaknesses in Böll's work, however, seem not to affect his popularity with a discriminating public. Already he stands in the company of two of his favorite writers: Dostoevski and Tolstoi. Like them, he has produced eminently readable work imbued with moral power. (pp. 196-97)

Robert C. Conard, in his Heinrich Böll *(copyright © 1981 by Twayne Publishers, Inc.; reprinted with the permission of Twayne Publishers, a Division of G. K. Hall & Co., Boston), Twayne, 1981, 228 p.*

RICHARD GILMAN

For a novel about terrorism, **"The Safety Net"** is remarkably deficient in suspense, of both the ordinary thriller sort and of any more complex kind, an imperiled progress toward wisdom, let's say. This is due in part to Böll's decision to keep the terrorists at the far edges of the story, so that we only know about them through the reports and musings of others.

But more responsible, I think, is Böll's wider intention, which is not only to examine the effects of terrorism on German life, but also to issue another *J'accuse* against the soullessness of present German life. To this end, he incorporates a half-dozen or more subplots, including a love affair between Tolm's daughter Sabine and one of the policemen guarding the family and an episode about a priest who leaves the church for a woman.

These subplots are presumably meant to provide a richer texture, a more varied perspective. They're intended, too, I think, to establish connections between ordinary, decent life, erotic and otherwise, and the extremism, social and political, that menaces it. But the connections are tenuous and, what's worse, arbitrary. . . .

One of the difficulties in Böll's fiction has always been his attempts to mingle or fuse orders of reality, to make the quotidian yield overarching truth. Another is his distribution of themes and points of view among so large a number of characters. The few novels in which he does allow a single consciousness to provide a focus are, I think, his best: **"The Train Was on Time," "The Clown"** and, especially, **"The Lost Honor of Katharina Blum."** Much of his best writing is to be found in his short stories, almost all of which are told in the first person; many of them are sharp, swift, even elegant. Stories such as **"The Man With the Knives"** or **"Children Are Civilians Too"** have none of the ponderousness, the murk and fuzz, the strained symbolism that mar nearly all Böll's self-consciously "major" novels.

In books like **"The Safety Net,"** Böll tries to do too much. One of his literary heroes is Tolstoy, whose scope and grandeur are a dangerous lure for any writer. Like Tolstoy, Böll believes strongly in committed literature, "useful" writing, and this helps account for his frequent moralizing tone and his scattering of ideas among too many characters and through as many aspects of social reality as he thinks will profit from being exposed.

This committedness also helps account for Böll's reputation, which is surely based less on purely literary strengths than on an earnest humanitarianism. His Catholicism, for instance, which is present as subject or coloration in nearly all his novels, is at bottom a type of Christian humanism that is opposed to the institutionalized authority and moral teachings of the church. Although Böll is more sophisticated and more "literary," the American writer he seems to me most to resemble, if only in his dogged quest for justice (and his occasionally deaf ear) is James T. Farrell. (p. 21)

Yet Böll's literary powers fall far short of those of an innovative writer like Grass or the late Arno Schmidt, whose "Evening Edged in Gold" is probably the most important novel published in any language in recent decades, with the possible exception of the Austrian Thomas Bernhard's "Correction."

For tugging against Böll's *prédilection d'artiste* is his obsessive dedication to a more humane society. The two urgencies aren't necessarily contradictory, but in Böll's case their clash has resulted for the most part in damaged art, something "**The Safety Net**" unhappily exemplifies. Still, Böll is a good man, a servant of values who deserves our respect. In an essay on Tolstoy he once wrote: "May every author be read word for word, may every author be allowed his tedious passages, his stubborness." While to grant Böll this isn't likely to make us enthusiasts of his writing, it doesn't seem to be too much to ask. (p. 22)

Richard Gilman, "A Novel of Terrorism in Germany," in The New York Times Book Review *(© 1982 by The New York Times Company; reprinted by permission), January 31, 1982, pp. 3, 21-2.*

ROBERT ALTER

The Safety Net is pervaded by a profound nostalgia, although it is Böll's great virtue here that he does not sentimentalize the past; he suggests only that we cannot dispense with it as the revolutionaries and the technological profiteers, in their complementary ways, would have us do: The aging Tolm and Käthe, his wife of thirty-five years, are deeply attached to their own origins, but their flashbacks to childhood, adolescence, and early adulthood do not soften the remembered contours of physical hardship, frustration, local jealousies, Church-induced hypocrisies and guilt. The past was far from utopian, and it of course included the twelve most ghastly years of German history, but it did sustain a humanly necessary sense of community—among neighbors, co-religionists, members of the extended family, and between generations.

By contrast, the essential trait of contemporary Germany as Böll conceives it is divisiveness. We are made keenly aware of the powerful momentum of class distinctions beyond the traditional and perhaps once cohesive society in which they originated. There is also a sense of vehement ideological divisions within the society unlike anything we have known in 20th-century America, including the turbulent 1960s. The terrorists are the most extreme manifestation of a general drive toward the denial of connection. Kinship and love must be allowed to mean nothing; Tolm can readily and realistically imagine his own grandson raised without feeling as a kind of human bomb directed to the destruction of his grandfather.

That bizarrely duplicated name Holger is said at one point to mean "island dweller with spear," and it is, presumably, to such a state of hostile isolation that the new order of terrorism would reduce every human being. The terrorists are, to borrow a phrase Leslie Fiedler once used for a rather different generation of rebellious youth, the "new mutants" who threaten the end of all traditional bonds and emotions. . . . (p. 32)

The other great strength of *The Safety Net* is that its unsentimental nostalgia is accompanied by a persuasive novelistic representation of the old-fashioned virtue of love. We see it exercised in several different ways among the two generations of Tolms, from the quiet love of the old couple to passion in the young, to parental and even filial love. The working out of this persistence of love amidst divisiveness in the denouement is somewhat problematic because rather too much is made to happen in the space of 48 hours and thirty or so pages, including a suicide, the apprehension and violent death of a principal terrorist, the reappearance of the missing grandson, the return (separately from the preceding event) of the prodigal daughter-in-law, and a dramatic act of arson. All this is managed with enough technical skill to rivet one's attention, but not without straining one's belief. In any case, what is most important about the final movement of the novel is the reconstitution in Rolf's two-room cottage of a community and of a family, his small haven, with its rough artisan's simplicity, becoming a kind of return to the warmth of the past for the main characters.

In the end, the tight meshes of the safety net cannot be pulled away; they are needed because the threat is still there—if not the specific threat that has been hovering ominously over the Tolms from the beginning of the novel, then some similar threat from another direction. But life, Böll wants to say, has to be more than the sensation of the net's reticulations, more than an endless naked shivering before telescopic lenses and electronic ears. There has to be some sustaining sense, even within the net, of a human community worth saving. Despite the flaws of the conclusion, Böll has managed through the characters etched in these monologues to evoke something of the ground of fellow feeling out of which community arises. The result is a novel that not only catches the scariness of living in a society lethally divided against itself but also provides a small intimation of how the perennial seeds of hope continue to grow in our climate of disaster. (p. 33)

Robert Alter, "The Shadow of Terrorism," in The New Republic *(reprinted by permission of* The New Republic; *© 1982 The New Republic, Inc.), Vol. 186, No. 9, March 3, 1982, pp. 31-3.*

JOHN UPDIKE

Though full of psychological insight, not to mention a noble and lofty sympathy for the human plight in general, "**The Safety Net**" moves its burden of circumstance minimally, and then by strange twitches of hearsay. Most novels give the impression of a tour too guided, the reader too purposefully led through a series of Potemkin villages and compressed encounters on the narrow trail the plot has laid out. The reader of "**The Safety Net**," on the other hand, is repeatedly and prolongedly situated in spots where the action is *not* occurring, though rumors of it can be faintly heard, and glimpses had as if from behind a broad post in the grandstand. There is something wrong with time and space in this book; though ostensibly about the highest realms of power, it mostly takes place in small towns, in manor houses and vicarages, and developments that feel leisurely turn out to consume less than a day—one person (Veronica) seems to be instantly transported from a hideout in Istanbul (more Turks!) to the German-Dutch border, riding an explosive-laden bicycle. How did she get there? What is going on?

Böll's realism, like that of Balthus, is stately, eerie, and surreal. The developments are set forth with a quiet and measured authority but have, as one character reflects, something "downright fantastic" about them. In this novel, several galaxies of concern seem to be in slow collision. Böll is better on sex and religion than on power and politics. The affair between Sabine Fischer and her bodyguard Hubert Hendler is given a nineteenth-century resonance by their both being serious Catholics; the possibility of guilt established, the novelist is able to do some lovely psychologizing (raising the question Can you have a psychological novel without religious consciousness? or, to put it another way, Are human souls worth reading about if there is no sin?). . . . The psychological weather within this triangle, so much more tenderly and reverently observed than in the case-hardened treatment of the same situation which we have come to expect in American fiction, would hold us longer than Böll permits it to; the clouds are quickly and oddly dispersed, as they are on the terrorist level of the action as well. It is as if Böll, having been seated long in the creation of this congested, repetitive work (the characters know each other too

well, and repeat in dialogue what the author has already told us), suddenly rose and gave an abrupt, abstracted blessing, like an elderly priest bored by too long and tangled a confession. (pp. 132-33)

The sense given in **"The Safety Net"** is of an interlocked society some of whose members fight claustrophobia with extremist visions and acts that the majority press themselves into an even tighter phalanx to combat. A number of characters escape this novel, and the reader escapes it, too, with relief but a fearful suspicion that its social gridlock is the shape of things to come. Our hero, the bewildered and diffident rich man Fritz Tolm, has this piquant exchange with his wife near the end:

> "You know I have always loved you. And there's something else you must know."
>
> "Yes, what is it?"
>
> "That some form of socialism must come, must prevail. . . ."

As if it had not already crushingly prevailed over hundreds of millions, and as if it did much more, at best, than make the squeeze official. (pp. 133-34)

John Updike, "The Squeeze Is On" (© 1982 by John Updike), in The New Yorker, *Vol. LVIII, No. 17, June 14, 1982, pp. 129-34.**

R(onald) S(almon) Crane

1886-1967

American literary critic, editor, and professor.

Crane's renown as a critic derives primarily from his astute defenses of pluralism, a critical approach whose basic premise is that "of the truth about literature, no critical language can ever have a monopoly." In contrast to critics who divide over the question of whether a work of literature should be studied as a self-contained aesthetic object or as one related to and affected by the world which surrounds it, Crane believed that valuable observations about a given work can be made from both perspectives. Basing his own criticism on the Aristotelian assumption that art is a representation of human experience, Crane was concerned with revealing in a work of literature "what kind of human experience is being imitated, by the use of what possibilities of the poetic medium, through what mode of representation, and for the sake of evoking and resolving what particular sequence of expectations and emotions relative to the successive parts of the imitated object." These critical aims are central to the work of a group of Neo-Aristotelians known as the "Chicago Critics," whose major figures, along with Crane, include Wayne C. Booth and Elder Olson.

Crane's best known and most influential works are *The Language of Criticism and the Structure of Poetry* (1953) and *The Idea of the Humanities and Other Essays Critical and Historical* (1967). These works contain the core of the thought and beliefs of the Chicago Critics and have been closely read by scholars and critical theorists. Both books are highly esteemed, even by some critics who do not share Crane's views. They are particularly acclaimed for their well-executed defenses of pluralism.

(See also *Contemporary Authors*, Vols. 85-88.)

RANDALL JARRELL

[*The Languages of Criticism and the Structure of Poetry* consists of] lectures about the two most influential sorts of contemporary criticism, and about a very different kind, an Aristotelian kind, which would supplement and counteract these.

This word *Aristotelian* will make some of us grunt, some of us beam, and some of us exclaim, "Oh yes, now I remember—Crane's the man that's been starting that neo-Aristotelian school of criticism." So far as most of us are concerned, to hear of such a project is to hate it. We feel, more or less: "If it's a good thing to do, surely in all this time somebody would have done it"; and we remember that during a surprisingly large proportion of that time somebody *was* doing it. Mr. Crane's school of criticism comes to bat with, so to speak, two millennia against it.

But as we read we see that Mr. Crane is persuasive and judicious and reasonable, that his arguments aren't lofty sneers, or rhetoric, or appeals to prejudice, but real arguments; we dismiss this general prejudice of ours, and try to make specific judgments worthy of Mr. Crane and of ourselves. Most of us will be pleased when he warns us of his anti-Hegelian turn of mind, delighted when we see that he really does believe in

seeing what great artists did, rather than in saying what they should have done. He is, most of the time, empirical. And he does not believe in some ideal form of criticism which has the virtues of all and the vices of none, but sees that the different ways of criticizing, languages of criticism, are themselves as different and contradictory as works of art are. (p. 191)

Mr. Crane divides modern critics of poetry into two schools: those who take an analytic, systematic interest in the language and meanings of poetry as these are differentiated from the language and meanings of prose; those who apply to poetry the insights of psychoanalysis and anthropology. Most of both sorts are New. Gazing at them from calm, distant, commonsensical eyes, Mr. Crane describes, with reflective detachment, his critics' midnight marches, routs, sieges, voyages, their allbut-mortal combats, their—I was about to say, their discoveries and victories . . . but these, alas! he does not describe. He does intelligent justice to their vices and exaggerations and absurdities—some of these pages are, in their mild, matter-of-fact way, crushing—but he neglects with methodical thoroughness the insight and imagination and affection that are so signally present in some of them, so signally absent in others. From his sensible, unfavorable, and rather unjust survey you can learn a great deal of what was wrong with the criticism of our time, and almost nothing of what was right with it.

And this is natural: Mr. Crane's analysis is, if not a vindictive one, a kind of preparatory one—he is setting the stage for his own special kind of criticism. He explains it, lists its limitations, honestly admits that it derives from a quite unorthodox interpretation of Aristotle; and then he talks, at length, with enthusiasm, about all that it would be, all that it would do for literature, criticism, education. (He can't talk about its faults because, after all, hardly any of it exists to be faulty.) Reading this celebration of the hypothetical virtues of an imaginary criticism, we smile, but it's a sympathetic smile; we all have a fellow-feeling for inventors, Utopia imaginers, and we enjoy Mr. Crane's enthusiasm and emotion—we had been troubled, earlier, by his calm tameness, his withdrawn, abstract, academic decorum. We wish him good luck with, good critics for, his new school of criticism. We wish it in a voice of perfunctory good will. (p. 192)

Randall Jarrell, "Aristotle Alive!" (reprinted by permission of Farrar, Straus and Giroux, Inc.; copyright © 1954 by Mrs. Randall Jarell, renewed 1982 by Mrs. Randall Jarrell; originally published in The Saturday Review, New York, Vol. XXXVI, No. 14, April 3, 1954), in his Kipling, Auden & Co.: Essays and Reviews, 1935-1964, *Farrar, Straus and Giroux, 1980, pp. 191-92.*

THE TIMES LITERARY SUPPLEMENT

[Crane's main subjects of inquiry are suggested by the title of his book, *The Languages of Criticism and the Structure of Poetry*.] In the phrase "the languages of criticism" he refers to the different methods of critical investigation, which (as he insists) are necessarily limited in their usefulness and their results by the terms in which they work. He begins by proclaiming himself a "pluralist" in this matter: it is not his view that any one sort of criticism is right, other sorts wrong. . . . [Crane's] interest in distinguishing between different sorts of criticism, different critical "languages," is one of the threads that run through the book. . . .

To a reader of *Critics and Criticism* it will come as no surprise that the critic to whom Mr. Crane and his friends most often look for guidance is Aristotle; and the second of his lectures is devoted to **"Poetic Structure in the Language of Aristotle."** . . . For Mr. Crane, interpreting the *Poetics* in terms of his own interests and needs, Aristotle is important primarily because he is concerned with "the structure of poetry"; more than any other critic, he believes, Aristotle avoids dealing with bits of poetry, and concerns himself with poems as organic wholes. No feature of this book, or of the writings of these critics as a school, is more welcome than this insistence on studying works of art separately, as things-in-themselves, in which no part can usefully be analysed without reference to the nature of the whole in which it occurs. . . .

Mr. Crane's insistence on criticizing a work of art as an organic whole is to be understood as a reaction against other kinds of criticism. One of these, of which he says little, seems to be incidental to the academic study of literature—the tendency to concentrate on one aspect of a thing at a time; which often leads to the critic's losing sight of the whole in terms of which alone this aspect has any meaning. An example, unfashionable at present, is the old-fashioned History of Versification, in which such entities as the Heroic Couplet, Rhyme Royal and the Alexandrine take on a strange phantom-life of their own, independent of the poems in which they occur. The study of poetic images, in isolation from the contexts in which they occur, is a more recent aberration of this sort. . . . Another

type of criticism in which the importance of the whole tends to be forgotten in the pursuit of parts and fragments, has spread more rapidly in America than here, although its origins may be found in the work of Dr. I. A. Richards and Mr. William Empson. This is the "concrete" or "practical" criticism in which the critic broods over a text—preferably with the minimum of "background" knowledge—and interprets it in terms of his own sensibility, with results that are frequently of more interest to the critic's own psychoanalyst than to readers interested in the poem. Against this last excess of romantic subjectivism—which seems to be spreading from one American university to another like bindweed in the garden, and which has already numerous proponents in this country—Mr. Crane's presentation of a neo-classical approach can only be salutary. He calls into question what is in effect the suppressed major premise of a great deal of modern criticism—that poetry is one and indivisible, something that can be recognized and judged by a trained observer, who need pay little if any attention (at least in the first instance) to questions of intention or *genre*. . . .

It is evident throughout the book that Mr. Crane wants literary criticism to emulate such branches of knowledge as physics, linguistics and psychology. Unless literary criticism has revolutions and crises like these other disciplines, he feels, it will fall behind in the competition for the attention of the public. . . . It seems to be modern philosophy whose achievements Mr. Crane views with the greatest admiration, and this influence may be to blame for some ugly and unnecessarily difficult language. . . . If [difficult language] is the price that literary criticism must pay for having "the same kind of history" as philosophy or sociology or physics—if such a phrase as "a process of dichotomous division within some general body of traits," and words like "satirization" and "compendent" become obligatory—then there may be something to be said for trying to keep the old edifice of criticism in repair, instead of running up a new building. To some of us, indeed, it is a little tempting to see the great emphasis on "new directions" in recent American criticism as an intellectual manifestation of the desire to "keep up with the Joneses." Nor should it be thought malicious if one sees a connexion between Mr. Crane's lack of interest in Hazlitt and Arnold and his lack of interest in writing well; or to relate an occasional lack of precision in his work (more noticeable in that of some of his fellow-Aristotelians) to the fact that the French masters of literary criticism, who surely have something to contribute to this debate, are hardly ever cited. Such "conspicuous consumption" of critical terminology as characterizes the weaker work of the Chicago critics is something that other writers will do well to avoid. . . .

When its faults have been perceived, however, this remains an important book.

"The Languages of Criticism," in The Times Literary Supplement *(© Times Newspapers Ltd. (London) 1954; reproduced from* The Times Literary Supplement *by permission), No. 2745, September 10, 1954, p. 572.*

NORTHROP FRYE

[In *The Languages of Criticism and the Structure of Poetry*] Mr. Crane speaks as though he were presenting a distinctive kind of criticism, recoverable from Aristotle, which has been submerged, practically since Aristotle's day, by the domination of rhetorical values. We are thus led to expect a fairly specific methodology in the last lecture; yet, on the other hand, we wonder how this can be consistent with his argument that all methodologies can find in poetry only what they have previously determined to look for. Much is claimed for his own method: it is even advertised with guarantees. "We can do all these things," he says, meaning the things other critics do; "but we can also do more, and as a consequence be able to do these things with greater precision and intelligibility. For we possess what these other methods have conspicuously lacked. . . ." But the principles, as well as the sparse examples from *Macbeth* and Gray's *Elegy,* remain very general in formulation. With the best will in the world it is difficult to see the practical application of, for instance, "the shaping principle of form and emotional 'power' without which no poem could come into existence as a beautiful and effective whole of a determinate kind," or "the assumption that the poet's end—the end which makes him a poet—is simply the perfecting of the poem as a beautiful or intrinsically excellent thing." (p. 94)

The fact is, I think, that what Mr. Crane is expounding is the norm of critical procedure, and his method is an exhortation to the critic to keep his mind on his job. He is urging the central and primary importance of the unbiased reading of the poem, and of the framing of critical hypotheses about it analogous, in what they stress and subordinate, to the actual proportions of the poem as a "concrete whole." He says, as clearly as his pythonic sentence structure will allow him to do, that the poem is its own object: that there is no end outside it, morality, truth, religion, or even beauty, to which it is finally to be related. In short, he is defining the aims and methods of the central practical activity of reading, studying, and evaluating poems which every sensible critic bases all his work on, whatever his special interests may be.

In revealing the conceptual barrenness, the circular arguing, and the errors of taste and perspective that result from neglecting this central activity, Mr. Crane has not only fully established his own point but performed a real service for all serious critics. I suspect, however, that the dialectic necessity of first defining an abstract "poetry," deducing *a priori* characteristics or values, and then making all poems the shadows of a Platonic Form, is in large part illusory—the illusion being not in Mr. Crane's mind but in the structures of what critics write. As I am included in the mythological group, I suppose my own methods are classed as deductive: actually they are inductive as far as my experience of them goes, generalizations shaped from a variety of individual contacts with literature. But I know that when I write them out they look as deductive as Euclid. Similarly, Mr. Crane usually examines the rhetorical critics when they are in a prefatory, harrumphing, what-after-all-do-we-really-mean-by-poetry mood which I think is generally expendable. The textual analysis that follows is their real contribution, and it is as often as not quite independent of such postulates. The main task of I. A. Richards' *Practical Criticism,* for instance, is surely to free inexperienced readers from exactly the kind of preconceptions that Mr. Crane condemns. And if the rhetorical critic tends to pass over plot-construction and "common sense apprehensions of his objects," he might retort that Mr. Crane's exposition of the *Poetics* also passes over the very emphatic statements in it about metaphor as the index of genius, the highest proof of the poet's mastery, and the one thing he cannot learn from others.

The real issue, then, is between criticism based on the central inductive operations of criticism, or what Mr. Blackmur calls "the enabling act of criticism," and criticism not so based, and consequently held captive by some kind of theory which

is sure to be either tautological or tendentious. But this is a straight issue between relevant and irrelevant criticism. If Mr. Crane is unwilling to push the issue so far, that is partly because he has a special job in mind for his "abstract" critics to do. We have seen that the latter often treat poetry as though all of it were didactic: now some poetry is didactic, and for such poetry their methods may be appropriate. Mr. Crane believes that didactic poems, which for him include the *Commedia* and *The Faerie Queene,* are of "another order" from mimetic poems, and that his Aristotelian method can be applied only to the latter.

I can see a general distinction between fictional and thematic literature, but I cannot understand how Mr. Crane's way of putting the distinction can be a functional or even a consistent part of his argument. First, it seems to me to rest on an inadequate analysis of didactic poetry. . . . Second, if Mr. Crane says, "a good poem can thus be said to have wholeness both as a *mythos* and as a *logos,*" he cannot very well go on to speak of "the most effective fitting of the *logos* as a whole to the *mythos.*" Nowhere else in his book does he talk of fitting two whole things together; besides, the difference between a real *mythos* (plot) and a mere sequence of events lies in the inseparably "logical" quality of the *mythos* itself. . . . Third, and most important, the quibbles involved in trying to apply the question "Is this poem mimetic or didactic?" would soon throw one back on a prior definition of "mimetic poetry," and so establish in Mr. Crane's method the very dialectical apparatus he is trying to avoid.

The main thing Mr. Crane does is to make a careful comparison of the poetic method of Aristotle with a modern method which sounds at first as though it were a monopoly of Mr. Crane and a few associates, but which, after all the qualifications are in, begins to sound more like the common practice or basic training of intelligent and candid critics everywhere. He does not rule out special critical interests, whether they are in archetypes or verbal texture or the history of ideas; all he rules out, in the long run, are quack formulas for discovering the secret of poetry or its "real meaning" in terms of something else. What he has done, then, if I am right, is to rehabilitate the common practice of criticism, dignify it with a tradition and a theory, and encourage it to feel strong enough to absorb instead of avoiding its more specialized and technical developments. And that is an essential task of enduring importance. (pp. 94-7)

Northrop Frye, "Content with the Form," in University of Toronto Quarterly *(reprinted by permission of University of Toronto Press), Vol. XXIV, No. 1, October, 1954, pp. 92-7.*

LAWRENCE LIPKING

The Idea of the Humanities has been designed to do justice to Crane as a humanist—a scholar not limited to any particular subject matter or set of problems. The range of the book is immense. First of all, it spans three (or four) separate fields: the humanities, the history of ideas, and literary criticism and literary history. Its essays (themselves written over a third of a century) travel in time from ancient Greece to the immediate past. . . . We see Crane in many fields, in many moods, in many circumstances. (pp. 455-56)

[The] exploratory nature of Crane's work, along with its abundance, is the main lesson this book has to teach. When we add Crane's various eminence as an editor, a bibliographer, an educator, and a reviewer to the command of many fields he demonstrates here, we have a diversity that few scholars can match. The point is important. Crane can be accused of having a limited sympathy for certain types of writing, or of being limited in his approach, but his activities, the reach and grasp of his mind, have not been limited. (p. 456)

The appreciation [Crane] brings to a text is adjusted to the nature of its art, the knowledge appropriate to it, and "the principles of its kind," and the necessity of making such adjustments is his constant theme. As a means of inquiry, criticism (Crane believes) must always demonstrate awareness of its own methods and processes. Just as the process of reading involves a constant accommodation of the expectations of the reader to the messages conveyed by the text, so the languages of criticism come to terms with the structures of poetry they half perceive and half create. The critic searches not only for the principles of construction embodied in works of art, but for the critical art which distorts least by its act of apprehension. Thus the besetting sin of criticism is to mistake its own operations for what it hopes to observe, or to consider itself a kind of knowledge rather than a mode of inquiry. (pp. 457-58)

[Whatever] one thinks of Crane as a critic or scholar, one can hardly deny his excellence as a reviewer. His capacity for summarizing an argument, and the methodological presuppositions that underlie an argument, amounts virtually to genius. During those days when Crane was reviewing regularly for this periodical, any candidate-scholar writing about the Restoration or Eighteenth Century ran the risk of having his assumptions, not merely those he had declared but those he had counted on concealing even from himself, ruthlessly exposed in public. Seldom have reviews been so rigorous, so searching. . . . In many ways Crane is an ideal reader: not the sympathetic, forgiving reader we fantasize about, but the scrupulous, demanding reader who forces us to be true to ourselves and still more true to hypotheses and facts that contradict our own cherished favorites. . . .

Reading Crane, one remembers that summary can be an art, and that any art on a level as high as this is rare. Many scholars, for example, have tried to summarize the organization of Locke's *Essay concerning Human Understanding,* but I know of none who rivals Crane in compactness, comprehension, and truth. Without ever divorcing Locke's ideas from their context, Crane patiently demonstrates how much of the *Essay* can be understood in terms of a central analogy: as motion is to the world of physical things, so thought is to the soul, and as the active arrangement of things by cause and effect is to the workman or artist, so the active arrangement of ideas by cause and effect is to the mind. (p. 459)

The summary of the *Essay* is a triumph not only of Crane's intelligence, then, but of his principles. Scrupulously accommodating his discussion to Locke's own problems and methods, he finds a coherence that has not hitherto been distinctly noticed, but now appears obvious. (p. 460)

Nevertheless, the method of analysis demonstrated by so much of **The Idea of the Humanities** is taxed for its strengths. It pays most severely with its prose style. While Crane's prose rarely becomes as murky as that of some of his Chicago colleagues, it seldom rises above dim twilight; it is a prose we read doggedly and put down readily and do not always pick up again. In some respects it resembles the style of the later Henry James. (p. 461)

Crane labors to leave nothing to the imagination, to specify every assumption, to name all the members of each category,

to restrain the very power of language to be allusive. In summarizing the beliefs of an age or the argument of a book, he surrounds the key terms with hedges of quotation marks and qualifying phrases that strive to restore the original context. His scruples are thus essentially uncreative. With a strict regard for the rules of evidence, with a determination not to be tricked by rhetoric into saying more than common sense warrants, Crane fashions a prose style that carefully adds nothing to his statements or his methods. (pp. 461-62)

Crane's prose style approaches an insuperable barrier. Short of quoting a literary work in its entirety, we can never completely recreate its context, and our most careful summary will be, after all, in a context of its own. A critical style which pretends to be non-existent will only surrender a degree of self-awareness. At times Crane seems insensitive to the whole spectrum of expressive possibilities. On the other hand, many of us may feel that a critic who errs on the side of structure rather than texture, of commonsense adequacy rather than ingenious subtlety, of selflessness rather than self display, still has something to teach us. (p. 462)

Crane's most influential contribution, however, has been to the history of ideas, to which he has brought the same rigorous concentration upon those methods and systems that regulate the internal structure of an argument. (p. 463)

Whether the history of ideas itself can survive this uncompromising insistence upon the unique meaning transmitted by each idea in relation to its context is an open question. Certainly Crane's methods do not allow for much intercourse between different periods or works. British scholars, used to an easier and more intimate conversation with the works of the past, are fond of saying that only a country as innocent of history as America could regard the Chicago critics as historians. Crane himself regards most of what passes for history of ideas as more properly "fashion of ideas," the reshaping of history to fit a model constructed *a priori.* For better or worse, he brings into sharp focus the evasions that sustain what we customarily think we know about literary history and ideas alike. Amid humanists who preach the interrelatedness of all human achievements, Crane is a humanist who shows that each human achievement is separate and complete in itself. (p. 464)

Perhaps the first qualities that should be noted in Crane as a critic of works of art are his geniality and his shrewdness. Having no single hypothesis or ingenious interpretation to force upon his audience, he can afford to be as genial, as modest, as any uncommonly intelligent common reader. . . . Having a keen eye for the process by which the author's choice of his subject and treatment leads to the choice of detail after detail, he seldom fails to be shrewd about the artistic problems that underlie specific literary effects. . . . One always senses that Crane has begun his analysis with a keen objective reading, not with a formula or a prejudice, and that his criticism is describing a recognizable work. It is not faint praise to say that he refuses to be too clever, or to be stupid.

Finally, however, Crane's writings on works of art lack something: they are not so intense, so interested, as we expect from our best critics. Partly this must result from his admitted preoccupation with theory, and consequent reluctance to spend much time on explication. Partly it must reflect . . . that his methods of analysis are best suited to "well-made" works whose principles of art admit of systematic formulation. But partly, I think, it stems from his scholarly suspicion of those explanations of works of art, and sometimes those works of art themselves, that tend toward the esoteric rather than the common understanding, toward brilliant texture or insight rather than steady professional competence. Crane has no great sympathy for the mysterious or the imperspicuous, even in literature, and therefore he discounts most criticism which centers upon the creative process or upon human experience, instead of upon the axis between the created and structured work of art and the audience it is meant to satisfy. . . . Crane's distrust of such mysteries and complexities (not only of chatter about them) sets radical limitations on his criticism.

These limitations are real and evident, and many critics will consider them all-important. The lot of a pluralist is hard. The disparity between his theoretical willingness to entertain any reasonable proposition or artistic donnée and his practical preference for some ideas over others must always be on display, and nothing is easier than to demonstrate that the pluralist lacks the universal sympathies and open-mindedness he recommends. Certainly Crane's pluralism can be faulted on this score. He has a taste for the literal and causal in criticism, and for Renaissance and eighteenth-century achievements in literature, and his taste for other critical languages or literary achievements sometimes wears thin. Nevertheless, when all the qualifications and rebuttals have been made, the genuine pluralism of Crane's analyses is remarkable. Anyone who doubts this should read the series of lectures on the humanities, with their clear descriptions and discriminations of, for instance, Quintilian, Vives, Bacon, Hugh Blair, and Arnold, each presented in his own terms and in a context adjusted to his own problems. Crane's limitations are not those of ego, not those of dogma. The characteristic pleasure offered by his best work is indeed pluralistic: the manifold joys of entering another man's mind or problems or arts and appreciating them for what they are.

How then to assess Crane's achievement? In the long run, his very ability to submerge his interests within those of the works he is studying may tend to hide his own individuality. Crane promulgates no single "approach," no pithy and memorable critical formula. The nearest one can come to such a mnemonic aid is the title of a lecture of 1956 (now first published): **"Every Man His Own Critic."** But this sort of phrase is calculated not to win disciples. Like other teachers of languages, Crane relinquishes his control when a student develops his own fluency. Rather than brand a small area of scholarship with his name, he has tried to keep many areas unbranded and open.

Of necessity, then, Crane's work has gone against fashions and fads. Insofar as his ideas have changed, that is because he has shifted to oppose whatever dogma was most popular at a given time. Indeed, one of the most striking qualities of *The Idea of the Humanities* is its timelessness. Since Crane's historical writings usually deal with primary sources, and represent them accurately, they are not likely ever to be obsolete. . . . Many of the scholars and critics with whom Crane shares an affinity—men like E. W. Dow and William Minto and C. A. Moore—belong (literally or figuratively) to an earlier century, when a breadth of reading and a modesty about the significance of one's own critical insights were more frequently met than now. If Crane's local reputation rests on his work as a founder of the Chicago school of critics, the effort of his career as a whole may serve to remind modern scholars and critics that their schools have supplemented, not replaced, the humanistic achievements of the past.

Nevertheless, almost in spite of himself Crane has influenced more than one generation of scholars, and that influence has not been at all conservative. Its full range can be appreciated,

I think, only by looking beyond Crane's immediate effect upon such works as Booth's *The Rhetoric of Fiction* to his less palpable effect upon the scholarly community at large, even (if I am not mistaken) upon scholars like M. H. Abrams and Northrop Frye whose work has gone in directions radically different from his own. (pp. 467-70)

Lawrence Lipking, "R. S. Crane and 'The Idea of the Humanities'," in Philological Quarterly *(copyright 1968 by The University of Iowa), Vol. XLVII, No. 3, July, 1968, pp. 455-71.*

BERT O. STATES

[*The Idea of the Humanities*] is perhaps the best argument in support of dogmatism (I would prefer another word) as a natural force in humanistic pursuits. Take, for instance, [Crane's] case against its most virulent form—"'dialectical criticism,'" or any criticism which sets up a "more or less elaborate pattern of logically contrary terms unified by a single principle of classification," such things as poetic versus logical discourse, the symbolic versus the realistic, the ironical versus the simple, and so on. It needn't even be an antithesis; any a priori premise will do because literature is "ambiguous" and will support even the most absurd hypothesis. . . . What this kind of criticism ignores, says Crane, is that literature is "a product of human invention and art," not a natural phenomenon, and is therefore "molded in countless unpredictable ways. . . . You can know what its nature is, consequently, only by finding out a posteriori what the men and women who have created it, through the ages, have made that nature to be; and there is no presumption that this can ever be reduced to a single set of logically symmetrical and necessary principles, such as these critics have attempted to formulate."

Granting the perils of "the high priori road," this seems to me a sweeping misrepresentation of what many of these critics are trying to do. I haven't checked out their "dogma" lately, but I don't recall that the best of them are under any illusion that they are saying the last word on their subject. Yet here and everywhere, Crane assumes—and I think in a very a priori way—that any critic who departs from anything resembling a general principle, or dialectic, has arrived at it almost by whim, or at least by inadequate examination of his texts and that he wants everyone else to employ his dialectic as the definitive "tool" for poetic analysis. In Crane's view, all these critics wear blinders by virtue of having a "special order of causes or theory . . . which [they] will habitually invoke, to the exclusion of others" (**"On Hypotheses in 'Historical Criticism'"**); they simply don't see the whole picture and as a consequence they see *no true picture*. Thus the Freudian critic . . . who gets only dream structures out of novels is falsifying them, the archetypal critic who gets only mythic structures out of poems is falsifying them, and so on, in the very act of "formulating and justifying his conclusions." Not once, in my recollection, does Crane suggest that there can be value or methodological integrity in concentrating a great deal of intellectual force on one narrow point. I think he is far more liberal than he argues, but in order to argue persuasively he must subsume *all* attempts to locate general principles under his derogatory heading: otherwise he is simply combatting individual abuses in a practice which might not be so bad in itself. (pp. 269-70)

Crane has a certain admiration for many of these critics (especially Lovejoy), but he always puts their left foot forward and his tone is ironical, flat. When he comes to discuss his ideal "historian of forms," however, his total critic-historian, the argumentative procedure changes abruptly. It is like coming off a bumpy country road onto the turnpike. (p. 270)

The New Critic, especially, looms monstrously to Crane. . . . He is willing, in one place, to credit [Cleanth Brooks and Robert Penn Warren's book] *Understanding Poetry* with an unexplained "great virtue," but immediately he leaps upon its "shortcoming"—that it "superimposes . . . a partial and one-sided theory of poetic form, with the result that the student is insensibly conditioned to see only those meanings and stylistic devices in poems which the theory selects as important." This is unfair—to assume that "the student" will read only this single book on poetic theory and no other, or that after sampling others he will, out of youthful impressionability, select this as his only model and imitate it to the letter. . . . Moreover, one might ask how *Understanding Poetry* could possibly have achieved its "great virtue"—which is surely connected with its special *intensiveness*—had it tried to satisfy all the other virtues of Crane's incredible program. Finally, there isn't the faintest suggestion that New Criticism, like any radical intellectual preoccupation since the sixteenth century recovered classical doctrine, may be running its "partial and one-sided" course out of sheer and undeniable curiosity with its own potentialities. Human revolutions are not well known for moderation and common sense.

What also qualifies much of Crane's admirable erudition for me (and I suppose I am carping about tone now, more than ideas) is . . . the author's conviction that the world more or less peaked with fifth-century Athens and has been going steadily downhill ever since. This is especially evident when Crane gets onto Aristotle. For instance, in **"Varieties of Dramatic Criticism"** his avowed purpose is to show how critics in all ages are "impelled to say the things they do" as a function of a set of historical conditions they themselves are in no position to assess. . . . One of his central ideas is that Aristotle's "inductive" method was reversed by the Renaissance critics, with the result that people began the practice of using the Aristotelian principles in a "quite un-Aristotelian way." Crane develops this idea very interestingly, but there is no denying that this event, in his eyes, stands as the Original Sin of modern criticism and he simply cannot keep his disappointment out of his supposedly historical "narrative." . . . This audible sigh of regret is symptomatic of Crane's general reluctance to extend to modern critical movements the same tolerance, the same involvement in historical necessity, that he automatically extends to criticism and literary movements he likes. . . . When he says "We are still largely under the influence of this characteristic nineteenth-century desire for maximum generality in the definition of literary forms," you know what his sympathies are. (pp. 271-72)

[There] is no doubt that Crane has put his finger on the right spot, and that we are once more abusing the texts with greater conviction than ever. The spirit of "synthesis" is upon us. We have this uncanny attraction to "raw form" today, as opposed to "content," and as Sir Kenneth Clark says in a recent essay, "content separates, form unites." Today when we say that something has form, or is structured, we are evidently conferring upon it the quality we admire most, as the Renaissance man . . . was conferring on a thing the quality he admired most by assigning it *a place* in the great chain. Perhaps the most dramatic difference between our brand of form-awareness and his is that ours is not so much hierarchical as integrative, not deterministic but coextensive—a fusion, as L. L. Whyte has said, of Platonism and process, of Eastern unity and Western diversity. Maybe this is the wrong explanation, or a simplistic one, but something like this appears to be forming our common intellectual denominator and, for better or worse, it is affecting everything we see in literature (I am tempted to say *can* see) and everything we say about it. To regret it seems, I think, hopelessly nostalgic; to do the job as sensibly as we can seems to be observing the goals of humanism in their most enduring aspect.

I think Crane will be most useful to us, however, if we put aside his impatience with us, considering it as the necessary bias out of which any critic writes, and take to heart the specific sense that he almost always generates. Our prejudice could use some shoring up and Crane has a way of finding its faults. . . . The range and seriousness of Crane's intelligence are staggering. I confess that reviewing him has been a matter of finding things I *am able* to talk about and pretending the rest belongs to somebody else's discipline. (pp. 273-74)

Bert O. States, "The Idea of the Humanities" (copyright, 1970, by Burt O. States), in The Southern Review, *n.s. Vol. VI, No. 1, January, 1970, pp. 267-74.*

Don DeLillo

1936-

(Also writes under the pseudonym Cleo Birdwell) American novelist.

DeLillo's novels examine American obsessions, manias, and the mythmaking process of various media in American culture. DeLillo experiments with form and structure and is known for deemphasizing plot. Through fast-paced, fragmented presentations and other stylistic techniques, he continually expands upon the implications of his themes. Because of his use of unconventional literary devices, critics place DeLillo in the developing postmodern experimental movement that includes the novelists John Barth, Thomas Pynchon, and Kurt Vonnegut.

DeLillo first gained wide attention with *End Zone* (1972), which was written from the perspective of a young man whose two consuming passions are football and nuclear warfare. Although generally recognized as a satire on the American obsession with the organized violence of football, *End Zone* also develops the idea of nuclear war as the climactic result of systems of ordered violence. *Ratner's Star* (1976), DeLillo's next major success, depicts a condition in which verbal ideas cannot compete with the clarity and order of mathematics. Like Pynchon, DeLillo believes that closed systems of energy in physics are related to closed systems of thought in metaphysics and that both create the illusion of an ordered universe. In DeLillo's work, knowledge is not static and finite but, like the modern scientific view of the cosmos, always in flux.

In *Players* (1977) and *Running Dog* (1978) DeLillo focuses on urban America, depicting pawn-like characters lost in a surreal, nightmarish existence. Although critics praised DeLillo's ability to evoke atmosphere, many readers found the novels excessively tawdry. *Amazons* (1980), a farce about the first woman to play in the National Hockey League and written under the pen name Cleo Birdwell, was praised primarily for its humor.

With his recent novel *The Names* (1982), DeLillo continues his examination of Americana, language, and learning and is hailed for his accurate characterization of American cultural values.

(See also *CLC*, Vols. 8, 10, 13; *Contemporary Authors*, Vols. 81-84; and *Dictionary of Literary Biography*, Vol. 6.)

MARTIN LEVIN

There have been many-too-many novels in which the protagonist tries to find himself: [in "**Americana**"] . . . he tries to *lose* himself.

"I'm trying to outrun myself," says ex-network executive David Bell (pausing for breath on an Indian reservation) and one must count his effort a success. There is no real identity to be found in this heaping mass of tossed word-salad. There are thickets of hallucinatory whimsy, an infatuation with rhetoric, but hardly a trace of a man.

© Thomas Victor 1983

The purple nightmares conjured up by Don DeLillo—in the form of various transcontinental interludes—are only fitfully interesting, although they do propose some curious images. . . . [The] most one can say for Mr. DeLillo's novel is that we're a bit closer to learning why Dave wants to lose himself.

Martin Levin, in a review of "Americana," in The New York Times Book Review *(© 1971 by The New York Times Company; reprinted by permission), May 30, 1971, p. 20.*

THOMAS R. EDWARDS

The writing in "**End Zone**" is continuously energetic, shifty, fun to watch for its own sake.

And, though the serious fan may care less about the final score than the quality of play, "**End Zone**" adds up impressively. DeLillo's first novel, "**Americana**" . . . , was also beautifully written and paced, but its materials seemed pretty familiar—the New York media man (TV documentaries in this case) alienated from work, family and love, who hits the road with a company of losers and drop-outs and, after seeing Middle America at its touching, exhausted worst, makes an ambiguous return to where he left off. If "**Americana**" was a savagely funny portrait of middle-class anomie in a bad time, it was also too long and visibly ambitious, and too much like too many other recent novels, to seem as good as it should have.

In **"End Zone"** DeLillo finds in college football a more original and efficient vehicle for his sense of things now. Gary Harkness, his running-back hero, comes to Logos after brief stops at four major football schools, which he left for reasons that suggest how the sporting life reflects the terms of our larger life these days: Expelled from Syracuse for a harmless escapade with a spaced-out coed, he quit Penn State because he couldn't see practice as character-building, Miami because he got too depressingly interested in a class in nuclear-warfare theory, Michigan State because he fatally injured an opponent. Yet he both loves football and can't think of anything better to do, and Logos, seeking big-time prestige under a famous coach now down on his luck, is his last chance.

The novel tells the story of his first season at Logos. Thanks mainly to a magical black runner named Taft Robinson, the team wins every game but the big one (described in loving and authentic detail) with West Centrex Biotechnical. But it's a season of losses all the same. A teammate dies in a car accident; an assistant coach shoots himself; Mrs. Tom's plane crashes; Coach Creed mysteriously declines into a wheelchair case; Gary's fat, sloppy girl friend (to whom he was first attracted because of the appliquéd mushroom cloud on her dress) slims down into a conventional and undesirable chicness, Taft Robinson gives up football in favor of ascetic mysticism. Gary, newly chosen as offensive captain for next year, ends up in the infirmary with a mysterious brain-fever, being fed through plastic tubes.

This isn't just a "football novel," that is. Gary's involvement with the sport is a version of his horrified fascination with the vocabulary, theory and technology of modern war à la Herman Kahn. From AFROTC Major Staley, a three-letter man and a veteran of the Nagasaki raid, he learns the larger play-book, whose rich and only too meaningful gibberish—"perimeter acquisition radar, unauthorized explosions, slow-motion countercity war, super-ready status, collateral destruction"—reverberates in DeLillo's lovely parodies of the argot of technical football: "Monsoon sweep, string-in-left, ready right, cradle out, drill-9 shiver, ends chuff." Or (as it were), Plutonium two thirty-nine, Cerium one forty-four, Strontium ninety, *Hup!*

The game, as DeLillo insists in an aside to the reader, isn't for either fans or players merely a covert form of war, a respectable outlet for animal violence. ("We don't need substitutes because we've got the real thing," as one of the wiser characters sensibly observes.) Rather, and more dreadfully, he makes us see football as an efficient illusion of order, a perfecting of reality through organized *language* ("impressions, colors, statistics, patterns, mysteries, numbers, idioms, symbols") whose complete and antiseptic coherence is the end of civilization itself, goal and cessation at once. (p. 1)

But as Freud finally had to tell us, the arguments for civilization are also arguments for death—the game stops in the end zone, and only the timekeeper, not the players, knows whether it will begin again. DeLillo, who's no easy parlor apocalypse-monger, permits his hero some small but enlivening resistances to cultural entropy, the tendency of political, social and intellectual systems to merge at dead center.

Gary accepts the captaincy while sustaining a savingly theatrical interest in whether or not he should wear his helmet for the coin-tosses, and even his fever, casually introduced in the

final paragraph, hints at the uncertain but possible value of vulnerability, persisting without certitude in a world where others accept defensive systems—technologies, religion, games, the large or small cultisms that flourish where fear is.

One of the Logos coeds is "into carrots pretty heavy," and everyone, young or old, does his or her thing with wonderful intentness upon its deflective complexity and subtlety; but if DeLillo allows no cozy up-beat victory to ironic unruliness, it remains a presence in Gary Harkness's helpless awareness of the deathly absurdity in the order he too desires but can't commit himself to.

DeLillo's vision of our lives is made of nightmare and disgust, but it's beautifully made; to see a strong, serious imagination discover and possess a potent metaphor, whatever its tendencies, is finally exciting and life-serving. In **"End Zone,"** more clearly than in **"Americana,"** this richly inventive new talent looks like a major one. (pp. 1, 14)

Thomas R. Edwards, "A Beautifully Made Football Novel about Thermonuclear War," in The New York Times Book Review *(©1972 by The New York Times Company; reprinted by permission), April 9, 1972, pp. 1, 14.*

SARA BLACKBURN

DeLillo's third novel ["**Great Jones Street**"] . . . is narrated by a revered and temporarily retired American rock star, so burned out and eaten up by the insanity of the demands upon him that he's holed up in a crummy room on New York's Great Jones Street until he somehow regains his will to go on. I wish this novel could be described fairly as a book set in the rock and drug world—as DeLillo intends—but it doesn't work that way, and the failure is just about fatal. (pp. 2-3)

DeLillo's descriptions of the pre-art-scene Bowery neighborhood are lovely; they evoke exactly the aura of quiet, desperate lives going on in an atmosphere of industrial emptiness that suits the events that promise to take place, a kind of eerie, post-destruction silence, pervaded by an air of panic.

The panic comes from some initial suspense about whether Bucky has really broken off relations with the national death cult, which DeLillo sees as youth culture at the end of the sixties; it comes, too, from Transparanoia, the giant (multinational, of course) conglomerate that manages Bucky and everyone else who matters, and from the menacing members of a loving country commune gone urban and brutal.

All of these parties are in a race for possession of a still-experimental version of a mind-boggling drug that will become the craze of the youth market, and the novel settles into a rather conventional race for the "product"—that is, whenever it remembers that it should have a plot. . . .

Cropping up throughout the narrative are a number of items that mark Bucky's recent passage: a series of powerful, satanic, destruction-haunted lyrics from the group's repertoire, now rendered slick and self-righteous; a transcript of Bucky's meeting with the leading members of a marvelously satirized liberal think-tank; the cameo appearance of Bucky's British counterpart, a Mick Jagger type who now devotes his full time to international business deals of a particularly vicious nature.

These features are sometimes intriguing, but they, along with a much longer string of Bucky-centered doomsday events, stay anecdotes that don't accumulate into much of a novel. In fact, we have a very hard time believing in Bucky as a character at all, let alone in either his recent past or his current desperation to survive.

The veracity of his character isn't helped by the fact that none of his friends or enemies seems capable of much motion or change. The absurd Texas football players of **"End Zone,"** infected as they were with racism and the worship of technocracy, were also weirdly capable of love, and DeLillo depicted them as salvageable—human and struggling victims of their time and place. The rock stars, drug dealers and hangers-on that populate **"Great Jones Street"** are so totally freaked out, so slickly devoted to destruction and evil, so obsessed with manipulating and acquiring, that they're beyond redemption. They're so evil that we don't care, and it's impossible to imagine that either Bucky or anyone else exists except as a mouthpiece for DeLillo's doomsday message. As for the wild excesses of the sixties drug scene itself, even DeLillo's skill at nightmare comedy doesn't begin to compete with what will long remain the last word on that subject: the frenzy and panic of Hunter Thompson's maniacal and hilarious "Fear and Loathing in Las Vegas."

For all of this, **"Great Jones Street"** is full of beautiful writing. . . . And this is DeLillo not nearly at his best, which usually combines . . . qualities of strong, clear imagery with a seemingly off-hand and piercing wit. There is a great deal of this kind of writing in **"Great Jones Street,"** but it doesn't save the book from being more of a sour, admirably written lecture than a novel, a book that is always puffing to keep up with the power and intensity of its subject.

Having savored its language and reported on my immense disappointment in this book (yes, people who haven't read DeLillo before will be disappointed too, if not so intensely as an admirer), I must now report that my enthusiasm for DeLillo has survived this near-disaster. I would still buy his next book the minute it appeared. Meanwhile, people who haven't already done so should read **"End Zone"**. . . . (p. 3)

Sara Blackburn, in a review of "Great Jones Street," in The New York Times Book Review *(© 1973 by The New York Times Company; reprinted by permission), April 22, 1973, pp. 2-3.*

J. D. O'HARA

Author of two fine novels, *Americana* and *Great Jones Street*, and one dazzling novel, *End Zone*, Don DeLillo [in *Ratner's Star*] writes the American version of a European novel of ideas. Perhaps he most resembles Thomas Mann, lacking Mann's mysticism and long-windedness but sharing his remarkable ability to evoke and evaluate the ideas, language and attitudes of a wide range of intellectual disciplines. DeLillo also possesses an undercutting skepticism proper to the age of Beckett and Borges, an eye for rational absurdity as keen as Barthelme's, and a sparkling comic inventiveness that fills his narratives with flashes of delight. He is already the writer Vonnegut, Barth and Pynchon were once oddly and variously taken to be, and he shows no signs of flagging, many signs of promise.

In *End Zone* one of DeLillo's many topics was the deceptive and incomplete nature of knowledge; another was the disparity between what we can manipulate intellectually, on the one hand, and "the untellable," on the other; a third was the contradictory temptations of complexity and simplicity; yet another was those unknowable, unspeakable fundamentals of existence,

excrement and death. These topics recur in *Ratner's Star,* where excrement is pervasive and infectious, and death takes many forms, including decay, shadows, flooding, historical reversal, and cosmological black stars and black holes, as well as the moral and cultural death implied by corporate greed.

The areas of knowledge central to *Ratner's Star* are astronomy and mathematics. DeLillo develops them brilliantly, so that the expert can wallow while even the layman can splash happily in the shallows or pick up pebbles on the shore. Billy Twillig, a 14-year-old Nobel-laureate mathematician from the Bronx, is summoned to Field Experiment No. 1, a huge think-tank, in 1979. A message has just been received from the vicinity of Ratner's star: 101 transmissions, 99 signals broken up by two pauses into 14 28 57. Mathematics is the only language potentially universal; Twillig must read this.

Field Experiment No. 1 provides characters whose elliptical speeches, cameo appearances, and odd behavior compose a fascinating, funny and unnerving picture of life as seen intelligently. "All I know is one thing doesn't lead to another the way it should," as one character complains. Even at its best, existence is repeatedly and disturbingly dual. The binary world of computers is divided into 1 and 0; Ratner's star is shadowed by a black dwarf; the rational Twillig is set against his antipodal opposite, a nameless and magical Australian aborigine; and the clear world of mathematics is undermined by violence in the Bronx, the subway where Twillig's father works, human passion and irrationality, the "void core" at the center of Field Experiment No. 1's "Space Brain," and the black holes of the universe. Worse, this antiworld infects the world of intellectual clarity. When Twillig makes an error he hears "keep believing it, s***-for-brains." Urine and feces become, as in grade school, "number one" and "number two"; and mysticism is wittily described as "science's natural laxative." Themselves decaying, the scientists here cannot face this world of corruption and excrement; they try to evade it with cosmetics and cute words. But words themselves are infected. Verbal ideas cannot compete with mathematical clarity; "the power of logic, so near to number and so distant," fills Twillig "with warped vibrations, as of a harp string plucked by monkeys." . . .

Unfortunately, DeLillo's choice of a science-fiction form ("fiction is trying to move outward into space, science, history and technology," he has said) obliges him to reach answers and to impose a dramatic conclusion on his discrete materials. The plot may be intended to appease those hominids still longing for the reassurance of cause and effect, but the many ideas so satisfyingly raised, developed, and clarified in this fine novel deserve a better fate. Still, what a mind-expanding trip to the finish line, and full of wit and slapstick as well. (There's a Fellini parade halfway through.)

J. D. O'Hara, "Your Number Is Up," in Book World—The Washington Post *(© 1976, The Washington Post), June 13, 1976, p. M3.*

GEORGE STADE

Don DeLillo's first three books had the feel of novels straining to be something else, of energies out of their element, tadpoles in a cocoon. If what novelists did was to round characters, set scenes and plot consequences, DeLillo was willing, but he did not seem happy doing it. He seemed happiest when careening off into a detour.

In "**Americana**" (1971), for instance, an executive at a TV network drops out of the rat race to drive cross country in pursuit of reality, America, himself. He finds them, but the news is not good. In "**End Zone**" (1972), a flakey halfback at Logos College in Texas jukes his way through a rough season. There are many references to war-games and to Vietnam. And in "**Great Jones Street**" (1973), a rock star, tout of rout and impresario of zonk, silences himself, retreats to a dingy tenement. His reputation catches up to him, with sinister effect. These plots, with all their insistent but familiar purport, don't count for much, even with the author. What counts is the aside, the digression, the excursus—the set-pieces of bravura craziness and inspired quackery, the rapid-fire dialogue of pointed indirection and baited indiscretion, the displays of learning twisted just enough to reveal the obsession behind it.

DeLillo's new book is the something else his others were straining to become. In "**Ratner's Star**" his energies are turned to Menippean satire—an ancient form invented by a Greek Cynic philosopher and ex-slave, developed by Lucian and Petronius and Apuleius, revived by Erasmus and Rabelais, preserved by Swift and Lewis Carroll, Americanized in "Moby Dick" and "Invisible Man" and "The Dream Life of Balso Snell." This last was written by Nathanael West, to whom DeLillo is very close in mood. He is close in subject matter to Thomas Pynchon, who seems to have learned how to use the form through a study of William Gaddis, a presiding genius, as it turns out, of post-war American fiction. The Menippean satire, in short, is the exemplary form of the moment.

It is the right form, that is, for fiction writers who have little interest in fitting together rounded characters, social relations and sequential plots—or who see little evidence of them in experience. It is the right form when experience seems to consist of discontinuous selves, collapsing institutions and arrested developments, which is how it seems to seem right now to our best fiction writers. In Menippean satires characters are reduced to the attitudes or theories for which they stand. Vice and folly are situated not in human nature or in social relations, but in distempers of intellect. Occupational bias and fantastic learning take the place of manners and morals. Plots are dislocated by juggernaut structures of ideas. Reality, social or other, is swallowed up by mind. And that is the way of things in Don DeLillo's new book. . . .

"**Ratner's Star**" is not only interesting, but funny (in a nervous kind of way). From it comes an unambiguous signal that DeLillo has arrived, bearing many gifts. He is smart, observant, fluent, a brilliant mimic and an ingenious architect. Too often, however, the razzle-dazzle seems that of a child prodigy, the conspicuous originality somewhat derivative, the dolar unearned, the desperation routine. And the flashbacks to Billy Twillig's family life seem vestigial remains, non-functioning traces of the novel this Menippean satire overgrew. All of DeLillo's books are in an anxious sweat for direct confrontations of the Zeitgeist—which, however, is like a nebula most clearly seen when you look past it or to its side. In "**Americana**," the narrator tells us that "one of my main faults was a tendency to get blinded by the neon of an idea, and there reaching truly inside it." and there is some of that in "**Ratner's Star.**" But the flashy neon seems pale amid the deep incandescence of this red giant of a book.

> George Stade, in a review of "Ratner's Star," in The New York Times Book Review (© 1976 by The New York Times Company; reprinted by permission), June 20, 1976, p. 7.

SARAH M. McGOWAN

The subtitle of *Amazons* [by Cleo Birdwell] is "an intimate memoir by the first woman ever to play in the National Hockey League." She is Cleo Birdwell, who was reared in Badger, Ohio, where, as a youngster, she spent a good deal of time playing hockey. Our story begins with Cleo signing a contract with the New York Rangers, the ensuing news conference and meeting with the Garden (as in Madison Square) president, James Kinross, a crude-mouthed alcoholic. Throughout the memoir we see glimpses of the hockey world which include Cleo's dressing room, which, though separate and of questionable sanctity, she considers unnecessarily discriminatory. For the most part the book does not deal with hockey but concentrates on Cleo's relationships with Floss, her agent who plays strip monopoly with one of her clients, her hippy brother who is an actor in blue movies, an assortment of men who flit across her sexual life, and Sanders, her lover, who is afflicted with jumping Frenchmen disease. . . .

Amazons is a light-hearted memoir in which most of the action apparently is happening now, and is merely spiced with reminiscences of her past. There are some humorous passages and a variety of sex scenes, but this book of fictional reflections provides no likeable characters, little character development and even less thematic development. Rather, it is an entertaining bit of episodic fluff that has its amusing moments as it attempts to parody people's neuroses and life styles. Some segments are well written and funny, but on the whole the writing is inconsistent. The title, which is explained at the end of the book, will attract some readers, but it left me with a prejudice I labored to overcome.

> Sarah M. McGowan, in a review of "Amazons," in Best Sellers (copyright © 1980 Helen Dwight Reid Educational Foundation), Vol. 40, No. 7, October, 1980, p. 237.

J. D. O'HARA

The title [of *Amazons*] is misleading. There is only one Amazon here, Ms. Birdwell, and her martial weapon is a hockey stick. *Amazons* is her autobiography, with appropriately heavy emphasis on last year, when she made athletic history by being the first woman to play in the National Hockey League. Fans now look forward to her return under the New York Rangers' interesting new management, about which she says some perceptive things. . . . But Birdwell does not write primarily for sports fans, among whom the literacy rate is low. She writes for a higher audience—us—capable of appreciating such subtlety as that of her dust-jacket photo. In the picture she wears her Rangers uniform, but her flowing hair and a businesslike skate cover the end letters and reveal her as (in French) an angel.

There is something unexpected about an autobiography written, even by an angel, at such a fledgling stage. After all, we do not read such works for mere names, dates and places. We seek insightful, amusing and thought-provoking observations arising from experience and bearing valuably on life as we know it. And what of all this can we expect from a 23-year-old native of Badger, Ohio, who has spent most of her recent years playing hockey in distant leagues? Face it, all pucks look alike.

But it figures that any woman who survives an N.H.L. season must have some extra smarts. (p. 385)

But Birdwell is not a professional author; her narrative follows no game plan. She experiences it as we do, moment by moment, and is sometimes equally surprised at the turns of events. Naturally, since she is a woman and full of small-town sociability, she writes mostly not about hockey action, in which every player is alone, or even about her happy youth. She tells about the people she lives among. And in the world of professional sport they are almost all men. . . .

The assurance of [her] generalizations [about men] and of the details given elsewhere indicates the modernity of these memoirs. Even her hymns to childhood include topics not traditional in the handling of that theme. Birdwell is a woman of the present. Many women are? Certainly lots of women publish books claiming that they are. But this is precisely where Birdwell differs. In such central areas as equality and sexuality, Birdwell . . . *Birdwell has no hangups. Nor has she overcome any.* This is not to say that she is a smug know-it-all. She is young. Much is new to her. She admits it. . . .

[She] is attractive and suddenly famous in New York; she can be used to make money. . . . She is besieged by lovers, promoters and other weirdos. All weirdos. Consider your own acquaintances. After narrating such encounters for a while Birdwell begins a chapter with the exhausted one-sentence paragraph: "All I wanted to do was play hockey."

She does not. In that chapter she leaves one man to visit another's apartment where she is phoned by a third. . . .

Well, Birdwell possesses many qualities undemonstrated here. She is perceptive, she uses language so well that one wants to read the whole novel to friends, even on the telephone, collect, and she is marvelously funny even in crises. . . .

The reader—you there—will have suspected something. A female hockey player? One would have heard, somehow. A funny female writer? Yes, it's possible; but her name is Ann Beattie. What's going on here? Who is this soloist really?

One can only intuit. Intuition reports that there are only two men alive capable of writing this book in English, and one of them didn't. So it must be the work of that terrific Athenian-American novelist Don DeLillo. Place your bets. And don't read the book in public if you have a shrill, whinnying laugh; people will complain. (p. 386)

J. D. O'Hara, "A Pro's Puckish Prose," in The Nation *(copyright 1980 The Nation magazine, The Nation Associates, Inc.), Vol. 231, No. 12, October 18, 1980, pp. 385-86.*

CHRISTOPHER LEHMANN-HAUPT

Not being much of a hockey fan, I thought for a couple of pages that Cleo Birdwell's **"Amazons: An Intimate Memoir by the First Woman Ever to Play in the National Hockey League"** was the real thing. After all, why not? A woman has played professional football—albeit for only one play—and another has scrimmaged with major-league male basketball players. And there's Cleo Birdwell in a New York Rangers uniform on the back advertisement of **"Amazons,"** looking big and raw-boned and every bit as tough as Anders Hedberg.

But the light began to dawn on me in the first few pages, when James Kinross, president of Madison Square Garden, says to the author: "Tell you the truth, Birdwell, I hate hockey. You don't have a black or Hispanic element. It doesn't reflect the urban reality. Who wants to see two white guys hit each other?"

. . . Besides, I know that the Rangers don't have and never had a general manager named Sanders Meade (Yale, class of '67), who is rendered impotent by the mention of Watergate, Vietnam and Iran. Or an announcer named Merle Halverson, who suffers from "a swimming-pool-shaped kidney." Or a coach with the name of Jean-Paul Larousse, who is periodically overcome by the need to speak long hours of French to Cleo, even though she doesn't understand a word of the language. Even I know that.

So, what is **"Amazons,"** if it isn't an actual memoir? It's a novel, obviously—a novel about Cleo's first year with the Rangers. (pp. 553-54)

It's about Cleo's agent, Floss Penrose, who lives to play strip Monopoly with a tennis pro named Archie Brewster. . . . And it's about Cleo's lover, particularly Shaver Stevens, a former hockey star who suffers from a mysterious disease called "Jumping Frenchmen," which compels him to keep checking the soles of his shoes and to do deep knee-bends.

Now I realize that none of the foregoing sounds particularly funny just lying there in naked summary. Nor does the fact that Shaver consults a doctor named Sidney Glass, who specializes in going on television talk shows and telling audiences, "We don't really know what disease is." Nor does the development in which the Saudi Arabians take over the corporation that owns the Rangers and reach a compromise whereby Cleo must wear a veil when she plays. (p. 554)

But even if it doesn't *sound* funny, it is. Cleo Birdwell has a way with the incongruous—which doesn't come as a surprise once you've learned that her name is the nom de plume for Don DeLillo, the novelist (**"End Zone," "Ratner's Star"** and **"Players"**). She has this talent for grabbing clichés by the throat and strangling them until they cough up meaning. She turns meaning inside out and exposes its nonsense. The funniest and most poignant scene in the book is the one in which she sexually stirs a sportswriter named Murray Jay Siskind by describing the Christmas ritual in her home town of Badger, Ohio, though the scene in which her father warns her about the dirty language she will hear in locker rooms takes a very close second. I can't describe them.

Does **"Amazons"** add up to anything more than a wonderfully funny string of gags? (pp. 554-55)

I'm not sure [Cleo] ever does turn [up the major thematical material she is looking for], unless you count her satire of big-time sports as major thematic material, or her eventual reduction of her lover to the status of a sleeping Prince Charming. (To cure Shaver Stevens of his Jumping Frenchmen, Dr. Glass puts him to sleep for five weeks in a container called a Kramer cube. Cleo isn't sure she wants him to wake up. He looks so "haunting.") But then I'm not sure if it matters. With all that's going on in **"Amazons,"** we really don't miss it. (p. 555)

Christopher Lehmann-Haupt, in a review of "Amazons," in The New York Times, *Section 3 (© 1980 by The New York Times Company; reprinted by permission), September 16, 1980 (and reprinted in* Books of the Times, *Vol. 111, No. 11, November, 1980, pp. 553-55).*

ROBERT NADEAU

[Nadeau is concerned with the linkage between revolutionary advances in physics in the twentieth century that have significantly

altered the "scientific" view of the universe and themes, presentations, form, and content in the modern novel.]

Not only are metaphysical assumptions . . . just as important and primary in the creative work of scientists as we have long known them to be in humanistic endeavors, [but also] the implications of new scientific theories . . . have often had unexpected impact upon those assumptions. It is . . . conceivable, although there is no precedent for it, that a radically new scientific paradigm, like that of the new physics, could prove so inconsistent with received metaphysical assumptions as to occasion a massive revolution in thought, out of which an alternate metaphysic would emerge. This is, I am convinced, our present situation. Not long after the publication of Einstein's special theory of relativity in 1905, many of the architects of what was fast becoming a revolution in scientific thought began to realize that they were not simply in the process of redefining concepts in a discipline, but were raising some formidable questions about the character of reality itself. They perceived, in short, that the revolution in physics seemed to be leading inexorably to a revolution in metaphysics, that a full acceptance of this new scientific view of the nature of things necessitated some profound changes in the conceptual machinery upon which an entire cosmos had been constructed. (pp. 2-3)

Once we perceive that the common-sense assumptions in [classical and Newtonian] science are not a priori truths, but rather a consequence of the experience of man in [a] particular culture, we should be better prepared to digest the concepts from the new physics that appear to undermine them. We should then be in a position to explore the mythopoeic function of this new science as it is now manifesting itself in the contemporary novel. Although most of the concepts from physics that have had an impact upon the novelists studied here can be traced to theoretical advances in physics made in the 1920s and '30s, we will also briefly review more recent controversies in quantum physics. Some of the novelists, like Pynchon and DeLillo, appear to have followed these developments rather closely, but the principal benefit of reviewing them is, I think, that they reveal a good deal about the fundamental organizing principles in the symbolic universe of Western man. (pp. 11-12)

· · · · ·

Although Don DeLillo's [first] six . . . novels are considerably more limited in scope of reference and range of implications than the three novels of Thomas Pynchon, there is remarkable similarity between these novelists' individual conceptions of the contemporary human dilemma. Both assume that the tendency of Western man to construct reality in terms of closed systems and symbolics is not only without epistemological foundation, but also functions as program and guide for the fragmentation of individual identity and the possible extinction of the entire race of man. They also share the conviction that the continued survival of human civilization is dependent upon a fundamental restructuring of the dynamics of our world-conceiving minds, and each favors a return to a more primal sense of being that allows for an enlarged awareness of self as manifestation of one unified process. Although DeLillo, like Pynchon, is preoccupied with exposing the [Aristotelian] principle of the either-or as the most invidious dynamic in the construction of closed systems and symbolics, the purging from consciousness of abstract systems definitions of reality is normally accompanied in his fiction by a renewed awareness of the denotative aspect of language. DeLillo apparently feels, more strongly than Pynchon, that by detaching ourselves from

the word as *Logos*, and placing greater emphasis upon the function of the word as concrete referent, we would be better able to construct an alternate reality more consistent with the metaphysics implied in the new physics.

The system under investigation in **Americana** is the electronic communications network, and the aspect of that system that receives the most careful scrutiny is the filmic image. David Bell, the youthful and thoroughly American protagonist, discovers in his work as a network producer that "words and meaning were at odds. Words did not say what was being said or even the reverse." This "child of Godard and Coca-Cola" . . . whose father and grandfather were both legends in the advertising industry, conceives of himself and others as little more than a compilation of images derived from a lifetime of exposure to movies and television programming. There is a tendency in this culture, speculates David early in the narrative, to regard the lens of the motion picture camera as "history. What the machine accepts is verifiably existent; all else is unborn or worse". . . . His belief that conceptions of self are increasingly the projections of identity marketed by commercial films and television leads to the conclusion that the authentic or unique self is being trivialized out of existence. (pp. 161-62)

Since the architects of this truth are the media managers who fashion images of the idealized self for the purpose of marketing products, the American dream, previously thought to be a function of received political and religious ideologies configuring in the lived experience of our cultural forebears, becomes increasingly the province of advertising. As David sees it, this new American "dream made no allowance for the truth beneath the symbols, for the interlinear notes, the presence of something black (and somehow very funny) at the mirror of one's awareness." Bombarded all of his life with the "institutional messages, the psalms and placards, the pictures, the words" of the advertising industry, he senses that "all the impulses of the media were fed into the circuitry of my dreams," and that he has become, finally, "an image made in the image and likeness of images". . . . (pp. 162-63)

Exposure to media entices Americans, suggests DeLillo, to view gratification of impulse in terms of the likeness or image of self that appears in advertising to have the most access to scarce commodities. . . . What is finally "merchandised," [explains David, through his home movie on American identity,] is the prospect of altering the image of the self for purposes of consumption, as opposed to refashioning, or reconstructing, the environment to create larger possibilities for growth and satisfaction. This segment of David's film also includes the comment: "Advertising discovered the value of the third person but the consumer invented him. The country itself invented him". . . . What this invention cannot represent, in that it reduces self to a set of single, composite, unidimensional images, is the richness and variety of experience in a diversified culture replete with contrasting life-styles and traditions. In the absence of extensive associations with the deep structure of received traditions and communal ethos that communicates the "truth beneath the symbols," the individual ceases to be highly individuated and also suffers the loss of any profound sense of relation to that which is *other*. (p. 163)

The reasons that this [film] is not likely to be successful are best understood by [the sculptor named] Sullivan. Like so many of DeLillo's characters, David is fascinated with numbers, assumes that "numbers have power," and also that the "whole country runs on numbers". . . . The attempt to recover an authentic self in the film is wrong-headed in Sullivan's view because it mirrors self through numeration, or through a vast accumulation of static frames of film. This obsession with numbers is, she tells David, "somewhat less than Euclidean in its sweep and purity; that one of my main faults was a tendency to get blinded by the neon of an idea, never reaching truly inside it; that to follow a number to infinity was not necessarily to arrive at God". . . . (pp. 163-64)

The collage of images that records the activities that represent, in David's perception, the life the culture deconstructs not into essences of identity, but rather into an ultimate cleavage between oppositions void of all signification. (pp. 164-65)

[And yet the] movie actually succeeds in the sense that it demonstrates, like the novel itself, the impossibility of imposing closed systems or symbolics, constructed in terms of the either-or, upon the essentially fluid and indeterminate life process. This is not, however, as DeLillo suggests in the conclusion of the narrative, a widely accepted truth in American culture. Ten minutes after David Bell, image and product of the "third-person singular," boards an aircraft to return to the mecca of the advertising industry in New York, "a woman asks for his autograph". . . . (p. 165)

In *End Zone* DeLillo is not, as some of the earlier reviewers presumed, drawing a simple-minded comparison between American football and modern warfare. What he has done in this narrative, with admirable ingenuity, is draw extensive parallels between the game as exemplar of all closed systems used in the construction of human reality, and the nuclear defense system. He then deconstructs the former in order to expose the latter as our most terrifying manifestation of the same habits of mind. Like Barth and Pynchon, who also dare to think the unthinkable in confronting the very real prospect of nuclear holocaust, the culprit for DeLillo is not the irremediable organization of our instinctual life, but the structure of our arbitrarily developed and potentially malleable symbolic universe.

Gary Harkness, the star running-back whose two major intellectual interests are the special character and appeal of football and the technology of nuclear war, attends four major universities before being recruited to play football for Logos College. The college, founded by a deaf mute, has undertaken an ambitious new football program under the direction of head coach Emmett Creed whose own illustrious career had been virtually destroyed when he broke the jaw of a second-string quarterback two years earlier at another university. The suggestion in the choice of names for coach and college that the game functions as emblem for systems definitions of reality is reinforced throughout the remainder of the narrative. Creed, "famous for bringing order out of chaos," conceives of football as a "complex of systems" which ideally "interlock" in some final "harmony". . . . (pp. 165-66)

[Gary's] deconstruction of the game reveals increasing resemblances between this system and the dramatically more lethal system of nuclear technology. . . . When the essential structure of football is bracketed out in the pick-up game in the snow through the elimination of huddles, customary gestures and postures, and even plays and opposing lines of players, what remains is the fundamental opposition between "man with ball" battling others "to keep possession of ball." The either-or as fundamental feature in the construction of systems is inescapable in football just as it is in all other systems and "double consciousness" . . . , as Gary's metaphysically minded fellow-player Bing points out, is just as inescapable here as it is elsewhere. Another player on this remarkable team, Ted Joost, even dreams about closure of the entire system of football with the use of a computer broadcasting "signals" to receivers in the helmets of every player in every game then being played. . . . (p. 166)

Gary's intense fascination with the "possibilities of nuclear war" begins with his exposure to a book assigned in a course on "disaster technology" at the University of Miami. . . . Even in the face of serious depression over his seemingly perverse interest in the subject, Gary is irresistibly drawn to this display of the "rationality of irrationality," in which "tens of millions die" and entire cities are destroyed. . . . Following a graphic description of the effects of nuclear blasts on cities and people, [Major Stanley, an AFROTC instructor,] comments that "war is a test of opposing technologies" configuring on such a high level of abstraction that "nobody has to feel any guilt. Responsibility is distributed too thinly for that". . . . It is, as Gary comes to view it, the underlying systems organization of the arsenal that sustains its growth, mitigates responsibility for its existence, and which may, as the mind that creates it hungers for closure, eventually lead us to the apocalypse. This last prospect begins to seem even more likely to Gary when the major, in another private conversation later in the narrative, tells him that the "big problem with war games, whether they were being played at the Pentagon, at Norad or Fort Belvoir, at a university or think tank, was the obvious awareness on the part of the participants that this wasn't the real thing". . . . The nuclear defense system becomes real, or ceases to function as simply an abstract schema of the possible, when, the major suggests, it is put into use. Closure in this system requires, in other words, the wedding of the ethereal war game, or war as unrealized possibility, with the war itself. (pp. 166-67)

Although DeLillo in *Ratner's Star* is definitely exercising poetic license in suggesting that human civilization originated at a much earlier date than can be supported by scientific evidence, we discover in this narrative not only an impressive acquaintance with concepts from the new physics but also the manner in which these concepts inform his artistic vision. . . . After discovering at an early age an extraordinary ability to conduct this internal dialogue in mathematical codes, Billy [Twillig, fourteen-year-old Nobel laureate in mathematics,] learns to take pleasure in inhabiting that "lonely place in his mind" where he is "free from subjection to reality, free to impose his ideas and designs on his own test environment. . . . This ardent disciple of the Pythagorean mathematical idea leaves his research post at "The Center for the Refinement of Ideational Structures" . . . to journey to a vast, internationally funded scientific laboratory and think tank called "Field Experiment Number One." It is the hope of the highly unorthodox directors of this project that Billy will succeed where others have failed in decoding radio messages emanating in space from the vicinity of the body known in astronomy as Ratner's star.

Billy, who reasons so thoroughly in the realm of the mathematical that he conceives of himself as "having two existences, right and left in terms of an equation," and who also fears that the mathematical side "might overwhelm the other, leaving him behind, a name and shape" . . . , functions in the narrative primarily as a vehicle through which DeLillo discourses upon the inability of closed scientific paradigms to fully contain or define natural process. Mathematical reasoning, with "its claim to necessary conclusions; its pursuit of connective patterns and significant form'' . . . , is premised upon assumptions, as Billy's mentor Softly points out in a ''work in progress,'' that are a product of an outmoded cosmology. (pp. 170-71)

Late in the novel DeLillo, as omniscient narrator, deals directly and at some length with the metaphysical implications of the new physics and draws some fairly definite conclusions. . . . The prospect that the mathematical coordinates can provide a direct transcription of self is doubtful, he notes, because ''in the wave-guide manipulation of light and our nosings into the choreography of protons, we implicate ourselves in endless uncertainty.'' DeLillo then asserts that this is ''the ethic you've rejected. Inside our desolation, however, you come upon the reinforcing grid of works and minds that extend themselves against whatever lonely spaces account for our hollow moods, the woe incoming. Why are you here? To unsnarl us from our delimiting senses?'' . . . This compulsion to define the essence of our being as mathematical or scientific entity will eventually, he concludes, ''make us hypothetical, a creature of our own pretending, as are you. . . .'' (pp. 172-73)

DeLillo, like Pynchon, is definitely not advocating an end to scientific investigation, nor does he mean to belittle the enterprise in the least. He is using present scientific knowledge to make the case that closed systems of abstractions that tend toward closure are not only invalidated by this knowledge, but provide a virtual guarantee that the entire human experiment will come to an abrupt halt in nuclear war. Although this is precisely what takes place at the conclusion of *Ratner's Star*, DeLillo is far more explicit here than in his other narratives in delineating those features of language, or those terms in the construction of the symbolic universe, that have driven us, in his view, to this absurd predicament.

The closure of economic and political systems that brings on the holocaust appears, first of all, to be the consequence of the effort by a bizarre business tycoon named Troxl to establish complete control over the international money market. . . . As the cartel [of which Troxl is part], renamed significantly ''ACRONYM'' . . . , begins to establish a monopoly over all ''model building organizations'' . . . , including Field Experiment Number One, it becomes increasingly more effective in moving the international monetary exchange system toward closure. As this movement occurs, global tensions increase proportionally. (p. 173)

The same compulsion to transform human reality into an idée fixe by containing it within abstract systems definitions is also at work in the effort to develop in the Logicon project a ''universal'' language that would facilitate communication with extraterrestrial beings like those initially thought to be transmitting the radio message. As Lester Bolin, who is most involved in the project, explains, this metalanguage cannot be spoken by a computer until they ''figure out how to separate the language as system of meaningless signs from the language about language'' . . . . The problem, as the anthropologist Wu realizes, is that such a metalanguage cannot ''mirror the world'' because it involves the ''impossible attempt to free reality from the structures it must possess as long as there are humans to breed it''. . . . Like any closed scientific paradigm that seeks to contain the open-ended, essentially indeterminate processes of nature, that which is finally mirrored is not the world but subjectively based human constructs. Since this mode of defining or explaining does not take into account the role of the observer in the participatory universe of the new physics, it communicates only itself.

The spokesman for the alternate metaphysics consistent with the new physics in this narrative is Shazar Lazarus Ratner, the impossibly aged and decrepit physicist after whom the star was named, who remains alive, ironically to be sure, only by virtue of an elaborate artificial life-support system. Ratner, like Whitehead, conceives of God, whom he refers to in the manner of orthodox Jews as ''G-dash-d,'' as identical with the endless process of becoming that is the life the universe. . . . Underlying the perceived world is, he says, the ''hidden. The that-which-is-not-there. . . .'' The inability to perceive, in normal states of consciousness, our proper relation to the ontological ground of Being is, suggests Ratner, largely due to the fact that ''everything in the universe works on the theory of opposites'' . . . , including language. The lesson learned in quantum physics that ''all things are present in all things. Each in its opposite'' . . . , has meaning, implies Ratner, only when we allow ourselves to ''go into mystical states'' and ''pass beyond the opposites of the world and experience only the union of opposites in a radiant burst of energy''. . . . Although transcendence of oppositions in language systems is a precondition for apprehending our actual condition in metaphysical terms, this does not, as Ratner sees it, diminish the power or importance of language. . . . The point of Ratner's somewhat rambling discourse is that although oppositions are both useful and necessary in the construction of our knowledge of the cosmos, and have real existence in the life of the cosmos itself, we must balance this understanding against the recognition that they are manifestations of one fundamental unity, and are, therefore, not absolute. (pp. 173-75)

When the scientists working on the Logicon project begin to sense that nuclear war is inevitable, they summon a ''woman from the slums'' who supposedly has ''unexplained insight into the future''. . . . After struggling through a series of violent contortions, Skia Mantikos, whose name means ''shadow prophet'' . . . , manages to utter a single, and from our perspective, very significant word: ''Pythagoras''. . . . It is important, of course, that the scientists, including Billy, who are privileged to hear this prophetic word do not have the first clue as to what it might mean. All of which serves to communicate DeLillo's fear that because language systems, particularly the mathematical, are assumed capable of revealing the immalleable essence of the real in an ordered, predictable, and closed totality the Western intellectual tradition might well be incapable of even questioning the validity of that assumption. (pp. 175-76)

Robert Nadeau, ''Preface'' and ''Don DeLillo,'' in his Readings from the New Book on Nature: Physics and Metaphysics in the Modern Novel *(copyright © 1981 by The University of Massachusetts Press), University of Massachusetts Press, 1981, pp. 1-16, 161-82.**

JONATHAN YARDLEY

Don DeLillo is a formidable prose stylist; as Fred Allen once said of another literary craftsman, ''He writes so well he makes me feel like putting my quill back in my goose.'' From time to time DeLillo thinks as keenly as he writes, and it is in these moments that *The Names*, . . . achieves its greatest power and interest. Unfortunately, though, these moments are concentrated in the first of the book's three principal sections, leaving the reader to plow through the remaining two-thirds with comparatively slight reward. *The Names* is an accomplished and intelligent novel, the work of a writer of clear if chilly brilliance, but it takes on too many themes and wanders in too many directions to find a coherent shape.

It is for his second novel, **End Zone,** that DeLillo is perhaps still best known. There his subject was the American propensity for institutionalized, ritualistic violence, and his metaphor for it was intercollegiate football. In *The Names* he is once again concerned with violence, but this time on an international scale. The narrator, James Axton, is a 38-year-old former freelance writer who now works out of Athens as "associate director of risk analysis, Middle East," for a group "writing political risk insurance in impressive amounts." His clients are large corporations who want to insure their investments against worldwide political turmoil, and his job is to evaluate the risks involved. . . .

In Athens, Axton is a member of a small community of Americans in similar lines of work, "the living to be made in terror." They are on the front lines, witnesses to and occasional victims of the seemingly endless process of disintegration and chaos. DeLillo describes their situation pungently. . . .

So long as DeLillo is describing this community and its perilous, morally equivocal position, *The Names* is entirely successful; his portraits of individual members of the community are sharp and true, his depiction of a world on the brink is wittily clinical, his dialogue is crisp and interesting. But he insists on going deeper than that, and when he does the novel drifts in various uncertain and not especially rewarding directions.

Axton is separated from his wife, who lives on "Kouros, an obscure island in the Cycladic group," with their 9-year-old son. There she works at an archaeological dig, and there Axton discovers evidence of cult murders. The murders come to obsess him. He believes that the cult, which seems to call itself "The Names," is "the only thing I seem to connect with." . . .

This—the mystery of naming, the mystery of language and words—is the theme to which DeLillo returns over and again. His Americans are people who are in the world yet unconnected with it because they have not bothered to learn any languages—which is to say any cultures, any realities—save their own. DeLillo asks the question, "How do you connect things?" and supplies the answer: "Learn their names." . . .

[That humankind can unite through language] is an appealing observation . . . , but DeLillo comes to it by so circuitous a route that many readers probably will lose patience along the way. To describe *The Names* as self-indulgent is perhaps unfair, but DeLillo allows Axton's quest to follow too many dead-end lanes and to wander too far from the subject about which he is most provocative, that of the rootless and cynical American internationalists.

> *Jonathan Yardley, "Don DeLillo's Terminology of Terror," in* Book World—The Washington Post *(© 1982, The Washington Post), October 10, 1982, p. 3.*

CHARLES CHAMPLIN

Don DeLillo is a mystery of a writer, one of the most critically acclaimed but narrowly known of all contemporary American novelists.

It is hard to say why. He is fearlessly original and uncompromising, but he is not an avant-gardist as I understand the term,

trying to see just how private language can be, or how ambiguous.

DeLillo is immediate, intense and, in a word that critics may like too well, accessible. He also creates glorious prose that in its freshness, precision and eloquence is continuously exciting to read.

His newest novel, "The Names," . . . may revise sharply upward the size of his readership. It stands above and out from any novel I've read in months: exotic, atmospheric, curiously suspenseful, full of characters at once unusual and fully realized.

But "The Names" is principally engrossing because it explores the American abroad and the American in this time, a citizen of the world who is by that definition also a citizen of nowhere, a stateless person more at home than ever in foreign cultures, although never able to be fully a part of them, more wistful than ever for the American past and the American home but cut off from them by the accidents and necessities of the present. . . .

DeLillo is his own unique voice, but for purposes of identification he can be triangulated by Lawrence Durrell in his poetic ability to catch the aromas, the look, the feeling of places and cultures alien to the reader; by John Cheever in his close familiarity with edgy modern relationships when neither surrender, rejection, joy or sorrow are ever quite total; and perhaps by John Fowles or Graham Greene, different as they are, in their characters' felt need for some sort of transcendence.

There is a quest in "The Names," a rather wispy, elusive quest, advanced by intuition as much as anything and at times seeming to be only a hypothesis. . . .

Things happen: There is movement and danger; there are minor flirtations and a major crisis or two. But DeLillo, who is said to have lived abroad for three years researching the novel, is obviously less concerned to tell a beginning-middle-end story than to set down a piece of our time, no longer Henry Luce's American Century but a time when Americans have become part of the world, linked deeply and inextricably with it.

DeLillo is by definition a serious writer, but like the three by whom he can be triangulated, he has a profound and restorative sense of humor, a vision of the ironies of situation, of the idiocies and fatuities of character.

"The Names" is full of set-pieces, on everything from film to second wives to language to belief, so that the novel has, chief among its excitements, surprise itself.

It is an extraordinarily original and enveloping piece of work and I hope that DeLillo of "The Names" becomes a name for a wider audience to conjure with.

> *Charles Champlin, "The American As Citizen of Nowhere," in* Los Angeles Times Book Review *(copyright, 1982, Los Angeles Times; reprinted by permission), November 7, 1982, p. 3.*

ROBERT TOWERS

Don DeLillo occupies a relatively sun-lit corner of that school of American writers who might be called Occultists—not because they deal with the supernatural (though some occasionally do) but because they see hidden correspondences between phenomena of the most heterogenous kind. Everything is in code; sometimes the code is to be compared, structurally, with other codes, all of them equally filled with, or devoid of, significance. John Barth's monumental *Letters* is a good example of the genre. So are Pynchon's *V, The Crying of Lot 49,* and *Gravity's Rainbow.* Often such fiction has a pronounced paranoid streak: not only codes but conspiracies abound, and for every conspiracy there is a counter-conspiracy and then a counter-counter-conspiracy that mirrors the first—and on and on in what can seem like an infinite regress.

Occultist novels provide engrossing games for the adept. For others, they are likely to seem static, even airless. From the start DeLillo's fiction has tended in the occultist direction, indulging obsessively in the creation or exploration of correspondences. From the start, too, his novels have been distinguished by a liveliness of style and intellect and an aptitude for vivid description that go far to compensate for the narrative inertia that has overtaken his earlier books. Since **Ratner's Star,** the apogee or nadir of his mirror-game experiments, DeLillo has opened his fiction to the possibilities of more extroverted action. The speeded-up pace in both **Players** and **Running Dog** seems to me all to the good. The two novels present a continually interesting, often entertaining texture, though they are likely to leave the reader eventually numbed by the unrelieved sleaziness and horror of the image of American life they project. The occult is to be found less in correspondences than in the preoccupation with covert organizations, plots, counterplots, spying, and terrorism.

In *The Names,* DeLillo has abandoned the dingy streets of lower Manhattan, where much of the earlier fiction is set, for the sun-struck, glaring landscapes of Greece and the Near and Middle East. The scene shift is dazzling: as always, DeLillo evokes his settings with such precision and sensuous detail that he runs the danger of having them assume a distinctiveness that his characters may lack. But we soon find that the familiar DeLillo weed patch of contemporary malaise, *Angst,* and planned or gratuitous violence is easily transplantable. The major occult element in the novel—there are other, minor mysteries—concerns a nomadic cult that appears variously on a Cycladic island, on a desolate, boulder-strewn peninsula in the Peloponnese, and in the tawny rubble of the Indian desert; earlier, the cult or one of its cells (there seem to be several) has sojourned briefly in Jordan and Syria. The cult is without a name, but is intensely interested in names—and in alphabets and inscriptions. Its supreme ritualistic observance involves the murdering—by hammer or sharpened stones—of some mentally or physically defective person whose name happens to have the same initials as the place where the murder is perpetrated.

Our guide to these arcana is James Axton, a late-thirtyish American "risk analyst" based in Athens. . . . [He] is part of a subculture of American "business people in transit" who may be interned in Tehran on one trip or feasted in Abu Dhabi on the next. . . . Axton drinks with his fellow expatriates in Athens, flirts rather chastely with their wives, and pays frequent visits to the island of Kouros, where his estranged wife Kathryn is working on an archaeological dig and his nine-year-old son Tap is scribbling away at a novel. It is on Kouros that Axton first hears of the dirty, bedraggled little group of cave-dwellers encountered in the upper reaches of the island by Owen Brademas, the archaeologist in charge of Kathryn's dig. Are they responsible for the bludgeoning, shortly afterward, of an old man—an event that sets the whole island talking? Brademas, whose major interest is epigraphy, is fascinated by the fragmentary evidence of an alphabet-obsessed cult of killers; so, for different reasons, is a maverick film-maker, Frank Volterra,

an old friend of the Axtons who arrives on the island and talks at length to Brademas; and so is Axton himself.

Brademas's own preoccupation with the letters (as opposed to the *meaning*) of inscriptions seems to have roots in a childhood spent in the prairie states, where he attended evangelical services that involved "speaking in tongues"—i.e., the utterance of nonsense syllables in an ecstatic state. As a boy, he resisted the efforts of his parents and the preacher to get him to participate; as a man of sixty he has in a sense despaired of meaning but longs to associate himself with the corrupted ecstacy of a meaningless act. Volterra, on the other hand, wants to film the cult as its members prepare for one of their murders. He is the ultimate voyeur-exploiter, a late twentieth-century sensationalist. The motives that impel Axton to follow Volterra and Brademas at a safe distance, gleaning what he can, are more nebulous. Though he too is drawn toward the deadly vacuum of the cult, he is not prepared to surrender his humanity to the nihilism that Volterra and Brademas in differing ways represent.

Much of this is interestingly and complexly conceived. But the very existence of the cult, which is crucial to the central action of the novel, is never made plausible—at least not to me. While one shouldn't expect a novelist as devoted to the elliptical as DeLillo to spell out all the answers, something more concrete and less arbitrary than what he gives is needed. One craves a bit of history: how did the cult, which, we are told, is not very old, begin? How did its polyglot members, who seem to be vaguely European, ever find one another? In a novel as essentially realistic as *The Names,* there is a limit to what one is willing to accept as "given." Similarly, Brademas, the Conradian figure who ventures furthest into the heart of negation, seems too willed or confected a character, his motivations too theoretical, his dark sayings too pretentious.

The Names is only intermittently compelling as a story, for DeLillo has chosen to pursue other concerns that lead away from the central action. Among the most rewarding of these are the long, somewhat oblique conversations with other members of the expatriate circle, particularly a middle-aged, half-British couple named Charles and Ann Maitland. The talk, revolving around aspects of their uprooted existence, is full of the unexpected and is often witty—as when Axton points out to the adulterously inclined Ann, whom he greatly likes, that love affairs may be functions of geography, of a woman's need to deepen her experience of a place to which her husband's job has taken her and which she will have to leave through no choice of her own. . . . Other diversions—invariably well written—include descriptive set pieces, episodes concerning Kathryn or Tap, chance encounters, random memories of Axton's; even a section from Tap's novel is inserted—its misspellings intact—at the end.

By thus breaking up the story line DeLillo has kept *The Names* from assuming the shape that we conventionally associate with novels of quest or revelation. What he achieves is a deliberate unshapeliness, a sense of fragmentation, menace, and loose ends that seems appropriate enough to our experience of the final, ominous decades of this extraordinary century. What he loses is some of the potential force that a greater concentration of his effects might have produced. I found myself reading *The Names* with much interest and with moments of high delight but with little sense of urgency. And I was left more hungry than gratified at the end. Nearly every page testifies to DeLillo's exceptional gifts as a writer—a writer who has not yet, in my view, published a novel whose total impact is equal to the brilliance of its parts. (pp. 32-4)

Robert Towers, "A Dark Art," in The New Republic *(reprinted by permission of* The New Republic; ©*1982 The New Republic, Inc.), Vol. 187, No. 3540, November 22, 1982, pp. 32-4.*

JOSH RUBINS

For Don DeLillo, . . . , the most convincing moves into the surreal have seemed to spring from necessity rather than whim. The violent, tainted face of Sixties-and-after America, the lurid emptiness of modern urban life: DeLillo responds to these with such intense loathing and despair that his inventions—from the enigmatic football teams of *End Zone* to the nude storyteller and Hitler home movies of *Running Dog*—carry a whiff of danger, of fury kept just barely under control by a shift to metaphor. The resulting imagery can sometimes be off-putting or self-defeatingly private; the cosmic perspective—with every personal dysfunction turned into a sociopolitical disease—can be schematic, even adolescent. But DeLillo's across-the-board revulsion has also drummed up disturbing, shattered-windshield worlds, with virtually every fictional convention infected, twisted askew. Characters who slide between cartoon and clinical report, bad-dream plots, switchblade-carved prose, and disjointed talk: in a novel like *Players,* all these elements, equally (just slightly) unmoored from reality, spin around each other like particles in solution, bouncing off a central alienation that DeLillo is too clever (or too angry) to take on directly.

In *The Names,* however, DeLillo is suddenly, eloquently, almost lumberingly direct—about the dynamics of alienation, about the corruption of the American personality. Instead of pawnlike, flyaway characters lost in a jigsaw nightmare, here is James Axton, a fulltime narrator-hero prone to measured pronouncements and near-Jamesian introspection. An American in Athens, working for a shadowy company that sells "political risk insurance" to corporations with foreign holdings, Axton may have an exotic trope of a job, but he has the most conventional of modern domestic crises: a communication problem with his estranged wife Kathryn, a late-blooming archaeologist who's now on a dig, with their precocious young son, on a desolate Aegean island. (p. 47)

[In Axton's] subsequent mild attempts at reconciliation, the role of conversation is made crucial. Indeed, throughout this novel the paradoxical nature of language—as a barrier, as a

way to "bridge the lonely distances"—becomes DeLillo's often-elegant vehicle for exploring Axton's alienation. (pp. 47-8)

Equally straightforward, and considerably more effective, is DeLillo's slide-show portrait of the American expatriate subculture that Axton edgily inhabits—those "business people in transit, growing old in planes and airports," thriving on the "humor of personal humiliation." Again, language is the sinuous motif: the ethnocentricity of English-speakers abroad, the fear and distortion that arise from Axton's limited Greek vocabulary, his faulty pronunciation, his concierge-phobia. . . . The novel's casual references to its international time frame—Iran and terrorism, 1979-1980—are sufficient to suggest global ramifications. An unsurprising revelation about Axton's accidental CIA connections . . . puts yet another thematic lid on.

For perhaps the first time, then, DeLillo has no apparent trouble making himself clear, pinning his vision down, through thoroughly traditional means. Yet he also fabricates a central plot that's closer to symbolic fable than to realistic storytelling; and this time the imaginative leap registers almost as an exasperating footnote, a leftover extra layer. Led on first by an archaeologist (his wife's mentor), later by a documentary film maker, Axton follows a blatantly implausible trail of cult murders from Peloponnesia to Jordan to India. What is this cult? Why do its unlikely killer members match up victims' initials with place names, cutting the initials into the blades of the murder weapons? Why have the world's semanticists turned so vicious? The answer, little more than another variation on DeLillo/Axton's philosophical drift, hardly justifies the side step into borderline fantasy. . . .

DeLillo, in fact, doesn't seem to need cults and spies and nude storytellers any more: Axton could have made his transformation—and might have made a more persuasive one—without the trek across an alien genre. And DeLillo's prose, though too often put in the service of Axton's magisterial ruminations, responds as securely to the fullness of intimate observation and psychology as it once did to the cool disjunctions of surrealism. This may not be DeLillo's farewell to CIA agents, mock-thrillers, and metaphoric violence; it may be merely a failed attempt to expand and explicate the old formulas. But there's more than a hint of a Prospero-like valediction here, and more than a hint that fantasy's loss could be realism's gain. (p. 48)

Josh Rubins, "Variety Shows," in The New York Review of Books *(reprinted with permission from* The New York Review of Books; *copyright © 1982 Nyrev, Inc.), Vol. XXIX, No. 20, December 16, 1982, pp. 46-8.**

Christopher (Ferdinand) Durang

1949-

American dramatist and lyricist.

Christopher Durang's plays satirize—sometimes with affection, sometimes with derision—the clichés and absurdities of daily life within the contexts of such disparate subjects as great literature in *The Idiots Karamazov* (1974); psychiatry in *Beyond Therapy* (1981); "serious" drama in *The Vietnamization of New Jersey* (1977); and Catholicism in the 1981 Obie award-winning *Sister Mary Ignatius Explains It All for You* (1979). His only Broadway production, *A History of the American Film* (1979), uses two hundred movie moments to burlesque sixty years of filmmaking. Durang's treatments are also diverse, ranging in tone from musical spoof or tongue-in-cheek farce to bitter ridicule. In one play his voice is that of the disillusioned Catholic, demanding, "If God is all-powerful, why does He allow evil?" and in another his persona is a dancing vegetable in a Busby Berkeley musical, singing "We're in a Salad."

Critics generally agree that Durang's principal stylistic weaknesses are his unsatisfactory endings and his preference for accentuating the joke rather than the issue, thus lessening the impact of his message. His alterations of classics into travesties have resulted in critical reception which has covered the spectrum from "witty and scholarly" to "lightweight and smart-alecky." Durang concedes that among both critics and theater patrons are some who will be offended by his irreverence; yet, he intends not to affront but to continue to interpret "the nature and purpose of the universe."

(See also *Contemporary Authors*, Vol. 105.)

© Thomas Victor 1983

MEL GUSSOW

["**The Idiots Karamazov**"] is, more or less, a musical comedy based on "The Brothers Karamazov," which is enough to make Dostoyevsky turn over in his grave. Actually there is nothing grave about this antic undertaking. A travesty by Christopher Durang and Albert F. Innaurato, . . . it is as precocious as it sounds but it also has moments of comic inspiration. . . .

The script is riddled with literary allusions and intellectual jokes. This is a lampoon not only of Dostoyevsky, but also of all Western literature.

The star role is the translator, Constance Garnett. . . . [She] is a daft old witch (the play is daft, too) in a wheelchair, attended by a butler named Ernest, who eventually blows his brains out. Absent mindedly, Miss Garnett leads us through the Karamazov saga, offering absurd footnotes and marginalia (such as the conjugation of the verb Karamazov).

The brothers' mother is named Mary Tyrone Karamazov. She wanders in from another play, shooting dope and confusing the saintly Alyosha with the sickly Edmund Tyrone. . . .

The brothers are more Marx than Karamazov, four pratfalling mad Russians. . . .

Textually the play occasionally smarts from its own archness, but musically it is right on its satiric target. If the authors are really as clever as they seem to be, they . . . will add songs and make it even more of a musical.

Dostoyevsky's Karamazov brothers enter like Chekhov's sisters, singing, "We gotta get to Moscow," and Grushenka . . . musically describes her romantic predicament, "Fathers and sons. I'm in love with fathers and sons." Eventually Alyosha is transformed into a pop star and plays the Palace, accompanied by a chorus of crazy ladies, Constance Garnett, Grushenka, Anais Pnin and Djuna Burnes. Later there is a send-up of L. Frank Baum, "Totem and Taboo and Toto Too," and Miss Garnett gets to yodel solo.

Everything is twitted, even the Yale Theater itself, with scenery removed by a black-shrouded stagehand, a creepy leftover from the company's last production. . . . One might say that "**The Idiots Karamazov**" is the flip side of Dostoyevsky.

I liked the all-nonsense attitude, but some of the humor seemed too facile. . . . [Instead] of building to a zany climax, the show dribbles off into a recitation by Miss Garnett of famous first lines (from Joyce to Melville) as if the playwrights felt a need to impress us. I was already impressed—with their wit as well as with their scholarship.

Mel Gussow, "'Idiots Karamazov', Zany Musical,"
in The New York Times (© 1974 by The New York

Times Company; reprinted by permission), November 11, 1974, p. 42.

EDITH OLIVER

The brief appearance last week of **"Titanic"** and **"Das Lusitania Songspiel"** was my first exposure to the comedy of young Christopher Durang. . . . From the evidence presented, Mr. Durang is a spirited, original fellow . . . , who brings back to the theatre a welcome impudence and irreverence. **"Das Lusitania Songspiel,"** which started the evening, and which was actually cabaret, was described in the program as "The Theatre Songs of Bertolt Breck," but Breck/Brecht really had very little to do with anything onstage, except for some offhand references to him and some fake attributions ("Swiss Family Trapp, from 'Mother Courage'"); in fact, one of the funniest routines was a tableau from "Barry Lyndon." (pp. 103-04)

"Titanic" was a merry and (innocently) obscene farce, with on-and-off good jokes and not a trace of boring camp, yet I ran out of laughter long before the actors ran out of steam. Few sexual perversions were neglected in a plot of blinding complexity, and there were many false alarms about icebergs. (p. 104)

Edith Oliver, "Young Blue," in The New Yorker *(© 1976 by The New Yorker Magazine, Inc.), Vol. LII, No. 14, May 24, 1976, pp. 103-05.*

ANTONIO CHEMASI

Christopher Durang is a young playwright out of Harvard and Yale who took the wrong turn at some point and wound up in comedy. While his contemporaries were grimly exploring the Vietnam experience or urban bleakness or poking through the ashes of burned-out lives, Durang was busy collaborating on a send-up of Dostoevski called *The Idiots Karamazov.* He was also turning out deliciously titled comedies like *When Dinah Shore Ruled the Earth, The Nature and Purpose of the Universe,* and *The Vietnamization of New Jersey.*

His latest is *A History of the American Film,* an elaborate spoof of more than a half-century of everything worth spoofing on the screen. The play . . . sprang Durang to national attention. But while the critics were generally delighted, there was a good deal of uncertainty about exactly what Durang's intentions were. Is the play an affectionate tribute to cinema or a bitter satire of popular culture? . . .

The uncertainty has something to do with the comedy's own flaws, but it has much more to do, I suspect, with the boldness of Durang's enterprise. He has done nothing less than to reclaim the movies as a topic for the theater. I don't mean the movies as a business or as a fabricator of glamorous lives or even as a source of theatrical plots. I mean the movies as an art and as an experience: For that the theater has hardly stirred at all. . . .

Whatever the reason for the traditional coolness, *A History of the American Film* may change all that—if for no other reason, ironically, than that it demonstrates that movies work on stage. (p. 66)

The result is a very funny and oddly moving play that is indeed a history—of sorts. It opens with a D. W. Griffith mother rocking a cradle and ends with a Sensurround earthquake rocking a stage audience off their seats. In between are a pell-mell series of parodies, in chronological order, of movie scenes,

stars, genres, styles, dialogue, and even lighting. . . . Appropriately, the scenes are linked by blackouts and are held together by a nutty plot that follows the fortunes of several characters—the great stereotypes of American movies—through the decades.

For his text, Durang has gone not to Lewis Jacobs or the other standard film historians, but to memory—his and ours. In fact, the play is less a send-up of the movies than of the detritus in our minds a few thousand movie-hours later. Not only the detritus of dialogue—"I came to Casablanca for the waters," "I coulda been a contender"—but of scenes and characters and plots and ways of looking at the world that have sunk into our minds for good, or bad. "Can you help me?" a girl asks. "I'm American, ain't I?" the man replies. So much for that burly chauvinism that the screen and the country once mirrored in each other.

A History of the American Film has the shape of a dream—or perhaps of a Marx Brothers film under the influence of drugs. Scenes melt into new scenes: A parody of *The Public Enemy* slips into a parody of *The Front Page,* then into a parody of a screwball comedy and of *The Grapes of Wrath.* ("We're the people," Ma Joad keeps croaking like a windup doll. She ends up as a hostile witness in a parody of a fifties' HUAC movie.) At the very center of the play are Jimmy and Loretta—the eternal James Cagney tough guy and Loretta Young innocent— the stereotypes that launched a thousand movies.

Jimmy's toughness is so quintessentially of the movies that it's hard to read his dialogue without falling into a Cagney tone. (pp. 66-7)

Loretta's innocence is so purely of celluloid that at one point she invokes the Production Code as if she were quoting a passage from the Sermon on the Mount. . . .

Together, Jimmy and Loretta dash through the decades of Durang's *History,* now slipping into the *Casablanca* roles of Humphrey Bogart and Ingrid Bergman, now as Marlon Brando and Eva Marie Saint, finally stopping—exhausted, bitter—as George and Martha of *Who's Afraid of Virginia Woolf.* . . .

[The] pleasures of watching Durang's play—at least a good production of it—are not in catching the references. They're largely in the experience of watching the great moments of the movies so expertly mimicked that even Gregg Toland's lighting from *Citizen Kane* is reproduced. There are instances where the sensations of watching a movie vie with the sensations of watching theater. It's at those very moments that we must face the fact—if we haven't faced it before—that the divide between film and theater is much less fundamental than used to be thought. The crowing by film's partisans died down long ago; today, superiority isn't being claimed by anyone.

The question remains: Why are the movies and the movie experience missing from the stage? What *A History of the American Film* demonstrates so well is that the memorable moments of the movies *work* on stage, have the weight to hold the stage, and demand a tribute—whether Durang meant one or not. (p. 67)

Antonio Chemasi, "Inner Circles," in American Film *(reprinted with permission from the September 1977 issue of* American Film *magazine; © 1977, The American Film Institute, J. F. Kennedy Center, Washington, DC 20566), Vol. II, No. 10, September, 1977, pp. 66-7.*

ROBERT BRUSTEIN

[*The Vietnamization of New Jersey*] is a satire of such ferocity that it runs roughshod not only through the conventions of [David Rabe's] *Sticks and Bones,* but through some of our most cherished liberal illusions.

Durang is a lineal descendant of Lenny Bruce, which is to say he is always trespassing on forbidden ground, skirting perilously close to nihilism. Still, Durang's nihilism is earned; like Bruce, he obviously suffers for it. The satire in *The Vietnamization of New Jersey* has been called collegiate, but it is rarely facile, and it is never self-righteous. Durang's comedy, at its best, has deep roots in a controlled anger, which can only be expressed and purged through a comedy of the absurd.

The Vietnamization of New Jersey is set in a suburban American living room, piled high to the ceiling with the detritus of our consumer culture: two hair dryers, three TV sets, an outsize rotogrill, sculptured ducks in flight over the fireplace. Seated at the breakfast table are Rabe's benighted family, now renamed Ozzie Ann, Harry, and Et, their teenage delinquent son. Et is pouring cornflakes down his trousers and eating his breakfast out of his crotch. Hazel, the black maid, clears the table by ripping off the cloth, dropping coffee, toast, and cereal into the laps of her employers who she proceeds to indict as malignant symbols of white America.

Into this disaster area comes David, home from the war, with his Vietnamese wife, Liat. Both are blind, which David demonstrates by walking into the refrigerator. Et moralizes: "The fact that they're blind literally in a way points to the fact that we and the American people are blind literally. We suffer, I think, a moral and philosophical blindness." Liat has married David because he is "the best damn stick man in the U.S. Army"—as a result, she can't remember if his name is Cholly or Joe. When they both fall into the family septic tank, Et draws the inevitable political conclusion that this symbolizes the way America is mired in the Vietnam War. Eventually, we learn that Liat is actually a girl named Maureen O'Hara from Schenectady, who went to Vietnam because she wanted to break into American musicals like *The King And I.*

David suffers a nervous breakdown when he learns that he can no longer use Liat to excoriate his parents' guilt, and spends the next four years hiding under the breakfast table. The coming of inflation reduces the family's fortunes: for Thanksgiving, they can only afford Campbell's Chunky Soup. Creditors repossess not only the furniture, but the walls of the set as well. Harry loses his job and shoots himself, ruining Ozzie Ann's nice new rug. The family is saved by Harry's brother, Larry, a Mafia hit man, who is also a sergeant in the Army reserves. Dressed like General Patton in jodhpurs and a bright chrome helmet, Larry brings order back into the household, teaching the family discipline, seducing Liat with chocolates and nylons, and catching David in a bear trap. At the end of the play, with everything having returned to normalcy, David decides to burn himself to death, and while Hazel regales the audience with ludicrous Bicentennial Minutes, the family admires the lovely orange glow that David is making in the sky.

Durang owes a certain debt to Ionesco in his manipulation of the absurd, but his style is peculiarly American. What he is obviously satirizing here is the heavy-handed symbolism, the fake piety, the smug self-satisfaction, the ponderous confrontations, demolishing the cliches about the Vietnam War expressed both by the right and the left. With *The Vietnamization of New Jersey,* Durang has declared a separate peace, and, as

far as American culture is concerned, has finally brought the Vietnam War to a close. (pp. 25-6)

Robert Brustein, "The Crack in the Chimney: Reflections on Contemporary American Playwriting" (copyright © by Theater, formerly yale/theater 1978; reprinted by permission of Theater and the author), in Theater, Vol. 9, No. 2, Spring, 1978, pp. 21-9.*

HAROLD CLURMAN

A History of the American Film is a great foolery. . . . It might also be described as a crazy quilt stitched together by a loose thread of a "story" and a shred of an idea. . . .

The vocabulary of American film, from the early days to more recent ones, is employed with especial reference to various news features or, if you will, historical events of the past sixty years or more. What we see is supposed to be a film (and people watching several different films), but the convention is not strictly adhered to. Everything goes: it is all slapdash improvisation, naively sophisticated, collegiate, smart-ass. One can think of it as vaudevillesque surrealism or self-congratulatory nonsense. If there is sense—and there is some—it may be thought of as cartoon commentary on the imbecilities of the passing scene.

There are allusions to both World Wars, to popular slogans, to period fads, to religious confusion, to divers political phenomena (radicalism, McCarthyism), and to tidbits that were grist to the journalistic mill over the years. It ends with the "prophecy" of a big bang-up, an all-devastating bellicose doom: the spirit is cynical. But we don't take it seriously—it is all for fun, and in this it is typical in several ways.

It certainly doesn't hurt, it tickles. It is significant only in that its significance is oblique. It leaves no enduring impression, except that we may remember some of its jokes and that we passed the time in momentarily delighted surprise. That's enough, isn't it, for an evening on the town.

An exemplary cuteness is *We're in a Salad,* a lampoon of a Hollywood production number à la Busby Berkeley, in which each girl represents a vegetable: Bean, Tomato, Celery, Cucumber, etc. There are nutty songs by Mel Marvin and all sorts of trick business and scenic stunts. . . .

The show might lend itself to study by film and stage historians, by journalists, and sociologists. Or it may be entirely dismissed by certain of the more serious-minded! On the whole I see in it something characteristic of the present (prosperous) theatrical season: it is animated, muscular, proficient and vain, not to say void. . . . [In A] *History of the American Film,* with its elements of satirical, perhaps even "intellectual," substance, all is forgettable mirth.

Harold Clurman, in a review of "A History of the American Film," in The Nation (copyright 1978 The Nation magazine, The Nation Associates, Inc.), Vol. 226, No. 14, April 15, 1978, p. 443.

JOHN SIMON

The idea of *A History of the American Film* must have seemed enchanting to its young author, Christopher Durang. It takes a few basic characters right through the typical genre movies—and others—from *Intolerance* to *Earthquake.* There is Loretta, the sweet girl from the orphanage, whom every kind of evil befalls without making her shed her innocence. She is part

Loretta Young, part Sade's Justine, and wholly in love with Jimmy, who goes from Jimmy Cagney to Bogart, from Jimmy Dean to Brando, always slapping Loretta around, ditching her, or making her equally unhappy by not ditching her. There is also Bette, who is Bette Davis and other tough and mean females, whose chief purpose is not so much to take Jimmy away as to make Loretta suffer more in the process. She is also Joan Crawford, Barbara Stanwyck, and Sade's Juliette among others.

Then there is Hank, the strong and silent yokel, who is Fonda, Stewart, and Cooper until he goes bonkers and becomes Tony Perkins in *Psycho*. And there is Eve (Arden), the perennial good-natured, wisecracking loser. Lastly, there are several Contract Players, doing various typical Hollywood parts. All of them, when not playing parodic movie scenes, become spectators at a typical Bijou, which is the main set of the show. . . . The symbiosis is complete: Audience and movie stars not only live off each other, they actually melt into each other. And on and on go the same basic idiotic relationships, through Westerns and war movies, thrillers and Busby Berkeley musicals. . . .

Durang's play is closet camp that needs to be much shorter, less elaborately bedizened, and fitted snugly into some intimate university theater. . . . [But] drawn out and overproduced in sundry ways, it sadly betrays itself as the campy, campus cabaret it is: bright and funny in places, but largely self-indulgent, repetitious, and sophomoric.

True, there are droll passages, like the takeoff on *Now, Voyager*'s notorious double-barreled cigarette-lighting scene, or a number of lusty sick jokes like this bit between a returning World War II veteran and the woman he left behind: "Michael, I've been promiscuous."—"*I* have no hands."—"Well, how promiscuous were you?"—"How much of your hands are you missing?" Durang also has a good ear for nomenclature: A spaceman arrives from the planet Zabar; a film is called *Seven Brides for Twelve Angry Men*. But at any moment things may collapse into "Don't sit under the atom bomb with anyone else but me," or "Jimmy, our vines have such tender grapes," where the references are either too obvious and crude, or too farfetched. After a while, the formulaic aspects become all too blatant; for example, simple inversion of a movie scene—as when the distraught heroine seeks disguised counsel from Piano Man, the wise and sympathetic black discreetly tickling the ivories to death. "If you were this friend," she asks after relating her own dismal story, "what would you do?"—"Ah'd kill mahself." (p. 100)

[Three] hours is too relentless for a simple and simpleminded joke. Durang finally says nothing beyond, ad absurdum, that the movies are absurd. (p. 101)

John Simon, "Film Flam," in New York *Magazine (copyright © 1983 by News Group Publications, Inc.; reprinted with the permission of* New York *Magazine), Vol. 11, No. 16, April 17, 1978, pp. 100-01.**

EDITH OLIVER

Christopher Durang has the wit, the high, rebellious spirits, and the rage of the born satirist. He is also one of the funniest and most original playwrights at work. His **"Beyond Therapy"** . . . could be considered his "Alice in Wonderland," . . . in a world run by psychiatrists and thick with their foibles and jargon. The play opens in a restaurant in [New York City]; a young man is seated alone at a table. Enter [the heroine] . . . , also alone; she has come in response to a personal ad that he has placed in a newspaper. "Are you White Male?" she begins. Her name is Prudence, his Bruce. They meet tentatively. Her arms get stuck as she tries to remove her knitted coat with appropriate sophistication (a funny piece of hokum that runs through the action). "I hope I'm not too macho for you" is his first bit of conversation, and "You have lovely breasts" is his second, and pretty soon he is telling her all about his male lover. Thus begins this whirligig of a show, which trips merrily along. . . . We meet, in their offices, Prudence's therapist, a tantrummy lecher, and Bruce's therapist, a clucking hen of a woman with a Snoopy hand puppet and a case of galloping aphasia, and, in Bruce's apartment, the nettled angry lover and (via a noisy, prolonged phone call) the lover's Jewish mother. As for Prudence, bewildered and confounded, every time she asserts herself she is out-argued or put down. There is a great scene back in that restaurant in which, her patience exhausted, she holds Bruce, his lover, and both therapists at gun point and, attracting the attention of a waiter for the first time in two acts, orders a steak for herself and menus for everybody. The lights dim, and we see all of them being served in semi-darkness. The effect is both beautiful and funny, and if that scene had ended the play (I reached for my coat when it was over) the audience would have left walking on air. As it was, Mr. Durang, in a misguided effort, I guess, to resolve the plot, added another scene or two and another character and several new jokes, letting the air out. Plot? Christopher Durang? What has he to do with plot or resolution or any other convention of the theatre? He goes his own way. (p. 91)

Edith Oliver, "O Frabjous Streep!" (© 1981 by Edith Oliver), in The New Yorker, *Vol. LVI, No. 48, January 19, 1981, pp. 90-1.**

FRANK RICH

Anyone can write an angry play—all it takes is an active spleen. But only a writer of real talent can write an angry play that remains funny and controlled even in its most savage moments. **"Sister Mary Ignatius Explains It All for You"** confirms that Christopher Durang is just such a writer. In this one-act comedy he goes after the Catholic Church with a vengeance that might well have shocked the likes of either Paul Krassner or Lenny Bruce, and yet he never lets his bitter emotions run away with his keen theatrical sense. . . .

[**"Sister Mary Ignatius"**] is both the most consistently clever and deeply felt work yet by the author of **"A History of the American Film"** and **"Beyond Therapy."** . . . [It] has the sting of a revenge drama, even as it rides waves of demonic laughter. The play is also terribly honest, for Mr. Durang knows better than to give himself a total victory over his formidable antagonist. With pointed rue, he must finally leave the church bloodied but unbowed. . . .

For about half the play's length, Mr. Durang uses his glibly dissembling protagonist to illustrate what he regards as church hypocrisies. Sister Mary must do some fancy and unconvincing footwork to explain how supposedly "infallible" dogma could have been changed overnight by her least favorite Pope, John XXIII. . . .

Eventually, however, we see that there is one question that does throw Sister Mary: "If God is all powerful, why does He allow evil in the world?" And the playwright forces the nun to confront that issue when four grown-up former students show up to stage a Joseph-and-Mary pageant, complete with camel, for her current flock. The visitors all hated their despotic teacher; they soon try to settle the score by making her defend God and His rules in a world where rape and cancer seem to justify such sins as abortion and agnosticism.

Mr. Durang successfully escalates this comic confrontation to a literally violent climax that strips the nun's moral authority bare even as it allows her to retain her crippling psychological power over her students, past and present. As the playwright sees his villainess, she will tolerate no failings in others—but will gladly use church law to rationalize even murder when it suits her own authoritarian purposes. . . . After her real—and insane—personality is revealed, she still remains all too frighteningly human. . . .

In [**"The Actor's Nightmare"**] the playwright gives us what his title promises—a hero, appropriately named George Spelvin . . . , who suddenly finds himself on stage in a play he has never rehearsed. The premise lets Mr. Durang show off his gift for theatrical and show-biz satire, for the play-within-the-play proves to be an ever-changing amalgam of "Private Lives," "Hamlet," "A Man for All Seasons" and the collected works of Beckett. Who but this writer would imagine that Godot will someday arrive—reeking of garlic and telling stewardess jokes? . . .

If **"The Actor's Nightmare"** finally runs out of jokes too early and fails in its effort to deepen its hero, it gets us as ready as possible for the unstoppably virulent comic nightmare that's soon to come [in **"Sister Mary Ignatius"**].

> *Frank Rich, "One-Acters by Durang," in* The New York Times *(© 1981 by The New York Times Company; reprinted by permission), October 22, 1981, p. C 21.*

ROBERT BRUSTEIN

[*Sister Mary Ignatius Explains It All For You* brings us close] to the truth, not through histrionic posturing, but through savage blistering satire. Durang is the American equivalent of an angry young man, his anger directed less toward social and political targets than toward the nightmares of his own personal history. These include the media, the middle-class family, and most of all, the Catholic Church, whose parochial school system Durang sees as an institutional conspiracy to suppress spontaneity and disseminate lies.

The play takes the form of an illustrated lecture by an aggressively rigid nun. . . . She is instructing a group of children—that is to say, the audience—about the canonical mysteries of Catholicism, and not since young Stephen Dedalus learned of the evils of self-abuse has there been an address designed to have a more corrosive effect on young minds. Aided in her efforts by seven-year-old Thomas—a boy "with a lovely soprano voice" ("which the Church used to preserve by creating castrati")—Sister Mary Ignatius embroiders on such appetizing themes as Purgatory ("You can expect to be in Purgatory anywhere from 300 years to 750 billion years"), Limbo ("where unbaptized babies are sent for eternity . . . before Pope John and the Ecumenical Council"), Mortal Sin ("murder, sex outside of marriage, hijacking a plane, masturbation"), and Sodom (every city with a population over 50,000 but especially Amsterdam). Her appetite for hell-fire is exceeded only by her passion for sweets, which she shares with Thomas when the goody two-shoes correctly answers a catechism.

The Sister then accepts questions from the children, some of which she even deigns to answer. The stickiest one is "If God is all powerful, why does he allow evil in the world?" This one she passes by with a glowering look. "Do nuns go to the bathroom?" "Yes." "Was Jesus effeminate?" "Yes." (Sadly.) And as her theological coup de grace: "God always answers our prayers. It's just sometimes He says no."

Later, she is visited by four former students who—as Joseph, Mary, and the two humps of a camel—enact a Christmas pageant. The players reveal themselves as anti-Sister rebels: a homosexual ("You do that thing that makes Jesus puke?"), a wife-beating alcoholic, an unwed mother, a girl with a history of abortions. It is the latter character . . . who has been nourishing the most hatred for Sister Mary Ignatius and her deceptions. She has seen her mother die, slowly and horribly, of cancer, which left her furious over having been made to believe in anything but the randomness of life. On the day of her mother's death, she was raped, which resulted in her first abortion; she went to a psychiatrist who seduced her, which resulted in her second. Having murdered her psychiatrist, she has now come to kill Sister Mary Ignatius, realizing it is childish to look for blame, "but basically I think it's all your fault, Sister." She expresses the inconsolable and irreconcilable anger of the disappointed believer.

The play ends in a comic massacre, as the Sister, aided by helpful little Thomas, blasts away at the four rebels with a concealed handgun. The ending has been criticized; I found it entirely appropriate to a work, as much Expressionist nightmare as satiric comedy, which has the Slaughter of the Innocent as its central metaphor. . . . I recommend the evening to you warmly. It represents another strong advance in the progress of a singularly courageous satirist, whose pen is dipped in venom and bile, and also in the blood of his own personal wounds. It is a solution of acid ink that cuts to sinew and bone, a rare mixture in a theater usually tinted with colored water. (pp. 24-5)

> *Robert Brustein, "The Naked and the Dressed" (reprinted by permission of the author; © 1981 The New Republic, Inc.), in* The New Republic, *Vol. 185, No. 23, December 9, 1981, pp. 21, 24-5.**

ROBERT E. LAUDER

[In the opening moments of **"Sister Mary Ignatius Explains It All For You"**] Sister Ignatius can seem to be a piece of humorous nostalgia recalling experiences in a Catholic grammar school and poking fun at some of the sisters who taught in those schools. A type of good natured humor highlighting eccentricities of some grammar school nuns when engaged in by Catholic adults, including priests and nuns, can co-exist with an attitude of both affection and gratitude and in a certain context even be a sign of faith.

Not so Durang's play. Until he frees himself from what he perceives as Catholicism his anger may strangle his creativity. In spite of all the attempts at humor in **"Sister Ignatius,"** Durang's attack on the church is dead serious. What he sets up to attack is less than a straw man. Thomas Wolfe's insight that you can't go home again may be true for most people, but some artistic ex-Catholics cannot seem to leave home. They have an obsessive preoccupation with a vision of Catholicism that is as trite as it is myopic. Durang's play is not so much a "Memories of a Catholic Childhood" as a "Memories and

Fantasies of a Catholic Angry Adolescent.'' The play reveals more about the marksman than the target.

There is a line in ''The Actor's Nightmare'' that sheds light on ''Sister Ignatius,'' its author and perhaps its audience, at least the group present when I saw the play. The main character struggling on stage for lines recites the act of contrition. He then explains to the audience that this is the prayer that Catholic children say when they go to confession. Though he muses that it is probably also the prayer that Catholic adults say when they go to confession he looks at the audience and says, ''I don't know any Catholic adults.'' The implication is that the adjective and noun are mutually exclusive. The line drew not only laughter but some applause the evening I attended the play.

I can not help wondering if vituperative attacks similar to ''Sister Ignatius'' against blacks, Jews or other minorities would be greeted with the same enthusiasm that the audience greeted ''Sister Ignatius.'' An observation of Peter Viereck's still seems to be true: Anti-Catholicism is the anti-Semitism of the intellectuals. Sociologist Andrew Greeley in his book *An Ugly Little Secret: Anti-Catholicism in North America* argues persuasively that the last remaining unexposed prejudice in American life is anti-Catholicism. The audience reaction to Durang's play bothered me as much as Durang's play. The evening I attended ''Sister Ignatius'' the ugly little secret was not a very well-kept secret. (p. 418)

Robert E. Lauder, "Theatrical Catholics," in America (reprinted with permission of America Press, Inc.; © 1981; all rights reserved), Vol. 145, No. 21, December 26, 1981, pp. 417-18.*

GERALD WEALES

In the curtain raiser to [*Sister Mary Ignatius Explains It All For You*], *The Actor's Nightmare*—a standard Durang parody pastiche which, against my better judgment, I often found funny—the baffled protagonist talks about having been an altar boy and about all the people he knows who went to Catholic school; he adds, almost as an afterthought, ''I don't know any Catholic adults.'' *Sister Mary Ignatius* explains why. I can imagine a devastating comedy about the worst aspects of Catholic education, c. 1950, but Durang is more cartoonist than comedian. His Sister Mary Ignatius . . . is pure caricature, and often very funny in the early sections of the play when she answers, edits, or ignores questions that have presumably been handed in by the audience. The scenes with the little boy are less successful whether she is surreptitiously fondling him or rewarding him with cookies for knowing his catechism; if it were not for Franz's air of unending surprise, the latter joke would have become tedious much earlier than it does. The play goes to pieces with the arrival of the accusatory former students, particularly the one who hates Sister Mary Ignatius because she believed the teacher; as presented here the nun has the credibility of Miss Piggy in love. Durang retreats from direct didacticism into black farce as the pistol-toting Sister Ignatius starts knocking off her pedagogical failures. It is possible that Durang believes that there is a mass murderer hidden in every knuckle-rapper or—to make a metaphor of his demonic finale—that Catholic education of this variety is destructive. I suspect something less serious. Judging by these two plays and the earlier *A History of the American Film,* Durang is a satirist whose vision is impaired by too many years of pop culture and

an impulse to go for the gag instead of the jugular. (pp. 50-1)

Gerald Weales, "Fr. Tim, Sister Sade: Anguish & Anger," in Commonweal (copyright © 1982 Commonweal Publishing Co., Inc.; reprinted by permission of Commonweal Publishing Co., Inc.), Vol. CIX, No. 2, January 29, 1982, pp. 50-1.

JOHN SIMON

It distresses me to have to report that Christopher Durang's *Beyond Therapy,* which was (in part) so funny off Broadway last season, comes off so leaden this year on Broadway. The explanation is not easily come by. Some of Durang's jokes were not funny then, but they were pleasantly overshadowed, or overlighted, by the ones that worked radiantly. Now, however, this play about a pair of unlikely lovers brought together by ads in the personal columns and kept apart by both their own and their therapists' hang-ups thuds with clinker after clinker: Even the lines that were riotously funny elicit only a wry smile or frozen silence.

Perhaps there is a kind of joke that does not bear repetition. . . . [A] good deal of Durang's humor depends on its shock value, and nothing is so shock-absorbent as a second hearing. The kind of humor that doesn't tarnish tends to be more intimately wedded to characterization, to figures that serve other causes besides the propagation of gags—say, those of ideas, pathos, credibility. Durang's characters are vehicles for highly diversified, often pointed but scattershot attacks; rather than building into funny flesh-and-blood creatures, they form witty clusters of grudges, sneers, and saucy iconoclasm. The laughs finally belong mostly to the playwright and not to Prudence or Bruce or the rest, and if, on top of that, they are hit-or-miss—as they are here—the failed ones have a way of undermining the good ones.

Then there is the rewriting. Durang, a clever writer, seems to be a lame rewriter. The first time round, the play was funnier in its devil-may-care fashion. Attempting to tighten and discipline it, the author has become more worried, less spontaneous, aware that he is going in no direction, and has conveyed his unease in a way guaranteed to choke off laughter. Thus the final scene, now much changed, shuffles hither and yon, marks time, repeats non-gags, and desperately waits for something to fall out of the air into its lap—if not comic inspiration, at least an ending. Endings have always been Durang's bane, but this embarrassment has never before been so apparent. How many times can the two main characters, left alone in a restaurant, call for a waiter they and we know isn't there? . . .

Perhaps we must blame the musical revue for not being around any more; this is the genre to which Mr. Durang would have contributed splendid sketches. It is when he has to flesh out and fill in things to full length that he becomes unsatisfyingly sketchy. Or perhaps he has since amused us so much more with his *Sister Mary Ignatius Explains It All for You* (though there too the ending is messy) that we now expect too much. Something gray seems to have fallen on Mr. Durang. . . . [It] drags him down. (p. 62)

John Simon, "Beyond Therapy . . . And Then There Were Nuns," in New York Magazine (copyright © 1983 by News Group Publications, Inc.; reprinted with the permission of New York Magazine), Vol. 15, No. 23, June 7, 1982, pp. 62, 64-5.*

BRENDAN GILL

It has been the ambitious dream of many an author throughout history to begin a piece of writing with a sentence—"Call me Ishmael," "For a long time I used to go to bed early"—so irresistible that his readers couldn't fail to proceed to the next sentence and then to the next and the next, pitching headlong as far into the piece as the author's literary ingenuity was able to entice them. This dream came true last week for Christopher Durang, at the opening of his delightful little farce **"Beyond Therapy"** . . . : the audience laughed at the very first line of the play, then at the second, and then at the third; I can bear witness to the fact that I wasn't alone in continuing to laugh with something like the regularity of a metronome through most of the rest of the play. Mr. Durang's earlier dramatic works have served to establish that he is one of the funniest playwrights alive; **"Beyond Therapy"** stakes new claims on our attention. . . . Our satisfaction with **"Beyond Therapy"** springs in large measure from the working out of a symmetrical process of inquiry on the part of a distraught young man and an equally distraught young woman; and the situation that they are distraught about—roughly, the difficulty they find in growing up and forming permanent relationships with their contemporaries—is the excuse for the play rather than the occasion for it. Farce requires only excuses; it is tragedy that requires occasions. (p. 112)

Brendan Gill, "Growing Up" (© 1982 by Brendan Gill), in The New Yorker, *Vol. LVIII, No. 16, June 7, 1982, pp. 112, 114.**

GERALD WEALES

Durang works at the level of acid cartoon, although he might not describe his method in those terms. "My sense of comedy comes from seeing a lot of things, things that are not just bad but very bad that, if presented boldfacedly on a stage, turn out to be funny." . . . [In *Sister Mary Ignatius Explains It All For You,* the] vividness of Sister Mary Ignatius as a likably malevolent lunatic depends as much on performance as it does on Durang's writing. In the opening part of the play, Sister Mary Ignatius answers questions, presumably submitted by the audience, in an often very funny session which makes the point that her assurance is a kind of ignorance by imprimatur. When her accusers turn up to illustrate the crippling results of her teaching (and when the play looks like it is in danger of succumbing to message), Durang has Sister Mary Ignatius whip out a pistol and bring the play to a grotesque comedy ending by killing off her failures.

It would be possible to read that ending seriously (Catholic education as a destructive force), but it does not play that way. Durang is essentially a lightweight dramatist, a comic writer who likes to frolic on the edge of potentially painful themes. His references most often are to the theater and the other popular arts rather than to life itself. *The Actor's Nightmare,* the curtain raiser to *Sister Mary Ignatius,* is pure Durang. A pastiche in which a man finds himself on stage acting in plays which he does not know and which keep changing as he performs them—Shakespeare to Coward and back—it is both a standard nightmare and an insider's joke, more amusing than I expected it to be. . . . The first act [of *The Vietnamization of New Jersey*] is a take-off on David Rabe's *Sticks and Bones,* mocking the didacticism that Rabe imposed on his Ozzie and Harriet parody, but Durang's working at that distance from a real subject is less a comment on Rabe or Vietnam than it is on Durang's oddly detached relationship to the society whose quirks and ills he seems to want to expose. As with the ending of *Sister Mary Ignatius,* one could take the second act of *The Vietnamization* seriously, viewing it as a comment on the militarization of America or the consequences of little wars in far places, but it seems instead a collection of gags that refuse to be weighed down by significance. If there is a dated quality to *The Vietnamization* (it is set in the years 1967 to 1976), *Beyond Therapy*—Durang's brief excursion into Broadway— is as immediate as this week's encounter with a therapy-obsessed bore. . . . [The] play has two professional caricatures— a seducing psychiatrist who suffers from premature ejaculation and a batty sugar-freak who seems to be a parody of the woman who treated Jill Clayburgh in *An Unmarried Woman,* although that creature (a real therapist with a brand-new book in the stores) was already parody enough. As for the central plot, in which Bruce and Prudence finally get together—despite the complications provided by their therapists, his male lover, and the bad service in the restaurant in which they meet—it is, as all Durang is, a thing of gags and patches. Durang is sometimes called a satirist, and so he is, I suppose. Yet, I see him as a man who gets up and says, "Let me tell you about Catholic education, Vietnam, the uncertainty of human connections, but first . . ." and then he pulls out the seltzer bottle and goes for the front of your pants. (pp. 523-25)

Gerald Weales, "American Theater Watch, 1981-1982," in The Georgia Review *(copyright, 1982, by the University of Georgia), Vol. XXXVI, No. 3, Fall, 1982, pp. 517-26 [revised by the author for this publication].**

Lawrence (George) Durrell

1912-

(Also wrote under the pseudonyms Charles Norden and Gaffer Peeslake) British novelist, poet, playwright, short story writer, travel writer, translator, editor, and critic.

Durrell is one of the most acclaimed novelists of the twentieth century. Continuing in the tradition of James Joyce and D. H. Lawrence, he has experimented with the structure of the novel while also probing the human psyche. His work is infused with observations on the nature of reality and sexuality, based in part on the ideas of Albert Einstein and Sigmund Freud. Durrell's rich, sensual style of writing is highly praised, especially for his vivid description of landscape, which evokes the spirit of a place and reflects it in the characters. In his novel *Justine*, for example, the exotic qualities of Alexandria, Egypt, are seen in the title character.

Born in India to Anglo-Irish parents, Durrell was sent away from the Himalayan region of his childhood at age eleven for schooling in England. He never felt comfortable there and eventually abandoned England for the Greek island of Corfu. He has lived and worked in various other areas within the Mediterranean world and now lives in southern France.

Durrell's early novels, of which *The Black Book* (1938) is deemed the most accomplished, rebelled against the sterility of English society, which he termed "the English death." Although his early novels met with little success, he developed through them the techniques which won him acclaim and recognition with *The Alexandria Quartet* (1957-1960). Composed of *Justine, Balthazar, Mountolive,* and *Clea*, the tetralogy offers several perspectives on events which involve essentially the same characters. The protagonist Darley, a novelist like many of Durrell's protagonists, attempts through art to rework reality in order to find patterns of significance and meaning. *The Alexandria Quartet* ranks among the major novelistic achievements of the twentieth century.

Durrell had originally planned to be a poet, but his voluminous output of verse has met with mixed critical reaction. His poetry blends the sensuousness of the Mediterranean world with the traditional form found in much British poetry in an attempt, in his words, to "match passion and clarity." Durrell's *Collected Poems 1931-1974* (1980) has prompted further study of his poetry.

Recent work by Durrell includes the three published novels of his proposed "quincunx": *Monsieur, or The Prince of Darkness* (1975), *Livia, or Buried Alive* (1978), and *Constance, or Solitary Practices* (1983). Set in southern France following the outbreak of World War II and echoing the successful strategy of *The Alexandria Quartet*, the novels and characters of *The Avignon Quintet* will be interrelated.

(See also *CLC*, Vols. 1, 4, 6, 8, 13; *Contemporary Authors*, Vols. 9-12, rev. ed.; and *Dictionary of Literary Biography*, Vol. 15.)

MARY WARNOCK

[*A Smile in the Mind's Eye*] must have been fun to write. Can it also be said to be fun to read? It is supposed to be for the

Photograph by Mark Gerson

smile of the title is partly the sign of an amused and detached attitude to life, while the 'mind's eye' suggests not only the images of memory, but the unity of mind and body, without which there can be no pleasure or enjoyment. It is a very short book, like the essence of a diary, kept with acute observation, and covering three weekends. It describes the swift flowering of two friendships, one with a Chinese Taoist, the other, chronologically earlier, with a French-woman, interested in Nietzsche. The link is a series of related recollections, themselves part of a lifelong but sporadic reflection on Tao.

Lawrence Durrell was born in India and was fascinated early by various forms of Buddhism. But he is not a religious man so much as an old-fashioned Thinker. Of course to write about a form of thought whose point is to be ineffable makes for difficulties. Like Kierkegaard, and indeed like Nietzsche himself, he hates theories, systems and the pretensions of science; and what emerges from these pages is more feeling than exact thought. This is why the quasi-diary form is so appropriate. Diaries are veridical, not systematic. They deal in physical details, not theories; and above all they distil atmosphere.

Jolan Chang, to whom most of the book is devoted, is a Chinese scholar who had corresponded with Durrell and who invited himself to stay in Provence. His weekend visit is so described that we can experience the heightened awareness, the concentration on the moment, the acute noticing and enjoying that seem to be the essence of Tao. Chang does not emerge as a very attractive guest. He came with a huge manuscript which had to be read and discussed; he never, or hardly ever, went to bed. He was bossy about cooking, did not like drinking, but every now and then took a swig of milk from his very small hot-water bottle. He was also liable to give his host long and quizzical *looks*. But Durrell liked all this, and was anxious to learn from the manuscript, since it fitted in with the vague thoughts about life he had entertained since he was a young man. The theme was old age, or rather immortality, since extreme old age and immortality seemed hardly to be distinguished. (pp. 411-12)

To approach immortality one must live in harmony with all nature; and this harmony can be achieved only by the avoidance of waste. At the heart of this belief lies a theory about sex. Men must economise, sexually, and avoid the wanton expenditure of sperm. This imperative is not prudential, it is moral. . . . The orgasm must no longer be thought of as the point of sexual intercourse. Instead a new closeness, physical and psychological (for the two cannot be separated), must become the central concept.

It may be that this view is most likely to appeal to the middle-aged or the old; it may be more attractive to women than to men, for women's sexuality was not much discussed in Chang's manuscript (and in any case they were permitted to have as many orgasms as they liked). But there is no doubt that it has charm. In particular the moral requirement that sexual partners should actually *notice* one another, should pay deep attention to each other's minds and bodies, though unlikely immediately to eliminate the vulgarising of sex or its violence, is an ideal none the worse for being romantic. And in the paradise of Tao the very old need feel no shame at the decline of their sexual powers.

So it is a lovely picture. Tottering always on the brink of absurdity, carelessly written, scattered thickly with exclamation marks, Durrell's book is undoubtedly a nice read. He describes things as they are. He is, after all, a proper travel writer. The weather, the sky, the stars, the food, the birds are all present to us. On the whole, then, it *is* fun to read, and even fun to think about. (pp. 412-13)

Mary Warnock, "Chang's Visit" (© British Broadcasting Corp. 1980; reprinted by permission of Mary Warnock), in The Listener, *Vol. 104, No. 2680, September 25, 1980, pp. 411-13.*

JAY L. HALIO

Livia: Or Buried Alive is the second in a "quincunx" of novels that [Durrell] began with *Monsieur* several years ago and that promises to become a tour de force rivaling *The Alexandria Quartet*. Concerned about fiction, particularly the novel, in a post-Einsteinian, post-Freudian age, Durrell makes a novelist a major character in his novels, someone writing about other characters who know what he is doing and who reflect, as the novelist does, upon what he has written. At times all this becomes a bit confusing, but the device provides several more or less simultaneous angles of vision, or rather different dimensions, in both time and space, for the action or events of the novels.

The novels may also provide different angles of vision, or dimensions of experience, for each other. Like *Monsieur, Livia*

opens with the death of a close friend but proceeds almost at once to a conversation between Blanford, the novelist and narrator in this book, and Robin Sutcliffe, the novelist in *Monsieur,* which both men claim to have written and have given different titles (Sutcliffe's is *The Prince of Darkness*). Their talk quickly gets around to discussion of two principal female characters: Pia, Sutcliffe's wife in *Monsieur,* whom Blanford has taken, in part, as a model for Livia, his wife in this novel, after making certain changes in her character and representation. They argue considerably about these differences between the two women and wives, noting their strengths and inadequacies as characters, and in the process informing the reader a great deal about themselves as husbands and novelists. Durrell claims that each of the novels in the quincunx will be independent of each other, though "roped together like climbers on a rockface," as Blanford, "squinting round the curves of futurity," describes them; they will be dependent upon each other "as echoes might be," not "laid end to end in serial order, like dominoes." But there are more than echoes that connect the first two novels; the first fifty pages of *Livia* lose, if not much of their intelligibility, then most of their point unless one has read *Monsieur*. It is one thing to recognize Lord Galen in *Livia* as an "echo" of Banquo, the wealthy banker of *Monsieur;* it is quite another to understand how Livia develops from Pia, Sylvie, and Sabine. Similarly, major locales resemble and differ from each other, as do incidents. If each novel enjoys its own integrity, as claimed, then each one also gains something from the other. Thus the whole group when it is finished may provide a means of viewing not only the same experience from different perspectives, but also different experiences that are related, especially the experiences of love (in all its varieties), death, and the nature of evil. At the same time, we may get further evidence of how a writer views his own work, even in the midst of writing it, particularly in the lively and sometimes whimsical style of an original and masterful novelist, which Durrell is. (pp. 231-32)

Jay L. Halio, "Fiction about Fiction" (copyright, 1981, by Jay L. Halio), in The Southern Review, *Vol. 17, No. 1, January, 1981, pp. 225-34.**

ALAN JENKINS

Durrell's "ideas" are in some ways the most dubious thing about him. They are seldom original or persuasive; they suggest, rather, a combination of half-digested gobbets of wisdom heavily seasoned with personal idiosyncrasy, or just plain whimsy. The same recipe provides most of the fare in *A Smile in the Mind's Eye,* a short account of Durrell's re-education in the disciplines of the Tao through the effect of two close personal relationships. One of these was with a Chinese scholar resident in the West who brought the manuscript of his work on the Taoist philosophy of love and sex for Durrell to read and criticize before publication; the other was a love-affair with the girl Durrell names as Vega. The book is full of memorable anecdotes—such as that of the two men spending Socratic evenings, after sharing the cooking and eating of a meal combining French and vegetarian Chinese cuisines ("the two greatest in the world"), discussing the prolonging of life through refinement and control of the male orgasm (fewer ejaculations, more years of life, runs the argument in crude form). There are some amazing records of personal achievement, both in the sexual takes and in the consumption of wine (which Durrell, under Chang's guidance, brings down to a manageable-sounding level). But for all this, the seductiveness of Durrell's evocation of the ravishing, mysterious Vega and the spruce, lively-minded and admirably self-disciplined Chang is not finally enough to persuade us of anything. Occasionally there is the excitement of a man wrestling with an overwhelming question or attaining some personal revelation, but the overall impression is of ideas being toyed with imaginatively, and being enjoyed for their suggestiveness and potency, rather than of an argument fully teased out.

This is of a piece with much of Durrell's work in prose, which confers an air of extraordinary significance on the mythical or imaginary ramifications of a place, a moment in history, a personage; yet we never feel that we come to understand in any depth what that significance is. This picking up and nourishing of potent connotations is Durrell's substitute (any really interesting writer must have one) for "method", yet it is constantly threatening to become a mere vice of style, one which allows his heady confections to take on an air of profundity, of serious purpose behind the surface dazzle. But just as Durrell could be accused of trivializing the material—Alchemy to Zen, sexual mysticism or Eleusinian mysteries—he picks up from ancient poetic traditions and religious disciplines, his "poetic" effects are often easily won, his fictions sustained by symbols, as he himself puts it with beguiling insight, "somewhat crudely objectivized". We may or may not be able to come to terms with the symbols . . . but Durrell is wrong when he says that these "have to be so"—meaning crudely done—since novels are "written to be read."

A "receptiveness to ideas", as a previous reviewer termed it, an atmosphere of weighty though vague symbolic meaning, and the imprecisions of a diffused synaesthetic excitement, are similarly the stock-in-trade of Durrell's poems, in which he himself finds, with some justice, "a very true and slender voice, rather Gautierish". There is little trace of Gautier's hard outlines [in *Collected Poems 1931-1974*], but we do find his rhythmical delicacy and firmness, and the linguistic verve which sustains a decorum of statement, of "things being said", yet is never without a whiff of "decadence", or a dandyish luxuriating in the way of saying.

We are usually aware of the shadow of the mythical and historical past falling heavily across Durrell's poetry; and we are always aware of the strong sense of place. But his gift for the echoing phrase is not always an effective substitute for structure. Faced with too much confectionery—such a profusion of the exotic, of the world of sun, sea, rock, olive and cypress, and of a language crammed with strangely generalized detail (the particulars dissolve in the heat-haze of a tremendous truth or in the *jouissance* of an irresistible conceit as often as they declare themselves in the hard-edged clarity of Aegean light), the appetite begins to cloy; we choke on such nutritious images. Behind the gorgeousness there is, perhaps, too much of a hint of picture-postcard or guide-book reality for unqualified assent. . . . The ambiguity of adjectives like "mythical" and "insoluble" is typical of Durrell's rather slapdash verbalism, his carelessness in spattering us with "effects", a word-drunkenness which is only intermittently telling or infectious. . . .

Yet elsewhere we come upon such images as "islands . . . / Struck like soft gongs in the amazing blue". . . . In these *trouvailles* we do see and feel the heart of Durrell's chosen world; as "the lucky in summer / (Tie) up their boats", they offer us a momentary and delicious anchorage in it, tempting us, as the Aegean itself does, "To enter April like swimmer . . .". Such temptations are everywhere in Durrell's poetry, and it seems pointless to argue that he might be a con-

sistently better poet had he resisted them more often. They should not, anyway, blind us to the vein of strong and pure lyricism that is tapped by sparer rhythms and more astringent structures. When this happens both setting and feeling are more sharply evoked. . . . Beyond the evidence of Durrell's exquisite ear there is the hardness and brilliance of the landscapes his imagination has "grown into"—what Peter Levi called the "mineral quality" of his words.

There is more, too, than visual impressionism; an attempt to "Match passion and clarity", which Durrell in a late poem calls "that hopeless task" but which his best pieces continue to do into the 1960s and 1970s. The later poems here introduce a darker, elegaic tone into what is, most memorably and insistently, an art of celebration—of places, certainly, but also of people, most importantly women. Durrell wrote in **"Logos"** (1939) that

> Woman
> Can be a wilderness enough for body
> To wander in: is a true human
> Genesis and exodus. A serious fate.

—and his poems chart the course of that "serious fate" with sharpness and poignancy; though to do it they have to get beyond his erotic sentimentality, and a Dali-esque surrealism of sinister, more or less sadistic associations. When Durrell tries to cross this half-hearted surrealism, all ellipses and outrageous juxtapositions, with the Elizabethans' violent metaphors, rapidity, roughness and density of texture, the result, though it yields the occasional bizarre or haunting line, has neither [immediacy nor graceful wit]. . . . But in lyrics such as **"Chanel"**, **"Episode"**, . . . or **"Notebook"**, Durrell is with Robert Graves as one of the finest love-poets of this century.

Echoes of Graves, and more insistently of Eliot, Auden, Yeats, do not merely signal Durrell's debts; they have stiffened and strengthened a "slender" voice which started with the fragile spell of late-Romantic incantations and phrases such as "those frail and tenebrous hands", into an art somehow akin to that building of dry-stone walls which Durrell so heartily recommends in [his published correspondence with Richard Aldington, *Literary Lifelines*]. There may be little "technique" (it is not hard to feel that some poems have a tendency to run on when the impulse behind them is gone) yet the finished thing can seem strangely solid and durable. (p. 1398)

Alan Jenkins, "Anti-Home Thoughts from Abroad," in The Times Literary Supplement *(© Times Newspapers Ltd. (London) 1981; reproduced from* The Times Literary Supplement *by permission), No. 4104, November 27, 1981, pp. 1397-98.*

PETER FIRCHOW

Some great novelists have also been great or at least very good poets. Scott, Hardy, Meredith, D. H. Lawrence spring immediately to mind. Other novelists, like Dickens or E. M. Forster, scarcely attempted to write poetry at all—that is, if we discount the often intensely purple passages in their prose. Finally, a few novelists have tried to write poetry but have succeeded only incompletely or intermittently. It is to this last category that Lawrence Durrell must be assigned.

Durrell's reputation as a novelist, based chiefly on the *Alexandria Quartet,* remains firm, though it is beginning to weaken a little at the edges. Durrell's reputation as a poet, on the other hand, is virtually nonexistent. In 1959 Durrell complained in an interview that "as for poetry, I haven't much reputation in England and can't even persuade my publishers to risk a *Collected Poems*." A year later his publishers took the risk; and they took it again in 1968 and now in 1980 [with *Collected Poems 1931-1974*]. But in terms of Durrell's reputation the difference these collections have made is negligible.

The reason, I think, for this critical neglect lies in the too rigorous application of Durrell's novelistic virtues to his poetry, where they turn into vices. His streak of bittersweet sentimentality, his love for exotica in places and people, his ironic pirouettes, his name-dropping, his portrayal of complex characters over the long haul—all these work in the novels as they do not work in the poetry. On the contrary, they irritate by raising expectations which they only rarely satisfy. So, for example, the **"Elegy on the Closing of the French Brothels"** (1947) arouses neither elegiac melancholy nor wicked joy—or anything really, other than the sad recollection of how differently a real poet like Villon handled similar situations.

Durrell's poetic is based on lines rather than on poems. He hopes for the "mantic line" in **"Poggio"** (1946) and "hunts" it in **"Style"** (1955). This poetic belongs to Dowson and to the early Yeats before the latter got it pounded out of him. This is why much of Durrell's poetry, despite the evident irony and sensuality and despite the frequent echoes of T. S. Eliot, has not yet entered the twentieth century. Too many poems end with punch lines, which is suitable for jokes but not for poetry. Too many poems originate—and end—in word-plays. . . . ["Song"] is ingenious, but it is ingenious in a way which leads nowhere. Ingenuity turns out to be not enough; it cannot take the place of inspiration.

Durrell's best verses are those which least conform to his own stated poetic, verses which do not pretend to be mantic and are content to be merely funny. His ballads of **"Psychoanalysis"** (1955), of **"Kretschmer's Types"** and of the **"Oedipus Complex"** (both 1960) cannot be termed serious poems; but then they are not bad poems either. They are, in fact, quite good light verse. W. H. Auden once observed that it is easier to be a good poet than to be a good novelist. The case of Lawrence Durrell does not seem to confirm this hypothesis. But then Auden was one of those poets who had never tried to write a novel.

Peter Firchow, in a review of "Collected Poems: 1931-1974," in World Literature Today *(copyright 1982 by the University of Oklahoma Press), Vol. 56, No. 1, Winter, 1982, p. 117.*

J. D. McCLATCHY

I have sometimes thought that Durrell is the last of the Georgian poets, that it may be a short step from Shropshire to Rhodes or Vaumort. His is no "weekend ruralism," but has always been a kind of delicate passion for the "natural." Most readers think of him as either a satirist or a love poet. He is actually to one side of either category. The droll imperatives of sex and conscience animate his poems—England at the end of its tether, tried to the Mediterranean pleasure principle. Durrell has wanted to write a poetry of the earth, and of the earthy. He is most at home in the Plaka, on the docks, at a brothel, his eye cocked for the *bas-fonds d'une ville,* by turns typical and grotesque and mythic. Even his later poems—occasional, listless—attempt their rueful celebrations. . . . (p. 170)

"I want my total poetic work," he wrote in 1943, "to add up as a kind of tapestry of people, some real, some imaginary." In fact, it adds up as more [as shown in *Collected Poems 1931-1974*]. He has a novelist's avidity for characteristics: features . . . , pretensions, and remoteness. His imaginary speaking-masks (**"Conon in Exile," "Eight Aspects of Melissa"**), the subjects of his epistles (**"Letter to Seferis the Greek"**), and his portraits (**"Eternal Contemporaries"**) are among his most subtle and convincing poems. But he has other, telling gifts. One is for the shaping pressure of narrative: **"Cities, Plains and People"** and **"The Anecdotes"** are especially fine examples of Durrell's ability to steer a true course through a swirl of details. At times, of course, he simply surrenders to local color—which he applies with a miniaturist's skill. But when he transcends the world's self-sufficiency, up toward the *idea* of places—a height rarely congenial to him—his poetry too rises to a pitch of sublimity. (p. 171)

This third edition of Durrell's *Collected Poems,* superseding those of 1960 and 1968, has been edited by . . . Canadian scholar James Brigham, who has added new poems (both early and late), appended to every poem dates of its various publications, and restored epigrams dropped from previous editions. Pronouncing himself pleased in a Preface, Durrell calls it "definitive and comprehensive." True, but I wish the same could be said of the poetry. Only the middle pages of this book speak memorably. Nearly all of Durrell's best poems were written in the 1940's. And even they have begun, alas, to curl around the edges. What is good in them is often a pastiche. One hears Eliot and Auden here, Graves and Cavafy there. That is no fault, but in the end one prefers the originals. Still, for that part of the world he has staked out, his poetry has always been, and will likely remain, a vibrant *Guide Vert.* (p. 172)

J. D. McClatchy, "All Told," in Poetry *(© 1982 by The Modern Poetry Association; reprinted by permission of the Editor of* Poetry*), Vol. CXI, No. 3, June, 1982, pp. 170-77.**

ANATOLE BROYARD

Is **"The Alexandria Quartet"** as good as we all thought it was when we first read it more than 20 years ago? I wondered about this when I saw that Lawrence Durrell has a new novel, **"Constance,"** coming out. Since nothing he published after the **"Quartet"** seemed to be in the same class, it occurred to me that we may have overestimated the books for which he is famous.

So I went back to the **"Quartet"**—like novelists, we have to keep revising ourselves—and read **"Justine,"** the first volume. I want to say immediately that it struck me as even better this time. It is, among other things, one of the great city novels, reminding us of Dickens's London, Balzac's Paris, Joyce's Dublin. Such books have a quality for which the Germans should have a word—something like "city-hunger," or "city-angst," a human tropism which makes us huddle or press together in the hope of intensifying our lives and crushing our loneliness. City-hunger is something like Freud's death instinct, an impatience to get to hell or purgatory, beyond the childish gratifications of the pleasure principle.

People are always saying—inaccurately—that something or another is like a dream, but Durrell's Alexandria *is* actually like the landscape of a dream. A hot, dry city, surrounded by desert, raked by winds and by contradictions. A relentless yet voluptuous city, beautiful and squalid, overcivilized and primitive.

There comes a time in the life of a great city when the place and its people exist in a kind of collusion or symbiosis, when they are unimaginable without each other, and Durrell's Alexandria had reached that condition. . . .

As I read . . . **"Justine,"** it seemed to me that no city would ever again allow us to look at it in such an intimate way, with so much complicity. **"Justine"** leaves you feeling that from now on we might have to live without this haunting sense of the city as a moral landscape. And this would be, if it happened, rather like living without a conception of guilt and innocence.

And how very advanced Durrell was, in his treatment of love. While almost every modern writer behaves as if we'd come to understand love only with his particular generation, some of Durrell's sentences sound as if they were written yesterday. . . .

Of course Durrell sometimes goes too far. Everyone in Alexandria is "exhausted," the canal is always "rotting." He keeps sniffing at death as if it were a bouquet and one suspects that he sees more colors and smells more odors than there actually are. But like Justine's sobs, his excesses have "a melodious density." . . .

A couple of years ago a critic named William Pritchard said of the characters in Ford Madox Ford's "The Good Soldier" that they are storybook people, impossibly pure as types. The same charge might be brought against Durrell's characters in **"The Alexandria Quartet"**—that they are impossibly pure in their stylized corruption. But I think that's the kind of frustrated remark that a critic sometimes falls back on when an author has made him uneasy with characters who challenge his boundaries. In his own wordy, romantic way, Durrell too challenged our boundaries.

> Anatole Broyard, *"Alexandria Revisited," in* The New York Times Book Review *(© 1982 by The New York Times Company; reprinted by permission), October 10, 1982, p. 39.*

FRANCIS KING

Laurence Durrell has used the word 'quincunx' to describe his plan of five novels, of which [*Constance*] is the third. 'Quincunx' means the arrangement of five objects in such a way that four of them are at the corners of a square or rectangle and one is in the centre; but whether *Constance,* one of its two predecessors (*Monsieur* and *Livia*) or one of its projected successors is to be regarded as the central work, is not clear. At all events, a prior reading of the first two volumes is not likely to be of much help in making sense of the plot of *Constance* or vice versa.

The first 156 pages of the 389 pages of this novel are, frankly, so dreadful that they might be mistaken for self-parody. When the narrative begins, Constance, her sister Livia, her lover Sam, her brother Hilary and a friend Aubrey, author of *Monsieur* (it will be apparent that Durrell is up to the old experimental-novel game of shuffling together separate packs of 'real' and 'imaginary' characters), are staying together in Constance's manor-house near Avignon. The detonation of the war blows them in separate directions. Hilary and Sam join up and Sam eventually finds himself in Egypt. Aubrey, a conscientious objector, also finds himself there, as part of the entourage of one of those immensely rich, immensely powerful, immensely cultivated Egyptians who appear in Durrell's novels but whom I myself was mysteriously and tantalisingly unable to locate

when living in Alexandria. Constance, a Freudian analyst, goes to work in a clinic in Switzerland. Livia, a character who bears some resemblance to Unity Mitford, assumes German nationality. At least three of these moves—those of Aubrey, Constance and Livia—would strain credulity in a realistic novel.

This whole section shows Durrell once again pampering his characters like some over-indulgent mother convinced that only the best is good enough for her children. When a woman goes mad, she is treated by Freud, no less. The Prince airily tells Aubrey before their departure for Egypt, 'You'll need some shark-skin dinner-jackets,' in the manner of a host telling a prospective guest, 'You'll need some shirts.' Subsequently, when Aubrey has arrived at his new home, 'palatial dispositions' enable him to occupy 'a veritable apartment with several separate but interconnecting bedrooms' and 'marvellous hieratic servants' present him with food 'on matchless plate.' . . . The yearning romanticism both of this imagined high life and of the style in which it is evoked reminded me of some novelist of the past, though I could not at first think whom. Then it came to me—Ouida!

Mr Durrell uses style in the manner of an aging woman using make-up. When he is discreet, the effect is enhancing; when he slaps it on, the effect is grotesque. Critics are always describing him as 'stylish' and whether they are using the epithet in its new sense of distinguished and elegant or in its old one of showy and pretentious, they have found the *mot juste.* When Durrell writes of 'soft, pornic clocks' (clearly a matter for Mrs Whitehouse to investigate) or of a 'ventripotent' banker, or when he compares a character to someone 'coming out of an epileptic "aura"' (the aura precedes an epileptic fit, it does not follow it), one can only squirm; but there are other passages of writing—for example one about Egyptian mummies in their sarcophagoi, worthy of Richard Burton—which make one want to cheer. (pp. 22-3)

Constance sets off, as a Red Cross official, from Switzerland to France, in the company of the Egyptian Prince. It is highly improbably that, even in this capacity, an Englishwoman would at that time have been admitted to the country, much less have been allowed to live in her former home; and it is even more improbable that she would have found her sister in the same town, nursing for the Germans. But once the god-like author has picked up these pieces from the chessboard and set them down where he wants them, there follow [many pages] of fiction of the highest quality. The sad humiliation of the defeated French and the brutal degradation of the conquering Germans are conveyed simply, strongly and compassionately. Typical of the French is the beautiful young woman who gives herself to the gestapo chief in return for favours for her dying husband, food for her children and the occasional reprieve of some member of the marquis. Typical of the Germans is the scholarly double-agent, in love with Livia, whom Hitler has despatched to locate the legendary treasure of the Knights Templar.

After the superb restraint of this section, the book once again descends into lurid vulgarity, like a train jumping points, running off the rails and crashing into a poster-paint factory. Constance, back in Geneva, starts a love-affair with a married Egyptian, who alternately penetrates her in a number of positions and produces statements like 'The poor little vagina must be likened to a little animal always eager for its nourishment', 'Sperm with no spiritual axis cannot feed the woman's ideas or her feelings' and 'The psyche is seriously ankylosed by the rigour of our *moeurs.*' That she does not jump out of bed and run, screaming, from the room is, presumably, intended as an indication of his prowess as a lover.

Half of this book is worthy of the Booker Prize, for which it has been listed. The other half is the sort of tosh that would give the Romantic Novelists Association a bad name. (p. 23)

Francis King, 'Stylishness,'' in The Spectator *(© 1982 by* The Spectator; *reprinted by permission of* The Spectator*), Vol. 249, No. 8049, October 16, 1982, pp. 22-3.*

STEPHEN BANN

[Among the English novelists who] have continually raised the stakes of a purely artistic ambition, Lawrence Durrell holds a secure and honourable place. The dedication of *Constance, or Solitary Practices* to 'Anais' and 'Henry' (and indeed to 'Joey') indicates the cosmopolitan range of his affiliations. Its last chapter, 'The City's Fall', evokes a dialogue with historiography which has become ever more explicit. The great French historian, Fernand Braudel, cited Durrell in the provocative conclusion to his study of the Mediterranean world, illustrating his concept of the *longue durée* with Durrell's claim that the Greek fisherman of today enables us to understand Odysseus. The last chapter of *Constance* reverts to this image of historical stasis. 'For the historian everything becomes history, there are no surprises, for it repeats itself eternally, of that he is sure.' As the German troops retire from Avignon in the closing stages of the Second World War, a stick of bombs falls upon the nearby asylum of Montfavet and liberates the insane—'The Crusaders of a new reality'. Filing out of the asylum into the festive town, they bear the names of the condemned Knights Templar of seven centuries before.

Several other indications point to Durrell's serious and intensive study, not only of the recent period in which the action of the novel is set, but also of the reverberating mythic structures which cast their patterns backwards and forwards upon the course of history. . . . Durrell utilises his filigree network of people and places (Avignon, Geneva, Egypt) for a kind of counter-strategy of offence against the paranoid potentate: he pits the Resistance against the Nazis, Cathars against Catholics, Templars against Monarchs and, above all, the ample, life-giving matrix of the Mediterranean against the sterile and destructive frenzy of invaders from the North.

Whether this very general gloss on *Constance* is plausible will be decided by the final appearance of the full 'quincunx' of which this is the third part. Three novels have now been published, and one assumes that there will be two more. But the primary sense of 'quincunx' is not, of course, the number five: it is the arrangement of points, or objects, in the same pattern as the black or white squares of a chessboard, or the 'five' of a pack of cards. Logically, this might imply that *Constance,* as the third element, has a central part to play, being the focal point through which all the remainder intercommunicate. However this may be, there can be no doubt that the reading of this superbly accomplished text offers the effect of an intricate and many-layered structure, whose overall laws of organisation can perhaps already be glimpsed through the imagination. The relations between male and female, between psychoanalysis and mystery cults, between fictional characters and their no less fictional authors—all have their special roles in structuring the symbolic space of Durrell's world. It is not the Treasure of the Templars (eagerly sought by some of the characters) which will be the promised reward of our reading. It is the no less

imaginary 'quincunx' of trees which marks the site of the treasure: in other words, the structure of freely circulating symbols which both creates the fictional lure and negates its reality. (p. 23)

Stephen Bann, ''Plots'' (appears here by permission of the London Review of Books *and the author), in* London Review of Books, *November 4 to November 17, 1982, pp. 22-3.**

ANNE TYLER

Lawrence Durrell refers to his current project of five interconnected novels—of which *Constance* is the third and latest—as a "quincunx." He might more aptly call it the Avignon Quintet. The fact that he has avoided doing so, and thereby forestalled associations with the Alexandria Quartet, seems significant.

The Alexandria Quartet is arguably his finest work, and certainly his most popular. With its labyrinthine twists of plot, its unexpected facets catching light from constantly changing angles, it has remained fresh and original for over twenty years. Who wouldn't long to repeat such a feat? The Avignon books, however, rely for their surprises upon trickery. It's the reader who is tricked, and readers are not a forgiving lot.

What we accepted in the first volume, *Monsieur,* was revealed toward its conclusion to be deception—not the interesting kind of deception practiced by true-to-life characters but the self-conscious, cerebral deception practiced by a writer pulling strings. It was as if, having created a successful illusion, Durrell could not resist showing how he'd done it. "Ha! Had you fooled, didn't I?" he says.

Livia, the second book, abandoned all pretense of verisimilitude and played throughout with questions of art versus reality. Were we intrigued by references to Pia in *Monsieur*? Well, there is no Pia. "It was cunning of you to make Pia a composite of Constance and Livia," a writer named Sutcliffe says in *Livia*. Sutcliffe is speaking to another writer, Blanford, who wrote a book called *Monsieur*. Blanford, by the way, has embarked upon a cluster of novels he refers to as a quincunx. This is something like those Quaker Oats boxes where the Quaker holds up an oats box that pictures a Quaker holding up an oats box, and so on into infinity.

After the intricate confusions of *Livia*—an annoying, tedious, and insulting book—it's a relief to find that *Constance* returns to a more accepted form of storytelling. Its story is that of Avignon at war—beginning with the last idyllic summer before the Nazi Occupation, ending with the ringing of the bells to signal the return of peace.

Writers still have a disconcerting way of turning up as characters here, meeting other writers whom they have invented and who are therefore characters once removed—the characters' characters, so to speak. The reader, like a slapped child, has trouble resuming his trustfulness and believing in what he's told. But it's a straightforward story, nonetheless. Constance, a loyal and kindhearted young woman, loses her new husband to a freak military accident, stays on in Avignon with the Red Cross during the Occupation, and combines her voice with a few others to deliver a sort of tone poem on the atmosphere in France during World War II. These voices give us a sense of the helplessness and despair experienced by the French in the presence of the Germans. They also bear chilling witness to the French complicity in the rounding up of Jews. (pp. 36-7)

There are flaws in *Constance.* One is the occasional lapse of ear. Words or sounds are repeated, as if the author had not thought of aural effect. . . .

Even more of a problem is the point of one is first grateful for the luxurious variety, then baffled, finally discouraged. "Here in this peaceful decor had walked Goethe and Eckermann of whom [Fischer] had never heard," we are told. If we are solely with Fischer at this moment (and we are), looking through his eyes alone, how do we ourselves know there was a Goethe or an Eckermann? . . .

Is this to say that the novel fails? No, not completely; for it's hard to imagine any work of Durrell's that is not ringingly evocative, full of character and possibility. There is always a sense of richness in his writing. Textures, smells, and sights tumble forth; he is a master at setting the scene. *Constance* carries enough conviction so that when, toward the end of the war, a woman proposes a trip around the world and a man asks, "What world?" we nod in agreement. We can bear witness to the desolation, the waste and hopelessness we've so palpably experienced during the course of the story.

This is a troublesome and often exasperating book, but it is above all else a book with a wealth of atmosphere, and in spite of its pretensions that atmosphere comes through with resounding clarity. (p. 37)

> *Anne Tyler, "Avignon at War," in* The New Republic *(reprinted by permission of* The New Republic; © *1982 The New Republic, Inc.), Vol. 187, No. 22, December 6, 1982, pp. 36-7.*

ALBERTO MANGUEL

Constance or Solitary Practices is a treasury of observations, the third in a planned series of five novels, set one inside the other like a set of Russian dolls. Each can be read independently, but the faithful reader who has followed the game step by step is rewarded by new-born images reflected in the other mirror-novels, each vaster in scope than the previous one, each acting on the others like a dream within a dream. *Constance* is the log-book of a poet.

Our times have not been kind to poets who venture into prose. Writing about Durrell in an essay precariously called "The Novel Today" (in *The Pelican Guide to English Literature*), Gilbert Phelps notes his dislike of him. He compares him unfavourably to Joyce Cary and Anthony Powell, complains about the superficiality of Durrell's characters, denounces the lack of sympathy between them and the reader, and finally credits Durrell only with "energy" that Phelps sees as "almost entirely cerebral." He says nothing of Durrell's poetic vision, nothing about Durrell's intention to create a picture of emotions ("not snapshots of people"), nothing about Durrell's concern with a clear vision of time, eternity, sexual longing, and the

artist's despair in his effort to portray all this. "It is not the meaning that we need," reads one of his poems written in the 1970s, "but sight." With *The Alexandria Quartet* Durrell achieved part of this purpose; with *Monsieur, Livia,* and now *Constance* his achievement becomes even more evident. More than Powell (because Durrell is a better man with words), more than Cary (because his scope is wider), Lawrence Durrell has set out to observe our recent past and capture its mood, its essence. (p. 11)

Durrell knows that a writer does not change the present; he changes the past. He educates our recollections, bullies the ghosts of things that were into giving accounts of themselves, organizes dates and events and places in what Durrell calls "the filing cabinet of his memory." Durrell the writer signposts the dusky regions gone by for us to revisit if not in safety, at least in a kind of order that the brain will grasp and the heart will bear.

Durrell's country is the world at war in the 1930s and '40s: Alexandria, Paris, Geneva, and especially Avignon, the city of Rabelais, whose two towers are called "He-who-speaks" and "He-who-grumbles." Through these ghostly cities—ghostly because Durrell describes them as they once were, in days gone by—move the passions and desires of men and women. Writers, Nazi politicians, women in love, spies whose knowledge of the Secret Service comes from the bad style (not the plot) of Sherlock Holmes stories, characters created by characters, are invoked to say their piece. The plot is complex, too intricate to summarize, and ultimately not essential.

The art of the novel and the erotic sciences are two related subjects with which almost all of these people are obsessed. There are wild theories about [women, Hitler, and sex. *Constance*] . . . mainly conveys a feeling of loneliness. . . . *Solitary Practices* (the subtitle) refers not only to the masturbatory (that is, fruitless, egotistic) pleasures; it describes men and women in their lonely quest, above whom hovers Freud, the god custodian, "Old Fraud" as one of the characters calls him.

But, as in *The Alexandria Quartet,* the convoluted, tortured characters are superseded by the writing, which acts as a distancing, wise hand between the reader and the novel. It has the abstract quality of music. . . . The language, however, can also be clean-cut and explicit. . . . Even the epigrams are so astounding they barely need a character to speak them. . . .

Henry Miller, who was Durrell's close friend, wrote his books out of his own immediate past, setting himself as an excuse for others to understand his age. Durrell chose to make up the characters that illustrate his subject. But the past they deal with is finally the same. What makes Durrell's exploration richer and more dangerous than Miller's is not the subject: it is the wonderful, neglected ability to put things into words, to spin webs of glass out of the language, to be that endangered species—a novelist of genius. (pp. 11-12)

> *Alberto Manguel, "The Novelist As Poet" (reprinted by permission of the author), in* Books in Canada, *Vol. 12, No. 3, March, 1983, pp. 11-12.*

John (Marsden) Ehle (Jr.)

1925-

American novelist and nonfiction writer.

Primarily a regional writer, Ehle realistically depicts the people and dialects of the South, yet centers his works around common human problems. Ehle is known for his nonstereotyped portrayals of black characters, particularly in his first novel, *Move Over, Mountain* (1957). His nonfiction *Free Men* (1965) recreates a little-known civil rights incident that occurred in Chapel Hill, North Carolina, in the early 1960s. The work is significant for the insights it gives into the civil rights movement as a whole.

Ehle is at his best when writing about the mountain people around his hometown, Asheville, North Carolina. His recent novel, *The Winter People* (1982), which takes place in that setting during the depression, is praised for authenticity of characterization and dialogue. Most of his other fiction is set here or in similar areas, though in different historical periods.

(See also *Contemporary Authors*, Vols. 9-12, rev. ed.)

PAUL FLOWERS

John Ehle has created a readable novel ["**Move Over, Mountain**"] about a Southern Negro, and if he deserves no other encomium, he should be praised for a fresh approach to the Negro's big problem, and his splendid avoidance of the trite theme in which Uncle Tom's great-grandson always must be the victim of a latterday Simon Legree. Mr. Ehle turns a spotlight on human beings in their struggle through a world where natural selection is the rule. The fact that the central character and nearly all the rest are Negroes is incidental. It is a story of struggle, determination, peculiar moral convictions and strange loyalties. . . .

Through travail, doubt, fear and frustration, Jordan moves to gain money and better position for his family; such obstructions as block his path are put there by others of his own race; in short, this is a success story in the familiar American tradition, and race has little to do with it beyond the frequently voiced theme of a promised land "up North." . . .

[It] is quite obvious that [Mr. Ehle] writes from a deep knowledge of his subject, and an understanding of technique rare in a first novelist. As we have said, he gives refreshing emphasis to a fact frequently ignored by "social problem" novelists—namely, that human problems in reality have little to do with geography or even race; that men, of whatever breed, who are tough and durable frequently triumph over adverse environments. No one will pity Jordan Cummings because he was a Negro. Readers will admire and respect him because he was a man.

Paul Flowers, "Jordan Cummings, Lord of Tin Top," in The New York Times Book Review *(© 1957 by The New York Times Company; reprinted by permission), April 21, 1957, p. 18.*

Photograph by Nicholas Dean; courtesy of John Ehle

COLEMAN ROSENBERGER

Mr. Ehle's "**Move Over, Mountain**" is an engaging book, a warm-hearted story of a North Carolina family which the author quite obviously respects and admires, told with insight and humor and a fine narrative sense. . . .

If Mr. Ehle rejects an easy stereotype of a Southern town for something more difficult to achieve, the realistic recreation of the kind of town which he has lived in and knows, his rejection of stereotypes in his characterizations is even more refreshing. It happens that Jordan and his family are Negroes. This fact involves them in some special circumstances, but the special circumstances are less momentous than those which are common to all the citizens, Negro and white of the community.

Jordan and his family are individuals. They are people with problems, but they are people, with all their various strengths and weaknesses, and not just problems. And the problems they have are those which, in one way or another, all human beings are likely to be heir to.

This is something rather unusual in a Southern novel. Perhaps Mr. Ehle, who was born in 1925, speaks for a new generation of Southern writers. In any event, to read "**Move Over, Mountain**" is a very happy experience.

Coleman Rosenberger, "Warm-Hearted Story of a Southern Family," in New York Herald Tribune Book

101

Review (© *I.H.T. Corporation; reprinted by permission), April 28, 1957, p. 6.*

ABRAHAM BARNETT

[*Move Over, Mountain*] is the story of Jordan Cummings, a North Carolina Negro who is able to triumph in business and preserve his family life when he gives up his desires to go North to seemingly easier success. The author's intrusive theme that a satisfactory economic and spiritual life for southern Negroes today merely awaits an inner resolution on their part is faultily based on the extremely simplified situation of the hero whose problems seem to have no important connection with racism but rather with his delusions about the North. The effects of Southern racism on Negro enterprise and migration are seriously underestimated. Although he resorts to the device of a dice game to bring the hero out of the nadir of his career, this white Southern author evidently respects his Negro characters. Despite the unrelieved colloquial style and sketchy characterization which add to the thematic flaw, the story of Jordan Cummings' travail and success holds our interest.

> *Abraham Barnett, in a review of "Move Over, Mountain," in* Library Journal *(reprinted from* Library Journal, *June 1, 1957; published by R. R. Bowker Co. (a Xerox company); copyright © 1957 by Xerox Corporation), Vol. 82, No. 11, June 1, 1957, p. 1536.*

HERBERT MITGANG

The hero of this biography ["**The Survivor: The Story of Eddy Hukov**"] is a former member of the S. S., one cruel arm of Nazi Germany's terror, but if he has acknowledged his past misdeeds or repented, readers will have a hard time finding where. John Ehle describes his story as a "heroic adventure on three continents" and Eddy Hukov as "one of the world's stateless persons." This language is an insult to the real refugees and displaced persons of war and a rephrasing of recent history.

Hukov was born in Lvov, Poland, of German parents. He joined the S.S., fighting bravely for them, winning the Iron Cross First Class. After learning that his family had been killed in an American bombing raid, the young Storm Trooper became a still more avenging fighter.

When Americans captured his unit Hukov asked another S.S. man to cut out from his skin the S.S. tattoo. . . . Hukov went underground, afraid to be discovered. He worked his way into a refugee camp, an oppressor among victims. Without papers, without the courage to face the peacetime consequences of his wartime affiliation, Hukov was ripe for the blandishments of a French Foreign Legion recruiter in Germany. . . .

Hukov and two Germans finally escaped from the Legion. They went to Thailand, and Hukov has remained there ever since. He is a man without a passport. Free Germany will not give him one and does not want him. . . .

Mr. Ehle, a novelist and teacher, first heard the Hukov story from a traveling friend and then pursued the story via the mails. He has done the difficult job of assembling a biography without ever meeting his subject, and has attempted to retain Hukov's style. Whether he has captured the true personality of his subject one can only guess.

> *Herbert Mitgang, "Looking Backward," in* The New York Times Book Review *(© 1958 by The New York Times Company; reprinted by permission), March 30, 1958, p. 31.*

ALLEN WARD

This dramatic novel ["**Kingstree Island**"] about fisherfolk who live on a wind swept island off North Carolina is remarkably like the scenario for a Hollywood epic. The year is 1938, but the people of Kingstree Island are cut off from the main stream of American life by a four-hour boat trip and their existence, as John Ehle describes it, is simple but violent in a way reminiscent of life in the old West nearly a century ago. Thus it is, perhaps, appropriate that this straightforward story is remarkably like a very good Western. Even the hero is the traditional wandering stranger.

Brandon Rhodes, a 24-year-old Southerner described as a "somber man, still holding traces of a distant aristocracy," has come to the island after many years of traveling the face of America. . . . [When] he first sets eyes on the island he decides he will make it his home.

This is not easy, for the island does not welcome strangers. The man who rules it—much as the rich old cattle baron traditionally rules the little Western town in the movies—is blind, aging Matt Tomlinson, boss of the fishing fleet and owner of the island's one store. Tomlinson has virtual power of life and death over the islanders, determining who shall work and who shall not. . . .

How Rhodes battles the old man for the right to stay on the island—and incidentally to free the fishermen from his grip—makes up the body of this picturesque tale. One never gets very deep inside the characters, but their actions give a fair idea of the turmoil underneath.

> *Allen Ward, "Offshore Nepenthe," in* The New York Times Book Review *(© 1959 by The New York Times Company; reprinted by permission), September 20, 1959, p. 50.*

FLORENCE HAXTON BULLOCK

A little more than a year after the crusade achieved its major goals, John Ehle tells, in "**Shepherd of the Streets**," the dramatic story of the Episcopal rector who became the fighting voice of the Puerto Ricans in New York's shockingly overcrowded West Side, and won for them, through his bold assaults on the city's Health, Sanitation, Buildings and Police Departments, something approaching protection under the law. . . .

Mr. Ehle based his fascinating story on close-ups of Father Gusweller at work and on the few statistics and sociological studies of the area which are available. It is an exciting, richly detailed portrait rather than a factual case history, with some of the pictures of the children and youth sentimentally shaded. Just possibly it results from Mr. Ehle's instinct to compensate for the woeful want of humane sentiment shown these newcomers to our city before Father Gusweller undertook to battle for their rights.

> *Florence Haxton Bullock, "Man of God in W. 84th St.," in* New York Herald Tribune Book Review *(© I.H.T. Corporation; reprinted by permission), July 10, 1960, p. 10.*

JOHN COOK WYLLIE

["**Lion on the Hearth**"] is John Ehle's third novel, and like its emotionally charged predecessors (the North Carolina Negro story, "**Move Over, Mountain**," and the story of the wandering stranger in "**Kingstree Island**"), it may be put down as a *succès d'estime.*

The story is of a Gant-like, Asheville, N.C., family, which worries as much as it can, but the differences between "Look Homeward Angel" and "**Lion on the Hearth**" are more striking than the similarities. The title-character is once more a wandering stranger, who, like Tom Wolfe, tried to go home again, to succeed only years later in death. But the central character, a young lad named Kin, is the sensitive soul isolated in a hostile world, struggling with sensual imagination against the malignancy of man.

The emotional intensity which Mr. Ehle exhibits is neither Caldwellian nor Faulknerian in quality. No powerful social or philosophical conviction charges it, and yet it has the merit of arising from a passionate consideration of the commonplace. The story of the Asheville family during the years of the depression opens with an account of a childbirth, ranges from a sweetheart-and-roses seduction, through a hotel-and-brothel scene, to a horse-trading deal de luxe, but the subject matter is a secondary consideration. The author is feeling the family's pulse with an audio-frequency amplifier, and his emotion carries him sometimes into the area of pathological inflammation of his conjunctives.

The book is in the mainstream of a worthy tradition of Southern fiction, and it can be read in the South as well as the rest of the United States as though it dealt with a foreign country. No one, unless it was Tom Wolfe, has ever before looked on Asheville with these elongated eyes any more than anyone else ever saw Jeanne Hébuternè with the compassion of a Modigliani. This is Parisian Impressionism, Tar-Heel Division, Asheville Section.

> *John Cook Wyllie, "Isolated in a Hostile World,"* in The New York Times Book Review *(© 1961 by The New York Times Company; reprinted by permission), October 15, 1961, p. 44.*

HAL BORLAND

America has had a succession of frontiers, each in turn a challenge to hardy, ambitious men and a trial to their women, each leaving its marks on the American character. History can only tell us what happened and when, but fiction such as this splendid novel can show how and why. "**The Land Breakers**" is one of the best recreations of our pioneer past that we have had in years, honest and compassionate, rich and true.

[Mr. Ehle] has many skills. His story moves—even when it seems to pause for sights and sounds and smells that taunt the senses, even when it deals with herbal lore. He has a sure sense of drama; the tension never falters, whether the immediate action is Lacey Pollard's return, a bear hunt, a livestock drive to market, or the birth of a baby. His characters are full-dimensioned, wholly credible. His dialogue, though it is often touched with poetry, sounds right as rain.

Often eloquent, it never moralizes. . . .

"**The Land Breakers**" has a rare degree of greatness.

> *Hal Borland, "On the Carolina Frontier," in* The New York Times Book Review *(© 1964 by The New*

York Times Company; reprinted by permission), February 23, 1964, p. 30.*

EDWARD MARGOLIES

Related in the first person by a North Carolina University professor, [*The Free Men*] traces in detail the genesis, development, and outcome of the civil rights disorders that wracked "liberal" Chapel Hill in the years 1963-1964. Professor Ehle focuses his main attention on three youthful leaders (two whites and a Negro), but gives ample coverage as well to other participants, white and Negro. . . . In his effort to be fair to all, there is perhaps an inevitable lack of passion and conviction in Professor Ehle's account—and some doubt as to where he himself stands, although, by and large, his sympathies lie with the demonstrators and their objectives. He employs novelistic techniques—sometimes shuttling back and forth in time, sometimes recording personal impressions, often reproducing verbatim newspaper accounts, conversations, letters and court proceedings to tell his story. All told, this is well worth reading. Chapel Hill's failure has larger national implications.

> *Edward Margolies, in a review of "The Free Men,"* in Library Journal *(reprinted from* Library Journal, *April 1, 1965; published by R. R. Bowker Co. (a Xerox company); copyright © 1965 by Xerox Corporation), Vol. 90, No. 7, April 1, 1965, p. 1733.*

THOMAS E. PORTER

Chapel Hill, N.C., is the home of the most liberal university in the South. In 1963, a colored face in the classroom or cafeteria caused no stir. But on an early April morning of that year, two white students began to picket a segregated restaurant on the main street—and the community caught its breath. For the next two years, there was never total peace of mind for those of us who lived and studied in that pleasant college town.

In *The Free Men,* John Ehle has documented those years in Chapel Hill, focusing on the experiences of the two students, John Dunne and Pat Cusik, who led the civil rights movement there. He tells the story with remarkable objectivity, neither canonizing the liberals nor castigating the town. (pp. 729-30)

This book adds a note to the history of civil rights movements. Unlike Mississippi and Alabama, Chapel Hill did not explode in violence. The university community and liberals in town government worked very hard to avoid showdown incidents. But the movement there, as reported in *The Free Men,* dramatizes a mystery: commitment to a cause. It was alarming to find that talk was not enough. Two dedicated students forced an issue—and you were either for them or against them. (p. 730)

> *Thomas E. Porter, in a review of "The Free Men,"* in America *(reprinted with permission of America Press, Inc.; © 1965; all rights reserved), Vol. 112, No. 20, May 15, 1965, pp. 729-30.*

PAUL M. GASTON

What may lie ahead for Mississippi—and the civil rights movement as a whole—cannot easily be predicted, but John Ehle's superb book, "**The Free Men**," should be read thoughtfully for clues. Mr. Ehle tells the story of the virtually unreported civil rights turmoil that gripped Chapel Hill, North Carolina, in 1963 and 1964. Home of the University of North Carolina, Chapel Hill is famed for its liberalism, Southern style, and was an unlikely place for the events described by Mr. Ehle. . . . [When] a small group of young people, dissatisfied with the "tokenism" which they felt characterized Chapel Hill, launched a movement for total desegregation of all public facilities, the community was unable to cope. There were extraordinary displays of civil disobedience, mass arrests, grossly unfair trials, and imprisonment and exile for the leaders. Intrinsically interesting, the Chapel Hill story is relevant to the rest of the South today for several reasons. One is that a split developed between radicals and liberals, shattering the liberal alliance that had accounted for previous progress in race relations. One wonders if this is a forecast of things to come elsewhere. There are signs that it may be. If so, we need to understand thoroughly the young militants in the forefront today. One of the major virtues of Mr. Ehle's book is the insight it gives into the young radicals who led the Chapel Hill movement. His portrait is certainly one of the most penetrating yet to appear. (pp. 617-18)

> *Paul M. Gaston, "Speaking for the Negro," in* The Virginia Quarterly Review *(copyright, 1965, by* The Virginia Quarterly Review, *The University of Virginia), Vol. 41, No. 4 (Autumn, 1965), pp. 612-18.**

PUBLISHERS WEEKLY

[*The Road* is a] long pastoral novel centered around the difficulties with nature and with people encountered in attempts to carve a railroad line around, over, and through a North Carolina mountain in the late 19th century. Weatherby Wright, the hero of the book, is a man driven by his dream of the economic and social advantages which completion of the railroad line will bring to his native mountain people, a dream strong enough to influence those around him. . . . The work is difficult, the book is long, and, unfortunately, the characters are not drawn sharply enough to interest the average reader. However, occasional passages show good insight into mountain people and their highly individual society.

> *A review of "The Road," in* Publishers Weekly *(reprinted from the November 7, 1966 issue of* Publishers Weekly, *published by R. R. Bowker Company; copyright © 1966 by R. R. Bowker Company), Vol. 190, No. 19, November 7, 1966, p. 60.*

JAMES BOATWRIGHT

["**Time of Drums**"] is a likable book—sober, honest, unpretentious for the most part—about a North Carolina colonel and his brigade during the Civil War, chiefly and climactically at the Battle of Gettysburg. . . . [It] should come as no surprise that [Mr. Ehle's] narrative has a certain sharpness and assurance about it. There's a wealth of rustic detail here, closely observed; a potentially arresting conflict between two brothers in love with the same girl; gory battle scenes; famous generals (Lee and Jackson in particular).

Ehle has Owen Wright, the colonel, tell his own story, for reasons Owen gives toward the end of the novel: "The notes about the war and my life in it I am writing for my children once they are grown should they seek an explanation for the reputation I have, for I am sometimes called a traitor and sometimes a hero by my own people." Owen's explanation of his motives, his hints at the ambiguity of his character, make him and the book sound interesting enough. Unfortunately, they promise more than is delivered.

"**Time of Drums**" is, in fact, a fatally flawed book. Reading it is hard going—there's no narrative thrust, no urgent, sustained rhythm—and this is largely the result, I think, of Ehle's method of getting the story told. What we are faced with is a first-person narrator who doesn't take advantage of the form—a chance to render events with vivid immediacy, say, or to develop a subtly ironic self-portrait—but doggedly insists on misusing the form; Ehle has Wright say and report all sorts of things that he just can't get away with.

The novel's solid virtues—its understatement, the characters' gritty integrity, Ehle's knowledge of place and historical event—are undermined by this failure of craft. In matters of fact, for instance, Ehle is determined that we know something of the sociology of the South, and he is forced to serve up huge gobbets of undigested knowledge in the unlikeliest ways. . . .

Ehle has Owen, a man in the thick of battle, view the proceedings with a panoramic eye, as if he were one of those foreign journalists perched in trees. After a rather lengthy historian's report on the defeat of various brigades (all somehow witnessed by Owen) Ehle attempts to justify Owen's remarkable vision: "There was Yank cannon fire now . . . and I was almost compelled to go to it; one is called, one can scarcely keep himself from running toward such challenging sounds and deeds. I moved along the ridge to be closer, to see it closer, to see it all." It's a brave attempt, but it doesn't convince. We end up witnesses to a conflict between narrative limitation and authorial desire.

There are less obvious failures of language and authenticity, which grow out of this same conflict. Whose language and sentiments are these, Owen Wright's or John Ehle's? "Most of my men don't need hate in order to be committed. They don't even need a political cause in order to be committed. What they need is each other and this regiment, they need being part of it; we need each other." To my ear, that comes perilously close to up-to-the-minute, contemporary cant. If we are going to have cant, let it at least be historical.

> *James Boatwright, "A Carolina Colonel in the Civil War," in* The New York Times Book Review *(© 1970 by The New York Times Company; reprinted by permission), September 27, 1970, p. 46.*

PUBLISHERS WEEKLY

["**The Journey of August King**"] is a tender, moving, but wholly unsentimental story that comes across like a classic folk tale. The simple but engrossing story revolves around a pious 19th century North Carolina farmer (middle-aged) named August King and a 15-year-old runaway slave girl, Annalees Williamsburg. . . . King is a simple, unimaginative man, not adventuresome, yet something in him longs to help the girl and he continues to do so, even though he is becoming more and more frightened, especially after he meets the girl's brutal owner. Gradually, rumors build that he is helping her and the suspense mounts. While all this is going on, August is tormented by doubts about his motives: is he doing it because of a sexual attraction towards the girl, or to atone in some way for negligence towards his dead wife? The conclusion is not only satisfying but uplifting, in a healthy, old-fashioned way. The novel is full of poetry and beauty in the style of its telling. It is also a brutal tale about human nature at its worst, and in August's case, at its best.

> *A review of "The Journey of August King," in* Publishers Weekly *(reprinted from the August 9, 1971*

issue of Publishers Weekly, *published by R. R. Bowker Company, a Xerox company; copyright © 1971 by Xerox Corporation), Vol. 200, No. 6, August 9, 1971, p. 40.*

PHOEBE-LOU ADAMS

Mr. Ehle always writes about the people of the North Carolina mountains in an unfussy style and with a sharp ear for local speech. His latest novel [*The Journey of August King*], set in the early nineteenth century, records the adventures of a law-abiding, grimly industrious farmer who, to his own bewilderment, risks his life and loses valuable property to help a runaway slave girl escape to the North. The work is notable for the contrast between the gentle tone of the narrative and the horrors it describes. A device which might have proved merely inappropriate actually creates a kind of eerie chiaroscuro.

Phoebe-Lou Adams, in a review of "The Journey of August King," in The Atlantic Monthly *(copyright © 1971, by The Atlantic Monthly Company, Boston, Mass.; reprinted with permission), Vol. 229, No. 1, January, 1972, p. 97.*

SAUNDERS REDDING

[John Ehle's *Time of Drums*] reminds me once again that one of the most talented of American regional novelists—and I do not use "regional" in a restrictive sense, but simply to indicate the author's concern with a particular region, which happens to be the South—has been shamefully and inexcusably neglected. . . . I know that this sounds exaggerated, but no living southern writer of whom I am aware has Mr. Ehle's sympathetic understanding of the "southern way of life" nor his deep and loving involvement in the people who live that life on either side of both the "color line" and the doctrinal line. His talents overwhelmingly support his emotional and intellectual commitment. His narrative skill, his projection of character, his sense of the dramatic and of the living realities are something more than first rate. (pp. 486-87)

Saunders Redding, in a review of "Time of Drums," in The American Scholar *(copyright © 1972 by the United Chapters of Phi Beta Kappa; reprinted by permission of the publishers, the United Chapters of Phi Beta Kappa), Vol. 41, No. 3, Summer, 1972, pp. 486-87.*

PUBLISHERS WEEKLY

["**The Changing of the Guard**" is a] thoroughly enjoyable novel, wry and witty, that really takes the reader out of himself and into the civilized world of banter and intrigue behind the scenes at the making of a perhaps great film. In Paris a famous film actor, his alcoholic actress wife who is making a comeback, an actress who is getting her first big break and a stinging, moody, deliberately insulting New Wave director are filming the last days of Louis XVI and Marie Antoinette. . . . The personalities of the historical figures are emerging and begin to have a fascinating effect on the 20th century people who are telling and acting out their story. The touching drama of Louis and his 'Toinette moves us deeply even as we laugh with delight at the very human peccadillos of the film people, on stage and off. This could be a real winner for the same audience that enjoyed "The War Between the Tates."

A review of "The Changing of the Guard," in Publishers Weekly *(reprinted from the November 25, 1974 issue of* Publishers Weekly, *published by R. R. Bowker Company, a Xerox company; copyright © 1974 by Xerox Corporation), Vol. 206, No. 22, November 25, 1974, p. 39.*

RODERICK NORDELL

As long as writers have ideas like Mr. Ehle's, the often predicted demise of the novel will have to be postponed. No other narrative form has the flexibility to permit such plausible trickery as the feat he brings off so well [in **"The Changing of the Guard"**]: merging the offscreen lives of movie actors with their on-screen roles to a point of bizarre fusion.

Taken literally, these stereotyped Hollywood lives of adultery, alcohol, and power ploys do not have much to recommend the reading of them. But Mr. Ehle weaves them into a timely image of what has been happening to moviemaking at a time of change from romantic glamour to gross realism. There are implications for a broader range of cultural values in such questions as whether candor has to mean the end of grace or the beginning of sensationalism.

Here the situation on a film set in Paris echoes the French Revolution which is the subject of the film. . . .

A concern for revolutionary nuance is not unexpected from the nonfiction observer of civil-rights activists in **"The Free Men"** of some years ago. The result is like a screenplay of 18th-century France imbedded in a 20th-century world where the test of revolution is whether it's good box office.

Roderick Nordell, "New Novel Merges Actors and Their Roles," in The Christian Science Monitor *(reprinted by permission from* The Christian Science Monitor; © 1975 The Christian Science Publishing Society; all rights reserved), January 10, 1975, p. 10.*

SHARON WONG

[In *The Changing of the Guard*] Richie Hall, a middle-aged English actor whose career and private life are on the decline, comes to Paris to star in a film based on the French Revolution. While Richie's egocentricity drives everyone around him wild, few realize how really insecure he is. Lamentable as the loss of youth may be, we are unmoved by this story. Reason: there is no propelling movement and even the writing is stagnant. Ehle frequently refers to actual celebrities in the attempt to create a realistic milieu. However this device fails because his characters have no substance of their own. The novel is on the whole a rather tiresome, humorless pastiche—a filmland fantasy that is lifeless and dull.

Sharon Wong, in a review of "The Changing of the Guard," in Library Journal *(reprinted from* Library Journal, *January 15, 1975; published by R. R. Bowker Co. (a Xerox company); copyright © 1975 by Xerox Corporation), Vol. 100, No. 2, January 15, 1975, p. 145.*

MARTIN LEVIN

Although [**"The Changing of the Guard"**] is set in the present, its heart belongs to the sixties, when films were in ferment and directorial style was a heavy subject. Consider the plight of

Richie Hall, a glossy international superstar who has come out of retirement from Beverly Hills to make a comeback picture in Paris. The script is something about the last days of Louis XVI and has been largely rewritten by the star himself; he sees it as a "vehicle" for his personality. But the director, a surly young brute arrogant with an *auteur* complex, has ideas that mingle naturalism with Grand Guignol. This is a conflict crying out for humor which is—sadly—an item in short supply here. . . .

John Ehle takes these two *poseurs* [Hall and Sigler] more seriously than they deserve and tells us far more about their film than we need to know.

> *Martin Levin, in a review of "The Changing of the Guard," in* The New York Times Book Review *(© 1975 by The New York Times Company; reprinted by permission), April 6, 1975, p. 16.*

DENISE P. DONAVIN

[*The Winter People* is a] beautifully woven story about North Carolina mountain folk. Ehle has avoided caricature in creating the Wright and Campbell clans—two mountain families who live in warily peaceful deference without hiding the scorn and animosity that has permeated their relationship for years. . . . The novelist produces splendid dialogue, climactic adventure scenes (especially vivid is an account of a bear hunt), and dramatic tension that is carried to the final page.

> *Denise P. Donavin, in a review of "The Winter People," in* Booklist *(reprinted by permission of the American Library Association; copyright © 1982 by the American Library Association), Vol. 78, No. 12, February 15, 1982, p. 744.*

JONATHAN YARDLEY

[John Ehle] has never quite managed to find the national audience he deserves.

In a just world, publication of *The Winter People* would rectify that; it is a lovely novel—quiet, forceful, serious but never solemn, old-fashioned in the best sense of the term. But this is not a just world, and there is simply no way of knowing whether Ehle will, with what is unquestionably his best book, at last be properly recognized. He is not a flashy writer, he deals with people and a place that may seem remote to many readers, he makes no gestures to literary fashion. He is merely good, which these days too often is not enough.

The Winter People is set in the mountains of North Carolina during the Depression. A clockmaker from the North, Wayland Jackson, 34 years old and recently widowed, is driving with his 12-year-old daughter to Tennessee, where he proposes to go into business. But he gets lost in the Carolina mountains, where he encounters a young woman named Collie Wright and asks her to "let us warm, and maybe feed us." . . .

She does, and so begins an involvement that soon becomes more intense and complicated than she had bargained for. Jackson and his daughter take up residence in an out-building on her place, and he sets up shop in a corner of her family's general store. He is powerfully attracted to her, and she to him, but she denies him her bed; she has borne one illegitimate child, she does not want another, and in any event she fears the reaction of the baby's father, a violent young fellow who is away but may return at any moment.

It is the prospect of the father's return that gives the novel its tension and sense of foreboding, that provides a dangerous presence even when the life of the little community seems most tranquil and happy. When at last he does return, he sets off a series of events in which many lives are altered. . . . (p. 3)

Collie, a strong and resourceful woman, feels an obligation "to complete what she had started." The action she decides upon entails considerable sacrifice and brings the novel to a surprising conclusion; yet it is one that most readers are likely to regard as entirely fitting, and consistent with the novel's themes.

But *The Winter People* is much more than the story of a woman and two men. At one level it is about the mountains, which are as vivid a presence in Ehle's work as any person. . . . At another it is about loss and renewal, as experienced by Collie and Wayland and ultimately the entire community. At still another it is about families, about the fragile yet durable ties that we establish among ourselves—a novel that says "the only choice a man ever had in life was to decide what sort of slavery to accept, and that determining to be free was the worst slavery of all."

Ehle's people, all of them, are splendid. Collie, her emotions seesawing as she tries with mounting frustration to keep her life on an even keel, is a person of striking good humor and endearing independence of mind. Wayland, gentle and decent and wry, has a strength that is as quiet as the novel's. Each of Collie's three brothers emerges, quickly yet subtly, as a clearly definable individual and, at the same time, a member of a family that is itself a clearly definable entity.

This is a novel about mountain people, with an absolutely sure grasp of mountain ways. . . . [Ehle] handles the Hatfields-and-McCoys feud between the Wrights and their neighbors, the Campbells, with a fine appreciation for nuance, a refusal to resort to quaintness or cliché, and a sure knowledge of the customs and subtleties involved.

Ehle's prose is exactly suited to his subject and setting. His people talk the way North Carolina mountain people talk; there is nothing stilted or artificial about his dialogue. And his descriptive prose is quite marvelous; it has an air of country formality and mannerliness that is thoroughly distinctive.

Like Ehle's other novels, *The Winter People* is modest in its claims; it is about ordinary (yet remarkable) people in an ordinary (yet breathtaking) place. . . . *The Winter People* is a very substantial piece of work: thoroughly rewarding and satisfying in every important respect. (pp. 3, 14)

> *Jonathan Yardley, "Love Affairs and Family Feuds in the Smoky Mountains," in* Book World—The Washington Post *(© 1982, The Washington Post), March 7, 1982, pp. 3, 14.*

EDMUND FULLER

["**The Winter People**"] is a splendid story of the clannish, fiercely independent mountain people and a newcomer among them. The opening tone is ominous but shifts quickly into a sustained, joyous lyricism, with the quality of "lilt and sway" that the stranger, Wayland Jackson, finds in the speech of a young mountain woman, Collie Wright. . . .

The cast is large, with memorably delineated personalities. Two compelling figures are the heads of the hostile clans. . . . The talk among all these people is extraordinarily rich, ranging from tones of rough humor and bawdiness to tenderness. Grimly threatening confrontations lead to hard negotiations that are like statecraft in miniature. No outside law is invoked; these families settle their own affairs.

There is a 39-page bear hunt in which the slight and gentle Wayland is tested, foreshadowing a graver testing he will face. Of bear-hunt stories William Faulkner is king, but Mr. Ehle can claim a dukedom. . . .

Edmund Fuller, "Feuding Mountain Clans and a Poignant Family Comedy," in The Wall Street Journal *(reprinted by permission of* The Wall Street Journal, © *Dow Jones & Company, Inc. 1982; all rights reserved), April 20, 1982, p. 30.**

IVAN GOLD

"The Winter People" is drenched in local wit and custom. . . . It is also filled with vivid evocations of the mountains and surrounding terrain, and alive with rounded, nuanced characters who appear to exist beyond the novel's covers.

John Ehle . . . has staked a serious, quiet claim to this profoundly American territory.

Ivan Gold, "Mountain People," in The New York Times Book Review *(© 1982 by The New York Times Company; reprinted by permission), May 9, 1982, p. 13.*

Gunnar (Bengt) Ekelöf

1907-1968

(Also transliterated as Ekeloef) Swedish poet, essayist, and translator.

Ekelöf is often described as the most important poet of modern Swedish literature. His work, which clearly reflects the influences of the mystical poetry of Persia and the Orient, Taoist and Indian mysticism, and French Symbolism and Surrealism, is both difficult and demanding. In the modernist aesthetic tradition, it challenges the reader to abandon conventional perceptions of both poetry and reality. As is true of the work of the Surrealists, Ekelöf's poetry also urges readers to explore the relevance of the subconscious to their thinking. In keeping with this aim, his work is often filled with fantastic, dreamlike images and symbols which mock rational thought. Against this background of thought, reality and self emerge as Ekelöf's major concerns, freedom from the dualistic moral conception of good and evil, his personal and poetic aim.

Ekelöf's first book of poetry, *Sent på jorden* (1932; *Late Arrival on Earth*), was an influential book of its time. Written in a period of the author's deep despair, it presents a bleak, nihilistic vision of a world hurtling toward destruction and employs techniques of French Surrealism. This work, Ekelöf's "suicide book," was written at a time when the bourgeois humanistic culture of Sweden was under fierce attack by Marxist and other groups and is considered revolutionary in that it attacked not only that culture but "the conventional structures of language and literature." Full of nightmarish imagery of death and decay, *Late Arrival on Earth* marks the beginning of Ekelöf's lifelong attack on traditional conceptions of both reality and poetry.

Dedikation (1934; *Dedication*), Ekelöf's second book of poetry, reflects the influence of French Symbolism in that the author portrays himself as an interpreter, or "seer," one whose vision and insight extends beyond the perimeters of surface reality. More positive than *Late Arrival on Earth*, this work shows the author groping towards the truth which he believes lies beyond reality. Ekelöf seeks a "oneness" that the dualistic moral conception of good and evil denies. He expresses if not hope, then at least a belief that one must not give up the struggle to transcend the limitations of reality as moralists have conceived it. Transcendence of such boundaries, Ekelöf believed, allows one to fully become "oneself." In *Sorgen och stjärnan* (1935; *Grief and Stars*), Ekelöf's third volume of poetry, the poet denies the existence of reality altogether: concepts, institutions, rules, and boundaries are seen as artificial, the mere inventions of persons struggling to impose order on the chaotic and unending struggle between good and evil.

Ekelöf considered *Färjesång* (1941; *Ferry Song*) the culmination of his thought. More intellectual than his previous works, *Ferry Song* in its style shows the influence of Symbolism and Romanticism. Attempting to reconcile the ideal and the real, Ekelöf here examines the natures of both self and reality and questions the validity of our traditional conceptions of them. He concludes that in a world where the forms of reality derive solely from the compulsions of persons caught in the mire of the imprisoning battle between good and evil, "only as a wit-

ness to this struggle does a person exist." Ekelöf then categorizes "witnesses": the innocent, whom good and evil play upon; the moralists, who propagate the dualistic system, taking sides and creating forms and structures to aid their cause; and the uncommitted, who recognize but refuse to participate in the war between good and evil. By withdrawing from the struggle that structures all cultures and societies, however, the uncommitted must pay the price of complete isolation.

Ekelöf's later poetry pursues themes similar to those of his earlier works, but in a rather different style and manner. In many of these works, there is an absurd element and an apparent attempt to shear his work of all but the most necessary words and images. On numerous occasions, Ekelöf himself denied that such works were even poetry. Critics nevertheless address them as such. The most renowned examples of this phase of Ekelöf's writing are *Dīwān över Fursten av Emgión* (1965; *Divan of the Prince of Emgión*), *Sagan om Fatumeh* (1966; *The Story of Fatumeh*), and *Vägvisare till underjorden* (1967; *Guide to the Underworld*).

Critics describe Ekelöf as a profound thinker and praise his ability to incorporate diverse influences into a coherent pattern of thought. Some also marvel that he remained, in spite of these influences, a distinctly Swedish poet in that the landscapes and aura of his native country haunt most of his work.

Ekelöf's poetry is described as innovative in form and technique, especially in its adaptation of musical forms to verse. His poetry, some feel, will have a lasting place in the history of modern literature because of its originality and its relevancy to the reader concerned with problems of the modern age.

(See also *Contemporary Authors*, Vols. 25-28, rev. ed. [obituary].)

ERIC LINDEGREN

Gunnar Ekelöf's poetry shows more sudden turns than that of any other poet in the Thirties' group [in Sweden]. In his five books of poems he appears in turn as saboteur, seer, romantic swan, blind beggar and ruminating ferryboat man on the river of death. But his personality is so strong in all these guises that we ought to speak of his different phases in the same sense that we speak of the phases of the moon. His books may also be compared with acts of a play: they develop out of one another in an almost dialectical way, bringing one another into relief, and supporting one another as do the poems of no other modern Swedish writer.

Ekelöf is a late romantic and a modern intellectual with a scepticism so deep that from the Western point of view he can be defined as an anarchistic mystic—one who doubts reality in the Eastern way. In fact, he is influenced by Persian, Indian and Taoist mysticism. At the same time, he is in the highest degree a product of European culture, both classical and modern. . . . The [Swedish] poets he reminds one of most are Stagnelius (in his romantic feeling for life), Almquist (in his mingling of *innocence and arsenic*) and Fröding (in his anti-moralistic thought). He further reminds one of these men in his remarkable gift for form, which shows itself above all in the fact that he is more self-reliant in form than any other living Swedish poet. This in turn is contingent upon his concern with music. Ekelöf does not so much write poems as compose books of poems. His greatest innovation in form is that he applied musical principles and forms in his poems, thereby creating a poetry that is no longer either speech or song, but both. Since music is above all the speech of the feelings, this conception of form has undoubtedly supported and strengthened the romantic tendency in Ekelöf's writing. In this essay I shall make no attempt to establish the exact correspondences between Ekelöf's poetry and the various musical forms underlying it, but only touch upon the way Ekelöf's typical themes are developed, contrasted, modulated—how they shift and change and yet always lead back to the same fundamental experience. (pp. 238-40)

The so-called *culture debate* was in full swing [when Ekelöf's first book of poems, *Late Hour on Earth* (also translated as *Late Arrival on Earth*) was published in 1932]: the bourgeois humanistic culture [of Sweden] was being attacked from three sides—by Marxism, by psychoanalysis, and by what was called primitivism. The voices of the propagandists broke against one another, and in this swarm of high, pugnacious words Ekelöf's *Late Hour on Earth* had the effect of an act of sabotage—long planned in silence and effective. Unlike the propagandists, Ekelöf used the secret approach of the saboteur. His aim was destruction of the "dead forms" in the culture, rather than salvation or proselytizing. At the same time, this book of poems represented the first personal application of the ideas of surrealism on Swedish soil.

Effective destruction rests upon thought and must be preceded by a thorough knowledge of both the objects to be blown up and the explosives to be used. Ekelöf's parodies of "classical masterpieces," executed with both scorn and hidden love, showed deep familiarity with the marbled layers of classicism. The dead marble became a threefold symbol for dead beauty, for what was dead in the culture, and for what was dead in people. The technique itself was partly inspired by surrealism, but it was far from the idea of "uninhibited inspirations" which outlawed any artistic refinement. Yet *Late Hour on Earth* was objective as none of Ekelöf's later books were. Harsh unsentimentality, self-analysis disguised as arrogance which handled the "I" with an impassive scientific tone: "I have sunk from the function of man to the function of the floor rug," indirect satire, psychoanalysis, surrealist methods, atonalism, and cacophony, all fused into a new whole—this was something new. With suicidal ruthlessness, the ego and culture were stripped of all their attractive disguises, of all possibilities of self-defense, and indeed almost of their very reality; what was left behind was a lost child on the shore of a sea where the bullet-ridden stage sets were burning. Personal dignity was sacrificed; exhaustion, disappointment, disgust appeared with naked and indiscreet clarity. . . . (p. 240)

But in the middle of this fragmented, and convincing contemporary chaos, Ekelöf's genuine romantic vein comes to the surface in his hatred of reality and, above all, in his identification with the child. . . . (p. 241)

For the romantic the helplessness of the child was a symbol of man's helplessness in the world of objects. Ekelöf is a potential Neoplatonist: the longing for purity, passionate and resigned, sounds again and again in his poetry. . . .

Two extremes of romanticism are on the one hand the assertion of self, which used to be called demonic but actually is human, and, on the other hand, the effacement of self, which is Christian or platonic—or Indian. The romantic swings easily from the feeling of being chosen to that of being a condemned man, god or leper. In his next book, *Dedication* . . . , which came out in 1934, Ekelöf appeared to some extent as the elect one, the representative of true existence—the dragonfly which flees from the poison of the gray ants, bringing with him a word like the seer. The epigraph of the book, *"I say that one must be a seer, one must make oneself a seer,"* was taken from Rimbaud. . . .

The seer here is neither the man who can gaze into the future nor the avenging prophet of the Old Testament, even though he shares certain features with the latter. Ekelöf's conception of the seer stems more nearly from Baudelaire and French symbolism. (p. 242)

[*Dedication*] was to be Ekelöf's positive proclamation, a half-magical attempt "to sing all death from his life," to save himself. While the surrealists committed only their "unconscious" in their poetry, Ekelöf, in keeping with his fundamentally religious nature, went back to Rimbaud and the symbolists. Not heeding Breton's warning to be cautious, he committed himself wholly to the attempt to arrive at a future "in which eternal oneness shall be ours." Even in Rimbaud the seer theory had taken on ominous accents, a consciousness of the task's unheard-of difficulty and weight; it took only a slight dislocation of his feelings for the seer to become the martyr of his own demands. One can follow this development in Ekelöf's *Dedication,* in which the seer ends as *the martyr in Caesar's orchard,* who ecstatically assents to his own death.

On closer examination, however, the seer theme is complemented in this book by something one might call a Parsifal-motif. What is imagined is not, as in Rimbaud, the demonic genius striving for oneness, the clear-sighted innocent nor the child ripened to an angel who will save the world, but rather:

> I am no human, I am an angel
> who has returned to earth in order to take hold
> of the throat of mankind with my hand!
> Evil has already burned away in me
> And the lie is not a remedy:
> I am too single-minded to cram life with lies!

But the road to single-mindedness is long. It begins with a frightening vision of life on earth as a dead man's dream, or something equally dead and eternal (**"Contra Prudentium"**); it goes on to visions of defeat, to Carl Frederik Hill's shattered kingdom of beauty (**"Fossil Inscription"**), to the **"Elegies"** with their great, though modern and fragmented, romantic voice and their meditations on mankind's eternally frustrated hope. (pp. 244-45)

[Even] the quiet, harmonious light with which the book closes cannot efface the ominous and unsolved conflicts. Yet, if one regards this book of poems in its entirety from the standpoint of its classical beauty (even though that is not the most significant standpoint), it is perhaps Ekelöf's finest volume. Like all proclamations, it is, as proclamation, only partly convincing; as poetry, it is always invocation, search, and struggle for solution. Both poles of Ekelöf's nature are clearly visible: *Late Hour on Earth* was the initial statement; *Dedication* is the reply.

In the first issue of *Caravan*, *(Karavan)*, . . . Ekelöf followed his anarchistic and individualistic line—the strong sense of self. In a highly polemical prose piece entitled **"Under the Dog Star,"** pointed and egocentric, society's frauds and lies and its blind belief in authority were attacked—with justice, certainly, though the mood reminds one of the Persian kings who had the angry and obstructing waters of the Hellespont beaten with chains. Against his picture of the rising flood of death, Ekelöf sets down the first precept in the seer's catechism: "I believe in myself, in the universe that is inside me." And as answer to the slanderers: "Those who doubt cannot judge me. I have faith." Whatever objections one may have to the arrogance or the substance of his piece, one must recognize the courageous consistency of Ekelöf's position. Such consistency can certainly lead to reaction and, at times, to collapse, but, in the best instances, it leads to new life and deepened insight.

For the next issue of *Caravan*, which came out in 1935, Ekelöf wrote a self-examination masked as an analysis of Rimbaud. Rimbaud, the titan of modernism, is seen as defeated, and Ekelöf's tone is entirely changed: Rimbaud wanted too much, his theory of the seer is now called *the great lunatic plan* and the infantile in his nature is underscored. Rimbaud is succeeded as an ideal by [the Swedish poet] Edith Södergran, "when she humbly returned to the tree of her childhood and all the simple inner realities on this side of the great visions." (pp. 245-46)

[In *Grief and Stars* (1936), a] changed mood carried with it a new artistic impulse beyond Södergran toward a more classical romanticism, particularly toward Hölderlin and Ekelund. At the same time, Ekelöf's application of musical principles in the composition of his longer poems reached its peak in such pieces as **"Summer Night," "Dithyramb,"** and **"The Singer's Song."** *Grief and Stars* marks a relaxation after the great tension; the singer sings neither to change himself nor to change the world, but only to be faithful to himself, like "the solitary swan." His courage lies in his belief in the meaningless beauty of song, and his song is a romantic swan song. **"The Singer's** Song" is the key poem of this book: a concealed self-examination and self-assertion which lead toward new avenues. The individualistic self-assertion is seen in a new and larger perspective. . . . (pp. 246-47)

But the will has splintered, the poet is sacrificed to his visions and is no longer their lord; he is what the world calls *sick*. . . . The old theme of the death-dream shifts and takes a more timely form:

> Hate's time has come,
> Murder's time has come
> but earth is slowly ruined
> by the poison of indifference.

This indifference destroys also the person whose entire strength was faith, but who has lost his stars. . . . And out of [the painful loneliness expressed in **"Summer Night"**] a conviction is born that what is deepest in man cannot be communicated to another person. Each soul is a "solitary star;" it is therefore natural and perhaps just that whoever pours himself out shall meet with indifference or hate. . . . (pp. 247-48)

But what faith can no longer create, the destructive lack of faith can. . . .

In the prose-poem called **"The Dream,"** the dissolution of the old Ekelöf idea of reality is made clear. In *Dedication* he had been able to reach reality by stretching out his hand to "lift a stone from the ponderous heart of the world," but in **"The Dream"** the theme of denial of reality is in full swing. . . . (p. 248)

It would be reasonable to assume that it is the intellectual illusions about reality which die [in **"The Dream"**]. However, since the 'dreamed' or mental reality has already completely penetrated the 'outer' reality, his thought becomes intelligible. . . . Only the poem called **"From the Foundry of the Soul"** hints at another insight, and at an alternative to dreams. (pp. 248-49)

Ekelöf's next book of poetry, ***Buy the Blind Man's Poem (Köp den blindes Sång,*** 1938) introduces no new themes, but offers instead a tremendously expressive picture of the romantic's winter, of his frostiness and isolation, and for those who feel that such expressiveness is the greatest value in a poem, the book is as interesting as his earlier ones. The experience of the unreality of life, now a part of Ekelöf's vision, is presented in a ballad tone. . . . The singer and visionary show traces of the shadows of unhappiness; he identifies himself now with the blind beggar whose arm has a warning band in contrast to the distinctive insignia of the seer or the political rebel. He is the man whom everyone slips past and tries to ignore. He stands speechless, waiting until everyone discovers what he has already discovered: that everything is illusion and fraud. . . . (p. 249)

In his next book, ***Ferryman's Song*** (1941; also translated as ***Ferry Song***), one can watch Ekelöf's distrust of reality extend to a distrust of our identity, our "I." ***Ferryman's Song*** is distinguished throughout by the battle within those "who want a purpose." The book is primarily a wrestling with a problem, a radical self-examination, at once more careful and more abstract than his earlier ones. One is reminded immediately of the later Eliot; however, the problem is entirely Ekelöf's own, and it is fascinating to watch how the feeling for life and the demand for truth, working together, drive him step by step along the narrow path of the mystic. At the same time, *Ferryman's Song* sharpens the problem of freedom to its point; its concern is to build the road which leads at once to personal freedom, destruction of dualism, true peace, and to the only true democracy. The key poem, **"Write, Then,"** is dominated entirely by this striking struggle of ideas. With the help of paradoxes, it attempts to wrest from words colored by dualism a meaning *beyond* dualism. The first assumption is the withdrawal from everything that stands within the code of power. . . . (pp. 250-51)

Ekelöf's demand for sacrifice, like all demands, claims a reward. The quietistic strain in Ekelöf arises from his conviction that mankind is only a battleground, "only as a witness does a person exist." (p. 251)

It follows from this that even the important ideas of culture, the positive concept of dualism, are regarded as false ideas, full of anxiety and fantasy, built on a mistaken picture of the "I." . . . [Fear and wishful] thinking together have built up illusion of a self, an I. But "the truth is you are no one. / A field, a piece of clothes, a name— / everything else is merely wishes."

One concept still remains; namely, truth in the sense of freedom from lies. Ekelöf uses this concept, now set free from dualism, as a battering ram, attempting to shake the whole building of dualism. We recognize once more the theme from *Dedication,* but here it is purified of the comparatively naive picture of the "I" which marked that book. (pp. 251-52)

On the whole, **"Write, Then"** indicates the defeat of something which one might call the atavistic romanticism in Ekelöf's work. . . . For this contemporary mystic it is the need for truth rather than the devotion to God which annihilates personality.

What we called the Parsifal-motif in *Dedication* turns up in ["**Write, Then**"] in a reverse form: innocence, which here is not identified with the ego but with life itself, is not that which saves but rather that which is continually sacrificed in the constant play of opposites. . . . (p. 252)

Good and Evil, though not in equal degree, are vampires upon innocence. The idea that instinct must be sacrificed during the continual civil war of moralism, and the dream of and compulsion toward a deeper insight into some plan beyond dualism finally led to the crystallization of three different human types. These are described in the important poem called **"Categories"** (**"Kategorier"**). The innocent and naive, the timid wild "creatures, who have not yet been confronted by the temptation of dualism," belong in the first category. In the second category are the countless moralists, those who always identify themselves with what they believe in, and who commit themselves entirely to the battle of the dragon and the knight, those not indifferent. . . . The third category includes the people who have advanced farthest, namely, those who have passed through the "Judaic law of rationalism." Those who are indifferent, anti-magnetic and odd, "those who try to go out as hostages from the heart, soul and destiny, taking with them only what was undefined and undefinable." In a note to the book, Ekelöf denied that this latter type of person should be thought of as an exclusive pacifist. The third kind of human being sees even ethics as a form of *totalitarian narcotics:* he is free to take a stand (for example, against Nazism) but also free with part of his being to refuse party identification. Simply expressed, one could say that this person is a rebel against the entire war mentality, and his hate and his battle are like heart and destiny—mere hostages.

The problem for this kind of man is, naturally, society. Society becomes for him the consciousness of the loneliness of all others. Men can only meet in reverence for one another's loneliness, based on the realization that all have in common what is best in human nature, that "what is ground in you is ground also in others." The mystic who takes "the inward and lower road" and who never renounces the condition of his freedom is in his way always loyal. . . . (pp. 253-54)

Ekelöf has arrived at this conclusion by accepting himself more fully than before, and by forging his weakness into his strength, in the true manner of the poet. What once stood out as "the hell of indifference" has been defeated and changed into the aristocracy of esoteric detachment. In the same sense, loneliness with its "infinite anguish" has been overcome by abandonment as the only possible form of life. The poet no longer underlines his abnormality; he is neither elect nor deprived— neither seer, blind man, nor clown. He can see himself from without with serenity and with the most unsympathetic eyes as "an absolutely useless person." (p. 254)

Eric Lindegren, "Gunnar Ekelöf—A Contemporary Mystic," translated by Robert Bly, in Odyssey Review *(copyright ©1962 by the Latin American and European Literary Society, Incorporated), Vol. 2, No. 3, September, 1962, pp. 238-56.*

ROBERT BLY

The inward thought of the Orient and the surrealist poetry of France have been [Ekelöf's] deep concerns, and have provided foundations for his own poetry. Yet his poetry is perfectly Swedish. His imagination in **"Trionfo della Morte"** for example reminds one strongly of his younger contemporary, Ingmar Bergman. There is a similar walk on the borders of religion and witchcraft, and inside the work of art visual images that seem to float.

In America, we assume that only a cracker-barrel sort of poetry can be popular. Swedish poets, particularly Ekelöf, do not follow this old rut of thought. Ekelöf is the most difficult Swedish poet, and yet his audience is large. . . . In his poetry there are linked successions of thoughts which are difficult to follow. These thoughts are embodied in high-spirited and colorful language. He is an uncomfortable poet, who tries to make the reader conscious of lies. His work attacks the moralistic personality. He divides all personalities into the innocent, the moralistic, and the uncommitted. The innocent temperament is primitive and intuitive; the uncommitted is the most highly advanced. The moralistic personality, overpowering today in numbers, sees in life only the fight between the dragon and the knight. It does not see the virgin at all. But the virgin who does not participate in the battle is life itself. What is behind and beyond the battle between good and evil is more important than either. As he says, "There exists something that fits nowhere." (pp. 546-47)

Robert Bly, "Translations from Gunnar Ekelöf," in The Hudson Review *(copyright © 1963 by The Hudson Review, Inc.; reprinted by permission), Vol. XV, No. 4, Winter, 1962-63, pp. 546-47.*

LEIF SJÖBERG

[Sjöberg is the principal translator into English of Ekelöf's work and has provided a significant amount of critical commentary on his poetry.]

When Ekelöf's *Färjesång* was published in 1941, it was in some respects a return to the sphere and manner of *Sent på jorden* with its use of thoughts and elements from various sources. This allusion technique has been extended and developed further in *Färjesång* where there are thoughts from Buddhism, Taoism, mystic writers, folklore, and modern rationalism. Partly because of this technique Ekelöf's name was linked with Eliot's. Some critics have attempted to establish Ekelöf's indebtedness to Eliot. . . . It is somewhat embarrassing for some Swedish critics that Ekelöf [himself had to point out the fact that what he has to say is entirely different from what Eliot has to say]. Ekelöf's art of pre-Christian and post-Christian mysticism, i.e., non-Christian, must of necessity differ widely from Eliot's meditations, which are clearly within the bounds of Christian thought, at least from his *Ash-Wednesday* on.

In *Färjesång* Ekelöf presents "a third position, the objective one." The key to this position, I think, can be found in the key poem **"Tag och skriv."** This poem, which consists of five movements, was conceived during the winter of 1938-39 at Hölö, outside Södertälje, where Ekelöf lived in great isolation in what was known as The Yellow Cottage. This was at the beginning of World War II and Finland's winter war, and was, personally, a "very trying time," according to the author. (pp. 307-09)

Through the poem Ekelöf uses antithetical technique. The title can be connected with the first half of the first movement. The second part can then be read as a quick response to the exhortation of the title. Even in the beginning movement, the first of a number of paradoxes is employed: by relinquishing one's self and one's claims one gains power. . . . (p. 314)

In the second movement the speaker rises out of his ashes, and once again hovers. There the "I" has taken the shape of the phoenix, the bird, which according to one version, lived to the age of five hundred years, according to another version to a thousand years or more, and at the end of its life span, built itself a nest of aromatic woods, settled on it, and set fire to it. From the ashes rises a new phoenix. (p. 315)

Although rising from his ashes can be read as "having got a long new life ahead of him, having been revitalised," the following line reads: "about to be engulfed by the formless swell." This indeed implies a deep concern with death: the realization of new life immediately becomes also the realization of death. *From* new life, *toward* a new death he hovers around. While hovering he can enjoy a bird's-eye view, and can take in man's total predicament: Man exists only in his capacity as a witness, an involved spectator, and because of this he has an obligation to record whatever his experience may be.

The rest of the movement does not need much comment. Both man's weakness and strength are subject to powers that are really outside his control. Man is nothing but a battlefield, where the two opposites fight it out. We might come to think of the two forces that Freud saw in human life, viz., the life instinct and the death instinct.

In fact, man is like a wanderer, whom we can meet in the folktale: there is a competition between the sun and the storm about who can take off the wanderer's cloak, either by strong winds, or by extreme heat. Both processes occur simultaneously, i.e., the strength as well as the weakness, which are both coming from the outside, are yoked together, just as the wanderer is beset by two phenomena which appear at the same time, the strong wind and the heat. This parallelism is employed throughout the suite, often as a unity of opposites or extremes.

Together they form the climate of Man's soul: Swedish April—unpredictable, with drastic changes, now hail, now sun.

The next movement deals with the nature of *self*. In the second stanza there is a reference to the competition of the sun and the storm that we have just mentioned: the wanderer may call himself "I" and he may say "it concerns me," but in reality he is no one. The "I" is explained as a projection of phantastic order, generated from fear. Commonplace abstract concepts such as justice, human dignity, freedom of will are seen as mere constructions, features in an ever-expanding system of beliefs in which each new extension will eventually be taken for granted, accepted and assimilated. As is indicated, these beliefs have grown, along evolutionary lines, during man's fruitless attempt to bridge the inescapable dualism of the self. A concept such as salvation constitutes the pyramid of these wishes, but this salvation has no existence except in highly developed human wishful thinking. "In reality you are no one." This statement runs through the whole movement like an echo, and it forms one of the easily recognized ways with which Ekelöf achieves his simple but effective rhythmic pattern that may suggest a Gregorian choir.

The first lines of the fourth movement touch upon the constant struggle between the most fundamental alternatives, these which Hindu religious thinkers called Brahma, the creator, and Shiva, the destroyer, and Freud the life and the death instincts. There is a beautiful truth in the observation: "But he who expects redemption, he is unredeemed. He who wills salvation, he is already damned." In his own development the author has reached above the concern about salvation, by courageously facing the human situation, as it is. He has arrived at a state of independence, so that he can claim: "I do not lie, there is no lying in me." The line has developed like this: I feel there is no lie in me; it is right; I am entitled to my objective contention having neutralized or devalued the "I"; this is how matters stand, i.e., the feeling or the thought-feeling rings true. An easily identified allusion which fits in admirably in the context is the suggestive, calamitous image of the balance, from the Book of Daniel.

While the "I" abandons itself, it is drawn and illuminated by the star of the secret battle, which is unseen and yet has more power than the sun and the moon. It has such paradoxical, opposing features as at the same time being simple and double, obscure and light.

Life is to the author the meeting of contrasts, but it is not one, pure component only, and it is definitely not what we are told in the folktales, that the dragon stands for all the evil and the knight for all that is noble. Nor is it in any way convincing to the poet to hear the talk about the Virgin's hope and trust. The struggle lasts forever—and the one to be sacrificed is neither projections like the knight, nor the dragon, but always the Virgin.

The poem could have ended here, and at one time did; however, in a fifth movement Ekelöf has followed up and further explored the superb poetical image of the Virgin. Her *inner* attributes are anguish and flight, but these are materialized as in a battle scene: the sword of the knight, and the claws of the dragon. Her *external* attributes, the crown, the mantle, and the clutched hands, are also attributes of the battle and as such can perhaps be termed inventions of the same type of wishful thinking as we have learned about in the third movement. (pp. 315-18)

[In] human life two forces are constantly at variance with each other; with our constant need for generalizations we call them good and evil. The continuous struggle between them is what produces the rhythm of life, or, if you please, evolution. The secret balance of these forces is seen by the poet as the Virgin. She can be called Virgin, because she is in no way yoked together with the stereotype opposites that we always are dealing with, i.e., life-death, east-west, good-evil. She is the third totally independent and unconnected point of view. That is why, to our eyes, she seems always to be wavering. She points to an absolute ideal, independence and freedom, far beyond good and evil.

In the last section—contrary to some interpretations—the author is still addressing the Virgin. She is not compared to a marionette but to a doll which is thrown about by children, compliantly resigning herself to the meaningless. Whoever can analyze the components of the combat as a struggle between the two forces, automatically discerns the balance point of the struggle, The Virgin. Whoever focuses on the Virgin (the balance) loses track of her, because she is part and parcel of the combat, and so disappears in the combat.

In the first movement then the poet makes a rational statement about his objectives. In the second he is using his imagination, and incarnates in the shape of a mythical bird, to suggest the mythological age, timelessness or a long-time perspective. If in the second movement the author speaks as an old sage from the mythological past, in the third movement he discusses the nature of the self from an entirely present-day viewpoint. In this view causality dominates, and one could expect little or no room for free will.

The next movement changes to a more lyric prophetic mood. There the poet reveals his own insight and belief, and he analyzes human life as seen in his own tragic predicament.

The concluding movement goes further into analysis of the mechanism of life, and leads to the discovery of its secret balance, The Virgin. In all we have had in this poem an intricate weaving together of statement, dialog, lyric, prophecy, meditation, analysis, and vision, and it all turns upon the question of "the only atonement, the only practical, for all alike," which is obliteration. Our only excuse is contained in a recognition of the fact that our nature conditions us to be greedy for power and to fail to realize that there is a higher type of power, a gentle kind, which fascinates the poet immensely. This power can be obtained only by renunciation of the self and narrow egotistical claims.

As with much of Ekelöf's poetry, if the reader lets the poem speak to him as a whole, the intricacies and details will grow clear, gradually, for beneath the complexity is a fundamental simplicity. (pp. 318-20)

> *Leif Sjöberg, "Gunnar Ekelöf's 'Tag och Skriv': A Reader's Commentary," in* Scandinavian Studies, *Vol. 35, No. 4, November, 1963, pp. 307-24.*

JOHN DEMOS

Ekelöf is a poet of surpassing stature, one of the masters of modern poetry, yet little known in America. [*Selected Poems,* translated by Muriel Rukeyser and Leif Sjöberg, 1967,] contains a wonderful selection of the Swedish poet's work. In it, three themes—time, death, and self—recur. In poem after poem, these themes are explored, expanded, and modified, but seldom is an idea, an image or an attitude repeated, so varied are Ekelöf's feelings and so skillful is his recording of them. His

poems seem grounded in a sub-atomic physics whose laws unfold in a resonance of wild and strange language.

> *John Demos, in a review of "Selected Poems," in* Library Journal *(reprinted from* Library Journal, *July, 1967; published by R. R. Bowker Co. (a Xerox company); copyright © 1967 by Xerox Corporation), Vol. 92, No. 13, July, 1967, p. 2584.*

MURIEL RUKEYSER

To find a new poet who speaks as we speak, who says the things we need to hear, but in another language, is to be filled again, to find the next place. And if he is a world-poet living in our time. And if he brings us a strange music, music of our own thoughts and nights, a sense of light-struck magnificence and of the horrors, of stubborn affirmation; and the filth of cruelty, death, and sexual madness. And if his poems fall into their riches, lyrics, long coherent processions, a kind of theatre, amazing new and sudden lyrics, reaching us in another way, like a new touch on us? This is Gunnar Ekelöf. (p. 5)

Fierce, magnificent music is given to us by Ekelöf, past the building of joy and the imperative which ends [the poem] **"Euphoria."** "He attempts to free himself from the dualistic moral conceptions," says Johannes Edfelt . . . , "and find a 'third' point of view."

If one climbed the hills to the top hills of a watershed and found there a yellow door, not set in a wall but standing free in air; if one could see the further hills and all the streams flowing away on the other side; but set hand to that door, opened it, and walked through, to find all different-colored, differently lit, otherwise, on the far side; that would be something of the change these poems make, that unique resonance of a new and formidable poet. (p. 8)

> *Muriel Rukeyser, in a foreword to* Selected Poems *of Gunnar Ekelöf by Gunnar Ekelöf, translated by Muriel Rukeyser and Leif Sjöberg (copyright © 1967 by Gunnar Ekelöf, Leif Sjöberg, and Muriel Rukeyser; reprinted with the permission of Twayne Publishers, a Division of G. K. Hall & Co., Boston), Twayne, 1967, pp. 5-8.*

LEIF SJÖBERG

It is true that Ekelöf occasionally may appear "absurd" in his later poetry, but to call him "absurd" is inaccurate. He is beyond categorizations of that type. Whether he would approve of the most recent offshoots of the "absurd school" is questionable. Whatever "absurdism" he has is by no means absolute. . . . Disbelief and skepticism are in fact more typical of Ekelöf than mysticism and absurdism. Skepticism requires an observant, analyzing mind, which is precisely what he has at his disposal. With all his outward success, and with all his analytical ability, however, he finds little but meaninglessness around him. (p. 18)

By being interested in fundamentals Ekelöf has had to make some painful reductions, he has had to start from scratch, without any expectations at all. . . . Instead of the superstructures, so typical of our civilization, he has often investigated substructures, basic conditions and concepts. The outcome is rather alarming, at least to those with fixed positions and values. In fact, he does not consider such rigid positions as real possibilities. He must have been struck by the many conflicting elements in his own personality which tended to cancel each other out. The extent to which he has experienced these conflicts has been so great that he has questioned the existence of the self. (p. 19)

As a consequence of [the] conviction [*"there is no I"*] the poet can go further in **"Open It, Write,"** which, according to some critics, can stand even a comparison with the high points in Eliot's reflective poetry. Ekelöf's pre-Christian and post-Christian, i.e. non-Christian, mysticism, however, differs widely from Eliot's meditations. In the third section of this long poem Ekelöf discusses the nature of *self*. The protagonist may call himself "I" and he may say "it concerns me," but in reality he is no one. The "I" is explained as a projection of fantastic order, generated from fear. Commonplace abstract concepts such as justice, human dignity, and freedom of the will are seen as mere constructions, features in an ever expanding system of beliefs in which each new extension will eventually be taken for granted, accepted, and assimilated. A concept such as salvation constitutes the apex of wishes, but this salvation has no existence except in highly developed human wishful thinking. "In reality you are no one." This statement runs through the whole movement like an echo, and it forms one of the easily recognized ways with which the poet achieves his simple but effective rhythmic patterns which may suggest a Gregorian chant.

In the last two movements of **"Open It, Write,"** he expresses the thought that in human life two forces are constantly at variance with each other; with our constant need for generalization we speak of good and evil. The continuous struggle between them is what produces the rhythm of life, or, if you prefer, evolution. The secret balance of these forces is seen by the poet as the virgin. She can be called virgin because she is in no way yoked together with the stereotype opposites that we always deal with, i.e., life-death, east-west, good-evil and so forth. She is the third totally independent and unconnected point of view, and points to an absolute ideal, independence and freedom, far beyond good and evil. This virgin is compared to a doll thrown about by children, compliantly resigning herself to the meaningless. Whoever can analyze the components of the combat as a struggle between the two forces, automatically discerns the balance point of the struggle, the virgin. Whoever focuses on the virgin (the balance), however, loses track of her, because she is part and parcel of the combat, and so disappears in the combat. Two of Ekelöf's most important concepts are "the virgin" and "nothing."

In Ekelöf's opinion it is thus "useless to sneak behind the cloth of human dignity and the spice-cupboard religion." What then can redeem this life? As seen from his poetry only, the answer seems to be—death. Death has apparently fascinated Ekelöf, since a number of poems deal with this subject. In fact, his first published book, **Sent på jorden** . . . he has himself called a "suicide book," or if you will, "a death book." (pp. 19-20)

[The volume **Färjesång**], which Ekelöf himself considers his real break-through, ends with **"Euphoria,"** presenting a sensation of almost ecstatic well-being experienced before a long one-way voyage. The poet appears thoroughly prepared for death. He is fearless, calm, almost happy. And in an early part of **En Mölna-elegi** (**A Moelna Elegy**) he recollects some of his relatives, their bad and good deeds in time gone by, as Yeats, Eliot and, later, Robert Lowell, James Wright, and others have done. (p. 21)

[Ekelöf's] brooding about death is no necrophilic endeavor . . . but springs from a synthetic tendency in Ekelöf's philosophy,

namely, that all things interact, that every object, including people and every concept, has a series of complex relations with its neighbors, and interpenetrates them. None of them can be fully understood until they are set in their proper environment, that is, relation to their past. Thus everything is dependent on everything, the lives of the dead ones is in a way relived by the poet, and their lives are his *raison d' être,* and at the same time excuse. This idea has been expressed in somewhat similar terms by him in **"A Dream (real)."**

Paradoxically, Ekelöf attributes to the dead ones even higher qualities than to the living ones. . . . Death nonetheless continues to haunt Ekelöf. Like an ancient Gilgamesh he constantly is frustrated in his ambitions to understand death. . . . (pp. 21-2)

Ekelöf's habit of looking at things as states or processes—perhaps inspired by his reading of ancient Indian literature, which also contains *The Book of the Great Decease*—makes it possible for him to embrace virtually everything as one and the same thing, one grand totality. He is no less aware than a scientist like Fred Hoyle that the basic cellular component of a human is no more remarkable in itself than the basic component of a turnip. A dog or a cat is perhaps as miraculous as a human being. This view of his explains how in his writing a tree can talk, and a stone can think. It is unlikely that the poet here has just borrowed ideas from folk tales. (p. 22)

Related to death is sleep, which can yield knowledge about the "inner" personality, "the inner cells." This is the important thing: to be oneself. . . . When he himself wants nothing higher than "to be or become himself," it is obvious that he normally endures great clashes in his personality. . . . [It] is implied in Ekelöf's poetry that *alone* is the only way a person can be himself, and *"individual* man" is the only person he can trust completely. No group or ruling majority, *only* the outsider, the individual, without loyalties, obligations and attachments can be free. (pp. 22-3)

If Ekelöf's staunch emphasis on the individual is founded on a personal need, his assurance "a world is every human being" is founded on his agreement with Stoic philosophers, Swedenborg, and a host of other thinkers. (p. 23)

If the pessimist Ekelöf expresses a considerable amount of dissatisfaction in general, he is dissatisfied in particular with certain aspects of life in the welfare-state. His book of poems, *Non Serviam* (1945)—with obvious references both to the literary tradition of Satan and Joyce's Stephen Dedalus—in effect states in the title poem that he will not serve that in which he does not believe.

A poet of such high sensitivity and deep cultural conscience would evidently be unhappy with many aspects of man's technical development. He reacts against the unnaturalness of the super-civilization which the Western world has created, as compared to a quiet, dignified life in meditation, which he much prefers. He also reacts against boastful talk about progress which often is superficial and no more than our ancestors have been doing all along, without boastful claims. His highly developed sense of cultural coherence and historical perspectives makes him also react against much publicized Western "discoveries" of what is no more than practices and phenomena of long standing in the Eastern world. He dislikes the artificiality, the *Ersatz* so common in our culture and hankers for the simplicity and joy of certain periods, like the baroque period of eighteenth-century Sweden, or Antiquity.

In **"The land of the Freeze"** Ekelöf pours out his criticism of a society which he has tried unsuccessfully to escape from three times during his years as a young man. . . . (pp. 24-5)

Right or wrong, Ekelöf is courageously standing up for his convictions and views. The matter is no doubt of great concern to him, but one may seriously question if he is ever on a par with his best achievements in these poems of love-hate to Sweden, and perhaps especially, Stockholm. (p. 25)

What Ekelöf primarily loves and enjoys is nature, and preferably the somewhat barren, yet idyllic, Lapland scenery. His other major love is the Mediterranean area, including its people, scenery, and culture. He has written numerous miniatures and nature impromptus, thereby joining the finest tradition in Swedish lyrical poetry, including such writers as Fröding, Heidenstam, and Strindberg.

To be sure, serious subjects are the main concern of Ekelöf, but particularly in the later volumes, beginning with *Strountes* (. . . 1955) he can be thoroughly humorous, frequently employing puns in a manner which may remind a reader of Desnos or Joyce. (pp. 26-7)

The course of Ekelöf's development will remain difficult to assess in detail, until the chronology of his work has been straightened out. Tirelessly he elaborates certain themes, as if never satisfied with his solutions. The confusion regarding the chronology has arisen because out of some kind of exaggerated need of honesty, the poet has published "initial drafts" and revised or retouched versions of certain poems in an order which is without doubt very different from the order in which they were written. Ekelöf is in this respect more like Auden than like Yeats. How complicated the situation can be may be ascertained from the fact that *A Moelna Elegy* was a work in progress for some twenty years or more, while sections of the poem were released for publication at various intervals.

Many of the poems published in 1955 and after have a prosy, anti-esthetic character which makes them read like brief essays, but Ekelöf is concerned enough about form to be extremely selective about words and sounds. Somewhat like Philip Larkin, who claims that "content is everything," Ekelöf applies the best of his art to the simple rhythms and cadences of his "statements," to which he attaches the greatest importance. His style appears as unadorned and unaffected as it could usefully be, and precisely for this reason it gets its character of genuineness and honesty as well as humility. It conveys adequately what Ekelöf is aiming at. (p. 27)

Leif Sjöberg, in an introduction to Selected Poems of Gunnar Ekelöf *by Gunnar Ekelöf, translated by Muriel Rukeyser and Leif Sjöberg (copyright © 1967 by Gunnar Ekelöf, Leif Sjöberg, and Muriel Rukeyser; reprinted with the permission of Twayne Publishers, a Division of G. K. Hall & Co., Boston), Twayne, 1967, pp. 13-29.*

ROBERT BLY

Many critics consider Gunnar Ekelöf to be the greatest living Swedish poet. He reached out early in his career to two sources outside the Scandinavian tradition: to the mystical poetry of Persia in particular, and the Orient in general, and to French poetry, especially the surrealist poetry of the late 'twenties. His poetry has deep roots also in Fröding, Almqvist, and the Swedish fairy tales.

In Swedish literature there is a much firmer division between the 'country' and the 'city' writing than there is in America or England. There has been a succession of great writers in Sweden each of whom has taken his place naturally in one of these two groups. Gunnar Ekelöf very clearly belongs to the second group, the writers that are Europeanized, ascetic, intellectual; and he is a supreme example of the greatness possible in that tradition.

Some of Gunnar Ekelöf's poems are made of linked successions of thoughts not easy to follow. We have no poet like him in English or American poetry. The subtle thoughts are embodied in high-spirited and eccentric language. . . . He is an uncomfortable poet; he tries to make the reader conscious of lies and of the unstable and shifty nature of the human ego.

His poems float along like souls above the border between religion and witchcraft.

We find him urging the reader to 'give up power', admonitions like those found in Persian mystics or in the *Tao Te Ching*. And it is clear Ekelöf understands very well the Eastern 'flavor of the infinite'. His poetry is constantly trying to hint to the reader the location of the road toward that transparent state of being the Easterners talk of.

At the same time, curious images slip into Ekelöf's poems from somewhere else. These other images have risen from the heathen Swedish ground, from old Finnish swamps and that part of the Northern unconscious still obsessed by shaman hallucinations, changing of bodies, journeys of souls during trance.

Ekelöf's poems are like a spider web strung between these two enormous trunks. (pp. 7-8)

Robert Bly, in an introduction to Late Arrival on Earth: Selected Poems of Gunnar Ekelöf *by Gunnar Ekelöf, translated by Robert Bly and Christina Paulston (this translation © 1967 Robert Bly), Rapp & Carroll, 1967, pp. 7-8.*

LEIF SJÖBERG

If there has been a major shift in poetic theory during the past two centuries, it has been *from* an emphasis on the external world (around us) *to* the internal, night world (within us). Thus, for a long time the consciousness of man has been the primary target for a vast number of writers and poets. The great many ways in which these consciousnesses are suggested may be illustrated by a brief consideration of three outstanding examples, in the works of James Joyce, T. S. Eliot, and Gunnar Ekelöf. . . . Joyce devoted more than a quarter million words to revealing the complexity involved in the passage of a single, ordinary day, and later, in *Finnegans Wake* (1939), used as many words to dramatize a single night as experienced by a single character. Eliot, on the other hand, limited his discussion of *The Waste Land* to just over four hundred lines. At about the time when Joyce began preparing *Finnegans Wake* for publication, Ekelöf began to write *En Mölna-elegi*. . . . [Ekelöf's] theme was a single, extraordinary moment. This moment of *Lebensstimmung*, this second, comprises images from a number of centuries and from various cultures and religions of the past and the present; it deals with the West as well as the East and with the primitive as well as the sophisticated, and it was "work in progress" for more than twenty years. (p. 9)

Some sensitive English-speaking readers of Ekelöf's poetry are put off, because he is allegedly "strange" or "weird." To use a phrase from *Finnegans Wake,* I think they feel "lost in the bush." In a way this is not surprising. Even in Sweden Ekelöf often had to "educate" his audience and initiate it into the new, before any meaningful form of communication could be established. Consider that Ekelöf "worked" on his audience for a whole lifetime—with sixteen collections of poetry (1932-68), translations of his elective affinities (including such writers as Baudelaire, Rimbaud, Apollinaire, Desnos, Breton, Tzara, Éluard, Whitman, Samuel Butler, Joyce, D. H. Lawrence, Auden, Hölderlin, Petronius, and others), three books of essays, numerous book reviews, articles on art, his participation in the debate on cultural questions, his poetry readings, etc., and you will see that the Swedish audience took its time before it gradually came to realize that Ekelöf often voiced precisely what so many had felt or experienced. In due course he was showered with prizes and literary awards, perhaps mainly as a result of his great appeal to the Swedish poets of the 1940s and the 1950s, whom he has greatly influenced. (pp. 9-10)

Ekelöf's situation in America is bound to be distinctly different, for numerous reasons. But I will venture the guess that had Ekelöf written in English he might have been regarded as one among many primary international influences on the current poetic climate. As things stand, Ekelöf has made modest headway in the English-speaking world. While there are readers of Ekelöf's work who in effect claim that they don't have the "poultriest notions what the forest he all means," I see this as a reason for optimism. Does it not indicate curiosity and awareness about Ekelöf as being unlike any other poet? That Ekelöf wants to reveal but also conceal, *simultaneously?* That in fact he "dives into the soul of the soul" and peers into the "reality behind the reality"? Like Auden's Double Man he was tormented by contrary impulses, which made him human in his fierce quest for independence. The Swedish poet Karl Vennberg summed it up neatly when he said that Ekelöf united "all those opposites that torture and elevate the poetry of our time" and could "take the guise of all those characters that still can entice those willing to risk their lives in the adventures of poetry." (pp. 10-11)

> *Leif Sjöberg, "Instead of a Foreword" (1970), in his* A Reader's Guide to Gunnar Ekelöf's "A Mölna Elegy" *(copyright © 1973 by Twayne Publishers, Inc.; reprinted with the permission of Twayne Publishers, a Division of G. K. Hall & Co., Boston), Twayne, 1973, pp. 9-13.*

VERNON YOUNG

[Ekelöf], the unique poet of his generation, led a self-tormented existence, to which his elegant, impersonal poems rarely furnish a clue. His family background, reminiscent both of Ibsen's *Ghosts* and Strindberg's *The Ghost Sonata,* left him to the mercy—one should perhaps say to the mercilessness—of the private pledge and the dream, to an obdurate alienation from his own culture. "I learned to hate Europe and Christianity," he confessed. By dint of application, he learned to hate a large surface of the inhabited globe, present and past. (This is the authentic, but concealed, virgin spring of the Swedish Middle Way.) Ekelöf's immersion in Oriental languages, from which derived the fabulous poems in [*Selected Poems,* translated by W. H. Auden and Leif Sjöberg, 1971,] was as ambivalent as his other commitments (e.g. his fine translations of French poets whom on principle he otherwise repudiated). . . . Such

wholesale immolation drove him to the border of suicide, in fact and artistically, when, in the Fifties, he fashioned a style of verse so exiguous as to be incommunicable—frozen, calligraphic, touched with obscenity—comparable in its way to the inhibited, self-abusing cinema of Bergman. In this frozen desert he nurtured a snowflush out of which incredibly bloomed the exotic penultimate poems, *Dīwān over the Prince of Emgion* and *The Tale of Fatumeh.* The first of these poems was allegedly inspired by a spiritualistic seance; its composition, begun in Constantinople, was dictated to him, the poet firmly believed, by an unseen medium. Take that or leave it: the *Dīwān* (it means simply a collection of poems) is an astonishing sequence of musical invocations, addressed by an 11th-century noble, captive and blinded, to a goddess, part-Madonna, part Earth-mother. (Ultimately, I am convinced, it is a parable of the tortured artist. "To be blinded sharpens the vision / Till all is light / the light of memory.") The other poem, likewise narrative-lyrical, which Ekelöf would have us interpret as a symbol of our interpersonal coldness, is told alternately in second-person and monologue form, the latter recited by the pathetic Fatumeh, reduced in her old age to the role of courtesan, after being abandoned by the Prince whose mistress she had been. Quite unlike any Western poems I can remember, these, punctuated by settings as solid and phantasmal as those of Chirico, are spiked with an odor of Eastern irony; their tone is Manichean, their dictation is crystal clear; they contain bizarre images of cruelty, passion and suffering which have a Sufistic resonance and calm. (pp. 671-72)

> *Vernon Young, "Nature and Vision: Or Dubious Antithesis," in* The Hudson Review *(copyright © 1972 by The Hudson Review, Inc.; reprinted by permission), Vol. XXV, No. 4, Winter, 1972-73, pp. 659-74.**

BRITA STENDAHL

One could speculate on Ekelöf's position among contemporary poets if his mother tongue had been English or any other "world-language," but one should then keep in mind the force of another, strangely similar Scandinavian, the Dane, Sören Kierkegaard. In due time Ekelöf will prevail and conquer. He stubbornly returned to the same themes with original imagination utilizing international and intracultural imagery. Much of what he has to say is placed on the sharp edge of paradox. Some music might be lost in translation but some might even be gained, for it is my experience that he is eminently translatable because the meat of his thoughts so often is merely suggested between the lines and in the clash of metaphors.

As a student of Ekelöf's works, it was only natural that I would devour his autobiography [*En självbiografi. Efterlämnade brev och anteckningar*] in search of clues to supposed riddles. I ran through it feverishly in order to get to know him better—but I put away the book with a feeling of disappointment. Upon rereading it I realize that the disappointment had its roots in my greediness for novelty and sensation. There is very little here that Ekelöf has not revealed earlier in his works. He was already transparent. What the book does is stress his sincerity. It is yet another Ekelöf volume bearing witness to his alienation in the modern, superficially structured world and to his familiarity with painful, passionate and basic existence.

It is of course a rich book full of ideas and poetry and as such a useful complement to much of what he has written. For years Ekelöf had contemplated writing some sort of autobiography but never brought it off. This volume is put together by his widow [Ingrid Ekelöf] from a mass of letters and notes that he had collected to that end. . . .

In selecting the material and adding just a few necessary comments, Ingrid Ekelöf has succeeded in giving us the picture of a man who lived according to his works and his words. Her evidence is overwhelming and overwhelmingly moving. For the autobiographical selections add little new—they merely prove the translucent consistency of a great poet. What he sees in retrospect was there from the first.

> Brita Stendahl, in a review of "En självbiografi. Efterlämnade brev och anteckningar," in Books Abroad *(copyright 1973 by the University of Oklahoma Press), Vol. 47, No. 1, Winter, 1973, p. 165.*

ROSS SHIDELER

Dreams are a central motif in the poetry of Gunnar Ekelöf, and throughout his writing he uses images from them to present insights unattainable through reason or conscious thought.

Ekelöf reflects qualities of both French symbolists and Scandinavian nature-lyricists. Rimbaud's famous declaration that the poet must make himself a *voyant,* a seer, affected not only the surrealists, but also led poets such as Ekelöf to explore the darkness within themselves. Ekelöf's fascination with Rimbaud was so profound that he translated a large selection of Rimbaud's prose and poetry and wrote a well-researched introduction for his translations. In this introduction Ekelöf suggests that we see Rimbaud as a sacrifice to the primitive dreams which modern man must retain if he is to stay in touch with his emotional life.

The surrealists also explored dreams, and Ekelöf had a clear affinity for those revolutionary writers living in Paris while he himself was there. Although Ekelöf disavowed much direct influence from the surrealists, some of his major themes parallel their obsession with the "unconscious." A major path to this hidden life, as Rimbaud had revealed, was through dreams. As an escape from oppressive reality, or as a return to the innocence and openness of childhood, dreams opened the doors, for all of the poets in this group, into the borders of a life often more confusing, but more meaningful, than daily conscious experience.

In "Solitude, Death and Dreams," a study of a series of themes in Ekelöf's writing, Bengt Landgren identifies a number of qualities attributed to dreams by Ekelöf. For an alternative to reality, the poet says, "Give me poison to die or dreams to live" (**"apotheosis"**). Dreams also offer a means of reaching some sort of unity with the universe, and they may represent a unique organ of knowledge. . . . This potential for knowledge moves either outward to the universe or inward to the unconscious self.

Ekelöf uses dreams, then, not as a standard fantasy, a harmless castle-building in the air, but as a tool for cutting away the superficial and everyday restrictive aspects of normal perception. Many of his images derive from this usage. Numerous variations on the contrast between everyday reality and dreams are present in Ekelöf's first volume of poetry [*Sent på jorden, Late on Earth*]. For example, the positive illumination offered by a dream in "sleep emptiness and even breathing" reverses to a negative fear caused by the loss of dream in the poem **"unrhymed sonnet."** . . . While "sleep emptiness and even breathing" moves from dark to light, from the loss of vision to the regaining of it, **"unrhymed sonnet"** moves from the

loss of dream to death. Landgren discusses a longer poem, **"cosmic sleepwalker,"** which further demonstrates Ekelöf's use of images from dreams. In **"cosmic sleepwalker,"** Landgren notes, the dream motif is linked with water and sea imagery. (pp. 531-32)

Reidar Ekner has also noted the significance of dreams to Ekelöf and discusses a passage from Ekelöf's prose where the narrator has a prenatal dream. Both critics relate these connections between dreams, water and mother figures to Ekelöf's personal experience with psychoanalysis. Ultimately, however, for Ekelöf, the emptiness of the world is broken not by psychoanalysis or by mother figures, but by dreams reflecting an identification with the animistic and organic in nature, with birds or stones, at best with children. . . . Blindness often characterizes Ekelöf's dreamer, whether it is the blindness of stones or the blindness of the Prince in his final trilogy.

In the 1930s, after Ekelöf's first volume, Landgren identifies a period in which Ekelöf, in the tradition of the surrealists, wants to use art as a means of uniting dream and reality. . . . This dream may relate to Rimbaud's ecstatic vision and his wish to create a universal language, but the wish to use art as a universal synthesizer faded for Ekelöf. (p. 532)

As he matured, Ekelöf continued to use the ability of dreams to offer new poetic images in which the unknown nature of the subconscious could be presented. Preoccupied through the war years with death and blindness, the poet tried to come to terms with man's condition. This effort resulted in a poetry often juxtaposing near and far, life and death, dream and reality. Two major poems written during the forties reflect two different ways of looking beyond the limitations of physical reality, yet both poems are inescapably dark and pessimistic. In **"Absentia animi,"** one of the finest poems in the Swedish language, the poet uses word-music to portray the meaninglessness in external reality. The poem suggests how through antithesis and contradiction one can see beyond the immediately visible. . . . [The poem delineates] the almost unique sense of "correspondence" between the depth of the self and the depth of the universe which characterizes Ekelöf's major poetry. For him, the cultivation of the emotional and subconscious aspects of the self is one of the prime functions of poetry. In the long poem **"Voices under the Ground"** the narrator seems to hear a dream dialogue within himself. By listening to the voices, he manages to explore, to experience time and the universe as one great continuous viscous substance.

Ekelöf's unique blend of humility and vision reached its peak in his final three volumes. Nearly every poem could be studied in relation to dream imagery, since the inspiration for the trilogy came from a vision that Ekelöf had during a visit to Istanbul in 1965. Ekelöf had studied Byzantine culture for some time, but his "vision" drew all of his lifelong concerns and energies together. The first volume [*Diwan över fursten av Emigón*] tells the story of the Prince of Emgion, brutally tortured and blinded, then left to wander during the collapse of Byzantium in the eleventh century. The second volume [*Sagan om Fatumeh*] concerns a young girl, Fatumeh, who is sister-mother-lover and guide to the mutilated Prince. The third volume [*Vägvisare till underjorden*] cannot be reduced to a plot, but it appears to be a series of dialogues, primarily between Fatumeh and the Prince.

The poems in all three volumes generally hover on the borders of the unreal, the allegorical and the unconscious. They often refer to dreams, a Shadow or images which suggest things present but invisible, or absent but visible. Occasionally they are quite straightforward. . . . Yet one senses even in [Ekelöf's simple poems] the imagery typical of dreams, the trivial object containing mysterious and significant connotations. Perhaps it is this quality in Ekelöf's poetry, listening to suggestive voices within himself, that has been most influential on modern Swedish literature. (pp. 532-33)

> Ross Shideler, " 'The Glassclear Eye of Dreams' in Twentieth-Century Swedish Poetry," in World Literature Today (copyright 1977 by the University of Oklahoma Press), Vol. 51, No. 4, Autumn, 1977, pp. 530-34.*

LEONARD NATHAN and JAMES LARSON

In both subject and style Ekelöf belongs among those poets we call "modern," that vague but handy term which allows so considerable a variety within a comfortably large category of likeness. Applied to poetic practice, "modern" suggests a deliberate rejection of or radical departure from convention, literary and social. The declared modern author characteristically addressed subjects that disturbed, when they did not offend or scandalize, most nineteenth-century readers, and not because such subjects sometimes violated sexual taboos, but because they would have seemed, by accepted standards, subliterary or, better, unpoetic. Modernist styles would have also seemed calculated to bewilder this same audience, denying them clear, orderly development of ideas, familiar cadences, and a common stock of allusion. (p. 6)

One of the marks of modernism is that it so easily crossed borders to create a sort of higher European intellectual culture to ward off what passed for barbarity. As a culture of opposition, European modernism drew much of its impetus from its adversary passion: the adversary—the *new* barbarism—was the middle-class society whose cultural strongholds were the established schools, academies, and museums; it is no surprise that these institutions, as well as the kind of art and literature they fostered, were the most visible targets of modernist mockery and outrage. Yet is it not ironic or paradoxical that many modernists, Pound and Eliot for example, summoned to their aid as witness and weapon cultural tradition itself, by which they meant not the debased nineteenth-century version but, depending on the writer, medieval Christianity, pre-Christian Greece, pre-Classical Greece, various primitive cultures, Hindu India, Confucian China, various combinations of these, and so on—that is, any period or culture remote enough in time and space to be safely idealized and held up as a shaming contrast to the current one, which they professed to despise and dread exactly because it lacked the attributes of real culture: true community, true faith, true taste, and other such elusive qualities, that modernists seemed able to find anywhere but in the present world.

If this description holds, Gunnar Ekelöf is surely a modernist. His subjects often violate traditional decorum, his style is determinedly eccentric, his lore frequently uncommon, at times exotic, and the feelings his poems are meant to elicit often display the gloom of someone facing a congenitally meaningless condition, a sort of cosmic barbarism. . . . [His] sometimes savage attacks on his homeland were launched in the name of some ideal culture or other, sometimes primitive; sometimes pre-modern; but always the target was the new barbarism, product of a vulgar, tasteless, rootless, dehumanizing mentality. This of course is a familiar target to the readers, say, of Eliot or Pound. And it is in the company of such that

Ekelöf belongs, another scarred warrior in the great cultural wars of this century. For him, the local or Swedish form of modern barbarism was the bureaucracy of the welfare state, the subject of some of his bitterest poems.

Having as it were put the poet in place, we must now qualify a little. For Ekelöf was also more (or happily, less) than a member in good standing of the European modernist culture. He was also very much a Swedish poet. If he writes sometimes of other landscapes—real or imagined—his native ones are always there in the background, at least as implicit contrast. And often he walks his readers through countrysides he knew by heart or makes them see through his exacting eyes the dreary and sterile spread of Stockholm. Nor did he have to cross the water or read Eliot to discover the pessimism that pervades so much modern literature. That has been a Swedish property since at least the time of the sagas. Melancholy is a nordic inheritance like long winters, to which it is probably connected.

Where Ekelöf shows himself most to be the poet of continental culture is in his style. Many of his poems share the surface obscurity associated with modernist literature. For all our experience with poets like Eliot, this obscurity is the thing most apt to deflect the contemporary reader's appreciation of Ekelöf. Yet Ekelöf's obscurity, like Eliot's, is less often an inherent property of the poetry than the result of an uncertainty concerning the poet's purpose. (pp. 6-8)

The power of [the poem "**Dordogne**" for example,] derives from a combination of particularly modernistic effects: stark, hauntingly fragmented details in violent juxtaposition, a development that keeps the reader slightly disoriented until almost the last lines, and the voice of the speaker—strangely detached, almost prophetic, but of a prophet whose utterance reflects the near unintelligibility of what he sees and whose revelation is full of dark surprises. All these effects are associated with modernist poetry. We have only to think of *The Waste Land* for example, even, as in "What the Thunder Said," for the practice of withholding punctuation to give the illusion of continuity of voice, the prophetic voice, almost hypnotically chanting its enigmatic revelation. "**Dordogne**" exploits these means not simply to conceal some otherwise available or obvious "truth" from the reader, but, in line with modernist aesthetics, to compel the reader to break beyond conventional perceptions and customary relations, in both poetry and ordinary experience. The view communicated in "**Dordogne**" is, after all, not far from Darwinian (Herbert Spencer's Darwin anyway); but it is more complex than that, than "nature red in tooth and claw." Ekelöf attempts to make us experience the quality of the primal chain of existence at the heart of all animal life, and, in the process, to make us perceive its almost ritual harmony, however brutal and pathetic from our point of view. It is thus he can call death and the dream or memory of eternal hunt and flight an Eden. The function of that paradoxical assertion, that violation of normal expectation, is to force us to see the subject anew. We are not to damn this Eden or, for that matter, admire it, only to *see* it, and thus see our own state as fallen from an essential understanding, the "secret" of those anciently interred under the mountain. (pp. 12-13)

["**Dordogne**"] also has an important link with an older tradition, that of the poetic quest, to which belong the *Odyssey* and *The Divine Comedy*, those poems that propose a journey or voyage to attain some truth or all-explaining experience. "**Dordogne**," a lyric quest, is built to a smaller scale and, therefore, more fittingly bears comparison with less epic adventures, for example Keats's "On First Opening Chapman's Homer" or Yeats's "Sailing to Byzantium."

"**Dordogne**" exhibits most of the stylistic means found in the other poems [in the collection *Songs of Something Else*] and one kind of subject—the paradoxical nature of the human condition—and one kind of voice, a quietly prophetic one that resembles incidentally the voice in more than a few of Rilke's poems. Ekelöf wrote many of this kind. They constitute a recognizable class, but not the only one. There is another fairly sizable group that address the objects of the poet's disgust and the voice in these is that of mockingly icy outrage. "**A Remark on Dedication**" belongs to this class; the first section catalogues the qualities of a resolutely sterile society that has bureaucratized all nature in its own image. . . . The hyperbolic description is a parody of high-toned advertising. Against this depressing vision of modernity, Ekelöf poses a startlingly burlesque counterforce. . . . So the poet, the anarchist poet—enemy of all this lifeless order—brings some hope, collecting, on behalf of the future, "fantasy slops," an ambiguous phrase, suggesting either the literary garbage of such a society or, ironically perhaps, the imaginative possibility given to a poet living in such a society. In either case—whether the poet purifies or transforms—the redemption hardly calls for wild celebration. It is a self-mocking triumph at best—the poet as garbage collector; but that's the way Ekelöf sees these matters. Though his inclination is toward strong opposition, strong contrast—"Life," he says, "is the meeting of contrasts" ("**The Beauty**")—he never gives the preferred side easy victories; more often it is defeated, if not by barbarism, then by time, which is quite enough to do the job.

But Ekelöf was not forever the grim or scornful adversary. Sometimes, as in "**Greece**," he is a poet of praise. The praise there is reserved for a far-off pre-modern world in which worship is accomplished in a whitewashed chapel which is compared to a sheep cote, by implication, the faith of the simple worshippers is compared to the innocent faith of animals. Ekelöf invariably treats animals (though not pets or monsters) with a kind of detached admiration perhaps available only to an urban poet—the geese in "**I heard wild geese**" are emblems of health and clean hope, in "**There are the steps**" thoroughbreds embody qualities—style, we might say—that provide the ultimate grounds for true calm, the calm perhaps of the shy and skittish poet; in "**A reality**" big cart horses are "pious." All these examples suggest that Ekelöf saw such animals as closely related to simple people, both sharing a faith in the earth merely by moving over it in a certain spirit, as if living itself were a kind of creed, though for human beings something more might be needed, a small chapel, say, in which to offer prayers and thanks to higher powers, human as they, as their icons plainly show.

Occasionally, Ekelöf could even find reason to celebrate a less simple condition, as in "**Euphoria**," where, in a beneficent mood, he can survey his own situation as a writer and discover in it a richness and power that make it seem a worthy occupation. (pp. 13-15)

There are among Ekelöf's works poems that can be called philosophical in that they directly engage the great questions: good and evil, reality, identity, time, purpose, and meaning.

Not that these matters are absent in one form or another in most of his poems, but in those like "**Ex Ponto**" and "**Torna Zeffiro**," he obviously struggles to find a language of large poetic statement, beyond what the brief lyric could manage. The strain of the effort is most noticeable perhaps in "**The Gymnosophist**"; here, risking a degree of abstraction that would daunt less daring poets, he almost stutters his way forward. . . . (p. 15)

[Ekelöf] is not really a personal poet; better, he is not a private one. There is no intimate revelation of his own life in the poems. He is not "open" or "naked," as we have come to know those terms. That does not mean his honesty is less harsh than more confessional poets. But when he is personal, talking about himself and/or to some "you," the voice is most often meditative and a little distant, as in the first of the elegies; or he shifts the subject from himself to his relation with his own art. Thus it is fitting that we should finish this discussion by commenting on a poem which Ekelöf declares with the precision of strong metaphor his justification for poetry and, by indirection, for himself. . . . The bird singing in winter [in "**Why do you Sing My Bird**"]—a little reminiscent of Hardy's darkling thrush—is a metaphor for the poet. The poet's song, a form of discontent, paradoxically reconciles, guides, and redeems. The song itself comes out of an inborn sense of decay, and, again paradoxically, is a hunger satisfied only when it consumes nothingness; for song seeks to hold the moment that "vanishes in the empty air." In this poem, contrasts are transformed from pure opposition into elements of a larger whole, the mysterious, all-including power of song itself, a song which exists between and yet contains both decay and silence.

The absence of the period after the last line lets the song itself follow the moment into stillness, so that the poem includes but is terminated by silence. This is Ekelöf's celebration of the power of poetry, and the function of the poet, but it would not be Ekelöf's if it did not celebrate with a muted affirmation; the last lines would hardly serve as the conclusion of a full-throated song of joy. Ekelöf would most likely agree with Auden that the poet must sing

> . . . of human unsuccess
> In a rapture of distress;

That is a modernist way of putting an ancient truth about poets and their work. Ekelöf was surely a modernist working in an ancient art, and when modernism is finally perceived as part of the tradition it often seemed to be struggling to overthrow, he will be read as an heir, not orphan, of that tradition. Then (and maybe this is already happening), his work will be seen not as part of a war against what preceded him (though that will be also true about it), but as having added something to it, as a type of transformation rather than rebellion. The discontent of the bird's song, after all, is only a by-product of its effort to reconcile. (pp. 16-18)

Leonard Nathan and James Larson, in an introduction to Songs of Something Else: Selected Poems of Gunnar Ekelöf *by Gunnar Ekelöf, translated by Leonard Nathan and James Larson (copyright © 1982 by Princeton University Press; excerpts reprinted by permission of Princeton University Press), Princeton University Press, 1982, pp. 3-22.*

Stanley (Lawrence) Elkin

1930-

American novelist and short story writer.

Elkin's purpose in writing, aside from indulging his love of language, is to offer different perspectives on, and new significance to, the unremarkable. He combines conventional and avant-garde elements in his stories to provide a freshness of image, character, and situation, and to demonstrate the value and interdependence of the traditional and the contemporary. His humor shows the often tragicomic nature and effects of obsession.

Elkin's heroes are bachelors and orphans who have sacrificed traditional family and community life for personal success. Though isolated by choice, these men attempt to compensate for their loneliness by substituting the love of crowds for personal relationships. Elkin's heroes are all salesmen in some way, often in transit, searching for fulfillment. Whether the protagonist is the franchiser Ben Flesh, the entrepreneur Leo Feldman, or the radio announcer Dick Gibson, America becomes a vast sales territory where one Holiday Inn is interchangeable with every other. The result is a feeling of being at home everywhere but having no real home anywhere. Success for Elkin's characters can range from James Boswell's wryly humorous determination to be a professional acquaintance of the famous to George Mills's thought-provoking intention to rise above the traditional ordinariness of his forebears and do something well in his lifetime.

Stanley Elkin won the 1983 National Book Critics Circle Award for his novel *George Mills* (1982). Some critics have called it a "breakthrough" book because of its potential for enlarging Elkin's readership. The many writers and reviewers who have admired Elkin throughout his career have expressed satisfaction that he is finally receiving the attention and acclaim he has long deserved.

(See also *CLC*, Vols. 4, 6, 9, 14; *Contemporary Authors*, Vols. 9-12, rev. ed.; *Contemporary Authors New Revision Series*, Vol. 8; *Dictionary of Literary Biography*, Vol. 2; and *Dictionary of Literary Biography Yearbook: 1980*.)

Photograph by Debra Bailin

ROBERT MAURER

Unlike his 18th-century namesake, the hero of this outrageous "modern comedy" [*Boswell*] is as undiscriminating in his admiration of great men as an autograph collector. His fate, he is told as a boy by an eminent psychologist (his first in-the-flesh celebrity), is to be a holder of coats, a sitter at the captain's table, a *persona grata*.

As a professional wrestler in a bout with The Angel of Death, Boswell suddenly realizes that everybody dies, and the knowledge propels him into a parasitic gluttony of the ego, a series of formless monomaniac adventures on a relentless search for VIP's, at whose feet he curls like a worshipful puppy. The world's richest man, history's first international revolutionist, a Nobel Prize-winning anthropologist, an Italian *principessa*— all these and others Boswell pursues even while he knows that the frailties of the great are as huge as the faculties that put them on top of the heap.

All of Boswell's mad frolics amount to very little, despite his inordinate tendency to philosophize, albeit tongue-in-cheekly, on the meaning of his bizarre existence. The novel becomes an over-long single joke, perhaps because most of us having adjusted to both our mediocrity and our approaching death in less frantic (and less interesting) ways than Boswell has, will find it impossible to project ourselves into the spot of a man admittedly so uncommon. "Do others feel their uniqueness as much as I do?" Boswell asks. *No.* "Mine is sometimes staggeringly oppressive." *Agreed.*

If Stanley Elkin ever dives into a subject more worthy of his talents, I hope that I am around to witness the splash. It should be a big one. For even as we detachedly read *Boswell,* it is clear that Elkin writes marvelously well. Humor explodes in bursts. Scenes crackle with gusto and imaginative fertility, and his people pop off the page with overabundant flesh. A book less atypical, more human, and he'll be signing autographs himself.

Robert Maurer, "Shaggy Doggerel," *in* New York Herald Tribune (© I.H.T. Corporation; reprinted by permission), June 21, 1964, p. 16.

MARCUS KLEIN

The fierceness in Stanley Elkin's *Boswell* is actually in some good part borrowed—not from James Boswell but from Saul Bellow. Mr. Elkin's character named Boswell speaks the wheeling, exuberant language of Augie March, and he has Augie March's penchant for metaphysical categories. Like Augie, too, he is submitted to a succession of tutelary "big personalities," and then he ends by asserting his own contrariety. Like Bellow's Henderson, Boswell is gigantic, ready to prove in the flesh the agonies of the spirit. The likenesses are unmistakable. And indeed Boswell—who like James Boswell is a collector of the great—in an instance invites Bellow to his wedding, along with Faulkner and Hemingway. It is a way of paying debts.

But despite dependency, and despite his cute trick in naming a character James Boswell, Elkin does have the talents of obsession. . . . The novel is credibly and cogently about Life and Death, nothing less. Elkin's Boswell goes roving among great men—rich men, geniuses, miracle performers, powers—with high spirits attuned to his despair, in desperate search for immortality. . . . Death is inevitable, but Life is better. The great thing, he decides halfway through, is to get as much as possible for one's death, to have one's history matter; by the time he is done he has discovered that the secret of greatness in life is the active, unreconstructed, insolent ego. There is something question-begging about both discoveries, to be sure, but Boswell in this comedy he plays out is an inventive man on the stretch, and his life is in him. (pp. 761-62)

> Marcus Klein, "Fiction North and South," in The Kenyon Review *(copyright 1964 by Kenyon College), Vol. XXVI, No. 4, Autumn, 1964, pp. 759-63.*

RAYMOND M. OLDERMAN

I don't know if *Searches and Seizures* . . . is Stanley Elkin's best book, but I'll tell you one thing—it's terrific. I feel as if I should write this in capital letters. No. Not capitals, headlines, maybe: READ ALL BOOKS WRITTEN BY STANLEY ELKIN. That's a little pushy; but if you want to learn to embrace multitudes, or construct catalogues of the crazy, lists of the looney, read Elkin. You'll learn to see pimples on the earlobes of the enormous, and to occasionally try and write bad imitations of Elkin just to touch the totem of his vitality. Elkin's works are profound and filled with stuff and ideas and visions and all the stimulations that make a critic want to examine him in depth, but above all he is a first-rate writer, a man of deep, almost Shakespearean compassion for the life of the individual no matter who he/she is, and he has one of the best eyes for detail of anyone writing now. (p. 140)

His books are filled with sustained comic and serious metaphysical flights of rhetorical salesmanship on people, on crayons, on consumer products, on the look of a hairdo, on one man's range of moving experiences, on hard luck, on low places and dirty deals, on high places and "plenty of plentitude." And the extent of his observations is matched by the genuine vigor of his descriptions. His work is filled with lust, with hunger, with hot juices burning his brain to know more, to see more, to live. Can you imagine Walt Whitman, Henry James, William Faulkner, Charles Dickens, and Woody Allen all pitching in?—Elkin is something like that.

Even when he contends with death, when he speculates on the future, when he examines the fuel that drives him, he doesn't think in terms of grand schemes and galactic dreams. He worries about all the details he hasn't seen. . . . Because Elkin's books have grown progressively more involved with wonder and mystery, they have continued, each in different ways, to grapple with death.

What is more important, for now, is to recognize that Elkin's love affair with life—in his novels—does not come out of political naiveté or faddish affirmation. It is wrung from a deep knowledge of human suffering given only to those who see in such detail that they are tortured into frantic searches and seizures. . . . It is hard to embrace a tortuous world. Few authors can look so closely at the texture of America and come away moved but still hungry for more. It is Elkin's great talent that when he sees plastic-motel America—consumer garbage, and piles of plenty, neon lips advertising the look of love, and all the detritus that most of us see and are repelled by—he also sees the human imagination, the human victims, the humans themselves standing somewhere behind the mess we all make. It can break your heart. But Elkin makes us embrace it all. (pp. 140-41)

The balance necessary for so close a look at contemporary life comes, in Elkin's books, from variations on his concept of style. On one level I mean that the energy of his rhetoric is not just manic; it is infectious. . . . In [another] sense, style has something to do with behavior. Everybody in Elkin's world seems to have some movie role in mind, but Elkin reveals these roles to us as a technique actor would reveal them—from accumulated outside detail that finally reaches inside. His best characters are not method actors—they are Olivier not Brando. But, the large supporting casts in his novels are often mediocre actors—types. We are given the set they work on, the costumes, the gestures, the clichés, grimaces, all the accumulated externals that shallow people mistake for inner personality or soul. Then we see them clearly: a mafia man who says softly, "it's Command Performanceville." We know how he looks, the gun under his camel coat, a businessman's look with only the minimum of lip movement. We have him. We've seen him in the movies, on TV—*Mission Impossible*. The Watergate Hearings, maybe. We really do see Elkin's characters everywhere, minor players, mostly letting their roles be thrust on them, never getting beyond the externals they imitate. They are Marcuse's one-dimensional humans, but to Elkin they are playing it the best they can.

On the other hand, Lawrence Olivier can play all the roles, and that is the secret of most of Elkin's manic heroes. They bear down on life by knowing all the roles, from outside in, from jargon to the edge of a breaking heart. Their energy comes from their drive to know all the movies, to shift roles as quickly as possible. They are acquainted with flux—who knows who'll come on stage next?—and they hunger for the challenge, for the knowledge. . . . Elkin's manic stars do, however, need strength. And, I'd like to talk for a moment about the evolution of style and its importance to his manic heroes, beginning with his first novel, *Boswell*. . . . (p. 142)

Boswell is literally a strong man, a weight lifter who turns his energy toward apprenticeship in role-playing. He is the most light-hearted of Elkin's manic heroes, but his range is terrific. He is a voyeur of everybody who plays their roles with gusto and style—the understudy for all the stars. He learns only from the best—"The Great," as he calls them. By the end of the book, the energy of his affirmation is still a strongman's energy. And so his major concern is: where does it end? how does he stop absorbing all the roles and expanding his ego?

Feldman, in *A Bad Man,* solves this problem, and presents the very best of Elkin's manic heroes. He confronts both the plenitude of suffering and the plenitude of strength. It is a moving book. It made me understand two gut level lessons: 1. Add my suffering to the suffering of others and you don't have compassion, you have added suffering. 2. We are not made of glass. I believe this is part of the politics of balance. But, in Elkin's third novel, *The Dick Gibson Show* . . . , the major character, also an apprentice role-player who wants to be the radio announcer with the perfect voice, is no longer troubled by the ego. The problem now is bad news, bad news everywhere. . . . By the end of the book we have been flooded with the bad news of everyday, the sour stomachs of love, the bad breath of the hopeful, the empty venom of the mediocre—all the flotsam and jetsam of misery that echoes from those call-in, late night radio conversation shows. Again Elkin's range in misery is as impressive as his range in strength. But all that grief has its effect. Some balance is lost. Gibson himself hunts for a styleless style, hungering no longer for the extreme that leads to knowledge, but courting the ordinary.

I keep wondering, how tired is Gibson? how tired is Elkin? How long can style overcome misery? Perhaps the answer is encoded in the response of one of the bit players in this book: a man with a perfect memory for detail, a photographic memory, who can literally recite every figure in the carpet of any room he has casually walked through. He learns style from a woman who trains him to be a polished performer. They fall in love. But career and love life are interrupted because he grows very farsighted. Glasses or contact lenses would ruin his style. So he can no longer see the small details—he memorizes mountain ranges, and he keeps his show biz polish. But he loses love—and his audience. *The Dick Gibson Show* ends with the once strong manic hero stopped by detail, seeing suffering everywhere. Perhaps, like the man with the memory, Elkin has seen too far, counted too much on style to bring balance. In any case, the energy in *The Dick Gibson Show* has shifted; the minor characters play their suffering, foolish, ugly roles too well, and perhaps the style of the manic hero has its limits.

That brings us back to *Searches and Seizures.* It is a collection of three very fine novellas, and it presents some new explorations for Elkin. I believe he is examining the former givens of style itself. How is it connected to taste, to behavior, to attitude, and to action? The first story picks up the manic hero once again, *The Bailbondsman,* hungrier than ever for the gusto of knowledge, but tiring. Better than Gibson, but ready to admit, ''I'm called on to make colorful conversation in my trade. Don't think I enjoy it. I'm a serious man; such patter is distasteful to me.'' But he does it well and although tired, he carries on to the end, both touched and touching, keeping the movie in motion. In the second story, Elkin departs somewhat, playing a little Henry James with *The Making of Ashenden.* Here, the hero is a man of exquisite taste on every level. Neither the most ardent leftist could fault his activism, nor could the moneyed-set fault his manners. He has style as balanced as the best of James' beautiful people. But when he meets the woman who is his match, he needs to purify himself of his discreet but nonetheless unvirginic past. So, of course, he goes into a wilderness that turns out to be like a series of art works . . . [and there] he lies down with a bear. Well, the rest is pure Elkin with a different style and the same wonderful embrace of life. Brewster Ashenden is purified, but while Faulkner might have loved the encounter, this is one he could never have written.

In the last novella, *The Condominium,* Elkin gives us another departure, a little bit of a Bellow-type character. I mean there is a little of that angst, a little of that lost diamond, scuffed by a bad old world. Here, style, place, and placidity are examined. . . . I believe Elkin is undergoing some change, and *Searches and Seizures* provides a great deal of provocation to understand his direction in depth. Read Elkin, please; he may come near breaking your heart, but you'll skip around too, right there in your office, on your rug—swinging and swaying right there as if you had hold of Melville's Catskill eagle, who ''can alike dive down into the blackest gorges, and soar out of them again.'' Because, even if you don't soar, you can certainly laugh. And you can wait till later to worry—like the hero of *The Condominium,* flying from the fifteenth floor—about ''the hole I'm going to make when I hit that ground!'' (pp. 142-44)

Raymond M. Olderman, ''The Politics of Vitality,'' in fiction international *(copyright © 1974 by Joe David Bellamy), No. 213, 1974, pp. 140-44.*

DORIS G. BARGEN

All of Elkin's fictions grow from the interaction of the protagonist and his professional role. Professional concerns are the basis upon which the literary structure is built. The fictional structure is not, however, the linear or curvilinear path of the protagonist's career, . . . but rather the cluster of episodes which dramatize the development of the protagonist's character. Plot is secondary. (p. 198)

The hero's occupation is important stylistically as well as structurally. It is common enough for novelists to place stress upon their protagonists' profession, but it is an unusual aspect of Elkin's fiction that the profession is so often one bound up with spoken English. All of Elkin's heroes, whether they are in business or in entertainment, share a passion for speechmaking. They oscillate between rhapsodic and rhetorical speechmaking, i.e., between speeches in which the speaker's love of literary elements, such as metaphoric patterns, becomes almost an end in itself and speeches in which literary devices are employed as a means of persuading the audience. Whenever the obsessed hero finds himself in rhapsodic ecstasy, he reminds himself of his need to communicate with others and thus to preserve himself from the isolation which threatens him. Once, however, he resumes his role as rhetorical speaker, he realizes that his speech, no matter how brilliant or persuasive it seems, is liable to fall upon deaf ears. The circle is completed when he withdraws again into rhapsody chiefly out of despair over his listeners' unresponsiveness. In self-conscious self-expression, he is both actor and audience. His progressive estrangement from the ordinary is mirrored in a linguistic shift from conventional to avant-garde modes of expression.

If Elkin's oscillation ended at the pole of rhapsody, if the circle closed in a kind of solipsism, his fiction would take on the darker tones of a writer like Samuel Beckett, whose comedy verges on tragic despair, but Elkin's heroes do *not* surrender to hopelessness. From the Boswell of his first novel to Ben Flesh in [*The Franchiser*], Elkin's protagonists tend to be stubborn believers in the possibility of communication. Some protagonists do give up the struggle, but most continue to speak and to argue that orphanhood is a fate we need not passively, wordlessly accept. (pp. 199-200)

Operating from a *gesellschaftlich* [modern society] base, Elkin's heroes find substitutes for lost *gemeinschaftlich* [traditional community] values compatible with their way of life. Their lack of roots in an organic community is symbolized by their literal or metaphorical orphanhood. Without families, his heroes are deprived of, or free from, the most important remnant of *Gemeinschaft* in the modern world. Besides this existential premise, their fate is also conditioned by urbane professions. Their life styles are based on a literal or metaphorical salesmanship. Through orphanhood and salesmanship they are marked as typical products of the modern *Gesellschaft*.

Critical of their own identity, they intuitively know what they lack—loving and lasting ties with family and friends. In their vain attempt to recapture values that vanished with the passing of traditional communities, they realize that they are deeply committed to modern society, i.e., to themselves as free individuals. They are, finally, unwilling to deny their orphan-and-salesman identity, difficult as it is.

Elkin's heroes are occupationally typical of modern society. . . . Because they are completely absorbed in their work, in their ambition to enhance their individual will in a mass society, they have lost the shelter of a community. (p. 201)

[In Elkin's novels] the heroes' conflict between *Gemeinschaft* and *Gesellschaft* is reflected by the contrast between their disappointed family life and their professional enthusiasm. Leo Feldman in *A Bad Man* . . . is in search for an absolute freedom of fixed relationships and a realization of his salesmanship. . . . [He] approaches the limits of his strength by having himself imprisoned in order to experience total isolation; he reviews his tense relationships with family, friends, and business partners; he fights the authoritarian power of the prison warden. Unwilling to play any ascribed role, only the role of his self-chosen profession, Feldman is inclined to overturn people's concepts of themselves and of himself by playing games in which roles are changed. . . . [Bad] man Leo sees more harm in the fixed, dull, lifeless, repressive relationships typical of a *Gemeinschaft* than in his competitive, provocative gambling. His salesmanship emphasizes such competition; he acts out his profession neither for profit nor for love but for the excitement of the unexpected, of feeling alive . . . and for the sake of intense communication. [He] repeatedly risks his life but is more conscious of the danger and more self-confident of his survival. (pp. 203-04)

[In *The Dick Gibson Show*] Dick Gibson's goal is pursued in comparative moderation. His broadcaster profession makes his interest in communication as prominent as Leo Feldman's investment in salesmanship. Yet, despite his work in a modern mass medium and his fight against authorities, he is in search of the ordinary, of family and love, perhaps all the more intensely. Paradoxically, radio, for all its modernity, seems to contain a potential for *Gemeinschaft*. Photographs of whole families united in front of the black box symbolize this to Dick Gibson. However, he distrusts the suggestive pictures and is not content with nostalgia. After a long apprenticeship, his discovery of an ideal format—the telephone talk show—finally furnishes him with an unprecedented, direct person-to-person radio contact with an invisible family of man. Radio, by definition a product of *Gesellschaft*, offers a satisfactory modern alterative to the conventional family. With his strong inclination toward the values of a *Gemeinscahft*, Dick Gibson, more than Leo Feldman, is prone to submit to the magic he is occasionally threatened by in his professional role—which in turn determines his identity. Like Leo Feldman, however, he consciously reveals the magic as a hoax. The two heroes resemble

each other most in their respect for communication and their implicit and explicit belief in a family of man.

The three heroes of *Searches and Seizures* . . . exceed Feldman's dangerous trial of his *gesellschaftlich* behavior and Dick Gibson's more moderate vision of his public and private responsibility. They seek the extravagant and the fantastic. In the novellas, the pulls of *Gemeinschaft* and *Gesellschaft* amount to almost superhuman, stylized polar forces. Archetypal phenomena seem to loom beneath the surface of modern society. In this decadent civilization, the bailbondsman, capitalist, and intellectual each discover that they must play the roles that are expected of them. Rebelling, Alexander Main goes on a man hunt; Brewster Ashenden, instead of marrying a rich dying lady, rapes a bear; and Marshall Preminger chooses death over life at the condominium as the more fitting response to his disappointed dream of *gemeinschaftlich* shelter. (pp. 204-05)

[*The Franchiser*] synthesizes elements from many previous works but comes to a conclusion of its own. Another of Elkin's orphan-salesman heroes, Ben Flesh, surprisingly, is adopted and a profession is ascribed to him. Yet his "family ties" are artificial and his franchiser project is a compromise between *Gemeinschaft* and *Gesellschaft*. From the beginning of his Finsberg heritage, his professional career is determined, his salesman's freedom limited by family responsibility. The family of man Dick Gibson strives for and eventually achieves with the finding of the ideal radio format, Ben Flesh inherits. Through the Finsbergs and the franchises, the brotherhood of man and the homogenization of America seem accomplished. When the energy crisis strikes, however, Ben realizes that his project, his American dream, had been doomed from the start. His adoption had only been a first symptom. Although he lovingly fulfills his obligations to the dying Finsberg family by selling his franchises, he knows that he is, ultimately, alone with his true orphanhood and the [multiple sclerosis] that is his very own energy crisis. Yet he does not—like Marshall Preminger—commit suicide when he is deprived of the hope for human shelter. He prepares for death by investing—independently—in yet another franchise, the Travel Inn. A monument to his changed life and a final symbol of *Gesellschaft*, it sells shelter to the homeless traveler.

The franchiser, more than any other hero, has witnessed his realization of family and also its tragic disappearance. He is thrown back upon his orphanhood—the proper symbolic role for a *Gesellschaft*. Although his experiment with the ideals of a community has failed, he continues the search for these ideals within society, where they appear on a transformed scale. . . . [The] spirit of *Gemeinschaft* does indeed continue to survive even in the most modern of societies. For Elkin to have realized this at a time when numerous novelists have chosen rather to cry out bitterly against an allegedly absurd universe, is a remarkable achievement.

The specific nature of this achievement becomes even clearer when one realizes tt Elkin has staked out a claim to an aspect of modern society which most writers have shunned in horror: popular and consumer culture. While subject matter and style of the Metafictionist have become increasingly elitist and esoteric, while Black Humorists are so emotionally involved in popular and consumer culture that they oscillate between loathing and adoration, Elkin has managed to occupy a middle ground between disdainfully ignoring and uncritically celebrating the contemporary commonplace. Like recent painters working with the visual environment of popular culture—comic books, advertisements, films, newspapers and magazines—

Elkin has exploited and illuminated the imaginative potential of institutions like Howard Johnson's and Holiday Inn. In his Whitmanesque catalogues of popular culture and its artifacts, he has achieved a poetic effect and discovered symbols appropriate to the age. By attaching aesthetic significance to phenomena which have been either scorned as subculture or mass culture or exalted as "the *real* America," Elkin has challenged contemporary clichés. (pp. 205-06)

> *Doris G. Bargen, in her* The Fiction of Stanley Elkin *(© Verlag Peter D. Lang GmbH, Frankfurt am Main 1980; a revision of a dissertation presented at the Universität Tübingen in 1978), Lang, 1979, 338 p.*

JOEL CONARROE

The heroes (or antiheroes) of Stanley Elkin's novels have Anglo-Saxon names like Dick Gibson, James Boswell, and George Mills, but once they start to talk any traces of British reserve disappear. And how they love to talk! Once an Elkin character starts a spiel, in fact, there is no stopping him. Not that anyone would want to—the monologues, even those of the shaggy-dog variety, are ebullient, funny, and filled with insights about the sad intricacy of things in this "griefhouse" we inhabit.

Who is this compulsive storyteller, this Niagara of words? If you are not yet acquainted with him you are certainly not alone—Elkin has always been a writer's writer, admired by his fellow craftsmen but undiscovered, for the most part, by a wider public. This obscurity persists even though he has been steadily turning out stories and novels for 25 years. . . . Blending farce and pathos, comedy and disintegration, he contrives, in book after book, to pluck laughter from despair. And he does so in some of the richest prose being written today. . . .

[The true hero of *George Mills*] is the English language. This is virtuoso writing, replete with verbal pyrotechnics, literary parodies and allusions, puns, calculated anachronisms, epic catalogues, and images as gorgeous as they are unexpected. When Elkin chose fiction as his medium the world lost a robust lyric poet; his language is fresh, quirky, original; his powers of invention seemingly inexhaustible. For all its air of improvisation, the book is *written,* and readers will want to move slowly through its more than 500 pages, savoring every rhetorical flourish.

A master of comic effects, Elkin is also our laureate of lamentation. Among the dominant motifs in his new book—as in the earlier work—are pain, isolation, missed opportunities, and the fear of death. "No one loved me enough, and I never had all the shrimp I could eat." The speaker, who typically undercuts her complaint with an ironic jest, is Judith Grazer, dying of cancer in a Mexican laetrile clinic. Elkin's female characters tend to be shadowy, but Judith is a complex woman who meets her fate in a moving manner. The Mexican scenes, written with dark humor, are terrifying. One senses that Elkin has stared death in the eye and somehow found a language to annotate the encounter.

Judith's chauffeur-confidant is George Mills, a man whose veins run with blue-collar blood, whose fate it is to be second fiddle, one of nature's born shipping clerks. Unlike those who inherit royal prerogatives, a millennium of Millses find themselves cursed to servitude, unable to break free of their class. In a dazzling opening chapter we meet the founder of the line, a stable boy who accompanies "a sissy sir" on a hilarious pilgrimage. We encounter other historical Georges along the

way, but the book's central character, the 42nd incarnation, is our contemporary, a St. Louis Everyman. George Mills, who takes what comes and who learns to live with what grace he has, should become a household name—at least in households with books—in the tradition of Sancho Panza, Leopold Bloom, and Rabbit Angstrom.

I will not attempt a synopsis of George's peregrinations in this thickly textured work. Let me simply say there is enough narrative invention here for several novels, and that the book, which takes place over a thousand-year period and in a number of settings, can be approached in several ways. Among other things, it resembles a collection of stories, the chapters having their own beginnings, middles, and ends. (pp. 1, 11)

[His novel] is much more than a compendium of delectable phrases and cultural trivia. Elkin brings news . . . of fathers and sons, mothers and daughters, of envy, poverty, love, bereavement, and fear, of the logistics of power and servitude, of faith and grace. The work, his strongest yet, will certainly evoke some smiles of recognition, and it will break some hearts too. It is the sort of rare novel one wants to read over and over. . . .

[Elkin] is one of our essential voices, and he deserves the widest possible audience. In a press release, his publishers suggest that *George Mills* may finally be his "breakthrough" book and liken it to *The World According to Garp.* The comparison doesn't do Elkin justice. He belongs in the company not of John Irving but of our great serious comedians, of Singer and Roth and Bellow. He's that good. (p. 11)

> *Joel Conarroe, "Stanley Elkin's St. Louis Everyman," in* Book World—The Washington Post *(©1982, The Washington Post), October 10, 1982, pp. 1, 11.*

CARYN JAMES

Stanley Elkin once described his literary taste as delicatessen rather than haute cuisine. "It's that yen for the salami sandwich at the gourmet dinner . . . it is for the disheveled, what the cat dragged in, the rumpled in spirit," he wrote. . . .

Elkin's taste, of course, is not as lowbrow as he claims. His greatest strength is the ability to combine high art and pop culture without shortchanging either one. His frequent subject is the regular guy with an all-American dream of making it big, but his sentences are often convoluted enough to give a Jamesian pause. This density of language may have kept Elkin off the best-seller list, but his natural audience is the one that appreciates John Irving and Kurt Vonnegut.

George Mills is not his most affecting book, and certainly not his funniest, but it is quintessential Elkin in style and substance. His five previous novels and two story collections not only capture Middle America; they embrace it. . . . Elkin deflates intellectual pretensions by recognizing that most people are perfectly comfortable in a fast-food world.

The Living End, Elkin's last novel, sets us up for *George Mills.* God puts in an appearance, and even he turns out to be a regular guy—part storyteller, part stand-up comic, part practical joker. *George Mills* takes this idea even further: it is about 1000 years of guys who are so ordinary they hand it down from father to son as a family tradition. From the first George Mills, servant to a nobleman during the Crusades, to the last, a working stiff in contemporary St. Louis, these are men who live under the curse of their "blue collar blood," pass on to their sons the story of this heritage, and always seem to be the butts of God's practical jokes.

Elkin focuses on the contemporary George and his upper-middle-class nobles and masters, intercutting George's story and the tales he has been raised on: those of his "Greatest Grandfather," of his own father, and of the 19th century English ancestor who landed in a Turkish harem. The novel is intricate, full of flashbacks, imagined conversations, and remembered family legends; it is also labored, brilliant in parts, and cumbersome as a whole. The historical sections often strain for laughs . . . ; Elkin's real gift is for depicting the plastic-coated world of today. Overall, this work is less humorous than most of Elkin's, for the Millses are obsessed with their fated family history, and their curse of ordinariness denies them the vitality and even the aspirations of Dick Gibson and Ben Flesh.

> *Caryn James, "Stanley Elkin's Deli Delight" (re-printed by permission of* The Village Voice *and the author; copyright © News Group Publications, Inc., 1982), in* The Village Voice, *Vol. XXVII, No. 43, October 26, 1982, p. 52.*

FRANCES TALIAFERRO

The short and simple annals of the poor have often been the starting point for Stanley Elkin's wild, raunchy imagination. *George Mills* is no exception, but Elkin strains the rather plotless framework of the novel by interpolating two long chapters that tell the stories of two historical George Millses: the first, who accompanies his noble master on the First Crusade and does some time in a Polish salt mine; and the forty-third, who (by chance) makes the acquaintance of King George IV and is sent on a diplomatic mission to Constantinople, where he happens into becoming a janissary and lives in a state of arrested horniness in the harem of Yildiz Palace. These two sections are not historical pastiche but contemporary Elkin, whether George Mills I is talking to his horse in the salt mine or George Mills XLIII is being fed a kosher lunch by the British ambassador to Constantinople. Both historical chapters stand well enough on their own to qualify as short stories, but as structural elements of the novel they seem as arbitrary and anomalous as flying buttresses tacked onto a split-level house.

Theoretically, the reader ought to care about George Mills: it's seldom enough that popular fiction turns to the working classes, and we ought to enjoy the opportunity for sympathy with the proles. In fact, Elkin spends his best energy not on his central character but on his digressions; George Mills, bland but observant, is a kind of Everyman-cum-Candide who visits whatever venue tickles his author's fancy. As a result, this overgrown, unpruned novel includes memorable, if erratic, sections on spiritualism and astral projection, King George IV's obsession with mother's milk, the protocol of the Ottoman court and of the American dance hall on Saturday night, the mores of the Mexican cancer clinic, and the dormitory-brothel of a medieval Polish salt mine.

Elkin's black humor generates some wicked portraits and throwaway scenes that would sustain another novelist for weeks. . . . (pp. 74-5)

Elkin has a special fondness for freaks, outsiders, and cheerful brutes; he is not without tenderness for the human condition, but even when he is being delicate he is grubbier, randier, more outré than most—a poet of orifices, a bathroom rhapsode. Readers of other Elkin novels will not be surprised to find that one of the most brilliant passages in *George Mills* describes

how the world looks . . . when you've just had handfuls of horse dung shoved in your face.

George Mills is Stanley Elkin's ninth work of fiction. It is billed as his "breakthrough novel"—which may be a reference to the amount of time and territory it covers, though it is less outrageous than *The Making of Ashenden*, the amazing novella in which a man makes believable love to a Kamchatkan brown bear, and less humane than *The Dick Gibson Show*, whose hero wends his picaresque way through the radio stations of America in search of his identity. No one should expect a serious novelist—especially a madly inventive one like Stanley Elkin—to keep writing the same book, but *George Mills* is so often rambling and tiresome that the reader thinks wistfully of earlier, pre-"breakthrough" novels by this eccentric virtuoso. (p. 75)

> *Frances Taliaferro, "Lyricist of the Lunch Pail," in* Harper's *(copyright © 1982 by Harper's Magazine; all rights reserved; reprinted from the November, 1982 issue by special permission), Vol. 265, No. 1590, November, 1982, pp. 74-5.*

THOMAS LE CLAIR

"George Mills" is a character and condition—"blue-collar blood"—beginning with an eleventh-century English stable boy pressed into the Crusades, reappearing in the early nineteenth century when George IV sends George Mills the forty-third as courier to a Turkish sultan, and ending, the line now defunct, with a middle-aged St. Louis furniture mover who, like the George Millses before him, listens to the hardships of the rich and searches for an audience to tell "the sad intricacy of things," all the protocols and sorrows his blood knows.

"Because I never found my audience"—that's the reason Stanley Elkin's God in *The Living End* gives for destroying the world. Ironically, this 1979 fable of an artist's final revenge became Elkin's most widely read work, bringing his other (and often better) novels back into print. Now in *George Mills* Elkin has written—like his extravagant God, like a whole P.E.N. of gods—his most ambitious and best novel, but I'm afraid its wealth of tale-tellers and listeners, all squeezing their exchanges for some D.N.A. of voiceprint, may overwhelm an audience not already confirmed in Elkin excess.

All the world as occasion for words, situations devised to circumstance and celebrate the tongue: it's an ample notion, broad and generous and passionate but more hazardous for fiction than Tinker Creek for travel or jails for journalism, a method that has let Elkin's books fall through the crack of reputation between realists (Bellow, say) for whom words serve the world and experimentalists (say Barth) whose words construct a world. Perhaps not *George Mills*, for here Elkin cinches the circle of his practice tight: the energy and precision of his language make real, even necessary and instructive, its odd occasions.

The "range of the strange," as an earlier Elkin character put it, is unusual in this novel, even for Elkin: wholly fabricated and persuasive tales of medieval salt mines, Janissaries, and eunuchs, a blacksmith's bad luck in small-town Vermont, Astral Projection in Cassadaga, Florida, and in the book's present a travelogue of Mexican laetrile cures and a choreographed funeral. Performances nested in performances, the stories are frames and analogs for the final George Mills, childless at fifty-one, living with a bad back and a dumb wife in a white backwater of South St. Louis yet convinced he is "saved," not by religion but by his certainty that nothing will ever be expected of him. (p. 37)

The St. Louis that envelops George Mills is daytime TV, the domestic melodrama of upscale sex and moneyed disasters. The lives are imposed on Mills by a minor novelist named Cornell Messenger whose costume-jewelry salesman father, like Elkin's, "compelled his arias," made him feel "obliged to take the stand from the time he had first learned to talk, there to sing, turn state's evidence, endlessly offer testimony, information, confession, proofs." Between Messenger's gossip and his own remembered adventure, two kinds of experience and perhaps two kinds of contemporary fiction, George Mills steers with humane resources to his conclusion, rather haplessly stated, that the point of life is "to live long enough to find something out or to do something well." George Mills is no artist, but his novel is high art, transformed like all of Elkin's books and sentences from the merely curious and sunken ordinary.

Elkin invents emotion. He sets up for wit and delivers instead some of the most moving scenes in contemporary fiction. They cannot be retold, but the means are no less than Faulknerian: the oral posing of alternatives, suspending resolution, spreading language to every corner of possibility, more suspension—then the brief, clean release of feeling. Still America's magnifico of metaphor, as well as alliteration, Elkin also remains a very funny man, adept at crazed monologue, goofy dialogue, and the exhaustive series. In *George Mills,* though, Elkin has powered his routines beyond comedy and beyond pathos to the emotional clarity that comes when the writer no longer worries about amusing and prompting his audience.

"George Mills" is a name for compromise. The novel does not. *George Mills* is a wonderful, grief-ridden, resisting, and finally—for Elkin—a pure book. (pp. 37-8)

*Thomas Le Clair, in a review of "George Mills,"
in* The New Republic *(reprinted by permission of*
The New Republic; © *1982 The New Republic, Inc.),
Vol. 187, No. 3545, December 27, 1982, pp. 37-8.*

Leslie Epstein

1938-

American novelist, short story writer, and essayist.

Epstein is a promising new writer whose fiction ranges from the farcical Russian spy spoof *P. D. Kimerakov* (1975) to the historical novel *King of the Jews* (1979). This latter, based on the Jewish experiences within the Polish ghetto of Lodz during World War II, examines the moral dilemma faced by the leader of the doomed population in his efforts to deal with the Nazi terror. Critics are divided in their estimation of the novel's place in Holocaust literature. While some critics have expressed admiration for Epstein's willingness to write about such a painful subject, others feel that his persistent use of satire creates an impression that he is trivializing the horrors of that time. Epstein has also drawn strong disapproval for failing to censure the Germans.

Epstein's recent novel, *Regina* (1982), deals with the spiritual crisis of a middle-aged Jewish woman. Regina resolves to free herself from those things and people that have restricted her growth in the past. In doing so, she finds herself and the solution to many of her problems.

(See also *Contemporary Authors*, Vols. 73-76.)

ANNE MARIE STAMFORD

If you can imagine a Woody Allen movie with the screenplay by Kurt Vonnegut, you'll have a good idea of what [*P. D. Kimerakov*] is like. Unfortunately for us, Mr. Epstein lacks the Vonnegut wit and the spontaneity of Woody Allen to pull it off.

It seems to me that Mr. Epstein has written a spoof on all the Russian spoofs of the sixties (pre-detente era). Pavel Donatovitch Kimerakov, "our hero," is a Russian scientist who is doing secret research on the aging problem that is afflicting Russian astronauts in space. He is sent to America for a gerontologists' convention. . . . Russian and American agents pop in and out in a myriad of unlikely guises, and some very funny slapstick scenes result. The problem is that these little comedy gems are buried in pages of interminable descriptions, such as two pages on a spider spinning a web, which reminded me of a physics textbook.

The book is narrated by an insidious Russian, who is never really fully identified. He constantly extols the virtues of Communism and spouts Russian wisdom, such as "A pig wearing trousers will roll in the mud." The narrator is good, and he preserves the absurd flavor of the novel, but he jumps around dizzily from one scene to another and at times becomes confusing.

My final verdict on this book is that it is funny, but simply not interesting. It might be enjoyed by adults who delight in a really nonsensical farce.

Anne Marie Stamford, in a review of "P. D. Kimerakov," in Best Sellers *(copyright © 1975 Helen Dwight Reid Educational Foundation), Vol. 35, No. 5, August, 1975, p. 162.*

DAVID BROMWICH

[In **"P. D. Kimerakov"**], a Russian scientist—like Nabokov's Pnin but even more muddled and less adept at concealing the muddle—finds himself drafted for cultural exchange and loses his heart to an American dancing girl who is managed by an improbable, mayhem-loving C.I.A. operative called L. T. Kapp. Hilarity is always ready to score in this sometimes over blown book, and it often sounds forced. This defect may be a sign of Leslie Epstein's honesty; he cannot hide the essential grimness of this particular corner of history, and he knows that pathos will be at war with buffoonery throughout his story. Unfortunately, the result leaves him with a narrative tone that is vague and in-between and not really comprehending. Yet there is an ease and warmth in the telling, and a nice crowding of the plot with minor characters, which make one read on. . . .

Kimerakov's oppressive life at home and his urge to invent models, religions, truths, his tireless and fascinated observation of spiders as they too grow old, his fiercely checked seduction of Larisa—comes through marvelously in the nervy and elegant style Epstein has chosen for it. He imparts a grandeur, not quite expressible, touchingly awkward, to this hero who "walked a bit like a waiter, smoothly, balancing instead of dishes a delicate heart."

The opening scenes in Russia show Epstein at the top of his form. And these are repeated, with something of their original force, near the close of the novel, when Kimerakov discovers his laboratory in disarray and finally is expelled from the Academy of Sciences, U.S.S.R. The American interlude, however—the experience of conversion, which ought to stand at the center of the story—is a disaster.

When in doubt, Epstein resorts to slapstick, though nothing could be less likely to refine his moral. In the background loom various menacing and ill-defined figures; dream and reality overlap, perhaps deliberately, but it is not clear why they should; Kimerakov's encounters with a nameless black prostitute (also C.I.A.?) are especially perplexing. L. T. Kapp for his part comes from a different sort of book, and the game he talks is pure Perelman, as when he parodies Stalin asking the intellectual to sign a confession. Confession of what? ''Your innermost thoughts that I happen to know from reading your mind. Go ahead, put your monicker down. This, by the way, is a real Dunhill pipe.'' Misplaced wit of this order, like its spawn, the harmless whacko violence, derives not from a cunning shift of gears but from an unwitting change of modes.

The narrator of ''**P. D. Kimerakov**'' is an insipid Party functionary: the hack-exhortations are in his mouth but, it would seem, so are the passages in which Epstein assures the reader of his own very considerable lyrical gift. Again, the confusion can hardly be called a fruitful mix—it's a mix-up—though the self-deflating rhetoric can be wonderfully funny in spots, as in a caveat against dreams. . . . Yet one would gladly sacrifice such outbursts for a narrative plan that truly licensed Epstein to deal with the full range of human feeling.

Isolated details in this novel have a deftness and charm of which the whole is unworthy. If only Epstein had let the story carry him where it would, and not decided, as he must have, to make a try at broad comedy under the oddest of handicaps. At all events this first novel should lead to others. Readers who enjoy its opening will be charmed by incidental virtues and forgive the mostly bumpy ride that follows. The echoes of Bellow here are so overt that Epstein can occasionally sound like Herbert Gold; and yet one senses in him what is rare enough at any time: the presence of a sly, appealing, grave and humorous talent that will eventually write its own rules.

David Bromwich, ''Pain Does a Ninotchka,'' in The New York Times Book Review (© 1975 by The New York Times Company; reprinted by permission), August 10, 1975, p. 6.

KATHA POLLITT

If writers got gold stars for the risks they took, Leslie Epstein would get a handful for the title story of this collection of short fiction. ''**The Steinway Quintet**'' belongs to that rare and difficult genre, the story that is in some sense ''about'' large intellectual and philosophical problems. Two gun-waving, pill-popping Puerto Rican J. D.'s break into the Steinway Restaurant on Rivington Street—once a favorite haunt of Sarah Bernhardt and Einstein, but now the lonely relic of a vanished Jewish community—and hold the aged waiters, patrons and members of the restaurant orchestra hostage for a huge ransom and a plane to China.

The setup is almost too convenient for the conflict Epstein wants to illuminate between culture and violence, but as narrated by the pianist Goldkorn, self-proclaimed free-thinker and occasional tippler, ''**The Steinway Quintet**'' manages to be

deft, original and very funny. At once shrewd and wide-eyed, Goldkorn is the perpetual optimist. . . .

Through Goldkorn, Epstein recalls with an affectionate but unsentimental playfulness the passionate intellectuality of the Eastern European Jews. But for Epstein the claims of reason, in which those Jews placed their faith, are of as little avail in the Steinway Restaurant as they were in Hitler's Germany. The puniness of reason in the face of horror becomes comic: ''What is the cause of this fear of death?'' asks one of the customers, a Freudian analyst, as the hoodlums prepare to murder everyone. ''Let us think of it in a rational manner. Is it not in reality the childish fear of losing the penis? Of being cut off from this source of guilty pleasure? Notice how when we recognize the source of our anxiety it at once disappears. Now we feel truly joyful.''

This is nonsense, of course. The truth is a darker but also more powerful talisman. When, for an audience of captives and thugs, the Steinway Quintet plays its last concert, Goldkorn feels himself to be ''no longer the separate citizen, but also a part of that ocean, like a grain of salt, no different from those other grains . . . yes, even—do not be alarmed by what I now say—even the two murderers, for they were a part of that ocean, too. That ocean. That darkness, friends. We know what it is, do we not?'' We do. It is the mystery of our common humanity and mortality, our means of embracing it neither the arid intellect nor the anarchic id, but music—the imagination, the heart.

Epstein has written a witty, moving story with a plot full of ''surprise'' turns, including a miraculous escape for the captives and just possibly for their captors as well. One regrets the more strongly those moments when, as though mistrusting the power of his art as Goldkorn never did that of his music, Epstein becomes self-consciously symbolic. For example, the Steinway could have done without its mural depicting the glories of ancient Greece, and the painfully tendentious conversations occasioned thereby. Surely, too, it is a lapse of taste to have the J. D.'s force their hostages to undress before they are shot, since the only reason for such a pointless request is to evoke in the reader thoughts of the showers at Auschwitz. These thoughts have already arisen quite naturally, however, and the direct pitch smacks of artistic manipulation.

I mention these instances of overstatement not to carp at a fine story, but because they indicate risks which the others do not surmount. Each begins with a complex situation, but is developed according to an overly intellectual schema. . . .

Even the best of these stories, ''**The Disciple of Bacon**,'' about an aging scholar who has wasted his life trying to prove that Mozart was a Jew, is marred by the overly literary gesture of defeat with which it concludes. It's a shame to see so much good writing (the vulnerable wit of the black children, the scholar's memories) marched, under protest, into formulaic oppositions and chicly doomful climaxes. For his next book, let's hope that Epstein takes that apostle of imagination and surprise, Leib Goldkorn, as his muse.

Katha Pollitt, in a review of ''The Steinway Quintet,'' in The New York Times Book Review (© 1976 by The New York Times Company; reprinted by permission), December 12, 1976, p. 7.

RUTH R. WISSE

Leslie Epstein's novel, *King of the Jews*, is loosely based on events in the ghetto of Lodz under the German occupation of World War II. (p. 76)

Although its central character, I. C. Trumpelman, is based on the actual chairman of the Lodz *Judenrat,* and though the book's descriptions of the local conditions derive from documented ghetto history, **King of the Jews** does not attempt a historical interpretation of either the ghetto Elder or of the ghetto itself. The book bears the same relation to the Holocaust as *M*A*S*H* does to the Korean war. Its flat caricatures, cabaret style of narration, and stylized theatrical staging for all the main events of the plot belong to the category of farce. Like other American war farces, Epstein's book isolates the moral *angst* of the situation from the historical conditions in which it originated: from the aggression of totalitarian regimes or, in this case, from the articulated program of genocide. True evil seems not to be a suitable subject for this genre. Thus the Germans, under euphemistic designations, remain outside the ''problem'' of this book, which concentrates on the destruction of the Jews as an internal Jewish matter. To use the kind of fairytale analogy in which Epstein delights, this is like the story of Red Riding Hood, but without the wolf. The wolf's lurking presence is admitted as part of the atmosphere, but the real subject is the credulity of Red Riding Hood, and the nature of her guilt in directing the wolf to granny's door.

The book's main thematic concern is with what the jacket copy calls the "excruciating moral dilemmas" of those charged with executing German orders, and of those not so charged whose initiatives had still to be weighed against the threat of collective reprisal. To dramatize this moral plight of the Jews, the book is studded with relevant debates. . . . There is even a debate . . . on whether children being deported to their death should be lulled with bright dreams or told that ''Oswiecim is the homeland of the Jews.'' Hannah Arendt's thesis of the banal inflexibility of the totalitarian mind during the Holocaust seems to have found its corollary in this presentation of the hyperactive Jewish moral imagination. But the debates, which include many classical ghetto arguments culled from various Holocaust anthologies, are phrased in snappy one-liners that make the ''excruciating moral dilemmas'' of the Jews sound like entries on a multiple-choice exam.

Had the novel engaged any of the issues it raises, it might have risked literary significance, for Epstein is a professional and engaging writer. But instead, the author has approached his subject with the deliberate naiveté of Dennis the Menace, and with a boyish nihilism that reduces the Jewish tragedy to a hollow metaphysical joke. The book's narrator is the key to its small success and larger failure. Presumably a survivor himself, this narrator speaks with touching intimacy about ''our town,'' lingering over familiar landmarks with unforced authority. At the same time, he assumes the currently fashionable pose of the literary impresario, offering his audience a tale he cannot undertake to judge: ''It is possible that everything would have happened just as it did, even if there hadn't been a terrible strike and even if the Elder had never arrived. Ladies and gentlemen, you decide.'' The idea that a ghetto survivor, in the face of his own remembered experience, would be subject to this degree of doubt about its meaning is an unintentional bit of farce at the author's expense. Such temporizing can only be the product of a tender, untried American imagination, masquerading as a ''survivor'' with about the same success as a child dressed up in his father's clothes. (It is also hard to trust a ''survivor'' who makes four mistakes in two quoted lines of Yiddish.)

This novel is narrated by a neutered survivor about a neutered people it calls the Jews. The family, which looms largest in authentic memoirs of the ghetto and is inevitably the source of the most wrenching pain, appears in this novel only in distorted and corrupted form. The book's characters are orphans, or representative types—the rabbi, the rich man, the thief. Lacking intimate bonds with one another, they move atomistically through the novel, arousing little compassion in one another, and even less in the reader. (pp. 76-7)

The Jewish polity is yet more seriously misrepresented. From the chaotic images of Jewish organizational life, one would never guess that the Jews were a people with a long history of communal survival, and that the Jewish political strategy of the ghetto had evolved through many centuries with not inconsequential success. The book's most conspicuous omissions are of Zionism, as both ideal and actuality, and of the secular and religious culture in which the Polish ghettos were steeped. Among Jewish political parties only the Bund and the Communists are mentioned, as though the author had deliberately expunged those elements of Jewish cultural and political life that have survived the Holocaust to give the lie to its finality. (p. 77)

Ruth R. Wisse, ''Fairy Tale,'' in Commentary *(reprinted by permission; all rights reserved), Vol. 67, No. 5, May, 1979, pp. 76-8.*

JANE LARKIN CRAIN

Fictionalizing the experiences of those 160,000 Polish Jews who were first herded into the ghetto of Lodz and later deported to the Nazi death camps, this novel rehearses yet again the question of Jewish ''complicity'' in Hitler's war against the Jews. In mannered and inflated prose, meant to evoke the narrative voice of Eastern European folklore, **King of the Jews** attempts to represent life inside the ghetto in terms that will fairly bristle with moral meanings and ironies. At the heart of this tendentious enterprise is one I. C. Trumpelman, head of the ghetto's Judenrat, a strutting, half-mad, power-hungry tyrant, and his cohorts on the council—venal, self-pitying, spineless Jews who at best passively acquiesce to the destruction of their fellows, and at worst, actively seek their own aggrandizement through betrayal and chicanery.

Masked by the author's stylistic tricksterism, the realities of ghetto life—the hunger, cold, filth, degradation, terror, and death, as well as the fellow-feeling and heroism—take on an air of pseudomytholgy. As one reads this book, it is as if 6,000,000 Jews hadn't really suffered and died at a particular time and place at all, but had merely been conjured up by Leslie Epstein as background for his fanciful exploration of the Eternal Enigma of the Jew.

''There is something in history that makes all men act the same!'' cries one of the characters toward the novel's close, implying that the ''persecuted'' and the ''persecutor'' are as one. Somewhere else, Trumpelman himself exclaims: ''This is what a Jew is. . . . A Jew is a shit like everyone else.'' It is in the service of this sort of vulgar perversity that the author has felt free to trivialize the Nazi Holocaust.

Jane Larkin Crain, in a review of ''King of the Jews,'' in Saturday Review *(© 1979 Saturday Review Magazine Co.; reprinted by permission), Vol. 6, No. 7, March 31, 1979, p. 53.*

NEAL ASCHERSON

The plunge attempted by Leslie Epstein in **King of the Jews** required not merely courage but a degree of self-confidence approaching the suicidal. Epstein has written a novel about the Holocaust, a monumental study of the leader of a *Judenrat*. The scene is the Ghetto of Lodz, in Nazi-occupied Poland, and the central character is based on Chaim Mordecai Rumkowski, that legendary figure who ruled the ghetto, terrorized its inhabitants into passivity and submission, and persuaded them that a policy of "co-operation"—of letting one category after another be rounded up and driven into the trains bound for the gas chambers—offered a chance of survival for the dwindling remnant.

It isn't overstating the matter to say that there is no more terrible story in the history of the world than this, and for more than thirty years the Jewish people have been trying to come to terms with it, sometimes by outright denial, sometimes by total condemnation, sometimes with mercy and understanding. But nobody, I think, has seriously tried to understand Rumkowski and his like, still less to find mercy for them. It is easier to accept a personality like Adam Czerniakow, head of the Warsaw *Judenrat,* who killed himself when he understood that he would have to hand over children for the next transport.

Epstein seems undismayed. His own background was remote from these events. . . . He has said that "it may take a third-generation Jew from LA to write a novel about the Holocaust," and seems well aware of the distaste which his enterprise may provoke. But that sally does him less than justice.

Isaiah Trumpelman, the main character, is brilliantly described. (p. 28)

The portrait of Trumpelman has great power. He is indeed a "King of the Jews." But the novel around him, vivid and engrossing as it is, remains a feat of pastiche. Epstein has drawn from the Jewish fiction of Eastern Europe, Yiddish or vernacular, the qualities of combined farce and horror, of stifling claustrophobia, and exaggerated them so that to turn for a moment to a page of Isaac Bashevis Singer or of Bruno Schulz is a relief, a contrast in its lucidity and even its calm. The introversion of the dying ghetto is heightened. Although these events are taking place in the midst of a large Polish industrial city, the Poles feature only in the occasional apelike shadow of a passing anti-Semitic peasant. The Polish resistance does not appear at all. And the Soviet failure to relieve the Warsaw Rising is tranformed and transferred into a deliberate Russian plan to let the Jewish partisans of Lodz be wiped out before the Red Army arrives in the city.

Epstein is in no way trying to make light of what took place; there is no question about his grief and passion—or of his talent. Satire was probably the only possible medium for his task. But finally one's conviction in the work stays suspended. Yes, but was it really that way? And Trumpelman/Rumkowski . . . is it possible, after all, that he was not a tragic figure but, like those whose orders he obeyed in the Final Solution, a demon whose moral features were banal? (p. 29)

Neal Ascherson, "The Damned," in The New York Review of Books *(reprinted with permission from* The New York Review of Books; *copyright © 1979 Nyrev, Inc.), Vol. XXVI, No. 5, April 5, 1979, pp. 27-9.*

ROBERT ALTER

Making novels out of the holocaust has proved to be a hopelessly self-contradictory enterprise for most writers. The conventional novel, with its formal coherence of beginning, middle

and end, betrays this subject, which by its nature destroys coherence in our understanding of history, theology, moral choice and human character. Leslie Epstein's quietly controlled, eerily lucid novel ["**King of the Jews**"] . . . . is remarkable for choosing an aspect of the subject and developing a special narrative mode that overcome the intrinsic difficulty of coping imaginatively with genocide. . . .

Mr. Epstein intelligently focuses his narrative not on the obscene mechanisms of mass murder itself, but on the morally ambiguous politics of survival of a Judenrat (Jewish Council) in a Polish ghetto.

Isaiah Chaim Trumpelman, the chief elder of the novel's Judenrat, is a figure clearly modeled on a historical personage, the megalomaniacal Mordechai Chaim Rumkowski, who under the Nazis ruled the ghetto of Lodz with a flamboyant combination of regal grandiosity and political shrewdness. But the town in which the fictional ghetto-suburb of Balut is placed remains unnamed and, in a related strategy, the words "German" and "Nazi" are never allowed to appear. Instead, the murderers are referred to as the Others or the Occupying Power; storm troopers become Warriors; the SS are called Death's-Headers. This manipulation of names contributes to the peculiar generalizing effect of the novel as a whole.

From the actual details of ghettos established by the Nazis as way-stations to genocide, Mr. Epstein has created a kind of grim moral fable that often reminds one of the fantastic yet profoundly historical narrative inventions that Kafka produced in short pieces such as "An Old Manuscript" or Nabokov in "Invitation to a Beheading." In this case, the effect of the fabulous is achieved through scrupulous adherence to historical fact, the one odd exception being the virtual exclusion of Zionism from the ghetto scene. . . . (p. 1)

Mr. Epstein's Trumpelman is a character of outrageous contradictions—which seems the only appropriate way to represent these Judenrat leaders who were both violently thrust and seductively drawn into a position of absolute power and absolute impotence in which no human being could continue to function with any moral coherence. A physician with dubious credentials and an insurance-swindler to boot, Trumpelman is something of a charlatan, but he is also in many respects a man of fierce integrity, devoted to his patients and paternally compassionate toward the children of the orphanage that he directs. (pp. 1, 44)

Trumpelman is a genius in the art of personal survival, and as the novel unfolds, he almost succeeds, as a grudging collaborator with the mass-murderers, in saving more of his people than could have been saved in any other way. No work of fiction has opened up so fully the unbearable moral dilemma in which the Judenrat members found themselves, governing with a pistol at their heads, administering the processes of death, corrupted of course by their awful power, yet trying to preserve life when there was no real way to preserve it.

"**King of the Jews**" is also noteworthy for the fine understatement and suggestive obliquity with which it tells its painful story. The announcement of the outbreak of World War II at the end of the first chapter is exemplary. As in a child's story (and the narrator is a survivor who might well have been a child at the time), a small speck is seen in the placid September sky, then the silver wings of a plane, which "lazily dropped," then bombs tumbling from it "all the way to the ground." Instead of the Hollywood-style hellish squadrons of more conventional writers, Mr. Epstein defamiliarizes the horror through this oddly idyllic perspective and thus reminds us sharply of the horrendously anti-idyllic nature of what is about to happen. It is a lesson in what artistic restraint can do to help us imagine the dark places of our history. (pp. 44-5)

> Robert Alter, ''A Fable of Power,'' in The New York Times Book Review (© 1979 by The New York Times Company; reprinted by permission), February 4, 1979, pp. 1, 44-5.

EDITH MILTON

[*King of the Jews*] is elegantly written, paced like a Burger-King commercial, and arranged with a very cunning eye for irony; its cumulative effect is that of an intricate artifice built on the grave of total horror. I am not accusing Epstein of bad taste; it is not really a question of that. Epstein's novel is somehow outside the range of taste, in the same way a novel might be if it were written by a dolphin. . . . Parts of the book are astonishingly beautiful; a scene, for instance, where doomed, starved boys act out, for a school exercise, the motion of the planets. Parts of it are disturbingly real; a game of naked leap-frog forced on the new leaders of the ghetto before they are shot. But I cannot recognize the experience which produced the book; it comes from an alien sensibility. . . .

The book has ample, documented foundation in fact. But it is written as a sort of folk-tale, a legend whose characters are caricature. Trumpelman has flowing white hair and wears a Dracula cloak; his wife, Miss Lubliver, favors skirts slit to the knee. The style is conversational, the tone of someone telling stories to children, but it sounds vaguely as though it is in translation, an English version of Sholem Aleichem. In the best Yiddish story-telling tradition, Epstein frequently stops to address us directly. (p. 94)

For me that sort of familiarity, not my favorite device even in genuine Yiddish fiction, here grates horribly against the enormity of the subject matter. Epstein seems constantly, quaintly, to be tugging at one's sleeve, demanding attention for himself, reminding us to admire his verve, his wit, the clever twists of his story line. The questions Epstein asks are very like [William Styron's in *Sophie's Choice*], existential questions of choice and the value of commitment to survival: what is collaboration? Is the choosing of who will die equivalent to murder? But Styron cares about his answers or his lack of answers, and lets his story grow from his own flawed perceptions and feelings in complex and sometimes messy grandeur. Epstein keeps things cool and tidy. One sees the creative writing class behind the brisk construction, which springs more from a talent for experiment than from the prodding of emotion and experience.

Well—the flaws of youth. There is in fact something green and adolescent in Epstein's writing. At its best this shows itself as a freshness of imagery so intense that it is poetic. At its worst, it appears as a total insensitivity to the textures of European life and Jewish ritual, which it reduces to an ethnic joke. The scene of a ghetto performance of *Macbeth* is *Tom Jones* with a touch of Molly Picon; rumors and rattlings of war seem made in Hollywood, circa 1943. (pp. 94-5)

There is one oddness of *King of the Jews* which seems worth the mention here: the Germans are never called the Germans—or the Nazis, or the SS, or Krauts, or any other name known to history. Epstein gives them names out of some comic-book Valhalla. They are ''the Others,'' ''the Blond Ones,'' ''To-tenkopfers.'' Hitler, in some pretty funny jokes about him,

becomes Horowitz. An eccentricity which Epstein explains as a game, unfortunately, works against the novel. By removing the Germans into comic abstraction, Epstein takes them away from serious participation in the action, and lifts their weight from the scale of responsibility. The novel becomes an angry fairy tale, an adolescent fantasy in which the outside world exists dimly, somewhere beyond the forest, and all guilt, all fault, and all control belong to the immediate family. In this case, using these materials, such distortion is an atrocity.

But one can scarcely fault Epstein for trying. Armageddon is hard to write about, especially these days when popular sentiment runs in favor of its being a civil war in the first place, and a bore as well. Epstein's novel, whatever its flaws and my moral qualms about it, tackles a ghastly subject and, God help us, makes it fun. (pp. 95-6)

> Edith Milton, ''Looking Backward: Six Novels,'' in The Yale Review (© 1979 by Yale University; reprinted by permission of the editors), Vol. LXIX, No. 1, October, 1979, pp. 89-103.*

KIRKUS REVIEWS

As critics have often noted, Epstein's fiction—especially **P. D. Kimerakov** . . . bears a large resemblance to Saul Bellow's. And this disappointing new novel [**Regina**] is the most Bellovian of all: a sociological/spiritual mosaic that could conceivably be subtitled *Mrs. Sammler's Revival*. Regina Glassman is a divorced, 40-ish movie-and-drama critic, in her youth an actress. On leave from her New York writing job at a magazine, she's unexpectedly called back to the stage: a revival of *The Sea Gull*, the play in which she'd had her tyro triumph. Blindly, vainly, she believes that she's been again tapped for the part of young Nina, only to arrive at rehearsal to find out that she's been cast, quite reasonably, as old Arkadina. And this initial scene of embarrassment is the novel's best, most affecting section, a play upon the shame of illusion. Thereafter, however, the book slips precipitously. Manhattan is experiencing a hellish, perhaps apocalyptic summer: drought, a rampaging rapist, little Hoovervilles along the Hudson that Regina can see from the West Side window; furthermore, Regina's son Ben seems to be undergoing a Karamazovian crisis of saintly transfiguration; ex-husband Davy is pressuring to be allowed to return; and, oddest of all, Regina finds herself repeatedly visiting the psychic surgery sessions of a Puerto Rican faith-healer and putting all her desperate spiritual chips on him. The mix, then—wacky spiritualism, art, social-fabric disintegration, pathetic family tableaux—is one we know from Bellow. The social-commentary style, too, is familiar. . . . But while Bellow's social/personal interplay is riveting at its best *(Sammler)* and thornily intense even at its weakest *(The Dean's December)*, Epstein's attempt seems second-hand and mechanical. And the result is a loosely-strung-together, ultimately unconvincing novel—from a writer with the talent (of *King of the Jews*) to be exploring more original territory than this. (pp. 1009-10)

> A review of ''Regina,'' in Kirkus Reviews (copyright © 1982 The Kirkus Service, Inc.), Vol. L, No. 17, September 1, 1982, pp. 1009-10.

GEORGE STADE

We know from Leslie Epstein's previous fiction—two novels and a collection of stories—that he has both a social conscience and masterly skills. We also know, especially from his last novel, **"King of the Jews"** . . . , that he has an imagination of catastrophe.

His new novel, **"Regina,"** is set in New York City in the 1980's, where inner catastrophes confront their external counterparts. One counterpart is the weather. It's midsummer; there's a heat wave and a drought. . . . Somebody in the neighborhood (the Upper West Side) is killing women who, as it turns out, remind him of his mother. He stabs each of his victims exactly 27 times. Relations between the sexes and among parents and children are awry. "It was a place as wicked as Babylon."

Theaters, restaurants, other entertainments—anything that might draw people to the city—are shutting down. And it's at a time like this that the 44-year-old Regina Singer, née Glassman, once a famous actress, now a film and drama critic, has been asked to perform in a revival of "The Seagull," the vehicle of her first triumph some 20 years earlier. . . .

The book abounds with correspondences, slight and substantial, which could easily have become excessively literary or Freudian or pat. They are not. For Mr. Epstein, nothing is neat; simple answers are a symptom of disease. . . . Mr. Epstein's dramatization of the relations between art and life, of the relations between how we are and how we see, of the ways in which we engulf and regurgitate each other, the ways in which we play parts that wind up playing us, is subtle and convincing. He illuminates these matters, and much of what he illuminates is their mysteriousness.

This kind of novel is risky, but Mr. Epstein's control is equal to his daring. He has even attempted to portray a character who is at once an intelligence, a body and a subconscious, all of which inform and are informed by an occupation, a family and a personal history that is simultaneously the history of our time. The minor characters are vivid; the blacks and Hispanics, the women and children in particular are drawn with imaginative sympathy. The white men tend to be wimps or schlemiels or worse.

In the last few chapters, set during and immediately after opening night, all of Mr. Epstein's motifs come together in a sequence of tremendous literary chords, hardly a false note among them.

George Stade, "Parallels Are Everywhere," in The New York Times Book Review *(© 1982 by The New York Times Company; reprinted by permission), November 21, 1982, p. 12.*

SUSAN LYDON

Despite the countless thousands of words expended on the soul of the middle-aged Jewish male (now plumbed nearly to exhaustion), his generational counterpart, the middle-aged Jewish female, has languished in a fictional limbo. . . . [She's] the last invisible woman. Or was until Regina Glassman sprang full-grown from the pen of Leslie Epstein [in *Regina*].

Regina would be the first to admit that her obscurity isn't due just to insensitive novelists: she has passed most of her life in a somnambulistic stupor, from which she is only now beginning to awaken. And her monkey-in-the-middle-age dilemma exists in life as well as art; caught between the intense egocentrism of her incorrigible teenage sons and the blind selfishness of her mother's senility, she hardly has time to find herself. But she's determined to try. . . .

With its many allusions to Chekhov, *Regina* is dense with symbolism; you can feel the weight of Epstein's literary predecessors. Regina is a flesh-and-blood character, but she's also Woman as barometer of social history—a time-honored tradition that includes Anna Karenina and Madame Bovary. In less skillful hands, Regina's story, with all its probing for answers to ultimate questions, might have seemed at best pretentious, at worst ludicrous. Epstein, however, maintains a tone that is neither too earnest nor too flip. And he manages to provide a few satisfactory answers: when the healer's "miracles" are exposed as mere conjurer's tricks, another version of mystical transcendence appears to take their place. In this case it's the transcendence of the ordinary, the beauty of the commonplace, the majesty of everyday, human reality. A hamische ending to a hamische story, but with enough substance that it lingers long after the last page has been read. Regina's soul is eminently worth illumination, for our sake as well as hers.

Susan Lydon, in a review of "Regina" (reprinted by permission of The Village Voice *and the author; copyright © News Group Publications, Inc., 1983), in* The Village Voice, *Vol. XXVIII, No. 3, January 18, 1983, p. 37.*

Ronald G(ilmour) Everson

1903-

Canadian poet.

Although Everson has been writing for more than fifty years, he has received little critical recognition. A number of critics who have reviewed Everson's work express bewilderment at his long neglect, for they feel that he is one of Canada's finest contemporary poets.

Everson's poetry is marked by strong images and pared-down lyrics. Most of his poems are short and display specificity of time and place. Everson often uses Canada as his subject and juxtaposes current scenes of rural Canada with historical and literary allusions.

Although Everson published four previous collections, he has received most critical attention for *Selected Poems 1920-1970* (1970).

(See also *Contemporary Authors*, Vols. 17-20, rev. ed.)

Courtesy of Ronald Everson

JAMES DICKEY

R. G. Everson is a Canadian poet, one of those almost-greatly-gifted writers from North of the Border, like Earle Birney, P. K. Page, Louis Dudek, A. M. Klein, and Irving Layton, who keep promising to give us a truly exciting national movement, and may yet. Everson at his best, is, I think, about as good as the best of these at *their* best, and since I like Birney, Miss Page, and Klein very much, I mean well by this. He is doubly interesting because he is in his fifties, and writes with the brashness and chance-taking-ness of extreme, belligerent, and intelligent youth. [*A Lattice for Momos*] brings to mind all sorts of remarks one could make about how poetry can furnish a second youth to people who discover that they are poets well on into life, and about how much this attitude and these qualities should be encouraged in those who have them. I prefer, though, to talk about Everson's particular case, and to say something about his hard-headed business-like way of getting his feelings down, and to let him show how surprisingly much this can yield in a short space. . . . Reading [his poetry], one declares eternal war against the weeping-willow-haired type of poet full of vague fantasies and admirable sentiments, like Shelley, and thinks of practicality as one of the greatest of the artistic virtues, and as underlying all real imagination. Even though Everson is practical in this way, he can also be very flat. But, as Louis Dudek says in a brief, sharp introduction, he also has a "sense of lived reality" in his poems, and that is what we want. As of now, Everson has just enough of the amateur about him to make his work interesting; I shudder to think of what might happen to him should he become a "professional poet." No matter what changes or developments he may go through, Everson has already said a few things uniquely and memorably. (pp. 666-67)

James Dickey, "The Suspect in Poetry or Everyman As Detective" (reprinted by permission of the author; © 1967 by James Dickey), in The Sewanee Review, *Vol. LXVIII, No. 4, Autumn, 1960, pp. 660-74.**

M. J. SIDNELL

[*Wrestle With An Angel*] is Mr. Everson's fourth offering. *Three Dozen Poems* (1957), *A Lattice for Momos* (1958), and *Blind Man's Holiday* (1963) received their due tributes for the precision, unity, wit and economy of the poems collected in them. The reader knowing and expecting this good craftsmanship and seeing it emerge so clearly from the present bouts with reality might take a sampling and see the collection as more of the same—a series of poems picking out in flashes of brilliance the involuted parts of a world. But a sampling could mislead. *Wrestle with an Angel* has a coherence as a whole which makes it a notable development from the earlier collections. There is throughout a sense of philosophical assurance; the images do not twinkle in isolation but as a galaxy whose shape is discernible. (p. 235)

Everson's beings have that loosely articulated unity within themselves that Golding's Pincher Martin has in the collection of lives that make his individuality: soul-life, nerve-lives of eye or finger-tip, will and mental-life. . . .

Everson constantly hints, sometimes more than hints, at horror, when, for instance, "The French are blowing up our mail-box duns" and in the same poem, "Sigmund Freud comes crawling through our bed." In **"With Burney and Dudek on Mount Royal"** the horror seems to triumph but in **"Daybreak at the** maternity ward'' the agony is glorious, stretching the imagination full of sky''—there, the possibilities of life seem not essentially or merely horrific but to extend beyond to tragedy.

Everson's spontaneity is unusually untempered in the one poem that seems to me to fail—**"In so sustained a remarkable amount of motion."** Elsewhere one finds very occasionally a stridency when he lets his guard down and loosens the tension of craft and thought. In **"The shared mystery,"** one of the several fine short narrative poems in the collection (how many poets can write narratives as compelling?), the last line in this stanza seems too shrill in a poet who is distinctively not vulgar:

> He did not again trudge the sky
> or plunge awkwardly on knock-about billows.
> He died all afternoon.

The death of the gull is the occasion for seeing "the whole sea flock" sharing "with children our common mystery." It is that common mystery, or rather Everson's sense of it, that binds his poems together. Behind the immediacy and brilliance of his apprehension of the animate world, picking its irrational and competitive way through matter, there is the shadowy outline of a plot linking the "immediate common-fact material / to gain ineffable meaning."

Mr. Everson's mind seems strangely modern for a Canadian poet, but he is in his mid-sixties. I hope he will hurry, to make up for the lateness of his return to poetry and come up with even more splendid trophies, for he is a rare poet whose art can bring us nearer to reality. (p. 236)

> *M. J. Sidnell, "Coherence," in* The Canadian Forum, *Vol. XLV, No. 540, January, 1966, pp. 235-36.*

ROBERT GIBBS

Going through [Everson's] four most recent collections I was aware of a true line of development. The poems of *A Lattice for Momos* (1958) are strong as individual things. They are occasional poems in the best sense. A bus ride, a lady stripper, a coffee with the poetry society, can start the Everson alchemy. Into the confined space of the occasion and the reduced physical form, he pours a disparate mix of associations, which in uneasy dancing suspension there (his kinetic jostling of word on word) fight it out. The encompassing spirit is still delight. (p. 118)

The view of things darkens and intensifies in *Blind Man's Holiday* (1963). The energy, now directed forward, is stronger and less overtly exultant. The poet still romps with the medium, showing a more than usual security in his craft. Occasions continue to give rise to poems, but the vision is more clearly a fusing one—the delight and fear or fearful delight of seeing all matters as inextricable. . . . The voice is pure Everson, though the wit and the close packing in of detail, often of a curiously unpoetic kind, is Marianne Mooreish.

Wrestle with an Angel (1965) doesn't wrestle as closely as *Blind Man's Holiday.* Something of the blessing won is here. The tone is more relaxed, the juxtaposing eye less astringent. The economy is still close, but there is a personal human voice and touch reaching through. (p. 119)

With *The Dark Is Not So Dark,* Everson moves on. His art opens up. The edges are hard but not so deliberately constrained. More important, his view of things has expanded and deepened. The space that surrounds his poems, geographical, historical, cosmic, is more continuous. The more important poems in the collection interact in a significant way, not just

to reinforce one another, but to complete one another, to enclose more of the whole imaginative life of the man. I am not meaning to indicate that Everson has suddenly become a great poet but that as one of few with a long and continuously productive career in Canada he is doing what a good poet should do—moving toward a more consolidated and complete expression of his vision.

His title indicates his stance as one of knowing the dark but of not being altogether confined by that knowledge. He celebrates in man what he himself has been, in Dickey's phrase, as a poet. . . . (pp. 119-20)

[The] geographical limits crack for an imagination that must range beyond them. The book is partly a naming of names, an examining of roots and surfaces, personal and national, but too aware of the limits of limits to stay inside. (p. 120)

The impulse is to . . . [quote] just to see how richly varied and how continuous the quality is. Some of the poems are slight, casual, playful. These keep the book from being too deliberate a thing. Everson has always ranged widely and freely. In this book more than in the earlier ones he gets far beyond the poem as gnomic artifact or tightfisted ironic complex. (pp. 120-21)

[Everson] is not a Canadian poet we need to make concessions to and apologies about. He belongs with our best. (p. 121)

> *Robert Gibbs, in a review of "The Dark Is Not So Dark" (copyright by Robert Gibbs; reprinted by permission of the author), in* The Fiddlehead, *No. 84, March-April, 1970, pp. 118-21.*

RALPH GUSTAFSON

Everson has been writing these how many years . . . quietly minding his poetic business at Montreal; making forays like Daniel into the prides of Canadian poets wherever gathered to decide the world and to read each other's latest; quietly publishing his poems in books published by the littler presses without what he is expert in and has always been retired from, fanfare.

Here, now, is the chance to get him straight in our minds: his *Selected Poems* of exactly fifty years. Good grief! We haven't acknowledged him in half a century, when he has been going so well, leading us into all sorts of actuality? (p. 65)

Whoever reads this poet is going to have to face up to it: the world is affirmative. The one great thing wrong with it, besides our own stupidity and the occasional hunchback, is that our time in it is too brief for us to get our fill of love. Everson is very out of fashion. He does not use the state of the world to exonerate his follies.

He just validates actual experience with significance; take it or leave it. He takes it with love. Plumed rhubarb blazes above his head; he suffers an apprehension of petals lest the mind open with intuitions and imaginings.

You can tell, leafing it through this book, that something vital is going on; something gay—like those wrinkled Chinese sitting looking at the lapis lazuli world; also something as dark as that light under that closed closet door. Like his housefly set free, he is blustering alive.

So filled with incidents is it, there is danger that the book will be judged a scrappy diary. I mind me of what Van Gogh told

Gauguin when Gauguin complained that Van Gogh painted too fast: "You look too fast."

There are many ways to get our inscapes. This is a poet who thinks in images. They are terse, hard, with their colloquial adjectives full tilt. No little "whimperings of wind". Their satisfaction is that of turning a nut neatly threaded on its bolt.

The imagery ranges from Hannibal and his elephant failure and Macbeth murdering for high-plumed sons, all the way from that to quasars and Iceland. But by and large (mostly large), the images concern farmland near Oshawa, Ontario, or dictaphone incantations and other urban exercises in Montreal. Everson is a sophisticate who knows about evening milking and spring ploughing. His rustic stuff is in a straight line from Raymond Knister's poetry. Everson, too, in his ploughing pauses to judge what he's done. You won't follow his rural history without ending up with some grand significances. (pp. 66-7)

The poems are all short. Switches of inconsequence occur, the space of the poem being too short for what Everson wants to put in it. Cloggings occur. But no matter for that. Only the mediocre are always at their best, as Maugham told me. Rural or city, two images per poem or six, what you will get is delight at Everson being delighted at being alive. The secret of that is that Everson has comedy up his sleeve, even though he is hurried among the generations. . . .

The old wait their customary predicament. But Everson doesn't grieve. The seasons turn cartwheels and he laughs while huge reality, a mindless lout, somersaults for his pleasure. Oh, he has an observation or two, this poet. . . .

I don't suppose he minds, knowing him as I do; but Canadians ought to be abashed that they have kept this poet in obscurity for so long.

There are far too many words around already, he says. Any poet who says that is worth reading. Certainly, Canada's present nests of singing birds ought to listen. (p. 67)

> *Ralph Gustafson, "Everson's Half Century" (reprinted by permission of the author), in* Canadian Literature, *No. 49, Summer, 1971, pp. 65-7.*

CHARLES MOLESWORTH

[It] is impossible to conceive of a reason to forge larger, more complex units out of R. G. Everson's brief, sufficient lyrics. [In his *Selected Poems 1920/1970,* this] Canadian gives us over one hundred poems in less than ninety pages. They are lonely poems, featuring a speaker who must face a new part of a familiar country, or who discovers a moment of historical consciousness buried below the mundane hours of commerce. If one assumes that a half-century of work is here arranged chronologically, Everson seems to have moved toward more open, but unsurprising, forms. He has not abandoned his essential lyric syntax: beginning with closely observed and deftly placed facts and remembrances, letting metaphoric structure occur casually, the poem takes a modest but firm jump onto the anagogic plane. . . . Like certain American poets such as David Ignatow, Everson engages a quotidian reality through the expressive gestures of idiomatic speech. His syntax, therefore, is not as careful, nor is his "analysis" of reality as polished as [Leslie] Norris's, or [Tony] Connor's, even. Yet through his poems we have a habitable space in which we can visit, catching ourselves in the traffic of the moment or snatching views of another time and another place. His poems are filled with Canadian landscapes, especially so in recent years, given a chronological arrangement, and though they sometimes wear their learning clumsily, as in *Report for Northrop Frye* or *Raby Head,* they more often move easily and gracefully. (pp. 111-12)

> *Charles Molesworth, "Some Locals," in* Poetry (© *1972 by The Modern Poetry Association; reprinted by permission of the Editor of* Poetry), *Vol. CXX, No. 2, May, 1972, pp. 107-13.**

LEN GASPARINI

R. G. Everson has been around for a long time, and he's as much a part of the Canadian poetry scene as maple trees in autumn. An inveterate traveller and raconteur, Everson makes poems out of everything. *Carnival* is his latest collection, and he's at it again, writing about a damselfly, his family tree, Oshawa weeds, a rainbow trout, gulls, and so forth. Many of the poems in *Carnival* are somewhat prosy, but the rich imagery is always consistent. . . .

On the whole, Everson's book is a bit uneven. It contains too many random observations that resemble unfinished paintings. If Everson had concentrated some of his energy on revision, *Carnival* would have been an exciting sequence instead of a collage.

> *Len Gasparini, "Pain, Thunder, and Rainbows" (reprinted by permission of the author), in* Books in Canada, *Vol. 8, No. 2, February, 1979, p. 24.**

Lawrence Ferlinghetti

1919-

American poet, novelist, dramatist, editor, and publisher.

Ferlinghetti was at the forefront of the literary phenomenon of the 1950s known as the Beat Movement. The Beat Movement, which began and was centered in San Francisco, attempted to expand the audience and appreciation of poetry by removing it from the exclusivity of the academic sphere. Ferlinghetti's most important contribution to this movement was his creation of a forum for Beat and other anti-establishment writers. In 1953, he founded City Lights Books in an avant-garde section of San Francisco. City Lights Books, the country's first exclusively paperback bookstore, carried works by counterculture writers that were, for the most part, unavailable elsewhere. In 1955, Ferlinghetti began publishing the City Lights Pocket Series, which included titles by Beat writers Jack Kerouac, Michael McClure, Gregory Corso, Allen Ginsburg, and others. Ferlinghetti's publication of Ginsburg's *Howl* in 1956 led to an obscenity trial which attracted national attention.

Ferlinghetti's own writing has brought him popular success but a lukewarm critical reception. Like that of other Beat writers, his poetry, which shows the influence of American idiom and jazz, stresses the oral aspects of literature and is written with performance in mind. Some critics have remarked that it is undisciplined and sentimental. Others praise what they see as his honest energy. General critical assessment of Ferlinghetti's writing seems to be that it contributed to the open, vibrant sensibility of the Beat Movement, but that unlike the work of Ginsburg or Kerouac, his writing was not particularly innovative.

Among Ferlinghetti's most important works is *A Coney Island of the Mind* (1958), his second book, which along with *Howl*, ranks as one of the most widely known volumes of American poetry published after 1950. In *Coney Island*, Ferlinghetti speaks of vanishing innocence and political radicalism, themes which become increasingly important in his later books. Ferlinghetti's concern with political issues led him to write about McCarthyism, the Vietnam conflict, and the Kennedy assassinations. The overriding message of his poetry is that he trusts neither the political Left nor Right. To date, Ferlinghetti has written only one novel, entitled *Her* (1960). It is a surrealistic autobiographical account of the pursuit of a woman who represents all women to the narrator. Because the novel was highly experimental and largely plotless, most critics found it baffling and difficult to appraise. Consequently, little criticism has been written on *Her*. Ferlinghetti has written two volumes of plays, *Unfair Arguments with Existence* (1963) and *Routines* (1964). Strongly influenced by the Theater of the Absurd, Ferlinghetti strives for an improvisational effect in his drama. Ferlinghetti's most recent book is *Endless Life: Selected Poems* (1981), a collection representing the past twenty-five years of his career as a poet.

(See also *CLC*, Vols. 2, 6, 10; *Contemporary Authors*, Vols. 5-8, rev. ed.; *Contemporary Authors New Revision Series*, Vol. 3; and *Dictionary of Literary Biography*, Vols. 5, 16.)

Photograph © by Gerard Malanga

JOEL OPPENHEIMER

["Endless Life" is assembled from Lawrence Ferlinghetti's] own choice of his work from the last 25 years. We can see the range of these poems spread out on the page, and they still hold.

Oh, yes, the influences leap out at you; E. E. Cummings and Kenneth Patchen ring from almost every page. And, fairly early on, when one can imagine Ferlinghetti realizing that all those young people were listening to him, the political rhetoric begins, and rolls on, muddled, to this day. But these are not terrible sins when the poetry sings; indeed, Cummings and Patchen and irate populist litanies might do us a great deal of good now.

In his poems there is also the quick pickup of—and slide away from—literary history, prefiguring a great deal of recent, less well done poeticizing by others. Ferlinghetti's poetic allusions are real parts of his poems and not just in jokes. . . .

One sometimes feels one is on a reading binge with Ferlinghetti, if not just inside his head where the lines he's read roll round. But it is a successful technique and it draws one in, makes one read. (p. 40)

There is [in Ferlinghetti's work], . . . a legitimate revisionism which is perhaps our best heritage from those raucous days—

the poet daring to see a different vision from that which the guardians of culture had allowed us. These days, of course, revisionism is all there is, but then it was a necessary cleansing. Ferlinghetti understood this and did not shirk. The other heritage from those days is a clear, objective eye. This, too, shines in these poems. (pp. 40-1)

Ferlinghetti himself, with his insistence on the "now," probably could not have believed [his] poems would weather so well. It's good to hear the voice still ringing in them. He's been lost a little to us lately; it has been to the academy's advantage to see him merely as a populist phenomenon, and the very poets he bred had been taught by him, and by their times, to ignore their past. One got the image of Ferlinghetti as Anthony Quinn in the film "La Strada," the aging strong man doing the one trick he's mastered.

But, indeed, he'd learned to write poems, in ways that those who see poetry as the province of the few and the educated had never imagined. That strength has turned out to be lasting. The poems have "Endless Life." (p. 41)

> *Joel Oppenheimer, "Weathered Well," in* The New York Times Book Review *(© 1981 by The New York Times Company; reprinted by permission), November 1, 1981, pp. 40-1.*

JOHN TRIMBUR

Lawrence Ferlinghetti, according to his FBI file, is a "Beatnik Rabble Rouser." Now I never thought that the Freedom of Information Act would advance literary studies, but after reading *Endless Life,* Ferlinghetti's own selection of his poetry from eight books and work in progress, I am reminded of the important conjunction between his poetry and the state. At home in the West Coast anarcho-pacifist tradition of Kenneth Rexroth and Kenneth Patchen, Ferlinghetti has written over the last quarter century a public poetry to challenge the guardians of the political and social status quo for the souls of his fellow citizens. A rebel rather than a revolutionary, Ferlinghetti has been generous in his support to the anti-war and anti-nuclear movements. . . . (p. 79)

But Ferlinghetti is more than a political conscience warning his brother and sister poets of unwitting collaboration and guilt by complicity. He is the self-described "Director of Alienation" seeking to coalesce a "collective subjective" of all of us—the "rabble" component of the FBI's equation—who take seriously the Beat generation's resistance to official culture and mores. This "collective subjective," as Ferlinghetti's **"Adieu a Charlot (Second Populist Manifesto)"** makes clear, comes from the "Little Man in each of us"—Ferlinghetti's identification with Charley Chaplin, the tramp drifting beneath city lights ("blinking in the neon"), entangled in the gears of the modern age. "It's not me It's Them out of step," Ferlinghetti's **"Director of Alienation"** says, "I came in looking for an angel." Which is hard to find these days, and at some expense to the poet. "Constantly risking absurdity" is the way Ferlinghetti characterizes his mission and the vulnerability of the poet, an acrobat "balancing on eyebeams." The task, Ferlinghetti says in the first **"Populist Manifesto,"** is not to apotheosize alienation in the self-referential, arcane, or occult salvation of "bedroom visionaries and closet agitpropagators." It is to direct that alienation to good use, in order to "speak out / with a new wide-open poetry / with a new commonsensual 'public surface'." Like the French poet Jacques Prevert whose work he translated, Ferlinghetti is most of all a see-er, not a

seer, whose call to "open your minds & eyes / with the old visual delight" is counterposed to the private sensibilities of the poetic schools and critics: "Poetry still falls from the skies."

So, the critics have never been particularly kind to Ferlinghetti, most often dismissing him as either sentimental or the literary entrepreneur of the Beat generation—judgments both inadequate and wide of the mark. In reverse order, it needs to be said that Ferlinghetti's City Lights publishing company is not simply a Beat clearinghouse but . . . has been instrumental in presenting new writing of many strains from many countries to the poetry public. . . . And then it needs to be said, as the Europeans have always recognized, that Ferlinghetti is a force in American poetry, a revisionist evaluation I think this collection will promote. His poems are strong and clear and deeply felt, inspired by the angel of lucidity. . . . Sentimentality, finally, is a bad rap, often pinned on poets whose work sells well, as Ferlinghetti's has, blaming the poet for his audience.

Kenneth Rexroth's judgment of the man and his work is a better one. "Many contemporary poets," Rexroth writes, "perhaps the most significant ones, have simply left the society, deserted it as doomed, or already dead. Ferlinghetti is very much inside it. He feels its evils as directed against him; as they say, he takes it personally." Ferlinghetti has risked the "absurdity" of his sentiments and his sanity, the "absurdity" of those who "Awake and walk in the open air." (pp. 79-80)

> *John Trimbur, in a review of "Endless Life: Selected Poems," in* Western American Literature *(copyright, 1982, by the Western Literature Association), Vol. XVII, No. 1, May, 1982, pp. 79-80.*

LEE BARTLETT

Ferlinghetti has published nine collections of poems, from which *Endless Life* draws its two-hundred pages. Ferlinghetti obviously thinks of himself as a political poet, in the tradition of the Russian Voznesensky, and as political poets go, he is not bad. Of course, like Lowell, say, or Levertov, he can get a little self-righteous and dull when he gets worked up. . . . Still, what often saves Ferlinghetti is his light touch, his fine sense of the comic. . . . (p. 277)

In *Endless Life* . . . we can see a distinct change in direction in Ferlinghetti's approach. The early poems (from *Pictures of the Gone World* and *A Coney Island of the Mind*), while slightly experimental in the unjustified left margins which we have come to associate with Ferlinghetti's poetry, are essentially traditional lyric poems dealing with the larger subjects: love, death, beauty, time. In other words, the poems often engage suffering (**"The World is a Beautiful Place"**), but it is a general suffering, a complaint about the human condition. It is not really until the 1968 **"Assassination Raga"** that many of the poems become occasional pieces dealing with specific political issues. From that point on, from poem to poem (and often within a given poem) Ferlinghetti seems to be at war with himself—is he a lyric poet, an Ausonius transplanted in the New World . . . with a touch of the wag, or is he a Beat *engagé*, chasing down men in gray flannel suits? And as with Pablo Neruda (who with Voznesensky ranks high in Ferlinghetti's poetic pantheon), it is when the lyric impulse wins out that he writes poetry we return to. (p. 278)

> *Lee Bartlett, in a review of "Endless Life," in* Arizona Quarterly *(copyright © 1982 by Arizona Board of Regents), Vol. 38, No. 3, Autumn, 1982, pp. 277-78.*

LARRY SMITH

Rarely has any poet's work received such wide popular acceptance and such limited critical appreciation as Lawrence Ferlinghetti's writing. While the public generally views the work as immediate, alive, and relevant, the academic and poet-critic generally attack it as being simplistic, sentimental, undisciplined, and in open violation of the conventional poetic form. Some critics, caught in the quandary of how to respond to the radically new values of this engaged poetry, have sought to detract from the writing by naïvely branding the poet as "one of those spiritual panhandlers" or "an egoistic trifler." Others such as Crale D. Hopkins and Vincent McHugh, who are more in tune with Ferlinghetti's methods and intent, respectively view the writing as "striking, powerful, convincing," and Ferlinghetti as "an original and a natural. A rare conjunction and in light of his astonishing gifts, correspondingly valuable." . . . Revolutionary in its form as well as its content, Ferlinghetti's writing is a deliberate and open challenge to the status quo of both art and life. As Hopkins points out, it is clearly based on a new definition of the very concept of "poetry." Apocalyptic in its conception, opposed to any traditional veneration of art, it is dedicated to no less than a radically new affirmation of the world and the word. Until we accept the genuine challenge of this poetry and deal with it earnestly and fully, we perpetuate the gap between experimental art and its critical appreciation. We labor in the dark. The existing art forms must bear the attack of experimentation if they are to remain vital. For Ferlinghetti they are clearly humanities which have failed to humanize us, and they are crying for reform. His art is most truly defined then by the protean forms which he has created to fulfill his revolutionary vision. (pp. 75-76)

[Ferlinghetti's] work is generated from the tension between things as they are and as they might become, the basic existential and romantic thrust of the work. He is both the realist and the idealist seeking to engage and regenerate life in his audience. Just as surrealist, expressionist, and naturalist painters have chosen to sacrifice certain "painterly" qualities for the immediacy of their art (the subject to artist to audience bond), so Ferlinghetti's engaged poetry sacrifices certain "poetic" qualities for its direct impact—its movement toward heightened consciousness that leads to action. Yet, while certain conventional poetic values are sacrificed . . . , not all are abandoned. Rather, they are *recast* with a more essential and deliberate molding of form to meet the goals of his vision. In fact, what emerges in Ferlinghetti's poetry is a more immediate rhetoric of form and function based on both its transparent values of essential action and its inner logic of emotion and thought. He thus develops methods to fulfill his integrated and tripartite vision of an art which is characterized as: 1) *authentic*—existentially true to the artist's candid sense of life; 2) *engaged*—grounded in broad and common human experience yet directed towards active transformation; 3) *visionary* in its pursuit of wonder—the positive potential of human existence. . . . More than any other contemporary poet, Lawrence Ferlinghetti writes truly memorable poetry, poems that lodge themselves in the consciousness of the reader and generate awareness and change. And his writing sings, with the sad and comic music of the streets. (pp. 76-7)

Three of the chief characteristics of Ferlinghetti's poetry—its oral basis, its satiric intent, its development of the authentic voice—are integrally bound. "The breath, response, the personal rhythm of Ferlinghetti's line—the immediacy, the directness of his style as he turns to tell you something. I don't

think anyone else has the tone of Ferlinghetti—the flat, dry, laconic and compelling tone-sound of his voice." Samuel Charters locates here the distinctive feature and the united effect of a Ferlinghetti poem in its personal, immediate, and expressive voice. Ferlinghetti creates a contemporary basis for the tradition of the Homeric, Celtic, and Druid minstrels. He becomes the contemporary man of the streets speaking out the truths of common experience, often to the reflective beat of the jazz musician. As much as any poet today he has sought to make poetry and engaging oral art. . . . (p. 77)

Surveying the gamut of Ferlinghetti's poetry convinces one of his visionary and engaged quest for the authentic. He is the public and personal poet of American consciousness whose work knows no boundaries of nationality or genre. His influences are internationally varied, yet they are directed through his personal dedication toward a common and vital art. . . . Whether it is in oral, satirical, open, abstract expressionist, surrealistic, filmic, or prose poem form, it is an authentic evolution of life and art reaching into each other. The development of his poetry through his various books and recordings thus provides a revealing summary of his poetic achievement.

Pictures of the Gone World (1955), both derivative and experimental, breaks new ground for what poetry could be while it also begins to build a Ferlinghetti style. Its self-declarative theme and form lay out the groundwork for Ferlinghetti as a writer. The "gone world" theme, a jazzman's analogy to Camus's "Absurd," lies before him, and he is in it and with it. It is reflected in his cultural mirrors, enlarged by his ready allusions, and sharply focused in the poem **"26"** declaration where he decidedly turns from thoughts of Yeats's Arcady to "all the gone faces / getting off at midtown places." His is to be an art deliberately engaged in life. For precedents in theme and form he has Americans E. E. Cummings and Kenneth Patchen, but more pronounced is the influence of Frenchmen Jacques Prévert, Guillaume Apollinaire, and Blaise Cendrars. He develops his own open-form, abstract expressionist mode while also reaching into speech forms for diction and style. Though some poems go flat from a too prosey form (either from ineptness, experimentation, or engaged stance), the work is an original and solid foundation for his later developments.

His translations of *Paroles* (1958), which he had been working on for some time, show Ferlinghetti as the perfect translator of Jacques Prévert. His coming to himself as poet, through Prévert, is revealed in their shared themes and forms (street and oral, slangy and surreal, with tones of the murder as well as the joy of life); the work is full of wit and love and caring. . . . (pp. 136-37)

When selections from *Pictures of the Gone World* were combined with the poetry-and-jazz experiments **"Oral Messages"** and the original poems of *A Coney Island of the Mind* (1958), Ferlinghetti had enlarged his stance and developed major themes of anarchy, mass corruption, engagement, and a belief in the surreality and the wonder of life. It was a revolutionary art of dissent and contemporary application which jointly drew a lyric poetry into new realms of social-and self-expression. It sparkles, sings, goes flat, and generates anger or love out of that flatness as it follows a basic motive of getting down to reality and making of it what we can. The book is a consolidation of themes and methods which brings together the surrealist images of the **"Coney Island"** poems, the abstract expressionism of the painting analogies (rendered in human effects), the oral style and cultural mirrors of the **"Oral Messages,"** the American sense of Imagism with a Joycean symbolism of subject and form. Loosely, the book forms a type of "Portrait of the Artist as a Young Poet of Dissent." There are some classic contemporary statements in this Ferlinghetti's—and possibly America's—most popular book of modern poetry. The work is remarkable for its skill, depth, and daring. (pp. 137-38)

Ferlinghetti's 1961 *Starting from San Francisco* followed Walt Whitman's lead in journeying outward as a means of expanding yet solidifying a stance. The personal and social involvements are broadened in these bold and bare poems directed toward a new engaged art for a new world. . . . The poems are direct in their content and in their violation of conventional form. An oral style predominates, often manifested in the deeply ironic voice and in his own heartfelt mixture of radicalism and innocence. The book was first issued with a recording of the poet reading key poems, and the book does contain some important statement poems . . . and some developments of the analogical method and the prose poem applied to engaged poetics. **"Berlin"** and **"Situation in the West"** were added later, rounding the collection to sixteen long poem confrontations which compose themselves in Ferlinghetti's evolving recognition of the evil and death in life.

The Secret Meaning of Things (1968) followed Ferlinghetti's period of experimental drama in the mid-sixties and reflects his stronger attention to irrational and intuitive analogy as a means of suggesting the "secret meaning" behind life's surface. Though the works are provocative, public, and oral, they are also more cosmic in reference, revealing a stronger influence from Buddhist philosophy. Despite the fact that the book appeared during the height of the Vietnam War, the writing is more in touch with life forces, mellowed by his attempt to be at one with his various feelings and places. The vision is both dark and hopeful in such apocalyptic statements as **"Assassination Raga,"** **"After the Cries of the Birds,"** **"Moscow in the Wilderness, Segovia in the Snow."** These six long poems continue the journey of *Starting from San Francisco* toward a deeper and clearer understanding in which the poet sees and records **"All Too Clearly"** the slow eternal progress of civilization.

Open Eye, Open Heart (1973) is Ferlinghetti's largest and most complete collection with material ranging from 1961 to 1973 included under four broad headings: **"Open Eye, Open Heart,"** poems of self and tributes to Patchen, Lawrence, Whitman; **"Poems in Transit,"** journey observations from around the world, including the impressionistic rendering of **"Russian Winter Journal"** and the surrealistic **"Trois Poèmes Spontanés,";** **"Public & Political Poems,"** various dated affirmations and tirades of his basic humanitarian socialist stance applied to new situations—Vietnam, Greece, Spain, and the poor; **"American Mantra & Song,"** American English chants of extreme open statement and lyric form. It is a big book with memorable poems reminiscent of *A Coney Island of the Mind,* but with a richer feeling and form and a finer, more matured voice. Like his cosmic journey toward understanding, this work contains diversity yet wholeness, held together by a composite of approaches and forms, attitudes and visions—the tried character of his life and its oneness with his art.

Ferlinghetti delineates the territory of his last three books of poetry in his open praise of the conscious and subconscious mind as "Maxims and legends of total reality, echoing and re-echoing there, . . . Visual beatitudes, landscapes of living and dying flashed upon the dark screen." . . . *Who Are We Now?* (1976) is a vision of the times translated into image-idea in a mythic earth-self quest. Though the collection is a little uneven, it contains the characteristic mixture of prose poems, tributes, filmic scenes, general views of life, art, politics, and society, and a return to three painting-poems for Gustav Klimt and Monet. It is, however, dominated by the momentous "Populist Manifesto," which contains all the best of Ferlinghetti—his particular angle of vision amidst a stark and dark reality, and all the care and calculation of his oral and rhetorical style. The poem is an explicit and artful delineation of the new essential poetry, a statement and demonstration of his engaged and authentic art.

Northwest Ecolog (1978) takes this urban poet into the wilderness where he is equally at home with earth-life concerns and able to meditate on life and age. It is a fine, mellow book full of quiet beauty and concern using imagist and open-form composition. Nature and consciousness come together in an epiphanous stillness in which the acts of perception and apperception unite. The journal prose and the original sumi drawings reinforce the transparent yet profound approach rendering the book as pure as a stream amidst the ecological destruction of encroaching civilization. The book has a rare wholeness of effect as autobiographical detail achieves universality through the meditative form brought on by a comprehensive consciousness of the ultimate limits of earth and life.

Following his populist directive, Ferlinghetti has published many of the poems in *Landscapes of Living and Dying* (1979) in newspapers. It too is a more mellowed, aged book, yet alive in its awareness of the times. The mythic reality of life is captured in various forms—the oral street observations of **"The Old Italians Dying,"** the satiric tirade of **"Home Home Home,"** the prose poem tributes of **"Look Homeward, Jack,"** the deep synthesis of political awareness and surrealist image in **"White on White,"** and the many mass culture filmic scenes. Possibly the strongest poem in terms of statement and form is his second populist manifesto, **"Adieu A Charlot."** Here Ferlinghetti strips away life's false myths (social and artistic) to arrive at the personal and universal myths that have been earned through the authentic. His characteristic engaged voice is heard loud and clear above the din of contemporary poetry and poetics. Through his vision, his ever-widening involvements, and his authentic search, he finds the essential stance and thus molds the creative forms to make him America's most public and personal poet. All of this is borne out in his recent journal poems published as *A Trip to Italy and France* (1980) and by his self-selected *Endless Life: Selected Poems* (1981), which is expanded by a third populist manifesto, **"Modern Poetry Is Prose (But It Is Saying Plenty)"** and by inclusion of a segment from his long work-in-progress, **"Endless Life."** Ferlinghetti is still very much at large, with us and of us, as he tells us in **"Endless Life,"** "For there is no end to the hopeful choices / still to be chosen . . . And there is no end / to the doors of perception still to be opened." (pp. 139-42)

Larry Smith, in his Lawrence Ferlinghetti: Poet-At-Large *(copyright © 1983 by the Board of Trustees, Southern Illinois University; reprinted by permission of Southern Illinois University Press), Southern Illinois University Press, 1983, 232 p.*

Timothy Findley

1930-

Canadian novelist, playwright, and scriptwriter.

With each of his books, Findley has more firmly established his place among Canada's important contemporary writers. Ambitious in his choice of themes and innovative in his handling of them, he writes of the human struggle against fate and questions the nature of self, love, and reality. Findley has examined these concerns from several different perspectives beginning with *The Last of the Crazy People* (1967). In this work, Findley portrays the life of a lonely and bewildered young boy whose tragic destiny is to murder his family.

Findley's most successful novel, *The Wars*, published in the United States in 1978, won the Governor General's Award in 1977. Written in a documentary style, it recounts the story of Robert Ross, an officer in the Canadian army during World War I. Findley here attempts to show that Ross's eventual death is both futile and triumphant. *The Wars* is described as a powerful account of how war simultaneously defines and destroys personality.

Famous Last Words (1982) is also related to war. In this novel, Findley molds Ezra Pound's poetic figure Hugh Selwyn Mauberley into a fully formed fictional character and traces his fascination with and involvement in fascist politics. Although described as flawed, many critics appraise *Famous Last Words* as an ambitious work that raises serious questions about the effects of political corruption and the meaning of history.

(See also *Contemporary Authors*, Vols. 25-28, rev. ed.)

Photograph by Robert Lansdale; courtesy of Nancy Colbert & Associates

ANTHONY BOUCHER

["**The Last of the Crazy People**"] is almost as pleasing as its odd title. An attempt to explain the far too frequent and inexplicable headline, " 'Nice Boy' Massacres Family," it is memorable not so much for its explanation (or for its gore) as for a surprisingly gentle, nostalgic quality which is wholly charming. Story and style may seem at variance, but I look forward to Findley's second.

> *Anthony Boucher, in a review of "The Last of the Crazy People," in* The New York Times Book Review *(© 1967 by The New York Times Company; reprinted by permission), July 16, 1967, p. 14.*

MARGARET PARTON

Like Ben Piazza, who three years ago wrote a moving first novel about boyhood called *The Exact and Very Strange Truth*, Timothy Findley is an actor. Again like Piazza, he is interested in boyhood and its relationship to the adult world, and he has an actor's ear for dialogue, an actor's eye for scenes. After three years, scenes from the earlier book remain vivid in the mind; it is probable that those created by Mr. Findley [in *The Last of the Crazy People*] will also linger for a long time, if less happily.

The first scene sets the mood, and almost—but not quite—tells us what is to happen. It is early September, after a rainless summer. An eleven-year-old boy carrying a box tiptoes out of his house in the dawn, crosses the back yard to the stable, climbs into the loft, and settles down in the straw by the half-open bale door overlooking the back of the house. The box is beside him, and so is his cat, Little Bones, whose "deadly, vibrant, yet clouded" eyes resemble his own. Together they wait and are still.

We gather from every careful word of this prologue that the boy is insane and about to do something terrible. The rest of the book, flashing back to the beginning of that hot Canadian summer, tells us of the events that have led inexorably to this September morning and of the people who contributed to them. And as we come to know the members of young Hooker Winslow's family and the middle-class community in which they exist, we begin to see that his inevitable tragedy is triggered not by one cause but by many, stress upon stress. (p. 36)

Only Iris, the Negro maid, takes any interest in the lonely boy or the pet cats who are his sole companions. But . . . not even Iris, with all her good will, can answer Hooker's inchoate questions; nor is there any help, he finds, in the bewildering adult world outside. "In all houses, all families, was it true that no one really loved?" Hooker wonders near the end. It is no surprise that his final act seems like ultimate sanity.

The Last of the Crazy People is not light summer reading. But it says something important, and says it with both craftsmanship and compassion. (p. 37)

> Margaret Parton, "A Sad Song of Eleven Summers," in Saturday Review (© 1967 Saturday Review Magazine Co.; reprinted by permission), Vol. L, No. 31, August 5, 1967, pp. 36-7.

PUBLISHERS WEEKLY

1930's Hollywood, with its overripe stars, larger-than-life styles, extravagant successes and even more extravagant failures, and the nightmare barbarities of Hitler's Germany, make a strange juxtaposition here. "The Butterfly Plague" is full of unlikely juxtapositions, but they work to make the book consistently interesting, often disquieting. Mr. Findley's novel is an ambitious one, for he has chosen to deal with the nature of reality, the meaning of life and death and love, and the future of the human race. Despite a style and setting that sometimes verge on the campy, his unique way of perceiving people and places gives his book considerable power. "The Butterfly Plague" is mostly populated by grotesques, including a former Olympic medal swimmer who is a carrier of haemophilia and who is married to a virulent master-race Nazi; her brother; a Hollywood director; and her mother, dying of cancer. All of these people and some other Hollywood types drift in and out of one 'another's lives and nightmares, and what emerges is a disturbing picture of man's despair.

> A review of "The Butterfly Plague," in Publishers Weekly (reprinted from the February 10, 1969 issue of Publishers Weekly, published by R. R. Bowker Company, a Xerox company; copyright © 1969 by Xerox Corporation), Vol. 195, No. 6, February 10, 1969, p. 72.

THE TIMES LITERARY SUPPLEMENT

[*The Butterfly Plague*] resembles an appreciative description of a fantastic film, the kind that depends on surrealistic images and a voguish "sense of period", more interesting to see than to read about. . . . A quick succession of intricate, brightly-coloured scenes must have been the aim; but Timothy Findley cannot, as a novelist, rival a film-director's pace. Instead of being fixed in cinematic images, the details of landscape, facial expression, physical appearance and (especially) clothing have to be set out in lists, as if they were instructions to the property department, the designer and the wardrobe mistress. Thus the novel proceeds more slowly than can have been intended.

The setting is Southern California, 1938, with flashbacks to Nazi Germany. The mood is one of fear, with epicene women and men wincing at hazards as normal as motor accidents or as nightmarish as Nazidom. . . .

[Many disasters occur to] bizarre characters. Miss Trainer, a motor-cycling nurse, discovers a lady in "rather old-maidish drawers" and lisle stockings, hanging from a tree, "with a black-handled knife inserted in her vagina". Miss Trainer swoons away—but the cold-blooded reader will be less perturbed, since this atrocity seems, like so much in the book, to be presented rather for its pictorial value than for any literary purpose. Occasionally there is a flicker of Firbank in the writing; but, generally, the book is too stodgy, long-winded and mirthless to make the comparison worthwhile.

> "Uncomic Strip," in The Times Literary Supplement (© Times Newspapers Ltd. (London) 1970; reproduced from The Times Literary Supplement by permission), No. 3549, March 5, 1970, p. 241.

MICHAEL TAYLOR

We no longer believe that some subjects are more appropriate for literary treatment than others: nowadays, every human activity, no matter how banal or disgusting, offers itself as legitimate material for the imagination to work on and turn into art. . . . There seem to be some subjects, however, which have a built-in intransigence to literary treatment because their historical reality, overwhelmingly banal, perhaps, or overwhelmingly disgusting, surpasses anything that the creative imagination can make of them. Writers instinctively shun these topics, it seems to me, and rightly so. It takes considerable nerve, therefore, to do what Timothy Findley has done [in *The Wars*]— to write a novel squarely about the unspeakable reality of the 1914-18 war in order to make that reality even more unspeakably real. Having read it, we're meant to put his book down angered and disgusted once again by the sheer futility of those four years, with the additional wrenching caused by our concern for the fate of the book's fictional Canadian hero, Robert Ross.

It's plain that Findley realizes he's dealing with intractable material because he camouflages the fiction of his story by pretending that the novel is a species of historical document, taking as its subject the life of Robert Ross, piecing it together from tape-recorded interviews, press-cuttings from the archives, old photographs, diaries, and the like. This technique enables Findley to intersperse his fictional account with grim and telling statistics about the war itself, though, in fact, the greater part of the book is a conventional third-person narrative, a novel, telling the story of its central character more or less straightforwardly as countless novels have done and will no doubt continue to do. But does the story of Robert Ross match, or add to, or make even more dire, the tragedy of which he is a tiny (though not necessarily insignificant) part? At best, it seems to only fitfully: there's frequently such a sense of strain in the telling of his tale that the insertion of those cold statistics from the greater drama makes his own biography seem forced and untrue.

Part of the trouble must lie in the clipped, portentous style that Findley chooses for most of the book's scenes whether or not they take place on the battlefield. . . . [The] dominant style of the book [is] obtrusively unobtrusive, especially in moments of crisis such as the death of Rowena, the revelation about Taffler and the Swede, or the various deaths on the battlefield. . . . At moments like these the book's Hemingwayesque style pitches over into sentimentality.

To describe the style of *The Wars* as sentimental is the closest I can come to conveying the cumulative effect of the novel's various crises rendered in this flattened, yet oddly apocalyptic, manner. Such a style takes its toll of the characters. Much of the time they exist in the shadows, wraiths, dream-figures caught fleetingly in various postures, their behaviour difficult to understand except that it in some way reflects the exigencies of their time. Distant eccentrics is the description that springs to mind—like Robert's mother and the appalling Lady Barbara d'Orsey with whom Robert falls in love. Robert himself is a hero in the silent tradition, more acted upon than acting, chief victim perhaps of the book's style. . . . [The] novel demands our anguished sympathy without really having done enough to earn it. (pp. 173-74)

Michael Taylor, in a review of "The Wars" (copyright by Michael Taylor; reprinted by permission of the author), in The Fiddlehead, No. 118, Summer, 1978, pp. 172-74.

THOMAS R. EDWARDS

Timothy Findley's **"The Wars"** is . . . elegantly written and structured and well aware of what can't be said about important human experiences. (Like other Canadian writers, such as Margaret Atwood, Robertson Davies and Marian Engel, Mr. Findley seems closer and more responsive to natural mystery than his peers south of the border.) (p. 14)

The book has flaws, certainly. Its rather poetic prose sometimes turns overripe. Its climactic moment—when Ross disobeys orders, shoots his commander and leads a herd of panicky horses to what turns out to be their death in a burning barn—is over-prepared for by insistent imagery of horses and fires. . . .

But for the most part **"The Wars"** is an impressively sustained meditation on how war crystallizes an unfinished personality even while destroying it, and on how the past remains available and valuable only in our ability to reinvent and reinterpret it. Ross's terrible story is also a terribly beautiful one, and it shows that Timothy Findley is a writer worth keeping an eye on. (p. 26)

Thomas R. Edwards, "The Grim War and the Great War," in The New York Times Book Review (© 1978 by The New York Times Company; reprinted by permission), July 9, 1978, pp. 14, 26.*

GARY T. DAVENPORT

[Brevity] is disastrous in the hands of Timothy Findley. In fact understatement of a very slick and ineffective sort is chronically recurrent in *The Wars*. . . . The story is well told, the scenes follow each other with sure logic, and, with one or two exceptions, the thematic interest arises naturally from the events instead of being forced.

The stylistic slickness of which I complained consists mainly of the frequent use of telegraphic one-liners (which one reviewer has associated—I think wrongly—with Hemingway) and typographical cleverness obviously calculated to bring the reader to the edge of his seat. (Two-word sentences. One-word paragraphs. Triple spacing. The works.) Another "special effect" is the studied sensitivity of the prose that occasionally emerges, especially toward the end of the book. . . . Cheap attempts to add intensity or beauty are never less welcome than when they are unnecessary, as they are here. When the author forgets to be "creative," his prose is entirely adequate to the task, and the intensity and beauty take care of themselves. The book is in any case a substantial performance, and I do not want to make it sound trivial. . . . [Findley] has overcome heavy odds by writing a convincing historical novel about an event which has been so momentous—and ultimately so inaccessible—as the war which all of us who call ourselves "modern" have come to see as our point of origin. (pp. xxi-xxii)

Gary T. Davenport, "A Canadian Miscellany," in The Sewanee Review (reprinted by permission of the editor; © 1979 by The University of the South), Vol. LXXXVII, No. 1, Winter, 1979, pp. xix-xxii.*

BRUCE PIRIE

In Timothy Findley's novel *The Wars,* Robert Ross, soon after arriving in Europe, finds himself leading a line of horses through thick green fog. The foul smell of the air puzzles him, but Poole, his batman, detects the odour of chlorine that has soaked into the ground.

The smell was unnerving—as if some presence were lurking in the fog like a dragon in a story. Poole was quite correct; the ground was saturated with gas. Chlorine and phosgene were currently both in use. Mustard gas was still to come.

This matter-of-fact chemical information is typical of the novel's verisimilitude. An almost documentary realism seems to seduce the reader into accepting the authenticity of the account. By mentioning "a dragon in a story," however, the narrator teases us with a glimpse of another, more truly seductive influence. Behind the elaborate realism of *The Wars* hides the beguiling shape of myth and legend—the dragon that lurks in the fog.

Northrop Frye finds the essential principles of story-telling in mythology; those structural principles are "displaced" from mythology to literature. What kind of displaced mythology would we expect to find in Findley's novel? *The Wars* is a work of irony; in it we see the attempt, as Frye says in *Anatomy of Criticism*, "to give form to the shifting ambiguities and complexities of unidealized existence." He goes on to say, "As structure, the central principle of ironic myth is best approached as a parody of romance: the application of romantic mythical forms to a more realistic content which fits them in unexpected ways." A dragon's proper home, of course, is the world of romance; if he can be displaced into the world of "unidealized existence," perhaps other aspects of his home-world have made their way with him. Following this lead, I intend to examine *The Wars* as a "parody of romance." (p. 70)

Adventure is the essential element of plot in romance, and in a naive form romance can be the story of a hero who dies in the glory of combat or who undergoes a series of exciting adventures and always comes back for more, like a comic book hero. There are plenty of children in the novel who see war this way. They range from Robert's younger brother, thrilled to announce at school that Robert would receive the Victoria Cross, to boys arriving at the front, exhiliarated by the "heaven-sent chance" to become men. (pp. 70-1)

The true romantic hero begins in innocence and journeys in quest of knowledge. A wise old guardian may supervise the initiation, as do Arthur's Merlin and Dante's Virgil. Robert's innocence lies in the fact that killing is "a foreign state of mind" for him. He needs "someone who could teach him, by example, how to kill" and thinks he has found such a person in the legendary Eugene Taffler, an older man who has already journeyed to war and back; ironically, this nearly mythic figure turns out to practise sexual perversions and later attempts suicide. . . .

Robert's initiations and loss of innocence remind us that we expect life to have four seasons—youth, maturity, age, and death—but part of the horror of *The Wars* is the realization that this natural cycle has been drastically accelerated. We expect young men in romances to face challenging ordeals and life-changing epiphanies, but in this novel too many men face dead-end ordeals and learn too much too soon. We see this in the constant emphasis on the childishness of the characters: ''men'' whose average age is nineteen, some of whom do not yet shave and whose voices still waver, who promise their mothers not to drink and who soil their pants in moments of crisis. (p. 71)

A variation of the innocence theme appears in the hero's pure love for a damsel—love, like adventure, being one of the key-notes of romance. In one version, the hero leaves a chaste lady, has adventures, and returns to marriage. In another form, often focusing on a sister or daughter figure, the journey ends in virginity. The chastity of the latter quest may thinly disguise a latently incestuous relationship; the chaste love of brother for sister may represent a lost Golden Age but may also hover near a moral taboo (virtue being most admirable when closely pressed by temptation).

In the case of Robert Ross, the catalyst for the story is his love for his sister Rowena; ''Rowena,'' we may remember, is the name of one of the heroines in *Ivanhoe*. Robert often remembers her in critical moments of the war. She represents a lost happy time: he remembers her with her rabbits, or the idyllic sound of lapping water as they vacationed at Jackson's Point. (p. 72)

Romances often begin with a knight riding off into a forest after an animal, an image which is never very far from meta-morphosis, the changing of the hunter into an animal. Near the beginning of the book, Robert goes for a long run with a coyote. The two enjoy a special communion, both drinking from a river in the prairie. Robert becomes oddly identified with the animal as he crouches ''on his haunches'' watching it. When confined to barracks for two weeks, he sits like a caged and lonely animal on the roof and stares across the prairie, ''wishing that someone would howl.'' Metamorphosis, or the union of human and animal identities, is an important theme in *The Wars*. . . . Metamorphosis in romance often in-dicates a lowering of human identity as the hero obscures the signs of original identity and joins a lower world of animals. In *The Wars,* it is a lowering in the sense that the humans are trapped and frightened like the animals, but the fellow-feeling with animals is also part of the human largeness and generosity of characters like Rodwell and Robert. To recognize oneself as an animal is to recognize one's kinship with and duty towards all life, a recognition threatened by the ''ethics'' of war.

The changing of humans into animals occurs specifically in those romances concerned with the descent of the hero, and *The Wars* is primarily the story of a journey into a lower world, although there are points of ascent. Ascents in romance typi-cally involve an epiphany at a mountaintop, tower, or staircase. Since the ascent reverses the Fall of Man, it is not surprising that the goal is often a new Eden, a *locus amoenus* or ''beautiful green world.'' (pp. 73-4)

[A] subtle image of ascent occurs when Robert and his men climb into a giant crater to cut gun beds. It is hard to find images of upward movement in the flatlands of Europe, and the crater is most obviously an image of descent, but Findley gets double service from this crater by making it an ironically inverted mountain. . . . As the men clamber out of the crater, they might as well be mountain climbing, with the ''sound of falling debris'' and the treacherous slipping backwards, ''slid-ing in the snow.'' At the top of this climb is a vestigial *locus*

amoenus, for in the midst of all the mud is a singing bird and an enemy soldier who has laid aside his weapon in order to watch the bird. At the peak, Robert shoots the soldier and then has a devastating epiphany: the man he has killed had no in-tention of killing him.

Images of descent are, of course, richly elaborated and to prepare for descent, one needs a talisman, such as a golden bough. For Robert it is his pistol, which gives him the ''ritual edge in authority,'' not so much from the enemy as from his own men in the nightmare world they enter. (p. 74)

The lower world is a form of hell, a night world, a subterranean world where the shapes of animals swarm upon the hero. . . . More than anything else, hell is full of dead people, and surely our main impression of the battlefront is that it is a world full of corpses. At times this vision of hell frankly becomes a vision of the Apocalypse, as when flame-throwers unleash fire storms, men explode from combustion, horses rear ''with their bones on fire,'' and the earth is ''seared and sealed with fire.''

Earth and air are man's natural elements. The romantic hero journeying to another world must pass ordeals of the other two elements, fire and water, just as Dante must pass through a ring of fire and the river of Eden. (p. 75)

The whole area of the battlefield is ''well below sea level'' and the men fight in ''a shallow sea of stinking grey from end to end'' where men and horses drown in mud. Robert's ordeal by water comes when he slips off a dike and nearly drowns. It becomes important to find ways of living with water. Robert appears to love Harris, who tells stories about feeling at home in water, and Rodwell's toad survives a gas attack by staying in a pail of water: ''It was a matter, Rodwell had said, of your element. The toad has a choice.''

The world of fire can be a destructive world of malignant demons, such as the enemy's fire storms, but it can also be a cleansing purgatorial fire. Both connotations apply to Robert's ordeal by fire in the burning barn. It shows the stupid destruc-tiveness of the war world; it is also a gateway by which Robert rises to a higher level of heroism. . . .

[The] life-assertive statements that appear throughout the book insist that there is . . . triumph in Robert's end: the epigraph from Euripides, for example—''Never that which is shall die''—or Rodwell's last letter to his daughter—''Everything lives forever''—or Robert's reply to the nurse who, ''ashamed of life,'' offers to help him die:

'Not yet.' *Not yet. . . .*

''Not yet'' are the words of a man who had been profoundly educated by his journey to the lower world. He fully knows the presence of death and he holds onto life. Knowledge of death feeds this human impulse to survive. When the hero fights the dragon to get at the secret treasure hoard, the real wealth is a wealth of wisdom, which is often wisdom about death. . . . (p. 76)

[Robert] finds a way out of the underworld, a way to survive: a radical act of individuality. The act leaves him physically scarred, of course, but heroes from Oedipus on have known that mutilation is often the price of great wisdom. Although the individualizing act, saving the horses, returns Robert to a full compassion for life, it necessitates the destruction of life—the killing of Captain Leather. This paradox is what Frye calls ''a return that achieves its recreation by a creatively negative act.'' . . . Unfortunately, ''creatively negative'' acts do not stand up well in the courts. One of the motifs of romance is the trial founded on a mistaken or narrow-minded charge or a wrong identity; the hero escapes by revealing his true identity. The Robert who shot Captain Leather was a man making a desperate last gesture to pull himself out of the lower world of war in order to recreate his own identity. Once that identity is recreated, he is no longer the same man. Thus, Robert's trial is, in fact, the trial of a "wrong identity" and it is poetically appropriate that he be tried *"in absentia"* and allowed to return to St. Aubyn's for convalescent treatment.

The return to St. Aubyn's is, of course, a return to Eden. As romance moves to a world of original identity, the symbolism of the garden of Eden reappears. . . . Robert can never return to his first Eden: Rowena and her rabbits are dead. The last picture taken during his life shows, however, that Robert has achieved a new Eden. Juliet d'Orsey loves him; they are together in St. Aubyn's; he holds her hand and "he is smiling." Juliet, who even as an old woman maintains a child's wisdom, becomes a substitute for Rowena.

This identification is made even more clearly in the epilogue. We see one more picture which echoes the earlier picture of Robert linked to Juliet, and this is "the last thing you see before you put on your overcoat":

> *Robert and Rowena and Meg:* Rowena seated astride the pony—Robert holding her in place. On the back is written: 'Look! you can see our breath!' And you can.

The hero brings the end of his quest in line with the beginning; the circle closes. (pp. 78-9)

[It] is clear that while *The Wars'* realistic details generate part of its appeal and effectiveness, the way in which those details are given imaginative impact goes beyond the effects of verisimilitude. We demand that historic and geographic "facts" be given a "shape" to contain them. The situation of the narrator in this novel mirrors this fundamental issue in fiction: he has only a few photographic images which, by themselves, say little. His task—"your" task—is to take those few facts and pictures and find their meaning. To find the meaning of the pictures, to discover the imaginative impact of realistic details, the story-teller must be a master of the basic principles of story-telling—principles which give shape to human experience, and which are as old as myth and legend. (p. 79)

> *Bruce Pirie, "The Dragon in the Fog: 'Displaced Mythology' in 'The Wars'" (reprinted by permission of the author), in* Canadian Literature, *No. 91, Winter, 1981, pp. 70-9.*

IAN McLACHLAN

[The protagonist of Pound's modernist poem "Hugh Selwyn Mauberley"] is the main character—initially, at least—in Timothy Findley's new novel, *Famous Last Words.* Immediately, one recognizes it as a brilliant idea that sparks a variety of possibilities in the reader's imagination. Findley has re-invented Mauberley for his own purposes, making him a younger man than Pound's, American, and a novelist. But any artist—according to Brecht, anyway—has the right to steal another man's work, provided he transforms it in the process. And it's in that transformation that the roots of our initial excitement grow. Pound's Mauberley was a symptom of a world that had apparently been wiped out by the First World War. Findley revives him and uses him to examine the way in which that

old world of class and style had not been eliminated after all, but went on clinging to its power with increasing avidity for another 20 years or more. (Even now, has its grip been broken?) Naturally enough, Findley's Mauberley, like Pound, is drawn to fascism, but a fascism attenuated and sweetened by the desire to reconcile itself to the pretences and subtleties of an older aristocratic tradition. The Duke of Windsor for Führer?!

The concept is a fine one. It affords Findley the freedom to move easily between the old hypocrisies and the new barbarism that was replacing them in the 1930s. In the process there's a lovely, wicked irony: that Pound's alter ego, whom he had used to liberate himself from the past, should now be used to expose the political falsehoods that he in his own due course was seduced by.

One's appreciation of Findley's cleverness may be so great that one suppresses the inevitable question that has to be put to it—at least, until much later in the novel. What is the necessary relationship of Findley to Mauberley? In Pound's case, the relationship was clear. Mauberley was the mask Pound might have become, and by writing about him, by making him a character in a poem that Mauberley could never have constructed in its entirety, Pound was able to make the separation complete. But why does Findley need this Mauberley he creates? Who is Mauberley to him? Or to us? It's only as the novel progresses, and as our dissatisfaction with it grows, that these suspended questions force their way back into our consciousness. . . . (p. 9)

At the start of the novel . . . there is [a] perfectly conceived metaphor for the role of the artist in a modern social context. It's a metaphor that is at one and the same time melodramatic and satirical, and it gives Findley a remarkable freedom to manoeuvre among the various trajectories of his narrative. Yet from that point on he seems to lose his grip on the intertwined themes that he has shown to be so potentially interesting. Or to be able to grip only one thread at a time while the others dangle loose.

I write those words hesitantly. This is an ambitious novel and Findley is a serious writer. The probability is that his readers will misunderstand what he is doing. A novel that starts from the intricate social and psychological puzzle of "Hugh Selwyn Mauberley" will be likely to mislead us, may do so even with glee. We cannot expect its fragments to build themselves brick by brick into a load-bearing arch. The arch will be an illusion created by contradictory free-standing shapes, and when we shift our position slightly it will disappear.

Moreover, a novel such as *Famous Last Words* is not simply an intellectual experiment. It has bifurcating purposes, taking as it does a tale of intrigue and wartime espionage and disrupting it so as to open it up to the light of analysis. The adventure novel is a form that reconciles a middle-class audience to the suppressed horror of the world it rests on. Findley is clearly concerned to break that form in such a way that the violence he so passionately abhors will flood back into it.

All that is clear. But not, finally, in this novel. I hold it up to the light and try to see through it. I look into it from different angles. I leave it on its own and walk out along the edge of the lake, turning my back on it, hoping to catch it off guard when I swing round and. . . . And still it doesn't work. A novel like this deserves the benefit of every doubt. Every doubt except the last. In the end the doubt envelops it all.

There are three main threads that Findley draws out of the superb symbolic knot he has tied for us at the beginning. One, recounted in the first person, is the strand of Mauberley's personal reminiscence as he recalls the bewildered way in which he shuffled headlong into the elegant and vicious half-world of right-wing politics. Mauberley himself is hollow, and there is little real interest either in his political conversion or in his belated consciousness of what it entailed. As the novel progresses, his plight loses much of our attention. That in itself is not necessarily a fault. There are many novels, after all, that have nonentities at their centres, and Pound's Mauberley was just such a devitalized bore. But Pound's Mauberley implied by indirection another kind of dynamics altogether. Findley's does not.

The second thread is the tale of botched high politics that Mauberley recounts: the plot to capture Wallis Simpson and her waxwork husband, the Duke of Windsor, and to transform them into the saviours of fascist Europe. The telling itself is suspect in that one never senses the presence of Mauberley the narrator behind it. But that would only be a significant fault in a realist novel, which this is not. The story, in some of its parts, is brilliantly handled with fine set-pieces of absurdity and flaring horror. The relationship between the ex-king and his despotic mother, Queen Mary, seems at times to be the one real emotional experience in the whole book. Yet one wonders constantly why it needs Mauberley to tell it at all.

The final narrative thread is the present description of the soldiers who occupy the hotel and of their conflicts and dreams about what they find there. In many ways, this is the most achieved aspect of the novel. It is surrealistic and satirical simultaneously, and one finds onself wishing there were more of it, since it might well provide the focus that could hold the novel's divergencies together. But Findley seems particularly constrained in these scenes, hardly ever giving them a free enough rein to establish a developed relationship with the rest of the plot.

So we are left with fragments, many of them very fine indeed, a few rather dull and pedestrian in their attempts at historical interpretation. But fragments, in sum, that don't mesh or even point significantly toward each other. There is neither a meaningful argument nor a convincingly imagined interdependence between them. The novel, in consequence, does not lead to any new insights either into the social and psychological forces that made fascism such a demanding necessity in the 1930s, or into the relationship of those forces to the pressures of our own world. Findley affords us some fascinating glimpses of the effects of political perversion; he leaves the causes hidden. (pp. 10-11)

Ian McLachlan, "Not the Full Smile" (reprinted by permission of the author), in Books in Canada, *Vol. 10, No. 10, December, 1981, pp. 9-11.*

ELSPETH CAMERON

Ezra Pound in his poem sequence "Hugh Selwyn Mauberley" claimed that "The age demanded an image / Of its accelerated grimace, / Something for the modern stage." With benefit of a hindsight denied to Pound, Timothy Findley in *Famous Last Words* takes up the challenge in a "prose cinema" of dazzling brilliance. Like his earlier novel *The Wars,* the story revolves around a man trapped in wartime events. Transforming Pound's poetic persona Hugh Mauberley into a plausible fictional character, Findley probes the meaning of history with such insight and skill that *Famous Last Words* becomes a leap forward in his work. . . .

Through his uncanny descriptive powers, Findley moves outward from a base of facts to convey an atmosphere in which the "porcelain revery" of Pound's Mauberley poems is finally shattered as the civilized world cracks apart. (p. 53)

In a novel of wider scope than anything he has yet attempted, Findley uses Mauberley to demonstrate that all it takes for evil to triumph is that men of conscience stand silent. Mauberley, like all men, must resist the evil he sees and feels not only around him but inside him. . . .

Although *Famous Last Words* is based on well-documented events gleaned from a range of sources—Frances Donaldson's *Edward VIII,* Hugh Kenner's *The Pound Era,* and James Pope-Hennessey's *Queen Mary,* among others—fact ultimately rallies to the side of fiction. What Findley knows defers always to what he has sensed. By according his own imagination the highest authority, he recreates history in terms that bring it uncomfortably close to us. But he keeps us always slightly off-balance, leaving us just uncertain enough to question our own hold on reality. Those electric moments of history, like blurred camera frames suddenly springing into focus, bring us face to face with our own souls. The result is a novel of the first magnitude: Sophoclean in power, certain in craft, and hauntingly beautiful. (p. 54)

Elspeth Cameron, "After the Wars" (copyright © 1982 by Saturday Night; *reprinted by permission of the author), in* Saturday Night, *Vol. 97, No. 1, January, 1982, pp. 53-4.*

Gabriel García Márquez

1928-

Colombian novelist, short story writer, journalist, and screen-writer.

Nobel laureate García Márquez is among the Latin American writers who rose to prominence during the 1960s, a flowering referred to as "El Boom." Like Julio Cortázar and Ernesto Sábato, García Márquez had been writing fiction for a number of years before gaining international attention. The almost simultaneous publication of major works by these three authors, along with the appearance of skillful first novels by Carlos Fuentes and Mario Vargas Llosa and the established importance of Jorge Luis Borges and Pablo Neruda, led to a recognition of Latin American letters as a potent force in modern literature. The enthusiastic popular and critical reception of García Márquez is based on the social realism and the political implications of his works along with his narrative technique of "magic realism." While setting his stories within a socially realistic framework, García Márquez embellishes them with surreal events and fantastic imagery, blurring the distinction between fantasy and reality.

García Márquez was born in Aracataca, Columbia, and lived there the first eight years of his life with his grandparents. The storytelling of his grandmother, the long decline and subsequent decay of Aracataca, and the myths and superstitions of its citizens all played roles in shaping García Márquez's imagination. While in college he became a journalist, which led to travels throughout South America, Europe, and the United States. During these years he composed short shories in which he laid the foundations of Macondo, a mythical village based on Aracataca. Macondo, with its richness of local color and characters, is comparable to William Faulkner's Yoknapatawpha County. Years later, in his acceptance speech for the 1982 Nobel Prize in literature, García Márquez acknowledged Faulkner as his master. García Márquez's early short stories, considered his least successful work, are experiments of a Kafkaesque nature that fail, according to Vargas Llosa, simply because they do not tell a story. But with "Los funerales de la Mamá Grande" (1962; "Big Mama's Funeral"), he successfully fused realism with myth and fantasy, lending a social and political dimension to fantastic events.

García Márquez first won critical recognition with *El coronel no tiene quién le escriba* (1968; *No One Writes to the Colonel*). This novella was especially praised for its insight into the condition of solitude as depicted in the character of a retired colonel who waits in vain but with unflagging determination for his pension, sustained by dreams which eventually become illusions. *La mala hora* (1962; *In Evil Hour*), García Márquez's first novel, was a major event in Colombian literature. Its montage-like presentation of a backwater town torn both by political oppression and moral corruption was an artistic success, while also documenting *la violencia*, a state of violence that raged through Colombia in the 1950s.

With the publication of *Cien años de soledad* (1967; *One Hundred Years of Solitude*), García Márquez won immediate international acclaim. The novel depicts the history of Macondo, from its founding by José Arcadia Buendía to its decline through

six generations of his descendants. *Solitude* presents Macondo as a microcosm of the country of Colombia, the continent of South America, and, by symbolic extension, as representative of the history of the world "from Eden to Apocalypse." As well as reflecting the political, social, and economic ills of South America, replete with fantastic events like the birth of a baby that has a pig's tail, the novel's labyrinthine structure, achieved in part by nonlinear development, long, free-flowing sentences, and epic scope, helped make *Solitude* a stylistic tour de force. *El otoño del patriarca* (1975; *The Autumn of the Patriarch*), his next novel, depicts the evils of despotism as embodied in a commanding and unloved dictator, with solitude again emerging as the theme. *Patriarch* proved to be a powerful political statement on totalitarianism. In addition, it was another stylistic triumph for García Márquez, presenting a phantasmagoric narrative through frequent shifts of viewpoint and extensive use of hyperbole to further enhance both comedic and horrific effects.

Following the publication of *Patriarch*, García Márquez vowed not to publish any new fiction until the Pinochet regime of Chile was either disbanded or overthrown. After six years, he published *Crónica de una muerte anunciada* (1982; *Chronicle of a Death Foretold*), a journalistic investigation of a murder twenty-seven years in the past that involved people with whom García Márquez was acquainted. With its constant juxtaposing of eyewitness accounts that ultimately prove unreliable, its shifting time sequences, and the surreal quality of its setting, *Chronicle* recounts the dreary presentiment of a tragedy that is fostered rather than averted by the inhabitants of a backwater community. Critics believe the novella reveals a people trapped in their own myths, unable to overcome the outmoded customs of their forebears or, perhaps, unable to triumph over fate. *Chronicle* provides another example of García Márquez's successful innovations in style and structure combined with the presentation of social realities.

With his successful fusion of social issues and magic realism, the universal implications he draws from events that occur in Macondo, and his successful experiments, García Márquez helped to reinvigorate the novel at a time when its death had been foretold.

(See also *CLC*, Vols. 2, 3, 8, 10, 15; *Contemporary Authors*, Vols. 33-36, rev. ed.; *Contemporary Authors New Revision Series*, Vol. 10; and *Dictionary of Literary Biography Yearbook: 1982*.)

GEORGE R. McMURRAY

At a time of dire predictions about the future of the novel, García Márquez's prodigious imagination, remarkable compositional precision, and wide popularity provide evidence that the genre is still thriving. Although his dramatizations of the sinister forces threatening twentieth-century life imply strong moral indignation, his works are illumined by flashes of irony and the belief that human values are perennial. The amazing totality of his fictional world is also achieved through the contrapuntal juxtaposition of objective reality and poetic fantasy that captures simultaneously the essence of both Latin American and universal man. (p. 6)

García Márquez's approach to fiction indicates that he has come full circle in at least one respect, namely, in his depiction of subjective states of mind reminiscent of surrealism. Thus, whereas his early short stories are characterized by hermetic morbidity and fantasy, his [*The Autumn of the Patriarch*] is the most lyrically conceived to date. During the intervening years he has sharpened his literary tools and emerged as a mature, consummate craftsman, the result of extensive reading and experimentation with a wide variety of styles and techniques. The vision of Macondo set forth in *Leaf Storm* reveals possible influences of William Faulkner and Virginia Woolf; Hemingway's aesthetic ideals are brought to mind by "**Tuesday Siesta**," "**One of These Days**," and *No One Writes to the Colonel;* other fine pieces such as "**Baltazar's Marvelous Afternoon**" and "**Big Mama's Funeral**" point the way toward the perfect synthesis of realism and fantasy displayed in the internationally acclaimed masterpiece, *One Hundred Years of Solitude;* and the most recent works depict a world in which lyricism and fantasy predominate.

García Márquez's fictional universe consists of three major settings: "the town," Macondo, and a seaside village, or, in the case of *The Autumn of the Patriarch*, a large seaport. Although solitude emerges as his most important theme, "the town" is also the scene of *la violencia*. The other two settings provide the backdrop for the recurring cycle of birth, boom, decay, and death. Time plays an important role in García Márquez's works, the horrors of lineal history serving to convey the failure of man's political, social, and religious institutions. On the other hand, the repetitive patterns and rhythmic momentum generated by mythical time create a mytho-poetic at-

mosphere that blurs sordid reality and thrusts the reader into a kind of temporal void where the laws of cause and effect tend to become meaningless.

García Márquez displays his mastery of irony and wry humor in *No One Writes to the Colonel,* the protagonist of which emerges as an absurd hero struggling against impossible odds. The subsequent works reveal a trend toward a more Rabelaisian type of humor, with greater emphasis on the absurdities of human existence. These attacks on the tenets of reason are more than likely intended to unveil the other side of reality and in this way question the outmoded conventions that have spawned the disasters of the twentieth century. An antirational outlook on the world is also expressed stylistically through the inordinately long, rambling sentences and jarring shifts in the point of view in "**The Last Voyage of the Ghost Ship**" and "**Blancamán the Good, Vendor of Miracles**." In addition "**The Last Voyage of the Ghost Ship**" presents a schizophrenic view of reality, depending primarily on contrasting images to reflect the protagonist's extreme alienation. The culmination of these tendencies is reached in *The Autumn of the Patriarch,* García Márquez's best portrayal of solitude and most lyrical novel to date.

The fact that many of García Márquez's characters reappear under different circumstances in subsequent works creates the impression that his stories and shorter novels are fragments of a more complete fictional universe. For example, Rebeca Buendía is first introduced in "**Tuesday Siesta**" as the widow who shoots the youth she believes is trying to break into her house. She is next seen as a rather eccentric character in "**One Day After Saturday**." Finally, in *One Hundred Years of Solitude* her entire life unfolds as an integral part of the Genesis-to-Apocalypse chronicle of Macondo. The colonels in *Leaf Storm* and *No One Writes to the Colonel* resemble each other in many respects, leading one to suspect that the protagonist of the second book is an extension of the portrait begun in the first. The mayor's brief appearance in *No One Writes to the Colonel* is a prelude to his major role in *The Evil Hour*. And the ineffectual Father Angel plays minor roles in *Leaf Storm* and *No One Writes to the Colonel* but emerges as one of the leading figures in *The Evil Hour*. (pp. 157-59)

García Márquez's fiction is also characterized by recurring episodes, details of which are altered in order to avoid monotonous repetition. For example, the extraction of the mayor's abscessed tooth by his enemy, the dentist, occurs in both *The Evil Hour* and "**One of These Days**." In the novel the episode represents a dramatic climax led up to by the mayor's vain efforts to alleviate his unbearable pain and his forced entry into the dentist's office at midnight with his armed guards. In the short story, however, the mayor arrives alone at eight o'clock in the morning threatening to shoot the dentist if he refuses to pull the tooth. Here dramatic tension is generated by the understated tone and the dearth of details, a technique intended to make the reader exercise his imagination. These successful, though widely differing, treatments of the same incident demonstrate García Márquez's skill as a practitioner of both genres of prose fiction. (pp. 159-60)

Although García Márquez's male characters have no monopoly on irrational conduct, his female characters are usually stronger, more down to earth, and less likely to be carried away by their emotions, whims, or abstract ideals. Indeed, in several of García Márquez's works the contrast between his male and female characters provides an important source of dramatic tension and irony. The most obvious case in point is José

Arcadio Buendía and his wife Ursula of *One Hundred Years of Solitude,* the former emerging as a rudderless dreamer and the latter as the mainstay, who, in spite of her husband's harebrained schemes, manages to hold the clan together for many generations. Similar contrasts between husband-and-wife figures exist in *Leaf Storm, No One Writes to the Colonel,* "There Are No Thieves in This Town," "Baltazar's Marvelous Afternoon," and "The Sea of Lost Time." And even in *The Autumn of the Patriarch,* Bendición Alvarado stands out as a pillar of strength for her wavering son, the patriarch, to lean on.

The reader of García Márquez's entire *oeuvre* may be left with the overall impression that today's world is doomed either to imminent annihilation or to entropic stagnation and decay. The fundamental reason for this pessimistic assessment would seem to be man's lost capacity for love, a defect underscored by his overwhelming greed for power and material gain. Nevertheless, ample evidence of eternal virtues is provided by such characters as the impoverished woman in "Tuesday Siesta," whose strength and dignity dominate every episode of the story; the courageous and idealistic colonels in *Leaf Storm* and *No One Writes to the Colonel;* Ursula, the archetype of feminine wisdom and stability in *One Hundred Years of Solitude;* her husband José Arcadio Buendía, who, though flighty and irrational, embodies man's heroic quest for progress and truth in a fathomless universe; their great-grandson Aureliano Segundo and his mistress Petra Cotes, whose sincere love makes them charitable toward others; Esteban, the messenger of hope, beauty, and human solidarity in "The Handsomest Drowned Man in the World"; and the generous protagonist of "Baltazar's Marvelous Afternoon," whose creative genius and private world of fabulous dreams represent the antithesis of despair and nihilistic destruction.

As best exemplified by *One Hundred Years of Solitude,* García Márquez's ingenious mixture of realism and fantasy has resulted in the creation of a total fictional universe in which the commonplace takes on an aura of magic and the impossible is made believable. His penetrating insights into the ambiguities of human nature are enhanced by a rich vein of anecdotes and leitmotifs he taps from his private mythology. Though he clearly implies moral indignation against brutality, exploitation, and degradation, he delights his readers with his deft fusion of tragedy and comedy and with his seductive powers of language. García Márquez is presently Latin America's most widely known living novelist. He is, in addition, one of the truly outstanding literary artists of our time. In its totality his work imparts not only the stark reality of an emerging strife-torn continent but, also, through the humanistic and universalizing elements of myth, imagination, and aesthetic perception, a highly original vision of man and his world. (pp. 160-62)

> *George R. McMurray, in his* Gabriel García Márquez *(copyright © 1977 by Frederick Ungar Publishing Co., Inc.), Ungar, 1977, 182 p.*

GREGORY RABASSA

When Gabriel García Márquez announced that he was abandoning literature for journalism until the Pinochet dictatorship disappeared from Chile, people expected him to keep his word, and many were surprised when he published *Crónica de una muerte anunciada (Chronicle of a Death Foretold).* He was not really breaking his pledge, however, as can be seen from what he said in an interview with Rosa E. Peláez and Cino Colina

published in *Granma* (Havana) and reprinted in *Excelsior* of Mexico City (31 December 1977). In the interview he is asked what aspect of journalism he likes best, and his answer is reporting. He is subsequently asked about the *crónica* genre and answers that it is all a matter of definition, that he can see little difference between reporting and the writing of chronicles. He goes on to say that one of his ultimate aims is to combine journalism and fiction in such a way that when the news item becomes boring he will embellish it and improve upon it with inventions of his own. So when he wrote this latest book of his, a short, tight novella, by his lights he was not returning to fiction but carrying on journalism as usual, even though his uncramped definitions could well apply to everything that he had written previously and supposedly had put in abeyance.

The chronicle has long been the primitive method of recording events and people and passing them on into history. Most of what we know about medieval Europe has come from chronicles, and in Africa history has been kept through the oral chronicles of the griots. In Latin America, Brazil in particular, the "chronicle" is a recognized and broadly practiced form, offspring of the more ancient variety, that lies somewhere between journalism and "literature." In the United States certain newspaper columns of a more subjective and personal nature correspond to the Latin American chronicle, which almost inevitably makes its first appearance in the press before going into book form. Therefore García Márquez is correct when he says that it is all a matter of definition in the question of whether or not he has abandoned literature and whether or not he has returned.

This new book shows many aspects of life and literature and how one is essentially the same as the other; life imitates art. It starts off in good journalistic style with the "when" and the "what."

> On the day they were going to kill him, Santiago Nasar got up at 5:30 in the morning to wait for the boat the bishop was coming on. . . .

This use of the temporal to begin the narration reminds one immediately of *One Hundred Years of Solitude,* which begins in a similar if not identical vein and sets the stage for the necessary retrospect. . . . The difference is that *One Hundred Years of Solitude* begins in medias res, in good epic fashion, while this "chronicle" opens almost at the end of the action, not quite so far as the end of life as in *The Autumn of the Patriarch,* but close to it. This might well show the influence of journalism in the direction that García Márquez's style has been taking through these last three longer works. The first is more legendary and historical as it develops toward its inevitable and fated climax, while the last two depend on journalistic investigation for their development.

Julio Cortázar has spoken about that nightmare for authors (and typesetters) in Spanish: *casualidad/causalidad* (chance/causality). There is no need to worry about such a slip in the interpretation of this story, as the two elements coincide quite neatly. It is known from the beginning of the tale that the Vicario twins are planning to kill Santiago Nasar for having deflowered their sister Angela, thus ruining her marriage to the strange but wealthy newcomer Bayardo San Román. Many people in the town are aware of the Vicarios' intentions, but through a concatenation of quite normal, even banal, bits of happenstance, nothing is ultimately done to stop them. Indeed, one gathers that even they have little heart for the dirty job that honor is forcing them to do and are only waiting for the authorities or someone to prevent them from bringing it off, since they are prevented by the code from backing down themselves. The title is quite fitting, therefore, in that the death in question has been announced and is foretold. García Márquez has managed to keep the shock and horror of surprise, however, by seeing to it also that the one person who is blithely unaware of what has been ordained, almost until the moment of the act itself, is Santiago Nasar. In the end chance has become the cause of the inexorable deed: *casualidad/causalidad.*

The format used for the narration of the tale is quite journalistic. The narrator, García Márquez himself, perhaps genuine, perhaps embellished, as he mentioned in the interview cited above, is investigating the murder some twenty years later in order to ascertain how such a thing could have happened, how in the end no one was in a position to stop what nobody, including the perpetrators, wanted to happen. The matter of imperfect memory (there are great discrepancies as to the weather) helps lend uncertainty to a tale or event that had become certain because of uncertainty itself. The narrator also relies upon his own memory; he was home from school at the time of the killing and was a friend and contemporary of Santiago Nasar, having caroused with him the night before the murder. In addition, he interviews the participants and several observers, tracking some of them down to more remote places. The narration is a kind of complicated act of turning something inside-out and right-side-out again in that it resembles the application of fictive techniques to the narration of true events in the manner of Norman Mailer and Truman Capote, but here fiction is treated like fact treated like fiction. This swallowing of his own tale by the snake gives a very strong feeling of authenticity to the story. (pp. 48-9)

Instead of giving us a linear narration of the episodes leading up to the final tragedy, García Márquez divides the novella into chapters, each of which follows the trajectory from a slightly different angle and involves a different combination of characters. The fictive structure is therefore a web of criss-crossed story lines, and in the center (or on the bias) is the hole of solitude and impotence where the killing takes place, uncrossed by any of the lines that would have plugged it and prevented the tragedy. This reminds one of the suicide attempt by Colonel Aureliano Buendia in *One Hundred Years of Solitude* when, in emulation of the poet José Asunción Silva, he asks his doctor friend to make a dot on his shirt where his heart is. We later find that the wily physician, on to the colonel's intentions, has designated the one spot in the area of the heart where a bullet can pass without being fatal. As in so many other aspects of this book when compared to the others, and as García Márquez does so many times with a technique that links all of his tales but at the same time differentiates among them, we have mirror images, reverse and obverse.

There is a richness of characters, as one would expect from this author. While he borrows some from his other books, as is his wont, he invents new ones that have great possibilities for expansion into tales of their own, the same as innocent Eréndira and her heartless grandmother, conceived in *One Hundred Years of Solitude* and developed at length in their own novella. As it is, García Márquez is adept at weaving different and seemingly unconnected stories together in order to make the webbing of his complete tale, and any of the tangents that he uses to devise the whole chronicle could be followed off into a separate narrative. There are also intriguing characters on the fringes that we hope to see more of. The wedding and

the murder coincide with the bishop's passage up the river (there are always rivers in García Márquez). This episcopal worthy was passing through early in the morning on the day after the abortive wedding and on the day of the killing. The atmosphere, rather than being tetric in advance of the slaughter (the brothers were butchers and killed him with their pig-sticking knives), is ludicrous; for it seems that the bishop's favorite dish is cockscomb soup, and the townspeople have gathered together hundreds of caged roosters as an offering to his grace. At dawn a cacophony ensues as the captive creatures begin to crow and are answered by all the cocks in town. As it so happened, and as predicted by Santiago Nasar's mother, the bishop did not even deign to stop, and his paddlewheeler passed by as he stood on the bridge and dispensed mechanical blessings to the sound of the congregated roosters. This was the comic atmosphere that would surround the death foretold.

What unites so much of García Márquez's writing is the sense of inexorability, of fatefulness. Things often come to an end that has been there all the while, in spite of what might have been done to avoid it, and often mysteriously and inexplicably, as with the death of José Arcadio, the son, in *One Hundred Years of Solitude.* Here the hand of doom is unavoidable, but the path is tortuous, as it would logically appear that there were ever so many chances to halt the assassination. There is a touch of mystery too, however, in the fact that the narrator-investigator was never able to find out if Angela Vicario and Santiago Nasar had been lovers. All evidence and logic said that the dashing young rancher, already betrothed to the daughter of one of his Arab father's compatriots, could not possibly have been interested in a brown bird like Angela Vicario. She had her own mystery, however, because in the end, years later, she and Bayardo San Román come back together again as strangely as they had been joined the first time. He appears one day at her new home in "exile" beyond Riohacha with a suitcase full of the letters she had been writing him—all unopened.

From the beginning we know that Santiago Nasar will be and has been killed, depending on the time of the narrative thread that we happen to be following, but García Márquez does manage, in spite of the repeated foretelling of the event by the murderers and others, to maintain the suspense at a high level by never describing the actual murder until the very end. Until then we have been following the chronicler as he puts the bits and pieces together ex post facto, but he has constructed things in such a way that we are still hoping for a reprieve even though we know better. It is a feeling that makes us understand why *King Lear* was altered in the nineteenth century in order to spare those sentimental audiences the ultimate agony of Cordelia's execution. García Márquez has put the tale together in the down-to-earth manner of Euripides, but in the final pathos he comes close to the effects of Aeschylus.

The little slips of fate that seem so unimportant until they end in tragedy are the blocks that he builds with. Coincidence or lack of it is not so patently contrived as in Mario Vargas Llosa's novel *The Green House,* where we have the same characters wearing different masks on different stages. Instead, the epiphanies mount up and reveal the characters and the circumstances (never completely; there is always something unknown) by a succession of banal delights and contretemps. (pp. 49-50)

"Chronicle of a Death Foretold" might well be the book that García Márquez was projecting in his Havana interview when he said that he wanted to write the false memoirs of his own life. He is not the protagonist of the story, but he is not only the author; he is the narrator. He even tells how he first proposed marriage to his wife and mentions her by name. In this way he is following the tradition of Cervantes, who mingled the real and the fictional to the degree that all levels came together in a time that only Proust could understand, and he is also very close to what Borges is up to in his story "The Other Borges." When Gabriel García Márquez said that he was abandoning literature for journalism, he probably did not realize the ambiguity of his statement, and since then, as he has done in his reportage, he has come to the conclusion that in technique at least—and possibly in many other ways as well—they are the same. (pp. 50-1)

> *Gregory Rabassa, "García Márquez's New Book: Literature or Journalism?" in* World Literature Today *(copyright 1982 by the University of Oklahoma Press), Vol. 56, No. 1, Winter, 1982, pp. 48-51.*

SALMAN RUSHDIE

[The opening sentence of Rushdie's essay purposely imitates García Márquez's writing style.]

We had suspected for a long time that the man Gabriel was capable of miracles, because for many years he had talked too much about angels for someone who had no wings, so that when the miracle of the printing presses occurred we nodded our heads knowingly, but of course the foreknowledge of his sorcery did not release us from its power, and under the spell of that nostalgic witchcraft we arose from our wooden benches and garden swings and ran without once drawing breath to the place where the demented printing presses were breeding books faster than fruitflies, and the books leapt into our hands without our even having to stretch out our arms, the flood of books spilled out of the print room and knocked down the first arrivals at the presses, who succumbed deliriously to that terrible deluge of narrative as it covered the streets and the sidewalks and rose lap-high in the ground-floor rooms of all the houses for miles around, so that there was no one who could escape from that story, if you were blind or shut your eyes it did you no good because there were always voices reading aloud within earshot, we had all been ravished like willing virgins by that tale, which had the quality of convincing each reader that it was his personal autobiography; and then the book filled up our country and headed out to sea, and we understood in the insanity of our possession that the phenomenon would not cease until the entire surface of the globe had been covered, until seas, mountains, underground railways and deserts had been completely clogged up by the endless copies emerging from the bewitched printing press, with the exception, as Melquiades the gypsy told us, of a single northern country called Britain whose inhabitants had long ago become immune to the book disease, no matter how virulent the strain. . . .

It is now 15 years since Gabriel Garcia Marquez first published *One Hundred Years of Solitude.* During that time it has sold over four million copies in the Spanish language alone, and I don't know how many millions more in translation. The news of a new Marquez book takes over the front pages of Spanish American dailies. Barrow-boys hawk copies in the streets. Critics commit suicide for lack of fresh superlatives. His latest book, *Chronicle of a Death Foretold,* had a first printing in Spanish of considerably more than one million copies. Not the least extraordinary aspect of the work of 'Angel Gabriel' is its ability to make the real world behave in precisely the improbably hyperbolic fashion of a Marquez story.

In Britain, nothing so outrageous has yet taken place. Marquez gets the raves but the person on the South London public conveyance remains unimpressed. It can't be that the British distrust fantasists. Think of Tolkien. (Maybe they just don't like good fantasy.) My own theory is that for most Britons South America has just been discovered. A Task Force may succeed where reviewers have failed: that great comma of a continent may have become commercial at last, thus enabling Marquez and all the other members of 'El Boom', the great explosion of brilliance in contemporary Spanish American literature, finally to reach the enormous audiences they deserve. (p. 3)

It seems that the greatest force at work on the imagination of Marquez . . . is the memory of his grandmother. Many, more formal antecedents have been suggested for his art: he has himself admitted the influence of Faulkner, and the world of his fabulous Macondo is at least partly Yoknapatawpha County transported into the Colombian jungles. Then there's Borges, and behind Borges the *fons* and *origo* of it all, Machado de Assis, whose three great novels, *Epitaph of a Small Winner, Quincas Borba* and *Dom Casmurro,* were so far ahead of their times (1880, 1892 and 1900), so light in touch, so clearly the product of a fantasticating imagination (see, for example, the use Machado makes of an 'anti-melancholy plaster' in *Epitaph*), as to make one suspect that he had descended into the South American literary wilderness of that period from some Dänikenian chariot of gods. And Garcia Marquez's genius for the unforgettable visual hyperbole—for instance, the Americans forcing a Latin dictator to give them the sea in payment of his debts, in *The Autumn of the Patriarch:* 'they took away the Caribbean in April, Ambassador Ewing's nautical engineers carried it off in numbered pieces to plant it far from the hurricanes in the blood-red dawns of Arizona'—may well have been sharpened by his years of writing for the movies. But the grandmother is more important than any of these. She is Gabriel Garcia Marquez's voice.

In an interview with Luis Harss and Barbara Dohmann, Marquez says clearly that his language is his grandmother's. 'She spoke that way.' 'She was a great storyteller.' Anita Desai has said of Indian households that the women are the keepers of the tales, and the same appears to be the case in South America. Marquez was raised by his grandparents, meeting his mother for the first time when he was seven or eight years old. . . . From the memory of [their] house, and using his grandmother's narrative voice as his own linguistic lodestone, Marquez began the building of Macondo.

But of course there is more to him than his granny. He left his childhood village of Aracataca when still very young, and found himself in an urban world whose definitions of reality were so different from those prevalent in the jungle as to be virtually incompatible. In *One Hundred Years of Solitude,* the assumption into heaven of Remedios the Beauty, the loveliest girl in the world, is treated as a completely expected occurrence, but the arrival of the first railway train to reach Macondo sends a woman screaming down the high street. 'It's coming,' she cries. 'Something frightful, like a kitchen dragging a village behind it.' Needless to say, the reactions of city folk to these two events would be exactly reversed. Garcia Marquez decided that reality in South America had literally ceased to exist: this is the source of his fabulism.

The damage to reality was—is—at least as much political as cultural. In Marquez's experience, truth has been controlled to the point at which it has ceased to be possible to find out what it is. The only truth is that you are being lied to all the time. Garcia Marquez (whose support of the Castro Government in Cuba may prevent him from getting his Nobel) has always been an intensely political creature: but his books are only obliquely to do with politics, dealing with public affairs only in terms of grand metaphors like Colonel Aureliano Buendia's military career, or the colossally overblown figure of the Patriarch, who has one of his rivals served up as the main course at a banquet, and who, having overslept one day, decides that the afternoon is really the morning, so that people have to stand outside his windows at night holding up cardboard cut-outs of the sun.

El realismo magical, 'magic realism', at least as practised by Garcia Marquez, is a development of Surrealism that expresses a genuinely 'Third World' consciousness. It deals with what Naipaul has called 'half-made' societies, in which the impossibly old struggles against the appallingly new, in which public corruptions and private anguishes are more garish and extreme than they ever get in the so-called 'North', where centuries of wealth and power have formed thick layers over the surface of what's really going on. In the work of Garcia Marquez, as in the world he describes, impossible things happen constantly, and quite plausibly, out in the open under the midday sun. It would be a mistake to think of Marquez's literary universe as an invented, self-referential, closed system. He is not writing about Middle Earth, but about the one we all inhabit. Macondo exists. That is its magic.

It sometimes seems, however, that Marquez is consciously trying to foster the myth of 'Garcialand'. Compare the first sentence of *One Hundred Years of Solitude* with the first sentence of *Chronicle of a Death Foretold:* 'Many years later, as he faced the firing squad, Colonel Aureliano Buendia was to remember that distant afternoon when his father took him to discover ice' (*One Hundred Years*). And: 'On the day they were going to kill him, Santiago Nasar got up at five-thirty in the morning to wait for the boat the bishop was coming on' (*Chronicle*). Both books begin by first invoking a violent death in the future and then retreating to consider an earlier, extraordinary event. *The Autumn of the Patriarch,* too, begins with a death and then circles back and around a life. It's as though Marquez is asking us to link the books. This suggestion is underlined by his use of certain types of stock character: the old soldier, the loose woman, the matriarch, the compromised priest, the anguished doctor. The plot of *In Evil Hour,* in which a town allows one person to become the scapegoat for what is in fact a crime committed by many hands—the fly-posting of satiric lampoons during the nights—is echoed in *Chronicle of a Death Foretold,* in which the citizens of another town, caught in the grip of a terrible disbelieving inertia, once again fail to prevent a killing, even though it has been endlessly 'announced' or 'foretold'. These assonances in the Marquez oeuvre are so pronounced that it's easy to let them overpower the considerable differences of intent and achievement in his books.

For not only is Marquez bigger than his grandmother: he is also bigger than Macondo. The early writings look, in retrospect, like preparations for the great flight of *One Hundred Years of Solitude,* but even in those days Marquez was writing about two towns: Macondo and another, nameless one, which is more than just a sort of not-Macondo, but a much less mythologised place, a more 'naturalistic' one, insofar as anything is naturalistic in Marquez. This is the town of *Los Funerales de la Mama Grande* (the English title, *Big Mama's Funeral,* makes it sound like something out of Damon Runyon), and many of the stories in this collection, with the ex-

ception of the title story, in which the Pope comes to the funeral, are closer in feeling to early Hemingway than to later Marquez. And ever since his great book, Marquez has been making a huge effort to get away from his mesmeric jungle settlement, to *continue.*

In *The Autumn of the Patriarch,* he found a miraculous method for dealing with the notion of a dictatorship so oppressive that all change, all possibility of development, is stifled: the power of the patriarch stops time, and the text is thereby enabled to swirl, to eddy around the stories of his reign, creating by its non-linear form an exact analogy for the feeling of endless stasis. And in *Chronicle of a Death Foretold,* which looks at first sight like a reversion to the manner of his earlier days, he is in fact innovating again. The *Chronicle* is about honour and about its opposite—that is to say, dishonour, shame. (pp. 3-4)

The manner in which this story is revealed is something new for Garcia Marquez. He uses the device of an unnamed, shadowy narrator visiting the scene of the killing many years later, and beginning an investigation into the past. This narrator, the text hints, is Garcia Marquez himself—at least, he has an aunt with that surname. And the town has many echoes of Macondo: Gerineldo Marquez makes a guest appearance, and one of the characters has the evocative name, for fans of the earlier book, of Cotes. But whether it be Macondo or no, Marquez is writing, in these pages, at a greater distance from his material than ever before. The book and its narrator probe slowly, painfully, through the mists of half-accurate memories, equivocations, contradictory versions, trying to establish what happened and why; and achieve only provisional answers. The effect of this retrospective method is to make the *Chronicle* strangely elegiac in tone, as if Garcia Marquez feels that he has drifted away from his roots, and can only write about them now through veils of formal difficulty. Where all his previous books exude an air of absolute authority over the material, this one reeks of doubt. And the triumph of the book is that this new hesitancy, this abdication of Olympus, is turned to such excellent account, and becomes a source of strength: *Chronicle of a Death Foretold,* with its uncertainties, with its case-history format, is as haunting, as lovely and as true as anything Garcia Marquez has written before. (p. 4)

Salman Rushdie, ''Angel Gabriel'' (appears here by permission of the London Review of Books *and the author; © 1982 by Salman Rushdie), in* London Review of Books, *September 16 to October 6, 1982, pp. 3-4.*

BILL BUFORD

Gabriel García Márquez has repeatedly expressed his surprise at being so insistently regarded as a writer of fantastic fiction. That exotic or ''magical'' element so characteristic of his work is, by his account, not really his own achievement. It is merely the reality of Latin America, which he has faithfully transcribed in more or less the same way that he might write about it in, say, an ordinary article written for a daily newspaper. On a number of occasions, in fact, Márquez has said that for him there is no real difference between the writing of journalism and the writing of fiction—both are committed to the rigours of realistic representation—and his own ideal of the novel involves as much reportage as imagination. Viewed in this way, Márquez can be seen as an inspired tropical reporter for whom the strange Columbian world—with its prescient prostitutes, benevolent ghosts, and an eccentric magician who refuses to die—is just his everyday journalist's "beat". The image is not entirely fanciful. In an interview published in last winter's *Paris Review,* for example, he says that the non-fiction account of contemporary Cuba that he is currently writing will prove to his critics "with historical facts that the real world in the Caribbean is just as fantastic as the stories in *One Hundred Years of Solitude.*" What he is really writing, he says, is good old-fashioned "socialist realism".

Chronicle of a Death Foretold is very close to Márquez's ideal fiction. Written in the manner of investigative journalism and in a conspicuously flattened, unadorned prose, the novel sets out to reconstruct a murder that occurred twenty-seven years before.

From the outset of Márquez's chronicle, everybody—including the reader—knows that the Vicario brothers intend to kill Santiago Nasar. Everybody knows how they mean to do it—with a pair of butcher's knives—and why. And they know so much because the brothers are dedicated to telling their plans to everyone they meet. The original Spanish title, lost in English translation, is important here. In *Una crónica de una muerie anunciada, anunciada* signifies not so much "foretold" as "announced" or "advertised" or "broadcast"—none of which, admittedly, makes for a very poetic title. The idea of an announced or broadcast death, however, is crucial. The brothers are committed to a course of action that has been determined for them—honour can only be redeemed publicly by their killing of Santiago—and they can only be relieved of their duty by the people around them. Once they have broadcast their intentions to the whole community, everyone, to some extent, by failing to stop them, participates in the crime. . . .

It is . . . obvious that this murder, for all the simplicity with which it is narrated, is no simple crime. Part of its significance is evident in the way it is understood by those of Santiago Nasar's generation, for whom the murder seems to mark the end of their youth and render illusory so much that was once meaningful. Flora Miguel, Santiago Nasar's fiancée, for example, runs away immediately after the crime with a lieutenant from the border patrol who then prostitutes her among the rubber workers in a nearby town. Divina Flor—the servant meant for Santiago's furtive bed—is now fat, faded, and surrounded by the children of other loves. And, finally, after more than twenty years, Angela Vicario is reunited with the husband whose affronted masculine pride was the cause of the crime. Overweight, perspiring and bald, he arrives still carrying the same silver saddlebags that now serve merely as pathetic reminders of his ostentatious youth. Márquez's chronicle moves backwards and forwards in time, and views the participants in a senseless murder long after the passion that contributed to it has died. In many ways, then, the novel offers itself as an icy demythologizing of both romantic love and the romantic folly it inspires; it is a debunking of dream and sentiment hinted at by the book's epigraph: "the hunt for love is haughty falconry".

But the real significance of the murder is much greater, and is felt by the entire community whose uncritical faith in its own codes of justice and spectacle is responsible for the crime. The weight of this responsibility is felt most, though, by the unnamed narrator; he returns because he is bothered not by an unsolved mystery but an unabsolved guilt, and the chronicle he produces is a document charting the psychology of mass complicity. It is interesting that Márquez, in developing a simple tale fraught with obvious political implications, chose not to fictionalize an actual political event—Latin America pro-

vides more than enough material—but to treat instead a fictional episode with the methods of a journalist. In so doing he has written an unusual and original work: a simple narrative so charged with irony that it has the authority of political fable. If not an example of the socialist realism Márquez may claim it to be elsewhere, *Chronicle of a Death Foretold* is in any case a mesmerizing work that clearly establishes Márquez as one of the most accomplished, and the most "magical" of political novelists writing today.

Bill Buford, *"Haughty Falconry and Collective Guilt,"* in The Times Literary Supplement (© *Times Newspapers Ltd. (London) 1982; reproduced from* The Times Literary Supplement *by permission), No. 4145, September 10, 1982, p. 965.*

DAVID HUGHES

One hundred pages of quality make [*Chronicle of a Death Foretold*] a fiction that reverberates far beyond its modest length. The story is a mere incident. In a waterfront town on the Caribbean a self-contained youth called Santiago Nasar will be, was, and indeed is being, stabbed to death with meat knives. This event takes place in gory detail on the last few pages. It is the sole preoccupation of the pages in between. And on the first we more or less know that it has already happened. So the suspense is not acute. . . .

Not so much marching forward as marking time, the narrative continuum continually drifts more back than forth, rescuing the story piece by piece from the memory of policemen, gossips, officials, shopkeepers, whores, whose 'numerous marginal experiences' are humanly unreliable. They can't even agree about the weather when the blows were struck. And that is the element that melts this strictly factual document (as it pretends to be) into delicious fiction: everyone in town regards his or her personal evidence as fact, whatever the contradictions. By exploiting the fallibility of his characters Marquez arrives at nothing but the truth.

The book's original touch is that these townspeople, deftly sketched without a word or image wasted, know before Santiago does, but without warning him, that he is on the point of being murdered. All have ostensibly cast-iron excuses, loss of nerve, forgetfulness, failing to take the threat seriously, not wishing to become involved. In their variety of selfish responses to foreknowledge, they bring on Santiago's death, as if secretly savouring it in prospect and relishing its aftermath. We are all to blame, mutters Marquez with good humour, because we all brainlessly share the eccentricity of common human feeling.

The book vindicates its brevity by an exactitude of detail that snaps a character to life without recourse to long or even direct description. To visualise a visiting bishop, all we need to be told is that his favourite dish—he discards the rest of the fowl—is coxcomb soup. The mayor's character is purely and simply conveyed when we are casually informed that a policeman is collecting from the shop the pound of liver he eats for breakfast. In these two images all authority, religious and civil, is nicely confounded, just because no heavy weather is made of confounding them. The reader is paid the compliment of being asked to respond imaginatively to the most delicate of hints and indeed to make his own moral structure from the ins and outs of the lack of narrative: to decide for instance, who is lying for good reasons, who being honest for bad.

One of the book's great virtues is self-containment. It presents a large world *in parvo,* without being selfconsciously a microcosm, framed in noble if miniature proportions, viewed by an aristocrat of letters whose attitude to the human lot mingles contempt and compassion in a witty blend. Nobody shows up either well or badly under the microscope. People are seen as wayward but pitiable cells in the body politic, preventing it from functioning properly but at the same time breathing an outrageous life into it.

Some days after reading this novella I am still in several minds as to what it is about. Just a faithful picture of a community living off shopsoiled machismo? An author's obsession with the dramatics of sudden death? The last drop of blood squeezed out of material better suited to a thriller? A neurotic treatise on the erotic corollaries of murder? Any or all of these perhaps—and more. And that's a healthy feeling of perplexity. If good books do furnish the imagination, they also echo on and on in its rooms.

David Hughes, "Murder," in The Spectator (© 1982 by The Spectator; reprinted by permission of The Spectator), Vol. 249, No. 8044, September 11, 1982, p. 24.

WILLIAM H. GASS

Chronicle of a Death Foretold does not tell, but literally pieces together, the torn-apart body of a story: that of the multiple murder of a young, handsome, wealthy, womanizing Arab, Santiago Nasar, who lived in the town where Gabriel García Márquez grew up. The novel is not, however, the chronicle of a young and vain man's death, for that event is fed to us in the bits it comes in. It is instead the chronicle of the author's discovery and determination of the story and simultaneously a rather gruesome catalogue of the many deaths—in dream, in allegory, and by actual count—that Santiago Nasar is compelled to suffer. Had he had a cat's lives, it would not have saved him.

It is his author who kills him first, foretelling his death in the first (and in that sense final) sentence of the novel: "On the day they were going to kill him . . ." We are reminded immediately of García Márquez's habit of beginning his books in an arresting way, perhaps a by-product of his long journalistic practice. "Many years later, as he faced the firing squad . . ." *One Hundred Years of Solitude* commences, and *The Autumn of the Patriarch* is no less redolent with death or its threats: "Over the weekend the vultures got into the presidential palace by pecking through the screens on the balcony windows." Santiago Nasar's death is first foretold in the way any fictional fact is, for the fact, of whatever kind, is already there in the ensuing pages, awaiting our arrival like a bus station.

Santiago Nasar also dies in his dreams—dreams that could have been seen to foretell it, had not his mother, an accomplished seer of such things, unaccountably missed "the ominous augury." Before the day is out, his mother will murder him again. Unwittingly, and with the easy fatality we associate with Greek tragedy, Santiago dons a sacrificial suit of unstarched white linen, believing that he is putting it on to honor the visit of a bishop, just as he has celebrated the day before, along with the entire town, the wedding that will be his undoing. So attired, he stands before his mother with glass and aspirin and tells her of the dreams she will misunderstand. Santiago Nasar is then symbolically slain and gutted by the cook as he takes a cup of coffee in her kitchen and has another aspirin for his

hangover. His father has mounted this woman, and she is remembering Santiago's father as she disembowels two rabbits (foretelling his disembowelment) and feeds their guts, still steaming, to the dogs.

The cook's daughter does not tell Santiago that she has heard a rumor that two men are looking to kill him, for he continually manhandles her, and she wishes him dead; the town, it seems, knows too, and participates in the foretelling. Attempts to warn Santiago are halfhearted: People pretend that the threats are empty; that the twin brothers bent on his death are drunk, incapable, unwilling; that it is all a joke. But Orpheus has his enemies in every age. Dionysus was also torn to pieces once, Osiris as well. The women whose bodies Santiago Nasar has abused (the metaphor that follows him throughout, and that appears just following the title page, is that of the falcon or sparrow hawk) await their moment. They will use the duplicities of the male code to entrap him. The girl whose wedding has just been celebrated goes to her bridegroom with a punctured maidenhead, and he sends her home in disgrace, where she is beaten until she confesses (although we don't know what the real truth is) that Santiago Nasar was her "perpetrator." And had not her twin brothers believed that the honor of their family required revenge, Nasar would not have been stabbed fatally, not once but seven times, at the front door of his house, a door his mother, believing him already inside, had barred.

The coroner is out of town, but the law requires an autopsy—the blood has begun to smell—so Santiago Nasar is butchered again, this time while dead. The intestines he held so tenderly in his hands as he walked almost primly around his house to find a back door he might enter in order to complete the symbolism of his life by dying in the kitchen he had his morning aspirin in—those insides of the self of which the phallus is only an outer tip—are tossed into a trash can; the dogs who wanted them, and would have enjoyed them, are now dead, too.

Santiago Nasar's mother's last sight of her son, which she says was of him standing in her bedroom doorway, water glass in hand and the first aspirin to his lips, is not, we learn, her last. Her final vision, which she has on the balcony of her bedroom, is of her son "face down in the dust, trying to rise up out of his own blood."

One man is dead, and hundreds have murdered him. The consequences of the crime spread like a disease through the village. Or, rather, the crime is simply a late symptom of an illness that had already wasted everyone. Now houses will decay, too, in sympathy. Those people—lovers, enemies, friends, family—who were unable to act now act with bitter, impulsive, self-punishing foolishness, becoming old maids and worn whores, alcoholics and stupid recruits, not quite indiscriminately. The inertias of custom, the cruelties of a decaying society, daily indignities, hourly poverties, animosities so ancient they seem to have been put in our private parts during a prehistoric time, the sullen passivity of the powerless, the feckless behavior of the ignorant, the uselessness of beliefs, all these combine in this remarkable, graphic, and grisly fable to create a kind of slow and creeping fate—not glacial, for that would not do for these regions, but more, perhaps, like the almost imperceptible flow of molasses, sticky, insistent, sweet, and bearing everywhere it goes the sick, digested color of the bowel. (pp. 83-4)

Chronicle of a Death Foretold, like Faulkner's *Sanctuary,* is about the impotent revenges of the impotent; it is about misdirected rage; it is about the heart blowing to bits from the burden of its own beat; yet the author, Santiago Nasar's first murderer, goes patiently about his business, too, putting the pieces back together, restoring, through his magnificent art, his own anger and compassion, this forlorn, unevil, little vegetation god, to a new and brilliant life. (p. 84)

> *William H. Gass, "More Deaths Than One: 'Chronicle of a Death Foretold'," in* New York *Magazine (copyright © 1983 by News Group Publications, Inc.; reprinted with the permission of* New York *Magazine), Vol. 16, No. 15, April 11, 1983, pp. 83-4.*

JOSEPH EPSTEIN

How good is Gabriel García Márquez? "Define your terms," I can hear some wise undergraduate reply. "What do you mean by *is*?" Yet I ask the question in earnest. Over the past weeks I have been reading García Márquez's four novels and three collections of stories—all of his work available in English translation—and I am still not certain how good he is. If I were to be asked how talented, I have a ready answer: pound for pound, as they used to put it in *Ring* magazine, Gabriel García Márquez may be the most talented writer at work in the world today. But talent is one thing; goodness, or greatness, quite another.

Valéry says somewhere that there ought to be a word to describe the literary condition between talent and genius. In writing about García Márquez, most contemporary American literary critics have not searched very hard for that word. Instead they have settled on calling him a genius and knocked off for the day. (pp. 59-60)

In sum, no novelist now writing has a more enviable reputation. His is of course an international, a worldwide reputation—one capped by the Nobel Prize, won in 1982 at the age of fifty-four. The Nobel Prize can sometimes sink a writer, make him seem, even in his lifetime, a bit posthumous. But with García Márquez it appears to have had quite the reverse effect, making him seem more central, more prominent, more of a force. . . .

In Latin America, Gabriel García Márquez has been a household name and face since 1967, when his famous novel *One Hundred Years of Solitude* was first published in Buenos Aires. This novel is said to have sold more than six million copies and to have been translated into more than thirty languages. . . . I thought it quite brilliant and stopped reading it at page 98 (of 383 pages in the paperback edition). A number of intelligent people I know have gone through a similar experience in reading the book. All thought it brilliant, but felt that anywhere from between eighteen to fifty-one years of solitude was sufficient, thank you very much. I shall return to what I think are the reasons for this. (p. 60)

Short of going to Latin American countries on extended visits, how does one find out anything about them? Whom does one trust? New York *Times* reporters capable of prattling on about fifty new poetry workshops in Nicaragua? American novelists—Robert Stone, Joan Didion—who have put in cameo appearances in one or another Latin American country and then returned to write about it? Academic experts, the kernels of whose true information are not easily freed of their ideological husks? Perhaps native writers? On this last count, I have recently read a most charming novel set in Lima, Peru, *Aunt Julia and the Scriptwriter,* by Mario Vargas Llosa, which gives us a portrait of daily life—corrupt, incompetent, sadly pro-

vincial though it is—very different from that which Gabriel García Márquez supplies. Whom is one to believe?

So many oddities crop up. How, for example, explain that García Márquez had his famous novel, *One Hundred Years of Solitude,* a book that he has claimed is an argument for change in Latin America, published in Argentina, universally regarded—to hear Jacobo Timerman tell it—as the most repressive of Latin American countries? How for that matter explain the emergence of Latin American literature to a place very near contemporary preeminence? How does one reconcile these various paradoxes, contradictions, confusions? It may be that finally, in reading about Latin America, one has to settle for the virtue which Sir Lewis Namier once said was conferred by sound historical training—a fairly good sense of how things did *not* happen.

Such a sense becomes especially useful in reading a writer like Gabriel García Márquez, who is continually telling us how things did happen. What he is saying is not very new. He speaks of the depredations upon the poor by the rich, upon the pure by the corrupt, upon the indigenous by the colonial—standard stuff, for the most part. But how he says it is new and can be very potent indeed. So much so that Fidel Castro is supposed to have remarked of him, "García Márquez is the most powerful man in Latin America." (pp. 60-1)

None of this power would exist, of course, if García Márquez were not a considerable artist. Literary artists make us see things, and differently from the way we have ever seen them before; they make us see things *their* way. We agree to this willingly because in the first place they make things interesting, charming, seductive, and in the second place they hold out the promise of telling us important secrets that we would be fools not to want to know. (p. 61)

Sweep and power are readily available to García Márquez; so, too, are what seem like endless lovely touches, such as a man described as "lame in body and sound in conscience." In **"The Handsomest Drowned Man in the World,"** a charming tale about a time when people had hearts capacious enough for the poetic, the way is prepared for a man "to sink easily into the deepest waves, where fish are blind and divers die of nostalgia." The movements of a woman in the story **"There Are No Thieves in *This* Town"** have "the gentle efficiency of people who are used to reality." A man in the story **"One Day After Saturday"** is caught at an instant when "he was aware of his entire weight: the weight of his body, his sins, and his age altogether." García Márquez's stories are studded with such charming bits: a woman with "passionate health," a man with a "mentholated voice," a town "where the goats committed suicide from desolation," another man with "a pair of lukewarm languid hands that always looked as if they'd just been shaved." García Márquez, as Milton Berle used to say of himself, has a million of them.

This fecundity of phrase was not always so readily available to García Márquez. Today his fame is such that his very earliest works are being reprinted and translated—most of them are in the collection *Innocent Eréndira and Other Stories*—and these early stories are dreary in the extreme: dryly abstract, bleak, cut-rate Kafka, without the Kafkaesque edge or the humor. As a novelist, García Márquez seems to have come alive when he began to write about the coastal town he calls Macondo and—the two events seem to have taken place simultaneously—when, by adding the vinegar of politics to his writing, he gave it a certain literary tartness.

García Márquez has claimed William Faulkner as a literary mentor, and the two do have much in common. Each has staked out a territory of his own—Yoknapatawpha County for Faulkner, Macondo and its environs for García Márquez; each deals lengthily with the past and its generations; and finally, each relies on certain prelapsarian myths (Southern grandeur before the American Civil War, Latin American poetic serenity before the advent of modernity and foreign intervention) to bind his work together. There is, though, this decisive difference between the two writers: Faulkner's fiction is almost wholly taken up with the past, while that of García Márquez, as befits a politically minded writer, generally keeps an eye out for the future.

Immersion in the work of such writers provides one of those experiences—perhaps it might be called moral tourism—exclusive to literature. By reading a good deal about a place rendered by a powerful writer, in time one comes to feel one has walked its streets, knows its history and geography, the rhythms of its daily life. Only certain writers can convey this experience through the page: Balzac did it both for Paris and French provincial towns; Faulkner did it; Isaac Bashevis Singer does it for Jewish Poland; and García Márquez does it, too. (pp. 61-2)

Viewed in retrospect, the Macondo stories—they are found in *Leaf Storm and Other Stories* and *No One Writes to the Colonel and Other Stories,* and the town is also the setting for the novel *In Evil Hour*—appear to be an elaborate warm-up for the novel *One Hundred Years of Solitude.* They seem to be sketches, trial runs, dress rehearsals for the big novel ahead. In these stories names will appear in passing—like Colonel Aureliano Buendía, one of the heroes of *One Hundred Years*—almost as if they were coming attractions. Then, working the other way around, incidents occur in *One Hundred Years* that have been the subjects of whole stories in the earlier volumes. To know fully what is going on in García Márquez one has to have read the author in his entirety. In these stories the stages in García Márquez's literary development are on display, rather like specimens inside formaldehyde-filled jars showing progress from zygote to fully formed human. One reads these stories and witnesses his talent growing, his political ardor increasing. In these stories, too, García Márquez shows his taste for that blend of fantasy and hyperbole, exhibited in a context of reality, that is known as magic realism. (p. 62)

"What I like about you," says one character to another in the García Márquez story **"The Incredible and Sad Tale of Innocent Eréndira and Her Heartless Grandmother,"** "is the serious way you make up nonsense." Serious nonsense might stand as a blurb line for *One Hundred Years of Solitude.* E. M. Forster remarked that at a certain age one loses interest in the development of writers and wants to know only about the creation of masterpieces. Certainly *One Hundred Years of Solitude* has everywhere been so acclaimed. The novel is a chronicle of six generations of the Buendía family, founders of the village of Macondo. It recounts such extraordinary happenings as Macondo's insomnia plague, its thirty-two civil wars, banana fever, revolution, strikes, a rain that lasts five years, marriages, intermarriages, madness, and the eventual extinction of the Buendía line with the birth of an infant who has a pig's tail and who is eventually carried off by ants.

"*One Hundred Years of Solitude* is not a history of Latin America," García Márquez has said, "it is a *metaphor* for Latin America." With that quotation we are already in trouble. What can it mean to say that a novel is a metaphor for a continent?

Before attempting to ascertain what it might mean, tribute must be paid to the sheer brimming brilliance of *One Hundred Years of Solitude.* "Dazzling" does not seem to me in any way an imprecise word to describe the style of this novel, nor "epic" any less imprecise a word to describe its ambitions. Its contents cannot be recapitulated, for in its pages fireworks of one kind or another are always shooting off. Disquisitions on history, memory, time wind in and out of the plot. Yellow flowers fall from the sky marking a man's death; a heart-meltingly beautiful girl ascends to heaven while folding a sheet, a girl whose very smell "kept on torturing men beyond death, right down to the dust of their bones." Everything is grand, poetic, funny, often at once. A man suffers "flatulence that withered the flowers"; a woman has "a generous heart and a magnificent vocation for love." (pp. 62-3)

And yet—why do so many readers seem to bog down in this glittering work? Part of the difficulty seems to me technical, part psychological. *One Hundred Years of Solitude* is peculiarly a novel without pace; it is, for its nearly four-hundred pages, all high notes, service aces, twenty-one-gun salutes. In a novel, such nonstop virtuosity tends to pall. To use a simile to describe a novel that its author describes as a metaphor, reading *One Hundred Years* is like watching a circus artist on the trampoline who does only quadruple back somersaults. At first you are amazed to see him do it; then you are astonished that he can keep it up for so long; then you begin to wonder when he is going to be done, frankly you'd like to see something less spectacular, like a heavy-legged woman on an aged elephant.

Unless, that is, you sense a deeper meaning beneath all this virtuosity. And here it must be said that there has been no shortage of deep readings of *One Hundred Years of Solitude,* a novel which, if critics are to be consulted, has more levels than a ziggurat. There are those who think that the true meaning of the novel is solitude, or, as Alastair Reid puts it, "We all live alone on this earth in our own glass bubbles." There are those who think that the novel is about writing itself. . . . There are those who are fascinated with the book's allusiveness. . . . There are those who believe that the stuff of myth ought not to be looked at too closely. . . . Then there is García Márquez himself, who has given a clear political reading to his own novel, commenting, in an interview, "I did want to give the idea that Latin American history had such an oppressive reality that it had to be changed—at all costs, at any price!" (p. 63)

Along with magic realism, Gabriel García Márquez has given us another new literary-critical label, "political realism," which, in its own way, is itself quite magical.

If *One Hundred Years of Solitude* leaves any doubt about the political intent of García Márquez's mature work, *The Autumn of the Patriarch* wipes that doubt away. When García Márquez says that *One Hundred Years* is a metaphor for Latin America, he is of course putting a political interpretation on his own novel. But *The Autumn of the Patriarch* is neither metaphor nor symbol but a direct representation of a strong political point of view. . . .

The dictator in *The Autumn of the Patriarch* lives for more than two hundred years, his demise, à *la* Mark Twain, being often reported but much exaggerated. He has been in power— he has been *the* power—longer than anyone can remember, and his is the greatest solitude of all: that of the unloved dictator perpetuating his unearned power. This man, who himself can neither read nor write, is described, examined, and prosecuted with the aid of a novelistic technique as relentlessly modernist as any in contemporary fiction.

The Autumn of the Patriarch is divided into six chapters, but that is the only division in the novel, and the only concession to the reader's convenience. The book has no paragraphs, and while the punctuation mark known as the period may show up from time to time, the novel's sentences are not what one normally thinks of as sentences at all. A sentence might begin from one point of view, and before it is finished include three or four others.

One of the small shocks of this novel is to see the most complex modernist techniques put to the most patent political purposes. Now it must be said that García Márquez did not invent the Latin American dictator. Trujillo, Batista, Perón, Hernández Martinez, Duvalier (dare one add the name Fidel Castro?)—one could put together a pretty fair All Star team, though these boys are bush league compared with what Europe and Asia in this century have been able to produce.

García Márquez's portrait of the dictator in *The Autumn of the Patriarch* is an amalgam of Latin America's dictators, minus . . . Fidel and with a touch or two of Franco added. As a picture of squalor, rot, and bestiality, it is devastating. The devastation is in the details, of which the endlessly inventive García Márquez is never in short supply. (p. 64)

The Autumn of the Patriarch is about more than politics alone—time and the nature of illusion are motifs played upon artfully throughout—but politics give the novel its impetus and are finally its chief subject. These politics are highly selective, predictable, more than a trifle clichéd. Octavio Paz has said that García Márquez, as a political thinker, "repeats slogans." As a novelist, he can make these slogans vivid, even funny, but they remain slogans. For example, the attacks on the United States in this novel come through the dictator's continuous dealings with a stream of U.S. ambassadors of perfectly Waspish and quite forgettable names—Warren, Thompson, Evans, Wilson—who in the end succeed in swindling him out of the very sea. Americans, the Catholic Church, politicians, all, in the mind and in the novels of Gabriel García Márquez, are swindlers. Liberals or conservatives, it does not matter which, they are crooks, every one of them. Which leaves—doesn't it?—only one solution: revolution.

So talented a writer is García Márquez that he can sustain a longish tale on sheer storytelling power alone, as he does in his most recent book, *Chronicle of a Death Foretold*. It has been said of García Márquez that he combines the two powerful traditions of Latin American writing: the left-wing engagé tradition of the Communist poet Pablo Neruda and the modernist mandarin tradition of Jorge Luis Borges. In this slender novel it is the Borges side that predominates. The book is about a plot on the part of twin brothers who are out to avenge their family's honor against a young man who they mistakenly believe has deflowered their sister, thus causing her husband to return her in shame to her family the morning after the wedding night. (pp. 64-5)

The tale is told with such subtle organization and such complete fluency that García Márquez can insert anything he wishes into it; and indeed the narrator does insert mention of his marriage proposal to his own wife and a brief account of his youthful dalliances with prostitutes. Such is the easy mastery of this novel that the reader is likely to forget that he never does learn who actually did deflower the virgin. *Chronicle of a Death Foretold* is a handsomely written and inconsequential book of a kind that offers ample leeway for deep readings, and one that could have been composed only by a hugely gifted writer.

"Intellectuals consider themselves to be the moral conscience of society," García Márquez is quoted as saying in the New York *Times Magazine*, "so their analyses invariably follow moral rather than political channels. In this sense, I think I am the most politicized of them all." Yet, oddly, in García Márquez's fiction morality is rarely an issue; García Márquez himself seems little interested in moral questions, or in the conflicts, gradations, and agonies of moral turmoil. The reason for this, I suspect, is that for him the moral universe is already set—for him, as for so many revolutionary intellectuals, there are the moral grievances of the past, the moral hypocrisies of the present, and, waiting over the horizon, the glories of the future, when moral complexity will be abolished. The moral question is, for García Márquez, ultimately a political question. Outside of his politics, García Márquez's stories and novels have no moral center; they inhabit no moral universe. They are passionate chiefly when they are political; and when they are political, so strong is the nature of their political bias that they are, however dazzling, flawed.

Thus, to return to where I set out, a short answer to my question—how good is Gabriel García Márquez?—is that he is, in the strict sense of the word, marvelous. The pity is that he is not better. (p. 65)

Joseph Epstein, "How Good Is Gabriel García Márquez?" in Commentary *(reprinted by permission; all rights reserved), Vol. 75, No. 5, May, 1983, pp. 59-65.*

ANTHONY BURGESS

I have two problems in assessing this brief work [*Chronicle of a Death Foretold*] by the latest Nobel Prizeman. The first relates to the fact that I've read it in translation, and any judgment on the quality of García Márquez's writing that I would wish to make is necessarily limited. Mr. Rabassa's rendering is smooth and strong with an inevitable North American flavor, but it is English, and García Márquez writes in a very pungent and individual Spanish. The second problem is the one that always comes up when a writer has received the final international accolade: dare one be wholly frank? Dare one set one's critical judgment up against what, though it is really only the verdict of a committee of literati in Stockholm, is accepted as a world consensus? I note, in [the publisher's] publicity handout, that we are to regard García Márquez as "South America's pre-eminent writer"—a view I cannot give accord to so long as Jorge Luis Borges is alive. I think, as is often the case with officially acclaimed writers of fiction, that the imputation of greatness has more to do with content—especially when it is social or political—than with aesthetic values. *One Hundred Years of Solitude,* a book which impressed me rather less than it seems to have impressed others, has undoubted power, but its power is nothing compared with the genuinely literary explorations of men like Borges and Nabokov. Now here is a new brief novel that is decent, assured, strong, but indubitably minor. I am not seduced by García Márquez's reputation . . . into thinking it anything more.

The minimal distinction of the novella lies in the exactness with which its author has recorded the mores of a community in which machismo is the basic ethos. The bishop is coming on a river boat to give his blessing, and sacks of cockscombs await him to make his favorite soup. The town swelters in morning heat and hangover. Sex is a weapon, not a gesture of tenderness. The atmosphere is visceral. Rabbits are being gutted by the beginning of the story; at the end the dying Santiago Nasar enters his house "soaked in blood and carrying the roots of his entrails in his hands." There is also an element of debased hidalgo refinement.

Before we get to the end, which is less an end than an initial theme to be embroidered with the views of citizens locked in a tradition that they see no reason to break, we are given a sufficient anthropological survey of a society that has never known the benefits of aspirant Protestant materialism and ambiguous matriarchy. It is the world of *Martin Ferrol,* the Argentine epic that glorified machismo and helped to keep South American literature out of the real world. The little novel is an honest record, cunningly contrived, but it seems to abet a complacent debasement of morality rather than to open up larger vistas. It is, in a word, claustrophobic. It does not induce a view, as better fiction does, of human possibilities striving to rise out of a morass of conservative stupidity. The heart never lifts. All that is left is a plain narrative style and an orthodox narrative technique managed with extreme competence. Perhaps one is wrong to expect more from a Nobel Prizeman.

> Anthony Burgess, *"Macho in a Minor Key," in* The New Republic *(reprinted by permission of* The New Republic; © *1983 The New Republic, Inc.),* Vol. 188, No. 17, May 2, 1983, p. 36.

SELDEN RODMAN

In much of his work [Gabriel García Márquez] has turned his hometown into a dream kingdom of shattered expectations built on nostalgia; Macondo is bereft of idealism, visions of a better world, calls to arms. These attitudes are seen as part of an old order that must be stripped away to get at the long-concealed truth. . . .

Before [*Chronicle of a Death Foretold*] came *The Autumn of the Patriarch,* a monologue of a dying tyrant based on the life of Juan Vicente Gómez of Venezuela, whose crimes had been magnified into myth in the mouths of refugees to Aracataca during the novelist's childhood. The book's highly praised style was baroque and convoluted. García Márquez implausibly defends his method by citing the supposed unreadability of *Ulysses* when it first came out, and claiming that "today children read it." Although an intellectual tour de force, *Autumn* lacks the endearing magic of the author at his best.

Chronicle of a Death Foretold, fortunately, brings García Márquez back on track. The setting is Macondo again, with many of the old faces reappearing in minor roles, including the author himself, his family and his wife. The mood is somber and tragic, for this is an account of a horrifyingly brutal and senseless crime. (p. 16)

Part morality tale, part fairy tale, *Chronicle of a Death Foretold* unfolds like a Greek tragedy. We know everything essential to the plot from the opening page, and yet García Márquez fills in the details with such masterful skill that we hang on breathlessly to the final paragraph, where the murder is described. As in all this writer's strongest work, the writing is lucid, factual, almost literary except for an occasional word or phrase in the vernacular ("rotgut," "eighty-proof hangover") to remind us that this is our world.

What is García Márquez trying to say in his books? I can hear him answer, amiably or scornfully depending on his mood, that he isn't trying to say anything, that he writes because he

must, that the words come out this way, virtually trancelike, dictated by his memory and edited by the sum of his parts. Which would be the truth.

Still, one searches for *some* connection between the public man and the artist. A typical Latin American liberal, the public man supports all Leftist causes, while shying away from justifying the Soviet Union's domestic atrocities and its more barefaced sandbagging of its weak neighbors. He hates Augusto Pinochet and reveres the memory of Salvador Allende, regardless of what Allende did in Chile during his reign. García Márquez excuses Latin America's political infantilism on the grounds that democratic institutions did not have centuries to mature as in Europe—ignoring the United States, which broke away from colonialism at the same time. (pp. 16-17)

As for the artist, Octavio Paz once tried to persuade me that García Márquez has not changed the language the way Pablo Neruda, Cesar Valléjo and Jorge Luis Borges have. "They started a new tradition, he comes at the end of an old one— the rural, epic and magic tradition of Ricardo Güiraldes, Horacio Quiroga, José Eustacio Rivera." I disagreed, comparing the Colombian Rivera's horrendous penetration of Amazonia with his successor's recreations of the past. One emerges from Rivera's desperate journey in *The Vortex* with a sense of suffocating depression, from García Márquez' strolls through Macondo with a reassuring conviction that a world so full of lusty adventurers, irrepressible louts and unconscious poets cannot be as bad as he says it is. The artist triumphs over the public man, over the sociologist.

In other words, whereas Rivera, the conscious artist, succeeded at what he set out to do—horrifying his readers—García Márquez, the unconscious artist and the better one, creates a realm that gives delight. His characters have lives of their own and they refuse to be manipulated. They may fulfill their tragic destiny, but they behave with so much spontaneity and good humor that we remember them as the better parts of ourselves and accept their world of irrational "happenings" as the real one. (p. 17)

> Selden Rodman, *"Triumph of the Artist," in* The New Leader *(© 1983 by the American Labor Conference on International Affairs, Inc.),* Vol. LXVI, No. 10, May 16, 1983, pp. 16-17.

D. KEITH MANO

[*Chronicle of a Death Foretold*] is, at one level, a simile for the fiction-making process. Here we are given events that, in some genuine sense, exist—lie formed by history—*before* they occur. And a townful of people—through their action, thought, custom, laziness, pride, willful negligence, through their unconscious art—create this plot-which-was-real. The irony is: that having created it, they cannot avert it. No second draft is possible: even in art, where free will would seem to be most free, a determinism, a manifest destiny, still presides. (p. 699)

A nameless narrator has come back. (Some 27 years, mind you, after Santiago Nasar was turned to human piecework.) Neither he nor the town can stop riding this hobbyhorse.

> For years we couldn't talk about anything else.
> Our daily conduct, dominated then by so many
> linear habits, had suddenly begun to spin around
> a single common anxiety. The cocks of dawn
> would catch us trying to give order to the chain
> of many chance events that had made absurdity

possible, and it was obvious that we weren't doing it from an urge to clear up mysteries but because none of us could go on living without an exact knowledge of the place and the mission assigned to us by fate.

Now that formulation, with all respect to García Márquez, is somewhat self-propelled. I don't believe it. No matter what the event, populations don't lie awake for a quarter-century grave-robbing their moral reminiscence. The linear habit will reassert itself. García Márquez's narrator—who previously has employed splendid sparse, aromatic, and elliptical prose—is indulging himself here. For one moment at least García Már- quez doesn't trust the event, its portentousness or imagic value.

Otherwise his attack is stark and, given García Márquez's pur- pose, proper enough. Because the narrator is examining an essentially novelistic occurrence, he has been sequestered as a juror might be. He cannot comment or probe: and this rather kiln-dries the novel. Angela, Bayardo, Santiago are left without development or chiaroscuro. They seem cryptic and surface- hard: film characters really. And there must be no surprise— art here lies in the event itself. That, to start with, is García Márquez's conceit. Angela, we don't know, might have taken her own virginity. Nor will we ever understand why rich Bay- ardo came to this unmarked burial of a town. *Chronicle* has become myth: as you don't ask for the psychohistory of Parsifal or Gawain, you must accept Angela, Bayardo, Santiago. But beyond García Márquez's glass-brick-hard style (redone bril- liantly, as usual, by Greg Rabassa in English), beyond a Warren

Report-meticulous detective reconstruction, it is hard to care much for these people. Emotion, you see, might skew our clarity. No character—even when he or she is presumed real— should elude an author's control.

The trial record will be introduced. An investigating judge "never thought it legitimate that life should make use of so many coincidences forbidden literature, so that there should be the untrammeled fulfillment of a death so clearly foretold."

García Márquez, I think, is over-indicating here. The events, though pretty sensational, aren't full of unbelievable coinci- dence. Life often has taken greater poetic license. What will distinguish this happening is the intensity of examination both by his townspeople and by his narrator. Intensity that seems somewhat forced. At one point the narrator, obsessive, will claim that he must put a "broken mirror of memory back together again from so many shards." But memory doesn't just reflect. In general, I wish García Márquez hadn't surren- dered so many of the devices and perquisites that belong to fiction: subjectivity, shifting POV, omniscience, judgment, plot surprise. Form is, of course, an artistic choice. García Márquez has given his choice excellent service. But more might have been essayed. After all every death is, to some degree, foretold. (p. 700)

D. Keith Mano, "A Death Foretold," in National Review (© *National Review, Inc., 1983; 150 East 35th St., New York, NY 10016), Vol. XXXV, No. 11, June 10, 1983, pp. 699-700.*

William (Gerald) Golding

1911-

English novelist, short story writer, dramatist, essayist, and poet.

Golding, who won the 1983 Nobel Prize in literature, is a widely read and seriously discussed author. His first and best-known work, *The Lord of the Flies* (1954), not only established Golding's reputation as a significant contemporary author, but also presented what has become his main theme: the conflict between the forces of light and dark within the human soul. Although it was several years after its original publication before the novel gained popularity in the United States, it has now become a modern classic, studied in most high schools and colleges. Set in the near future, *Lord of the Flies* revolves around a group of school boys abandoned on a desert island during a global war. They attempt to establish a government among themselves, but without the restraints of civilization they quickly revert to savagery. Similar in background and characters' names to R. M. Ballantyne's nineteenth-century classic *The Coral Island, Lord of the Flies* totally reverses Ballantyne's concept of the purity and innocence of youth and humanity's ability to remain civilized under the worst conditions.

Although none of Golding's subsequent works achieved the success of *Lord of the Flies,* he has continued to produce novels that elicit widespread critical interpretation. Within the thematic context of exploring the depths of human depravity, the settings range from the prehistoric age (*The Inheritors,* 1955) to the Middle Ages (*The Spire,* 1964) to contemporary English society. This wide variety of settings, as well as the vastly different tones and surface structures of his novels present dilemmas to critics attempting to categorize them. Nevertheless, certain stylistic devices are characteristic of his work. One of these, the use of a sudden shift of perspective, has been so dramatically employed that it both enchants and infuriates critics and readers alike. For example, *Pincher Martin* (1956) is the story of a naval officer who is stranded on a rock in the middle of the ocean after his ship has been torpedoed. The entire book relates Martin's struggles to remain alive against all odds. The reader learns in the last few pages that Martin's death occurred on the second page, thus transforming the novel from a struggle for earthly survival into a struggle for eternal salvation.

Golding's novels are often termed fables or myths. They are laden with symbols (usually of a spiritual or religious nature) so heavy in significance that they can be interpreted on many different levels. *The Spire* is perhaps the most polished example, equating the erection of a cathedral spire with the protagonist's conflict between his religious faith and the temptations to which he is exposed. *Darkness Visible* (1979), Golding's first novel after a silence of twelve years, continues to illuminate the universal confrontation of Good and Evil. Golding was awarded the James Tait Black Memorial Prize for this novel in 1980.

Golding's experience as a member of the Royal Navy during World War II informs many of his novels, most notably the recent *Rites of Passage* (1980). This allegorical work, set in

the early nineteenth century, takes place on a ship en route from England to Australia. The voyage serves as a device to isolate a microcosm of British society, allowing Golding to further develop his theme of the darkness inherent in human nature. *Rites of Passage* earned Golding the Booker McConnell Prize in 1980. Although Golding has ventured into other literary forms including the recently released collection of miscellaneous essays, *A Moving Target* (1982), his reputation derives from the strength of his novels.

(See also *CLC*, Vols. 1, 2, 3, 8, 10, 17; *Contemporary Authors,* Vols. 5-8, rev. ed.; and *Dictionary of Literary Biography,* Vol. 15.)

EDWARD BLISHEN

Few in recent years can have written better than William Golding about the sea and bullies. *Pincher Martin,* that terrifying metaphysical sermon, was marvellous about the action of water, the way it moved in the sun or under rain, when lapping that awful rock or being hurled at it in a storm. As for bullies, *Lord of the Flies* is a sort of treatise on the variety in which they come: and *The Inheritors* a statement about the supersession of an earlier, gentler human being by Homo Sapiens, your original hooligan.

Rites of Passage brings these strands together in a new fashion. Some time early in the nineteenth century, Edmund Talbot, a young man of aristocratic background, is on his way from England to Australia. It's an odd ship he's on: a man-of-war switched to passenger-carrying. He's keeping a journal for the eye of his godfather, a peer and man of influence, who's asked that it be kept frankly: he hopes to relive his own youth through it. . . .

[On board the ship there] are emigrants, the people, at one end, and gentlemen and ladies at the other: with a white line on the deck to keep them apart. It's an allegory, already, of Regency Britain, and made more powerful by the construction of various devices for bringing about blindness. That's to say, the reader shares the gentlemanly blindness of never actually witnessing the world at the people's end, and the young toff, who's clearly going on to govern the British Empire, is blind to much that is going on under his own nose.

He understands perfectly well the nature of Miss Brocklebank, who is to be taken in a quick disgusted flurry in his cabin—or hutch, as he calls it. He can identify, if not understand, Mr Prettiman, the social philosopher. But he mistakes at first the character of Summers, who has risen from the ranks to be an officer, and sets Talbot a puzzle: how can someone ill-born be a man of honour and a gentleman? Talbot, however, is a rapid learner: he is passing, Mr Golding seems to suggest, through a youthful phase of acute sensitiveness and quick and even generous understanding.

But the crux of it lies with the Captain, who hates parsons; and the young, not very worldly, inexperienced parson who is travelling on the ship, uneasily at the gentlemanly end. We see the appalling tragedy of the Reverend James Colley through Talbot's eyes, blindfolded and then horridly wide-open. Through a letter written by Colley—begun as a letter to his sister, but soon becoming one he could let no sister see—we reinterpret the events which Talbot has so wittily misconstrued: the elegant amusement of the young diarist turns to horror. But Talbot recovers. The novel is clearly, in part, about the human capacity to climb back to the levels at which shoulders are gracefully shrugged.

It's beautifully done: because that side of Mr Golding's gift that has sometimes accorded ill with his sombre moralities—the element of the eighteenth-century wit—is here given appropriate employment. It's a novel that shows how the sheer panic of being human moves about, sometimes hideously, under the skin of that pretence of being at home in the world that we call civilization.

Agree with Mr Golding's view of things or not, it's marvellous to see how such a gift (which I've always thought of as metaphysical—his novels remind me of Donne's sermons) is now enjoying a harvest as fruitful as the one a quarter of a century ago. It may even be richer than the first. Here, in Colley, is Piggy of *Lord of the Flies,* dying again: and Pincher Martin's unworldly friend. Here again is the shuddering surmise that to be human is perhaps to be monstrous. Here is the perception, deeply written into Mr Golding's work, that "Men can die of shame". But here, too, is the quietly excellent Lieutenant Summers, who is plainly unmonstrous and at the same time is not to be bullied. He is, I think, the author's most convincing attempt to portray a good, strong human being.

Edward Blishen, "Sheer Panic of Being Human," in The Times Educational Supplement (© *Times Newspapers Ltd. (London) 1980; reproduced from* The Times Educational Supplement *by permission), No. 3357, October 24, 1980, p. 18.*

ROBERTSON DAVIES

The deep satisfaction we feel in reading and reflecting on William Golding's novels rises from his power to isolate, describe and make real to us moral problems that concern us all. The notable moralists of our day are novelists and poets. Philosophy is remote from the average intelligent person and the churches rarely command his allegiance, but for all that he is eager to come to grips with serious problems of morality. Much popular fiction offers him nothing but a reflection of the easy, fashionable despair of those who paddle timidly in the shallows of experience, but William Golding tackles moral problems head on, and wrestles them to the floor.

How does he do it? His mind possesses a coherent, compassionate but unsentimental attitude toward life and mankind, and his scale of values, though not inflexible, is firm. In the broad sense of the term it is a religious mind, because it is engaged with the great themes of our existence and will not be content with easy, pessimistic approaches to them. Too often pessimism is achieved by ignoring whatever cannot be made to fit its needs. His reflections present themselves to him in the form of fiction, and here again he is not satisfied with the bonelessness that contents those contemporary writers whose novels remind us of Edward Lear's flopsican mopsican Bear. He brings a formidable professionalism to his writing, and his novels have the completeness that marks them as works of art. . . .

[In his latest book, *Rites of Passage,* Golding's] splendid professionalism shows in the skill with which he takes the device of the personal journal and the letter, so familiar from the fiction of the period he has chosen for his story, and gives them convincing period quality, while at the same time insinuating into them a kind of insight which is post-Freudian. But these insinuations are never obvious; we never feel that the 20th century is nudging the 19th or that our age is pretending to some absolute superiority in judging human affairs.

One of the marks of the novelist of the first rank is his capacity for what might be called impersonation, the ability to speak through a character in such a way that more is revealed than the character is directly aware of; young Mr. Talbot, who writes of himself as if he were a silly, snobbish young ass, comes off rather better than he could know. Colley, who writes as a man who has removed himself from all that is dark in man's nature, provokes our pity. He is a man who has never seen his Shadow, and who is depending on his clerical rank and his feverish piety to overcome an inborn inferiority. He hopes to attain gentility through sanctity, an idea that could only occur to a fool.

Here is where Golding will rub some of his readers raw, for it is not a fashionable attitude to suppose that some people are naturally inferior, not in birth but in character. But this book anatomizes snobbery, that peculiarly English trait, in a manner that hints that snobbery may sometimes be a response to a genuine intuition, as is the case with Talbot.

Although there is plenty of ambiguity in this novel, there are no loose ends: everything is present that enables the reader to draw extensive and possibly profound conclusions about what happened, and why, and whether or not it was inevitable. The whole book is written with a fine economy. It seems to move easily and, when Talbot is writing, somewhat self-indulgently, but there is nothing unnecessary at any point; every joke, every scrap of flattery addressed by the godson to his noble patron, tells us something we need to know. The minor characters are drawn with a certainty of line and occasional enriching with color that reminds us of the pen and red chalk drawings of the period in which the story is set.

This is very good Golding, and good Golding is among the best fictional currency we have. Its hallmark is a suggestion of hope, and that is a rarity in serious modern novels, so many of which are blighted by what old theologians called ''wan-hope,'' by which they meant despair of salvation. But not William Golding: he is not so Graham Greene as all that.

> Robertson Davies, ''William Golding: Voyage to the Center of the Self,'' in Book World—The Washington Post (© 1980, The Washington Post), November 2, 1980, p. 5.

MICHAEL WATERHOUSE

Although *Darkness Visible* (1979) is one of [Golding's] most forceful novels and it is certainly one of his most ambitious, it is surprisingly disorganized. Here we have the moral discussion placed right at the heart of society in the nineteen-sixties, as made familiar by the hallmarks of decline we read about in our newspapers: marital breakdown, sexual promiscuity and deviation, prejudices of all kinds and an attempted kidnapping. Some of the book is reminiscent of *The Pyramid;* the crises of youth experienced by both Matty and Sophy are told with the same witty compassion that tracked Olly through his adolescence. But there is also a far more sinister element. The first part of the narrative is primarily concerned with Matty, the second with Sophy, and in the third they, and most of the subsidiary characters, come together in the kidnapping with which the plot climaxes. That might appear taut enough, but although the events seem to follow a plausible sequence, there is a disparity between the characters and all they do, and a sense that underlying this crammed package of incidents there is an area of character interest which is touched on but which never surfaces. The Miltonic title seems to authorize this reticence. *Darkness Visible* begins and ends in flames and in between all we do see is hellish 'sights of woe', on which little light is shed, morally or psychologically.

As a child Matty was discovered in a Blitz fire, horribly disfigured and retarded, and he spends his early years moving from one job to another, ostracized and unloved. He travels to Australia, has his genitals crushed by an aborigine, and returns to England, obsessed with religion and convinced of his 'vision' (reminding us of Jocelin and Simon). Sophy, on the other hand, is very attractive, brought up in a comfortable middle class home, and bored. She experiments with sex and petty thieving, and then plans to kidnap—as much for reckless enjoyment as the promise of wealth—a young boy at the school where Matty works in the garden. The attempt fails, Matty dies in the fire which results, and Sophy flings about, desperate and unsure what to do. Golding draws no conclusions. Matty's vision that his 'mission' has something to do with the school and something to do with Sophy is proved correct, but then his prediction that the world will end on 6/6/66 is not. That the novel lacks a direction for its moral discourse may be to its credit; the experience it recounts is formless and Matty and Sophy are necessarily inarticulate. But for the novel to have succeeded as the *tour de force* it could have been, it needed to establish

more firmly a causal connection between the degeneracy and the violence, and the society which bred them. For Golding, explanation and understanding strengthen a fiction; the novelist must search out plausible explanations for actions, no matter how thin they are. As it is, many of the characters and events of *Darkness Visible* seem to be on the periphery—Matty, handicapped and fanatical, Pedigree the pederast, the dropouts with which Sophy surrounds herself, and the whole alien world of the sequence in the Australian outback. The jumble of too many events clogs the novel and leaves us with an impression of bleakness that is essentially unintelligible.

It is tempting to argue that the new novel solves all the problems, but that would be to overstate the case. *Rites of Passage* is not as ambitious a novel as *Darkness Visible* and the journal format would have been inappropriate, as demonstrated by the constraints of the short section devoted to Matty's diary in *Darkness Visible*. It does, however, resolve the difficulty of finding a suitable setting in time and place and the shift of perspective has found its proper position within the novel's structure. Although the reader must make some effort to follow the 'tarpaulin' language and the period conventions of speech (indeed, part of the book's quality lies in its sophisticated use of what, at times, approaches pastiche), it has nothing like the remoteness of *The Inheritors* or *The Spire*. The isolation of these characters is determined by the fact that they are confined to a ship at sea, but the novel differs from *Lord of the Flies* in that the social conventions are not stripped away. It is true that they break down when the 'Badger Bag' episode gets 'out of hand', but the Captain, however reluctantly, has to reinforce conventional proprieties by issuing apologies. Similarly, the licence allowed the common sailors and emigrants 'in their cups' is limited and when exceeded, is seen to be corrected by a formal enquiry into Colley's death. We may be sceptical about the motives behind the Captain's apology and enquiry, but the order of the ship does not collapse.

Unlike in the earlier novels, the moral issue is not invoked until the shift of perspective occurs. Admittedly, Talbot's seduction of Zenobia and his irreligious contempt for Colley are morally dubious, but these are secondary to the substantive questions raised by Colley's letter. The letter evokes compassion and respect for his obvious devotion and sincerity. We may notice his admiration for Rogers's body, suspect it even, but is spoken in a spirit of innocence which precludes the possibility of deliberate self-deception. His 'fall from grace', homosexuality released by drink, is a natural urge unchecked by the moral considerations that would otherwise have inhibited him; it was through no fault of his own. Like Talbot's, Colley's system of morality 'owed less to feeling than to the operations of the intellect' and the shame which kills him appears a disproportionate punishment.

If we exonerate Colley, with whom does the moral issue lie? Talbot? Captain Anderson? Both are guilty of negligence. Talbot might be reproached for his bigotry and thoughts of implicating Colley with Zenobia, Anderson for his victimisation of Colley, but strong judgements on these men are curbed by other, mitigating considerations. Anderson's resentment of Colley derives from his view that but for the clergyman who married his mother, he might have had higher expectations. Talbot has a position to protect; it is expected of him that he will stand aloof and his peremptory response to Summers's injunction that he should do his duty smacks more of a failure of understanding than of any more serious shortcoming. Having aligned ourselves with the narrator, we share, in some measure, Talbot's loss of dignity after the perepeteia.

So the moral issue is confused and complicated by the roles these characters play and the notion that the world of the ship is a stage becomes an increasingly dominant theme of the book. They literally tread the boards. The Captain's orders are to be learnt by heart, like any stage part. Zenobia's makeup is designed to show her at her best under the lights of Colley's service. These theatrical aspects to their drama, when added to the formal difficulty of access to authoritative information, inhibit our capacity to appoint blame and may make us wonder whether such an experience as this is susceptible of moral judgement.

The disconcerting implication of this uncertainty is that the pleasure we have taken in following the events is somehow culpable. Talbot's journal ensures that our distance from his point of view is slight and that we can enjoy the comic entertainment of Colley's servility and mortification at the Captain's hands. (We may remember that Talbot's purpose in writing the journal is entertainment.) It was Stevenson who said that to centre our notion of morality on forbidden acts introduced 'a secret element of gusto' into our judgements; our eagerness to discover what happened in the fo'castle betokens not merely a desire for completeness but a fascination with that aura of the unknown and forbidden which surrounds the event.

Such a manipulation of the experience of reading seems less an indictment of society than a misgiving about the presuppositions which underpin moral values. The novel is being pulled in two directions. The journal involves us in the world of the ship, whilst the theatrical aspects insist that the characters are playing out a drama and, but for the luck of casting, they could equally appear in different roles. We are made aware of the book as a fiction and of the shortcomings of fictions as they are traditionally told. The scattered references to, amongst others, Richardson and Coleridge, ground the novel in a point of view that is morally sure, but too limited to grasp those refinements of behaviour which elude moral consistency. Talbot is forever being proved wrong in his estimates of other people; his reading has not equipped him to avoid mistaken judgements of Deverel, Mr. Prettiman and, of course, James Colley. The moral stance in *Rites of Passage* is tentative, because we cannot with certainty decide what the moral issue is.

Golding in 1980 is less certain about the validity of his own opinions. The moral convictions with which he began have matured into a recognition that whilst human beings may treat each other with immeasurable cruelty, their actions often spring from a complex of history and motivation that engages the very sources of ignorance and belief which prompt morally endorsable actions in others. It is not a question of which direction to take; nor is it that these characters are blind to the distinction between good and evil. Rather it is that in obeying the dictates of conscience, social man has no guarantee that his actions will be uniformly good. 'Any human endeavour can never be wholly good; it must have a cost in terms of people.' Jocelin's religious obsession is not dissimilar to Matty's. Which is the better man? In the 1965 essay on Fable, Golding wrote that he might still believe in the perfectability of social man. I wouldn't care to say whether he still does. He considers that man is a little more 'sensible' than he thought, but not any 'better'. The evidence of *Darkness Visible* does not tend to corroborate this cautious optimism, but the intelligent stoicism that is a part of the beauty of *Rites of Passage* might well do. (pp. 10-14)

Michael Waterhouse, ''Golding's Secret Element of Gusto,'' in Essays in Criticism, *Vol. XXXI, No. 1, January, 1981, pp. 1-14.*

WILLIAM BOYD

Towards the end of William Golding's latest novel—*Rites of Passage*—its protagonist Edmund Talbot remarks to a naval lieutenant that 'life is a formless business, Summers, Literature is much amiss in forcing a form on it!' The notion is a central one in Golding's work and also in any appreciation of it, for literature, we are now fully aware, cannot do else other than impose a form, even when aping life at its most random and contingent. From one point of view Dean Jocelin's vision and construction of his cathedral spire is a prolonged debate on the futility of the entire purpose of trying to shape and create something out of redoubtably intractable material—the writer's problem no less than the medieval architect's. Golding goes further than this. Not content with the struggle to shape and form he also seeks answers to grave and essential questions about the human condition: 'the unnamable, unfathomable and invisible darkness that sits at the centre.' . . . This overall seriousness of intent on Golding's part—the sense that his novels are meditations on or dramatisations of life's most seminal concerns—is at once his great strength and his weakness, an advantage and a constraint; some of his novels are immeasurably enhanced by it, others find the freight of significance too much to bear.

Perhaps the problem can be conveyed more precisely by recording a remark Graham Greene made. Greene complains that 'I would like to ascend into myth but find my books so often muddy with plot'. This, I suspect, is not only a piece of self-criticism (misguided, in my opinion) but also a wishful indication of the way Greene would like his books to be read. It's a plea for less popular assessment, a desire to be rated—or to write—on a deeper more elemental level. Golding, on the other hand, suffers from the opposite reaction. Not only in the reverential, solemn way people approach his work but also, from his fourth novel onwards, in some impulse governing the way he writes.

Most novels tend inevitably towards what we can call the world of history—the rich infinitely varied world of phenomena, of appearances and details. Indeed, it can be argued that there is something in the novel form itself that fosters and encourages this inclination. This is what Greene is bemoaning—the pull is too hard for him to resist. Golding, alternatively, has determinedly steered his fiction towards the other pole: that of myth, and all the more single-mindedly since *Free Fall*. Of course, in most serious fiction both elements co-exist, but in varying degrees and, by and large, the mythic features are subordinate, the *referential* aspects of the form claiming most of our attention. This duality also applies to Golding. *Lord of the Flies,* he has related, started out primarily as an attempt to portray what children are really like, in opposition to the anodyne Victorian image in *Coral Island*. However, the novel is more than that, clearly—or at least became more than that—developing into the first exploration of now familiar Golding themes: an examination of innocence, the dark truth about human nature and a delineation of his particular Manichean vision of the world.

But what made Golding's first three novels so remarkable (and I would rate *Pincher Martin* as high as any) was the extent to which he managed to introduce the mythic element without threatening the tenuous equilibrium that has to exist between the specifics of history and the generalities of myth. *The Inheritors* captures with marvellous ability a wholly realistic sense of the Neanderthal world as well as reenacting on the wider level the confrontation between Innocence and Experience. So too *Pincher Martin* is at once the story of a real man marooned on a rock in the middle of the Atlantic as well as an elaborate parody of the Creation, an illustration of man's immense ego and his futile heroism.

Many commentators see Golding's first five novels as forming a homogenous unit, but I would be inclined to mark the division after *Pincher Martin*. Both *Free Fall* and *The Spire* significantly tip the balance towards myth and concentrate attention rather more on the solution of what might be termed spiritual or aesthetic dilemmas. Significance is no longer tethered to fact. One is too conscious of the huge abstractions bulking beneath the narrative and its surface details. There is, at the back of the reader's mind, an overpowering, and at times enervating, awareness of correspondence: the fact that nothing in these novels is offered for its own sake, but is there to serve the rhetoric of the mythopoeic impulse. In *Free Fall* and *The Spire* the mythical *sous-texte* of the novels dominates the detriment of the fiction. There is on occasion a certain inflated, striven-for trenchancy in the prose (a failing Conrad was also prone to), as well as passages of great power. There simply isn't enough 'muddy plot' obscuring the vision. Not that the vision is ever crystal clear—Golding's answers are never unambiguous and succinct—it is instead that one knows one should always be seeking the analogical matrix that lies beneath the prose, striving all the time to 'see into the life of things'.

The two books that followed *The Spire*—*The Pyramid* and *The Scorpion God*—represented a hiatus in the Golding oeuvre. *The Scorpion God* consisted of three novellas and *The Pyramid* was an untypical, Trollopian novel recrafted from some early short stories. It wasn't until the publication of *Darkness Visible* last year—after a self-confessed eight-year block—that the sequence of Golding novels proper continued. To put it at its most simple, *Darkness Visible* is an uneven, strained attempt to reconnect the twin worlds of muddy plot and myth that had diverged since *Pincher Martin*. To some extent it succeeds brilliantly, as in the opening chapter dealing with the blitz and the simple hero Matty's exposure to the pentacostal firestorm, and the later chapters treating his life and education. However there is something disconcerting about the book's self-conscious modishness—terrorism, paedophilia—and for once Golding's superb organizational grasp of his material seems to have deserted him almost completely. There is no doubt that the writing of the novel was something of a purgative experience—Golding has stated that he has refused to read a single review of the book—and it will come to be seen, I suspect, as something of a curiosity—an aberration in what is otherwise a career of masterly technical control and authorial self assurance. Its, so to speak, emetic properties have clearly proved efficient, and we now have, a year later, a novel which . . . reaffirms a memorable return to form and the literary stature of its author.

Many reviewers of *Rites of Passage* have qualified their praise, ranking it with *The Pyramid,* seeing it as something of a perfect minor work. It is far more than this: rather it's a return to tried and tested techniques; in many ways a look back at what has come before and a summary of the preceding novels' achievements. Golding's best novels take place in a confined world: the island in *Lord of the Flies*, the rock in *Pincher Martin*, language in *The Inheritors*—further confined by the characters' vastly limited conceptual boundaries. Similarly, *Rites of Passage* takes place on an aging man-of-war, en route with a party of emigrants for Australia, at some point towards the end of the Napoleonic wars. The main burden of the narrative is taken

up by a privileged young passenger called Edmund Talbot, who is recording the events of the passage in a journal for the benefit and amusement of his aristocratic patron. This journal in itself is a superb example of literary mimicry on Golding's part, a feat of imaginative sympathy with the early-nineteenth century that comes close to the intellectual efforts required to render Neanderthalers' world-view in *The Inheritors*. . . . The narrative point of view shifts and the events of the voyage are retold by Colley. This change in perspective completely alters our conception of events as Talbot has thus far related to us. Colley has been the victim of callous persecution at the hands of the officers of the ship and the captain himself. He has been humiliated in front of the ship's company during the traditional crossing-of-the-equator ceremony. Colley's idea of his own nature and his standing in the eyes of his fellow passengers is revealed as hopelessly and tragically inaccurate. Talbot's journal and narrative have also to be reassessed and he sees himself as being unwittingly responsible for Colley's bizarre demise. This sudden, final change of viewpoint causing a reanalysis of all that has passed before is a feature that occurs in all of Golding's first three novels. Here it is handled with great skill and deftness, used not only as an instrument of humourous irony and a subversive literary technique (as remarkable as Conrad's similar exercise in *Under Western Eyes*—a writer to whom Golding comes to bear more and more resemblance) but also as a means of focusing on the themes of guilt, persecution and delusion which were only intermittently apparent in Talbot's self-opinionated journal. Now Talbot is able, with the aid of Colley's letter and the impromptu inquest held after his death, to fill in the gaps in his own defective and subjective account of what has been going on in the ship. The hidden and unknown act which brought about Colley's insupportable shame and eventual death is suddenly made clear.

Rites of Passage and *Pincher Martin* are the only two Golding novels where a revelation of what takes place at the end will completely ruin the reader's enjoyment of the book—a sufficient testimony to the renewed status of muddy plot. However, *Rites of Passage* contains greater riches than pure narrative entertainment. Riches which, on the basis of only two readings so far, I can only hint at. Like *Lord of the Flies, The Inheritors* and *Pincher Martin, Rites of Passage* has 'at its back' another text. (For the preceding three, they are, respectively, *The Coral Island,* Wells's *Outline of History* and *Robinson Crusoe*). In this case it is Coleridge's 'The Rime of the Ancient Mariner'. . . . Just as Golding challenges the dogmas of his literary starting points in his first three novels so he 'deconstructs' Coleridge in *Rites of Passage*. To put it at its most brief, Colley is at once Mariner and Albatross, and the purgatorial sufferings which lead to redemption in the poem are pointedly, and with wicked irony, eschewed here. In the poem the Mariner confers his blessing on the water snakes and is freed from the albatross by his unselfish act. Colley, re-enacting the Mariner's part with a more literal accuracy goes on from this point to assume an albatross which leads to his squalid end. His geographical passage across the equator, his physical move over the white line painted on the deck to separate 'gentlemen' from 'people' symbolises his own transit from the factitious world of civilized appearance to the darker realms of the unconscious, which ultimately brings about his doom. This is a multi-layered and marvellously intelligent novel with endless subtle allusions and reverberations and effortlessly marshalled cross-references. It is also a witty and solidly realistic account of life on a sailing ship at the beginning of the last century. There is an exuberance and confidence about the book that signals the author's own awareness of his return to former strengths. The balance is triumphantly right. (pp. 89-94)

William Boyd, "Mariner and Albatross," in London Magazine *(© London Magazine 1981), n.s. Vol. 20, Nos. 11 & 12, February-March, 1981, pp. 89-94.*

DAVID MONTROSE

Just as Eliot's criticism is read more to learn about Eliot than, say, Marston or Massinger, so [*A Moving Target,* a] collection of lectures, essays, reviews, and travel articles, will be read primarily for sights of the author rather than in expectation of intrinsic merit. Golding will not be pleased with this state of affairs . . . he dislikes 'value by association', disparaging in 'My First Book', the situation whereby his *Poems,* published in 1934, 'has been on offer in the United States at 4,000 dollars'. The dislike is at least partly justified; like Eliot's essays, some of Golding's occasional pieces—as *The Hot Gates* (1965) demonstrated—repay perusal on their own account.

The best things about *The Hot Gates* were the childhood reminiscences, 'Billy the Kid' and 'The Ladder and the Tree', with the travel articles a close second. While there is nothing so directly autobiographical in *A Moving Target,* places are again impressively represented. What elevates this aspect of Golding's artistry above the routine is his profound sense of history and, indeed, pre-history: landscape is not, for him, a simple here-and-now, but a cultural palimpsest, the sum of its centuries. This sense is strongest in English climes: *The Hot Gates* splendidly evoked the Channel, Stratford, the South Downs; *A Moving Target* celebrates Wiltshire, Golding's home county; and the cathedrals of Winchester and Salisbury. Here, the author tunes into the *mana* of a location, looking through the contemporary to reconstruct the past. 'Tourists will not see what I see,' he writes in 'Wiltshire', 'for it is invisible.'

The benefits yielded by this awareness are most evident when the present collection's English epiphanies are stood alongside its articles on Holland, Greece, and Egypt. Golding's historical sense does not travel well: 'Through the Dutch Waterways', the piece where it is wholly absent, is the least successful. (p. 23)

Turning from the 'Places' section to 'Ideas', one encounters pieces that score rather lower on the intrinsic merit scale. The shining exception is 'Intimate Relations', an essay on journal-keepers even better—because longer and wider-ranging—than Alfred Kazin's exposition in *The Inmost Leaf.* Kazin confined himself to literary diarists—Emerson, Thoreau, Gide . . .— but Golding reaches from Jimmy Mason, an obscure Essex villager, to Queen Victoria, encompassing Pepys, Samuel Johnson, and Admiral Hervey *en route.* Himself an inveterate journal-keeper, Golding achieves an empathic understanding of the diarists' varying motivations, from 'the pleasure principle' of Mason and Pepys—keeping memories fresh by suspending them in prose—to Victoria's sense of duty.

The book reviews . . . have some points of interest, not least Golding's refusal to be impersonal; were it not for the author's identity, though, they would probably receive few second glances. The lectures are notable chiefly for the sidelights they cast on their deliverer. (pp. 23-4)

David Montrose, "Half-light," in New Statesman *(© 1982 The Statesman & Nation Publishing Co. Ltd.), Vol. 103, No. 2672, June 11, 1982, pp. 23-4.*

FRANK KERMODE

William Golding is evidently a bit fed up with being the author of *Lord of the Flies.* It was greeted with proper applause when it came out in 1954, but soon became the *livre de chevet* of American youth, and, worse, a favoured text in the classroom in the years of the great boom in Eng Lit, when a sterile popular variety of the New Criticism was encouraging all manner of dreary foolishness; whereupon the cognoscenti turned away, and called the book naive. Yet it was indeed a noble and a novel performance, to be followed in quick succession by two even more remarkable books, *The Inheritors* (1955) and *Pincher Martin* (1956). . . . The powerful, idiosyncratic voice came through again—always on new and unpredictable subjects—in *Free Fall* (1959) and *The Spire* (1964). But there was less excitement than before and also the rate of production slackened. In 1972 there were, among the three *novelle* of *The Scorpion God,* two of Golding's best things, exhibiting his extraordinary blend of intensity and remoteness, that central inexplicitness within the explicit for which he is always trying. And *Darkness Visible,* three years ago, seemed to indicate a continuance of the old powers, perhaps augmented (as sometimes happens) by an audacity that comes as a grace to some artists in old age. Like Matty, hero of *Darkness Visible,* in his happy time, Golding holds that there is nothing hid which shall not be manifested, and nothing kept secret but that it should come abroad. He will utter things which have been kept secret from the foundation of the world, as many of them as he can: for this is what he takes novels, like parables, to be *for.* The effort involved is extraordinary; he has grown more willing to discuss it, but no more able to say exactly what it entails.

This new book [*A Moving Target*] is his second collection of occasional pieces, and in the Preface he remarks that when asked to speak about his own work he has always tried to resist, but 'has always given way in the end so that at last I find myself talking about myself with the grossest liberality'. But his own work is not the only subject of this book, and some of the other pieces—though not, by any means, all of them— give one no less useful insights into his unique yet traditional talent. . . . [One] always senses behind the novelty of Golding's achievements something that is not quite of his moment.

In reviewing *The Spire* [see *CLC,* Vol. 17], I was trying to get at this quality when I compared the novel to Vaughan Williams, and especially to *Job,* and I still think the comparison useful: Blake's *rifacimento* of the Bible itself transformed in an idiosyncratic modal music with saxophones thrown in. But the tone of these essays has less heroic antecedents. It brings to mind the Forster of *Abinger Harvest:* 'the moment we landed two Nubian gentlemen in full ethnic costume leapt out from their place of concealment and began to sing, the one meanwhile playing a gusli, the other beating a drum. We paid them to stop, which they did.' A bit joky, but it isn't so committed to the facetious that it can't modulate at once into seriousness.

The book starts with a collection of pieces on Places. . . . The second section is labelled Ideas, though Notions would have suited some of the essays better. . . . [The] writing here is often more than agreeable. Reviewing a book about high-altitude photography, Golding remarks that 'if the whole round earth did not appear, still great cantles of it . . . became visible'; and my guess that 'cantle' had probably not been used in precisely that sense since *Antony and Cleopatra* III.x is confirmed or anyway supported by the *OED.*

And indeed this review is a remarkable piece of writing, very properly saved from oblivion. One of Golding's strengths has always been that he strives to see the individual human being against long perspectives, cultural, geological, cosmic. And so he ends his high-altitude review with a genuine *O altitudo,* touched by his characteristic religious feeling: 'Surely, eyes more capable than ours of receiving the range of universal radiation may well see her [the earth], this creature of argent and azure, to have robes of green and gold streamed a million miles from her by the solar wind as she dances around Helios in the joy of light.' He has the same sense of numinous remoteness in contemplating the statuettes of the Earth Goddess at Delphi, far older than the oracle; or a footprint in a cave in the Auvergne, or a lateen sail of a Nile riverboat; or Homer, who is repeatedly and lovingly invoked or remembered.

Wonder is Golding's mode of knowledge. 'The bare act of being is an outrageous improbability,' he says, describing himself as a man prone to 'a sense of continual astonishment'—rather like St Mark. And at his most serious: 'What man *is,* whatever man is under the eye of heaven, that I burn to know and that—I do not say this lightly—I would endure knowing.'

The novels are his way of finding out. . . . The reason why he can freely discuss the craft of his writings but say nothing much about the secrets they may make manifest is that the form of knowing is not the same as understanding; like the spire in his book, the novels, if they are any good, get their glory from elsewhere.

Of course the mason or carpenter must know his job, but the glory is beyond him. The novelist will detect a truth or a relevance; it may be indicated only by an enigmatic sentence that 'will lie in the bed of the river of words like a stone, itself invisible but making a swirl on the surface'. It is the power to make such sentences that gives the great novelists an affinity with the saints; and that affinity explains why it cannot be talked about. The truth of fiction lies, says Golding, not in its representation of the phenomenal world, but in its 'fitness with itself, like the dissonances and consonances of harmony'. Seen from a long way off, it might appear a creature of argent and azure.

This is a mystical view of the novel, one which is as different as possible from the long perspective of Shaw (the final section of *Back to Methuseleh* 'is called "As Far as Thought can Reach''; and has left at least one reader thinking that if that is as far as thought can go, the sooner it comes back the better'). Golding wants to be here as well as elsewhere, out in violet space or in a future which produces men from eggs.

He is a conservative anarchist, he says, stuck in his human time and place, but dealing in human creativity, which he takes to be an aspect of an 'ultimate Creator'. For our creativity, he says on his last page, is 'a sign that beyond the transient horrors and beauties of our hell there is a Good which is ultimate and absolute.' He is better at his religious exercises than at being a theologian; better at the holy than at the idea of the holy. But in the end *A Moving Target* tells one more about this one-man marriage of heaven and hell than we might think we have any right to know; and for all its obviously secondary quality it deserves the study of all who value proximate creation.

Frank Kermode, ''Cantles'' (appears here by permission of the London Review of Books *and the author), in* London Review of Books, *June 17 to June 30, 1982, p. 12.*

IAN GREGOR AND MARK KINKEAD-WEEKES

The first impression of [*Rites of Passage*] is its 'immediate accessibility'. Not since *Lord of the Flies* has a Golding novel

enjoyed such happy recognition, indeed it is difficult to resist the thought that part, at least, of the success of *Rites of Passage* came in the form of re-assurance, that the author of the earlier novel was alive and well, and that the quarter century which separated the two books had not diminished his narrative power. There was a similar recreation of detail and atmosphere, the south sea island replaced by a ship of the line. The smell, the cramped quarters, the clanking pumps, the sand and gravel in the bilge, the constantly tilting decks, the wind in the ropes—the cumulative effect is to make us think not so much of vivid description as an 'on the spot' report. This, Golding makes us feel, is just what it must have been like to have been aboard such a ship at the turn of the last century.

But what gives these details their vividness is that they are continually at work in making us aware of the presence of a whole society, or more exactly, of two. There is the society of the officers, essentially an extension of the land society, ever mindful of rank, courtesies, amorous strategies, and the obligation to unseen paymasters. Below decks, there is the society of the sailors, crowded, noisy, dangerous when roused, and (for those on the upper decks) living a life as remote as any native tribe. Between the two, marking the deck, is the white line. What is so striking—and 'the line' is a good instance—is how effortlessly the precisely observed detail releases the wider perspective—so we can discern in the microcosm of the ship, a wider society: an age of revolution, and of ideas about Reason and Order, Feeling and Freedom. Though the reference is oblique, it is not difficult to infer that the name of the ship is *Britannia*.

These details, these perspectives, would count for little if it were not for the language in which the novel is written. Corresponding to the two societies, there is a double idiom—Talbot's late Augustan idiom of Taste and Enlightened Good Sense, Colley's Romantic idiom of the Man of Feeling. What is extraordinary about the language of the book, however, is how completely Golding is in command of it, so that there is no suggestion of pastiche or professed imitation; on the contrary, it is the language of the book which is the source of its energy and exuberance, and hence its individuality. With considerable ingenuity Golding makes Talbot self-consciously acquire a third idiom—Tarpaulin language—so that its phrases, deliberately arcane and archaic, throw into contrast Talbot's own 'natural' mode. In this way, Golding boldly heightens our awareness of the language, but only in the interests of making us feel it to be a homogenous part of the world it seeks to communicate.

The observed life of the ship, the wider perspectives the voyage affords, the language—all these elements gradually converge and make for a strong total effect. The difficulty arises when we begin to put that into words. It is not just a question of the drastic simplicities entailed in any formulation of complex imaginative effects, but more disturbing than that. It is an uneasy feeling of responding so sharply to certain features of the book as to be lured, like Talbot, into false 'understanding'. The very clarity of the undertaking would seem to lead to a position where we not only have to revise our interpretation, but more radically, to ask what is the nature of interpretation. We can feel the ground beginning to shift uneasily as soon as we put the question which, from one point of view, seems so appropriate. What is at issue in *Rites of Passage?* How Mr. Talbot went to sea and learned to know himself? How Mr. Colley was made to encounter the 'reality' of his own temperament and was overcome? As soon as the questions are put, we seem to hear that hidden laughter which echoes in the novel, and feel that we have been tempted into a kind of 'understanding', a kind of interpretation, which it is the veiled purpose of the novel to subvert. In a rather curious way, *Rites of Passage* seems to reverse the experience of being in a maze. We enter full of purpose and interest and are delighted immediately by the precision and variety of the detail, by prospects, far and near; we expect to be taken further in—then, quite suddenly, we find ourselves on the outside. We seem to have taken a wrong turn, a re-entry seems called for, and perhaps that is also part of this particular maze. (pp. 112-14)

When 'the end' of the novel comes, it is headed simply with an ampersand; this is a novel which resists conclusion. Yet depth is dramatically defined by the surface which encloses it.

For Golding the resources of art have to be drawn upon to communicate 'a truth' more mysterious than Talbot's, more provisional than Colley's; they have crossed the line too easily. Golding's novel is a rite which 'holds the line' itself in respect—ever mindful of the depths, but no less mindful of the human need for passage, for survival.

Yet Golding has always been committed to exploring beyond the line, into the depths, where the world of social behaviour and character gives way to hidden dimensions of good and evil, joy and horror—which *Rites of Passage* refuses to explore but will only call attention to, as a stage defines an open trapdoor, or a picture-puzzle the shape of its missing piece. It is that 'darkness' that [*Darkness Visible*] insists must be made *visible*, cost what it may in a different kind of art that may be caviare to the general. Now author and reader must cope from the start with visions of extremity, beginning with the twentieth century experience of inferno. The exploratory imagination is careless of elegance, willing to risk the outrageous, the obscure, the contorted, the farcical, in order to reveal not a brightly-worked surface but the underside, "the seamy side where the connections are". Where *Rites* woos us through a charming worldling like ourselves, the other novel seems to need distorted lenses—a saintly idiot, a pederast, a terrorist—to overturn our ordinary sense of human nature and make its warp and woof unmistakeable. Whereas *Rites* delighted in language, *Darkness Visible* calls language itself in question. Above all, where *Rites* depended on artful *juxtaposition* of scenes and pictures, it is only a continuous process of deeper and deeper *exploration* that can hope to make darkness finally visible, beyond paradox and different points of view, through some sequence of focussings. (pp. 118-19)

It would seem that the two novels in tandem enabled Golding to express different potentials of his art more fully than had been possible in any single work. One book is the most powerful of all his metaphysical explorations, seeming to contain and extend the whole *oeuvre* since *Lord of the Flies*, an astonishingly original work but difficult, contorted, obscure. The other dances along, light, bright, and sparkling, artful, literary, linguistically inventive; the work of a master-craftsman and a comedian who has always been around, if overshadowed by the metaphysician—yet the missing piece of the jigsaw, the dark hole in the stage, are all the more 'there' for the colour and animation which surround them. One artfully disposes scenes on the surface to define a gap; the other plunges beyond the line, over the edge, into the very depths—Rembrandt to Brocklebank or Picasso. One is predominantly social, a comedy of manners albeit with a dark dénouement, which sees writing as itself a rite of passage enabling worldlings to *negotiate* dark initiation and death: to cope with the "monstrous" which comes

up from underneath, to get past 'the horror' of the dying in the darkness, and the human shape all alone in a wide wide sea. The narrative is "sewn up," the cover story prepared, the ship goes on, the reader returns to the world. The other *begins* by insisting that we stare into holocaust, and pursue to the end the metaphysical questions raised by tragedy and apocalypse. Its protagonists are extra-ordinary—saintly idiot, terrorist, pederast—and they are taken to points of no return. The reader, too, is taken to where ultimate questions cannot be negotiated or sailed past. One book delights in languages and affirms the power of writing as a rite of passage. The other calls language in question, and strives to open up the mysterious space between words and make what is hidden there visible, wordlessly. Each tries for a different way of being true to the paradoxes of Golding's imagination and his truth-telling urgency: how from the real and the clear, contradictions always (for him) spread and proliferate into multiplicity, opacity, mystery; but how art must continually find ways to clarify, to focus into unity. . . . [By giving us these two novels] almost simultaneously, Golding has achieved an extraordinary effect. It is not that we can possibly think of them as somehow one work, for each is too uniquely itself. Yet manifestly they deepen the focus on the same area of preoccupation, by coming from such different angles. And they seem to have liberated each to be *more* itself, its kind of thing, than it could have been if it had simultaneously been trying also to be the other.

And this has liberated readers too, who may have found in one or the other book more of the Golding they really like, in a purer state than usual. The reception was certainly very different. In England one novel instantaneously won widespread praise and a major prize, the other remained relatively unheralded, apparently unprized. In America it was the other way round.

It seems likely that the newly 'extreme' art, refining out elements first one way, and then another, will divide Golding's admirers in their preferences, without preventing a common recognition of what has been achieved. (pp. 128-29)

Ian Gregor and Mark Kinkead-Weekes, "The Later Golding," in Twentieth Century Literature *(copyright 1982, Hofstra University Press). Vol. 28, No. 2, Summer, 1982, pp. 109-31.*

VIRGINIA TIGER

The fiercely obdurate quality of Golding's imaginative achievement—what has been called his poetic intensity—derives from his ability to construct solidly patterned novels on foundations of the most daring verbal modes. His technical range is great, encompassing material as diverse as a sailor's sea-washed body, the befuddled encounter of prelapsarian creatures with rapacious interlopers, an 18th-century sea voyage across the equator. Yet, however, heterodox his fictional topographies may be, his seminal themes, like those of other obsessional artists, are limited and homogeneous. Each of Golding's novels represents another face carved from his earliest, most deeply held conviction that the two signs of man are his belief in God and his capacity to kill. (p. 217)

Golding has taken upon himself the formidable task of arousing the religious impulse and restoring to this recalcitrant time the spiritual dimension which is the stuff of vital religious mythopoeia. The problem for the novelist is to portray his notions about mysterious and multiple modes of spiritual life in concrete novelistic terms. To this end Golding early devised an ingenious narrative form: the ideographic structure.

Controlling each Golding novel is a narrative technique whereby two points of view are turned on one situation. In *The Inheritors,* for example, events are viewed first from the perspective of the Neanderthal mind, a mind that cannot reason beyond sense data. Golding gives us, first a primitive world to inhabit, a world where ideas are images; then, abruptly, he places us in the world of the pragmatic logical mind of the Cro-Magnons. In *Pincher Martin,* we move from the necessarily solipsistic world of a shipwrecked sailor struggling for seven days of ever diminishing strength to maintain his sanity on a barren rock to a remote island in the Hebrides where we discover to our existential alarm that the corpse that has been rotting for a week bears the identity disc of the shipwrecked sailor.

The overall intention of Golding's ideographic structures is to make his readers embrace paradoxes of existence which his own characters cannot recognize. In the final scene of *Darkness Visible,* for example, where the dying Mr. Pedigree imagines golden light emanating from the disfigured face of Matty, Golding means us to intuit that even as debauched a creature as Pedigree can be granted the possibility of salvation. It is not the least of the difficulty in reading Golding that he expects his readers to reassemble narrative images, reconcile apparently opposing points of view, build bridges between contradictory perspectives—all in the service of imaginatively participating in his religious construct. *Rites of Passage,* Golding's eighth novel, raises the same difficult questions for the reader as does *Pincher Martin,* his third: do the many obstacles to intelligibility, indeed to clarity, posed by the formal device of the ideographic structure reward or retard the reader's progress to final understanding? For *Rites of Passage* is a canvas of grids, elusive shapes, and obscurities as puzzling at first as any painting from Picasso's Cubist period. (pp. 217-18)

As readers of Golding's *Scorpion God* and *The Hot Gates* will well remember, this novelist has always been much absorbed by history, cutting sweeps wide and assured into distant times, shaping and fitting historical detail like the timbers of a great ship, to a moral purpose.

To this end, Golding in *Rites of Passage* once more adopts his characteristic paraphrase of the Old Masters. In varying degrees, the novels have all had as part of their genesis a quarrel with another writer's view of the same situation. Golding, by deliberately subverting literary models, intends his reader to judge the moral distance between, say, Ballantyne's complacent view of small boys in *Coral Island* and his own somber recasting in *Lord of the Flies.* In *Free Fall,* this sublative technique underwent something of a sea-change, but even there Golding used Dante's *Vita Nuova* as an ironic model for Sammy Mountjoy's love of Beatrice Ifor.

There is no such simple scenario underpinning *Rites of Passage.* Its provenance is Wilfrid Scawen Blunt's two volume work, *My Diaries: Being a Personal Narrative of Events, 1888-1914,* wherein Blunt mentions an acquaintance's reference to an episode in the 1790's involving the "iron" Duke of Wellington. En route to India, Wellington boarded an adjacent convoy, having been requested to buoy the spirits of a fellow seafarer sunk in a deep lethargy. The iron Duke's effort apparently failed—the man died. "I don't understand it. But it's something that deeply interested me," Golding has said of the incident which clearly constitutes an intriguing, because inexplicable, determined death. "*Rites of Passage,*" Golding

continued, was "an attempt to invent circumstances . . . where one can see that this kind of thing can happen: that someone can be reduced to the point at which he would die of shame."

Of course, sea mysteries such as this have long fascinated and appalled Golding; indeed, in both *Lord of the Flies* and *Pincher Martin* the sea lurks as a palpable presence and atavistic force. The ocean is no imaginative stranger to the Golding who commanded a British Navy rocket cruiser during World War II and participated in the sinking of the *Bismarck. . . .* So the life and literature of sea voyages, *The Odyssey* and *The Aeneid* and the poetry of salt water, naval logs, sea shanties, memoirs, navigation manuals, accounts both fictional and real, have—to use a figure of speech with which he would feel at home—mulched down. In their rich coalescence, *Rites of Passage* germinated.

Here he has reworked not so much the nautical literature of Melville, Stevenson, and Conrad as the travel literature of Smollett and Marryatt. These very British books, bombastic accounts of shipwrecks, mutinies, and murders, demand an innocence of approach which, as Golding noted in a review of Jules Verne, "while natural in a child amounts to a mark of puerility in an adult."

Peter Simple, Frederick Marryatt's 1834 tale of a fool who rises to become a gallant and capable officer in His Majesty's Service, may be one of the literary models Golding recasts in *Rites of Passage.* For Marryatt's portrait of the frank, open-hearted tar whose fun-loving temper buoys him up in a sea of hard knocks is, as Golding has said of Wells' view of Neanderthal man, "too neat, too simple." Literature may have it that the jolly tars of the fo'castle with their practical jokes were a fun-loving lot. In actuality, they were probably as ignorant, superstitious, and unruly as the tars Golding portrays in *Rites of Passage.* In his paraphrase of Marryatt's resolute, generous ever-courteous Captain Savage and the frigate world he commands (both a nursery and a school of the true spirit of British seamanship), Golding shatters once again a smug view of human nature. His cleric-hating Captain Anderson—who licenses the tars' persecution of poor parson Colley—is a genuine, not a counterfeit, Savage. And Golding's sea story has, as Talbot himself writes: "never a tempest, no shipwreck, no sinking, no rescue at sea . . . no thundering broadsides, heroism, prizes, gallant defences, and heroic attacks." . . . It does, however, sight an enemy, dark on the horizon: the guilt and shame gripping the heart of man. (pp. 221-22)

As a rule, in Golding's novels, the sheer magic of the story-telling lulls us into unguarded enjoyment. Our innocent delight is then darkly undercut by an abrupt shift in narrative viewpoint; new revelations force us to modify our earlier sympathies and reconsider what—to our untutored hearts—had previously seemed innocuous. And *Rites of Passage* is no exception. Talbot's journal—which frames the story—disarms almost totally. . . . (pp. 222-23)

The ideographic habit—with its practiced technique of calculated obscurity—is very much in evidence in *Rites of Passage,* where often we must piece together—even deduce—information which the self-absorbed Talbot simply does not apprehend. His myopia is with us from his first journal entry. . . . (p. 223)

Golding's novels never conclude with one unequivocal meaning . . . ; they insist upon the intermingling of the visible and the invisible, the physical and the spiritual, the world of the burning candle and the burning bush, the cellarage and the spire. In the eschatology of *Free Fall*—as in that of *Pincher*

Martin—Mercy does operate in the world, although it may be hidden from the eye of those who reject goodness. The drowning Pincher imagines that he faces a bully and an Executioner while Sammy despairs of the Judge, who he imagines stands on the other side of the cell's door preparing to punish him for his guilt. Yet both novels suggest that the punishment which each protagonist posits is the projection of his darkness. ("It's a whole philosophy, in fact," Golding explained, "suggesting that God is the thing we turn away from and make a darkness there.") When the dying Jocelin is granted a momentary glimpse of a kingfisher and an appletree Golding intends the reader to see the two emblems as symbolizing the "my-godness" of man.

Rites of Passage hints that Colley might have been granted release from the cellarage of his deep sense of self-degradation. Recall, first, that Colley has in his library a copy of Baxter's *Saints Everlasting Rest,* devotional meditations on sudden death. Also, Colley fears "the Justice of GOD, unmitigated by his Mercy!" . . . ; he believes that "the power of Grace is infinite" . . . ; he believes that the "happiest outcome" of all his "distress and difficulty" is "OUR REDEEMER" . . .—indeed, these are the last words of his testament. Turning to Talbot's description of Colley's posture in dying where his hand is barnacled to a "ringbolt" . . .—"one hand still clutched what both Falconer and Summers agreed was a ringbolt" . . .—one may surmise by way of the nagging, reiterative (though unexplained) reference to the ringbolt that Golding intends us to inspect it as a symbolic shorthand, like the verbal paradox of Jocelin's "upward waterfall." Falconer may explain that a ringbolt "has several uses . . . but particularly hooks the tackles by which the cannons of a ship are secured." We may (if we are spiritually inclined) imagine another "use" and interpret it as that bolt from the blue—God's grace—which hooks the penitent believer into the ring of God's everlasting Mercy.

Just as *The Inheritors* proffered the hint of sanctity on the level of the plain beyond the Fall where the artist, Tuami, sculpted the death-weapon into a life image, just as Pincher Martin is offered the chance to "die into heaven," just as Mountjoy and Pedigree are mysteriously released from the cell of their own unendurable identities, so too Colley may have been granted everlasting rest. (pp. 229-30)

In *Rites of Passage* Golding has again provided plunder enough for a whole shipload of critics. Once again, he has constructed a religious mythopoeia, the spur of a spiritual dimension—at least in the imaginative realm—in which the reader can participate. For *Rites of Passage* is, among many other things, about last rites. The novel's structure—with its partial concealments, oblique clues, delayed disclosures—forces us to bring into focus Colley's conduct in the fo'castle farce as well as Talbot's role in Colley's final and appalling disgrace. We discover that it was Talbot who catalyzed the whole sordid sequence of humiliations, ending in the parson's death. Had Talbot not flaunted his rank, thus undermining the captain's sense of his own authority, the captain, in turn, might not have countenanced Colley's persecution. The final effect of *Rites of Passage* is to implicate the reader in the responsibility for the loss of innocence: Talbot's belated sense of shame becomes our shame, our guilt. We rest at one with him in the final entry he makes in his journal: "With lack of sleep and too much understanding I grow a little crazy, I think, like all men at sea who live too close to each other and too close thereby to all that is monstrous under the sun and moon." . . . (p. 230)

*Virginia Tiger, "William Golding's 'Wooden World':
Religious Rites in 'Rites of Passage',"* in Twentieth
Century Literature *(copyright 1982, Hofstra University Press), Vol. 28, No. 2, Summer, 1982, pp. 216-31.*

GABRIEL JOSIPOVICI

In his preface [to *A Moving Target*] Golding explains that five of the pieces included began life as lectures. And he says: "When you get down to it, what an audience wants to hear from a novelist is how he writes. Since how he writes is in intimate association with what he is and how he lives the novelist finds himself in danger of being his own raw material." He goes on: "I have always tried to resist this and have always given way in the end so that at last I find myself talking about myself with the grossest liberality. This leads to nothing but self-disgust." I find the tone of this disturbing. If the self-disgust is genuine, why agree to give the lecture? Even more to the point, why publish such pieces between hard covers? I feel there is a confusion here which is not the bafflement of wonder such as Golding felt in Delphi or Egypt, but a Protestant sort of confusion about guilt and honesty. And the lectures themselves too often reflect this, unfortunately. The tone is both humble and hectoring, it both seems to despise its audience and seeks to woo it. The last lecture is a case in point. Entitled "Belief and Creativity" it is full of such remarks as: "Marx, Darwin and Freud are the three most crashing bores of the Western world." This may be Golding's view, but it does nothing for us except to tell us that it is his view. Should it interest us for that reason? . . .

Fame seems to have got at Golding. To judge from these lectures he cannot get over the fact that he is known from Iceland to the Cape and from Timbuctoo to San Francisco. If he has not read he has at least examined every single book that has been written about him. And though part of him dismisses it all as nonsense, another is impressed. "Ladies and gentlemen," he begins one lecture, "you see before you a man, I will not say more sinned against than sinning, but a man more analysed than analysing." And the title of the whole collection, which is also the title of one of the lectures, refers not to the novelist's quarry but to himself: "It was not long ago that I received a letter from a young lady at a famous English university. . . . She was, you see, looking for a subject for her thesis." Her professor had recommended that she write on a subject connected with Dr Johnson, but "she was not going to write a thesis on anything as dull as a dead man. She wanted fresh blood. She was going out with her critical shotgun to bring home the living. She proposed I should bare my soul. . . . I wrote back at once, saying that I agreed wholeheartedly with her professor." Someone who had known Dr Johnson, and so was safely dead, he suggests to the young lady, would make a much better target, for he would stand still. "But as for me, I am a moving target."

In one sense this is true and right and proper. But the person who writes: "I am a moving target" is in imminent danger of becoming nothing but a monument. To use this as the title of the entire collection suggests a degree of self-regard which can only be dangerously stifling to the development of the man and the author.

Of course the old skills have not deserted him; but there is a difference. The earlier novels stemmed from bafflement. The experience of the Second World War, he remarks in a review reprinted here, "are like black holes in space. Nothing can get out to let us know what it was like inside. It was like what it was like and on the other hand it was like nothing whatsoever. We stand before a gap in history. We have invented a limit to literature.'' This is not a modish bowing before the horrors of Belsen and Hiroshima. It suggests at the same time the impossibility of comprehension and the need to comprehend, and this is what the early novels use every skill at the artist's command to convey. Those skills were dredged up under the pressure of a violent reality. "The theme of **Lord of the Flies** is grief, sheer grief, grief, grief, grief.'' But in **Darkness Visible** and **Rites of Passage** the skills seem to be used only to make the audience gasp, to make the reader say: ''What a powerful, deep writer Golding is!''

The difference is brought out in almost allegorical style by a peculiarity of this book. After a lifetime of wondering about Egypt Golding finally went there. The essay he subsequently wrote about his visit is a marvel. But he felt that it would be valuable to include one essay from his previous collection **The Hot Gates,** ''Egypt from My Inside'', which would enable the reader to compare the imagained and the real. This was an excellent idea and the two form a fascinating diptych. But it was also a dangerous one. In ''Egypt from My Inside'' there is a central episode in which the little boy, wandering about the Egyptian rooms of the British Museum, is befriended by a curator who invites him back behind the scenes to help unwrap a mummy. This is more than the boy had ever dreamed of, it brings him to the height of rapture. Having described the whole episode Golding writes:

> Now it is important to realize that I remembered and still remember everything in vivid and luminous detail. It became the event of my life; and before I returned to the museum I talked the thing over passionately, with my parents and myself. I suffered the terrors of bed. I wrote an essay describing the episode when I went to school, and got extravagant praise for it. I brooded constantly about the lid of the sarcophagus with its hidden face. Yet it is important to realize that none of the episode happened at all.

The writer's cunning, his skill, is here at the service of a truth: the child's passion for all things Egyptian. In order to convey this he has to draw the reader in, to make him too take part in the adventure. In this way the reader will discover how powerful a force desire is, and what an instrument for the fulfilment of desire is the imagination. This is the stuff of the earlier novels. Contrast an equally cunning opening to a later lecture: ''Mr Chairman, ladies and gentlemen, It gives me particular pleasure—I might say peculiar pleasure—to address you today in Germany, home of exact scholarship, because it was a German reference book which announced my death in 1957.'' The writer's cunning is here used to make us applaud him for his humour, insult his audience and point out the extent of his fame. It's a queer mixture, and it is in this vein, it seems to me, that the last two novels are largely written.

This volume is fascinating then because it gives us a glimpse of two Goldings. The pieces about place, about Homer, about fairy-tales, convey the power of his imagination, his extraordinary ability to enter into and convey to us the strangeness and incomprehensibility of the world we live in. The lectures, on the other hand, give us a glimpse of the writer turning into a monument, not graciously but uneasily. It is sad to think that it is we, the reading public, the academic institutions, who

have done this to someone who has given us so much. Let us hope it is not irreparable damage we have done. ''It is a fine thing to be able to write to an author while he is still alive. If you are still alive will you answer these questions?'' wrote a little boy to Golding recently. I very much hope the answer to that question is yes, but it's by no means a foregone conclusion.

Gabriel Josipovici, ''A Pragmatist and His Public,'' in The Times Literary Supplement *(© Times Newspapers Ltd. (London) 1982; reproduced from* The Times Literary Supplement *by permission), No. 4138, July 23, 1982, p. 785 [the excerpts of William Golding's work used here were originally published in his* A Moving Target *(reprinted by permission of Farrar, Straus and Giroux, Inc.; in Canada by Faber & Faber Ltd, London; copyright © 1982 by William Golding),* Farrar, Straus and Giroux, 1982, Faber & Faber Ltd, 1982].

SAMUEL HYNES

I may as well begin with a flat proposition: I think William Golding is the most interesting English novelist now writing. . . . I'd be rather surprised if [that proposition] were widely accepted; my impression is that Golding tends to be overlooked when the Novelists' League Standings are made up, as though he was known to be good, but at some other game. The rank-ordering of artists is, of course, unimportant—it's only a book reviewer's parlor game; but it is important to ask why a novelist of such extraordinary originality and power has somehow reached old age without having become an acknowledged classic. (p. 36)

[Golding's] interest has always been in finding possible forms for his moral vision, and not in the forms themselves. The forms have changed from novel to novel because the vision demanded new paradigms, but the vision has remained constant: man is fallen, evil is actual, suffering is certain, redemption is necessary but unlikely. It is a bleak reality that Golding goes on reimagining, but not an empty one; and better a bleak world containing good and evil than a cheerful one containing neither.

An art of moral parables is emphatically unmodern, and so are other aspects of Golding's life and career: his reclusiveness, his indifference to contemporary public issues, his distaste for his own fame, and his unwillingness to perform as a literary journalist/celebrity, or as anything else except what he knows himself to be. The latter point shows clearly in [**A Moving Target,** a] modest collection of Golding's recent nonfictional writings. These few essays, book reviews, and lectures are apparently the whole of his occasional work from the past twenty years. Many were pieces reluctantly taken on, as Golding rather ungraciously tells us in his preface: lectures given to earn American dollars so that he could quit teaching, or as a civic duty (English novelist lectures in France, trade follows the flag); reviews written of books of no particular interest to Golding; travel pieces written because a travel magazine had asked for them. Only a few of the writings collected here come near to his heart's concerns, and even these seem guarded and self-conscious.

No one is likely to read this collection out of a passionate love of essay-reading; in our time there is no such taste. No, if you take up the book it will be because you think I might be right about Golding—that perhaps he *is* important. And if you do take it up, what will you find that might affect your understanding of the writer? Two things, I think. First, the ''author.'' I put the term in quotation marks because writing is always role-playing, and Golding in his occasional pieces assumes a distinct and rather odd role. He is The English Man of Letters, a bookish, old-fashioned man, comfortably familiar with the classics . . . , knowledgeable about Pepys and Dr. Johnson and Jane Austen, the sort of writer who quotes from examples that we all should recognize, but who never identifies the hard ones. His prose style is straightforward and fluent, though it gets a bit sludgy when he dwells on something he loves . . . , and clogs up altogether when he attempts abstract thought (the same is true of the novels). He is comfortable in his study with his books, but ill at ease at the lectern, where he is likely to lose control of his argument, and slither to the end of a talk in a tangle of disclaimers and apologies: "I find I have entered an area to which my powers of description are inadequate," "I have given much bumbling thought to the question," etc. He is safest when most solemn; when he attempts a joke, as he does now and again, the effect is disastrous, like a bishop trying to put an audience of Rotarians at their ease. And the jokes are terrible.

What one feels most of all about this Man-of-Letters Golding is that though he may feel at home in Wiltshire, he is not at home in the twentieth century. Or perhaps I should put that slightly differently, and say that he is as much at home in his time as he thinks any man should be: it isn't man's fate to be at home in the world, and anyone who thinks he is doesn't understand the human condition. For those features of modern civilization that most of us would consider definitive—the ideas, the social structures, the institutions—Golding has only a sour disdain. . . . [He] distrusts the experimental method—it has begotten "that lame giant we call civilization"; he dislikes television, tourists, and Macy's parade. About politics he has only one contribution to make: "With bad people, hating, unco-operative, selfish people, no social system will work. With good people, loving, co-operative, unselfish people, any social system will work." This is the politics of the Change of Heart; it is fundamentally conservative, and it is religious, and Golding is both—half Christian, half curmudgeon.

This is Golding the Essayist. . . . A somewhat different Golding speaks in the lectures when the novelist, speaking self-consciously *as* a novelist, tries to explain what he does, and how it works—not because he wants to, but because that's what his audiences expect of him. At first he seems a disap-

pointing figure, this novelist—conservative and commonsensical. . . . But here and there a more personal and more revealing voice breaks through, at the places where Golding speaks of himself not in terms of his craft, but in the more fundamental terms of his beliefs.

The last piece in the book, a lecture delivered in 1980 titled "Creativity and Belief," is the most interesting example of this. Here Golding offers a curious image of modern civilization as like a Macy's parade—a procession of human beings dwarfed by the vast plastic figures that float above them. The balloon figures are our modern totems—Marx, Darwin, and Freud again—and rather than march in their shadows, Golding chooses to leave the procession, and look for his own belief. The belief he has found is straightforward enough: he believes, he says, in God. But he also believes that the ground of believing is mysterious and irrational, and always will be—that we must base our knowledge of ourselves and our world on a ground of unknowing. This is not a surprising statement for a Christian to make; but it is surprising coming from a major modern novelist. And it does point to a quality of his novels that makes them unique among modern works: they are about belief, and not about the loss or the lack of it. This doesn't make them optimistic. Quite the contrary: Golding defines the theme of *Lord of the Flies* as "grief, sheer grief, grief, grief," and the other novels share that theme. But, as a character in one of Faulkner's novels says, "Between grief and nothing, I will take grief." And so will Golding.

For a man like Golding, without any particular philosophic or speculative gifts, without even much evident knowledge of the systems that he is rejecting, to set himself imaginatively against the current of his century is an extraordinary gesture: an act of hubris, perhaps, but also of courage. And an act that was necessary to create the conditions of his art. If that art is unimportant, then these writings, mostly minor as they are, are a waste of anybody's time; but if it is important, then the essays and lectures are important, too, and valuable for even the scattered insights that they give to the odd, grieving, parable-making mind behind the art. (pp. 36-7)

*Samuel Hynes, "Grief, Sheer Grief, Grief, Grief,"
in* The New Republic *(reprinted by permission of*
The New Republic; © *1982 The New Republic, Inc.),
Vol. 187, No. 11, September 13, 1982, pp. 36-7.*

Graham (Henry) Greene

1904-

English novelist, short story writer, dramatist, children's author, writer of travel books, essayist, and editor.

Greene has been a widely acclaimed and popular author throughout most of his long career. His prominence derives mainly from his novels, most of which pursue his obsession with the darker side of human nature within the context of a spy thriller or adventure story. Greene is described as a Catholic writer: the human struggle between faith and doubt and the despair and alienation of modern humanity are constant themes in his work. In spite of his many decidely Catholic concerns, Greene is an intellectual nonconformist. He rejects systematic adherence to the precepts of any contemporary religion or institution.

Greene is a skillful storyteller whose novels are suspenseful and entertaining. They swiftly move the reader into the physical action and moral conflict of the story. Greene's best-known work, *The Power and the Glory* (1940), is representative of his treatment of character and theme. Here, as in all of his fiction, thematic concerns are worked out more through characterization than through plot. In this story of the persecution of a priest by a police lieutenant, Greene pits political and secular conventions against spiritual and religious ones. Effectively avoiding the use of stereotype, Greene portrays both men as whole persons. The priest, like the police lieutenant, is a complex character capable of both good and evil acts. Critics consider such characterization as evidence that Greene is a writer of great depth. For him, the sinner is often the saint, the idealist, a danger.

Although there seems to be little contention about the significance of Greene's earlier work, in more recent years his status has been questioned. His recent novel *Monsignor Quixote* (1982) has been cited by some critics as an entertaining and well-constructed novel with a powerfully realized atmosphere. Other critics of the novel question its merit. Paul Fussell, commenting on Greene's esteem suggests that it is "only the current absence of Faulkner and Waugh and even Hemingway that makes Greene seem a novelist of consequence instead of, say, a fourth-rate Conrad."

(See also *CLC*, Vols. 1, 3, 6, 9, 14, 18; *Contemporary Authors*, Vols. 13-16, rev. ed.; *Something about the Author*, Vol. 20; and *Dictionary of Literary Biography*, Vols. 13, 15.)

The Bettmann Archive, Inc.

PAUL FUSSELL

It might be thought that it's only the current absence of Faulkner and Waugh and even Hemingway that makes Greene seem a novelist of consequence instead of, say, a fourth-rate Conrad. Is Greene not really a writer whose conceptions, plots, and style are, if the truth were told, as seedy as his famous settings? Can he construct? Can he imagine plausible characters and deliver believable images of their behavior in an efficient style? Is not his melodramatic, Manichean vision of life less a sign that he is "a Catholic novelist" than evidence of a coarse intelligence? Are not his psychological studies of fear and guilt forced and fraudulent? Is there the qualitative difference he imagines between his novels and his "entertainments"? Does not his instinct for spy and detective adventure betoken a literary sense considerably less than subtle? These are the troubling questions that arise whenever Greene is put forward as a major writer. They arise anew with [*Ways of Escape*, the] second volume of his memoirs.

The first volume, *A Sort of Life*, appeared in 1971. It dealt with his life only up to his 20s. Here we have the rest of it, from 1929 to 1978. As Greene admits, "rather less than half" the book has been cobbled together from the introductions he's provided for the collected edition of his works. These bits are now arranged chronologically and bridged by new passages. There is thus an air of pastiche and incoherence about the whole, although the parts are often attractive.

"I grew clever at evasion," Greene wrote of his youth in *A Sort of Life*. . . . This action of repeated escaping is now promoted to the theme, or pseudo-theme, of *Ways of Escape*. Travel is an escape from boredom and England; novel-writing, an escape from newspaper work; film-reviewing, an escape from novel writing; the short story is an escape from longer fiction; playwriting is an escape from filmscript writing, etc. Here escape is like other big "themes" in Greene: it seems to illuminate and unify, but actually it's just another way of escaping—escaping precision. (pp. 33-4)

But if Greene's run-through of his literary career is dominated by this kind of thematic hokeyness, when he forgets his fake unifying theme he offers some fascinating things. Like his account of libeling Shirley Temple. . . . Valuable too are his accounts of anti-colonial uprisings he has seen, in Malaya, Kenya, and Vietnam. His interpretation of what happened at Dien Bien Phu is masterly. So is his version of being deported from Puerto Rico as a onetime Communist during the days when the McCarran Act was still without loopholes. He is startling and funny on Batista's Havana, in its day porn capital of the free world, startling and not so funny on Papa Doc's Haiti. There are hints that he's been engaged in more espionage than we have known about, for sometimes he has the greatest trouble indicating his motives for being in a certain crucial place at a certain crucial time, and has to fall back on his "escape" explanation. . . . And he ends with a characteristically melodramatic account of "the Other"—an imposter calling himself "Graham Greene" who pops up all over the world, introducing himself as the famous writer, making time with women, and borrowing money. Greene's closing words constitute a final whiff of evasiveness, and they lodge with us the suspicion that perhaps his problem is that he has the soul of a spy: "I found myself shaken by a metaphysical doubt. Had *I* been the imposter all the time? Was I the Other?"

Who is he anyhow? He seems by this time so conspicuously an international figure, with his Harry Limes and Orient Expresses and Stamboul trains, his travels everywhere, his exotic locales, his residences abroad in Antibes and Anacapri, that it's surprising to be reminded by this book how intensely British he remains. . . . Greene's subject is justice, and he comes from the very British world of Fielding and Blackstone, Cobbett and *The Secret Agent* and Orwell. He writes in that quintessentially British genre, the detective story, only once-removed.

His frequent success with the nasty has tended to conceal the terrible truth that he's seldom written carefully. The very first sentence of *A Sort of Life* offers a freshman howler: "An autobiography is only 'a sort of life'—it may contain less errors of fact than a biography, but it is of necessity more selective. . . ." For "less," read "fewer." But Greene's winning quality is his modesty. He knows he doesn't write very well, although he thinks his trouble is ineffective metaphor and blurred visual perception. Actually it is his inability to master English syntax and the fine points of English sentence structure. (pp. 34-5)

Paul Fussell, "A Gentleman's 'C'," in The New Republic *(reprinted by permission of* The New Republic; © *1980 The New Republic, Inc.), Vol. 183, No. 26, December 27, 1980, pp. 33-5.*

CHRISTOPHER LEHMANN-HAUPT

Why do we read "Ways of Escape" with such absorption, if it is nothing more than a collection of occasional pieces written "as a form of therapy"? The most obvious answer is, because Mr. Greene could take the entries in a plumbing manual, tie them together gracefully and make them seem coherent and interesting. Furthermore, "Ways of Escape" is decorated with striking physical descriptions of the many corners of the world to which Mr. Greene escaped. There are enduringly penetrating analyses of political crises that occurred where he was escaping.

And if Mr. Greene is reticent about betraying the privacy of others, he is almost swaggeringly willing to inform on him-

self—his suicidal moods, his manic-depressive swings, his attraction to drugs, sex, liquor and physical danger—in sum, his many "ways of escape." . . .

Yet what I found most consistently interesting about "Ways of Escape" is Mr. Greene's running commentary on the craft of writing. The book could well serve neophyte authors as an instruction manual on writing and reading fiction—on the distinction between prose and poetry, on how to develop imaginary characters from real ones, on how to give the Unconscious sufficient sway, on researching exotic locales, on distinguishing between what a book is saying and what its characters are saying, on the art of developing a story from fragmentary impressions—all related to specific incidents in Mr. Greene's own writing career.

But there's a deeper, less practical point to all the talk about art. What "Ways of Escape" is really about is how the author's experience gets translated into fiction. And in a way this is a good deal more personal and revealing than the most intimate autobiography he could have written.

Christopher Lehmann-Haupt, in a review of "Ways of Escape," in The New York Times (© *1981 by The New York Times Company; reprinted by permission), January 8, 1981, p. C22.*

JAMES ATLAS

"A Sort of Life," the first volume of Graham Greene's autobiography, was not equivocal in its title alone. Depicted there was a typical Georgian childhood among the British intellectual middle class, a world of nannies, eccentric aunts and uncles, doting if remote parents who fostered an early love of literature, unhappy school experiences followed by an Oxford education: in short, the world depicted—with some variations—in Cyril Connolly's "Enemies of Promise," in Evelyn Waugh's "A Little Learning," in Peter Quennell's "The Marble Foot." Typical, perhaps, yet hardly complacent; on several occasions in his youth, the author claimed, he had played Russian roulette with a loaded revolver discovered in his brother's cupboard.

No self-respecting writer would lay claim to a happy childhood, but the image of a 19-year-old boy wandering out to a meadow and applying a pistol to his head has always seemed to me implausible, melodramatic in a way Greene's novels rarely are. Yet reading ["Ways of Escape," the] sequel to "A Sort of Life," I found myself persuaded by his claim to a flirtation with suicide. The figure portrayed in "Ways of Escape" is a "manic-depressive temperament" who "enjoyed" the London blitz because it provoked a "sense of insecurity"; who found in Indochina during the troubled 1950's "that feeling of exhilaration which a measure of danger brings to the visitor with a return ticket"; whose incessant quest for adventure has served the same purpose as those suspense-charged afternoons when he spun the chamber of his revolver and waited for a click or an explosion: "escape from boredom, escape from depression."

Greene's compulsion to visit the most troubled corners of the world—Vietnam in the years of French occupation; Malaya in the early 1950's, during the Communist insurrections against the British; Kenya during the Mau Mau rebellion; a leper colony in the last days of the Belgian Congo—may have been a way of "tempting the end to come," but it had a literary motive as well. Just as Dostoyevsky seemed to draw inspiration from the threat of financial ruin, Greene has drawn his best material from these arduous voyages. Tranquil domestic environments don't interest him; even **"The End of the Affair,"** a tale of adultery set in London, unfolds against the backdrop of the blitz.

A master portraitist of the dreary, Greene returns in **"Ways of Escape"** to the sorry realm of his novels, those exotic, shabby outposts in Africa, Haiti, Latin America, the Far East. . . . The narrative voice—guarded, laconic, world-weary, depressed—is the voice of Greene's protagonists; of Fowler, the British journalist in **"The Quiet American";** of Bendrix, the tortured novelist in **"The End of the Affair";** of Querry, the famous architect who escapes from the pressures of celebrity in **"A Burnt-Out Case."**

But where the novelist's versions of himself are men confused by their own contradictory impulses and humbled by the savage events they witness, men unnerved by the pitiless waste of history, the autobiographer disposes of the crises in his life with the bland dispatch of a civil servant out of one of Greene's own novels rubbing his hands and efficiently resolving some difficulty over a passport. Despite his persistent intimations of despair, the dour, death-haunted novelist is less in evidence than the club man dining out on well-rehearsed anecdotes. (pp. 1, 28)

What Greene has decided to offer his readers in **"Ways of Escape"** is a desultory chronicle of the events that inspired his plots and the people on whom his characters were based (a chronicle, it should be noted, that draws liberally upon various prefaces to his novels). . . .

Candid about his literary problems, Greene is resolutely impersonal about everything else. **"Ways of Escape"** is one of the most evasive autobiographies I know. . . . In 1946, he reports, he was suicidal—"at a loss," a "carrier of unhappiness to people I loved"—and briskly moves on to the political situation in Malaya. Twenty years later, he confides, "a difficult decision in [his] private life" prompted him to leave England and settle in France—and there he leaves the matter.

His descriptions of others are no less grudging: Herbert Read, an admired mentor, invites the young novelist to dinner with T. S. Eliot—and that is the last we hear of them, apart from the disclosure that the company "talked of Arsène Lupin." In Hanoi, Greene obtains an interview with Ho Chi Minh and goes on at great length about his efforts to procure the beer and opium that gave him "the energy to meet Ho Chi Minh at tea." Of the interview itself, not a word. The failure to explain verges on provocation.

Well, never mind, one is tempted to say: The truth is that novelists are seldom great autobiographers. . . . The autobiographer discovers some necessity to chronicle his life, and usually does it only once; the novelist does it in every novel. Greene has recounted in his work the crucial episodes of his life. Anyone acquainted with his principled, arrogant, suffering protagonists already has an autobiography of their creator. (p. 28)

James Atlas, "A Sort of Autobiography," in The New York Times Book Review *(© 1981 by The New York Times Company; reprinted by permission), January 18, 1981, pp. 1, 28.*

DENIS DONOGHUE

Ways of Escape makes one feel, yet again, how much a writer of the Thirties Greene is. The work he did in that decade, from *Stamboul Train* (1932), *England Made Me* (1935), *A Gun for Sale* (1936) to *Brighton Rock* (1938), *The Lawless Roads* (1939), and *The Power and the Glory* (1940), is not his best; much of it is overwritten, besotted with a rhetorical extravagance taken over from Conrad's *The Arrow of Gold.* But if not his best work, it is his most typical, producing his major themes, situations, and images.

Greene's mind, like Auden's during the same decade, was appeased mainly by lurid occasions. The imagery common to Greene, Auden, Isherwood, MacNeice, and Spender is of frontiers, maps, passports, an atmosphere not of death, Juliet's tomb, but of terror, mostly sought for its *frisson.* . . . The enjoyment of insecurity, fear, and terror, sought as an escape from boredom and depression, is one of Greene's themes in *Ways of Escape.* When we accept the force of it in him, we find ourselves revising our sense of Auden and his friends; reading *Look, Stranger!* and *Letters from Iceland* as rituals against boredom, not merely against the public nightmare, dread, and war.

Greene's themes in *Ways of Escape* are also retained from the Thirties. Betrayal, it is true, is perennial, but Greene's sense of it issues from a set of circumstances, conventions, and assumptions peculiar to the English Thirties; and shared by many bright young men who entered upon their careers with a view of life largely provided by their experience in such institutions as Berkhamsted and Balliol. Such men had their first experience of betrayal in school; a friendship spurned, a secret disclosed. . . . [As] Dr. Plarr says in *The Honorary Consul,* "caring is the only dangerous thing." . . .

My argument is that Greene, coming of age in the Thirties, defined his art mainly in melodramatic terms, with corresponding themes of betrayal and equivocation. After *The Power and the Glory,* he put his talent on a thin diet, got rid of Conrad, and took his themes more casually. *The Heart of the Matter* (1948) and *The End of the Affair* (1951) are just as serious as the earlier novels, but they don't proceed upon an assumption of universal menace. And they have moments in which the ironies of *The Comedians* (1966) and *Travels with My Aunt* (1969) are anticipated. But they are still derived from gestures which were already habitual to Greene in the Thirties. It has always been the habit of Greene's intelligence to seek menacing occasions; of his morality to lure temptation; of his body to seek danger; and of his convictions to long to be undermined. Even in his later years, his exploits have often retained a trace of adolescence. In *Ways of Escape* his account of being deported from Puerto Rico has every sign of being a prank on his part, and, worse still, a Balliol prank. (p. 15)

One of the many interests of *Ways of Escape* is the question of character. Greene has always been more concerned with character than with action or plot. He has referred to "the abiding temptation to tell a good story," and has often yielded to it, but only to give a character room to move. . . . (pp. 15-16)

In all his novels, Greene's procedure, he tells us, is to begin with a hunch, an intuition of a person, a character. The book then goes in search of him. The object is to achieve virtually complete knowledge of this character. Greene explains in *Ways of Escape* that few of his characters were based upon people he knew; the reason being that, even in the case of an old friend, he knew him only well enough to realize that complete knowledge of him was impossible. With an invented character, complete knowledge is, at least in theory, possible. . . .

Greene's assumption of complete knowledge of his invented characters may explain, incidentally, one irritating feature of his novels, his relation to a character called God. Greene has often written as if he had complete knowledge of God, knew what he would forgive, and so forth; since God is by definition an invented or imaginary character, the assumption doesn't seem preposterous, though its reiteration is tiresome. Anyway, when the novelist has achieved complete knowledge of his character, he is in a position to lavish his sympathy upon him, even if to more disinterested eyes he seems, like Kim Philby, a liar and a scoundrel. . . .

Complete knowledge makes possible complete compassion. The purpose of the novel, I infer from Greene's account of more immediate issues, is to enable the novelist and his readers to practice complete compassion, an impossible task in real life, since we can never know enough. . . .

But even if a novelist knows the worst and the best and everything in between, he is not obliged to make his disclosures as full as his compassion. There is more to Colonel Daintry than sardines. Greene's way is to seek complete knowledge of a character, and then to disclose enough about him to keep his secret, while convincing the reader that the character has one. Opening a tin of sardines implies all the other things Greene knows of Colonel Daintry: it is the novelist's privilege to keep most of them to himself. (p. 16)

A character begins to form when the novelist senses that he is being solicited by a person, a figment as yet, a phantasm. For the reader of *Ways of Escape* and *A Sort of Life,* the character is one Graham Greene. There is reason to suppose that the novelist Greene was solicited by the character eventually named Greene. The novelist has a novelist's interest in this person. He seeks complete knowledge of him, and sends him into several remote corners of the world partly to try him out, make him disclose himself: more exploits, more knowledge. The process is one by which a something vague becomes a something more definite, comes from mere potentiality into being. Or comes from one phase or mode of existence into another. A type becomes a character.

It seems feasible to think that the novelist Graham Greene saw himself as a type, to begin with, and that the particular type was the spy, the confidential agent so congenial to the English Thirties. (pp. 16-17)

The purpose of *Ways of Escape,* as of *A Sort of Life,* is to transform a type, the spy, into a character continuous with the type, the novelist as spy. Greene's travels become secret missions, carried out ostensibly for *The Sunday Times* but in truth for himself, to acquire complete knowledge of himself. . . .

Ways of Escape ends with a bizarre Epilogue called **"The Other,"** about another man called Graham Greene, or at least a man who has been using various names, including John Skinner, Meredith de Varg, and Graham Greene. Our man in Antibes, our Graham Greene, proposed to *Picture Post* that they send him to find and interview the other joker, then in jail, apparently, in Assam. The plan didn't work out, because the Other had by then jumped bail, and there was a risk that our man might be arrested in his place. The story has more plot than novels by Graham Greene tend to have; and the characterization is thinner than usual. I take **"The Other"** as Greene's version of Conrad's "The Secret Sharer." And I do in part believe it.

The book, then, is interesting, enjoyable, and informative. But it does little to remove one's misgivings about Greene's entire

work, misgivings which I have suggested by describing him as very much a novelist of the English Thirties. My implication is that he settled for themes all too congenial to that decade, and for a melodramatic assumption of their significance. The later novels toned down the portentousness and assimilated their style to a more accomplished urbanity, but they did not question, in any radical way, the melodramatic privilege. Greene's fiction is, at the very least, memorable: to advert to the novels is to recall scenes, characters, atmospheres, and to renew one's sense of having felt their force, mostly as incrimination and conspiracy. But I find a residual feeling in myself of dissatisfaction, reflecting an achievement on Greene's part limited to the possibilities indicated by my reference to melodrama. His novels have always had an insecure sense of how seriously they should take themselves; an insecurity not at all stabilized by Greene's tactical division of his fiction into "novels" and "entertainments."

A case in point: several pages of *Ways of Escape* deal with Greene's experience of smoking opium in Hanoi. These pages are related to Fowler's opium-smoking in *The Quiet American.* But neither in the novel nor in the memoir is there an indication of what the experience comes to, or what value the reader is invited to give it. Does it stand for the *"huxe et volupte"* to which Greene refers in *Ways of Escape,* with a claim for significance lodged by further reference to Baudelaire's *"L'Invitation au Voyage"*? Or is it to be read as merely exotic, part of the wisdom of the Orient which the reader is not required to receive? In the novel, as in the memoir, it seems to veer between triviality and ominousness. In the memoir, these pages have an air of significance, but only the air is conveyed, not the significance. Greene's novels, too, leave it open to question whether, in his relation to his perceptions, he is a native or a tourist. (p. 17)

Denis Donoghue, "Secret Sharer," in The New York Review of Books *(reprinted with permission from* The New York Review of Books; *copyright © 1981 Nyrev, Inc.),* Vol. XVIII, No. 2, February 19, 1981, *pp. 15-17.*

DON COLES

[Graham Greene's *Monsignor Quixote* is] a curious little book, which reminds one, unpromisingly, of so many approximate models. Quaint and ingenuous priest, lusty and Communist mayor, set down together among Spain's dusty roads and hostelries—such an odd couple, whatever in the world will *they* get up to? Except that of course you *know* what they will get up to, these two good ole' boys together, because not only has Giovanni Guareschi long ago identified the two principal roles in his resistably heartwarming *Don Camillo,* but the theme has been beaten within an inch of its life by too many others, has it not?

Well, yes, I would say. I don't think Graham Greene really wins out over his rusting *dramatis personae* with any sureness, not even when their story's over. What can he do with these two bearers of such familiar burdens? St. Francis de Sales and Karl Marx, the Bible and the Manifesto? It is sobering news that, as well, our priest is now closely identified with the Knight of the Sorrowful Countenance ("How can he be descended from a fictional character?", asks his bishop, thereby instantly earning a minor commission among Greene's legions of the quasi-damned), and our Mayor is nicknamed Sancho, and their ancient second-hand car is Rocinante, and a faithful housekeeper is intermittently Dulcinea. . . .

Well, it's very, very difficult, all this ballast. The story heaves over its shiftings down there, rolls about, barely stays afloat. For some readers, it will probably capsize. . . .

[But on the other hand there are passages like] this one, where an undertaker has been badgering Father Quixote to hear his confession concerning the theft of two brass handles from a coffin: "You have stolen two brass handles," says the priest, "don't feel so important. Say you are sorry for your pride and go home."

The artist, in other words—the author of the marvellously skilled and affecting *The Human Factor,* which I think to be the most near-perfect novel in English of the last 10 years and his own best—still has his gifts. He appears intermittently, providing moments that please and move, and I think that on balance these moments justify the book. . . .

It's a close-run thing, though. If I am to come clean with my feelings about this latest Quixote, they would be this: that as a fiction this works very ill, the characters are stalking horses (lovely, opaque phrase!) for a lot of ideas concerning church and state which are often familiar, sometimes shallow, usually boring; and that what makes it work, *if* it works, is the long life-in-art of its maker, whose mind even in its off-moments cannot forbear to cast off glints and half-glints of those small, considered, human details that have always been the centre of his work.

The other fortifying thread shows up when the man who has written 20 novels, travelled the world, and spent most of his time outside any domestic shelter, out in the open, (very admirably so in my opinion) speaks in his own voice. We know it is his voice and are therefore untroubled by any developing sense of dissatisfaction with the characters in this twenty-first novel. Typical is the priest, after a conversation with his Dulcinea, saying to himself, "how is it that when I speak of belief, I become aware always of a shadow, the shadow of disbelief haunting my belief?" . . .

Lines like these would seem fraudulent in the mouths of most people, fictional or otherwise, but anyone who has read Graham Greene knows that they represent probably the least-ambivalent article of faith he owns.

> *Don Coles, "Articles of Faith," in* The Canadian Forum, *Vol. LXII, No. 721, September, 1982, p. 32.*

JULIAN SYMONS

[Graham Greene] has often been praised for the quality of his observation, but this lies in the creation of an atmosphere appropriate to period, place and characters rather than in what things actually look like.

There are few detailed descriptions of people in the novels: lips, noses, figures are rarely made explicit, and the description of Father Thomas's nose in *A Burnt-Out Case* has the shock of rarity. Places give off an exotic feeling that is almost invariable, whether it is the river down which Querry moves in the same novel, or the view of boat passengers crossing a "grey wet quay," over a wilderness of rails and points" on the first page of the early *Stamboul Train.* The river, the quay, fifty other scenes in the novels, have a cinematic effect that is brilliant yet general, offering an overall scene rather than particular observation of the details within it. In small matters Graham Greene is often a faulty recorder. When he says that the Berkhamsted of his childhood contained "pointed faces

like the knaves on playing cards", he must have had a special pack, for in standard packs two knaves are shown full face; when he recalls a chess player saying "I open with Queen's Pawn Two" memory betrays him, for the Queen's pawn will be on the second square before the game begins. . . .

[But it is] the ambiguity rather than the accuracy of [these observations that] is important, for the ambiguity reflects his belief that "to a novelist his novel is the only reality". One is in no doubt here that the writer means just what he says. The novels have reality, truthfulness and meaning for their author in a sense that life does not. In one of his fine essays about Henry James, Greene plausibly suggests that the ruling passion in James's work was the idea of treachery. There is a ruling passion in his own work too, the idea of faith and its betrayal. This is the subject that he has approached over and over again, turning it so that it sometimes shines dazzlingly and is at other times much blurred, considering its application to a variety of characters and circumstances, but driving always towards that point at the dangerous edge of things where an extreme situation demands a decisive action. So Jones in *The Comedians* moves into the guerrilla world of which he is ignorant, Querry dies to preserve the secret that he did not commit adultery. Father José in *The Power and the Glory* leaves a place of safety to say Mass for a dying gangster, and in *The Honorary Consul* the atheist Doctor Plarr and the former priest Leon both make sacrificial gestures leading to their deaths.

There are several other themes in the novels and entertainments (a word used "to distinguish them from more serious novels", perhaps misleadingly used, since it seems wrongly to imply that the other books are not entertaining), just as James is involved in many subjects other than treachery; and indeed for both writers treachery often seems inextricably linked with heroism, and a kind of love. From the beginning, Greene's links with the thriller have been close. As he has said, his first published novel, *The Man Within,* began with a hunted man, and the idea of hunter and hunted persists, often in a more sophisticated form. Querry, for instance, may be said to be hunted down by the public world from which he has tried to escape. . . .

The early Greene was very much a novelist of the 1930s. The symbols of the decade came naturally to him, the railway station and the frontier, suggesting arrival, departure, the difficulty of human communication. . . . Whatever may be missed by the Greene eye, his ear was perfectly tuned to the slang and songs of [the] time. . . .

[The typical Greene protagonists] are figures doomed by the machine age, by monopoly capitalism, above all by their own weakness. Anthony Farrant in *England Made Me,* D working faithfully for what he knows to be the losing side in *The Confidential Agent,* Pinkie in *Brighton Rock,* all in a sense forecast the inevitable war that lies ahead. They are no-hopers, people unable to accommodate themselves to the way life is lived, as Anthony's sister Kate is able to do in one book, the exuberant big-breasted Ida Arnold in another. These early books are as good an introduction as could be wished to everyday feelings in the decade, offering a much wider social range than the novels of Waugh and Isherwood during those years. . . . The effect achieved is not one of literal realism. It is rather that fragments of reality are wonderfully magnified through the glass of a strange, powerful imagination. These novels have what Wilkie Collins called a whiff of the Actual, but they also transform the actual, giving the Brighton sea front, a train journey through Europe, a modern office building in Sweden, a significance that in drab reality they hardly possess. Within the limits of what is attempted, these are almost wholly successful books, novels using the framework of the thriller for serious purposes.

Flickers of doubt arise only when the author is moved to draw the character up to his own level of intelligence and knowledge. D wonders whether a picture is by Etty when he is unlikely ever to have seen an Etty, Pinkie's language occasionally outstrips his semi-literacy. There are also immensely enjoyable inventions . . . which occasionally affect that important whiff of the Actual, and moments of more private joking. What, for example, is a ''buer'', the name used more than once by Pinkie for what would now be called a slag? . . . It seems highly unlikely that *buer* was used by pre-war Brighton racecourse gangs. Does this matter? In a book like *Brighton Rock* which depends so much on our belief in the setting and the language, yes, marginally it does. . . .

[Greene] deprecates the label of ''Catholic writer'' which has been attached to him since *Brighton Rock*. He is, he insists, ''not a Catholic writer but a writer who happens to be a Catholic''. Yet one surely does not ''happen to be'' a Catholic, any more than the present reviewer happens to be an atheist. For a writer to be a Catholic, particularly in a society where Catholics are a small minority, must be important, and it is inevitable that for Graham Greene as for Evelyn Waugh his beliefs should have affected the standpoint from which his novels were written. All of the important books written after ·*The Power and the Glory,* including *The Honorary Consul* which the author prefers to all the others, could have been written only by a Catholic. The lighter and more thrillerish works of these later years, such as *Our Man in Havana* and *The Human Factor,* are uncertain about places and people in a way that the early novels are not, or move into a flippancy that seems only part intended.

It is on the finest of the later novels—*The Comedians, A Burnt-Out Case* and *The Quiet American,* as well as *The Honorary Consul*—that Graham Greene's reputation will chiefly rest, and they gather power and beauty from complexities in the personal faith of one who has ''an intellectual if not an emotional belief in Catholic dogma''. It is noticeable that in them Graham Greene is strenuously determined to play fair. An opposition is set up between those with faith and those who lack it, and the unbelievers are often given the best lines, sometimes even the best actions. That is wholly in contrast to *Brighton Rock,* where we are in no doubt that Pinkie's view that life for the wicked must end in damnation is infinitely preferable to Ida Arnold's delighted acceptance of physical enjoyment. (p. 1089)

In the later books the approach is much more subtle, and the message is not the same. Often they look towards the possibility that faith and reason may be united. . . . The progress has been one from Catholicism to humanism, a differentiation Graham Greene would be unlikely to accept.

Yet to insist on a single theme is pressing too hard, ignoring too much. . . . [It] is doing Graham Greene much less than justice to make these novels seem nothing but moralities, even complex ones. Much else goes into them: most immediately an overwhelming attraction towards scenes exotic to the stay-at-home reader; not only a love of Indo-China . . . but also affection for Haiti and Puerto Rico and Santo Domingo, Argentina, the Congo, West Africa. Why, Scobie wonders at the moment when he is swerving in his car to avoid a dead pye-dog in the road, why do I love this West African state so much?

And since there are not only dead pye-dogs in the road but live rats in the bathroom and cockroaches around everywhere, the question seems a good one. For the central Greene character, however, these are almost recommendations, testimony to the fact that they are living on the dangerous edge of things and have reached a point from which there is no turning back. Boredom for them is suburban life, the train to the office, the meat in the fridge, the wife in the bed.

There is a level on which these books may be taken as adventure stories. . . . It is [his] skill in shaping and telling a story, astonishingly rare in modern fiction, that has been primarily responsible for winning Graham Greene so many readers. The organization of plots—the decision, for example, to show us almost at the beginning of *The Quiet American* that Pyle is dead—and the placing of scenes is done with supreme skill. On another plane, the power in creating atmosphere that earlier gave memorable views of unfashionable bits of London, is now used to show an empty hotel in Papa Doc's Haiti, the confusions of Saigon during the French Indo-China war, the details of a *léproserie*. And on another level still, the later novels delight by an irony now beautifully understated, where in the early books it was sometimes too pungent for full effectiveness. (pp. 1089-90)

[The] separation between early and late Greene is not by any means total. An ascetic distaste for human greed and desire runs through all the work. . . .

Monsignor Quixote is important in showing what may be the last stage of the novelist's long argument with himself about the needs, nature and effects of faith. This, it must be said, is almost the extent of its interest. . . .

The tone throughout is lightly whimsical. . . .

The book will not weigh heavily in the scale of Graham Greene's achievements. The parallel with Cervantes has little point, the humour is much more like that of the unsuccessful plays than that of the successful novels. . . . Yet *Monsignor Quixote* is important, because it carries the author's humanism to a point where religion seems a secondary consideration to improving social conditions. The whisky priest exhorted his flock to suffer, but Quixote (also a heavy drinker, but feeling no need to make apologies for it) reads Marx in the brothel. ''Perhaps a true Communist is a sort of priest'', Quixote says to Sancho, but it seems as clear that a true priest is a sort of Communist. . . . The priest and the Communist debate on equal terms, and the author seems to sympathize with them both. . . .

Graham Greene . . . has found strength in his later work through a Manichaeism that balances faith against works, passivity against action, pleasure against goodness, detachment against involvement. Sometimes the balance tips one way, sometimes the other. ''Action is dangerous, isn't it?'' Martha says, and her lover Brown agrees, but they are condemned by inaction. What is said in the dedication of *A Burnt-Out Case,* that the book is ''an attempt to give dramatic expression to various types of belief, half-belief, and non-belief'', is true of all his finest novels. Their beauty and effectiveness spring from the fact that as a novelist Graham Greene is able to transcend whatever, as a human being, he may believe in a dogmatic sense. His characters exist in their own right, not as creatures of religious or social propaganda. Through them is expressed not certainty but doubt. They struggle, and fail or survive, in a world where good and evil, in themselves and in society, are locked in an unending struggle: the world of the Manichee. (p. 1090)

Julian Symons, "The Strength of Uncertainty," in The Times Literary Supplement *(© Times Newspapers Ltd. (London) 1982; reproduced from* The Times Literary Supplement *by permission), No. 4149, October 8, 1982, pp. 1089-90.*

SAMUEL HYNES

Graham Greene belongs to the category of obsessive artists: all of his writing life he has seen the world in essentially the same way, and he has written his novels—twenty-four of them now—to give forms to that vision. This is in no sense a pejorative, or even a limiting judgment: some visions are important enough to demand, and to justify, a lifetime's attention, and Greene's achievement as a novelist is surely a function of his obsessive single-mindedness.

Greene's world has always been a battlefield on which two contrary principles—call them The Power and The Glory—eternally confront each other. The Power is all the world's big-battalions—all governments, police, organized crime, big business, political parties; it is always corrupt, and it always prevails. The Glory has been represented in the novels mainly by individual instances of Christian faith, though it has also appeared as political idealism, and even occasionally as love. Greene has never represented it as a counterpower in the world: the *ecclesia triumphans* has never been a part of his vision, and he seems equally unable to imagine an actual government that would be Glorious. Faith is not for him a way of winning, but a way of living with defeat. . . . (p. 32)

Monsignor Quixote is yet another restatement of Greene's obsession, this time in a short and parable-like form. The source of the parable is obvious in the title, and Greene has taken pains throughout the book to keep *Don Quixote* in the reader's mind. . . . The linking to Cervantes isn't systematic, but you're not likely to miss it.

Along the way Father Quixote's faith collides with the powers of the society through which he travels: the power of the Church, in the person of his bishop, and the power of the state, mainly in the members of the Guardia Civil. Like his namesake, he is threatened, beaten, taken for a madman, and locked up; and in the end, like the Don, he dies.

One can imagine how such a book might have come to be written. Greene goes on a tour of Spain with some Spanish friends (he names them in his dedication) and no doubt he reads *Don Quixote* as a preparation, as conscientious tourists do, in the hope that somehow that national classic will reveal something to him of the essential nature of Spanishness. And having made the journey and read the book, he decides to put the two together.

Described in that way, *Monsignor Quixote* sounds like an elderly *jeux d'esprit,* just an old novelist fooling around, keeping his hand in. And certainly the book does seem to be rather casually put together, though that is appropriate, after all, to the picaresque tradition to which it belongs. But what it has to say about Greene's obsessive themes is not casual, and certainly not fooling.

Greene has always located his novels out at the dark edge of human existence, somewhere between doubt and despair. But his most recent books, especially *The Human Factor* and *Dr. Fischer of Geneva,* seemed to me almost to go over that edge, into absolute despair. That despair was perhaps reasonable enough if you consider that these two books were about South African politics and the power of capitalist wealth; still, despair is beyond the limits of a religious perception of the world, and calls that perception into question. So I'm relieved to see that *Monsignor Quixote* is a swing back, away from despair toward doubt. Indeed, doubt is a principal topic of discussion in the book; and more than a topic, it is a value. Both the priest and his friend, the Communist, doubt the absolute systems to which they have committed themselves; and because they doubt, they are humane and decent men. . . .

Clearly *Monsignor Quixote,* like most of Greene's other recent novels, is at once religious and political, though orthodox in neither. Greene's politics have always been hard to define: left-wing, certainly, and sharply critical of Western capitalism and imperialism, but distrustful of the left when it sought or seized power. There is no precise term for such an essentially critical political position, but perhaps Christian Anarchist comes as close as any for a world view that sees all human institutions as instruments of power, and all power as corrupt. (p. 33)

Sancho, who has the last word, ends the novel with two questions. He has been thinking that he had come to love Father Quixote, and that his love has survived the priest's death: "for how long, he wondered with a kind of fear, was it possible for that love of his to continue? And to what end?" This may not be everybody's idea of an upbeat ending, but it is, like the whole novel, a kind of doubting affirmation: a world in which faith exists, even quixotic faith, is not a world to be despaired of, though one may—and indeed one *must*—doubt.

Don't take this positive note to mean that Greene has grown benign in his old age: the world he sees around him is still a fallen world, as his other recent publication shows. *J'Accuse* is a pamphlet that denounces the cruel injustices inflicted on a family of Greene's friends, who live near him on the Côte d'Azur. Greene finds in their daughter's extremely unpleasant divorce case evidences of police corruption, judicial malfeasance, and the influence of the Mafia. The pamphlet names names and makes explicit accusations, and Greene's publisher must have waited in some anxiety for the libel summonses to arrive, though I gather that all that has happened is that the pamphlet has been suppressed in Nice, and Greene has been fined for distributing it.

J'Accuse adds nothing to one's understanding of Greene's work, but it does offer an appealing view of Greene as Quixote, charging windmills of power in Nice. And knowing, of course, that he will fail, for what does power care about pamphlets? The case he reports is involuted, and the dark side of Nice remains murky; but I'm glad he wrote it, whatever the results. For it confirms the morality of his novel: it is better to be angry, even ineffectually angry, than to be indifferent, better to have faith in justice, even a doubting faith. Better windmills than nothing. (p. 34)

Samuel Hynes, "Greene in Winter," in The New Republic *(reprinted by permission of* The New Republic; © 1982 The New Republic, Inc.), *Vol. 187, No. 17, October 25, 1982, pp. 32-4.*

Geoffrey H. Hartman

1929-

German-born American literary critic.

Hartman, a renowned critical theorist, is noted especially for his early critical analyses of Romantic poetry. His *Unmediated Vision* (1954) and *Wordsworth's Poetry, 1787-1814* (1964) are both judged by many critics to be classics in that field.

In his later work, particularly *Beyond Formalism* (1970) and *The Fate of Reading* (1975), Hartman reevaluates traditional methods of literary criticism. In these books, he critiques the "close reading" method of criticism advocated by the New Critics, describing it as limited. Hartman calls for more creative methods of literary criticism and for literary critics to broaden their aims. In *Criticism in the Wilderness* (1980) Hartman urges the modern critic to "view criticism . . . as within literature, not outside of it looking in."

CHRISTOPHER RICKS

Among the things which Coleridge "lamented" about Wordsworth's poetry was that "his genius was not a spirit that descended to him through the air; it sprang out of the ground like a flower." Geoffrey Hartman might have taken this remark as an epigraph for his fine book [*Wordsworth's Poetry, 1787-1814*]. His argument is that it is just exactly here that Wordsworth's true genius lay: in his ability to respect the earth and the air, to hold nature and imagination in balance, indeed in magnanimous reciprocity. If Wordsworth's poetry reaches great heights, it is as an arch does, by stresses that meet and support each other in loving opposition. . . . In his important, various, and stimulating book, Mr. Hartman shows conclusively that Wordsworth's progress was towards a true understanding and expressing of [the true relationship between nature and imagination, each respecting the other, each inexorable yet gentle in its power], and that his decline (notably in *The Excursion*) must be connected with his inability to maintain any longer this fatiguing and precarious balance. *The Excursion* sells the visible world grievously short—and in doing so, makes imagination not more but less effective. . . .

Mr. Hartman offers some extremely revealing comparisons, for example with Milton and Virgil; but the real battle, as he shows, is between Wordsworth and Blake. If Wordsworth were to be thought to triumph, that would be because in the end his sympathies and ideals were more inclusive, more hospitable, than those of the poet who was compelled to say: "Natural Objects always did and now do weaken, deaden, and obliterate Imagination in Me." Mr. Hartman's formulation is excellent: "beyond but not away from" nature. The relationship has the inseparable interdependence which we find both in the poet's largest conceptions and in, say, a true metaphor: vehicle and tenor, perhaps, but the vehicle is not a cab which you can curtly pay off when it has served your turn. Wordsworth's poetry respects the dignity of all things . . . , including "unknown modes of being," and, in so doing, it creates for itself respect and dignity.

But Mr. Hartman's book is implicitly an attempt to right a balance. What ever disturbed it? The fact that the modern reader

 is now far less sensitive to beauties of literalness than to beauties of imagination. The reciprocity of the visual and the visionary is certainly Wordsworth's theme and his achievement. And it is natural enough that Mr. Hartman should not think it necessary to go on laboriously about Wordsworth's triumph of literalness—natural, but also dangerous, since our own imbalance, our own blindness to the literal and our hyper-sensitivity to the significant, is now likely to distort our reading of Wordsworth. (p. 10)

The legitimate concern with the poetic imagination has now reached so engrossing a stage as to make me think that Mr. Hartman has underrated his duty to help a modern reader to see how beautifully effective Wordsworth's literalism is, how strong and how worthy a partner for his imagination. (p. 12)

*Christopher Ricks, "The Greatness of Wordsworth," in* The New York Review of Books *(reprinted with permission from* The New York Review of Books; *copyright © 1965 Nyrev, Inc.), Vol. III, No. 12, January 28, 1965, pp. 10, 12.*

THE TIMES LITERARY SUPPLEMENT

To call Professor Hartman's new book ***Wordsworth's Poetry, 1787-1814*** is about as relevant as squeezing the late C. S. Lewis

Photograph by T. Charles Erickson, Yale University; courtesy of Geoffrey Hartman

178

between the covers of an Oxford History. Those who come to it expecting the survey its title implies will find instead a series of insights, stimulating, personal, not to be relied on. Apart from moments of chronological vagueness Professor Hartman's scholarship is exact, but his approach sometimes seems strangely beside the point as one returns to the poetry itself. . . .

The correct title for the book would undoubtedly be *Wordsworth's Apocalyptic Imagination*. In *The Unmediated Vision* of 1954 Professor Hartman "glimpsed" "a paradox inherent in the human and poetic imagination: it cannot be at the same time true to nature and true to itself". Now he goes much farther. We are presented with "the drama of consciousness and maturation", shown a Wordsworth "plagued" by the fear "that nature is not enough, that his imagination is essentially apocalyptic and must violate the middle world of common things and loves". "The poet's later strength", it is asserted, "has its origin in experiences that intimate (negatively) a death of nature and (positively) a faculty whose power is independent of nature". Despite the occasional reassuring summary, it is not easy to isolate the stages of Wordsworth's alleged development. Professor Hartman treats *The Prelude* as if it recorded historical fact, and often seems to be discussing the child in terms far more relevant to the poet of twenty years later. The early poetry, too, is wrenched to fit the pattern of Wordsworth's progressive alienation from nature. . . .

The author's central position is much weakened by his refusal to take seriously Wordsworth's belief in the One Life. In *The Unmediated Vision* he went to extraordinary lengths to deny that there was pantheism in "the light of setting suns", and here the question is passed over with the odd contemptuous reference to Wordsworth's "mild anima mundi religion". This is not merely an omission. In 1798-99—the period of "Tintern Abbey" and the early parts of *The Prelude*—apocalypse meant for Wordsworth not self-consciousness, autonomy, but communion. The two things are radically opposed. . . .

Always at the back of Professor Hartman's mind is the Apostrophe to Imagination in *Prelude* Book VI. . . . Certainly the mind is autonomous but is the passage the climax of a prolonged struggle towards consciousness, or merely an isolated moment of imaginative power? There were after all seven Books of *The Prelude* to go when it was written, and yet there is no sequel. And what of Professor Hartman's admission, courageous if not wise, that it is difficult to know whether Wordsworth's imagination had in fact become fully independent before this point? His book is often dangerously far from the poetry as such, but it would be hard to feel much impressed by an autonomy reached after all but a handful of Wordsworth's great poems had been written.

The importance of Professor Hartman's central thesis may be open to doubt, but his detailed criticism can be very good. . . . A great deal of thought too has gone into the notes and critical bibliographies, which are well worth reading in their own right.

> *"Apocalyptic Imagination," in* The Times Literary Supplement *(© Times Newspapers Ltd. (London) 1965; reproduced from* The Times Literary Supplement *by permission), No. 3296, April 29, 1965, p. 332.*

LAURENCE LERNER

[Geoffrey Hartman] doesn't believe that mere brute life can be art. "Forms are a betrayal of life": hence they are necessary. (Mr Hartman calls his collection *Beyond Formalism*, but "be-

yond" doesn't imply rejection; the truer your allegiance to it, the better you will transcend the apparent limits of formalism). Only the writer who is restrained by form, held at a distance from sheer experience, can perform the significant act of breaking out of it. Mr Hartman is not worrying here about the classical realists . . . : they had social and rational norms that kept them at a necessary distance from the flux of experience. He is concerned with the impersonal modern novelist who, by not allowing us to perceive his judgment on his characters, could be accused of not being able to handle his world—if it were not that his mode of distancing himself is not that of judgment but that of creating heroes. Modern realistic fiction, threatened by the all-engulfing democratic embrace that Whitman used to boast of, stands back and becomes art by means of its attachment to romance and myth.

Such at any rate is my account of Mr Hartman's suggestive but maddeningly elusive argument. If I have understood him right, then I rejoice to concur. If Stendhal was in danger of turning art into mere life, how much more is beat poetry or the fiction of the inarticulate. To attack form and insist on plain reality can, at a given moment of literary history, be exhilarating because of the tearing sound as it breaks free of a convention that had clearly begun to lie. Art *turning into* life can be marvellous, as in Wordsworth, Stendhal, George Eliot. But then, when it's happened, we have to step back again, take our distance, perceive in a structured way—if only for the sake of being able to break out again. (p. 64)

Mr Hartman is a man of . . . [great] learning, whose mind never keeps still, so that the very subject he is writing about seems to change from sentence to sentence. **"The Heroics of Realism"** is almost the clearest essay in this book: many of the others are totally opaque. I read him with a kind of bemused admiration, but to learn anything from a critic I need to understand a rather larger fraction of what he says. (p. 66)

> *Laurence Lerner, "Stendhal's Mirror," in* Encounter *(© 1972 by Encounter Ltd.), Vol. XXXIX, No. 6, December, 1972, pp. 62-6.**

JOSEPH N. RIDDEL

Though there is evidence here and there that [*Beyond Formalism: Literary Essays 1958-1970*] is a kind of housecleaning before a new start, Professor Hartman has indeed rendered a "book"—a statement from mid-career, Janus-faced, a summary and a prospect. It is also a major critical statement, made with an indirectness and a sense of the problematic of all such statements that seem to be Hartman's especial contribution to the critical project: that open, tentative, endless, self-contradictory violation by the mind of the very object of its love. *Beyond Formalism* is a confession of American roots and European efflorescence, the statement of one critic's education in the necessity and perverseness of the word and therefore his embodiment of the paradox of man, the myth-maker condemned to unravel (demystify) his own enchantments in order to begin again.

At first glance, *Beyond Formalism* is a classic example of the arbitrary, an accident of some twelve years, a multiple of interests, and not a few commissions. At the second, it has all the coherence of a single consciousness exploring the problematic of consciousness, questioning itself, seeking, and holding final answers at a distance. To be sure, the twenty-one essays and reviews, divided for the purposes of the book into four untitled and somewhat arbitrary subdivisions, ranging from practical exegesis to the criticism of criticism and from masters like Milton to moderns of questionable repute, present a very tentative order. The order it has is more like a tapestry than a narrative. In fact, the weaving of the tapestry is the metaphor to which Professor Hartman finally turns as the "figure" of literary language, "The Voice of the Shuttle." But the book also has a "theme," a "subject." For Professor Hartman, the scholar of comparative Romanticism, that "theme" is Romance—Romance as the story of story-telling, the "myth," if only because life depends on the reciprocal and continuing activity which allows the telling to begin again and throws man into his historicity. (p. 178)

For Hartman, literature, like human culture, is inexplicable without some understanding of Romance (the world of man's imagining, myth-making). If, therefore, the historical period of the great Romantic poets brings that activity to a focal point, the history of literature itself is the history of the Romantic, of the crisis of self-consciousness. (p. 179)

Readers of these provocative essays will remark the contrary pull toward theoretical statement and a resistance to leaving the text. This is especially evident in the practical criticism in the essays on Milton and Marvell, on Wordsworth and on the explorations of Romantic anti-self-consciousness and the "genius loci." Hartman distrusts the authoritative and privileged detachment of even those critics he admires—like Frye and Blanchot—just as he resists the kind of intimacy with the text evident in the criticism of Georges Poulet, whose singular preoccupation with consciousness he finds a particular kind of "formalism," the concern with greater as opposed to lesser forms, with the authorial *cogito* rather than the particular work. In a sense, Hartman is commenting on the "blindness" (as Paul de Man calls it) implicit in any critical holism. The act of criticism for him must above all resist its own consuming desire for reification.

For Hartman, in the end, poetry is the best commentary on poetry (as Romantic poetry, in its self-reflexiveness, often makes evident), for it recognizes the necessity of enchantment in its own activity. But if criticism cannot be poetry, if interpretation cannot ultimately resist its demystifying function, it can refuse to accept the illusion that it recovers an ultimate truth and value from the text. If criticism must play its inevitable role, of making exoteric the esoteric or hidden or "sacred" silence of the text, it needs to make clear that such "profanations" are in the nature of poetry itself, the bringing to "word" of some sacred mystery. In his practical criticism, Hartman tends to be a kind of allegorist, weaving in a texture of metaphors about metaphors his story of the poetry's story, the drama of mediation or, in Heidegger's terms, of the fall into language.

Hartman proposes no "anatomy" (of either literature or criticism), then, but an activity which will make poetry talk about itself, as Romantic and post-Romantic poetry habitually does. . . . The metaphor of the precarious journey, which can end at no truth, is the figure of both poetry and criticism for Hartman. The function of criticism, like that of the poetry it explores, is not to deliver some final truth or enlightenment, but to keep all forms open. (pp. 180-81)

Hartman's theory, and even his practical criticism, does distract one at times with its own resistance to the inevitable "opening" of interpretation, its persistence in trying to sustain the enchantments of the text. This hesitance to demystify produces a critical text that punctuates its usual clarity with areas of strategic opaqueness, as if the criticism grown doubly-self-

conscious could at will escape its own mediating force and reaffirm presence at the center of the imaginative event. Hartman will not go as far as Blanchot, nor even his colleague Paul de Man, in confronting the nothingness at the center of fictions. He still holds out for the possibilities of transcendence, for the transport of Romance from self-consciousness to imagination. But as Wallace Stevens, the poet who provides Hartman with a running series of metaphors about metaphors, wrote: "the absence of imagination had / Itself to be imagined." That opens upon a world beyond formalism, but it also throws us back into the problematic of imagination, that it may be our last fiction. If it is, can we refuse to demystify it, as a part of our living the fiction itself? (p. 181)

Joseph N. Riddel, in a review of "Beyond Formalism: Literary Essays, 1958-1970," in Comparative Literature *(© copyright 1973 by University of Oregon; reprinted by permission of* Comparative Literature*), Vol. XXV, No. 3, Spring, 1973, pp. 178-81.*

RICHARD POIRIER

[In **"The Fate of Reading and Other Essays"**], there emerges a consensus view of a possibly coherent theory of poetics. This is . . . validated by some extraordinarily deft analyses of Wordsworth, Keats, Collins, Valéry, Goethe and Christopher Smart, and much briefer but equally brilliant illuminations of a number of other writers. . . .

"The Fate of Reading" is much more intensely speculative than [**"Beyond Formalism"**] and so much more anxious for patterns that every analysis of a writer or a work is made continuous with literary theory, every poem is shown to be an act of criticism, every act of criticism a poetic one.

Extremely difficult, extremely burdened by "anxieties" about critical influences, and in many ways a sectarian inquiry into the hazards and hopes of contemporary theories of literature, this is even so a peculiarly non-academic, even anti-academic book. Hartman is against both the polemical and the pedagogic inclinations of academic interpretation; the first, because it prevents what he calls in the title essay "universalizing scrutiny"; the second, because the pedagogue as reader tends to retreat from what is most astonishing in literature into what is most susceptible to structured analysis. Who, then, is the imagined audience for this book, what kind of reader is conjured by its style?

The style here and in the work of Hartman's associates is intentionally difficult, as if they want to exclude that general public who might otherwise join—but would as surely corrupt by simplification—their effort to restore to literature and to reading the awe and mystery which have apparently been taken from them by various efforts at popularization. For the restoration of mystery is Hartman's most pervasive ambition. His is a sometimes gleeful unintelligibility, not unlike Lacan's, combined with some of the prophetic preciosity of Bloom—"the eristics of interpretation are its eros."

Much of the difficulty is made necessary, of course, by the theories among which Hartman adjudicates, but a good part of it is addressed to an Elect for whom obscurity is at least the initial evidence of a trip in deep water. (p. 21)

I should say that these remarks on Hartman's style are not meant to give comfort to those who would be incapable under any circumstances of appreciating the enormously impressive intelligence at work here and the selfless energy with which

Hartman addresses inherently complicated matters. Most other critics avoid the essential questions he asks about the representation of the self in acts of writing and reading, questions made all the more difficult by his choosing to ask related ones about the places where this representation occurs—not only within known conventions of literary form but in that mysterious area where the so-called text and the so-called context of writing, or of reading, blur into one another. His basic concern, described in words of one syllable, is like Arnold's when, in "Stanzas From the Grand Chartreuse," he falls under the shadow of his mentors and cries "And what am I that I am here?"

At issue is not the legitimacy of this question but the quality of response to it. My complaint is that, like de Man and Bloom, Hartman wants to assert his critical presence as if contending for the role of poet-priest. . . . [His] ideal critic is, to use one of his Hegelian phrases, capable of "hermeneutic heroism." The implication is that there must be an answerable style, sometimes afflated, sometimes even bullying, and very often displaying the large-mannered motions of a mythy mind.

For all this, Hartman's book does demonstrate the advantages as well as the dangers of stepping across the line that customarily separates literary from literary-critical discourse. It allows him to show, for one thing, and more eloquently than anyone has before, that if critics are poets then poets are often the very best critical historians—*in* their poetry. The influence of one poet on another has not always been the occasion for "anxiety," and not conspicuously till after Milton. But the idea that it was at any time fraught with feelings of competitive repulsion as well as gratitude was brought to the fore by Hartman and Bloom, following on the work of W. J. Bate, and ought to invigorate everyone's sense of what otherwise has been a benign notion of literary transmission—except, it should be said, in the study of American literature. Hartman's capacity to elicit history from modifications in poetic forms and images is masterful in a number of these essays. . . . (pp. 21-2)

Another advantage stemming from the confusion of poet and critic is that the recognition in poetry of a subliminal anguish about its own history calls into question the more stubborn kinds of literary idealism. The idealization of the autonomy of the literary text becomes, for critics like Hartman and de Man, an intolerable estrangement. Furthermore, the rather smugly confident privileges accorded literature as a result of a belief in textual autonomy—including the assumptions that there can be no such thing as unmediated expression and that the self cannot hope to break through the determinants of form—are privileges which literature itself, if read intently, does not choose to claim.

Thus, while Hartman, like Bloom and de Man, is essentially conservative about the possibilities of ever getting "beyond formalism," his conservatism is extremely agitated and complex. On the one hand, Hartman is rightly dismissive of theories which make literature into an allegory of possible escapes from the past or which try to claim that literary forms are always alternative to social ones in their hospitality to irrational, sublime or visionary states of consciousness. On the other hand, it is nonetheless incumbent on Hartman, given his notions of the critic's proper role, to question most existing poetic theories of closure, of the poem as resolved and self-contained. Sense—the meaning, so-called—can be one form of closure, the "triumph of form" another, and Hartman is unhappy about both of them. (p. 23)

Hartman wants to believe that the history of poetry as a continuing and essentially self-critical enterprise might show us how to deal with the larger stresses of contemporary culture. But unlike most other literary-cultural élitists he has a very troubled vision of poetry and of his own possible relations to it. He insists that our poetic inheritance can be useful only if we learn to give fuller acknowledgment to that demonic side of the psyche which his kind of interpretation can find even in the most unruffled texts—as in his too audacious reading of Keats's "To Autumn."

The problem, however, is that Hartman's critical daring actually strengthens conservative illusions about the power of education by poetry. He encourages us to suppose that threatening fractures in the general culture can be understood by studying supposedly analogous threats that have in the past issued from the psyches of individual poets as challenges to poetic form. Hartman's desire to read poetry as in large part a continuing struggle with the demonic thereby becomes politically significant and is to some extent politically motivated. His work tends, that is, to locate in the psyche those horrors which issue more deviously still from social, economic and political rather than poetical institutions. Even assuming that high literary culture could adequately teach us to cope with the culture in general, it would have to be a literary culture defined far more broadly than it is in a book devoted to a poetic line, and a very selective one at that.

With what cannot be a wholly conscious political shrewdness Hartman thus excites the imagination of poetical-critical power even while ignoring our prosaic powerlessness; anxieties about poetical-critical form are substituted for anxieties about forms of political and economic authority which also shadow literature and the imagination of the self. That is why the tone of the Elect which can be found in criticism of this kind, based as it is on the appropriation by the critic-poet of unprecedented cultural authority, has disturbing political implications. (pp. 24-5)

Criticism of literature or of literary theories is never purely literary or unbiased. Hartman knows this, but he has not been nearly theoretical enough in asking where his investigations into a comprehensive theory of literature would lead him if he opened them to forms more responsive than poetry to social and political and economic factors. The history of poetry is not the same as the history of literature. And the history of consciousness inherent in literary forms can't be accounted for by any number of interpretations, however masterful, when these are confined mostly to poetic texts. Hartman's theories are hobbled when it comes to any kind of writing—like novels and plays—where form embodies collective, social and not merely poetic consciousness. It is enormously difficult to locate the history of consciousness imbedded in literary forms because novels and poems (particularly poems written under the stress of specific historical occasions) are notoriously insidious in their ideological content—in their capacity, that is, to universalize certain norms which in reality are the product of class or other special interests.

It may seem ungrateful to bring up these objections of so potentially political a nature, but to do so is, I hope, further evidence of the thresholds to which Hartman brings us. If he aspires to any kind of thorough-going theory involving the dramaturgy of forms with the self, then he should now be especially cautious that a theory merely of poetry does not gel into a prematurely complete theory of literature. Otherwise he will encourage unfortunate inferences about his omission of recalcitrant and latently political aspects of literary form. (pp. 25-6)

Richard Poirier, "A Star Trek in the Theory of Poetics," in The New York Times Book Review (©
1975 by The New York Times Company; reprinted
by permission), April 20, 1975, pp. 21-6.

DENIS DONOGHUE

The Fate of Reading is a new selection of Geoffrey Hartman's writings, from work published during the past five years. Many essays resume the themes of an earlier selection, *Beyond Formalism* . . . , extending their implications or exacerbating them as the mood of Hartman's mind requires. A reader who does not already know Professor Hartman's work should repair that deficiency before tackling the new book. Otherwise, *The Fate of Reading* would appear a random miscellany of fugitive pieces caught and held for trial merely because Professor Hartman had an interest in their capture. In fact, the book is most compelling as evidence of the range and quality of Professor Hartman's mind and of the point it has reached in a causerie set astir in his first book, *The Unmediated Vision*. . . .

Two verses from Deuteronomy made an epigraph for *The Unmediated Vision*. Moses says to the people of Israel: "The Lord talked with you face to face in the mount out of the midst of the fire", and then, "I stood between the Lord and you at that time, to shew you the word of the Lord; for ye were afraid by reason of the fire, and went not up into the mount." In the first, the people have an unmediated vision of the Lord; in the second, Moses places himself as mediator, critic, and linguist between the people and their Lord. Three verses later the Lord forbids the people to make graven images "or any likeness of any thing that is in heaven above or that is in the earth beneath or that is in the waters beneath the earth". It is my impression that Professor Hartman has been pondering these verses for their bearing upon the nature of poetry: his books are meditations upon visions mediated and unmediated, graven images, the status of presentation and representation, likeness and language.

The book of evidence consists of *The Unmediated Vision*, the analysis of action and history in *Malraux* . . . , the brooding upon imagination and nature in *Wordsworth's Poetry 1787-1814* . . . , considerations of the sinister aspect of mediation as trespass and transgression, most clearly produced in "The Voice of the Shuttle" and an essay on Blanchot in *Beyond Formalism*, and now the anxious pages on "the living, ancestor-haunted consciousness" in *The Fate of Reading*. The argument of these books does not make an impeccable logic. There are signs of internal contradiction, and especially of a moment which I think of Professor Hartman as having reached in 1969 when he found himself losing faith in every doctrine which declares that an unmediated vision is possible. In 1967 Paul de Man asserted that sign and meaning can never coincide, and that literature is defined by this tragic knowledge: "it is the only form of language free from the fallacy of unmediated expression". I cannot see how Professor Hartman could have read that assertion without a shudder, unless he rushed back to Deuteronomy and renewed his faith in Moses as a sounder critic than de Man.

Professor Hartman's early books assume that poets seek and sometimes achieve an unmediated expression. Written in the spirit of literary idealism, these books declare the possibility of "a constitutive self" capable of breaking through "social

veils and similar determinants". To Professor Hartman, an unmediated vision is a vision of life free from the restraint of a canonical text: the modern poet "passes through experience by means of the unmediated vision; Nature, the body, and human consciousness—that is the only text". He speaks again of "a vision unconditioned by the particularity of experience", and in the study of Wordsworth he refers to the poet's urge "to cast out nature and to achieve an unmediated contact with the principle of things". . . .

An unmediated expression is a desire congenial to poetic genius, and in *Beyond Formalism* Professor Hartman opposes genius to Genius, "the personal 'ingenium' in its unmediated, forgetful vigour" to the starry guide "whose influence accompanies us from birth but is revealed mainly at crucial historical or self-conscious junctures". In another version the unmediated vision is given as the authority of a poet's voice, not a Mallarméan vibration but the spirit's audible presence to itself. Every version is animated not only by Deuteronomy but by that passage in the *Confessions* in which St Augustine, praying to his God, says that "what I know about myself I only know because your light shines upon me, and what I do not know about myself I shall continue not to know until I see you face to face and my dusk is noonday". Professor Hartman's books are therefore odes to the poetical character construed as an embodiment of the sublime.

The unmediated vision, Professor Hartman's supreme fiction, is menaced or compromised by the loss of Eden—the substitution of an arbitrary for a natural language, and the rift between consciousness and experience. But he maintains as a perennial desire or a mythology of self what de Man and other critics have set aside as a fallacy, the unmediated character of the poet's gibberish, the magician's abracadabra. He is stubborn in associating art with freedom, seeing art as an unmediated virtue thriving in the throes of mediation. In the study of Malraux he returns to Malraux's reflection upon Goya, a painter who represents the unusual, the terrible, the inhuman, not by depicting an actual or imaginary spectacle but "by inventing a script capable of representing these things without being forced to submit to their elements". If art can do that, surely the idiom of genius, spirit and voice is justified.

I cannot find in *The Fate of Reading* conclusive evidence that Professor Hartman has either given up or renewed his faith in the unmediated power of imagination. He is impressed by de Man's assertion, but he has not fulfilled its logic. Meanwhile he reveals the poet living in the indeterminate middle ground which is human life, a space marked if not filled by "boughten mercies and mediations". If the middle ground cannot be held, it collapses into "a direct, unmediated confrontation of the individual and his God". While the going is good, the world mediates between man and God: the paradigm for this happiness is another passage in the *Confessions* where the earth, interrogated, says "I am not God, but God is He who made me". Another version is Wordsworth's faith, reached in *The Prelude*, that Nature suffices the energies of consciousness, a faith which Professor Hartman in *The Fate of Reading* presents as the consummation of Wordsworth's "spousal verse", a vision of Nature as "recreated rather than consumed by the demands of consciousness". Art is a process by which feeling, instead of consuming itself in use, is recycled in an endless restoration. Professor Hartman does not haggle over the nature of Nature, whether it is substance or sign, appearances or the codes we impose upon them. In the study of Malraux he votes for styles, forms, and models rather than "the seductive and hypnotic realm of appearance'', and speaks of the artist accepting a system of received signs until he finds his own. But he does not fret, he continues to believe in the transforming power of imagination. With such a faith, he can see with equanimity the mediating role of nature and the proliferation of its defects: all will be well.

Professor Hartman quotes with pleasure a passage from the *Histoire de France* in which Michelet says that Rabelais collected wisdom from the old, popular idioms, from sayings, proverbs, school farces in the mouths of fools and clowns, ''but mediated by follies of this kind the genius of the age and its prophetic power are revealed in their majesty''. In this quoting mood Professor Hartman is ready to accept the fact of mediacy, if only as a curse; it is ''the inveterate mediacy of the word'', the darkness of mediations in which Coleridge's mariner finds himself. He then takes the risk of mediation by translating it into the idiom of trespass, transgression, estrangement and interpolation. But he never takes pleasure in the sheer resourcefulness of language. At one point he refers to Stevens's ''lingua franca et jocundissima'', but the only passage I can recall which responds to the jocund spirit in language is a few pages in *Beyond Formalism* where he writes of puns as interventions—two meanings jostling for the space of one and making a room wide enough to accommodate both. Otherwise he writes of language as if it were a desperate expedient and never a joy. . . .

Twice in *The Fate of Reading* he quotes the passage in *The Philosophy of History* where Hegel describes the Greek character ''transforming the merely Natural into an expression of its own being''. The Greek spirit ''knows itself free in its productions'', and respects and venerates them. . . . (p. 934)

I am surprised, therefore, that [Professor Hartman] does not resort to Hegel rather than keep up the strain of mediating between situations mediated and unmediated. In the preface to *The Phenomenology of Mind* Hegel, speaking of the magical power of mind which converts the negative into being, says that it ''cancels abstract immediacy, i e immediacy which merely *is,* and, by so doing, becomes the true substance, becomes being or immediacy that does not have mediation outside it, but is this mediation itself''. Again, in the *Logic,* Hegel says that nothing is absolutely immediate in the sense that it is in no way mediated; and nothing is mediated in the absolute sense that it is in no way immediate. . . . I am not saying that Hegel ends the matter, but that Professor Hartman should have pressed the argument of immediacy and mediation a good deal harder before relying upon its service in five books. The trouble with the distinction between visions mediated and unmediated is that if it is confused it spreads confusion further into its critical consequences, making distinctions without real difference.

When Professor Hartman writes brilliantly, as he often does when the occasion is a poem by Wordsworth, Valéry, Keats, Smart, Goethe, Milton, or Marvell, his mind surges beyond concepts and theories into the poetry itself. Nearly everything he writes in this mood could be sustained, if it needed any support beyond its own justice and coherence, by one sentence from Hegel, namely, ''Greek freedom of thought is excited by an alien existence, but it is free because it transforms and virtually reproduces the stimulus by its own operations''. This is enough to be going on with, and to allow Professor Hartman to appeal to art as ''a reservoir of resonances''. Clearly, his heart is in the right mood in *The Fate of Reading*. He wants poetry to tell the time of history without sinking into historical determinism, he insists on ''the sense of an informing spirit''

in art, the source of its authority; and he has many important things to say about myth, depth psychology, the poet's identity, the psychology of art. But I am not convinced that he has found for his perceptions the appropriate ''lingua franca et jocundissima'' which he associates with ''vernacular perception''.

Professor Hartman's theory of art is basically simple: it is Art as Philomela. Tereus having raped Philomela cut out her tongue to prevent discovery, but she wove a tell-tale account of the crime into a tapestry, and there is magic in the web of it. What Professor Hartman calls ''the thaumaturgic Word'' could not be silenced; the truth must emerge, consciousness struggles to appear as form and not as consciousness. So we come to the truth-telling power of fiction. Professor Hartman quotes in summary a story by S. Y. Agnon which endorses the magic of Philomela's tapestry. . . . (pp. 934-35)

It is a beautiful, happy ending, and I am sure Professor Hartman believes in it, at least on the Sabbath. What he believes on other days is not clear. Is language great because it tells the truth? Or a cheat because it cannot do what it offers to do? Are words, as Feste claims, ''very rascals'', Cretan liars? In *The Fate of Reading* Professor Hartman never gives himself space or time to answer these questions, though they break into his pages when given half a chance; naturally, since his essays are meditations upon Keats, Wordsworth, Goethe, I. A. Richards, Harold Bloom, Valéry, and the mystery story.

There is a particular impediment in *The Fate of Reading* and that is Professor Hartman's style, or rather its present phase. He can write as lucidly as any critic, and more powerfully than most, but his current mood is aggressive. ''I admit to a variable style'', he says, ''which consists mainly of a playful dissolving of terms and abstractions, but one that seeks to bring out their creative force as unrecognized 'poetic dictions'.'' He argues that criticism should not be a yea yea, nay nay affair conducted in dry prose. Why should not the critic be ''divers et ondoyant''? ''We should not see the things of this world under the species of a false objectivity, or of its killing nomenclature.'' True, but these arguments can easily serve a bad cause, an equally corrupt subjectivity. Professor Hartman seems to me to have moved into the decadent phase of his mind, having left behind, unresolved, many fundamental problems. . . .

I could be more patient with . . . [certain of his] sentences if I thought . . . [they were] sustained by a coherent theory of literature, by sound principles cogently maintained, and a sense of literature as far more important than anything that can be said about it. Professor Hartman probably thinks of his work as *l'écriture* rather than as criticism. Under any name I think his current style too self-regarding to be wholesome; it compels his intelligence to feed upon high-jinks and rascality.

The essays on Keats are the most important things in *The Fate of Reading,* and the most remarkable, but even in these triumphs Professor Hartman's wilfulness is a nuisance. Eloquent on the anxiety of influence, ''the burden of authorship'', and Keats's ''shame at self-assertion'', he has little to say of the other power, Keats's self-confidence, his buoyancy even in the Hyperion poems. What Professor Hartman says of Keats's burdens and compulsions I do in part believe, but I wish he would make his account truer to the poems by sensing everything the poet received from the gods, the muses, the poetic forms. The anxiety of influence is not merely angst. Professor Hartman knows this, but the excess of his style does not allow him to say it. His work is most valuable when it is possessed by a force more thoughtful than its decadence, and speaks with that authority;

this, for instance, on Keats: "Most of the Odes", Hartman writes, "are a feverish quest to enter the life of a pictured scene, to be totally where the imagination is." I am content with that. (p. 935)

Denis Donoghue, "Mediate and Immediate," in The Times Literary Supplement *(© Times Newspapers Ltd. (London) 1975; reproduced from* The Times Literary Supplement *by permission), No. 3832, August 22, 1975, pp. 934-35.*

JONATHAN CULLER

[Geoffrey Hartman] repeatedly proves himself a subtle analyst of genres, though he usually prefers to invent or discover his own. Several essays in *The Fate of Reading* illustrate the kind of criticism he now does best: the grouping together, as a sub-genre, of a series of thematically linked poems which, when arranged in this way, come to manifest different degrees of consciousness and self-consciousness (consciousness of the group in which they find themselves) and thus tell a tale of the adventures of Poesy or of the trials of the Poetical Character. The best of these, "Evening Star and Evening Land," invokes poems addressed to the evening star and explores the way in which the investigation of poetic consciousness and its development arises as a solution to the problem of how to narrate Nature.

Expert in the perception of self-reflexive figures, Hartman discovers, as the preoccupation of most sub-genres, the task of continuing poetry and the difficulties of emerging as poet through a representation of self in poetic language. . . . Literary history is the history of fictions and of the anxieties which accompany fiction: fear of a decline in poetical energy, concern with the impossibility of achieving unmediated presence through fictive representation, anxiety about the authenticity of the self that emerges through poetic representation.

There are real problems here, real opportunities for literary history, which Hartman explores with a cunning elegance. But his historical project has a perverse accompaniment which ultimately hints at an ahistorical nostalgia: the revival of late eighteenth-century critical discourse as the privileged metalanguage. Notions of the poetical spirit and the poetical character may well be apposite figures for the problems of poetic reflexivity, but this supposed historical fidelity is finally part of an escape from real literary history. Hartman seems uncertain whether to reconstruct historical series and modes or to play the role of gloomy oracle, announcing cultural decline, the intolerable burden of history and the necessity of error; and his language assists a studied equivocation. It is sad when so talented a critic evades problems he could treat so well, and one may be forgiven for supposing that he feels pursued by a demon. Certainly here, in the glorification of Romanticism's impossible calling, in the surrender to the temptations of the gnomic, one recognizes the debilitating influence of Harold Bloom, a true anxiety of influence. (pp. 90-1)

Jonathan Culler, "Reading and Misreading," in The Yale Review *(© 1975 by Yale University; reprinted by permission of the editors), Vol. LXV, No. 1, Autumn, 1975, pp. 88-95.**

DONALD MARSHALL

Formalism—called "New Criticism" when it was still young, aggressive, and ambitious—seems to have died from its own

success. Any ordinary modern critic can read with unprecedented sensitivity to nuances of meaning and to the delicate formal economy of part and whole. More important, the critic's language can report the subtlest reading in terms of precise textual details. This habit of rigorous reading is evidently indispensable for modern poetry. But earlier texts—from Shakespeare and the metaphysicals to the romantics—also profited from formalist analyses. These replaced an older style of literary study, personified in the "gentleman scholar" who combined sensitivity with broad learning and good taste with sound memory. Early formalists trusted that the *Oxford English Dictionary* contained enough history to let an explicator get on with his real task: reading. And instead of basing critical judgments on personal taste or on unquestioned community standards, explication itself, shrewdly conducted, was expected to lead from neutral description toward the exhibition of complexity and internal coherence, these two constituting a double and virtually self-evident criterion for excellence. But despite the multiplication of subtle readers, the problems of literary history and evaluation have proved intractable. And these problems are the core of . . . [Geoffrey Hartman's effort] to get beyond formalism. (p. 131)

[In *The Fate of Reading*] Hartman's ambition, I think, is to recover the possibility of writing literary history after the devastating gain of consciousness and self-consciousness brought about by formalism. The days are gone when a poem reduced itself to a few brisk commonplaces that could be catalogued in a score of texts, ancient and modern. After formalism, any decent poem seems an abyss of complication. Equally, literary history can no longer content itself with external narrative patterns unthinkingly borrowed from Darwin or Hegel. Hartman's solution to the difficulty is to transfer historical consciousness from the literary historian to the poets themselves.

Hartman may have the most acute consciousness of form in modern criticism. But the form he studies is itself a rise or intensification of the poet's consciousness as it confronts literary tradition, including the state or spirit of the language. Form is a delicate balance between individuated self-consciousness and a medium preserved by the saving acknowledgement of its objectivity. The readings of Keats in this volume trace with moving subtlety his search for something "to set a bottom for inwardness, to limit an endless and corrosive self-concern." The ode "To Autumn" is Keats's triumphant discovery of the answer. Hartman's uncanny talent is to make literary history rise out of the poet's own effort to focus the revel of inherited forms and conventional topics. Literary history does not go on behind the poet's back, but precisely through the thoughtful labor of his creation. Form is not fixed beyond history; nor is it the organic economy of the unique poem. Form *is* history—or at least it is so in literary history. The tension between literary historian and critic dissolves; for the critic reading the poem's form has to see that form as the shadow cast by the poet's own historical consciousness. . . .

Despite the differences, Hartman in a sense complements Bloom. While Bloom strides across the bridge of tradition from strong poem to strong poem, Hartman is willing to work more patiently through the smaller fry, the Grays and Collinses. His reward is a more varied and less anxious sense of the poem's relation to tradition. Our reward as readers is to find in *Beyond Formalism* and *The Fate of Reading* a few anticipatory sketches for that history of the "spirit of romance" from Milton through the English romantics that Geoffrey Hartman—and, I believe, only he of all living scholars—has it in him to write. That history could triumphantly disclose in poetry and testify by its own existence to the power of a rememorative word. Such a word would augment us all. (p. 134)

> Donald Marshall, ''Beyond Formalism,'' in Partisan Review *(copyright © 1977 by* Partisan Review*), Vol. XLIV, No. 1, 1977, pp. 131-34.**

GERALD GRAFF

Insofar as I could discern a thesis in this diffuse book [*Criticism in the Wilderness: The Study of Literature Today*], I took it to go something like this: Anglo-American literary studies have come to be dominated by a dull and demeaning ideal of ''practical'' criticism. For a number of reasons, critics have narrowed their aims. . . . [The] dry, utilitarian spirit of Locke has triumphed over the more daring, speculative spirit of Hegel, Nietzsche, and Heidegger. A prime expression of this practical bias of literary studies is the tendency to regard criticism as an austere science, holding itself pure of any imputation of literary character lest it compromise its objective authority. This bias has made Anglo-American professors suspicious of the free-ranging inquiries of Continental philosophers and critics, particularly as pursued by recent avant-garde thinkers like Jacques Derrida. What, then, is to be done? Without abandoning the close analysis of concrete literary works, criticism, Hartman urges, must open itself to theoretical inquiry. It must overcome its fastidious insistence on purity and acknowledge its communality with literature, especially with literature's impulse to call all things into question, including the premises of literature and criticism themselves.

Hartman connects the narrowly utilitarian view of criticism and the ''defensive partition of the critical and creative spirit'' with a more pervasive fear of self-conscious thought. He has written frequently on this theme in culture and literature, as for example in his useful essay, ''Romanticism and Anti-Self-Consciousness.'' His basic notions, indeed, would seem to be an extension of the ideas of Romantic philosophers such as Schiller and Hegel: since the dawn of the modern age our culture has been so overwhelmed by its sense of the multiplicity and complexity of experience and the plurality of possible points of view that it has come to see the fully conscious pursuit of knowledge as leading not to enlightenment but to skepticism and paralysis of the will. . . .

I have inferred the above summary rather than taken it directly from *Criticism in the Wilderness,* since Hartman does not choose to present his ideas in a linear fashion. Part of the problem is that this book is essentially a collection of disparate essays unconvincingly posing as ''chapters'' in a unified work. But I suspect the lack of linear exposition may itself be an attempt to make a point, to exemplify the ''literary'' conception of criticism that Hartman is recommending. Only the introduction and final chapter (''A Short History of Practical Criticism'') yield incisive generalizations. The 265 pages between presumably justify inclusion as a series of show pieces demonstrating the proposed reunion of theory and explicative criticism. (p. 34)

In treating his variety of topics, Hartman all but comes to the point of asserting something. Instead of arguments, one gets wry remarks, witticisms, puns, allusions, and quotations, lots of allusions and quotations. In order to make sense of this long section, one has to watch for repeating motifs—repression, purification, etc.—as one would in taking in *The Waste Land* or a Wagnerian opera. Sometimes one encounters a passage that sounds so much like thinking that one rereads it four or

five times in search of the sense, but with limited success. . . . Possibly in defense of this kind of writing, Hartman observes that ''no one would argue that all subjects can be made easy.'' This is true, but we tolerate difficulty when we judge the results to be both worth the trouble and producible in no more simple way. That is not clearly the case here.

More serious an impediment than out-and-out opacity, though, is Hartman's habit of taking essential definitions and explanations for granted, as if it can be safely assumed that the reader is already so familiar with them that he would be bored by having them spelled out. . . . Such allusive writing both flatters and intimidates the reader. He is credited with inside knowledge but made to feel anxious if he reflects that he may not have it. Hartman no doubt knows what he means, but his technique of non-definition—taken in itself—encourages bluffing. It leads to a familiar kind of pseudo-communication in which all parties pretend to know what is going on while none of them really does for sure.

Hartman's most sustained piece of analysis comes in an interesting section on Walter Benjamin. He shows how the repressed ghost of theology persistently erupts through the intended Marxist sociology. What limits the exercise is that whereas Benjamin aspires to be profound, Hartman is seemingly content to be clever. Here and in other chapters, Hartman surrounds his topics with a tone of sophisticated irony that forbids the crudity of making a commitment or even stating a proposition. Again, it is a case of criticism aiming to be literature—according to a certain conception of literature, it should be noted—by making itself resistant to paraphrase, by turning itself into a dramatic ''process'' of thought rather than a chain of reasonings leading to a conclusion, by seeking to ''be'' rather than ''mean,'' and by ironizing out of existence anything that threatens to become a conviction. (p. 35)

The trouble with Hartman's view lies not, I think, in his conflation of the critical with the literary, or his wish to merge literature, philosophy, and history. He is right in thinking that the isolation and compartmentalization of these subjects has had much to do with impoverishing literary discussion in the last 20 years. The trouble lies rather in Hartman's conception of what is ''literary,'' a conception that excludes the making of statements. One assumes Hartman is not incapable of consecutive argument, but that he has decided that if it's consecutive argument you want you should have gone into electrical engineering or zero-sum accounting. Despite his repeated emphasis on the need to put our concepts in question, one feels Hartman has never questioned this very common view of literature as the antithesis of and antidote to positive science. Reacting against the dominance of commercial and technological institutions, one defines the literary (and often the humanistic in general) as everything that science and technology are not, which is to say, as non-logical, non-conceptual, non-objective, non-verifiable, and not open to refutation. This slanders literature in the process of celebrating it.

In Hartman's case, this attitude produces an instructive contradiction. Although, as we have seen, Hartman wants criticism to overcome its defensive aversion to philosophy, his own conception of criticism (and perhaps of philosophy too) is so defensively anti-scientific as to cause him to purge his writing of assertion. He himself complains that we define literature as whatever is left over after subtracting everything else, yet he falls for another version of this negative dialectic. Aiming to inject a vital impurity into critical discourse and to ruffle complacency, Hartman ends up keeping his own discourse pure of anything anybody could argue with. (p. 36)

None of my objections should distract us from recognizing the justice and importance of many of Hartman's criticisms of established literary studies. I agree with him that criticism has been made monotonous by the mass production of explication for explication's sake; that important theoretical questions about meaning and interpretation posed by avant-garde critics have been ignored or relegated to specialists; that the severance of literary studies from history, philosophy, and theology is a disaster, as is the estrangement of all these studies from the larger public culture (save where they filter down in a debased, therapeutic form). I think Hartman exaggerates the Anglo-American indifference to Continental ideas; existentialism, for example, has had great vogue here and influenced the New Criticism and other schools. But Hartman does not have his eye on many of the central problems of his discipline, and it is no doubt significant that a scholar of his stature should now speak out about them. Still, insofar as Hartman's own work is proffered as a model, it submerges us deeper into the "wilderness" mentioned in his title rather than showing a way out. I doubt if anybody but those already committed to avant-garde literary criticism will be moved by Hartman to think better of it than before reading him. The curious inquirer will get a clearer sense of the implications and uses of the newer critical theories from Jonathan Culler's *Structuralist Poetics,* from Culler's more recent essays in defense of deconstruction, and from Stanley Fish's theoretical papers, collected in his forthcoming *Is There a Text in This Class?* He may want to argue with much these writers say, but it is one of their strengths that what they say can be argued with. What is finally disappointing about Hartman's book is not that it renders its subjects obscure but that it renders them inarguable. (pp. 36-7)

> *Gerald Graff, in a review of "Criticism in the Wilderness: The Study of Literature Today," in* The New Republic *(reprinted by permission of* The New Republic; © *1980 The New Republic, Inc.), Vol. 183, No. 18, November 1, 1980, pp. 34-7.*

TERRENCE DES PRES

Criticism in the Wilderness may be the best, most brilliant, most broadly useful book yet written by an American about the sudden swerve from the safety of established decorum toward bravely theoretical, mainly European forms of literary criticism. There are, however, immediate reasons why this book, when you first take it up, will disturb and put you off. Professor Hartman's style, for example, is always elegant but relies deliberately on puns, allusions, jumbled language levels, wild quoting, moments of self-parody and splashes of arcane terminology. Hartman also moves back and forth at lightning speed from thinker to thinker, leaping prodigiously from one incisive insight to the next. And the book's basic structure is hard-line *and* oracular, rational-empirical *and* theoretical-mystical. All of this is by way of demonstration, Hartman showing us the kind of thinking he wishes to defend; and all of this, if you hang on, turns out to be great fun and cause for high intellectual excitement.

Hartman is one of our smartest scholars; he knows as much about modern culture as anybody and says lots fast, yet not without a meditative undertow. . . . His method is playful, for reasons he clearly sets forth, but his message is deeply in earnest. He defines a kind of critical thinking which he calls "speculative," "philosophical," "theoretical," a kind of lit-

erary criticism which refuses the subordinate position assigned to it by Anglo-American practice, a criticism which would engage rather than serve its object, or, put another way, which presumes to serve literature best by becoming a counterliterature of its own.

I do not say that if you read Hartman you will be converted. The ideas of critics like Harold Bloom and Jacques Derrida are hard to love. But the predicament of literature will appear more racked with riddles than most of us dreamed, and those of us who think steadily about literature, about culture, about the toils of interpretation, must at least test the strength of our positions against the challenge Hartman offers.

To dismiss Continental thinkers as theory-mad is no solution. And here Hartman is especially helpful. The likes of Heidegger, Lukacs, Benjamin and Derrida are suddenly articulate. The rites of revisionism and deconstruction are revealed in a bright sweep of formulations, some as simple as saying that criticism "discloses the iconoclastic within the iconic." (pp. 471-72)

It will be objected that Hartman has been at pains to glorify his own profession and lift a second-order activity to the commanding status of art. Yes and no. Criticism gains a new dignity from boldly confronting its relation to literature, and by sacrificing the security of mere commentary, it extends the borders of literary experience. But it remains tied to a text and inherits that pathos. . . .

A more serious objection is that by refusing to remain subordinate, criticism runs the risk of irresponsibility, promoting chaos and breaking norms. Again, yes and no. If the norms are false, they must go. And we are already deep in chaos; "tradition" is the euphemism we use to cover arbitrary order, and all critical theory stays rooted in what Hartman calls its "text-milieu," the very limited number of books we happen to know. As for responsibility, cant and posturing are always with us; but we don't have to read far, in a given case, to sense which way the wind blows.

We have only to see the remarkable things Hartman can say about specific poems—by Yeats, Dickinson, Williams—to realize that such insights simply cannot be had within the confines of practical criticism. As always, the proof is in the pudding. Revisionist criticism, which uses ideas freely, which dares to speculate, which exploits its own predicament and conducts itself in accord with its new sense of import, enriches the study of literature immensely. It keeps the mind's options open, turning now toward theology, now toward politics, expanding the reach of the art which remains at its center. (p. 473)

> *Terrence Des Pres, "Continental Drift," in* The Nation *(copyright 1980 The Nation magazine, The Nation Associates, Inc.), Vol. 231, No. 15, November 8, 1980, pp. 471-73.*

DENIS DONOGHUE

"**Criticism in the Wilderness**" is concerned with many of the same questions that troubled its predecessors, but it differs from them in one respect: to a well-defined problem it suggests a bizarre solution.

The problem is: What good is literary criticism in a time of mass education? The normal answer is that a critic can show what it means to read well; to read a poem or a novel, for instance, in such a spirit as to make the reading a valid experience, valid in intellectual, emotional and moral terms. When we read a work of art, we study the human imagination as a form of freedom: We think of the imagination as the mind in the aspect of its freedom. If the literary critic is employed to teach in a classroom, he regards teaching as the civic form of his skill: In teaching, he speaks, argues, persuades and practices the decency of communication. That is roughly the rationale of criticism.

Mr. Hartman is not content with such a program; he finds it constricting. He resents the convention by which criticism is deemed to be a secondary activity, subservient to the poems and novels we read, the primary texts.

In his early books, and even as late as **"Beyond Formalism,"** he was content to practice literary criticism and literary history, conventionally defined. But in recent years he has lost faith in literary history and now he is demanding that criticism transform itself. Into what? Into literature: he wants to veto the conventional distinction between literature and criticism. The critic should produce not an essay in the interpretation of, say, Yeats's "Leda and the Swan" but a piece of prose, unconstrained by its ostensible object: call it prose, writing, *lécriture* or work, as in a work of art. Criticism should give up its service, which Mr. Hartman regards as servitude. (p. 11)

In a gruff moment he asks whether any critic has value who is only a critic. To which I answer: Maybe not, but the critic can't repair his disability by pretending to be something else, a Romantic poet, for instance.

What has this to do with literary criticism in a time of mass education? One of the oddities of **"Criticism in the Wilderness"** is that it is dedicated "to my students," because it gives an extraordinarily gloomy account of university teaching. . . .

Mr. Hartman's argument is wild and vehement. Where other teachers find difficulty in communicating with their students, Mr. Hartman wants not to solve the problem but to transcend it. . . . The interpreter enters the text, making his entry as bold and violent as the text itself. I am content to wait for the result of these crossings and entries, but I must declare a prejudice: A critic who determines to make himself a sublime poet is likely to make himself a failed poet and an unhappy wretch. . . .

[Hartman's] own style makes me wonder. In one mood, he is a vigorous, witty, trenchant writer, formidably lucid and polemical. Many of his sentences make me feel: I wish I had said that. But some of them make me feel: I wonder would that be worth the labor of understanding it? . . .

Readers have often wondered aloud why Mr. Hartman, whose early books were unfailingly lucid, seemed to go out of his way to make his later work cloudy and threatening. I have heard it suggested that he had merely fallen in with bad companions and corrupted his style. The new book provides a different explanation: His style is a desperate attempt to prevent his work from being prematurely assimilated. Demanding for criticism the latitude of style readily given to poets and novelists, he is also demanding that a critical essay be read in the same way as a poem or novel; and, in our time, with the same readiness to confront its difficulty. . . .

Mr. Hartman thinks that criticism can escape from the mass mind by taking to the higher hills of poetry and fiction; by cultivating dictions and syntaxes the mass mind has no hope of catching. It is pointless. Any text, however wild and vehement, can be incorporated. In **"Criticism in the Wilderness"** Mr. Hartman is virtually infatuated with Derrida's "Glas," a

wild text even by wild standards. . . . But "Glas," too, can be incorporated; it lives only to the extent to which it has been incorporated. What form of existence has it, except as a text on some smart university courses called Contemporary Thought 405 or the like?

If Mr. Hartman wants to write sublime prose, he is free to write it. But he should not lead his readers to believe that the field of criticism is held by purveyors of a genteel or neoclassic tradition. (p. 32)

Denis Donoghue, "Reading about Writing," in The New York Times Book Review *(© 1980 by The New York Times Company; reprinted by permission), November 9, 1980, pp. 11, 32-3.*

FREDERICK CREWS

There can be no mistaking the fact that the study of meaning has now been vigorously contested. Some theorists hold that such study is always marred by a simplistic equation of meaning with the mental states of authors before or during the act of composition. A preoccupation with meaning, they say, leads to an undervaluing of conventional elements that are crucial to the way literature is perceived. But that cogent point is in itself no menace to academic business as usual. The real challenge comes from theorists—let me call them *indeterminists*—who argue that meaning is conferred not by authors but by readers, and that a work's meaning is therefore constantly subject to change. If that position is accepted, meaning ceases to be a stable object of inquiry and one interpretation is as lacking in persuasiveness as any other. The inevitable corollary is that debates among critics are entirely pointless. Such is the conclusion urged by the most influential of contemporary schools, Jacques Derrida's "deconstructionists," who claim that the "evidence" marshaled for any given interpretation is simply an artifact of that interpretation. If the deconstructionists are right, the greater part of our criticism has consisted of exercises in self-delusion. (p. 65)

[Hartman's] *Saving the Text: Literature/Derrida/Philosophy* strikingly exemplifies the frothiness of "theory" in the Derridean mode. But the earlier one, *Criticism in the Wilderness: The Study of Literature Today,* is even more telling, for as a highly defensive reply to opponents of "the hermeneutical Mafia," it places on view all the hostilities and confusions that go to make up the full-blown indeterminist spirit. These books, moreover, invite study because their author . . . has long been recognized as a preeminent American critic. His own progress, which I will not pause to recount, from historically informed interpretation to vapid attitudinizing could stand for the fate of much "advanced" academic discourse over the past two decades.

Hartman is quite aware of belonging to a movement of resistance to a continued concern for meaning. He even gives the movement a name, *revisionism,* which points to its essentially oppositional purpose. In championing the revisionists, he has in mind chiefly himself and his Yale colleagues Paul de Man, J. Hillis Miller, Harold Bloom, and Jacques Derrida. . . . But lest he be thought parochial, Hartman admits as tentative members such further enemies of "objective" reading as Stanley Fish . . . , Fredric Jameson . . . , Hans-Georg Gadamer, H. R. Jauss, Wolfgang Iser, and Norman Holland. If he is only lukewarmly supportive of this secondary group, it is not because he specifically disputes their ideas, but because he fears they have not altogether forsworn the quest to discover what literary works are about. Through precept and example Hartman urges us not to "methodize indeterminacy" by merely shifting the source of meaning from authors to readers. As he says in an untypically straightforward sentence, "contemporary criticism aims at a hermeneutics of indeterminacy." . . .

[Hartman] strives unabashedly to keep conclusions at bay. The critics he admires are those whose language is "curiously unprogressive or exitless." Their work "reveals contradictions and equivocations, and so makes fiction interpretable by making it less readable. The fluency of the reader is affected by a kind of stutter: the critic's response becomes deliberately hesitant." And the prince of stutterers is . . . Derrida, whose "exhibitionistic" and "interminable"—these are terms of forgiving fondness—treatise called *Glas* supplies us not with anything so vulgar as ideas, but with "a chain of secondary elaborations stretching to infinity."

Hartman himself is never more at home than when recapitulating the "sense of débris" that pervades *Glas* or in trying his own hand at the recommended form of verbal doodling:

> That the word "knot" may echo in the mind
> as "not" is one of those small changes that
> analyst or exegete are [*sic*] trained to hear.
> "When thou hast done, thou hast not done."
> There are so many knots: Donnean, Penelopean, Lacanian, Borromean, Derridean. . . .

(p. 69)

Here is a self-congratulatory hermeticism whose purpose seems to lie somewhere between the dropping of names, the displaying of tidbits of esoterica, and the muddling of agency. In this ghostly prose, sounds echo, similarities appear, a text is almost signalling its intention, the Lacanian primal process hums along, and a series of slippery signifiers establishes itself—as if neither Hartman nor Derrida had anything to do with these stage effects.

Given Hartman's aspirations toward inconclusiveness, it may seem anomalous that in *Saving the Text* he also puts forward a general theory of literature. But there is little danger of his being too easily understood. At times he appears to be proposing that literature originates in "a primal word-wound" which, conveniently for the theorist, has undergone such transformation that its traces are no longer available for study. Elsewhere he hints that literary form "saves the text" from the maddening openness, the impossibility of closure, that Derrida ascribes to language. But then again, the main idea of his book, "inspired," as he confides, "by French reflections," may be that "literature is the elaboration of a specular name"—whatever *that* means. It would be tacky to ask for specifics from a writer who disarmingly announces, "I cannot find it in myself to worry the question of the relation of empirical evidence to theory. . . ." According to revisionist etiquette, theory "should not impose or lacerate but *allow in others—in the world itself—an unconstrained response*" (emphasis added). One must cultivate an exquisite vagueness if such a response is to be achieved. . . .

In *Criticism in the Wilderness* [Hartman] sets out to repeal "[t]he automatic valuing of works of art over works of commentary," to lift criticism from its "second-class status in the world of letters." As opposed to Matthew Arnold, who called the epochs of Aeschylus and Shakespeare "the promised land, toward which criticism can only beckon," Hartman suggests that perhaps "we are forerunners to ourselves"—that is, that criticism is already our outstanding literary genre.

In order to match "the primacy of art," Hartman believes, critics must marshal a "near-daemonic" force, an extravagance or "brilliance" which "liberates the critical activity from its positive or reviewing function." The criticism he admires is therefore that which deserves to be called "digressive," "outrageous," "freakish," even "ridiculous," for that way lies the Sublime. . . . If readers fail to appreciate the steely courage of critics who dare to navigate this void, it must be because they find "a possible loss of boundaries" to be just "too threatening." Even boredom, it seems, is a form of defensive homage to the extremity of revisionist heroics.

What readers may think, however, is of less moment to Hartman than what critics require for themselves. On that subject he is cryptic but usefully suggestive. . . .

Our problem today, Hartman opines, lies with those who would "separate out, *bureaucratically*, the functions of critic and artist" (emphasis added). The idea of acquiring definite knowledge of literature conjures to his mind the specter of "technocratic, predictive, or authoritarian formulas," of a "monumental, totalizing system," even of "a managerial society full of technicians, operators, language therapists, a department of discourse control and emendation." . . . [Hartman implies that] elite critics must become Luddites in the factories of meaning production. By staunchly refusing to reach conclusions about literature, they will help to preserve "inwardness" from the ravages of middle-class rationality and homogeneity. (p. 70)

Yet revisionists with power can at least decline to be "hired grammarians" for those semi-literates who have been, as Hartman puts it none too delicately, "dislocated into institutes of Higher Education." And they can keep 'em guessing about the mysteries of criticism. If "[t]he 'service function' imposed on English departments . . . contributes to dividing literary studies into the grind of 'communication' or 'rhetoric' courses as against high-stepping intellectual entertainment"—why, Hartman simply opts for the entertainment.

Despite its arrogance, however, *Criticism in the Wilderness* is a distinctly melancholy collection of statements. It abounds in references to "resentful and lonely" critics whose colleagues misunderstand them and who are paid too little for undergoing "a routine that can seriously hamper self-development." Although Hartman repeatedly disparages what he elsewhere calls "academic-rotarian" professors who crave definite ideas, he complains bitterly against critics who "carp at critics" and who "bite or bark at their own kind." And his concluding proposal that students of law and medicine be required to study literary interpretation, presumably along the lines of the "hermeneutic highjinks" that he favors, is as wistful as it is devoid of a rationale.

Thus Hartman's campaign against isolation does not as yet appear to be a notable success. Nor could it be, given his renunciation of rationally based choice between competing theories, hypotheses, and interpretations. The vision of a community of investigators, whether within or between disciplines, is a phantom unless the parties involved acknowledge grounds of evidential appeal. And the fact that Hartman hasn't quite decided what he wants—is it fraternity, recognition, or mere exemption from the "service" that underlings will still be required to perform?—only renders his situation more pathetic. His tentative brief for boldness, his decorous critique of decorum, his politics of educational disdain—what are they, if not the marks of a mandarinism whose intellectual pretexts have dropped away? . . .

[By] now it should be clear that despite the variety of its moods, indeterminism as a movement bears implications that are both irrationalist and undemocratic. To be sure, not every indeterminist matches Hartman's sarcasm in speaking of the deteriorating "varnish" and "veneer" of "this ideal of a freemasonry or grand democratic concourse of polyphonic yet pacific persons." But in disparaging the evidential grounds on which scholars and critics can address one another's ideas, indeterminists create a vacuum that can only be filled by cliquish power. A whole department or university operating without regard for independent rules of judgment would be barbaric in principle if not in outward demeanor.

I do not mean to suggest, however, that indeterminists amount to some sinister public force. . . . On the contrary, the indeterminists are for the most part mild-mannered professors who are trying to fend off discouraging thoughts about the waning importance of criticism. They have much in common with those colleagues who greet their movement not with eagerness to test its cogency, but with bland, incomprehending gratitude that *something* is still happening within a comatose field. For on one side and the other—that of "philosophical" affectation and that of routine exegesis—assumptions remain largely unexamined. If shopworn ideas about nothingness and meaninglessness are still allowed to pass for breakthroughs in theory, the fault may lie less in our superstars than in ourselves. (p. 71)

> *Frederick Crews, "Criticism without Constraint,"*
> in Commentary *(reprinted by permission; all rights reserved), Vol. 73, No. 1, January, 1982, pp. 65-71.*

BERNARD BERGONZI

Hartman's *Saving the Text* shows him at one and the same time engaging with Derrida, succumbing to him, imitating him and resisting him. His writing is determinedly playful, recalling Helen Gardner's sharp comment about playfulness being a synonym for critical activity; witness his extreme verbal self-consciousness, his frequent puns and his jokey chapter headings: "Monsieur Texte", "Epiphony in Echoland", "How to Reap a Page", "Psychoanalysis: The French Connection", "Words and Wounds." . . .

Hartman's book presents a multiple perspective of texts: there is extended comment on Derrida's book *Glas* (= "knell", and also, punningly, *glace* = "ice or mirror") which is itself a parallel collage, with Derrida's commentary, of texts by Hegel and Genet, enacting the juxtaposition of philosophy and literature briefly indicated in Hartman's subtitle. For someone who does not believe in the self or in presence Derrida is a central enough presence in this book, as in many others; perhaps, thinking of him as a bare name and no essential thing, and bearing in mind his own taste for distancing quotation marks, one should present him as "Derrida." His historical masters are Mallarmé and Nietzsche; thus do the tormented culture heroes of one *fin de siècle* return to haunt the next.

In more than one sense Hartman "goes along with" Derrida, but his book hints at an underground yearning for voice and presence, which surfaces in the final chapter, "Words and Wounds." *Saving the Text* contains elements of both criticism and philosophy but it exemplifies the deconstructionist tendency for such kinds of writing to turn into modes of fiction. Read as a work of fiction it is dense and cloyingly arch. In addition to the word-play there is a crooning, caressing quality in Hartman's prose, the tone of a man talking quietly and earnestly to himself rather than trying to communicate to others; an example, perhaps, of the loneliness of the American academic pontiff. (p. 62)

> *Bernard Bergonzi, "A Strange Disturbing World: The Conflicts in Criticism,"* in Encounter *(© 1982 by Encounter Ltd.), Vols. LVIII & LIX, Nos. 6 & 1, June-July, 1982, pp. 58, 60-7.*

John (Clendennin Burne) Hawkes (Jr.)

1925-

American novelist, short story writer, dramatist, poet, critic, and editor.

Hawkes is an extraordinary stylist whose primary interest is the psychic and imaginative processes of human beings. His work is difficult and demanding, full of scenes intended to startle and even repel the reader. By "violating" his audience's sense of normalcy and propriety, Hawkes hopes to jar it into new levels of awareness of the beautiful and dangerous capabilities of the human imagination. Hawkes himself describes his fiction as travels through the landscape of the psyche. He emphasizes its brutal and absurdly comic aspects in order, conversely, to understand what it means to feel compassion.

With the publication of *The Cannibal* (1950) and *The Beetle Leg* (1951) Hawkes gained a reputation as an eccentric, avant-garde novelist and a radically innovative stylist. Set in desolate waste lands and full of sadistic violence, these two novels depict the human attempt to impose order on chaotic reality with such things as art, religion, and love. These forces prove powerless, however, against the violence that emerges as the prevailing reality in these novels. Hawkes's theme of the beauty and horror of the human imagination is considered most developed in *The Lime Twig* (1961). Compared to the earlier works, this novel has a more conventional structure, but the prose is still considered experimental even though it is less fragmented and surreal. *Second Skin* (1964) marks Hawkes's more extensive use of artist-heroes and their attempts to enforce their vision upon the world.

Hawkes's "comic triad" of the early 1970s—*The Blood Oranges, Death, Sleep, & the Traveler*, and *Travesty*—helped solidify critical opinion of him as one of the most important novelists of the twentieth century. The protagonists of the triad, in their attempts to simultaneously experience and control reality, reflect the human desire to find order and harmony in the world. The novels are farcical in their portrayal of ambitions fulfilled or denied, yet poignant in their observations of how sexuality defies the control of individuals. *Travesty* has won special attention for its satire on the human need to organize and explain. Hawkes's recent works, *The Passion Artist* (1979) and *Virginie: Her Two Lives* (1982), further his examination of the psychic process.

(See also *CLC*, Vols. 1, 2, 3, 4, 7, 9, 14, 15; *Contemporary Authors*, Vols. 1-4, rev. ed.; *Contemporary Authors New Revision Series*, Vol. 2; *Dictionary of Literary Biography*, Vol. 2; and *Dictionary of Literary Biography Yearbook: 1980*.)

ALBERT J. GUERARD

[*Guerard, often considered the most knowledgeable critic on Hawkes, has had a lengthy literary and social relationship with Hawkes. The two met at Harvard in the late 1940s when Hawkes was enrolled in Guerard's writing class.*]

Without question Hawkes has been, like Faulkner, one of the great liberating maieutic influences on contemporary literature,

Photograph by John Forasté; courtesy of John Hawkes

in the astringent bite of his psychology and the audacity of his invention. But I would like to make a case for the primacy of poetry, of language—language in the largest sense to include intricate structure and what Hawkes calls "chordal insistences", but also language as simply rhythm and words, words from which the strangeness has not been rubbed away.

One of the obvious things any academic survey might undertake would be to compare the themes of wartime violence and corruption and degradation, of *The Cannibal* and *The Goose on the Grave* and *Second Skin*, with the intricate ballet—the sinuous repetitive saraband of sexual experiment—in *The Blood Oranges, Death, Sleep & the Traveler, Travesty*. Those who feel betrayed, or who feel Hawkes has betrayed his origins, as they look from *The Cannibal* to *Travesty;* those who want a writer to be true always to his first vision and first modes of distortion, would do well to consider how often major writers have refused to settle down. There are writers who, like Faulkner and Joyce, begin fairly conventionally and move toward more and more audacious, even perverse experiment. But there is also Melville, writing for a time *in nomine diaboli*, and ending in classical if embittered serenity.

I know, however, of no such radical innovator as Hawkes in his twenties (very nearly a generation ahead of his time), possessed of an absolutely original style and dynamic vision, becoming such a suave master of the traditional resources of the novelistic art. (pp. 2-3)

In 1948 I wrote, in my introduction to *The Cannibal,* that it was less surrealist than *Charivari,* and that I suspected Hawkes would move still further toward realism; and that how far Hawkes would go as a writer "must obviously depend on how far he consents to impose some page-by-page and chapter-by-chapter consecutive understanding on his astonishing creative energy; on how richly he exploits his ability to achieve truth through distortion; on how well he continues to uncover and use childhood images and fears." In my 1962 addendum I could remark that the "predicted movement toward realism has occurred, but chiefly in the sense that the later novels are much more orderly and even in pace, and distinctly less difficult to read." Yet I could also say that Hawkes's position was an unusual one: "that of the *avant-garde* writer who has imitated no one and who has made no personal gestures of defiance". He could move "toward realism"—in pace, in the timing of scenes, in the subtle manipulation of the reader, in overall control, in language—without becoming banal. And if he ultimately came to parody other writers—Ford Madox Ford in *The Blood Oranges,* Camus in *Travesty*—it was with a Nabokovian joy in aesthetic play. *Travesty,* for all its seriousness, is in the highest sense a playful book. It is well to remember how some of the greatest writers, indeed some of the most ponderous, have ultimately allowed themselves comedy, even farce. . . . (pp. 3-4)

I would like to stress not the movement toward *realism,* which is obvious, but rather the movement toward a more conscious and more suave psychology and art. Psychology *and* art. The movement is from a Freudian wit, deeply dependent on unconscious understanding as well as conscious; from extremely powerful *condensation,* from multiple instances of *overdetermination,* to fully conscious, sophisticated, suave, even delicate manipulation of sexual materials. But this movement in psychology is accompanied by an increasingly sinuous and polished rhetoric, by finely controlled periodic rhythms, by language used in a very precise denotative as well as connotative sense. The Hawkes of *The Cannibal* was by far the most interesting eccentric stylist of his time; the Hawkes of *Travesty* (no less subversive, it may be, deep down) is one of the purest masters of classical English (or even classical French) prose.

A few familiar moments of horror will illustrate the movement toward more conscious (and more serenely comic) psychological content, with sexual disturbance even serving as rhetorical embellishment, though not only rhetorical embellishment. . . . I find several such [moments of horror] in only eight lines of *The Cannibal:* the fingers of a dead defender that spatter a wall; the flesh hanging from hooks in a butcher shop, "the plucked skin and crawling veins"; the legs and head "lopped" from the horse statue . . . all this under an "evil cloaked moon." Wire, in these eight lines, catches the knee of Jutta's child, who in the guise of a fox will presently be dismembered, beginning with the fox's brush cut in half. That appalling surgical operation, which is closely paralleled by the skinning of a white rabbit in *The Painted Bird,* involves totally conscious displacement. Between the early evocation of fingers spattering a wall and the later one of the unfortunate child/fox are two other powerful evocations of castration fear, reflecting, it may be, different degrees of authorial consciousness. The dead Merchant wedged between two beams may evoke an additional sexual anxiety, with the cocoon in the mouth anticipating the bat in the mouth of *Second Skin.* . . . (pp. 4-5)

Much of *The Cannibal* operates through obscure, half-censored suggestion. . . . The power of these scenes lies in their evocation of anxieties suggested but not defined; of displacements felt but not immediately seen.

No doubt someone somewhere is presently engaged in writing an article on "Orality in Hawkes". The iconography of fellatio, more and more explicit as we move through the novels, might provide him material for a chapter. Thus Luke treating the child bitten by a snake, in *The Beetle Leg,* sucking the wounds, a comic yet sinister evasion. . . . The displacements in *The Lime Twig* are invariably powerful: Thick's rubber truncheon and the beating of Margaret, more sinister than explicit rape, or Sybilline and her stocking made into a ball, and "thrust against the depths of his loin . . ." The prolonged injection administered to Sparrow by Larry suggests a generalized homosexual violation, with fellatio perhaps implicit as the needle is withdrawn, "a tiny heart of blood on the tip of it". The injection scene, some five hundred words of very precise writing, arouses the fears any person experiences, facing the needle; but surely a good deal more. The tattooing of *Second Skin* is comparably detailed, but with the needle now involving the attacker's tongue. Skipper's scream in turn, "clamped" between his teeth, is "a strenuous black bat struggling, wrestling in my bloated mouth". The tattooer's punctures lead to uncensored recollection of his homosexual violation at the time of the mutiny. . . . The scene, already pleasingly complex, is further overdetermined when the tattoo is revealed: the name of the dead Fernandez with whom, on that Dickensian honeymoon, Skipper hoped to share his daughter. Even did share her, given that minute inspection of her purse.

With the trilogy of sex [*The Blood Oranges, Death, Sleep & the Traveler,* and *Travesty*] (though I hope literary historians will find a better phrase), these genial materials are frankly brought to an often comic surface, wholly displaced. . . . The writing—throughout the trilogy—is suave, controlled, fully conscious; and in *Travesty* relatively chaste, though the conceptions are complex enough, with the narrator sharing both wife and daughter with his shadowy double Henri. There are, however, as in a loving recognition of the iconography, comparable to Chagall's introduction of a donkey's head, the prolonged perversities of the carrot game at *Chez Lulu*'s, the blindfolded girls fishing "desperately for the fat carrots with their glistening tongues". It "was Chantal, of course, who finally understood the game," while her father watched in fascination.

The exquisite rhythms and formal control of *Travesty* are those of true classical art; and the penis can now be, altogether openly, a "great bird". To say classical is of course to evoke, for certain minds, the Oedipus complex, and the destiny onto which Oedipus blindly stumbled. Nowhere in literature is the triangle more deliberately evoked than in a late scene in *Travesty,* but the story told from the threatened father's vantage. . . . (pp. 5-7)

Obviously John Hawkes's progress toward a conscious classical art is not confined to oral pleasures or Oedipal anguish. Leslie Fiedler's view is that Hawkes's art has become more private [see *CLC,* Vol. 3]. My own is that Hawkes has, without sacrificing his unmistakable personal vision and perverse tonality, achieved a very much larger view of human difficulties: a classical view. Of my Old English studies nearly a half-century ago I retain only one line that recurs to me as I shave—*Grendel gongan, goddes yre baer,* and one of the very beautiful metaphors in English literature of the brevity of life—Bede's bird that flies into the mead-hall and out again. But no more beautiful than the sudden deepening of the car's journey in *Travesty,* and our recognition that it too can be read in the largest terms of our human journey. . . . *Travesty* is a masterpiece of wholly conscious and controlled, truly classical art. (pp. 7-8)

Albert J. Guerard, "John Hawkes: A Longish View," in A John Hawkes Symposium: Design and Debris, edited by Anthony C. Santore and Michael Pocalyko (originally a symposium at Muhlenberg College on April 9 & 10, 1976; copyright © 1977 by New Directions Publishing Corporation; reprinted by permission of New Directions Publishing Corporation), New Directions, 1977, pp. 1-13.

HELEN S. GARSON

In *Pornography and the Law,* a book written by two psychologists [Eberhard and Phyllis Kronhausen], eleven "major criteria" for obscene books are listed. Of the eleven, eight are applicable to the work of Hawkes, especially to his plays and to the novels *The Lime Twig, Second Skin*, and *Blood Oranges*. Those eight ingredients are: seduction; defloration; incest; the permissive-seduction parent figure; supersexed males; nymphomaniac figures; homosexuality; and flagellation. . . . But although Hawkes does meet those criteria and frequently another requirement that a book is aphrodisiacal which keeps "before the reader's mind a succession of erotic scenes," he does not attain what are considered all the structural requirements of pornography. For example, the "true" pornographer, if he uses background scenery, treats it erotically. Hawkes' scenic descriptions, though sometimes highly suggestive or filled with sexual symbolism, are often also non-erotic.

The plot of a Hawkes play or novel may be simple or complex but almost always sexuality in multiple forms is focal. Plotting in his work is so unlike that of most writers that there are few ways to get a handle on the material. (p. 152)

If motivation for behavior is also lacking, there is yet one instance of the similarity to pornography where character depiction is extremely limited. Once again Hawkes' work falls on both sides of the line. Although *Second Skin* and *Blood Oranges* have at least one character, the narrator, who is shown in depth, this is not true of *The Lime Twig,* in which all the characters possess a flatness, a stereotypical quality that is characteristic of the pornographic film or novel.

The narrator and major character of *Blood Oranges* calls himself a "sex singer"; his very existence depends on the sexual act, which is intended to obliterate time, to negate dissolution and death. His sexual exploits rival those of any supersexed male of pornography. However, he is not singular in his pursuit and desire. His wife has sexual cravings at least equal to his own. She is the nymphomaniac par excellence. She must have him—and others, just as he must have her and others. Any man or woman in their seasonless, timeless land of Illyria may be their prey. The sexual act is the charm against death. His world, then, seen through the narrator's lens, is a succession of voluptuous scenes and actions; the scenery is lush, ripe, warm, flowing, in a word, erotic; birds, animals, snakes, flowers, and fruit are an integral part of this country of desire. But pain, mutilation, and brutality also of sexual nature invade Illyria and bring death with them.

The linkage of sex and death is as old as primitive literature. Hawkes uses this liaison far more savagely in *Second Skin* and *The Lime Twig.*

From first page to last in *Second Skin,* sex and death are central. The narrator of this novel is a man who has lived his life with suicides, his father's, his wife's, his daughter's. He has also lived in a sex immersed world (though he, himself is somewhat asexual), where sex is degenerate, vicious, and omnivorous. (pp. 152-53)

A major event in the novel is one in which the narrator himself is tatooed, a tableau which appears to be lifted from a pornographic film. . . . The significance of the scene is that it serves as a metaphor for all that has happened to and yet awaits the narrator: pain, loss, suffering in dark and sordid surroundings where sexuality is absolutely evil. . . . Where can such a victim finish out his later years but on a "sun-dipped wandering island in a vast baby-blue coral sea," a place where he is the artificial inseminator of cows. On the strange, seasonless island, bereft by death of everything except one friend and a shared illiterate island mistress, he finds the ultimate sexual fantasy come to life. . . . Yet the knowledge of death is always with him, even in his select paradise. (p. 153)

In *The Lime Twig,* the most brutal of all Hawkes' work, gothicism, decadence, and pornographic elements are brought together in a terrifying vision of death and nothingness.

The Lime Twig is filled with symbols of darkest desire: brute sexual power is represented by the animal—horses, "the flesh of all violent dreams," and the mechanical by cars, steel guns, and steel vests. Secret male fantasies are realized in orgies of lust and beastiality. A beautiful insatiable temptress destroys the human quality and turns men into swine. All women suddenly become available as dreams of passion are gratified. (pp. 153-54)

People are abducted, are mutilated, abandoned, and forgotten; a throat is cut; a man is kicked to death by a horse; others die on the track. Bees sting sparrows to death. Houses are ransacked—all traces of the occupants are removed. Mortuary bells sound, as well they might. They toll for all of us. . . .

To label John Hawkes as a pornographic writer would be as naive as it was to so classify D. H. Lawrence and James Joyce. Yet both Lawrence and Joyce had far fewer elements of pornography in their work; furthermore they drew characters who searched for meaning, and existences that had creeds. But writers do utilize pornography as a means of revealing their perceptions of life. . . . John Hawkes uses the elements of pornography to show us a world bereft of light. Like a progenitor of black humor he perceives twentieth century life to be absurd, and in its absurdity obscene. By definition, that which is obscene is pornographic. (p. 154)

Helen S. Garson, "John Hawkes and the Elements of Pornography," in Journal of Popular Culture (copyright © 1976 by Ray B. Browne), Vol. X, No. 1, Summer, 1976, pp. 150-55.

DONALD J. GREINER

John Hawkes occupies a peculiar place in contemporary American fiction. He is one of the few truly gifted writers in the so-called black humor movement which has flourished since 1950, but he lacks the renown enjoyed by less talented authors. In the years since World War II innovative American fiction has turned from the documentation of social forms and the use of realistic technique to an evocation of nightmare and fear. The feeling of disruption left from the war, the specter of atomic catastrophe so vividly objectified at Hiroshima, the tensions of the cold war, and the spread of random violence in everyday life have all contributed to the conviction that chaos rather than order dominates day to day living.

The most exciting of today's novelists reflect this sense of the fractured life in their fiction, but, significantly, the prevailing tone in most of their work is not the gloomy pessimism which might be expected but a shocking sense of humor. Shocking because it encourages laughter at events which are, more often than not, horribly violent, the modern comic novel often meets the general feeling of doom with humor. We need only recall Kurt Vonnegut's Bokonon thumbing his nose at You Know Who while the world around him solidifies into ice (*Cat's Cradle*) or Joseph Heller's Yossarian walking naked around the air base because Snowden's guts spilled on his uniform (*Catch-22*) to understand how a different kind of humor, often grotesque and violent, comments on the world's absurdities.

Some readers may protest the use of the term "black humor," claiming that it is either a cliché or a catch-all phrase which attempts to accommodate too many diverse literary works. The sheer terror which accompanies Hawkes' comic episodes, for example, seems unrelated to the humanity of Vonnegut's comedy or the antics of J. P. Donleavy's Ginger Man. For this reason a variety of descriptive terms has been proposed. Robert Scholes calls some of these novelists "fabulators." Richard Poirier, in *A World Elsewhere,* speaks of "comic-apocalyptic writers," while Conrad Knickerbocker suggests "humor with a mortal sting." Perhaps we should settle for Richard Kostelanetz's more conventional phrase, "American absurd novel." It makes little difference what we call this recent movement in American fiction—I am content with "the modern American comic novel." The point, of course, is not the relative blackness of the comedy, but rather the general vision which most of these authors share. (pp. xi-xii)

Taken together, the novels of Hawkes, Vonnegut, Heller, John Barth, Donleavy, Friedman, Thomas Pynchon, Ken Kesey, James Purdy, and others suggest a type of fiction so refreshingly different from the conventional novel that one suspects the prophets of the novel's death to be wrong. What these authors do have in common is a vision of their world as chaotic and fractured. How can one affirm order in a world which is fragmented—and violently so? But though the disoriented quality of modern life prevents the black humorist from celebrating order, it does not propel him to nihilism. The fact that *Catch-22, Giles Goat-Boy,* and *Second Skin* have been written, published, and read suggests the authors' hope for meaningful communication at the very least. (p. xiii)

[In] many modern fictions, form dominates content; technique is more important than social or moral commentary. And when the demands of structure are considered superior to the matters to be expressed, the pattern of fiction assumes primary significance. Hawkes has this problem in mind when he declares plot, character, setting, and theme to be the novel's enemies. The subordination of these traditional features encourages the author's concern with pattern and structure. If my remarks have merit, then a lot of us are going to have to change our customary criteria for judging a novel: by the validity of the moral vision it communicates, or by the proximity to felt life it reveals. The modern American comic novelist is not sure that a verifiable moral vision exists, or that life can be ordered long enough to approximate it. At the risk of oversimplification, I suggest that these authors refuse to verify a moral code because verification would allude to order and sanity in a world which they see as fractured and absurd. Thus these writers underplay the tradi-

tional interests of the novelist. Their common concern is not with morality or reality but with technique.

No one would argue that the black humorist is unusual because he laughs at man's absurdity. Many writers of the past have couched their awareness of their time's chaos in shocking, grotesque images. In the English tradition alone one need think only of Pope, Swift, and Sterne. The ancestor of the modern American comic novel is satire. . . . Hawkes and his contemporaries show an irreverence, ranging from playfulness to the most sardonic criticism, toward traditionally venerated norms like science, religion, and patriotism. But unlike the traditional satirist—and the distinction is crucial—most black humorists reject the satirist's faith in the ability of satirical laughter to reform man's follies. Even the most elaborate definition of satire must emphasize the author's use of laughter not so much to tear down as to encourage a rebuilding. . . . The traditional satirist and the contemporary comic novelist meet primarily in their shared confidence in the value of laughter, but each puts laughter to work differently. For the modern humorist, the ridiculous joke called life must be laughed at if sanity is to be maintained. Most of these novelists show a love of humanity instead of the scorn often found in standard satire.

Black humor is not a conscious rejection of satire as much as a matter of simply not writing it. If modern comic fiction has a literary target, it is realism. Too many readers continue to associate fiction with realism—we have all heard the exclamation that a particular novel was enjoyed because it was "so real." In realism, representation of life is more important than art. But in black humor, with its emphasis on technique, the use of words to explore and express the imagination outstrips the description of things. . . . To appreciate what Hawkes is doing with fiction, we must slough off our traditional notions of what makes a novel. Popular opinion to the contrary, realism is not the sole way of looking at life truthfully. It is no more than another literary device, an outdated one at that. Given the fragmentation of the twentieth century, realistic depiction of it does us little good. We already know that things are bad. Life cannot be made to seem reasonable if it is ridiculous. The more important question posed by a black humorist is how to live with one's self and with others in a fractured world. Laughter may not save the world, but it can help us live our lives. . . . When reading Hawkes it must be remembered that his characters do not discover absurdity or chaos or meaninglessness. Rather, these qualities are the given factors. His novels *begin* with the probability that Michael Banks, or Margaret, or Skipper will meet defeat; whereas traditional fiction usually details the process of the protagonist discovering the possibility of defeat and death. Finding out that life is cruel is often the crucial experience for the characters in conventional novels—think of *What Maisie Knew,* say, or *A Farewell to Arms*—but Skipper or Yossarian or the Ginger Man expects cruelty. Their problem is not how to avoid defeat but how to live with its probability.

John Hawkes is very much a part of this trend in recent American fiction, but when placed beside his colleagues, he is undoubtedly the least known. If it were not for the fact that Hawkes' fiction is of such high merit, his lack of readers would not be deplorable. But because Hawkes is one of the two or three most talented of all American writers who have matured since 1950, his obscure reputation is a cause for concern. Incredibly, readers who pride themselves on a knowledgeable awareness of recent trends in fiction either dismiss his work as too difficult or ignore his comic vision to stress his truly grotesque horrors. In most cases, however, he remains unknown and unread. (pp. xiii-xvi)

When he is read at all, his fiction excites both high praise and strongly worded negative criticism in nearly equal amounts. . . . Yet it seems to me that many of the adverse evaluations and misreadings result from both ignorance about Hawkes' aims and misunderstanding of his often militant experimentation with humor, narrative voice, and structure. . . . Hawkes considers himself foremost a comic novelist, but evaluations of his fiction typically concentrate upon the nightmarish events, failing to discuss how the consistent use of humor affects the terror. . . . I do hope that what I have to say will encourage more serious readers to pick up his novels. A writer of Hawkes' genius deserves a wider hearing. (pp. xviii-xix)

> *Donald J. Greiner, in a preface to his* Comic Terror: The Novels of John Hawkes *(copyright 1978 © by Memphis State University Press), revised edition, Memphis State University Press, 1978, pp. xi-xix.**

PAUL ROSENZWEIG

With the publication of *The Passion Artist* (1979) John Hawkes completed a decade of writing that marked a clear, if subtle, change of direction in his fiction. Most apparent and controversial was the emergence of a highly explicit and, in a manner, titillating sexual content, dominating all four novels written by him in the seventies [*The Blood Oranges* (1971); *Death, Sleep, & the Traveler* (1974); *Travesty* (1976); and *The Passion Artist*]. Combined with the gothic strain that has characterized his writing from the beginning—his fascination with violence and cruelty and death—both the explicitness and the untraditional nature of the sexual concerns have tended to overshadow the less striking but as essential evolution in his use of form and pattern. Hawkes's structures seem to have become more severely controlled in these four novels, his style more classical, his manipulation of his material far more noticeably self-conscious. His characters emerge more sharply from the novels, in large part because they are more simply and essentially patterned. The fragmented images and events of his earlier novels have been consolidated within a more traditional plot sequence, while at the same time the multiple points of view of the earlier narratives have been incorporated into an all-encompassing single point of view. Such an inclusive perspective more immediately invites comparison with the artistic vision of the author himself, particularly when it takes the form of first-person narration, as is the case with the first three novels.

In general, Hawkes's writing seems to incorporate a general awareness of itself as esthetic pattern, a tendency which may in part explain Hawkes's admiration for the more explicitly self-referential fictions of John Barth, with which Hawkes's fiction of this period bears an affinity not at first apparent. . . . All the major male characters in the four novels are in some manner artists, either by vocation or avocation; they are poets, photographers, artisans, musicians, or collectors of erotica. More important, however, than the ubiquity of such concrete artistic pursuits is their link with a more pervasive obsession with pattern and order which Hawkes shows to lie at the heart of man's psychology in general. The novels of this period seem to demonstrate an awareness of a basic correlation between both the subject and form of man's various patterned versions of reality and his psychology.

In his treatment of this relationship, Hawkes seems to have come to terms with his own preoccupation with the formal aspect of his writing, with pattern and structure, and at his best in so doing he has achieved a unified vision, uniting form and substance in a manner he had not formerly achieved. Where in his earlier novels, the esthetic logic that dictated the portrayal of his dark vision of violence and death in highly labored, even tortured, structures remained unclear, at times seeming forced or arbitrary and all too often inaccessible, in his latest works Hawkes seems to have realized the inner logic that dictated such a union. The psychology of esthetics—indeed, the basis of human motivation in general—is portrayed in these four novels as primarily a psychology of control, formed in reaction to the passivity and impotence which is forced upon man by the prevailing reality of chaos and dissolution. The central concerns of Hawkes in these four novels, sexuality and death, are depicted as the primary forces causing such chaos: man's confusion, violence, and ultimate destruction. (pp. 69-70)

While Hawkes seems increasingly fascinated with this realm of artifice, it is a measure of his realism that his characters' means of control are shown to be illusory, reality proving less malleable in actuality than it seems when transformed by the imagination. In all four novels, sexuality and death prevail as the ultimate realities, reasserting their independence by refusing to pattern themselves in accord with the fiction of harmony by which each of Hawkes's male characters attempts to palliate the alien environment.

The exploration of this relationship between manifest esthetic vision and the underlying psychology which helps produce it is most completely and complexly treated in the first three novels Hawkes published in the seventies, comprising a triadic unit of their own. It is not by accident that they, particularly *The Blood Oranges* and *Travesty,* most perfectly balance form and substance, employing their own structure and pattern to reflect in a crucial manner the intricacies of the relationship between esthetics and psychology. Narrated by their central characters, all three novels are carefully crafted monologues whose form, no less than substance, is inseparable from the highly problematic personalities of their fictional creators in a manner reminiscent of Nabokov in such a novel as *Pale Fire.* Hawkes's verbal artistry, like Nabokov's, at first seems only a reflection of the author's own penchant for pattern, an objective means of shaping the novel's content, but gradually such pattern-making is implicated as well as a product of the subjective needs of a highly distraught narrator, using esthetics to shape the narrative toward his own subjective ends. However, while for Nabokov the psychological aspect is primarily a means to further artifice, Hawkes seems equally interested in exploring the psychological depths of the mind in its own right. By being thus internalized by the first-person narrative form, the relationship between each novel's manifest subject matter of violence, sex, and death (inchoate and anarchic) and its highly stylized structures (inherently orderly) is made an appropriate exemplification of the novel's central theme, the fullest and most immediate reflection of the general rage for order, characteristic of all the major male figures in the triad as well.

The episodic structure of all three novels, in which the temporal flow of the traditional narrative is forced into nonchronological tableaux by the exigencies of the narrator's mind, reflects the more general tendency of Hawkes's estheticians to restructure the unwieldly and amorphous flow of time in order to deny the specter of such inevitabilities as aging, impotence, and death. This rewriting of events is also reflected in the double-time sequence of each novel: a static present interwoven with highly edited memories of the volatile past which has brought the narrator to his present impasse. Such editing, only one of the less explicit aspects of an attempt to control, is reflected most graphically in *The Blood Oranges* in the absence of any but the most fleeting mention of the narrator Cyril's past before coming to his idyllic Mediterranean retreat, in the refusal of Allert, the narrator of *Death, Sleep & the Traveler,* to describe, perhaps even to remember, the centrally symbolic act of murder which he has committed, around which the other events of the narrative cohere, and, in the most explicit editorial tyranny of Papa's monologue in *Travesty,* in which no other voice but his is allowed to be directly heard.

While the three monologues are manifestly presented as personal exemplars of universal truths, of theories and ideologies, they serve as well as justifications of the narrators' own lives and the sad predicament in which they all find themselves. Each narrator describes an intricate complex of events centering about his open marriage in which both he and his wife engage in various other sexual relationships which in each case lead to disaster, including the death of at least one participant and the isolation of the narrator himself from all the people for whom he professes to care most deeply—not merely his wife, but his mistresses and wife's lover, the latter a supposed friend of his as well. Despite the facade of disinterested inquiry and analysis and avowed "clarity" of vision, each narration is inescapably a subjective fiction which the narrator composes in order to temporarily stay or disperse the loneliness, guilt, and confusion to which he has succumbed. By means of these monologues, the narrators attempt both to justify events by giving them a clear and comforting meaning and at the same time exonerate themselves from any responsibility for them by seeing them as a product of an unfortunate congruence of impersonal forces beyond human control. . . . Yet all three narrators are motivated as fundamentally by both revenge and the pathetic attempt to control those persons and aspects of their lives over which they have lost all control.

At the same time, the visions of Hawkes's narrators can hardly be dismissed as merely products of aberrant minds, something Hawkes himself has made clear in various remarks about the triad in which he strongly suggests his own identification with both the narrators and their visions. Cyril's monologue with its inclusive criticism of the life-denying aspects of Christianity is, after all, at heart merely a highly personalized version of a traditional Dionysian perspective. Even Papa's more extreme vision, attempting to justify both murder and suicide through esthetic principles of cosmic dimensions, possesses an insightfulness and cogency which suggest it is only an exaggerated version of more traditional esthetic and existential approaches to life—to be taken on one level, therefore, at face value.

It is not primarily in Hawkes's ability to shock or stun us with man's fundamental and primitive sexuality and violence or in his ability to dazzle us with the artifice of his intricate kaleidoscope of patterns that his artistry of this period shines brightest and most profoundly; rather it is in this simultaneous expression of these two contradictory functions of esthetics as both clarifier and obfuscator. The fertility of his characters' imaginations functions simultaneously as the means by which the varied richness of reality can be adequately captured and, paradoxically, as the intricate maze by which the fundamentally unpleasant aspects of that reality can be artfully avoided. Hawkes's triumph in the works of this period is that his own ambivalence not only allows both interpretations (seeing his characters as both psychopaths and seers), but at some point

forces us to confront the contradictions and oversimplifications involved in either version by itself. Moreover, he makes us aware of the possibility that for all our elegant rhetoric, the truth may be merely something we stumble upon in our flight from it, while at the same time demonstrating that the inescapability of reality, of loneliness and death, of violence and sexuality, is what forces us to be such craven, half-blind purveyors of truth.

Despite its clear differences in plot and structure, *The Passion Artist* is also imbued with a sense of the fundamentally paradoxical nature of man's condition. The central metaphor of the novel, the prison, is used to suggest that each man and each woman is simultaneously both the oppressed and the oppressor, jailer and prisoner, in relationship both to others and to himself. (pp. 71-4)

While throughout Hawkes's corpus the primary manifestations of man's need to control are abstract, those conscious and unconscious patterns which man imaginatively imposes, from the first Hawkes has shown his interest in the link between such internal structures and the harshly imposed external ones by which the authoritarian personality imposes its fictions upon others. In his first novel, *The Cannibal* (1949), by recording events in postwar Germany through the narratorial perspective of the neo-Nazi Zizendorf, Hawkes suggests a parallel between Zizendorf's attempt to reimpose authoritarian rule on Germany and his imposition of an intricate yet ruthless verbal order on his narration. In that novel, too, the central feature of the surrealistic landscape is a prison of sorts, an insane asylum, appearing as well in each of the three novels of the triad. While this "political" side to fiction-making is relatively muted throughout the triad, it is increasingly evident in each of the three novels—Papa proving the most overtly and consistently tyrannical, and Cyril, the least physically intimidating, able to rely instead on the power of his demagogic oratory in order to rule. In *The Passion Artist,* however, this aspect of Hawkes's obsession with order and control reemerges fully. The woman's prison, like the insane asylum, connects those actual prisons which authoritarian regimes impose upon their dissidents and minorities with the internal prisons of the mind.

As its title also indicates, *The Passion Artist* is thus a less abrupt departure from the triad's concerns than its central plot suggests. By telescoping an authoritarian regime's repression of its dissidents with man's domination of woman and her subsequent retaliation, Hawkes manages to emphasize the sexual politics and internal dimensions of all controls. (pp. 74-5)

In such clearly delineated patterns of causality, however, the novel proves disappointing, its vision oversimplified. If in Hawkes's earliest works there was an excessive imbalance between form and content—the plot too severely dislocated, resulting in obscurities which suggested an author not fully in command of shaping his material—in *The Passion Artist* the seeds of an opposite danger lie. The precise patterns of the novel too tightly restrict the inherent complexities of the material. Thus, through his own artistic interpretation of his material, Hawkes exerts the same excessive control that the novel's content explicitly depicts.

As I have suggested, such clearly conceived interpretations are not new with *The Passion Artist;* they were an increasingly dominant thematic concern of all three novels of the triad, becoming in *Travesty* a highly ironic satire of such tendencies to organize and explain. The psychoanalytic causalities, which appear only implicitly in *The Passion Artist,* were made an explicit concern of *Death, Sleep & the Traveler*. However, the psychoanalytic theory and dream interpretation, which each of the major characters employs to explain Allert's personality and actions, functions in part ironically in a way the form of the later novel does not allow. The crucial difference is determined by the differing form of the two works; the first-person narrations of the triad, unavoidably subjective, contrast with the more "objective" third-person narrative of *The Passion Artist*. The triad's form prohibits any too simple, one-dimensional interpretation of pattern, for each theory—indeed each pattern within the novel—can be as validly interpreted as a reflection of the narrator's own self-justifying need to pattern by selecting events to corroborate his own predetermined perspective, while in *The Passion Artist*'s third-person narration, the selection of events and images is attributable only to the author himself. (pp. 75-6)

Whether Hawkes was aware of how his adoption of the first-person narrative stance would affect the ambiguities and resonances of the three novels in the triad is unclear. Although the ironies which each of the narrators in the three successive novels unwittingly creates become increasingly broader and more evident, Hawkes's own comments suggest (as does his subsequent less deft use of third-person narration in *The Passion Artist*) that he may in fact be more oblivious to such formal ironies than his fascination with form and irony would otherwise indicate and that his adoption of first-person narration was a fortuitous choice in both senses of the word. In contrast to such possible lack of understanding and control of his material, Hawkes's apparently more clearly directed patterns of meaning in these later novels may reflect a type of increased understanding of his material which suggests another potential danger for his writing. The manner in which he formally adopts such recognitions may hold the key to the future quality of his art. (pp. 76-7)

Paul Rosenzweig, "John Hawkes's Novels of the Seventies: A Retrospective," in Arizona Quarterly *(copyright © 1982 by Arizona Board of Regents), Vol. 38, No. 1, Spring, 1982, pp. 69-77.*

CHARLES CHAMPLIN

[John Hawkes, a] prolific, well-regarded author of modernist fiction, has in "Virginie: Her Two Lives" written what is at once a parody, pastiche and examination of erotic prose, the literature of arousal.

It is an indubitably original and inventive undertaking, superbly written by a man totally in control of his effects. In one fundamental way it is different from the genre it is founded upon; examining the difference is, I think, the object of the exercise. At its center is an untouched innocence, close to but independent of the prevailing debaucheries. (But *debaucheries*, I see, is as loaded a word as *pornography*, which is in turn as dangerous, imprecise and explosive as a sawed-off shotgun. Make that the prevailing erotic goings-on.) . . .

It needs to be said that this is literary sexuality whose tanglings are so swaddled in crypto-poetical prose that the arousal factor is significantly below that of an issue of Good Housekeeping. . . .

A major theme in erotic writing is the despoilation of innocence, the taking of virgins, the falls from grace of priests and nuns. It is as if to prove that there is no one left to judge the despoilers, no one sin-free and able to throw stones. The eroticism floats free of duty, or morality.

Hawkes may be making no more moral judgment than to say there is another way to tell it all. But with the character of sweetly caring and untouched Virginie herself, he gives his **"Virginie: Her Two Lives"** qualities of poignance and perspective that erotic fiction, constructed as such, never has. . . .

"Virginie" could probably not have been written a half-century ago except as an act of defiance or of commercial exploitation (it is neither). In 1982 it is a brilliant exercise in style and invention, an ironic and frequently amusing parodic tribute to a genre and an implicit commentary on changing times.

Charles Champlin, "An Innocence at Play in Erotica," in Los Angeles Times Book Review *(copyright, 1982, Los Angeles Times; reprinted by permission), May 9, 1982, p. 6.*

BERTHA HARRIS

While most novelists are still slouching down the overmarked trails of human experience (including the trail of erotic experience) like bored guides hustling us on to the next souvenir stand, John Hawkes has a seemingly endless capacity to make fresh wilderness out of every new work he writes. The trouble, for his readers, is that wilderness is not like home: there will be natives who don't speak our language; beasts, perhaps, with a taste for human flesh. Almost certainly, we will get lost. And how can we trust a guide who doesn't know how to act like a buddy? Or a lover? . . .

Most of us can at least nod knowingly when we hear his titles dropped (*The Blood Oranges, The Cannibal, The Lime Twig, The Passion Artist*). But few have actually read his work. Hawkes's unpopularity has been ascribed to the difficulty of his vision ("modernist"), to his discomfiting refusal of received ideas ("eccentricity") and to his making "terror rather than love the center of his works." This last assessment, by Leslie Fiedler, comes closest to describing why the fainthearted avoid Hawkes and why his intrepid followers celebrate him. I would, though, quarrel with half of Fiedler's evaluation—which implies that Hawkes deliberates over love as subject before he rejects it. Like the Grand Canyon, Hawkes's fiction tells us, love's landscape has been littered by too many tourists. We can be shocked into pleasure now only by nightmare.

John Hawkes is not read because he is feared, and he is feared because his subject is in direct opposition to our yearnings for hygienic, daylight safety at all costs—even at the cost of passion. In *Virginie, Her Two Lives,* Hawkes carries terror into the erotic and offers us a nightmare preceded by a half-comic, half-cruel pornographic illusion. Happening, as it does, in a series of dreamlike episodes, *Virginie* is less novel than illusion: objects, symbols, images appear and disappear as if by magic; female characters are reduced to wish-fulfillments. Virginie, the heroine, represents Hawkes's sole intellectual assertion in the work, *Virginibus puerisque*, the apotheosis of her name, she serves to tell us that without Innocence we are bereft of appetite. . . .

In classic pornographic (and dream) tradition, the world beyond the illusion falls away. Reading Hawkes, we are as we are when we approach orgasm if we are compelled by him. Yet this is not real sex; it's an invocation to sex, cloaked in ritual and disguise. Hawkes is an imperious manipulator: we cannot look away even when revulsion or excess or bafflement demands that we rest. We feel all in Hawkes's dream, even while we resist understanding all we feel. But this is the nature of dream, of nightmare, and sometimes of sex. . . .

In his brief preface, [Hawkes] tells us he conceived this work "in a reverie about de Sade." But that solemn and terrifying old Master of the Revels is only superficially recalled in Seigneur and not at all in Bocage. Otherwise (especially when he is instructing his disciples in the rigors and delights to come) he reminds me of nothing more than W. C. Fields at his most absurdly pontifical. His "regimen of true eroticism" reads like a combination Eighth Avenue boot camp, medieval convent, and Virginia finishing school: getting up early in the morning to take music lessons and being kept from writing verse is unquestionably doing hard time, but not exactly life-threatening, not from the Sadean viewpoint.

It is Hawkes's comic subtext that prevents his illusion from being a turn-on. . . .

As adults we can laugh and so end, at any moment, slavery to feeling. Children, incapable of detachment, cannot. Virginie's unwavering loyalty to her masters' dreams of sex is the death of her. Because she is trapped in centuries of innocence, her servitude cannot mature into revolt. Virginie will never be a woman, and this is her nightmare. Feminism is coiled beneath Hawkes's sensuous images, his occasions for belly laughs. . . .

Hawkes seems to crave neglect. He is a loner; he does not attempt either relevancy or communication. His literary elitism ultimately excludes the reader, and no matter how much I admire his eloquence, I am angry at him for shutting me out. *Virginie* is like a visit from the supernatural, a hair-raising but unprovable encounter, rather like some kinds of sex. Entrenched, however, in *Virginie*'s erotic illusion is pornographic revisionism. While Hawkes would agree, I think, that a girl is never ruined by a book, he would add: nor *in* a book. There are no women in pornography. Only the erotically able-bodied (men, that is) romp in the minds of fantasists, brimming cap-à-pie with all the refinements—finesse, colère, magie, volupté, bel esprit. For the sake of convention, the able are put on the page veiled in female disability; ideas of the feminine are played with as though they were men.

> *Bertha Harris, "Sade Cases" (reprinted by permission of* The Village Voice *and the author; copyright © News Group Publications, Inc., 1982), in* The Village Voice, *Vol. XXVII, No. 20, May 18, 1982, p. 46.*

ANGELA CARTER

There is considerable resistance in the Anglo-Saxon, Protestant tradition to the notion that sexuality might involve more than the sum of the relevant parts. Since John Hawkes' novel, *Virginie: Her Two Lives,* is set squarely in the context of a quite other, Mediterranean tradition of metaphysical eroticism in which sex is seen as a profound metaphor for the more bewildering aspects of the human condition, it is possible that this glittering, tender, extraordinary parable may be misconstrued in our pragmatic latitudes.

Indeed, although Virginie's two lives expose her to a vast number of complicated sexual games and she witnesses all kinds of exhibitions of sexual activity, Hawkes' novel may not "really" be about sex at all. It might, at bottom, be about our relations with that indefinable part of experience which the

adored lord and master of her life in the 18th century evokes, when in extremis he calls Virginie his "soul."

The troubadours believed the sexual act was the living image of a transcendental state of being; so did the surrealists, always a potent influence in Hawkes, and so, too, did that de Sade to whom Hawkes pays a number of sly homages. Therefore, *Virginie: Her Two Lives* may be intended to be read, in some degree, as allegory. Certainly it demands careful reading; but it gives such pleasure to read this novel carefully!

It is an audacious book, both in style and content, and it is written with breathtaking grace. Reading it is like watching a great trapeze artist perform without a safety net.

Formally, it comprises the juxtaposed first-person narratives of two lives of the same young girl. (p. 1)

In both her lives, Virginie is in a state of suspended prepubescent unawareness. With living, innocent admiration, she observes the rituals by which two men, one an aristocrat, one a taxidriver, attempt to transform the occasionally intractable raw material of femininity into their own idea of woman. The raw material is in both cases a random harem of women picked up in the hedgerows or on the streets; the ideal woman is a being devoted to, disciplined into, giving pleasure to men. Woman as magic, sexual other, in fact.

Both aristocrat and taxi-driver are in the business of "creating" women. Which, as it happens, is the business of any male writer when he sets out to invent a female character. Is there some key to a possible allegorical meaning, here, perhaps?

But Virginie, although she is Hawkes' invention, knows she exists for herself. And also for her mother, as well as for her father and father substitutes; her mother exerts an absolute dominance on both narratives. Not content with the rule of other, Virginie asks herself; "What is the other's sense of itself? Not as other, my object is your subject, and vice versa." Never allowed to participate in the rituals by which women are created, she knows she is ["doomed to eternal childhood"]. . . . (pp. 1-2)

She wonders, eventually, if these men who create women would be "so sorely missed if they gave up their art" and what Hawkes calls the "magnificent mirage" of the phallus turns out to be just that—a mirage. A mirage of what he calls, in a preliminary note, the "shell-pink space of the pornographic narrative."

If the novel ends with the immolation of Virginie's precious innocence in both her lives, with her death or deaths, in fact, there is a suggestion it was only her innocence that made her, in the first place, the "phantom accomplice" (her own phrase) of these artists in flesh, her phallic masters.

Hawkes' serene, inviolable prose is so precise, luminous and evocative as to make this novel seem dreamed rather than read; it is as inscrutable and as capable of as many interpretations as an enchanted mirror, troubling, strange, a marvel. (p. 2)

> *Angela Carter, "John Hawkes' Dialogue of Sex and Soul," in* Book World—The Washington Post *(© 1982, The Washington Post), May 30, 1982, pp. 1-2.*

JAMES WOLCOTT

With *Virginie: Her Two Lives,* Hawkes is once again playing the keeper of the crypt, decorating the sarcophagi with amorous doodles. The novel, narrated by a tremulous waif named Virginie, shuttles like a time-machine from a castle of regimented decadence in rural France (the year—significantly—is 1740, the year of Sade's birth) to a low-rent house of bawdiness in Paris (1945). Under both roofs Virginie flits about on her errands like a nest-tidying bird, bearing rapt witness to the debaucheries and sadistic rites of all these devoted sensualists. She's the Eternal Child, enveloped in a milky glow of unsullied innocence. . . .

[Although] John Hawkes is often touted by his admirers as a comic writer, his touch is far from nimble, his manner seldom slangy or racy. Steeped in a cultured funk, his novels strive to be erotically rich and dark and Continental—pillow books for postmodernists. . . .

Not surprisingly, then, the sex in *Virginie* is seldom affectionate or carefree: it becomes another futile scrape of the fingernails against the walls of nothingness, an orgasmic death rattle. In Hawkes's previous novel, *The Passion Artist,* the finale of a bout of fellatio is described as "a long uncoiling of the thick white thread from the bloody pump," an unappetizing discharge. . . . Set in a European urban deathscape, *The Passion Artist* is awash with psychic slime, its surfaces sticky with mold and caked semen. If the phlegmatic nausea of *The Passion Artist* seemed indebted to the French New Novel (Nathalie Sarraute, particularly), the pornographic lyricism of *Virginie* summons up the ghost of Anaïs Nin, a writer Hawkes is on record as admiring. Not only does Nin's pet word "labyrinth" turn up with telling frequency, but the book's claustrophobic eroticism recalls the clamminess of Nin's posthumous bestsellers *Delta of Venus* and *Little Birds.* Indeed, Virginie is Hawkes's little bird, beating in the void her feverish wings. . . .

For all its humid to-do, Nin's erotic writing tended to be cosmopolitan and domestic, with Colettish schoolgirls in white socks bouncing on their lewd uncles' knees. Hawkes's recent erotic writing has gone in for a more bucolic kick. In *The Passion Artist,* Hawkes's unfortunate protagonist was hosed down with a shower of horse urine ("So, little Konrad Vost, you have shamed the horse!" shouts a tormenting ogress), and in *Virginie* a horse receives unwanted dental work at the clamping end of Seigneur's pincers. . . . Later, a dog and a pig form a squealing, grunting threesome with a maiden named Colère as Virginie secretly watches from behind a curtain of black netting. Perhaps a new ark ought to be built to shelter the innocents of the animal kingdom from the lunging advances of Hawkes's characters, who somehow believe that a horse's bleeding gums offer the key to a woman becoming A Woman.

Of course, these bestial interludes aren't there for cheap, sordid effect. No, the point of these incidents is to illustrate that old pornographic wheeze about submission being the true source of sexual transcendence. . . . John Hawkes's fiction is heavy on debasement, but the adoration comes in stray, feeble glimmers; it's really the pulping of flesh and not its sanctification that engages his imagination. (p. 14)

No matter what riotous coupling is taking place in barnyard or boudoir, one is always aware of Hawkes conducting the action from the pit, at a sluggish tempo. A slogging, death-haunted determinism rules Hawkes's fiction—every kiss threatens to turn into an invitation to cannibalism, every caress a prelude to bondage. John Hawkes has a flair for stirring up queasiness, and his lyrical touches often have a sweet dying fall, but he's become so snug and smug in his role as the Prince of Mortification that his sadomasochistic episodes are turning into a

tired riff, like the suicides in Joyce Carol Oates's novels. (When Oates's characters open the medicine cabinet, it's usually checkout time for their stay on earth.) Despite the ogress's cry in *The Passion Artist,* it's really John Hawkes who insists on shaming the horses. (p. 16)

James Wolcott, "Straw Dogs," in The New York Review of Books *(reprinted with permission from* The New York Review of Books; *copyright © 1982 Nyrev, Inc.),* Vol. XXIX, No. 10, June 10, 1982, pp. 14, 16-17.*

ALAN FRIEDMAN

[In] conception and execution ["**Virginie**"] has a certain grandeur and an impressive flaw. . . . "**Virginie**" is an ambitious enterprise, an eclectic anthology of erotica, a reckless attempt to embrace irreconcilable forms, from medieval love poetry to modern pornography. The resulting flaw is forgivable. So many "sources and influences" have been assembled here like pearls on a narrative string that even as the author strains to close the clasp, his necklace comes apart. But it would be swinish to complain.

The author tells us in a prefatory note that the book was "conceived in a reverie about de Sade." Immediately thereafter, before the novel opens, we come upon a longish poem, an ancient and pleasant debate on the game of love, triumphantly asserting that love is revealed, not through touches or glances, but through love letters. No great ingenuity is required to understand that the book that follows is itself a kind of love letter addressed to admirers of Hawkes's own, often sinister work.

Subtitled "**Her Two Lives,**" the book has two plots. In the first chapter the time is 1945, the place France and the heroine an 11-year-old girl named Virginie. The personification of erotic innocence, she's the reincarnation of another 11-year-old named Virginie whom we meet in chapter two, also in France, but in 1740. The modern Virginie, as the novel begins, is about to be burned to a crisp. Nevertheless, before she is quite burned up, she manages to tell us how her older brother (in 1945) assembled a troupe of libidinous women and men. These free spirits, 10 in all, engage in a variety of sexual shenanigans. In keeping with the spirit of the age, the erotic episodes in 20th-century France are sensual, tawdry and egalitarian. Also, often plain silly. (Some of his material has been adapted, Hawkes notes, from that marvelously silly writer, Georges Bataille.)

More central to the book, and far more fascinating, is the 18th-century plot. The earlier Virginie tells the story of a nobleman named only Seigneur, whose vocation it is to create "Noblesse" (specifically, erotic nobility) in female volunteers of a lower class. A creative artist, he shapes and refines women, esthetically, spiritually and sexually, for the requirements of aristocratic patrons. Five at a time, these upwardly mobile women are sequestered in Seigneur's castle until they have completed his course in post-Renaissance love. An arduous course: Each one, by the time she graduates to Noblesse, will have "known the fire, taken up the bees in her bare hands, watched the agony of animals for her sense of pride, aroused even the sacred father in his confession," and so on.

Now this is the stuff of fable and romance, whereas in the modern period the amorous details (concerning corsets and toilets, G-strings and tattoos) are apt to come from such lowly mimetic forms as the ribald tale and the long filthy joke. Through all of this, Hawkes remains an elegant parodist of porn. In both plots, the eroticism is choreographed. Passion is rhetorical. Sexuality is emblematic of spiritual virtue. Lust is satisfied in a Gallic never-never land.

John Hawkes may yet become a French novelist. This metamorphosis has been going on apace, partly a matter of style, partly a matter of the products of his imagination. One thinks—too automatically—no good can come of this. But in what way can it do him harm? A taste for Hawkes, among his American readers anyhow, is probably an acquired taste. . . . (pp. 20-1)

[Works such as this], which perpetuate the tradition of sadism, are at best misguided, at worst contemptible. It should be sufficient to reply (though it won't be) that [this book] is, in its own way, a celebration of the decay of love. (p. 21)

Alan Friedman, "Pleasure and Pain," in The New York Times Book Review *(© 1982 by The New York Times Company; reprinted by permission), June 27, 1982, pp. 3, 20-1.**

PATRICK O'DONNELL

To "place" any contemporary author in a literary context or tradition is a hazardous affair, especially when, as is the case with Hawkes, that author continues to write novels which intentionally disrupt both the singular contexts his fictions create and the traditions of the novel in general. . . . [In novel after novel Hawkes] forces us to reassess the role of the artist and the fiction-making process, often rendering ironic the portrait of an artist in an earlier work, so that his fiction as a whole presents us with a fluid, self-parodic, generative vision of consciousness and artistry. (p. 143)

If any one thing can be said to characterize the fiction produced and worth considering since World War II, it would be that writers, disenchanted with tradition, even the recent traditions of modernism, create works that ironize, parody, reject, and annihilate the boundaries set forth by those traditions. Contemporary fiction is by turns apocalyptic, exhaustive, thoroughly antimimetic, and disruptive, even of itself, depending upon which critic one reads—but clearly it, like Hawkes's fiction, is impossible to classify in any sense; it is self-consciously atypical. Thus it defies tradition and categorization, and implicitly argues that it is in the nature of fiction to do so.

Given these risks and cautions, and given the fact that the act of placing an author within a generalized context is fated to be reductive, it is of interest and importance to compare Hawkes with other important contemporary authors. The comparison may shed a contrasting light on Hawkes's work, showing its unique, singular qualities as well as showing what, by chance, Hawkes shares with other novelists of his generation. Like many of his contemporaries, Hawkes is a "postwar" novelist in that much of his fiction uses war as a background upon which a particular landscape is painted, as a symbol for the social and historical catastrophes that his heroes either authorize or transcend. *The Cannibal, The Lime Twig,* and *Second Skin* refer directly to World War II, while other fictions, such as *The Owl* and *The Blood Oranges,* refer obliquely to the eternal barbarism in which mankind continually engages. While none of his books are as directly about war as Mailer's *The Naked and the Dead* or Heller's *Catch-22,* Hawkes shares with these writers the implicit recoil from mass violence and a simultaneous fascination with it. Mailer's monotonous, "objective" voice in *The Naked and the Dead* parallels, to some extent, Hawkes's own concern for distancing himself from terror so

that it may be described and circumscribed by language. Hawkes has been compared with Heller, with the Pynchon of *Gravity's Rainbow,* and with the Vonnegut of *Slaughterhouse-Five* as a "black humorist" who is able to defend us from and control the horrors of reality through the absurd or comic perspectives of fiction. While this is a loosely defined category at best, Hawkes does share with Heller, Pynchon, and Vonnegut a propensity for the incongruous, the horrific, and the obscene, placed within the thematic framework of transcendence and escape that a laughable, minute, parodic descriptiveness brings about. The scene of Brigadier Ernest Pudding's scopophilia in *Gravity's Rainbow* or of Yossarian's discovery of the mortally wounded Snowden in *Catch-22* is similar to that in *The Cannibal,* where Jutta's child is hacked to pieces by the mad Duke. In all these instances, the authors are attempting to disrupt our conception of normalcy, to confront us with the world's violence, and to provide us with a means of responding to it as we gaze upon the horror or madness. Along with these novelists, Hawkes seems appropriately apocalyptic in the face of mass violence and its nihilistic results; detachment and laughter seem the only feasible antistrophes to the warlike chorus that finds its way into much of contemporary fiction.

More important than Hawkes's stance as a postwar novelist is what we have seen as his evolving concern with the role of artist, who must create out of the blasted fragments of history and "reality," an aesthetic realm where the power of style holds sway. Often, the quest for an aesthetic escape fails as the artist-hero is subsumed by the disasters of the psyche and of personal history. . . . For Hawkes, the ability to *see,* in Conradian terms, to imagine the depths and heights of human potentiality, to fulfill dream, nightmare, or prophecy is menacing and dangerous. The enforced power of the imagination in his fiction more often leads to annihilation, as in the case of Konrad Vost in *The Passion Artist,* or to the stultification of time and vision as in *The Beetle Leg* and *Death, Sleep & the Traveler,* than to the temporary escapes, undermined by absurdity, which take place in *Second Skin* or *The Blood Oranges.*

Hawkes's concern with aesthetic power and its discontents is one shared most notably by a contemporary who is only marginally "American," Vladimir Nabokov. While it is true that he is more interested in the playful aspects of language than in the psychological intensity which Hawkes achieves, Nabokov, too, is concerned with the power of the artist to create a world of aesthetic harmony and unity that allows the maker to escape time or destiny. The heroes of *Lolita* and *Pale Fire,* Humbert Humbert and Charles Kinbote, construct entire worlds that may be merely the shadows cast by their injured, grotesque imaginations. . . . Both authors demonstrate the fragility of language as well as its comic, dark, or graceful uses; both see, at the heart of language and fiction, a failure and a lack, embodied in the personages of their protagonists who, despite their brilliant, commanding, hyperbolic, even courageous imaginations, are failures, scapegoats and criminals, paranoids and dictators.

This concern with fictionality is one Hawkes shares with many contemporary writers who are primarily interested in the self-referential, circular, tautological nature of language. Hawkes's heroes often become lost in or destroyed by the dreams, visions, and fictions they create. In Hawkes's work one often senses, despite its brilliancies and stylistic disruptions, a kind of linguistic fatalism in which events, symbols, even syntactic fragments endlessly repeat themselves, as in a dream, the dreamer condemned to what Fredric Jameson cites as "the prison-house of language.'' Language as repetition, fiction as recurrence are concepts that Hawkes enforces in his work, thematically and stylistically; in this, he bears resemblance to John Barth and William Gass, among many others. . . . What these writers hold in common with Hawkes is a paradoxical interest in the capacity of language to expose imaginative extremities, and a belief that language always hedges itself, creating its own systematic boundaries and horizons, such that the imaginative quest is undermined by the vehicle of its own enterprise. So we have Skipper or Cyril or Vanderveenan, whose very language determines their limitations as well as their extraordinary artistic capabilities. This, it is true, is the case for any fictional hero, but in Hawkes's work the imaginative vision is so extreme, so dependent upon the primacy of language, that the failure of vision is all that more devastating. Hawkes thus makes a significant contribution to the current effort by contemporary writers to explore the nature of fictionality and the power of language. (pp. 143-47)

[In] Nathanael West's *The Day of the Locust,* there is a memorable scene wherein Tod Hackett witnesses the killing and gutting of several birds which will be served for dinner, rendered in the precise and ''objectified'' details that Hawkes presents in his own scenes of victimization. The bird-killing scene in West's novel is emblematic of the inherent sadism and hatred for life that pervades the apocalyptic Hollywood of the 1920s which he portrays. Flannery O'Connor, upon whom Hawkes has written a significant critical essay, uses a similar method of detachment in describing her Southern grotesques, her ''good country people,'' itinerant preachers, and displaced persons. In the case of each of these writers, as for Hawkes, whatever the subject of a given fiction or its social or historical context, the primary artistic effort is to describe and distance, through a clearly conscious stylization of the world, through parody, ridicule, and exaggeration, that which is ''abnormal,'' tabooed, usually unacceptable or indescribable. The effort, too, is to bring us as readers into a dark or unfamiliar world and, by victimizing us, to confront us with the human potential for failure and lyricism within ourselves.

There are many other influences that bear upon Hawkes's work, as there are many other possible comparisons to contemporaries: the murky surrealism of Djuna Barnes's *Nightwood,* Conrad's voyages to the interior, Faulkner's stylistic experimentation, the sensationalistic, disruptive, mythic violence of Jerzy Kosinski's *The Painted Bird,* or the lyrical dreams of Stanley Elkin's fiction provide only a few examples. However, it is best to conclude a discussion of this crucially important and disturbingly enigmatic writer by insisting upon that which is unique in his body of work. As we have seen, even referring to the collection of Hawkes's novels as a ''body'' assumes a false continuity and categorization, for each new novel seems to shatter the contexts and horizons of vision produced by the former so that, having gotten ''used'' to one of Hawkes's novels, we must be prepared to be usurped from our comfortable place as readers by the next. Thus, to typify his work in any way does it some injustice, especially when we consider the eventuality of the future novels that Hawkes will write. A few things can be fairly asserted: Hawkes is, above all, a stylist, concerned with the elasticity of language and the power of metaphor to accommodate his envisionings of psychic processes and imaginative projections. His drastic, bleak visions are accompanied by a comic spirit, a sense of irony and ridicule in the face of failure, and this integration of comedy and disaster allows Hawkes to fictionalize the unbearable, to perform the artistic act. For him, the act of making the world fictive can

only occur through a kind of phenomenological bracketing and detachment which, rather than miming ''reality,'' cause to appear out of the fog of dreams and the psychic cesspool the sharp, cutting edge of that which has been forgotten or repressed. In his way, Hawkes serves as a conscience for the contemporary reader, not in any traditionally moral sense, but there to remind us of that which causes fear, anxiety, or repulsion. In a time when, too easily, we project the sources of our anxiety onto exterior pressures and forces, we have Hawkes to remind us that the true horror, as well as the ''saving beauties,'' lie within. (pp. 148-49)

Patrick O'Donnell, in his John Hawkes *(copyright © 1982 by Twayne Publishers, Inc.; reprinted with the permission of Twayne Publishers, a Division of G. K. Hall & Co., Boston), Twayne, 1982, 168 p.*

PETER KEMP

John Hawkes's new novel, *Virginie,* is a book about eroticism that seems more concerned with doubling than coupling. Taking pains to mirror earlier models—from the troubadours to Georges Bataille—it also offers matching narratives: both recounted by Virginie, a girl in her eleventh year and at the eleventh hour of her innocence. . . .

Between the two narratives, parallels proliferate. Lines and images recur. The culmination—havoc wreaked by an avenging mother—is the same in both. And the women involved in the erotic tableaux likewise seem counterparts across the centuries. In the 1740 story, they are endowed with allegorical names, Finesse, Colère, Magie, Volupté, Bel Esprit: and delicacy, anger, magic, voluptuousness and wit are, respectively, the main qualities displayed by the five modern women.

The chief difference between the two stories is one of tone. Exuberant and surreal, the contemporary episodes are livelier. The eighteenth-century story, invested with an emblematic eroticism, is governed by rigid protocol. Virginie speaks of the ''passion for symmetry and need for order'' shown by Seigneur, the master of the Chateau Dédale. And within this labyrinthine dwelling, life is elaborately patterned. . . .

Visual rhymes and chromatic echoes . . . constantly pull the book's material into shapes of weird beauty. And they also harmonize with the novel's insistence on balance as the essence of the erotic. Many of the disciplines Seigneur imposes are designed to curb excess in one direction or another: careless power is rectified by careful domination; the poetic is pushed instructively amongst the animal; debauchery is played against religious repression. In keeping with this concern for equilibrium, the prose often has the poise of a *pensée:* ''Innocence is the clarity with which the self shows forth the self. Love is the respect we feel for innocence.'' And there are some very formal fables, such as Seigneur's allegory about the lover's progress from the Plain of Indifference to the Citadel of the Desire to Please. . . .

Not that the book is thinly diagrammatic. It is saved from this by the lush accuracy of Hawkes's prose. . . . This microscopic receptivity—fresh, inventive, and alert—pervades the book. It gives everything an unusual immediacy, whether Hawkes is writing of [red roses] . . . or of a mass of intestines slithering from a disembowelled deer. . . . Precise and resonant, delicate even in its accounts of the grossly physical, *Virginie* is not only a shapely erotic fantasy; it is also a work of potent poetry.

Peter Kemp, "Doubling the Ecstasy," in The Times Literary Supplement *(© Times Newspapers Ltd. (London) 1983; reproduced from* The Times Literary Supplement *by permission), No. 4165, January 28, 1983, p. 79.*

LORNA SAGE

Hawkes's *Virginie* is a series of interwoven erotic tableaux, very deliberate, intensely artificial, conceived as he says in a reverie on de Sade. . . . In each, an 11-year-old Virginie, little sister of the master of ceremonies, plays the part of accomplice, voyeuse and narrator. And though one narrative is heraldic and archaic, while the other is slatternly and burlesque, Virginie's constant presence draws them into a single focus.

The point being, for Hawkes, that speculations on the art of pleasure can only take place via an 'innocent consciousness,' one that banishes time past and future, and concentrates with ruthless single-mindedness on the present moment. His characters are subsumed into their roles, and become actors in lust's timeless allegory: big brother, little sister, the five women who exchange and combine the aspects of female sexuality (Colère, Bel Esprit, Volupté, Finesse, Magie), and—in the background, waiting to pounce on her erring son and daughter, and demolish the pleasure-pavilions—formidable Maman, who represents marriage, procreation, time's vengeance. . . .

The pursuit of pleasure (as commentators on pornography have often remarked) is an arduous rather than ardent business, and requires a systematic deformation of style, which Hawkes here painstakingly replicates. The pleasures 'Virginie' offers are hedged around with rules that squeeze all but the last breath of life out of the subject.

Lorna Sage, "Spoils of Erotic Parody," in The Observer *(reprinted by permission of The Observer Limited), January 30, 1983, p. 47.**

Kazuo Ishiguro

1954?-

Japanese novelist and short story writer.

Ishiguro was born in Nagasaki and grew up in England. His debut novel, *A Pale View of Hills* (1982), has drawn favorable response from critics who describe his writing as subtle, graceful, and full of promise.

A Pale View of Hills focuses on the private despair of Etsuko, a young woman who survived the bombing of Nagasaki and moved to England after the war. In a broader sense, the bombing symbolizes the loss of a culture and the alienation of a people trying to cope with the modern world.

KIRKUS REVIEWS

[*A Pale View of Hills* depicts the] present-day troubles and dark memories of Etsuko, a Nagasaki woman now living alone in England—in a strongly moody but ineffectually structured first novel. Etsuko is now alone, divorced; one daughter, Keiko, has committed suicide; the other, Niki, English-born, lives unmarried with a man in London. And these very un-Japanese social circumstances direct Etsuko's musings back to the time in Nagasaki, a year or so after the Bomb, when things started to unravel. . . . [Even] more disturbing [is the] anarchic story of Etsuko's friend Sachiko—who accepted the lies and evasions of an American boyfriend, even though this led to the horrendous maltreatment of her little girl, Mariko. (Mariko, emotionally battered by neglect, wandered the canals at night, unmissed, a walking symbol of victimized Nagasaki.) Throughout the novel there's a distant overtone of destruction hovering— pieces of lives that can never be rejoined. But Ishiguro, who writes in English, pulls things seriously out of kilter with . . . bad weighting of flashback/flashforward technique: the doses of memory are numbing, hard to swim free from when the book attempts to pitch ahead into the present. And the result is evocative but oppressively unfocused fiction.

A review of "A Pale View of Hills," in Kirkus Reviews *(copyright © 1982 The Kirkus Service, Inc.), Vol. L, No. 4, February 15, 1982, p. 224.*

JAMES CAMPBELL

One of Kazuo Ishiguro's themes . . . is the conflict between the traditional and the modern worlds. [In *A Pale View of Hills*] it is set against the background of the bombing of Nagasaki. . . . I first came across Mr Ishiguro's work in Faber's *Introduction 7*, where his story 'A Strange and Sometimes Sadness' impressed me as the work of a delicate and imaginative mind. *A Pale View of Hills* certainly fulfils the promise. The narrator is a middle-aged Japanese woman who, having lived through the bombing, is now resident in England. Her narrative switches in time between the present and the period just after the war, when the dust raised by the bomb is still very much in the air, and when she was in the role of a subservient wife. In the eyes of everyone, and in all senses, she appears to have survived. Nothing is necessarily as it seems, however; the terrible events prove to have had more than just

a physically destructive effect, and Mr Ishiguro's double-barrelled narrative device enables him to show the past determining the present. In Etsuko's present life as much as in her past, she is encircled by a chain of death which has its beginning in the war. The Japanese sections centre around some mysterious killings and Etsuko's uneasy relationship with her friend's daughter; things begin to look sinister when, in the present, she starts dreaming about a little girl 'swinging'. What is most impressive about this novel is the way in which the author manages to blend the historical and psychological dimensions, so that his protagonist is a creation of her times. It is all done with subtlety, but if there is a fault it is that the incidental detail is not sufficiently filled in. Some characters are rather faceless, and the dialogue is vapid in places. Perhaps after this fine first novel, Kazuo Ishiguro will risk a little more in the realm of style.

James Campbell, "Kitchen Window," in New Statesman *(© 1982 The Statesman & Nation Publishing Co. Ltd.), Vol. 103, No. 2657, February 19, 1982, p. 25.**

PAUL BAILEY

Kazuo Ishiguro has written a first novel of uncommon delicacy. *A Pale View of Hills* is an extremely quiet study of extreme emotional turbulence, which summons up the various nightmares of a survivor of Nagasaki in a manner that will probably perplex those readers who like to swallow their horrors whole or enjoy being told the worst, at length. It is not Ishiguro's intention to "do" Nagasaki, as other novelists have recently "done" Buchenwald and Babi Yar. Far from it; his commitment in this book is to a private desolation, and he honours that commitment to the letter. . . .

The greater part of *A Pale View of Hills* takes place during that immediately post-war summer in Nagasaki. Etsuko remembers a woman called Sachiko, who lives with her daughter, Mariko, in a wooden cottage that "had survived both the devastation of the war and the government bulldozers". Sachiko is to all intents and purposes a vagrant, ekeing out an existence on the money she scrounges off gullible people like her new friend, Etsuko. She has immense pride, and cannot disguise the fact that she was born considerably higher up the social scale than her present life would indicate. Etsuko is intrigued by this aloof and elegant outcast and her strangely alienated offspring, and allows herself to be used by Sachiko for their benefit. Sachiko, with her talk of the American lover, Frank, who is soon going to return to the United States with a Japanese wife and stepdaughter, is a vivid presence. Her relationship with the dull, solicitous young housewife who helps her when she is at her most distressed is beautifully suggested in a series of decorous conversations that become increasingly revealing as the story develops. It is what happens to poor little Mariko, however, that is at the heart of the novel and gives it its resonance, and this too is suggested with great attention to the effect it had, and has, on Etsuko's life. Ishiguro very cleverly shows a person exploring the unhappiness of her own past by concentrating on other people. . . .

A Pale View of Hills works largely by inference. My only criticism is that at certain points I could have done with something as crude as a fact. Almost nothing is said, for example, about Etsuko's second husband, who would appear to have been a man of some intelligence. [Her daughter] Keiko's withdrawal from him, and consequently from her mother, is only hinted at, yet it would seem to be the most traumatic event in the whole sad story. It is very skilful of Kazuo Ishiguro to leave out, as it were, the major part of the tragedy in order to examine its origins, but the absence of the successful journalist and lecturer who whisked Etsuko off to England becomes worrying towards the end of the narrative. In all other respects though, this is a bravely reticent novel, courageous in its self-effacement, its honourable—and unfashionable—refusal to show off the possibilities of the Novel. *A Pale View of Hills* is concerned with more important matters.

Paul Bailey, "Private Desolations," in The Times Literary Supplement (© *Times Newspapers Ltd. (London) 1982; reproduced from* The Times Literary Supplement *by permission), No. 4116, February 19, 1982, p. 179.*

FRANCIS KING

Although Mr Ishiguro has spent most of his life in England and has even acquired an MA in Creative Writing at the University of East Anglia, [*A Pale View of Hills*] is typically Japanese in its compression, its reticence and in its exclusion of all details not absolutely essential to its theme. It might, one feels, be some apprentice work by Kawabata or Endo, its dialogue rendered slightly stilted by translation. It is a memorable and moving work, its elements of past and present, of Japan

and England held together by a shimmering, all but invisible net of images linked to each other by filaments at once tenuous and immensely strong. (pp. 24-5)

Francis King, "Shimmering," in The Spectator (© *1982 by* The Spectator; *reprinted by permission of* The Spectator), *Vol. 248, No. 8016, February 27, 1982, pp. 24-5.*

EDITH MILTON

["*A Pale View of Hills*"] is narrated by a Japanese woman, Etsuko, who, like the author, was born in Nagasaki and lives in England. Widowed by the death of her second, English, husband, and mourning the suicide of her first, Japanese, daughter, Etsuko finds herself recalling random moments of a summer in Nagasaki during the 1950's. It was the summer of her brief, enigmatic friendship with Sachiko, the woman next door, and the time of her meeting with Sachiko's disturbing and troubled child, Mariko. . . .

Etsuko's memories, though they focus on her neighbor's sorrows and follies, clearly refer to herself as well. The lives of the two women run parallel, and Etsuko, like Sachiko, has raised a deeply disturbed daughter; like her, she has turned away from the strangling role of traditional Japanese housewife toward the West, where she has discovered freedom of a sort, but also an odd lack of depth, commitment and continuity.

Still, this is no indictment of the unhappy changes which have drowned an old culture. In fact, Kazuo Ishiguro suggests that the honor of the past was itself more than a little tarnished. . . . As for the future, it appears to belong to Etsuko's second daughter, Niki, a hybrid of East and West, loyal to nothing, attached to no one, ignorant and disorganized; she is also, however, entirely honest and admirably free of prejudices and compulsions. She may, the book suggests, be the best of an indifferent bargain; then again, she may not.

A delicate, ironic, elliptical novel, **"A Pale View of Hills"** means much more than it says. Etsuko has been a musician, and in her mind themes and images echo and repeat in a contrapuntal arrangement of increasing power. Sachiko's failed motherhood resonates against Etsuko's. The two women mirror each other's ambivalence about having abandoned the accepted modes for Japanese wives and widows. The images of kittens being drowned, a rope twisted around Etsuko's sandal, a girl dangling from a swing, the reappearing phantom of a long-dead woman who has killed her baby and the haunting absence of the lives and customs blown away by the war reverberate and multiply, suggesting by repetition a scale much larger than that implied by any individual image. Sachiko and Etsuko become minor figures in a greater pattern of betrayal, infanticide and survival played out against the background of Nagasaki, itself the absolute emblem of our genius for destruction.

The story, following its narrator's memory, begins after the bombing of Nagasaki, but that event lies at its center. Barely touched upon, mentioned only by innuendo, the destruction of Nagasaki appears as a vacuum defined only by the misplaced lives and the disjointed modes of survival which derive from it. But in this book, where what is stated is often less important than what is left unsaid, those blanked-out days around the bomb's explosion become the paradigm of modern life. They are the ultimate example of qualities which the novel celebrates: the brilliance of our negative invention, and our infinite talent for living beyond annihilation as if we had forgotten it. (p. 13)

Edith Milton, "In a Japan Like Limbo," in The New York Times Book Review *(© 1982 by The New York Times Company; reprinted by permission), May 9, 1982, pp. 12-13.**

JONATHAN SPENCE

A Pale View of Hills has caught the loss and uncertainty of modern Japan. . . . (p. 266)

[It] is a beautiful and dense novel, gliding from level to level of consciousness as it slips between the narrator Etsuko Sheringham's widowed life in the English countryside and her days as a young pregnant wife in the suburbs of Nagasaki, where she managed to find one important friend. The atomic bomb had fallen not long before, but, as the author drily observes, "Memory, I realise, can be an unreliable thing"; in *A Pale View of Hills* the memory of the bomb and what it did to a city is at one with the memory of Mrs Sheringham's daughter, Keiko, a suicide in a Manchester rooming house. Just as centrally to the novel, the memory of a little girl, beside a muddy Nagasaki river, watching the drowning of her pet kittens, is at one with that same girl some years before, watching a mother in the dying embers of Tokyo, drowning her baby in another river.

The pale hills of the novel's title are, in a literal sense, the slopes of Inasa that rise tranquilly above the city of Nagasaki, and would be seen from the narrator Etsuko's house as she carried her unborn child. Yet they are also evocations of a fading life, of a Japanese world where one's own dead children and their sufferings blur with the impact of other people's dislocated lives. (p. 267)

Jonathan Spence, "Two Worlds Japan Has Lost Since the Meiji," in New Society *(© New Society; reprinted by permission of the publisher), Vol. 60, No. 1017, May 13, 1982, pp. 266-67.**

PENELOPE LIVELY

The impact of *A Pale View of Hills* . . . is out of all proportion to both its length and its slight plot. The narrator, Etsuko, resident in England, recalls her relationship with another woman in Nagasaki many years before, and the odd and slightly sinister events surrounding it; her recollections take place during a visit from her daughter by her English husband, her elder, Japanese, daughter having recently committed suicide. The daughter leaves; the recollection ends without any actual completion of the brief tale of the mother and child with whom it is concerned. And the novel finishes on a dying fall that is both unsettling and a little baffling—which indeed has been its effect throughout. For its strength is a remarkable quality of style in which dialogue and narration are unemphasised and yet oddly powerful. It is the kind of writing in which one searches in frustration for the source of its effects; sparse, precise and plain, the language has a stealth that leaves you with images that are suggested rather than stated. Trying to pin this down, I turned back through the pages looking for the description of a certain room: it was not there, was a product of my own imagination. And this is a subtle power for a writer to have—the ability to prompt a creative response in the reader, to arouse reactions which must be quite individual, so that the book takes as many forms as it has readers. It can only be done by means of this stylistic negativism, and the danger of course is that it overreaches itself and lapses into blandness. Once or twice *A Pale View of Hills* threatens to do this, but on the whole the effect is one of extraordinary tension, of implied griefs and evils.

The setting of Etsuko's recollection of her Japanese past is not arbitrary. It is Nagasaki, and the shadow of the bomb lies over the place and the people. The sad, wild, neglected child—Mariko—of Etsuko's friend Sachiko has seen "terrible things." A new Japan is emerging from the ashes of the old, and the conflict between the two generations is neatly and economically presented in the frustrated confrontation between Etsuko's father-in-law, a retired teacher, and the young colleague who has attacked his old-fashioned teaching methods. . . .

But the real subject of Etsuko's recollection is Sachiko, the woman who has fallen on hard times and who preys on Etsuko's good nature—borrowing money, dumping her child—while with quiet desperation she pursues the American GI who may be her passport to better things. Sachiko is an elegant opportunist, and her conversations with Etsuko are masterpieces of Ishiguro's loaded writing: dialogue of wonderful delicacy in which Sachiko bolsters up her own *amour-propre*, keeps the younger woman in her place, and conceals—almost, but not quite—her bitterness and panic. . . . Behind the unadorned narrative, so deliberately devoid either of explanation or of descriptive indulgence, lurks a sense of menace and of sadness. As a first novel this book is remarkable; its control and economy look like the work of a much more experienced writer. (p. 90)

Penelope Lively, "Backwards and Forwards," in Encounter *(© 1982 by Encounter Ltd.), Vol. LVIII, No. 6 and Vol. LIX, No. 1, June-July, 1982, pp. 86-91.**

(Patricia) Ann Jellicoe

1927-

English dramatist.

Jellicoe is an experimental playwright who works in the "theater of demonstration" where action is considered more important than words. Her visceral approach to drama emphasizes movement and sounds rather than language in its traditional communicative sense. Jellicoe's plays reflect her belief that humans are ruled more by emotion than intellect.

Jellicoe's first play, *The Sport of My Mad Mother* (1958), which centers on a group of teenagers given to outbursts of violent behavior, sparked interest because of its fragmented structure, and the extensive use of chants, drumbeats, and meaningless phrases. Critics found little substance beyond the novelties of the play. Her next play, *The Knack* (1961), however, proved to be a popular and critical success. The play revolves around three intelligent young men who become ruled by their sexual feelings when an attractive young woman enters their lives. Most critics felt Jellicoe's non-narrated action worked well in this comedy of manners.

Since *The Knack*, Jellicoe has concentrated on directing community and children's theater groups, although her somewhat conventional biography play *Shelley, or The Idealist* (1965) met with modest success. In all her works, Jellicoe stresses improvisation and free form as she attempts to expand the possibilities of theater.

(See also *Contemporary Authors*, Vols. 85-88 and *Dictionary of Literary Biography*, Vol. 13.)

© Jerry Bauer

THE LONDON TIMES

[In *The Sport of My Mad Mother,* Ann Jellicoe] gallantly attempts to give poetic expression to the predicament of a generation ruled by fear. It is unfortunate that she appears to see life in a series of newspaper *clichés*.

A world of fear, she insists, must develop the Teddy Boy mentality. The grown-ups play with atom bombs, the kids with knives and guns. The kids are violent, they are cruel, and to find themselves "killers" would give them a moment of proud ecstasy. But they are always looking over their shoulders, hopeful that someone strong enough to lead them will appear, fearful lest their eyes should encounter not the wished-for leader but some truly awful surprise.

This kind of aimlessness is not easy to dramatize; and Miss Jellicoe, though she is not without skill in working arresting rhythms into the basic English of her dialogue, gives us a rather gritty evening of expressionism which sheds no special illumination on its theme and is not particularly entertaining.

The fundamental trouble is that the theme itself can be adequately expressed in a very few words, and when they have been said it only remains for them to be amplified by a number of bleak diagrammatic indications. Miss Jellicoe has denied herself anything in the way of a story and the characters have no power to develop, except as part of a moving diagram.

Some of these movements are surprising enough to hold the eye, but they do not often get through to the mind.

"Court Theatre," in The London Times, *February 26, 1958, p. 3.*

ALAN BRIEN

Miss Ann Jellicoe in *The Sport of My Mad Mother* has written what might be called 'a modern surrealist fantasy': an exercise in theatrical *collage*. Just as the painters tacked scraps of newspaper and torn menus on to their canvas, she has worked into her text the chanted directions from a home permanent-wave kit and a pastiche of a rock-'n'-roll song. The intention in each case is presumably the same—to prove that the most intractable gobbets of the real world can be transmuted by art into art. And she has similarly taken the surface appearance of some contemporary characters—an American social worker, an Australian hell-cat, two South London Teds and their doxy—and pressed them into service as symbols. . . .

Unlike some critics I see absolutely no objection in principle to mixing in every kind of stage convention. The characters talk sometimes to each other, sometimes to the audience, sometimes to a drummer on the side of the stage, and sometimes to the stage-hands and electricians. They sing, dance, chant in unison, moan in couplets. They mime, mug and declaim. It is all rather like the last drunken night of University revue—full of old jokes, crude props, high spirits and low comedy. And often the effect is very funny—sometimes even rather eerie and arresting. But as a play with any precise relevance to any human problem, dilemma or situation, *The Sport of My Mad Mother* is a flop.

The production is not at fault. Miss Jellicoe has devised some ingenious and spectacular methods of keeping her ideas juggling in the air like Indian clubs. But the clubs are invisible or else so hollow and light that they go up in the air and are carried off by the wind. With the best possible will in the world, I was unable to discover what she had to say. The clues which were underlined, both in text and production, with the heaviest black pencil were exactly those which were most cryptic and impenetrable. Why should Greta (according to the programme note 'an irresponsible life-force') be a raucous Australian with long hair dyed the colour of dried tomato ketchup? What purpose was there in wrapping Caldaro ('Knowledge and Science') as a newspaper parcel? Who is the fieldmouse of a waif in the old army greatcoat who mutters lines of almost Wordsworth silliness which go something like 'Me all soft and loose I lie, Looking empty at the sky'?

Miss Jellicoe has been compared to Ernst Toller, Thornton Wilder and T. S. Eliot. There seem to me to be nearer and less ponderous influences at work a lot of the time. The human parcel, and the parade of the Guys, the unexpected bouts of song and dance, the infectious spurts of make-believe which become reality, are like half-memories of John Cranko. The parody of the schoolroom ('Please, may I be excused?' 'No. Stay behind and fill up the ink-wells') might be word for word from an old Will Hay film. The perming instructions which turn into a jolly concert party chorus derive from *At the Drop of a Hat.* It is possible to practise *collage* so passionately that there is no room left on the canvas for any of your own paint. Miss Jellicoe does not carry her magpietude quite to that extent. But it is noticeable that where her observation is most direct and naturalistic—as in the earlier scenes of the Teds' squabble for power—symbol and reality chime most resoundingly together. Conversely, where the symbols get out of hand and start bossing around the characters who embody them, her imagination is at its weakest and her dialogue at its dullest.

Alan Brien, "Tinkling Symbols," in The Spectator *(© 1958 by* The Spectator; *reprinted by permission of* The Spectator), *Vol. 200, No. 6767, March 7, 1958, p. 296.*

T. C. WORSLEY

[In *The Sport of My Mad Mother,* Miss Jellicoe] is attempting to evoke the world of adolescence in a modern city setting, and she succeeds by a variety of wholly acceptable non-naturalistic devices. The two boys and girls go through their motions of boredom, swagger, funk, hate; they seem to exist in some limbo of unformed fantasy, without any specific myth to give their fantasy shape: they are filled with an undirected aggression for which their setting provides no outlet; they are waiting for something or someone to provide them with some reason—any reason at all—for doing the next thing. And since there is nothing in the ethos of contemporary life to provide this reason, they seize on any—even the slightest—pretext for galvanising themselves into some activity. These spasmodic bursts of action Miss Jellicoe works up very well; most of

them—since the aggression in these children has gone sour for want of using—are acts of cruelty or violence. Sometimes they break into a spontaneous dance, but more often they turn on each other, or persecute the local half-wit, or, in the most sustained sequence of this first half, set on a clean-cut, clean-limbed young American who is wandering round their city streets, 'innocently' trying to find the reason for their state of mind.

These staccato outbursts may be accompanied by a young man on the forestage with a set of drums, and the dialogue is vibrant and taut, but as repetitive, too, and as banal as the lyrics of their favourite songs. So, Miss Jellicoe does succeed in giving us intensely and vividly an image of the world she wishes to portray: and it is not difficult to follow her exposition of it so far. It is what she does with it once it is evoked that both puzzles and, frankly, disappoints. We move deeper into a world of symbols which have, I suppose, some private, but not enough public, meaning. A brilliant, vital young creature with blood coloured hair comes in proclaiming herself an Australian (the Life Force, explains the programme); she is the leader of the gang to which the youths belong, but having got herself a child in the belly by the leader of an opposing gang, is abandoning the leadership of her own and dedicating herself (are we meant to gather from her postures?) to the pure pleasure of fertility. Now all this seems to be unnecessarily muddled and unworked out. For, you see, the plain fact is that . . . Miss Jellicoe has at this point slipped in a story, and has, quite simply, told it very badly. Nor is this the only muddle point. She also throws in the garlic of yet another style. There are 'alienation effects'—asides to the electrician off-stage working the lights, direct appeals to the audience and so on.

T. C. Worsley, "Adolescents," in New Statesman *(© 1958 The Statesman & Nation Publishing Co. Ltd.), Vol. LV, No. 1408, March 8, 1958, p. 301.*

THE TIMES, LONDON

Whatever one expected next from the author of that strange and disturbing play *The Sport of my Mad Mother* (the piece itself permitted an infinitude of speculation) it would hardly have been a comedy of manners. And yet that is precisely what Miss Ann Jellicoe's new play [*The Knack*] is. . . .

No dramatist depends less than Miss Jellicoe on the actual words used and more on the circumstances of their using. The texts of her plays are scarcely more than blueprints for the cast and director, for in the "theatre of demonstration" she has evolved what happens (emotionally as well as physically) counts for much more than what is said. This seems at first to make her works difficult and remote from the traditions of the British theatre (certainly it accounts for the mystification with which *The Sport of my Mad Mother* was greeted) but on reflection she turns out simply to be doing much the same as Mr. Noel Coward, for example, did many years ago when he allowed the hero and heroine of *Private Lives* to play what was in effect a passionate love scene while apparently discussing the possible resemblance of the Taj Mahal to a biscuit box. The only difference is that what in Mr. Coward was an incidental effect is here used continuously, to create a play beyond and virtually independent of most that the actors actually say.

What *The Knack* says, then, is often insignificant; what it is about is quite a different matter. Briefly (for it is a brief though close-packed play) it is about three men who do respectively too well, all right, and not well enough where women are concerned, and about the effect that the arrival in the house (rented by the least successful) where they all live of a *jolie-laide* innocent looking for the Y.W.C.A. has on their relations with each other. The various tensions and jealousies set up are cunningly mapped out by Miss Jellicoe. . . . [The] whole evening is so funny that the audience forgets to think it advanced, which must surely be exactly what Miss Jellicoe always intended.

> *"Drama beyond the Spoken Word," in* The Times, *London (© Times Newspapers Limited 1961), October 10, 1961, p. 16.*

BAMBER GASCOIGNE

The Knack provides a fascinating comparison with *Play with a Tiger*. . . . Both plays are written by women, both of whom can be described as 'new wave' dramatists; and both are about sexual callousness. Yet the two plays could hardly be more different. In *Play with a Tiger* Doris Lessing has a story to tell about one particular love affair and the pain of it. She wants to tell it naturalistically, but she also wants her play to have the clear markings of wider 'significance.' . . . We have to know the exact relationships between the minor and major characters—where did they meet, how long ago, why are they here now? We have to know in detail what is causing the representative noises in the street. Even the dramatic pool of orange light has to be explained (it comes from the street lamp shining through the window when the interior lights are off). . . .

Ann Jellicoe is a more instinctive playwright. In *The Knack* she also wants to write a play of general significance, but she decides for this reason to make its whole tone general, almost abstract. But since she doesn't want her play to seem arty or expressionistic—as it would if presented, say, on three stilted rostra of differing heights and one kidney-shaped podium—she, too, makes her naturalistic excuses. But she makes them briefly and economically at the very beginning of the play and then never needs to return to them. Her permanent setting is a bare room, with the walls and ceiling covered in light splurges of colour. The reason, we immediately learn, is that a charming young man, the tenant, is in the middle of painting himself some murals; and, since he likes space, he has moved everything into the passage except a bare metal bedstead and two chairs. We soon meet the two men he shares the house with, both of whom are obsessed by sex—one because he can never get too much (he needs it as other people need sleep, five hours a day), the other because he can't get any. Given this universal trio—supersex, sex and subsex—all we need now is a girl. One soon passes the window and, though a stranger, scrambles in. Thus, amusingly and most acceptably, Miss Jellicoe has provided herself with an abstract setting and with a cast of four which hasn't an ounce of overlap or wastage. . . .

All the many relationship-games which develop out of the situation are extremely funny because Miss Jellicoe writes them brilliantly; but they are also very frightening, since one recognises consistently their reality in everyday life, their cruelty, their harm. Laughter surf-rides through the audience on the crest of a shudder, and Miss Jellicoe's harsh *jeu d'esprit* proves itself more true, more angry and more moving than all Miss Lessing's weightiness.

There are elements in the play which could be improved. Some of the arias of verbal ping-pong are too artificial, some of the set speeches too set; and it is a mistake to present Tolen as a jack-booted automaton just because he is a sexual Fascist—

there are enough of them around to justify a more familiar presentation. . . . [But everyone] should see this play soon. . . . (p. 445)

> *Bamber Gascoigne, "With a Bare Bedstead," in* The Spectator *(© 1962 by The Spectator; reprinted by permission of* The Spectator*), Vol. 208, No. 6980, April 6, 1962, pp. 445-46.**

JOHN RUSSELL TAYLOR

[*The Sport of My Mad Mother*] was a complete commercial disaster; from the critics it received slightly more approval than from playgoers, but on the whole not very much. Even so, one or two critics recognized that Ann Jellicoe was trying, not yet with complete success admittedly, to do something quite new in the English theatre: to make her play primarily something which happened in front of its audience and made its effect as a totality, rather than a piece of neatly carpentered literary craftsmanship which would 'read well' and work only by way of its dialogue's appeal to the mind.

The script of *The Sport of My Mad Mother*, in fact, makes very little sense just read cold: it is simply the short score from which a full orchestral sound can be conjured by a skilled musician, or the scenario for a ballet waiting for a composer to write the music and a choreographer to stage it; it is, not surprisingly considering the circumstances of its writing, 'director's theatre' to the nth degree, clearly seen by the author mainly as an *aide-mémoire* in the transference of her initial conception from the stage of her own mind to a real, physical stage. Consequently when staged it makes extraordinary demands on the playgoer schooled in the traditional techniques of the English stage: he expects the play he sees to be, in effect, written mainly for the ear, with the eye required to act on its own just once in a while, when it may note a bit of business and aid the mind to deduce some logical significance for it. But here is a play which assaults (the word is used advisedly) both eye and ear, and makes very little appeal to the intellect at all.

It is about a group of teddy-boys, whose behaviour throughout is instinct with a purely arbitrary spirit of violence, one or two outsiders who become involved mysteriously with them (Caldaro, a young American; Dodo, a retarded 13-year-old) and Greta, their spiritual leader, a legendary figure of destruction and in the end, when she gives birth to a child, of creation too, who corresponds presumably to Kali, the Indian goddess of creation and destruction who is the 'mad mother' of the title ('All creation is the sport of my mad mother Kali'). Much of the dialogue, most of it, in fact, is almost entirely incantatory in effect, with a minimum of analysable sense; just enough to create the atmosphere of menace and violence always on the point of being unleashed, without ever defining the nature and purpose (if any) of either too exactly. Quite a lot of the 'dialogue' indeed, is merely sound—cries and ejaculations, repeated monosyllables shorn of any associative effect and used entirely for their tonal qualities. On the page it looks as intimidating and uncommunicative as the hieroglyphs of some unknown tongue; in the theatre it all surges over and around one, a strange, disturbing pattern of sights and sounds which produces a corresponding series of emotional reactions from which gradually a total picture of a violent, instinctive way of life emerges: it is about people who are for the most part inarticulate and uncommunicative, and instead of trying to externalize their emotions and reactions in necessarily stilted and artificial words it creates in the theatre a sort of symbolic equivalent of the mental climate in which they live and thrusts us willy-nilly into it.

But it can do this only so long as we abandon ourselves to the experience instead of stopping to question it. As soon as we deliberately extract ourselves from participation in what is happening and ask what any particular line or section *means,* we are lost and the play is lost to us. In an interview in the *New Theatre Magazine,* published by members of the drama faculty of Bristol University, Ann Jellicoe herself put all this very clearly:

> I think the word 'meaning' shows exactly what is wrong with people's attitudes. If they were to ask 'What is the play about?' it would be a better approach. This is a new kind of play, which demands a new approach. Most play-goers today are not used to taking anything direct in the theatre. What they do is transform it into words and put it through their brain.
>
> (pp. 65-7)

> You see, so many plays tell you what is happening the whole time. People don't act angry; they tell you they're angry. Now, my play is about incoherent people—people who have no power of expression, of analysing their emotions. They don't know why they're afraid; they don't even know that they are afraid. So they have to compensate for their fear by attacking someone else; they're insecure and frustrated, and they have to compensate for that by being big, and violent. And all this is directly shown, instead of being explained; if you're content to watch it without thinking all the time 'What is the meaning?' so that you don't even see or hear, you're so busy thinking—then you will get what it's about.

The Sport of My Mad Mother might well appeal to a variety of people for a variety of reasons, but the Girl Guides Association is about the last body one would expect to find its attitudes, its tone or its style palatable. Yet shortly after it was produced Ann Jellicoe was commissioned by them to write a show for staging . . . , the only conditions being that it should be 'of interest to youth', have a 'positive ending', make room for some foreign guides, and have a cast of about 800 girls, 100 boys, and possibly some adults. (The most likely explanation of the commission seems to be that they had heard she wrote 'interesting plays about teenagers'.) Her imagination fired by the possibilities inherent in the form of presentation, she decided to accept the commission and produce something personal which at the same time satisfied all these conditions. The result, *The Rising Generation,* was rejected out of hand by the committee, even after complete rewriting and conventionalization, but the original text was later published in *Ark,* the magazine of the Royal College of Art.

From this it emerges as by far the most interesting and imaginative work ever written in the simple but spectacular form of the youth pageant (though that, admittedly, is not saying very much). It is a story about intolerance and totalitarian rule, told in parable form, though a parable, surely, little calculated to appeal to the Girl Guide ideal: it postulates a conspiracy by the monstrous regiment of women, headed by Mother, 'an enormous woman half-masked with a padded headdress and

shoes', to dominate the world and exterminate men. Men are banished and expunged from history; girls at school have to repeat religiously 'Shakespeare was a woman. Milton was a woman. The Black Prince was a woman. Robin Hood, she was a woman. King John was a woman. Newton was a woman'; while their teacher firmly indoctrinates them: 'Men are black. Men are thick. Men are tall. Men are strong. Men will tear you, beat you, eat you. When you're older, you will know.' But finally the girls get together with the boys to rebel against the tyrannical domination of Mother, and though she puts into operation her final threat, the Bomb, they survive and as the show ends the whole vast arena is transformed into a flying saucer to carry them all to a new life somewhere in space. Throughout, the piece not only says something, and says it clearly enough to 'appeal to youth', but it also uses the wide open spaces of the Empire Pool [where it was to be performed] and its resources brilliantly: the spotlit pursuit of the boy Stephen, the triumphal progress of Mother, her opponents held at bay by a battalion of charladies with flaming mops, and the great final transformation could hardly fail to make their effect. It was perhaps too much to expect the Girl Guides Association to see the singular merits of *The Rising Generation,* but by refusing it they rejected the most interesting work they are ever likely to receive in response to a commission, and incidentally deprived the 7,000 Guides who fill the Empire Pool every night when such a show is on of a strikingly effective piece of spectacular entertainment, to put it no higher.

If *The Rising Generation* suggests in some ways a re-handling of themes from *The Sport of My Mad Mother* in a rather different context, Ann Jellicoe's next play, *The Knack,* . . . shows a complete departure in subject-matter, allied with a remarkable consistency in form and style. (pp. 67-9)

[*The Knack*] is a comedy about, as far as can be seen, normally intelligent, articulate people caught at precisely the point where the image of rational, intelligent man breaks down just because they are completely ruled by their emotions, their fears and insecurities. The subject of these feelings, naturally enough, is sex—where else is the normally civilized man more subject to non-civilized, indeed anti-civilized, influences? (p. 70)

Whole sections of the text make no noticeable sense in themselves, because it is always what is going on, and what the audience apprehends from participating in what is going on, that counts. Often the dialogue is simply a series of disjointed *non sequiturs* or uncomprehending repetitions, and in one key scene, where Colin and Tom gradually draw Nancy into their fantasy that the bed in the room is actually a piano, of 'pings' and 'plongs' variously distributed and extending virtually uninterrupted over some three pages of the script. The most remarkable quality of the play, in fact, is the sheer drive of the action, physical and emotional, right through its three acts in one unbroken movement; in the theatre not only does the play not demand rationization on the part of its audience but, unlike *The Sport of My Mad Mother,* which is by comparison sometimes uncertain and immature (the last act in particular fails to cap the previous two conclusively), it positively forbids it: the spectator is carried along irresistibly by the verve and ebullience of the play, and at the end, even if he does not know what, stage by stage, it means, he certainly knows vividly what it is about.

In the five years between *The Sport of My Mad Mother* and *The Knack* Ann Jellicoe has matured and developed extraordinarily as a dramatist while continuing obstinately to plough her solitary furrow. . . . Her plays are quite unlike anyone else's, and even in a generation of dramatists distinguished above all else for their sure grasp of practical theatre her work stands out by virtue of its complete command of theatrical effect. Her plays are difficult to stage, undeniably, since they depend so completely on their theatrical qualities and the sensitivity and accuracy with which the director can cover the bare framework of mere words with the intricately organized architecture fully drawn out in the creator's head. But once staged, and staged well, they infinitely repay the trouble; one only hopes it will not be another five years before she chooses again to face some director with such a challenge. (p. 71)

> *John Russell Taylor, "Presented at Court: Ann Jellicoe," in his* Anger and After: A Guide to the New British Drama *(© 1962 by John Russell Taylor; reprinted by permission of A D Peters & Co Ltd), Methuen & Co Ltd, 1962, pp. 65-71.*

HAROLD CLURMAN

[*The Knack*] is a ripple in that "new wave" of English writing which has enlivened the London stage since 1956. To say the least, it is fun.

I identify it in this unassuming fashion because, as with many plays of its kind, there is a temptation to treat it as esoteric. It might be preferable, to begin with, to view *The Knack* strictly as entertainment—as one might judge an extended but on the whole well-sustained revue sketch. (p. 88)

The play is what the French might call a clown show; it never states a case. It is "crazy"; yet its characters' eccentricity—for example, when three of them enact the playing of a piano on a bedspring—is not so remote from the actual behavior of young folk today who will beguile themselves in some such way to fill the emptiness of the hours.

The talk is both terse and loose, epigrammatic and repetitive, extravagant and dry, pointed and inane. We laugh and at the same time ask ourselves, "Where are we?" We are here and now, very much in the midst of today's bewilderment (especially in certain English circles): sportive, "civilized," spiritually null and void. There is a faint odor of homosexuality on the premises.

The play has something of Harold Pinter's weird bleakness, together with the variety-hall travesty of London's "Crazy Gang." It hovers about the Theatre of the Absurd but never really enters.

Finally, it is a clever stage piece. It lives on action—sound, speech and movement—all of it zany yet never less than lucid. One need not concern oneself with how "good" the play is nor how seriously one has to take it. As spoof or symbol it has unmistakable merits. (p. 89)

> *Harold Clurman, "The Playwrights: Ann Jellicoe" (1964), in his* The Naked Image: Observations on The Modern Theatre *(reprinted with permission of Macmillan Publishing Company; copyright © 1958, 1959, 1960, 1961, 1962, 1963, 1964, 1965, 1966 by Harold Clurman), Macmillan, 1966, pp. 88-9.*

THE TIMES, LONDON

Ann Jellicoe's play [*Shelley*] . . . will come as a surprise to those who associate her simply with verbally experimental studies of the teenage scene.

But, like her two previous plays, it is the work of a writer mainly concerned with overhauling theatrical form. In *The Knack* content took second place to speech rhythms; and in *Shelley* she seems much less concerned with saying anything of interest about the poet than with putting Victorian melodrama back on its feet.

It is a rather self-conscious exercise. Actors in the programme are listed as "heavy", "walking gentleman", "general utility", and other Victorian theatrical categories.

Some of the straight melodramatic effects come off—such as the overbearing Westbrook's plot to snare Shelley into marrying Harriet, and the subsequent episodes of marital estrangement and suicide (not Harriet's actual dive into the Serpentine, though). What is missing is boldness of construction and the sheer sense of energy. Miss Jellicoe seems to have lost confidence in her chosen form, and written instead a documentary melodrama.

It thus becomes hard to tell how the play is meant to be understood. Sometimes it sticks exactly to the facts. Even Shelley's expulsion from Oxford by a tribunal of ludicrous pedagogues is given in direct quotation; and for his death Trelawny (hastily donning a yachting jacket) simply steps forward and delivers the appropriate passage from *The Last Days of Shelley and Byron* to the assembled cast.

On the other hand, to create a melodramatic scene, Miss Jellicoe involves Mary Godwin in fierce jealousy for Jane Williams—when, by all accounts, the historical Mary regarded Jane as one of the few comforts that life at Lerici had to offer.

Shelley himself . . . goes through the action in the obligatory white shirt displaying a swan-like neck; but the writing offers no interpretation of him. At one moment he seems a noble idealist and at the next a monster of self-deception.

The play is at its best in the occasional passages of old-fashioned psychological drama. These do not light up the protagonist, but they do provide powerful moments for . . . [the] gently hypocritical Godwin, and . . . [for Mary Godwin], who has one speech, blaming Italian exile for the death of her children, that has the true voice of feeling.

> *"Documentary Melodrama of Poet's Life," in* The Times, *London (© Times Newspapers Limited 1965), October 19, 1965, p. 16.*

IRVING WARDLE

Until last night this was just a funny story: a classic comedy of misunderstanding between an avant-garde artist and a blinkered institution—as if someone had commissioned Baudelaire to write a book on gardening. [But the new production of *The Rising Generation*] has now shown that Miss Jellicoe, at least, knew exactly what she was doing. The events are monstrous—but so are those that children imagine for themselves: and the way they develop amounts to a projection of childhood free-association in broad-scale theatrical terms.

The production (cut down to a mere cast of 150) opened with an assault on the audience by an army of cleaning ladies who then formed up on stage raised Nuremburg cheers for their leader—the nightmarish "Mother", carried in on a litter, voluptuously cajoling them into man-hatred with a skeleton swinging over her head.

The atmosphere takes one back to the heyday of C.N.D., but it is still heady. The writing is boldly mapped out into sections of plot development and crowd rhythm. Its simple, magnified technique would clearly have a far greater impact in the setting for which it was first intended, but even at close quarters it is great fun.

Irving Wardle, "Ghoul the Guides Missed," in The Times, *London (© Times Newspapers Limited 1967), July 24, 1967, p. 6.**

IRVING WARDLE

Ann Jellicoe's new play [*The Giveaway*] is a farce about a family who win a ten years' supply of cornflakes as a competition prize and there are two ways of looking at it: either as the calculated attempt of an experimental writer to turn out a commercially profitable piece: or as an honest and logical effort to extend her work into popular territory.

I have no hesitation in taking the second view. Miss Jellicoe, whatever her critical reputation, has never sought out the avant-garde public. Her interest, among other things, is in the traditional broad theatrical categories, and when she is on top of her form (as in *The Knack* and *The Rising Generation*) there is no one like her for flooding the place with joy. Unfortunately there remains the well known split between intention and range of talent; and while *The Giveaway* shows her still in command of the comic techniques with which she made her name, it does not show much aptitude for conventional farce.

There seems no doubt that this is what she meant to write. Her characters, who inhabit three adjoining houses, have been assembled strictly with a view to farcical development. The prize-winning Mum . . . is simply a compulsive tea-drinker and an inexhaustible source of middle-aged female inconsistency. Jim, her honest mechanic son . . . , dotes on the dumb-blonde lodger, who favours sharp-suited Cyril next door: while on the other side dwells the scatty Daisy Wink . . . , who pines for Jim. There are also the eight huge mobile crates in which the cornflakes arrive; and to begin with it seems that these are to be the real actors in the comedy.

However, no such development ensues. Perhaps Miss Jellicoe imagined what Ionesco would have done with them, shuddered, and decided that crates should know their place. So although the cast play hide and seek round them, play rhythms on them, and address them as domestic pets, they take on no theatrical life of their own. Nor does Miss Jellicoe intend any social comment on the free-gift business and its clients. The crates and the characters are there simply for laughs; and not many people laughed last night.

One reason for this lies in the characterization. It may be true that farcical character cannot accommodate any complexity. But simplicity is not the same thing as simple-mindedness; and Miss Jellicoe's people are so dim that, far from permitting rapid action, they slow it down to a crawl in which everything has to be explained to them in one-syllable words. Together with this, there goes a deficient instinct for how long suspense can be sustained. Not only do you see the next development coming; by the time it arrives you have lost interest.

What pleasure the piece offers comes from Miss Jellicoe's old games with nonsense language and physical rhythm; and from one passage where Daisy (attired as a schoolboy) bursts right out of character for a series of crazy parodies of television commercials.

Irving Wardle, "Effort to Extend Scope," in The London Times, *April 9, 1969, p. 6.*

JOHN SIMON

The English theater has developed a brand of Absurdism of its own, more socially conscious, more concerned with quaint but real types, more prosaic than its French counterpart. In the plays of N. F. Simpson, Henry Livings, Ann Jellicoe and a few others, the Absurd has been domesticated: it has been swathed in flannels and tweeds, a pipe has been stuck in its mouth, and it has even developed a taste for tea. Certainly the amount of tea consumed in Ann Jellicoe's *The Knack* compares favorably with the quantity ingested in a play by James Bridie, J. B. Priestley or whoever the current West End favorite may be. But Miss Jellicoe strains her tea through some curiously barren, bizarrely monochromatic, almost basic-English dialogue, but an always slightly off-base basic.

She gives us three young men in a lodging house: one a sort of Soho satyr who measures out his life with petty seductions; the other a foolishly likable ninny, starved for women; the third an *homme moyen sensuel,* full of outrageous fancies but quite sensible underneath. The teddy-boy picks a little provincial guinea pig for the teddy bear to practice on under his sinister guidance. The nice chap tries to humanize the experiment. The guinea pig revolts. There are all kinds of crosscurrents, cross purposes, double crosses, and minor mayhem. Amiable decency seems, in the end, to assert itself.

Miss Jellicoe has said in an interview that "people should forget their intellect for a while and lead fuller and richer sensory and emotional lives," and *The Knack* certainly capitalizes on the most visceral aspects of conversation, so to speak, garnished by charmingly feminine flights of comic fancy. Her play is a kind of good-natured fat lady, naked but wearing a funny hat— a daintily comic cloche over a Gaston Lachaise body. Typically, the girl's dialogue for half a page or more consists of the word "Rape!" Simple but not ordinary: she is screaming about a rape that hasn't been committed, though she wishes it had; and calling for help which, however, she doesn't want to come. It is the victim raping the rapists, who are really rapists in spite of themselves. It is a topsy-turvy world, seen upside-down through an old-fashioned camera, but all the time we know that we will get from it a picture that is comfortingly right-side-up. I found *The Knack* amusing and endearing. . . . (pp. 55-6)

John Simon, "Autumn, 1964: 'The Knack'," in his Uneasy Stages: A Chronicle of the New York Theatre, 1963-1973 *(copyright © 1975 by John Simon; reprinted by permission of Random House, Inc.), Random House, 1975, pp. 55-6.*

ALLEN SADDLER

Community Theatre is one of those new concepts where a critic treads warily, if at all. Is it to be judged as a piece of theatre, or does it come under the Arts Council dictum for community arts, 'participation more important than the product?' How can you view a piece of work when the quality of performance is a secondary consideration?

The Reckoning succeeds on both counts and spoils the discussion. As a piece of theatre it is exciting, dramatic and experimental, and as a piece of community art it seems to have involved at least 200 people directly in performing and backstage functions and to have aroused the interest of a large section of the population of Lyme Regis.

The difference in this piece of community art from others I have seen is that the professionals have not taken a back seat, but have acted as a catalyst, with the energetic Ann Jellicoe taking a positive lead in writing, directing and organising. . . .

The Reckoning deals with a brief period in the history of Lyme at the time of the Monmouth rebellion. Young Sam Dassin rode a series of sweaty horses to London to warn the king. Dissenters were hung, drawn and quartered and families split asunder. . . .

The form is action on three stages, with the audience swivelling round in the middle and often involved in crowd scenes. At first it is disconcerting when the man standing next to you is violently hauled off to face the dreaded Judge Jeffreys, but after a while the interest in following the progress of events overcomes shyness.

The play is a series of short sharp scenes. Melodramatic, violent and moments of crude, even zany, humour, I would say it was a good deal more theatrical than historical. No doubt the people of Lyme know their local history, but an outsider would do well to bone up before arrival. The performance is preceded by a carnival purporting to be an Elizabethan market known as Cobb Ale. (The Cobb is a harbour and the ale was sold, although not in plastic cups, to pay for its upkeep.) This half-hour of local colour does certainly set the scene. From then

on it is all action. The mayor and his cronies scramble around in a frenzy, people rush by in terror, beg for mercy or confide strange secrets into your ear. A girl who is pregnant by a Catholic finds herself in a strange dilemma, proclamations are read from all parts of the hall. Soldiers burst in. Bands parade. Prisoners are dragged off screaming. Brawls break out just where you are standing. Events proceed so quickly that there is no time to examine the Catholic or the Protestant case. The quiet periods, (very short), are dour predictions of family troubles. Of course, it is a bloodthirsty period and to encapsulate all the drama and violence into about two hours leaves little time for debate.

When all the colour has dimmed what is the future for this type of theatrical enterprise? This massive effort ran four nights in Lyme Regis and was sold out for every performance. It is unlikely to be produced elsewhere. No doubt that Lyme is a warmer community as a result and it is the effect on the community that is important. Amateurs acted with professionals, scores of children had an experience to remember, a local writer achieved total integration with the community, but, overall, *The Reckoning* remains a very enclosed local event. If shorter working hours and micro-processors do make the inroads that have been predicted, local theatre of this scale and quality may be the concept of the future, but I think that this experience has shown that it will need professional vision and expertise.

Allen Saddler, "The Reckoning" (© copyright Allen Saddler 1979; reprinted with permission), in Plays and Players, *Vol. 26, No. 6, February, 1979, p. 29.*

Pamela Hansford Johnson

1912-1981

English novelist, essayist, critic, dramatist, poet, and mystery writer

Johnson was a prolific writer whose novels defy rigid categorization. This is perhaps because her style ranged from early twentieth-century experimentalism to the third person narrative typical of nineteenth-century British novelists. Her plots, themes, and settings varied with each work. Johnson's variability is also indicated by the fact that her first novel, *This Bed Thy Centre* (1935), an immediate critical and popular success, focused on ignorance of sexuality and was viewed as rather "permissive" in its day; years later, in the tract "On Iniquity" (1967), she questions the mores of permissive society.

In the mid-1930s Johnson was briefly engaged to Dylan Thomas, who suggested the title of her first novel and with whom she shares similar literary devices, such as the use of interior monologues and the "stream of consciousness" technique. Johnson married Neill Gordon Stewart, though, and collaborated with him on two murder mysteries under the joint pseudonym Nap Lombard. The stories were written as escapist fiction and are not representative of her oeuvre. Subsequently, Johnson married C. P. Snow and together they composed several short plays which they both later dismissed as frivolous. Her novels have always received the most attention.

Although Johnson wrote two trilogies and has several characters appear in more than one volume, each of her novels is unique, differing from the others in some way, whether in presentation, resolution, or character types. In general, her characters attempt to achieve a balance between their inner and outer lives. Her comic touch helps to ease her studies of modern morality.

(See also *CLC*, Vols. 1, 7; *Contemporary Authors*, Vols. 1-4, rev. ed., Vol. 104 [obituary]; and *Contemporary Authors New Revision Series*, Vol. 2.)

Photograph by Mark Gerson

DESMOND SHAWE-TAYLOR

Miss Johnson is distinguishable from the many intelligent novelists of the day by the fact that she is not in the least afraid of people who are ordinary and good. Most writers would run a mile to avoid such people as material for fiction, partly for fashionable reasons (someone might murmur "Priestley," and then where would they be?), but principally because the virtuous are so very difficult to do well. But characters of simple goodness, when realised in fiction without either insipidity or sentimentality, are encountered by the reader with a delight that is quite unforgettable. What a pleasure it is to think of Trollope's Mr. Harding, or of Peter Schulz, the old Professor of Music in Romain Rolland's *Jean Christophe*. Miss Johnson attempts nothing on that level, but her new book [*World's End*] shows that she is sensitive to the quality of natural goodness and can present it to the reader when she sees it. And yet the world which she depicts is one which many novelists would have wanted to cram with nicely touched-up iniquities: a needy, uncertain, semi-artistic group living at World's End, Chelsea. The most disreputable of them are the drink-soaked pianist Sipe and his worthless wife, Irene, about whom there is something of the flavour of an early Huxley (Coleman or Spandrell): but, if they are less witty and horrifying, they are also more real. At the heart of the book is a love-story, although the lovers are seen nine years after marriage, not a few months before as usual. Arnold Brand is middle-class, intelligent, wanting to write, often unemployed and generally depressed: the footling jobs that do come his way—snobbish little travel agencies and so on—bore him to death. Doris is humorous and good-tempered and wretchedly overworked in a draper's shop. Brand is miserably conscious of failing to provide for his wife, indeed at times he is kept by her; his shame makes him unkind to her and drives him into a flirtation with a second-rate dancer named Rosary, who hovers pathetically on the edge of the stage world. He does not want Rosary when he is happy; but when he is unhappy she represents for him a different world, a world in which he need feel no shame. That is well observed. Arnold and Doris live in a top-back room which they rent from Ma Hogben, and in this character, which might easily have become a shapeless receptacle for traditional Cockney good nature, the author has been uncommonly successful. . . .

Round these figures the story moves with easy command of dialogue and invention of incident; and all the time we hear rumbling in the background the Big Noises and the Big Guns; wars and rumours of wars; the hateful mass-cruelties and stupidities. All the World's End people (except Macdonald, the Communist downstairs) are of the sort which for generations has regarded foreign affairs as something to be read about in the papers after breakfast and then left to their betters; and now they are caught in that terrible problem of our day: that the precise moment when we all feel that we can no longer afford to remain idle spectators should also be the moment which demands, even of the experts, more experience and knowledge and judgment than ever before. What sane idealist in England would not feel less sure of his own wisdom after being Foreign Secretary for a week? Ma Hogben is of course resolutely iso-lationist; Sipe shrugs his shoulders and retires, desperate but undeceived, to Montparnasse; Brand, broken but also strength-ened by the loss of his wife in childbirth, leaves with Mac-donald to join the International Brigade in Spain. He is doing what he believes to be right; but *is* it right? and, if so, for how many? As a novelist, Miss Johnson is not obliged to deliver judgment; it is a tribute to the sincerity of her book that it raises the whole question (without in the least solving it) of the relationship between "the world of the street corner and the world beyond the horizon."

Desmond Shawe-Taylor, in a review of "World's End," in The New Statesman & Nation *(© 1937 The Statesman & Nation Publishing Co. Ltd.), Vol. XIV, No. 346, October 9, 1937, p. 567.*

EDITH H. WALTON

Partly due to her precocity—her first book was published when she was only 22—but more to the fact that her talent is gen-uinely individual, Pamela Hansford Johnson has attracted con-siderable attention in England. She has never, I believe, had an equal success here [in America], nor up till now has she deserved it. Although full of vitality and color, **"This Bed Thy Centre"** was a confused and ill-organized story, while **"Blessed Above Women,"** its successor, had a morbid, macabre quality which was definitely unpleasant. Skillful technically, it was mainly a tour de force. With **"World's End,"** however—a very moving though quite unpretentious tale—Pamela Johnson has suddenly acquired a new depth and maturity.

By one definition—the simplest—**"World's End"** is a love story, dealing with a struggling young couple, Arnold and Doris Brand. . . .

As to their personal story, it is so ordinary, so unexceptional that the book can barely be said to have a plot. . . .

As the story progresses from one small crisis to another, the emphasis remains constant upon the relationship between these two. Their quarrels and reconciliations, the ebb and renewal of their passion, the moments of pain and delight which checker the course of their love—this is the essential stuff out of which **"World's End"** is fashioned. . . .

Due to its very simplicity, it is hard to explain why **"World's End"** is so exceptionally good. For one thing it is a novel unspoiled by trickery and artifice. These young people, Arnold and Doris, are presented with scrupulous honesty. Their mo-ments of pettiness and weakness, their rather pitiful frailty, serve somehow merely to heighten the poignance of their pas-sion. The English critic who likened Miss Johnson's novel to Hemingway's "Farewell to Arms" was not so far astray as one might think. It gives one the same live sense of an over-mastering love.

Finally, by deliberately stressing the odds which the Brands and their kind must face, Miss Johnson has greatly sharpened the contemporary significance of her story. Her lovers are sym-bols of all the frightened little people who do not know, these days, where security may be found.

Edith H. Walton, "A Moving Tale of Simple Folk," in The New York Times Book Review *(© 1938 by The New York Times Company; reprinted by per-mission), February 27, 1938, p. 6.*

JANE SPENCE SOUTHRON

"The Monument" is a novel reflecting a world on the brink of unimaginable disaster. If you had not before read a word by this young English novelist you would only have to get well away into the opening paragraph to realize that here is a writer of fiction who should matter. There is a sudden downward sweep into the heart of a widely comprehensive subject. There is plain, pregnant wording. There is realism. There is poetic thought. There is a warmth of feeling that embraces mankind not only in the individual but in the aggregate. And there is directness. The story that follows bears out the expectation aroused.

Miss Johnson's first novel, **"This Bed Thy Center,"** gave promise that has yet to receive its complete fulfillment; which is better than if, at so young an age and with all life before her, she should have been able to crystallize her possibilities into too small and too neat a success. **"World's End"** estab-lished her securely among those contemporary fictionists whose appeal is, to a large degree, quietly emotional. In **"The Mon-ument"** she has essayed a more ambitious task—one not only calling for an intimate acquaintance with conditions that, ul-timately, underlie most of the unrest of our time but demanding, also, an uncommon endowment of courage.

She deals uncompromisingly with the appalling poverty and sordidness behind the façade of London's dignity and wealth, and is not content with showing us what is wrong. She gets down among it, fighting. Annie Sellars, a young married woman of the working class, one of the four main characters chosen, we are told, as representative of the world visioned from the top of a tower overlooking London, is a passionately convinced member of the Labor party. She is also, definitely, a woman whose young, ardent love for a man developed, after marriage and the births of her two children, into a devotion to home and family which she succeeds in reconciling with wider duties.

Annie's story is a tenderly human one with no "Party First" touch about it. Bob, her husband, hates her being jailed, march-ing in "Save China" parades and leading processions for the lifting of non-intervention. So does her young son. But Annie has humor, and she jollies them along with her. She has grit too; working her fingers to the bone when Bob is incurably hurt and she must fend for the lot of them.

A similar lack of one-sidedness characterizes the rest of the narrative. Another of the four "representatives" is a young and highly cultured Jew, Raphael Barrandane, born to affluence and surrounded by overmuch love and care by a doting father. Contrasted with him is Albert Whye, whose tentative gropings after the beautiful in life and art have been perpetually thwarted by extreme poverty. . . .

"The Monument" is as close to today's news as it is possible for a work of fiction to be, but there is no conspicuous absence of perspective, since the issues dealt with, notably the wars of aggression now in progress or being contemplated, have been so long and so intensively with us. One of the two major themes, and one which is intimately connected with the stormy love story of Raphael and Mary Captor, the fourth "representative" of the time and place, is the anti-Semitism shown as having grown up lately, owing to fascist propaganda, among a particular class in London. Against this class the author wages no uncertain war.

Mary herself, a novelist with a book banned by the public prosecutor, is, to this reviewer, the least interesting figure of the score or so delineated. Her ultra-modernism cannot compete with the plain humanity that makes Jenny, Albert's frail sweetheart; Teddy, his wayward brother; Jim, his nearly blind old tyrant of a father, and many another of the lesser characters so satisfyingly pleasing. Perhaps Miss Johnson's strength lies in depicting not the sophistications but the simplicities of human living.

Jane Spence Southron, "A World Stands on the Brink of Disaster," in The New York Times Book Review *(© 1938 by The New York Times Company; reprinted by permission), September 11, 1938, p. 7.*

JOHN KENNETH MERTON

Miss Johnson is a young English writer who already has produced five novels and who with her **"World's End,"** published early this year, achieved a certain amount of success. The facility with which she writes, combining with the praise she has received (in England there is a disposition to rank her rather highly) seems to have gone to her head. For in her latest [**"The Monument"**] she has attempted something beyond her powers, and in her youthful overconfidence has even attempted to show off. The result is not merely a failure but a muddle.

Her idea is good enough. It is that of carrying forward simultaneously four separate stories, and of letting them all be seen against a background of the most up-to-date contemporaneousness. Unfortunately we gather the impression that Pamela Johnson's characters are concerned only with Spain and are hardly aware that such a person as Hitler exists. As for the separate stories, each is too unsubstantial to make up, even when combined, a web of sufficient firmness. Good scenes are to be found, but the general effect is vague.

John Kenneth Merton, in a review of "The Monument," in Commonweal *(copyright © 1938 Commonweal Publishing Co., Inc.; reprinted by permission of Commonweal Publishing Co., Inc.), Vol. XXVIII, No. 26, October 21, 1938, p. 680.*

JANE SPENCE SOUTHRON

[**"Too Dear for My Possessing"**] is a book of queer enchantment; of strange, astringent realism; a book stripped utterly of sentimentality but deep with feeling that is both psychic and sensuous. You are not rushed into anything. You drift along as quietly, at first, as did 13-year-old Claud Pickering in his little old boat on the stream that opened out of the Bruges Canal. A boy's world; but an exceptional boy. A boy with an unordinary endowment of sensibility, of artistic perception.

The pace quickens imperceptibly. The boy is a youth; a young man. He is married, is successful; but haunted, always, by a dream, a vision, a reality that life—or he himself or the girl who was the heart of the dream—forces into the background. Suddenly you are in the grip of tragedy, poignant, silent tragedy

that makes no show; and you realize how very far Pamela Hansford Johnson has come in the few but pregnant years that separate this beautiful, pain-dogged book from her promising first novel.

This also is a young book; but it is not youthfully tentative. The dream was youth's prerogative. The tough, clear-eyed decision that gives the finale its strength and special significance is the writer's answer to the challenge of contemporary events. Pamela Johnson, looking back on her own generation's less than thirty years, has taken stock of them, given them their meed of due, nostalgic longing and swept them into the discard. With quiet confidence she speaks here—and not the less effectively because she speaks in fiction—for the young intellectuals of her day and country. . . .

Miss Johnson has never done anything finer than the brief, episodic scenes that carry . . . [the story of Claud's] life from boyhood in Bruges to London and Paris and that link [Helena Shea], the gifted stage and cabaret star and the budding London-Paris art critic in a passion of young love that feeds on frustration.

It is a story with heartbreak in it; mystery, the mystery of personality, of spirit, before which science has nothing to say, and the occasional aching loveliness that is art's greatest gift to life. For Miss Johnson is a young artist but a real one, with the artist's unceasing dissatisfaction as insurance.

Jane Spence Southron, "New Work by a Brilliant Writer," in The New York Times Book Review *(© 1940 by The New York Times Company; reprinted by permission), July 28, 1940, p. 7.*

DESMOND HAWKINS

Pamela Hansford Johnson belongs, with R. C. Hutchinson and Romilly Cavan, to a new generation of respectably popular novelists who are just arriving, or have just arrived. In [***Too Dear for My Possessing***] she writes in the first person, as a boy and later as a man: a difficult feat of male impersonation which is strikingly successful and which must inevitably be labelled *tour de force*. . . .

This is a full-fathoms-five novel to drown in, ample in dimension, leisurely and detailed in development, packed with carefully elaborated characterisation and incident. The recollections of a boyhood in Bruges have an individual atmosphere and a sharpness of vision which carry full conviction, and it is in describing these early years that Miss Johnson is most satisfying to read. But there is a disturbing undercurrent, even in the best of the opening chapters: a portentousness of address and a further vagueness beyond each attempt at precision, which remind one increasingly of Charles Morgan. The young artist in a luminous afterglow of reminiscence, already shadowed with philosophising—it is *Portrait in a Mirror* which comes to mind as the most apt comparison. And sure enough, with Claud's puberty accomplished, Miss Johnson can find no objective but the agonised adultery of morganatic marriage. Cecil, the magnetic cabaret-singer, embodies nothing more than the Tin Pan Alley truism that Glamorous rhymes with Amorous. Claud, deliciously motionless between his *Fata Morgana* and the kind crumbs of dull marriage, reduces both his women to tears and offers a pocket-handkerchief. This is, of course, a tragic human situation—or at least a pathetic one—and I do not belittle it. But the novelist who is satisfied with it in terms of the *mystique* of Romance is merely adding density to an existing fog. . . . [Miss Johnson's] conception of character and moral situation is entirely commonplace. There are good moments in *Too Dear for My Possessing,* careful observation, moments of insight into human behaviour, promising scenes; but they all wash down to a couple of novelette profiles moaning over an investigation of former lovers. . . . (p. 214)

> *Desmond Hawkins, "The Ladies," in* The New Statesman & Nation *(© 1940 The Statesman & Nation Publishing Co. Ltd.), Vol. XX, No. 497, August 31, 1940, pp. 212, 214.**

R. ELLIS ROBERTS

Sidney Nichols was the hindquarters of the famous horse which, with his partner Benny Castelli in front, paraded the musichalls of England in the years after the last war. The act was called The Trojan Brothers, and the farcical, impudent animal was brought on to the stage by Benny's wife, known in the profession as Miss Maggie. Sid came of a family long connected with the stage: Miss Johnson, in this brilliant and moving story ["**The Trojan Brothers**"], is extraordinarily successful in her description of the variety world. The bars and eating-places between Glasshouse Street, back of Piccadilly, and the Roman's in the Strand; the glare and smell of hot dressing-rooms; the generosity and pettiness and childishness of the artists; the excitements and depressions; the extreme chances and changes—all of these are given with ease and assurance. In the overall picture of one aspect of London life "**The Trojan Brothers**" is in the true Dickens tradition, and can stand with Mr. Patrick Hamilton's incisive etchings of the darker corners of the great city. . . .

All the main characters are astonishingly life-like; and Miss Johnson shows unusual skill in giving the reader, by a phrase or an incident, a key to the nature of these people—the primness and possessiveness of Maggie, the humility and occasional fury of Benny, the greedy, self-pitying lust of Betty and her essential vulgarity, the tender understanding of Hockaby, the female impersonator, the simple, anxious goodness of Mrs. Nichols, Sid's mother. Sid himself, the widower who, since his wife died in childbirth, thinks of himself as her murderer, Sid with his wild gaiety, his audacity, his self-confidence is admirably portrayed throughout the book, and not least when his infatuation for Betty drives him over the edge of control and leads to her death and his own. Miss Johnson's only failure, I think, is the portrait of Anna. Up to the last book she is beautifully drawn. . . . But Miss Johnson wavers into uneasy melodrama when she drives Anna into the position of a half-unconscious accessory to Sid's murder of Betty. Anna is too imaginative, too brave to allow herself thus to drift into this role. Still, in so ambitious and successful a novel as "**The Trojan Brothers**" this hurried disposal of a character who, I fancy, grew more important than her maker intended, is a small fault.

> *R. Ellis Roberts, "The Rear End of the Act," in* The Saturday Review of Literature *(© 1945, copyright renewed © 1972, Saturday Review Magazine Co.; reprinted by permission), Vol. XXVIII, No. 24, June 16, 1945, p. 28.*

JANE MARTIN

For the purposes of "**The Trojan Brothers**," her latest novel, Miss Johnson has given up the wholesale manufacture of character types in favor of a well-constructed plot. The result is the most tightly knit and satisfying narrative she has yet produced.

In a London music hall her English *Pagliaccio* moves toward tragedy in the hindquarters of a horse. . . .

While doom is still rumbling off stage Miss Johnson gives her own best performance. There are authentic outlines of drab, matter-of-fact lives behind the honky-tonk of the music hall; the miasma of jealousy and intrigue hanging over backstage like a queasy cloud; sounds and smells of plain homes; acrid flavor of small, nagging worries. Paradoxically, so long as she is concerned with life around and about the theatre, the author gives us reality; it is only when she probes into the everyday impulses and motives of her actors that a sense of the theatrical begins to overwhelm us.

For Sydney, the protagonist, is believable only so long as he sticks to his normal role: a squat, freckled man with a clown's face and a philosopher's mind. When he gives way to his obsessive love for cousin Betty Todd, who married out of her class, his behavior needs more explaining than is to be read into Miss Johnson's rather misty analysis. (p. 15)

Miss Johnson seems more shrewd than deeply perceptive, so that her characters are of a first-degree subtlety not calculated to stand the strain of tortuous analysis. With precision and skill she can touch off the seamy side of a jealous, plain wife, a playboy husband, a shrill gossip. There are sharp, vivid scenes throughout the book which are effective and memorable; the cocktail party where Betty Todd serves humiliation to the Trojan Brothers, the week-end gathering where a shiny half-world attains a sub-Hollywood atmosphere; a theatrical row in a dressing room, frivolous and fateful. These are the highlights which the author creates with ease and proficiency.

But the case of Betty Todd and Sydney calls for more penetrating scrutiny. Betty must seem sharp and greedy enough to be a minor vixen, yet too confused and meager to have undermined the integrity of a natural philosopher. Always we will think of Sydney as an exceptionally nice man who had a bad dream about a murder. The book remains an excellent story which need never have wandered into the substratum of neopsychiatry. (pp. 15-16)

> *Jane Martin, in a review of "The Trojan Brothers," in* The New York Times Book Review *(© 1945 by The New York Times Company; reprinted by permission), July 1, 1945, pp. 15-16.*

D. S. SAVAGE

An Avenue of Stone is a skilful piece of contemporary reporting about our post-war lives, or the lives of a few selected personages whom Miss Johnson happens to have had, it would seem, under her observation. Her central character is a reluctantly ageing, but still captivating, beauty whose last bid for youth and life takes the form of a pathetic attachment to a spineless young man who apologetically sponges on her until he finds the girl to make him the kind of capable and dominating wife he requires. It is an authentic piece of observation, with few false notes, and has the unintense interestingness which the opportunity of peering into other people's lives, so like our own, and so unlike, always carries. The fact that it hasn't any other qualities, that the whole thing is flat observation without background or depth, is in one way rather . . . frightening? . . . depressing? . . . while at the same time it sharpens the factual authenticity of the tale as a depiction of contemporary life. Miss Johnson puts the whole thing together with the most expert unobtrusiveness, so that one reads rapidly to the end, to find the story has merged imperceptibly, as it seems, into the world around.

D. S. Savage, in a review of "An Avenue of Stone,"
in The Spectator (© 1947 by The Spectator; *reprinted by permission of* The Spectator), *Vol. 178, No. 6205, May 30, 1947, p. 634.*

THE TIMES LITERARY SUPPLEMENT

The elderly beauty who cannot quench her desire for love is a stock figure of fiction, though no doubt the theme still contains unexplored possibilities. Unfortunately Miss Hansford-Johnson, who does not seem to feel any compelling interest in her subject, has treated it in a mechanical way [in her novel *An Avenue of Stone*]. . . . One is not quite sure whether Miss Hansford-Johnson fully realizes that the woman who cannot grow old is a pathetic rather than a tragic figure. The attitude of the devoted though impatient stepson who tells the tale suggests that the reader is meant to see a grandeur in Helena which cannot possibly be there. The young protégé who leaves her without warning and the friends who gossip about her are too severely condemned for an inevitable attitude.

Sympathy with the heroine could have been won only by an extraordinarily vivid and vital presentation of someone who was an exception to all the rules. This Miss Hansford-Johnson does not achieve. Judged by her conversation and behaviour, Helena is a tiresome, egocentric and devouring personality from whom it would be a duty to flee at any price. Nor does the stilted dialogue of the other characters contribute anything to the desired illusion. Miss Hansford-Johnson has been most successful with her portrait of the neurotic young man who has to be propped up by some woman in order to survive. His combination of slyness and charm, devotion and complete unreliability is well conveyed.

"Enigmatic India," in The Times Literary Supplement (© Times Newspapers Ltd. (London) 1947; *reproduced from* The Times Literary Supplement *by permission), No. 2365, May 31, 1947, p. 265.**

JOHN RAYMOND

Catherine Carter once again raises the question of the historical and the "period" novel. Where does the one end and the other begin? One thinks of a "period" novel as an artificial, impressionistic potboiler and the majority are little better than that. Indeed, Miss Hansford Johnson's book bears signs of the atmospheric writing that we associate with the film script. Yet, long before we have finished this 460-page evocation of the Victorian theatre we realise that this book is far from being a potboiler. It is, rather, a clever writer's purple indiscretion. Miss Hansford Johnson is an accomplished novelist who has surrendered to the impulse to hurl her creative bonnet over the windmill. Her gaslit heroine and twopence-coloured background lie outside the diocese of the critical conscience and one must read her book in the spirit in which she appears to have written it. Certainly, it is an indiscretion that I thoroughly enjoyed sharing. The author has visualised the Belvedere Theatre and its inmates with such a passionate imagination (and, in the case of some of her characters, with a perceptive sharpness that recalls her earlier novels) that one forgives her for modelling her hero's traits on Irving and basing incidents on

theatrical history. One even forgives her for rewriting Clement Scott's notices and getting Mrs. Charlotte Charke's name wrong (but would Cibber's disgraced daughter ever have adorned a green room picture gallery?) Miss Hansford Johnson's vision only fails her in the case of the Irvingesque Peverel himself. She is unable to communicate the man's greatness as an actor. Her heroine is enchanting but her hero leaves one feeling, as Hazlitt said of Kemble, that though the temple is unimpaired, the divinity is sometimes from home. (pp. 132-33)

John Raymond, in a review of "Catherine Carter,"
in The New Statesman & Nation (© 1952 The Statesman & Nation Publishing Co. Ltd.), *Vol. XLIII, No. 1091, February 2, 1952, pp. 132-33.*

JAMES KELLY

What could be a more satisfying antidote for today's literary malaise than a lovingly executed Victorian novel of the London theatrical world in the Eighteen Eighties? A distant, gas-lit, perfect period it was, more antique and fustian for most of us than the Elizabethan. On deck to shape its historical personality were Ouida, Wilde, Henry James, George Moore, Gilbert & Sullivan. . . . The Impressionists were stirring and a fresh wind was blowing through the arts, but the decade must have seemed comfortably stable to most extant adults. In **"Catherine Carter,"** the youngish, London-born author brilliantly reconstructs this time and mood, amply fulfilling the promise of **"World's End," "The Trojan Brothers,"** and five or six lesser works which she has sent us since 1935. With her new novel, Miss Johnson has unmistakably arrived.

Remarkable for its poetic sweep and penetration, **"Catherine Carter"** unfolds most of its action at London's Belvedere Theatre, where a repertory company headed by the rising young actor-producer Henry Peverel is putting on Shakespeare and contemporary plays. Egocentric, dedicated to greatness, surrounded by carefully selected mediocrities, Peverel tolerates no rival for his place at center stage. Certainly he does not suspect that 22-year-old Catherine Carter, the worshipful, fervent child to whom he patronizingly gives acting lessons, will one day reach his own eminence.

Peverel has missed his cue. The passionate conflict between these two determines the course of both lives just as it gives the novel its focus. . . . It is a climactic moment in a performance of "Antony and Cleopatra" when [Catherine] and Sir Henry at last face each other as equals, tying together the contrapuntal themes of a plot which has seemed to flow naturally and unhurriedly from events.

Isabel, Sir Henry's motherly mistress, and Willy Palliser, his malevolent factotum, would be memorable in any company, as would Mrs. Carter, Catherine's scheming mother, and Malcolm Rivers, her conjugal experiment. Proof of Miss Johnson's craftsmanship lies in the fact that she can portray love at many levels, conduct excursions into the minds of actors wrestling with Shakespeare, compile an impressive documentary of the theatre, and provide a historical period piece—all without confusion or lapse from serenity.

Some readers may feel that **"Catherine Carter"** is too special, too much of the theatre. But even these dissenters will be hard put to name a pleasanter way to step out of 1952 for the duration of 478 pages.

James Kelly, "Peverel Misses His Cue," in The New York Times Book Review (© 1952 by The New York

Times Company; reprinted by permission), July 20, 1952, p. 4.

THE TIMES LITERARY SUPPLEMENT

Miss Pamela Hansford Johnson is a very cool and intelligent writer, and if she always promises a little more than she performs, her performance is still well out of the range of most novelists. She writes very carefully, building up a character with small, ingenious strokes; her observation of social and intellectual nuances is acute; yet in the end much of her work is softened by an emotionalism which blurs the outlines of character and weakens the story.

The Last Resort [published in the United States as *The Sea and the Wedding*] is about a well-to-do girl who is rejected by her lover after the death of his invalid wife, and marries a homosexual in the desperate need to obtain at least a new name and an unseparate life. All the minor figures in the story are wonderfully well done—the heroine's rude old father and leech-like mother, the lover's dying wife, the impersonal narrator who provides an undistorting mirror through which the story is seen.

At the heart of the book, however, is Celia; and Celia's small passages of arrogance and uncertainty, her devouring love for Eric Aveling and her last throw for happiness when he rejects her, are somehow not acceptable in Miss Johnson's terms. A compromise has been made somewhere in the course of writing, by which the severely realistic conception in her mind has been sentimentalized; with rather confusing results, because our original idea of Celia as upon the whole an unsympathetic character is not easily countered by the later attempt to give her a cloak of pathos. To say all this is to judge *The Last Resort* by the highest standards—those, say, of George Eliot. On any lesser level it can be praised as a most penetrating and intelligent novel.

"The Bond and the Free," in The Times Literary Supplement *(© Times Newspapers Ltd. (London) 1956; reproduced from* The Times Literary Supplement *by permission), No. 2855, November 16, 1956, p. 677.*

ELIZABETH JANEWAY

How long have unmarried British females in their thirties suffered from stifling family relationships and anemic love affairs? Is it only since World War I slaughtered thousands of potential husbands? Or does it go further back, to Victorian papas a là Mr. Barrett, and fiancés dead of fever on the North West Frontier?

Celia Baird, the heroine of Pamela Hansford Johnson's new novel [*The Sea and the Wedding*], is one of the most convincing, as she is one of the most pathetically repellent, of the whole genre. She has achieved, indeed, a semi-escape from it. That is, though she spends week-ends with Mummy and Daddy at a gruesome seaside hotel, she occupies a flat in London during the middle of the week, runs a typing bureau and has a lover. Yet it is only too evident, as she stalks through these pages of understated prose, jangling her bracelets, buying company but not companionship, that her emancipation only enslaves her more. Despair and ineptitude have somehow got into the marrow of her bones, as if a Bad Fairy had presided over her christening to insure that all the good wishes made

there should come true unhappily, to no avail, or after a corkscrew twist into mockery, like the wedding of the title.

Does it sound a depressing tale? Well, so it is, in a way, but Miss Johnson's crisp prose, her observant, satiric eye, and her gift for the smaller prickles of suspense keep the reader going. What I did miss, I confess, was the larger kind of suspense, the kind that entangles one in hope for and sympathy with the characters, the kind that depends not on plot but on immediacy of feeling. This is not here.

In part, I think, the trouble stems from the way in which Miss Johnson . . . has chosen to tell her story. Celia's situation— her loneliness, her bitter and hated dependence on her parents, her late precarious love which is mangled rather than cut off, her struggle to survive honorably and, finally, the fantastic solution she seizes upon—can be seen as tragedy; in which case it demands a warmer, more immediate telling than it gets. Or it can be turned into satire by a colder, crueler, recounting. But Celia's history is narrated by that troublesome, ubiquitous "old friend" who infests English fiction of the middle range, the "I" who is an observer but not a participant. . . .

This tidy narrator is unimportant as a person; but as a device, she thoroughly hampers the story, for she not only forces it one remove away from the reader. She also narrows the range it can move through to what is seen by one pair of eyes, and to a rather narrow reportorial realism.

The result is a curious, almost exact reversal of the standard, well-constructed "happy ending" novel. The climax is supplied by the death of a love affair instead of its growth, by Mr. Wrong instead of Mr. Right, by irony instead of sentiment. Very well. The trouble is that the dénouement can be foreseen and the plot seems as relentless as if Celia were going to live happily, instead of unhappily, ever after. Miss Johnson has stood the happy ending on its head and done it with considerable skill. She has contrived a believable gallery of characters, pathetic, horrible, funny and touching—some of them all at once. Many of the scenes are distressingly real enough to make one's skin crawl. But her very success at this reversal of the "happy ending" novel involves her in the use of its technique. And in this technique there is no room for the surprise, the vitality, what British novelist Rex Warner recently called "audacity," which could have turned a competent and interesting book into a moving and absorbing one.

Elizabeth Janeway, "Unhappily Ever After," in The New York Times Book Review (© 1957 by The New York Times Company; reprinted by permission), February 24, 1957, p. 4.

WALTER ALLEN

The Unspeakable Skipton represents a new and perhaps unexpected development in Pamela Hansford Johnson's talents. Together with *The Last Resort,* which appeared in 1956 and is surely one of the best novels of our time, it shows that there can no longer be excuse for failing to recognise that Miss Hansford Johnson is as good as any novelist writing in this country today. She began her career as a novelist when very young, and from the beginning she has been admirably professional; she has always known how to make the most use, in the most economical way, of her material. Short of the daemonic genius of an Emily Brontë, there is in the long run no substitute for professionalism. But it has its attendant dangers. It can degenerate into formula. The professional novelist's besetting sin is always what Norman Douglas called 'the novelist's touch', the falsification of life through failure to realise the 'complexities of the ordinary human mind'. It is not a failure the novelists we read and re-read are guilty of; and one of the inspiriting qualities of *The Last Resort* was precisely Miss Hansford Johnson's skill in rendering the complexities, the contradictions, the discontinuities of behaviour, so that in the end the action she described could stand as a satisfying image of life itself, one rendered with a sad, lucid, honest acceptance that made it not silly to be reminded of George Eliot.

There was something else, too. It became slowly apparent that, very quietly, Miss Hansford Johnson was extending the territory of the novel. It was not that the types she was describing, or their milieu, were exactly new; but she had made them new: the retired, angry, self-absorbed doctor, his wife neurotically possessive of their daughter, the 'camp' architect, and the rest. She had seen all round them and caught them in a new light, in a new significance, so that in the end they were somehow bigger, richer as emblems of the human condition, than one might have expected them to be. 'The novelist's touch' was conspicuously absent from their delineation. So with *The Unspeakable Skipton*.

Here, Miss Hansford Johnson takes as her subject a type much more common in the arty pubs and clubs of Soho than it has been in fiction: the paranoiac artist. Until now, treatment of him has been marginal: one recalls Mercaptan in *Antic Hay*, and there are entertaining sketches in the early novels of Anthony Powell. The great exemplar in life is Frederick Rolfe, 'Baron Corvo', and Miss Hansford Johnson has admittedly drawn partly upon him for her full-length study of Daniel Skipton, Knight of the Most Noble Order of SS. Cyril and Methodius. But Rolfe has been no more than the starting-point: Skipton exists in his own right and in our time. . . .

Skipton is a superb comic creation, and the final impression he makes is that of truth. Without sentimentality, without for a moment abating the rigour of her sardonic comedy, Miss Hansford Johnson brings out the full pathos of the poor wretch and his fate, which in essence is that of the dedicated artist without talent. And she embodies his fate in a plot marked by continuous and delightful invention and a set of characters that are wonderful foils to Skipton. The chief of these is the poetic dramatist Dorothy Merlin, author of *Joyful Matrix*, prophetess of the womb and a fertility goddess in theory and in practice. She is as magnificent a monster, almost, as Skipton himself; and the remarkable thing is that, though I can think of no one in contemporary literary life even remotely her counterpart, she emerges, with her hangers-on, as an acceptable symbol of the literary world and the literary values that Skipton in his dotty way is fighting. The setting—Bruges with its bells and its canals—adds a dimension of poetry to the comedy. *The Unspeakable Skipton* is a brilliant piece of sustained writing, which, as an original and successful comic work, challenges and compels us to revise our former notions of the nature and scope of Miss Hansford Johnson's talents.

> *Walter Allen, "Portrait of a Paranoiac," in* New Statesman *(© 1959 The Statesman & Nation Publishing Co. Ltd.), Vol. LVII, No. 1452, January 10, 1959, p. 48.*

THOMAS F. CURLEY

[In *The Unspeakable Skipton* Miss Hansford Johnson proceeds to a] celebration of Daniel Skipton's doom. That is what the novel is about. From the very beginning, from the time Skipton hears and sees, through his pocket mirror, Dorothy Merlin say of him, "*Why* is that man like a carrion crow," you know Skipton is lost. Not that you care. Insufferable in victory, magnificently spiteful and enraged in defeat, Skipton on his death bed conquers, but only esthetically, his gross tormentors.

It's amazing how well all this is brought off. At first reading, I put the book down as a better than competent but not a great work. It is not great but it is so very accomplished that any comparison with the competent is an injustice.

Skipton is presented as unspeakable but we are persuaded, though never told, to like him. And yet never once, no, not for a sentence, does the author entice our sentiments or our emotions. You could not care less what happens to Skipton or the rest but you thoroughly enjoy reading about him and them. Now that is an achievement worthy of unqualified praise and admiration. I don't know of an American who is capable of it.

As for engaging the affections, well that is something, as Miss Hansford Johnson no doubt knows, that is beyond the reaches of art. At least it should be. (pp. 549-50)

> *Thomas F. Curley, "Celebration of an Author's Doom," in* Commonweal *(copyright © 1959 Commonweal Publishing Co., Inc.; reprinted by permission of Commonweal Publishing Co., Inc.), Vol. LXIX, No. 21, February 20, 1959, pp. 549-50.*

WHITNEY BALLIETT

Two recent English novels—Pamela Hansford Johnson's **"The Unspeakable Skipton"** and Penelope Mortimer's "Cave of Ice," . . . are forceful suggestions that perhaps the irrepressible magnetism of the novel lies, when all is said and done, in its elusiveness, its basic indefinability. Miss Johnson's book, which has been described in the English press as a remarkable work that enlarges the boundaries of the novel, appears to have changed shape in crossing the water, for here it seems only a highly skilled imitation of a conventional novel. . . . (p. 167)

"The Unspeakable Skipton" has everything that Mrs. Mortimer's book hasn't, and nothing that it has. From its beginning one is conscious of being in the presence of a Novelist at Work. Indeed, the book's structure, prose, settings, and characterizations have been exquisitely handmade, and they emit a fat, pleased Currier & Ives glow. . . . (p. 169)

The hero-villain is a penniless English writer, Daniel Skipton, who, the author of a once mildly celebrated avant-garde work, lives in self-imposed exile in Belgium, where he passes his time in writing scurrilous letters to those who support him, and in pimping, lying, cheating, boasting, and being generally execrable. Miss Johnson slowly circles Skipton, covering every inch of him with the thick blue paint of her prose, but, just as day and night would be meaningless without each other, Skipton, too, is meaningless, for she has forgotten—unlike Mrs. Mortimer, whose subject matter is equally unappetizing—to offset his wretchedness with any of its opposites, which would make him pitiable, and thus meaningful. Instead, in Medealike fashion, the book drones flawlessly along in a nasty, high-pitched whine, which is only intensified by the people who surround Skipton, all of them variations of him. The result resembles the sensation one might have after abruptly realizing that a beautifully finished cigar-store Indian is, after all, just a block of wood. (p. 170)

*Whitney Balliett, "Now You See It, Now You Don't,"
in* The New Yorker *(© 1959 by The New Yorker
Magazine, Inc.), Vol. XXXV, No. 5, March 21, 1959,
pp. 167-70, 173.**

GERALD SYKES

Quite possibly a portent of stiffening literary morality, this
excellent novel ["**The Humbler Creation**"] reverses two of
the major trends of good modern fiction. It shows almost none
of the frank subjectivity, the recognition of imaginative limitations that so frequently make the modern novelist more interesting than his characters. It also breaks sharply with the
bohemian attitudes of those writers who seem to secede from
their society in a way that Pamela Hansford Johnson . . . most
clearly does not. . . .

Miss Johnson writes so well in a traditional vein (one obvious
ancestor is Trollope) and at the same time shows such an
intimate realistic grasp of modern minutiae that she suggests
a comparison, if only for purposes of historical elucidation,
with the British woman novelist generally regarded as the best
of our times, Virginia Woolf. Miss Johnson justifies the comparison, not because she possesses anything like Mrs. Woolf's
verbal magic—she does not, though she writes with masterly
precision—but because she goes deeper, knows her people
better and faces up more squarely to their problems. If Mrs.
Woolf was a Bloomsbury stylist reacting against the crudities
of H. G. Wells and Arnold Bennett, Miss Johnson is a post-
imperial social scientist reacting against the elegant estheticism
of Bloomsbury.

In "**The Humbler Creation**" she considers the overworked,
underpaid, middle-aged, tone-deaf, unimaginative vicar of a
London parish who has the misfortune, when his icily handsome wife turns away from him, to fall in love with another
woman. He does nothing improper, he only pours out his heart
and kisses his beloved on the neck, but the mere existence of
his unfulfilled emotion is sufficient reason to haul him before
his bishop and threaten his suddenly obstinate passion with
general ruin. In this unlikely material, free of any poetry,
animal joy or religious ecstasy, Miss Johnson has had the
novelistic prescience to see a rare opportunity. While presenting her wretched vicar against a humdrum background of
church bazaars, organ practice, family quarrels, well-meaning
officials and cheerless sinners, she has cannily dramatized the
path of duty that is still for so many dogged, long-suffering
Britons the only way to glory. She has created a symbolic
portrait of Britain today.

Those of us who have not followed such a narrow path, who
imagined such rigors had ended forever with the coming of an
economy of abundance and a well-known trend toward ethical
relativity, will yet be held by this story. It is no mere anach-
ronism. Beneath each line it asks: "What happens to nations
when they lose this despised mechanical morality? And how
many individuals can live without it?" The book is a kind of
"Pilgrim's Progress" for our times, except that this pilgrim
makes no progress, but simply tries to carry on.

The novel is not grandly conceived; it is content to make its
tough, neo-Puritan point, to tell its single story and be done.
But it makes that story indirectly so pertinent, and tells it with
such an effortless flow of flawless detail, that unless I am
mistaken it is going to enter the small pantheon of the significant books of our day.

Gerald Sykes, "Pilgrim without Progress," in The
New York Times Book Review *(© 1960 by The New
York Times Company; reprinted by permission), Feb-
ruary 28, 1960, p. 4.*

SUSAN M. BLACK

[In *The Humbler Creation*] Miss Johnson's style and her material are in tune—almost too much in tune. Only her descriptive, figurative and symbolic use of light and color call attention
to the prose. The author writes of skies that are transparent,
violet, cobalt, brilliant with stars and lime-green. She described
blazes, bubbles, gleams and lozenges of light that may be pale,
deforming, dull, reflected, lemon, sallow, torporous or sour
and that comes from fire, lamp, sun and moon. Characters
radiate light figuratively: there's the "so inhumanly bright"
assistant vicar whose romance "suffered from the limelight of
a parish" and who was wont to send "an azure gleam of
amusement in Maurice's direction." Fisher's principles are
"illuminating," Libby "glows" only at bazaars and as Alice's
father-in-law lies dying in "moneyed brightness" the author
takes us into the "stained-glass windows of his mind." Alice's
room is literally and symbolically the brightest spot in the book.
Maurice comes to adore the light she is so fond of.

The Humbler Creation is dominated by the themes of resignation, renunciation and unhappiness. It has been written without the touches of humor evident in other novels by this prolific
writer; smile we may but laughter would be inappropriate. But
although it so colorfully pictures people who are content if they
can "cope" with life, not to mention enjoy life, this is by no
means a despairing book. That the members of a parish feel
compelled to put an end to a platonic affair that offers their
vicar his only chance for happiness seems wrong, but the author
insists on the rightness of their motives; their actions indicate
largeness rather than smallness, strength and not weakness,
and a sense of duty rather than whimsy.

Susan M. Black, "Virtue inside the Rectory," in The
New Republic *(reprinted by permission of* The New
Republic; *© 1960 The New Republic, Inc.), Vol. 142,
No. 12, March 21, 1960, p. 19.*

THE TIMES LITERARY SUPPLEMENT

One need not be a Christian to believe in Hell—to be aware,
that is, of an irredeemable blackness of soul from which there
is no escape, for which there is no consolation. The central
character of *An Error of Judgement* is an agnostic, to all appearances a wise and unusually good man, but he is obsessed
by the idea that deep inside he is vile, cruel, and forever
damned. *Corruptio optimi pessima* might have provided Miss
Hansford Johnson with one suitable motto for her new novel,
though the tortuous and startling series of circumstances she
has devised suggest a moral complexity which should challenge
most conventional Christian or, indeed, humanist ethical judgments.

William Setter is a distinguished Harley Street consultant married to a big, gay, gadabout wife called Emily. Gradually,
through the mild, quizzical eyes of a decent little man called
Victor, who somewhat improbably becomes Setter's confidant,
the anatomy of a tortured soul takes shape. Because he has so
far restrained his perverted urge to cruelty, has, in fact, turned
it to virtuous effect, Setter cannot accept the idea of a God
who will judge him worthy of salvation; the only hope, he

believes, is to do nothing, to alleviate the strain of hypocrisy by abnegating moral responsibility. . . .

Miss Hansford Johnson spares us none of the agonized soul-searching which must attend the predicament in which Setter [finds himself when it becomes clear to him that his friend Sammy has murdered an old woman], but she is far too accomplished a novelist to offer simple answers or even to hazard faith. By choosing as narrator a man who, with ironical detachment, is half-convinced Setter is insane or at least a freak, she makes the whole nasty business a nightmare barely credible in the respectable, educated *petit-bourgeois* world he and stupid little Jenny inhabit; Miss Hansford Johnson sets her often lurid moments of horror against a sane and humorous domestic background. To be sure Victor, with his hypochondria and his mother-in-law troubles, is a bit of a bore, and his worries often seem chiefly an excuse to show Setter's personal charm and magnetism. Although Setter's story is made to seem more convincing by being scrappily recalled, the jigsaw is sometimes clumsily obvious.

But Miss Hansford Johnson becomes with each novel both more complex and more assured a writer. Plot and character are subtly embroiled and observed; there is plenty of meaty, provocative thought underlying the smooth surface style. *An Error of Judgement* is her most ambitious and serious novel so far. But it is a pity that, perhaps for the sake of the paradoxical doubt implied by the punning title, she has this time failed to make us care much about the fate of her characters, although they certainly succeed in shocking one into admiration.

> *"The Road to Hell?" in* The Times Literary Supplement *(© Times Newspapers Ltd. (London) 1962; reproduced from* The Times Literary Supplement *by permission), No. 3151, July 20, 1962, p. 521.*

EDMUND FULLER

Pamela Hansford Johnson's distinguished body of work is characterized by the range and diversity of her subjects and treatment. Alike in a high, and developing, quality of workmanship and human feeling, they are immensely varied otherwise. She does not repeat; she is always trying the unexpected. **"The Unspeakable Skipton," "The Humbler Creation,"** and this novel [**"An Error of Judgement"**] suffice to demonstrate the point.

Here she examines the complex nature and abruptly terminated career of a successful Harley street consulting physician, William Setter. He is drawn in depth, and one of the adroit aspects of the portrayal is that he is seen wholly thru the eyes of a narrator, Victor Hendrey, who is likable but not notably discerning. The author makes us see Setter thru a combination of what Hendrey sees and a realization, from the bare facts, of aspects that he does not see. . . .

The core of the book is Setter's abrupt decision to abandon his practice. It is a shock to everyone and undermines his own already weakened marriage. He takes the drastic step because of his conviction that there is an ineradicable streak of sadism in him to which the practice of medicine offers too many subtle temptations; he has become a consultant to get away from the simpler physical ones of inflicting pain legitimately. In his newer role the temptations are more complex and psychological.

Is Setter right? That is the enigma which makes the book's fascination. He is an honorable, self-judging man, but how to judge ourselves is a universal problem. . . .

There are memorable scenes, even peripheral to the main thread, such as a week-end at Setter's. Well-realized secondary characters include Jenny's mother and the Anglican priest, Malpass, also involved in the problem of Sammy. This is a remarkable and disturbing book with broad applications.

> *Edmund Fuller, "Remarkable, Disturbing Story of Self-Judgment" (© 1962 Chicago Tribune; reprinted by permission of the author), in* Chicago Tribune, *September 16, 1962, p. 3.*

GERALD SYKES

Early in 1960 Pamela Hansford Johnson . . . published a remarkably effective novel called **"The Humbler Creation."** It was written in the Victorian tradition of Trollope, and it read somewhat like an imaginative social worker's report on the joyless career of a London clergyman whose acceptance of his frustrations made him seem to symbolize a middle-class British preference for public duty over private fulfillment. Now, two and a half years later she has published [**"An Error of Judgement"**], a more ambitious but artistically less successful study of a London physician who behaves quite differently, kicks over the traces when he makes an unpleasant discovery about his wife, stops practising medicine and finally commits murder. Miss Johnson has turned away from sociology to metaphysics; she is now examining evil.

In doing so she has put aside her talents of empathy, style and structure. It is difficult to identify oneself with Dr. Setter, who does his work with conspicuous—if literarily unconvincing—skill until one day he is obliged to recognize that his wife loves another man. . . .

Miss Johnson has chosen to study an irrelevant kind of evil. Setter possesses no general or symbolic significance; he is an unappealing crank who raises expectations he does not fulfill. Excessive preoccupation with one's own sinfulness does exist, and the Calvinist mentality is far from departed from the modern world; but as treated here, it seems more like a personal obsession of the author's than an analyzable force that we can study with profit or enjoy esthetically. The thought and the culture that should have gone into the underpainting of an ambitious canvas are simply not there.

This has led to frequent faults of structure and to a painful inadequacy of style. Unmotivated encounters abound, and dramatic surprises fail to surprise. Scenes are set with no sensuousness at all, and the story is told in a graceless language.

Miss Johnson threw away a great deal when she threw away her old-fashioned Victorian crutch. She is trying bravely to stand on her own feet, and we must applaud her courage, but she gives us nothing like the pleasure she once gave. Now this popular novelist faces the stern problems that more advanced novelists have long faced. We can only hope that she will be able to solve them with the new skills she now requires.

> *Gerald Sykes, "Dr. Setter's Obsession," in* The New York Times Book Review *(© 1962 by The New York Times Company; reprinted by permission), September 16, 1962, p. 5.*

KENNETH GRAHAM

There is nothing of the fantastic in Pamela Hansford Johnson. *The Survival of the Fittest* is wholesome and sustaining and dramatically un-American. It describes the lives of a group of friends, all of them in or close to 'the literary world', during the 1930s, the war years, and, briefly, up to the Sixties. . . . [They] become entangled with one another in various love-affairs and animosities, marry unexpectedly, or divorce, or fail to marry; come to tragic ends, or flourish in middle-aged prosperity beneath the apple-trees in Sussex. Technically, the book is impeccable—except for one disruptively high-pitched excursus to the Russian steppes, where the real writer of the group dies dramatically in picturesque surroundings. The book's quiet, even tone, though monotonous, allows for a certain cumulative strength, and there are places where the very usualness of the human cycle of grief and reconciliation gives dignity and feeling to the otherwise flimsy characters. The historical events are just sufficiently seen and no more: they are not allowed to create any panorama, but only to intensify or to weaken the various relationships that are established within the group.

I suppose the book offers a fair picture of the lives of certain middle-class and lower middle-class London types (there are a few shadowy proles who, unlike the others, have not read their Donne and Proust). But does the narration really rise above the essential callowness of the characters in it? It is all rather genteel and rather complaisant. Even the tragedies, the strife, the waste and futility, the elegiac ironies, are easily absorbed into a general well-bred cosiness that suddenly becomes openly offensive in the picture of the group and their precocious children in later life: Eton, Winchester and the Sorbonne; champagne-and-pâté picnics in Richmond Park; brave regrets for the snows of yesteryear; and the son James, the Masterful Young Wykehamist who dresses so well, knows his Proust, and marries the girl who acted Rosalind for OUDS. Mummy, meanwhile, as good a socialist as the others, is marching to Aldermaston. It is such a twittering world, and it could only have happened in the south of England. (p. 640)

> *Kenneth Graham, "Varieties of Picaresque"* (© *British Broadcasting Corp. 1968; reprinted by permission of Kenneth Graham), in* The Listener, *Vol. LXXIX, No. 2042, May 16, 1968, pp. 639-40.**

A. S. BYATT

Reading [*The Survival of the Fittest*] is a curious experience; vague and casual from moment to moment, it is nevertheless compulsive and cumulatively gripping. Its mood is elegiac: characters, places, periods, history, are evoked, suggested, rather than solidly dramatic. There are moments of drama—Polly's terror, the richly amoral Georgina's blank and intense misery over a one-page divorce, her convincing and detailed discovery after remarrying her husband of a sexual satisfaction that precludes the need for further exploration.

But events are subordinated to a sense of the long emotional shifts and structures of whole lives, and the group's corporate life. All the time tone and style are muted, close to cliché, never sharp. In her wartime trilogy Pamela Hansford Johnson created in precise detail a whole world of black market, shell shock, rationing, requisitioning, button-polishing. Here she builds with a few light touches, appealing to the memory of 'those days' (the 'wild' Fitzroy Tavern, firefighting, Spain, Hiroshima), giving the reader a sense of remembering, even where

he cannot, fictional characters and real events. Pure states of emotion stand out as they do in memory, intense, detached from all but the most significant (and usually stock) objects and descriptions. There is a general feeling only to be fully grasped at the end, of a world, people and relationships that really aged and changed, yet still contain their original force. (p. 655)

> *A. S. Byatt, "Elegiac Saga," in* New Statesman (© *1968 The Statesman & Nation Publishing Co. Ltd.), Vol. 75, No. 1940, May 17, 1968, pp. 654-55.**

JOHN KNOWLES

Miss Johnson's is the humanistic, not the satirical, eye. . . . [In "**The Honours Board**"] she gives us telling portraits of the people in and around [a] small, not very distinguished, upper-middle-class school (all of the characters begin by saying that class distinctions don't matter in Britain any more, and end by suspecting that they do). Central are Cyril and Grace Annick, the aging headmaster and his wife, devoted equally to the school and to each other, and the much longed-for and at-last acquired truly scholarly student, Peter Quillan. It is on him that they fasten their hopes to put their preparatory school on the map intellectually, by his winning a scholarship to one of the great schools on the next rung in the English private educational ladder, Eton or Winchester or Harrow. The peculiar intimacy, even devotion, which develops between masters in schools like this and their wives on the one hand, and certain students on the other, is affectingly shown—the way in which these people whose lives are devoted to their schools watch students come, help them to flourish, and watch them go, rarely to return. The depiction of this rich, poignant and true relationship instead of the usual brutal, uncomprehending clichés is enough to lend distinction to the novel.

The essence of prose fiction is particularity, concreteness, the portrayal of a world about which the reader, largely ignorant of it, will say, "Yes, it must be like this, that's the way it has to be." At this Miss Johnson excels. All the tensions of faculty in-fighting are brought into the pitiless daylight, the most intimate secrets of each master and wife are shown to be the casual small change of everyone else's daily conversation, seams of adultery, kleptomania, lesbianism, alcoholism and most of all strangling loneliness are traced through the school, all set forth in a relaxed, clear, conversational prose.

Miss Johnson's aim in "**The Honours Board**" is limited, and perhaps because of that, very accurate. Her characters suspect that in the far off world people like themselves and private schools such as this have a small and steadily shrinking place. But just as they finally conclude that class distinctions may be durable, they conclude that the kind of education they offer may prove durable too. This kind of novel, with its author's implicit claims to omniscience about her characters, its conventional structure and attention to nuance, has a shrinking place in literary fashion today. But I suspect it will prove very durable too. (pp. 4, 42)

> *John Knowles, "At Last a Truly Scholarly Student," in* The New York Times Book Review (© *1970 by The New York Times Company; reprinted by permission), September 20, 1970, pp. 4, 42.*

DOROTHY L. PARKER

[In "**The Honours Board**"] as in so many middling-good English novels . . . , a tidy group of characters has been summoned for some contrived, artificial reason made recognizable immediately by a series of deftly executed but superficial gestures—and assigned roles to play, virtues to represent, some outlandish deviancy to display or endure ("kleptomania!" "suicide!" "alcoholism!") without their really having much to do with each other—a congeries of ciphers to be pointed at, exhibited, stage-managed. Even a character whose part is thoroughly ordinary—the Annicks' daughter Penelope, for example, a nice girl really, has an antique shop, recently lost her husband, you know—has a large pasteboard sign suspended from her neck reading "Indecision," with subtitle: "Young widow, may try one or two men, this or that job, or even toy with the notion of a luxurious titled marriage, before making the right choice." (Who is, of course, the terribly devoted young master of obscure origins, a rough exterior and a heart of gold.)

All the same, there are modest rewards in this unassuming little novel, small touches that persuade absolutely by their accuracy of insight. The only schoolboy who is realized as a character (the rest being merely plastic fixtures) goes through a cruel battery of qualifying exams while ill, and both his agonies and those of Annick, suffering along with him, are compelling. But the fine moments are too few, the faultless observations too minuscule, and though admirable, altogether unsurprising.

That's the source of disappointment. In addition to being a critic who has seriously pondered the nature and mysteries of the novel, Miss Hansford Johnson has been an accomplished practitioner of the art, the author of eight previous novels, the most recent of them a novel of impressive range and some depth. Yet here she takes no chances, and in consequence achieves no surprises—which is to say no illuminations, nothing that extends her scope or our awareness. Everything is exactly where it should be, where we knew it would be, because that's where we last saw it, where it has always been.

Dorothy L. Parker, "Rites of the English Schoolboy," in The Christian Science Monitor *(reprinted by permission from* The Christian Science Monitor; © 1970 The Christian Science Publishing Society; all rights reserved), October 22, 1970, p. 8.*

JULIAN SYMONS

[Pamela Hansford Johnson's *Important to Me*] is basically an autobiography, done with an apparent casualness that conceals a brilliantly skilful shaping and placing of material. Behind headings like 'Education', 'The Liberal Package-Deal', 'Instructions on the History of Art', 'Edith Sitwell', there is a self-portrait and the account of a life. Without dramatic revelations, but with no great reticences either, she tells us about childhood, parents, two marriages, children, times of depression and times of anguish like those of her husband's (C. P. Snow's) two eye operations, during the second of which he suffered cardiac arrest. Within the limits of being well-mannered, she is straightforward and admirably candid. She understands, but does not stress, the limiting influences on her own life, the necessities imposed by her own character. Was it remarkable that her mother should live in the same house with husband and wife during both marriages? To me yes, but she makes it seem inevitable although, as she says, perhaps unwise. The memoir of her mother is beautifully done, perhaps the most tender and delicate thing in the book.

The portrait that emerges is of a very intelligent and humane woman whose commonsensibleness conceals a powerful ro-

mantic idealism. She never cared for arty bohemianism. . . . She admired Edith Sitwell, wrote a book about Thomas Wolfe. She loved in Dylan Thomas the romantic boy, not the boozy teller of tall stories. There must have been for a while a considerable struggle between these two sides of her personality, but the sensible pragmatist triumphed. Certainly the pragmatist is in charge in the sizeable part of this book that discusses today's and yesterday's problems of What To Do about This and That.

What do the rich (and the not so rich) pay for in their children's education? 'Small classes and good manners.' A pretty good nutshell answer, and what do reformers offer but larger classes in any near future? What do opponents of 'streaming' want? Total fairness? But 'What is "fair"? And whom are we to be fair to?' Sometimes she is naïve—as about Orwell and Spain, or about the law's attitude to offences against property—but more often sharp. Liberals, Women's Libbers and total opponents of censorship get their knuckles rapped. The pragmatist is a good person to have around, although she is a bit schoolmistressy for my own taste. The autobiographer is more complex and more interesting, reading Herbert, Vaughan and Crashaw, enjoying the lusciousness of Renoir and feeling that Etty had 'a very rapturous time of it' with his nudes, making an Arabian Nights fantasy out of a smoky sunset seen on Battersea Rise. Such passages remind us that, although the pragmatist is dominant in the excellent realism of her novels, the best of them (*The Unspeakable Skipton* for example) have gained a depth and resonance of which she was perhaps not fully aware herself when writing, from her lifelong feeling for the strange, the excessive, the dark side of the moon.

Julian Symons, "Vintage Years," in New Statesman *(© 1974 The Statesman & Nation Publishing Co. Ltd.), Vol. 88, No. 2270, September 20, 1974, p. 386.*

GILLIAN WILCE

Already widely praised, *A Bonfire* does possess those qualities noted by others—a modest style conveying an honest perception of the way things were in the Twenties and Thirties. This much-remarked-upon feel for period is perhaps not as impressive as the psychological accuracy. After all, it has been possible much more recently for a young woman to feel the same half-real fear of the eternal bonfire at the end of the primrose path of sexual self-indulgence that lurks in Emma's consciousness during the three marriages and one one-night stand which occupy her up to age 26. The fondness, irritations and fluctuations of influence between mother and daughter are also faithfully reflected. Life is about making do. Money has to be earned, accommodation sought, envelopes addressed for the Labour Party. A more complete world is mirrored here than the slimness of the book might suggest. The craftsmanship can't be faulted, and yet . . . And yet dissatisfaction lingers. It is a good train read (and, goodness knows, quality entertainment isn't to be sneezed at) but this reviewer anyway, recognising it all so well, longed for just a little fresh illumination. (pp. 20-1)

Gillian Wilce, "Fiction and the Railway Public," in New Statesman *(© 1981 The Statesman & Nation Publishing Co. Ltd.), Vol. 101, No. 2615, May 1, 1981, pp. 20-1.**

MARIGOLD JOHNSON

A Bonfire is an odd novel and its mix of memory, morality and mundane fancy is finally less than satisfying. It is like a plot retold by a child who sees quite clearly a detailed pattern but hasn't been warned against starting sentences with "And then". But it has the same sort of direct appeal, plunging matter-of-fact into emotion and event with brisk and plangent language. Emma is full of innocent yearnings when her father dies the night of the Guy Fawkes party, which is also the night her mother Agnes has explained to her the meaning of adultery and Emma, aged fourteen, thinks she'd prefer being a nun. Can it be this chance but traumatic conjunction which leads to the poor girl's final conviction that her sexual gratifications, blessed or unblessed, have irrevocably destined her for "the everlasting bonfire"? . . .

The cynic might comment that if Emma had been less preoccupied with her own sins of the flesh—and with the wagging finger of suburban disapproval—she could not have complained of an unhappy life: her innocent blinkers, briefly cast off in 1936 when, "despite her own troubles, the events of the previous year had not left her unmoved" and she addresses envelopes pleading for "milk for Spain", are there to protect her against the greater sins of envy and pride, and the author clearly wants us to admire in Emma the guts and defiance of convention so lacking in her dreadful mother Agnes.

But what should we make of a bizarre excrescence on the day-to-day events here recounted? At several of the important junctures in her young life, Emma is sent nasty (though not very nasty) anonymous postcards suggesting that she and Mum are scheming females who deserve all the bad luck coming to them. We are meant to speculate as to whether the villain is sharp-tongued Miss Plimsoll, a sour old family friend given to saying that more or less everything is a waste, and even to "tushing" girlish good news; but no detective skill is needed to guess that her brusque and gaunt person conceals a heart of golden generosity. The final truth about the poison pen pal is a big disappointment, and seems extraordinarily irrelevant.

Gratuitous and trivial as much of the detail may seem, however, it is here that Miss Hansford Johnson's old and welcome flashes of wit suddenly enliven the book. When Emma, aged sixteen, saves for a permanent wave, "which meant being strung up by the hair to a machine for three hours", her Aunt says "'Look at the curled darling' quoting from something or other"; when they discuss the American Stock Exchange crash, Miss Plimsoll speculates whether "all those men killing themselves know it's a mortal sin"; on the baby's first visit to the seaside Nanny remarks that "small boys always know just what to do, they throw stones at it." It is very nearly worth the platitudinous padding to happen on Miss Hansford Johnson's wry and wise comments. . . .

Marigold Johnson, "Clapham Junctures," in The Times Literary Supplement *(© Times Newspapers Ltd. (London) 1981; reproduced from* The Times Literary Supplement *by permission), No. 4074, May 1, 1981, p. 484.*

JAMES LASDUN

Pamela Hansford Johnson is an expert at lulling her reader into a cosy sense of security, and then rudely shocking him out of it. Sections of *A Bonfire* are pure domestic idyll, and one could imagine finding them in women's magazine stories of the period between 1924 and 1937, in which this novel is set.

Emma, the heroine, grows up doing and feeling all the things one expects from a girl in that safe, middle-class world: she loves Rochester in *Jane Eyre* and hates brussell sprouts, she goes to parties where well-behaved young men make remarks like, 'This is a boopsy tune eh?', and she marries a man who is almost too good to be true.

Placed in the background of this blissful world are certain undercutting details that hint towards the introduction of a less idyllic tone. Hitler is rising in Germany, the family parrot indulges in some vicious behaviour, and a prim old lady is embarrassed by a broken loo-flush. Then suddenly the bombshells begin to fall, turning Emma's life into a catalogue of catastrophes.

Why do these things happen to a nice girl like Emma? That is the mystery that keeps one reading this book. Emma herself seems to think she is being punished for her sexual appetite which has set her on 'the primrose path to the everlasting bonfire.' As no other explanation is given, one is left with the conclusion that the author either shares Emma's belief, or that she is suggesting that Emma's feelings of sexual guilt have somehow made her into what D. H. Lawrence would have called a 'murderee'. However, the tenor of the book bears out neither the authorial prudishness implied by the former, nor the ambitious psychological subtlety of the latter, and this failure to provide an adequate solution to the central question is the one major flaw in an otherwise well-observed and unsettling piece of fiction. (p. 26)

James Lasdun, "Axis Echoes," in The Spectator *(© 1981 by* The Spectator; *reprinted by permission of* The Spectator*), Vol. 246, No. 7977, May 30, 1981, pp. 26-7.**

ISHRAT LINDBLAD

Any critic faced with the task of defining the nature of Pamela Hansford Johnson's novels finds that, like many of her characters, it belongs to a class that is extremely difficult to label— too good to belong to the middle range but not good enough to belong among the really great. Yet, if, as Iris Murdoch firmly maintains, "it is the function of the writer to write the best book he knows how to write," there can be little doubt that Pamela Hansford Johnson has more than fulfilled her function as a writer. Throughout her long career as a novelist she has demonstrated the seriousness of her commitment to her art and explored those aspects of life that touch upon the experience of most readers with a great deal of lucidity and humaneness. (p. 175)

Gradually her interests seem to have developed from the general toward the particular, and in the novels that she wrote during the 1940s she analyzes man's romantic nature and his tendency to fall in love with an unobtainable dream. In the novels of the 1950s she becomes more preoccupied with the workings-out of an enduring relationship and turns her attention to the circumstances that cause it to disintegrate. Truly successful relationships are rare in her fiction and suggested rather by a promise of their being so than by their actual attainment. *Catherine Carter* and *The Honours Board* are the only two novels in which she describes a successful union between her major characters. In general her real gift lies in her ability to analyze pain and loss. *The Humbler Creation* is an example of how well she is able to convey such emotion and relate it to moral necessity. The novels of the 1960s seem to be characterized by a preoccupation with the problems of good and evil.

Ironically enough, two of the novels where she is most clearly concerned with the evil in man are ostensibly comic in mode. Her most recent novels are her most assorted since they seem to represent a return to forms and ideas she has tackled before and wishes to approach once more in depth and with maturity. Thus *The Survival of the Fittest* is a mature version of the early panoramic novel; *The Honours Board,* a well-balanced study of the personal relationships in a closed community; and *The Holiday Friend,* an exploration of the individual's ability to suffer through passion. *The Good Listener* is reminiscent of *The Unspeakable Skipton,* with its cadging hero, and it also indicts the society that permits such people to flourish. (pp. 175-76)

In spite of the seriousness of her commitment Pamela Hansford Johnson's books are never without humor. She writes with irony and compassion and does so with such skill that most situations in her novels are permeated with an ironic vision.

Some of the situations in her novels recur with enough frequency to draw attention to themselves as characteristic. Thus her protagonists are usually intelligent young men and women from the "middle-middle" class, with literary or artistic ability, whose experience has much in common with her own. She also makes frequent use of a dominant mother and a weak or absent father, and the relationships between mother and child, teacher and pupil are among the most poignantly drawn in her fiction. At the same time she displays an interest in the bizarre and abnormal: nymphomaniacs, homosexuals, old men and women painfully in love with the young, crazed passion, and murder all fall within her range.

In terms of technique Pamela Hansford Johnson has moved away from the experimental toward the traditional. Early in her career as a novelist she favored the form of the psychological novel and made repeated use of counterpoint, stream of consciousness, and interior monologues. Toward the 1940s, however, she seemed to settle for an objective narrator, and many of her best novels employ this device. Her use of it exploits the perspective that distance and the passing of time lend to an experience, and it is this aspect of her work that

most readily comes to mind as evidence of her debt to Marcel Proust.

Since the 1960s she has not made use of an objective narrator and instead has moved over to the method of the great nineteenth-century novelists with an implied third-person narrator and a traditional chronological sequence of events. This technique has enabled her to explore character fully and to comment on the action without seeming to intrude. The increasing sophistication of her use of images and symbols as devices for structural unity is also evident in her mature work. Whereas, in her early fiction, images were evocative and profuse, in her later novels they are chosen with care and usually contribute to the total meaning. (pp. 176-77)

[At] present in Britain, writers like John Fowles, Malcolm Bradbury, and Christine Brooke-Rose reveal a renewal of interest in experimentation. Pamela Hansford Johnson reflects the pattern of her age in the development of her fiction, with the effects of the experimental period evident in the early novels, and the gradual acceptance of well-tried and tested techniques in the main body of her work. However, in some of her latest novels—for example, *The Unspeakable Skipton, An Error of Judgement,* and *The Good Listener*—there is evidence of a fresh search for new forms to express her particular requirements and a sign that her talent has by no means stagnated or become conventionalized.

Even the novel she was working on at the time of her death and which she intended to call "Adelaide Bartlett," represents a new departure in that it is based on historical material in a way that none of her other novels has been. It is clear that she made a significant contribution to the art of fiction, having written at least a dozen novels that will continue to demand respect. (pp. 177-78)

Ishrat Lindblad, in his Pamela Hansford Johnson *(copyright © 1982 by Twayne Publishers, Inc.; reprinted with the permission of Twayne Publishers, a Division of G. K. Hall & Co., Boston), Twayne, 1982, 204 p.*

Ward S(wift) Just

1935-

American novelist, short story writer, nonfiction writer, and journalist.

Just's writings reflect his experiences as a journalist in Washington, D.C. and as a war correspondent in Vietnam. His nonfiction includes *To What End: Report from Vietnam* (1968), an impressionistic record of that conflict; and *Military Men* (1970), a study—based largely on interviews with professional soldiers—of the American army of the 1970s.

As a fiction writer of terse prose, Just has established a favorable reputation for capturing the ambience of a place. Particularly notable in this regard are his novel *Stringer* (1974), which evoked the nightmare of Vietnam, and his short story collection *The Congressman Who Loved Flaubert and Other Washington Stories* (1973), which depicted the political crosscurrents within the capital of an America at war. A later novel, *A Family Trust* (1978), reveals Just's midwestern roots in its portrayal of a small town dominated by a patriarchal editor-publisher of a local newspaper. Returning to the Washington milieu, his recent novel, *In the City of Fear* (1982), is set in the present-day capital. The story shifts back and forth in time to evoke the long shadow of Vietnam.

Although critical reception to his work is uneven, Just is commended for being a serious writer who accepts the difficult challenge of writing about contemporary politics.

(See also *CLC*, Vol. 4 and *Contemporary Authors*, Vols. 25-28, rev. ed.)

© Nancy Crampton

JOHN SACK

Firepower, air power, American tolerance of the slaughter of innocents—war in Vietnam has escalated even more things than these. In the spirit of the times the Saigon press corps has added to the press' own artillery, now often sending us the screeching statistic, the lachrymal adjective, the sentence that practically tears at readers' eyes and ears until we are cowed into one close corner of certitude. There are even reporters (and mind you, I don't imply they are *wrong*) who apparently deplane at Saigon with a soapbox as well as an Olivetti packed in their 44-pound allowance.

Not so Ward Just of the *Washington Post*. Finishing up a brilliant year as its correspondent in Saigon and in some of its scary environs and sitting down to write his Vietnam report [*To What End: Report From Vietnam*], he went to extreme lengths—he went, in fact, to Ireland—lest he let analysis escalate to advocacy and advocacy undermine his good faith. Mr. Just anticipated that on the shores of the Shannon, Vietnam's daily calamities and Washington's almost imbecile unawareness of them would be miles enough away to inform his prose without purpling it. Just was right. His book is beautifully restrained, innocent of all polemics and still irresistibly persuasive, a panorama of Vietnam's people, politics and meaningless disasters in a picture built of the most delicate of pointillist dots. Even as one began to think that the only alternative

to passionate intensity was Washington's platitudes, one is recalled to gentle reason.

"Friends who have read the manuscript tell me it has the tone of a late-night confessional," says Mr. Just. Never does he raise his voice in writing it; neither does he allow himself the indulgence of irony, the stage-whispered shout. And quite remarkably, never does he write of anything so insufferable as refugee camps, Vietnamese corruption, napalm burns and senseless death. Let others tell of Vietnam's seamiest side— Just has recognized that the bright side of Vietnam's war is wretched enough. He accords a chapter to Ky's incorruptibility but only allows a footnote to his "business activities," and that suffices. While other writers rage at Vietnam's indifference to Vietnam's war and at Vietnamese as straddlers of electrified fences, in Just's compassionate chapter they are seen simply trying to fit their lives to their philosophies: to the Mandate of Heaven. . . .

He must be the only reporter who doesn't do a set piece by going into the paddies with the Vietnamese army and writing of its incompetence, loud transistor radios, siestas, cowardice and stolen chickens, a catalogue that can be differentiated from one to another reporter's story only by the decibels of the reporter's snorts or the deliciousness of his cool understatement. Instead, Just passes an afternoon with the Vietnamese ruff-puffs or regional and popular forces, a jayvee army of "indifferent leadership, ancient weapons, inadequate pay, dreadful housing, and absolutely no motivation," an army, though, that no Pentagon press release has ever insisted was Asia's white hope. Clearly, Just isn't in a vast conspiracy to discredit the Pentagon's optimism when he writes of the ruff-puff company resting in a paddy, cooking half-a-dozen liberated chickens, laughing, ladling soup, and, as a sort of after-dinner entertainment, actually getting the American Air Force to shatter a quite inoffensive hamlet at the paddy's edge . . . .

Just's method is the moral: eliminate everything that can shriek of the war's insanity, and what is left still moans of the war's futility. The only editorial comment is left to Thucydides' *Peloponnesian War:* "They endured no small sufferings, to no end."

> *John Sack, "Vietnam without a Soapbox," in* Book World—The Washington Post *(© 1968 Postrib Corp.; reprinted by permission of* Chicago Tribune *and* The Washington Post*), April 7, 1968, p. 3.*

SAUL MALOFF

[Ward S. Just's **"To What End"**] pleads no cause, and argues no case. It does not even take a position. It records and describes, evokes and portrays, with the fine eye of a good, skeptical but feeling journalist trying to make sense out of his experience. Just found that quest elusive and mystifying; and that is the book's theme. (p. 126)

Just is at his best and most effective in writing about the utter futility and despair of the quagmire that is Vietnam. He is also fine, in the Hemingway tradition, in his descriptions of actual combat, including, and especially, the patrol in which he was himself wounded. There are vivid tales of dogged determination; the unerringly recorded bawdy humor of men in combat, revelations of impressive courage. Yet somehow they fail to inspirit, hearten, reassure. Though sometimes unintentionally, it is testimony to Just's fidelity as a journalist and to his sensitivity as a man that his report from Vietnam should be overwhelmingly depressing. (p. 126A)

> *Saul Maloff, "The Absurd War," in* Newsweek *(copyright 1968, by Newsweek, Inc.; all rights reserved; reprinted by permission), Vol. LXXI, No. 15, April 8, 1968, pp. 126, 126A.*

ROBERT B. NORDBERG

Ward Just, after eighteen months as a correspondent in Vietnam, wrote a critique of the war, **"To What End?"** Some of the same concern for social justice appears in his first novel [**"A Soldier of the Revolution."**]. Its rather wooden hero is Michael Reardon, a former monk who works for a foundation in an unnamed Latin American country. . . .

Reardon is kidnapped by a group of guerrilleros plotting to overthrow the government. They are all the more determined for knowing their chances are about nil. Reardon is necessary to them because they wish to seize the radio station he supervises long enough to broadcast the news of revolution to the Indians. Reardon is captivated by the dedication and resolve of the guerrillas and their leader, El Jefe. He finds himself, not simply going along with a situation he cannot help, but doing everything he can to help them in their madcap scheme. The author seems uninterested in the success of the venture.

The twelve (significant?) revolutionaries are shot up and running off in all directions as the story ends. One is not told whether Reardon and El Jefe will survive and, if so, whether they will fight another day.

The story is worthwhile as an illustration of the way a man's behavior can be transformed when he finds something he believes in. The motivation of the hero is incomprehensible, though. Why would a man who has seen through the pretensions of foundations and do-gooders suddenly become a zealot for the proposition that all will be well if all foreigners leave the country? One suspects that Reardon was just bored. He is also boring. The man is supposed to live an intense inner life of conflict and search, but none of it comes through to the reader. The other characters are equally flat, except for one Brother Bicker, who believes to the end that the country can be saved if enough holy cards are distributed. This reviewer believes that a novel ought to point a theme or, failing that, at least present some interesting people. This one does neither. One feels that Mr. Just feels something very intensely and wants to say it, but either there isn't much to it or he can't get it said.

> *Robert B. Nordberg, in a review of "A Soldier of the Revolution," in* Best Sellers *(copyright 1970, by the University of Scranton), Vol. 30, No. 8, July 15, 1970, p. 153.*

L. J. DAVIS

When a journalist writes a novel, he has at least two clear options. The one most commonly taken is to fictionalize events and institutions—a runaway bombing plane, the United States Senate—of which he presumes to have some special knowledge. With significant but exceedingly rare exceptions, the results generally range from ridiculous to just plain dumb. The second option is to abandon "fictionalization" either wholly or in part and attempt the novel as an art form. [With *A Soldier of the Revolution*] Ward Just . . . has taken the latter course, and in the measure that his novel succeeds, it does so because he is rather a better novelist than most of the members of his profession. Unfortunately, that is not saying much. He is an intelligent and sensitive craftsman reaching—somewhat self-consciously—for the level of Graham Greene. It is as though a highly competent draftsman were suddenly to aspire to Cézanne: a noble aspiration that usually results in a doomed attempt. Just makes a commendable but far too strenuous effort that leads him to commit the cardinal error of the ambitious amateur novelist: He seems to feel that if his characters are saying something profound, they don't have to be doing anything believable.

Just's writing possesses certain of the solid virtues of his trade: clarity of style if not always of content, brevity, and a good eye for detail. His descriptions of the high plain of South America, the Indians, the government, the American Catholic mission, and the mechanics of American aid are infallibly interesting and doubtless accurate. And yet, despite moments of real descriptive power, it is impossible to escape the impression that one has heard it all before, perhaps in *The New York Times Magazine*. It is a world observed with intelligence and humanity, but not penetrated in any true sense with artistic perception.

In the manner of Graham Greene, the main character is very much a burnt-out case. . . . It goes without saying that he is at the end of his tether—in fact, it goes so much without saying that it scarcely gets said at all. Obsessed with the failure of religion and the futility of his life, he is rather *too* obsessed. Thinking in a kind of feverish shorthand, serving as the author's eyes while trying to establish himself as a character in his own right, Reardon finally becomes positively opaque.

In the end the novel is torn apart by its own internal contradictions. The main action of the book—the abduction of Reardon by the insurgents—is simply unbelievable in commonsense terms, which is the same thing as saying it is unbelievable in novelistic terms too. Reardon's long interview with the guerrilla chief reads exactly like a reporter's interview—if, in fact, it had been presented as a reporter's interview there would have been absolutely nothing wrong with it—but on the level of a simple encounter it is absolutely ridiculous. There is no reason why everything that happens couldn't have happened in an entirely different way: motivation becomes arbitrary and totally at the author's mercy. Things work out the way they do solely because he wants them to and not for any reason of their own. On the level of a newsreel, the subsequent raid on the radio station is okay, but on the reflective and human level, point of view suddenly comes unstuck and swerves wildly from character to character, while Reardon himself seems to be thinking about nothing much but the history of the Sten gun as a weapon of war. I could think of a lot of things he should have been thinking about instead, such as life and death. He might just as well have been thinking about the history of the button, for all the good it does the reader.

So the novel fails because Just doesn't really know what a novel is or how it works. His view is too exalted and far too abstract. He would have written a much better book if he had followed his instincts and stuck to the facts.

> L. J. Davis, "A Tourist in Greeneland," in Book World—Chicago Tribune (© 1970 Postrib Corp.; reprinted by permission of Chicago Tribune and The Washington Post), July 19, 1970, p. 13.

PAUL DENISON

[In "Military Men"] Ward Just takes the empathic approach to the men of the army. Thus he makes possible a fuller understanding of the "military mind" than one can gain from either the army's passionate critics or its champions, or even from dispassionate observers.

Mr. Just's style is both impressionistic and precise—James Joyce read by Walter Winchell. Hypersensitive military men may detect undertones of chic cynicism; to other readers the line between sarcasm and sympathy may seem blurred.

But on the whole the book rings true.

Mr. Just has touched all the obvious bases: cadets and professors in the "beautiful ghetto" of West Point; draftees leading lives of "unspeakable, stupefying boredom"; sergeants who make up the army's "single relentlessly subtle element"; . . . utility infielders known as officers; nonconformist officers who "exist like beached fish within the system."

With an empathic ear, and perhaps a tape recorder, Mr. Just carefully records the words and thoughts of soldiers as they retreat and regroup. The first five chapters sound like stanzas of a swan song, sung by entertainers who don't know when the act went stale.

> Paul Denison, "The Army—and How to Survive It," in The Christian Science Monitor (reprinted by per-

mission from The Christian Science Monitor; (© 1971 The Christian Science Publishing Society; all rights reserved), February 11, 1971, p. 11.

THE VIRGINIA QUARTERLY REVIEW

[**Military Men,** the] fast-paced but episodic account of the "new" American army, is journalese at its best. Too thin to be history and too unsystematic to be sociology, it is nonetheless a document of considerable authority. Though the widely known chapter on West Point is in some respects the most interesting (and frightening), those on Fort Hood and Fort Lewis are equally penetrating and considerably more graphic. The author draws no general conclusions, but the men who train, fight, drink, love, gripe, and mark time through these pages do. The picture they paint is one of an army in deep trouble over discipline, race relations, the intrusion of changing civilian values, and, above all, an unpopular war. (p. cxxxii)

> A review of "Military Men," in The Virginia Quarterly Review (copyright, 1971, by The Virginia Quarterly Review, The University of Virginia), Vol. 47, No. 3 (Summer, 1971), pp. cxxxii-cxxxiii.*

L. J. DAVIS

Locked within almost every first-rate journalist there seems to be a third-rate novelist fairly shrieking to be let out. It is a familiar phenomenon, rather along the lines of an occupational disease, and if I pause here for a moment to dwell on it, I do so in part to put off the dread moment when [**Nicholson at Large**], Ward Just's second third-rate novel in five years, will have to be discussed. It is not a prospect to be looked forward to. . . .

They have such high hopes—the Ward Justs, the Joe Flahertys, the Harrison Salisburys, the Jimmy Breslins, to name but a few. Their earnestness, their dedication, their *devotion* is graven large on every opaque sentence they write, on every paragraph that never seems to come out right, on every lugubriously cumbersome chapter as their books shamble on toward a Bethlehem forever beyond their reach. There is a kind of ghastly aura about such novels that reduces the reader to a state bordering on stupified pity. (p. 24)

As for **Nicholson at Large,** about the best that can be said for it is that it occasionally rises to the level of Michael Mewshaw on a bad day. As a novel it begins in the air, proceeds to Maine, and ends up in Maryland. In the course of these wanderings we are treated to a feast of clichés, a plot that could be comfortably inscribed on the back of a postage stamp, and a single burning question that I seriously doubt will set tongues to wagging from the Sunrise Highway to the Golden Gate. To wit: what the hell is going on here, anyway? A middle-aged reporter quits his job and takes up with a younger woman. Just is at pains to suggest that the two events are unrelated; unfortunately, he is at no pains whatever to tell us why not, and he never gets around to doing so. The affair ends for reasons similarly shrouded in mystery (Just's explanation for this event being about as clear as the words of a man strangling on false teeth) and so, for all intents and purposes, does the book, although it lingers on for a chapter or two in a kind of twilight sleep. We are also treated to quite a lot of garbled vaporing on the nature of journalism, government and Che Guevara. There is also a reasonably competent description of a funeral. It does little to clear the air.

The desire to write a novel may very well be a valid excuse for producing one. It is, however, no excuse for publishing it. Ward Just by any other name would be nothing but another addressee on a form-letter rejection slip. It would have been a mercy to us all.

L. J. Davis, in a review of "Nicholson at Large," in The New Republic *(reprinted by permission of* The New Republic; © *1975 The New Republic, Inc.), Vol. 173, No. 14, October 4, 1975, pp. 24-5.*

ARTHUR COOPER

Like many novels about Washington, ["**Nicholson at Large**"] is both an attack on the abuses of power and a skillfully camouflaged roman-à-clef. . . . (p. 92B)

There·is about Just's work an ironic detachment, a gelid intelligence. Like Harold Pinter, whom he admires, he knows how to achieve artistry through cryptic ambiguity. The reader has to peer hard at the spare, lean prose: his characters deceive each other—and themselves—not by what they say but by what they don't say. And while self-deception may be the book's apparent theme, Just, as in his previous novel, "**Stringer,**" works on other levels. Allegorically, "**Nicholson at Large**" is also an understatement about the deferred dreams and foreclosed possibilities of post-Camelot America. With this book we can drop the adjective "promising" about Ward Just as a novelist. He is rapidly moving into the heavyweight class. (p. 96)

Arthur Cooper, "A Reporter's Exorcism," in Newsweek *(copyright 1975, by Newsweek, Inc.; all rights reserved; reprinted by permission), Vol. LXXXVI, No. 15, October 13, 1975, pp. 92B, 96.*

DORIS GRUMBACH

We often talk about the old-fashioned novel, a genre that has all but disappeared from the lists of quality fiction. What we mean by the term is a storytelling novel, peopled with characters who are quickly established in our minds: No ambiguity exists about what is happening or who is acting or why. The old-fashioned novelist tells us everything he knows about his story, and it is usually enough to satisfy our curiosity. His narrative has a beginning, a middle, and an end that strikes the reader as both inevitable and complete. Old-fashioned fiction is "well-made," to use a term often applied to the plays of the French dramatist Sardou.

Ward Just writes this kind of novel and has apprenticed himself to his craft in the traditional way. . . . [A Family Trust] is his latest, fully realized old-fashioned novel. It remains to be seen whether he can restore our taste for its special kind of pleasure. . . .

The narrative often moves slowly, almost ponderously—though it is always very thorough in detail—as it goes through three generations. The novel has at least three "heroes"; the newspaper itself, the town of Dement, fighting against the advances of progress and development; and the Rising family, held together for a while by Amos's powerful conservative dicta until without the founder's unilateral vision, it finally disintegrates. A fourth hero is perhaps the individualistic Middle West, holding out against the little foxes of commerce and the blandishments of the corporate East.

The essential conservatism of the heroes makes *A Family Trust* a story of American values in the tradition of the early twentieth-century American novel. Its moral roots are strong, and the reader finds himself on the side of Amos Rising and Dement and furiously opposed to the evils of encroaching Chicago, its "aggression, its heat and energy and money." We pull along with Townsend and Amos for small-town honor and virtue. . . . Against all logic we find ourselves hoping that Charles (the son who's taken over the *Intelligencer*) will not sell the paper to outside interests and that Dana (the novel's beautiful and intelligent heroine) will somehow give up her unconventional life as a New York editor and take on the running of the paper. But of course it cannot be. The old order is defeated, the town has been permanently invaded by development and big business. The picturesque old bog becomes a housing development, and the newspaper loses its independence.

I have called *A Family Trust* old-fashioned. It is, not only in form and in character but also in its defense of the old American virtues—decency, honesty, smallness, independence, faithfulness to family, trust in friends, and patriotism for town and country. These things are past worrying about: For many of us the battle has long since been lost. For towns like Dement, the war against ugliness and bigness is over, but we can enjoy accounts of the battle in novels like Ward Just's.

Doris Grumbach, "The Familiar Virtues of an Old-Fashioned Novel," in Saturday Review *(© 1978 Saturday Review Magazine Co.; reprinted by permission), Vol. 5, No. 14, April 15, 1978, p. 87.*

THE NEW YORKER

[*A Family Trust* is a] slow-moving but eloquent book about a Midwestern family, the Risings, and their feelings for and connections with the small Republican town whose newspaper they run. In describing the lives of several generations of newspapermen and their families from the nineteen-thirties to almost the present, Mr. Just really gives us a subtle mid-century profile of the Midwest (where he grew up). From the family patriarch, Amos Rising, whose shadow dogs his three sons even after his death, to the independent-minded, freedom-loving daughter of the newspaper's last family editor and publisher, all the Risings are touching in their struggle to come to terms with their region's "landlocked sense of inferiority and rejection coupled with an equally strong sense of virtue and destiny." Mr. Just's prose, like the people he writes about, is plain, controlled, and brimming with energy, and it is no small mark of his skill that he constantly elicits strong sympathy from the reader for even the most hidebound of the cramped, rigid, conservative characters with whom his book overflows.

A review of "A Family Trust," in The New Yorker *(© 1978 by The New Yorker Magazine, Inc.), Vol. LIV, No. 9, April 17, 1978, p. 136.*

JONATHAN YARDLEY

The prevailing subjects in Ward Just's fiction . . . are politics, war and, more recently, the Middle West. His view of all three is bleak and ironic, yet it is tempered by affection: Mr. Just genuinely likes politicians, understands the appeal of warfare and loves his native Middle West . . . even as he despairs of what has happened to it. Thus his fiction has an ambigious quality that is most effective, providing as it does an underlying tension and an appreciation of complexity.

"Honor, Power, Riches, Fame, and the Love of Women" is a collection of six stories, two of them rather long, the others little more than extended vignettes. All are fine, for the simple reason that Mr. Just is a fine stylist. He is clearly an admirer of Henry James, whose novels are likely to be found on the bookshelves of his characters, and he writes in a leisurely, reflective manner that is faintly reminiscent of James.

All of these stories deal, directly or indirectly, with relations between men and women in times of stress. The four shorter pieces are "war stories," exploring from different angles the fragility of such relationships in the unreal circumstances of war—the Vietnam War, as it happens, though it is not specifically mentioned. (p. 13)

Mr. Just hands out no victories, offers no moral judgments. He understands that people respond to stress in different ways, and he is content merely to observe them, sketching their twists and turns for our consideration. Some of his best work is in this collection, which I read with unwavering admiration. (p. 34)

> *Jonathan Yardley, "People in Stress," in* New York Times Book Review *(© 1979 by The New York Times Company; reprinted by permission), September 9, 1979, pp. 13, 34.*

D. KEITH MANO

"Media" is one of those prodigal words: long ago it left home to set up a bachelor loft in SoHo. Yet the progenitorial meaning deserves regard. "Medium. 1. a middle state or condition; mean." E.g.: steaks done media rare.

Media people inhabit a forlorn *sheol*: homeless, separate, strung between fact and fact-chosen-for-public-edification. . . .

Ward Just, who has been a war correspondent, can appreciate the media between-world. His arresting, cohesive collection [*Honor, Power, Riches, Fame, and the Love of Women*] (two novellas, four short stories) will modulate and vary this distinctive theme. There are six people: all have been, in some degree, detached or bereaved by an intermediate environment. Three war correspondents, one CIA operative, one truce-negotiator, one congressman. (p. 1374)

These men and women are no longer fit for quotidian existence. Most have families in abeyance somewhere: but they know the trans-oceanic telephone operator more intimately. . . . [The] past will threaten a well-articulated public persona (try bragging in front of somebody who has known you since childhood). . . . Truth about the self must be revisionist. Yet none of Just's six is foolish: they understand. And they survive by mobilizing a pragmatic cynicism. Irony is their separatist nation. . . . The crucial act is mediation: parable, image can be more efficient than shortshrifted truth. Would you care to know everything about a senatorial candidate: the state of his digestion; his cracked slipper soles; his dismal midnight fear?

Yet, at some point in each narrative, authentic passion—usually sensual—will rear its charming head. Contradiction: a correspondent cannot cover his own affair. Genuine emotion—unedited, felt—jeopardizes irony. The media careerist is uncomfortable; it dishevels his mind. And he must either scrap romance or turn in his press pass to the realm of quick, synoptic truth.

Just writes a demure prose: as though he didn't want "writtenness" to distract from detail. Oddly (or not so oddly), when romance intervenes the style and dialogue become turgid by comparison. Nonetheless, this is an affecting book: it thumbs

down a crucial issue honestly and with strong, professional insight. That issue being: To what extent can reality be condensed and still remain valid? And: What effect does such constant abridgment have on the jobbers of truth?

Considerable effect, it would seem. The stories are frail. They end abruptly, like broken transmissions from some vague front line. Or, with more aptness, they end like a new event that can no longer divert its readership. (pp. 1374-75)

> *D. Keith Mano, "Media-tion," in* National Review *(© National Review, Inc., 1979; 150 East 35th St., New York, NY 10016) Vol. XXXI, No. 43, October 26, 1979, pp. 1374-75.*

PUBLISHERS WEEKLY

[With **"In the City of Fear,"** Just] has produced another fine novel about the Washington scene, one so authentic and honest in its portrayal of the political era of the past 20 years that it reads like fact not fiction. The three central figures are Congressman Piatt Warden, ambitious and ready to compromise his integrity if it will help him get ahead; his wife, Marina; and Sam Joyce, the colonel whom she loves passionately, and who has given his life to living up to his duty in Washington and in Vietnam. They come across as a very real and believable human beings, as do the dozens of friends and colleagues whose own stories interlock with theirs. The terrible pressures and fears that are always a part of the Washington scene are brought vividly to life, as is the loneliness that haunts even those in high places. The shadow of the Vietnam War looms over all of them and takes its own tragic toll. Whether he is writing about a cocktail party or mourning the sudden death of a good man, Just writes with a passionate conviction that keeps the reader's attention riveted.

> *A review of "In the City of Fear," in* Publishers Weekly *(reprinted from the August 13, 1982 issue of* Publishers Weekly, *published by R. R. Bowker Company, a Xerox company; copyright © 1982 by Xerox Corporation), Vol. 222, No. 7, August 13, 1982, p. 67.*

JONATHAN YARDLEY

Ward Just's new novel [*In the City of Fear*], like the eight works of fiction and nonfiction that preceded it, is preoccupied with two subjects: Washington and Vietnam, which happen also to be where Just spent most of his career as a journalist. Its characters, like those in his previous work, occupy the upper and upper-middle tiers of the power structure; its settings are the corridors and salons of power that they inhabit; its themes, though addressed from various directions and angles, involve the ways in which power is exercised and the moral dilemmas it poses.

Beyond any doubt, *In the City of Fear* is Just's most ambitious attempt to grapple with these matters. It is not a work of great length, but it embraces a large cast of characters and a formidable array of themes and variations—too large and too formidable, in fact, for the book to succeed as fiction. *In the City of Fear* is a novel of ideas and opinions; given that its author is Just, these are usually interesting and always elegantly stated. But its structure is oddly misshapen and uninviting, its characters are less appealing than Just appears to believe them to be, it contains too much brittle talk, and its doggedly solemn atmosphere is ultimately exhausting. There's much in the book to admire, but little in it to like.

Though the novel moves back and forth in time, from the first pregnant moments of American involvement in Vietnam to the final hours of indecision and withdrawal, its principal activity takes place during the time of the nation's most intense and divisive committment there. . . . [Piatt Warden, his wife Marina, Colonel Sam Joyce] and their closest friends, among whom are an influential journalist and an official of the Central Intelligence Agency, reside in a tiny corner of Georgetown that they know as Shakerville from "their half-joking description of themselves in the old days, 'movers and shakers.'" It is a dinner party to Shakerville that provides the core around which the novel is constructed, a party at which many hard truths are painfully exposed.

As the party begins, Marina reflects upon the mood of the day. . . . "Washington now was like a family suffering terrible, unspeakable illness. It was an illness that could not be described to outsiders, so the family, once so cocky, was now subdued and defensive. It was family trouble, and they were all part of it." The dinner party is, in microcosm, a gathering of that family—a domestic battle mirroring the real war being fought several worlds away.

Though a great deal is going on in this little battle, the central struggle is for Piatt Warden's soul. He . . . has cautiously, carefully stayed on the fence in the Vietnam debate—a position that makes him the subject of intense wooing by the White House, the occupant of which Just brilliantly portrays. As the evening wears on, as whiskey and fatigue do their work on the diners' inhibitions, the full panoply of moral and political questions confronting Piatt—as well as Washington itself—is gradually, remorselessly brought to light. It is a process that leaves only one participant on fully defensible moral terrain: Sam Joyce, the good soldier, drawn back to Vietnam over and again not out of love for combat but out of loyalty to his fellow soldiers—his fellow men.

Sam Joyce is the novel's central character, if indeed it can be said to have one, and when he first appears in it he establishes its central metaphor. His war is over now and he is in a Washington hospital, the victim of a corrosive disease. . . . The metaphor—disease eating up a man, war devouring a nation—is painfully obvious, and symptomatic of the difficulty Just creates for himself in the novel: he is so intent on proving his thematic points that he takes the life right out of it. *In the City*

of Fear is more successful as editorial commentary than as fiction. . . .

From the first page of *In the City of Fear* to the last, you can see the machinery cranking. The novel has many fine moments, but it is simply too programmatic to sustain attention or genuine interest.

> *Jonathan Yardley, "Washington's Drawing-Room War," in* Book World—The Washington Post *(© 1982, The Washington Post), September 26, 1982, p. 3.*

JACK BEATTY

"The security system was on the blink." Thus the first sentence of [*In the City of Fear,* a] fine novel about a highly placed set of Washingtonians after, during, and before the Vietnam War. The sentence refers to a burglar alarm but its connotations reach to the war, as do so many seemingly quotidian images, details, and events in this novel. Wallpaper in a Georgetown dining room, for example, alludes to the war by depicting a battle of the American Revolution, the imperial British in full retreat. Or a man, a staffer of the Kennedy National Security Council, is killed, run over by a drunk driver on busy Eye Street; this connects to the war by being an absurd death, a man in his prime, no meaning to it at all. These and like details fill a space of allegory, connecting the texture of the novel not only with the fate of the characters but with the fate of the nation. . . . I should make clear, however, that Ward Just has not written a disguised essay on What Vietnam Did to America. In fact, though it carries historical allegory, his novel is a solid fiction in its own right about a handful of government insiders caught up in a war that got away from them.

A Washington novel, then, the kind of fiction that is not considered serious, not in the same class with Philip Roth's memoirs of whacking off, or Ann Beattie's tales of how Nick met Debbie at a Stones concert. America is about power, but make this a theme in fiction and you will be taped: genre writer; can't be profound. Next. To be sure, Just is no Dostoevsky; public personality is his beat, not the depths. Still, he manages the trick. With a touch of cliché here, a dab of knowledge there, a little mystery over on this side, he peoples a fictional world with credible characters and makes us believe in it and care about them. (p. 40)

> *Jack Beatty, "The Home Front," in* The New Republic *(reprinted by permission of* The New Republic; *© 1982 The New Republic, Inc.), Vol. 187, No. 17, October 25, 1982, pp. 40-3.*

Thomas (Michael) Keneally

1935-

Australian novelist.

Keneally is one of his country's most prolific contemporary writers. He is of Irish-Catholic descent and spent several years studying for the priesthood. Unable to accept traditional Catholic doctrine, Keneally left the seminary, but his writing is pervaded with his continuing concern with human conscience and moral principles. Early novels such as *The Place at Whitton* (1964), a gothic horror story set in a seminary, and *Three Cheers for the Paraclete* (1968), which features a liberal Catholic priest, directly reflect his religious experiences.

Many of his later novels, however, center on historical incidents. Peter Ackroyd has commented that, "In Keneally's hands the historical novel is redeemed as the raw materials of the past are turned into a kind of fable." Most critics agree that Keneally offers a fresh perspective to historical events by focusing on the people involved and their struggle with moral choices. Critics praise his narrative voice, his careful characterization, and his sense of place.

Bring Larks and Heroes (1968), described as the historical novel that "made his name," depicts social interaction within the early convict society. Another important novel, *The Chant of Jimmie Blacksmith* (1972), offers insight into Australia's race relations by reforming the story of a half-breed turned outlaw. The Joan of Arc legend and the horrors of fifteenth-century warfare are the subjects of Keneally's *Blood Red, Sister Rose* (1974). Other novels dealing with war include *Gossip from the Forest* (1976) (the Armistice of 1918), *Season in Purgatory* (1977) (the partisans of Yugoslavia during World War II), *Confederates* (1979) (the American Civil War), and his recent *Schindler's Ark* (the survival of thousands of Jews from the Holocaust due to the efforts of a German industrialist). *Schindler's Ark*, which won the prestigious Booker McConnell Prize in 1982, exemplifies Keneally's skill at personalizing history.

(See also *CLC*, Vols. 5, 8, 10, 14, 19 and *Contemporary Authors*, Vols. 85-88.)

PETER KEMP

[Thomas Keneally's *Schindler's Ark* (published in the United States as *Schindler's List*)] deals with Europe during the Second World War. . . .

Schindler's Ark is largely documentary: the account of a Sudeten German industrialist who saved at least 1,300 Jews from the extermination camps. Based on interviews with those who knew him, it aims 'to use the texture and devices of a novel to tell a true story'. What makes this approach peculiarly appropriate is that Schindler's life frequently resembles something from fiction. Running an armaments factory that produced nothing, playing cards with a demented Nazi for a Jewish girl's life, he seems a blend of Good Soldier Svejk and Scarlet Pimpernel.

A large, easy man, convivial, womanising, Schindler moved into Cracow in 1939, looking—in the wake of the Nazi oc-

© Jerry Bauer

cupation—for commercial opportunities. What he encountered was a different kind of opportunity: that of snatching lives from liquidation. To his eternal credit, he responded with energetic enterprise. Schindler's *bon viveur* good nature had ensured him a wide network of friends, drinking cronies, mistresses. When he saw what was happening to the Jews, this same good nature impelled him to turn the network into a (usually unrealising) rescue organisation. Bribes and bluff, cognac and con-man effrontery won him permission to run his own camp for the Jewish workers in his factory. Here, with heroic chicanery, he defended them against the Nazis. . . .

Examining in detail Schindler's extraordinary oasis, Keneally surrounds it with a panorama of enormities. The Nazi shambles is meticulously reconstructed; each stage in the persecution of the Polish Jews is sickeningly charted, from the first sporadic houndings to the chemical abattoirs and fuming crematoria of Auschwitz. The book looks at both the feverishly sub-human and the freezingly dehumanised: on the one hand, SS psychopaths barking out brutalities as their wolfhounds rip at prisoners; on the other, a macabre bureaucracy of Holocaust-efficiency experts, debating whether each 'death case' need be filed under eight different departments, or circulating memos about the formalities to be observed when flogging female inmates.

The latter combination of pathology and protocol is typical of the stark contrasts that Keneally keeps finding in his material. . . . The book's main contrast, though—making it at once harrowing and heartening—is between the heaped-up horrors of the camps and the very individual decency of Schindler with his wily pluck, life-saving bonhomie, altruistic black-marketeering. . . .

Keneally's portrait of Schindler is inspiriting and carefully unidealised. It scrupulously avoids all temptation to mawkish hagiography. Likewise, in the retailing of SS degradations, he keeps clear of the pitfalls of sensationalism, handling the almost unbearable with the tough delicacy it demands.

Peter Kemp, "Prize Fighters" (© British Broadcasting Corp. 1982; reprinted by permission of Peter Kemp), in The Listener, *Vol. 108, No. 2782, October 14, 1982, p. 31.**

LORNA SAGE

Documentary is a way of interrogating the world of fact, and of reintroducing us to the value of the craft that creates characters and narrative.

Thomas Keneally in *Schindler's Ark,* which salvages the stories of 1300 survivors of the Holocaust, and attempts to characterise their improbable preserver Oscar Schindler, is deliberately entering a territory that, notoriously, still beggars imagination. The story he reconstructs is one that goes against the grain of the general horror, and reinstates a degree of freedom and choice in a context where such things were, seemingly, impossible. . . . In characterising Schindler, and in making his particular choices plausible (as opposed to merely factual: the historical record does that), Keneally is reopening the question of how adequately we have imagined what happened.

What the book addresses is the imagination's apparent addiction to the worst: 'novelists spend most of their time writing about the fairly predictable triumph of malice over good,' Keneally suggests in a preface. The Schindler material drew him because it was in this sense deeply 'embarrassing,' an unpredictable triumph of good. As Keneally presents him in the novel Schindler becomes, by almost imperceptible stages, a three-dimensional 'good' man, at once alive and in love with life, without ever seeming 'fated' or heroic or unnatural.

He is a businessman . . . , an opportunist. The greed for life which leads him to join the Abwehr intelligence service to avoid the army, and to follow the army into Poland to establish his profitable enamel business supplying army kitchens, leads him too into race-blindness, 'Jew-loving.' . . .

It's by juxtaposing suggestions like these from the record that the book builds a character compounded of hail-fellow-well-met generosity, possessiveness, ingenuity and stubbornness. Schindler's obsessively convivial style means he can neither retreat into domesticity to avoid what is happening, nor identify with large-scale dreams of resistance. Instead he saves 'his' Jews, the slave-workers he accumulates in his factory and retrieves from death-camps, and does it by the means he knows—corruption and wheeler-dealing—and ploughs back his enormous profits into what increasingly becomes for him a factory for lives. . . .

[The book] addresses itself as much to the reader's present as to the past, in asking how far we can make sense of the intricate process by which its unheroic hero made his own sub-plot in history. Thus even the inevitable loose ends serve their purpose. Our times drive us to the boundaries of fiction . . . , and the ambiguities of documentary symbolize our problems very exactly.

Lorna Sage, "A Factory for Lives," in The Observer *(reprinted by permission of The Observer Limited), October 17, 1982, p. 33.*

PAUL ZWEIG

History would not normally be concerned with such a man as Oskar Schindler, a mere minor player in the sybaritic night life of a small Polish city during an unspeakable war. But history is not an exact science, and Oskar Schindler is remembered, as few men have ever been, in the testimony of 1,300 Jewish workers who escaped Poland's cities of death because Schindler, against every probability, became a possessed man, ready to risk everything in a daring, almost flaunted mission of rescue.

The versatile Australian novelist, Thomas Keneally, tells the true story of Schindler's rescue effort in this remarkable book ["**Schindler's List**"] which has the immediacy and the almost unbearable detail of a thousand eyewitnesses who forgot nothing. The story is not only Schindler's. It is the story of Cracow's dying ghetto and the forced labor camp outside of town, at Plaszow. It is the story of Amon Goeth, Plaszow's commandant and Schindler's dark twin. (pp. 1, 38)

In his 1980 novel, "**Confederates,**" Mr. Keneally recreated the American South during the Civil War in all its concreteness and lilt of language, surely a stunning feat for an Australian Irishman. Now he has accomplished a similar feat even more tellingly. "**Schindler's List**" reads like a novel: Its voices are thick with living tissue; its scenes are so vivid they appear to result from a kind of ventriloquism. Perhaps after 37 years, it has become possible to write of such things without the cry of anguish, the testimony of rage. Perhaps by choosing to write about Amon Goeth's reign of deadly caprice—a measurable horror beside the obliterating fact of Auschwitz—Mr. Keneally has chosen a subject that art can contain. Today the *Schindlerjuden* are scattered from Israel to Los Angeles, and Mr. Keneally has gathered their testimony. . . . Because of their memories, he has grasped not simply the "holocaust"—that end-of-world fire—but the fragile daily acts of survival and death which human beings manage, even in the mouth of hell. He has given Oskar Schindler the stunning reality of a man who was neither "good" nor "virtuous" but a genius of life, a savior.

In the old epics a character is occasionally inhabited by a god, and then he acts beyond himself, living on the edge of wonder. When the god leaves him he becomes ordinary once again. (pp. 38-9)

For three years during the war Oskar Schindler was inhabited by a profound moral passion, and then the god left him. When the war ended he drifted from one failed business to another. Eventually he arranged to live part of the year in Israel, supported by his Jewish friends, and part of the year as a sort of internal émigré in Frankfurt, where he was often hissed in the streets as a traitor to his race. After 29 unexceptional years he died in 1974.

There is a mystery here, and Mr. Keneally is too good a writer to try to explain it. He leaves us with the remarkable story of a man who saved lives when every sinew of civilization was devoted to destroying them. (p. 39)

Paul Zweig, "A Good Man in a Bad Time," in The New York Times Book Review *(© 1982 by The New York Times Company; reprinted by permission), October 24, 1982, pp. 1, 38-9.*

D. J. ENRIGHT

It is easy, Thomas Keneally remarks prefatorily, to chronicle the victory that evil generally scores over good, but "it is a risky enterprise to have to write of virtue". And *Schindler's Ark* is "'the story of the pragmatic triumph of good over evil, a triumph in eminently measurable, statistical, unsubtle terms". As if to palliate this artistic offence, Keneally hastens to assure us that "virtue" is not quite the right word for Schindler. True, he was generous to all his women and they all remained fond of him—but *all* in this context is scarcely a pointer to virtue. Keneally really needn't have worried. We are happy to hear of a triumph of good over evil once in a while, and in particular a pragmatic and unsubtle victory as distinct from the type called "moral". Given the circumstances, we would not want to hear about it if it were totally fictitious, of course, for that would only be the cruel, mocking triumph of a money-making lie. But we are assured that it is true. And Keneally's defensive or ironically deprecatory prolegomena are part of that assurance. A saintly Schindler we might find hard to take; and a saintly Schindler could never have deceived the Army, the SS, the ministries, into believing that—apart from an odd partiality for Jews, but then, some Jews were women, and they knew about old Oskar—he was one of them. . . .

Schindler's Ark is not a great literary novel in the class of Thomas Mann's *Doctor Faustus,* not the kind of book that Grass or Böll might have created out of similar material. It is nearer to the documentary-style adventure stories of Hans Hellmut Kirst (*Officer Factory, The Night of the Generals*), though less of an "entertainment", far more powerful and more significant in its theme. For better or for worse, symbolic overtones are rarely to be detected, and individual characters have little depth or definition. Schindler himself, while we follow his antics with greater fear and trembling than the Scarlet Pimpernel could ever command, remains an uncertain figure. Was he moved by compassion, by disgust with the Nazi regime? By (to begin with, at least) a capitalist's natural urge to do business freely? Was he a blend of gambler, sentimentalist and anarchist? Or motivated by a stubborn determination to keep his word to "his" Jews and preserve his honour as a good sport, a determination strengthened by three arrests and interrogations? Was it a zest for excitement, compensating for the flatness of life with an ascetic (though morally admirable) wife? . . .

Something of all these, perhaps. Certainly he derived huge satisfaction from getting the better of pompous jacks in disreputable office. It occurred to me early in the proceedings that there was something of Hašek's Švejk in Schindler—when Keneally was describing the air of innocence that enveloped his sexual peccadilloes. . . . This absence of certainty is as it should be. Only if Keneally had been writing total fiction could he have given us a total and authoritative interpretation of Schindler's behaviour. . . .

[The account] seems too neat to be true. But since no self-respecting writer of fiction would indulge in so arrant an im-

probability, it can only be true. *Schindler's Ark* deserves to have won the Booker Prize—as long as it isn't *really* a novel.

D. J. Enright, "Fouling Up the System," in The Times Literary Supplement *(© Times Newspapers Ltd. (London) 1982; reproduced from* The Times Literary Supplement *by permission), No. 4152, October 29, 1982, p. 1189.*

MARION GLASTONBURY

To conceive of the unendurable present as part of a story with a significant plot and uncertain outcome presupposed an outside world of shared meanings and moral continuity. It assumed human recognition; a day of reckoning. Because the Holocaust provides an objective correlative of Hell, outstripping the craziest nightmares and the cruellest dreams, the imagination is constantly challenged, and soon exhausted, by the effort of grasping it. As we know from government archives, Whitehall officials refused to credit what were described as 'the exaggerations . . . of these wailing Jews'. In the face of strained credulity and closed minds, new words are always needed. But any novelist who attempts to do justice to these facts comes up against the limitations of his own creative vision and energy, while feeling confined by the limitations of literature itself. . . .

Schindler's Ark is based on the wartime recollections of 50 Jews, now living in Israel, America, Australia and Europe thanks to their timely transfer as slave labour to a factory where 'the soup was thick enough to sustain life'.

The joint testimony of these survivors has been tirelessly researched, skilfully assembled, scrupulously checked. The narrative sequence of flashbacks, clues and forecasts mingles suspense and shock with an immediacy unattainable through the settled hindsight of history. In delivering successive moments of experience, the novelist selectively defers the realisation of where they lead. . . .

The strength and purpose of the book lies in what the victims have to tell us. . . .

All the memories of Keneally's informants converge in the person of Oskar Schindler, and it is here that misgivings arise. The author portrays the hardware manufacturer not only as the centre of the action but as the natural heir to an apocalyptic destiny: a life-enhancing figure. .

Keneally specifically denies any intention of canonising Schindler and claims to be on his guard against retrospective myths. But, by identifying Schindler with redemptive virtue, casting him in the balance against monstrous evil, citing the Talmud's 'Righteous of the Nations', Keneally turns chronicle into panegyric and elevates the Direktor to a dignity unsustained by evidence. Indeed, he repeats only grudgingly the allegations of former shopkeepers that the usurper beat them up. . . .

The real Schindler owed his reputation for mercy and munificence to the company he kept. In the society of mass-murderers, the racketeer passes for a man of principle, distinguished only by the enormity of *their* crimes. These continue to defy analysis. 'Is there any cause in nature that makes these hard hearts?' Understandably at a loss, Keneally reverses the question and proposes, in effect, his own enigma: 'What lies behind this daring conscience, this exceptional compassion, this marvellous lack of race-hatred and blood-lust?' From here it is a short step to the mystic notion of divine grace working through the usual Catholic channels: a childlike hedonist, wayward prodigal, sensual adventurer and whisky-priest-equivalent is seized with a desire for souls 'in the absolute passion that characterised the exposed and flaming heart of the Jesus that hung on Emilie's wall'. Sceptics may regret this apotheosis as another defeat for rational enquiry.

Marion Glastonbury, "Too Grateful," in New Statesman *(© 1982 The Statesman & Nation Publishing Co. Ltd.), Vol. 104, No. 2694, November 5, 1982, p. 25.*

A. N. WILSON

There can be no doubt that the story of Oskar Schindler is one of the more remarkable to emerge from the Second World War. . . . He was a swindler, a drunkard, and a womaniser. And yet, had he not been these things, he would not have been able to rescue hundreds of Jews from the concentration camps.

Keneally is quite understandably fascinated by this story. And he writes a very vivid book about it. But a narrative is all it *is,* laced with anecdote. . . . The story is so important to him that he has shrunk from the task of turning it into a novel.

Schindler is conceived as a very competent journalist would have conceived him, not as a novelist. There is nothing wrong with this. *Schindler's Ark* is not a novel. It is a highly competent, workaday piece of reportage. The feeling is therefore irresistible . . . that it represents a great lost opportunity. Presented with the bare outline of Schindler's career and character, the reader finds it too odd to be fully comprehensible. He remains a two-dimensional character because Keneally describes him so realistically. Had he been a character in a Graham Greene fiction, Schindler might have seemed more real. And we might have come closer to understanding the fundamentally theological paradox of his nature: that all his petty vices were serviceable for the cause of good; that in the ghastly world Schindler inhabited with such a buccaneer mixture of heroism and the gambling instinct, good could grow out of evil. (p. 71)

A. N. Wilson, "Faith & Uncertainty," in Encounter *(© 1983 by Encounter Ltd.), Vol. LX, No. 2, February, 1983, pp. 65-71.**

W(illiam) P(atrick) Kinsella

1935-

Canadian short story writer and novelist.

Kinsella, a native of Alberta, received favorable critical attention for his first collection of short stories, *Dance Me Outside* (1977), and has been hailed as one of Canada's most talented fiction writers. In *Dance Me Outside*, Kinsella introduces a Cree narrator named Silas Ermineskin who appears in Kinsella's second book, *Scars* (1978), and in his most recent collection of short fiction, *Born Indian* (1981). Critics find his realistic depiction of North American Indian culture balanced in its judgment and effective in its combination of pathos and humor.

In *Shoeless Joe Jackson Comes to Iowa* (1980), Kinsella focuses on characters who have vivid imaginations and creative means for coping with life's disappointments. *Shoeless Joe* (1982), based on the title story in *Shoeless Joe Jackson Comes to Iowa*, is a comic fantasy about an Iowa farmer who builds a baseball stadium in his backyard and anxiously waits for Shoeless Joe to return and play. Most critics were enchanted by the novel, which combines fictional and autobiographical perspectives.

(See also *Contemporary Authors*, Vols. 97-100.)

Photograph by Hogan's Studio

GEORGE WOODCOCK

[Readers of Canadian literature] have had a plethora of guilt-ridden fiction written by white authors about Indians, and a little fiction written by Indians and Metis in which blame is laid on the whites with unconvincing stridency; the truth lies somewhere lost between them. W. P. Kinsella has found a way out of this impasse in a comic approach that restores proportion and brings an artistic authenticity to the portrayal of contemporary Indian life which we have encountered rarely in recent years. Indians living on reservations, Kinsella suggests to us, are not entirely pitiful victims, nor are white men always bullying tyrants. On the contrary, the Indians of *Dance Me Outside,* with their own strange leaders like the medicine woman Mad Etta, have managed to create on their reservations and in the corners of the prairie towns where they feel at home a life that may be full of moral and physical pitfalls . . . but which is at the same time a life of their own, held together by a traditional mutual aid that makes the reservation a refuge where any person belonging to the group can return and expect support with no questions asked. Beneath all the comic situations that arise out of the incompatibilities of white and Indian attitudes towards life and its objectives (for only alienated Indians have ambitions in our sense), it is this solidarity of family, clan and tribe that in the end makes us feel that the Indians are in fact more self-integrated than the frenetic officials who attempt to turn them into imitation white men. Yet the saddest characters in all the stories are not the white men, but the Indians who willingly imitate them, and these include not only the would-be establishment politicians like Chief Tom, who becomes successful only when his wife publicly performs a traditional dance he detests, but also the verbose Red Power agitator, Hobart Thunder, who becomes the victim of his own inflammatory propaganda, misunderstood by the Indians who

listen to him. Laughter and evasion have always been excellent means of cultural survival, and in the stories which form *Dance Me Outside,* W. P. Kinsella deploys these elements with a virtuosity that reminds one of Hasek's use of fictional mockery as a social weapon in *The Good Soldier Schweik*. Survive, evade, remain yourselves, was Hasek's message to the Czechs, and that is not far from Kinsella's message to the Indians. (pp. 100-01)

> George Woodcock, "Oberon's Court," in Wascana
> Review *(copyright, 1976 by* Wascana Review*), Vol.*
> *11, No. 2, Fall, 1976, pp. 98-102.**

ANTHONY BRENNAN

When I learn that a book is populated by characters called Robert Coyote, Frank Fence-Post, Sadie One-Wound, and Poppy Twelvetrees, my response is usually a groan in anticipation of an attempt to make restitution for or to make me pay for Wounded Knee. Dee Brown's work seemed to call forth lost tribes of white men who discovered roots they never knew they had. The Great Spirit moved within them, and they felt, or at least suspected, a tickle of feathers down their backs. Kinsella's book *Dance Me Outside* is all the more refreshing because it quite consciously eschews ersatz heroics and any kind of nostalgic, mythopoeic reflections on a technicolour golden age.

This collection of almost a score of stories gives us wry, picaresque vignettes of life on an Albertan Reserve near Wetaskiwin. A teenager, Silas Ermineskin, recounts to us, in a syntax that has stubbornly survived the tinkering of school-teachers, the adventures of his friends and relatives. The book is held together by a sardonically amused response to the mysterious habits of the white men. We learn how confidently Wilbur Yellowknees handles his stable of whores, how skillfully Old Joe Buffalo takes revenge on a white farmer, how relieved Annie Bottle is when the child she gives birth to in a barn dies, how the gargantuan Mad Etta makes magic in trying to solve Rider Stonechild's amorous problems. The stories are low-key, deliberately unspectacular, full of rueful mirth and a carefully accumulated wisdom, as Silas learns the ways of his world. They are as far as can be imagined in mood and intention from the souped-up mythology and hokey gibberish that Carlos Castaneda peddles.

The book very effectively illustrates the variety of ways in which Indians are not merely vicitimized but are conditioned to expect and accept victimization. . . . The narrator enjoys stealing the white man's best lines and forking them back mockingly, as when he defines a prosperous Indian: "The house is painted and they got a car that runs." Kinsella does not, however, set up the whites as straw-men. One of the absurdest figures in the book is Hobart Thunder, a militant Indian who comes to spread the gospel of violence and becomes a victim of it. Silas and his friends cast a shrewdly sceptical eye on politicians, both red and white, who seek to use them. Their posture is stoical rather than aggressive. Any casual violence they happen to unleash on their enemies must give the impression of being caused by dumb foolishness rather than by calculation. Kinsella's people have developed many of the strategies found in concentration camps. There is no celebration here of noble, old-fashioned heroism. The best we can ask for, as in such a vast range of modern literature, is the ethics of the survivor. But the Indian paradoxically has an advantage over many other survivors. The reserve, which is in so many ways a trap, is also the source of strength: "With us here, it don't matter what you done, it always okay for you to come back home." Kinsella makes it clear in many of his stories that the Indian harbours a kind of bewildered contempt for the white men who so consistently cast aside the comforts of this refuge.

One of the best stories in the book, **"Ups and Downs,"** recounts the roller coaster adventures of Silas and his friend on a trip to Las Vegas. Whether they are winning a thousand dollars and living in a suite or broke and sleeping on a golf course, the next day they manage to maintain an air of imperturbable, cocky amusement. They have what Kinsella in another story calls panache. It is an error to think that this results from having nothing to lose. Even as they take advantage of the white man's stereotypes, they refuse to submit to them. They manage effortlessly to "live on the edge," as the west coast hipster would phrase it. In reading this picaresque account of violence and mayhem, I was inevitably reminded of Hunter Thompson's *Fear and Loathing in Las Vegas*. On reflection what seems remarkable is the self-conscious lengths Thompson has to go to in breaking away from up-tight white society. He invokes the whole self-destructive mythology of the romantic hero; he invents a monstrously berserk alter-id-Dr. Gonzo; he blows his brains out on a smorgasbord of drugs—*then* he can feel free enough to tear through the straight world like one of the horsemen of the apocalypse. Kinsella's characters do not melodramatize themselves. They are aware that Indians have been

treated like dangerous children for at least a hundred years. When an opportunity arises to fulfill the image in spades, it seems churlish to pass it up.

One of the advantages of having these stories gathered together in a collection is that one comes to enjoy the flavour of the characters in a wide variety of situations and to appreciate their ingenuity in honing the art of the survivor. One of the disadvantages is the repetition and the sense that too many of them are pitched to achieve a similar impact. There is no really outstanding story in the collection, none which reveals a great reach or power in reserve, or which takes any great risks. Many anthropologists have begun to use the methods of the short story writer in accumulating anecdotal case studies. The stories here are thoroughly enjoyable, but Kinsella will have to reach out a little more if he is to avoid being crowded off his turf by sociologists. But it is pleasant to find a man who can mock the pathetic attempts of the 'apples'—those with red skin desperate to be white inside—and who would surely be able to nail those white writers who desperately try to invent a new identity as red warriors. (pp. 137-38)

Anthony Brennan, "Down and Out in Montreal, Windsor, and Wetaskiwin" (copyright by Anthony Brennan; reprinted by permission of the author), in The Fiddlehead, *No. 115, Fall, 1977, pp. 137-40.*

TERRY ANDREWS LASANSKY

Dance Me Outside is a vibrant and funny collection of stories. . . . Written in the first person in a lean style, they concern an eighteen year old Indian named Silas Ermineskin who lives on a reserve just south of Edmonton, Alberta.

Silas is an impassive and resourceful kid, who, intent on his future, trains doggedly at a government technical school to be a mechanic. He shrugs off an ever-present prejudice that looms large as the distant Rocky Mountains. Traditionally, education is his only out, but English is a foreign language and he still hasn't got all the verbs right. He is also highly inexperienced with the white man's ways and getting someone who calls him a "wagon-burner" to tell him the time of day is like making the earth turn the other direction.

Kinsella, however, knows both sides well. **"Feathers,"** for instance, is a comic, skilled portrayal of the ménage à trois, climaxed by the omnipotent Indian dance. . . .

Many of these stories have appeared previously in Canadian magazines. Gathered here, they represent a strong first collection.

Terry Andrews Lasansky, in a review of "Dance Me Outside," in Western American Literature *(copyright, 1978, by the Western Literature Association), Vol. XII, No. 4, February, 1978, p. 328.*

CHOICE

W. P. Kinsella is a gifted Canadian writer who chooses rather oddly to present his stories through the persona of a Cree Indian, Silas Ermineskin. [In *Scars*, the] narrator's English is fractured in syntax but vivid in image and metaphor. Kinsella manages to provide a tragicomic perspective on the white and Indian worlds as they collide in a series of extravagant misunderstandings. The book gets off to a slow start, but the stories pick up with **"John Cat,"** and the rest of the book is fine indeed, especially **"Goose moon"** and the title story. This is the second collection of Kinsella's Indian stories, and the reader cannot help wondering how long he will continue to write in this way. While the writing shows more skill than *Dance me outside* (1977), Kinsella does repeat himself a bit and might do well to turn his satirical eye on white Canadian society from a vantage point within it. All in all, *Scars* is a good collection of stories and a strong antidote to the rather toxic myths about the Mounties and the supposed racial harmony of Canadian society. (pp. 79-80)

A review of "Scars: Stories," in Choice *(copyright © 1979 by American Library Association; reprinted by permission of the American Library Association), Vol. 16, No. 1, March, 1979, pp. 79-80.*

FRANCES W. KAYE

W. P. Kinsella is not an Indian, a fact that would not be extraordinary were it not for the stories Kinsella writes about the Cree Silas Ermineskin; and his sister Illiana, who moved to the city and married a very straight white man; and his friend Frank Fencepost; and the medicine lady, Mad Etta, who wears dresses made from five flour sacks, with ermine tails fastened along the sleeves, and the rest of a Cree world. Kinsella's Indians are counterculture figures in the sense that their lives counter the predominant culture of North America, but there is none of the worshipfully inaccurate portrayal of "the Indian" that has appeared from James Fenimore Cooper through Gary Snyder. Kinsella writes about Indian men who get drunk and beat their wives and children, women who run away to be prostitutes, an Indian used-car salesman who has an inside track on cheating Indians, and a chief who uses his Indianness only for the political leverage it gives him to be more white. Yet it is only in the face of these defeated people and these betrayals that the significant victories of the other characters and the real strength of the lives they have created and salvaged become apparent.

Scars is Kinsella's second collection, and readers of the first, *Dance Me Outside,* will be glad to see the development of earlier characters and themes, although this collection, and each individual story, stands on its own. **"Fawn"** is a sequel to the earlier story **"Butterflies,"** in which a white girl finds a refuge which her own society couldn't give her. **"Mr. Whitey"** is a further exploration of the need for but defeat of a genuine messianic force, first stated in **"Penance."** In *Scars* it is again the women who bear the brunt of living in a culture that keeps from being crippled only by its sense of being alive. Silas, who is studying to become a tractor mechanic and also studying with Mad Etta to become an assistant medicine man, continues to serve as narrator. His voice unifies the stories as his life unifies at least some of the paradoxes of his culture.

Yet finally what makes Kinsella's stories work is his eye for detail and his sense of how a few remembered images come together to create a place and a people that compel belief. Kinsella's Indians wear the counterculture uniform of jeans, yet in Kinsella's hands this is no uniform but a theme on which to compose variations. The Indians confuse some visiting Italian film makers. "They say you Indians are all dressed up in denim like cowboys supposed to be. They want to know if cowboys dress up like Indians." The used-car dealer is dressed like an imitation cowboy, too, with his "old cowboy boots" and "wide brown belt." A girl who has struggled to acquire seeming security and a decent life wears a white sweater and "clean jeans." A woman in jeans and running shoes lacerates

her arm in mourning for her child which her husband has given away, and the blood drips "from her fingertips into the fine grey dust and onto her running shoes." Yet for all their ubiquity, jeans can't be fully adapted to the old ways of the Cree and thus are a compromise part of the culture. (pp. 84-5)

Scars is an excellent book: moving, funny, often brutal, yet joyously affirming sex and life and honor and responsibility, and handsomely produced withal. (p. 86)

Frances W. Kaye, " 'Don't Freeze Off Your Leg'," in Prairie Schooner *(reprinted from* Prairie Schooner *by permission of University of Nebraska Press; ©1979 by University of Nebraska Press), Vol. 53, No. 1, Spring, 1979, pp. 84-6.*

ANTHONY BUKOSKI

[The ten short stories in *Shoeless Joe Jackson Comes to Iowa*] mark a considerable change in direction for W. P. Kinsella whose first two collections, *Dance Me Outside* and *Scars,* deal with life in and around a Cree Indian reservation. The stories here, most of them successful, are set in such widely differing places as Disneyland; an Iowa cornfield (more than one Iowa cornfield actually); Maintoba Street in Victoria, known as "The Pit," Kinsella says; a whorehouse in Edmonton, "jumping-off place for American troops going and coming on the Alaska Highway"; and a forlorn San Francisco bar, looking "as if it had endured a century of continuous Monday nights" where the protagonist in the story **"Last Names and Empty Pockets"** drinks with Janis Joplin.

In addition to these rich and varied land-and-cityscapes (the people inhabiting them are just as diverse), Kinsella's stories constantly change mood and tone, divided as they are almost equally between the fantastic and the real. **"Fiona the First"**—accorded an Honourable Mention in *Best American Short Stories 1980*—is one of the fantasies. It deals with a sort of Ancient Mariner doomed for eighty years now to wander airports and railway stations picking up girls. The title story, **"Shoeless Joe Jackson Comes to Iowa,"** is another fantasy story, this one concerning a farmer who constructs a ballpark in his backyard in order to witness the return of the legendary Shoeless Joe Jackson. . . . These are fanciful, entertaining stories.

The realistic ones—the very fine **"Waiting for the Call,"** for instance, or **"Mankiewitz Won't Be Bowling Tuesday Nights Anymore"**—are even better. Told in the terse, clipped speech of a street-wise juvenile, **"Waiting for the Call"** is an affirmation of the power of love to survive in the face of hardships, while **"Mankiewitz Won't Be Bowling . . ."** chronicles the lonely death of a taxi driver. In another realistic story, **"A Picture of the Virgin,"** the central character is forced to admit to himself and to his friends that he had fallen for a prostitute's story, paid her simply to hear her troubles. In a scene reminiscent of the disillusionment at the end of Joyce's "Araby," Charles recalls looking up at a frosty streetlight: "Soon the taunting voices were far behind me, and there was only the cold and the stars and the sounds of my feet on the frozen sidewalk."

Aside from **"A Picture of the Virgin,"** what is most refreshing in these ten stories is their emphasis on hope and regeneration. In Kinsella's world when physical survival is impossible, one often survives in the works of others. In *Shoeless Joe Jackson Comes to Iowa,* other people are the means of our redemption, our salvation. Through them, the dead are reclaimed, exonerated of past misdeeds. In **"First Names and Empty Pockets,"** the doll maker retools Janis Joplin's image in his workshop, building a testament to her. In **"Mankiewitz Won't Be Bowling Tuesday Nights Anymore,"** Bert, the fellow taxi driver, plans to name the league's bowling trophy after his deceased side-kick, Manny. And in **"Shoeless Joe . . ."** that fabled ballplayer is exonerated of wrongdoing in the 1919 World Series when an Iowa farmer toils three summers to build a place for him to play again. It is this act of believing that makes Kinsella's characters appealing—no easy task in fiction. The breakdown of the act of faith, on the other hand, makes **"A Picture of the Virgin"** all the more disturbing.

If there are disappointments among these stories, they are modest ones. **"A Quite Incredible Dance,"** for instance, is too much "a story." Intended as an account of the psychological torment a father undergoes when his daughter marries a man "even more loathsome than he [the father] anticipated," the ending is contrived, I think, the characters unconvincing finally. One anticipates the story-teller here. Another piece, **"Sister Ann of the Cornfields,"** seems incomplete, a fragment, an exercise in descriptive prose and little else. Nevertheless, W. P. Kinsella's *Shoeless Joe Jackson Comes to Iowa* is worthy of our attention. An important change, it represents a branching out from the so-called "Indian" stories of Kinsella's first two collections. There is no telling where this masterful writer will find the characters for his next book. Wherever it is, I want to be there to meet them. (pp. 126-27)

> *Anthony Bukoski, in a review of "Shoeless Joe Jackson Comes to Iowa" (copyright by Anthony Bukoski; reprinted by permission of the author), in* The Fiddlehead, *No. 129, Spring, 1981, pp. 126-27.*

MARK CZARNECKI

[The stories in] *Born Indian* are cleverly written in a freewheeling style. . . . This is Kinsella's third collection of funny-sad tales about white-Indian confrontations, most of them narrated by Silas Ermineskin, a young Cree from a central Alberta reserve. It's cowboys and Indians in reverse, with the stupid, bigoted whites outfoxed, outjoked and outsexed by crafty salt-of-the-earth natives. Unquestionably, white racism deserves all this and more, but the crude articulation of stereotyped emotion glossed over with aw-shucks moralizing . . . adds up to submissive politics and punching-bag art.

Kinsella's difficulties with perspective are unfortunately abetted by his greatest strengths. To a remarkable degree, he invests his characters with credible speech patterns, behavior and ideas. But because the narrator Silas has no distance on his own stories, the result is a puppet show, realistic and detailed yet devoid of insight. . . .

The format of *Born Indian* is questionable too. Most of the stories have been published on their own in various literary magazines, thus genealogies, marriages, professions and so on have had to be re-established each time. No allowance has been made in this collection, however, for the fact that the cast of characters varies little from story to story, making much of this explanatory information redundant and irritating. All they add up to is an extended sitcom—why not fess up and present them as such? (p. 61)

> *Mark Czarnecki, "Schemers and Redeemers," in* Maclean's Magazine *(© 1981 by Maclean's Magazine; reprinted by permission), Vol. 94, No. 19, May 11, 1981, pp. 58, 61.**

IAN PEARSON

In *Shoeless Joe,* Kinsella is boxed in by his own inventiveness. Having J. D. Salinger sleuth around a baseball mystery is a delightful idea, but a difficult one to execute. The writer has to recite such lines as: "It's a sad time when the world won't listen to stories about good men." Of course, this is W. P. Kinsella, not the real Salinger speaking. To put your own words into a living person's mouth is merely presumptuous, not clever.

Similarly, the flights into fantasy are too easy and obvious. The author wants us to release our reason and break down the barriers between the living and the dead, the prosaic and the mystical. But Ray's alternate universe of baseball is too contrived to be seductive, and the pace is too sluggish to work as a madcap picaresque. Kinsella reaches for the otherworldly magic of Gabriel García Márquez. What he achieves is the limp fancy of Richard Brautigan. (pp. 59, 61)

> *Ian Pearson, "Fantasy Strikes Out," in* Maclean's Magazine *(© 1982 by Maclean's Magazine; reprinted by permission), Vol. 95, No. 16, April 19, 1982, pp. 59, 61.*

TERRANCE COX

Shoeless Joe is a novel from left field: a unique left field on the Iowa farm of Ray Kinsella. One night Ray hears a voice say, "If you build it, he will come," and knows that "it" refers to a baseball park and "he" to Shoeless Joe Jackson. Most prominent of the Chicago Black Sox, Jackson in 1919 was banned for life from baseball for throwing the World Series.

W. P. Kinsella pursues baseball, most literary of sports, to the anagogic and still manages to write a humane and comic book. His manner recalls Marquez, Jack Hodgins and, not accidentally, J. D. Salinger.

Ray builds his magic stadium and while watching Shoeless Joe and others play ball, hears the voice again, this time saying, "Ease his pain." The mission clearly means kidnapping J. D. Salinger and taking him to Fenway Park for a Red Sox game. . . .

A clipping that Ray carries extols Salinger's ability to make readers love his characters: "They are so real, so vulnerable, so good, that they remind me of that side of human nature which makes living and loving and striving after dreams worth the effort." Kinsella shows the same ability in *Shoeless Joe.* His novel celebrates imagination and effort, wittily posits serious theses on the role of baseball and other art forms and provokes various kinds of laughter.

I'm not, like Ray and W. P. Kinsella, sentimental about baseball, but *Shoeless Joe* makes me wish I were.

> *Terrance Cox, in a review of "Shoeless Joe," in* Quill and Quire *(reprinted by permission of* Quill and Quire*), Vol. 48, No. 6, June, 1982, p. 32.*

IAN B. McLATCHIE

In *Born Indian,* Kinsella creates the composite impression of a carnivorous, overtly hostile white society: "the daughter, who was named Dora, went off to Edmonton, got swallowed up by the city and it be just the same as if she died." . . . On one hand, the sheer absurdity of racial oppression becomes almost a liberating force: as one character says, "When we're down as low as we are on the totem pole then the only thing there is to do is laugh.'' . . . Balanced against the humour of the stories, however, is the sense of dangerous unpredictability which generally prevents the narratives from lapsing into the seductive category of the formulaic short story. For Kinsella's longtime narrative *persona, Silas Ermineskin,* any tendency towards artistic complacency is prevented by the constant evidence of his ''beneath the underdog'' role as an Indian and a creative artist. . . .

As in the case with most single-author story collections, a successive reading of the fourteen stories in *Born Indian* accentuates certain narrative and structural deficiencies. Most notably, Silas occasionally seems little more than a mouthpiece for his author; at these moments, the charge of Kinsella's presumptuous liberalism seems justified. And yet, it is a tribute to Kinsella's story-telling ability that, overall, the stories benefit from placement in an anthology. In particular, the subject of cultural, rather than economic, poverty emerges as the most important and convincingly stated theme of the collection. The surprising shift, in the final piece of the collection, to magic realism, however, radically affects the significance of this theme. The process of cultural degradation is momentarily reversed as Silas realizes, in his ability to create fictional worlds, a far greater power than that of his antagonists. The story, **''Weasels and Ermines,''** is one of the more impressive pieces of short fiction to appear in Canada in recent years. (pp. 146-47)

Ian B. McLatchie, in a review of ''Born Indian'' (reprinted by permission of the author), in Canadian Literature, *No. 93, Summer, 1982, pp. 146-47.*

MAGGIE LEWIS

To say W. P. Kinsella's **''Shoeless Joe''** is a book about resurrection and baseball makes it sound foreboding and silly, and sometimes it is, but that doesn't matter at all. . . .

Kinsella does wonders in this book: The visual fantasies are so rich that whether you believe them or not, you can't help imagining them. There is no resisting Ray Kinsella—the protagonist—and his first vision of baseball past. . . .

Ray Kinsella is a fervently enthusiastic character. You might get tired of mawkish and too physical descriptions of his love for his wife and his insistence on the kittenish cuteness of his daughter. But when he's talking baseball, the enthusiasm is catching. In fact, it was enough to make this reviewer, whose only contact with the game is the memory of being hit on the head with a softball she was supposed to catch, love baseball herself for a while. This is a convincing novelist.

Even when Ray Kinsella kidnaps J. D. Sallinger (yes, J. D. Salinger), the novel keeps you believing. It's not so much believing: it's wishing. Things that happen in this book are so wonderful, you feel that if they didn't happen, they should have. Baseball players who had vanished into mythology keep turning up, one by one, night after night. The long-reclusive J. D. Salinger speaks again. The fantasy just keeps getting better. There is no lurking dark side of the story to instruct the reader not to ask too much.

The book must have been pure wish fulfillment for its author, who is described as spending his summer touring US baseball capitals. He has a rare talent for conveying pure joy. He waxes corny and nostalgic, but it doesn't matter, because by then the thrill of seeing all the old baseball stars is yours, too. It gets harder to put the book down as your expectations get going for the next great happening.

The descriptions of landscape are poetic, and the baseball details will warm fans' hearts and not get in the way of mere fantasy lovers. This book would make great reading on a summer vacation. In fact, this book *is* a summer vacation.

Maggie Lewis, ''A Fantasy for Baseball Lovers,'' in The Christian Science Monitor *(reprinted by permission from* The Christian Science Monitor; © *1982 The Christian Science Publishing Society; all rights reserved), July 9, 1982, p. 14.*

Brad Leithauser

1953-

American poet.

Hundreds of Fireflies **(1982), Leithauser's first book of poems, has been very well received by critics. He is described as an important new poet whose work is amazingly polished and, unlike much contemporary poetry, life-affirming. Critics compare Leithauser with poets of distinction, including Robert Frost and Marianne Moore, among others.**

Leithauser is concerned with craft and formal construction. He is an observer and precise recorder of tiny details, especially in nature. His poetry, critics observe, is fresh, humorous, and exuberant in an appealing way. Leithauser also has the gift, it is noted, for speaking plainly and for pointing to beauties and pleasures often overlooked.

JOEL CONARROE

Auden once said that the more conscious writers are of inner disorder the more value they place on tidiness in their work as a way of controlling their emotions. Perhaps it is inner chaos, even dread, that accounts for Brad Leithauser's fascination—almost obsession—with technique and with orderly, complicated structures. I suspect, though, that Leithauser is simply inventive by nature, playful, and in love with language.

His *Hundreds of Fireflies* . . . is a veritable anthology of verse forms, all manipulated with dexterity and verve. The effects are always calculated—every syllable counted and patted into place (a seven-line stanza, for example, with seven syllables per line), every complex rhyme scheme worked out to the last detail. Not surprisingly, too, for someone so conscious of weights and measures, he is given to gleeful wordplay. . . . And whether he is annotating a firefly's "arythmic light," a bat's "gimpy flight," or a bullfrog's "harsh gravelly notes," his verbal poise is always in evidence.

His muse, it is clear, is Marianne Moore, and a few of the poems, **"Giant Tortoise,"** for example, do explicit homage. . . . He also shows his debt to Frost, trying his own version of **"Birches"** and offering a handful of those couplets that Frost was partial to, as in lines on a Venus' flytrap: "The humming fly is turned to carrion. / This vegetable's no vegetarian."

That last line, come to think of it, sounds like Howard Nemerov, and apparently he too is deposited in Leithauser's memory bank, as are W. H. Auden, Anthony Hecht, Richard Wilbur, and many others. But the book is no mere echo chamber; Leithauser has a distinctive voice, an altogether appealing one.

> *Joel Conarroe, in a review of "Hundreds of Fireflies," in* Book World—The Washington Post *(© 1982, The Washington Post), February 21, 1982, p. 13.*

BRUCE BENNETT

The hallmark of **"Hundreds of Fireflies"** is meticulous examination of particulars. So uninsistent is Brad Leithauser's

voice, one at first assumes that what is being offered is simply what meets the delighted eye. His poems depicting landscapes, habits and movements of creatures and "personalities" of celestial objects give pleasure and testify to the credo in the title poem:

> Merely
> to watch, and say nothing,
>
> gratefully,
> is what is best, is
> what we needed.

But such a bearing scarcely prepares one for the urbane self-scrutiny of the long two-part poem **"Two Summer Jobs."** There the self-conscious, Harvard-bound youth of the early 1970's and the disaffected, ironic graduate at decade's end form a composite, with Mr. Leithauser's technical skills everywhere evident. The first part, **"Tennis Instructor,1971,"** unfolds through intricately rhymed 11-line stanzas; the poet uses the Rubaiyat stanza for **"Law Clerk, 1979,"** and plays on it brilliantly.

Yet the best work comes at the end of the book. Poems like **"Birches," "Duckweed," "Along Lake Michigan"** and **"The Ghost of a Ghost"** transport the reader to realms of suggestiveness involving time, nature and mystery that could never be encompassed by cleverness, sheer skill or mere observation. (p. 12)

Bruce Bennett, "The Work of Four Poets," in The New York Times Book Review *(© 1982 by The New York Times Company; reprinted by permission), March 14, 1982, pp. 12, 16-17.**

JAY PARINI

Brad Leithauser's *Hundreds of Fireflies* brims with simple, sensuous poems that are, in a sense, eclogues and elegies. . . . [The] pastoral poet, a Virgil or Frost, typically gathers metaphors from the countryside to take with him back to the city. Thus Leithauser, perhaps alluding to Frost, writes a poem called **"Birches"** and another about a Michigan ghost town where, "Had I not been told / Where to pick out the vined / Roots of settlement, I might / Have seen no trace at all," calling up Frost's "Directive." Yet none of his master's wayward ambiguities or gnarled syntactical routing make their way into Leithauser. His poems rush like water down hill, luculently fresh, as in **"Dead Elms by a River."** . . .

Some of [Leithauser's] poems read like exercises in descriptive poetry and have less imaginative pressure than one expects in serious work, but unevenness of this sort often plagues first books. The good news is that Leithauser has a clear eye—an unclouded vision of the world. . . . He ruthlessly avoids the showy surrealism and unnatural (and unconvincing) metaphors that have given much of contemporary poetry a bad name. Still better, he has respect for what is called "craft"—the workmanship that saying things plainly requires of even the most exalted genius. I venture that Brad Leithauser will find poems closer to himself, and truer, as he grows. Meanwhile, *Hundreds of Fireflies* makes good reading. (p. 38)

Jay Parini, "A New Generation of Poets," in The New Republic *(reprinted by permission of* The New Republic; *© 1982 The New Republic, Inc.), Vol. 186, No. 15, April 14, 1982, pp. 37-9.**

PHOEBE PETTINGELL

Brad Leithauser seems to be at home anyplace. For several years I have been following his poetry with delight whenever it appears in magazines. His first book, *Hundreds of Fireflies* . . . , confirms my sense of pleasure. Among the often strident clamor of youthful poetic voices, Leithauser's stands out for its rare combination of exaltation and skillful control. Usually, he concentrates on small subjects, miniature perceptions. . . .

Leithauser's ideas are effervescent with optimism. The most somber spectacle can still provoke his hopeful imagination to a vision of rebirth. A dead deer on the beach **"Along Lake Michigan,"** for example, merely fills the poet and his companion with disbelief—death simply cannot exist in this place. . . . For Leithauser . . . , as for Shelley, death itself is a dream from which we awaken into the white radiance of eternity.

Perhaps the most impressive and developed part of *Hundreds of Fireflies* is a section entitled **"Two Summer Jobs."** These sustained narratives depict the unfolding portrait of the artist as a budding poet. . . . **"Law Clerk, 1979"** (Leithauser is now a lawyer) traces the subtle development of a mature poetic sensibility. The young man works his way through writer's block by staying late at the office, and while there, attempting

parodies of famous poems—an interesting peek at how he acquired his easy grace with forms. A scene of the conventionally dressed law clerk encountering a bluejeaned former classmate from Harvard, also an aspiring poet, now rusticated to the country to make pots, is a sly parody of the usual clichés about nonconformist poets. As Leithauser becomes increasingly comfortable with the legal world, "the whole courtly game / of claim and counterclaim," he discovers as well the actual nature of his poetic gifts. Looking out at a Manhattan illumined by the dying light, Leithauser feels that it "seems to say we come / through drudgery to glory." Here as elsewhere in *Hundreds of Fireflies,* many disparate worlds are reconciled. This is an exciting debut from an ambitious and brilliant poet. (p. 15)

Phoebe Pettingell, "Reconciling Disparate Worlds," in The New Leader *(© 1982 by the American Labor Conference on International Affairs, Inc.), Vol. LXV, No. 9, May 3, 1982, pp. 14-15.**

SVEN BIRKERTS

[*Hundreds of Fireflies*] is an overtly formal book. . . . It is marked by extreme control, personal reticence, and a calm, confident virtuosity that makes us think of Elizabeth Bishop or [Richard Wilbur]. And more remarkable than the style is the subject matter. Leithauser writes almost exclusively about the natural world—not the implacable Nature of Jeffers or Frost, but the benign, pastoral, optically infinite nature of the Dutch landscape painters. His poems are so detailed and unemphatically lucid that we cannot help but wonder where and how the poet weathered the experiences of the past decade. . . .

We have been schooled to approach poetry in a certain way, taught to extract content, a message, and then to summarize and report. Leithauser's poems resist these tactics. His lines embody the perceptual experience, *are* that experience; they hug their content and will not give it up. The poems are not about anything. Their meaning consists of the progress of the eye across the texture of the page, the movement through beautifully patterned clauses. The formal underpinning is clearly not gratuitous. It is there because attentiveness of such high degree discloses order. Yielding to the exigencies of form we become tensed and alert. The eye slows down, starts to move on tiptoe. And when we come to the end of the poem there is closure, the obscure, half-unconscious appeasement of our appetite for balance and clarity. The qualities of the poem become—briefly—our qualities. . . .

Leithauser's work is proof that the heritage of formal verse is more arsenal than obstacle, that the problem, where there is a problem, lies not in the rigidity of the forms but in the rigidity of their user. Here is a clear case of a supple and subtle intellect deriving maximum benefit from its interaction with formal strictures. The maturity of these poems is to some extent derived from the maturity of poetic form itself. And as for the criterion of relevance—any doubts we may have vanish as we begin to read. . . .

Hundreds of Fireflies is not without its weaknesses. At times the reader will long for greater variety of subject matter or a less imperturbable tone. Also, it might be argued that the poet falls victim to his own skill in places—his knack for pure resolutions sometimes limits his access to less predictable sideroads. In the same way, there could be more burr, more rasp, more protrusion of recalcitrant fiber: in other words, less smooth precision. But this is quibbling before a stunning maiden voyage. We would do better to break a champagne bottle belatedly against the hull, to praise the courage and obstinacy required to stand so far apart from gangs and trends. Here is a man with a love of the world and its words and the exceedingly rare capacity to express the first by means of the second.

Sven Birkerts, in a review of "Hundreds of Fire-flies," in New Boston Review *(copyright 1982 by Boston Critic, Inc.), Vol. VII, No. 3, June, 1982, p. 29.*

HELEN VENDLER

[Brad Leithauser] has learned from Marianne Moore a form of compressed emblem description, from Elizabeth Bishop an un-assuming visual scanning, from Robert Frost a love of rural scenes, from A. R. Ammons a telling use of modesty of voice, and from James Merrill a worldly form of narrative verse. [In *Hundreds of Fireflies* these] lessons have been assimilated beyond pastiche, on the whole, and have been brought into a tone distinguished by its mildness. Mildness is in fact Leit-hauser's chief personal form of stylization. Mild poets are rare. There is a welcome lightness and sweetness in Leithauser rec-ommending him to readers whose tastes bring them to Herbert and Schubert. And (another form of stylization) he likes, like Herbert, the compression of the proverb or the riddle. . . . [The eleven **"Astronomical Riddles"** in this volume, for ex-ample, bring] the unwieldy planets into the surprising styli-zation of brief self-description. . . . (pp. 41-2)

Leithauser's quick sympathy, his humor, and his love of an elusive playfulness appear in these trifles. He is not unaware of what such orderly compressions of phenomena leave out in their will-to-stylization: another of his short poems [**"The In-tegers"**], muses on the neatness of the procession of the in-tegers vis-à-vis negative and irrational numbers and nonre-peating decimals. . . . A mind wishing to write such **"Minims"** (as Leithauser calls them) is of course in danger of forgetting the swamp in its passion for "neatness of finish! neatness of finish!" (Marianne Moore). However attractive the self-effac-ing quality of such polish may be in this era of lugubrious self-exposure in verse, it cannot be the only ingredient a poet has to offer. Leithauser branches out in two directions when he forsakes his *jeux d'esprit.*

One (in **"Two Summer Jobs"**) is a believable form of stylized autobiography (borrowed from James Merrill). . . . Though expertly enough done, these poems are finally poems finding no stylization beyond what is offered by Merrill—his airy glit-ter, his penchant for puns, his jewelled effects, his tinge of evening nostalgia, his dying fall after a sparkling trajectory, his light ironies. Leithauser's other venture is far more his own—a series of poems on animals or natural scenes, poems formed in stanzas with a pattern of delicate and unemphatic rhyme. These poems have titles like **"Giant Tortoise"** or **"Daybreak"** or **"Dead Elms by a River"** or **"Birches."** Their chief form of stylization is the framing of a scene stripped to essential detail and seen in a moment of insight. . . .

In [**"Birches"**] Leithauser is writing in syllabics, but his seven-syllable line breathes with the life of the English trimeter and tetrameter and the French octosyllabic line of the *lais,* even allowing itself from time to time (as "in the overhanging leaf-age," the last line of the poem) to subside into that pleasant eight-syllable cadence. This meditation on birches expresses gratitude for the lightening of forest darkness offered by a stand of birches; they bring clouds into the forest, they are the fem-inine to the forest's masculine, they siphon down the sun's

light, they are "becomingly multiform," and they suggest a mild prehistoric beatitude.

The poem hints rather than declares; but we do know, by the end, that the slender birches, though not entirely gentle (they can evoke lightning on stormy days) are nonetheless a youthful presence relieving the forest's immobility and gloom. Leit-hauser's concentration of attention makes the birches pliant to his imaginative will; it is he that sees their bark as "tattered but immaculate bandages." This is the stylization of anthro-pomorphism; but the birches are no sooner thus made human than they are made saurian in Leithauser's flexible handling of their appearance.

The mystery Leithauser sees in appearances is of course a reflection of his suggestive mind, which turns things over in attraction and fear. Each of his poems repays rereading; most have a shapeliness of evolution that pleases all by itself; and on many pages the reader is struck by the writer's interest in playing with scale, a resource frequently ignored by poets. (p. 42)

Helen Vendler, "The Creeping Griffon," in The New York Review of Books *(reprinted with permission from* The New York Review of Books; *copyright © 1982 Nyrev, Inc.), Vol. XXIX, No. 14, September 23, 1982, pp. 41-4.**

ROBERT B. SHAW

Leithauser seems . . . the sort of poet who collects and assim-ilates, giving each inconspicuous detail its due without inflating it, piling up exact observations with a freshness and prodigality like nature's own. He is one who, in Yeats's phrase, has at-tained "right mastery of natural things." One is reminded of earlier inspired accumulators: of Moore, of Bishop, perhaps most of Wilbur. In these poets description can become almost microscopic; [in *Hundreds of Fireflies*] Leithauser emulates and even may outdo them at this. . . . (pp. 179-80)

The poet sees the lustrous surface of things but also penetrates it. . . . The awareness of a submerged darkness—[in **"Duck-weed"**], and in **"The Return to a Cabin," "The Ghost of a Ghost,"** and others—lends a needed gravity to Leithauser's writing. But it is not usually what he chooses to dwell upon. He is like Wilbur particularly in this, I think: the vision of the world remains, against odds scrupulously taken into account, an affirmative one. More than affirmative—celebratory. The poems communicate delight as much through their alertness of style as through their keenness of perception. There must be very few poets as young as Leithauser in such absolute com-mand of their instrument. In particular his handling of rhyme, sometimes in extremely intricate patterns, is remarkable in avoiding distortion of diction or syntax.

It is difficult to single out titles for specific notice in a collection of such consistent quality. Except for a few dispensable epi-grams, all of the poems aspire to and many of them attain true distinction. I should mention **"An Expanded Want Ad,"** for its enticingly casual but faintly haunted scene-setting, **"Ca-noeing at Night"** and **"Along Lake Michigan,"** for their calm and ample rendering of experience. At the center of the book is a pair of poems, **"Two Summer Jobs"** which successfully strike quite a different note from the rest of the book. These are poised, rueful, autobiographical vignettes: amusing and touching memories of working as a tennis instructor and, eight years later, as a law clerk, Leithauser is normally so careful not to obtrude his personality in an obvious sense that it is

surprising, and somehow liberating, to see him here commanding center stage. Too elaborate in design to summarize,
these two poems have a lot to say not only about Leithauser
himself, but about coming of age in the Seventies. There is in
them a personal warmth and charm that is a match for the
poet's considerable technical skill. Like any good book of
poems, **Hundreds of Fireflies** is capable of arousing in readers
any number of responses. I would like to note in closing one
immediate effect of the book upon me, because it is one that
few books have lately offered. Reading it made me happy.
(pp. 180-81)

Robert B. Shaw, "Fireflies and Other Animals," in
Poetry *(© 1982 by The Modern Poetry Association;
reprinted by permission of the Editor of* Poetry*), Vol.
CXLI, No. 3, December, 1982, pp. 170-81.**

Siegfried Lenz

1926-

West German novelist, short story writer, dramatist, and essayist.

Among the foremost authors of contemporary German literature, Lenz is known for expressing humanitarian concerns in his fiction. Although his works maintain a distinctly German identity, their themes are universal, presenting current issues and problems.

Lenz's novels *Das Feuerschiff* (1960; *The Lightship*) and *Stadtgesprach* (1963; *The Survivor*) were translated into English in the early 1960s but did not receive a significant amount of critical attention in the United States. *Stadtgesprach*, however, is now noted as an important introduction to Lenz's recurring themes: duty, and the causes and nature of inhumanity and guilt. With the publication of *Deutschtunde* (1968; *The German Lesson*), Lenz gained international recognition. Most critics judge this novel to be Lenz's masterpiece. Here he fully develops early themes and examines how the lives and minds of Germans were changed by World War II.

Lenz's short stories are noted for their concise style and credible characterizations. In many of these tales, Lenz analyzes the discrepancy between appearance and reality. The same theme emerges in such later novels as *Das Vorbild* (1973; *An Exemplary Life*) and *Heimatmuseum* (1978; *The Heritage*).

All of Lenz's work displays his subtle sense of humor and perceptive sense of detail. Though critics consider his recent book, *Der Verlust* (1981; *The Loss*), slightly mawkish, they agree that its subject, the loss of speech, leads to an insightful study of language and silence.

(See also *Contemporary Authors*, Vols. 89-92.)

© Lütfi Özkök

skeleton of *The Survivor,* it does little to strengthen it as a work of fiction.

Kenneth Lamott, "Thinking a Good Fight," in Book Week—The Sunday Herald Tribune (© 1965, The Washington Post), June 20, 1965, p. 18.

KENNETH LAMOTT

[In *The Survivor* Siegfried Lenz] created a dilemma of a not unfamiliar sort. The Resistance in a Norwegian village has tried to assassinate a German general. In retaliation, the local commandant has taken 44 hostages—the leading men of the town—and intends to shoot them if the leader of the Resistance does not give himself up.

Which is more important, continuing the Resistance or saving the lives of the hostages? Accepting the hypothesis that the cause of the Resistance was just in an absolute sense, there really is no question, but the right decision is the one that raises particularly painful questions of individual morality. The exploration of these problems is the main business of *The Survivor.*

I wish I could say that Mr. Lenz has been entirely successful, for he brings to his book both intelligence and sensitivity. I was not, however, really moved by it, and I think the trouble is that in spite of all the vigorous action that takes place, this story is essentially an intellectualized version of something experienced at second or third hand. Mr. Lenz has a tendency toward moralizing aloud, often in the form of rhetorical questioning. While this technique may help lay bare the moral

C.A.H. RUSS

[While so many of Siegfried Lenz's stories are] firmly set against the background of modern Germany, he is not just a chronicler of his country's recent history and present society, important as this function of the contemporary German writer continues to be. He sees himself as a reformer, but he insists that his protest is subordinated to, and conveyed by, his art. . . . Lenz, we may add, although delineating German scenes and situations so vividly, tries to look beyond them to more universal issues. This may be illustrated by his tale *Stimmungen der See,* which depicts the clandestine attempt of three men to cross the Baltic. On internal evidence alone, it is hard to decide whether the action occurs during the war or afterwards, whether, in other words, the fugitives are trying to escape from the Nazi police State or from communist East Germany. Now what Lenz is doing in *Stimmungen der See* is to concentrate on psychological tensions set against the background of the sea that he knows and describes better than any other German writer of our time. The 'Stimmungen' are human as well as natural. The story's historical point of departure is, in the final analysis, irrelevant to its timeless themes: tension between the generations, the interplay of hope and fear, and man's cruelty to man. (p. 242)

Lenz's concern, then, is with generally valid, universal themes which, as in *Stimmungen der See,* transcend any purely historical context. Indeed, the timeless figure of the loser, the man who fails to survive the moment of truth, the fallen idol, dominates Lenz's fiction. Sometimes the character is trapped by external forces, or by the action of others, but sometimes, too, his own failings are unmasked. Whether he be tycoon, farmer, athlete, journalist, or teacher, his status—his security—will be demolished. The techniques with which Lenz handles this simple theme in his tales repay closer study.

We may first consider five of the 'Ich-Erzählungen' which form a substantial proportion of Lenz's short stories. Each of the five employs a narrator-observer who records the 'fall', or defeat, that he has witnessed. In *Die Festung,* a son recalls how his father, a dispossessed East Prussian farmer, finding his tenure of new land cancelled, in turn, by an army requisition, ensconced himself in an improvised fortress as futile as the son's sandcastle. In *Risiko für Weihnachtsmänner* and *Ein Haus aus lauter Liebe,* a hired outsider stumbles on a travesty of family life. . . . [In] *Der grosse Wildenberg,* the narrator is confronted in the great man's sanctum with a lonely figurehead who is delighted to receive a visitor. . . . (pp. 242-43)

The narrator-observer of *Der seelische Ratgeber* is also a narrator-victim. The idol falls, but so, in a sense, does his admirer: the effect is all the sharper in that his disillusionment, although constantly implicit, is not articulated until the final sentence. Narrator-victims appear in other tales. Lenz again shows us characters who, through their own fault or not, emerge as vulnerable or unable to fulfil expectations. In the narratives to which we now turn, however, the 'ich' himself is exposed. Thus, in *Lukas, sanftmütiger Knecht,* a white farmer recounts his desperate journey terminating in the discovery that the Mau Mau had reached his home before him. The narrator of the lighter *Mein verdrossenes Gesicht* cannot sustain the gloomy expression on which his career as a photographer's model depends. The 'Amüsierdoktor' suffers even greater discomfiture, and nearly goes the way of all fish. Once more, then, the commercial world comes under Lenz's scrutiny, as in the first group of 'Ich-Erzählungen'. However, whereas the great Wildenberg's powerlessness is seen through the eyes of his visitor, the model and the 'Amüsierdoktor' themselves retail their misadventures. Narrator-victims have replaced narrator-observers. In *Lieblingsspeise der Hyänen,* on the other hand, we find both devices. They are not here combined, as we have seen them to be in the figure of the editorial assistant of *Der seelische Ratgeber.* Instead, the narrative structure, one 'Ich-Erzählung' inside another, entails a situation in which the first narrator—the observer—listens to the second, American narrator—the victim—lamenting that his womenfolk's obsessive visits to shoe-shops throughout the family's European tour have prevented his re-visiting the scenes of his wartime experiences.

Schwierige Trauer requires separate attention. It is an 'Ich-Erzählung' in the form of an apostrophe to a dead member of the narrator's family: the mayor of an Eastern border town preoccupied, on the flight to the West, with saving trivial documents, whatever the human cost. Here the 'ich' is not so much the observer, or victim, but rather the agent of the denunciation directed against the mayor, who is, of course, in

the terms of our discussion, the idol with feet of clay. Personal anger may explain the, for Lenz, unusual technical choice of a dynamic fictive narrator, for the writer was an eye-witness of the flight from the East.

We turn to stories outside the 'Ich-Erzählung' category. As we have seen, the latter includes tales dealing with inadequacy or defeat, observed by the narrator in others or himself. Now, in further works, characters observe *each other's* failure to meet a challenge. We might term this the device of the character-observer. The observed challenge arises, in each case, on the physical plane, but its implications transcend that level. Like *Stimmungen der See,* these stories marry physical action and psychological reaction in a manner typical of Lenz's work. In *Drüben auf den Inseln,* a young man drowns as his sweetheart looks on helplessly—the intruder into a closed world has succumbed to the elemental forces within it; and in *Das Wrack* a son observes his father's frustrated exhaustion as he dives repeatedly, and fruitlessly, to search a submerged wreck. *Silvester-Unfall,* another of Lenz's many explorations of close relationships, shows a family watching its head, who is doomed by disease, during the forced festivities of his last New Year's Eve. Here, as in *Das Wrack,* the act of observation is underlined by repeated allusion to it. In such other tales as *Der Läufer, Ball der Wohltäter* and *Jäger des Spotts,* the witnesses of defeat are multiple, although Lenz's victim-figure in the latter story may (almost literally) snatch some measure of victory from its jaws.

In these narratives, employing character-observers, the agent of man's failure is nature itself, represented by the sea, by animals, and by the vulnerability of the human body to exhaustion, age and disease. Even the deed which leads to the athlete's disqualification, in *Der Läufer,* seems more a reflex action, or bodily accident, than wilful. Elsewhere, however, Lenz portrays the victims of *other characters.* The latter engage in more than observation, are less passive than most of the narrators of the 'Ich-Erzählungen' (recalling, rather, the opponents confronting some of the narrator-victims), and may therefore be termed character-agents. Thus, *Der längere Arm* and *Nur auf Sardinien* each portrays a wife's undermining of her husband's self-respect. (pp. 243-44)

Lenz the realist reveals a keen eye for visual detail, from the momentary flash of the sun on an aircraft cockpit high above the fugitives' boat in *Stimmungen der See*—an elusive symbol of liberty (or danger?)—to the effects of heat on lead, conveying both the suspense generally inherent in the context of 'Bleigiessen' and the menace latent in the particular setting of *Silvester-Unfall.*

Lenz's description of nature also testifies to his accuracy as an observer. . . . And the variety of settings . . . is, of course, articulated in specific local colour. (p. 247)

The fusion of physical sensation and psychological process becomes, in *Der Anfang von etwas,* an aspect of human communication: 'Hoppe spürte, wie sich Paulas Finger um seinen Unterarm schlossen, ihr Erschrecken sich im wachsenden Druck der Finger Fortsetzte.' The proferred hand conveys false feeling in *Ein Haus aus lauter Liebe* and genuine distress in *Die Festung.* Everyday gestures are endowed with meaning.

To return to *Der Anfang von etwas,* this story also exemplifies Lenz's realistic treatment of *sound.* As Hoppe prepares to cast his belongings into the river, the privacy and secrecy of his intended action are conveyed by the distance and impersonality of the sound that he hears: 'Er . . . spähte die Pier hinab, musterte die Luken der Speicher, stand und lauschte auf das schleifende Geräusch einer feren Strassenbahn'. . . . The enormous care devoted to realistic detail in Lenz's stories may be finally illustrated from this same tale by the accumulation of visual and acoustic elements relating to the fruit-machine.

For his descriptive material, then, Lenz draws heavily on the sights, sensations, gestures and sounds of everyday life. Yet, as we have noticed, the descriptive elements in question often carry some deeper implication. Even in that highly documentary account of the operation of a fruit-machine, unexpected abstract nouns link the mechanical process and the feelings of the players. . . . Lenz is not, therefore, a mere chronicler of surface reality. What we have seen to be true of his themes is true also of his style. He is neither merely polemical in his approach nor merely naturalistic in his technique. (pp. 247-48)

[Lenz has] been termed the most conventional writer of his generation in his use of language. On the other hand, there are signs that Lenz's inquiries may now be leading him to a greater degree of technical experiment. His latest novel, *Stadtgespräch*, represents an attempt to practise on the grand scale the form of the narrative apostrophe, or harangue, already adumbrated in *Schwierige Trauer*. A recent short story, *Der sechste Geburtstag*, essays the—for the male writer—difficult task of employing a female fictive narrator. We may hope that other experiments will follow in the years to come. For, if Lenz succeeds in fusing experiment with the traditional narrative virtues which are his already, he may emerge as a major artist. (pp. 250-51)

> *C.A.H. Russ, "The Short Stories of Siegfried Lenz" (a revision of a lecture originally delivered at the Institute of Germanic Studies, University of London, on May 20, 1965), in* German Life & Letters, *n.s. Vol. XIX, No. 4, July, 1966, pp. 241-51.*

THE TIMES LITERARY SUPPLEMENT

Herr Lenz is perhaps regarded most highly for the distinction of his contributions to the short story and the novel; it is in these fields that his major publications have so far lain. His most recent book, this collection of four radio-plays [*Haussuchung*], illustrates something of the imaginative range to be found also in his prose fiction. Precision, care and felicitous craftsmanship reveal themselves in the neatly rounded construction of these works, where dialogue and scene-sequence are presented economically and convincingly. . . .

The author has the gift of making his reader feel quickly at home in his imagined world and of proceeding without further delay to sustaining our interest in this world by a sequence of surprises and a continuity of tension. His sympathies are with the oppressed and frustrated, but can extend also to the representatives of a society that he is satirizing (*Das schönste Fest der welt*). The author's approach is cautious in the judgments it encourages us to make, while urging us on to concern and compassion.

> *"Guilty Couples," in* The Times Literary Supplement *(© Times Newspapers Ltd. (London) 1967; reproduced from* The Times Literary Supplement *by permission), No. 3435, December 28, 1967, p. 1260.*

THE TIMES LITERARY SUPPLEMENT

Siegfried Lenz's latest novel, [*Deutschstunde (The German Lesson)*], may well be the most successful work of fiction to appear in West Germany since the war. . . . The book has attracted both the public's interest and an almost universally favourable critical reception. *Deutschstunde* is neither a simple nor an inexpensive book and its impact represents a very interesting phenomenon indeed. It shows, for example, that "Bewältigung der Vergangenheit" is still a living issue in West Germany, despite the desire to "forget it all", of which we often hear. On another level, the success of *Deutschstunde* also demonstrates, as does so much of Herr Lenz's work, that the trend to "documentary" literature in Germany has not rendered obsolete the quite different approach of a writer who has always insisted, and proved, that he is a story-teller, a lucid exponent of the *craft* of fiction. *Deutschstunde* is the longest and, at the same time, the most ambitious of his novels.

Siggi Jepsen, the narrator, is the inmate of an institution for juvenile offenders, set on an island in the Elbe. Unable to produce for his German master an essay in praise of duty, he is placed in solitary confinement in order to perform the task at leisure. He plunges into it, and we read his essay as he writes it. The account of his past life, which the essay represents, turns on his medial position between his father—a policeman in the northernmost part of Germany—and the painter Nansen, who has been forbidden by the Nazis to continue working. . . . The policeman's fidelity to his meaningless duty, involving the surveillance of the painter, the resulting estrangement of father and son, as the latter turns to Nansen—the father-figure frequent in Herr Lenz's work—and Siggi's obsessive desire to protect paintings on public display by taking them away and concealing them, even though the Nazi era is ended, leading him to acts of "delinquency", form only some of the strands in the texture of an exceptionally rich novel.

This material could well have been treated in a documentary manner. It is, in fact, presented in a tentative, inquiring and provisional way. Siggi constantly corrects himself, revising his choice of words as he tries to tell his story. Sometimes a self-deprecating turn of phrase or studied casualness will suggest that the task is beyond him; but he keeps at it until it is successfully completed. Then we see that the search for language has also been a quest, across the years, for the identities of the characters, including the narrator, and for the identity of their country, scrutinized in that—or this?—"Deutschstunde". The heading of the fourteenth chapter—"Sehen"—has implications for the novel as a whole. Not only is Nansen a painter, but the book teems with motifs related to sight and visual perception. In this world of inarticulate or uncommunicative people, the characters constantly watch each other, and seek, or avoid, each other's gaze. Everyday objects—a clock, a mirror, a photograph—are scrutinized, the very word "Bild" repeatedly appears in both literal and metaphorical application, and imagery drawn from the world of the cinema reminds us that we, too, are watching, and trying to decipher, the German past.

Deutschstunde is rich too in finely observed details of the regional setting. The evocation of domestic atmosphere, the scenes of provincial life, and the sidelights on Siggi's routine in the institution (presented in splendidly satirical terms) represent other factors which certainly bring the reader close both to the narrator's past and to his life now. Yet to describe *Deutschstunde* as a realistic novel would be a curious half-truth: the data, so to speak, are *not* given. The presentation of Siggi's story is, as we have seen, tentative. Yet, however cautious his inquiry, its findings are unambiguous.

Siegfried Lenz's favourite theme of the precariousness of status and power has found its most extended and impressive articulation to date. The figure of authority, the policeman, like his counterpart in the short story **"Der Verzicht"**, is weaker than his victim. He can offer no more than the confident cliché of "duty", typifying a kind of frozen language which obstructs the path to truth along which, in contrast, his son gradually, if uncertainly, progresses.

"German Lessons," in The Times Literary Supplement (© Times Newspapers Ltd. (London) 1969; reproduced from The Times Literary Supplement by permission), No. 3500, March 27, 1969, p. 317.

MICHAEL HAMBURGER

The immediate appeal of *The German Lesson* . . . has a good deal to do with the strict limits Lenz observed in writing it. . . . [He] is a master of minutely observed detail. . . . [He] has confined himself to a single setting, deliberately excluding all reference to anything outside the experience and consciousness of the characters—provincial characters at that, even though one of them is a painter with an international reputation.

The greater part of the action takes place during the last two years of the Second World War, at and around Rugbüll in Schleswig-Holstein, close to the Danish border. It is narrated in retrospect by Siggi Jepsen, who has been told to write an essay on "The Joys of Duty" at the school for juvenile delinquents to which he was remanded after the war, for reasons bound up with the story he tells: an account of the conflict between his father—the local policeman—and the Expressionist painter Max Ludwig Nansen. . . . (p. 71)

The reader expecting a heroic confrontation between the forces of good and evil in Nazi Germany will be disappointed: this novel avoids histrionics. Jepsen does his duty; Nansen applies a related stubbornness and cunning to the business of getting on with his work. If *The German Lesson* is a political novel at all—and it can be read as though it were not—what we learn from it is that the Nazi regime was upheld by "decent" and conscientious executives, little men like Jepsen or—as Hannah Arendt showed—like Eichmann. The demons of earlier fictions about the Third Reich are absent here. The nearest thing to an irrational compulsion in Jepsen is his inability to leave Nansen alone after the end of the war; yet such behavior could also be attributed to his stubbornness, narrow-mindedness, and inflexibility. Similarly, Siggi cannot break the habit of concealing Nansen's paintings even when, after the war, Nansen has been rehabilitated. It is for removing paintings from a Hamburg exhibition of Nansen's work that Siggi is institutionalized as a delinquent. His father remains the policeman at Rugbüll, and we can be sure that Jepsen will serve the Federal Republic just as loyally and meticulously as he had formerly served the Third Reich.

Siegfried Lenz learned from American writers such as Hemingway the discipline of understatement. Since such realities as concentration camps, "the final solution," or other major horrors of the war do not impinge on the awareness of his provincials, they are not mentioned in the novel. At one point Nansen is summoned to an interrogation by the Gestapo, but Siggi—who knows or imagines all kinds of things that he has not witnessed himself—is as reticent about this experience as is Nansen himself. . . . Rarely does the narrator draw a moral or generalize, and when he does, the effect—within the context of this book whose ironies and satirical strands are as unobtrusive as its seriousness—is almost startling.

The seriousness, in fact, comes over not as a quality of the writer's mind but of the persons in the novel, including the many subsidiary local characters whom I have not mentioned. That is one reason why *The German Lesson* has a density and solidity reminiscent of nineteenth-century novels about provincial life. (p. 72)

Whatever political allegory may have been worked into the realistic fabric of *The German Lesson,* it is not a simple or unambiguous one. If we read the book as a novel about the Nazi era we are bound to object that rural Schleswig-Holstein was not Germany, that the new technology of destruction is scarcely hinted at, that the conflict between a policeman's ruthless devotion to duty and a painter's devotion to the freedom of his art does not and could not possibly convey either the banality or the monstrosity of evil that distinguished National Socialism from other authoritarian systems. Nansen, we are told, had once been a supporter of the regime; and he is among those members of the community who are called upon to form a last-minute home guard when the war is lost. Since he remains part of the community to the end, he cannot represent the victims of Nazism, who ceased to exist not only as artists but as human beings.

Yet political allegory, as I have suggested, is not essential to *The German Lesson,* which excels as a novel about people, places, and things, rather than as a novel of ideas. The issues involved in the clash between Nansen and Jepsen remain of urgent relevance not only to Germany, with its tradition of rigidly obedient officialdom, but wherever duty conflicts with judgment, conscience, or independence of mind. What is more important, Nansen does not merely stand for the freedom of self-expression. His function in this novel is closely related to that of Siggi as narrator and witness: it has to do with seeing—the title of one chapter in the book—and the necessary interaction between imagination and outward reality.

As a painter Nansen sees and interprets the world around him. Jepsen, on the other hand, is blinkered both by his servility and by his authoritarianism, self-deceived even about the desire for power that motivates his obedience, so that duty yields joys. This ambivalence comes out in Jepsen's dealings with his young son, the narrator, whom he thrashes for going out of the house without permission, yet also makes use of for his own professional ends, revealing an almost abject dependence upon him. As for his older son, the deserter, Jepsen no longer sees him as a son or as a human being, but is prepared to hand him over to the "authorities" for punishment. In all such dealings Jepsen receives the passive support of his wife, whose love for her children is never in doubt.

Lenz excels at the rendering of these family relations between people who are laconic, humorless, and trapped in a patriarchal order that it never occurs to them to question. We get to know them intimately not so much through what they say as by what they do, what they look like, what they eat; by the gestures and movements that express what they feel and think.

It is left to each reader to draw his conclusions about this patriarchal order which—at least among the peasantry and petty officialdom of provincial regions—remained almost intact behind the political and military machinery of the Third Reich. That the "joys of duty" were still a fit subject to be assigned for a German essay in the progressive, seemingly benevolent institution in which Siggi is being reformed after the war is one of Lenz's pervasive but unobtrusive ironies. Another is Siggi's relationship there with his guard or warder, Joswig, who constantly reminds Siggi that smoking is forbidden in the cells, yet provides him with cigarettes. If we insist on finding allegories in the book, and Joswig may be taken to be a postwar variant of the policeman father figure, there is also room for comforting inferences about the future of the Federal Republic.

American and English readers of this book will be confronted with a world that few of them will find easy to reconcile with what they know about Nazi Germany. Moreover, they may be astonished that Siggi's narrative, so packed with the almost palpable details of day-to-day experience, scarcely touches on sexual love. Siggi's story, after all, spans his puberty; by the time he has finished telling it he is twenty-one. Yet sexual experience or even sexual fantasy would have been out of place not only in his essay on "The Joys of Duty" but in the ambience which his story evokes and captures. Instead, we get Siggi's and Nansen's emphasis on seeing, so that there is no lack of sensuous substance but an extraordinary abundance of it. Certain episodes, like that in which Siggi and his sister wade out at low tide to catch flatfish with their hands and feet stick in one's mind with the persistence of lived experience. So, too, does the whole natural setting, with its changing light and winds, its harshness and heaviness. (pp. 72-3)

Siegfried Lenz himself may well have transported certain recollections of his childhood in what was East Prussia to the vicinity of his West German home. The concreteness of many descriptive passages suggests as much; and in an autobiographical sketch, written well before the publication of this novel, he mentioned that his father was a "patient official." If he did transpose parts of his story from the Baltic to the North Sea, the imaginative graft has taken, and the effort required of an English or American reader is very slight compared to that feat. In any case, Lenz has succeeded in writing a consistently gripping novel about normal life in a provincial outpost of Nazi Germany—without melodrama, demonology, or a pretentious superstructure of allegory and symbolism. And he has done what many realistic writers have tried and failed to do: sustained his readers' interest in characters who are not outstandingly attractive, sensitive, or articulate. The key to that achievement is the gift of seeing. (p. 73)

Michael Hamburger, "A Third Reich with No Demons," in Saturday Review (© 1972 Saturday Review Magazine Co.; reprinted by permission), Vol. LV, No. 10, March 18, 1972, pp. 71-3.

CHRISTOPHER LEHMANN-HAUPT

I'm finding it very difficult to choke back hostility to Siegfried Lenz's "The German Lesson," to resist complaining that a certain ponderousness weighs it down, a certain unwillingness to come to the point, a certain metaphysical elusiveness. I want to indulge my prejudice against the Teutonic imagination, to agree with a not unperceptive student I once knew, who in a fit of exasperation with Johann Fichte (I believe it was) scrawled at the bottom of a term paper the message that "GERMANS CAN'T WRITE." . . .

My inclination is to sum up Mr. Lenz's plot and theme with a series of questions that may make his work sound somewhat less than compelling. Why is the story's hero, Siggi Jepsen, locked up in a prison for juvenile delinquents on an island in the river Elbe? Why has Siggi been assigned by prison authorities to write an essay on "The Joys of Duty"? Why is Siggi troubled by this assignment, and why does he insist on carrying it out by filling one thick copybook after another with

his life story (which becomes the book we are reading) until his keepers grow exasperated and practically beg him to desist?

What is Siggi getting at with this lengthy account of how his father, a rural policeman, becomes obsessed with acting on an order from Berlin to prevent an expressionist painter living in his district (an old friend who once saved him from drowning, of course) from producing any more "degenerate" art? Why, if Siggi has taken the artist's side, did he start stealing the paintings produced in defiance of the ban? And what the devil does the fish imagery have to do with it all?

I'm urged to answer these questions derisively—to sneer that the conflict between the policeman devoted to his duty and the defiant painter dramatizes nothing less obvious than the divided German spirit, conflicted in its longing for authority and culture. Something tells me that Siggi himself is supposed to represent the twisted outcome of that character conflict: a boy who—heavy irony here—ends up in prison for stealing the artist's paintings to safeguard them from his father's zeal to do his duty. I'm afraid that the novel's final irony is that Siggi learns nothing from his punishment. He has simply written his interminable analysis of "The Joys of Duty" in response to yet another sense of duty. And apparently the point of the biological imagery—all the details of aquatic species and the references to Darwin—is supposed to be that fate would not have allowed Siggi's story to be otherwise—that the fate of Germans, past, present and future, is locked in the steps of determinism.

And yet I am nagged by the feeling that this treatment is not fair to Mr. Lenz's novel. For the truth is that while I was often tempted to put it down, I had to keep reading "The German Lesson." There was something pictorially irresistible about the North Sea coast in which the story is set. It was a relief to read a novel set in wartime Germany in which no storm troopers march or Nazi slogans are shouted, yet in which we could never doubt where we were. That expressionist painter was a powerfully attractive figure, with his greatcoat patched with bottomless pockets, his stolid imperturbability and the comic dialogues he indulged in with an invisible esthetician named Balthazzar. The policeman himself was not unappealing . . . not at all . . . in fact, it was hard not to sympathize with his slow-witted sense of loyalty and his crude peasant instincts. If ever the Third Reich was pictured in microcosm, with its prejudices against people not rooted in the land, and its tiny spasms of nationalistic fervor that added up to an irrational howl only in final sum, then Mr. Lenz has done it . . . has surpassed it.

"The German Lesson" will not go away. The solemn drollery of its narrative voice has gotten under my skin, I see; and I suspect that its German original is even more infectious. I can't get out of my mind the scene in which Siggi's older sister, Hilke, goes hunting for seagull eggs with her boyfriend, Addi, and, suddenly, the sky becomes a feathered mass of screaming birdclouds, and Addi collapses in an epileptic fit. I remember the old doctor who must pause to catch his breath after every half-dozen steps he takes, and who gives his patients a multiple choice of diagnoses to pick from. I can't shake off the feeling that if Mr. Lenz's footsteps are just as heavy as the doctor's, the imprints they leave are indelible.

So where does all this leave us? With feelings mixed to the extreme, obviously. This is not a novel over which to enjoy the passage of spring to summer, or a bag of potato chips. It is probably not a book that will appeal at all to an American audience at this late date in the century. But I keep thinking of Van Gogh's "The Potato Eaters"—its gnarled figures crouched in dark earthen space, consuming their meager fare with resignation and tragic hope. One does not wish to enter that world or even to linger with its image. Yet the power of its crude composition remains unforgettable.

> *Christopher Lehmann-Haupt, "Figures in a Dirty Ground," in* The New York Times *(© 1972 by The New York Times Company; reprinted by permission), April 5, 1972, p. 43.*

KINGSLEY SHORTER

There was little in Siegfried Lenz's two earlier novels published here [*The Lightship* and *The Survivor*] to herald the beauty and richness of *The German Lesson*. Both struck me as heavily upholstered short stories. . . .

Both books were well written, but neither amounted to more than its synopsis; one feels that the author conceived the theme first, and only then clothed it in incident. In *The German Lesson* it is the other way about: The theme grows irresistibly out of the material. Since the theme is the joys of duty as experienced by a law-abiding, indeed law-enforcing, German under the Nazi regime, Lenz takes us to the heart of the 20th-century agony. This is, then, an ambitious book.

What is unusual about it is that Lenz has chosen to deal with issues of universal significance in a setting so apparently peripheral, so local, that a mere outline of the novel must make it sound like a genre work—closely observed but minor, miniature; or an exercise in nostalgia. In fact, it is neither. Set amid the peat bogs, dykes and desolate water meadows along Germany's North Sea Coast, *The German Lesson* is so powerful an evocation of place that I found myself combing the map of Schleswig-Holstein for the villages that stud the narrative.

Some are real, some are fictitious; for like everyone's childhood in retrospect, Lenz's landscape is a haunting superposition of precise coordinates on the inner world that only in childhood is coextensive with actual fields, actual woods. Through the eyes of the 11-year-old Siggi we come to know the ever changing cloud formations, the dramatic play of light over the sea, the omnipresent force of the wind; through his eyes the characters, too, take on an inevitable, almost elemental force. (p. 9)

Reading Lenz makes one realize the extent to which grotesquerie has been a substitute for feeling in postwar German writing. It is as if what happened under Hitler was so dreadful that art is impotent to represent it; as if everything now must be ghoulish, a dance of death on the ruins of sensibility; as if we'd been numbed by the sheer scale of the disaster, to the point of believing the facts to be beyond human reckoning, incomprehensible. Lenz deals with this by narrowing the scope but at the same time hugely increasing the magnification, cranking his lens down into the culture where the protozoa of totalitarianism thrive and multiply. Instead of inventing bizarre incidents, Lenz brings a naturalist's attention to bear on the minutiae of "ordinary" behavior, the microevents that cumulatively produced the megalomania, the camps, and all the rest of it.

The story is seen through the eyes of a child, but recounted when the narrator is already a young man. The immediacy of the one qualified by the ironic perspective of the other gives the book both freshness and great depth. A child does not theorize; he experiences and feels accordingly. Reconstructing the events 10 years later, Siggi seeks the meaning of his ordeal in a painstakingly minute examination of his memories.

Precise observation is the key. . . . [The] insistence on the exact time of day, the exact configuration of the heavens, the exact wind strength and direction—and the corresponding exactness of observation about persons and their movements, gestures, speech—powerfully recreates the feel of childhood, the directness of the child's experience.

Lest this weight of circumstantial evidence oppress the reader, Lenz has perfected a totally opposite technique for rendering it more manageable: the cartographer's schematization. (pp. 9-10)

Siggi is reassuringly anchored in his cell, whose contents lend themselves to finite inventory; the reader can breathe with him there, between dives to his private Atlantis. The breathers help, for what Siggi fetches up from under 10 years of silt is depressing stuff. (p. 10)

Siggi's excavation is thorough. But meaning is not so easily come by: The brute facts of experience have a way of surviving all explanations intact. Siggi shows in great and compelling detail how his father and the painter behaved the way they did, how it was inevitable that they should have done so, and how their conflict partially unhinged him; he is unable, however, to understand why.

As if to illustrate the intransigence of experience, the futility of explication, Lenz introduces a young psychologist who visits Siggi in his cell and reads him excerpts from a clinical study of his "case." Like Siggi-the-narrator's own map-making simplifications, this "objective" commentary is reassuring because it appears to make sense of otherwise senseless phenomena. Siggi knows better: "No, Wolfgang Mackenroth! It was like that and yet it was not like that at all."

The German Lesson is in the end tragic, not so much because of the events themselves but because of their resistance to interpretation, because they cannot truly be grasped. And if they cannot be grasped, neither can they be transcended. . . . Why, he asks, why, why, why are they the way they are, the people "down our way." "And I put my questions to their way of walking and of standing, to their glances and their words. And whatever I learn from any of it does not satisfy me." The tone is so fresh and youthful throughout, and the conclusion so despairing, that one is quietly appalled.

There is much more to be said in praise of *The German Lesson*. But perhaps Tolstoy's dictum about happy and unhappy families applies to art, too: All good novels resemble one another, every bad novel is bad in its own special way. A list of Lenz's achievements in *The German Lesson* would surely be as dull as the book itself is enthralling. It isn't perfect; occasionally— very occasionally—Lenz lapses into archness, or sentimentality, or preachiness. Yet these are minor flaws in a major work. Let me simply say I was really sorry when I got to the end, and leave it at that. (pp. 10-11)

> *Kingsley Shorter, "Germany Under the Lens," in* The New Leader *(© 1972 by the American Labor Conference on International Affairs, Inc.), Vol. LV, No. 10, May 15, 1972, pp. 9-11.*

PHILLIP CORWIN

Rarely is a novelist able to operate successfully in several simultaneous dimensions—personal, historical, and esthetic— without resorting to allegory, artifice, or just bad writing. In *The German Lesson,* Siegfried Lenz turns the trick. He has created characters with profound political and artistic significance who never lose their credibility as people. . . .

The implications of this story are so broad that they form a kind of invisible picture of the most fundamental characteristics of the modern age: the conflicts between art and totalitarianism, between blind obedience and the dictates of conscience, between family and society, between freedom and responsibility, between the writer and his audience. And the amazing thing is that no matter which way one reads *The German Lesson,* there is something to be learned.

> *Phillip Corwin, "Read Him Any Way You Like, Mr. Lenz Scores," in* The National Observer *(reprinted by permission of* The National Observer; © *Dow Jones & Company, Inc. 1972; all rights reserved), May 27, 1972, p. 21.*

D. KEITH MANO

The German Lesson is good, but not nearly so good as it appears. Siegfried Lenz writes in what I'd call the accretive style: sentences go three steps forward, two steps back. There is an illusion of lush detail, great perception, but the novel is like a box of cornflakes: it tends to settle in transit. . . . *The German Lesson* reads like old Dr. Kildare dialogues, not memorable, but very memorizable. . . .

Lenz imitates—but seldom approaches—really hard and incisive writing.

This, of course, is the Gunter Grass style. Siegfried Lenz does seem awfully derivative. If either novelist should happen to pass, say, a paint factory, there will follow one chapter, perhaps two (called probably "The Joys of Paint"), complete with brochures, specifications and color charts. The digressive method has its venerable ancestry: *Jacques le Fataliste* out of *Tristram Shandy.* In *The German Lesson* we have predictable devices, "How shall I describe his hat?" "I must stop here and set the scene." It puts a MAN WORKING sign over the author's head. These phony associations are a substitute for the business of metaphor making. And the reader, with noticeable condescension, is made to participate in, to be present at, the artist's great moment of creation.

Grass and Lenz share the same concern: Germany and It Can't Happen Here But It Certainly Did, Didn't It? The first person protagonist is ordered to write a German essay on Duty. The essay becomes a novel about his duty-mad policeman father and a great painter forbidden by the Nazis to paint. *The German Lesson* means, transparently, the Lesson of Germany. It celebrates the free mind's triumph in a totalitarian state, tries to clamp half-nelsons on the German character. But where Grass uses immense, loud, mesmerizing emblems, Lenz is matter-of-fact. . . . Lenz's moralizing, like his style, is full of air, pretentious, over-simple. . . . Lenz is a talented writer. The book has sold a quarter of a million copies in Germany alone. But not for its literary excellence—rather for its very proper and expiatory response to the national guilt. (p. 646)

> *D. Keith Mano, "When They Are Good . . . ," in* National Review *(© National Review, Inc., 1972; 150 East 35th St., New York, NY 10016), Vol. XXIV, No. 20, June 9, 1972, pp. 646-47.**

THE TIMES LITERARY SUPPLEMENT

Das Vorbild [*An Exemplary Life*] tells the tales of a small but ill-assorted official committee in search of a model (potential *idols* appear along the way, but a model is what is wanted), an agreed example of estimable attitudes and behaviour which, if suitably written up, might be included in a textbook for use in German schools.

Lenz is an accomplished short-story writer, and any quest for neatly depictable episodes which demonstrate the ways in which more or less admirable people think and act would give his talents scope. The scope in this case is vast, since the stories under scrutiny are presented not with their inventor's commendation but, in essence, as the choices made, the models proposed by three highly disparate educationists. And each of these in turn has a history, a far from exemplary domestic background, which emerges as yet another semi-independent narrative within the whole. All told, then, *Das Vorbild* is a rich plum-pudding of a book: whether it can be said to hold together is debatable; certainly it is hard to digest. . . .

Despite its distinctively German features, *Das Vorbild* raises questions and hints at messages of wide concern. The problematic urge to seek, follow, set, propagate, or impose shiny examples is not of course peculiar to this or that nation. . . . Nevertheless, the appeal of Lenz's book is strangely limited. It reads well; the author handles language with remarkable precision and an unobtrusive panache which his more flamboyant German contemporaries have reason to admire. It is funny, witty—the writer has an eye for comic detail, a gift for straight-faced irony, for amusing formulation which can be a delight. And it is packed with characters, incidents, and observations that command attention. And yet the whole is disappointing, flawed by what might be an inherent weakness. In view of the possible importance of the job in hand, those tackling it appear implausibly lightweight, as do their arguments and their space-consuming proposals, their "models", on occasion.

If this is one of Lenz's points—that serious tasks are sometimes given to the wrong people—he is an unconscionable time making it; but, whether it is or not, it is hard to escape the conclusion that the cast of *Das Vorbild* has been chosen arbitrarily. That this casting has contributed to the overall inconclusiveness of the work is clear: readers are likely to be left not merely with queries which deserve to remain unanswered but also with a feeling that, on the moral and educational issues to which so much space is devoted, Lenz is incongruously reluctant to take a stand.

> *"The Perfect German," in* The Times Literary Supplement *(© Times Newspapers Ltd. (London) 1973; reproduced from* The Times Literary Supplement *by permission), No. 3745, December 14, 1973, p. 1547.*

DAVID PRYCE-JONES

[*An Exemplary Life*] is an exemplary novel. It is on the abiding subject of all good fiction—how should one live now?

Three people have met in Hamburg to edit an anthology for children, and in order to fill one chapter they must find some life-story which will serve as a suitably inspiring model for the young. These three consist of Pundt, an ageing schoolmaster, Rita Sussfeldt, a freelance busybody, and Heller, a trendy growing a little long in the tooth. Although they have been somewhat stylized respectively as conservative, shambolic liberal and progressive, they are scrupulously characterized as well. . . .

Not surprisingly, no single piece of anthology prose can be accommodated to such differing tastes. Siegfried Lenz has fun with that, having constructed the splendid position whereby he can sit in literary judgment on his own material. . . .

Slowly the European novel is reviving the old central belief that fiction's purpose is to illuminate people and the choices they make. Siegfried Lenz, with his gifts, is himself a fine and encouraging example.

David Pryce-Jones, "How to Live Now," in The Times, London (© Times Newspapers Limited 1976), November 18, 1976, p. 10.

LOTHAR KAHN

Despite his major reputation in Germany, Siegfried Lenz remains virtually unknown in the United States. . . . Perhaps this can be traced to his lengthy descriptions of unknown German landscapes, both physical and cultural. His lingering on Frisian village scenes and, even more, his plumbing of the German soul may have left Americans at a loss. In this country we have moved so drastically from even minimal concepts of duty and discipline that the representation of their misuses in German life apparently failed to strike a meaningful chord.

That was one of the central messages of *The German Lesson*: how duty, often a desirable quality, was converted into a fatal political liability as loyal Germans carried out dehumanizing orders under Nazism. . . . Lenz' book was a truly frightening picture of the Third Reich in microcosm. . . . The novel enabled the author to probe the whys, the implicit guilt, the missed options of the Nazi years. It was search without breast-beating but with a persuasive moral earnestness; a return to the past to investigate the values that—exaggerated and perverted—had led to monstrous and destructive behavior.

Now, in *An Exemplary Life*, Lenz anchors himself in the present. Again he uses a bleak North German landscape, this time the metropolis of Hamburg on gray and rainy November days. Again, too, he confronts his characters with the social and individual choices that may elevate or debase a human being. For the new work addresses itself to a simple question: Given a free hand to come up with "an exemplary life," a perfect model of conduct for youngsters to emulate, could we produce such a life, whether real or fictional?

A committee of three, charged by the Ministry of Education for North German lands with finding a paradigmatic story for inclusion in a school reader, meets in a run-down Hamburg hotel to exchange the results of their respective searches. The three had experienced no difficulty with the first two sections, one on Work and Festivals, the other on Home and Abroad. But here they encounter problems. They read their stories to each other; they dissect them; they do not find any suitable.

At least part of the trouble rests with the people selected to compose the anthology. . . . As they read and reject each other's suggestions, they not only recognize the shortcomings of their proposals but become aware of the paucity of their individual lives as well—revealed to us by Lenz in between consideration of their proposals.

Old Valentin Pundt thinks about his single son, who for no apparent reason killed himself shortly after brilliantly passing his examinations in Hamburg. Trying to understand the tragedy, Valentin begins to see his own existence in a new and frightening light. (pp. 9-10)

Yet Pundt, a man of the old school, performs perhaps the most exemplary act in the book. He hears some whimpering sounds and comes upon two helpless people being trampled by mem-

bers of a vicious gang. In his strictest schoolmaster's voice he bids them stop and is stopped himself, his limp body set adrift in a boat on the Alster. Saved through a miracle, Pundt lies in a hospital room questioning his worth and decides to quit the project.

Dr. Suessfeldt, part of an ill-defined *ménage à trois*, is forever ignoring traffic regulations as she flits from one cultural meeting to another. Her role is never made clear, however; Lenz did his novel no favor in creating her. Janpeter Heller, by contrast, is a vital part of the plot and a foil to Pundt. In a foolish effort to be one of the youthful crowd—he knows every phase of The Scene—he has alienated his wife and ruined his marriage. Heller is not aware of it, but his brand of modern cynicism barely conceals his disenchantments and inner bankruptcy, and his gestures of idealism are pathetic and amusing.

How were these specimens of human failure, who started out barely suspecting their inadequacies, chosen to prepare a chapter to mold the young? Lenz gives no answer but, as in *The German Lesson*, he skillfully explores the dichotomy between the purity of an ideal and its application in human practice, or, from another vantage, the distance between precept and preceptor. . . .

It is easy to sense Lenz' distrust, once again, of moral absolutes, especially in the political sphere. He does not claim inspirational examples do not exist, rather that every human life is suspect in some quarters, and all are potentially dangerous, futile or self-destructive. More than any other writer today, with the possible exception of Saul Bellow, Lenz is frightened by the intellectual, cultural and political clutter of our times, and by forces so complex and contradictory that simple solutions are beyond reach. Yet Bellow always salvages a remnant of hope through some prescriptive formula; Lenz does not. If this work nevertheless avoids generating black despair, it is because of his subtle humor, his dexterous use of unobtrusive irony, his amusing situations.

An Exemplary Life is a fascinating but tricky and ambiguous novel. It is also highly readable for a deeply philosophical work, thanks in large part to Lenz' admirable tendency to let his characters be defined by what they are doing and how they do it. We know them through the way they eat, drink and drive, the places they visit, their actions in the face of old and new situations.

True, the exemplary lives rejected by the trio are invented by Lenz in a manner that allows him to stack his case, and the many stories and the novella within the book occasionally distract. But if this novel is not quite on the level of *The German Lesson*, it nevertheless confirms Lenz' place alongside Gunter Grass, Heinrich Böll and Uwe Johnson as one of the top writers in Germany today. (p. 10)

Lothar Kahn, "A German Master," in The New Leader (© 1976 by The American Labor Conference on International Affairs, Inc.), Vol. LIX, No. 24, December 6, 1976, pp. 9-10.

G. P. BUTLER

["**Die Phantasie**"], the last, longest, and most recently written of the thirteen pieces which go to make up this collection, *Einstein überquert die Elbe bei Hamburg*, is, if not the best, certainly the clearest single illustration of [Siegfried Lenz's] thematic inventiveness that one could hope for in what is still, after all, a shortish story of some forty-five pages. Three writers of differing artistic persuasions meet in a pub and agree to show each other their paces by improvising tales which might explain the presence there of the unknown couple in the corner—their only fellow customers. All three are, of course, Herr Lenz: Klimke, who is "convinced that one can only reveal reality with the aid of the fantastic" . . . ; Gregor, who insists that "invention must always be authenticated by reality" . . . ; and the first-person narrator of the tales' framework, who is accused—justly—of inconclusiveness: "That's typical of you . . . with you everything ends in the air, because you consider solutions impolite."

Impolite or not, openendedness, fantasy, imaginative realism and occasional flashes of critical commitment, of liberal stance-taking, are indeed all characteristic of Lenz's storytelling, no matter how the stories are assembled . . . and no matter what their ideal medium: he is, of course, a dramatist, too, with a keen ear and an acute sense of situation, . . . and several of the items gathered together in his new book might be even more enjoyable performed than read. **"Fallgesetze"**, for instance, a slightly implausible and perplexing story of intrigue and skulduggery among stone-fishers (or pearl-fishers), is told by the three voices, in a repeated sequence, of the drama's principal figures and is virtually a script for radio. . . .

Lenz's inclination to end "in the air", to leave the reader wondering what happened next, is arguably one of his strengths; but unfortunately it belongs to those features which, if recurrent and encountered in quick succession, can irritate—even though, as here, they appear in essentially discrete units which deserve to be assessed as such. **"Die Wellen des Balaton"**, for example, describes a rendezvous, on more or less neutral territory, of two related couples: a prosperous pair from Bremen (he is a refugee from the GDR) and a poorer but none the less self-assured one—likable enough, rather stolid, understandably defensive—from across the border. Will the twain ever really manage to meet? What takes place is a brief and fruitless encounter. And the reader finds himself asking the questions he would commonly ask, and to which he can normally find some kind of answer, after dipping into a novel or reading an excerpt. They concern not only matters of detail (How did Trudi get that scar on her cheek?), but the place of the episode in the whole from which it has apparently come. Curiosity is similarly aroused and left unsatisfied by the everyday story of student folk with which the collection opens (**"Das Examen"**— a well-captured glimpse of the stresses inherent in the German examination system, and in examination candidates' marriages), by the account which follows it (**"Ein Grenzfall"**) of an eventful day in the seemingly humdrum life of a harassed customs officer, and by much else besides.

In other words, as his record to date has indicated, Lenz is first and foremost an anecdotalist whose ambitions and abilities as novelist are sometimes in conflict with what he does best. A lack of economy, for instance, to which in a novel there are few legitimate objections—Günter Grass's stress on the importance of "incidentals" comes to mind—can and does occasionally mar the narratives in *Einstein*. At his best, on the other hand, Lenz is superb. The book's title story is a short piece of virtuoso whimsicality . . . , "a photograph to be read" in which the theory that all motion is relative is translated into mundane yet phantasmagoric practice—imaginings catalysed by the presence on a Hamburg ferry of Albert Einstein. But in spite of his wit and generally admirable lightness of touch, the author is perhaps most impressive—at least in this volume—when he is most sombre: the savagery of **"Die Augenbinde"**, an eerie, allegorical comment on the levelling processes to which society subjects its more gifted members; the

fearful bitterness of **"Die Schmerzen sind zumutbar" (The Pain is Not Excessive),** a military dictator's conclusion after undergoing—voluntarily, in the interests of his regime's image—a selection of the interrogation techniques of two of his henchmen; the sadness of **"Wie bei Gogol"** of an incident which epitomizes the plight of West Germany's illegal guest-workers—these are evidence of a rare and versatile talent, and, praise be, of one still vigorous enough to express concern through literature. One hopes that there is more to come, even if more means no better.

G. P. Butler, "Destination Unknown," in The Times Literary Supplement (© *Times Newspapers Ltd. (London) 1977; reproduced from* The Times Literary Supplement *by permission), No. 3920, April 29, 1977, p. 538.*

BRIAN MURDOCH AND MALCOLM READ

The basic theme of [the novel *Stadtgespräch (The Survivor)* and the story **'Das Feuerschiff' ('The Lightship')**] is the choice of evils imposed when hostages are taken for any purpose. That they come to different conclusions—insofar as they come to conclusions at all—is probably inevitable. The increase in kidnapping as a political weapon over the past few years has, moreover, sharpened the sensitivity of the reader to the problems inherent in this kind of theme, but an increased awareness of the possibilities of such a situation has not made the possibility of a general solution any more likely. Lenz does, of course, treat the theme in his drama *Zeit der Schuldlosen,* and the 'experimental' situation set up there is echoed in these works, too. There is some justification for treating the stories not in the order of composition but in that of the events told in them. *Stadtgespräch* is set—in spite of efforts to make the time and place deliberately vague—in Norway during the Second World War. **'Das Feuerschiff'** is set after the war, although there is still a link with it. (p. 40)

Stadtgespräch is potentially a war-time suspense story. A Scandinavian country is under enemy occupation, and in the town at the centre of the story, an enclosed, small community, a resistance group is formed only after two years, under the leadership of Daniel, a one-time student who has broken off his studies. (p. 41)

The tale is told by a first-person narrator, not Daniel, but one of his followers. It is, moreover, an address *to* Daniel, a statement to the effect of 'this is the story as *I* remember it—you must tell it from your side.' Further, there is no suspense as to whether Daniel actually does give himself up. (p. 42)

The narrative strategy of the novel is for the most part successful. Sometimes it is stretched, as indeed it is in *Deutschstunde,* where the narrator has to be made to be present to overhear a conversation. Here, there is a vital conversation between two of the hostages, and the narrator has to be placed in a position to eavesdrop and report. Sometimes, though, the omniscient narrator intrudes willy-nilly: this is clear in the description of the death of the hostages. The resistance fighters hear the shooting and imagine what is happening, and the narrator imagines it in great detail, but he does so through Daniel. . . . The vividness of this incident, where the imagination overtly takes over, makes more real the supposedly involved narrative of the rest. The problem of narrative reality becomes more acute if we compare the shooting with the hurried flight of the resistance fighters from their camp, something which presumably did have witnesses. . . . (pp. 42-3)

Lenz builds upon the fundamental dichotomy between good and evil, a basic contrast between occupiers and occupied which is clear, and against which the more complex problems of how a single community responds may be set. To draw overtly on the historical opposition in Nazi-occupied Norway would seem to have been more appropriate.

The occupiers are portrayed negatively. . . . One man's (or one epoch's) partisan is another man's terrorist, and Lenz would presumably not want any confusion of loyalties to occur later. (pp. 43-4)

The story . . . recalls the basic tenet of the heroic epic, which shows a human figure struggling against a destiny which is inevitable, and since it *is* inevitable, can be told from the beginning. *Stadtgespräch* reverses the fate of the medieval hero, however: it is Daniel's fate to survive, not to die. When a hero of the Germanic epic died in an inevitable struggle, he found glory, and was aware of this. Daniel's fate in surviving is to find accusations and whisperings against him—a *Stadtgespräch*, not an heroic poem.

The opening of the work does not preclude tension within the story, of course: the incidents that arise from the basic situation have an inner tension that contributes towards the readability of the work. These incidents sometimes take the story in unexpected directions, but all are related to the central theme of Daniel.

Daniel is doomed to failure from the beginning. The resistance started too late:

> Everyone knows that it came late, the town had been occupied for two years, we had come to terms, subjected ourselves, got used to it; we had discovered that it is possible to live without justice. . . .

What Daniel demanded was a different attitude, and his transformation into the embodiment of resistance becomes clear in the more philosophical portions of the novel. (p. 44)

Daniel's efforts, however tragic they might appear, are the imposers of the necessary moment of truth, the urge to make those involved state what is right and what is not. The pastor's notions of forgiveness might be sincere, but ultimately they are flabby. The irony is that the central figure here—Dr Lund—and the one who understands, has to die. The rest of the people in the town do not understand, or if they do, they do not remember when the state of injustice is passed.

Daniel himself is a passive figure, and the echo of the 'lions' den' is presumably intended. The forces are beyond his control and he becomes aware of his own impotence. . . . Daniel does not develop in the work, but the awareness of the passive nature of his own suffering constitutes an anagnorisis. (p. 46)

The work has implications for the single individual in an extreme situation, and it has links with the earlier novels. For Dr Lund, the fact that he is faced with death forces his awareness of existence. Indeed, the whole incident in the town is testing:

> A line ran through the town, a shadow-line, a line of decision. It was visible and palpable already, it concerned everyone. . . .

Daniel forces the people of the town to stand on one side of the line or the other.

The second set of problems in the novel concerns historical objectivity, and added to this is the notion of overcoming the

past by remembering it. Lenz illustrates here the basic lesson of history; that men never learn lessons. It is not the forces of evil that are castigated, but those who forget afterwards the whole necessity of resistance to an evil force, but rather remember only the concrete losses of forty-four men and a ferry. Those lives must also be set against humanity, not against Daniel.

The problem of objectivity takes the novel beyond its chronological limits, into historiography itself. In a short time the sequence of events becomes distorted, and even Daniel hears from the prison guard at the end a version of one incident that contrasts with what has been told us by the narrator as an eye-witness. This brings about the ultimate paradox: the story has to be reiterated, in order to keep it fresh. (pp. 49-50)

Stadtgespräch is not paradigmatic in any practical sense. In a passage which, in this novel, is unusual in its sententiousness, we are told that:

> Past credit-marks don't let anybody off the responsibility for a present action. For us, all that counts is how we survive and the one thing that tests us daily: the present. . . .

Recent experiences with terrorism have shown all too clearly that every case is different. In 'Das Feuerschiff', however, Lenz does seem to be setting up a political or at least an ethical paradigm. This time the forces of terrorism make an attack from outside on to the picture of order, and the black and the white are clear again from the beginning. The problem is not in determining who is the terrorist, but rather how one is to react to terrorism. More even than in *Zeit der Schuldlosen,* we are presented here with a test-tube situation, an experiment, an exploration.

Freytag is captain of a lightship at anchor in a channel which has been dangerous because of the mines and wrecks left from the war. It is about to be withdrawn from service, however, and this is the last spell of duty. Freytag has on board with him not only his small crew, but also his son Fred, who despises him, for reasons which are not immediately clear, and which form the sub-plot of the work.

A small boat is spotted by the son and its crew rescued, but it turns out to contain an unlikely trio, two thugs and the sinister Dr Caspary, who have just committed a major robbery. They are armed, and have effectively taken the lightship hostage. Their threats of violence ensure that the police are not called, and Freytag, to avoid hurting any member of his crew, agrees to their demand that their boat be repaired. The crew, however, will not do this and eventually it is cut free. This forces a showdown: Caspary demands that the lightship be loosed from its moorings to take them to freedom. Here, however, Freytag stops. He faces the gun aimed at him and is wounded, but does not give way. By now the police have been alerted, however, and the remaining two criminals—one has been killed, as has one member of the crew—are taken prisoner. The order of the sea has been maintained.

The sub-plot is concerned with the attitude of Freytag towards violence. Until the ship itself is threatened, and thus the whole concept of order at sea, he gives in to the demands of the three terrorists rather than risk harm to his crew. His son demands action, and reveals that his distaste for his father stems from tales of an incident in which his father was involved when in command of a sea-going ship. The ship had been lying off a Greek island with a cargo of grain, forbidden by the shipping company to put in and unload, in spite of famine, until the price could be forced up. The father and two others were held when the grain was eventually unloaded, were tortured, and only two returned to the ship. Freytag had refused to risk the entire crew to return for one man. The son understands neither this nor the attitude Freytag adopts towards Caspary and his accomplices, and the point of 'Das Feuerschiff' is precisely to explain that attitude.

Freytag realises that individual heroics are unsatisfactory, and acts—heroically—only when the entire concept of order is threatened. . . . (pp. 50-2)

'Das Feuerschiff' fits well into the mould of the nineteenth-century novella. There is a concentration of space, time and action, a limited cast, a 'remarkable incident' and a dominant symbol. The symbol is that of the lightship, there all the time, lighting a path through the treacherous waters, embodying *Ordnung* (order). The phrase 'bounden duty' takes on a new meaning here, and Lenz develops the paradox that the ship is tied—a prisoner to duty. Yet freedom is, for the ship, illusory—to unmoor it would mean to destroy the order of things.

The parable-like nature of the story as a whole is underlined in the character of Caspary. . . . The seamen are real: Freytag has been at sea for many years, has learned much and has realised the rôle of order and fixedness; and if the rest of his crew have some memorable attributes, such as Gombert with the crow as a pet, they are none the less real. Caspary is not a caricature, although the thugs who accompany him are more or less so. . . . [The] interest is in any case on Caspary, who is characterised (as Lenz so often does his sinister figures) with a gesture—here polishing a large ring—and with his dark glasses.

He is, of course, an allegorical figure: the force of evil itself. He has assumed the identity of his twin brother, a lawyer (another favourite theme of Lenz), and has also been a large-scale blackmailer. Lenz places him in opposition to, and in discussion with Freytag: the seductive force of evil is set against the principle of order. This is the experimental centre, the philosophical thesis of the work. For Caspary's activities as a blackmailer have a philosophical basis. . . . Original sin, or perhaps in a nontheological context 'original evil', does not demand cynical acceptance, it demands an imposed order. Caspary sneers at this: 'Order, Captain, is the triumph of a lack of imagination', . . . 'Phantasie'—the imagination that Caspary is so proud of, but which is such a danger. Imagination is a dangerous thing after all, and we recall that another German word for imagination is 'Einbildung', which can also be a 'delusion of grandeur'.

Here as in so many of his works, Lenz is writing about guilt as a state of being. Paradise may be an ethical prison, but it is still Paradise, and the way to return to Paradise is to impose on oneself the prison of order. The lightship has to be tied, and this is the basis of the work. It is—sneers Caspary—'a born prisoner' . . . , as is Freytag. But

> if a ship goes down, then it is a single tragedy,
> and is part of the price that you have to pay
> when you follow the sea. But if a lightship
> leaves its post, the whole order of the sea is
> finished. . . .

For this reason, when that seems possible, Freytag *does* act heroically. His last words in the story are addressed to his son: 'Everything in order?' . . . —and it is. This applies to the ship and now to his relationship with his son, who now understands him.

Given the strong allegorical mould of the work, it must be stressed that the tale is again a gripping one—more so perhaps than *Stadtgespräch*. Here we have too the superficial showdown tension, a German *High Noon*, and a narrative where the philosophical interludes—the debate between Freytag and Caspary—are less obtrusive. Elements of real tension are built in: one of the two criminal brothers is killed, and Caspary is taken prisoner, but released. One of the crew is also killed. There is an attempt on the part of the criminals to suborn a member of the crew, and, towards the end, a storm blows a live mine towards the ship. Freytag utilises the weapons and skill of the criminal Eddie to fire on and detonate the mine, thereby saving ship and pirates, and the political implications are interesting: a man without weapons has saved a situation by using the weapons and the force of evil. The concepts of the greatest good and the end as justifying the means are invoked. The incidents must be taken as they come, but order must prevail over all else. (pp. 52-4)

Brian Murdoch and Malcolm Read, in their Siegfried Lenz *(© 1978 Oswald Wolff (Publishers) Limited), Wolff, 1978, 157 p.*

THOMAS HAJEWSKI

In his weighty book [*Heimatmuseum,* Lenz] tells the story of a Masurian *Heimatmuseum,* from its creation by an uncle of the narrator Zygmunt Rogalla, through its sixty-year history up until its deliberate incineration by the narrator himself. Like the situation in Böll's *Billard um halbzehn* in which Robert Faemel blows up the monastery built by his grandfather, Rogalla's *Akt der Befreiung* is similarly motivated, even though the reasons for the museum's destruction are several and fundamentally more complex than in Böll's book. They generate the overall suspense of the novel and are only revealed at the book's end.

Heimatmuseum should appeal most favorably to those intimately familiar with the German-Polish area it so vividly describes—i.e. Masuren, a region of thick forests, glistening lakes, strange wildlife and mystical folk customs. In fact the initial half of the novel is a collection of tales, all of which taken together make up a loose cultural history of the area and its inhabitants. . . . Of less interest to the uninitiated reader is Lenz's liberal use of regional dialect.

The speed of the narrative picks up appreciably around the novel's midpoint. The Nazi takeover is experienced in this corner of Europe with the same apprehension as elsewhere, within as well as beyond the borders of the Reich. . . . A crisis is reached when the museum, whose custodianship Rogalla has inherited from his deceased uncle, is to be converted from a regional museum of Masurian culture and history into a *Grenzland-Museum,* a restructured showcase emphasizing Nazi ideals and dedicated to visually justifying German as opposed to Slavic ownership of and rights to the region. The richness of the Masurian past as symbolized by the museum's contents and the near-mystical intermingling of "Geschichte, Heimat, Erinnerung" run like a current through this book, and the attempt at prostituting this relationship by the Nazis (and later by more contemporary factions) implants in Rogalla the idea of the museum's destruction a generation later. . . . After concluding that recent history has essentially not instructed, due to its cyclical nature, and has been grossly misused at the expense of home, family, tradition and memory, Rogalla destroys his beloved structure.

The novel is not without flaws. Lenz has attempted to give his long, often fragmented story more cohesion by having each part narrated by Rogalla as he is lying in a hospital bed recovering from burns received during the museum fire. A certain Martin Witt, presumably the reader, comes to visit him on more than a dozen occasions, each time being treated to another lengthy chapter of the narrative. This situation in itself, together with the sterile hospital surroundings and the initial confused state of the badly burned narrator, tends to opaque the work and presage the less-than-optimistic "moral" of the novel following the museum's destruction. The near daily, almost automatic appearance of Herr Witt and Rogalla's continued referral to him as simply "mein Lieber," take on a ritualistic tone which only anesthetizes the reader further.

In addition to a short-circuited attempt at giving this long book more cohesiveness, Lenz seems to have deviated little from his own earlier themes of guilt and atonement, duty and conscience, freedom and moral responsibility. While reading this novel, I kept fighting off the impressions that it had all been told before, in the so-called "Verlorene-Heimat" novels by other German writers and in more polished prose by Grass and Böll. Yet the clarity with which Lenz describes events from the Masurian past and his undeniable gift for storytelling (i.e., *short story* telling) demonstrate that the main problem with this novel lies more in form and structure rather than in literary relevance or content. Visitors to the *Heimatmuseum* will undoubtedly have more controversial, diverse opinions regarding its contents than would be the case with most bestselling German novels. (pp. 497-98)

Thomas Hajewski, in a review of "Heimatmuseum," in World Literature Today *(copyright 1979 by the University of Oklahoma Press), Vol. 53, No. 3, Summer, 1979, pp. 497-98.*

SALMAN RUSHDIE

"A detestable word? A word with a dark history? . . . I realize that the word has a bad reputation, that it has been abused, so seriously abused that one can hardly use it nowadays . . . But for that very reason, could we not try to rid the word of its bad connotations? Give it back a sort of purity?"

The word is "homeland," and the speaker is Zygmunt Rogalla, master weaver of rugs and the narrative of Siegfried Lenz's new epic fable ["The Heritage"]. Its original title, literally translated, was "The Homeland Museum," and its theme is the vast gulf between Germany's past and present: a gulf created by the Nazi's unscrupulous use of the idea of homeland, heritage and history to justify and legitimize xenophobia, tyranny and the doctrine of ethnic purity. "The Heritage" is, among many other things, an attempt to rescue the past from its exploiters: a fable of reclamation, the very writing of which entails a kind of heroism that reveals Siegfried Lenz . . . to be much more of an optimist than his narrator.

The novel begins when Rogalla deliberately burns down the museum in which, for most of his life, he has tended the relics of his homeland's past. His arson, we finally learn, is motivated by a desire "to bring the collected witnesses to our past into safety, a final, irrevocable safety, from which they would never again issue forth, but where they could never again be exploited for this cause or that." This would seem to be a deeply pessimistic act; but then again, through a feat of total recall that makes up most of the novel, Zygmunt Rogalla restores to us the history of his lost homeland, neither sentimentalized nor

distorted, made neither quaint nor risible; the heritage is given back its innocence, because, as Rogalla knows, "in our memory things lead a purer existence."

Siegfried Lenz's novel is a colossal achievement. It contains a seemingly endless parade of striking images and characters who seem larger than life precisely because they are so beautifully rooted in life. . . .

The homeland of **"The Heritage"** is an East Prussian province called Masuria, and it is made as real to us as Günter Grass's Kashubia. . . . The prevailing mood of **"The Heritage,"** however, is more somber than Günter Grass ever gets. Which is not to say it is less memorable. Anyone who reads Siegfried Lenz's description of the evacuation of Lucknow in the last dark days of the Second World War will find it hard to get it out of his head. . . .

The English-language edition of **"The Heritage"** has been "shortened with the co-operation of the author"; perhaps this accounts for the occasional jerkiness of the storyline, and for certain unsolved mysteries, such as why Zygmunt calls Conny "the great Konrad Karrasch" without really justifying the epithet. It seems a shame to have gone at this book with scissors; it's like arbitrarily removing some exhibits from a museum.

Never mind. The book has survived the surgery. It remains a genuinely fabulous tale, another demonstration that the fable is now the central, the most vital form in Western literature; and it should be read by anyone who takes pleasure in entering a world so beautifully and completely realized that, for all its apparent alienness, it rapidly becomes our own.

Salman Rushdie, "A Fable of Reclamation," in The New York Times Book Review *(© 1981 by The New York Times Company; reprinted by permission), July 19, 1981, p. 6.*

S. N. PLAICE

The concept of "Heimat" has no adequate equivalent in English because German history has charged it with such disreputable connotations. The Nazis appropriated the word for ideological purposes. . . . The concept of a traditional, regional home was already strongly rooted in popular consciousness, and it was not long before the word "Heimat" no longer implied sentimental feelings towards one's own homeland, but rather patriotic feelings towards the "völkisch" element of the rural past, a reverence for all things that purported to be of ethnic German origin. . . .

This atavistic "heimat" ideology was naturally of great significance in East Prussia, a province separated from the fatherland for a second time by the establishment of the Polish Corridor in 1919. It is East Prussia, more specifically the dreary swamps and lakes of Masuria, which provide the setting for Siegfried Lenz's historical novel [*The Heritage*]. The original title of the book was *Heimatmuseum,* and it seems faint-hearted of Krishna Winston, the translator of this otherwise admirable American version, to abandon the German and opt for the unappealingly general title of *The Heritage*. This sacrifices the two central ideas of the book at a stroke. For Lenz must surely have intended the museum not only as a metaphor for the whole ideology of "Heimat", but also as a metaphor for his own novel. *Heimatmuseum* is itself a work of restoration and preservation, an anecdotal, folkloristic and historical archive of the vanished culture of Lenz's native province, which was wholly incorporated into Poland at the end of the Second World War.

The book is a spoken memoir. From his hospital bed, Zygmunt Rogalla, the rugmaker, relates his former life in the Masurian town of Lucknow to a silent listener, Witt. . . . The constant asides to Witt are tediously artificial and intrusive upon a narrative that really needs no framework. They show up glaringly in translation. The narrator-rugmaker analogy is carefully exploited, however. Zygmunt weaves the events of his own life, the semi-magical cultural heritage and the political history of Masuria into a single tapestry.

The narrative begins exuberantly with Zygmunt's childhood. . . .

In adulthood, as Zygmunt learns the art of rugmaking and inherits the museum, Conny [Zygmunt's childhood friend] becomes a free-thinking journalist, championing the Polish minority and opposing the increasingly Nazi local Homeland Association. Adam Rogalla had originally described his collection of Masurian relics as "unimpeachable witnesses", but Conny is by now fully aware of the sinister purpose to which they might be put. . . . A visit from a Nazi official to effect the removal of all non-Aryan exhibits confirms Conny's suspicions and obliges Zygmunt to close the museum to the public.

With the advent of National Socialism, the narrative no longer has the same exuberance. The impression is of individual destiny giving way to remorseless historical forces and collectivist ideology. In keeping with this, perhaps, the characters that now crowd the book grow blander, and the historical events are reported in a more conventionally realistic style. The final, inevitable flight from Masuria is a rather tired inventory of the deprivations of war. It is tempting to reproach Lenz for allowing the narrative to flag, but the shift in style does reinforce the cultural argument of the book—that the creative individualism of regional Germany was swamped by a centralized ideology proclaiming the very values of "Heimat" it was actually destroying.

There is no suggestion that post-war German democracy reversed this cultural decline. At the end of the war, with the help of other Masurians in exile, Zygmunt reconstructs the Heimatmuseum in Schleswig, in the Bundesrepublik. His subsequent decision to destroy the collection is largely influenced by Conny's sudden and rather implausible volte-face. Uprooted from Masuria, the journalist falls into the sentimental trap he had once so sardonically criticized. He begins to write nostalgic pieces on "the lost homeland", and becomes deeply involved with the Lucknow Homeland Association, reformed in exile. . . .

Zygmunt's ultimate realization is that the only way of making relics of the past safe from present exploitation is to destroy them. But the extension of this paradox is that Lenz has preserved the relics of the Masurian past in his own Heimatmuseum, the novel, and written a work that cannot disguise its nostalgia for a lost homeland and for a vanished epoch of regional German culture. Thus, on one level, *The Heritage* is propagating the same values of "Heimat" that Lenz has seen so ruthlessly distorted and exploited in Germany. A hankering for the things of the past and a desire to preserve them is, he believes, a human weakness to which not even the most critical intellect is immune. The past refuses to be obliterated, but in his own book Lenz has at least managed to press it into the service of enlightenment rather than reaction. The feeling remains, however, that the past cannot be presented impartially: its retrieval must always serve an ideological purpose.

The Heritage deserves comparison with *Dr Faustus* and *The Tin Drum* as a comprehensive analysis of Germany's cultural

disintegration. Zygmunt may not have quite the naive humanity of a Zeitblom or the charisma of an Oskar to make a memorable narrator, but Lenz has nevertheless managed to put Masuria on the literary map forty years after it ceased to exist politically.

S. N. Plaice, "The Masurian Museum," in The Times Literary Supplement *(© Times Newspapers Ltd. (London) 1981; reproduced from* The Times Literary Supplement *by permission), No. 4089, August 14, 1981, p. 928.*

WES BLOMSTER

The complex and still-youthful hero of Lenz's novel [*Der Verlust*] suffers from aphasia, the loss of speech. Through the elevation of this affliction to metaphor Lenz transforms his narrative into an essay upon language and silence, grounding it firmly in territory explored by Wittgenstein, George Steiner and Peter Handke.

Uli, the central figure, is a gifted and charismatic person, rich in imagination but unable to make final decisions about his life. He exists as a drifter, keeping all options open. His failure is expressed most intensely in his tenuous relation with the major female figure of the work; here the ultimate breakdown of communication manifests itself. With subtle care, Lenz allows his observations upon man and language to emerge as the major theme of the work. Through the loss of speech the hero grows inaccessible even to himself. The novel ends with cautious optimism, indicating that, while there might indeed be no solution to today's problems, everyone stands nonetheless at a beginning, where he must learn to give voice to his being. The imperative is hailed as the only proper and possible approach to life.

The control which Lenz exercises over his low-keyed narrative offers at the outset little hint of the intensity which it will soon achieve. Subplots reflecting the troubles of everyday people— the eviction of a retired couple from their dwelling, the violent death of a teen-ager—give the book that rootedness in reality which has always distinguished Lenz's product. The most powerful moments in the book are those in which the speechless hero attempts to express himself—only to produce incoherent and meaningless sounds.

Wes Blomster, in a review of "Der Verlust," in World Literature Today *(copyright 1982 by the University of Oklahoma Press), Vol. 56, No. 2, Spring, 1982, p. 327.*

HANNA GELDRICH-LEFFMAN

The image of blindness, actual physical blindness, appears in literature from the earliest times to our days. When we confront the image, a bewildering array of possible interpretations leads into seemingly different directions. On the surface, blindness, like any other physical or mental impairment, has a negative meaning. Yet, on closer examination, another, positive, side appears and, in turn, suggests an ambivalent, two-sided structure of the symbol. It is perhaps the richness of allusive meanings which accounts for the fascination it holds for writers and which makes it a most appropriate symbol for our times. (p. 671)

For the writer Siegfried Lenz art is responsibility and commitment and the artist . . . cannot shed his obligation to make these problems of his fellow men his own. . . . (p. 689)

Light as the symbol of intellectual clearsightedness and mastery is stressed as being a positive quality. Blindness in such a context can have only a negative value and will stand for the intellectually closed world of a society that is not free. The existence of such totalitarian states is a deep preoccupation of Lenz; conflicts of responsibility and the question of guilt, as well as the theme of conflict between the individual and power or between the human and the inhuman are constantly reappearing in his works.

Two works of Lenz depict just such a totalitarian society, the short story, **"Die Augenbinde"** . . . and the apparent reworking of the same theme in the play also entitled *Die Augenbinde*. . . . In the short story three men who play cards together during their ride home on a commuter train talk about the serial story one of them had read in his local newspaper about the happenings in a small town called Tekhila. . . . The story describes how the whole town, led by the mayor who has a leather eye-cover, goes to the school-house to capture the son of the teacher for his "crime" of being able to see. The father tries to protect his son by denials and justifications, but the young boy freely admits his newly gained sight.

He pleads for his freedom by telling the townspeople that precisely because he can see, he could be useful to them since he could show them the economic possibilities of Tekhila. But they do not react. . . . So he is captured, taken out of town and bound to the one end of the water-wheel drawn around in a circle by a mule, and the cover is put on his eyes. Everything is done without hesitation, without words, as if it had been done many times before, and the man who binds the boy seems to do it out of a sense of personal experience. . . . The one word which is never mentioned throughout the whole story is "blindness!"

In the play, *Die Augenbinde,* a similar theme is presented. Here it is a scientific expedition stranded at a place called Mallidor, where everybody is blind. The members of the expedition are called upon to join the community, and it becomes increasingly clear to them that they will not be allowed to leave. But the price to join life at Mallidor is conformity with life there, blindness. In contrast to Tekhila, physical force is applied only as a last resort. The first approach is persuasion, persuasion to put on the eye-cover or mask. . . . Should they not "choose" to take the eye-cover and accept the life of the community, they are faced with total abandonment and eventual death. (pp. 689-90)

Slowly the forces of Mallidor seem to win, and one by one the members of the expeditionary group choose the security of submission and acceptance, take the cover, and go to town just as in Eugène Ionesco's *Rhinoceros* and Max Frisch's *Andorra* the characters opt for conformity. First they see the rule of blindness as a sickness that permeated everything in town. . . . Later Carla, the only woman of the group, and one who . . . constitutes the pivotal center and the core of resistance, analyzes it more correctly saying that it is fear that made these laws, the fear that light should fall into a "diseased" eye. . . . It is a rule that fears the light because it could not prevail over people with open eyes. It will therefore use whatever means it can to establish its control over people. One means was violence, the other persuasion. Convenient slogans were used to brain-wash the population and give this ultimately anti-human rule a cover of respectability, even of humanitarian-

ism. . . . And it is again Carla who rebels against them. It is Carla who recognizes the diabolical reversal of values which prevails in this society where insight is negated and blindness is used for its own distorted aims. . . . Only the blind can be led by such words. Blindness then stands here as the symbol of ignorance and evil, the counterpart of enlightened knowledge symbolized by light.

The ultimate irony in the situation at Mallidor is the fact that the rulers, the mayor, are themselves not blind. When he is confronted by the strangers who can see that he is not blind, the mayor justifies himself by saying that he has to be different to ensure balance. . . . But Mircea confronts his father when he suddenly realizes the deception. . . . The ultimate crime in this deception, Mircea feels, is that his father has left them all in ignorance and made them deceive themselves. . . . But even armed with this knowledge no revolution happens and Mallidor continues as it is. It is the now blind Alf, the real "seer," who, aided by Carla, who is now called a Kassandra, will continue the resistance, since the only road to salvation is seen in rebellion and the opposition to force.

The play has been called a simple political parable of opposition to a dictatorship, a parable of the vulnerability and power of free men; sight is a symbol for contact with reality, discernment, and the ability to choose, and conversely, blindness is the absence of all of these. It has received relatively poor critical reaction, yet it does embody thematically some of the central preoccupations of Lenz: the problems of freedom, power, tyranny, and humanism. (pp. 691-92)

The startling fact about the image of blindness . . . is that it can stand for seemingly contradictory aspects of reality, i.e. the negative aspect of lack of knowledge and insight, as in Lenz, or the positive aspect of a deeper understanding and truer knowledge of life. . . . [It] is used to distance the audience from the play so that a critical attitude becomes possible. It also makes it possible for . . . Alf in *Die Augenbinde* to become to a certain extent [a sacrificial victim] whose death or sacrifice brings about the resolution of the conflict. . . . [Blindness is] used to symbolize the ambiguity of language, its possibilities to mask and hide as well as to reveal and communicate truth so that blindness becomes a most appropriate symbol for the paradox of language, truth and life itself. There is a constant shifting between two levels of sight and blindness: physical sight representing the visual aspect of reality stands as a limiting factor for the literary artist and is combined with intellectual, spiritual blindness; whereas physical blindness representing the non-visual, imaginative, mystical and spiritual aspects of reality stands as the liberating, open, non-limiting factor for the creative imagination and is therefore combined with deeper intellectual and spiritual knowledge and insight. Sight and blindness are used as the metaphor for language in its double aspect of revealing and hiding, limiting the truth, not only in the outright negative abusive use of the lie or the premeditated un-truth but also in the fact that as soon as language is uttered or made seen a limiting factor comes into play masking the total reality of the statement. (p. 693)

Hanna Geldrich-Leffman, "Vision and Blindness in Dürrenmatt, Buero Vallejo, and Lenz," in MLN *(© copyright 1982 by The Johns Hopkins University Press), Vol. 97, No. 3, April, 1982, pp. 671-93.**

C(live) S(taples) Lewis

1898-1963

(Also wrote under pseudonyms of Clive Hamilton, Nat Whilk, and N. W. Clerk) English novelist, essayist, critic, autobiographer, poet, and short story writer.

Lewis is considered one of the foremost Christian authors of the twentieth century. Indebted principally to the works of George MacDonald, G. K. Chesterton, and Charles Williams, and to ancient Norse myths, he is regarded as a formidable logician and Christian polemicist, a perceptive literary critic, and—most highly—as a writer of fantasy literature. Among the imaginative works for which he is best known are *The Screwtape Letters* (1942), the series of children's books collectively called The Chronicles of Narnia, and the science-fiction trilogy comprising *Out of the Silent Planet* (1938), *Perelandra* (1943), and *That Hideous Strength* (1945). The conflicts presented in Lewis's fiction evoke the cosmic struggle between good and evil, and evidence the Christian vision which informs his literary and critical works.

An acknowledged authority on medieval and Renaissance literature, Lewis taught at Oxford and Cambridge. A traditionalist in his approach to life and art, he opposed the modern movement in literary criticism toward biographical and psychological interpretation. Instead, Lewis practiced and propounded a theory of criticism which stresses the importance of the author's intent, rather than the reader's presuppositions and prejudices. In his Christian polemics, notably *Mere Christianity* (1952), *The Abolition of Man* (1943), and *The World's Last Night and Other Essays* (1960), Lewis's renowned wit and reason serve to defend the faith he embraced in 1931 and to attack the modern social/religious trend which equates change—no matter how foolish or destructive—with progress. Ever popular, Lewis's books continue to attract a growing readership and are the subject of increasing critical study.

(See also *CLC*, Vols. 1, 3, 6, 14; *Children's Literature Review*, Vol. 3; *Contemporary Authors*, Vols. 81-84; and *Something about the Author*, Vol. 13.)

THE TIMES LITERARY SUPPLEMENT

[*An anonymous critic provided the only review of Lewis's first book, a collection of traditional poetry written under the pseudonym "Clive Hamilton" and titled* Spirits in Bondage.]

These lyrics are always graceful and polished, and their varied themes are chosen from those which naturally attract poets— the Autumn Morning, Oxford, Lullaby, The Witch, Milton Read Again, and so on. The thought, when closed with, is found rather often not to rise above the commonplace. The piece which most arrested us was **"The Satyr."**

A review of "Spirits in Bondage: A Cycle of Lyrics," in The Times Literary Supplement (© Times Newspapers Ltd. (London) 1919; reproduced from The Times Literary Supplement by permission), No. 897, March 27, 1919, p. 167.

THE TIMES LITERARY SUPPLEMENT

[The long narrative poem **"Dymer,"** written by C. S. Lewis under the pseudonym of Clive Hamilton] is notable because it is in the epic tradition and yet is modern in idiom, and reflects a profoundly personal intuition. . . . [Doubtless] the prejudice which exists against the epic as a modern art form is due to a belief that in civilized hands it must prove an impure form, a form in which substance and idea are not necessarily related.

Mr. Hamilton has disproved that belief by showing that, in the modern epic, the spiritual may be translated into terms of the physical as inevitably as, in the primitive epic, the physical was translated into terms of the imaginative. He has shown this more convincingly than Mr. Masefield in "Dauber," with which his poem may be usefully compared, because Dymer's experience is throughout metaphysical. His ordeal is not on the high seas but in the swamps and arid places of his own soul-making. To embody such an experience in action is very difficult. For realism is unequal to its complexity, while fantasy easily tempts into regions picturesque but remote from reality. It demands, in fact, a symbolism in which adventures, essentially abstract, are made concrete and physically convincing. And it is such a symbolism which Mr. Hamilton has achieved, not by occult brooding but in response to immediate and commanding intuitions. Consequently the adventures of his hero, though fantastic, are entirely real. They are wholly relevant to the spiritual history of which they express the stages. And this history, though intensely individual, has also a universal significance. It is that of a youth who rebels against the discipline of life and claims his birthright of natural liberty, only to discover that the instincts which he has indulged and sanctified are brutal in origin and fact. . . .

So brief a summary does scant justice to the subtlety with which Dymer's pilgrimage is traced, the impressive rapidity of the action in all its fluctuations, and the frequent beauty of the imagery. Mr. Hamilton is equally successful in communicating both the horror of his hero's realization of the animal grossness which underlies the nature that he embraced as a "breaker of bad laws" and the lyrical ecstasy of instinctive self-abandonment. The sprawling thing with "pale hands of wrinkled flesh" by which he images the former is indeed akin to the monster of the primitive epic, but it is so drawn as to inspire spiritual as well as physical revulsion. Similarly the brooder over dark magic . . . in whom he personifies the temptation to withdraw disillusioned from the actualities of life, has perhaps his parallel in such a figure as Merlin. But both are wholly original projections of Mr. Hamilton's own distinctive intuition of the abysses into which a man may fall in his search for a perfectly expressive life.

"A Modern Epic," in The Times Literary Supplement *(© Times Newspapers Ltd. (London) 1927; reproduced from* The Times Literary Supplement *by permission), No. 1302, January 13, 1927, p. 27.*

ALBERT GUERARD, JR.

Too frequently the professional historian is not a good scholar because he wholly ignores esthetic considerations. Mr. C. S. Lewis, in his study of allegory and courtly love ["**The Allegory of Love**"], shows himself to be even more a man of letters than a literary historian. But as a literary historian he suffers from the defect of his qualities. Time and again he deserts his real subject, the history of allegory as a form and courtly love as a sentiment, for long excursions into pure esthetic criticism. He feels it incumbent upon him to indicate all the scattered felicities in even such a poet as William Nevill. Mr. Lewis has tried to rescue something from the dust of each of the long allegories he examines.

Thus "**The Allegory of Love**" is in reality two books—both excellent, but each vitiating the other. The purely historical study of the growth and decline of allegory and courtly love is a careful piece of scholarship, and the first and second chapters are excellent essays in comparative literature. With the third chapter, however, it is evident that the author has become more interested in individual poets than in historical tendencies, and at this point the thread of the "story" is lost. . . .

The incidental merits of this book, while detracting from its value as scholarship, are very great. I suspect that Mr. Lewis is more interested in literary theory than in history: an abstract of his preliminary analysis and definitions would constitute a valuable little book on the criticism of poetry, as well as a thorough introduction to the study of late medieval literature.

Albert Guerard, Jr., "Courtly Love," in New York Herald Tribune Books *(© I. H. T. Corporation; reprinted by permission), October 18, 1936, p. 14.*

J.R.R. TOLKIEN

[Tolkien, author of The Hobbit *and* Lord of the Rings, *was one of the "Inklings," a group of friends who met weekly in Lewis's rooms to discuss literature and to read works-in-progress to each other. During the few years of its existence, the group included Lewis, Tolkien, Charles Williams, Owen Barfield, W. H. Lewis, and several other noteworthy regulars. Tolkien, a man of strict and very conservative literary standards, frequently disliked Lewis's imaginative works. But in the following letter to his publisher, Stanley Unwin, Tolkien defended his friend's novel* Out of the Silent Planet. *On 2 March 1938, Unwin had sent Tolkien an excerpt from a reader's report, which had disparaged as "bunk" the inhabitants of Lewis's planet Malacandra. Unwin asked Tolkien for his thoughts on Lewis's book.]*

Lewis is a great friend of mine, and we are in close sympathy (witness his two reviews of my Hobbit): this may make for understanding, but it may also cast an unduly rosy light. Since you ask for my opinion, here it is.

I read [*Out of the Silent Planet*] in the original MS. and was so enthralled that I could do nothing else until I had finished it. My first criticism was simply that it was too short. I still think that criticism holds, for both practical and artistic reasons. Other criticisms, concerning narrative style (Lewis is always apt to have rather creaking stiff-jointed passages), inconsistent details in the plot, and philology, have since been corrected to my satisfaction. The author holds to items of linguistic invention that do not appeal to me (Malacandra, Maleldil—eldila, in any case, I suspect to be due to the influence of the *Eldar* in the Silmarillion—and Pfifltriggi); but this is a matter of taste. After all your reader found my invented names, made with cherished care, eye-splitting. But the linguistic inventions and the philology on the whole are more than good enough. All the part about language and poetry—the glimpses of its Malacandrian nature and form—is very well done, and extremely interesting, far superior to what one usually gets from travellers in untravelled regions. The language difficulty is usually slid over or fudged. Here it not only has verisimilitude, but also underlying thought.

I was disturbed by your reader's report. I am afraid that at the first blush I feel inclined to retort that anyone capable of using the word 'bunk' will inevitably find matter of this sort—bunk. But one must be reasonable. I realize of course that to be even moderately marketable such a story must pass muster on its surface value, as a *vera historia* of a journey to a strange land. I am extremely fond of the genre, even having read *Land under England* with some pleasure (though it was a weak example, and distasteful to me in many points). I thought *Out of the Silent Planet* did pass this test very successfully. The openings and the actual mode of transportation in time or space are always the weakest points of such tales. They are well enough worked here, but there should be more narrative given to adventure on Malacandra to balance and justify them. The theme of three distinct rational species *(hnau)* requires more attention to the third species, *Pfifltriggi.* Also the central episode of the visit to Eldilorn is reached too soon, artistically. Also would not the book be in fact practically rather short for a narrative of this type?

But I should have said that the story had for the more intelligent reader a great number of philosophical and mythical implications that enormously enhanced without detracting from the surface 'adventure'. I found the blend of *vera historia* with *mythos* irresistible. There are of course certain satirical elements, inevitable in any such traveller's tale, and also a spice of satire on other superficially similar works of 'scientific' fiction—such as the reference to the notion that higher intelligence will inevitably be combined with ruthlessness. The underlying myth is of course that of the Fall of the Angels (and the fall of man on this our silent planet); and the central point is the sculpture of the planets revealing the erasure of the sign of the Angel of this world. I cannot understand how any one can say this sticks in his gullet, unless (a) he thinks this particular myth 'bunk', that is not worth adult attention (even on a mythical plane); or (b) the use of it unjustified or perhaps unsuccessful. The latter is perhaps arguable—though I dissent—but at any rate the critique should have pointed out the existence of the myth. Oyarsa is not of course a 'nice kind scientific God', but something so profoundly different that the difference seems to have been unnoticed, namely an Angel. Yet even as a nice kind scientific God I think he compares favourably with the governing potentates of other stories of this kind. His name is not invented, but is from Bernardus Silvestris, as I think is explained at the end of the book (not that I think that this learned detail matters, but it is as legitimate as pseudo-scientific learning). In conclusion I might say that in designating the *Pfifltriggi* as the 'workers' your reader also misses the point, and is misled by current notions that are not applicable. But I have probably said more than enough. I at any rate should have bought this story at almost any price if I had found it in print, and loudly recommended it as a 'thriller' by (however and surprisingly) an intelligent man. (pp. 32-4)

J.R.R. Tolkien, in an extract from his letter to Stanley Unwin on March 4, 1938, in The Letters of J.R.R. Tolkien, *edited by Humphrey Carpenter with Christopher Tolkien (copyright © 1981 George Allen & Unwin (Publishers) Ltd. Reprinted by permission of Houghton Mifflin Company. In Canada by George Allen & Unwin (Publishers) Ltd.), Houghton Mifflin, 1981, Allen and Unwin, 1981, pp. 32-5.**

ALISTAIR COOKE

There must be profound reasons why wars spawn so many quack religions and Messiahs, but to discover them would require an exhaustive psychological study of the relations of war and peace to personal insecurity. On a lower level, we may wonder at the alarming vogue of Mr. C. S. Lewis, whose harmless fantasies about the kingdoms of Good and Evil (**"Out of the Silent Planet," "The Screwtape Letters"** and now **"Perelandra"**) have had a modest literary success, while multitudes of readers, and in Britain radio listeners, succumb to the charm of his more direct treatises on Christian conduct.

It may be that a war in which our own shining ideology is so blurred by political trickery, cowardice and double-talk, puts a desperate premium on believers from 'way back, so that we gain confidence from hearing them preach as gospel what we have heard ourselves saying faintly since September, 1939. . . . It must be the same impulse that has pitchforked Mr. Lewis into the limelight, for in doubting times completely unremarkable minor prophets are pressed into making a career of reassurance.

In the days before radio, Mr. Lewis' little volume [**"Christian Behavior"**] would have been reviewed politely in the well bred magazines and no harm would have been done. But the chief danger of these homilies on behavior is their assumption of modesty. They are talks given over the radio by an Oxford don fairly recently converted to Christianity. From the way they were received in Britain, and from the eagerness of American networks to have Mr. Lewis shed the light on our own dark continent, it may be assumed that the personal values of several million Britons and Americans stand in imminent danger of the befuddlement at which Mr. Lewis is so transparently adroit. Mr. Lewis has a real radio talent. . . . He knows it is the first task of radio to make difficult ideas honestly clear. Since his subject is morality, or as he calls it "directions for running the human machine," and since this is the topic above all others that has exercised the finest agonies of the saints, and the best skill of poets, philosophers and psychiatrists since the beginning of time, he is tackling about the toughest assignment ever known to radio. He has to explain the Beatitudes in words of one syllable.

These noble limitations, of which he seems so conscientiously aware, would throw a better man than Mr. Lewis. That they produce in him a persuasive pseudo-simplicity, giving smooth reassurance on questions that are for most men matters of profound concern, would be unimportant if the radio did not encourage its acceptance as the sort of redemption we have all been waiting for. The exposition of every fundamental human problem from "Social morality" to "Marriage" and "Charity," comes out with a patness that murders the issues it pretends to clarify. Thus you learn (though it doesn't help) that in making a moral choice "two things are involved. One is the act of choosing. The other is the various feelings, impulses and so on which his psychological outfit presents him with, and which are the *raw material* of his choice." (What do you choose with?) Mr. Lewis' use of italics here is quite characteristic. It is a frantic make-weight used to tip the scales of an argument that will not conform to the easy balance he has arranged ahead of time. Talking of the sin of Pride, he says, "The other, and less bad, vices come from the devil working on us through our animal nature. But this doesn't come through our animal nature at all. It comes *direct* from Hell." How much more intriguingly might this discussion have been prolonged if Mr. Lewis could have arranged for it to come *indirectly*. These italics remind me of the British use of such adverbs as definitely, really, *ac*tually—they are testy emphases masking indecision about something that should be plain enough.

But the vortex in which Mr. Lewis flounders, while keeping up the same simple pretense of doing an easy and muscular crawl, is sex and marriage. He allows that as a bachelor it is possible he may be prejudiced, but his deep distaste (and fear?) of the whole subject reduces him to the convictions that because a young man might by a single act "populate a small village," the appetite "is in ludicrous and preposterous excess of its function"; that there is something "wrong" with the "sexual instinct" of present-day humans; that being in love was never intended to last; and that extra-marital sex is monstrous because "it isolates one kind of union from all the other kinds of union which were intended to go along with it" (by the same reasoning, it must be equally irresponsible to lunch with friends you don't live with). This is exactly, Mr. Lewis might be appalled to discover, the Puritan's view of sex, as it is the rake's. This frightened dualism is further demonstrated by a brilliant Freudian slip, revealing an unconscious identification of two nouns that bare Mr. Lewis' worst suspicions: he says, "If anyone thinks that Christians regard unchastity as *the* great vice, he is quite wrong. The sins of the flesh are bad, but they are the least bad of all sins. All the worst pleasures are purely spiritual." No wonder "pleasures" is not in italics. For this idea can lead only to Mr. Lewis' secret fear that unchastity is the best pleasure.

"**Perelandra**" appears superficially to be a bracing holiday from these grave matters, for it is another adventure of Dr. Ransom in search of his unearthly utopia. But it is the natural, and arid, counterpart of "**Christian Behavior**," for it is a fantasy compensation for Mr. Lewis' deep dissatisfaction with mankind and the world he inhabits. . . . In "**Perelandra**," which is Mr. Lewis' name for the more embarrassing planet Venus, Dr. Ransom-Lewis swims in oceans of unsalted water ("It was drinkable"!), rushes deliciously into gaping valleys, wins the battle of Temptation against the spirit of evil (not a gigantic cat but as grisly, and known as the Un-Man), and—if it is not too bold a word—conceives bliss in the scene of himself standing in an enchanted wood discussing loneliness and death (he had traveled from earth in a coffin) with a beautiful girl who is "totally naked" but sexless, because on Perelandra they blessedly do not know about sex.

It is at this point that an earthly book-reviewer must uncross his gross legs and tiptoe out, leaving Mr. Lewis to the absorbed serenity of his dreams. (pp. 578-80)

Alistair Cooke, "Mr. Anthony at Oxford," in The New Republic *(reprinted by permission of* The New Republic; © *1944 The New Republic, Inc.), Vol. 110, No. 17, April 24, 1944, pp. 578-80.*

W. H. AUDEN

The pedagogic purpose of "**The Great Divorce**" is to correct a misunderstanding of a misunderstanding of the Christian doctrine of Hell, to clarify what Dante saw written over the gates of the Inferno: "Justice moved my High Maker: Divine Power made me Wisdom Supreme, and Primal Love." The original misunderstanding was to think of the Law of God in terms of the laws of men, that is, as something He imposes on individuals, with or without their consent, and for breaking which He imposes, without their consent, an eternal penalty. If this were true, it would really imply that there were two Gods, an imminent God the Creator, and a transcendent God the Judge, and against such a dualism liberal theology very properly reacted—Blake's "The Marriage of Heaven and Hell" is one of the great polemics in this reaction. In adopting in its stead a doctrine of inevitable progress, however, liberalism denied freedom in another way, for, if the Love of God is omnipotent in the sense that sooner or later I shall be compelled to recognize it, then my present freedom to refuse is only apparent, and when my sins get me into trouble I may reasonably complain that it was very unkind of God not to exercise his omnipotence earlier. If I am not eternally free, I am not free at all. . . .

Like an increasing number of modern works of art, "**The Great Divorce**" revives the medieval literary device of the dream and, since Mr. Lewis is a distinguished medieval scholar, revives it with unusual ease and facility. There is a celestial bus which visits the Grey Town, where the streets are endless, sinister, and mean, "always in the rain and always in evening twilight," to pick up any passengers who wish to visit the Green Plain. . . . One of the ghosts asks the driver when they have got to be back and is told: "You need never come back unless you want to. Stay as long as you please." To the ghosts everything seems unbearably solid, the flowers hard as diamonds, the leaves heavy as sacks of coal, but to the solid people who come to meet them, since they are equally real, nature is natural.

The latter have known the ghosts on earth and have come to try to persuade them to stay, but, in all but one case, without success. . . .

Meanwhile, the spirit of George Macdonald plays Virgil to Mr. Lewis's Dante and explains to the dreamer some of the mysteries of choice and time. . . . (p. 22)

I think it unlikely that if other books as generally entertaining as "**The Great Divorce**" appear this year, they will be as generally instructive, and vice versa, so that it seems ungracious to ask for more, but I cannot help wishing Mr. Lewis were a little less energetic or a little less patient. He might then give us fewer books, which would be a pity, but our satisfaction in the books he did write might be more lasting and complete. Thus, there are a number of little points in his latest volume which I am sure he would have modified if he had taken more time. For example: However unjust it may be, however the regionalists may resent it, provincial dialects belong, like mothers-in-law and boarding-house food, to a farce convention, and George Macdonald's occasional lapses into Doric are, to this reader at least, shymaking. Again, in his treatment of the sins which tempt the artist, he tries to combine in one figure two mutually exclusive idolatries: the pride from which some artists, usually the bad ones, suffer is of demanding public recognition; the pride of others, usually the good ones, is of not caring whether the public "gets" their vision or not, but I do not believe the two can coëxist in the same person, as they do in Mr. Lewis's painter.

Finally, in a book which sets out to explain orthodox doctrine to the laity, it is very important that there should be no possibilities of heretical misunderstanding, and I think I have detected two. Dante or no Dante, it is theologically not in order to present a historical character, in this case Napoleon, as a lost soul; only fictional characters like Othello, who have no life outside our knowledge, can be so presented. We have no right to believe, far less to hope, that even Hitler is in Hell. Secondly, in his account of the conversion of the young man, Mr. Lewis symbolizes the transformation of lust into sanctified desire by the transformation of a red lizard into a white stallion. Now a horse may be a more complex creature than a lizard, but it is not a better one, and a universe in which all lizards were horses would be a less valuable universe. Mr. Lewis may have a personal antipathy to reptiles, just as I have a nervous horror of insects, but such feelings are accidental and have certainly no theological validity.

But such reservations are minor indeed in comparison with all the positive merits of "**The Great Divorce**." As a last word to those who, like myself, take delight in Mr. Lewis's writings, I should like to recommend the works of the late Charles Williams, a writer as unjustly ignored by American publishers as Mr. Lewis is widely and deservedly recognized. (pp. 22-3)

W. H. Auden, "Red Lizards and White Stallions," in The Saturday Review of Literature *(© 1946, copyright renewed © 1973, Saturday Review Magazine Co.; reprinted by permission), Vol. XXIX, No. 15, April 13, 1946, pp. 22-3.*

JOHN WAIN

This author is of course well known as a controversialist—indeed my view is that the death of George Orwell left Mr. Lewis standing alone as our major controversial author—and while controversialists are common enough in the world of letters, they do not usually get asked to contribute to a 'safe' academic series like the Oxford History of English Literature. So it is important to begin by saying that the controversial nature of the book [*English Literature in the Sixteenth Century,*

Excluding Drama, volume III of *The Oxford History of English Literature*] does not make it any the less helpful as a literary history. The chief functions of a literary history are fulfilled: the names are strung together, the historical and biographical information is given, and the bibliography shows us how to set about more detailed study. What is more, the book is a very pleasurable one to read. Mr. Lewis is today the only major critic of English literature who makes a principle of telling us which authors he thinks we shall *enjoy*: this may not sound much, but most dons have moved a long way from any recognition that literature is something that people used to read for fun. Mr. Lewis, now as always, writes as if inviting us to a feast: not in the take-it-or-leave-it Saintsbury way, but always giving his reasons, and frequently warning us to stay away from this or that boring writer who is only included because the *Oxford History* can't leave him out. He quotes, for instance, a few good things from one William Warner, and adds, 'But no one should be deceived by these quotations into reading Warner.' This is sense; pleasure is a major motive in reading anything, and if the fact is tactfully suppressed by most academics, that is because they don't enjoy their work and ought really to say so. This is all I have to say about the literary qualities of the book, but I assure you that the whole review could easily be given over to praising its wit, its pure and strong prose (what they used to call 'nervous'), and the general high spirits of the performance. Mr. Lewis is the virtuoso of literary history; he is like a violinist who makes up his own cadenzas.

I must now turn to the elements in the book that make it controversial. These, as everyone will know, are in the parts which treat of the concept of the 'Renaissance.' Mr. Lewis is, broadly speaking, 'against' the Renaissance, in the sense that he thinks its importance as a factor in causing things has been exaggerated. What he is attacking is the view, common for the last three centuries, that the Renaissance was a great 'liberation' to which we Owe Everything. Mr. Lewis claims that this estimate of the Renaissance achievement is simply their own valuation of themselves, which we have not yet got rid of, and that in fact the period witnessed (whether or not it 'caused') as many deaths as it did births. Certainly the Renaissance, on its literary side, stands for the acceleration of classical studies, the rejection of the Middle Ages, the discrediting of scholastic philosophy; and Mr. Lewis, however he looks at these things, cannot see that they did any good to the English literary mind. (p. 403)

On the side of the book that can more precisely be described as literary criticism, I hardly know where to start: *inopem me copia fecit*. Perhaps the most balanced and just section is that on Elizabethan satire (a good corrective to Allen Tate's essay), the most original—suggesting a new attitude—that on Shakespeare's sonnets, and the most provocative, that on Spenser. I select the last. Mr. Lewis, living through the period which has seen Spenser take his first real toss, has always been very keen on helping him up again; sometimes this has involved him in being less than fair to the very real objections that can be made. In this book he does not launch any broadsides, probably not having space for them, but gives the *Faerie Queene* the best possible hand-up by explaining its essential structure and showing us what to look for. These pages sent me back to the poem, and certainly it is by no means bad, but I felt Mr. Lewis was going a little far in claiming that Spenser is bound to be popular with anyone who has any feeling for the English tradition. 'Among those who shared, or still share, the culture for which he wrote, and which he helped to create,

there is no dispute about his greatness.' But now 'His world has ended and his fame may end with it.' So if you don't like him you must be one of the modern barbarians. But come now, there must always have been readers who found the dreadful silliness and perfunctoriness of parts of the *Faerie Queene* a barrier to their enjoyment. (p. 404)

But . . . I for one feel quite positive that [Mr. Lewis's] book will be read, and will deserve to be read, by a lot of people for a long time. (p. 405)

John Wain, "Pleasure, Controversy, Scholarship,"
in The Spectator *(© 1954 by* The Spectator; *reprinted*
by permission of The Spectator*), Vol. 193, No. 6588,*
October 1, 1954, pp. 403-05.

KATHRYN ANN LINDSKOOG

[C. S. Lewis's] Narnian series hinges upon the acceptance of supernatural phenomena. . . . (p. 33)

There are, of course, skeptics in these books. In *The Lion, the Witch and the Wardrobe* the children did not accept Lucy's tale about discovering Narnia when they first heard it. They consulted the wise old professor about her strange story. They complained that when they looked in the wardrobe there was nothing there, asserting that if things are real they're there all the time. "Are they?" the Professor said. The time element also bothered the children. During less than one minute, Lucy claimed to have spent several hours in Narnia. "That is the very thing that makes her story so likely to be true," said the Professor. He explained that if there really was a door in his house that led to some other world, it would be very likely that the other world had a separate time of its own so that however long one stayed there it would never take up any time on earth. (pp. 33-4)

When the children had had actual experiences with the supernatural, the concept of other worlds was much easier to accept. Once they had been out of their own world, they could conceive of many others with comparative facility. The idea came to Digory in *The Magician's Nephew:* "Why, if we can get back to our own world by jumping into *this* pool, mightn't we get somewhere else by jumping into one of the others? Supposing there was a world at the bottom of every pool!" (p. 34)

The philosophy underlying this structure of multiple natures is clearly explained in a speculative passage in *Miracles.* . . . Lewis begins with the supernaturalist's belief that a Primary Thing exists independently and has produced our composition of space, time, and connected events which we call nature. There might be other natures so created which we don't know about. Lewis is not referring here to other solar systems or galaxies existing far away in our own system of space and time, because those would be a part of our nature in spite of their distance. Only if other natures were not spatiotemporal at all, or if their space and time had no relation to our own, could we call them different natures. This is important in Lewis's literary theory:

> No merely physical strangeness or merely spatial distance will realize that idea of otherness which is what we are always trying to grasp in a story about voyaging through space: you must go into another dimension. To construct plausible and moving 'other worlds' you must draw on the only real 'other world' we know, that of the spirit.

The only relationship to our system would be through common derivation from a single supernatural force. Here Lewis resorts to the figure of authorship discussed by Dorothy Sayers in *The Mind of the Maker*. The only relationship between events in one novel and events in another is the fact that they were written by the same author, which causes a continuity in his mind only.

There could be no connection between the events in one nature and the events in another, by virtue of the character of the two systems. But perhaps God would choose to bring the two natures into partial contact at some point. This would not turn the two natures into one, because they would still lack the total reciprocity of one nature, and this spasmodic interlocking would arise, not from within them, but from a divine act. Thus, each of the two natures would be "supernatural" to the other. But in an even more absolute sense, their contact itself would be supernatural, because it would be not only outside of a particular nature but beyond any and every nature.

When this philosophical speculation is geared to a childhood level of interests, delightful possibilities for story situations appear. One of these, [introduced by the prince of Narnia to a young English guest aboard the "Dawn Treader," is] the concept of our world being known elsewhere as a myth. . . . (pp. 34-6)

Just as our world bears aspects of a fairy-tale world from the Narnian point of view, so the Narnian world is rich with figures of earthly folklore. . . .

In Narnia, giants, centaurs, dryads, fauns, dwarfs, sea serpents, mermaids, dragons, monopods, and pirates live in an environment of castles, caves, magic whistles, golden chessmen, and enchanted gardens. The implication is that all elements of myth as we know them are shadows of a foreign reality. (p. 37)

C. S. Lewis is known for opposing the spirit of modern thought with the unpopular Christian doctrines of sin and evil. He considers evil not as a nebulous abstraction but as a destructive immanence which should be openly recognized and not complacently ignored, even though such recognition is disquieting. This principle is the major element in Lewis's otherwise happy concept of nature. In his own words, "We find ourselves in a world of transporting pleasures, ravishing beauties, and tantalising possibilities, but all constantly being destroyed, all coming to nothing. Nature has all the air of a good thing spoiled." In *The Magician's Nephew* original sin enters Narnia: ". . . before the new, clean world I gave you is seven hours old, a force of evil has already entered it; waked and brought hither by this son of Adam." . . .

Throughout the rest of the series, this element of evil manifests itself in Narnia in various forms, always subjugating and trying to destroy the goodness in nature. (p. 38)

In *The Silver Chair* [a] witch has assumed power . . . by suppression of the glad natural order of the world beneath the surface of the earth, reminiscent of Wagner's Nibelheim. There she enchanted merry dwarfs from the deep land of Bism and brought them up near the surface of the earth to Shallowlands to work for her in a state of glum amnesia. She is planning a great invasion of Narnia. The idea of invasions and battles is basic to those books.

"Enemy-occupied territory—that is what this world is," Lewis plainly states in *Mere Christianity*. Yet he consciously avoids slipping into dualism, which he defines as "the belief that there are two equal and independent powers at the back of everything, one of them good and the other bad, and that this universe is the battlefield in which they fight out an endless War.". . . (pp. 39-40)

Lewis makes it clear in *The Lion, the Witch and the Wardrobe* that the power of evil is inferior to the power of good. The power of good is that of the great King. . . . (pp. 40-1)

The limitations of evil are discussed in *Mere Christianity,* where Lewis states, as he does in *The Screwtape Letters,* that wickedness is the pursuit of something good in the wrong way. One can be good for the sake of goodness even when it hurts, but one cannot be bad for the sake of badness. One is cruel for the pleasure or usefulness of it, not for the sake of cruelty itself. Badness cannot be bad in the way that goodness is good, for badness is only spoiled goodness. . . . (p. 42)

Spoiled goodness is illustrated in the beginning of sin in Narnia, as related in *The Magician's Nephew.* Digory had been sent to a distant garden to fetch a silver apple. On the gate was written this verse:

> Come in by the gold gates or not at all,
> Take of my fruit for others or forbear.
> For those who steal or those who climb my wall
> Shall find their heart's desire and find despair. . . .
>   (pp. 42-3)

Digory was just turning to go back to the gates when he stopped for one last look and received a terrible shock. There stood the Witch, throwing away the core of an apple which she had eaten. The juice had made a horrid dark stain around her mouth. Digory guessed that she must have climbed in over the wall. He began to see the truth in the last line of the verse, because "the Witch looked stronger and prouder than ever . . . but her face was deadly white, white as salt.". . .

The King explained the result of this act to the children later. The Witch had fled from the garden to the North of the World, where she was growing stronger in dark Magic. She would not dare to return to Narnia so long as the tree was flourishing there, because its fragrance had become a horror to her. "That is what happens to those who pluck and eat fruits at the wrong time and in the wrong way," the King concluded. "The fruit is good, but they loathe it ever after.". . . (p. 43)

The preponderance of dark magic and witches in Lewis's books gives the impression that he is greatly concerned with demonology. However, the overall tone of his work echoes the glad assurance of St. Paul, "For I am sure that neither death, nor life, nor angels, nor principalities, nor things present, nor things to come, nor powers, nor height, nor depth, nor anything else in all creation will be able to separate us from the love of God in Christ Jesus our Lord" (Romans 8:38).

In contrast to the everlasting quality of God's love, which is his principal message, Lewis reminds us that the physical world is in a process of disintegration. He seems to agree with the concept of Sir James Jeans, that "If the inanimate universe moves in the direction we suppose, biological evolution moves like a sailor who runs up the rigging in a sinking ship."

In Lewis's opinion, the modern conception of progress, as popularly imagined, is simply a delusion, supported by no evidence. Darwinism gives no support to the belief that natural selection, working upon chance variations, has a general tendency to produce improvement. Lewis asserts that there is no general law of progress in biological history. He calls the idea of the world slowly ripening to perfection a myth, not a generalization from experience. He feels that this myth distracts us from our real duties and our real interests.

This attitude is illustrated by the depressing picture of [the dying world of Charn] given in *The Magician's Nephew*. . . . (pp. 43-5)

In *The Last Battle* Jill declares, "*Our* world is going to have an end some day. Perhaps this one won't . . . wouldn't it be lovely if Narnia just went on and on . . .?"

"Nay," she was answered, "all worlds draw to an end; except Aslan's own country." (p. 46)

The destruction of Narnia began with the invasion of commerce and the plunder of nature by greedy men. The idyllic forest was ruthlessly destroyed in a sacrilegious turmoil by crowds of imported workers, before the rightful owners realized what was happening. This is an exact parallel to the development of the near-fatal dangers in Lewis's adult book about Britain, *That Hideous Strength*.

The actual end of Narnia was a dramatic pageant of mythical splendour. It concluded with the moon being sucked into the sun, and the world freezing forever in total darkness. Here Lewis follows the tradition of the North rather than the conventional Christian concept of destruction by fire. Peter, High King of Narnia, was given the key to the door of heaven, and locked out the cold.

Lewis's response to nature, then, is threefold. First is romantic appreciation and idealization. Second is analysis leading to an acceptance of the supernatural and to speculation about it. Third is moral awareness of the force of evil in nature and of the temporal quality of our world. Each of these responses is basic to Lewis's Christian philosophy and is an important influence upon his books for children. Nature is more than a background setting for the action of his characters. "Either there is significance in the whole process of things as well as in human activity, or there is no significance in human activity itself." (pp. 46-7)

> *Kathryn Ann Lindskoog, in her* The Lion of Judah in Never-Never Land: The Theology of C. S. Lewis Expressed in His Fantasies for Children *(originally a thesis presented at Long Beach Teachers College in 1957; copyright © 1973 by William B. Eerdmans Publishing Co.; all rights reserved), Eerdmans, 1974, 141 p.*

FRANK KERMODE

[*While serving as a professor at Cambridge, Lewis wrote* An Experiment in Criticism *in response to the increasingly popular critical theories of his fellow Cambridge don, F. R. Leavis. Lewis believed that Leavis wrongly placed critical emphasis on the subjective extraction of meaning from literary texts, rather than on simply receiving and evaluating them according to the authors' own purposes. Kermode, himself a distinguished critic, saw much to Lewis's approach.*]

Modern criticism, perhaps because it is multitudinous and arcane, is often thought, by modern critics especially, to be very valuable. Now Professor Lewis does not think so; he has an air of strenuous disinterest, but one comes to see that the *cause* of his book [*An Experiment in Criticism*] is disquiet at the possible fate of literature when it falls into the wrong hands. Not until the end does he, with much art, reveal that he has had in his sights a particular school of critics, and even then—

shrinking a little, it may be, from their 'insular ferocity'—he refrains from naming them.

The main argument is that one can best sort out books by sorting out readers. Broadly, there are the Many who use, and the Few who receive, works of art. This is not to say that the Many are vulgar or immoral or immature compared with the Few, but only that they want very little from art: pictures *of* something, music with tunes, books with stories. In so far as the work of art offers more than this very little it becomes less useful to them. The Few also need this element, but much more besides. Unfortunately their ranks are swollen with impostors—academic careerists, culture-men, improvers of themselves or of others. But when you get down to the genuine Few you find they have complex needs and abilities of a kind that distinguish them very sharply, as readers, from the Many. . . . [With] this basic distinction between two kinds of reader as a tool, one can proceed to divide good books from bad: what satisfies *only* the Many is bad, what satisfies the Few, or even some of the Few, is good. Thus you might condemn the Tarzan books, but not Milton, or anyway not until you have shown that his admirers all read him in the manner of the Many. 'The ideally bad book is the one of which a good reading is impossible'—of course you must try to give it a good reading before you can say this. On the other hand, a good book 'permits and invites' good reading.

This summary does little justice to a vigorous and schematic essay, which is diversified by subsidiary treatments of other topics germane but not central, and given exceptional authority by Professor Lewis's vast and ordered reading. Perhaps he underestimates the number of ways in which a genuine member of the Few might be induced to err, especially in the direction of eulogy. But by and large his distinctions are well made and acceptable, I should have thought, to most. In considering what follows from them, he comes to what I have called the cause of the book.

For it seems to follow that we must question 'the utility of strictly evaluative criticism, and especially of its condemnations'. And indeed, says Professor Lewis, it is the least of all the kinds of criticism. Perhaps he makes this point a little too sharply, or perhaps he has no need of that illumination of the familiar which is sometimes a product of this kind. But his purpose is the admirable one of courteously assaulting what he calls 'the Vigilant school of critics', those honest witch-hunting hygienists whose 'conception of what is good in literature makes a seamless whole with their total conception of the good life' and who 'admit no such realm of experience as the aesthetic'. Their suspicious attitude to all books save those which appear in a small approved list precludes all possibility of their making the necessary 'surrender', and they may do great harm to the practice of good reading.

This is urbanely said; there is no specific mention of that dreadful Vigilant arrogance which corrupts pleasure and judgment, and which is now available in paperback. Professor Lewis thinks a literary work is impossible of access, let alone of evaluation, to him who cannot in the first place receive it with love. So received it is an 'enlargement of being'; like love, it 'heals the wound, without undermining the privilege, of individuality'. He does not add this: only after such an experience can great criticism be written; which is why it is so rare. (pp. 658-59)

> *Frank Kermode, "Against Vigilants," in* New Statesman *(© 1961 The Statesman & Nation Pub-*

lishing Co. Ltd.), Vol. LXII, No. 1599, November 3, 1961, pp. 658-59.

CHAD WALSH

It is not hard to enumerate the assets that Lewis brought with him when he set out to be a writer. First of all, intelligence. His mind, sharpened by lifelong training, was formidable in its power and precision. One can disagree with him to the point of fury, but not condescend. Coupled with the superb mind was solid erudition. He was master of classical, medieval, and Renaissance literature, so much at home in it that he could make use of its symbols and themes with unconscious ease and grace. Greek and Roman mythology and the legends of the Celts and Germanic peoples were as much a part of his literary frame of reference as the Bible. His books grew out of the collective memory of Western mankind.

Lewis brought to traditional mythology as much as he took from it. His vivid imagination could transport his mind to the floating islands of a distant planet, and from there he would evolve the story of Paradise Retained. This absolute clarity of visual imagination is one of the main appeals of his more fantastic books. Anyone reading, say, *The Lion, the Witch and the Wardrobe* is given so distinct a picture of Aslan's death that he could reproduce the scene on canvas with photographic detail.

Lewis's intelligence and his imagination, taken together, are more than equal to the sum of the parts. In his fantasies one always senses barely beneath the surface a powerful mind controlling the movement of events. In the expository and argumentative books, when the tools of logic are at full strength, there are sudden epiphanies of ''Joy,'' so that the rules of reason are sweetened by fragrances from a different land.

Lewis brought another asset to his writing. Conviction. . . . The content of Lewis's conviction—traditional Christianity—may seem to many readers a misplaced loyalty, but when it is encountered as transmitted through his mind, it cannot be dismissed as superficial. And in ways his readers may not consciously recognize, it gives strength to all that he wrote.

No matter what great use he makes of pagan mythology, Lewis's central symbol system is biblical. The pagan gods must fit themselves into Jehovah's universe. It is easy to observe how, about the time he wrote *The Pilgrim's Regress,* he had come to view all experiences through the eyes of the Christian faith and to express them through its symbols. The advantage of a traditional symbol is that it is always rooted in the eternal archetypes. Lewis's older contemporary, William Butler Yeats, regretfully found he could not believe in Christian doctrine, and as a substitute devised his own mythology and metaphysics, writing his book *A Vision* to explain it. His system worked well for his own creative imagination, giving him ''metaphors for poetry,'' but most readers find something contrived about it. It does not resonate in the same way that Lewis's symbols do. From a purely literary point of view, the most fortunate thing that ever happened to Lewis was his embrace of Christianity in his early thirties.

Finally, to conclude this inventory of assets, there is Lewis's style. It can be seen evolving from two sources in his boyhood writing. There is first of all the ''Boxen'' style—brisk and businesslike, not poetic, but capable of irony and wit. The other source is represented by ''Bleheris,'' with its euphuistic delight in fancy language and flowery turns of phrase. From the marriage of the two styles came [his] remarkable flexible and gracious style. . . . It is straight to the point, lean, free of inflated language and the technical jargon of the professions. At the same time, thanks particularly to the use of exact metaphors, it is capable of modulating into highly poetic effects—more poetic, in fact, than most of Lewis's verse. It is a modest style, summoning the reader to go beyond the exact words and to retain in his memory not the words but what they point to. (pp. 243-45)

Lewis's career as a published author began with two books of poetry, *Spirits in Bondage* and *Dymer.* He subsequently relegated verse to a corner of his life, making no serious attempt to bring out further books of poetry. Only after his death were two additional collections published.

His short poems frequently attempt to do in verse what he learned to accomplish equally well in prose. More problematical are the long narrative poems. *Dymer* is hopelessly confused and confusing, though with sections of brilliant writing. When it is compared with *The Queen of Drum,* the progress Lewis had made in a few years is startling. He was very close to becoming the modern Chaucer, though less tolerant of the foibles of daily existence. He backed away—perhaps as much because of public indifference as anything else.

One postscript on his poetry. It is strongly visual, turned outward, objective, far removed from the confessional tradition as represented, say, by Robert Lowell and Sylvia Plath. Such objectivity, though Homer would have understood it, is rare in modern poetry and not greatly in demand. All Lewis's qualities, handicaps today, could become assets if some vast psychic shift, a movement from subjectivity to objectivity, realigned the landscape of poetry. Lewis's verse, including the short poems, might suddenly speak with a much stronger voice. But no signs of such a psychic mutation are visible.

I come now to his achievements as a literary scholar. (pp. 245-46)

Lewis was as much out of step in his criticism as in his poetry. At times, it is true, he talks like a New Critic, emphasizing the need to concentrate on the text itself and not become bogged down in biographical and historical details. But he seldom undertakes minute *explications de texte.* He also shows little interest in other modern critical approaches, such as the psychological or the archetypal. He is that type of scholar least in fashion—the appreciative critic, whose great gift is to whet a reader's appetite for a particular book and to give him just enough practical guidance so he can find his way through it.

Few major reputations are based solely on criticism and literary history. Stubbornly and perhaps rightly, readers think of writing about writing as a secondary thing. There is nothing secondary about the next category of Lewis's books—those dealing directly with religion, metaphysics, and ethics. The continuing popularity of these works, particularly *Mere Christianity,* is emphatic evidence that they speak to listening ears.

Perhaps part of the secret has been explored by Lewis in his doctrine of ''great nouns'' as contrasted with the ''adjectival'' role of mere literature (''Christianity and Literature,'' in *Rehabilitations*). The overpowering effect of a book like *Mere Christianity* reflects the way it transcends itself and its author. The uncanny literary skill moves the reader's thoughts beyond the gleaming metaphors and directs them to concepts and hopes that leave language behind. It is as though all the brilliant writing is designed to create clear windows of perception, so that the reader will look *through* the language and not *at* it. It is a kind of kenosis. Lewis withdraws himself so that he will not distract the reader from that which is visible through the clear panes of the writing. Any literary critic determined to concentrate on purely literary considerations constantly finds himself analyzing and debating Lewis's *ideas* and has to struggle against recalcitrant forces if he wants to keep his analysis on purely literary tracks.

Another source of power is Lewis's ability to use Aristotle's tools to maximum effect. Here a hypothetical shadow hangs over these books. Only the future will tell whether this kind of logic will continue to seem as much a part of the structure of the universe as it has long appeared to Western man. (pp. 246-48)

The solid core of Lewis's achievement, however, consists of those more imaginative and mythological books in which his ability as a writer and his sensibility as a Christian are fruitfully wedded. These books are the space trilogy and Narnia, together with *The Pilgrim's Regress, The Screwtape Letters,* and *The Great Divorce. (Till We Have Faces* is a special case, to be discussed later.) In these books he puts to work every talent he possesses and raises to a high literary level the serious fantasy. The schism between logic and romance is healed, and myth, fact, and truth are revealed as mere interim categories.

Lewis is not the first writer to attempt serious fantasy, but he is one of the most powerful, haunting, and successful. Endowed with a tremendously effective visual imagination, he creates other worlds, including that supernatural realm where Maleldil reigns supreme, to set in juxtaposition with our familiar Tellus. He makes of this genre a means of dramatizing the human condition and posing the everlasting questions. He converts fantasy into a presentation of philosophic and theological insights. (p. 248)

What does he do for us in his fantasies? He creates new worlds, and in creating them he sets Tellus in sharper relief. We see it almost for the first time as we compare it with Narnia, Mars, or Venus. *Mere Christianity* may become less compelling if the canons of logic change, but this would not cancel out the imaginative reality of Lewis's worlds. Time cannot destroy them. We now know that Venus has a temperature of 900° Fahrenheit, and that Mars is a nightmare of desert and monstrous volcanoes. No matter. Any reader of Lewis, by the magic of his vision, explores not the spheres of the astronomers, but the planets of the restless spirit. Meanwhile, he comes to understand his own provincial planet more precisely because it is not the only theater of Maleldil's cosmic drama. Lewis's particular way of relating imaginary worlds to our empirical world—through theology and mythology as well as actual voyages back and forth—is distinctive and gives him a central claim to being master of this literary form.

In *The Pilgrim's Regress* we explore a parallel world of the spirit which illuminates the familiar world that cameras can photograph. In *The Great Divorce* the gray town, familiar here and now to us earthlings, is seen in contrast to the borderlands of heaven. In *The Screwtape Letters* we behold our world through demonic eyes and understand better each passing moment.

At any rate, these three books plus the trilogy and Narnia constitute the most distinctive achievements of Lewis's visionary mind. They shape the reader's consciousness to entertain thoughts of a dynamic cosmos in which supernatural dramas are acted out. These books take their places as a subdivision of the great mythologies that have supplied meaning to so many

civilizations. Lewis is a myth adapter and a myth maker, expressing his mythology through the pageants enacted first in the theater of his own imagination and then on the stage of the reader's mind.

I have so far said nothing about *Till We Have Faces.* Its differences from the fantasies are much more striking than the similarities. True, mythology plays a key role, but not the same role. The Venus symbolized by blood-stained Ungit is more like a psychological or spiritual force surging inside the individual than the gloriously objective Venus of *Perelandra* and *That Hideous Strength.* In *Till We Have Faces,* Lewis turns to traditional mythology as a way of saying something about those depths of heart and soul that he had previously left alone. This book is not a fantasy. It is a realistic novel. It is closer in insight to Dostoevsky than to the ancient myth of Cupid and Psyche from which the narrative springs. If Lewis had lived longer, he might have explored these depths further. It is another "might have been."

As it is, the fantasies must be the centerpiece of his achievement. It is easy to point out their occasional defects and limitations. There is sometimes the playing for cheap effects as in the dunking of Weston, and some details of the N.I.C.E.'s downfall. Certain of the characters are close to straw men. The narrative is often interrupted by editorializing and sermonizing. But how petty this list seems. The clarity and majesty of Lewis's vision, and the literary skill with which he expressed it, engulf the minor defects.

Lewis fits so oddly in our accustomed literary categories that it will be a long time before we can see him in proper perspective. But as we meanwhile read him, our spontaneous responses tell us much. In a world where the sacred groves are being felled to make way for airports, he conjures into existence other worlds corresponding to the intuitions of mankind's mythological dreams. Choosing not to seek originality, he produces some of the most original books of the century. In him is combined the sophistication of an Oxford don and the primal intuitions of a shaman. The roots of his vision lie in the unconscious mind where we are still one with the caveman painting sacred pictures on the wall. Thus Lewis, far from being an escapist, is a writer who renews our contact with the ever-present but often ignored sources of our psychic life. His visionary books are destined to survive, as much in our collective memories as in the footnotes we dutifully add. (pp. 249-51)

Chad Walsh, in his The Literary Legacy of C. S. Lewis *(copyright © 1979 by Chad Walsh; reprinted by permission of Harcourt Brace Jovanovich, Inc.), Harcourt Brace Jovanovich, 1979, 269 p.*

NEIL RIBE

Lewis talks about male and female so often that it is hard to know where to begin, or indeed what to leave out [of an essay on his view of the subject]. . . . Why does this theme appear so often, and in so many different guises—as poetry, essay, fiction and myth? For Lewis, the reason is simple. Masculine and feminine are not merely curious facts about biological existence; they reflect the very structure of the universe. To understand the enigma of masculine and feminine is to have approached the mystery at the heart of creation where symbol and reality are one. . . .

In the preface to *That Hideous Strength*—which he calls a "modern fairy tale for grownups"—Lewis notes that his story follows the method of the traditional fairy tale. All fairy tales begin, he says, not with the proverbial witches and ogres, but with "humdrum scenes and persons". In the same way, Lewis begins his profound meditation on masculine and feminine by asking us first to look closely at what we already know—real men and women. . . .

To many readers, it will seem [at the outset of the novel] that Lewis has presented [in Jane Studdock] a rather biased portrait of a woman who has neither the ability nor the enthusiasm for a career, but stubbornly refuses to devote herself to her duties as wife and mother. But before we pass judgment, let us remember Jane's husband. Mark is a young Fellow in Sociology at Bracton College who is on his way up: he has been admitted to the "Progressive Element" of the College and offered a post with the prestigious National Institute for Coordinated Experiments, or N.I.C.E. Mark sincerely believes in the goals of these groups: to combat "reactionism" and "blind traditionalism" in any form, and to eliminate social backwardness and unrest through scientific reconditioning. Mark's success, however, is due less to intellectual ability than to his eagerness to please and willingness to put politics before principles. He finds irresistably attractive the knowing conversations, the insolent exercise of power, the "fine, male energy" of the society in which he has recently begun to move. He conquers his instinctive distaste for his new colleagues with the thought that now—at last—he is really on to something big.

Neither Jane nor Mark expects what happens to them next. Jane is scared out of her wits by vivid dreams which come true, and discovers that she has the gift of prophetic vision. Mark loses his Fellowship at Bracton College almost without knowing it, and is dragged ever deeper into the dark world of the N.I.C.E. at Belbury. Husband and wife are set on opposite sides in a battle to decide the fate of man.

Many readers, having gotten this far, may find themselves both fascinated and repelled by Lewis's views on the nature of man and woman, uncongenial as they are to the modern temperament. No doubt Lewis would have taken this as a compliment. We would do well to examine more carefully what he has to say by taking a closer look at the Studdocks.

Jane and Mark could hardly be more different. Although Jane has hopes for a career as a scholar, her real nature is intuitive and emotional. She sees through Mark's new friends immediately—one look at Feverstone's face tells all she needs to know. More important, however, she has dreams which really do come true, and this frightens her very much. She resents these dreams as a threat to her freedom, as interference with her internal affairs. Her anger is only increased by her tendency to break into tears at difficult moments, to behave like the "little woman" in need of male protection whom she so detests. What Jane fears most is dependence and entanglement—hence her resentment not only against her dreams, but against Mark and even love itself. She feels, rightly, that her sensitivity meets only callous disregard from her husband. But as we turn to Mark, we see that his wife's feelings are not the only things he disregards. He has pretensions of being an intellectual, of a modern sort which Lewis describes as follows:

> His education had been neither scientific nor classical—merely 'modern'. The severities both of abstraction and of high human tradition had passed him by: and he had neither peasant shrewdness nor aristocratic honour to help him. He was a man of straw, a glib examinee in subjects that require no exact knowledge.

Mark lives in a bloodless world of his own making, in which words like "vocational groups" and "classes" have more substance than real men and women. (pp. 2-3)

Mark and Jane are not wicked, of course, but merely young and immature. Their problem, in Lewis's eyes, seems to be that they have denied their true natures as male and female. Lewis's view here is decidedly traditional and unmodern. The proper sphere of man's activity is, for Lewis, intellectual and political; his is the realm of abstract thought and the exercise of power. Such a life tends to face not inward towards the self and its intimate relationships, but outward towards abstract concepts and the world of human affairs. From this orientation arise some of the cardinal sins which beset the male sex: the tendency to substitute abstract concepts for the reality which grounds them; to treat men and women as objects to be manipulated for personal or political gain; and to forget that compromise, while a necessity in political affairs, does not apply to moral principles. For Lewis, it would seem, a man's exercise of his true function carries with it the possibility, even the likelihood, that it will be abused. (p. 3)

Jane . . . understands human character and motivation intuitively—she could never live in a world of abstractions as her husband does. Nonetheless, Lewis seems to suggest that she, too, is denying her true nature. A major part of woman's role is, for Lewis, the nurturing of children and the preservation of the values of the home against the often amoral world outside. A woman's nature is thus directed inward, not outward towards the world. Jane resents this traditional notion and seeks to escape it by pursuing her career and putting off childbearing. She fails to see that her true strengths are intuitive and emotional, not rational or political. Jane's failure to accept her own nature is shown not only in her angry reaction to her dreams, but even in the disdainful attitude she assumes towards her housekeeper, Ivy Maggs. Lewis seems to identify this kind of haughtiness as a peculiarly feminine temptation. (pp. 3-4)

Gradually the picture widens. First we meet the Dimbles, Dr. and Mrs. Dr. Dimble has been Jane's tutor in college, while his wife serves as a kind of "unofficial aunt". From what Lewis tells us, we can gather what his opinion of the Dimbles is: they are Mark and Jane as they ought to be. Dr. Dimble is a scholar of Celtic languages, sober and forthright in speech; an intellectual who is nonetheless a man of introspection and moral courage. His thought—even when it flies over everyone's heads, like his discourse on Merlin—remains always concerned with human reality. His wife, whom everyone calls "Mother Dimble", is the very personification of what we would call "woman's intuition". She understands Jane's feelings and problems immediately, and Jane often finds herself taking comfort in Mrs. Dimble's ample arms. . . . To the reader, though, the best thing about the Dimbles is their good humor. They are not the kind of people one laughs *at*, of course, but *with*—and what a delightful change after Mark and Jane, who take themselves too seriously. (p. 4)

That Lewis means us to note the contrast between the Dimbles and the Studdocks is clear from the scenes where we see them together. At the Dimbles' house, Jane immediately suspects that Mrs. Dimble's motherly concern has an ulterior motive: "She's dying to know whether I'm going to have a baby. That sort of woman always is." Later, when Mark storms into Dr. Dimble's office, the contrast between his irrational blustering and Dimble's moral self-awareness is painfully clear.

Lewis proceeds to introduce other pairs of characters, and each sharpens his portrait of male and female by allowing us to recognize the true nature by the presence of its opposite. First we accompany Jane on a mysterious journey to visit an even more mysterious person, Grace Ironwood. Miss Ironwood, dressed all in black, is austere and inscrutable as she records Jane's dreams. She is unmarried, and we find out later that she is a doctor—surely proof that Lewis respected women's ability. Miss Ironwood is a puzzling figure, but her opposite number in the story is all too clear. I refer, of course, to Fairy Hardcastle, the head of the secret police of the N.I.C.E. Her similarities to Miss Ironwood only serve to make their differences more apparent. Like the latter, Miss Hardcastle too is dressed in black—black leather—that is. Like Miss Ironwood, Fairy Hardcastle also "interviews" Jane—but with the aid of a smoldering cigar. . . . In Fairy Hardcastle, Lewis has portrayed the very inversion of womanhood, whose brutal masculinity has distorted her nature beyond recognition.

Not long afterwards, Jane meets the Dennistons. They are about her age, and Arthur is a former friend of Mark's. . . . But Jane notices strange things about them. The Dennistons say they "belong" to a Mr. Fisher-King, the Director of a small company with some kind of odd spiritual mission. (pp. 4-5)

And so we come to the last pair of characters we must consider: Ransom, the Director of the company of St. Anne's, and Wither, the Deputy Director of the N.I.C.E. We had best look at Wither first. . . . For Lewis, as we have seen, the exercise of rationality and abstract thought is a true fulfillment of man's nature—but only if held in check by constant commerce with human reality. Wither has abstracted himself out of all human sentiment, indeed human existence. To say that Wither's personality is like the smile of the Cheshire cat conveys everything but the horror of it.

Lewis describes the progress of Wither's "unsentimental education" thus: "He had passed from Hegel into Hume, thence through Pragmatism, and thence through Logical Positivism, and out at last into the complete void." Let no one imagine that Lewis is talking about something which happens only to evil men; Wither himself in his youth was probably much like Mark is now. Rather, Lewis seems to say, it is only a man who can be capable of this kind of evil. The officials at Belbury—Frost, Straik, Filostrato, Feverstone—have exchanged their humanity for the "complete void" of abstraction. It is no accident that all these officials are male—such a radical denaturing of the self is, for Lewis, almost unthinkable in a woman.

Finally, however, Jane meets the Director himself: "For the first time all those years she tasted the word *King* itself with all linked associations of battle, marriage, priesthood, mercy, and power." Jane's world is unmade in an instant.

The conversation that follows is one of the high points of the book. Jane, who so easily sees through the outer shell of human pretension, now finds her inmost self laid bare to a man unlike anyone she has met before. . . . She confesses that she no longer loves her husband. . . . For Jane, marriage is an association grounded in freedom and maintained by sentiment. For the Director, however—and for Lewis—marriage is a continual reenactment of the hierarchy at the heart of creation. But we should never think of the hierarchy of obedience and rule as a joyless affair, as Lewis shows by means of a rather droll example. As the Director blows a note on a silver whistle, three plump mice sally forth to gather up the crumbs he has left for them on the carpet. "'You see,' says the Director, 'obedience and rule are more like a dance than a drill—specially

between man and woman where the roles are always changing.'" (pp. 5-6)

Later, when she moves into the manor at St. Anne's, Jane sees the "dance of obedience and rule" lived out in the daily existence of the company. The name of the manor is most appropriate: St. Anne is the patron saint of housekeepers. Jane is surprised to find her old housekeeper, Ivy Maggs, treated as a spiritual equal, but even more that the men and women take turns doing the dishes! Rather than deny the differences between the sexes, the company celebrates them with grace and wit. (p. 6)

Meanwhile, Mark too is undergoing a change of heart. The threat of death, as someone has said, "concentrates the mind wonderfully", and as Mark sits imprisoned in Belbury his life passes before his eyes. Then, with a shock he remembers Jane. . . . Something like love for her wells up in Mark's heart.

All the pieces are now in place; battle is about to be joined. No longer will the struggle be with flesh and blood, but with the powers and principalities: "they have pulled down deep heaven on their heads." In the same way, it is not simply man and woman, but Masculine and Feminine themselves in their awesome reality, which are revealed as the story approaches its climax.

Just before the storm breaks, we see Jane and Mrs. Dimble preparing the cottage for Ivy Maggs and her husband, who is to be released from jail that day. For Mrs. Dimble, the task is "something between a game and a ritual," and Jane feels herself left outside of an archaic world of which Mrs. Dimble is a part. . . . Then, as she muses in the hot sun, she sees the visitor and understands. A strange woman stands before her, dressed in flaming robes, bare-breasted, half-mocking; as Jane watches, she wreaks havoc on the trim little room, and everything she touches bursts forth with luxurious vegetation. For this is the earthly Venus, Fountain of all that grows and desires, Earth-mother herself. . . . The Director explains that Jane had met the Feminine itself, but raw and demoniac; Mother Dimble has that same power, but has transformed and baptized it. And that transformation can take place not by surrender to her husband, nor to the Director, but only to God Himself, the Masculine who is the ground of all. . . . Even as she leaves the Director, though, Jane's old fear of being possessed contends with her new-found understanding of the "world beyond Nature". The Director remained still on the other side of an unfathomable abyss; her dream of finding a man who "really understood" had been let down. Religion, she thought, ought to mean "a realm in which her haunting female fear of being treated as a thing, an object of barter and desire and possession, would be set permanently at rest and what she called her 'true self' would soar upwards and expand in some freer and purer world." But a strange and terrible thought comes into Jane's mind: "Supposing one were a *thing* after all—a thing designed and invented by Someone Else and valued for qualities quite different from what one had decided to regard as one's true self?" But then the great change comes—and none of these thoughts matter any more: "She had come into a world, or into a Person, or into the presence of a Person." And so the real battle of *That Hideous Strength* is won.

In discovering the true meaning of male and female, Jane has found her Lord and Creator. For Lewis, these two discoveries are really one and the same. At last, we can see why male and female was a theme of such overwhelming importance for Lewis: nothing less is at stake than our understanding of the nature of God and of His relationship to His creation. (pp. 6-7)

After Jane's conversion and the finding of Merlin, Belbury's downfall is a foregone conclusion: "And the rain descended, and the floods came, and the winds blew, and beat upon that house; and it fell; and great was the fall of it." Those who would have abolished man are themselves abolished. The *hubris* of Belbury and its project of scientific reconditioning holds for us yet another lesson on the nature of male and female, which Lewis certainly implies but never explicitly states. Lewis was by no means the first to understand that the modern scientific world-picture represents an extreme masculinization of nature and a banishing of the feminine. Throughout history, mankind has always conceived of the processes of living nature—engendering and birth, decay and death—as feminine. It is no accident that in most languages the words for "mother" and for "matter" are etymologically related. Modern science, on the other hand, tends to conceive of nature as dead matter in motion, which can be analyzed and recombined at will.

Even its methods are largely masculine, rather than feminine, in character: science focuses on *parts* rather than *wholes*, looks *at* rather than *along*. Lewis makes the same point in *The Abolition of Man,* where he envisions a new science which "would not do even to minerals and vegetables what modern science threatens to do to man himself". The men of Belbury, by denying nature and the feminine, reap what they have sown and are destroyed. . . .

Lewis's tale ends as it began, with "humdrum scenes and persons". Yet how different they are now! Jane and Mark have been given wisdom beyond the measure of their years—and so, perhaps, have we. They never knew that in discovering themselves as male and female, they would discover as well the awesome reality of God. They learn, as we do, that male and female are but shadows of a glorious strength. (p. 9)

Neil Ribe, "That Glorious Strength: Lewis on Male and Female," in The Bulletin of the New York C. S. Lewis Society *(© 1983 New York C. S. Lewis Society), Vol. 14, No. 1, November, 1982, pp. 1-9.*

Jakov Lind

1927-

(Pseudonym of Heinz Landwirth) Austrian novelist, short story writer, dramatist, and scriptwriter.

Lind is a powerfully expressive writer who is best known for his horrific portraits of human depravity. His is a bleak vision of the world, one in which there is no morality or reason and in which the bizarre is commonplace. As evidence for the truth of this vision, much of Lind's fiction points to and chronicles the Holocaust and the tragic events that occurred in Central Europe during World War II. He sees the mass extermination of the Jews and the horrors of the war as proof that cannibalism is basic to human nature and that humans crave violence and death. In works that are said to go "beyond nihilism," Lind combines realism with black humor and the grotesque to portray the modern individual as one who seeks neither to redeem or be redeemed.

Lind's own wartime experiences as a Jew form the basis of his vision and are recorded throughout his fiction. Born in Vienna, he lost his parents during the Nazi invasion of Austria and at the age of eleven was sent to Holland by a Zionist refugee group to escape persecution. After the Nazis invaded Holland, he obtained false documents and fled to Germany where he successfully masqueraded as a Nazi. After the war, Lind emigrated to Palestine. He returned to Europe in 1950 and wandered there for several years. Since the late 1950s, Lind has lived primarily in England. These travels and experiences weave their way in and out of Lind's work. His viewpoint is that of the alienated outsider, an exile forced by fate to witness a civilization devolving into madness. Fluent in six languages, Lind abandoned German to write in English in the late 1960s. Critics view this as evidence of the ambivalent feelings he has for Germany and for his past.

Lind's most renowned works are the short stories collected in *Eines Seels aus Holz* (1964; *Soul of Wood and Other Stories*) and his first novel, *Landschaft in Beton* (1966; *Landscape in Concrete*). In both of these works, Lind uses the grotesque in a Kafkaesque fashion in combination with realism to demonstrate the barbarism of the Nazis and the events of World War II. Lind's dark vision of the world is fully developed in these books which have cannibalism and perversity as their recurring themes. Critics praise the vivid imaginativeness of *Soul of Wood* and *Landscape in Concrete* and respect their depth of feeling. Lind's later work includes a three volume autobiography and the recent novel, *Travels to the Enu* (1982). The latter, the first of Lind's novels to be written in English, is reminiscent of Jonathon Swift's *Gulliver's Travels*. It satirizes postwar Western civilization.

(See also *CLC*, Vols. 1, 2, 4; *Contemporary Authors*, Vols. 9-12, rev. ed.; and *Contemporary Authors New Revision Series*, Vol. 7.)

FRANK TUOHY

Travels to the Enu, Jakov Lind's first novel to be written in English, is described by his publishers as a "funny and fantastic satire on modern European life", and it is dedicated to "all

seafaring travellers into unknown worlds, above all to our Master, Jonathan Swift." Claims like these encourage the reader to pull up his socks; even to get out his disbelief suspenders, dated and frayed though these may be, from the back of the drawer.

Jakov Lind's command of English is impressive though not impeccable. A native speaker would not have referred to "lapidary wisecracks". Like Vladimir Nabokov and Joseph Conrad, he makes use of the word "pal" (though not "chum")—which must reflect some felt inadequacy in our language. Where the dialogue sounds peculiar ("Cut the shit, you alien devil") he has at least the excuse that it is being spoken by the half-human species he has invented. Of his powers of invention there can be no doubt.

Orlando, the narrator, signs up for a cheap cruise on the SS Katherine Medici, a true *Narrenschiff* whose surly and rebellious crew, gluts of food and periods of famine, mutinies and piracies, make her into an image of economic life as we know it. The ship blows up and our hero thinks, wrongly as it turns out, that he alone has survived to tell the tale.

Once on shore he is surrounded by the Enu, monstrous painted creatures whose heads are crowned with arrangements of hair which turn out to be birds' nests. . . . The sea is tabu to the Enu, and Orlando and the other survivors who turn up are denied the chance to build a boat. Instead they are transported to a city in the interior where Enu civilization is described in detail (mostly scatological, as with Lind's mentor Swift) and compared by implication with our own.

With fables like *Travels to the Enu* there is a conflict between the writer's concerns and those of his readers. The writer is fuelled by his own ideas or obsessions, but his readers are less interested in disentangling an allegory than in finding images which have a strong imaginative authority. . . .

Travels to the Enu suffers from an absence of ground rules. Where reality could be easily established, it is ignored. The Enu were visited by a Portuguese explorer, but he writes incorrect Spanish: they were taught English, including recent slang, by two ''newly-wed socialites'' whose plane crashed there in 1937, and who were friends of D. H. Lawrence and Frieda. And who could walk about with the weight of a flamingo or a vulture on his head? Here, powerful vision collapses into arbitrary fantasy.

Modern European life offers rather too broad a target. Swift's contemporaries regarded themselves as highly civilized: he told them they stank. Orwell's *Animal Farm* was rejected because it went against current orthodoxy. Jakov Lind's imagination is in good order, his fable is intelligent and enjoyable. He has, unlike other younger writers, earned his pessimism. But he may be telling us something we already know.

> *Frank Tuohy, ''Among Feather-Brains,'' in* The Times Literary Supplement *(© Times Newspapers Ltd. (London) 1982; reproduced from* The Times Literary Supplement *by permission), No. 4119, March 12, 1982, p. 289.*

MELVIN MADDOCKS

In 1938, when Jakov Lind was an eleven-year-old schoolboy, the Nazis goose-stepped into his home city of Vienna, sending him fleeing to Holland and a lifetime of Diaspora. Something more than a Jew without a country, Lind became a displaced artist as well, without a sure tradition or even a language. He wrote at first in German; now he uses English. . . . He has variously conducted his literary experiments in short stories (*Soul of Wood*), novels (*Landscape in Concrete*), autobiography (*Counting My Steps*) and even scores of radio plays. Yet few contemporary writers have been so single-minded. During all his wanderings he has clung obsessively to the original question from that day when Vienna became ''one big swastika.'' How does a witness register the madness of his times without going mad himself? . . .

Lind has evolved less an answer to lunacy than a technique for exposing it. In every work he manages to reduce history to a wild nightmare from which one wakes up laughing. In his latest novel, with a nod to Jonathan Swift, grand master of the savage laugh and the surreal voyage, Lind sets sail on one of his most inspired trips.

A certain disgruntled writer, Orlando, and half a dozen other tourists find themselves shipwrecked on the island of the Enu, a very odd little South Pacific island. . . .

[On Enu there] is no place to go, no work to do. Physical labor is a status symbol that an Enu pays to perform. An Enu need not raise a sweat even for food. The natives and their inadvertent guests eat excrement processed to look like conventional food. Ambrosia comes from the sewers. Guano is refined to an elixir of life. . . .

Sex is free, abundant and pointless. Death has no sting. It is the custom for an Enu to go out of sight to die—conveniently underground. From sheer boredom the inhabitants invent their wars, like board games. They do not even care if they win. Winning can be a problem. ''Win a war and you have to make the enemy do your will,'' the Enu Defense Minister complains. ''What will? We have no will. We even lack a will to live. We no longer need it.'' . . .

The one unforgivable sin in any Lind world is logic. Are the Enu a race of mutants—survivors of a nuclear bomb experiment? Or are they the missing link—a throwback to the age of reptiles? Is the island paradise or purgatory? At different times, Lind has it both ways. Consistency, as he sees it, is the hobgoblin of those without other hobgoblins.

The only real drama on the Enu island is leaving it, and even that may not count. Orlando decides to return to London because it really does not matter whether he leaves or not. His companions decide to stay for the same reason. So the Lind anti-hero trudges on—a pilgrim making no progress, a permanent refugee moving from one no man's land to another. Bring on the next clowns! Bring on the next cannibals!

Lind is nothing if not uneven. Weirdness follows weirdness, vision succeeds vision, sometimes worthy of a Hebrew prophet, sometimes no more than a gag-writer's whimsy. But *Travels to the Enu* adds up to far more than a tour de force. It takes true stamina to be so profoundly lost. After all these years on the road, Lind is no more bitter and no less funny than when he started, an impressive feat given the course of history in the meantime. His mind may swarm with hoofed and steaming demons like a phantasmagoric painting by Pieter Bruegel, but he can still grin at the bared fangs of his own beasts. He has not become a beast.

''A writer,'' he says, ''is someone who hates himself and loves the world.'' In Jakov Lind's game, one out of two is not bad.

> *Melvin Maddocks, ''Tourist Trap,'' in* Time *(copyright 1982 Time Inc.; all rights reserved; reprinted by permission from* Time*), Vol. 119, No. 17, April 26, 1982, p. 84.*

JOHN LEONARD

Mr. Lind is playing Jonathan Swift. His original island was Vienna, and his own original speech was German. **''Travels to the Enu''** is the first book he has written in English. After all the jokes—at the expense of the Portuguese, logical positivists, thinking in French, ''human engineering,'' Ionesco and the origin of the species—he is being very serious about language and literature. He is a Swift who, disconcertingly, giggles and then gargles.

Language is garbage; the Enu eat pages. Someone observed: ''We are choking to death on verbs and nouns.'' Someone else reminds himself, ''But I am talking to the wrong ears,'' Algebra is understood to consist of ''incomprehensible numbers and letters no one can decipher.'' Nobody among the Enu can manufacture the paper on which he might write. These refugees are estranged from ''the elementary prose of existence, like eating, drinking, and excreting.'' We are told, ''Stupid thoughts may cost you your life.''

You will want to know what happens in **''Travels to the Enu,''** and I'm not going to tell you. Yes, there is sex, and yes, there are Nazis, and the ship that goes down is called Medici, and the American philosopher will astrologize, and when everybody grows paws we know for sure we are dipping our tongue in myth, but this book is really a romance with language. It is about finding "reasons and imagination" in a vocabulary that seems cannibalistic. It has its doubts about abstraction, and it may even object to culture. It wonders, who is fit to survive? It will marry the typewriter and the night. Every story is a small death; every word is a wound. . . .

[Lind] is a writer—one of the best—who has chosen to speak in a different tongue. It is amazing that he is witty; it is not at all surprising that he is profound. One welcomes him to our island.

> *John Leonard, in a review of "Travels to the Enu,"* in The New York Times (© 1982 by The New York Times Company; reprinted by permission), May 14, 1982, p. C29.

THE NEW YORKER

In imitation of Jonathan Swift (as is acknowledged at the front of ["**Travels to the Enu**"], Jakov Lind shipwrecks his narrator on a remote island, where he is obliged to explain western civilization to the natives and the natives' civilization to his civilized Western reader. He suggests that mankind's prospects are pretty dim. . . . The narrator has a difficult time explaining to the islanders the power of the written word (that a scribble can trigger mass destruction boggles his own mind), while his account of the causes and effects of their chief affliction—boredom—seems unpleasantly familiar. The natives' treatment of the narrator, alternating between brutality and obeisance, and their own social rites (including the worship of birds, which roost in their coiffures, and the manufacture of edibles from excrement), as well as their earthy English, give Mr. Lind ample opportunity for sadistic and scatological digressions. Sometimes his narrator says something original and surprising—his description of a jet plane as a dangerous bird is good—but on the whole this is heavy-handed stuff. (pp. 139-40)

> *A review of "Travels to the Enu,"* in The New Yorker (© 1982 by The New Yorker Magazine, Inc.), Vol. LVIII, No. 13, May 17, 1982, pp. 139-40.

THOMAS W. GERRITY

A curious little fantasy, [*Travels to the Enu*]. Its plot is the merest peg from which hang the author's crowded thoughts on life's futility. The narrator, Orlando, recounts his adventures aboard an absurd, "no frills" cruise ship, S.S. Katherine Medici, out of Southampton bound for Sarawak. Once at sea, the crew of cutrate cutthroats set about robbing and murdering passengers, an amusement halted when this ship of fools suddenly founders. Orlando and several other passengers survive to reach an island inhabited by naked cannibals who strongly resemble "hominid baboons"—the Enu. . . .

The portrayal of the male Enu's easy life and the female's easier virtue affords occasionally clever swipes at just about everything and everybody, including the CIA, the KGB, Opus Dei, abortion, Margaret Thatcher, the Royal Navy, and of course, nuclear armament. With marvelous irony, the author quotes Von Clausewitz' sincere belief in the humaneness of modern warfare. After enduring at the hands of the Enu enough degradation to daunt even the heroine of *L'Histoire d' "O"*, Orlando eventually escapes back to England.

Deep inside each artist . . . lurks the urge to perpetrate satire. A few succeed: e.g., Swift, Orwell, Waugh, and Firbank, whose spirits lightly echo, here and there, in Lind. But where in Lind are the real fun, the bits, the truth, and the humanity of these originals? Lacking in such glories, his effort often seems a ponderous pastiche, a scatalogical cheap shot, and, ultimately, heartless.

> *Thomas W. Gerrity, in a review of "Travels to the Enu,"* in Best Sellers (copyright © 1982 Helen Dwight Reid Educational Foundation), Vol. 42, No. 3, June, 1982, p. 90.

PAUL ZWEIG

"**Travels to the Enu**" is not very long, yet somehow, after its brilliant beginning, it drags. The Enu are marvelously grotesque Swiftian creatures, but after a while the joke wears thin. Orlando's irony and King IT's jerky humor begin to sound like an angry tract. Lind starts out as Swift, and ends up on a soapbox complaining about skyscrapers, nuclear war, racial bigotry, international cartels and the cynical collaboration of the working classes. He calls this rotten state of affairs "the Fourth Reich." But by now the hard satirical edge is gone. This isn't satire anymore, it is bitching on a large scale, and we have heard it before. That is a shame, for there is an angry genius at work in "**Travels to the Enu**," although it doesn't quite manage to control its materials.

> *Paul Zweig, "Modest Proposals,"* in The New York Times Book Review (© 1982 by The New York Times Company; reprinted by permission), June 20, 1982, p. 10.

JAY TOLSON

The plot [of *Travels to the Enu*] like that of *Gulliver's Travels*, is built around a sea journey, a shipwreck, a mysterious island and its even more mysterious inhabitants. Mr. Orlando, a London writer, unappreciated and therefore mildly bitter, signs up for a South Seas cruise on the S.S. *Katherine Medici*, a ship operated by Cosmic Ltd., "pioneers in social tourism." Once out of port, this little floating metaphor of the socialist experiment turns into a nightmare. Passengers are forced to serve the crew, possessions "disappear," and a few unfortunate souls are tried and executed for their most unsocial resistance. Through it all, Captain Gilbert Cook, convicted for gassing his entire family back in Jolly Old, exhorts the passengers to sacrifice everything for the good of the "entire community."

With a cruise like this, it seems like a positive stroke of good fortune when, late one night, the *Medici* enters "her final port of call, a permanent darkness eight thousand feet below the surface." The survivors—our narrator Orlando and a few others—are washed ashore and wake up the next morning to find themselves at the mercy of the Enu, the most outlandishly got-up crew of crazies to be found outside Andy Warhol's Factory. . . .

[It] turns out that the natives speak English, several varieties in fact (though Cockney is the dialect of choice), picked up, we learn, from an English couple stranded on the island some years before. Talk is high sport among the Enu, and the banter in the initial interrogation of the survivors provides the comic high point of the novel. "What you and I speak here I won't call 'English,'" IT explains to Orlando. "You are strange to me and I am a stranger to you. We speak. Let's say we speak 'strange,' and let's see who can speak stranger, you or I?'' Lewis Carroll would recognize his spiritual son in the maker of these sentences, with their weird, yet undeniable sense. (p. 6)

Lind's comic and satiric gifts are best deployed in the boat scenes and in these playful, oblique exchanges on the beach. By not trying so hard, by appearing to enjoy the strangeness of language itself, he says more than even he, perhaps, thinks he does. Unfortunately, Lind feels compelled to take on the Great Issues, and as the novel advances he abandons his strong suit in favor of a clunky symbolism. (pp. 6, 15)

One of the problems of this book, in addition to its polemical excess, is the character of Orlando. Characters in satire are traditionally thin creatures, attitudes on legs, roving preconceptions of how the world should be. The Gullivers and Candides of fiction are genial, trusting fellows who end up duly chastened by their experiences. But Orlando, in addition to being thin almost to the point of nonexistence, goes nowhere in his travels. He sets out disillusioned with the world and mankind, and he returns with his cynicism confirmed: a spiritual journey from A to A. And that might explain the dramatic slackness of this novel.

The question must be asked: Why did Lind bother to write this kind of book? He is a gifted storyteller (his *Soul of Wood,* a short-story collection, stands in my opinion as his best work to date) and an immensely interesting person. A Jew born in Vienna in 1927, he not only survived the Holocaust, he managed to work in the very heart of the beast, posing for a time as a simple (and properly Gentile) deckhand on a Rhine river barge. Unlike most other novelists who survived this horror, Lind . . . , has resisted writing thinly disguised novels about the experience. Indeed, in his actual autobiography, *Counting My Steps,* he makes relatively little of those years of danger and hardship; he seems, rather, to have enjoyed them—as though they confirmed his childhood sense of the absurdity of human affairs.

But that is precisely Lind's weakness as a satirist: There is no suggestion of disillusionment. He expects only stupidity, pettiness and evil of man. Always an outsider (he even disliked his fellow Jews in Vienna), he appears to view the holocausts of our century as vindication of his darkest suspicions. No one can fault Lind for believing what he believes; but one can fault him for attempting satire, which needs, at the center of all its "savage indignation," some little naive faith that man could—yes could—be better. (p. 15)

Jay Tolson, "Shipwrecked on the Island of the Bird People," in Book World—The Washington Post *(© 1982, The Washington Post), August 29, 1982, pp. 6, 15.*

John D(ann) MacDonald

1916-

American mystery and science fiction writer.

Among the most prolific and popular writers of detective fiction, MacDonald is also one of the most highly praised within this genre. Although his stories are formulaic, they are well-crafted, featuring artfully devised plots and a wide diversity of crimes and characters. Within the framework of solving mysteries, MacDonald has shown a deftness for capturing the local color of various American communities, especially of those in Florida, and his stories offer keen social criticism on environmental concerns, business and government corruption, and the artificiality of commercial culture.

MacDonald is best known for his Travis McGee series. McGee, a husky and virile "salvage expert," lives on a houseboat away from commercialized Florida, coming ashore only to aid victims of crime—in much the same manner as Robin Hood—for a fifty percent commission. McGee salvages both the material loss and the emotional state of his characters and then returns to his boat. *Cinnamon Skin* (1982), the most recent addition to the McGee series, is representative of MacDonald's successful blend of machismo, local color, and social criticism.

(See also *CLC*, Vol. 3; *Contemporary Authors*, Vols. 1-4, rev. ed.; *Contemporary Authors New Revision Series*, Vol. 1; and *Dictionary of Literary Biography*, Vol. 8.)

© Jerry Bauer

DAVID A. BENJAMIN

[Travis McGee] has the hint of meanness and suggestion of illegality that made Sam Spade such a fascinatingly ambiguous character; he has [Phillip] Marlowe's sense of self-directed irony, his striking physical presence, and though more open to sensual experience, he shares in main his moral outlook; and finally he has Lew Archer's sensitivity and interest in others, a willingness to get involved with people, probably more involved than Archer himself.

Yet if McGee's character relates in part to an illustrious tradition, much of his personality as well as the basic ingredients of the novels must be traced to MacDonald's earlier suspense novels. (pp. 29-30)

The basic plot of a McGee adventure usually begins with the interaction of a girl (either an old friend or friend of a friend or kin to one) in trouble, and a large sum of money (missing, stolen or buried). Travis swallows the bait and sets off on his mission of rescue, either by land (in Miss Agnes, his faithful Rolls pick-up truck), or by sea (in the Busted Flush, his elegant houseboat that he won in a poker game from a Brazilian playboy). Usually he is accompanied by Meyer, the hairy and brainy economist-cum-pal also living in quasi-retirement on a houseboat (in Bahia Mar, Fort Lauderdale, Florida). Meyer rarely has a major role in the subsequent action (the major exception to this being *The Long Lavender Look* [1970] where his role is vital), serving instead as a useful convention, the idiosyncratic buddy, a bright Watson to McGee's earthy Holmes. McGee, like the Hemingway hero, is someone to whom things happen, and who also manages to make things happen. Once

he has supplied sufficient pressure, the local scene explodes, and Travis then fits the pieces into the right slots. Usually the mystery-adventure involves a gang of con artists of one sort or another: smuggling, thievery, bamboozling, all types of chicanery. Rarely are we ever confronted with murder just for murder's sake: the profit motive is writ large in John D. MacDonald's world, as is only fitting of a novelist with an M.A. from the Harvard Business School.

Travis tracks down the gang through a tenacious process of elimination (usually literal); he somehow survives a grotesque assortment of killings and general mayhem, although his friends often aren't as lucky. The climax of the novels involves a ferocious mano-a-mano between Travis and the killer, invariably an upwardly mobile sadistic psychopath. In this struggle, Travis is almost killed, but recovers amazingly (lucky breaks seem to fall his way), gains the upper hand, relaxes (stupidly) and, then is attacked once again by his now totally crazed adversary, who gets a death grip on McGee, but never manages to consummate the act. Usually he ends up killing himself while trying to escape (thus saving Travis the responsibility for his death).

The closing scene usually finds Travis returning to the Busted Flush for some badly needed R & R with a playmate in tow (if she has survived the above carnage). If not, sometimes a playmate from an earlier tale will pop in to console McGee. Or at worst there is always the amusing comradery of the sympatico Meyer.

The success of this formula over the span of 16 books is due to more than simplicity. One obvious factor is the characterization of Travis McGee: a bundle of contradictions, brutal yet likable, fairly honest, with a Marlovian sense of humor and honor. Another ingredient is MacDonald's peculiar genius in creating with several swift sure strokes highly believable and interesting subsidiary characters, who take on a real life of their own and interreact convincingly with Travis, whether for him or against him. . . . MacDonald displays equal skill in creating fascinating vignettes of the towns and cities where these adventures take place (often sociological documents in their own right), and equally interesting details concerning whichever con is being played, from stamp collecting (*The Scarlet Ruse*, 1973) to the old badger game (*Darker Than Amber*, 1966) played for deadly stakes, to pornographic blackmailing in Hollywood (*The Quick Red Fox*). Finally there is the writer's Poeish knack for creating an atmosphere of elemental nightmarish terror, in generating the "smell of fear," as Chandler put it in discussing the *Black Mask* writers, a magazine for which MacDonald wrote several short stories.

This smell of fear relates directly to MacDonald's ability to create believable characters with whom we can identify as victims and equally convincing and frightening villains. Although Travis himself is as indestructible as most mythic heroes, we realize that his friends are less immortal. Often we meet them first after they have already been victimized, and are fully aware of how much they have suffered, and how cruel and destructive any further suffering would be. We are therefore almost as psychologically vulnerable as they are themselves to the idea of further pain, and we cringe when such violence recurs. In *Bright Orange For the Shroud* (1965), Vivian Watts is raped by the animalistic yet shrewd Boone Waxwell. She is ravaged not only sexually, but also psychically, a cruel abasement that leaves her no choice but suicide.

The McGee novels (and in fact almost everything written by MacDonald) are morality plays: Travis engaged in an endless struggle on behalf of defenseless victims, a force of Good against the multifarious Evil rampant in our harsh society. Though protean in their form the MacDonald villain is generally greedy, sexually twisted and amoral; in short, a sociopath, total madness only a flicker away. MacDonald's moral vision is conservative and manichean: McGee strives to preserve traditional values which he honors as an act of social good.

Yet in some of the recent novels one senses a certain ennui creeping into Travis' soul. He seems to be more remote with his friends, his women, even his enemies. In *The Dreadful Lemon Sky*, he turns down Carrie Milligan's offer of herself for no apparent reason except indifference, he remains strangely distant with Cindy Birdsong, in spite of himself; he can't make up his mind whether the clearly amoral Freddy Van Harn is really such a bad guy; and finally when his cop colleague, gutsy Captain Harry Max Scorf, has his head blown off by Hascomb, McGee uses Hascomb's moment of stunned "incredulous horror" to win the shootout, but then passes over Captain Harry's death without even a word of tribute.

Perhaps Travis and John D. both need a vacation, a time for McGee to savor his putative retirement, and a chance for MacDonald to work on a different type of novel for a while,

to freshen his extraordinary narrative gifts. One remembers McGee's lament early in *The Dreadful Lemon Sky,* that his favorite Plymouth gin is no longer bottled in England: ". . . it isn't the same. It's still a pretty good gin, but it is not a superb, stingling dry, and lovely gin." (pp. 30-1)

David A. Benjamin, "Key Witness," in The New Republic *(reprinted by permission of* The New Republic; *©1975 The New Republic, Inc.), Vol. 173, No. 4, July 26, 1975, pp. 28-31.*

JONATHAN YARDLEY

Like the other McGee novels, *The Empty Copper Sea* is a Cook's tour of the shadier side of the Sunshine State. We meet its Sun Belt aristocracy of bankers, contractors, insurance agents and big-money operators, and its confused underclass of retirees in mobile homes and condos, drifters with dark tans and darker notions, and the restive, frustrated middle class. Most of all, we meet people who in one way or another are sticking it to other people. . . .

[MacDonald's] is not a cheerful view of the world. Everywhere he turns he sees crooks, corruption, venality, selfishness, stupidity—above all, the conscienceless rich socking it to a defenseless society. The disappearance of Hub Lawless, the yachting businessman, sets off a chain of events that affects almost everyone in Timber Bay; the novel is really about "all the people who get hurt when somebody sets up a conspiracy to defraud."

That may explain why, apart from the pure entertainment he provides, MacDonald has such a large and loyal following: under all the cynicism and violence, the cheap sex and the plastic motels, there is a strong streak of compassion. He cares far more about the victim than the villian. He would also doubtless argue, as the surprising conclusion of *The Empty Copper Sea* attests, that we are all victims. Whatever the case, what matters is that without any pretensions he has serious things to say, and he says them uncommonly well.

Jonathan Yardley, "Travis Triumphs Again," in Book World—The Washington Post *(©1978, The Washington Post), September 10, 1978, p. E3.*

JOHN CASEY

"Cinnamon Skin" is as good as, or perhaps even a little better than, the standard Travis McGee.

In this quest McGee and his eccentric economist friend Meyer are attempting to track down a man who has had several identities and several consorts whom he has killed. Bluebeard, in a word. The quest is, as it should be, the chief pleasure in a McGee mystery, but Mr. MacDonald also has a reporter's ear for odd facts and arresting tones of voice. McGee and Meyer get people talking about their work, and we hear good on-the-job briefings from a geologist, a real-estate tycoon, a farm-equipment salesman, a cafe waitress, a west-Texas police sergeant and others.

For those John D. MacDonald fans who stay the course, there is an additional element—an autumnal wistfulness in the maverick McGee. His current ladylove, whom we meet in the beginning, opts for a promotion in her career that takes her away from Florida and McGee. He muses about what it would have been like to have children. He sighs about the despoiling that has occurred in Florida (he used to be angrier that it *was* happening).

But the essential elements of the series remain: The bad guy operates not only out of greed but out of sexual villainy. Many of Mr. MacDonald's villains have a dangerous power over women, to which the reader, along with McGee, is a sometime voyeur. The brute can make them cry for more, as if he has an instinct for that piece of original sin in even the best woman that can undo her, if not against her will, against her better will. One could question this point: Is this a male fantasy, a veiled delight in female vulnerability? Or is it a male fear of another male's power? In any case, the good woman undone by her sexual vulnerability to a bad man is a recurring theme, and we get a couple of versions of it in **"Cinnamon Skin."** In what may be the other side of the coin, we also get, in this story, a bad older woman undoing an adolescent boy.

There are other recurrences that MacDonald fans will enjoy: a fight in which McGee bests a practitioner of the Oriental martial arts with good old American horse sense and bulk, the unmasking of the last alias of the bad guy living in tropical splendor, a shoot-out in the Yucatan jungle. At the conclusion McGee ends up again with vengeance for a friend and yet another beautiful woman temporarily aboard his houseboat, The Busted Flush.

John Casey, "Thrillers Three," in The New York Times Book Review *(© 1982 by The New York Times Company; reprinted by permission), August 22, 1982, pp. 10, 22.**

DAVID GEHERIN

The two most obvious statements that can be made about John D. MacDonald as a writer are, one, that he is prolific (sixty-three novels and hundreds of short stories to date) and, two, that he is immensely popular (at least twenty-six of his titles have sold more than a million copies each). While popularity is certainly no assurance of quality, neither is it necessarily evidence of inferior work. What is readily apparent to any reader of MacDonald's novels is that he is a writer of great versatility and talent whose high standards have combined with high productivity to produce a significant body of outstanding fiction.

Slip F-18, Bahia Mar, Ft. Lauderdale, Florida, has become as famous an address as Sherlock's Holmes's 221b Baker Street flat or Nero Wolfe's West 35th Street brownstone. . . . Travis McGee has joined the small but select company of fictional characters who manage to transcend the boundaries of the books in which they appear. However, thanks to MacDonald's care in creating a character with substance as well as stature, McGee has also become an effective spokesman for public and private themes. An endlessly fascinating man, his growth, development, and faithful adherence to principles of moral behavior in an increasingly amoral world are sources of continuing interest. Equally important, he serves as a prism through which MacDonald is able to reflect his own views and opinions on dozens of issues of contemporary relevance. Whether assailing the venality and corruption he sees around him, bemoaning the regrettable decline in the quality of much of our contemporary culture, or deploring the shameless assaults on the environment, McGee has become an impassioned commentator on the way we live today—a feature that elevates his exciting adventures to a level of seriousness beyond mere escapist entertainment.

In an impressive body of fiction, which comprises considerably more than the Travis McGee novels, MacDonald has shown that writing for a mass-market audience (most of his books have first appeared as paperback originals) and adhering to the general patterns of genre fiction—activities that some would dismiss as second-rate—are in his case no impediments to the creation of first-rate work. His widespread popularity attests to the fact that he knows how to entertain his readers, but even a cursory examination of the novels themselves shows that he also has important things to say about contemporary America, and that he says them uncommonly well. Combining readability with serious intentions, MacDonald enjoys the enviable status of a writer who appeals both to those readers who claim they never read mysteries and to the legions of devoted fans who do. (pp. vii-viii)

MacDonald is a gifted storyteller. . . . Neither as byzantine as Ross Macdonald's nor as loose and desultory as Raymond Chandler's, MacDonald's plots are well-woven, artfully constructed arrangements of action sequences. They are neither needlessly complex nor do they exist simply to obscure the identity of the villain until the final chapter. A master at creating and sustaining mystery, suspense, tension, and drama, MacDonald understands all the tricks of readability; turning the pages in one of his novels is always a pleasure, never a duty. And although each of the McGee books adheres to the general outlines of a simple recurring pattern—McGee is roused from *The Busted Flush* to retrieve or restore some valuable item for a person in distress, usually a woman, and then retires to his boat again at the completion of his mission—MacDonald is skillful enough to avoid duplicating situations. Finally, his plots generate enough narrative energy to keep the reader moving at a brisk pace throughout the books, yet are flexible enough to allow for the inclusion of quiet, gentle scenes, as well as the many mini-sermons that have become such a characteristic feature of the McGee books. (pp. 171-72)

As important as story is, however, it isn't everything to MacDonald; his novels always feature believable characters about whom, thanks to his skill in making them real as well as interesting, the reader comes to care deeply. His success in achieving such credibility in his characterizations can be traced to the same feature that makes his prose so effective—concretization of detail. Normally he introduces a character by focusing on a single vivid detail in order to give that figure a substantial presence on the page. (p. 172)

Although one encounters the full spectrum of humanity in his novels, it is possible to divide his characters into two main groups: manipulators, usually men, who are driven by the need to accumulate, compound, launder, or extort money; and victims, usually women, who are conned, abused, and mistreated by them. By concentrating on these two types, MacDonald is able to examine in novel after novel two of his primary interests: the focus on victimized women allows him to display the wondrous variety of the female species while exploring the ecstasies of male-female relationships; the focus on the manipulators allows him to depict in gloomy detail the moral grubbiness of everyone from unsavory con men and common swindlers to respectable real estate agents and fast-buck merchants who are out to cheat the unwary, defraud the unsuspecting, exploit the consumer, ravage the land, and debase the quality of modern life.

But whether they be heroes or villains, saints or sinners, featured performers or background figures, MacDonald's characters are invariably believable and interesting. Thanks to his instinctive choice of the right gesture, mannerism, speech pattern, quirk, and tic, even the most insignificant character is allowed his brief and shining moment in the limelight before being retired to the obscurity of the background once more. In the richness of his characterizations and the perceptive delineation of their innermost selves, MacDonald creates a world of recognizable beings who are driven by the same emotions—fear, love, hate, greed, loneliness, compassion—that compel us all. More than any other feature, it is MacDonald's skill in creating credible and convincing characters that gives his work the look and feel of solid reality. (pp. 173-74)

Neither as characteristically lean as Hammett's prose nor as extravagantly colorful as Chandler's nor as elegantly poetic as Ross Macdonald's, MacDonald's prose is an effective blend of elements of all three styles. By combining concrete details, unpretentious diction, colorful images, and rhythmically balanced sentences, MacDonald produces a zesty and energetic prose that is enlivened by one of the most authentic and distinctive voices in the genre. As imposing as the figure of McGee is, as exciting as his adventures are, and as socially relevant as his commentaries are, it is MacDonald's crisp, clean prose that gives the books their distinctive flavor. The sheer quantity of his fictional output is evidence that MacDonald is a hardworking writer; the exceptional quality of his vigorous and energetic prose (whose appearance of effortlessness should not lull us into taking it for granted) is evidence that he is a superior craftsman. Only a writer in love with words and enamored of the particular beauties of the language could have produced the richly textured, supple prose that is one of the special pleasures of each MacDonald novel.

In the final analysis, however, MacDonald is no mere storyteller, psychologist, social critic, philosopher, or poet; he is a *novelist*, who combines all these separate interests and talents into works of art that capture and evoke the spirit of his age as effectively as those of any other contemporary writer. . . .

For the past three decades, in dozens of novels, MacDonald has been an acute chronicler of the American Dream as it has moved south and taken up residence in the Sun Belt. If his works can be said to have a central theme, it is money: there is perhaps no writer who knows better than he how money works and how it weaves its magic spell over people. His concern is not with the very rich or the very poor but with that segment of the populace driven by avarice to accumulate, often by shady means, all it can. It is such con men, swindlers, and hustlers who provide him with his plots, serve as his villains, and produce the victims for his keenly observed chronicles which, thanks to his concentration on the human factors of each situation, achieve a powerfully compelling emotional resonance.

Like many of his mystery-writing colleagues, MacDonald is ultimately interested in something more than mere escapist entertainment. Flatly rejecting Jacques Barzun's notion that "anyone who attempts to improve on the mystery genre and make it a real novel suffers from bad judgment," MacDonald asserts with confidence and ample good reason that "No one can tell me that it is not within my authority to try to move my suspense novels as close as I can get to the 'legitimate' novels of manners and morals, despair and failure, love and joy." Whether for the sake of convenience one categorizes his works as mysteries, adventures, or thrillers, it is clear that such labels are inadequate in conveying the full extent of his accomplishment. By creating a substantial body of thoughtful and provocative entertainment for an enormously diverse and widespread audience, MacDonald has justly earned for himself the right to be considered a serious American novelist worthy of the highest distinction. (pp. 180-81)

David Geherin, in his John D. MacDonald *(copyright © 1982 by Frederick Ungar Publishing Co., Inc.), Ungar, 1982, 202 p.*

Helen MacInnes

1907-

Scottish-born American novelist.

Helen MacInnes writes novels of international intrigue based upon a pattern of traditional characters, values, and elements of suspense. Her standard conflicts take the form of opposing ideologies: America and the West versus the Nazis and, later, Communists and terrorists. The lines of good and evil are clearly drawn in her work and it is understood that good will triumph. Accordingly, her amateur heroes consistently emerge unscathed from the most danger-fraught situations, after first thwarting their professional antagonists. *Above Suspicion* (1941), a tale of espionage set in pre-World War II Germany and Austria, begins the roster of MacInnes novels. Her most recent, *Cloak of Darkness* (1982), is a thriller about international terrorism and munitions trafficking.

While most critics praise the accuracy and detail of her narratives, many have called her characters innocuous, interchangeable, and unrealistic—types rather than individuals. Others observe, however, that her lack of introspection contributes to the light, readable pace of her books. Critics also note that MacInnes's books could be more concise, though their length derives more from her frequent digressions than from inflated writing. Because her professionalism and story-telling ability are widely acknowledged and respected, it has often been suggested that she write books with a greater variety of subjects and plots. MacInnes attempted to do so in *Friends and Lovers* (1947) and *Rest and Be Thankful* (1949), but when both books received lukewarm critical reception, MacInnes returned to the formula responsible for her books being consistent best sellers.

(See also *Contemporary Authors*, Vols. 1-4, rev. ed.; *Contemporary Authors New Revision Series*, Vol. 1; and *Something about the Author*, Vol. 22.)

© Nancy Crampton

ROSE FELD

To say that "Above Suspicion," by Helen MacInnes, is an excellent first novel is not enough. It is a great deal more than that. It tells an exciting story with the technical smoothness of an accomplished writer; it creates a mood of suspense which carries through to the end of the volume, and it possesses what is rare in a book of this sort, a subtle note of humor which contributes to the distinction of the job. . . .

The plot gets increasingly feverish at the end and a little incredible but it makes good reading. But convincing and real as the morning sun is the feeling Miss MacInnes has for the Germany and the Austria of pre-war days. She writes of people and places with a nostalgic knowledge and tenderness. Against the rhythmic tread of boots, of military marchers and salutes, she limns the twisted lives of simple men and women who know they are powerless to do anything but accept the rule imposed upon them. She contrasts beautifully a woman who approves the new order of things, Frau Koppler, and one who cannot, Frau Schichtl. Each leaves her mark on the destiny of

the Myleses. And as excellent as her portrayal of the German people and psychology is the author's development of her two main characters, an English pair who have their own brand of humor and gayety and courage to see them through a harrowing experience.

Rose Feld, "Peril in Pre-War Germany," in New York Herald Tribune Books (© I.H.T. Corporation), July 13, 1941, p. 2.

MARGARET STERN

"Above Suspicion" is another of those ingenious spy stories which are by-products of the war. The formula, though familiar, seems to have unlimited possibilities, and Miss MacInnes has turned out a first novel which moves lightly and swiftly. The impact of nazism on the easy-going world of liberalism has to some extent jarred literary production out of its self-conscious introspection to forms that are more external. It is paradoxical that it should take a war to restore a sense of the ordinary, everyday lives of men and women. But the present war does seem to have produced this effect. . . .

The author obviously has a very definite attitude toward the régime in Germany, but her reactions remain external, never marring the sparkling surface of the narrative. So too her characters, German and English alike, are simplified black and white portraits, types that never become individuals. Only Frances Myles occasionally comes alive with a touch of feminine insight or feminine observation. But the lack of depth keeps the action moving rapidly and induces in the reader very much the same state of mind produced by a detective story. Perhaps, in the last analysis, the closest parallel is a Hitchcock film, which has the same one-dimensional portraiture, the same pervading atmosphere of suspense, the same Englishness.

> *Margaret Stern, in a review of ''Above Suspicion,'' in* Commonweal *(copyright © 1941 Commonweal Publishing Co., Inc.; reprinted by permission of Commonweal Publishing Co., Inc.), Vol. XXXIV, No. 16, August 8, 1941, p. 378.*

ROSE FELD

Again Helen MacInnes has done it and this time in a more complex and ambitious work than her first espionage novel, **"Above Suspicion."** The new book, **"Assignment In Brittany"** leaves small doubt as to her creative powers. She is more than the weaver of an exciting tale of war intrigue; she is a novelist who can hold her own on literary grounds. Her background, her characterization, her detail of plot and dialogue possess finesse and subtlety and reality. And just as she brought the feeling and atmosphere of Germany into her first book, so does she capture and translate for the reader the strength and the spirit of the land and the people of Brittany. . . .

Brilliantly Miss MacInnes develops and expands the complexities of her plot. But even better than her plot is her description of the Breton countryside and its natives. She writes about them as one who knows them and loves them. The Corlay farm might be a place she has lived for years; the tiny seacoast hamlets with their fishermen, who were willing to risk their lives to carry the enemies of the conquering Nazis to safety, communities and people she has always known. A Frenchman could not write about them with greater personal warmth and regional design. . . .

There is a love story woven into the tale, and wisely Miss McInnes gives it second place. But even in second place it rises to distinction by virtue of her subtle and restrained writing. And like a murmuring accompaniment to all that happens in the four weeks of Hearne's stay in Brittany is the restless ferment of a proud people who are only temporarily conquered. Before long, one is certain, the murmur will rise to a shout. **"Assignment in Brittany"** is more than good entertainment; it is a war book that carries the lift of faith and of ultimate victory.

> *Rose Feld, ''Brittany Parachute Adventure,'' in* New York Herald Tribune Books *(© I.H.T. Corporation), July 12, 1942, p. 2.*

JOHN C. CORT

Don't be scared away by the unfortunate title. **"While Still We Live"** . . . is another successful effort by Helen MacInnes, who proved in **"Above Suspicion"** and **"Assignment in Brittany"** that she has a happy flair for combining exciting fiction with her own personal war against the nazis. . . .

You get the feeling that Miss MacInnes is straining a bit, trying to do something more important than just another good mystery thriller about fighting Hitler. For such heavy-duty stuff it doesn't appear that she has quite enough artillery. She is always intelligent and interesting—well, nearly always—but outside the heroine, who is obviously Miss MacInnes and very charming, the characters are just a little too simple, a little too much like the people you meet in good mystery thrillers.

But Miss MacInnes's talent is considerable and for a vivid picture of Polish resistance and a most sympathetic reminder of the virtues of that embattled people, we must certainly be grateful. And as for her detailed account of the activities of the Polish underground, I can only say that if it isn't actually like that, it certainly ought to be.

> *John C. Cort, in a review of ''While Still We Live,'' in* Commonweal *(copyright © 1944 Commonweal Publishing Co., Inc.; reprinted by permission of Commonweal Publishing Co., Inc.), Vol. XL, No. 6, May 26, 1944, p. 140.*

ROBERT W. ANDERSON

Miss MacInnes's narrative [in *While Still We Live*] does not carry much conviction or real interest, for she is working out an elaborate exposition and a rather unconvincing background of war-torn Poland. But then suddenly she doffs pretentiousness and gets down to the hunter and the hunted, a type of tale which she tells with consummate skill. . . .

Like a well-dressed bride, Miss MacInnes's story wears something old and something new—with just enough of the new to keep the reader moving on through a great deal that has become old hat to followers of spy romances. The characters are well known and well worn, the action unashamedly melodramatic. It is a personal story of an individual's adventures, and it is at its best when it is not making pretenses at representing the indomitable spirit of the Poles. The tragedy of Poland and her people has been so expertly and vividly presented to the world by factual accounts that Miss MacInnes's somewhat generalized panorama suffers by comparison. But if you accept the novel for what it really is, a romping, melodramatic tale, there can be no quibble about its effectiveness.

> *Robert W. Anderson, in a review of ''While Still We Live,'' in* The Atlantic Monthly *(copyright © 1944, by The Atlantic Monthly Company, Boston, Mass.; reprinted with permission), Vol. 173, No. 6, June, 1944, p. 129.*

JAMES MacBRIDE

Five years after its publication, this reviewer still has affection for Helen MacInnes' first novel, **"Above Suspicion."** . . . Miss MacInnes has published three novels since that event—and, in every instance, slickness has replaced real drama, and technical competence has atoned for warmth. Their author is by now a dependable performer, in The Saturday Evening Post sense of that dubious phrase. . . .

"Horizon" is Miss MacInnes' current contribution to the still fashionable—and still perfunctory—probing of the POW's psyche, before and after his escape from the barbed wire. Peter Lennox, her hero, is one of the most taciturn Englishmen we have ever encountered in a novel. To make matters worse, virtually nothing happens to him after his carefully muted escape from an Italian prison camp in '43, and his flight to the mountains of the South Tyrol. . . .

The author has prepared her scenery with loving care, but it is scenery without actors.

At times, "**Horizon**" shows signs of life—and then nose-dives into vagueness again as the novelist struggles with frustrations too heavy to handle. Dramatized in exterior terms, it might have done well as a short story. As a scamped novel, that locks itself deliberately in the brain of a dull young man, it is worse than disappointing.

> *James MacBride, "No Action," in* The New York Times Book Review *(© 1946 by The New York Times Company; reprinted by permission), May 26, 1946, p. 22.*

MARY McGRORY

The grace and good breeding that made other MacInnes novels a delight have gone into ["**Friends and Lovers**"]: but, since it lacks the suspense and the compensating psychological excitement of her earlier books, its good qualities are not quite enough to sustain its thinly plotted narrative. The author has obviously intended a touching picture rather than a profound one. The story is told almost entirely in dialogue, which affords little opportunity for probing. . . . As a novel, "**Friends and Lovers**" is talky, uneventful and pieced out with extraneous matters. As a romance, however, it should appeal to those who have won out over just such opposition and who . . . think that love is a serious matter. That takes in a lot of people.

> *Mary McGrory, "A Variety of Hammock Companions for the Late Vacationer: 'Friends and Lovers'," in* The New York Times Book Review *(© 1947 by The New York Times Company; reprinted by permission), August 17, 1947, p. 16.*

GEORGE CONRAD

Helen MacInnes has published five novels of life abroad. In "**Rest and Be Thankful**" she not only taps the American scene for the first time but seeks the very essence of it in the cattle lands of Wyoming. To that end she has shaped a story with precision, fine tolerance and manifest skill. If it displays more facility than force, and is sometimes tentative when it should have been trenchant, one must admire her resolution in the choice of theme. This was not a lazy self-assignment.

What the author has undertaken is a sharp, ironic juxtaposition of Eastern culture and Western customs, not only in relation to each other but in contrast with European life. In passages of barbed humor, weathered wranglers and hard-muscled ranch owners take the measure of literary drones and novelists in embryo. Here is a precise differentiation between breeding as applied to manners and breeding as applied to steers. What is mainly lacking is a boiling point; the novel does not stir the pulse because it does not reach the bedrock of reality. . . .

Miss MacInnes does not get much beneath the surface of most of her characters. . . . Possibly "**Rest and Be Thankful**" is a bit too concerned with the tea-cozy relationship of two heroines for whom life is so nicely smoothed. Next time, perhaps, the brew will be stronger.

> *George Conrad, "World Travelers in Wyoming," in* New York Herald Tribune Weekly Book Review *(© I.H.T. Corporation), August 7, 1949, p. 7.*

CONSTANCE MORGAN

[*I And My True Love*] is a smooth, readable story of love and espionage in contemporary Washington. It is so contemporary that one would not be too surprised to find any or all of the plot's many ingredients in today's headlines, and the characters are neatly chosen for a combination of plausibility plus drama. Start with a member of a Czechoslovakian mission who returns from behind the Iron Curtain to revive a love affair with the beautiful wife of a consultant to the State Department. Juxtapose against this triangle a young niece from California and a lieutenant from Korea. Flank them all with solid friends on the one hand, and sharp, untrustworthy young men on the other, and you have provided your reader with a generous number of possibilities for emotional and political excitement. With her practised hand, Helen MacInnes develops these possibilities one by one against the background of that small but famous section of the nation's capital called Georgetown.

She does it skilfully. Descriptions of one's own town are as difficult to acknowledge as recordings of one's own voice, and to this reviewer the Georgetown of Miss MacInnes seems somewhat overvarnished, but her scenes and figures are recognizable. The heroine's crowded engagement pad, her small dinner party and those who attend it, including the chic, dubious, not-so-young bachelor and his antithesis, a nice, unfashionable, reliable servant of the government, are all standard Washington features. (The heroine's husband is an exception. He is so unpleasant that it is difficult to understand why the State Department or his wife accepted him.) Better than standard is the author's knowledge of the problems of security which enables her to demonstrate lucidly and effectively the amount of damage done by an apparently "tiny" leak of information. By connecting this leak to a question of trade rather than defense, she brings it home to the conscience of the citizen who deals with less spectacular secrets than the Atomic Energy Commission.

After this, it may seem captious to complain that the love story is far less convincing than the political one, but the author devotes more than half of her novel to the emotional problems of her main characters and it is the poorer half. The characters are not big enough to fill the roles so carefully prepared for them. The young do better than their elders because their dilemma is far from tragic and their tentative approach to love is described quite touchingly, but the supposed mature love affair does not rend the heart as much as the situation warrants. Helen MacInnes can invest a shabby room off lower Connecticut Avenue with the menace of an occupied country; her terse recital of what her heroine does in the last pages of the novel is sharp and telling; but there are long passages when the conversation of her characters falls flat. (pp. 64-5)

> *Constance Morgan, "Under the Capitol," in* The Saturday Review, New York *(© 1953 Saturday Review Magazine Co.; reprinted by permission), Vol. XXXVI, No. 7, February 14, 1953, pp. 64-5.*

ROBERT PHELPS

An exceptional suspense story is always a matter of how it's told, of the fine art of unravelling—if that word doesn't impute too haphazard a character to a process that is very precisely controlled; and no one in the business today knows and practices its secrets with more finesse than Helen MacInnes.

The scene of ["**Decision at Delphi**"] is Greece, and the goings-on have to do with an extreme anarchist minority, whose leader, an ex-guerrilla fighter, known only as Odysseus, is plotting an assassination which could lead to political chaos. But a former comrade, Stephanos Kladas, has photographic evidence which will identify him, and is smuggling it into Greece in the luggage of Kenneth Strang, an unsuspecting young American assigned to sketch Greek ruins for a travel magazine. When Stephanos disappears, Kenneth becomes involved, and it is then that Miss MacInnes' technique takes over, teasing and tautening the suspense until almost the final page.

Characterization under such circumstances is relatively unimportant; indeed, anything very interesting in itself would only get in the way. So Kenneth is a nice, intelligent, hard-working hero, an architect who is enough of a poet-maverick to prefer free-lance illustrating to designing office buildings, and boyishly manly in the way ladies love to imagine men to be, and in which they almost invariably are not. . . .

The remaining personae and situations are standard: the masterful police inspector, the shady travel agent, the stuffy British diplomat and his indiscreet wife; a beautiful dark girl who dashes in and out with flurried warnings, and a mysterious white yacht which meets an American ocean liner at Gibraltar and carries away certain even more mysterious passengers; and of course murder, kidnaping, secretly delivered letters, shadowing policemen, and enough puzzled, questioning dialogue to make it all sound like a quiz show much of the time.

To all of this, Miss MacInnes also has added a glamorous gratuity: landscapes from Taormina to Sparta, all freshly observed and deftly sketched into the background. . . .

> Robert Phelps, "Suspense Artist at Work," in New York Herald Tribune Book Review (© I.H.T. Corporation; reprinted by permission), October 30, 1960, p. 12.

JOHN L. BROWN

Helen MacInnes has been providing literate entertainment for readers who fancy cultured British chat with their manslaughter. Her formula has seldom varied: civilized travelogue plus melodramatic espionage plus a generous dusting of powdered-sugar sex. In her later books (has she been told that readers of thrillers want lots and lots of action?) this basic plot has sometimes grown so complicated that one is hard put to figure out the details. "**The Venetian Affair**" is a case in point. Despite a straightforward beginning, the intrigue soon becomes as ingeniously convoluted as a baroque facade. . . .

Devotees of this author's work will know how to skip the purple patches, the political sermonizing, most of the romance. I enjoyed "**The Venetian Affair**." I'd like Miss MacInnes even better if she had more concision. . . . A question of taste, I suppose.

> John L. Brown, "Bang-Bang All The Way," in The New York Times Book Review (© 1963 by The New York Times Company; reprinted by permission), September 29, 1963, p. 48.

JANE SOUTHERN

Helen MacInnes has written a new novel of international espionage and has called it "**The Venetian Affair**." It starts in Paris and ends where the title promises. It involves a divorced drama critic and a pretty young widow, experiencing the less sordid thrills of the Cold War, and takes them to many places of interest, two or three good restaurants, and more than one dark alley. The widow has tasteful clothes, and the critic possesses more intelligence and courage than is usual for his profession. This is probably all the information that a great many readers will require. The brand name is on the package, and it would be churlish to examine the contents before purchase.

However, Miss MacInnes' status as a dependable treat deserves some study. There are many accomplished ladies writing about the more domestic and cozy forms of murder, but few who have made a name for themselves in the frontier lands of the secret agent. . . .

Miss MacInnes is no emancipator. She has simply transferred her nesting instinct to a more exotic environment, like a sparrow in no-man's-land between the trenches. She employs all the usual decor of the spy thriller: last-minute planes, long distance trains, microphones concealed for surveillance and boutonnieres displayed for identification. . . .

But though violence and its thwarting is the basis of her story, it remains mostly in the background. Murder occurs nearly always off stage, and sex, usually its constant companion in this genre, hardly appears at all. (p. 20)

It is with . . . miniature conflict that Miss MacInnes is most skillful at creating tension and alarm in the reader. She is excellent at observing how raincoats can get switched at airports, and thus change the history of nations, or how the decor of an apartment reveals its absent owner. She also believes that character creates plot, and neatly dovetails the experience of her personalities into the action they take under crisis. This is a welcome change from the arbitrary nature of cause and effect in most spy novels. . . .

The book is rather long for its kind—more than 400 pages. She might have maintained her effects with more cunning if she had left out at least some of the passages of stern warning about the ubiquitous bogey of the Communist menace. After all, anyone who likes this kind of book already knows cowboy from Indian. (p. 21)

> Jane Southern, "A Gun in Her Handbag," in Book Week—The Washington Post (© 1963, The Washington Post), October 20, 1963, pp. 20-1.

ROBERT NEVILLE

It ought to surprise no veteran reader of spy stories that in Helen MacInnes's latest book ["**The Double Image**"] American, British and French counterintelligence (assisted by the Greeks) is still struggling valiantly against the machinations of a resourceful, far-flung Soviet espionage apparatus. For a while the numerous knock-out blows, abductions and murders are even-handed, but in the end the Allied agents prove their mettle and track down their prey. Yet another victory is chalked up for the Free World.

In other words, in "**Double Image**" Miss MacInnes has stuck close to the tried-and-true formula she so successfully exploited in "**The Venetian Affair**." (p. 4)

As is usual with thrillers by Miss MacInnes, this story is told with a cast of characters so large it is sometimes difficult to remember just who is who and on what side. The Russian agents are apparent newcomers to Miss MacInnes's novels, but some of the Allied agents are old-timers from previous works. (pp. 4-5)

Miss MacInnes has also once again taken an honest, hard-working American newspaperman . . . and converted him, temporarily at least, into an Allied agent. Here is a bad habit which the author should break. . . .

The plot of **"The Double Image"** is detailed and complicated, and only the attentive reader will keep everything straight. The reader who regards spy fiction as light bedside reading had better beware in this case or he will find himself hopelessly confused. A book with all the intricacies Miss MacInnes commands needs to be read carefully or not at all.

Her forte is authentic background. Other authors may be as well versed in espionage methods, but few can surpass her in describing the smells, the tastes, the looks, the ambiance of diverse European locales. . . .

The novice in international skullduggery may well ask if all of the elaborate feinting, disguising, backtracking and tailing so painstakingly described by Miss MacInnes is truly fundamental to good spying. . . . Miss MacInnes's characters are all well-grounded in the most modern forms of recording information; but they all seem hopelessly old-fashioned when it comes to communications. To an outsider unversed in the folkways of spies, Miss MacInnes's world of espionage seems badly in need of streamlining. (p. 5)

> Robert Neville, "Spies and Super-Spies," in The New York Times Book Review (© 1966 by The New York Times Company; reprinted by permission), January 9, 1966, pp. 4-5.

P. L. BUCKLEY

[The formula for Helen MacInnes's novels, a quarter century after she began writing them and most recently in *The Salzburg Connection*,] remains much the same, a couple of non-professionals inveigled into taking a hand from—hold your breath—patriotic motives with the good guys against the bad, the adventure taking place in some attractive foreign part—Venice, Delphi, in this case Salzburg. In the waning days of World War II, the Nazis sank a chest containing the names of important collaborators into a remote Austrian lake and set up a ring of fanatic agents to guard it—shades of the Rheingold. Twenty years later, it is brought to the surface and everyone wants it: the Nazis, the KGB, Peking, and of course the Austrian, British and American secret services. Into the churning situation walk a young American lawyer and an attractive publisher's representative (female) and, after assorted kidnapings, murders and associated skullduggeries, the compromising papers end in the right hands. A warning: Helen MacInnes demands a lot of her readers these days—her plots are intricately woven—so read with attention. The slightest lapse may cost you the clue that should tell you at the very end on whose side the key character is. (p. 35)

> P. L. Buckley, in a review of "The Salzburg Connection," in National Review (© National Review, Inc., 1969; 150 East 35th St., New York, NY 10016), Vol. XXI, No. 1, January 14, 1969, pp. 34-5.

JOSH RUBINS

The MacInnes political antennae, always tuned in to the latest international headlines, have proved more reliable than ever.

At the center of ["**The Snare of the Hunter**"] is writer Jaromir Kusak, a Nobel prize nominee in voluntary exile from Czechoslovakia. An amateurish but valiant Anglo-American quartet resolves to effect the reunion of Kusak with his daughter Irina—without leading the Secret Police (in hot but secretive pursuit) to the writer's Swiss hideway.

Any serious contemplation or extended examination of the mainsprings of this story's narrative would reveal gaping chasms in logic and raise foolish but fundamental questions for which Miss MacInnes furnishes no answers.

Of course, there'd be no story if logic were triumphant and, happily, the pace and rich texture of the MacInnes style leave few moments for question-raising contemplation.

Like its predecessors, **"The Snare of the Hunter"** is part travelogue. Without even setting off for an airport, we can gawk at Vienna's Opera House, lunch at Grinzing, glance at the grim Czechoslovakian border, and then head west for Italy and Switzerland, where the ultimate in sophisticated tourguides will lend us a green Mercedes and send us off on our own. The terror of the chase only seems to intensify the beauty of the landscape, and none of the characters ever wonders if he'll have enough money to pay the bill.

Beyond vicarious tourism, a MacInnes novel offers characters who are decent human beings, with inner thoughts that emerge and recede as the author's stream-of-consciousness roams from mind to mind.

The occasional excesses of this technique generate faint echoes of the Ladies' Home Journal, but enough ironic and hard-edged sentiments keep that impulse in check.

More recklessly, Miss MacInnes allows her mind-excursions to extend to the hidden traitors of the piece, making us aware of their evil intentions too soon, sacrificing possibilities for climactic revelations.

Suspense survives, however, and, as the hunters and the hunted finally converge on a dot on the map, it is almost embarrassing to discover how much we've come to care about Irina and her brigade.

And there is strong satisfaction in knowing, without the ambiguities fostered in recent novels of political intrigue, the heroes from the villains—and in witnessing their just deserts.

> Josh Rubins, in a review of "The Snare of the Hunter," in The Christian Science Monitor (reprinted by permission from The Christian Science Monitor; © 1974 The Christian Science Publishing Society; all rights reserved), March 27, 1974, p. F5.

THE TIMES LITERARY SUPPLEMENT

Helen MacInnes's new novel [*Agent in Place*] opens with the theft, by Chuck Kelso, a foolish and idealistic young American, of a top-secret Nato memorandum. Part of this is leaked to the press; the far more important second half, however, falls into the hands of a Soviet agent, and the rest of the novel concerns the efforts of English, French and American intelligence departments, with some amateur assistance, to repair the huge breach that has been blown in their security. The motive behind

Chuck's action is his belief that there is a need to know, a "moral obligation to publish and jolt the American people into the realities of today".

Some writers might have used the clash between two moral obligations as the theme of their novel; Helen MacInnes's scheme of values, however, as Chuck finds to his cost, is as black and white as the shadow and sunshine of her favourite mise-en-scene, the Mediterranean—here the locale is Menton. Miss MacInnes is not interested in achieving even a semblance of authenticity in her novels, and it is hard to take her clean-cut young Americans and sinister East Europeans seriously.

> *A review of "Agent in Place," in* The Times Literary Supplement *(© Times Newspapers Ltd. (London) 1976; reproduced from* The Times Literary Supplement *by permission), No. 3890, October 1, 1976, p. 1260.*

SARA TERRY

Time and again Helen MacInnes has proved herself a master of novels of intrigue and suspense. But while she once more has employed all the ingredients that have worked so successfully for her in the past, her eighteenth book falls just short of the mark.

MacInnes novels are known for their colorful settings, tightly-paced action, and plots which dovetail neatly with the international and political headlines of the day. At least in the first and third categories, **"Prelude to Terror"** follows suit with its predecessors.

The plot revolves around New York art consultant Colin Grant, who is commissioned by an eccentric millionaire to purchase a Ruysdael painting at an auction in Vienna.

Grant quickly finds there is more to his task than purchasing the painting and soon is involved in a web of terrorism, laundered money, and intelligence agents.

As always, MacInnes paints a wonderfully vivid landscape, from the busy streets of Vienna to the quaint chalets and woods of the surrounding countryside.

Although she wastes no time plunging her readers into the action, there are, as with most novels of foreign intrigue, wide gaps in the story line. It is simple enough to grasp the heart of the affair, but the minute the reader looks too deeply into the plot, logic goes awry.

However, it is easy to overlook such gaps if a novel is fast-paced enough to sweep its reader along without giving him time to ask too many questions.

This novel partially succeeds in avoiding pitfalls in the plot but tension slackens mid-way through the story following a taut, climactic episode in which Grant purchases the Ruysdael painting.

From that point on, the reader is left with plenty of time to ponder loose ends and the story begins a slow unraveling which leads to an ending that should have been a bang but unfortunately is only a pop.

The author develops her characters with compassion, but there is a predictability here that is unsettling: once the lines are drawn between the good guys and the bad (which occurs early in the story), there are none of the unexpected twists and double-crossings that suspense readers find so fascinating.

The story makes a concise, full-circle swing, picking Colin Grant up in New York and a few, short, action-packed weeks later leaving him as he prepares for his return trip.

But Grant starts and ends in the same dismal emotional predicament—contemplating the murder of a woman he loved—and the closing message that all any of us can do "is just keep going" is a weak finish for a lofty plot.

"Prelude to Terror" at its best moments is an extremely well-paced, absorbing work that promises much. But although it makes for some lively reading, that promise never is fully realized.

> *Sara Terry, "Prelude Ends on Weak Note," in* The Christian Science Monitor *(reprinted by permission from* The Christian Science Monitor; *© 1978 The Christian Science Publishing Society; all rights reserved), September 27, 1978, p. 19.*

ANATOLE BROYARD

I underestimated the mystery reader, and I apologize. I realize now that it takes much more commitment—character, even—to read Miss MacInnes than it does to go through Thomas Mann or Marcel Proust. There is so much to remember that isn't memorable.

Secret drops, code names, cover techniques, labyrinthine motives, alternative procedures, espionage bureaucrats: one needs energy, patience, doggedness, a photographic memory. One needs a reason, too, not the get-away-from-it-all impulse I naïvely supposed, but the determination of a man working for a Ph.D.

Why do they do it? . . . Perhaps a Helen MacInnes novel is the mental equivalent of jogging.

I was struck by the familiar warning after the title page: "The characters in this novel are completely imaginary. Their names and experiences have no relation to those of actual people." . . . It's absolutely true in this case. I have never met any actual people who talked or behaved like those in **"The Hidden Target."**

What does one famous terrorist do when he meets another famous terrorist? He congratulates him on his somber gray jacket and dark shirt, that is to say, his inconspicuousness. It seems that terrorists are awful fussbudgets. They are always asking themselves: "Is anyone loitering around, waiting to follow me? Will that cabbie remember my face, my destination? See what excellent cover those tourists in the church provide all the way into the street." Another terrorist is caught red-handed and finds "his show of righteous indignation to no avail."

Mystery novels may be written in a mysterious language. Kiley the terrorist is ordered to be "circumspectly dressed," to make "a complicated arrival" in Bombay. Perhaps it is the tension under which the characters labor, but they do make very small small talk. The daughter of a high American official remarks that he hates bulky briefcases. "Spoils the silhouette," replies the head of an antiterrorist organization in all seriousness. When the handsome young terrorist manhandles the rich American girl before running off, her first words are, "He took all my money."

The plot of "**The Hidden Target**" has to do with two young terrorists taking two American girls and two other couples through Europe and Asia in a camper as cover while they finance and recruit terrorists in these places. Apparently, their plan involves bypassing all the major attractions, and there are quite a few contretemps with the passengers about the itinerary. The principal girl is subjected to an unspeakable ordeal: forced by a terrorist to walk through the red-light district of Bombay. Miss MacInnes's decency and restraint should be weighed against her literary transgressions. (pp. 577-78)

> Anatole Broyard, "Two Recent Thrillers," in The New York Times, Section 21 (© 1980 by The New York Times Company; reprinted by permission), September 7, 1980 (and reprinted in Books of the Times, Vol. III, No. 12, December, 1980, pp. 577-79).*

NEWGATE CALLENDAR

Every two or three years along comes a Helen MacInnes spy story, and just off the presses is "**The Hidden Target**" . . . . Her latest effort follows the familiar MacInnes formula.

That means spies, the good versus the bad, a clean-cut American type, an attractive female, a romance, a great deal of double-dealing, the evil Russians somewhere around, Us against Them. Why change a good formula? It so happens that in "**The Hidden Target**," the evil forces are exponents of international terrorism. But there are hints that the Russians are pulling the strings. Otherwise the book contains no surprises. . . .

If the action of "**The Hidden Target**" is entirely predictable, it is at least a tribute to the storytelling skill of Miss MacInnes that one gets involved in the book. She is a real pro. But perhaps the time has come for her to sit back and try to think of something a *little* different. Miss MacInnes is not as prolific as Vivaldi, who has been accused of writing the same concerto grosso 500 times, but in her 18 novels she also can be accused of adhering too closely to a formula.

> Newgate Callendar, in a review of "The Hidden Target," in The New York Times Book Review (© 1981 by The New York Times Company; reprinted by permission), January 11, 1981, p. 22.

KIRKUS REVIEWS

[*The Hidden Target*], one of MacInnes' least persuasive efforts, hardly cried out for a sequel. But here [*Cloak of Darkness*] is anyway: a drab terrorist-hunt that doesn't even feature the vast scenery or the damsel-in-distress setup that made *The Hidden Target* fairly readable. Robert Renwick of "International Intelligence Against Terrorism" (Interintell), who saved lovely young Nina—now Mrs. Renwick—from super-terrorist Erik in *The Hidden Target,* is on Erik's trail again: Interintell has received information that Erik's on the loose in Africa. Furthermore, Interintell has learned that two corporations are involved in illegal arms deals—*and* that these villains have drawn up a "Minus List" (nine enemies to be assassinated) and a "Plus List" (the bigwigs who are secretly funding international terrorism). Interintell, then, has three new missions to accomplish: track down Erik; warn the people on the Minus List (Renwick himself is one of them); and somehow get hold of the Plus List before it falls into the hands of the USSR or other terrorist-deal-makers. Meanwhile, too, it becomes clear that there's an informer somewhere in the Interintell organization. Unfortunately, however, despite all these Missions Improba-

ble, the plotting here is limp and suspenseless—as Renwick and his cronies wander around (Ethiopia, New York, Paris, Switzerland), find a few bodies, exchange a few shots, knock off Erik, and eventually locate the chateau of super-villain Klaus Sudak. And, though everybody constantly *worries* that Nina *might* get kidnapped, she remains a bland, inactive mini-matron throughout. So, with no imperiled heroine to identify with and no conviction in MacInnes' sluggish, comic-book terrorism, this is her weakest work ever—but don't underestimate the obliging nature of a long-time, loyal readership. (pp. 755-56)

> A review of "Cloak of Darkness," in Kirkus Reviews (copyright © 1982 The Kirkus Service, Inc.), Vol. L, No. 13, July 1, 1982, pp. 755-56.

MICHELE SLUNG

In Helen MacInnes's novels—"**Cloak of Darkness**" is her 20th—every cafe and konditorei in Europe is a launching pad for terrorist activity, funded, encouraged and often directly organized by that source of all global evil, the K.G.B. The hand that brushes the Sacher torte crumbs off a lapel may shortly be carrying a Russian grenade. For many years Miss MacInnes has been the Claire Sterling of fiction; not even détente thawed her cold-war message. In "**Prelude to Terror**" (1978), the heroine, a Western agent, summed up the prevailing attitude: "There's a job to be done, a necessary job. Someone has to do it; we can't all sit back and watch the totalitarians take over." She goes on, "I know it has to be done. Or else we'll all end up regimented nonentities, scared to death to step out of line or raise our voices. Everything and everyone in place according to the book of Marx." (p. 15)

Actually, the characters in all of Miss MacInnes's books, especially the last three decades' worth, are interchangeably innocuous. Good guys are good, bad guys bad, with descriptive seasonings omitted. If writing were a salad bar, Helen MacInnes would be iceberg lettuce, bland but serviceable. (pp. 15, 33)

While [espionage writers such as John le Carré] dwelt on the modern spy's ambivalences, emotional paralyses and other assorted neuroses, Miss MacInnes, her formula pretty much intact, continued to see the enemy with single-minded revulsion.

But it's not her refusal to go "modern" and "psychological" that's wrong. . . . The problem is rather her lack of verve, the way in which her books are as chill as the war she's depicting. It's enough to make one long for temperature-raising doses of sex and sadism, although the readers who have made Miss MacInnes a best-selling writer would no doubt disagree. A cross between Ayn Rand and Phyllis Whitney, without the redeeming excesses of either, Miss MacInnes has built an *oeuvre* of strangely funless thrillers.

"**Cloak of Darkness**" is no exception. . . .

On the one hand, it's hard to fault Miss MacInnes for portraying a normal-seeming guy with the good manners to call his wife so she won't wait dinner. But the effect of these details is to let in an odor of bygone days—not wholly gone, but not retrievable either, even during a period of sociopolitical recidivism. For Miss MacInnes, the C.I.A. and related bodies will always be on the side of the angels, and the dress code in heaven specifies button-down collars. . . .

Murder and mayhem occur, but no really likable character meets his maker, which has not always been the case in Miss MacInnes's previous books. The end, which arrives long after one is ready for it, is tidy and aseptically romantic; more MacInnes novels than not are sealed with a kiss after the Iron Curtain has once again closed on its own.

Intelligence work probably is dull and conventional. One should be grateful that Miss MacInnes's characters don't keep office hours and play golf on the weekends—on the reader's time, so to speak. **"Cloak of Darkness"** is not a dreadful thriller; it simply doesn't thrill. And the suspense, where it exists, is inserted like toothpicks in a club sandwich; it could be extracted entire, leaving the plot unchanged. (p. 33)

Michele Slung, "Good Guys, Bad Guys," in The New York Times Book Review *(© 1982 by The New York Times Company; reprinted by permission), September 26, 1982, pp. 15, 33.*

Derek Mahon

1941-

Irish poet, editor, critic, and essayist.

Of the several skillful poets who emerged in Northern Ireland during the 1960s, Mahon is considered the most eclectic in themes and technique. Unlike his compatriots Seamus Heaney, John Montague, and Michael Longley, who focus on Irish history, society, or culture, Mahon is more detached. Born in Northern Ireland to Protestant parents, but distressed by the violence and unrest within Ulster, Mahon lives and writes in England. A sense of exile pervades his poetry.

With his first two volumes of poetry, *Night Crossing* (1968) and *Lives* (1972), Mahon came to be regarded as a gifted craftsman. When *The Snow Party* (1975) and the "selected collected" *Poems: 1962-78* (1979) were published, however, Mahon developed a stronger reputation as an important poet. These works present what have come to be Mahon's primary themes: the decay of civilization and the alienation and isolation of the modern individual. Mahon explores these concerns from the standpoint of an outsider, sorrowfully observing the winding down of order and meaning in the world. His finest achievement to date, "A Disused Shed in Co. Wexford" in *The Snow Party*, has been described as one of the finest British poems to have been published during the 1970s. Its description of a shed wherein hundreds of mushrooms are huddled has led to various interpretations concerning human aspirations.

Although Mahon's subjects are usually serious and his outlook bleak, his verse is consistently balanced by wit and a sharp sense of life's ironies. These qualities, along with Mahon's tight linguistic control, appeal to both critics and readers. Having "tidied up" and collected his early verse, Mahon has embarked on a new phase characterized by a wider imaginative range and including the recent volumes *Courtyards in Delft* (1981) and *The Hunt by Night* (1982).

ROBIN SKELTON

[Derek Mahon's collection *Night Crossing*] suffers from gentility. . . . He writes deftly, levelly, subtly, reminding one of the controlled mild ironies of Larkin, though he lacks Larkin's nostalgia and Larkin's particular usage of ennui and anxiety. Moreover, he does, from time to time, edge into romanticism and, in his *Legacies, after Villon,* he reveals considerable rhythmical vitality and some sardonic gusto. This is a good book, but a safe book. It was the Choice of the British Poetry Book Society and some of the poems won an Eric Gregory Award. One can see why, even while yet again realizing that the very coherence and control which makes the book an award winner is also that which makes one restlessly wish for poems whose idiosyncratic originality would make for more excitement and more controversy. (p. 400)

Robin Skelton, "Five Poets and Their Stances," in Poetry (© 1969 by The Modern Poetry Association; reprinted by permission of the Editor of Poetry), Vol. CXIV, No. 6, September, 1969, pp. 397-401.*

Photograph by Michael K. Barron; courtesy of The Gallery Press

THE TIMES LITERARY SUPPLEMENT

No one has satisfactorily explained how it is that a whole young generation of Irish poets—Heaney, Mahon, Longley, Muldoon and others—is apparently devoted to the well-made poem at a time when their English, Scottish and to a smaller degree Welsh contemporaries have almost entirely thrown it overboard in favour either of grim fragments or of vapid maunderings. The longest poem in Derek Mahon's [*Lives*], **"Beyond Howth Head"**, is of a shapely fluency which set the pattern for the verse-letters of Seamus Heaney and Michael Longley: behind it all there is perhaps the shadow of the Robert Lowell of "Near the Ocean" and "Waking Early Sunday Morning". Whatever the explanation, these new poems of Mr Mahon's have an attractive suppleness and wit. What stops them from going beyond that is a common quality of being marginalia, literary notes (**"An Image from Beckett"**, **"J. P. Donleavy's Dublin"**, **"After Cavafy"**, **"Edvard Munch"**). Not that one pays much heed to those remarks of Kingsley Amis's years ago, about all the topics and subjects one shouldn't write about; but "secondhand" often implies "shop-soiled", and Mr Mahon's eyes and words are so fresh that it seems a pity to let them steam up with literariness. . . .

"Moving Around," in The Times Literary Supplement (© Times Newspapers Ltd. (London) 1972; reproduced from The Times Literary Supplement *by permission), No. 3667, June 9, 1972, p. 651.**

ALAN BROWNJOHN

Between *Night Crossing* in 1968 and his new collection, *Lives,* Derek Mahon produced a very promising . . . pamphlet called *Ecclesiastes.* It now looks like a bridge between a pleasant but slightly too romantic and too tidy early style and something much tougher and more ingenious. *Lives* is a very good book, difficult and cryptic, but far more versatile and skilful technically, and managing to be both original and moving about his troubled Irish settings without being derivative or simplistic. There is no comfort in his new poems, very little of the nostalgia he was once prone to. 'Entropy', the title of one of them, might be said to be a central theme: modern society, with its fitted carpets, 'ploughshare factories', 'bright cars' and 'ditched bicycles', is running down in this bleak, brooding landscape where the past offers no valid illusions to live by and a poet's 'germinal ironies' offer the only kind of (very marginal) hope. (p. 842)

Alan Brownjohn, "Change Direction," in New Statesman *(© 1972 The Statesman & Nation Publishing Co. Ltd.), Vol. 83, No. 2152, June 16, 1972, pp. 842-43.**

P. N. FURBANK

The first poem in Derek Mahon's *Lives* is about arriving home in Dublin, distraught, after a Transatlantic flight: and something like the time- and place-confusion of jet-travellers gives the book its theme. The poems, written from that Atlantic island whose aerials are turned towards Britain and America, are about wanting to locate oneself, to decide to what parts of the human inheritance to direct one's aerial. Are signals still to be received from Raftery, the saints or Stone Age man? Or does the poet, like the anthropologist,

> know too much
> To be anything any more?

A beautiful poem, 'In the Aran Islands', turns, in construction as well as in thought, on this axis. Witnessing a pub-singer, one of his hands 'earthed to his girl', the other cupping his ear to hear his own song, the poet sees it as what he longs for himself—to be doubly located, in the here and now and elsewhere. . . . It is a reassuring vision, cancelled simultaneously by a less comfortable one: a solitary seagull, going out like the song into the Atlantic night, reminds him of the wildness he must always lack. There is tact and precision in Mahon's rendering of such turning of his thoughts upon themselves, such tentative trying-on of different lives (the 'lives' of his title). There are, as well, fine intellectual high-jinks in the long verse letter 'Beyond Howth Head'—'Dover Beach' done over by Auden—in which he reviews his theme more discursively. This is a sparse and not very ambitious collection, but the work of a sure talent. (p. 375)

P. N. Furbank, "Knockabouts" (© British Broadcasting Corp. 1972; reprinted by permission of P. N. Furbank), in The Listener, *Vol. 88, No. 2269, September 21, 1972, pp. 374-75.**

DOUGLAS DUNN

If events in Ireland have been thought malefic in their relations to the art of poetry (as they are to almost everything else) then that may be the reason why Heaney and Derek Mahon have both maintained two distinct styles apiece. One can be used for the racial-*cum*-archaeological manoeuvres of their imaginations, or simply the lyricism towards which they are drawn by temperament, and another for more direct utterance, for the kind of poem which, in their Irish circumstances, is expected of them.

The formula is too simple, and suggests a similarity between Heaney and Mahon which doesn't exist. Mahon's art is one of elegance, in which the assurance of his skill aspires to suavity, to an ease of writing in which the labour of making will be inconspicuous but impressive. Heaney's poems on the other hand are hewn, as if he wants to give the impression that, like Gaelic poets of old, he composes in the dark with a boulder on his chest. Mahon is also less immersed in the culture and history of Ireland. He appears to be re-enacting the Irish gesture of flight from possible parochialism towards a more sophisticated milieu of Europe complicated by home-looking, by the love-hate affections of the literary exile.

Yet it is these glances towards home, or, rather, intense stares productive of irascibility or melancholy, that, at present, predominate. This happens virtually on account of the over-literariness of many of his other poems. "**Hommage to Malcolm Lowry**", "**After Nerval**", or "**Epitaph for Flann O'Brien**" are examples. No matter the sincerity of these genuflections, Mahon's cleverness, wit, and grace are preferable when working against less literary subjects. "**Cavafy**", for instance, though literary enough in its origins, is an exhilarating series of poems.

Mahon's image of enchantment is summarised for him in the life of the gipsies. He has written about this in his earlier books. In the new collection [*The Snow Party*] he imitates a poem by Philippe Jaccottet, "Les Gitanes." A world of bandana and banjo, sing-songs under the stars at places with no disheartening historical associations—it looks like self-indulgence, though Mahon is too alert to allow his writing to create anything so inept.

Mahon's consciousness controls his imagination, as it must, to save the integrity of imagination and prevent it from being the repository of mere longings. (pp. 78-9)

The finest poem in *The Snow Party* is "**A Disused Shed in Co. Wexford.**" The poem starts with a literary occasion, but Mahon leaps over the possible limitations of that; the poem blazes off the page, and is the consummation of his writing so far, simply one of the finest poems of the decade. There is nothing wrong with it; and the same can be said for "**The Banished Gods.**"

To say of a poem that there's "nothing wrong with it" might sound as grudging as the terms of praise said to be characteristic of the great jazz player, the late Pee Wee Russell—"it doesn't bother me." But I think it's true praise. Neither Mahon nor Hugo Williams, though, is a poet of negative virtues, writing tight little syntactical perfections which protect, lovingly, a single precious image. Mahon's "elegance" is more significant than that; he is not playing for safety but living up to a subjectively formed stylistic ideal within which he can be seen to *perform* in language without sacrificing what he feels for his concerns. (pp. 80-1)

Douglas Dunn, "Mañana Is Now," in Encounter *(© 1975 by Encounter Ltd.), Vol. XLV, No. 5, November, 1975, pp. 76-81.**

ANTHONY THWAITE

In a verse letter by Michael Longley, a fellow Ulsterman, Derek Mahon is addressed approvingly as one of the "poetic conservatives''. He might well take umbrage; for the spirit that emerges from his poems is one which, while it hungers for ceremony and inherited order, has only the wannest faith that ceremony survives or that such order has relevance. Wistful, reticent, resigned, the poems in *The Snow Party* sound like the fastidious reflections of self-imposed exile. . . .

Lost futures, rather than Mr [Seamus] Heaney's lost pasts, are the substance of Mr Mahon's poems. **"The Last of the Fire Kings"**, **"Thammuz"**, **"The Banished Gods"** and (a beautifully judged stroke of minimalism) **"Flying"** are all hesitant reachings forward to possibilities just beyond the range of understanding. In these, and in other poems such as **"The Snow Party"** and in parts of the **"Cavafy"** sequence, there is a sardonic aestheticism, a diffident acknowledgment that art can arrest and fix at least something in what would otherwise be mere noise and flux. Two prose-poems, **"A Hermit"** and **"The Apotheosis of Tins"**, play humorous variations on the theme. . . .

For all its circumstantial wryness, this is tenuous stuff, however, and it seems to me, reading *The Snow party,* Mr Mahon's third book, that there is some danger of his talent thinning itself away into arbitrariness and whimsy. As if to show that he can indeed manage something more solid, he ends the collection with its most impressive poem, a meditation with the bleak title **"A Disused Shed in Co. Wexford"**. Here "A thousand mushrooms crowd to a keyhole", and are celebrated as dumb survivors whose tenacity spells out a hard-won lesson. . . .

[With] Mr Mahon one senses a pressure of events behind the taut evasiveness. . . .

Anthony Thwaite, "At the Point of Speech," in The Times Literary Supplement *(© Times Newspapers Ltd. (London) 1975; reproduced from* The Times Literary Supplement *by permission), No. 3843, November 7, 1975, p. 1327.*

TERENCE BROWN

In Derek Mahon's poetry it is possible to see what can be made of the Irish urban and suburban experience. . . . [Mahon] has produced a small body of remarkable verse, developing out of a sense of the complex, aesthetically uninspiring tensions of Northern Protestant middle-class identity. Mahon has spoken of the difficulties of writing out of such a background, from a 'suburban situation which has no mythology or symbolism built into it'. . . . (p. 192)

In 'Glengormley' and 'As It Should Be' Mahon considers the implications of suburban existence in a country whose past has been heroic, dramatic, mythological. 'Glengormley' recognises the new heroism of suburban survival, contrasting it, a little too predictably, with Ulster's prehistoric titanism. . . . The tone throughout is ambivalent, suggesting only partial acquiescence in suburban order. . . . The quality of life has no doubt superficially improved . . . but the poem concludes with ironic deflation. . . . For Mahon is no eulogist of suburban possibilities nor of industrial society's blessings. He cannot even rise to [Louis] MacNeice's excited response to its bright surfaces, sensing rather a new barbarism beneath a façade of materialist disregard for ideology, social hierarchy and commitment. . . . (pp. 193-94)

An antipathetic reaction to the conditions of advanced capitalism is, of course, a fairly commonplace response in modern poetry. Often the poet who responds in this fashion turns to a local tradition in quest of roots, identity, fragments that he

may shore against what he feels is the contemporary ruin. Mahon rejects such a strategy, such imaginative Jacobinism, since the local tradition he knows in his bones is not one with which he feels much ready sympathy. Mahon's 'hidden Ulster' is no Gaelic pastoral-aristocratic idyll, but the Protestant planter's historical myth of conquest, and careful, puritan self-dependence frozen to a vicious, stupid bigotry which constricts personal identity, crippling the possibility of change, growth and excellence. . . . So 'Ecclesiastes' is a powerful, impassioned rejection of the tradition that lies beneath the surface life of Belfast's superficially emancipated suburbia. It is a denunciation of the Northern Protestant's self-understanding and a call to him, to abandon a stance of intolerant rectitude and ridiculous isolationism which is the fruit of an assertive, black-minded self-dependence. . . . (p. 195)

Recognising, as [Roy] McFadden did before him, the impossibility of any simple regional loyalty Mahon, like McFadden, is drawn to romantic outsiders, individuals, who assert their individuality not in dour, provincial self-satisfaction but in bohemian excess, rhetorical panache, by style in the face of metaphysical bleakness. So he celebrates De Quincey, Van Gogh, Dowson and the tragic generation, a forger who works in agony and fanaticism. . . . There is something in [his] poems of that fabricated cosmopolitanism we have detected in earlier poets, suggesting Mahon's insecurity, caught between a narrow society he dislikes and the larger world outside his province, where he must make his life. What is not fabricated is the note of loneliness, bordering on terror, that informs his work. Some of his poems treat journeys by car, train and plane, as essentially solitary, if not quite so finally desperate, as those in MacNeice's late work. . . . [Like MacNeice] Mahon not only experiences cultural dislocation, but moments of metaphysical *frisson.* . . . Like MacNeice also, he senses an interdependence of dark and light knowing that life's moments of vision and ecstasy are set against the dark and cold. . . . (pp. 196-97)

History, it is important to make clear, does not mean for Derek Mahon that complex of Irish linguistic, ethnic, religious and geographic truths sensed as permanencies which it is in the poetry of John Montague or Seamus Heaney. History for Mahon is no saga of land and people but a process, 'the elemental flux' ('**Rocks**') which casts one man as coloniser, another as colonised, and man in innumerable roles. So . . . [*Lives*] must be read as a series of experiments in perspective, in which modern Irish and European political and historical experience are viewed from different spatial and temporal angles.

'**Edvard Munch**,' for example, contemplates one of the Norwegian artist's canvases, considering the mysterious relationship of material things to historical and political process—comparing the relationship implied in the painting to that in experience itself. '**The Archaeologist**', '**What Will Remain**' and '**Entropy**' step into post-history and into gigantic landscapes to see man's life *sub specie aeternitatis,* the planet littered with capitalism's banal bric-à-brac. . . . '**Consolations of Philosophy**' and '**Gipsies Revisited**' balefully regard the assumed security of modern bourgeois life from the grave and from the tinkers' roadside, while the bright searching images of '**An Image from Beckett**' reveal a landscape and city of some unlikely human future hopefully immune to death, irony and absurdity. . . . '**A Dark Country**' tests the possibility, by contrast, of local, personal attachments in a lyric of moving, tentative affirmation . . . while '**Lives**' is a witty series of perspectives on Being itself, in its unlikely manifestations.

Two things raise these perspectivist experiments above the level of clever mannerism: the poet's depth of humane feeling and his imaginative range. In these poems the poet has made a virtue of necessity. Accepting a dissociated sensibility as the inevitable possession of a Protestant Ulsterman, he has exploited his understanding of fragmentation and flux in a series of richly imaginative poems, in which confusion or triviality might so easily have resulted. Derek Mahon has expressed admiration for writers of the American South, who managed to write, as he sees it, good poems out of a 'morally ambiguous situation'. In *Lives* and in his more recent poem **'A Disused Shed in County Wexford'** Mahon has given good grounds for belief that he has the necessary imaginative and intellectual gifts to emulate them. (pp. 198-200)

Terence Brown, "Four New Voices: Poets of the Present," in his Northern Voices: Poets from Ulster *(© Terence Brown, 1975), Rowman and Littlefield, 1975, pp. 171-213.**

SEAMUS DEANE

[Mahon's] imagination seems to be at once haunted and attracted by the thought of a total apocalyptic disaster which would wipe out the mess of the modern world and leave instead only the ticking of "a slow clock of condensation." Yet his other favorite scenario, "the ideal society which will replace our own," is as elusive and as ironically observed as the apocalypse. For between these two falls the shadow of Belfast, the dark industrial waste in which Mr. Mahon goes time and again to seek what he calls "the original poetry of our lives." The violence of recent years and the weight of the north's urban and spiritual dreariness have increasingly left their imprint on Mahon's work. From one point of view which he assumes, Belfast is the wasteland, the terminal point, the very antithesis of what a culture might be. But it is also the poet's own territory, his community, lost, but still passionately wishing to be found again. . . . The struggle between community and wasteland which consumes so much of Mr. Mahon's writing is not resolved in favor of either. More subtle than a resolution, there is an interweave, so that often we find the longing for community, "the ideal society," spoken by those who are most utterly victimized by the wastage of modern existence. In fact, as in **"After Nerval"** and **"The Apotheosis of Tins,"** it is the very wastage which speaks or is spoken for. The rubble contains within itself the heavenly city we failed to realize.

No modern Irish poet has taken the weight of responsibility with so much elegance and panache. The very nature of Mr. Mahon's language . . . works, in its eloquence against the bleak content. His style is at war with his meaning, for the tight linguistic control and the clipped, educated vocabulary evoke a sense of rationality in contrast to the irrationality or apocalyptic nature of the experiences they render. One means by which Mr. Mahon sharpens this paradoxical effect is by the cancellation of time. His poems have a locale, but their voice is that of **"The Last of the Fire Kings,"** the voice of one who is "through with history." . . . History, especially in its Irish form, but not only in that, is a kind of dream, a communal symbol of what we are, reduced by the author to an arid nonidentity in the actual world of the present. But we remain aware that Mr. Mahon remains haunted by the fragile possibilities of what the dream might, in another world than this, have become.

Two poems in particular in [*The Snow Party*] retain that fragility—the title poem and the final one, **"A Disused Shed in**

Co. Wexford." This latter is dedicated to the English novelist J. G. Farrell and owes something to his novel *Troubles*. . . . In a disused shed, locked in darkness since the days of the (last?) Irish civil war, a forest of mushrooms has been growing, straining toward the minimal light of the keyhole. The "We" of the poem, inquisitive tourists with their flash cameras, open the door, and in a burst of light the weak lost souls of the past are exposed, pleading, to the vacuous present. . . . Here again Mr. Mahon reaches out to rescue the lost history of the victimized, the lost possibilities of the silent, of the inanimate, of the history in which a future other than the one which we now have once resided. In the other poem, **"The Snow Party,"** we meet again with an image of stillness and pale fragility, a Japanese snow party, as fixed in its odd silence as a Japanese print, while beyond, in the contemporaneous European world, "they are burning / Witches and heretics / In the boiling square." One image is out of history. It is a dream of civility and perfection. The other is in history, savage and barbarous. They are interwoven with one another as the imagination, enduring, is interlocked with time. In this fashion Derek Mahon takes the burden of his culture. Along with the element of repudiation there lives the element of involvement. (pp. 205-07)

But what we recognize finally is that the inflection of these poems is toward silence, a home "safe from the historical nightmare." In that respect Mr. Mahon's poetry often reads, with its bitter courage, like the last will and testament of a dying culture. (p. 207)

Seamus Deane, "The Appetites of Gravity: Contemporary Irish Poetry," in The Sewanee Review *(reprinted by permission of the editor; © 1976 by The University of the South), Vol. LXXXIV, No. 1, Winter, 1976, pp. 199-208.**

BRIAN DONNELLY

With three published volumes of poetry behind him—*Night-Crossing* (1968), *Lives* (1972), *The Snow Party* (1975)—Derek Mahon has now clearly emerged as one of the most talented of the present generation of Northern Ireland poets. Indeed, in the wider context of English poetry of the last ten years, his work has retained qualities that looked increasingly likely to disappear with Auden's death—qualities of wit and wry humour in poems that reveal a lively and quirky intelligence. He has early shown a technical mastery in poems where humour and a lightness of touch often combine to achieve an unexpected seriousness. Taken as a whole, one can discern in his work a preoccupation with man's spiritual loneliness and isolation which is reflected in the large number of poems that deal with individuals or groups forced by temperament or circumstances to live outside the normal social framework. At its most sombre, Mahon's verse reveals an acute awareness of the brevity of all human life and the futility and pathos of man's existence as a finite being. . . .

As a northern Irishman Mahon has, on several occasions, dealt with the state of the Six Counties in his poetry. These handfuls of poems are, in their way, as valid and moving as many of the more historically conscious probings of Seamus Heaney and John Montague, poets who have made the evolution of the province their chief concern as artists. These poems are, moreover, part of Mahon's preoccupation with the individual's sense of isolation, for in them the speaker is usually looking at events in his native place from the outside, at a safe, if uncomfortable, vantage point. In **'Glengormley'** *(Night-Crossing)*, a poem written before the present unrest began, Mahon celebrated the then unheroic quality of life in a Belfast suburb. The tone and humour of the opening lines recalls to mind much of Mac-Neice's verse. . . . (p. 23)

Viewed in retrospect, few utterances by Ulstermen can have proven so ironic given the course of events in the province over the past six years. When Mahon has confronted the troubles in his subsequent collections it has been as an exile (he has resided in England for several years) and the state of exile, of being isolated in place and time, is a condition which he explores over and over again in his verse. (p. 24)

[The] specific instance of a general feeling of being cut-off from the goings on of the majority of men occupies a central place in Mahon's poetry. In many of his best and most characteristic poems the speaker or central character is a lonely, isolated figure, an odd man out. We encounter him in all three collections, in such poems as **'Grandfather'**, **'My Wicked Uncle'** *(Night-Crossing)*, **'The Last Dane'**, **'A Dying Art'** *(Lives)* and in **'A Refusal to Mourn'** *(The Snow Party)* in which Mahon memorably recreates the life of an old man living alone in the small but telling details of his lonely existence. . . . (pp. 24-5)

However, it is those characters who are totally alienated from any form of normal social life and aspirations that he has so vividly given voice to in his poetry. His affinity with Beckett in this respect is first made apparent in the fourth section of **'Four Walks in the Country near Saint Brieuc'**, entitled, **'Exit Molloy'** *(Night-Crossing)*. . . . In this short monologue Mahon has succeeded in capturing the tone of the Beckett hero, a tone of bewildered and resigned detachment from the sufferings of the body heightened by characteristic pedantry.

Life's failures appear again and again in all three of his collections. Yet, no matter how bleak or desolate man's fate seems, the verse usually displays a grim, ironic wit and humour which holds final despair at arm's length. Sometimes, however, this proves almost malicious as in the address to the poets of the 'tragic' generation in **'Dowson and Company'** *(Night-Crossing)*. . . . (p. 25)

But it is in the dramatic monologue that Mahon's alienated characters come most fully and convincingly to life. The monologue is a form that he has perfected and which allows his wit full play behind the mask of the speaker. **'Legacies'**, the final poem in *Night-Crossing*, is a case in point. This poem is a free imitation of François Villon's 'Le Lais' in which the poet, cold and destitute, writes a will which pours scorn on the world which has rejected him. The measure of Mahon's achievement is that he succeeds in vividly recreating the mood and spirit of the original French, a task that defeated Robert Lowell in his rendering of Villon in *Imitations*. (p. 26)

In a poem like **'Legacies'** Mahon is restoring to English poetry qualities which are rare at the present time—conversational narrative combined with wit, intelligence and humour capable of realising a deep seriousness. The fact that **'Legacies'** and many other poems have a literary basis (often in foreign literatures) is not a limitation, as some critics and reviewers have suggested. What is important is that Mahon almost always transcends the merely literary which can be seen to serve as starting points for his exploration of important human conditions and concerns.

The skill and ease in handling a colloquial narrative apparent in **'Legacies'** is seen to good advantage in the long verse letter **'Beyond Howth Head'** which concludes *Lives*. In this poem Mahon's wit is given wide scope. The form of the verse letter allows him to relax and to be discursive in his comments on life in general and Irish life in particular, much in the manner of Auden in his *Letter to Lord Byron*. Here Mahon is less intense in his view of life than in many of his other poems, although the swiftly moving narrative, carried along in neatly rounded couplets, contains a good deal of trenchant criticism of such issues as American involvement in south east Asia, the depopulation of the west of Ireland and Irish sexual morality. Yet, overall the mood is light as, for once at least, the poet has managed to put his more usual apocalyptic view of life into perspective, allowing that 'the pros outweigh the cons that glow / from Beckett's bleak *reductio*'. The poem ends on a well judged note of self-mockery which succeeds in keeping its comments on life from appearing pretentious. . . . (pp. 26-7)

The lighthearted mood of **'Beyond Howth Head'** is atypical of the prevailing atmosphere of *Night-Crossing* and *Lives* which in general create sombre visions of the human condition. This view of man's fate is extended and deepened in *Lives* as in **'Gipsies Revisited'** in which the life of the homeless and social outcasts is used as a metaphor of the real fate awaiting us all, only thinly disguised by the veneer of domestic well-being. . . . The projected vision of the world returned to its most primitive state is one that haunts Mahon's imagination. In **'Entropy'**, **'What Will Remain'** and **'Consolations of Philosophy'** *(Lives)* he approaches the bleak and unappealing negations of Beckett's *Lessness*. (p. 27)

Lives also includes poems that are sheer *tours de force* of the imagination. Such is the title poem, a play on the doctrine of reincarnation of the body. . . . Taken together, *Night-Crossing* and *Lives* show Mahon exploring and dramatising an attitude to life in a variety of forms. There is less a sense of development between them than a growing awareness on the part of the reader that the two parts of a single whole have been completed. In his most recent collection, *The Snow Party,* he has succeeded in moving far beyond the achievement of the earlier works. His central preoccupations remain the same, but there is clearly an attempt to encompass more in a wider diversity of forms and situations. Some of the poems in this collection would fit unobtrusively into either of his preceding volumes—**'Afterlives'**, **'The Gipsies'**, **'Epitaph for Flann O'Brien'**, **'September in Great Yarmouth'**, **'A Refusal to Mourn'** and the amusing concrete poem, **'The Window'**. But in the poems that give *The Snow Party* its distinctive mood and character there is reflected a significant deepening of the imaginative range of the earlier work.

Poems such as **'The Last of the Fire Kings'**, **'Thammuz'**, **'Matthew V. 29-30'** and the title poem all dwell upon the inability of the individual to escape from violence. (p. 29)

[Perhaps] the most curious preoccupation in *The Snow Party* is the attitude to the world of inanimate objects which, because they are the paraphernalia of everyday life that we take for granted and discard after they have served their purpose, can be seen as an extension of Mahon's concern with the plight of the human outcasts in the earlier collections. These poems are not all meant to be taken wholly seriously as in **'After Nerval'**. . . . **'The Apotheosis of Tins'** is in a similar vein, one of the two delicately organised prose poems in the book, in which a tin in a rubbish heap asserts the independence of the world of objects against human 'patronage' and 'reflective leisure'. This poem is skilful and clever, and Mahon is able to use the occasion to poke fun at aesthetic pretentiousness. The stilted academic jargon of the speaker, the mocking allusion to *Hamlet,* the threatening tone are all controlled in beautifully balanced periods. . . . (pp. 31-2)

These poems are, admittedly, lighthearted and quirky. Yet readers who may be prepared to dismiss Mahon for entering such quaint and obscure corners of the imagination will have to pause for further reflection on the poet's imaginative processes at the final poem of this kind, **'A Disused Shed in Co. Wexford'.** This is the concluding poem in *The Snow Party* and in it Mahon once again brings the inanimate world to life—in this instance 'a thousand mushrooms' locked away in a shed of a derelict country hotel. His evocation of their plight builds up into a convincing and moving metaphor of all the persecuted and forgotten peoples in human history. . . . Most critics, even those who see Mahon's poetry as 'tenuous stuff', the result of a talent 'thinning itself away into arbitrariness and whimsy' [see excerpt above by Anthony Thwaite] are agreed that this is an impressive achievement. Indeed, one reviewer regarded it as 'the consummation of his writing so far, simply one of the finest poems of the decade' [see excerpt above by Douglas Dunn]. Whether or not one is prepared to agree with this placing of the poem in a hierarchy—and I for one am—it is right to stress that **'A Disused Shed'** is the culmination of Mahon's work to date and not an isolated and fortuitous success. It treats that theme that has been central to his work since *Night-Crossing*—exclusion from ordinary life and harrowing solitude—in a way that reveals one of the undoubted strengths of his poetry which is its ability, because of its eccentric perspectives on the world, to offer a fresh view on central human concerns.

It would be a mistake to conclude an evaluation of Mahon's poetry by claiming for it a narrow seriousness. His work is serious, as I have attempted to suggest, but it contains, too, a good deal of whimsy spiced with intellectual mockery and word play which is none too common in English poetry today. Yet, it is when this lightness, or seeming lightness, and quirky vision combine with his assured technical mastery to create a poem like **'A Disused Shed in Co. Wexford'** that the full potential of Derek Mahon's poetic talent becomes apparent. (p. 34)

> Brian Donnelly, *"The Poetry of Derek Mahon," in*
> English Studies *(© 1979 by Swets & Zeitlinger B.V.),*
> *Vol. 60, No. 1, February, 1979, pp. 23-34.*

PETER PORTER

It is especially good to have Mahon's carefully edited 'selected collected' [*Poems: 1962-1978*]. It may be a little dismaying to find a poet under 40 devoting more time to tidying the drawers of his wardrobe than to adding new garments to it, but Mahon warns us that he may revise his poems still further, in the Auden manner. Mentioning Auden acts as a reminder that he and MacNeice issued their 'Collecteds' before their fortieth birthdays, and that precocious writers may have considerable achievements to their credit while still young. Mahon certainly has, and the fastidiousness which keeps his collection short also ensures that each poem is a properly accomplished work of art.

Mahon is not a characteristic Ulster poet: his version of lapidary is closer to Robert Graves's than to Yeats's. Yet childhood and adolescence in Ulster have left their mark on him—in poem after poem, he traces his wariness and refusal to be betrayed into easy afflatus to Irish distortions of reality.

Much of his work is pervaded by a sense of exile, and remembering the past becomes for him a matter of emblems and symbols. He is attracted to artists who have the power to make things from their various losses. . . . Mahon is a practitioner of the carefully stylised poem-as-letter, usually to Ireland from Europe or vice versa. **'Beyond Howth Head'** shows him tooling up for his own 'New Year Letter,' . . . but there is more awareness of unease, of being farther into a dangerous century, than there is in Auden.

> Peter Porter, *"Voices from Ulster," in* The Observer
> *(reprinted by permission of The Observer Limited),*
> *No. 9831, January 27, 1980, p. 39.**

BRIAN DONNELLY

In 'Tradition and the Individual Talent,' T. S. Eliot warns against the tendency to single out and praise those aspects of a writer's work 'in which he least resembles anyone else', adding that 'the most individual parts of his work may be those in which the dead poets, his ancestors, assert their immortality most vigorously'. This dictum is relevant in the case of Derek Mahon whose new collection, *Poems 1962-1978,* includes most of his previously collected work, as well as some twenty-three new poems, most of which are printed in the latter part of the book.

Many of the poems assert the immortality of MacNiece and Auden and reveal the powerful presence of Samuel Beckett. The influence of non-English speaking poets, especially the French, is also evident, both indirectly and in the fine imitations such as **'The Condensed Shorter Testament'**, a reworking of his earlier rendering of Villon in **'Legacies'** (*Night-Crossing,* 1968). Yet it is a measure of Mahon's true originality that he impresses us as being a uniquely individual voice in whom all influences have been melted down and absorbed in the crucible of his own quirky and fertile imagination. The sense we get from reading *Poems 1962-1978* is of being shown aspects of life from new angles that are at first disquieting and, finally, compelling. The vision of reality is often at odds with our normal perceptions and if it fails to illuminate it almost always amuses. In **'Glengormley,'** for example, Mahon celebrates the hum-drum existence of a Belfast suburb in a manner that is both gently mocking and affectionate. . . . His fascination with the ordinariness of the place is typical too, for he is, above all, a poet who imbues the prosaic with a tinge of romance. (pp. 131-32)

Much of Mahon's poetry is preoccupied with decay. His is an imagination that almost habitually conceives the impermanence of all human endeavour. In such poems as **'Entropy,' 'The Golden Bough'** and **'Consolations of Philosophy'** he imagines the world returned to its primal state, a wasteland of random matter, vegetation and silence. The trappings of civilised life are viewed as a thin veneer concealing the void into which all life will finally descend. (p. 133)

His most memorable poems are those in which [an] awareness of human destiny is charged with controlled pathos, as in **'A Disused Shed in Co. Wexford'** *(The Snow Party,* 1975), his finest single achievement so far. . . . [This poem] shows the imaginative richness and superb technical skill of this poet. The language is subtly evocative of a slow and lonely decay; the images are haunting. . . . (pp. 133-34)

Although Mahon comes from Belfast the civil disturbances of the last twelve years have not forced themselves directly upon his imagination. From time to time he has expressed unease with the business of writing verse while the bombs go off and innocent people die. . . . Yet the deepest impulse in his verse is to escape the claustrophobia and nightmare of Northern Ireland and to flee into the solitude of the self. The tension in his work, which has led to some of his best poems, is the realisation that one is inevitably caught up in history and that no release may be possible. (p. 134)

In spite of the fact that Mahon has not confronted the historical evolution of Irish violence in the direct manner of some of his contemporaries, he has, nevertheless, written poems in which his attitude to the ambiguities of life in the North is implicit rather than explicit. A case in point is **'The Snow Party'** in which Mahon succeeds in expressing the awful paradox that affronts the normal scale of human values: the coexistence of gross inhumanity with a civilised and decorous culture. His achievement is that his small stanzas obliterate the gap in space and time that allows us to conceive of these two orders of existence as being mutually exclusive. (pp. 135-36)

Most of the new poems [in *Poems 1962-1978*] are typical Mahon and, as well as the marvellous **'The Sea in Winter,' 'The Chinese Restaurant in Portrush'** and **'Heraclitus on Rivers'** are particularly fine. So, too, is the short and haunting **'Penshurst Place'** in which he evokes the elegance and barbarity of the high Renaissance in two beautifully cadenced stanzas.

Yet all is not well. Most of the earlier poems have been revised, some very slightly and a few substantially. Many have been given new titles. By and large I feel that the revised titles were unnecessary. . . . But the revisions bother me more and this is only partly owing to a dislike of the familiar being tampered with. In **'Matthew V. 29-30,'** for example, the larger stanzas seem to me to slow down the breathtaking pace of the original which is so much a part of this poem's total effect. . . . One could go on weighing the relative merits of the original versions of poems with these later ones. Suffice to say here that *Poems 1962-1978* is a splendid book. (pp. 136-37)

Brian Donnelly, "From Ninevieh to the Harbour Bar," in Ploughshares *(© 1980 by Ploughshares, Inc.), Vol. 6, No. 1, 1980, pp. 131-37.*

JACK HOLLAND

Since the mid-1960s, several Northern Irish poets have made their presence felt in the English literary world. The most praised, Seamus Heaney, has been hailed by some critics as a major poet—the most important since William Butler Yeats. There is now a growing interest in his work in America. Like Heaney, Derek Mahon has established himself in England as a considerable talent. His three volumes of poems have now been gathered into *Poems 1962-1978,* which will serve as a good introduction to his work for American readers.

There they will find a poetry that is poised, scrupulous and reserved. Irony is generally on hand to prevent escape into confessional self-indulgence. Like all good Irish poets, he does not fear artifice, nor does he eschew the offhand, conversational tone. He is very much a poet of light and form, at times pursuing a definition of Stephen Dedalus's "Ineluctable modality of the visible," as in the series **"Light Music."** . . . (p. 260)

Technically, Mahon's work is varied. He handles the long line with dexterity, as he does the octosyllabic couplet; he can rhyme unobtrusively, without jarring syntax, and can produce

the sorts of matter-of-fact prosy poems more in keeping with contemporary taste. His early mentor was Louis MacNeice—like Mahon, a Belfast-born Protestant. Though his occasional flights of flamboyant rhetoric are generally more successful than MacNeice's, Mahon shares his honest skepticism; both, when at their best, also share the urge to pay homage to the object as it is, to refine perception of the thing down to an ingenuous clarity.

In spite of his background, Mahon has little to say about the position of the poet amid Northern Ireland's troubles, except the occasional ironic comment. . . . His restraint of the issue is as refreshing as the lack of it in so many other Irish poets is nauseating.

Part of the reason that Mahon is not better known here is that he belongs to an Irish literary tradition not much appreciated in America—or England, for that matter. It is an urban tradition, as indubitably Irish as James Joyce or Samuel Beckett or Sean O'Casey. It shares the prevailing moods of Irish poetry—bitterness, melancholy, tenderness; but it has a powerful ironic edge to it and a searing objectivity. Its esthetic and ontological complexities do not fit in with the rural/pastoral stereotype of the Irish poet dear to certain cultural circles—a stereotype that would lead, say, to a preference for Heaney's work. It is to be hoped that Mahon's poetry will introduce that other—urban—tradition of Irish writing to new readers, who will find it a challenging and sometimes radical one. (pp. 260-61)

Jack Holland, "A Searing Objectivity," in The Nation *(copyright 1980 The Nation magazine, The Nation Associates, Inc.), Vol. 231, No. 8, September 20, 1980, pp. 260-61.*

ANDREW MOTION

Two years ago Derek Mahon published what he called the 'selected collected' edition of his poems. It was, he said, 'in some senses, a first book, the kind of thing you put behind you before proceeding to the real business of learning and trying to create'. Understandably, he was uncertain about what this 'real business' might produce. Apart from outlawing 'impertinent rhetoricism', he was content simply to advertise himself as being 'at last in a position to *begin*'. *Courtyards in Delft* contains the first 14 results—and it's perhaps not surprising that their concerns are strikingly similar to those of his earlier work: the Troubles, the nature of human survival, the obstinate durability of 'mute phenomena', and the value of personal relationships. There is, though, a marked change in the manner of his new poems, if not in their matter. In the past, he has invariably worked best in one of two distinct styles: the cryptic-imagistic—often using details and devices reminiscent of Beckett—and the candid-explanatory. By combining the two in his most successful poem, **'A Disused Shed in Co Wexford',** he made an exception to prove the rule: its images retain their elusive mystery in spite of being subject to his lucid analysis.

Most of the poems in *Courtyards in Delft* attempt to recreate this balance and fusion. But while still flickering quickly and wittily from image to image, they also tend to use longer and more elaborate verse forms, and to argue their themes with greater deliberation. . . . The danger of this development, obviously, is that the poems will diminish the resonance of their themes by spelling them out too clearly. . . .

There are a number of moments when Mahon seems, tacitly, to be asking himself whether he should persist with this line of development, or revert to the strategies and strengths of his earlier work. . . .

Noticing this dilemma helps to explain why three of the most arresting new poems deal with paintings. By depicting fixed moments in time, they offer refuge from flux at the same time as they highlight its difficulties. That is to say, they help him moderate his need to 'begin' again, and encourage him to write—in the title poem for example—without any sign of self-conscious striving. . . . (p. 20)

Andrew Motion, "Facing Two Ways," in New Statesman *(© 1981 The Statesman & Nation Publishing Co. Ltd.), Vol. 101, No. 2618, May 22, 1981, pp. 20-1.**

JOHN MOLE

Derek Mahon's new collection [*The Hunt by Night*] contains several poems good enough to place alongside his **"A Disused Shed in Co. Wexford"**, a justly celebrated piece. . . . It is not only in his confident use of the familiar stanza form that Mahon can be seen as the Marvell amongst his contemporaries and compatriots. He is a truly witty writer, and his recent work reminds me of T. S. Eliot's observation that all too often one is confronted by "serious poets who seem afraid of acquiring wit lest they lose intensity." That this is a genuine risk is illustrated by numerous, honourable present-day poets, but in Mahon's case what Eliot calls "wit's internal equilibrium" is immediately evident. Whereas there has always been a tough reasonableness behind his sometimes very slight lyric grace, there are all the signs that the lyric grace in itself is becoming tougher. . . . (p. 71)

Mahon's poems are full of radiant objects which shine all the brighter for their setting in a dark, chilly universe of exile and unrest, and a hard, crystalline energy informs the measured verse.

Mahon can, at times, appear a solemnly playful, self-aware doomsday dandy, and in **"Another Sunday Morning"** he simultaneously assumes and is amused by the stance. The echoes of Robert Lowell are unmistakable and, given the title, clearly deliberate, but the sardonic viewpoint is more reminiscent of Louis MacNeice in Regents Park than Lowell in Central. (pp. 71-2)

John Mole, "Respectable Formalities," in Encounter *(© 1983 by Encounter Ltd.), Vol. LX, No. 4, April, 1983, pp. 69-75.**

Bernard Malamud

1914-

American novelist and short story writer.

Malamud ranks as one of the most significant contributors to contemporary American literature. His fictional world, most often urban and Jewish, is formed around the struggle for survival of characters who face the particular hardships of modern existence. Their survival depends upon their ability to combat life's inevitable suffering by breaking through the barriers of personal isolation and finding human contact, compassion, and faith in the goodness of others. The typical Malamudian hero stumbles through this process in a tragic yet comic way, invoking both pity and humor. Although Malamud is a prolific writer and the recipient of many prestigious literary awards, he is perhaps best known for his novel *The Fixer* (1967), which was awarded both the Pulitzer Prize and the National Book Award.

The Natural (1952), Malamud's first novel, is perhaps his most symbolic. On the surface, the novel explores the life of an American baseball player; yet, as with all of Malamud's works, there are various interpretations of the deeper levels of meaning. For instance, some critics cite evidence of the Arthurian legend of the Holy Grail, while others apply T. S. Eliot's "wasteland" myth in their analysis. In many ways it foreshadows predominant future concerns: a suffering protagonist struggling to reconcile moral dilemmas, to act according to what is right and good, and to come to grips with his existence. These themes recur in Malamud's second novel, *The Assistant* (1957), in the portrayal of the life of Frank Alpine, a cynical anti-semitic youth who goes to work for a Jewish grocer. Through this contact Frank learns to find grace and dignity in his own identity. Described as a fable, as are many of Malamud's stories, this novel affirms the redemptive value of maintaining faith in the inherent goodness of the human soul. Malamud's first collection of short stories, *The Magic Barrel* (1958), was awarded the Pulitzer Prize. Like *The Assistant,* most of the stories in this collection depict the search for dignity and meaning within the grim entrapment of poor urban settings. They often resemble the Yiddish folk tale in their humor and their use of character-types drawn from Hasidic traditions. Many of Malamud's short stories have been reprinted recently in *The Stories of Bernard Malamud* (1983), a collection which includes two new stories.

Based in part on Malamud's teaching career at Oregon State University, *A New Life* (1961) superimposes the hero's quest for significance and understanding on a satiric mockery of academia. Malamud's next novel, *The Fixer,* is one of his most powerful works. Derived from the historical account of Mendel Beiliss, a Russian Jew who was accused of murdering a Christian child, and also drawing on East European Jewish mysticism, *The Fixer* turns this terrifying story of torture and humiliation into a parable of human triumph. *The Tenants* (1971) returns to an urban setting, where the theme of self-exploration is developed through the contrast between two writers, one Jewish and the other black, struggling to survive in a New York City ghetto. Within the context of their confrontations, Malamud also explores the conflict between art and life. The protagonist of *Dubin's Lives* (1979), as with Harry

Lesser and Willie Spearmint in *The Tenants*, attempts to create a sense of worth for himself, both as a man and as a writer. A biographer who escapes into his work to avoid the reality of his life, William Dubin bumbles through comically disastrous attempts at love and passion in an effort to find self-fulfillment.

God's Grace (1982) differs from Malamud's earlier works in its scope and presentation of subject matter. Set in the near future immediately after a nuclear disaster which leaves only one human being alive, *God's Grace* explores the darkness of human morality, the nature of God, and the vanity and destruction which has become an integral part of the human race. Critical reception to this work varies immensely: some critics feel that the contrast between the serious moral fable and the humor of a situation, in which the protagonist alternately converses with God and a group of apes, provides a uniquely intriguing narrative. Others, however, feel the structure of the novel does not support the seriousness and ambition of its themes. But in common with his other works, *God's Grace* expresses Malamud's intensely humanistic concerns, along with the humor and insight that have made him a leading American author.

(See also *CLC,* Vols. 1, 2, 3, 5, 8, 9, 11, 18; *Contemporary Authors,* Vols. 5-8, rev. ed.; *Dictionary of Literary Biography,* Vol. 2; and *Dictionary of Literary Biography Yearbook: 1980.*)

SHELDON J. HERSHINOW

Writing in a parable mode that uses (to varying degrees) his own distinctive mix of realism, myth, fantasy, romance, comedy, and fairy tale, Malamud has continued to grow artistically. Always a writer willing to take risks, he has freely experimented with new themes and techniques, especially in his short stories. He has over the years developed considerable stylistic range and has often attempted to move beyond the pale of his "Jewish" humanism. These efforts are always interesting, frequently successful. Yet his great achievement, as an artist and as a moralist, has come from his success in creating a distinctive fictional world that is the embodiment of his "Jewish" humanism.

Central to Malamud's moral sensibility is his positive, pragmatic attitude toward suffering. . . . His fiction suggests that life—at lease for goodhearted, humane people—is a search to make unavoidable suffering meaningful. Nearly all of his novels center on the suffering that results from the conflict between human freedom and human limitations, with the stress on the latter rather than the former. Frank Alpine (*The Assistant*), Sy Levin (*A New Life*), Yakov Bok (*The Fixer*), Arthur Fidelman (*Pictures of Fidelman*), Roy Hobbs (*The Natural*), and Harry Lesser (*The Tenants*), all strive to escape an ignominious or unfulfilling past and to achieve a new life of comfort and fulfillment. All six are defeated in their ambition, but the first four achieve a new dignity, turning defeat into victory by assuming a burden of self-sacrifice. (pp. 136-37)

Malamud characteristically develops the idea of the regenerative power of suffering by using the Jew (specifically the schlemiel figure) as a symbol of conscience and moral behavior. . . . In a celebrated statement, Malamud once said, "All men are Jews except they don't know it." By this he meant that the Jew can serve to represent the individual's existential situation as an isolated, displaced loner who has the potential for achieving moral transcendence through suffering that engenders insight and a commitment to love. All people, Malamud implies, have a common identity as ethical beings. . . . (pp. 137-38)

In Malamud's fiction, the Jew as a symbol of ethical man is joined by another pervasive symbol—that of life as a prison. When Morris Bober [in *The Assistant*] resents his bad fortune, he sees his grocery store as a "prison," a "graveyard," a "tomb." The store is the source of his bitterness, suffering, and frustration—evidence of the limitations of the human condition on earth—and at the same time it symbolizes Morris's every existence, embodying the source of his moral strength. *A New Life* moves Malamud even closer to an explicit existentialist viewpoint. Sy Levin chooses a future "chained" to Pauline Gilley. With her he might appear to be a free man, but really he will be locked inside "a windowless prison" that is "really himself, flawed ediface of failures, each locking up tight the one before." In other words, Levin has exercised the freedom to choose his own "prison." Similarly, Yakov Bok finds spiritual peace only after choosing to remain in the tsar's prison, with no guarantee of ever being released. Harry Lesser voluntarily emtombs himself in what he likes to think of as a "sacred cathedral" of art, but which turns out to be the prison of his own divided soul.

Yet one must ask whether Malamud's metaphoric use of the Jew to represent the good man struggling for a meaningful existence in the prison of life is convincing. Certainly the European Jews, throughout the Middle Ages and again in the nineteenth and twentieth centuries, experienced an extraordi-

nary amount of suffering, but in elevating their hardship to the level of an ethical symbol, Malamud, in spite of his characteristic irony, sometimes borders on sentimentality. For example, near the end of *The Fixer* Yakov Bok's lawyer proclaims to his client, "You suffer for us all. . . . I would be honored to be in your place." Seen in this light, Malamud's famous statement, "All men are Jews," implies that it is the human lot to suffer, that suffering is potentially beneficial, and that we should therefore learn to accept our burdens and see in them the promise of growth and fulfillment.

Critics often talk about the theme of redemptive suffering in Malamud's works. This terminology can be misleading, since it has the effect of suggesting a specifically Christian view of salvation that is present but peripheral in Malamud's fiction. It should be emphasized that his vision has its roots in the Old Testament, while the Christian idea of salvation derives from the New Testament. This point is fundamental to an understanding of Malamud's work. In his fiction, he unrelentingly asks what might be called Old Testament questions: Why do good men suffer while evil men frequently prosper? Why should we be good, when there is no reward for goodness? How can we have faith when there are no signs to confirm our faith? Why should we love, if our love is met only with scorn? Malamud's perspective on these age-old questions is heavily influenced by the somewhat fatalistic Old Testament story of Job, a pious man who suffers unjustly without ever understanding why. He knows only that it is God's will that he suffer. To the man who suffers without any apparent reason, God's ways seem harsh and unjust, but Job does not attempt to rationalize this injustice; rather, he acknowledges this as part of the mystery of life. It is simply the way of the world; the sun shines as brightly on the wicked as it does on the good and just.

The suffering of Morris Bober and Yakov Bok is not redemptive in the Christian sense. For them as Jews, the concepts of heaven and hell do not offer a solution to the dilemma of existence. They have no sense of individual salvation; they do not believe that their suffering in this life will be rewarded in the next. Malamud's view is rather that goodness is its own reward while evil inflicts its own punishment. This is why love and compassion—and schlemiel heroes—are so important in Malamud's fiction. No suffering can be redeemed by any act of God or the State. The only "solution" possible for the problem of evil is for people to respect and nourish each other now, during this life. And only a schlemiel would choose the intangible spiritual rewards of goodness over the material benefits of narrow self-interest. Thus, Malamud's association of suffering with Jewishness is not merely sentimental. It also contains a hardheaded realism.

Suffering, however, does not interest Malamud for its own sake. It is, rather, a corollary to his real concern, one that can easily be missed: what he primarily wishes to explore and express is the sheer terror of existence in the twentieth century. The horrors of Verdun, the Great Depression, Dresden, Auschwitz, Hiroshima, Vietnam—the world's "uncertain balance of terror," as President Kennedy expressed it in his inaugural address—these have their counterparts in Malamud's fiction. Backdrops of Depression hardship, symbolic landscapes of garbage-filled back alleys and collapsing buildings, McCarthyism, and anti-Semitic injustice on a massive scale—these settings cast their dark shadows over all of Malamud's fictional world, serving as constant reminders that we are faced with malevolent forces so powerful that they threaten our very existence as thinking, feeling, moral beings. Thus it was understandable that Malamud should choose the Jews as symbols of suffering, for they have lived through the Holocaust, the most horrifying campaign of terror in human history. In Malamud's works the Jew becomes an isolated loner who represents the hopes, fears, and possibilities of twentieth-century humanity.

Suffering in Malamud's fiction, then, has two aspects, one somewhat sentimental, the other more fatalistic, full of terror. To the extent that Malamud's writing romanticizes suffering, it is dangerous and destructive. Morris Bober and Frank Alpine are masterful creations, but for people actually to submit to similar suffering in their own lives, acting on the belief that their suffering will somehow redeem them, would be fruitless and masochistic. Similarly, Yakov Bok becomes a powerful example of a human being's ability to grow spiritually in the face of injustice, but the hard fact is that most poor people unjustly imprisoned—even "political prisoners"—simply waste away without ever being allowed to serve the cause of justice, no matter how noble their suffering might be. But Malamud surely never intended anyone to take his metaphoric treatment of suffering literally, as a life model. Nonetheless, the literal implication is there. For the most part, however, the hard-headed attitude toward suffering prevails in Malamud's fiction. In this respect his writing provides a sort of strategy for living with the terror of modern life on an everyday basis. This is the source of both the power and the importance of his fiction. *The Assistant* and *The Fixer* are Malamud's strongest novels largely because they capture most effectively our existential sense of terror in the modern world. (pp. 138-42)

In the world of Malamud's fiction compassion, love, and understanding—the humane values—rather than physical circumstances give meaning to one's life. It is a world that blends hope with despair, pain with possibility, and suffering with moral growth. Out of the everyday defeats and indignities of ordinary people, Malamud creates beautiful parables that capture the joy as well as the pain of life; he expresses the dignity of the human spirit searching for freedom and moral growth in the face of hardship, injustice, and the existential anguish of life in our time. (p. 146)

> *Sheldon J. Hershinow, in his* Bernard Malamud *(copyright © 1980 by Frederick Ungar Publishing Co., Inc.), Ungar, 1980, 165 p.*

JAMES M. MELLARD

[The] work of Bernard Malamud seems very much to exhibit [a] strain of naive-modernist fiction, though, like Bellow's, it is largely a work of critical consolidation. If Bellow is in the "hotter" tradition of James, Malamud takes the "cooler" modes of an early modern like Anderson, assimilates them, and makes them his own, though he does not really (nor does he need to) transform them. But Malamud's best work is no simple art. He uses as effectively as any critical modernist the basic epistemological mode of the lyric novelist in order to treat themes of alienation and suffering, at the same time that he uses the modes—which he begins to parody—of comedy and tragedy, the ironic and the romantic. In *The Natural* he draws upon the tradition—largely popular—of sports fiction in America, one seen or felt vividly in Anderson, Ring Lardner, Hemingway, Fitzgerald, and even Faulkner. In *The Assistant*, as Malamud creates an urban landscape as vital but threatening as any from the naive tradition of American naturalism, he also creates a hero who is as powerless, as psychically indeterminate, and

as bent upon self-definition as one of Bellow's "dangling men." In *A New Life* Malamud writes yet another of those "academic novels" with which American fiction abounds; in *The Fixer* he turns to the treatment of an actual historical crime and punishment, similar in some ways to *An American Tragedy* and *Native Son; Pictures of Fidelman*, like *Winesburg, Ohio* and several works in Faulkner, is a cycle of stories focusing upon the development of one character. *The Tenants* seems to owe less to other fictions than to the allusively poetic world of Shakespeare's *The Tempest*, yet it, too, depends upon the sort of intellectual, physical, even erotic conflict between Black American and White that we see in Faulkner, Warren, Baldwin, Styron, and Updike.

The tradition in Malamud, as it had been for the naive modernists, becomes epistemological and ontological, the performative and pastoral elements providing both a way of knowing and a content to be known. The mode of perception that the performative voice gives Malamud allows him to exploit fully the resources of the pastoral as a content. Through it Malamud can employ very simple people as his protagonists, antagonists, and supporting characters; these people can accept their own most foolish, as well as their own most heroic, actions in the most matter-of-fact ways; and they can talk about themselves, their world, and its values in the most uncritical vocabularies available to the popular mind. Moreover, the pastoral mode permits him to structure his plots as if they belonged to the *mythoi* of tragedy and comedy. But, while Malamud's voice seems to validate the ways in which his characters see the world, in his best novels—*The Natural, The Assistant, The Fixer*—there is always a note of parody that comes out of his use of popular "myths" such as the tragedy of the ball player Shoeless Joe Jackson, the ecstatic romance of St. Francis of Assisi, and the nightmare terrors of Russian Bolshevism. That undercurrent of parody, as one expects in a modernist work, leaves forms and meanings subtly indeterminate. Like Faulkner, Malamud is disposed—as the Russian formalists say—toward "baring his devices," as he forces us to study his fictive worlds at the same time that we regard his epistemological and ontological modes, but less like early Faulkner than like the critical modernists, he opts for formal openness rather than for formal pluralism. Malamud's exploiting the possibilities of pastoral and the naive popular consciousness, however, pushes him slightly closer than, for example, Saul Bellow to the late modernism of Vonnegut and Brautigan; still, one would not wish to overstate their differences. One must agree with Max Schulz's views of Malamud and the modern Jewish novelists in general: ". . . willingness to accept the world on its own terms—disorderly, incoherent, absurd—'without any irritable reaching after fact and reason,' and yet without losing faith in the moral significance of human actions, underlies the confrontation of experience in the best of the contemporary Jewish American novels." (pp. 152-54)

> *James M. Mellard, "The Sophisticated," in his* The Exploded Form: The Modernist Novel in America *(© 1980 by the Board of Trustees of the University of Illinois; reprinted by permission of the author and the University of Illinois Press), University of Illinois Press, 1980, pp. 125-74.**

DOROTHY SEIDMAN BILIK

No contemporary American writer has written about immigrants and survivors more frequently or more imaginatively than has Bernard Malamud. His fictional world is peopled with

Diasporans of all kinds but, unlike [Abraham Cahan's assimilated protagonist in his *The Rise of David Levinsky*], Malamud's characters embody significant fragments of the Jewish past. Most frequently Malamud portrays remnants of the earlier generation of immigrants, unwilling refugees from American Jewish affluence, survivors of an older Jewish community who retain unassimilated Jewish values and who do not relinquish their accents and their anachronistic occupations. Although Malamud includes some survivors of the Holocaust in his fictional Ellis Island, he has not yet directly portrayed a survivor as central figure. In *The Fixer,* however, Malamud depicts an earlier survivor of anti-Semitic persecution. . . . (p. 53)

With the exception of *The Fixer,* which is historically distanced from the Nazi period, Malamud's allusive, indirect, parablelike tales of Jewish life do not confront the Holocaust experience. Nevertheless, Malamud's immigrant characters, even when they are not survivors, frequently have the insubstantiality of remnants or of dream figures. Insofar as they embody the modern sense of dream-made-real, Malamud's immigrants resemble the European survivors discussed by Lawrence Langer [in his *The Holocaust and the Literary Imagination*]. However, only in *The Fixer,* where the dream is a nightmare indeed, does Malamud's world contain the horrors that Langer includes in the aesthetics of atrocity. In Malamud's other fictions the grotesque elements are countered with the possibility of realizing the Diaspora dream of earthly redemption. In addition, Malamud's modern adaptation of the traditionally ironic tone of the Yiddish story teller distances and ameliorates some of the grimmer implications of his fiction.

The dreamlike insubstantiality, the redemptive vision, and the irony are frequently manifested in Malamud's modern counterparts to the East European Hasidic *rebes* and *tsadikim*. Malamud's modern *tsadikim* are considerably less saintly than their historic predecessors, but their very susceptibility to the modern world allows them to be more effective as teachers—the essential task of a *rebe*. Fictional antecedents for Malamud's *rebes* are Henry Roth's Reb Yidel Pankower and Isaac Rosenfeld's Reb Feldman. In Rosenfeld's novel the relationship of the *rebe* to the young seeker is shown as anachronistic. In the writings of Malamud, the teacher is both more ambiguous and more effective, yet the ancient Jewish paradigm is discernible. The pupil-teacher relationship may be of a younger, assimilated Jew to an older, more traditional Jew; sometimes the relationship is between Jew and gentile; usually the relationship is between a more callow seeker and one more experienced in suffering. Frequently Malamud develops the quester and the teacher as dual protagonists or *Doppelgänger* (*The Assistant,* "The Magic Barrel," "The Last Mohican" . . .). The immigrant figure is the keeper of the Jewish past, a past that is transmitted in much the same way that the Hasidic masters passed on wisdom and lore to their pupils. Indirectly by means of parable, sometimes fragmentarily, sometimes inadvertently, unlikely modern Hasidim like Morris Bober, Pinye Salzman, Shimen Susskind, and others pass on meaningful fragments of Jewish ethics and collective Jewish history to questers and novices who are even more unlikely and unaware than their teachers.

The Malamud novice or quester is frequently in error at the beginning of his quest. Sometimes he attempts to make a new life of his past (*Pictures of Fidelman* . . . , "Lady of the Lake" . . .) or attempts to live a life in terms of false goals (*The Assistant,* "The Magic Barrel"). Through his encounter with an immigrant or exile, the quester once more confronts his own

historic past or reforms his goals and sometimes, in classic style, achieves recognition and reversal. The contact between quester and immigrant *Doppelgänger* at times results in the quester's seeming to incorporate the older figure. The older figure may wane, even die, but some of his spirit or knowledge lives on in the now-changed quester. [One] of Malamud's most widely known works [*The Assistant,* is an example] of this pattern. . . . (pp. 53-5)

Frank Alpine, the assistant in the novel, is a climber, a man clearly destined for higher things. Unlike many of Malamud's protagonists (Fidelman, Levin, Freeman, Lesser, Bok), Frank is not Jewish, at least not at the beginning of the novel. Although an American, Frank feels alienated because he is an orphan, a Catholic, a drifter. What he learns from Morris Bober is how to be a Jew, which in Malamud's terms means how to be a human being.

It has been common to stress the ecumenicalism of Malamud's concept of Jewishness. But to stress the universality and Christianity of Malamud's "conversions" and reversals is to ignore the concrete Jewish particulars in which those universals are grounded. Bober's Judaism, particularly in its unorthodoxy, in its flawed state, is thereby more relevant to the flawed seeker. Of all Malamud's immigrant *rebes,* Bober comes closest to secular sainthood. Morris is a Jobian sufferer as well as a Sabbath-breaking, ham-eating sage. In his insistence on scrupulous honesty in a dishonest world, Morris Bober is a true follower of the Torah in modern dress. Malamud evokes with loving irony, older, folkloric Jewish themes transformed by the passage of time. This occurs in the oft-quoted passage where Morris, self-conscious and under stress, explains to Frank that to be a Jew one must suffer for the Law. For Morris this does not mean Sabbath observance, or adherence to Leviticus, but rather "this means to do what is right, to be honest, to be good. This means to other people." Some have been offended by the simplicity of the reductivism; others have noted the resemblance to the Sermon on the Mount. But the steadfastness is Jobian and talmudic.

Malamud is reaching back to a well-known Jewish anecdote about the great Rabbi Hillel (first century B.C.E.). The rabbi was challenged by a heathen who said he would become a Jew if the wisdom of the Torah could be expressed while standing on one foot. Hillel had no difficulty in replying, "That which is hurtful to thee do not do to thy neighbors! This is the entire Torah, all the rest is commentary. Go and study it." The sources do not tell us whether the conversion took place; but in Malamud's novel the seeker, perhaps more sincere than his ancient predecessor, by action, experience, and precept does indeed become Jewish. (pp. 55-6)

The presence of history is . . . dramatically rendered in the form of the novel. Frank Alpine is converted from a conventional Jew-hater, who admits that he "didn't have use for the Jews . . . ," into a definite Jew-lover, who first craves Morris's daughter carnally and then loves Morris filially. The ultimate action, almost a ritualized punishment for lust, is Frank's circumcision, which "enraged and inspired him." . . . Significantly it is spring when Frank becomes a Jew. Though the Easter story of death and resurrection is surely part of Malamud's rich allusiveness, Malamud's text says "Passover," which celebrates redemption from pagan bondage and anticipates the giving of the Law. In addition, the ironist in Malamud should never be dismissed. Passover is the traditional time for anti-Semitic blood-libels and persecutions of Jews in Eastern Europe, a theme Malamud pursues pointedly in *The Fixer.* Spring renewal with its pogroms and suffering often has a bitter taste in Yiddish literature. Morris has been sacrificed and Frank has metonymously taken part in his sacrifice through the ritual of circumcision. (pp. 57-8)

The Fixer . . . is relevant to the discussion of postwar immigrant fiction because of the novel's evocation of the Holocaust in the oblique manner of some Jewish American writers. Malamud says that the story of Mendl Beilis, the history upon which the fiction is based, was paradigmatic for him: "Somewhere along the line, what had happened in Nazi Germany began to be important to me in terms of the book, and that too is part of Yakov's story." To include the Jewish catastrophe, Malamud confronts it indirectly, in microcosm, in the past. For what actually happened to Mendl Beilis is far less important than what the fixer and the reader experience of the condition of Jewish life in Eastern Europe. In addition, Malamud avails himself of the reader's knowledge of the contemporary Jewish tragedy to illuminate both past and recent history. The fact that there was a Beilis case allows Malamud to ignore its historic particulars and thereby create an imaginative truth that is more effective than fictionalized history. (p. 64)

In Malamud's fictional world, with its emphasis on the unexpected, Jewish characters do not enjoy an innate moral superiority. Some, like Julius Karp and Nat Pearl in *The Assistant*, are demonstrably inferior, especially to the gentile Frank. But history, economics, circumstances, and the unsought experience of suffering are what define the Malamudian teachers and *tsadikim*, and Malamud's Jews qualify. Even among the less admirable, like Karp, Feld, and the appropriately named Harry Lesser of *The Tenants*, there is a potentiality for moral growth. The reader is induced to see embodied in the most unlikely spirit a spark of righteousness. Only the ambitious accountants and lawyers, those who follow the American Dream of worldly success, are refused Malamud's mercy and are denied possibilities for moral development. (p. 70)

Robert Alter, among others, complains of Malamud "that nowhere does he attempt to represent a Jewish milieu, that a Jewish community never enters into his books except as the shadow of a vestige of a specter." Clearly it is not because Malamud cannot write realistic, socially and historically rooted fiction. *The Tenants, The Fixer,* and *A New Life* are all strongly rooted in history, event, and social milieu. But in the immigrant stories the particular strength of these Diaspora Men resides in their not being rooted in space, in their unassimilated, alien transcendence of milieu. Unlike the prewar immigrant, Malamud's Jews do not perceive of America as a "promised land." Alfred Kazin complains of Malamud's "abstractness" and contrasts him to the Yiddish masters who "gave the earth of Russia, the old village, a solid reality, as if it were all the world they had to cherish." But Malamud, although close to them in spirit according to Kazin, does not show "the world, but the spectral Jew in his beggarly clothes—always ready to take flight." Is this not precisely what Malamud intends? The setting, like the language, attempts to capture that which is essential, that which can be distilled into something ultimately portable.

Malamud is not, as Kazin avers, abstract out of despair; rather, he attempts in language, setting, and character to preserve what is most ephemeral and yet what can best be preserved. That which an immigrant can carry with him may be nonmaterial, may suffer a sea change, may even be debased, but it is transmittable, capable of living under the most adverse conditions, and hence the only heritage worthy of transmission. It is am-

biguously compounded of common suffering, common humanity, common responsibility, and common peril. And how well Kazin (still carping) sees what Malamud is trying to do with his surreal language: "He makes you think not that Jews really talk that way but how violent, fear fraught, always on edge, Jewish talk can be." (pp. 74-5)

The essentially comic form, albeit qualified, of Malamud's work points to the distance that separates America and Americans from much European experience of the Holocaust, although Malamud, like other Jewish American writers, is in the position of a "witness-through-the-imagination," one who has "(merely) 'heard the terrible news'." And news of such magnitude has considerable effect as Malamud's prose shares with the "schizophrenic art" of the Holocaust a metaphoric language employed to "sustain the tensions that inspire it" rather than to resolve those tensions. Like the "literature of atrocity," Malamud's works are characterized by "irrealism"—'a reality whose quality is unreal. The line between the comic and the tragic often becomes blurred as the authors struggle to express the inexpressible." (pp. 75-6)

Dorothy Seidman Bilik, "Malamud's Secular Saints and Comic Jobs," in her Immigrant-Survivors: Post-Holocaust Consciousness in Recent Jewish American Fiction (copyright © 1981 by Dorothy Seidman Bilik; reprinted by permission of Wesleyan University Press), Wesleyan University Press, 1981, pp. 53-80.

ALAN LELCHUK

How often is it that a major contemporary novelist opens his latest book with a dialogue between God and man? Or employs for his main characters one human being and a chimp, with an assortment of gorillas and baboons for other dramatis personae? Or seeks to conceive a fable for the future—man after the nuclear "Devastation"—that is nothing less than a retelling of the Old and New Testaments, complete with the author's views on man's (and God's) nature, good and evil, cause and effect, fall from grace? Odd stuff for a novel, no doubt. Yet these are the materials of Bernard Malamud's latest book, **"God's Grace,"** a fable by turns charming and foolish, topical and far-fetched, provocative and innocent.

Certain questions immediately strike the reader. Is the boldness of the attempt at neobiblical wisdom and prophecy paid for at too high an artistic price? Are there enough effective scenes and moments to cancel out the troubling elements and the borderline risks?

Constructing fables, we should remember, is nothing new for Malamud. As far back as his first novel, **"The Natural"** . . . , his best novel, **"The Assistant"** . . . , and many of the splendid short stories in **"The Magic Barrel"** . . . and **"Idiots First"** . . . , Malamud has been in the fable business, so to speak. . . . Unlike Bellow and Roth, writers with whom he is mistakenly aligned, Malamud has always had a fondness for telling tales arranged for the purpose of a specific moral lesson; for a story surface deceptively simple, a prose style artfully direct; for an atmosphere marked by the childlike and pristine, even the religious. Moreover, he has not been averse to presenting animals that speak—witness stories like **"Talking Horse"** or **"The Jewbird."** I mentioned a fondness for such tales, but I must add, of course, an excellence in execution too, for Malamud, at his best, is a kind of folk artist of genius. Despite his intellectual ambitions, his strong suit has always been writing from the gut, a kind of literary primitivism. Neither realism nor surrealism has been his forte through the years, but the fable, the parable, the allegory, the ancient art of basic storytelling in a modern voice; through this special mode he has earned his high place in contemporary letters.

"God's Grace" is the most up-front fable he has yet written, complete with a defensive Yahweh, an ironic Moses, Jesus, talking chimps and perverse gorillas, biblical rites of sacrifice, plus, of course, the pointed moral wisdom—this time full of dark prophecy. Does the darkness emerge from the author himself growing older, facing his own end, or his living in an age of crisis, when civilization is facing its own possible end? Whichever, there are in this novel moments of lucid beauty beside moments of harrowing blackness—Eden and Apocalypse between two covers. The result is an odd, fanciful book, a mixed bag of surprise characters and enchanting emotions that sometimes jar alongside unlikely happenings and obvious artifice. In part because it emanates from authentic strains in the author's imagination, "God's Grace" yields certain mainstream Malamudian pleasures. In part because it attempts to be a prophetic allegory, it suffers as a novel from the nature and burden of that beast. (pp. 1, 14)

> Alan Lelchuk, "Malamud's Dark Fable," in The New York Times Book Review (© 1982 by The New York Times Company; reprinted by permission), August 29, 1982, pp. 1, 14-15.

EDMUND FULLER

"Man had innumerable chances but was—in the long run—insufficient to God's purpose. He was insufficient to himself."

That theme is variously expressed in Bernard Malamud's extraordinary fable, "God's Grace," . . . which manages the rare feat of being a post-nuclear-holocaust story both somber and sometimes very funny. . . .

Weighing the ever-difficult problem of how much to disclose, I cannot conceal that the fable which, for a time, seems ebulliently hopefilled, abruptly clouds over. Aggressions more brutal than that of Cain against Abel break out. The animal world is not to be sentimentalized. Mr. Malamud, whose mood had seemed hopeful, suddenly makes it clear that if the late great human race is to have successors, they too will be fallen, they too expelled from the Garden.

I can't deny that from a highland of delight, as his reader, I found myself plunged into a chasm of depression that disappointed me sorely, making the title of the book, "God's Grace," and of its last chapter, "God's Mercy," seem harshly ironic. Jonathan Swift excoriated our kind as "the most pernicious race of little odious vermin that nature ever suffered to crawl upon the face of the earth," but at least kept his noble horses noble.

A few hours of reflection and a rereading of the end softened my reaction. There is a kind of painful majesty to his closing pages, with their inversion of the Abraham and Isaac story, also with their hint of Babel. In the last line, George, the gorilla, is the key to a hope, a grace, a mercy, not easy, not sentimental, not guaranteed, yet the stronger for its austerity. In the inventive, reflective, tragicomic, ultimately reverential fable of "God's Grace" Mr. Malamud may have created his most lasting work.

> Edmund Fuller, "After the Holocaust: A Somber and Funny Fable," in The Wall Street Journal (reprinted by permission of The Wall Street Journal, © Dow Jones & Company, Inc. 1982; all rights reserved), September 13, 1982, p. 30.

ROBERT ALTER

Bernard Malamud is a writer who early on established an emphatic paradigm for his fictional world and who ever since has been struggling in a variety of ways to escape its confines. His latest novel [God's Grace] is his most strenuous strategem of escape, moving beyond the urban horizon of his formative work into an entirely new mode of postapocalyptic fantasy—with intriguing though somewhat problematic results.

When I say "paradigm," I am not referring to the explicit Jewish themes or to the morally floundering Jewish protagonists that have been trademarks of Malamud's fiction, with the exception of his first novel, *The Natural*. In fact, God's Grace is the most self-consciously Jewish of all his books. Its hero, Calvin (née Seymour) Cohn, the son of a rabbi and himself a former rabbinic student, carries his dog-eared copy of the Pentateuch into the strange new world in which he finds himself, tries to transfer its ethical teaching to the new reality, conducts inward arguments with God, sometimes even alluding to rabbinic texts, and, above all, broods over the awesome story of the Binding of Isaac and wonders what it might suggest about God's real intentions toward humanity. What I mean by "paradigm" is, in essence, the phenomenological substructure of Malamud's fictional world—its constant tilting of its protagonists into narrow enclosures, preferably cluttered and dirty, and ultimately with no real exits. The novelist has repeatedly sought to give his own claustrophobic sensibility a moral as well as thematic justification by intimating that these sundry traps, prisons, and living graves in which he places his protagonists (Morris Bober's grocery store, Yakov Bok's cell, Harry Lesser's condemned tenement) are the harsh limits within which a true moral life of commitment is realized. But . . . this is precisely the least convincing aspect of Malamud's work.

God's Grace, as a future fiction, sets to one side—without, however, entirely suppressing—the Malamudian vision of cluttered incarceration by sweeping the global slate clean. . . . By an absurd oversight of God—or is it, Cohn wonders, a new twist of His inscrutable design?—Cohn alone of all humanity is saved in the insulated roundness of his deep-sea submersible. Up to this point, the plot follows a familiar enough route of reasonably plausible science fiction, but by rapid stages, uninhibited fantasy takes over. Summary is bound to be a little unfair to the novel because Malamud makes it far more engaging than will be suggested by the bare fictional data. . . .

Cohn's island might of course be construed as another version of the Malamudian prison, but it has a speciousness, a paradisiacal sense of benign nature, absent from the characteristic roach-ridden cells, literal and figurative, of Malamud's previous fiction. Even the Crusoesque cave that Cohn makes into his home, complete with rough-hewn furniture, shelves, and a rolling wooden barrier at the mouth, is more cosy womb than tomb. This mode of fantasy, moreover, releases an element of exuberance in Malamud's writing that was exhibited in some of his most attractive early stories, like "Angel Levine" and "Idiots First." The opening chapter, in which Cohn, in his dripping wet suit, discovers that, despite the promise recorded in Genesis, the Flood has come again, and then finds himself addressed from above by an impatient Lord of Hosts, is a bravura performance. Many of the pages that follow are informed by a winning zaniness of invention. Modulations of tone are always essential when Malamud's writing is working well, and the quality of wry bemusement, hovering between sad reflection and self-ironic laughter, lends a certain emotional authority to the fantasy. (p. 38)

Malamud has described his own novel as "a visionary tale with a prophetic warning." Some of his efforts, I fear, to convey a visionary argument through the story betray an underlying weakness, and the prophetic warning at the end, though it may seem to the author to serve a moral purpose, is a painful illustration of how Malamud's materials can go wildly out of control. Let me first address the visionary argument. Given the calamitous state to which humankind has brought the world, and, if you are a believer, to which God has permitted humankind to bring the world, Malamud not only questions human nature but also the nature of the God who allows His own handiwork such a cruel genius for self-annihilation. This theological inquiry is focused chiefly through a confrontation between Jewish and Christian views (in the persons of Cohn and Buz) of the story of the Binding of Isaac, the compelling and baffling parable of how God might seem to require the slaughter of His human sons. Christian tradition calls the story the Sacrifice of Isaac because it is taken as the typological intimation of the Crucifixion; Judaism calls it the Binding because the actual denouement of the story is stressed, in which the angel's voice stays the sacrificial knife just before it plunges. Cohn is led to speculate, considering what has happened to his own century from the Holocaust through Hiroshima to the ultimate devastation, that the Lord who oversees this world might in fact want an actual immolation of humanity.

Struggling to perpetuate a humane Jewish ethics, Cohn promulgates to his fellow primates what he calls the Seven Admonitions (in deference to his Mosaic predecessor, he avoids the term commandment), which reflect a cautiously hopeful, pragmatic view of the necessity for altruism and of man's small but real potential for good. The Second Admonition reads: "Note: God is not love. God is God. Remember Him." This Jewish theological emphasis, it might be observed, reverses certain subterranean Christian motifs that can be detected in the earlier Malamud. . . . Late in the book, at a point when Cohn's hoped-for new covenant is manifestly disintegrating, Buz, who has played a shadowy role in the process of disintegration, makes bold to erase the word "not" from the Second Admonition. The theological assertion, thus Christianized, that God is love, might seem benign enough, but in view of what is afterward perpetrated by the hand that has revised the Admonition, an anti-Christian polemic is clearly implied. Those who make such an ideal claim about God, we may infer, are the most likely to slip into the abyss of the anti-ideal; or, alternately, a God who is supposed to be love in a world where so little of it is in evidence may also enact the outrageous paradox of sacrificing mankind, His only-begotten beloved son, in the most ghastly way to demonstrate that He is love.

Malamud's theological argument, unlike the tonality and humor of his fantasy, is not misrepresented by summary. It is, in other words, schematic, sketchy, lacking weight of experience and density of intellectual texture. One symptom of this lack of anchorage is that Cohn's abundant references to Jewish tradition are patently secondhand and in some instances misinformed. More serious is the fact that this polemic with Christianity in the end contradictorily reimagines a doctrine of Original Sin, the plot concluding with an irresistible assertion of the Old Adam. There is an ambiguity here that is confused rather than fruitful: a reader, contemplating the conclusion,

could easily turn the whole book around, something I doubt the author intends, and claim that Cohn's guarded Jewish optimism about humanity was all along a superficial view and, worse, an abysmal delusion.

The denouement involves a horrific orgy of infanticide and cannibalism and then dire consequences of a rather strained symbolic character for Cohn himself. Malamud wants this to be taken as prophetic warning, but it seems far more like sheer punishment inflicted by the author on his protagonist and thus implicitly on the reader as well. Punishing his incarcerated characters has been a temptation to which Malamud has of course succumbed again and again. The feel of the ending here is unfortunately very like that of the ghastly ending of *The Tenants,* when Harry Lesser sinks an ax into the skull of Willie Spearmint at the exact moment his black rival lashes off his testicles with a razor-sharp knife. Even without pursuing psychoanalytic conjecture, we may note that there is a palpable gap between such unleashing of aggression against characters and readers, and the moral claims made for the fictional expression of all that rage. (pp. 38-40)

The moral message [in *God's Grace*] is unexceptionable, but the vehemence with which the brutish counterforce to kindness and pity is imagined at the end is disquieting. Instead of holding a prophetic mirror to the contorted face of mankind, the novelist—at least so it seems to this reader—has once again taken his lovingly fashioned creatures, bound them hand and foot, and begun to play with axes, knives, tearing incisors, and other instruments of dismemberment. (p. 40)

Robert Alter, "A Theological Fantasy," in The New Republic *(reprinted by permission of* The New Republic; © 1982 The New Republic, Inc.), *Vol. 187, Nos. 12 & 13, September 20 & 27, 1982, pp. 38-40.*

MORRIS DICKSTEIN

At first glance, *God's Grace* looks like an improbable novel to come from Bernard Malamud. In fact, it is an odd book, period. . . .

The book is clearly a version of *Robinson Crusoe,* updated to the age of total war. Malamud has written about talking animals before—in **"The Jewbird"** and **"Talking Horse."** But those stories, like all of Malamud's best fiction, are hard as diamonds, tight and spare rather than verbose, and with no overt moralizing. In *God's Grace,* Malamud's sententious side takes over—even one of the chimps complains that Cohn's homilies insult his intelligence. Unlike the great fabulists, whose art is playful rather than ponderous, Malamud no longer trusts the tale to carry its own meanings. Cohn, a self-anointed prophet bursting with conventional wisdom, is constantly telling the beasts to surmount their animal qualities. Yet he does a bit of surmounting himself—of the only girl chimp, a charming creature named Mary Madlyn, in the hope of "depositing in her hospitable uterus a spurt of adventurous sperm" to carry the seed of his future order.

Cohn tries in bizarre ways to teach Judaism to the animals. . . . But the chimps rebel against him, turn into Christians (of a sort), and make him the object of a little pogrom. Malamud would have us see Cohn as a classic Jewish victim—first a survivor, then a bearer of enlightenment, then a martyr for the cause of intellect and civilization. But the reader may feel that Cohn's own failings have helped precipitate disaster. Cohn plays God with his charges, but they tire of his moral superiority and reassert their own nature.

God's Grace is Malamud's most pious and most literary work, in some ways closer to Cynthia Ozick's territory than to the marvelously earthy fiction he once wrote. Its style is a dour pastiche of biblical English, especially the Book of Genesis. The novel echoes and retells the stories of Noah and the Flood, Adam and Eve, Abraham and Isaac, and the sufferings of Job. Its hero even has occasional dialogues with God, who speaks in a weird mixture of solemn cant, tangy Yiddishisms, and bureaucratese. (p. 54)

The book gets stronger when it puts this feeble humor aside and builds starkly toward catastrophe. What begins as a fable about survival gets transformed, like other late Malamud novels (*The Fixer, The Tenants*), into a study in isolation, anti-Semitism, and futility. In his great early stories, collected in *The Magic Barrel* and *Idiots First,* Malamud wrote about the tensions—moral, personal, generational—among Jewish characters, about the problematic nature of Jewish identity, quite apart from religion. Starting with *The Fixer,* though, Malamud shifted his attention to the confrontation between Jews and goyim; his work began to deal in victims and villains, became more predictable, and lost some of its inner richness. *God's Grace* follows this pattern. For the brutal Russians in *The Fixer* and the wary, hostile blacks in *The Tenants,* Malamud here substitutes a small society of animals, gratifyingly malleable at first but ultimately vengeful and destructive, as in the other books.

Instead of giving us "a complete departure from his previous novels," . . . Malamud has rewritten his racial fable, *The Tenants,* substituting atomic apocalypse for urban disintegration, a remote island for an abandoned tenement, and a batch of chimpanzees for the angry blacks of the sixties. The New York of his earlier book is a kind of jungle. Dense foliage sprouts in vacant apartments, and the physical devastation resembles the effects of nuclear war. . . . A Jewish writer, explicitly compared to Robinson Crusoe, is the last inhabitant of the empty tenement ("the only man on the island") until a black writer takes refuge there. Their tentative friendship, fostered by a devotion to craft that transcends their difference of background, eventually turns to bitter animosity, for reasons that recur exactly in *God's Grace:* the hero's incessant preaching, which demoralizes and finally unhinges his listeners, and a sexual conquest that deprives them of their women. These may seem contradictory, but both acts arise from an unconscious sense of racial superiority, which the author himself scarcely acknowledges. Sex and race show up the narcissism that can lie concealed in "higher" values.

God's Grace is marred by a sloppiness of detail in the way the fable is worked out. Malamud, hurrying toward his larger moral, shows little patience for the particulars of the acquisition of language, the practical problems of survival, the aftereffects of nuclear war, and Cohn's former life as a scientist. But these harm the novel less than the blinkers that restrict its vision. Malamud portrays his protagonist, as he did in *The Tenants,* as a kind of alter ego: a troubled, thoughtful, well-meaning man who tries—as this novel itself does—to bring a gleam of moral truth into a benighted world already far advanced in destroying itself. But his heroes, wrapped up in their exalted aims, rarely see the futility of their well-worn message or notice their own lapses into hypocrisy. (pp. 54-5)

Morris Dickstein, "The Sedulous Ape," in New York Magazine *(copyright © 1983 by News Group Publications, Inc.; reprinted with the permission of* New York *Magazine), Vol. 15, No. 38, September 27, 1982, pp. 54-5.*

JOSEPH EPSTEIN

When do we give up on a novelist? Sometimes, if it be foul enough, a single sentence will do the job. . . .

But what if the writer has acquired a reputation as a serious and highly accomplished artist, thought in some quarters to be a major novelist, a modern master even? What if, more complicated still, he has given you pleasure, insight into the working of the human heart, and other novelistic rewards in the past? What if he writes one poor book, then a second, then yet a third? At what point do you concede, however regretfully, that this writer no longer speaks to you, and walk away? (p. 49)

[Bernard Malamud's first novel], *The Natural,* plays off all the old baseball legends against Arthurian and other myths, and does so in a way that is both charming and serious. Although it was a first novel, the book sets out most of the themes, motifs, and character types its author would work with over the next few decades. The hero of *The Natural,* Roy Hobbs, is a loner, the first in what will be a fairly heavy traffic in Malamudian hard-luckers who can usually be counted upon to fade and fall within sight of the finish line. Suffering is at the heart of this novel, its point and its purpose. . . .

While there was more than a dash of Ring Lardner in *The Natural,* and a touch or two of Nathanael West, the dominant style was Malamud's own, and this was most impressive. Anchored in realistic detail, it yet was able to fly off into the regions of the fantastic at the drop of a comma. By means of this style Malamud could see the comedy of his characters while retaining his—and engaging our—sympathy for them. . . .

There are no Jews in *The Natural;* or at least no Jews to whom being a Jew has any importance. The point is worth making because being a Jew, its responsibilities and the consequences of not living up to those responsibilities, became central to Malamud's work over the next decade or so. . . .

The Assistant, Malamud's novel of 1957, is about little other than the question of what it means to be a Jew. I won't recapitulate the details of this carefully made yet exceedingly cheerless novel, except to say that it is saturated with pain and filled with the dignity of suffering. To be a true Jew, for Morris Bober, the book's exemplary character, is "to do what is right, to be honest, to be good." It is also, according to the rabbi who delivers the eulogy over the dead Bober, to suffer and endure, "but with hope." (p. 50)

The importance of suffering, the need for hope no matter how heavy the burden of suffering, the necessity of not shutting one's heart to the suffering and hopes of others—out of these cards Bernard Malamud built the splendid literary house that is *The Magic Barrel.* . . . Each story in the book shimmers with implications. Malamud seems to have found the perfect plots to give unforgettable flesh to his themes. Comedy and grief rub shoulders, as when an immigrant Jew addressed the Lord: "My dear God, sweetheart, did I deserve that this should happen to me?" Malamud's stories come out of the Yiddish tradition of storytelling, from the way they open . . . to the way they can ignite suddenly into fantasy . . . to the way their particulars rise off the page into universal significance. And, finally, the book reveals Malamud to be a moralist, an intricate and subtle and unpredictable one—which is to say, a moralist of the most interesting kind.

A New Life, Malamud's novel of 1961, exhibited both a continuation of and a number of departures from his previous work. Among the notable departures is the fact that this novel is more firmly anchored in time and place than Malamud's earlier books. . . .

But [it is] not, alas, much of a tale—or not as impressive a tale as one might have hoped for from the author of *The Magic Barrel.* . . . Bright patches there are in *A New Life;* laughs, too. Yet the novel seems, for the first time in a work by Bernard Malamud, thin. It sags in its middle. Lengthy though *A New Life* is, its substance feels light, while the stories in *The Magic Barrel,* though brief, have ballast. . . .

If there is something a bit trivial and finally clownish about *A New Life,* no such thing can be said of *The Fixer* (1966). This novel, it will be recalled, is based on the 1913 Mendel Beiliss case. . . . [In] the pathetic person of Mendel Beiliss, the Russian Jewish community, indeed all Jews everywhere, stood on trial.

There is a natural gravity to this subject, and Malamud proves in every way up to it. The difficult materials of *The Fixer* are handled with great artistic tact. So serious is the subject that there isn't room for the least literary exhibitionism, and none is allowed. The phrase *tour de force* for once applies. (p. 51)

The Fixer was not only an artistic but a critical and a commercial success. . . . If Malamud was not yet hanging around the house awaiting a call from Stockholm, he nevertheless had every reason to think himself among the major writers of our day. . . .

[The] first novel that Malamud produced after *The Fixer* was *The Tenants.* . . .

Such as it is, the drama of *The Tenants* mainly has to do with whether the two writers [Harry Lesser and Willie Spearmint] will complete their manuscripts. Racial feelings mix with rivalry and these are further complicated by Harry Lesser's interest in Willie Spearmint's white lady friend. Whatever the novel's symbolic intent, it is spoiled because the details seem so wrong. . . . More, though, than small details are off. Tonally, the novel sound wrong. Malamud does not quite seem up to the violence of his black writer. No character in the novel is worthy of one's sympathy, so among them all one divides one's antipathies. Saddest of all, for the first time in a book by Bernard Malamud, you don't want to turn the page.

How can a really good writer write a really bad book? He can choose the wrong subject. He can—which is much the same thing—misgauge his own talent, and allow his literary ambition to exceed his literary equipment. He may become unfocused morally, the world suddenly seeming more complicated to him than once it did and hence less susceptible of being dealt with by his art. However serious he is as an artist, he may nonetheless come to take himself too seriously. In the case of Bernard Malamud, with *The Tenants* a new heaviness set in, and it was not the weight of authority.

Dubin's Lives (1977), Malamud's next novel and also his longest, is about a professional biographer, a husband and father who in his late fifties has a bout of eleventh-hour adolescence and sets out to prove the adage about there being no fool like an old fool. Which is to say, at fifty-six William Dubin falls in love with a girl of twenty-three. There is every reason to think that Bernard Malamud would not agree with this brief summary of his nearly four-hundred-page novel. My guess is that he views this novel as a profound investigation of middle age, and that he sees his biographer, William Dubin, as a quester, a man ardent not to let life slip away from him. . . .

The earlier Malamud would have made fine ironic hay of this, and spun it into interesting moral material. The late Malamud takes it straight. . . . Cliché of clichés, we are talking, in *Dubin's Lives,* about a bloody mid-life crisis. But the crisis is not only William Dubin's; it is also Bernard Malamud's as a novelist. Signs of this novelist crisis are that Malamud's language has begun to fall apart—"presently" is misused, "into" (as "into an affair") crops up again and again, "experience" is used as a verb—his self-indulgent and boring descriptions of landscape go well beyond the permissible, and winters in the novel seem longer than they do in life; Malamud's writing about sex, earlier always witty, here becomes chiefly embarrassing. Worst of all, William Dubin is a selfish, charmless man, and it is far from clear that Malamud is aware of this. This is what makes reading *Dubin's Lives* such a chore. As Jane Austen puts it in *Mansfield Park:* "The indignities of stupidity, and the disappointments of selfish passion, can excite little pity." And, one might add, less interest.

Why do novelists seem to feel the need always to be changing—to be, in the cant word, "growing"? Did Tolstoy feel this? Did Dickens? Is this a contemporary phenomenon? Is it chiefly an American one? No one, surely, can accuse Bernard Malamud of disobeying the dictum to change, of ignoring the urge to innovate. Now, after the straight realism of *Dubin's Lives,* he has turned, in his latest novel, *God's Grace,* to fantasy. (p. 52)

The novel's early pages have some of the pleasing excitement of Robinson Crusoe, with Cohn setting up house on the island. Then Cohn discovers that the chimpanzee Buz has been trained to talk. Soon the other chimpanzees show up, attesting to God's "cosmic absent-mindedness" and, more important, the novelist's need to keep his story going. Cohn sets out to renew life by establishing a community among the chimpanzees and the ape and himself—one that is more civilized, founded on sounder principles, than the one that has just destroyed itself, apparently with God's willingness, in a nuclear devastation.

Naturally, this plan will come to grief. Despite Calvin Cohn's lecturing the chimps on the best thought of the Bible, Freud, Kierkegaard, Ortega y Gasset, despite his holding a *seder* for them to honor God and his impregnating of the one female chimpanzee on the island, the animals revert to type—human type, that is. They become, in other words, competitive, aggressive, divisive, finally vicious. But the novel goes bad before the chimpanzees do. Once the chimpanzees are allowed to speak, *God's Grace* takes on something of the quality of a television situation comedy, with symbolism added. Much of the humor in the novel is of the kind known as faintly amusing, but then chimp humor, on the scale of wit, is roughly three full rungs down from transvestite jokes. Someone once defined charm, negatively, by saying that if you think you have it, you don't. In *God's Grace* one feels Malamud thinks he has it.

Poor Malamud, the larger he strains to become, the smaller his talent begins to appear. In *God's Grace* he sets out to understand the ways of God, which is quite a project. In his earlier fiction, when a shoemaker, a grocer, a "fixer" spoke, one felt one could hear God in the background; in this novel, where God does speak, all one can hear is the reedy voice of a novelist. (p. 53)

Joseph Epstein, "Malamud in Decline," in Commentary *(reprinted by permission; all rights reserved), Vol. 74, No. 4, October, 1982, pp. 49-53.*

ALVIN B. KERNAN

[The] confrontation of text and society is the subject of Bernard Malamud's *The Tenants* . . . , which portrays very clearly the nature of traditional romantic beliefs about the reality of the literary text and the breakdown of these beliefs when they are confronted by social realities which directly contradict and confront them with an aggressive urgency and power born out of suffering and a need for help from all institutions, including art. I would not argue that *The Tenants* is one of the greatest of modern novels, but it is extraordinarily powerful and compelling in its realization of the view that is central to the conception of literature as a social institution: that literature and the arts are inescapably a part of society, and that the central literary values, though they are not totally socially determined, do respond in a dialectical manner to what takes place and is believed in that society.

Bernard Malamud, a writer with a strong investment in the craft tradition and the literary work as object, has dramatized the deconstruction of the literary text in a way which makes clear why it is becoming impossible for the writer any longer to believe that literature can remain independent of the world. Malamud begins with an image of what he considers the present situation of the writer. . . . [The] House of Fiction built by Flaubert and Henry James, has degenerated in *The Tenants* into a squalid New York City tenement inhabited as the story begins by a solitary writer. Once there had been a small garden on the roof where the writer often sat after a day's work, looked at the sky and the clouds, "and thought of Wm. Wordsworth." . . . But those recollections in tranquility have passed, along with Wordsworth's belief that poets make the world in their poetry, and now the garden is sterile, and unvisited. Below the garden, the building is untenanted except for a solitary person, the latter-day writer Harry Lesser, who lives, with many locks on his door, as high up in the building as he can, but without a view. The landlord Levenspiel has found the old-style tenement unprofitable and, in order to tear the building down and replace it with a more economical structure of modest size with stores on the bottom floor, has evicted all the tenants except Lesser, who refuses to go. But he is prevented from carrying out his practical plans by Lesser's refusal, protected by various laws on tenants' rights, to vacate. The House of Fiction has been invaded by the world and has degenerated into a fearsome place of decay and terror. (pp. 76-7)

The Tenants is a carefully constructed parable in which every detail has meaning on at least two levels, and the tenement is not only a realistic depiction of the desperate state of much of New York City, particularly such areas as the South Bronx, but of the wasteland of modern western society and the incursion of this reality into literature toward the end of a terrifying century. The battered fragments of an older, better-ordered society, it is now foul, barely functioning, its corridors filled with darkness and terror, the temporary shelter of wounded, homeless, indistinguishable men and animals, haunted by nightmare visions such as the hermaphroditic Hitler and the scapegoat-eating flower. Responsibility for this invasion is divided between the profit-seeking capitalist landlord with his dream of wealth and the artist who by refusing to leave when the capitalist landlord tries to empty the old building for the wrecker, keeps it standing and therefore subject to the forces which reduce it to a grotesque chamber of horrors. Perhaps, *The Tenants* suggests, it might be better for the artist to move on and let the old culture and the old art end rather than to try to keep them standing in a world in which art has no function and against which it therefore no longer has any real defenses.

Levenspiel's new world, his building in which the apartments above rest on the shops below, both architecturally and economically, might be preferable to the monstrosity that has resulted from the artist's stubbornly trying to work amid the ruins.

The artist, however, supported by the tangled laws of the old liberal society which ignore economic realities to protect the tenant from the owner, keeps the old building standing, trying to maintain the old literary values in the midst of the wasteland world. Lesser the novelist "squats"—Malamud's world is an intensified realistic version of Eliot's wasteland and frequently refers to it—in a few gray and cold rooms on the top floor which contain the minimal necessary furnishings of the old culture, the bookshelves with the patiently assembled library of cherished books, the hi-fi equipment and a few jazz and classical records, the desk, the typewriter, and the notes and files. The arrangements for eating, sleeping, and washing are rudimentary, but these matters of the flesh are not of much concern to the artist Lesser. . . . Behind the many locks on his door, he lives out the ultimacies of the totally dedicated romantic artist in a hostile world, a parody of Flaubert at Croisset or Proust in his cork-lined room of silence exploring his memories, of Joyce in his exile of silence and cunning creating a great work in the smithy of his soul.

Lesser reasons that he must stay on in the old building, despite the dangers and discomforts, because it is here that he began the book he is presently working on, and it is therefore here that he must finish it, if it is to be finished at all. He has written two earlier books, the first a *succès d'estime* which pleased him despite its small sales, and the second, in his opinion a poor book which nevertheless did well and was bought by the movies, providing him with enough money to live, very frugally, for a number of years while working on his third novel. . . . Lesser is now deep into this third book which will, he hopes, prove to himself and to the world that he is a true writer; but he has been at it, like the Greeks before Troy, for over nine years, and the book is in deep trouble, for he cannot find the necessary ending for the already-written beginning and middle. Levenspiel cannot understand, of course, either why the book should take so long—"What are you writing, the Holy Bible?" which is what a craftsman-artist like Lesser thinks he is writing—or why it cannot be written in another, more comfortable place just as well. But Lesser knows that it must be finished here where it was begun because, on the surface level, only here can he find that complete isolation needed for the intense effort of completing the book. On the allegorical level the meaning would seem to be that only in this particular romantic stance of isolation from and antagonism towards a broken and ugly world is the concentrated, introspective, priestly work of the Dedalian artificer possible. His art is not possible in a setting, or condition of being, other than that which the scene of *The Tenants* realizes, for another setting would necessitate a different kind of art. He needs the ugliness of the world as a foil against which to create the beauty of the perfectly articulated work.

For Lesser art is "glory," a "sacred cathedral . . . with lilting bonging iron bell," . . . and he is its high priest or rabbi, whose service is a willing servitude. He is a professional writer, a workman who lives for his work. He rises in the morning eager to begin writing, and he falls asleep each night planning the work of the next day. (pp. 78-80)

Lesser not only has the compulsive work-ethic his art requires, but he has the technical skills and tools of the verbal craftsman as well. Words, language, grammar, rhetoric are his tools, and he can "no longer see or feel except in language." . . . He prefers a sharp, precise, sparse, clear style, the exact style of Flaubert, *le mot juste,* and he finds that writing flawed which contains irrelevancies, repetitions, or underdeveloped possibilities. He avoids the blurred image or the "shifting effect," and finds meaning in sharp focus, careful arrangement of the parts, in proportion and orderly development. . . .

For Lesser, art is finally "a matter of stating the truth in unimpeachable form" . . . , but the truth is always determined by language and form, not by any reference to the world. . . . Thus Lesser turns inward away from the world, living his solipsistic priestly life, ignoring the devastation around him, and trying to meet the merciless formal demands of a book which asks him by its own structure to "say more than he knew." "Form sometimes offers so many possibilities it takes a while before you can determine which it's insisting on," . . . and so the writing goes on for nine long years. (p. 81)

The Tenants opens with Lesser waking to work on his book and "catching sight of himself in his lonely glass," and the book he is writing is another mirror, for its subject is a writer created in almost the exact image of Harry Lesser, who is in turn writing a novel about love, hoping that the book will create the love he cannot find in or feel for people. Art seems to stretch out to infinity, pre-empting reality by simply duplicating itself, a perfect realization of the claim of the romantic literary text to depend on nothing but itself. Malamud's novel about a writer trying to write a novel about a writer trying to write a novel is a wilderness of mirrors, a completely enclosed and infinite world of formalistic art. (p. 82)

The title of Malamud's novel, *The Tenants,* suggests that Lesser is but a temporary resident in, not the owner of, the House of Fiction, and reminds us as well that there is more than one resident. The other tenant is a new arrival, the Black, Willie Spearmint—an obvious and not very happy reference to Shakespeare—who represents in the novel a view of writing which is the antithesis of Lesser's formalistic tradition of art for art's sake. Willie's life recapitulates the primitive phases of the development of the poet as romanticism hypothesizes it. His "election" takes place in prison where, suffering primal fear and bewilderment, he first begins to sing the blues and then finds in the song both comfort and his own identity as lyric singer: "he listens and hears, 'Willie Spearmint sings this song.'" He then begins to read and gradually begins to feel that he too can write. . . . Once out of prison Willie continues to write, and his stories, in contrast to Lesser's involuted and isolated self-reflecting novel about a writer trying to write a novel, are almost unbearably painful reflections of the most terribly immediate aspects of life in Harlem, of wretched jobs and beaten children, of drugs and whores, of men cornered and shot in alleys and women who in despair drink lye and hurl themselves off buildings, and above all of the hatred and violence between black and white, a violence which culminates in the story "No Heart." . . . (pp. 82-3)

But Willie Spearmint's writing is in trouble too, for all the power that drives it. He cannot find the form which adequately expresses his experiences and feelings, and so he too comes to the isolated tenement to find the distance from himself and the world his writing also requires. If Lesser's work lacks reality and energy, Willie's suffers from the absence of what Lesser has too much of, art and form. (p. 83)

In Malamud's romantic view, art is the work of the outsider, in this case the Jewish writer and the black writer, and these marginal men need one another, for each has what the other lacks. . . . If Willie introduces Lesser to some of the vitality and passion his life and work lack, Lesser in turn introduces Willie to the concept of literary craft, reads and criticizes his manuscript, gives him a dictionary and a handbook of grammar. . . . At first the results of the relationship seem ideal, for Willie begins his story again as a novel, moves into the tenement, and sweats the necessary long hard hours over his writing. But the attempt to become a craftsman destroys his writing, for he begins to overwrite in a florid, rhetorical style, employing a pressured stream-of-consciousness technique with elaborate mechanical connections between its various parts. This grotesque "arty" style conflicts directly with the "tensile sparseness" of Willie's "sensibility" and the raw facts of a tale of a black mother trying to kill her son with a breadknife before drinking lye and "throwing herself out of the bedroom window, screaming in pain, rage, futility." . . . Under the weight of Willie's rhetoric, the characters turn into zombies, and the language becomes "a compound of ashes and glue." When Lesser is forced by his own honesty and craft responsibility to tell Willie these truths about his work, Willie is nearly destroyed and vows to quit writing forever, turning to direct action to relieve his frustrated feelings and further his revolutionary cause.

Without art or self-conscious literary technique, *The Tenants* shows, literature lacks meaning and effect, remaining only a crude unmediated egoistic cry of rage and the satisfaction of hatreds, but craft, when applied, seems to desiccate all that it touches, destroying the artist and making it impossible for him to complete the work.

In Malamud's view, Flaubert is wrong: a book cannot be written "about nothing," form cannot complete itself, for writing is in the long run dependent upon the world in which it exists. Western poetry has traditionally expressed this interaction of life and art by marrying the craft of the poet to the love story, for love expresses in physical terms the beauty, completeness, and harmony of being which the craft of the poet also creates in his art. . . . The love story the poet tells, and the skill he uses to tell it have traditionally been but two aspects of the same desire for the beautiful which art seeks to create as an ideal in an ugly and fragmented world.

But earthly physical beauty, which Irene Bell (née Belinsky), represents in name and person, and the beauty of artistic form, which Lesser pursues, are separated in the grotesque world of *The Tenants.* At the beginning of the novel, Lesser lives a loveless existence, unmarried, without family relations. Seizing rare opportunities for occasional, and usually unsatisfactory, sex, he pursues an abstract Flaubertian beauty exclusively. Irene Bell belongs to Willie Spearmint, who frees her from her middle-class life and teaches her the power and pleasure of sexual love. But he finds that he cannot write near Irene, near the actuality of beauty, and so in order to complete his story he begins to work in the House of Fiction. At first he spends only weekdays there, but as his involvement with his craft becomes more intense he moves out of Irene's apartment and spends longer and longer periods in the tenement, foregoing all the physical pleasures of life, food, warmth, and love. But the farther he drifts away from physical love and its embodiment of beauty, the more difficult and less effective his writing becomes. At the same time, Lesser, who has gotten to know Irene through Willie, begins to love her and find comfort with her, and as he does so, his writing improves and moves easily and powerfully towards the promised end.

The point could not be made more clearly: the beauty of art depends upon the real beauty of flesh and the world, even as art rests inevitably upon an experienced reality. To write about nothing is not only cruel indifference but an impossibility. The "knot intrinsicate" of the form of art and the act of human love is drawn even tighter by the involvement of the two writers who need one another. Willie Spearmint has all the primal energy, the ego, the moral passion, and the deep involvement with the world which Lesser's writing lacks; Lesser has all the dedication, concentration, and formal skills Willie's writing lacks. They need each other as writers, even as in their circumstances as Black and Jew they need each other as men. But despite early uneasy movements toward brotherhood, to the apparent benefit of both men and both books, the relationship breaks down because of an insurmountable antagonism. Lesser steals Irene from Willie, who has already more or less abandoned her, and Lesser's attempts to improve Willie's writing destroy it. In fury at the knowledge that he has been cheated in both senses, Willie tries to kill Lesser, beats Irene, and in a culminating act which explains all the others, he breaks into Lesser's apartment and burns all his manuscripts. Since Lesser, close to the promised end, has removed the copy of his book from the safe deposit box for corrections, this means that his book is destroyed, even as Willie's has been, and both writers must either abandon their work or start over again. The mixture of art and life is, apparently, an ideal no longer available to the modern writer as it was to his predecessors. Art and life have become separate and the literary text cannot be written any longer, or if it is it is destroyed. Abandoning art and returning to the world seems to be the only answer, and Willie storms off proclaiming "Revolution is the Real Art," while Lesser considers marrying Irene and going with her to San Francisco to begin a new life. But the power of writing over the writer is absolute, and both men drift back to the tenement. . . . The writers seldom meet, but each avidly reads the scraps of writing the other discards in the ashcans, each hoping that the other will both fail and succeed. But the writing of both degenerates in hatred of the other. Having rejected form, at least outwardly—though he still endlessly rewrites and constantly changes subjects—Willie's writing grows more incoherent, and its formlessness is reflected in its themes, self-loathing and obsessed hatred of all whites, particularly all Jews. . . . In the end, his writing, unable to become anything more than his own raw feelings and his own actual experiences, reduces itself to pages of paper which begin with two opposing words, BLACK-WHITE, and gradually eliminates WHITE, letter by letter, until only the single word BLACK appears over and over again. As Willie's writing realizes the tendency of a number of modern writings, such as Beckett's plays, to disappear into the vortex of a single word endlessly repeated, Lesser's skill gradually dies and he, the man of words, becomes "nauseated when he wrote, by the words, by the thought of them." . . . [As] their books are drawn down into silence, Lesser and Willie are consumed by their hatred for each other. (p. 87)

Levenspiel, the owner of the house, is the appropriate person to put the question that society from Plato to the present has asked of poetry: "What's a make-believe novel, Lesser, against all the woes and miseries that I have explained to you?" To which the craftsman-artist had once answered proudly with Nietzsche, "No artist tolerates reality," or had pointed to Joyce's "luminous silent stasis of aesthetic pleasure" as the true reality redeeming a fallen world. But Malamud speaks for a later generation of authors. Art depends upon the world, and its values must be lived out in the world. It cannot generate its

own conclusion but must find that conclusion in actual experience; that experience, however, is not satisfactory by itself, and if it is to live and have meaning it must take the shape and form that only art can give, transforming particular facts into believable and effective truths. Malamud cannot find any way of bringing these seeming opposites together to a promised end. Instead, art and experience seek their extremes, and in this extremity love dies and the art which seeks love's end through skill and form expires into silence or a single obsessive word sounded over and over again. Having failed to reconcile its artist protagonists, Malamud's own novel cannot reach the promised end but dies away with another word repeated hopelessly, "Mercy, mercy, mercy." Art no longer has the power to bind together a world of racial and class hatred, of decayed cities, individual isolation, of endless war and the broken forms of a former civilization. Nor can it any longer create, as the romantics believed they could, an abstract image of perfect beauty in words which will outlast the world. As its texts lose their power, unable to overcome any longer the destructive forces represented by the tenement and the racial hatred it contains, they lose their reality and become only unfinished manuscripts, a single word endlessly repeated, scraps of yellow paper in the garbage can. (p. 88)

Alvin B. Kernan, "Battering the Object: The Attack on the Literary Text in Malamud's 'The Tenants'," in his The Imaginary Library: An Essay on Literature and Society *(copyright © 1982 by Princeton University Press; excerpts reprinted by permission of Princeton University Press), Princeton University Press, 1982, pp. 66-88.*

ROBERT ALTER

[None of Bernard Malamud's] longer fictions has the absolute rightness of tone and invention of his best short stories [collected in *The Stories of Bernard Malamud*].

His real gift is for the short story, for the spare, rigorous etching of solitary figures caught in the stress of adversity. When Malamud translates such figures into the novel, whose ampler dimensions lead us to expect development, he has difficulty in making his personages go anywhere except deeper into disaster. The plots of his novels tend to devolve into extended fantasies—sometimes lurid, sometimes just depressing—of mutilation and interment. By contrast, his stronger stories exhibit exquisite artistic tact, a remarkable intuition for saying a great deal with the most minimal narrative gestures, and a delicacy of feeling about the characters that cannot be reduced to any simple technique. (p. 1)

[The typical protagonist]—the isolate pensioner as everyman—is more often than not a Yiddish-speaking immigrant Jew who seems to have known little in his life but hard work and hard times. He is typically beset with painful and humiliating ailments—hernia, bad back, weak heart, arthritis, a veritable cornucopia of the physical ills flesh is heir to. He is also typically on the brink, or below it, of poverty, counting pennies in the back of his rundown grocery store or in his dingy rented room, wondering where next month's rent will come from, perhaps dreaming sometimes of a sufficiency he knows he will never enjoy. (Malamud's vision is pre-eminently that of a writer whose formative years were spent in the Great Depression.) Finally, the characteristic Malamud protagonist often proves to be desperate for love. In several instances, it is a father whose love for a rebellious child has soured into a resentment bordering on hatred. In other stories, it is the pathetic love or mere erotic longing of an older man for a younger woman which will get him nothing but mockery and frustration.

As my composite portrait of the Malamudian hero may suggest, this is bleak and narrow stuff for the making of a fictional world, but in his stories Malamud has often been able to transform this material into the most arresting images of the human predicament. There is no single formula that will explain how this transformation takes place, but I think it has a good deal to do with the laconic lyricism with which his prose evokes loneliness and abandonment and poverty. For such subjects, too little stylistic elaboration would produce mere flatness, too much, insistent pathos or masochistic self-indulgence. But in his best stories Malamud works in a perfect middle register that elicits compassion through its very terseness. . . .

Rereading these stories, I am surprised to find that the tautness of the prose owes something to a writer radically removed from Malamud in sensibility and values—Ernest Hemingway. In his fondness for sequences of short sentences and monosyllabic words, the shifting of much of the emotional burden to strategically chosen physical objects rendered with flatly descriptive terms . . . , Malamud shows at least an affinity with the writing in perfect Hemingway achievements like "A Clean, Well-Lighted Place" and "Old Man at the Bridge." The difference, of course, is that Malamud does not hesitate to point directly to Davidov's limp and his weariness, or to Rosen's "wasted" appearance and "despairing" eyes, though he is prudent in simply stating these attributes of adversity and then allowing Rosen's dreadful room to speak for itself. Also unlike Hemingway is the interpolation of a bit of interior monologue. . . . (p. 35)

Perhaps one of Malamud's difficulties as a novelist has been that anxiety deployed over 300 or more pages begins to rasp, the anxious characters often driving themselves in the end to some orgy of self-immolation. In the short stories, however, where the writer can catch a revelatory moment of distress that intimates a lifetime, Malamud has been able to become the bard of anxiety, making the more successfully realized of his protagonists large and resonant in their smallness and their plaintive groans, allowing us as readers to see the fears and uncertainties of our lives figured, however grotesquely, in theirs.

The actual fictional rendering of these eternal flounderers is often a good deal less bleak than any summary of their predicament might lead one to suppose. In this regard, what I have said about the "Hemingwayesque" aspect of the style is a little misleading; though the prose is usually not very metaphorical and certainly avoids pyrotechnic effects, there are little eruptions of figurative perception that are funny or mysterious or magical, tokens of an imagination outside the grimy walls of the trap in which the protagonists are typically caught. . . .

[In] the most memorable of Malamud's stories there are often significant glimpses of a shimmering horizon of fantasy beyond the grim scenes of impoverishment and loneliness in the foreground. The fantasy can enter through an image, a dream, a hallucination, or occasionally through the configuration of the whole story, as in **"The First Seven Years"**; for all its realistic depiction of immigrant existence, it is a touching fairy tale of an apprentice winning the master's daughter, with an echo of the Bible (Jacob working seven years for Rachel) and perhaps a reminiscence of I. B. Singer. . . .

Of all these stories, it can be said that only Bernard Malamud could have written them. They are neither imitative nor imita-

ble. Not every story in the selection is equally strong, and there are four or five pieces that strike me as flat or even abortive. But this volume includes stories like **"The First Seven Years," "The Magic Barrel," "The Last Mohican," "Idiots First"** and **"Angel Levine,"** which I think will be read as long as anyone continues to care about American fiction written in the 20th century. (p. 36)

Robert Alter, "Ordinary Anguish," in The New York Times Book Review *(© 1983 by The New York Times Company; reprinted by permission), October 16, 1983, pp. 1, 35-6.*

JOHN L'HEUREUX

"Art lives on surprise," Bernard Malamud once said. "A writer has to surprise himself to be worth reading." Over the years Malamud has provided surprise, and more: brief tragedies laced with wit and irony, full-length portraits of our inhuman condition, novels and stories that explore the longings, frustrations, failures, defeats, and—sometimes—the miraculous resurrection of the human spirit. . . .

What immediately strikes the reader [about *The Stories of Bernard Malamud*] is how quickly and completely Malamud compels our belief in the reality of his fictional world, even when that world includes angels, a talking horse, a magic crown. We believe even his ghetto Jews—who seem to inhabit a time and place solely of Malamud's contriving—because, with his deft prose, his flat and funny dialogue, his absolute authority as storyteller, he makes us believe. These are odd, taut, tortured stories, and not all of them work—**"Take Pity"** and **"The Mourners,"** for example, ask the reader for an emotional response that neither the characters nor their situation has earned. But at their best they achieve something rare and wonderful. . . . In the witty **"Rembrandt's Hat,"** in the magical **"Silver Crown,"** in the heartbreaking **"My Son the Murderer"** suffering becomes a function of personal choice, of the unwillingness or inability to communicate, of fate modified by free will. Surprise here takes the form of irony, elevated and sweetened by Malamud's intelligence and sensitivity.

All of Malamud's stories are shot through with feeling and fantasy. The hard, observed images of real life combine with the passionate thrust of his imagination to produce for the reader wondrous impossibilities. . . . The depth of feeling in these stories, the breadth of life lived, is not undercut but enriched by the evident fantasy. . . . Fantasy is made to bear witness to the unfathomable mystery at the heart of all suffering and desire.

Malamud's best stories surprise and illuminate; the great ones redeem. **"Angel Levine," "The Magic Barrel," "The Last Mohican"** are, by any standard, great stories. They are more than magical; they are mystical. In each of them an overwhelming need—ostensibly physical, but ultimately spiritual—propels a man into a preposterous relationship with someone who pursues him. . . .

From each of these relationships the pursued character flees into the darkest recesses of his own soul, and there he encounters an overwhelming question. Unless I become a whole man, can I claim to be a Jew? Do I truly love God if I do not also love people? Am I my brother's keeper? If I give the beggar four dollars, why not five? If five dollars, why not my suit? If my suit, why not my life? In his response to the terrible question, the pursued becomes the pursuer, joyous now, hopeful, because in his pursuit he loses everything he thought had mattered and wins the one thing he valued least: his possible self. Suffering here is at once personal and cosmic. . . . These stories anatomize our human isolation, and redeem it.

And everywhere there is that funny, inflected, fatalistic voice. ''My dear God, sweetheart, did I deserve that this should happen to me? . . . .''

Here is Malamud in all his richness, humor, pathos, heartbreak. An analyst of suffering, a moralist with a ripe sense of irony, Malamud finally is a pessimist who nonetheless believes in the possibility of redemption. *Stories* is a surprising and welcome book indeed.

John L'Heureux, "The Angel of Life," in New York Magazine *(copyright © 1983 by News Group Publications, Inc.; reprinted with the permission of* New York *Magazine), Vol. 16, No. 41, October 17, 1983, p. 94.*

PAUL GRAY

Sprinters do not ordinarily sign up for marathons, nor do lonely long-distance runners enter the crush of 100-yard dashes. But some authors perform an analogous feat by writing both short stories and novels. Instead of being complimented on their versatility, though, they frequently encounter a peculiar problem: facing themselves as competitors. . . .

Under such difficult conditions, [Bernard Malamud] has been racing himself for a long time. . . . *The Stories of Bernard Malamud* includes 23 pieces selected by the author from . . . past assemblages, plus two previously uncollected stories. The book not only offers substantial evidence that Malamud's stories are better than his novels; it makes the distinction seem irrelevant. In sufficient concentration, small objects achieve critical mass, enough fast victories add up to a triumphant long haul.

Malamud's world reveals itself bit by bit: a place of stony certainties and infrangible laws, brightened occasionally by

enclaves of unexpected magic. Those who live here are predominantly poor, oppressed by hard work. Most are men without women. More than half the heroes in these stories are bachelors or widowers. . . . The main character in a story called *The Model* speaks for most of Malamud's men: ''Is there nothing more to my life than it is now? Is this all that is left to me?''

These people must bear Old Testament burdens, punished not just by life but by the suspicion that they somehow deserve all the troubles heaped upon them. . . .

In *Idiots First,* Mendel has been approached by Ginzburg, a messenger of death, and warned that his life expires at midnight. Mendel must somehow raise the train fare to send his son Isaac, who is 39 and unable to care for himself, to an uncle in California. He succeeds, and the fierceness of his determination frightens even death himself. . . .

This is one of the handful of happy endings in Malamud's stories. Yet all the tales radiate a joy that has nothing to do with consequences. The author consistently portrays a kind of heroism devoid of self-consciousness or sentimentality. Convinced that their fates have already been determined, characters go on stubbornly behaving as if their actions mattered. . . .

Malamud is probably the most severe writer of his generation, a trait that may explain why his work has been extensively admired but less widely loved. Still, the gathering of these stories reveals a gentleness in Malamud's art that was not always clear before. He admires the sheer cussedness of his characters, their backs to the wall, squabbling in the maw of annihilation. He relishes the cranks and eccentrics who, destined to suffer and die, still insist on making noise in a vast, indifferent universe. Mendel, grappling with his fate, screams, ''You bastard, don't you understand what it means human?'' This book offers 25 vivid and unforgettable answers.

Paul Gray, "Heroism without Sentiment," in Time *(copyright 1983 Time Inc.; all rights reserved; reprinted by permission from* Time*), Vol. 122, No. 18, October 17, 1983, p. 92.*

Paule Marshall

1929-

Black American novelist and short story writer.

Although her fiction was long neglected in scholarly literary circles, Marshall is now considered an important writer in contemporary black literature. Her work depicts the emotional growth and newly found independence of black women who have discovered and accepted their heritage. Although some may be tempted to label Marshall a feminist writer, critics feel that her work, in a general sense, depicts the individual's search for a secure identity in an uncertain world.

Marshall's parents immigrated to New York City from Barbados in the 1920s. This West Indian influence is prevalent throughout her work. Her first novel, *Brown Girl, Brownstones* (1959), tells of a young Barbadian immigrant girl whose parents are caught in the conflict between ethnic autonomy and assimilation. *The Chosen Place, the Timeless People* (1969) is a symbolic novel about the inhabitants of a small, underdeveloped Caribbean island and their refusal to accept modernization. Her recent work, *Praisesong for the Widow* (1983), is the story of an unhappy, affluent American woman who experiences a spiritual rebirth while vacationing in the West Indies.

Marshall's novels are praised for their rich characterization and descriptive power. Many critics agree that her strength as a writer lies in her usage of West Indian idioms and dialect. It has also been said that Marshall is the first contemporary novelist to fully explore the psyche of black American women. The author herself defines her works as an attempt to "trace history," because "as a people we have not as yet really engaged our past."

(See also *Contemporary Authors*, Vols. 77-80.)

© *Thomas Victor 1983*

CAROL FIELD

Rarely has a first novel come to hand which has the poignant appeal and the fresh, fierce emotion of **"Brown Girl, Brownstones."** . . .

Racial conflict and the anger and frustration it nurtures are part of this tale, but equally, if not more, important are the personal conflicts of men and women making roots in a new land, of men and women caught in duels of love and hate, of ambition, envy and failure.

While Selina is the heroine of this novel, it is her parents who give it and her its depth and color. Through them, through their passions, their clashes, their hopes, the girl assumes shape and meaning.

To Silla, gaunt and strong, the brownstone house in Brooklyn which she leased represented a giant step from the slavish toil she had known in Barbados. To own the once elegant building, to cut up its enormous chambers, to have a houseful of well-paying roomers was her dream. Other "Bajuns" were doing it, making money, getting ahead in the new world. With a little help from her husband she could swing it, she knew, but Deighton was no man to depend on. . . .

He was handsome; he loved good clothes; he had ambitions for getting on in the world but they were woven of the stuff of dreams. Starting correspondence courses, he saw himself successful as a radio mechanic, an accountant, a trumpeter in a jazz band and then, realizing his limitations, he dropped them. How he willfully and wantonly checkmates Silla in her illegal efforts to capitalize on Barbados land he unexpectedly inherited makes the heart-stirring climax of the book.

Wonderfully, in incidents and scenes that hold the nuances of character as well as language rich with Barbados locution, Mrs. Marshall puts the quickness of life into these two. The tortured Silla, remembering her wretched childhood, spells out its details in anguished words for Selina, seeking to explain her ambition and hardness. But it is the dream-bemused Deighton, with his charm, his good clothes, his fancy woman, his rosy-hued tales, who is closest to the girl's heart. While she inherits some of her mother's iron, she is, in her love of poetry and fantasy, of people and adventure, the daughter of Deighton. . . .

["**Brown Girl, Brownstones**"] is an unforgettable novel written with pride and anger, with rebellion and tears. Rich in content and in cadences of the King's and "Bajun" English, it is the work of a highly gifted writer.

Carol Field, "Fresh, Fierce and 'First'," in New York Herald Tribune Book Review (© I.H.T. Cor-

308

poration; reprinted by permission), August 16, 1959, p. 5.

THE NEW YORKER

When Mrs. Marshall writes about those she truly loves, she cannot be resisted. Her singularly talented first novel [**"Brown Girl, Brownstones"**] describes the childhood and adolescence of a Brooklyn girl whose parents, both Barbadian immigrants, share an unhappy marriage and a memory of their native island. . . . To Selina's mother, Silla, the island represents poverty, oppression, and a poetry and beauty that she misses and despises. To her father, Deighton, the island is his heart's desire, and he longs to return to it. When an unexpected legacy gives Deighton two acres of island land, he begins to make plans to return home and build a house. Although he has never succeeded at any of the various trades he has taken up in his efforts to raise himself in life, he believes he can make the money to go home and claim a splendid place for himself in his own country. . . . [Silla] covets her husband's two acres not for themselves but for the price they will bring, and she schemes to get his inheritance away from him and sell it. The climax of the novel, when the struggle between Deighton and his wife reaches its peak, marks a turning point in the great creative impulse that carries Mrs. Marshall so triumphantly through the first half of her work. From this scene on, although her writing continues to be interesting, it loses in emotion, and therefore, because she is an intensely emotional writer, it loses in power. Selina, who is ten years old when we first meet her, and who remains always at the front and center of the story, is an appealing figure, but even more appealing and memorable are some of the many other figures Mrs. Marshall introduces into this crowded, resounding novel. (p. 179)

> *A review of "Brown Girl, Brownstones," in* The New Yorker *(© 1959 by The New Yorker Magazine, Inc.), Vol. XXXV, No. 31, September 19, 1959, pp. 179-80.*

VERNON HALL, JR.

["**Soul Clap Hands and Sing**"] is something of a renaissance in authentic feeling for real men, women and life. Named for its geographic setting—Barbados, Brooklyn, British Guiana and Brazil—each story describes in terms of natural action and reaction how an aging and dying man attempts to face up to the decline of his virile powers. Each man portrayed is conceived in terms of his relationship with a woman; in fact, Mrs. Marshall—herself the mother of a male child to whom this volume is dedicated—is saying that a man is truly a man when he commits himself to a genuine, creative love, and that a woman realizes her womanliness through her man. And she etches character and setting with descriptive power and insight. . . .

Paule Marshall's art is serious, wholesome and strong.

> *Vernon Hall, Jr., "A Stellar Performance," in* New York Herald Tribune *(© I.H.T. Corporation; reprinted by permission), September 17, 1961, p. 6.*

ROBERT BONE

Paule Marshall, who is something of a *cuisinière*, specializing in Barbadian dishes, has concocted a novel of West Indian life that will greatly enhance her reputation. Not to mince words,

"**The Chosen Place, the Timeless People**," in my opinion, is the best novel to be written by an American black woman, one of the two important black novels of the 1960's (the other being William Demby's "The Catacombs"), and one of the four or five most impressive novels ever written by a black American. (p. 4)

"**The Chosen Place, the Timeless People**" is a parable of Western civilization and its relations with the undeveloped world. The setting of the novel is a Caribbean island—and, more precisely, its most "backward" and unassimilable region, called Bournehills. Bourne Island, as the name implies, forms a symbolic boundary between the cultures of Europe and Africa, between the forces of progress and tradition, between town man and countryman, rich and poor, white and black.

To the island comes a team of social scientists from an American research-and-development foundation. . . . As the characters acquire symbolic resonance, we see that Allen represents an effete civilization that has pledged its soul to the gods of technology. Harriet embodies the suicidal impulse of the Western psyche: its unyielding racism and will to dominate, despite a superficial liberalism. Saul represents the possibility of transformation and renewal, providing only that fate will overtake him with a blinding vision.

At the center of the novel is the magnificent figure of Merle Kinbona: part saint, part revolutionary, part obeah-woman. A creation worthy of Camus, she commands the loyalty of the villagers by virtue of the obeisance they accord her suffering. Her devastated life emerges with the ravaged landscape and economy of Bournehills; her toughness and resiliency contain intimations of the new beginning. She is the challenge and testing-ground for the white characters; an agent of destruction or catalyst of growth.

It is Merle who fortifies the village in its special mission, its determination to bear witness to the past. Every year at carnival, the Bournehills band undertakes the ritual enactment of a slave revolt, to remind the people of their painful history and strengthen them against the future. This annual ceremony justifies their daily hardships, gives meaning to their barren lives, and explains their obstinate resistance to the modern age.

The concluding section of the novel is ironically entitled "Whitsun," a holiday that celebrates the descent of the Holy Ghost to the Apostles, bringing them the gift of prophecy. Mrs. Marshall's heroine is likewise cast in the prophetic role. In her confrontation with Saul's wife, she breaks the chains of psychological dependency. She thus prepares the way for a second coming—not of Jesus meek and mild, but of Cuffee Ned, the slave insurrectionary. (pp. 4, 54)

["**The Chosen Place, the Timeless People**"] is a compendium of the old-fashioned novelistic virtues. Four massive structural blocks support the weight of the plot and of the author's epic intentions. The characterization, no less imposing, rests on solid foundations; the style is as delicate as the architecture is massive. Mrs. Marshall is the master of a trim and sprightly prose. She has a good eye for detail, and there is no descriptive passage that does not contribute to the psychological development, or advance the symbolic action.

Not the least of her achievements is a viable solution to the problem of dialect. The flavor of West Indian speech is conveyed by an occasional pungent idiom or a striking departure from normal syntax: for the most part, she leaves accent and intonation to our imagination. By suggesting rather than transcribing living speech, she preserves the flesh and sting of it, without impeding the flow of her narrative.

Her most impressive feat, however, is the transformation of politics and history into ritual and myth. . . . As in the Yeats poem, "Two Songs From a Play," Athena bears away the beating heart of the slain Dionysus, so the timeless people will assist at the demise of the Christian West, gaining sustenance for the future from the brutal past.

Such is the substance of Paule Marshall's myth. It is a myth of survival. . . . (p. 54)

Robert Bone, "Merle Kinbona Was Part Saint, Part Revolutionary, Part Obeah-Woman," in The New York Times Book Review (© *1969 by The New York Times Company; reprinted by permission), November 30, 1969, pp. 4, 54.*

RICHARD RHODES

Paule Marshall has written a monumental book. [*The Chosen Place, the Timeless People*] is by no means an unqualified success, but it has the virtues of its length of story and depth of commitment: complexity, the evocation of a people, characters whose lives we can follow long enough to see them through major decisions and major life-changes.

Set on a fictional Caribbean island, *The Chosen Place, the Timeless People* concerns the lives of blacks there who would like to move beyond the old strictures of birth and caste, and of whites who accept the conditions—and the conditioning—and of those who do not. Among those who do not is an expedition of social scientists from the United States—Saul, his patrician wife Harriet, and his assistant Allen. Dominating them all once they have settled in to begin studying the island's problems—dominating the novel, for that matter—is Merle. . . . Merle attracts Saul to a serious commitment to Bournehills. She leads the poor of the district in a near-revolt when their cane factory is closed down. She is, in her sensitivity and her violence, the poor of the district, and against her Harriet finally throws all her WASP force and is destroyed.

At the same time, Merle is the reason why Mrs. Marshall's novel does not entirely succeed: The whole book, though written in the third person, judges its characters as if from Merle's point of view. Saul is too plastic to believe; Harriet too thin-blooded to be real; Allen more spineless than even a frightened latent-homosexual could be. Merle dominates it all as if she were larger than life, which in Mrs. Marshall's telling she is, though she does not seem so to the reader. Yet, if the characters are faulty and the story sometimes ponderous, it is also sometimes unforgettable. . . .

Richard Rhodes, "A Serious Matter," in Book World—The Washington Post (© *1969 Postrib Corp.; reprinted by permission of* Chicago Tribune *and* The Washington Post), December 28, 1969, p. 10.

HENRIETTA BUCKMASTER

Paule Marshall is, I think, one of the best novelists writing in the United States. She has form, style and immense mastery of words. She writes with all her senses as well as with her acute and probing mind. Sometimes I feel she is almost too gifted—or rather, that this plethora of riches is a bit too much on display and needs a sharper restraint. . . .

In "The Chosen Place, the Timeless People" she is writing about an island in the Caribbean which is a piece of land but also a state of mind. To the demographer, the anthropologist, the sociologist, who have come to carry out a research development project, the island is a challenge to their best technical training, to their enlightened expertise, and to their humaneness which is very much engaged in action.

But there is an element here which the whites from the United States can only attempt to understand with their heads, and that is what the past has done, what being black has meant. . . . In fact the past is barely mentioned, though it lives in the gnomic recollections of a slave rebellion. These timeless people in this chosen place survived because they understood through a deep reflex that they could only prove their humanhood by survival. What happens to them now, in the present, is another thing. The Americans talk about the developed countries helping the undeveloped, of the fusion of tradition and progress. But these are words and attitudes which have not been tested by the island, and the island persists in saying, "I'm somebody now. Recognize me."

[Merle Kinbona] is a bridge between past and present, attitude and action. The island is her bone and breath. But she knows what other worlds are like. She has lived in England; she now runs a guest house and has no illusions. She is a remarkable character. Her spiritual intuitions are negligible, her human understanding profound. . . .

This is a long novel, sparing of plot. Peoples' lives twine and knot, while the island and the sea and the sun make different and relentless demands. . . .

[Mrs. Marshall] is writing about people who are disengaged at a profound level of being, very much engaged at the level of doing. She is saying their efforts to draw together never go back far enough, never draw nourishment from their sources. The island is that moment when a human being is required to look at himself but nine times out of ten turns away.

["The Chosen Place, the Timeless People"] is a high achievement within the goals set by the author. My reservations are a measure of my respect.

Henrietta Buckmaster, "'I'm Somebody Now. Recognize Me'," in The Christian Science Monitor (*reprinted by permission from* The Christian Science Monitor; © *1970 The Christian Science Publishing Society; all rights reserved), January 22, 1970, p. 9.*

JANET BURROWAY

I would have made more space for Paule Marshall's *The Chosen Place, The Timeless People* if the author herself had made less. This is a depth-study of a remote Caribbean village, 'chosen' by a benevolent American organisation for a rehabilitation scheme. The inhabitants of Bournehills are timeless in the fierce pride with which they hold to their customs and their history, but also because the time for their way of life is running out. Paule Marshall's great strength is characterisation, and she gives us dozens of telling portraits, catching the haggard unease of the Jewish social scientist with as much accuracy as the headlong chatter of the black hotel matron, the stiff pseudo-Englishness of the local grandees. Unfortunately these characters are so numerous, and their confrontations developed at such length, that the significance of their story is partly lost.

This is an impressive fat book with a superb thin book inside trying to get out.

Janet Burroway, "Golden Pulp," in New Statesman *(© 1970 The Statesman & Nation Publishing Co. Ltd.), Vol. 80, No. 2063, October 2, 1970, p. 426.**

BELL GALE CHEVIGNY

A novel that harbors an intelligent revolutionary politics and a compassionate, penetrating humanism is an event in any time. If the time is now, if the revolution is black, if the compassion transcends race, it is a freak or a miracle, depending on whether or not you trust it. I trust **"The Chosen Place, the Timeless People."** I think it is an important and moving book. And Paule Marshall seems to me as wise as she is bold, for in compromising neither her politics nor her understanding of people, she makes better sense of both. . . .

I was surprised at the quiet of this novel's reception until I discovered how difficult it is to write about. In many ways that matter to me, it is not extraordinary, but in two months I haven't stopped recommending it and—daily—thinking about it. Its form is in no way original, but the old bottle is blown wider to hold more kinds of wine: through the consciousness of its major characters the Jewish novel and the black novel meet, and the WASP gets almost equal time. I know of no serious contemporary novel attempting this synthesis—it almost constitutes a new form. The prose is workmanlike and rarely soars, but marvelously evokes West Indian place and speech and provides an unusually haunting experience. And although it does not forge a new black sensibility, neither is it a white folks' story. . . . It deals with all of us, in all our kinds, where we are now and how we stand with each other. It sums up. It casts some things we know intermittently in a durable mold so we can know them better. The Invisible Man of Ralph Ellison says, contrasting blacks to whites, that blacks are "older than they in the sense of what it took to live in the world with others," and in this sense only a black author is old enough to dispense this vision. It is a ripe, ripe book—I guess it is a classic. (p. 6)

I want to say this book is mellow and I want to say it expresses throughout the need for revolution. This will seem a contradiction to those whose revolution harbors none but militant feelings. But it is not a contradiction if we see—and this is the book's achievement—that revolutionary ideas are coming of age. (p. 31)

Bell Gale Chevigny, in a review of "The Chosen Place, the Timeless People" (reprinted by permission of The Village Voice *and the author; copyright © The Village Voice, Inc., 1970), in* The Village Voice, *Vol. XV, No. 41, October 8, 1970, pp. 6, 30-1.*

LEELA KAPAI

Paule Marshall is the author of *Brown Girl, Brownstones; Soul Clap Hands and Sing; The Chosen Place, The Timeless People;* and a few short stories and articles. With a remarkable maturity in her work, she displays a subtle understanding of human problems and a mastery of the art of fiction. Some of the major themes in her works concern the identity crisis, the race problem, the importance of tradition for the black American, and the need for sharing to achieve meaningful relationships. In her technique she blends judiciously the best of the past tradition with the innovations of recent years. (p. 49)

Quest for identity is a perennial theme in literature. There is no age when a sensitive soul has not been troubled by questions about the meaning of his very own existence and his relation to the world around. The identity crisis assumes even more gravity for the minority groups who were either brought to this land or who came of their own accord in search of greener pastures. Lost in a new cultural environment, such people need more than ordinary effort to recognize and keep their identity alive. However, such self-questionings are not the prerogative of only the members of a particular group based on race, sex, or age; therefore, Miss Marshall concerns herself with people of all ages, of all races, and of all strata.

Miss Marshall's first book, **Brown Girl** . . . , is a *Bildungs-roman*, in which the trials and tribulations of growing up are complicated by the fact that Selina, the protagonist, is the daughter of Barbadian immigrants. Selina is caught between the conflicting attitudes of her parents, though she sympathises clearly with her father. . . . Selina shows her defiance and anger by her affair with an unsuccessful artist in her community. Since an inevitable part of growing up in America is coming to terms with racial conflict, Selina cannot escape it either. Her moment of revelation comes through Mrs. Benton, a typical "liberal" Northerner. To show her broad-mindedness, Mrs. Benton showers Selina with tales of her generosity to her "girl," who was "so honest too." She compliments Selina for her poise and speech, adding "it's just wonderful how you've taken your race's natural talent for dancing and music and developed it . . .". . . . So Selina realizes that she is, after all, set for the stereotype role of an entertainer. And as if to confirm it, Mrs. Benton requests her to say something "in that delightful West Indian accent." This first exposure to racist attitudes forces Selina to see the life around her in a new light.

In the moment of her need, Clive fails her too, and Selina has to fall back upon her inner strength. She realizes then that despite her differences with her mother, she is very much like her. She also learns to value her people; "they no longer puzzled or offended her." She admits, "they had bequeathed her a small strength. She had only this to sustain her all the years." . . . (pp. 49-50)

[The next book, *Soul Clap Hands and Sing,*] is, as a critic put it, held together not by mere alliteration but by theme. In contrast to the first novel, these novellas deal with old men who, approaching their end, realize that they have failed to live. (pp. 50-1)

In both **"Barbados"** and **"Brooklyn,"** the protagonists learn the truth about themselves through two young girls. In the former, the aging farmer Watford, who returns to his home rich after fifty years of toil in Boston, keeps himself aloof, disdaining others and assuming the superiority of his masters. When at last he turns to a young woman for affection, he is spurned mercilessly. . . . In **"Brooklyn"** Max Berman, a teacher of French literature, not only fails in his attempt to seduce a fair Negro girl and sees the futility of his life, but also enables her to see where she belongs. All her life Miss Williams had been sheltered by her parents from the white people as well as from the darker members of her race. She had thus grown up belonging to no world. Max's behavior makes her accept her blackness with pride.

The old men of the next two novellas are Gerald Motley in **"British Guiana"** and Heitor Baptista Guimares in **"Brazil."**

A descendant of Hindu, Chinese, and Negro ancestors, Motley does not know who he really is. He tolerates Sidney's arrogance and contempt because he serves as a constant reminder of what he could have been. Seeing Sidney's pain he feels glad that "he is old and would never know pain again." Death is perhaps the only merciful end of his state. In "**Brazil**" Guimares, the night-club entertainer, known by his assumed name O Grand Caliban, finds himself "lost in the myth he has created." On the eve of his retirement, he realizes that his white partner has robbed him not only of his years of glory, but even deprived him of his very name. He too perhaps has no chance to retrieve his lost identity.

Thus in all the four novellas, the old men finally come to see the truth, but their time is gone. Out of the ashes of the old, a new phoenix arises, and it seems that the nameless young girl of "**Barbados**" with her politically aware boyfriend, Miss Williams of "**Brooklyn**," Sidney Parrish of "**British Guiana**," and the madonna-like wife of Caliban bearing his child in "**Brazil**" are the heralds of a new future.

The question of identity is brought to the fore again in *The Chosen Place*. . . . Merle Kinbona is an enigmatic woman who, in the words of Allen, "somehow is Bournehills." Merle's traumatic experience in childhood when her mother was shot by her white father's lawful wife haunted her all her life. Even though her father never acknowledged her, he arranged for her schooling; however, material comforts have never compensated for love and understanding. Merle is now in her hometown after a long stay in London where she had a nervous collapse after her marriage with a young African broke on his learning of her past relationship with a white woman. At Bournehills, she is trying to forget her hurt and misery behind the facade of endless chatter and assumed indifference. By the end of the novel, she has learnt she must go back to Africa to pick up whatever broken pieces of her life remain. (pp. 51-2)

The search for identity of all educated black women seems to be Miss Marshall's concern in "**Reena**" [a short story published in *American Negro Short Stories*, edited by J. H. Clark]. Reena, obviously the writer's alter-ego, is an intelligent girl who gradually grows aware of the acute injustice of the society. After her struggle at college and two abortive affairs with young men who use her for their own ends, she faces the problem of finding a suitable mate. The educated black men are either settled or they prefer white women. Her marriage to an aspiring photographer does not last too long, for he resents Reena's success. Reena resolves to bring up her children fully aware of their own personalities and race and plans to take them to Africa to show them black men living with pride in their heritage.

Closely connected with the question of identity is the race issue. In *Brown Girl* . . . the racist attitude of White America looms large in the background. Selina's cry of anguish voices the feelings of all people of all minorities. Her desire for violence, "to grab the cane and rush into some store on Fulton Street and avenge that wrong by bringing it smashing across the white face behind the counter" . . . is not uncommon too. In "**Brooklyn**" the life of Miss Williams is an evidence of the ambiguous identity experienced by many blacks. She succeeds, however, in accepting herself as a proud member of her race and thwarts the centuries old pattern of seduction and exploitation. Motley and Caliban in "**British Guiana**" and "**Brazil**" respectively suffer on account of the white power structure that encouraged no individualism.

The Chosen Place . . . weaves in the race issue subtly in the entire story. Harriet represents the spirit of the white world. She is only a step ahead of the Bentons of this world. When she fails to comprehend why a woman would sell the eggs to someone else rather than feed her own family, she takes it to be another backward streak of the incorrigibles. Her impotent anger and frustration come out vividly in the carnival scene where she realizes that the reign of people like her is over and a new generation is emerging. Her death seems to be a symbolic end of all that white America stands for and the ever-mourning waves of the ocean perform the ablution of the old sins of the past. Perhaps a new race of active men like Saul and sympathetic ones like Allen will create better understanding between the races.

This new world, Miss Marshall feels, will be created only through an acute awareness of the past. . . . Since Miss Marshall believes that without tradition one has no real existence, she has all her major characters go back to their ancient heritage. (pp. 53-4)

Miss Marshall says, "My concern has always been not only with content, what is being said, but also the way it is being said, the style." This concern shows in her craftsmanship. She uses a judicious mixture of the old and the new in fictional tradition. The plots of her novels are unambiguous and interesting containing conflict and suspense to keep the reader engrossed. But she uses liberally symbolic language to heighten the meaning; thus her stories are very often capable of being taken on different levels of meaning. At one level, *Brown Girl* . . . is the story of Selina's growing up, but on another level, it is also the story of "any people undergoing fundamental change and disruption." . . . *Soul Clap* . . . deals with the identity crisis of the protagonists, but it also represents the passing away of the old order and the time for the new. *The Chosen Place* . . . at one level deals with the problems of its characters, but on the other level traces the history of black-white relationships. (pp. 55-6)

Paule Marshall excels in her character portrayals, but one must confess that she is partial to her women. They receive more careful attention, but that too is for a certain end, for she believes that the Negro woman has been neglected in literature. (p. 56)

Her women are complex characters but with hidden reservoirs of strength, which they need in order to survive. The mother in *Brown Girl* . . . is presented sympathetically despite her harshness; it is because the writer sees her as a product of her environment. If she is ruthless, it is understandable, if not excusable. Merle also is strong; her suffering has neither bent nor broken her. With her incessant chatter she may seem out of her mind at times to some, but that is her way of letting off her steam and diverting others from her sorrows.

In her attempt to battle with the old stereotype of the strong mother portraiture, Miss Marshall becomes unduly harsh with all mothers. Silla destroys her man and alienates her children by her very strength; Clive's mother keeps him tied to her apron-strings. In "**Brooklyn**" the mother of Miss Williams shares the responsibility in creating the ambiguity in her life. Similarly, in *The Chosen Place* . . . the mothers or the mother-figures, black or white, fail miserably. Harriet's obsession with meaningful life grew out of her mother's passivity; Leesy, the mother-substitute for Vere, cannot understand the new politically conscious modernized young man. In short, there is no mother who is depicted favorably.

Among men, Selina's father is portrayed well enough though he loses our sympathy eventually. The character studies of the men in **Soul Clap** . . . also succeed in capturing their despondent states of mind. Saul, however, is the best creation of her fictional world. He is strong, yet has his weaknesses too and is very much aware of the common bond that unites all human beings. Thus he is a very human character.

Even though the writer does not use Joycean style of stream of consciousness technique, she frequently focusses on the subconscious mind of the characters. Combined with the editorial omniscience, her method succeeds in giving us an insight into the characters. In her first novel, the problem of the point of view is somewhat simplified, for we see the action mostly through the protagonist's eyes. But we do see the events from Silla's angle and also from Deighton's perspective. In her novellas most of the narrative is seen through the consciousness of the protagonists. Her last novel shows an adept handling of the point of view. She makes use of the mystical quality of the island where in the solitude each of the major characters faces his past and the flashbacks assist us in understanding his motivation.

Like Ralph Ellison Paule Marshall believes that the "Negro American writer is also an heir of the human experience which is literature. . . ." From Eliot and Joyce she has learned the value of tradition. And then she does not forget the value of folk material. She tells us that she learned the first lessons of the narrative art from listening to her mother and her friends. After their hard day of scrubbing floors, they had to talk out their hurts and humiliations. Their acute observations about the people they worked for and their vivid portrayals filled their young listener with awe and admiration. Miss Marshall sees their gift as a part of the great oral tradition. . . . She feels that the mysterious element that held her spellbound has its source in the archetypal African memory. She uses it time and again, but it is at its best in **The Chosen Place**. . . .

Through Miss Marshall's comments and, best of all, through her works, one can attempt to formulate her aesthetic beliefs. She seems to be quite in agreement with some of the tenets of the much discussed black aesthetics, and yet she differs too. Miss Marshall also stresses the need for identity. She too believes in understanding of one's past, both individual and historical. She too stands for reviving the African cultural heritage which gives supremacy to man over the machine. She too believes that the black writer owes a great responsibility to himself and to his world, to express his views to the world through his art. But here she diverges. Her works show that she does not believe that the art of the black writer should serve only one end. Like several other writers, she knows that the American writer cannot deny his Western heritage. She is equally proud of her black heritage but believes that her art should be devoted to showing the relationship of an individual to the other inhabitants of this world, no matter what their color, race, or geographic location is. She writes of blacks, very often of West Indians, simply because a writer writes best when he makes use of what he knows best. Her characters are, therefore, human beings first; their racial identity is secondary so far as the art is concerned. This fact does not make her any less believer in black pride; in fact, her pride stems out of her deep confidence. (pp. 57-9)

> *Leela Kapai, "Dominant Themes and Technique in Paule Marshall's Fiction," in CLA Journal (copyright, 1972 by the College Language Association; used by permission of The College Language Association), Vol. XVI, No. 1, September, 1972, pp. 49-59.*

LLOYD W. BROWN

Apart from the usual review notices in the usual periodicals, there has been no noteworthy discussion of Paule Marshall's major works. . . . This neglect is unfortunate, because Paule Marshall's major themes are both significant and timely. Her West Indian background (Barbadian parentage) enables Paule Marshall to invest her North American materials with a Caribbean perspective, and in the process she invokes that Pan-African sensibility which has become so important in contemporary definitions of Black identity. Secondly, her treatment of the Black woman links her ethnic themes with the current feminist revolt. Finally, the ethnic and sexual themes are integrated with the novelist's interest in the subject of power. This interest is the logical outcome of her preoccupation with groups—women and Blacks—whose roles have been defined by powerlessness. But her treatment of this subject is complex and innovative because she analyses power not only as the political goal of ethnic and feminist movements, but also as social and psychological phenomena which simultaneously affect racial and sexual roles, shape cultural traditions, and mould the individual psyche.

Indeed, Paule Marshall's style invariably includes images of power-as-experience. She is a good example, in this regard, of those novelists in whom the recurrence of major themes imposes a distinctive iconography on their narrative forms. We can trace throughout her fiction rhythms of movement and sound which symbolically dramatize the dynamics of power in several forms—physical force, will power, political and sexual power, and so on. This power symbolism imparts a distinctive rhythm to her fictional forms as a whole: the narrative opens and closes with identical or similar symbols of power; or her themes present certain forms of power, such as death and the life-force, as alternating cycles in the cosmos. Paule Marshall's style therefore defines her themes. It fulfills the concept of fictional style not merely as a "mode of dramatic delimitation, but more precisely, of thematic definition."

One of her short stories, **"To Da-duh, In Memoriam,"** is typical of her rhythmic use of symbols for "thematic definition." Briefly, this is the auto-biographical story of a young girl from Brooklyn on her first visit to her parents' family in Barbados. During the visit her spirited clashes with her grandmother, Da-duh, dramatize the conflict of two life-styles: the rural traditions of the old woman's pre-technological society versus the young Brooklynite's machine culture. After the visit Da-duh dies when the British air-force "buzzes" her village during anti-colonial riots. And years later her grown-up granddaughter keeps her memory alive: "She died and I lived, but always, to this day even, within the shadow of her death. For a brief period after I was grown I went to live alone, like one doing penance, in a loft above a noisy factory in downtown New York and there painted seas of sugarcane and huge swirling Van Gogh suns and palm trees striding like brightly plumed Watussi across a tropical landscape, while the thunderous tread of the machines downstairs jarred the floor beneath my easel, mocking my efforts."

The opening statement ("She died and I lived") presents the life-death antithesis which the subsequent rhythm symbols explore. The "swirling" suns and "striding" palm trees of her tropical landscapes evoke the rhythmic movements of dance—

the rhythm of life. But this life-rhythm is counterbalanced by the thunderous "tread" of the machines. On the whole, the passage opposes the power of life to the power of death. Thus the earlier, personal conflict between the narrator and Da-duh is part of a larger confrontation between the pastoral innocence of the old woman's dying world, and the invincible power of a machine age which triumphs, in turn, through the brassy arrogance of the granddaughter, the Royal Air Force, and the machines of the New York factory. . . . The granddaughter's sentimental gesture as a painter may be mocked by the all-powerful machines downstairs, but the very attempt to recapture the essence of Da-duh's world is itself an assurance that the humanist principles which Da-duh embodies have replaced the narrator's earlier brassiness, and have survived, once again, to challenge the mechanical wasteland. Moreover, the opening statement of the paragraph places the life-death antithesis on a metaphysical plane. The reflection, "She died and I lived," is more than an exclamation of remorse and self-pity. It is a reminder of the universal life-death cycle—the cycle which is initiated by the alternating phases of destruction and re-creation on physical levels of experience. Consequently, the symbolic rhythms of power in the painting paragraph define the cycles of power as a universal principle.

The rhythms of machine power, and all the forces which they symbolize or oppose, are just as pervasive in Paule Marshall's first novel, **Brown Girl Brownstones**. . . . As in the short story, the rhythm symbol is explicit. When young Selina Boyce visits her mother at a factory she notices the rhythmic noise and movement of the machines. They "seemed forged into one sprawling colossal machine. This machine-mass, this machine-force was ugly, yet it had grandeur. It was a new creative force, the heart of another larger form of life that had submerged all others, and the roar was its heartbeat—not the ordered systole and diastole of the human heart but a frenetic lifebeat all its own." In effect, the rhythm of the machine represents the technological life-form which (as in Da-duh's death) has submerged the human values represented by the heartbeat. And this analysis of the machine culture leads to Silla Boyce's relationship with that culture. . . . (pp. 159-61)

Machine-force, Silla's force, the synchronized movements of machine and hands—all these are the rhythms of a culture that is defined by power. Silla and other Barbadians who share her ambition to succeed in that culture manifest the "mechanical rhythms" of an awesome power of purpose. Appropriately it is Silla who describes this purpose as an ethic of power: "No, power is a thing that don really have nothing to do with color. . . . nobody wun admit it, but people got a right to claw their way to the top and those on top got a right to scuffle to stay there." . . . The thoroughness with which the Barbadians have adopted this ethic is also emonstrated by the symbolic rhythms of the calypso. Silla's husband Deighton is despised by the community when he "squanders" away his family's share in a Barbadian land-sale, and the calypso celebrations at a wedding party become the community's ritual of punishment and exclusion: "the dancers turned in one body and danced with their backs to him . . . their voices rushed full tilt at him, scourging him and finally driving him from their presence with their song, 'Small Island, go back where you really come from!'" . . . When Silla eventually has him deported to Barbados, her bitter words echo the calypso refrain: "'Let him go back where he came from!' and a passing train lent the words a thunderous emphasis." . . . The machine-like force of the immigrants' inflexible purpose has really mechanized the calypso. The calypso is, intrinsically, a rhythm symbol of the life-force. But

the ritual expulsion at the wedding party (in effect an exclusion from the sexual rites of the life-force) transforms the calypso into an instrument of the immigrants' determination to secure the material rewards of a power-oriented culture. When Silla echoes the calypso refrain at the time of Deighton's arrest, she helps to transform the calypso from its vital function into a manifesto of machine power. Appropriately enough, the cadence of the original refrain has now blended with the mechanical rhythms of the passing train, with the same "thunderous" emphasis that one hears in the short story, **"To Da-duh."**

On the other hand, those immigrants who reject this "machine-force" use the calypso rhythm to express their vitality. Suggie Skeete, a maid in the White suburbs, demonstrates this meaning of the calypso rhythm when she dances in her apartment. . . . It is significant that Selina Boyce joins Suggie's calypso dance when rebelling against her mother's ruthless ambition. Eventually the rhythms of Selina's love-making dramatize her own celebration of life. Indeed, her lover Clive becomes part of the cosmic rhythms of the universe. . . . (pp. 161-62)

The confrontation between these powers, the machine-force and the life-force, is crystallized in the conflict between Silla, on the one hand, and Selina and Deighton on the other. The reader's initial reaction to this conflict is largely controlled by Selina's earlier perspective, since we view the narrative events through her eyes. . . . [Selina] retains her sympathy for Suggie and her father while recognizing them as weak-willed individuals whose "failure" is defined, not so much by Silla's excessive materialism, as by her iron will. As for Silla and the Association, Selina eventually learns to comprehend and admire their "sources of endurance . . . their purposefulness—charging the air like a strong current." . . . But if she admires their purposefulness she remains alienated by their insensitivity to values or persons outside their machine-mass; and, in the final analysis, she herself emerges as the power of will, or purposefulness, made human and functional in a power-oriented culture, without becoming mechanized or brutal. (p. 162)

Lloyd W. Brown, "The Rhythms of Power in Paule Marshall's Fiction," in Novel: A Forum on Fiction *(copyright © Novel Corp., 1974), Vol. 7, No. 2, Winter, 1974, pp. 159-67.*

WILLIAM BRADLEY HOOPER

Praisesong for the Widow, Marshall's third novel, is uncomplicated yet resonant. The main character, Avey Johnson, a late-middle-aged black woman, widowed but secure in a civil-service job in New York, decides to cut short a Caribbean cruise and return home as speedily as possible. Avey is suffering from some "odd discomfort," more psychological than physical; it seems she has lost a firm grasp on the meaning of her past. But rather than going directly back to New York, she is convinced by an old man she meets after disembarking the cruise ship to take a side excursion to an out-of-the-way island. There, she achieves a renewal of her sense of place and significance—as a black, as a woman. There is no limit to the kind of readership to which this novel will appeal; with deft exploration of character, Marshall speaks to anyone interested in thoughtful fiction.

William Bradley Hooper, in a review of "Praisesong for the Widow," in Booklist *(reprinted by permission of the American Library Association; copyright ©*

1982 by the American Library Association), Vol. 79, No. 7, December 1, 1982, p. 466.

ANNE TYLER

["**Praisesong for the Widow**"] rings with the same music and some of the same lilting Barbadian speech [as "**Brown Girl, Brownstones**"], but it is a firmer book, obviously the product of a more experienced writer. It lacks the soft spots of the earlier work. From the first paragraph, it moves purposefully and knowledgeably toward its final realization.

The widow of the title is Avey Johnson, black and middle aged, decorous to a fault in her tasteful dress, her long-line girdle and her underarm shields. The praisesong is performed by a group of dancing natives on the tiny island of Carriacou, and how Avey Johnson comes to be there—how she leaves her luxurious cruise ship and her two staid women friends—is a story that's both convincing and eerily dreamlike. . . .

The reader knows before Avey what her trouble is. Secure in her middle class life, her civil service job, her house full of crystal and silver, Avey has become sealed away from her true self. Her dreamy intimations of something gone wrong will have to become near nightmares—with Avey stumbling disheveled down a burning stretch of sand, then succumbing to a mortifying siege of illness in front of strangers—before she fully comprehends.

There are times when her ordeal makes us slightly uneasy. She seems consciously set up for some of her embarrassment, uncharacteristically willing to prolong it, as, for instance, when she submits to a sponge bath even after she is well enough to take herself in hand again. For the most part, though, we are borne along by Avey's story without question—first, because of the subtle, intriguing aura of mystery, with scenes proceeding unexplained and strangers appearing to know and welcome her, and, second—much more important—because that true self of Avey's is described by means of breathtakingly vivid glimpses of her first years with her husband.

If there is a clearer evocation of early marriage anywhere else in literature, I can't think what it would be. Avey recalls her young husband, Jay, in the finest detail—that startling kind of detail that comes only when a buried memory is unexpectedly recovered. . . .

What is touching is not that Avey's husband is now dead but that he died long before his physical death. He was done in by poverty and racism and the constant pressure to succeed. By the time his family had "arrived," Avey's husband was another person entirely. (p. 7)

Jay Johnson became the more somber Jerome, endlessly pushing ahead. At his funeral everyone "congratulated her on how well she had held up in the face of her great loss."

Will black Americans, reading of Avey Johnson's rebellion against her homogenization, sympathize with it? Will they willingly accompany her on her journey backward to find her own "tribe"? I can't answer that. All I'm sure of is that her other journey—her wistful journey to her younger self—is universal, and it is astonishingly moving. (pp. 7, 34)

Anne Tyler, "A Widow's Tale," in *The New York Times Book Review* (© 1983 by The New York Times Company; reprinted by permission), February 20, 1983, pp. 7, 34.

DARRYL PINCKNEY

Paule Marshall does not let the black women in her fiction lose. While they lose friends, lovers, husbands, homes, or jobs, they always find themselves. The precocious heroine of **Brown Girl, Brownstones** . . . comes of age and rejects the class aspirations of her tightly knit Barbadian community in Brooklyn. The willful teacher of **The Chosen Place, The Timeless People** . . . is middle-aged and heading toward a sharp turn in her rocky road, one that will take her into battle with developers on her Caribbean island, and then to the unknown in Africa. The well-heeled woman approaching old age in **Praisesong for the Widow** finds spiritual renewal on a remote island in the Caribbean.

In exploring the stages of black women's lives, Marshall insists that the woman with enough nerve can win even when the deck is stacked and the other players are hostile. Nerve, here, means making radical choices, and though the liberating destinies Marshall gives to her heroines are often unconvincing, the attraction of her work lies in a deep saturation in the consciousness of her characters and the ability to evoke the urban or tropical settings in which they toil. (p. 26)

The journey into the past, moving closer to one's cultural background, is a recurring theme in Paule Marshall's fiction. Discovering the Caribbean or Africa has, for her, the properties of psychic healing. In her latest novel, **Praisesong for the Widow,** this pilgrimage serves an almost exorcistic function. It is a quest for purity and release. (p. 27)

The renewal that Avey Johnson, the widow of the title, finds in the Caribbean may be ambiguous because of the awkward construction of the novel. It is an interior monologue told in the third person. The narration wanders from the inside of Avey Johnson's dreams to speculations more proper to an omniscient voice. Moreover, much is told in internal flashbacks, and this makes for a cumbersome reliance on the past perfect to keep chronology straight. The curious monotone in the writing is a disappointment, considering the animation Marshall is capable of giving exotic settings, as she did in a collection of short stories, **Soul Clap Hands and Sing**. . . . **Praisesong for the Widow** hasn't much substance, though we review with Avey Johnson her steep climb of years, and we get a sense of endless procrastination waiting for her to get to wherever she is going. (pp. 27-8)

Avey cannot explain to her friends or even to herself why she wants to leave the cruise. . . .

Avey is, one assumes, on the verge of a nervous breakdown. She has the withdrawn tendencies of someone in a paranoid state. She is repelled by people and things, anxious to keep her mental balance. But Marshall cannot make very vivid or menacing Avey's nightmares involving the old woman from her childhood. She spends paragraphs describing the ship, the meals, the routine, the pointless consumption and idle luxury in solemn detail that becomes both tedious and laughable.

Avey's panic does not abate once she is ashore. There are no taxis in sight and Avey spends several paranoid pages wondering why there is such a huge crowd on the Grenada wharf and why they were all speaking a strange language and why they were well dressed but ferrying in decrepit craft and where they were going. She is told by a sneering taxi driver that it is the season of the annual "Excursion." People from the out-island of Carriacou prepare all year for the festive return home. . . .

Carriacou is the island where Avey undergoes her transformation—but not until we are given the story of her life, a story of working for and getting everything she wanted only to wonder about the cost. (p. 28)

The outline of Avey's story is familiar. But instead of blaming the years for Avey's disappointments, Marshall leaves us with the impression that it was somehow Jay's fault. Unlike Deighton [in **Brown Girl, Brownstones**] who, by his temperament, was the architect of his own ruin, Jay completed his night courses. He worked overtime and remained faithful to his wife. Yet there is a faint note of condescension toward his ambition to get his family from the five-floor walk-up to the house and garden in North White Plains. This seems to be a favorite notion of Marshall's: the price of pulling up one's bootstraps is the soul, and men are more likely than women to sell theirs. The trade-off is particularly damaging to blacks since they can never belong to the white world, but that world forces them to give up the culture that is their only possibility of redemption.

Avey's trip to Carriacou is occasioned by an improbable meeting with an old man, Lebert Joseph, in a rum shop down the beach from the hotel where she is staying until she can get a flight out. She confides her unease immediately, and this is peculiar, given the code of propriety by which she has lived for so long. But Marshall means to present a woman who is desperate, although we never get more than the sense of a bored, somewhat frightened tourist. Joseph invites Avey to make the Excursion with him. He has known many who suffer from her ailment: "People who can't call their nation. For one reason or another they just don't know. Is a hard thing. I don' even like to think about it. But you comes across them all the time here in Grenada. You ask people in this place what nation they is and they look at you like you's a madman."

Slavery always seemed a fairly reasonable explanation of why most black people cannot name their tribe, but Lebert Joseph is a creation of unforgivable sentimentality. . . . The odd notion that south of the border, in the Caribbean or Africa, the elderly among the people will come forward to lead their lost brethren back to their roots can only result in sentimentality.

Avey is taken ill during the crossing—strange that the description of vomiting in this novel is as off-putting as the descriptions of sex—and this makes her more vulnerable. She is open to the ministrations of Joseph's large family who welcome her as one restored to them. Avey participates in the rituals of the homecoming, which climax in a dance and a prayer addressed to the ancestors and called the "Beg Pardon.". . . The ceremony stirs in Avey memories of the church services she attended with her old aunt in South Carolina and helps her to make sense of her recent dreams. She returns to New York resolved to "spread the word" about her discovery of the "Beg Pardon."

Such romanticizing of black culture in no way honors it. Romanticization has been constantly debated among black artists, its practitioners claiming that one must know the past in order to shape the future. The question is, what value has the past when it is so reduced? It is, at best, a kind of overcompensation. Paule Marshall has throughout her work pitted a mystical, lyrical African past against the evils of the West. Such an easily conceived idea of the cultural past does not increase our understanding of it. (p. 29)

Virginia Woolf once observed that when women come to write novels, they probably find themselves wanting to alter established values, to make important what is insignificant to men and to make trivial what men think essential. Marshall shares this subversive inclination and sometimes it brings satisfying results. But Woolf also warned against a distorting element that can enter the fiction of those who are painfully aware of their "disability," and in Marshall's case the distorting element is not only a simplistic view of culture but also a simplistic idea of strength. The women in her novels are meant to seem courageous but they have more of the manic certitude of religious fanatics. They have an almost narcissistic appreciation of their own states of mind but little is revealed about the complicated forces against which they claim to struggle. This limited picture of the world is what sets Marshall's women apart from those of Zora Neale Hurston, whose women are more tolerant, forgiving, and, one might say, truly experienced.

Perhaps this one-dimensional approach comes from current strains in black feminism. To counter the image of the black woman as victim, a different picture is deemed necessary, one that inadvertently makes such words as "nurturing," "positive," and "supportive" unbearable. One is constantly aware of a manipulation of reality at work in Marshall's fiction and this causes us to distrust it. (pp. 29-30)

Darryl Pinckney, "Roots," in The New York Review of Books *(reprinted with permission from* The New York Review of Books; *copyright © 1983 Nyrev, Inc.), Vol. XXX, No. 7, April 28, 1983, pp. 26-30.*

Colleen McCullough

1938?-

Australian novelist.

McCullough is best known for her popular novel, *The Thorn Birds* (1977), a generational saga set in Australia that was made into a television miniseries. Because of its romantic nature and entertaining narrative, *The Thorn Birds* has been termed an Australian *Gone with the Wind*.

McCullough's first novel, *Tim* (1974), sensitively explores a love relationship between a spinster and a younger retarded man. Although well received critically, it did not attain the best-selling status of either *The Thorn Birds* or *An Indecent Obsession* (1981), her third novel.

McCullough admits that she does not strive to create great literature, and most critics agree that the value of her fiction lies in its ability to entertain. They find her plots engrossing although somewhat contrived, her characterizations adequate, and her descriptions of Australian life and landscape skillful. Her thematic concern centers on the conflict between love and duty.

(See also *Contemporary Authors*, Vols. 81-84.)

© Jerry Bauer

A review of "Tim," in Best Sellers *(copyright 1974, by the University of Scranton), Vol. 34, No. 4, May 15, 1974, p. 97.*

PUBLISHERS WEEKLY

This first novel of awakenings [*Tim*] is a lovely and refreshing addition to tales of love. It is also, however, a story with a difference, one that might be characterized as love triumphant, but not love without its bittersweet shadings. Mary Horton is a middle-aged, successful businesswoman, a spinster. Raised an orphan, she has lived her life alone, has relied on her own discipline and self-sufficiency—until Tim comes along. He is 25, an Adonis in body, a child in spirit. . . . Colleen McCullough's telling of the story of Tim and Mary—how they meet and what happens—is accomplished, sensitive and wise.

A review of "Tim," in Publishers Weekly *(reprinted from the February 18, 1974 issue of* Publishers Weekly, *published by R. R. Bowker Company, a Xerox company; copyright © 1974 by Xerox Corporation), Vol. 205, No. 7, February 18, 1974, p. 67.*

BEST SELLERS

The course of this novel [*Tim*] is rather predictable and the bitterness of the last two pages does not restore realism to what is basically a very romantic tale—but it is a good, warm, rather lovely story with some delightful characters. And the slang of Australia in the somewhat idealized dialogue is spicy and, to northern-hemisphere ears, fresh and pleasant. . . .

[The] plot is not only idyllic, it is a little too pat. Yet, it is worked out with skill and the people are real, made all the more real by their speech, much of it earthy slang. Some of the characters and some of their conversations are sheer delights.

MARGARET FERRARI

Tim is a simple, effective first novel by Colleen McCullough whose native Australia serves as the book's setting.

The novel is direct rather than subtle. It tells a gentle, spare story of a growing relationship and a mutual awakening of Mary Horton, a 45-year-old spinster who has never paid any attention to her own emotional needs in her climb from orphanhood to financial success, and Tim Melville, a strikingly beautiful, 25-year-old, mentally retarded boy whose innocence and gentleness are still intact.

Well into the novel, a specialist in the problems of the retarded voices what might be the book's central thrust: "Not one of us is born without something beautiful and something undesirable in us." . . .

Tim is a manual laborer "without the full quid," who catches Mary's eye and unsettles her world. . . .

Each of the two people become the center of the other's life, partly because of their growing love for one another, and partly because Tim is being left without family to care for him.

Mary would never think of marriage as a solution, even though she is aware that she has awakened previously unfelt emotions in Tim, but when the suggestion comes from a qualified, objective source, she realizes that this would be one of the few ways in which Tim might actually enjoy his full manhood. The delicacy with which their strange love story is handled peaks here, because Mary admits to herself that she is not an unconventional woman and, though she clearly loves Tim, she is concerned about what people will say.

There are many genuinely touching moments in the novel. . . . (p. 59)

The novel moves quickly. Its language is clear and direct, full of colorful Australian slang. McCullough's feeling for character, from major to minor, is compassionate yet concise. They are without exception well-rounded and believable. Her delicacy is perfectly suited to the story.

A criticism: the novel really ends before Colleen McCullough ends it. It is an anticlimax when Tim cuts himself badly. Perhaps she means it to show that his beauty can be marred or that he truly needs taking care of and cannot survive on his own. Perhaps she means it to give concrete evidence of the way the world will always misconstrue this strange looking relationship. But nevertheless, it seems superfluous.

Still, *Tim* is a warm book to read, reassuring about goodness in human nature and about the power of love to overcome worldly obstacles and to make us care more for another person's interests than for our own. (p. 60)

Margaret Ferrari, in a review of "Tim," in America *(reprinted with permission of America Press, Inc.; © 1974; all rights reserved), Vol. 131, No. 3, August 10, 1974, pp. 59-60.*

ELIOT FREMONT-SMITH

The Thorn Birds is the saga of the Clearys, primarily of Fee Cleary and her daughter Meggie. It is also the story of an ambitious Catholic priest, Ralph de Bricassart. . . . And it is, first and last, the story of Drogheda, this book's Tara. Land-in-the-blood is a major and vivid theme; it works here, it is not obnoxious.

The novel opens—and it opens slowly—in New Zealand in 1915, then switches to the ranch in New South Wales that the Clearys make their home. It's a setting the author knows in detail and describes with considerable force. . . .

The plot creaks at times, and McCullough isn't above exploiting coincidence. . . . But one marvels much more than minds. McCullough does make her characters and their concerns come alive; she gives them (the leads particularly, and Ralph most of all) intelligence and complexity and dimension. Even the minor characters are not dull.

What holds the book together, however, is not the characters alone, or Drogheda, or even its rather refreshing wholesomeness, but McCullough's slightly quirky, very spunky style. Her prose, even when stately, owes little to any formula; it is driven by a curiosity of mind, a caring for the subject, and some other great energy within the author that in turn, at one remove, spurs the reader on. *The Thorn Birds* didn't make me laugh and weep, and I could put it down. It is, after all, a romance, and very long. But then I kept picking it up again, more times than can be accounted for by any sense of duty. A fine book.

Eliot Fremont-Smith, "The Book: Romance with Spunk" (reprinted by permission of The Village Voice *and the author; copyright © The Village Voice, Inc., 1977), in* The Village Voice, *Vol. XXII, No. 13, March 28, 1977, p. 94.*

ALICE K. TURNER

"Happy families are all alike," wrote Tolstoy at the beginning of *Anna Karenina,* "but each unhappy family is unhappy in its own way." . . .

At the beginning of *The Thorn Birds,* its author, too, establishes firmly that unhappiness is to follow, though she lures us with the promise of at least one good time as well. She recounts a little parable, the legend of a bird that sings just once in its short life before proceeding to impale itself on the longest, sharpest thorn it can find: "For the best is only bought at the cost of great pain."

It all sounds promisingly dreadful, if a little corny (rhymes with thorny) . . . [but] I am here to testify that *The Thorn Birds* is a success both in terms of unhappiness and of uniqueness.

It is set in Australia, which, just for starters, is a change. I had thought that the remoteness of the Australian landscape might be a liability, but it turns out to be quite marvelous. At the time that the Cleary family arrives at Drogheda, the Victorian manor in New South Wales which is to serve as their Tara, the author, Colleen McCullough, takes a few pages to record their reactions to Australian wildlife. . . . Once she has set the scene, the author moves on, preferring to emphasize the dreariness of sheep, flies and dust, but for the reader that strange environment is established, and, like the other strangenesses of the book, accepted.

The story is that of Fiona and Paddy Cleary and their nine children, particularly of their only daughter, Meggie. There are very few outside characters . . . [among them Father, later Cardinal, Ralph de Bricassart]. . . .

Very few novels spotlight a Roman Catholic priest as a sex symbol, but Father Ralph's bravura performance in this one rivals the landscape for originality. Father Ralph is simply yummy. . . . And, of course, he is out of the running, which gives the author plenty of opportunity to dangle him as an erotic tease. (p. E1)

The third unique quality of this novel lies in the astonishing sexual deprivation which is the lot of every character in it, except, by necessity, for the parent Clearys, who make the novel possible. Priests and widows are more or less celibate in many novels, but McCullough is ruthless even with characters who might reasonably be expected to get a little fun out of life. . . .

[In the long wait for the] moment of supreme whoopee, we get many other treats—violent deaths, cunningly crafted betrayals, womanly self-sacrifice, manly valor (and vice-versa for both), and a lot of good, solidly intriguing information about Australian life. . . .

To expect *The Thorn Birds* to be a Great Book would be unfair. There are things wrong with it, stock characters, plot contrivances and so forth. But to dismiss it would also be wrong. On its own terms, it is a fine, long, absorbing, popular book. It offers the best heartthrob since Rhett Butler, plenty of exotic color, plenty of Tolstoyan unhappiness and a good deal of connivance and action. Of its kind, it's an honest book. (p. E2)

Alice K. Turner, "Cardinal Sin," in Book World—The Washington Post *(© 1977, The Washington Post),* April 24, 1977, pp. E1-E2.

WEBSTER SCHOTT

Miss McCullough's plan [in "**The Thorn Birds**"] is to trace three generations of a New Zealand family, especially the Cleary women: Fee, Meggie and Justine (grandmother, mother, granddaughter) through poverty and wealth, loving and dying and all the emotional terrain in between. She takes her title from a Celtic legend about a wondrous bird that sings only once in its life. . . . (p. 13)

Miss McCullough wants us to see that her characters experience great joy bought with equally great suffering. The question along the way is not whether they will hurt as much as how and when the blows will come, and who will take the meanest cut.

Though "**The Thorn Birds**" is much more compelling entertainment than the popcorn novels waiting down at the neighborhood Safeway, it still shares the company of fiction so machined with plots and outfitted with colorful characters that even when it achieves conviction—mostly in landscapes, natural disasters and first-time sex—it seldom expands our knowledge of what we have to do to get through life, or what the source of our eternal struggle may be. Miss McCullough isn't that kind of writer. She doesn't intellectualize. She narrates. She makes things happen to people. And so often that you don't drop her lightly. Later you wonder whether all the excitement meant anything. (pp. 13, 18)

While Miss McCullough's vocabulary isn't any wider than her reservoir of ideas, her memories of Australia and her imagination never run dry. She reads easily. Her characters are credible, if interchangeable. She writes as if to improve on life. And if we read fiction to fill the boring spaces left by reality, then "**The Thorn Birds**" fits our need. It runs like a dream factory. (p. 20)

Webster Schott, "Golden Fleece," in The New York Times Book Review *(© 1977 by The New York Times Company; reprinted by permission),* May 8, 1977, pp. 13, 18, 20.

AMANDA HELLER

[*The Thorn Birds*] promises romance, sentiment, history, the appeal of a faraway setting.

You may ask: Is *The Thorn Birds* a good book? No, it isn't. It is, in fact, awesomely bad. The writing is amateurish, all adjectives and exclamation points. The dialogue is leaden. . . . The characters are mechanical contrivances that permit the plot to grind along without encountering much resistance.

To its credit, *The Thorn Birds* is as easy to absorb as an hour of *The Bionic Woman* and as addictive as popcorn, if you like popcorn. . . . (pp. 91-2)

Amanda Heller, in a review of "The Thorn Birds," in The Atlantic Monthly *(copyright © 1977, by The Atlantic Monthly Company, Boston, Mass.; reprinted with permission),* Vol. 239, No. 6, June, 1977, pp. 91-2.

PAT CAPLAN

Promoters are calling [*The Thorn Birds*] the Australian *Gone With The Wind*.

The Thorn Birds does resemble *Gone With The Wind* in containing a feisty Irish paterfamilias, a long-suffering mother, and a set of red-headed twins. It also features a sexy priest, a huge fortune, and three generations of family on a sprawling estate. And how little it makes of these possibilities!

In scene after scene, McCullough moves to the edge of conflict, peeks over, then shies away. The book opens on Meggie Cleary's fourth birthday, when her brothers wreck her new doll. The parents admonish the boys not to misbehave again. They never do. Paddy Cleary's sister summons his family to live on her Australian sheep station, Drogheda, because she has $13 million she might leave them when she dies. Father Ralph de Bricassart takes away most of the Clearys' inheritance, and how do they react? "We're going to live in the big house . . ." says Paddy. "Let the church have Mary's money and welcome."

The Clearys redecorate the house, stay friends with Father Ralph, and never have any money problems. Father Ralph goes to Rome for an uneventful rise through the church hierarchy.

Meanwhile, back at the sheep ranch, Meggie Cleary has fallen secretly in love with Father Ralph and won't marry any of the neighbors' sons. She marries a shearer because he looks like Ralph, but soon spurns him with a crushing, "You can't kiss for toffee!" Drogheda endures a 10-year drought, but nothing happens because they have enough water tanks. The Clearys install screens on the windows to keep out the flies, and Archbishop Ralph notices them when he comes to visit.

When the characters are good they're goody-goody, and when they're bad they have a good excuse. Ralph confesses a dalliance with Meggie to his mentor, who says: "I am not shocked, Ralph, nor disappointed. . . . Humility was the one quality you lacked, and it is the very quality which makes a great saint . . ." McCullough allows her wayward priest to cop out of his spirit-flesh dilemma by deciding of Meggie that "she, too, was a sacrament."

Meggie bears Ralph a son, but nobody even guesses who the father is except Meggie's mother, and she never tells anybody. The insipid boy grows up to be a perfect priest, enjoying several tea parties with the cardinal.

The Thorn Birds does include a nifty fire and some colorful landscape. Punched up and rewritten, the story could make a passable motion picture. The book is definitely no page-turner, though. Instead of villainy, intrigue, or danger, McCullough offers silliness and easy resolutions:

> *A baby would solve everything so please let there be a baby. And there was. When she told Anne and Luddie, they were overjoyed. Luddie especially turned out to be a treasure. He did the most exquisite smocking and embroidery*
> . . .

Don't we get enough of this sort of thing in real life? For escape and fun, we crave the exotic, the risque, the novel! How disappointing that the only interest *The Thorn Birds* can sustain is curiosity about its fate as a publishing venture. Confirmed in our dratted cynicism, we put down this mediocre book and wait to see how far the bally-hoo can carry the ho-hum.

Pat Caplan, "Everyone's Nice, Life Goes On—A Page-Turner?" *in* The National Observer *(reprinted by permission of* The National Observer; © *Dow Jones & Company, Inc. 1977; all rights reserved), June 20, 1977, p. 18.*

RUTH MATHEWSON

[The success of **The Thorn Birds**] seems to reflect the accuracy for most readers of the jacket-blurb assurance that "there is simply no way to put it down once you have begun it." The declaration has been echoed by so many commentators (as if other words had failed them) and used with such extravagance (one of them "scarcely ate or slept for two days") that it has become a phenomenon of its own. (p. 15)

[Eliot Fremont-Smith] found **The Thorn Birds** "a fine book," with a "refreshing wholesomeness," but it didn't make him laugh or cry, and he *could* put it down, he said, "because it is, after all, a romance." At the same time, he acknowledged that something "spurs the reader on" specifically, a style "driven by a curiosity of mind, a caring for the subject, and some great energy within the author" [see excerpt above].

While the book certainly has these qualities, I would not link them to its style, or styles—which seem to derive from (and sometimes unwittingly to parody) a great many old-fashioned novels. Nor would I attribute the smashing success of **The Thorn Birds** to its bringing an unknown continent to life. The author is at her best in describing the swarming fauna, the dramatic monsoons and droughts, the floods and fires of her native Australia. She succeeds as well in communicating her extensive knowledge of work processes [such as sheep shearing]. . . . Ultimately, though, I think that what "spurs the reader on" is nothing more than the conventional plot.

Popular fiction, Northrop Frye has said, is "stylized and conventional to a very marked degree. We know in advance the kind of story we are going to read, and . . . we find the continuity of reading easier because of an exceptionally vigorous pacing supplied by the convention. . . ." (pp. 15-16)

[In *The Secular Scripture*] Frye elaborates on his theory of popular literature. The bulk of it, he says, he would describe as "sentimental romance," a category that extends and develops the "naïve" formulas found in folk and fairy tales. The many variations of romance make up a structure that Frye sees as constituting an eternal vision of the world—a secular parallel of sacred scripture. And his further observations would seem to explain the qualified responses to **The Thorn Birds** that I have cited.

Because this kind of fiction is designed to entertain, he believes, "guardians of taste" consider it a waste of time. . . . Great literature, Frye contends, is "the genuine infinite" as opposed to "the phony infinite, the endless adventures and the endless sexual stimulation of the wandering of desire." He then adds a crucial qualification: "But I have a notion that if the wandering of desire did not exist, great literature would not exist either."

No one claims **The Thorn Birds** is great literature, yet it does raise some interesting questions about this "wandering." The central liaison in the three-generation epic is between a handsome, ambitious priest, Father Ralph de Bricassart, and the beautiful, spirited Meggie Cleary. . . . [The young priest first thinks] of 10-year-old Meggie as "the sweetest, most adorable little girl he had ever seen, hair . . . not red, not gold, but a perfect fusion of both . . . eyes like melted jewels."

Whoever gets this far will not be put off by the prose, and knows what will happen. He will read on simply to find out how the inevitable will take place—how the priest's tenderness for the child will become passion for the woman, how his ambition will result in his becoming a cardinal. (Interestingly, the actual sex is not unusually titillating: McCullough is explicit only when encounters fail; when they are blissful she tends toward a rhetoric of "melting bones" and "roped limbs.") The story sets up a curious sequence of expectations during the "continuous" experience of reading that is not clear until the novel is over, and the "discontinuous" process of criticism (the distinction is Frye's) has begun. Then one sees that for half the book one has waited for the illicit love to be consummated, and for the other half one has waited for it to be punished. Thus the narrative serves both the rake and the censor in the reader, whose returning sense of discrimination makes him wonder at his easy surrender to each.

More than the fact of wish fulfillment, the atavistic quality of the wishes fulfilled are disconcerting to sober second thought. For example, the priest privately curses his aging patroness—"wicked old spider. God rot her!" If she dies soon afterward, and her corpse does rot in the summer heat, what satisfaction have we derived? A licensed voyeurism? A hint that a priest's curses are efficacious? We are distressed, too, by the free-floating mythic suggestiveness that plays throughout, most of it having to do with symbolic incest. Love for a priest is love for a "father"; there are strange understandings between mothers and sons, between sister and brother. . . .

Only once the tale has been told does the kill-joy in the reader emerge, making him recognize that the force carrying him along has been the momentum of conventions. McCullough's accomplishment lies in her large acquaintance with them, and in her skill at exploiting the "wandering of desire" while keeping inhibitions (and ordinary skepticism) temporarily at bay. To say that one cannot put this book down is really another way of saying that it is the most conventional novel to appear in a long time. (p. 16)

Ruth Mathewson, "Putting Down 'The Thorn Birds'," in The New Leader *(© 1977 by the American Labor Conference on International Affairs, Inc.), Vol. LX, No. 14, July 4, 1977, pp. 15-16.*

ANITA BROOKNER

"Something I can get my teeth into", the woman in the library said to me the other day. The analogy with eating is fairly important, as is the grass-roots conviction that novels should be long, pleasurable, and nourishing. **The Thorn Birds,** a saga of love, money, adventure and disaster in the Australian outback, has arrived in time to save a sizable part of the population from malnutrition.

Of course it will be publicized as Australia's answer to *Gone with the Wind* and of course it contains vast areas of tosh, although those interested in role reversal will notice that the petulance and whimsy that made life at Tara so taxing have taken an unexpected turn. "I'll make you writhe", says malevolent chatelaine Mary Carson to her parish priest, Father (later Cardinal) Ralph de Bricassart . . . : "You're the most fascinating man I've ever met. You throw your beauty in our teeth, contemptuous of our foolishness. But I'll pin you to the wall on your own weakness, I'll make you sell yourself like any painted whore. Do you doubt it?''

This is not merely bad writing; it is true innocence, and it should be respected. For Colleen McCullough, who is not yet a professional novelist but is every inch a storyteller, shares the same appetites as the average reader and indeed does much to satisfy them. Innocence and generosity transform this chronicle of three women into something that is very close to compulsive reading. And it is the sort of reading that kept people happy before the advent of the television serial, a blockbusting yarn that has very little to do with the way we live now. For all its lavishness, the underlying ethic is a stern one. Miss McCullough is at her most authentic when she describes the vicissitudes of work and the character of landscape. . . . Ralph is a dead bore; the love scenes have the awesome imprecision of Lord Peter Wimsey's honeymoon and it is clear that they have been imposed on a story which is mainly a territorial rather than a sexual odyssey. When describing the eminent churchman's escapades, which somehow do not stand in the way of his career at the Vatican, Miss McCullough seems to be leaning rather heavily on *La Faute de l'abbé Mouret;* when describing the agonies of cane-cutting in North Queensland, she is most vividly herself.

The novel is a weird mixture of unusual description and concocted incident. No summary could do justice to the plot and might in any case lend itself too easily to parody. Suffice it to say that the women are indomitable, the men unreliable, the territory formidable, and the cash turnover immense. We are allowed the comfort of a complete disregard for the norm. . . . It is something of an achievement—in fact it is a considerable achievement—that no one could read this book simply for an easy laugh. Discrepancies of scale disappear in the relentless onward march of the narrative and at the end, which, it must be said, is far too long delayed, are not much remembered. It is in fact a good bad book, and it deserves a suspension of the critical faculties. It will give the woman in the public library something to get her teeth into at last.

And I suspect that it is not exclusively a woman's book. . . . Despite Miss McCullough's scorn for her male protagonists, there is no sexism in her argument, and there may indeed be a kind of homestead revival in her readership. . . . I suggest we all stick with her. She is clearly extraordinary in a way both men and women can admire. . . .

Anita Brookner, "Continental Drift," in The Times Literary Supplement *(© Times Newspapers Ltd. (London) 1977; reproduced from* The Times Literary Supplement *by permission), No. 3941, October 7, 1977, p. 1135.*

WILLIAM A. NOLEN

[In *An Indecent Obsession,* the] second world war is winding down. On an unidentified island in the Pacific, in a hospital to which wounded Australian soldiers have been evacuated is a special ward—Ward X—reserved exclusively for those soldiers whose wounds are not physical but psychological. They are "troppo," the Australian word for soldiers who have broken under the stresses of warfare. . . .

Sister (Australian for nurse) Honour Langtry, a 30-year-old unmarried woman from an upper-middle-class Australian family, is in charge of Ward X. Since the ward is physically separated from the rest of the hospital and since there is no staff psychiatrist, Honour takes, by default, full responsibility

for the five patients who remain there as the war ends and the book begins. . . .

To this relatively stable mini-world, another patient, Sergeant Michael Wilson, is introduced. As the reader might guess, Wilson upsets the precarious balance. . . .

An Indecent Obsession is never boring. Colleen McCullough has created fully drawn and believable characters, and she keeps her plot moving along nicely—though I do wish she could have introduced a bit of levity. There isn't a laugh in it. But the author also delivers a message, intended or not. It is that happiness, contentment and tranquility depend to a great degree on how we manage our relationships with our families, friends, lovers—all those who are close to us. . . . We're not always as sensitive as we should be to the effect that any one of our relationships may have on another; our worlds are too large. Fortunately, most of those with whom we come in contact have the basic emotional stability to understand or overlook moderate shifts in our emotions. But in the microcosm of Ward X, with all its inhabitants already on the thin edge, the delicate balance of interwoven lives, and their frightening fragility, becomes terrifyingly apparent. In fact, if Edward Albee hadn't already appropriated the title, *A Delicate Balance* would have been a more illuminating title for McCullough's book than is *An Indecent Obsession.*

Finally, the question a lot of potential readers will want answered: Is *An Indecent Obsession* as good as McCullough's *The Thorn Birds?* The question can't be answered. It's like asking if a nice, ripe orange is as tasty as a nice, ripe apple; it depends on your mood and your taste buds. I enjoyed both books, but I thought *An Indecent Obsession* was more intriguing, more thought provoking than was *The Thorn Birds.*

William A. Nolen, "By Love Possessed, by War Obsessed," in Book World—The Washington Post *(© 1981, The Washington Post), October 11, 1981, p. 6.*

JOANNE GREENBERG

Ward X [the setting for **"An Indecent Obsession"**] has reached a certain balance with the help of a nurse-catalyst, Sister Honour Langtry, who initially emerges as almost a stock character in British fiction—a combination of Jean Brodie and Mary Poppins. Into this stabilized environment comes a new element: a soldier named Michael who has been placed on Ward X for no discernible reason. . . .

The environment is one of the chief villains in this novel. Half the action is concerned with warding off the elements and the pests that inhabit the hospital: keeping dry, keeping cool, keeping free of mildew, keeping flies and mosquitoes and roaches out. Everyone on the ward is obsessed with this. The heat and humidity are pervasive and oppressive, and in Mrs. McCullough's hands are a constant reminder of the claustral feeling of the hospital itself and of the souls imprisoned there. (p. 14)

Thematically, **"An Indecent Obsession"** is a very old-fashioned novel, with its focus on the conflict between duty and love, a rare concern in contemporary fiction. It's not strange that the character of Honour Langtry, the quintessential nursing sister, has a powerfully Victorian flavor.

But there is a chilly wind blowing off Honour Langtry, and she is perhaps not as sympathetic a character as the author intended. Her commitment to duty seems less than righteous.

She allows no other nurse on Ward X, on the grounds that it would confuse and tire these war-weary men, but one feels that her obsession is basically selfish. She wants the power to herself; she wants to be the center of their lives, and her lack of awareness of the part she is playing in her patients' dependency strains one's sympathy for her. Later, after the war and the horrible climax of the book, Sister Langtry goes into "mental nursing" because of her experience on Ward X. She does this, we are told, at considerable sacrifice in prestige, out of compassion and dedication for those patients who go into Australia's mental hospitals never to leave. But her "compassion" seems disinterested, impersonal, and I doubt that Mrs. McCullough meant to leave this cool impression.

Although much of this material has been treated before, Mrs. McCullough brings an immediate sense of time and place to her portrayal of Ward X, and her attention to detail makes one feel the discomfort of the sweltering tropical nights as well as appreciate the awesome beauty of the sea, the torrential rains and the sunsets.

The last lines in the book read: "Nurse Langtry began to walk again, briskly and without any fear, understanding herself at last. And understanding that duty, the most indecent of all obsessions, was only another name for love." Neither the sentiment expressed nor the suggestion that Nurse Langtry finally understands herself is convincing; nevertheless, Colleen McCullough is able to make the reader care about Sister Langtry, who, despite herself, is a vibrant enough character to make the book enjoyable and worth reading. (pp. 14, 54)

Joanne Greenberg, "Love and Duty," in The New York Times Book Review *(© 1981 by The New York Times Company; reprinted by permission), October 25, 1981, pp. 14, 54.*

CAROL RUMENS

Belying its label, Colleen McCullough's new chart-topper [*An Indecent Obsession*] is in the mould of one of those improving tales for young ladies with which our grandmothers were expected to educate their souls. "Or, Sister Langtry chooses the Path of Duty" would have made an excellent sub-title, containing enough of a clue perhaps to save the reader from spending the whole volume worrying mildly about the identity of the "indecent obsession" and drawing various, consistently wrong, conclusions. In fact, McCullough scatters clues liberally throughout, though that "indecent" has served to throw us off the scent. In the last paragraph she spells it all out; "duty" is the obsession in question, though McCullough adds, in an attempt at profundity, that "duty is only another name for love". Is that why it is indecent? There seems to be no other justification in the novel's pages for this brand of heavy irony. Irony, in fact, begins and ends with the title, though a dose of it would have been beneficial to the character of Sister Langtry, seemingly an amalgam of every screen and pulp-fiction Supernurse who has confronted the world of suffering manhood with a starched breast and soft, susceptible heart. . . .

Despite the idealism her author wishes upon her, Sister Langtry spends a great deal of her time sexually sizing up her patients. Michael, whose arrival the first section of the book laboriously charts, is of immediate fascination, although "Sis", we learn, is already involved with another patient, Neil (officer-class, like her), and has been on the verge of succumbing to the beautiful but psychopathic Luce. For love and duty it is clearly going to be a long war. . . .

McCullough touches on some interesting areas of ambiguity: between sane and insane, hetero-and homosexual, lust and bloodlust, male and female attitudes to sex, but fails to explore them in the depth they merit. She is far more interested in her heroine's state of romantically polarized conflict between Neil and Michael, love and duty. Her attempts at showing us the self-questioning side of Langtry produce some feeble interior monologue which reveals little more than the authorial strings at work.

Too many of the other characters (hypochondriac Nugget, crusty misogynist Colonel Donaldson) seem to be out of the Hospital Writer's Casebook; Luce, however, is convincing, with his veneer of swaggering machismo and his bitter social resentments. His death occurs offstage and its unpleasantness is handled with restraint. However, there is surely a missed opportunity here; McCullough might have involved the reader with the one character of tragic potential. Nor does the "whodunnit" *frisson* amount to very much. So manipulative a writer is unwilling to leave her readers the space in which to form their own doubts and draw their own conclusions.

The least one might expect from a best-selling author is the ability to tell a gripping story, but McCullough's narrative is often slow, plodding and short on surprise. The argument between love and duty becomes increasingly banal after the climax of Luce's death. . . . But at least the last, postwar section with Sister Langtry permanently committed to psychiatric nursing in unidealized surroundings attains a sober realism between the bouts of moralizing, and the avoidance of wedding-bells and happily-ever-after comes as a pleasant relief.

Carol Rumens, "Within the Starched Breast," in The Times Literary Supplement *(© Times Newspapers Ltd. (London) 1981; reproduced from* The Times Literary Supplement *by permission), No. 4106, December 11, 1981, p. 1448.*

THOMAS E. HELM

One would not describe *An Indecent Obsession* as spellbinding, nor think of Australian novelist Colleen McCullough's treatment here of an army nurse assigned to oversee a half-dozen mentally disordered patients at the end of World War II as in any way comparable, let's say, to Ken Kesey's *One Flew Over the Cuckoo's Nest.* Her book has neither the emotional power nor the intellectual toughness associated with that American novel. Still, like her earlier work *The Thorn Birds,* this is a fairly well-crafted piece of fiction with a good story line and, for the most part, convincing characters.

Honour Langtry stands at the storm's eye, shepherding men whose lives are at loose ends, suffering from battle weariness and jungle fatigue but also, the reader is led to believe, something more serious, more troubling. The suffering of Ward X is not medical; the pain signals rather a malaise of mind and spirit, at once amorphous and sinister. One hopes to learn more of this peculiar pain not susceptible to the ministrations of the medical physicians, and one expects too that Honour Langtry, with sensitivities and an intelligence above the common sort, will penetrate its mysteries. Would that that were the case.

Honour does her duty, does it lovingly and, with but one important slip, does it without lapse. Yet she does it without profound reflection on the human misery around her. Even the malevolent Luce, with whom she is matched early on, as good against evil, makes no significant impression on her. . . . Luce is dispatched in a bloody scene well before the novel's end, and, while the circumstances of his death bear significantly on the plot, his character does not, nor does the fact of evil he apparently represents.

Love, it turns out, is the indecent obsession, and not just love in general, but love seen as duty. Here we are into something. Good for McCullough! With the contemporary abandonment by church and society of the idea that love can be, perhaps ought to be, duty, we have a novelist calling attention again to what is central to the love commandment of the New Testament: love as vocation, love as a claim on the will amid real possibilities and real limitations, love as an obedient service to others. These qualities define Honour Langtry's devotion to nursing, to Ward X and, above all, to the men who are her patients. One wishes only that the problems associated with evil or with the malaise of the human spirit might either have been integrated into the story or jettisoned. These secondary themes clutter the fiction, distract from its real point, and raise expectations that go unfulfilled. The net effect is that Honour Langtry's final discovery about herself and her work loses some of its force. (pp. 383-84)

Thomas E. Helm, in a review of "An Indecent Obsession," in The Christian Century *(copyright 1982 Christian Century Foundation; reprinted by permission from the March 31, 1982 issue of* The Christian Century), *Vol. 99, No. 11, March 31, 1982, pp. 383-84.*

Larry (Jeff) McMurtry

1936-

American novelist and essayist.

Larry McMurtry has been called the best regional writer that the Southwest has produced, yet his novels are the antitheses of *Shane, The Virginian,* and other classics of the Western genre. While earlier "cowboy" novels were idealized epics of courage and nobility, McMurtry demythologizes the West. He uses satire and black humor to portray people who share the basic human experiences of dissatisfaction, frustration, loneliness, and loss.

In his earlier books such as *Horseman, Pass By* (1961) and *Leaving Cheyenne* (1963), that loss includes the disappearance of traditions embodied in the "code of the West," the disintegration of the family, and the disillusionment produced by unfulfilled hopes and dreams. Hypocrisy and stagnation in small-town life are exposed in *The Last Picture Show* (1966), as the adolescents and the adults in a dying Western town attempt to escape boredom and find some sense of identity in their preoccupation with sex. *Cadillac Jack* (1982) features another of his drifter-hustlers in an aimless quest for the meaning of life.

McMurtry has been faulted for inflating insignificant plots. It has also been noted that, while he poses important questions in his work, he does not follow them through, preferring instead to pursue the entertainment value of a situation. He is consistently praised, however, for his skill in using language to evoke memorable people and places in painstaking, realistic detail. While McMurtry's strongest writing has been about place, specifically, his native Texas, his later books have grown away from that base, especially with *Moving On* (1970), *All My Friends Are Going To Be Strangers* (1972), and *Terms of Endearment* (1975), "urban Westerns" which some critics believe may be his most important contribution to changing the Western novel. In his collection of essays, *In A Narrow Grave* (1968), McMurtry indicated his intention to be free of the subject matter and language restrictions which limited his predecessors. As a result, his innovative approach to the Western novel has indeed flouted tradition, even while he has paid homage to its passing.

(See also *CLC*, Vols. 2, 3, 7, 11; *Contemporary Authors*, Vols. 5-8, rev. ed.; *Dictionary of Literary Biography*, Vol. 2; and *Dictionary of Literary Biography Yearbook: 1980*.)

CHARLES D. PEAVY

Larry McMurtry recently published his first non-fiction book [*In a Narrow Grave*], a collection of essays on Texas customs, beliefs, and cities. It will be interesting to compare this book with his novels, all of which display a knowledge of and respect for the land. But McMurtry displays no sentimentality or nostalgia for the country, however descriptively he has written of it. . . . McMurtry has written about life in the country and in the dead or dying little towns from first hand experience. In doing so, he has chronicled what becomes a major theme in his fiction: the initiation into manhood and its inevitable corollaries—loneliness and loss of innocence.

© *Jerry Bauer*

McMurtry's first novel, *Horseman, Pass By* . . . examines the initiation theme that is developed further in his later novels. A general feeling of loneliness permeates this first book. (pp. 171-72)

Lonnie's loneliness, however, is different from that of the adults in the book. . . . [It] is that strange mixture of restlessness, longing, and frustration so typical of the male adolescent. The same train that depresses his grandfather fills Lonnie with *wanderlust*. . . . (p. 173)

Lonnie's expressions of discontent and restlessness are, of course, symptomatic of his awakening sexuality, catalyzed by the presence of the brown skinned Halmea. . . . The primary motivation for Lon's wanting to escape the confines of the ranch, of Thalia itself, is to discover himself through sexual experience. . . . (p. 174)

Neither Updike nor Salinger has been as successful as McMurtry in describing the gnawing ache that accompanies adolescent sexuality. It is this same awakening sexuality that racks the boys in *The Last Picture Show*. Sex dominates their thoughts and their conversations, and it is the motivation for many of their actions (both foolish and violent). . . . Halmea [in *Horseman, Pass By*] understands men, and she understands the adolescent male—she knows how sex can drive a man, causing him to be clownish, lovable, or vicious. She has been amused by Lon's sexual awakening, by his obvious and bungling overtures; now she can sympathize with his frustration and anxiety. In this she somewhat parallels Molly in *Leaving Cheyenne,* who realizes the importance of sex to a man: "it was because a man needed it, and had it all tangled up with his pride." . . . Indeed, it is only with the magnificently realized character of Molly that any of McMurtry's males find happiness, fleeting though it may be. Lon, in *Horseman, Pass By,* remains unfulfilled, and in the "Epilogue" it is apparent that he must flee Thalia and its environs. . . . But he is not going past Wichita, where his friend is hospitalized. He was correct when he sensed the futility of himself and of his friends: "All of them wanted more and seemed to end up with less; they wanted excitement and ended up stomped by a bull or smashed against a highway; . . . whatever it was they wanted, that was what they ended up doing without."

In McMurtry's second novel, *Leaving Cheyenne* . . . , the characters are equally bound to the town of Thalia and its environs; the Cheyenne of the title is Thalia (that is, Archer City), but no one leaves. Yet in this novel McMurtry is not so much concerned with adolescence as he is with the interactions of his characters. . . . The book is structured in four parts: the first section is Gid's narrative, the second Molly's, the third Johnny's, and the fourth the inscription on their tombstones. Both Gid and Johnny have loved Molly since they were boys, and the forty year span of the book traces their strange relationship with her. Much is revealed about Molly in the first and third sections; since she is the most important thing in the lives of the two men, it is quite natural that their narratives are predominantly about Molly. It is in Molly's own section, however, that the reader is given the greatest insight to Molly's personality. Although Molly's narrative is concerned with her memories of father, sons, and lovers, the section is really about her; in the account of her love for these men Molly seems to epitomize the Sanskrit message spoken by the thunder in Eliot's *Waste Land: datta, dayadhvam, damyata* (give, sympathize, control). Molly has indeed given *all* for love; her life has been dedicated in unselfish giving. Unlike Gid, she has not been afraid to be "whole hog in love." . . . (pp. 174-76)

Ironically, despite her complex motivation for doing so . . . , Molly marries the wrong man. The result is that her husband Eddie grows to hate her, and the lives of Gid and Jimmy are ruined. Nevertheless, Molly is a remarkable heroine in a book that recounts one of the strangest relationships in literature.

McMurtry is not as successful with his protagonists in his third novel, *The Last Picture Show.* . . . McMurtry has said that part of the concern of *The Last Picture Show* is to portray how the town is emotionally centered in high school—in adolescence. As a result, the protagonist of the book is somewhat inadequately developed. But *The Last Picture Show* is weaker than McMurtry's first two novels in other ways than characterization. For one thing, McMurtry seems to write better when he writes of the country. He hates the stultifying atmosphere of the small town, and his antipathy shows in *The Last Picture Show.* McMurtry says that the emotions at work in *Leaving Cheyenne* probably reflect his marriage rather than his adolescence, and are more complex, while the emotions underlying *The Last Picture Show* are distaste, bitterness, and resentment against the small town. . . .

The Last Picture Show, employing the third person omniscient point of view, records the emotional experience of several adolescents (Sonny, Duane, Jacy, and Joe Bob) and indicates how the town (as opposed to the country) complicates their coming of age. (p. 180)

The main action of the novel is concerned with the emergence into manhood of a high school senior named Sonny Crawford. His sophistication (or loss of innocence) as well as that of his peer group, is accomplished through sex. It is through the medium of sex that the inhabitants of Thalia seek (and find) their identity. (pp. 180-81)

The earliest treatment of sex in *The Last Picture Show* is the description of the adolescent sex play of Sonny and his "steady" girl, Charlene Duggs. . . . Charlene allows Sonny a little "above the waist passion," but nothing else. Their love making has become a dispassionate ritual which, at best, is frustrating; ultimately, and inevitably, it becomes boring. . . .

Duane is also having trouble with his girlfriend Jacy. Jacy, a spoiled and egotistical rich girl, has no intention of ever marrying Duane, who roughnecks on the night shift with a drilling crew. Jacy equates sex with popularity and performs most passionately when before an audience. (p. 181)

Jacy's theatrical passion actually enhances her reputation at Thalia's high school. Most of Thalia's adolescents seem to have been affected by the movies; even Sonny's girl, Charlene, is most passionate in a theatrical setting. . . .

Though their sexual experience is somewhat broader than that of the girls, the boys of Thalia also often base their notions of love, beauty, and passion on what they have seen in the movies. (p. 182)

The closing of the movie theatre, which had exerted such an influence on the town's adolescents, marks the end of innocence (symbolized by Billy's death) and the emergence into adulthood by the town's youth (the last picture show was "The Kid from Texas").

Billy, the idiot boy who swept out the pool hall and the movie house . . . , symbolizes innocence. He is often the brunt of cruel pranks played by the boys, but he always remains trusting and loving. He cannot accept the fact that the movie is closed forever; "for seven years he had gone to the show every single night." . . . As a result of a fight over Jacy, Sonny has lost the sight of one eye, and when Billy is killed he has both his eyes covered with Sonny's eye patches. McMurtry told me that the blindness motif that runs throughout the book symbolizes the "sightlessness of life in a small town." The picture show is what the inhabitants of Thalia see beyond the town; when the show closes, what is beyond the town also closes for them.

The loneliness that was such a dominant leitmotif in McMurtry's first two novels is omnipresent in *The Last Picture Show,* which begins "Sometimes Sonny felt like he was the only human creature in the town." Sonny's loneliness is echoed in the lives of the adults: Ruth Popper, Genevieve Morgan, Sam the Lion, and Lois Farrow. The loneliness of the adults is underscored by their realization that they are growing old. (p. 183)

The loneliness felt by most of the characters in the book combines with the boredom of the small town to cause them to seek an escape in sex. (p. 185)

[Small] town life is what [*The Last Picture Show*] is about; specifically, small town sex life. It is not by any means a "western" novel—McMurtry's Thalia could have been located in Sherwood Anderson's Ohio or William Faulkner's Mississippi. *Book Week* reviewed *The Last Picture Show* as "a retreat into the literature of nostalgia," "a kind of Huckleberry Finn after the fall." This is, of course, not quite accurate—McMurtry is certainly anything but nostalgic in this book. . . .

McMurtry's portrayal of male adolescence is realistic, if frank. If the book seems obsessed with sex it is only because the adolescent male is typically preoccupied with the subject himself. (p. 186)

McMurtry's male protagonists discover, or come close to discovering, the meaning of life through women who are much older than themselves—in many ways even Molly is a woman when Gid and Johnny are still boys. . . . The themes of loneliness and lost love are recurrent themes in McMurtry's novels, but the most important theme is the achievement of manhood (with its accompanying loss of innocence) by the various protagonists of the novels. (p. 188)

Charles D. Peavy, "Coming of Age in Texas: The Novels of Larry McMurtry," in Western American Literature *(copyright, 1969, by the Western Literature Association), Vol. IV, No. 3, Fall, 1969, pp. 171-88.*

L. J. DAVIS

The principal trouble with Larry McMurtry's [*Moving On*] . . . is that it is about 500 pages too long. His characters are too amiable and ordinary, his action is too slight, his psychology is too shallow, and his incidents are just too damn *normal* to justify the incredibly extended treatment he has given them. There is simply not enough material here to cover the ground, and the result is a book that is fidgety, diffuse, and keenly disappointing.

From a summer in the rodeo circuit to a year in graduate school in Houston, the book follows the lives and declining personal fortunes of an attractive but bland pair of wealthy young Texans named Jim and Patsy Carpenter. McMurtry is dealing with some important themes, among them the decline of the old pioneering virtues and the role of women in a basically masculine society, but more often than not he ends up striking nothing but air. The Carpenters don't have any real problems, they have pretend problems. The unreal nature of their problems—and their very real anguish in dealing with them—is, of course, part of McMurtry's point. It is a point that is sufficiently blunted by 794 pages of repetition to make one wish that his characters were poor or crazy or something so that we could at least get some action. Patsy's love affair—which takes up the middle third of the book—has simply got to be one of the dullest on record, and it is not helped by McMurtry's tendency to use three paragraphs of description where one would do as well. His obsession with the banalities of everyday experience is maddening. . . .

The book has some solid qualities. At his best, McMurtry writes with intellect, compassion, and considerable skill. Patsy Carpenter is real, even if her problems aren't, and no matter how tired I got of her . . . I never stopped believing in her or caring about what was going to happen to her. The book is filled with memorable cameos—a rodeo clown, an elderly rancher, a cowboy who drives the zoo train in the off-season, graduate students—and McMurtry has a superior sense of place and time and the way the land sits. Yet the prose is full of white space and the plot is full of missed opportunities. One can scarcely comprehend Jim Carpenter at all, except in the simplest of terms, despite all the effort that is lavished on him.

L. J. Davis, "Daily Life in Texas," in Book World— The Washington Post *(© 1970 Postrib Corp.; reprinted by permission of* Chicago Tribune *and* The Washington Post*), June 21, 1970, p. 6.*

JAMES K. FOLSOM

The different treatments of the same story in the novel *Horseman, Pass By* and the film *Hud* . . . show clearly the difficulty of translating the "mood" of a work of fiction into film and the necessity imposed by a visual medium of having characters act as visible foils to each other. . . . [The] film closely follows the plot of the novel, both in specific incident and in general intent. *Horseman, Pass By* . . . is remembered in retrospect through the eyes of Lonnie, its now older boyhood observer, who reflects upon the significance of a series of events that had happened on the ranch of his grandfather, Homer Bannon. Homer, a man past eighty years old, his wife, and Hud, her son by a former marriage, live on a ranch in Texas together with Lonnie and Halmea, the black cook and housekeeper. At the beginning of the novel a dead heifer has been discovered that turns out to be a victim of hoof-and-mouth disease. Homer's cattle must all be destroyed in order to halt the spread of the disease, and the reactions of the characters in the novel to the worst disaster which can strike a cattleman, form both the conflict in the novel's plot and the catalyst for Lonnie's transition to adulthood.

In a sense the differences between the two treatments of the story are indicated by the change in title from *Horseman, Pass By* to *Hud*. (pp. 365-66)

For the motion picture concerns itself with Hud in a way the novel does not, Hud becoming if not the film's moral hero very definitely its focal character. . . . [The] film has had to make specific the various generalized aspects of the novel's "single image" of the cowboy and to present them in terms of direct foils. Hence the values that in the novel are scattered among a number of characters, in the film are polarized between Hud and Homer Bannon, both of whom come to represent two distinct and mutually exclusive models for adult life. Rather than having a general view of the adult world as presented retrospectively through a number of characters, the film Lonnie must make a specific choice between two models who are conceived of as being directly opposed to one another. Though at the beginning Hud seems to Lonnie more attractive, by the end of the film Homer has replaced him as the desirable model.

This overly schematic analysis of *Hud* may give the quite erroneous impression that it is less subtle than *Horseman, Pass By*. Such is most emphatically not the case. The difference is rather, that in the film subtlety is expressed through the nuances of conflict between the two major characters, Hud and Homer, while in the novel subtlety is expressed through proliferation of characters and . . . through the retrospective musings of Lonnie himself upon the meaning of his own experience.

Horseman, Pass By is quite consciously conceived of as a mood piece and McMurtry does a brilliantly effective job of presenting, through Lonnie's thoughts, the inchoate but very real yearnings of adolescence for something, it knows not what. In *Horseman, Pass By*, then, Lonnie's adolescent perspective may effectively be presented in terms of his yearnings for some kind of escape from the world in which he finds himself. (p. 367)

Quite the opposite is true of the symbolic pattern of *Hud*, in which, if only because we must see both Homer and Hud, we understand very clearly what Lonnie is drawn *toward,* and not so clearly what exactly he is reacting *against*. The respective endings of novel and film emphasize the point: for while the metaphor of the novel is of escape, that of the film becomes exile.

Again, the very real difference between the two versions of the story may best be seen by analysing some of the changes from the novel made in the film. First of all is the fact that Halmea is changed in *Hud* from a black to a white woman, and Hud's rape of her, successful in *Horseman, Pass By,* is abortive in the film. Though this change originally may well have been prompted by non-esthetic considerations, it is nevertheless an effective one. The rape of Halmea in the novel is accomplished by Hud while Lonnie, who loves her, stands passively by. Though thematically this may make good sense, it is impossible to visualize except upon the screen of retrospective memory. In the novel Lonnie can tell us that this is what happened, without further explanation, and we accept his statement, though not without some mental reservations. But when the scene is actually presented to us we withhold our assent. When we must actually see the scene rather than having it reported to us, the basic improbability of the action becomes evident.

A more important change in the film is in the development of Hud's character. In the novel Hud's attractiveness to Lonnie as an image of successful sexuality is not really insisted upon until the rape of Halmea, while in the film this aspect of Hud's character is emphasized from the beginning. Early in *Hud* Lonnie is seen searching for Hud, whom he finds in the house of a married woman whose husband is away. The adolescent devil-may-care attractiveness of Hud to Lonnie is clear in this scene, which stands in clear symbolic contrast to the unattractive aspect of the same side of Hud as presented through the attempted rape of Halmea. In *Horseman, Pass By* the contrast can be, and is, more abstracted.

The necessity in the film to place Hud and Homer Bannon in direct contrast issues in one other really major change, the almost total omission of Jesse, the ranch hand. In *Hud* Jesse's role is reduced to that of a walk-on part, while in *Horseman, Pass By* he is a major character.

The reason behind the change is again visual. In the novel both Hud and Jesse act as direct comparisons to Homer. Hud's morality is placed in specific contrast to Homer's, in both novel and film, in terms of the two men's different reactions to the discovery of hoof-and-mouth disease in their cattle. After the initial shock has worn off, Homer realizes that the only moral choice open to him is to have his cattle slaughtered, and he accepts the necessity for the destruction of his entire herd. Hud, in contrast, proposes to Homer that they sell the cattle before the disease is diagnosed and the herd quarantined. If someone is "stupid enough to buy" the cattle, Hud sees no objection to selling them. In short, *caveat emptor*. "That ain't no way to get out of a tight," Homer says, and refuses.

Jesse, in contrast, acts as a foil to Homer in terms of the theme of escape. For he has been everywhere, Lonnie thinks, and Lonnie's own yearnings for distant places are gratified by listening to Jesse talk of his experiences. . . . (pp. 367-69)

Hud eliminates the theme of Lonnie's yearning for escape that is central to *Horseman, Pass By,* and therefore of necessity decreases Jesse's significance and eliminates the minor subplot of the Thalia rodeo and Jesse's failure to perform creditably at it. The need inherent in a visual medium to establish an explicit polarity between Hud and Homer is again the explanation. While in the novel both Hud and Jesse may act as contrasts to different aspects of Homer, in the film the distinction between Hud and Jesse must inevitably be blurred because of the fact that since Homer must be visualized as a person they must be seen in contrast to all of him rather than to specifically differentiated qualities of his character. Therefore Hud and Jesse, had they remained of equal importance in the film, would inevitably have become redundant rather than complements to each other. The difference between them, in short, which is of basic importance to the novel, would have appeared less striking on the screen than their overpowering similarity in terms of their not being Homer. (p. 369)

Again, the film has concentrated its effect rather than spreading it out over a number of characters, since visually the most important thing is not which particular character makes the suggestion [to let the cattle infected with hoof-and-mouth disease run wild, instead of destroying them], but that the suggestion itself is one totally antithetical to Homer's own values. In the film Lonnie has received a direct lesson in terms of two diametrically opposed characters; in the novel, by contrast, the same opposition can be expressed without redundance by more than one character, if only because each character, if not seen, is visualized by the reader as representative of a more or less isolated point of view rather than as a person of flesh and blood, someone who stands in opposition to relatively specific qualities in Homer Bannon rather than to his entire character.

This necessity to condense all the foils to Homer in the character of Hud inevitably implies the one major change between novel and film—a total reversal of the ending. Lonnie learns, through the action of *Horseman, Pass By,* the futility of his own generalized longings for escape. The world, he discovers, when viewed with, in Yeats's phrase, "a cold eye," is not the romantic place he had thought it was at the beginning of the novel. Captive at the beginning of the story of the common adolescent belief that somewhere there must be more "life" than there is in one's own environment, Lonnie learns the truth symbolized by the name of the town—Thalia—where the story's action has taken place: that the stuff of life and history and epic poetry may be discovered in one's own surroundings if one has the intelligence to know where to look for it.

In the novel, then, Lonnie's education culminates in his acceptance of the world for what it is and his rejection of the unreal attitudes toward it he had held at the beginning of the story. (pp. 369-70)

In *Hud* the ending is quite different. Here, Lonnie's newly won maturity has taught him not to accept the world as it is, but rather to see the validity of Homer's attitude toward life and to reject the tempting but ultimately immoral standpoint represented by Hud. . . . [And] so at the end of the film he sets out to make his own way in the great world he has rejected in the novel. While the ending of *Horseman, Pass By* showed Lonnie's new maturity by emphasizing his realization of the flimsiness of his adolescent longings for escape, the ending of *Hud* shows it in terms of his symbolic acceptance of Homer's attitude toward the world and his rejection of Hud's.

The major differences between [the novel, *Horseman, Pass By,* and the film *Hud*] . . . are largely implicit in the very different points of view required by the two media. The primacy of vision in the film, though perhaps an obvious point, cannot be too strongly insisted upon. It results first of all in the necessity for an almost complete denial of both the retrospective mood and the nostalgic point of view upon which the [novel relies heavily]. . . . The internalization of the fictional point of view implied by the reminiscences of an older hero reflecting upon his past is simply impossible to achieve with either success or consistency upon film for two reasons: first of all, the narrator of the novel must inevitably become one among many characters in the film; and secondly, the action of the story when seen must be seen as occurring in the present.

An equally important, and less obvious, difference between novel and film also follows from the primacy of vision implied by the latter. For although the phrase "cast of thousands" has become a cliché for describing the so-called "epic" film, in fact the necessity for externalization implicit in the film results in an overwhelming tendency to simplify by reducing the number of characters. (pp. 370-71)

For all their specific differences, however, both media have in common one basic attitude toward their material.   This attitude comes ultimately from an environmentalist belief, inherent in primitivism, that man reflects in moral terms the physical nature of his environment. This belief, which is in fact nothing more than an assumption, is treated as though it were axiomatic for interpreting the materials of the great American epic. (p. 371)

The great problem, then, shared by both the Western film and Western fiction is the problem of presenting man against the landscape. What is the landscape, first of all: the beauty of the Grand Tetons or the ugliness of the Bannon ranch? And how does man stand against it: does he stand *for* it, symbolizing in detail what it expresses in general? or does he stand *in contrast to* it, repudiating everything it represents? There are of course no simple answers to these questions, all expressions of a basic ambiguity in the American identity; no answers, that is, except for the statement of the metaphorical problem and of its ritual solution. (p. 372)

> *James K. Folsom, "'Shane' and 'Hud': Two Stories in Search of a Medium," in* Western Humanities Review *(copyright, 1970, University of Utah), Vol. XXIV, No. 4, Autumn, 1970, pp. 359-72.**

LARRY GOODWYN

One of the most interesting young novelists in the Southwest—and certainly the most embattled in terms of the frontier heritage—is Larry McMurtry. He should be examined in some detail for a review of his literary inquiry serves to summarize both the uses and dangers of the frontier inheritance as it affects the newest generation of southwestern writers to toil under its shadow.

McMurtry's first two novels, *Horseman, Pass By* and *Leaving Cheyenne*, were promising efforts to put the materials of frontier culture to serious literary use. . . . [Both books] are in-the-grain novels of people striving to live by the cultural values of the legend. An authentic mood is further heightened by the voice of the narrator. McMurtry speaks through a narrator who is frontiersman enough to move with ease through the tall-in-the-saddle milieu, but sensitive enough to note the ritualized energy and directionless fury surrounding him. In these two novels, one sees a writer laboring, desperately laboring, to transcend his heritage by finding something in it beyond the limits of the unexamined legend. There are values to be ad-

mired: a code of generosity in personal conduct, an intact ability to act. But (McMurtry gives us occasional reason to believe), there is something disturbing at the center of the world. The generosity is applied only to certain kinds of people, and the ability to act—untempered by reflection and introspection—can easily degenerate into mindless tyranny. McMurtry does not consciously underline this critical response, but it is clearly present within his material. (pp. 200-01)

His third novel, *The Last Picture Show*, represents a turning away from this kind of questioning, and . . . the recently published *Moving On* accelerates this movement. *The Last Picture Show* is about the transitional generation of frontier people who were raised in town. The novel avoids the obvious pitfalls: it is no panting pastoral lament for a lost wilderness, no brooding documentation of the disarray of misplaced agrarians baffled by the corrupting metropolis. Rather, what is missing is a sense of narrative control, as if the characters are "at home" but the author is not. The first person narrative voice is gone, and with it vanishes much of the power that characterized McMurtry's first two books.

The feeling is therefore induced that we are in the presence of a skilled craftsman who is uncertain what he is trying to portray. Is the legacy from the past too powerful to bear investigation? In the privacy of the author's mind, in what is *not* written in *The Last Picture Show* as well as what is, the frontier seems clearly to be winning the test of wills.

Moving On vastly increases the suspicion that McMurtry—like so many of his literary forebears in the Southwest—has turned from the effort to employ the frontier heritage in a way that, for example, William Humphrey utilizes the "Old South." Eight hundred pages long, *Moving On* is a repetitious book about a young couple bickering away their lives. The narrative voice is again missing, and, again, the loss of dramatic power is evident. The conjunction of these two facts may point to McMurtry's dilemma. Relying, in his first two novels, on the literary device of the provincial narrator, McMurtry found a voice that seemed to serve well as a strengthening connection between himself and his sources. In turning to new sources . . . McMurtry departs from a proven technique in a way that seems to have cost him a sense of literary focus as well.

In a book of intensely personal essays revealingly entitled *In a Narrow Grave,* McMurtry provides an absorbing insight into his own sense of dilemma as a writer and as a Southwesterner. One of these essays, entitled **"Take My Saddle from the Wall: A Valediction,"** purports to be Larry McMurtry's personal declaration of independence from the frontier mystique. . . . One comes away with the feeling that, despite its title, **"Take My Saddle from the Wall"** is not a work of apostasy at all. What is ominous is the beguiling simplicity with which McMurtry takes down his saddle in his mind while his heart immediately replaces it. He can do one or the other, and put either to dramatic use, but one would suppose he would have the distinctions well in hand; a writer simply cannot afford such innocence in respect to his own point of view, at least not in an essay entitled with such precision. One senses the same ambiguity at work in his last two novels: the frontier ethos, removed from the center of his work, continues to hover around the edges—it surfaces in minor characters who move with purpose through novels that do not.

Literary critics of the future will, when pausing to focus on the Southwest, probably bless Larry McMurtry for his presence. . . . Larry McMurtry's literary life reveals the forces at work in the dominant culture patterns of the Southwest: the anguish of those of its artists who are searching for firm ground upon which to stand within the ethos of the western legend, and the difficulty of their psychological effort to break through the limitations of frontier affirmation in order to achieve a critical focus on their material.

The creative agony of Larry McMurtry is, in its own complex way, a benchmark in the literary evolution of the southern frontier. His disarray is more visible than most of his predecessors because he is sufficiently armed, in a skeptical age, to ask questions that intimidated them. (pp. 201-03)

> Larry Goodwyn, "The Frontier Myth and South-western Literature" (originally published in American Libraries, Vol. 2, No. 4, April, 1971 through special arrangement with the author and the ALA Editorial Committee), in Regional Perspectives: An Examination of America's Literary Heritage, edited by John Gordon Burke (copyright © 1971, 1973 by the American Library Association), American Library Association, 1973, pp. 175-207.*

REED WHITTEMORE

[*All My Friends*] focuses almost exclusively on sex for the first few chapters, then dwindles for a long stretch into life and literature, as if even McMurtry had grown fatigued by coition, but finally returns determinedly but tragically to the sexual theme when the hero Danny Deck, having discovered that the girl with "the clearest eyes, the straightest look, the most honest face" of *all* the girls won't—or maybe the word is can't—have him decides to commit suicide. . . .

If *All My Friends* is made into a movie, perhaps again a shift in the story's focus will occur, which would be for the best. The story has many good characters; McMurtry comments wittily on the contemporary writing scene; and he displays a masterly ease in handling narrative and dialogue. But he has been told by his muse or his bank of the positive virtues of sexual activism, so that much that he says about the meagerness of Texas small-town life—or, in the middle of the novel, about the meagerness of the artisty life in California—is undercut by his obsession. (p. 28)

Yet McMurtry does catch some of the quality of that life, those lives, despite his obsession, and if he were Sinclair Lewis or Hamlin Garland rather than Texas's Henry Miller a reader would come away astonished by what his poor beaten-down characters have been driven to in their various crummy refuges from the American dream. They never speak or think beyond their immediate experience. They seem never to have heard of governments, war, values, progress, god. With the exception of a drunken English sociologist who likes to talk big and literary (and thereby to discredit the big and literary), the range is from orgasms to Uncle L's goats. The talk about goats is comic, and so are Uncle L's manhole covers and camels (it seems that he collects these), but even such diversions, which indicate that McMurtry clearly felt the need for diversion, don't get us out of the small-talk small-scene small-soul rut that Texas seems to have dug for its people. They are just there in the dust, the wind, the tenements and the car back seats, living their unilluminated existential privacies. (pp. 28-9)

Of course it may be I who am in the minority in imagining that many American lives do contain, or should or could contain, more than McMurtry finds in his land of oil derricks, pool halls and Mexican whore houses. Maybe what he has found there is in fact our country's still center. . . . But McMurtry's commitments are not that clear; in the first place he does not come at sex, as did Lawrence, as a holiness, but is instead matter-of-factly physical about it; and in the second place his social consciousness—or whatever that larger awareness is that I have tried to describe that makes for what some still think to be civilization—is unquestionably present and at work in him. He is not a primitive by inclination or god's order; he is only driven into mimicking a primitivist ethic by the current demand that a novel be sex and by the apparently very real absence of alternative pleasures and pastimes in his homeland (and in the Californian writer-culture that succeeded it for him). In other words there seems to be a sort of negative rationale at work in the man at the moment making him the novelist he is. And he is so good at being the novelist he is that it may be ungrateful of me to wish he would discover some new country; but I do. (p. 29)

> Reed Whittemore, "Texas Sex," in The New Republic (reprinted by permission of The New Republic; © 1972 The New Republic, Inc.), Vol. 166, No. 14, April 1, 1972, pp. 28-9.

JANIS P. STOUT

Northrop Frye writes in *Anatomy of Criticism*, "Of all fictions, the marvellous journey is the one formula that is never exhausted." I would add that the aimless journey, wandering, is also a timeless formula and one with a relatively constant meaning. This archetypal structure, the journey, variously pervades and controls the novels of Larry McMurtry and extends their import beyond the limits of a regional commentary.

McMurtry's five novels have not generally been considered in relation to archetypes but rather in relation to the more limited patterns afforded by their Texas setting and its distinctive heritage. Regarded in regional terms, the novels show considerable variation, as the impulse to mythicize the forebears and to assess present life by its departure from their model, evident in *Horseman, Pass By* and *Leaving Cheyenne*, yields, in *The Last Picture Show*, to a virtually unrelieved distaste for the moribund small-town life which succeeded that austere heritage and, in the last two novels, to a radical dissociation from any cultural heritage. This growing disaffection is fittingly manifested in the successively greater predominance of journey structures which, increasingly, describe the circuitous patterns of aimless wandering.

In a comment appended to *Horseman, Pass By* McMurtry said, "In my own generation of adolescents the shakeup [of an urbanizing society] manifested itself as a consuming restlessness—an urge to be on the move." . . . *Leaving Cheyenne* shows the strongest attachment to place and to a stable and traditional pattern of life, ranching. To the adolescents of *The Last Picture Show* and to Hud, of *Horseman, Pass By,* the automobile offers escape. But to the characters of the two novels of contemporary urban life, *Moving On* and *All My Friends Are Going to Be Strangers,* neither the goal nor the repellent impulse for escape is clear. . . . In simple uncertainty, they practically live in their cars. This growth in the dominance of the automobile, as well as the varying modes of the journey motif in the novels and the cultural dissolution they signify, can be seen to occur in three distinct phases, and it is in this sequence that I would like to consider McMurtry's work. In the first two novels, the impulse to journey is chiefly a desire for experience, and the more fully a character identifies himself with the ranching way of life the less he travels. The journeys of *The Last Picture Show* are sporadic and frustrated expressions of an urge to find an alternative to an empty and deadening life. But the last two novels share a use of journeying as a metaphor for modern life itself, which is seen as being impoverished by the demise of the old traditions and the lack of new structures of meaning and allegiance.

The youthful protagonists of the two early novels, which chronicle the decline of the ranching tradition, keenly feel the urge to be off, to broaden their horizons. To them, journeying means adventure. But both are caught between this urge and the equally strong allegiance to values represented by their ranch homes. Thus, Lonnie, of *Horseman,* is caught between loving admiration for his grandfather, Homer Bannon, and a reluctant attraction to his stepuncle, Hud.   Lonnie's restlessness manifests itself in his driving fretfully between ranch and town, but there is nothing new he can learn in Thalia and almost nothing to do. It is not that Lonnie is a rebel against his origins; he "really liked" Thalia but "just didn't want it for all the time." . . . What he does want is acquaintance with the wider world, that essentially represents adulthood.

The catalyst for this wish is Jesse, a forlorn drifter, whose talk makes Lonnie "itch to be off somewhere . . . to go somewhere past Thalia and Wichita and the oil towns and Sno-Cone stands, into country I'd never seen." . . . But Jesse explicitly warns him against a rootless life. . . . [Finally however, with the departure, destruction or death of everything that had meaning to him,] Lonnie sets out, apparently, to follow Jesse's nomadic example.

The implications of this concluding departure, however, are not entirely unambiguous. Certainly he has lost his cultural roots, but it is implied that personal allegiances may nevertheless provide him a secure sense of identity. (pp. 37-40)

A similar theme appears in *Leaving Cheyenne* as McMurtry moves back to give, from the carefully distinguished points of view of his three central characters, an account of the regional development from the relative stability of the early twentieth century to the town-centered transience of approximately the same period as that of *Horseman, Pass By.* Against a background of the move away from the land, he projects a drama which affirms allegiance to one's own place. (pp. 40-1)

In the long opening section—which pointedly antedates the local impact of the automobile though not the impulse of youth to venture from home—Gid and Johnny are eager to see new places. Like Lonnie in *Horseman,* they have an initiation into the "sophisticated" adult world when they take cattle to market in Fort Worth. . . . But for both—Johnny, who "didn't feel like he belonged to any certain place," and Gid, who "was just tied up with" Archer County . . .—the venture to the plains is presented so as to debunk the romance of journeying. After Gid's feat of breaking nineteen wild horses in one day come a dull round of work and simple homesickness, and Gid returns home because, he says, "home was where I belonged" and "it was my country and my people." . . .

After this trip to the plains, both Gid and Johnny stay close to the ranch which Gid has inherited from his father. For Gid, this is largely because he has been bitten by "the land bug." . . . But Johnny's true "blood's country" or "heart's pastureland" . . . is cowboying itself, rather than any particular place. He is held to Archer County by love of Gid and Molly. It is largely because of this difference in motivation that Johnny

(who appropriately has the last word in the novel) is most nearly the ethical center of the book. (p. 41)

The Last Picture Show is dominated tonally not by nostalgia, but by McMurtry's antipathy to the small town life he describes. Thalia has become a place to be escaped, and restlessness dominates. Sonny, another late-adolescent, who is the nearest in the book to being a central character, first appears in the opening chapter struggling to get his old pickup to run. It is a prophetic detail, for Sonny will never be able to escape. But during the novel he and various other adolescents of Thalia travel [continually] . . . in their search for amusement. (p. 42)

Their circuitous travels, always ending in Thalia again, are parallel in futility with their ventures into sex. (p. 43)

By the end of the novel, a few have escaped, but Sonny, physically crippled by his past and emotionally dependent on an older woman, is left in dusty Thalia. . . . Sonny's last act is to start out of town in his truck, but finding nothing but emptiness all around answering the emptiness within, he returns. . . . (pp. 43-4)

Sonny lacks a past which can provide him an identity and a role in his shabby present. The most visible sign of his regional past in the entire novel is the cattle truck that kills [the retarded boy who was left in his care] Billy. The basis of Sonny's problems, that is, is a radical cultural discontinuity. It is this lack of a meaningful past, present, or future that creates the restlessness increasingly evident in McMurtry's adolescents. (p. 44)

In *Moving On* and *All My Friends Are Going to Be Strangers,* McMurtry has moved even further from the traditional cultural roots of his region. None of the characters in these two novels has any sense of a usable past, and none is purposefully directed toward the future. They inhabit the burgeoning cities of Texas with no apparent means of orienting themselves and nothing to engage them but endless, unsatisfying motion—as the title *Moving On* well indicates. The problem, of course, is that they are not moving on toward anything. The journey pattern so insistent in McMurtry's first three novels has in these become dominant, as the characters drive endlessly and pointlessly around the country chiefly between Texas and California. Not surprisingly, novels so constituted lack cohesive form; or rather, their forms may be described as being imitative to a radical and destructive degree.

The primary action of both novels is completely divorced from ranching, the traditional, land-based way of life that provides a relatively stable background for the first two novels. In *Moving On,* ranching is transformed into rodeoing, itself a transient way of life. Real ranching appears only in the small spread of a stepuncle of the heroine Patsy's husband and in a vast domain, like an industrial complex, whose owner shares, in a scarcely lesser degree, the wanderlust of the main characters. Only Roger Waggoner, the elderly stepuncle, never travels. Waggoner is an embodiment of lost but still respected virtues; a parallel figure in *All My Friends,* the narrator's Uncle L, is a ludicrous eccentric running an insane parody of a ranch. But either way, both are vestiges of the past, unable to hand on its values. (pp. 44-5)

Aside from these ranching relics, the two novels are populated by nomads. In both, university life is a way-station for academic migrants and those who have not yet decided where they want to go. Both casts of characters are quite large, since people drift into and out of the main characters' lives, seemingly for no particular reason, as they wander. . . . They are as fully cut off from the moral past as they are from the ranching past. Action develops as encounter, involvement (often sexual), and estrangement. Danny Deck, narrator and hero of *All My Friends,* is hopelessly subject to random emotional entanglements, all of which prove destructive as well as transient, because he has no basis for judging others or the quality of his own response to them. Like the journey structure of which it is a function, this pattern of emotion-laden encounter that litters the novel with undeveloped characters can be seen as a functional form clearly and poignantly indicative of the protagonist's cultural malaise. He feels, he says, "dislodged," . . . and stability in his personal relationships is as impossible as fixity in place. (p. 45)

None of the characters in either novel travels with fixed purpose—their wanderings are not quests—nor is even the motive of escape clearly defined. Rather, like Patsy's husband Jim, they travel out of vague dissatisfaction with life as they find it and uncertainty as to what they want to do. (p. 46)

Similarly, McMurtry's construction of novels by no apparent principle but random accretion appears to be a self-defeating enterprise. The pattern of transient involvement in both these late novels is brilliantly indicative of the cultural shortcoming McMurtry indicts . . . ; unfortunately, this expressive form, by its very nature, is destructive of the overall novelistic structure and renders the work a chronicle of tedium. One thinks, by contrast, of the tight structures of *Horseman, Pass By* and *Leaving Cheyenne.* McMurtry seems to be saying that their kind of neatness is available only to an art of nostalgia, that an art honestly treating the present flux, at least as he experienced it in Texas, is foreordained to fragmentation. If so, he is offering a bleak aesthetic vision.

The ending of *All My Friends* is problematic but clearly related to McMurtry's use of journeying as a metaphor for cultural loss. The puzzle is that Danny apparently drowns himself in the Rio Grande, but his death would violate all conventions of first person, past tense, narration. (p. 47)

The sense of finality, hence of death, is accented by the preceding abandonment of his car, which itself seems near death. . . . The implication is that by giving up his means of journeying, Danny is giving up living.

The quality of Danny Deck's journeying, as of Patsy's and the journeying of numerous minor characters in the earlier novels, has been circuitous wandering. In *Leaving Cheyenne,* Gid and Johnny travel only to learn the lessons proper to youth; they have a source that draws them back and a feeling of belonging when they get there. In *The Last Picture Show* only Sam the Lion knows his place and keeps it. In the last two novels figures out of the Texas past who bear marginal resemblance to Sam, the old ranchers, are anachronisms. The young central characters of all five novels have either loose ancestral ties or none at all, as fathers or father surrogates die partway through the action of all except the last novel. Lacking any sense of continuity with the past or of belonging to the life of any particular place, McMurtry's protagonists are, to a progressively greater degree after *Leaving Cheyenne,* left to wander inconclusively. (p. 48)

[McMurtry's] choice of allusive and thematic patterns extends the significance of his work beyond the scope of documentary or localized satiric interest. The initiation patterns of his novels, for instance, are universalizing, as are the literary allusions which link the personal emotions revealed in *Leaving Cheyenne*

to those of people far removed in time and place. In that same novel, the structural indications of a cyclical vision of human life also extend the reverberation of the drama beyond its indisputably pungent localization.

McMurtry's recourse to the archetype of journeying is another, and a more significant, resonating device. As we have seen, the journeying impulse is closely related to the specific cultural impoverishment McMurtry exposes. But through the journey pattern these novels join a longtime tradition of literary journeys, a tradition which has appeared in epics of all literatures but has been a particularly characteristic American form because of the peculiarities of the nation's history. Indeed, the insistence with which McMurtry's characters strike out . . . links these novels to the heritage of westering and to the great California dream. Like other Americans throughout our history, these Texans define their values spatially. The loss of traditional values involves his fictional people in fruitless geographical search and a permanent restlessness. (pp. 49-50)

> *Janis P. Stout, "Journeying As a Metaphor for Cultural Loss in the Novels of Larry McMurtry," in* Western American Literature *(copyright, 1976, by the Western Literature Association), Vol. XI, No. 1, Spring, 1976, pp. 37-50.*

BRINA CAPLAN

Somebody's Darling has an interesting story to tell: Hollywood has chosen Jill Peel, a shy, witty, work-obsessed animator and cinematic technician, to be America's first woman film director. Her initial effort, *Womanly Ways,* is successful, so successful that it sends her on to the New York Film Festival, an Oscar, and the direction of a second film, this one a Western, to be shot on location in Texas. Jill's success, however, proves insistent; it places her in the confidence of a dying mogul; it ensnares her in a brutal love affair. It sets her at odds with a vengeful, female superstar and enforces a nearly disastrous distance between her and her oldest friends. At 37, Jill Peel must struggle to reclaim herself from Hollywood's entangling system of rewards and punishments, and from the contradictory demands of love, work, friendship and fame.

McMurtry has divided *Somebody's Darling* among first-person narrators, a design that necessarily tests his technique as a storyteller. There are three sections, three different points of view. Jill's protector, Fitzgeraldesque adviser, and closest friend, Joe Percy, speaks first. The second section is recounted by Owen Oarson, ambitious, violent and emotionally numb, the lover whom Jill acquires during her stay in New York City. And Jill herself tells the last part of her story.

Since self-disclosure is the method of the novel, *Somebody's Darling* opens appropriately, in mid-conversation. . . . McMurtry issues an invitation to eavesdrop which, if we accept it, ought to draw us into the nature of his characters and set us within the bounded and carefully crafted world of the good novel. (pp. 121-22)

Through several of his novels now, Larry McMurtry has been charting a fictional world, extending its boundaries, populating it with recurrent characters. . . . The geography of this world is the author's own: humid Houston, intellectual Austin, Hollywood's hills and movie-lots, an outsider's-become-insider's New York. McMurtry has tenanted this landscape with Texans and Californians, with film people and book people, with eccentrics and hustlers, with artists and movie technicians, housewives and academics. When a fictional world accretes in this way, novel by novel, it allows its author time to cast over his landscape for meaning, pattern, value. There is a promise made . . . that as the author slowly structures his fictional world, he will invest its architecture with a significant interpretation of inner and outer life. . . .

Somebody's Darling hints at themes that McMurtry has suggested previously in earlier novels: the terror underlying all relationships between men and women; the paradoxical isolation that shadows a woman's growing strength; the difficulty of saving one's soul in a culture as nourishing as a greasy hamburger, as anonymously formed and fatally sterile as a styrofoam cup. Relentlessly pursued by a "how" or a "why," any of these themes would become substantial, an "important question," the material of a good novel. But once again, as in his previous fiction, McMurtry refuses to track down the game he has startled from the bushes. And so, despite Joe Percy's advocacy of "loyalty," of the persistence essential to craft, the hunt is lost. "Important questions" slip off into the woods while McMurtry entertains us with easy sentiment and instant laughs.

The dialogue of *Somebody's Darling* is consistently clever; but it is also uniformly clever and, therefore, finally, wearyingly clever. The three narrators of the novel, in fact the entire populace of McMurtry's world, speak a California variant of American Wiseass. . . . Joe, debonair and death-haunted; Jill, desperate and struggling; Owen, tightlipped and deliberate, all sound alike. They are facelessly funny, as interchangeably voluble as the writers of Johnny Carson's monologues.

Since the joyful and the suffering, the stupid and the sensitive all express their feelings casually in one-liners, no character in *Somebody's Darling* articulates an independent inner life. Moods remain causal unknowns, motives are as remote and unsummonable as ghosts at noon. Somehow or other, people simply feel this way today, that way tomorrow. . . . Conceivably the man with the map might be McMurtry himself, were he to cease sketching funny lines long enough to create fully dimensional portraits. He does not lack observational talent. But in spite of his awareness that craftsmanship requires patience, McMurtry remains obsessed by pace. He continues to be a quick-sketch artist who insists upon completing every picture within the moment.

As a result his novel trades away substance for speed, a costly bargain. "Important questions" give way to an easy existential shrug. Life, we learn, is not as good as the movies; or, as one character succinctly sums it up, "life is a mess.'" If McMurtry had solidly invested his world with necessity, then such a conclusion might ring true. . . . But Larry McMurtry's world is not intractible, complex and baffling; it is simple, clever, and timed for a laugh. (pp. 122-23)

He is an extremely talented writer, funny, skillful, observant. But he must constantly arrive, and so he is unable to journey. Although McMurtry sets *Somebody's Darling* on the road to Wessex, he cannot steer it to its destination, because he insists on stopping off for a snack at every Dairy Queen along the highway. (p. 123)

Brina Caplan, "Existential Shrugging," in The Nation *(copyright 1979 The Nation magazine, The Nation Associates, Inc.), Vol. 228, No. 4, February 3, 1979, pp. 121-23.*

JOSEPH J. ESPOSITO

Somebody's Darling employs some of the conventions of aesthetic realism and employs them well; the characters are rounded and believable and the story line involving. . . .

A complex narration, similar to that of *The Sound and the Fury,* interestingly complicates plot and characters by showing them through overlapping and frequently contradictory lenses. (p. 181)

McMurtry's is to my mind the most mature of several recent novels by men that consider the current status of women in American society, yet it is bound to come under criticism from a certain quarter. Why make [the protagonist] Jill Peel a film director with only modest talent? Why make her fall in love with cruel men? Why make her incapable of sticking up for herself? I think McMurtry would here invoke his realist aesthetic: he can only paint what he sees and the world as he sees it unfortunately provides more material to create a Jill Peel than, say, "the woman warrior" of Maxine Hong Kingston's fascinating book of that title.

But, putting sociology to the side, realism is no excuse for artistic dullness. An interesting character is one thing, an effective narrator something else entirely. All of the book's narrators are unreliable, but the men manage to be authoritative even when they lack any credentials other than the will to impose their voices upon the world. Jill lacks that will. She can't quite cut it as a director, and she can't cut it as a narrator. Her material resists her. When she sympathizes with [movie queen] Sherry Solare, who kills her own son and steals Jill's man, she thereby denies herself an exploration of a deeply evil character. [Her close friend] Joe Percy's narration may, through his self-absorption, cut him off from the present tense of the novel, but nostalgia belongs to a powerful literary tradition which Percy can conjure easily and effectively. Owen [Jill's unsavory lover] does hide behind cynicism, but in the world of *Somebody's Darling* it is hard to locate the tender feelings he misses out on. In the voice of a different narrator than Jill Peel, or perhaps in a book by a different novelist . . . , the evil of a Sherry Solare could achieve tangible and fearsome proportions. . . . But *Somebody's Darling* is not that kind of book and McMurtry not that kind of writer. Thus what we are left with is a novel whose narration partially falters due to the author's strict adherence to aesthetic realism. (pp. 181-82)

Joseph J. Esposito, "Faltering Realism," in Prairie Schooner *(reprinted from* Prairie Schooner *by permission of University of Nebraska Press; © 1979 by University of Nebraska Press), Vol. 53, No. 2, Summer, 1979, pp. 181-82.*

KIRKUS REVIEWS

McMurtry's down-home fictions have always been juiced up with side-orders of raunchy charm and beer-barrel comedy—but this time [in *Cadillac Jack*] he tries, with middling results, to make an entire novel out of such enticing (yet ultimately wearying) trimmings. Narrator-hero "Cadillac Jack" McGriff is a onetime rodeo bulldogger who now travels the country, in his pearly Cadillac, as a super-duper dealer/scout—picking up antiques and other collectibles (e.g., a load of gem-encrusted cowboy boots), buying at garage sales, selling to the super-rich. . . . McMurtry does a dandy job with Jack's business doings here: his highway world of garage-sale finds, auction fever, and obsessive acquisition is captured in rich, economic detail. And the quieter comedy . . . often scores. But the supposed center of this novel, Jack's romantic quandary, is uninvolving throughout, thanks to the thin characterizations—while the broader [Washington] D.C. farce clashes badly with the tough-guy sentimentality. An idle mix of charm, noise, and hoke, then: far too long . . . , fitfully endearing, and especially disappointing after the textured comedy/drama control of *Somebody's Darling.*

A review of "Cadillac Jack," in Kirkus Reviews *(copyright © 1982 The Kirkus Service, Inc.), Vol. L, No. 15, August 1, 1982, p. 894.*

JOHN BROSNAHAN

[Cadillac Jack, a] rambling drifter of a man—an antiques spotter who travels the country searching for collectible treasures and who acts as a middleman between seller and dealer—can't quite find the key to his own life. What Jack does find is himself in love with two women, and he's unable or unwilling to choose between them. While the plot often seems to be going nowhere at half-speed, McMurtry injects some marvelously comic poignancy into Jack's purposeless meanderings and creates a number of memorable characters in the bargain. A natural for fans of the author's wistful brand of soul-searching.

John Brosnahan, in a review of "Cadillac Jack," in Booklist *(reprinted by permission of the American Library Association; copyright © 1982 by the American Library Association), Vol. 79, No. 1, September 1, 1982, p. 2.*

PETER PRINCE

It isn't entirely Larry McMurtry's fault that his new novel [*Cadillac Jack*] gives off a strong sense of *déjà vu*—there has been a surfeit of C&W/good ol' boy themes in fiction and movies lately. The smirking shade of John Travolta's urban cowboy seems to hover over most of Cadillac Jack's mild adventures, though Travolta would be far too young to play in the film version. Even Willie Nelson—and this gets closer to the area of McMurtry's culpability—would be far too young. For Cadillac Jack is carrying around in his peach velour interior a case of apathy, depression and world-weariness that would seem to need at least 150 years of bitter and dispiriting living to engender.

In his fine novels of the Southwest, McMurtry appeared to invest great stores of emotional sympathy in his characters. They were often not particularly strong or admirable people, yet the loving, intense way the author followed them and their doings rendered them touching, interesting, always alive. It's hard to see any trace of that generous intensity in *Cadillac Jack.* Once in a while the book quickens into life—usually when Jack has made a profitable or peculiar antique trade—but for the most part the writing feels flatter than the landscape around Lubbock. Regrettably, the novel is written in the first person, and thus the mournful, jaded outlook of Jack is the only vision we get. And Jack, with his small, fruitless love affairs and his long, boring hours behind the wheel of his Cadillac, is the man to squelch everything down to the level of his own deep ordinariness.

As an antidote to my feelings of depression over the book, I picked up McMurtry's earlier *Moving On* and was again quickly drawn in by the enlivening corespondences this writer can so well reveal between characters he cares about and the vast, dominant scenery in which and against which they struggle. It does seem that McMurtry's shift of focus to the Eastern megalopolis has been no more successful than has Cadillac Jack's. And, strangely, McMurtry seems to have lost in transit his generosity toward the failures and strugglers in life. Little peo-

ple, it seems, are all right if they are Texas rodeo riders or gas station mechanics, but when they reveal themselves as Washington office clerks, they merit nothing but crisp disdain. . . . Sweep 'em away. (pp. 536, 539)

In the heart of the book there is something not uninteresting struggling to get out, some parallel between Cadillac Jack's function as a middleman between sellers and buyers of treasures which he never allows himself to possess and his similar inability to hold fast to human relationships. And McMurtry is always readable; the pages turn easily enough. Moreover, he is a canny craftsman and must have been aware of the flat tone that enfeebles this book. Unfortunately, his efforts to liven things up take the form of extended, wild fantasies about Washington high life, which, though energetic, give the impression of a society observed purely through a keyhole. Certainly it can be read by the rich and powerful with perfect equanimity. Off-target burlesques will not bother them very much. A cold, hard, unforgiving stare at their activities might have been another matter.

It is difficult for a reviewer to know quite what to do when a favorite author disappoints so keenly. Certainly there is no temptation to utter sharp, impertinent cries of "Shape up, McMurtry!" Probably the best thing is to bow the head, avert the gaze and hope for better things—perhaps a swift, safe return to Texas for this often excellent writer. It is a bold thing to try for, but it should be possible to make an effective story in which the central character is an apathetic, exhausted bore. . . . Just to write an apathetic, exhausted novel about him, however, seems an easy way out. (p. 539)

Peter Prince, "A Good Ol' Antique Dealer," in The Nation *(copyright 1982 The Nation magazine, The Nation Associates, Inc.), Vol. 235, No. 17, November 20, 1982, pp. 536, 539.*

EDEN ROSS LIPSON

By his own account, Cadillac Jack McGriff, 6 feet 5 inches of Texas manhood without his boots or Stetson, 35 years old and twice divorced, is a natural scout and a natural womanizer. Having done a stint as a bulldogger on the rodeo circuit, he retired to roam the country in his big pearl-colored Caddy with peach velour interior. He now spends his days scouting—exploring back roads for antiques and collectibles, buying and selling what strikes his fancy, "too curious, too restless, too much in love with the treasure hunt" to specialize.

The double conceit of scouting and that fancy vehicle allows Larry McMurtry . . . the peculiar luxury of a rambling, often incoherent, frequently entertaining tale. . . .

But every time Mr. McMurtry threatens to get into something like substantive plot or character development, Jack jumps into that dad-blamed car and drives off somewhere. The cruising is endless and serves only to connect the short, affectionate, sometimes hilarious vignettes of Americans trading and swapping that give the book its genuine eccentricity. (p. 13)

Larry McMurtry is a problematic figure. His second and finest novel, **"Leaving Cheyenne,"** threatens to become an acknowledged classic. . . . With his third novel Mr. McMurtry found cars and the possibility of escape; then came Houston and after that the open road. Lately, as the author has drawn on his experiences in Hollywood and in Washington, . . . his fiction has been increasingly satirical and cartoonish. (p. 20)

Eden Ross Lipson, "A Cast of American Originals," in The New York Times Book Review *(© 1982 by The New York Times Company; reprinted by permission), November 21, 1982, pp. 13, 20.*

JOSEPH BROWNE

Like most "antique" collections, Larry McMurtry's eighth novel [*Cadillac Jack*] is actually two or three valuables and a whole lot of junk. This is especially disappointing because McMurtry is too good a novelist . . . to believe that dozens of one-dimensional albeit eccentric characters, a protagonist who exists only to concatenate these eccentrics, and a theme and plot that remain forever incipient constitute literary art.

Cadillac Jack McGriff, antique scout extraordinaire, has a recurring dream of driving backward down the highway of his life. This surreal element permeates the novel like a crazed Pac-man munching away at everything resembling sustained characterization and meaningful plot. Although he seems dedicatedly ignorant of most things, McGriff does know "the power of things." Just name your "thing," and this modern day picaresque prostitute will find it, buy it and sell it to you faster than a maniac auctioneer's spiel.

Jack McGriff, however, is no itinerant flit frolicking about America emitting high-pitched squeals of delight over each newly discovered antique treasure. He's obviously meant by McMurtry to be all man, viz., a six-foot-five Texan, ex-world champion bulldogger, twice-divorced womanizer who spits out, John Wayne style, such philosophical aphorisms as "Truth can be counted on to arrive under its own power, where women are concerned." . . .

Reading *Cadillac Jack* is like walking through a labyrinth of side-shows or, much worse, like watching 30 or 40 television sitcoms and soaps in rapid succession. Having read the book, having escaped from the maze, having turned off the television, readers/viewers are bound to exclaim incredulously, "I pay $15.95, and that's it? No main attraction? No feature-length special? What a rip-off; this was supposed to be a novel by Larry McMurtry!" Several entertaining characters (really more flagrant caricatures than they are characters) do momentarily entertain and demand some attention, but ultimately readers will empathize with Jack when he laments midway through the novel that he seems to have "wandered into a garden of grotesques." (p. 179)

Somewhere beneath this novel's nonsense and scattered among its outlandish flotsam and jetsam lies a legitimate story about understanding America's spiritual and aesthetic values by examining what we keep as treasures and discard as trash. McMurtry himself may have sensed this, but the story remains hidden, and *Cadillac Jack* is, finally, as they say in Texas, all hat and no cattle. (p. 180)

Joseph Browne, in a review of "Cadillac Jack," in America *(reprinted with permission of America Press, Inc.; © 1983; all rights reserved), Vol. 148, No. 9, March 5, 1983, pp. 179-80.*

Yukio Mishima

1925-1970

(Pseudonym of Kimitake Hiraoka) Japanese novelist, short story writer, dramatist, film director, and essayist.

Mishima was one of the first Japanese writers to achieve international attention. He was obsessed, both in his life and his art, with what he called "my heart's leaning toward Death and Night and Blood." Mishima combined elements of both Eastern and Western literature, but his respect for Japan's imperialistic past is an essential hallmark of his work. He created a literature, often autobiographical and darkly sensual, in which he attempted to deal with the meaninglessness of life; he was especially distressed by the materialism of post-war Japan. As a dramatist, he is noted for the skillful way he wedded elements of the ancient *Noh* tradition to contemporary themes.

Since his ritual suicide, Mishima's critics have attempted to explain his action through his work. Mishima may have felt that committing *seppuku* would affirm his personal convictions and would remind the Japanese of their lost ideals. His last work, a tetralogy known as *The Sea of Fertility*, is based on reincarnation. It was completed on the day of his death and many consider it the author's masterpiece.

(See also *CLC*, Vols. 2, 4, 6, 9 and *Contemporary Authors*, Vols. 97-100, Vols. 29-32, rev. ed. [obituary].)

© Yoko Mishima

NANCY WILSON ROSS

The Temple of the Golden Pavilion [*Kinkakuji*], based on an actual occurrence in recent Japanese history, deals with the complex pathology and final desperate crime of a young Zen Buddhist acolyte, in training for priesthood at a Kyoto temple.

In 1950, to the distress and horror of all art-loving and patriotic Japanese, the ancient Zen temple of Kinkakuii in Kyoto was deliberately burned to the ground. (p. vi)

But although Mishima has made use of the reported details of the real-life culprit's arrogant and desperate history, culminating in the final willful act of arson, he has employed the factual record merely as a scaffolding on which to erect a disturbing and powerful story of a sick young man's obsession with a beauty he cannot attain, and the way in which his private pathology leads him, slowly and fatefully, to self-destruction and a desperate deed of pyromania. (p. vii)

[The] author of *The Temple of the Golden Pavilion* does not give the impression that he is in any way concerned with voicing a philippic against Zen Buddhism. Yukio Mishima appears chiefly interested in the imaginative re-creation of a psychotic acolyte's obsession and a detailed portrayal of the steps that led to his last desperate, destructive act. The emphasis falls on the individual. Even the sociological factors are made subservient to young Mizoguchi's pathology. (p. viii)

The Temple of the Golden Pavilion has around it an aura of Dostoevskian violence and passion. I found many reminders of Dostoevsky's involved and tortuous struggles with the age-less questions of "forgiveness," "love," "mastery." Yet as

the story of *The Temple of the Golden Pavilion* fatefully un-winds, one is strangely free of emotional identification with any character—and here, certainly, the Dostoevskian comparison sharply ends.

This freedom from emotional identification does not, however, lessen the book's power. It seems, in a singular way, to intensify it, almost as though the stuttering Mizoguchi's murky analyses of the nature and conduct of the people he encounters in his daily life become the reader's own astigmatism. The "moral" position from which we, as Westerners with a Puritan tradition, are accustomed to judge behavior both in life and literature is missing from these pages. The episodes are, for the most part, presented free of judgment. In fact there seems to be little, if any, stress on familiar "values." Those dualisms of black and white, body and soul, good and evil that we take so for granted are not found in *The Temple of the Golden Pavilion*. Evil is represented, to be sure, but never with comment direct enough to suggest a tangible attitude toward it. (p. xi)

The Temple of the Golden Pavilion is rich in scenes, incidents, episodes which, though developed in great detail, often leave the reader uncertain as to their meaning and portent in relation to the story's main line. There is in this a similarity to life itself, where the threads of relationship are never neatly woven into a clear and fixed pattern. In reading Mishima's novel, one is not so much baffled as frequently *suspended*. (p. xii)

Through the pages of a novel like Yukio Mishima's, one is able to perceive some of the elements that have gone into the creation of this rare, paradoxical, and long-enduring civilization; elements which well may, in the modern world, face final dissolution. In *The Temple of the Golden Pavilion* a fragment of contemporary Japanese life, with its roots still deep in the culture of the past, is presented not for our judgment but for our observation. The opportunity offered here by Yukio Mishima's special insight and fictional talent is one for which to feel properly grateful. (pp. xviii-xix)

> *Nancy Wilson Ross, "Introduction" (reprinted by permission of the author), in* The Temple of the Golden Pavilion *by Yukio Mishima, translated by Ivan Morris, Alfred A. Knopf, Inc., 1959, pp. v-xix.*

ANTHONY WEST

The subject of **"Kinkakuji"** is one that lies close to Mishima's heart, and the book is written with great intensity and passion, though without any trace of incoherence. It is the imaginary autobiography of an actual person who in 1950 committed a crime that shocked all conventional Japanese. This was the burning of the Kinkaku, the Golden Pavilion of the Rokuon Temple, the sole survivor of a group of palace buildings erected in Kyoto between 1395 and 1397. (p. 113)

For Mishima, the Kinkaku affair became symbolic of the situation of his generation as he saw it. The Kinkaku itself, the elegant folly that had by dint of survival become a holy object, stood for the irrelevant cultural legacy his generation had inherited from feudal Japan, while its resurrection, intact, perfect, and meaningless, from its own ashes provided a perfect allegorical representation of the sacrifice of the living present to the dead past. He accordingly wrote this novel, an extraordinarily convincing and extremely moving reconstruction of the life and the emotional development of the young man who came to loathe and love the original Kinkaku so passionately that he could escape from its domination only by destroying it. . . . The growth of his hero's obsession is described by Mishima with the economy and force of a writer of the first rank so that in the end the reader shares his agony and recognizes the absolute necessity of his bizarre crime. With its psychological penetrations and its vivid evocation of the life of Kyoto in Japan's cruelly testing years of defeat and occupation, **"The Temple of the Golden Pavilion"** has substantial claims to be considered one of the most interesting novels of the decade. This would not be the case if Mishima were writing about a wholly Japanese problem, but he has touched on one of the major discomforts of his generation in every country—the feeling that the modern world is so different from the old that the greater part of its cultural legacy has become merely an irrelevant burden, inhibiting and stifling the creativity of those who wish to deal with life as it is, and not as it was, or is supposed to have been. This forceful and exciting novel has the widest possible frame of reference and is in no sense either exotic or parochial. (pp. 113-14)

> *Anthony West, "An Arrival, a Departure," in* The New Yorker *(© 1959 by The New Yorker Magazine, Inc.), Vol. XXXV, No. 18, June 20, 1959, pp. 113-16.**

D. J. ENRIGHT

Unfortunately Mishima gives the impression [in *The Temple of the Golden Pavilion*] of striving to be simultaneously a very Western novelist (philosophical disquisitions and conscientious documentation) and a very Eastern novelist (symbols galore) . . . But this novel is a caricature of post-war Japanese fiction. Mizoguchi is the typical hero; unhealthy, nastily *conscious* about his perversities, alternately arrogant and self-abasing, an inveterate intellectualiser yet contemptuous of reason. The incidents are similarly typical. . . .

Despite its *nominally* powerful incidents, I would say that the novel is conspicuously lacking in power—and precisely because it is devoid of moral sensibility (which, by the way, is not exclusively a 'Puritan,' or even Western, accessory). Consequently nothing really matters: the trampling of the prostitute is unpleasant, not powerful; the burning of the Temple is shocking and ridiculous (in the way that the price of tobacco is), not powerful; the hero could eat his mother raw and we should only feel a faint disgust with the author. We have established no moral connection with Mizoguchi; as a character he is rather less 'powerful' than Alice's Red Queen. The episodes are gratuitous, just as the recurring 'symbols' omit to symbolise.

> *D. J. Enright, "Graces and Disgraces," in* The Spectator *(© 1959 by The Spectator; reprinted by permission of* The Spectator*), Vol. 203, No. 6849, October 2, 1959, p. 450.**

TAKASHI OKA

["**After the Banquet**"] bears the unmistakable Mishima stamp in its flawless construction, its delicious evocation of atmosphere. Like so much of modern Japanese literature, however, it is essentially an indoor type of writing—fragile, sensitive, intelligent, but somehow lacking the full-blooded vigor, the loamy richness of the greatest western masters. . . .

There is no question that as a novel **"After the Banquet"** is always fascinating and frequently brilliant. The author's intent is clear—to convey what the dust jacket calls his heroine's "blazing vitality." The celadon fineness of Mishima's writing, however, gets in the way of his intent, as if an artist who excelled in watercolors and line drawings had decided to experiment in oils.

> *Takashi Oka, "Novels from India and Japan: 'After the Banquet'," in* The Christian Science Monitor *(reprinted by permission from* The Christian Science Monitor; *© 1963 The Christian Science Publishing Society; all rights reserved), February 14, 1963, p. 11.*

WILLIAM BARRETT

At first glance there might seem to be a certain naïveté about *After The Banquet* . . . , as if the author, in writing a novel, were imitating an alien idiom. But this initial reaction . . . quickly vanishes; the apparent naïveté turns into a style all its own, direct yet allusive, poetic without being gushing, and we realize that the author has accomplished the amazing feat of making his novel entirely successful by Western standards and yet never losing contact with his own great tradition of Japanese poetry. (p. 162)

The plot is slight; the novel triumphs as a character study of a couple past their prime caught in the toils of a hopeless marriage. In Kazu, particularly, Mr. Mishima has caught the pathos of the middle-aged woman fluttering in love with the impulsiveness and abandon of a young girl as we have not had it in fiction since the best of Colette. (p. 163)

William Barrett, "Autumn Love," in The Atlantic Monthly *(copyright © 1963, by The Atlantic Monthly Company, Boston, Mass.; reprinted with permission), Vol. 211, No. 3, March, 1963, pp. 162-63.*

EARL MINER

[The theme of] *The Sailor Who Fell from Grace with the Sea* [*Gogo no Eikō*] is at once special in character and an outgrowth of motifs developed in earlier books. . . .

Inherent in this story are two artistic difficulties which the author does not entirely overcome: the credibility of the love affair between two characters with such widely differing backgrounds, and the credibility of the boys' inhuman sophistication and actions. Mishima seeks to transcend these problems by his emphasis on the symbolic. While the adults represent irrational ardor succumbing to practical reality, the boys represent "absolute dispassion" grounded in naïveté. What relates the two is death: in literature death is often the accompaniment of passion or the result of sterile abstraction.

The novel is profoundly, even beautifully macabre, especially in its reversal of the usual images of child and adult. In its portrayal of adult passion and its manipulation of narrative points of view, it recalls Henry James, while in its picture of childhood, and its almost allegorical approach, it reminds one of William Golding in *Lord of the Flies*. . . . If the sailor's stories of life at sea seem to the boys "too typical to be true," the novel itself is perhaps too disturbing to be false.

Earl Miner, "A Failure of Feeling," in Saturday Review *(© 1965 Saturday Review Magazine Co.; reprinted by permission), Vol. XLVIII, No. 38, September 18, 1965, p. 106.*

HAROLD CLURMAN

Superficially *The Sailor Who Fell from Grace with the Sea* . . . is a horror story of juvenile delinquency. (pp. 171-72)

We are reminded, to begin with, of the children in Dostoevsky and Gide whose crimes express the innate evil of mankind, gratuitous and mindless. But in Mishima's novel the children are nihilists because they are absolute idealists. . . . Sex itself for them is not only an unworthy but an insignificant activity. The sailor of the story—he is an officer on a merchant ship—is a hero to them so long as he remains one, free from the taint of mundane commerce. When he consents to join the commonplace citizenry, he must be done away with as a traitor.

Curiously, the sailor himself shares his assailants' sentiments. He too feels that his marriage entails a corruption, a descent into the sloth which his killers call "impermissible things," the ordinary traffic of life. . . .

Dense in substance, far-reaching in allusion, this novel is brilliant in the conciseness of its narrative line. The imagery is marked by a sort of impersonal sensuousness, a graphic and colorful precision. The verbal means employed are spare; one is aware of a dominant control. . . .

Mishima's posture is one of apparently imperturbable contemplation, something between anguished awe and puzzled serenity. (p. 172)

Harold Clurman, "Mad Old Man and the Sea," in The Nation *(copyright 1965 The Nation magazine, The Nation Associates, Inc.), Vol. 201, No. 9, September 27, 1965, pp. 171-72.**

EDWARD SEIDENSTICKER

["Forbidden Colors"] insists upon comparison with an even earlier Mishima novel, "Confessions of a Mask" ["Kamen no Kokuhaku"] . . . , and it is inferior to the earlier novel in most respects save price and bulk. Both works have as their heroes handsome young homosexuals. Both contain a strong element of narcissistic subjectivity, not to say self-gratification; in both there is a great deal of sadism and masochism, quite at home in a flamboyantly amoral world; and in both a denial of intellect and glorification of the senses, fundamental to all of Mishima's writing, is incongruously combined with rather a lot of quite strained intellectualizing.

One would expect the more subjective and autobiographical of the two, "Confessions of a Mask," to make one more uncomfortable; but such is not the case. It is not easy to say why, unless perhaps the point is that the hero of "Confessions of a Mask" is in the hands of nature and is able to convey to us what it says and does to him, whereas the hero of "Forbidden Colors" is essentially passive in the hands of an abstraction, and is himself an abstraction, an assertion of beauty (with what frequency the author uses the word!) that goes unrealized.

The other abstraction comes nearer having life. Early in the book, in a somewhat improbable scene, the young hero is impelled to confess his proclivities to an aged, ugly and very famous novelist. Thereupon he becomes the device through which the older man has his revenge upon the female sex, and becomes at the same time a sounding board and proving ground for his theories of art. . . .

At moments when there ought to be conflict and exchange between the two, the older man has a way of vanishing in a flood of words and the younger into a vortex of silence. . . .

But one must go a little further in trying to define why this is, in the end, a cold, repellent book. At one point, perhaps a quarter of the way along, when revenge upon the female sex is proceeding nicely, the older man writes of the younger in his diary: "To have found such a perfect living doll as this! Yuichi is truly exquisite. Not only that, he is morally frigid." One wonders again: can a morally frigid novelist really be much of a novelist at all?

Edward Seidensticker, "Yuichi Was a Doll," in The New York Times Book Review *(© 1968 by The New York Times Company; reprinted by permission), June 23, 1968, p. 32.*

THE TIMES LITERARY SUPPLEMENT

Yukio Mishima's *Madame de Sade* [is] a Japanese study of the enigmatic marquise who remained constant to her husband during his imprisonment and abandoned him when he was released during the Revolution. Mishima's explanation is that the lady could put up with Sade's actions, but not with his literary work which, in her view, forecast the emerging social order. . .

Apart from the historical snag that Sade himself proved a moderate when entrusted with revolutionary authority, this conclusion comes over as the mechanical dislocation of an exclusively schematic action. All the characters stand for some abstract quality: law and order, religion, carnal desire, female guile, &c. The Marquise herself represents marital devotion and, as such, cannot change her mind without doing violence to the play's structure. As the work of a Japanese author, *Madame de Sade* shows considerable skill in its handling of the surface manners. . . . But real feeling only breaks through in the gloatingly detailed accounts of Sade's pleasures.

> *"Pie-Eaters, Scroungers, Assassins & c.," in* The Times Literary Supplement *(© Times Newspapers Ltd. (London) 1968; reproduced from* The Times Literary Supplement *by permission), No. 3473, September 19, 1968, p. 1052.**

MASAO MIYOSHI

Mishima's first volume, *The Forest in Full Bloom* (*Hanazakari no Mori* . . .), is a collection of precociously decadent and detachedly romantic stories, many of which recollect a colorful but boring upper-class life long gone even then. Also they provide a heavy dose of nationalistic rhetoric glorifying the beauty and elegance of the Imperial past—a fact interesting in view of their author's later works. The elaborate and archaic vocabulary and general aloofness to the drab and wretched scenes of wartime Japan similarly foreshadow his mature works, whose motifs, images, and themes are already apparent. With *Confessions of a Mask* . . . , Mishima entered the forefront of the Tokyo literati. (pp. 145-46)

Overall, the progress of the plot [in *Confessions of a Mask*] follows the protagonist's growing-up years with no temporal disruption. Structurally, however, there is no clear beginning, middle, and end, nor is the division into four [chapters] marked by any discernible stages. It is notable, too, that the narrative tempo slackens considerably as the work proceeds.

In the earliest part, the "I's" memory is spotty. . . . The references are all in quick succession in the first ten pages with little analysis from the narrator. As the "I's" self-awareness develops, there is an increase in frequency of more analytic comments which connect the episodes. Also, as he grows older and the distance between experiencing self and narrating self diminishes, the narrator begins to concentrate on his sexual impulses, which focus alternately on Sonoko and his own body. There is now a full analytic commentary on each episode, retarding the passage of time and intensifying self-consciousness. The change in narrative style of course underlines the changes that occur between childhood and youth, in the perception of time and the self, but more importantly it dictates a change in the modality of the work from that of a highly imagistic, "poetic" narration to a more novelistic one. The gain in psychological fullness appears to be at the expense of lyrical intensity. (pp. 146-47)

The narrator's story is often in the present tense, which essentially obscures the distinction between time past and time present. Where this happens, the narrative sequence following the "I's" chronology does not easily yield a thoroughgoing consequentiality which arranges events into a plot, nor does it suggest an overall connected meaning. The power of the work arises instead from intensity and concentration of feeling. In this sense, *Confessions of a Mask* takes rather the form of a lyric than of a novel. (pp. 148-49)

Throughout the book, there is only the "I" who feels and does not feel, thinking about himself, looking at himself. This "I" fills the whole story, leaving no room for anybody else. Where then does the intense lyricism, the almost moving sadness, come from?

There is nothing about narcissism which is essentially antithetical to lyricism. . . . With Mishima, however, the narrator seldom lets himself go with his powerful emotions. As soon as they are registered, loneliness and despair—or joy and pleasure on a few occasions—are intelligently outlined and effectively dealt with. (pp. 152-53)

In this book of confessions in which almost everything is taken note of and accounted for, there is one thing the narrator leaves largely unanalyzed, and this is the gradual change in the attitude of the "I" toward his self-understanding. In the first chapter the story is wholly episodic, and the "I" understands, in his own way, what he is doing. But he is never self-conscious about his mode of self-understanding. His reaction to the night-soil man and other physical workers; his fascination with the picture of a knight on a white horse (ending abruptly when he is told the knight is a woman); his excitement at smelling soldiers' sweat; his early transvestitism . . .—these spots of time are arrested in cold clear pictures. And there is little intervention by the narrator as he records these scenes from his childhood, or what he calls his "preamble to [his] life.". . . (pp. 153-54)

It is absurd to see *Confessions of a Mask* as simply a record of a young homosexual, almost as absurd as calling *Lolita* a memoir of a child molester. There is a certain aspect of loneliness that only a sexual pathology can accurately shape. Thus homosexuality and autoeroticism in Mishima's work are not allowed to be the end-meaning of the story, but are made to serve as metaphors. What is more, the worry over one's perversion can serve as a fit metaphor for a knowledge, only gradually and painfully attained, of the transience of childhood and the passage of time. There is an intense sadness to this loss reverberating far beneath and beyond the author's personal life. (pp. 154-55)

[*The Temple of the Golden Pavilion* is also written] in the first person. Whereas *Confessions of a Mask* somehow maintains the form of a "confession," the narrator confiding his inner events as if in a diary, *The Golden Temple* is a much more indefinite soliloquy. Here the arsonist Mizoguchi is presumably telling his story after having committed the crime. But nothing is said about his present whereabouts (is he in prison?), his listener's identity, or about the circumstances giving rise to his soliloquy. . . . Such vagueness in Mishima's central conception of the narrative situation says a good deal about the work. (p. 159)

What was said as regards the *Confessions* must be repeated here, and even more emphatically: this work, too, evades consequentiality by the most subtle means. What happened earlier is connected with what comes later only thematically, not novelistically—that is, not historically, psychologically, or causally.

For evidence of this, it is notable that the narrator's sophisticated aesthetics has no endorsement in his experience. Nothing thus far in his background would have been likely to develop such a high degree of articulation on the meaning of beauty. (I am not insisting that Mizoguchi's aesthetics is "incredible," given his origins and education, but am arguing that *The Golden Temple* simply disregards the job of making it appear probable or even feasible in the light of his background.) The limits of his knowledge and consciousness are quite arbitrarily drawn according to the situation at hand. (pp. 159-60)

It is tempting to generalize here and talk about Mishima's overall failure in characterization. There is no question that he created very few memorable characters. Perhaps he is "too much himself" to feel with other people, to become them, as a character-novelist might do. But to point out what a writer cannot do very well is only a very small part of criticism. He is what he is because of other things which he does uniquely and other writers may not do nearly as well or at all. We must look elsewhere than in characterization for Mishima's accomplishment. (pp. 160-61)

For a true reading of *The Golden Temple,* one must resist the impulse to see it dramatically. Mizoguchi's tale is not a dramatic monologue; nor is it a clinical self-observation of a schizophrenic. But his view of beauty, which recurs in one form or another in all Mishima's works up to the very last, may safely be taken for Mishima's. (p. 162)

Whereas *Confessions of a Mask* mourned over the passage of time that erodes the experience of beauty, here it is the anticipation of the soon-to-come destruction that intensifies it. (p. 164)

Several nagging questions need to be heard. What happens to beauty by the burning of the Golden Temple? And how does it affect the future of the "I's" relationship with the outside world? Also important, in what way does the arsonist "symbolize the artist"?

That no beauty exists without constant threat of perishing is a given of this book. As long as the bombing continues, the "I" is at ease with the Golden Temple—in love with it, really—feeling no gap between the mind's image and the actual structure. The moment the danger disappears, beauty loses its evanescence, and it now belongs to a different order. The "I" must restore the danger so that equilibrium can be restored between external beauty and his inner world in all its vulnerability.

There is also the problem of beauty's destructive force over life. Because the Golden Temple is ordered into an exquisite form, it rejects the chaos that life is. And the perceiver, if unable at the same time to bear with the disorder and shapelessness of life, must either reject experience totally or shut his eyes to the form that exists only in lifeless art. To escape the paradox, the "I" finds another way: he will destroy the form in order to be released from its spell; in this way he feels he can at least live, even if his life is consequently disordered and unbeautiful. Action, whatever its particular nature, at least has this faculty of reclaiming life over sterile order. (pp. 167-68)

[Mizoguchi] imagines his act of destruction may do something to change other people's awareness of beauty. Since the order that makes beauty possible consists in the end of disordered matter, the reduction of the form to its chaotic components ought to make people realize beauty's ultimate nothingness. Indeed, it should make the artist himself realize that his efforts to prove that his vision is more than nothing are also futile. Meanwhile, the Golden Temple is something: an obese pig that grows and grows inside him, feeding on what remains of his isolated self.

Finally, the portrait of the artist emerging from *The Temple of the Golden Pavilion* is almost totally negative, with little in it to justify either the artist's craft or his vision. Only the near-mad act of total devastation generates any meaning for the

artist. But then, Mishima's art is seldom a cheerful one. He raises questions, disturbing, destructive ones, for which he is uninterested in finding answers. *The Temple of the Golden Pavilion* is a dangerous, disturbing, and beautiful book mostly because beauty really is dangerous, existing only where life itself is threatened with annihilation. (pp. 168-69)

> *Masao Miyoshi, "Mute's Rage," in his* Accomplices of Silence: The Modern Japanese Novel *(copyright ©1974 by The Regents of the University of California; reprinted by permission of the University of California Press), University of California Press, 1974, pp. 141-80.*

HISAAKI YAMANOUCHI

[Mishima's suicide] was rooted in what may be called his personal and aesthetic motives. No explanation, in either purely political or aesthetic terms, is adequate: the truth may be seen only from a due balance between the two. For Mishima's whole career was one of paradox built on an extraordinary tension between spirit and body, words and action, and artistic creation and commitment to the world. (p. 138)

Mishima's contribution to modern Japanese literature was immense. In embracing both traditional Japanese literary sensibilities and knowledge obtained from European literature he was as masterly as Sōseki and Akutagawa. In Mishima's case, however, the mode of amalgamating the two elements was far more complex than in his predecessors. The philosophy underlying his *seppuku* was definitely Japanese. The last phase of his vindication of Japanese cultural identity was fanatically nationalistic. The literary past and present, or Japanese tradition and Mishima's individual talent, were superbly synthesised in his *Five Modern Noh Plays (Kindui Nōgaku Shū . . .).* On the other hand Mishima was well versed in European literature. Raymond Radiguet and François Mauriac, for instance, are among those writers to whom the young Mishima looked for inspiration. Again, one of his plays was adapted from Racine's *Phèdre.* It is easy enough to detect in his work literary elements of European origin, such as the Greek idealisation of physical beauty, sadism, satanism of Baudelaire's type, and so on. Further, in its logical clarity and rhetorical richness his prose style is by far the most distinguished in modern Japanese literature; he is one of the few Japanese writers whose prose can equal the best of European prose in these qualities. In his achievement, after all, Mishima surpassed many of his Japanese predecessors.

Mishima's place in the history of modern Japanese literature may best be clarified if we compare him with the I-novelists [who wrote autobiography in the guise of fiction] and especially with a typical example of their kind, Dazai Osamu (1909-48). (pp. 138-39)

The almost deliberate morbidity in Dazai's real life was unforgivable to Mishima. And yet Mishima shared with Dazai certain characteristics such as physical frailty, in his youth at least, and a sense of enmity towards the world. Mishima, however, differed from Dazai in that he was a man of extraordinary stoicism who continually transformed his own self into its opposite. Furthermore, Dazai's confusion between life and art led to the failure of the latter. This had a curious result. First, a sensitive and frail young Mishima tried to disguise his real life under a mask of wholesomeness. Secondly, he allowed room in his work for the gloom of his mind's abyss, but made every effort to make the created world of his work independent of his life. It will be my purpose to trace in Mishima's work a hidden morbidity somewhat like Dazai's, and to see at the same time how he succeeded, unlike Dazai, in maintaining the autonomy of his work through his perfect artistic method.

Confessions of a Mask . . . is a short example of a *Bildungsroman,* in which the hero's personal history is traced from his childhood to his adolescence. One of its peculiar features is the author's uninhibited treatment of sexual perversion. What matters, however, is not sexual perversion as such, but its wider implications. (pp. 139-40)

It is worth noticing that the hero's sexual perversion is curiously connected with his attraction to death. . . . The references to death are legion. . . . One may find here the elements that recurrently constitute the trinity in Mishima's novels: death, love (either perverted or not) and eternity.

The hero's obsession with death, furthermore, is placed in a historical setting. He feels his future to be a burden. Accordingly the prospect of death on the battlefield and even in an air-raid is attractive to him. Ironically enough, however, he is dismissed from the army on the very first day of recruitment. This intensifies his desire for death: he looks forward to the time when the American troops will land and devastate his native soil. The defeat in the war therefore deprives him of his hope and brings him back to normal life. Thus for the hero of *Confessions* there are antithetical values: war against peace, abnormality against normality, and inability against necessity to love women. One constitutes reality and the other mere fiction. In other words the hero stands at odds with the society of postwar Japan, which is fictitious only; reality lies in the products of his own phantasy. (pp. 140-41)

In a word the hero is a nihilist who cannot find any meaning in life and in a sense inherits the characteristics of the I-novelists in general and Dazai in particular. What then is the relation between the hero and the author? Is the former a mere reflection of the latter and, if so, would it follow that there is little to choose between Dazai and Mishima and that Mishima's dislike of Dazai is that of one's own counterpart? The question leads us to consider the meaning of the title of the novel: *Confessions of a Mask.*

At first sight the title appears self-contradictory. A confession must be the true voice of feeling, which indeed was the case with the I-novelists, but in Mishima's case it is spoken by a mask. What then is the meaning of the mask? Is it merely a device for the author to disguise himself? If so, the confession would be made by the disguised self of the author. But this author-hero identification does not explain the self-contradiction of the title. There must be something more in the implication of the mask. First, in the context of the novel, the mask could mean the hero who is unable to, and yet pretends to, love a woman. . . . It seems irrelevant to identify the hero with the author and to consider whether or not Mishima himself was homosexual. Certainly homosexuality in itself is an important theme, but it is also the means of presenting a larger theme. The stoicism of the hero who tries unsuccessfully to love a woman becomes a stoicism in putting up with the existing order of the world which he actually does not accept. The second meaning of the mask therefore, is the disguised self of the hero who is at odds and yet must somehow come to terms with the world. It is not the first but the second meaning of the mask that makes possible identification of the hero with the author and hence the third meaning of the mask. So long as Mishima shares with the hero nihilism and stoicism, the

hero is the mask of Mishima himself. But the author is so well disguised under the mask of the hero that the confession is not as straightforward as that of the I-novelist. Viewed in this way, the title is not self-contradictory at all, but is a superb artistic device which made it possible for the author of this novel to detach his work from life as the I-novelists had never done before. And yet the fact remains that the nihilism of the hero inevitably reveals the abyss in the mind of the author himself, which made the artistic device all the more necessary. The author's own nihilism and his urgent need to disguise it under the highly artistic device were to become Mishima's major preoccupations.

Mishima's aim in *The Temple of the Golden Pavilion* . . . was to show the logical consistency of the protagonist's act of setting fire to the Golden Pavilion by enriching his character. On the surface the protagonist looks so defective that one might well call him an anti-hero. Nevertheless he is equipped with some important qualities. The theme of alienation from society is as dominant as in *Confessions.* (pp. 141-42)

From [an] analysis of *Golden Pavilion* there emerge such important features as the protagonist's estrangement from life, his nihilism or inability to find any positive meaning in life, and his obsession with beauty as an absolute value. In fact, these are all relevant to Mishima himself. And yet Mishima's art is so perfect that the created world of *Golden Pavilion* is completely autonomous. The work certainly reveals Mishima's own preoccupations, but there is no confusing the world of art with Mishima's own life. The world of his work in itself is a reality, perhaps even more real than life, and by attaining such a reality Mishima is able to survive his own enmity towards life. In simplified terms phantasy dominates over reality.

Nihilism or the concept of life as fiction still continues in Mishima's work in the 1960s. The precocious boy of thirteen and his companions in *The Sailor Who Fell from Grace with the Sea* . . . despise life as boring, hypocritical, sentimental, fictitious and ultimately meaningless. . . . [The] nihilism of the boys is the obverse of their cult of physical strength. The novel is an autonomous work of art detached from Mishima's own life even more perfectly than *Confessions* and *Golden Pavilion* and yet the curious fact is that worship of physical power is exactly what Mishima had been practising since the mid-1950s in order to transcend his fundamental nihilism.

What is particularly interesting about Mishima is the extraordinary tension between his life and works. In some of his works, such as *Confessions* and *Golden Pavilion,* the major characters, handicapped in various ways, cannot accept the external world except as mere fiction, and their hunger for eternity, coupled with their death-wish, makes them desire the end of the existing order of the world. In others, for example, *The Sound of Waves,* the major characters embody the fullness of life through their ideal physical strength. Here we have in fact the two sides of one coin: the former represents Mishima's own nihilism disguised under the highly artistic device of fiction and the latter Mishima's wish-fulfillment or search for his anti-self. In both cases it is characteristic of Mishima that in contrast to the I-novelists there is no simple confusion between his own life and the artistically created world of his work. Mishima was successful in creating a world of fiction not only as real as life, but even more real. To create such an autonomous world of fiction was the means of compensating for his sense of enmity towards the external world and hence of mastering life. In a word, writing novels as a kind of phantasy-making was for Mishima a means of survival and salvation.

There is no doubt that Mishima conceived of *The Sea of Fertility* (*Hōjō no Umi* . . .) as the culmination of his creative work. (pp. 143-45)

The Sea of Fertility is much wider in scope, both thematically and structurally, than *Confessions* and *Golden Pavilion*. But it readily links up with the earlier works. The theme of alienation from life is represented even more dramatically by being reduced to the antithesis between life and death. Such characters as Kiyoaki and Isao, although one is socially immoral and the other a criminal, seem to demonstrate that death is absolute, eternal and pure, whereas life involves absurdity, banality and impurity. Honda, on the other hand, is essentially a rationalist, succeeding as a lawyer and attaining wealth. But he is also under the spell of the irrational: his faith in the idea of reincarnation and interpretation of Kiyoaki's diary and dreams. The ultimate physical decay of Honda and the futility of his life throw into relief the absoluteness of dream and death, which can be even more real than life itself.

The obsession with death and apocalyptic vision of the end of the world are pervasive elements in Mishima's novels. However, if we adopt the view that Mishima's work constitutes an autonomous world, these elements in themselves do not account for his own tragic death. What of the trilogy that deals with the coup d'état of 26 February 1936 ['**Patriotism**' '**Kiku on the Tenth**' and *The Voices of the Heroic Dead*]. . . . [In these works] we should notice a change in the relation between Mishima's life and art. In his earlier works the apocalyptic wish for the end of the world is conceived by negative characters who are handicapped in various ways and cannot master life. In the army mutineer, however, Mishima represents a character who is no longer handicapped but fulfils his personal integrity through physical strength. Curiously enough, this is exactly what Mishima practised in his own life.

In the last years of his life, martial activities were becoming conspicuous. . . . The remarkable fact was that Mishima's physical training proved useful for his mastery of life as much as the act of writing his novels. Thus Mishima came to find complementary to each other those things which had originally seemed antithetical: the world and words, life and art, body and spirit. As a corollary to this Mishima asserted the Japanese tradition of the union of literary and martial arts and Wang Yang-ming's concept of the unity of knowledge and action. Formerly, the created world of Mishima's art was a compensation for his disenchantment with his unmanageable life. Now Mishima was the master of both spheres of art and life, and, paradoxically enough, the two spheres came to encroach upon each other in a way they did not with the I-novelists. Now the muscular and masculine Mishima could realise his desire for an apocalypse in the sphere of action, and did so in his final attempt at a coup d'état and his own suicide. (pp. 148-50)

Mishima's death . . . was no mere passive defeat since he had the will to control his own life. The situation was one of paradox. If Mishima had remained the type of writer who, as in his earlier years, felt handicapped in life but compensated for it by creating his work, he would have kept on living in that mode. Now he had acquired physical strength, by means of which he could extinguish his own body so that his soul could live. It seems likely that for all his success as a great literary figure the external world remained alien to him and that the content of his life, even including his last attempt at a coup, was a product of his phantasy. He lived all along in a phantasy world, which could never be authentic except through

serving the ultimate purpose of being transformed into an art form. (p. 152)

Hisaaki Yamanouchi, "A Phantasy World: Mishima Yukio," in his The Search for Authenticity in Modern Japanese Literature *(© Cambridge University Press 1978), Cambridge University Press, 1978, pp. 137-52.*

GWENN BOARDMAN PETERSEN

[Problems] of interpretation abound [in the four novels of *The Sea of Fertility: Spring Snow, Runaway Horses, The Temple of Dawn,* and *The Decay of the Angel*]. . . . [The] prevalence of Mishima's hybrid personal symbolism leaves the reader uncertain of the correct context in interpreting Mishima's fictional—and philosophical—approach to Reincarnation. Like the characters in Mishima's play *Dōjōji*, we are faced with sounds simultaneously identified as Nō chant and "a noisy factory." We only know that we are participating in Mishima's "beautiful, sweaty, intricate choreography of death." (p. 289)

[In] view of the care with which Mishima completed his manuscript [for *The Sea of Fertility*] hours before the action of his *seppuku*, we are surely justified in seeking clues to his death by sword in these four novels. At the same time, the tetralogy reexamines Mishima's earlier literary preoccupations, ideas beautifully and ironically resolved in that area of the moon from which the novels take their name, the arid *Sea of Fertility*.

In these four novels, familiar Mishima settings, recurrent characters, and obsessive themes, symbols. and images all make their final appearance. The recurrent image of sweating flesh is even elevated to a metaphysical sign foreshadowing decay— just as these four novels foreshadowed Mishima's own death. (pp. 290-91)

At the simple narrative level, *The Sea of Fertility* presents a four-part chronicle of the reincarnation of a beautiful boy, Kiyoaki. . . . (p.291)

[But it] is impossible to read these novels in the simplistic terms of plot: ultimately, the reader must face the metaphysical implications. At the same time, the novels of the tetralogy are linked—by character, symbol, and incident—to earlier fictions, essays, drama, even musical comedy lyrics. Mishima did indeed include everything of his life and thought in *The Sea of Fertility*.

Even the nagging voice of the pedagogue-author occasionally seems to be that issuing from behind the masks of earlier characters. Once more, Mishima's characters are not permitted well-developed individualized voices; the reader may well grow tired of the excess of aphoristic commentary. To replace such earlier (and unlikely) mouthpieces as a thirteen-year-old boy discoursing on "the chaos of existence" in *The Sailor Who Fell from Grace with the Sea,* Mishima produces extraordinarily varied figures in his final work, however.

Mishima's earlier tetralogy, *Kyōko no Ie (Kyōko's House. . .),* had failed largely on account of its excess of philosophy over (literary) art. . . . And the reader not inclined to philosophical speculation finds much of *The Sea of Fertility* as arid as its namesake on the moon.

In *The Sea of Fertility,* the reader is offered a four-part education not only in reincarnation but also in the meaning of Free Will; in Hindu belief. . . ; in esoteric elements of Buddhist belief. . . ; in the Sutra of the Peacock Wisdom King; in a world survey of theories of transmigration. . . . (pp. 295-96)

Whatever the meaning of *The Sea of Fertility* as a whole, it is appropriate that the most insistent of the recurrent themes is *seppuku,* the action with which Mishima achieved his *bumbu ryōdō* [unity of spirit and action]. *Seppuku*—"beautiful" death by the sword—is muted in the first volume, where Kiyoaki specifically reacts against "militarism." In the second volume, sword and *seppuku* and the ideals of past warriors provide a gloss on all of Mishima's work. There are links not only with the treatment of *seppuku*. . . in his films, dramas, and fictions, but also with his discussion of the samurai code in *Hagakure Nyūmon,* the voices of spirits of the war dead in *Eirei no Koe,* and other untranslated discussions of the Japanese Spirit. . . . (pp. 298-99)

As the catalogue of *seppuku* and other deaths by sword continues . . . , the reader hears echoes of Mishima's voice in a hundred other settings. Isao declares: "Once the flame of loyalty blazed up within one, it was necessary to die"—the words sound like a preliminary script for Mishima's own death-scene *Geki* (Appeal). References to disemboweling and a dagger in the throat described as "graceful" or "brave" further suggest the language of "**Patriotism.**" And when even the rather phlegmatic Honda dreams of "the supreme bliss of the moment of suicide," we hear once again the voice not of created character but of creator-author.

A substantial portion of *Runaway Horses* is a treatise on "lost" Japanese values as well as on the sword and noble death—again reminiscent of Mishima's aesthetic and his repeated references to the role of the sword in exalting the Japanese spirit. (p. 299)

In *The Temple of Dawn,* however, death by sword takes its metaphysical aspect from the ritual slaughter of goats, sacrifices to the Hindu Durga (Kali). And images of beautiful death by sword cannot convey the theme of decay in the final volume. In the account of *The Decay of the Angel,* with its metaphysics of sweating flesh, the noble image of suicide is flawed. . . . [For example], Tōru believes he will find true perspective "on the far side of death"; he thinks of the sexual fullness of love-suicide and foresees death in terms of pain. Mishima's words, perhaps—but ambiguous, especially when we consider Tōru's signs of decay.

The theme of beautiful death is also carried in imagery of swords—whether in a "sharp" blade of grass or the "stabs" of a cold shower. (p. 300)

Throughout *The Sea of Fertility* . . . images of beauty and beautiful death are linked to the ideally beautiful male figure that moves through all of Mishima's fictions. In *Spring Snow,* Kiyoaki is described in terms that show he is exceptionally beautiful, a doomed figure with "smooth" back, "grace," and "firm masculinity." . . . Once again, we meet a man "afflicted" by true beauty, with a predilection for suffering and an incapacity for friendship. . . . (p. 302)

Images of beautiful death are oddly resolved in the final volume with the Beauty—and Decay—of Tōru, another of Mishima's many sea-linked hero-gods. Tōru is linked with the sea at the most literal level. . . . It is fitting that this sea god should be discovered by Honda: Honda is the unifying figure who moves through each narrative to simultaneously identify the lovely Kiyoaki and speak the words of Mishima's philosophy. (p. 304)

Honda's thoughts on suicide . . . may hint of a deeper symbolism in Mishima's many deaths by water. . . . Through Honda, Mishima suggests that Time should be cut short just before the waterfall's plunge—at the pinnacle of physical beauty. (p. 306)

The dominant colors of blood, sun, and fire had been muted in *Spring Snow*—as in the golden sheen and scarlet reflections of the mother's fan. Garden settings in that novel provided a traditional (red) flower-in-the-mirror or moon-in-the-water image, too: the reflection of red maple leaves in the pond (although, as so often in Mishima's fictions, that image set up ripples of disquiet). In *Runaway Horses,* the blood red of heroic death is linked with the vermilion and gold of the symbolic sun, the "true image of His Sacred Majesty." (p. 308)

In *The Decay of the Angel,* Mishima uses the same palette. . . . The Robe of Feathers myth blazes with golden fire imagery, as Honda meditates on the *tennin* and the Five Signs of Decay. And the fire—like the sea—merges with images of cruelty and with sexual associations even while it hints of metaphysical meaning.

Fire, blood, and sea are simultaneously setting and symbol. So too the metaphysical sweat that marks the decay of the heavenly being is accompanied by real sweat throughout the entire tetralogy. (pp. 308-09)

[The] hints of sweating bodies move from erotic to metaphysical meaning. . . . In *The Decay of the Angel,* the sign begins as "cold sweats," with a glimpse of Tōru continually washing his armpits. Later, Honda sweats profusely as he puffs uphill to the mystic, sunlit garden. But by then the scene of Tōru's decay—the five signs now shown in his soiled, smelly appearance and flower-decked hair—has already signaled the passage into Nothingness.

Thus *The Sea of Fertility* seems to end. Yet its timing does not quite coincide with the dramatic ending of Mishima's own life, in spite of his assertion he would realize his *bumbu ryōdō* in this dual performance. For although the fourth novel opens in the year of Mishima's death, its narrative carries us into the future, four years hence. We are thus reminded of Mishima's comments on his inability to imagine a world continuing beyond the world of his novel. There is also a profound paradox: a tetralogy taking reincarnation for action, theme, characters, and imagery simultaneously presents "words" (spoken by a woman, though!) to suggest that perhaps the beautiful Kiyoaki had never "existed."

Paradoxes, however, are characteristic of all Mishima's work—including the odd "Greek" way that he identified with noble samurai ideals of his own nation's past and his search for a renewal of Japanese "spirit" by means of such foreign devices as body-building and weight-lifting. Moreover, the values that Mishima so often said that he wished to "restore" are values that receive scant support in his imagined universe.

In all his work, there are problems of setting. Even when his characters are not moving in an exotic world of Brazilian coffee plantation, ancient Leper King court, or modern political arena, they seem to be blind to the Japanese aesthetic. In Mishima's theory of fiction, dramatic necessity does not justify a character's ignorance (even of so small a matter as the correct name for traditional furnishings). Why then, is so much of his fictional world profoundly foreign? Why are his characters so consistently blind to every imaginable Japanese value?

Mishima himself attempted to revive the spirit of *Young Samurai* while living in a Western-style Tokyo house filled with

Greek statuary, European furniture, and the works of foreign authors. The characters in his fictions sleep not under soft Japanese quilts (*futon*) on the *tatami* but in Western twin beds, in brass beds imported from New Orleans, or in double beds whose squeaking springs are lovingly detailed. Underfoot there is parquet flooring or Persian carpeting, while crystal chandeliers dangle from the ceiling. When lovers write, they do not inscribe poems on fans or use a brush and delicate Japanese paper: they use a ballpoint pen on stationery embossed with a design from Walt Disney. (pp. 309-10)

As these characters smoke their brand-named American cigarettes or drive their (branded) American cars, they do indeed suffer those "symptoms of the disease of modernity" mentioned in *Forbidden Colors*. Like the boy in *The Sailor Who Fell from Grace with the Sea*, they appear to break "the endless chain of society's taboos." They reject the Japanese sense of *aware* and share with Shunsuke the experience of "Ionian melancholy."

This world seems entirely divorced from the lyrical Japanese feeling of Kawabata's. (p. 311)

The reader who responds to Kawabata's delicate brush strokes while being repulsed by the harsh lines of Mishima's world might at this point recall some aspects of Japanese history. For instance, readers disturbed over Mishima's enthusiasm for Western body-building techniques as a first step on the route to Japanese spiritual regeneration might well recall that Japan's traditional arts were for some years proscribed by the MacArthur regime. Along with that temporary loss of the spiritual elements of their martial arts, the Japanese also suffered a separation from Shintō (blamed for "nationalistic" fervor, although it is an inseparable element also of modern attitudes toward sex). They suffered an even more terrifying loss when their Emperor—a figure whose Divine Majesty is in direct descent from the (Shintō) Sun Goddess Amaterasu—was suddenly presented to them as a man who appeared in department stores, carrying his soft-crowned hat.

This is the lost postwar world appearing in so many of Mishima's fictions. It is a world we must understand in Japanese terms if we wish to know how men as apparently unlike as Kawabata and Mishima can describe their work in terms of postwar nihilism. This is the world whose inhabitants live in the "spiritual vacuum" to which Mishima so often referred in his last years—the world he described in *Taidō* as one where, thoughtless, "we are rushing headlong toward fragmentation, functionalization, and specialization . . . toward the dehumanizing of the human being."

These are the dehumanizing crannies that Mishima explores with such obsessive vigor—unmasking all the inhabitants. . . . He drags them out of the soft light of a moon-viewing party into the glare of neon and the brilliance of crystal chandeliers. He shows them viewing cherry blossoms that resemble "undertaker's cosmetics" or that are only discarded paper decorations. . . . (pp. 311-13)

Mishima and his characters alike seem to deny many aspects of their past, but they cannot escape its meaning. (p. 313)

Thus Mishima prepared for his final union of spirit and action through the writing of four novels reexamining events and meanings of Japanese history. . . . If the conventional Japanese symbols appear but rarely in his pages, and seem to deny this past, we should recall the seemingly flawed maple-viewing incident at the opening of *Spring Snow*. Discovering a dead dog in the waterfall would seem to be a disastrously "wrong" version of autumn's traditional maple-leaf viewing. Yet it is worth noting that for the abbess of Gesshūji this does not spoil the occasion. On the contrary, it stimulates thoughts of *yuishiki*—of awareness or consciousness—the thread of meaning that runs through the bewildering reincarnations and transformations of Mishima's beautiful boy(s).

However barren *The Sea of Fertility* may seem to be, in Mishima's version it is fed by the purifying waterfall, moves with the passions of his sea imagery, is illuminated by the colors of sun and fire, and is part of the mythic memory of the life-giving (Hindu) Sea of Milk. However ugly the businessmen, the politicians, the housewives, the lovers, the priests, and however decayed the bodies of young sea gods, there is Beauty—to be glimpsed but never grasped. It is to be found in the Golden Pavilion of the imagination: not in the peeling paint of a neglected and flawed building. Thus it is fitting that Mishima's own death was a return to the past, as he performed the act of *seppuku,* the warrior's ultimate gesture.

That bloody, beautiful ritual death, however, can be understood only if it is recognized as a gesture linked with Mishima's view of the "heroic" and "beautiful" death in *Sun and Steel,* with his belief that the most profound depth of the imagination lay in death. And of course the gesture takes on added significance when it is seen as Mishima's own way of finding that "endless beauty"—cutting time short in that instant of the "radiant pinnacle"—described in the waterfall and flowing streams, the images of *The Sea of Fertility.* (pp. 313-14)

> *Gwenn Boardman Petersen, "Mishima Yukio," in her* The Moon in the Water: Understanding Tanizaki, Kawabata, and Mishima *(copyright © 1979 by The University Press of Hawaii), University Press of Hawaii, 1979, pp. 201-319.*

BETTINA L. KNAPP

The Damask Drum has maintained the formulae of Noh theatre in its spiritual outlook, its themes, characters, relationship to nature and use of symbol. Like Zen Buddhism and Taoism, *The Damask Drum* is meditative, introspective, slow-paced, subtle and suggestive. The depth and meaning of Iwakichi's love may be apprehended in sudden flashes of illumination; it is not brash or aggressive, but turned inward, felt, sensed. [Iwakichi is an old janitor who eventually commits suicide because of his unfulfilled love for a woman in a dressmaker's establishment.] Like conventional Noh drama, *The Damask Drum* has no real plot, and therefore it may take an infinite amount of patience for a Westerner to understand the series of complex images which make up its song-and-dance sequences, tonalities and the inflections included in its choral and orchestral accompaniments. Of import are Iwakichi's sensations; the feelings evoked during the course of the performance; the tensions aroused by the images implicit in his discourse, his gestures and pace. . . . All aspects of Iwakichi's stage life, as well as that of the other protagonists, are stylized and predetermined: spatial patterns woven about the stage, poses, interpretations—all add to the fascination of the theatrical experience.

Important in *The Damask Drum* as it had been in ancient Noh theatre, is the relationship between the stage proceedings and nature. Although the play takes place in two office buildings, there is a symbolic correlation between Iwakichi's feelings and attitudes and nature in general: a correspondence between the cosmic domain and its interaction with regard to the individual in the phenomenological world. These two realms inspire resonance and infinite patterns and distillations of sensations and moods.

The notion of timelessness and eternal becoming implicit in traditional Noh drama is clearly discernible in *The Damask Drum.* Iwakichi lives in a three-dimensional as well as in a four-dimensional sphere. He experiences these worlds interchangeably. In the phenomenological domain, matter and spirit only seem to operate antithetically; in reality, they are manifestations of the Taoist's yin/yang principles, a single universal cosmic force. Since matter and spirit are one in the atemporal sphere, death and life coincide, as do image and reality, fiction and fact. Duality and multiplicity exist only in the existential domain, in Iwakichi's world. The conflicts which arise are stressed by Mishima throughout *The Damask Drum* not only for dramatic purposes, but also for metaphysical reasons: age as opposed to youth, inanimate and animate objects, life and death, outer and inner domains, solitude and society, business and poetry. . . . The continuity of this duality expresses the eternal play of conflicting forces which must be endured in life. (pp. 384-85)

That Mishima has situated his drama on the third floor of two office buildings is not surprising. Verticality was always an important factor in Noh drama. The height of the office building corresponds to the mountains which figure so prominently in early Noh theatre. Motionless, still, mountains represent ethereal spheres: heaven, spirit, light circulating about the universe. So the office building in *The Damask Drum* reveals Iwakichi's vision: his love which is too absolute; his desire, overly encompassing; his idealization. The dichotomy between the purity of this image—that is, his ladylove (height)—and the earthiness of the woman of reality (ground) is too great to take on existence in the phenomenological sphere. It can only come to life in the imagination. Iwakichi's earthly fall in suicide at the conclusion of the first part of *The Damask Drum* compels him to take stock of the polarities between fantasy and reality and to rework his vision. Only in death does divergency vanish and oneness prevail.

In the collective and cosmic world of Noh theatre, nature is neither crushed nor violated, nor is it used exclusively for man's benefit, as is so frequently the case in the Western world. In *The Damask Drum* nature is experienced as part of a whole. . . .

In accordance with the close correspondence between man and nature characteristic of Noh drama, Mishima's use of natural forces is implicit in his work. Wind, for example, to which Iwakichi alludes when he opens the window, is alive; it enters into the stage ritual as a turbulent force, a catalyst. (p. 385)

Inasmuch as Noh theatre is archetypal and bathes in the collective domain, specifics such as characters and sets are to be considered symbolically. Characters in traditional Noh theatre are fixed for the most part. Iwakichi, the Old Man, corresponds to the *shite,* the main actor. Although he does not wear a mask (nor does he under certain circumstances in ancient Noh plays), his face itself remains expressionless: it virtually becomes a mask. . . . Iwakichi's expressionless face severs him from the outside world. He must therefore look inward. In so doing, he injects his part with "emotional coloring" by means of a variety of poses of the head and neck and by downward or upward glances and intricate gestures. (pp. 385-86)

Iwakichi in many respects is reminiscent of a Zen Buddhist priest who is detached from the material world, which he con-

siders meaningless. He has swept it all away, symbolically speaking, and has rid himself of the dross, the material encumbrances which tie him to life. His inner riches—his fantasy world, his dream—the realm of the absolute, are of higher value to him. . . .

Kayoko, the young letter-carrying clerk, may be considered a kind of contemporary *waki,* a wanderer throughout the temporal and atemporal realm. She sets up the dialogue or chemical interchange between the two views of life. . . .

The dancing master, the young man, the government official and the owner of the dressmaking establishment are ironic, satiric and humorous in a rather grotesque manner. They are modern counterparts of the *kyogen,* those ancient clowns who kept audiences amused by their farces and laughable ways. Anonymous beings who emerge from nowhere and vanish into darkness, they serve to heighten tension, to explain the stage happenings in less than poetic language. They infuse comedy as well as cruelty into Iwakichi's poignant love situation. . . .

Although only a stage prop, the damask drum, as a symbol, is steeped in tradition. It is representational and yet remains functionless. Comparable to the *koan,* a device used by Zen Buddhists to banish rational and syllogistic reasoning (techniques so dear to Western mentality), it serves as a basis for experience. It allows Iwakichi to become exposed to the mysteries of existence, to intuit undreamed-of truths, to transcend individual understanding. . . .

As stage property, the drum belongs to the logical and rationally oriented universe, the intellectual sphere and not the archetypal realm. In that it was sent to Iwakichi by those living in the temporal world, the drum represents formalism, convention, geometrical and causal reality. The dimensionless universe sought by Iwakichi and implicit in Zen Buddhism and Taoism implies a world *in potentia*—the notion of perpetual becoming. . . .

In keeping with Shinto belief, everything in nature, whether animate or inanimate, is alive. Shinto deities (*kami*), in the form of spirits of trees, mountains, flowers, ancestors, heroes, the sun or the moon, breathe, act and react in the existential sphere. Man approaches the *kami* without fear and in friendship. A force or *kami* therefore inhabits both the essence of the drum and the laurel tree. Although the drum did not respond to Iwakichi's pleadings, the laurel tree does. . . . All the poetry, sensitivity and creative impact of [Iwakichi's] feelings emerge in this one symbol. Its beauty and gentleness become consoling forces for Iwakichi, who feels his loneliness with such desperation.

The laurel and the moon are recurrent images in Iwakichi's world: they usher in a mood of melancholy. The moon, symbol of transformation, represents biological rhythms and cyclical states. Frequently evoked by Japanese poets, the moon is associated with indirect rather than direct experience and knowledge. . . . (p. 386)

For the Westerner, *The Damask Drum* may lack action and conflict. For the Oriental, tension is concentrated and distilled in the images, poetry, gesture and plastic forms which move about the stage. The spatial compositions create the mood, develop and pursue the single emotion which is the sine qua non of Noh theatre.

Just as the Zen painter uses the fewest possible brushstrokes to express the world of multiplicity, so Zen poetry is also known for its sparseness. Mishima maintains this tradition. A word in *The Damask Drum* stands alone, bare, solitary, divested of adjectives and adverbs, and becomes an entity unto itself. . . .

It is the intensity of sustained emotion in *The Damask Drum* which moves audiences and not the realistic portrayals. . . . (p. 387)

> Bettina L. Knapp, ''Mishima's Cosmic Noh Drama: 'The Damask Drum','' in World Literature Today (copyright 1980 by the University of Oklahoma Press), Vol. 54, No. 3, Summer, 1980, pp. 383-87.

NORIKO MIZUTA LIPPIT

[When] Mishima stated that he had ''somehow conquered his inner monster'' by writing *Confessions of a Mask,* it did not mean merely that he had finally confronted his homosexual temperament, but also that he had found the way to deal with his desire to express his temperament in literature, the way to fictionalize his temperament.

Besides being a confessional novel, *Confessions of a Mask* is a novel about Mishima's method for the novel; indeed, it is as significant to Mishima's novel as *The Counterfeiters* is to Gide's. If the temperament and ''sensuous perception'' underlying his metaphysical and aesthetic world are poetry, this novel is the logical architecture of that world and the means to give it logical form (by fictionalizing it). For Mishima, the novel meant the method, and the question of the novel and the question of methodology were inseparable. Indeed, for Mishima, who preferred masks to real faces, structure to lyricism, and artificial effects to real facts, ''fiction'' was the key term.

When it first appeared, however, *Confessions of a Mask* was considered solely as an openly autobiographical work, an I-novel in which a bold confession of the author's homosexuality takes place. In fact, the protagonist of the novel is meticulously presented as identical to the author insofar as his biographical data are concerned. If the novel is a confessional I-novel, then the identification of the protagonist with the author is not in doubt, and the confession of the protagonist is the confession of the author. The novel must be understood accordingly as the removal of the protagonist-author's social mask, an exposé of the real face hitherto hidden behind the mask. (pp. 182-83)

There is no doubt that Mishima meant the protagonist to be taken as the author himself, as his meticulous effort to make the protagonist identical to him indicates, and it is also evident that Mishima intended to make his homosexuality public by writing this novel. Indeed, confession exists at the core of modern fiction, and the modern novel is a means for ''confession.'' (p. 183)

What did Mishima intend to do by letting his protagonist confess, and what did he want to reveal by wearing the mask of the homosexual protagonist? Mishima was not like Shimazaki Tōson and Tayama Katai, writers who were urged on in their art by a desire for self-revelation for ethical or artistic reasons; nor was he like Shiga Naoya, a writer for whom the search for self provided the structure and the materials for his novels. Yet in creating his prototypal, ideal heroes, Mishima was almost exclusively involved in creating heroes who reflected various aspects of his own personality. Whether Mishima was an egomaniac seeking to express himself in terms of his heroes or merely tried fastidiously to identify himself with the heroes he created, there is no doubt that the protagonists' worlds were what inspired Mishima's dream and passions as his own inner world.

Mishima's well-known dislike of Dazai Osamu certainly reflects on the surface his criticism of those I-novelists who use openly their own weakness and desperation as subjects of literary pursuit. Yet one cannot but feel that Mishima's dislike of Dazai is due to his disgust at seeing in Dazai his own egotistical inclination exposed so defenselessly. Mishima's attack on confessional I-novels and their authors—brooding, self-destructive intellectuals who could be interested only in their own inner agonies—and his criticism of the tendency among Japanese writers to identify life and art, can best be understood as paradoxical rhetoric used to hide his egotistical involvement in himself. (pp. 183-84)

Although there is no doubt that *Confessions of a Mask* is about himself, what is revealed by the confession is not the real face of Mishima; the novel is another ''masked play,'' enabling him to survive not as a writer who lives in daily social life, but to survive as a writer.

Prior to writing *Confessions of a Mask,* Mishima wrote several nihilistic aesthetic works which appeared anachronistic in the postwar literary atmosphere. He had already discovered his central theme, the life whose beauty and brilliance are supported by its impending annihilation. His ''sense of ending'' had already found the metaphors of summer and sea, metaphors which were to occupy an increasingly important place in his later works. Mishima started as a writer with his ''aesthetics of annihilation (ending)'' serving as the raison d'être for both his life and his art. Just as Mizoguchi in *Kinkakuji* . . . felt threatened when he learned that the temple had escaped, now that the war was over and destruction no longer seemed inevitable, Mishima felt threatened by having to face the postwar era of peace in which a long life seemed assured to him, thus depriving his art of its basic metaphysics. The tragic stance which Mishima and his protagonists could assume when confronted by predicaments in which their death seemed assured would no longer be possible for them, and Mishima had to create new predicaments which would enable them to be tragic heroes, heroes in the world of his ''aesthetics of the ending.''

In this sense, *Confessions of a Mask* is his successful attempt to create a new ''fate'' for his hero, a fate that would condemn him to inevitable ''destruction.'' In the novel, his destruction or death is only a social one, taking the form of absolute alienation in a spiritual sense from peaceful, ''everyday life.'' The novel is a deliberate declaration of the identity of the author and his hero as masochistic homosexuals. The declaration is a challenge to society, but not a challenge to accept the protagonist-author as a homosexual. Rather, establishing his ''abnormality'' was an attempt to separate himself absolutely from the world of daily life and to force society, therefore, to condemn him.

The novel is, therefore, a rational articulation of his relation to the world and to the age. It is a novel in which Mishima made a statement about his ''being in the world,'' to use Sartre's phrase, attempting thereby to retain the possibility of being identified as a tragic hero and thus to maintain his aesthetics of death. If Mishima ''confessed'' in the novel, he confessed his deep-seated fear of living in the peaceful postwar world where his raison d'être as a man and as a writer no longer existed. (pp. 184-86)

Mishima's homosexuality was a ''fate'' which he deliberately chose, a fate which separated him (and his protagonist) from ordinary life. . . .

In order to make his homosexuality "fate," it was necessary for both society and Mishima himself to condemn his trait or temperament. (p. 186)

Defining oneself as an outsider, a "pagan" who cannot occupy a place in a normal, humane life, is one of the singular means artists have used for self-definition in modern industrial society, a utilitarian society hostile to art. . . .

In modern Japanese literature, such I-novelists as Katai and Tōson converted their failure in everyday life into privileges of the novelist which would enable them to concern themselves exclusively with their isolation and to write about it. Dazai Osamu also deliberately acted out the role which others forcibly imposed on him. In Mishima's case, homosexuality presented a stronger rationale for the protagonist's isolation and uniqueness, for the isolation is physically real rather than just mental. As for Mishima himself, in like fashion precisely, his "abnormality" was the license for his art, his license for writing. (p. 189)

Confessions of a Mask is the story of the birth of an artist, that of Mishima himself. The homosexual protagonist who at once fears and aspires for pure flesh is a metaphor for the writer who, belonging to the world of intellect, writes because he aspires for the tragic intensity of life. In this sense the novel is about himself, about the search for the author. The self-search of the protagonist is identified with the self-search of the author, his ontological quest for what he is; it is the self-search of "a creature, non-human and somehow strangely pathetic." In this sense the novel can be called truly confessional.

The novel is, however, a fictional work and not a real account of Mishima's life. In his notes for *Confessions of a Mask,* Mishima wrote that true confession is impossible ("the true essence of confession is its impossibility"), for only a mask with flesh can confess, and that he intended to write a perfect fictional work of confession. In order to pursue the ontological quest of the mask, a mask must deliberately be worn. If Mishima's mask were forcibly taken away, we might discover that there is neither a face nor any naked facts at all behind it; there would be nothing, or at best abstract passion, which was for him the substance of life. (pp. 189-90)

Noriko Mizuta Lippit, "'Confessions of a Mask': The Art of Self-Exposure in Mishima Yukio," in her Reality and Fiction in Modern Japanese Literature (copyright © 1980 by M. E. Sharpe), M. E. Sharpe, 1980, pp. 181-90.

Michael (John) Moorcock

1939-

(Also writes under pseudonyms of Bill Barclay, E. P. Bradbury, and James Colvin) British science fiction and fantasy writer.

As a writer and editor for *New Worlds* magazine, Moorcock played an important role in the development of the New Wave movement in science fiction and fantasy which began in England in the 1960s. This movement was formed in reaction to the "pulp" image of science fiction and fantasy writing and against the widely held belief that the genres had little, if any, literary value. Moorcock and other writers of the New Wave urged science fiction and fantasy authors to use a wider range of subject matter and styles in their work and to be more concerned with structure and technique. At the time of its inception, *New Worlds* magazine was the only outlet available to science fiction and fantasy writers who were experimenting with form and technique in the manner advocated by the New Wave leaders. Moorcock, a frequent contributor to the magazine, is renowned for his unorthodox variations on traditional science fiction and fantasy themes and techniques.

Moorcock is an extremely prolific author whose work is not easily classified into traditional science fiction and fantasy categories. Like other New Wave writers, he has a tendency to merge genres. His works blend science fiction, heroic fantasy, elements from the sword and sorcery tradition, and techniques commonly used in avant-garde literature. Perhaps the most popular of Moorcock's work is his series revolving around a character named Jerry Cornelius. Cornelius, like other Moorcock protagonists, travels not only through time and space, but also has multiple identities; he has the ability to change physical characteristics, personality traits, and gender. Through the creation of characters like Cornelius, Moorcock developed the idea of "multiverse," a metaphysical concept which posits that various levels of reality coexist within one universe. By proposing alternative forms of history and reality and by breaking traditional conventions of content and style, Moorcock has both pleased and baffled his critics. Some praise his work for its vivid, energetic, and highly imaginative landscapes and structural techniques; other critics find Moorcock's work unnecessarily obscure and lacking in substance.

(See also *CLC*, Vol. 5; *Contemporary Authors*, Vols. 45-48; *Contemporary Authors New Revision Series*, Vol. 2; and *Dictionary of Literary Biography*, Vol. 14.)

JANICE ELLIOTT

[*Behold the Man*] is wildly ambitious, irritating, uneven, and very promising for [Michael Moorcock's] future. As a temporarily exhausted science-fiction addict, I have been waiting for a long time for the form to grow up, to achieve the leap from entertainment to art. There have been signs lately that this might be happening and Mr Moorcock, in *Behold the Man*, comes tantalisingly close.

The theme is fascinating, a genuine attempt to marry the orthodox novel of psychological investigation with science fiction and historical speculation. Karl, your well-known hero with

© *Jerry Bauer*

identity problems, travels in a time machine to ancient Palestine. He falls in with John the Baptist, seeks Christ and finds him as a hunchbacked congenital imbecile. This passage, and Karl's subsequent assumption of Christ's identity, passion and Crucifixion, could have been ridiculous, even offensive. It says much for Mr Moorcock that they are not.

Less successful is Karl's own psychological history shown in flashbacks which rudely interrupt the far more gripping narrative of his adventures in Palestine. Childhood experiences, seduction by a naughty vicar, a superficial equation of sex with religion and (naturally) a disastrous later love life, are undercooked Freudian ham. *Behold the Man* is an ambitious failure, patchy, skimped and exciting. There is a powerful imagination here and an original, disturbing point of view.

Janice Elliott, "Present & Past," in New Statesman *(© 1969 The Statesman & Nation Publishing Co. Ltd.), Vol. 77, No. 1986, April 4, 1969, p. 486.**

ROBERT NYE

Michael Moorcock, at 30, begins to stand in relation to the world of science fiction much as Poe stood in relation to the Gothic novel. That is to say, he is an ingenious and energetic experimenter, restlessly original, brimming over with clever ideas, whose exploitation of a certain form is so thorough that one almost smells a whiff of parody at the root of it. Again like Poe, if Mr Moorcock set out half-inspired by a need to mock the conventions he was using he soon lost that cynicism. His albino prince, Elric, hero of the early short stories collected as *The Stealer of Souls,* is mastered by the sword *Stormbringer* in the novel of that name. . . . Elric's handling of Stormbringer has things in common with the author's handling of SF. The weapon comes alive in his grip. Mr Moorcock began with fancies and conceits, which increasingly assumed a weight or aspect of true myth. That aspect is nearly complete in [*Behold the Man*]. . . .

[In this novel] Mr Moorcock has gone farther in point of imaginative outrage than ever before and farther—in my limited experience—than any previous writer in the genre. This is all to the good. What's the use of having men on the moon unless they're men who've read *The Naked Lunch*? Mr Moorcock's Karl Glogauer travels backwards in time in search of the truth about the Crucifixion. He finds more than he bargained for: a drooling idiot Jesus confined to a back room of the carpenter's shop, an animal Mary, Joseph on the make. . . .

Some will protest that his writing is still not up to his theme, and that the book to this extent is sensational, a parcel of blasphemies and conjuring tricks lacking a final seriousness of style to string it together. In my opinion it would be fairer to say that here is an author of rare talent who has stumbled rather too early on an idea so dangerous and brilliant that scarcely any living writer could do justice to it.

> Robert Nye, "Naked Lunchers on the Moon," in The Guardian Weekly *(copyright © 1969 by Guardian Publications Ltd.), Vol. 100, No. 15, April 10, 1969, p. 15.**

MAURICE CAPITANCHIK

[*Behold the Man*], which sets out to show that Christ could have been almost anyone who came from the future, might have made a remarkable novel, but this one, predictable in its progression and uncongenial in technique, flags badly. The mixture of psychology and religion, and the tone, are slightly reminiscent of early Colin Wilson, but the book's greatest flaw is the portrayal of the 'actual' Christ, which is tasteless and insensitive almost beyond belief. Mr Moorcock is a talented man, but his ability to write with pseudo-seriousness about serious things belongs to the genre of science fiction proper rather than to a Faustian spiritual search.

> Maurice Capitanchik, "Over-Exposed," in The Spectator *(© 1969 by* The Spectator; *reprinted by permission of* The Spectator), *Vol. 222, No. 7346, April 11, 1969, p. 476.**

THE TIMES LITERARY SUPPLEMENT

[*An Alien Heat* is set] in the twilight of human history (many thousand centuries hence), where a refined and decadent society, equally reminiscent of Wilde's aesthetes ("The party was absolutely perfect. Not a thing went right.") and the colourful, androgynous Eloi of Wells's *The Time Machine,* passes its days in extravagant and inconsequential amusements.

The world we know has long since passed into remote history, but is not entirely forgotten. Jherek Carnelian, a sort of Algy Moncrieff of the period, takes a special interest in nineteenth-

century England, from which (as indeed from all other known epochs) time travellers occasionally arrive—to be locked up, as often as not, in someone's private menagerie of anachronistic grotesques. . . .

It's a clever and entertaining fable, memorable and provocative in its surface texture, and not without its serious side. The ironic, Swiftian vision of the contemporary world, albeit distorted by Victorian caricature, is handled with admirable lightness of touch, though it's the casual details of Jherek's *fin du globe* society which give the book its distinctive flavour. An enjoyable piece of work by a writer of unusual inventiveness.

> "Fin de Everything," *in* The Times Literary Supplement *(© Times Newspapers Ltd. (London) 1972; reproduced from* The Times Literary Supplement *by permission), No. 3686, October 27, 1972, p. 1273.*

ALAN BURNS

The War Lord of the Air is one of Michael Moorcock's best. His ingenious and original notion of an *alternative* history enables him to reconstruct the twentieth century rather than just go SFing off into the blue. . . . There's a great Boy's Own adventure on the North-West frontier to counterpoint and contrast with the good old space/time continuum. But again the packaging is overdone. There are three layers to unwrap before we get to the hard stuff in the Himalayas. Within the fiction titled *The War Lord of the Air* is another fiction narrated in an Editor's Note which describes the discovery of a manuscript said to have been written by Moorcock's grandfather. Grandpa's manuscript introduces another book-within-a-book, a story told by Bastable, a washed-up Englishman living on an island in the Indian Ocean. . . . And so to the triple coda. . . .

Moorcock also overdoes his attempts to rationalise the time-shift fantasy. Bastable constantly doubts his own sanity; he ascribes his fantasies to the effects of opium; he asks himself if he's dreaming. I prefer my fantasy neat, without elaborate frameworks or naturalistic justifications. But there is no doubting Moorcock's skill. . . .

> Alan Burns, in a review of "The War Lord of the Air" *(© copyright Alan Burns 1974; reprinted with permission), in* Books and Bookmen, *Vol. 19, No. 8, May, 1974, p. 87.*

THE TIMES LITERARY SUPPLEMENT

[*The Land Leviathan*] is a fantasy about how, in an alternative twentieth century, Black Power finally ends up ruling the world. Stated thus the story would sound to have, if not high seriousness, then at least a compelling tendency towards significance. Its effect is very different, however, being at the same time vivid and wayward. This arbitrariness is the fault of Michael Moorcock's chosen mode of narration: as the sequel to *The War Lord of the Air* the book is presented as the personal diary of one Captain Oswald Bastable, a soldierly adventurer of the late nineteenth century in the tradition of those English travellers whose lack of imagination was to be transmuted into fearlessness or eccentricity by a later age. Mr Moorcock does this well: he has managed a stylish pastiche of those first-person accounts of adventure on the fringes of the Raj. But the style has its own fatal consequences in that the narrator—half naive, half secure in his Britishness—seems to wander through the story while things happen around him in a haphazard and patternless way. He makes sense of nothing, and can but turn it all into a rip-roaring yarn.

It is all a harmless fable, and, discounting mild irony, quite lacking in import. Captain Bastable's vacillations about whether to side with the Whites or the Blacks are typical of his class and type, evincing nothing but uneasy humanitarianism. This is no mode for viewing anything, much less world cataclysm; and because Bastable takes no properly reasoned stand and because his narrative *is* the book, *The Land Leviathan* is nothing more than the romance its subtitle modestly claims it to be.

> *"An Alternative Now," in* The Times Literary Supplement *(©Times Newspapers Ltd. (London) 1974; reproduced from* The Times Literary Supplement *by permission), No. 3769, May 31, 1974, p. 577.*

RON KIRK

Is [Michael Moorcock's *The Lives and Times of Jerry Cornelius*] the overdue last instalment of the Cornelius saga (*The Final Programme, A Cure for Cancer, The English Assassin*)? . . . Can *Lives and Times* be a transmogrification of what admirers and cultists have been awaiting under the provisional title of **"The Condition of Muzak"**? Probably not; names are one of the few near-constant things as our hero changes sexuality, sex, colour and condition at the drop of an acid, fleeing down the labyrinthine ways of uncountable alternate presents or near futures. Michael Moorcock gives no clue, but I think this must be seen as a spin-off, like the Jherek Carnelian of *The Alien Heat.* . . .

What is Jerry Cornelius? A hero for our time, a man without qualities or with all of them—which amounts to the same thing. . . . His loyalties are partly given to the shadowy Time Centre, an organization dedicated to knitting up the ravelled web of time, ironing out bulges in the seamless garmet. His missions take him to scores of possible twentieth centuries, unruly and catastrophic, but none more so, I am sure, than Mr Moorcock's view of Original Reality. . . . His objectives are obliquely described, often to the point of impenetrability; his techniques range from necromancy to murder. . . .

Some commentators have seen Cornelius as an ugly portent of the nihilistic world he inhabits. . . . This is a little like denouncing a policeman for an unwholesome interest in crime—which is not to deny that Mr Moorcock, like some coppers, may like his work too much. But the ironic distancing is mostly convincing: "Irony is no substitute for imagination", remarks Cornelius, smugly, knowing that his creator has, if anything, a surplus of both.

Below the irony and the ambiguities are some surprisingly old-fashioned decent liberal certainties: much the same could be said of James Bond and Cornelius's resemblance to a hyperkinetic Bond is more than parodic. He's a sentimentalist, more freely moved to tears than any character in literature since Lord Lundy. Under the pansexual permissiveness he's a fighter for order.

> *Ron Kirk, "Love and Entropy," in* The Times Literary Supplement *(© Times Newspapers Ltd. (London) 1976; reproduced from* The Times Literary Supplement *by permission), No. 3869, May 7, 1976, p. 561.*

NICK TOTTON

[*The Adventures of Una Persson* . . .] is all resonance: like the whole 'Jerry Cornelius' sequence of novels and stories, it is an attempt at portraiture of the twentieth century in its essence. An ambitious project: and all Mr Moorcock's previous attempts have been dreadfully flawed. But in the light of this novel they can be seen as necessary preliminaries: here, he at last succeeds—not, of course, in totalising the twentieth century; but in showing us a great deal that we already know in our bones, but have perhaps not yet articulated, about where and when 'here and now' is.

Mr Moorcock's great gift is for synthesis. He has a strong sense of the cultural moment, the coherence and intelligibility of fashion, music, literature, politics, and every other human activity. Often his representations of such synchronicities have been forced, over-experimental. The effort has been too visible for harmony; and harmony is essential. In *The Adventures of Una Persson* . . . there is a new relaxation to Mr Moorcock's writing: he can afford the time to take care over its fine texture, and the time to feel for his characters, and to give them feelings.

There is a lot of time to play with, in fact. Mr Moorcock's highly effective way of looking at here and now is to look everywhere else. His characters are time travellers, who can move not only forward and back (though temporal inertia keeps them pretty much to this century) but also sideways, into alternative histories. One might describe the whole thing as a dramatic extension of mood décor. Instead of just altering the thematic era of one's decorating to suit a mood, one can actually travel there, and stay until one's mood shifts. Like most people with such exaggerated resources, Una and Catherine are looking for something worth doing. They try activist manipulation of history and hedonist retirement by turns; trapped always in the ambiguity of (partial) omniscience without omnipotence. Understanding a problem does not always imply solving it; and it is increasingly clear that the twentieth century is one big problem. Mr Moorcock knows no more than the next person about solutions; but his new book is, finally, that elegant, informative and enjoyable statement of the problem which he has for so long failed to achieve. (p. 22)

> *Nick Totton, "Polarities," in* The Spectator *(©1976 by* The Spectator; *reprinted by permission of* The Spectator*), Vol. 237, No. 7743, November 20, 1976, p. 22.**

NICK TOTTON

'This was a gift-wrapped, throwaway age, Mr Cornelius. Now the gift-wrapping is off, it's being thrown away.' And through the debris stalks Jerry Cornelius: assassin, *bon vivant,* universal idiot genius, specialist in the resurrection gimmick, protagonist of many novels and stories by several hands and central character of the tetralogy now completed by *The Condition of Muzak.* His secret, though, is that he has no character at all in the normal sense of the word. He is a nomad of the territories of personality; even his skin colour and gender are as labile as his accomplishments ('Jerry could rarely speak German'). He is a set of co-ordinates: a peg on which to hang the costume of one's choice. A potentially infinite manifold of stylistic gestures—so long as they have style.

So he represents the zero-point of the novel: either its transcendence or its decomposition. Not only character is abandoned—consistency as a criterion of plot depends formally and actually on consistency of character. These four books employ at least a dozen major alternative universes, a dozen different histories of the twentieth century, as backdrops; and it is doubtful whether any of these is internally consistent. Many of the main protagonists die repeatedly, their resurrection usually going quite unremarked. If a protagonist's death carries no finality, then where are we to look for it? And without finality of any kind, what is left of plot?

The parodied Pater epigram in the title of the last novel gives at least one game away. If Mr Moorcock's art aspires to the condition of muzak, then it aspires to endlessness rather than the more conventional goal of eternity; and the difference is immense. The primary qualities of muzak are repetition, blandness, and consistency in the special sense of continuity, homogeneity. Mr Moorcock swings his glove in the face of Western culture's most central values. (pp. 21-2)

[The novels] are pulp-writing of a very blatant and conscious sort. There is nothing in Mr Moorcock's huge *oeuvre* to suggest that he is capable of orthodox characterisation and plotting at all. When he writes a conventionally structured book, it is two-dimensional and third-rate, bearing all the marks of honourable, in-it-for-the-money deadline work.

What he has contrived to do in the Jerry Cornelius books (some of the best of which are actually outside the tetralogy) is to make a virtue of his incapability. Out goes fuddy-duddy consistency, and associated values like depth, three-dimensionality and so on; in comes the new pragmatism of a surface excitement intended to take over from form and content altogether. . . . And there is a tremendous surface excitement here: dialogue worthy of the great Hollywood sophisticated comedies—from which it occasionally borrows—and scenery which changes too fast to become boring. . . .

One can see Mr Moorcock as a gifted populariser of avant-garde techniques. . . . It is certainly true that he is a populariser rather than an original artist: a magpie of *anschauungen* who beautifully represents our culture's current eclecticism. But what concerns me is the actual nature of the trinkets that he assembles. A populariser is a bringer of news; and Mr Moorcock brings news of massive alienation. . . .

He is right: the novels do tend towards the condition of muzak. Even the end of the world begins to pall when there are eight alternative versions in a single novel. To recapitulate the conditions of our suffering in an endless melisma of formal variations, an endless permutation of pseudo-insurrections, this is muzak. Perhaps one day a different message will crackle out of the loudspeakers, inflaming the supermarket shoppers.

But I do not think that Michael Moorcock will provide it. (p. 22)

Nick Totton, "Culture Shock," in The Spectator *(©1977 by* The Spectator; *reprinted by permission of* The Spectator), *Vol. 238, No. 7762, April 9, 1977, pp. 21-2.*

BOB SHAW

The Condition of Muzak—like *The Final Programme, A Cure For Cancer, The English Assassin* and some related works—continues Moorcock's harlequinade theme and brings it to a climax, though climax may be too simplistic a term in the Cornelius context of a universe in which time and location are wild variables, where endings are hardly ever final, and where the characters have a Tom-and-Jerry-like capacity for resurrecting themselves from personal calamity.

In *The Condition of Muzak* the Cornelius family—plus the enigmatic figures of Una Persson, Bishop Beesley, Miss Brun-

ner and the others who make up their circle of friends/enemies—are shown again performing all the gyrations of the Entropy Tango, but this time we are aware of the dance slowing down. Jerry Cornelius himself begins to lose his vital force, and near the end of the book the death of his mother is presented as a real and final demise, in a scene which derives considerable power and emotion from that very fact.

This break with the spirit of the original *commedia dell'arte,* in which the characters are immortally free to appear in any time or place, probably reflects the decline of harlequinade itself—to Moorcock's sorrow. . . .

It is impossible to summarise briefly the plot of *The Condition of Muzak*—were it possible the author might feel his achievement had not equalled his intent—but the inventive, image-sparking quality of Moorcock's writing is there on every page as the spotlight darts relentlessly from scene to scene. . . .

Throughout the book there is great visual emphasis on dress and details of uniforms and brand names, which is entirely appropriate to its theme, and after a while the reader comes to see and accept that the costume and the mask have a profound influence on the wearer. The chaos that ensues—as chaos must do when the accepted invariant points of time, location and identity are discarded—is well portrayed by Moorcock. . . . (p. 50l)

Bob Shaw, "Tango Time," in New Statesman *(© 1977 The Statesman & Nation Publishing Co. Ltd.), Vol. 93, No. 2404, April 15, 1977, pp. 501-02.*

PETER ACKROYD

Michael Moorcock specialises in fantasies, but his aren't of the jubilant human variety which the Christmas fairy loves. His universe is one which possesses neither meaning nor logic, and human beings can play only a minimal role in it. *The Knight of the Swords* is a science fiction of the past—'science' in the sense that Man and all his works are not at its centre. It's really a novel about changing perceptions, about evanescent technologies and star-crazed soft-ware that escape the usual boring traps of 'the individual' and 'society'. Prince Corum—not a human being but some creature of a greater destiny—goes on a quest to destroy the thing he most fears. And in the process the book adopts the sacramental language of Malory, and combines it with the special effects of a *Dr Who* script. . . .

The narrative might be set in the remote past or in some unimaginable future, and this peculiarly disembodied quality allows Moorcock to concentrate upon the thing itself: the telling of a story, so that each element becomes outrageously predictable and everyone's fantasies are satisfied. It has, in other words, to be written like a children's story or a newspaper report.

It needs an imagination that is visual rather than literary (which is why so many of *The Knight of Swords'* effects have been borrowed directly from the cinema): to deal directly with sensations and to transfer them to the page without embarrassment. This means, of course, that the prose can work freely in only two directions. In its odd encounters of the third kind—when it veers towards 'meaning'—it can become heavy and unnecessarily crude: 'Upstart Man was beginning to breed and spread like a pestilence across the world.' In a work of pure sensationalism, this needn't be said. It is only necessary that power, and powerful effects, should win in the end. (p. 29)

Peter Ackroyd, "Out of Sight," in The Spectator *(© 1977 by The Spectator; reprinted by permission of* The Spectator*), Vol. 239, No. 7799, December 24, 1977, pp. 29-30.**

ALASTAIR FOWLER

[*Gloriana, or the Unfulfill'd Queen*] represents something of a new departure for Michael Moorcock. Those who admire his ingenuity and creativity but deplore the lax forms in which he has often indulged them will at the outset be favourably disposed towards a Moorcock work that claims to "have some relation to *The Faerie Queene*". It seems to offer a change from those interminable gothic or barbarian intrigue fantasies; taking a new start, perhaps, from Sprague de Camp's and Fletcher Pratt's Spenserian fantasy *The Mathematics of Magic.* Besides it promises a definite *mise-en-scène,* instead of the vacuous elasticities where Moorcock's stories have usually been sketched.

However, the world of *Gloriana* turns out to be Tudor England and Faeryland with a difference. Some characters' names and motifs are drawn from Spenser; but the action takes place—or fails to—in the Elizabethan court of some other time line than ours. . . .

Far from being romance, *Gloriana* . . . is intrigue fantasy: improbable plot versus implausible counterplot, with characters almost uniformly flat and villainous. The heroine is a discontented giantess (at six foot six outtopping de Camp's and Pratt's six-foot Britomart), who vainly searches for fulfilment in polymorphous sexual adventures and orgies with a seraglio of monsters. This unvirgin queen has nine illegitimate children; yet her court's tone is more cliquishly homosexual than even its historical model. Gloriana's Albion contrasts with her tyrant father's. It purports to enjoy a golden-age idyll free from violence and war. . . . But it is a pleasure-obsessed society, not specially attractive even on the surface; while underneath, the official pacifism is sustained by ruthless secret action organized by a machiavellian establishment statesman, Montfallcon.

His agent Quire, a villainous antihero, makes an art of "spying, murder and betrayal" and seeks only "to amplify and define [his] senses". Yet loving him somehow helps Gloriana to advance from regressive sexuality to maturity. Quire corrupts the court, is briefly outwitted, and then becomes Gloriana's Arthur in an ending that solves everything and nothing. For Moorcock's platitudinous allegory has little to say about its great abstracts—open government, ideals and means, the balance of reason and romance. When Quire (Reason) provokes Gloriana to say "You taught me to love only myself" the *significatio* is both trite and morally dubious.

Fortunately the true meaning of *Gloriana* is of another order. Its main achievement is a symbolic place reminiscent of the neogothic *carceri* of Mervyn Peake (to whose memory Mr Moorcock dedicates his book). Secret passages in Gloriana's palace lead into closed-off ancestral parts, shadow palaces below or behind the obvious ones. . . . This subliminal life-house is an authentic creation, and might have made the setting for a powerful fantasy. Its Morlockian inhabitants not only represent an unassimilated political element that threatens the peaceful state, but also enact Freudian mysteries. The deeper story has to do with uncovering evil that comes from the walls, and with suppressing or releasing the shadow fringe and the primitive forms of life. *Gloriana* thus attempts inwardness,

even if its intimations of immorality remain unrealized by adequate fiction.

Full of plots as the book is, it has little story. It remains mosaic fiction, capsule narrative alternating with static displays of elaborately described clothes whose colours and materials it meticulously inventorizes until their brilliance turns dull. . . .

The words seldom convince. As the embarrassing imitations of occasional verse show, Mr Moorcock is word-deaf. . . . The diction leaps between stools of fustian and cliché, with falls into sheer tastelessness. . . .

In a period extravaganza we expect manneristic exaggerations of style. And sometimes Moorcock supplies these, as in the amplifications of an intellectual London where 'rats wrangle over such profundities as which came first, the baker or the bread". But most of his imagery is remorselessly visual; while time and again a single formal strategy, the list, does duty for all the variety a rhetorical age might have furnished.

Yet again, Mr Moorcock's over-abundant creativity has outstripped his narrative powers. This is especially true of the book's denouement, a series of unbelievable *volte-face* in which the villains are supposed to turn out only apparently evil. What then of their murders? Perhaps some fictive subtlety is intended, having to do with the allegorical status of the earlier events. If so, the writing fails to express it; so that all collapses in ludicrous melodrama. . . . Surely fantasy has outgrown this kind of writing.

Alastair Fowler, "Queening It in Albion," in The Times Literary Supplement *(© Times Newspapers Ltd. (London) 1978; reproduced from* The Times Literary Supplement *by permission), No. 3978, June 30, 1978, p. 742.*

PAUL ABLEMAN

The trouble with a first-person narrator is that once he is set in motion ('I am a child of my century and as old as the century') he chugs on under his own steam and both author and reader are stuck with his manufactured personality, however bumpy the ride it produces. Since [*Byzantium Endures*] only takes the narrator up to the age of 20 and we are promised further instalments [to] bring the story up to date, it is prudent to ask how roadworthy Colonel Pyat really is. Michael Moorcock has, in fact, lumbered himself with a pretty ungainly and rickety hero, both from the point of view of character construction and the more delicate one of literary convention.

Pyat is supposed to be an engineer with a 'poor, baffled, terror-ridden mind'. He is endowed with three distinct literary styles. The first is a perfectly serviceable narrative prose which carries the bulk of the story. . . . But, to express the alleged demonic side of his nature, he periodically bursts into black rhapsodies. . . . And an appendix gives samples of the polyglot raving into which he supposedly plunges from time to time. . . .

The three modes do not fuse convincingly into the evocation of a human mind. But an even bigger impediment to belief arises from Pyat's alleged racial origins. He is portrayed as being violently anti-Semitic but inadvertently reveals that he is the illegitimate son of a dead Jewish father. Since the reader has no difficulty in interpreting the clues that Pyat uncomprehendingly relays, and the man is credited with shrewdness as well as high intelligence, his stubborn naivety strains our credulity. He looks Jewish and is circumcised. Almost everyone he meets assumes he is a Jew but he blunders on serenely unaware of his Semitic blood. (p. 24)

The sad truth is I found Colonel Pyat a bore and his odyssey unconvincing. Michael Moorcock, fortified by deep research, strives to bring a historical epoch to life but almost any single page of Isaac Babel's *Red Cavalry* conveys more of Russia's revolutionary agony than the whole of this book.

Oddly enough, Mr Moorcock's third-person Jerry Cornelius novels are, in their quirky, free-wheeling way, truer and more moving than this massive fiction. There is here a sense of over-exertion, as if Mr Moorcock were striving to demonstrate that he is not just the thinking hippy's bard but, as Mrs Cornelius might have put it, a 'jenewine orffer'. His Ukraine is conceived as the central arena of history where Rome, Carthage, Greece and Israel pursue their ancient struggles in modern permutations. But this ambitious notion is both too schematic and too diffuse to serve as a satisfactory basis for fiction. Byzantium may indeed endure but *Byzantium Endures* does not, alas, live. (pp. 24-5)

Paul Ableman, "Unagonising Saga," in The Spectator *(© 1981 by* The Spectator; *reprinted by permission of* The Spectator*), Vol. 246, No. 7981, June 27, 1981, pp. 24-5.*

PENELOPE LIVELY

Michael Moorcock, author of over fifty books, is known mainly for his science fiction works. *Byzantium Endures* is an historical novel: long, complex, richly peopled, as confusing, turbulent and intense as the events it describes—the factional fighting in the Ukraine in 1917-18. Moorcock purports to be presenting the recollections of one Colonel Pyat, an émigré washed up in the Portobello Road area in the Sixties and Seventies. . . . (pp. 85-6)

Pyat is an unlovable character, to put it kindly: a zenophobic anti-Semite with Pan-Slavic ideals, bombastic, insensitive, opinionated, a braggart. . . .

And while he brags and proclaims, his brash and opportunistic personality shines through the lush precipitate prose, alternately exasperating and amusing. . . . He becomes a cocaine addict and discovers women and is imprisoned by the Bolsheviks and escapes death by good luck and by good management. And as the country seethes and boils around him he pontificates on life and on history and on ideas—with, presumably, the wisdom (if that is the right word) of hindsight. We are, after all, reading the memoirs of an old man, selected and slanted as they may be.

The novel must, I think, be reckoned a *tour de force*. I have to admit that I never really felt engaged, reading it; Pyat's deficiencies of personality, the enormous cast of characters bouncing in and out of the pages, the welter of places and bewildering shifts of fortune all contribute to confuse rather than compel. . . . It is inconclusive, like history; the reader is left with a feeling of anticlimax which is acceptable in an account of facts but not so in a work of fiction. But, that being said, one cannot but admire the pace of the book, the virtuosity, the descriptions of people and of places. . . . For many it will be a robust, absorbing read, even if it is difficult to emerge with a clear picture of what has been happening to whom, and why. (p. 86)

Penelope Lively, "Wisdoms of Hindsight," in Encounter *(© 1981 by Encounter Ltd.), Vol. LVII, No. 5, November, 1981, pp. 84-8.**

GREGORY SANDOW

No writer who lists 12 of his books and then accounts for the rest with a weary "etc. etc." can be all bad. In fact, Michael Moorcock has written far more than a dozen good books, ranging from entertaining to profound; in his native Britain, he's taken quite seriously. It's wonderful to see Moorcock grow from a genre writer into, simply, a writer, which he officially does with [*Byzantium Endures*[, the first of his books that's not science fiction or fantasy.

Here Moorcock has the audacious idea of telling—in this and further projected volumes—the story of the 20th century as it appears to one of its victims. The victim in question is Colonel Pyat, a charming, confused, and unscrupulous Ukrainian. (p. 42)

Pyat appeared earlier in Moorcock's four Jerry Cornelius novels as a diplomat, moving with world-weary skill through a globe in such disarray that the British Empire is under joint attack by Scotch rebels and Cossacks. *Byzantium Endures* is supposed to be his true story—his autobiography, in fact—and the scrupulously researched, vivid picture of Russian society collapsing during the Revolution and civil war turns out to be a more poignant image of the fall of the west than any of Moorcock's alternate or future worlds: a mainstream novel gives him far more scope to nourish the obsessions (and also the passion, zaniness, and eye for detail) that made his science fiction both fun and worthwhile. And there's no denying his literary skill, particularly when he describes a journey by train through the frozen Russian winter in oddly comforting imagery of deep black and cold white, reminiscent of Nabokov.

If *Byzantium Endures* has any problem, it's that the fantastic events of Pyat's life and the even more fantastic tone of his desperate commentary don't quite match. Moorcock's vision of our world's destruction may not be specific enough to ground the wild growth of his literary invention. (p. 43)

Gregory Sandow, in a review of "Endures" (reprinted by permission of The Village Voice *and the author; copyright © News Group Publications, Inc., 1982), in* The Village Voice, *Vol. XXVII, No. 9, March 2, 1982, pp. 42-3.*

CHOICE

Best known in the US as a science fiction and fantasy writer, Michael Moorcock proves in *Byzantium Endures* both his versatility as a fiction writer and the mastery of his craft. He achieves a fine and penetrating irony in the creation of his narrator, an anti-Semitic Jewish-Cossack Russian expatriot picaro. . . . More than just a readable historical novel—although it is that too—*Byzantium Endures* is a portrait of war from its chaotic and senseless underside and a humane, if often comic, anatomy of what it takes to survive in wartime as well as of the costs of such survival.

A review of "Byzantium Endures: A Novel," in Choice *(copyright © 1982 by American Library Association; reprinted by permission of the American Library Association), Vol. 19, No. 9, May, 1982, p. 1242.*

Alberto (Pincherle) Moravia

1907-

Italian novelist, short story writer, essayist, critic, playwright, scriptwriter, travel writer, editor, and journalist.

Moravia is one of the foremost literary figures of twentieth-century Italy, certainly the most widely known internationally. His use of existentialist themes, based on mass indifference and the selfish concerns of the bourgeois world, predate the writings of Sartre and Camus. In his exploration of the human relationship with reality, Moravia presents a world of decadence and corruption in which humans are guided primarily by their senses and where sex is valued over love. These themes have been repeatedly explored and reworked in all of Moravia's writings.

Moravia's sensibility was shaped in part by a painful battle with tuberculosis that left him bedridden and isolated during his adolescent years. He spent the time reading and writing avidly and then achieved major success with his first novel, *Gli indifferenti* (1929; *The Time of Indifference*). The novel depicts sex as the basic psychological principle and most significant activity of modern humans. In a world of isolation and apathy, the characters in *The Time of Indifference* use sex (or money, or politics, in ways that relate to sexual obsession) as a means toward achieving happiness, but are doomed because their sex is loveless. The novel drew praise for its psychological insights and its portrayal of a world approaching total disillusionment.

As an antifascist during Mussolini's regime, Moravia came precariously close to being labeled an enemy of the state. In the fiction he wrote at this time, he depicted people using others as a means of self-satisfaction but cloaked what could be seen as allusions to fascist politics in allegory and satire. During this time he traveled extensively as a journalist. He was forced to flee Rome in 1943, living for several months among peasants in rural Italy. His fiction became more socially conscious and Marxist-oriented at this time. In the long short story *Agostino* (1947), widely regarded as a classic of the genre, an adolescent becomes aware of sexuality and also the plight of the lower classes in a story of deep psychological probings and social implications.

During the 1950s Moravia turned from Marxism, advocating instead intellectual solutions to world problems. He began writing "essay novels" in which ideology plays as important a role as the story itself. He also abandoned use of an objective, third-person narrator in favor of first-person narration in order to depict the world subjectively. The two volumes of short stories that make up *Racconti romani* (1954 and 1959; *Roman Tales*), contain many of Moravia's best works. Because of his repetitive themes and his journalistic style of writing, many critics have concluded that Moravia is most effective when writing within the short story framework.

Moravia's concerns in more recent years have been the dehumanizing effects of society and technology, the human psyche, and the breakdown of communication. With the recent novels *La vita interiore* (*Time of Desecration*, 1980) and *1934* (1982), Moravia again concentrates on the obsessive qualities of politics, money, and sex. *Time of Desecration* examines mod-

ern day terrorism while *1934* takes place during Mussolini's regime at the time of Hitler's rise to power. The critic Stephen Spender views *1934* as a brilliant work, especially in its contrasting of Germany's active and Italy's passive acceptance of totalitarianism.

That all of Moravia's work is essentially an extension of themes presented in *The Time of Indifference* has led to contrasting critical opinion of his oeuvre. Some critics judge him an artist of limited range who has contributed no stylistic or structural innovations to the novel or the short story and who covers the same ground over and over. Most critics, however, appraise Moravia as an artist who is exploiting the full potential of his concerns, using classic storytelling devices to present the preoccupations of modern human beings. Indeed, Moravia's work displays many of the leading schools of thought of the twentieth century: existentialism, Marxism, psychology, phenomenology, and the role of the artist. Moravia himself is oblivious to charges of monotony, believing that all artists must pursue the single problem they are born to understand.

(See also *CLC*, Vols. 2, 7, 11, 18 and *Contemporary Authors*, Vols. 25-28, rev. ed.)

JOAN ROSS AND DONALD FREED

First, and foremost, Moravia is a storyteller and human behavior is at the core of his fictional world. Though at times

353

the writing is tedious, a little contrived, or a little too polished, it is always very much alive. At his best, Moravia emerges as a rare cynical genius who illuminates his world with a penetrating psychic understanding. Indeed, his insights are handled with the depth and subtlety of a master psychologist. As his characters reveal their needs; our own necessities are disclosed. To understand Moravia fully is to lose our "intolerance"; he makes us aware, conscious, knowing. We cannot escape facing the challenge to be compassionate and different. In Moravia's work it is always the individual that counts. (pp. 151-52)

Moravia's view of life emerges as essentially tragic. His great fear is that man has become a machine, an automaton or "thing," more fearful still, a means. "The use of man as a means and not as an end is the root of all evil." He has said, "Man is automatically not to be happy, that is the human situation." However, it is out of this very morbidity, this unflinching courage in portraying man as he is, that Moravia's vision becomes heroic. Faced with the absurdity of life, an absurdity which equals suffering, his characters nevertheless survive. Mán can rise above adversity. . . . Man does not have to be destroyed by circumstances; he has the inner resources to conquer defeat and avoid destruction. Whatever the horrors, man can survive.

Over and over Moravia uses crime and brutality to illuminate man's absurd condition. Violence and crime make man aware of the other extreme he is capable of through love; hence, a higher existence is revealed. Compassion, that capacity to feel sorrow, solidarity, sympathy—to suffer, not only for your own predicament but for that of others—is the key to Moravian love. To be willing to assume the sorrows of others and to suffer because of (and with) others is the challenge which Moravia would demand us to accept. Instead of the old pity and terror of literature, the existentialists present us with anguish and radical solidarity.

Moravia has gone beyond the bleak, sordid vision of [his first novel] *Time of Indifference*. In subsequent works his perception has deepened and matured. Out of this intense vision we sense a true empathy for the condition of modern man. This growth toward understanding and compassion is that factor which earmarks Moravia's greatness; he has gone beyond the existential nausea of *Time of Indifference* to existential compassion in the later works.

The author has made the statement that, "The writer's task is to perfect the one problem he was born to understand." Certainly, he himself has taken this task seriously. Over and over in his desolate, gloomy, ironic world, the central theme that emerges is the relationship between man and reality. Further, as Moravia's world is a carnal one, his characters most often establish their own reality through a relationship with the opposite sex. As this is accomplished, all other relationships fall into proper perspective. . . . Moravia's preoccupation with the sexual motif is not carried to the point of abuse as some critics feel. He, himself, is willing to clarify this motif.

> My concentration on the sexual act, which is one of the most primitive and unalterable motives in our relation to reality, is due precisely to this urgency; and the same can be said of my consideration of the economic factor, which is also primitive and unalterable, in that it is founded on the instinct of self-preservation that man has in common with animals . . . sex in the modern world is synonymous with love.

Who can deny that love is a very frequent subject in the literature of all times and all places? But, someone will say, has love been transformed into sex in modern literature . . . has it lost the indirect, metaphorical and idealized character it had in the past, and so ended up by being identified with the sexual act? The reasons for this identification are many; the chief one is the decline in the taboos and prohibitions which too often compelled false idealizations of the erotic act in an artificial way.

In this existential framework of Moravia's, the quartet of love, existence, reality, and suffering are irrevocably joined. They interlock, interrelate, overlap; they are interdependent. Without love man does not really exist—"he is a mere dehumanized item of existence." Existing implies a new perception and enlargement of reality. As the struggle to exist (conversion) defeats the forces of nonexistence, nihilism, and absurdity, everything changes. *All* things are seen in a new way—a new reality emerges. Camus, too, seems to traverse this same path back to life via the absurd and suicide. He would have us jolted from the monotonous pattern of our everyday lives. . . . A new vision is the beginning of *revolt* for Camus, as therapeutic in its consequences as *conversion* is for Moravia.

Moravian reality, as we now understand it, is inextricably linked to love, to compassion: that capacity to feel anguish, solidarity, tenderness, and sympathy. Further, through this love, this compassion, man suffers; not only out of his own predicament but for the predicament of others. He must be willing to assume the sorrows of others—to suffer because of, and with others. This reality is filled with pathos as it is intimately merged with the sense of experience as suffering. It is through love that man suffers. Suffering becomes the contingency of love. Man is exalted through love when he can face this contingency; when he has the courage to commit himself to love even though he knows that this exposes him to the possibility of great suffering. Commitment to love, without the possibility of overlooking the risks, is what makes man, fine, elevated, superior, the overman.

Man establishes the sense of his own identity, his own reality, *becomes* himself in the most profound terms when he loses himself in a love relationship. As man loves, he transcends the banal, the common, the narcissism of everyday existence; he experiences that which is better than himself. His perception of himself, of objects, of nature, of the world around him becomes valid and meaningful. Through love he suffers, and by suffering he can understand, he can know, he can experience, he can feel, he can act—he is alive.

Reality is coeval with love. As man loves he gains the sense of reality. But love is fleeting, this is the paradox. Man is expelled from the world (reality) through loss of love. He can find ways of loving—never permanently, but he is sustained by the memory of love; hence, exile then return through memory to love. (pp. 152-56)

There is in *Luca* a long dream passage of exquisite nature imagery [in which a character dreams he is a tree]. This passage might be interpreted as a hymn to the totality of Moravia's life-view. It is, at the same time, a summary of the lyric existential reality. (p. 156)

Like a tree, man, too, springs from the earth and is nurtured by it. Man, his arms raised to the sun, is free—he captures that sense of "aggressive freedom" and "unlimited exploration." He may be limited by the bounds of his own imagination, but Moravia sets him free to exploit these bounds. Man must live his life to the fullness of his freedom and his imagination. In reading this dream passage we feel the rush and joy of life pulsating in *our* veins, I-Thou.

Moravia is wholeheartedly committed to the writer's greatest task, that of explaining the condition of man in a chaotic universe. From the very start of his literary career Moravia has always asked the fundamental question—how is man to deal with reality? How is he to conduct himself in a world which has become "dark and unplumbable—worse still, had disappeared"? To that singular problem Moravia addressed himself in his first novel and continues the quest to this day with a deepening understanding of man's predicament. Propelled by this quest he endeavors to give us as complete a picture of man as possible. And always, the cause and cure of problems must be found in man's inner self. As if he were born to write endless variations on one story, his style is persistent. Persistence of style—that is the existential equivalent to the old "character."

Moravia comes to grips with the torments, the pettiness, the emptiness, and the hollowness which plague contemporary humanity. He does feel compassion for man's lot and he has intimate knowledge, through personal deprivation, of man's suffering. And the perceptiveness and penetration with which he delineates man's suffering is a measure of this radical solidarity. He opts, finally, for love, but like the older *Mediterraneans* he knows that Eros, as Hesiod wrote, breaks the bones. He is able to stand this risk. He instructs us that if man is to sustain himself in a brutal society he must do so by love—a total commitment to another human being. Moravia speaks to us of ourselves. He is truthful, he is authentic. Is not authenticity the highest praise we can accord any artist in these times or, for that matter, any man? (pp. 158-59)

> Joan Ross and Donald Freed, in their The Existentialism of Alberto Moravia *(copyright © 1972 by Southern Illinois University Press; reprinted by permission of Southern Illinois University Press), Southern Illinois University Press, 1972, 172 p.*

MICHAEL WOOD

Albert Camus suggested that suicide was the only philosophical question, and Alberto Moravia's new novel ["**1934**"] centers on a character who thinks of little else. More precisely, he wonders whether suicide is the only solution to despair or whether despair may not, as he puts it, be stabilized, accepted as "the normal condition of man . . . as natural as the air we breathe." "What did I mean by 'stabilize'? Somehow, imagining my life as a Nation, to institutionalize despair, recognize it officially . . . as a law of that same Nation."

Lucio is a young Italian hanging about Capri, peering into the melancholy eyes of Beate, a German woman he has met there. He is a student of literature, a translator of Heinrich von Kleist, the German dramatic poet whose short life ended in a double suicide, and he sees in the girl's "unhappy and stubborn look" not only a trace of moody German Romanticism but also "the sorrow of the world." Sure enough, Beate is contemplating suicide and would like to make Lucio a partner in a pact. High tragedy and silliness mix here—"It's all bad literature," Lucio thinks—and there are wry, awkward jokes. . . . Then Beate leaves Capri with her husband and is replaced in Lucio's *pensione* by her twin sister, who is also her moral opposite, full

of sauciness and life. After that the plot takes a couple of fancy twists it would be unkind to reveal. (p. 11)

In 1934, the time of the novel's title and action, Mussolini had been in power for 12 years and Hitler for one. Hitler speaks on the radio and is heard by eager German holidaymakers— "He was not a concise speaker," Lucio laconically says—and word of the Night of the Long Knives reaches Capri by telephone. We are meant, I take it, to connect what Lucio calls his "psychological adventure" with the larger shifts of history. But how? Beate says her husband "horrifies" her, because "his hands are stained with blood." Does she simply mean that he is a Nazi and she is not? Or has she more specific violences in mind? Does she mean anything at all, or is she playing a gloomy game for Lucio's benefit?

There are, I think, two major implications in the novel. The first is that Fascism creates a world of salutes and gestures, a bullying theater where people either perform or are persecuted and where, therefore, many of the performers are merely hiding behind the tokens of loyalty. It will be hard to tell believers from pretenders in such a world, and zeal itself will begin to look like a parody, since, as Lucio slyly says, there are "things too true not to be feigned." At the same time, as is made clear by a story Lucio gets from a Russian exile he has run into, dictatorships need not only spies but *agents provocateurs*, who can tamper with reality more substantially. "An informer seeks the truth; the provocateur constructs it."

Despair is especially relevant in this context, because it is what must be concealed in forward-looking epochs. "What . . . could be more authentic than despair in times of terrorist dictatorship, and what, in the same times, less authentic than a healthy joy in living?" We are given a striking image of this treacherous, distorted universe very early in the book, when Lucio describes the landscape of Capri as "lying": The mountain looms, menacing, while the sea looks calm and reassuring, yet the sea is in fact the more dangerous. Which is realer, Beate's romantic sadness or her twin's hearty appetite for food and sex? Which is more German? What if both are only disguises?

The other implication is subtler and more profound. Lucio wants to "institutionalize" his despair. We may feel he is not thinking of despair at all, merely flirting with some distant relative of it, and indeed another character says to him that "true despair is not talkative." But then Lucio's doubts actually reinforce the sinister point. To glorify a despair that is less than real is frivolous as well as morbid. And either way the whole procedure plays into Hitler's hands, makes Lucio, the declared anti-Fascist, the unwitting accomplice of his enemies. He wants what they want. They too want to institutionalize despair, except that they are calling it joy.

The novel raises good questions and shows that Moravia, at 75, is far from flagging. It is perhaps a little too tricky for its own good, and Lucio is something of a stooge, as characters in Moravia's works often are, a creepy, cerebral fellow who is always several steps behind events. Moravia has craftily built ratiocinative, literary habits of mind into Lucio's character, and I suppose this disarms the critic. Or maybe not. Lucio thinks like a book. Perhaps his being in a book is not the perfect alibi. (pp. 11, 30)

> Michael Wood, "Desperate Remedies," *in* The New York Times Book Review *(© 1983 by The New York Times Company; reprinted by permission), May 8, 1983, pp. 11, 30.*

JOHN SHEPLEY

Durer's famous angel, *Melencolia,* has a way of alighting in some unexpected places. One of these is the first page of Alberto Moravia's new novel [*1934*] . . . , where the symbol of intellectual depression turns up as a passenger on a boat from Naples to Capri. . . . If [the narrator Lucio] can plausibly contrive the suicide of his novel's hero, he thinks, there will be no need for him to follow suit: "I would save myself through writing."

The sight of the woman on the boat overturns this resolution. Lucio embarks on a prolonged flirtation with her, endures the insults of her husband and pursues the couple (who turn out to be Germans) to a *pensione* in Anacapri. So attuned is he to the situation he has created that he even guesses their name out of thin air: Müller.

Before long, he is attributing to Beate Müller, with apparent confirmation forthcoming at every step, the motives of Heinrich von Kleist, and casting himself as a male Henriette Vogel, the woman with whom the German Romantic writer carried out a double suicide pact. The game is suspended only temporarily when the Müllers leave the island to return to Germany. They will be replaced by Beate's mother and twin sister, Trude, with whom, Beate explains, she and her husband will cross paths in Naples.

It is soon obvious, of course, that the twin sisters are a fiction: Beate and Trude are the same woman. The problem is which, if either, is the "real" one—the melancholy, suffering, suicidal Beate, or the vulgar, gluttonous "life-loving" Trude, an exuberant Nazi. From then on, nothing is quite what it seems. Lucio, in fact, is the victim of a hoax. Mother and daughter turn out to be a lesbian couple. A package containing shoes is replaced by one with a bomb, and before it has a chance to go off, the package is found to contain shoes after all. . . .

[Lucio] undergoes humiliation and sexual manipulation. An anti-Fascist, he is conned by Herr Müller into giving a Fascist salute in the dining room of the *pensione.* On a boat with Trude, she obliges him to lower his bathing trunks so that she can inspect him and be sure he is not circumcised. She then uses his foot to masturbate herself. One grows a little impatient with this fellow; he seems a poseur, a prig and a fool. The project for "stabilizing despair" that he describes to everyone seems all too literary and artificial, especially since he acknowledges his "familiar mood of despair at not being in despair."

Yet it is precisely this ambiguity that enables him to carry out his assigned role: to interrogate himself and others, to probe, to ask what are often the wrong questions and thereby elicit lengthy confessions. Capri itself—at first an unlikely setting for the somber thoughts and morbid impulses accompanying an examination of political sadism—suddenly becomes the ideal stage for this masquerade and the proper destination for Dürer's gloomy angel. The sphinx that overlooks the sea as Lucio follows Sonia up the steps of Shapiro's villa ensures that although a charade is being enacted, the right questions will ultimately be asked.

It takes the intrusion of Hitler (talking on the radio) to restore these actors—and the reader—to reality. In a brilliantly executed and appalling scene in the stuffy, oppressive, 19th-century parlor of the *pensione,* the German guests gather to listen to their *Führer,* while an animated argument breaks out between two of them over the supposed virtues of the traditional German student duel. This is too much for Lucio, who for the

moment abandons his efforts to separate the personae of Beate and Trude. The art collector Shapiro (clearly modeled on Bernard Berenson) is trundled on stage to impart a cynical and ironic bit of advice to the younger man on how to overcome despair: "Get rich." Then Hitler is heard congratulating himself on the crushing of a "conspiracy" in Germany—it is the Night of the Long Knives. A double suicide takes place on schedule, and a tragic dimension is restored.

John Shepley, "In the Fascist Shadow," in The New Leader (© 1983 by the American Labor Conference on International Affairs, Inc.), Vol. LXVI, No. 10, May 16, 1983, p. 21.

JOSHUA GILDER

Alberto Moravia's *The Conformist,* perhaps his most famous novel, was in many ways a convincing portrait of fascist psychology, but I for one never understood what lesbianism had to do with it all. . . . Still less could I make out in Moravia's last novel, *Time of Desecration,* what mother-daughter incest, troilism, and sodomy had to do with terrorism in present-day Italy. Now *1934* returns us to the lesbian-fascist nexus (again with incestuous overtones), and in a subplot we hear about two sodomitical Trotskyites in pre-revolutionary Russia. Don't Christian Democrats ever get kinky?

Moravia's earlier stories were often brilliant little studies of erotic compulsion. But the erotic component has steadily drained away, until all we are now left with is the compulsion. *Time of Desecration* read less like a novel than a case study of sexual pathology, and one notices an almost clinical quality to Moravia's writing in *1934* as well. . . .

[The novel] proceeds through a number of *Magus*-like changes of identity, leaving Lucio bewildered and the reader, unless he is a Fowles fan, increasingly irritated. The most frustrating aspect of it all is the feeling of having ended up precisely where one began. The revelations of identity beneath the disguises don't add up to revelations of character, and Lucio, for all his psychic turmoil, never seems to change.

The connection between sex and politics remains just as much a mystery as ever. Perhaps they're both just plausible motivations for an obsession that, by this point, seems to have taken on a life of its own. Moravia writes with a fetishistic intensity that, for a while at least, draws you in and carries you along. But one soon realizes that the logic of his obsession has brought him full circle, and that he's traveling in a tighter and tighter orbit around an ultimately inaccessible center. The third or so time around, one begins to weary of the trip.

Joshua Gilder, "Love on the Right: '1934'," in New York Magazine (copyright © 1983 by News Group Publications, Inc.; reprinted with the permission of New York Magazine), Vol. 16, No. 21, May 23, 1983, p. 88.

STEPHEN SPENDER

The contrast between the Italian and the German temperament is a central theme of [*1934*]. Since in 1934 both countries were under dictatorships that distorted the way people behaved, the contrast is seen ultimately as one between different styles of playacting: Mussolini-style fascism, which for the Italians was a matter of rather superficial conformism, and Hitler-style Nazism, which for the Germans demanded a total submergence of all individuality within the party, and which dragged the Italians down with it. Lucio and Beate are both opposed to the dictatorial regimes of their countries. Yet when Lucio is greeted by Herr Müller raising his arm vertically in the Hitler salute, he gets a sign from Beate and raises his arm horizontally in that of the Italian fascists.

The point surely is that all personal values, even those of the opponents of totalitarianism, are falsified by such dictatorships. (p. 25)

The year 1934 is the year of the falsification of everyone's values, the dissolution even of his or her personal identity, the destruction of personal relations. Lucio discovers that in his love for Beate he is forced into the role of playacting when—Beate and her husband, Herr Müller, having returned to Germany—they are replaced by Beate's twin sister, Trude, and her mother. Trude is in every way the opposite of Beate: instead of being doomed and intellectual, she is frivolous and vulgar, indeed obscene. Beate was anti-Nazi, just as Lucio is antifascist (despite, as we have seen, his having given at a sign from her the Fascist raised-arm salute).

Beate, in their one snatched conversation, has told Lucio that she detests her husband because ''his hands are stained with blood.'' Trude talks with religious fervor of the bliss of submerging one's identity in the party. She contrives a situation in which Lucio exposes his penis in order that, before making love to him, she may discover whether he is circumcised. It would be blasphemy against the party for her to sleep with a Jew. But after all this, she reveals to Lucio that in fact she is not Beate's twin. She is, in fact, Beate. Nor is her mother her mother. Both of them are actresses who have been playing roles in order to teach a lesson to Lucio whom, in his harassment of Beate and her husband, they take to be, like all Italians who go to resorts in order to seduce girls, a Casanova.

The reader, like Lucio, may disbelieve all this, except that at the end the story takes a tragic turn, which is perhaps evidence of the truth of one relationship—that of Beate/Trude with the fellow actress who has been playing the role of her mother. The morning after Hitler's speech Paula and Beate telephone Germany, and learn that Beate's husband is one of the victims of the Hitler purge of Roehm's followers. On hearing this, they go to a place called La Migliara and commit suicide by swallowing cyanide tablets which Beate has stolen from her husband. Thus the German lesbian couple achieve the double suicide which is the logical conclusion of Kleist's double suicide with Henriette Vogel.

To convince the reader a story such as this, with a plot so full of seeming improbabilities, has to be a tour de force, written with great virtuosity—and Moravia succeeds triumphantly in this (he is also beautifully supported by his translator, William Weaver). The reader has to be kept not just looking forward while following a story which, like the one of Kleist that Lucio is translating, seems always to be thrusting him on, but also looking back so that every new and unexpected turn of events

elucidates what has happened before. For instance, when Trude explains that she is really Beate and has no twin sister, the reader has mentally to reinterpret Beate's behavior from the moment when Lucio first sees her on the ship going to Anacapri. When he does so, he finds that everything Beate has done, which perhaps he took at face value, is indeed elucidated by the revelation that she has, in the opening scenes of the novel, been acting a role. The difficulty produced by the narrator, of course, is that the reader does not know what to believe. And this is the truth of the book: that within the external situation of the Italian fascist-German Nazi relationship it is impossible to accept as authentic virtually anything people do.

This is underlined by a curious episode—the relationship between Lucio and a character extraneous to the rest of the action, a Russian refugee, a woman of middle age, who sleeps around with waiters, sailors, everyone who will have her. Lucio goes to her with the intention of working off some of his repressed sexual energy reserved for Beate. In fact, at the last moment (a very depraved one) Sonia rejects him, saying that there is something about him that is cruel and that scares her. She then tells him her story: she was a Russian revolutionary who disobeyed orders to kill her lover, a double agent. The episode, which took place when she was twenty-seven, killed her, she says. She is really a living corpse. The character and her situation underline what must certainly be taken as the moral of Moravia's book, but Sonia seems superfluous to the story of Lucio and Beate/Trude. The insistence on political truth intrudes on the truth of the imagination.

Another episode that seems extraneous occurs in the penultimate chapter when Lucio visits the famous art dealer and collector Shapiro, who is Sonia's employer, in order to discuss with this wise and famous art historian the problem of his despair. The evocation of Bernard Berenson, very exactly described, is wholly enjoyable, even though it has little to do with the rest of the novel. Shapiro/Berenson's advice to Lucio illuminates Berenson's cynicism more than Lucio's despair. It is, quite simply, ''Get rich.'' He then launches into a description of his Latvian childhood that Moravia must surely have heard from Berenson himself.

The episode of Sonia is perhaps too politically schematic, identifying Russian communism with Italian and German fascism; and that of Shapiro/Berenson is perhaps too journalistic. Nevertheless, *1934* is a wonderful invention. It starts with Kleist and Kafka and never loses its sense of them; but it is also a book in which fantasy, reality, and some deep truth about how personal relations are disfigured by the loss of freedom are all fused with Italian bravura. (p. 26)

Stephen Spender, ''Victims of Politics,'' in The New York Review of Books *(reprinted with permission from* The New York Review of Books; *copyright © 1983 Nyrev, Inc.),* Vol. XXX, No. 11, June 30, 1983, *pp. 25-6.*

Amos Oz

1939-

Israeli novelist and short story writer.

Amos Oz is acclaimed for his stories of Israeli life, particularly those set in the kibbutz, which he writes with critical affection, having been a kibbutznik himself for many years. His first book, *Makom aher* (1966; *Elsewhere, Perhaps*), is a look at the singular problems and relationships experienced in such a community. It was followed by *Mikha'el sheli* (1968; *My Michael*), a psychological profile of the fantasy life of an Israeli housewife, which introduces Oz's controversial contention that Jews and Arabs have ambivalent, rather than purely hostile, feelings for each other.

Oz's themes include the destructiveness of Judeophobia upon both the hater and the hated, the interrelationship of all human experience, tensions between community and individuality, and the shifting border between the real and the surreal. *La-ga'ath ba-mayim, la-ga'ath ba-ruah* (1973; *Touch the Water, Touch the Wind*) develops his ideas of reality. The characters are always in search of the elusive ideal, something to be found only in "another place," never here and now.

Oz creates his fiction from the political and historical heritage of Israel and its traditional relationships with surrounding lands. A repeated motif in his novels is that of borders which keep people both together and apart. Oz longs for the union of disparate peoples, though he understands the improbability of his wish. In a recent book of short stories, *Where the Jackals Howl* (1981), he uses his recurring symbol of the jackal to represent the ever-present threat to Israel from beyond its borders.

Many critics insist that Oz should be recognized as a writer of international stature, not only for his revealing portrayal of Israel, but also for the outstanding artistry of his fiction.

(See also *CLC*, Vols. 5, 8, 11 and *Contemporary Authors*, Vols. 53-56.)

© *Thomas Victor 1983*

A. G. MOJTABAI

"Elsewhere, Perhaps" was a book full of unease that was not allowed to surface, the tension smoothed over by the voice of the narrator, a voice level and interminable, sometimes smug or starched with disapproval, but always composed, never shaken. The unidentified narrator was a man soberly respectful of the principles of collectivism upon which the kibbutz was founded, yet cognizant of the difficulties in living up to these standards, a spokesman full of injunctions to will power and exemplary tales of changes of heart. Any unsettling doubts were contained and tempered by irony. Why, for example, the narrator asked, can't a man of sound principles control his nightmares? Wherever one went, the narrator stood between the reader and the unfolding drama, much as a tour guide stands before, and defends against, a visitor's direct contact with a foreign scene.

"Where the Jackals Howl" is, in many respects, the double, the darker brother of "Elsewhere, Perhaps." This collection of stories [originally published in Hebrew in 1966], is only now appearing in English. It is, by far, the stronger book. It is also far more troubling. Here, the unease is directly confronted; there is no mediation, no muting, no equable light. This is a book of dark shadows and glare and, through the shadows, in and around and through each story, glides the jackal. As a literary artifice, the jackal—or the dispossessed-turned-jackal—is overdone, but as an ever-present feature of the geographical and psychic landscape, the jackal cannot be too attentively heeded. There were jackals, too, in "Elsewhere, Perhaps," but they were neatly fenced off. . . . (p. 3)

What makes the jackal so very menacing a presence here is that the threat is no longer simply external. . . .

"Where the Jackals Howl" is a collection of eight stories, a few of them with a shared cast of characters, the rest with apparently nothing in common. But the absence of a common thread is only apparent. There is a consistent inwardness, and a curious, but necessary, lack of resolution to all these tales; they are closely linked by the way the author's mind works in each of them, turning and turning upon some question that yields no answer—a desertion, a hunger never to be sated, an unjust preference, God's inexplicable favor. The most haunting issue raised is that of exclusion, dispossession—the question of Isaac and Ishmael, why one son is favored and the other not. The issue crops up in many guises; it might be something as seemingly mild and commonplace as an elderly bachelor in

358

the midst of families, or a son who can think of no way of distinguishing himself before his distinguished father, or a passionate suitor passed over for a heedless one. Placed together as they are here, these apparently disparate situations can be seen as having mutual bearing upon one another.

In **"Upon This Evil Earth,"** the story of Jephthah is imaginatively re-created. Jephthah beseeches God for love: "God love me and I will be your servant, touch me and I will be the leanest and most terrible of your hounds, only do not be remote." Jephthah tries to think of himself as someone like Isaac and Jacob, who were also sons of their fathers' old age, but is continually reminded that he is "the son of another woman, like Ishmael."

Judges II tells us that Jephthah was the son of Gilead, the Gileadite, and a harlot; here he is presented as the son of an Ammonite harlot. The particularity of this detail gives the story of a divided man an even sharper focus.

We know how Jephthah was told he would not inherit his father's house, how he was driven out by the sons of his father's wife, how he came to live in the land of Tob, how the elders of Gilead sought him out as their captain in repelling an Ammonite invasion, and how Jephthah finally consented, vowing to sacrifice whatsoever first came forth from the doors of his house to meet him on his victorious return. And who could forget the terrible unfolding of that vow? . . .

We know the story, but perhaps we have not properly savored its bitterness. Nor have we truly reflected on the bitterness of Ishmael, of whom Jephthah, the perpetual stranger, is perpetually reminded. In Islamic tradition, significantly, the fate of Ishmael (Isma'il) has been pondered and somewhat ameliorated, and there is even a popular belief among Moslems that Isma'il, not Isaac, was the beloved son whom Abraham offered up in sacrifice. These rancors have not abated over the centuries: The children of Isaac and the children of Ishmael are today still locked in enmity.

The enmity takes many forms. It may be the friction between tillers of the soil and wandering herdsmen. **"Nomad and Viper"** starts out as the tale of such a conflict, but slowly changes shape.

As the story begins, conditions of drought and famine have forced the military authorities to open the roads leading north to the Bedouins. Foot-and-mouth disease, crop damage, and a rash of petty thefts follow in the wake of the nomads—also a mysterious music from the encampments at night. Geula, a not-so-young unmarried woman living on a kibbutz, stumbles into a Bedouin on one of her solitary walks. She is repelled and strangely fascinated by the man's dark beauty; she is touched by his elaborate courtesy; what she cannot seem to feel is the full measure of his humanity. Together, they share a smoke. Then the man begins to pray. Geula persists in interrupting him with impertinent personal questions; the Bedouin flees. Afterward, alone in the shower, shivering "with disgust," she experiences the strange recoil and twisting of her own thwarted desires:

> "Those black fingers, and how he went straight for my throat. . . . It was only by biting and kicking that I managed to escape. Soap my belly and everything, soap it again and again. Yes, let the boys go right away tonight to their camp and smash their black bones because of what they did to me."

Notice the easy shift from "he" to "they"—hatred is a great simplifier. And yet, later, lying among the bushes, watching the planes overhead and listening to the sounds borne by the night winds, Geula is overcome by another feeling, a longing to be healed: "How she longed to make her peace and to forgive. Not to hate him and wish him dead. Perhaps to get up and go to him. . . ."

"Where the Jackals Howl" is a strong, beautiful, disturbing book. It speaks piercingly—whether wittingly or unwittingly, I know not—of a dimension of the Israeli experience not often discussed, of the specter of the other brother, of a haunting, an unhealed wound; it reminds us of polarizations everywhere that bind and diminish us, that may yet rend us. (p. 35)

> A. G. Mojtabai, "Perpetual Stranger in the Promised Land," in The New York Times Book Review (© 1981 by The New York Times Company; reprinted by permission), April 26, 1981, pp. 3, 35.

LESLEY HAZLETON

Most of the stories in [*Where the Jackals Howl and Other Stories*] were written in 1962 when Oz was in his early 20s. To someone unacquainted with *My Michael* or with the later stories, particularly those in *The Hill of Evil Counsel*, they are a fascinating introduction to an excellent writer. But to those who expect the later Oz, they will for the most part be a disappointment. They foreshadow much of his later work in theme, in imagery, and particularly in the evocative use of climate and landscape. But they suffer from the light of the midday sun. They seek the shadows too obviously, and too often cast none.

Oz knew what he was talking about a decade later. These early characters are indeed sometimes grotesque, their emotions too crude, their tales too obviously biblical in intensity. In the title story, as a jackal cub resigns itself to death in a trap, a founding member of a kibbutz rapes a young woman, then tells her that he is her natural father. In **"The Way of the Wind"** an inhumanly ideological father abandons his son in disgust when the son fails to show the courage his father expects of him—and the son kills himself rather than live with the shame of it. In **"Strange Fire,"** a woman tries to seduce her prospective son-in-law; she reveals that his father was also the father of her daughter, and now she seeks in him that same brief flame that she found in his father a generation before.

They are savage and ruthless emotional beings, this founding generation, playing out their lust and bitterness on the flesh of their children. One longs for some subtlety in them, some sense of identity in their offspring. But the writer was still young, and could allow none.

There is one story, however, in which this theme works superbly: the longest and most recent one, **"Upon this Evil Earth."** . . . It is the story of Jephthah, the warrior judge of the desert who figures in chapter 11 of the biblical book of Judges, and who swore that he would sacrifice the first thing to greet him on his return home if he were given victory over the Ammonites. The first thing to greet him was his only child, a daughter, and he sacrificed her.

Oz tells the story in the style of the desert: first the tale in brief, taking it for granted that everyone knows the bare bones of it but introducing it in any case as a matter of form and graciousness; and then the whole story, from before the beginning to the very end, told at length with a luxurious feeling for detail even in the sparse desert lives of its protagonists. And Oz adds one particularly terrifying detail to the original tale: the daughter hears her father make his oath, and purposely comes out of the house to be the first to greet him, wearing a bridal gown. Thus, she forces him to kill her, ensuring that no other man will ever be able to claim her. It is a grand and chilling tale, magically told, and makes one long to see Oz take more of the old legends and imbue them with the complex shadows of humanity.

Another Oz theme in these stories is the complex of Jewish emotions about Arabs. Oz's portrayal of this ambivalent attitude created a furor in Israel when *My Michael* was published, because in it the heroine has sexual fantasies about the Arab twins with whom she played as a child and who are now grown, in her mind, into terrorists. In the earlier story "**Nomad and Viper**," included here, a woman fantasizes about a Bedouin encountered in the kibbutz orchard, the fantasies moving from rape to seduction as hate and a vision of possible peace flow through her mind. It is a cruel, contorted vision of sexuality, set against a background of violence, in which the kibbutz men set out armed to teach the Bedouin a lesson, to stop the nomads from raiding their orchards and stealing from the kibbutz. But the story as a whole is a vivid and accurate portrayal of the conflict between the Jewish settlements and the Bedouin, a conflict still being played out today, 20 years later.

All the stories in this collection are powerful, in the way that the midday sun is powerful. But if you find yourself looking for the shade, for a cooler place from which to look at the emotional struggles of a country in the making, then you must go to *My Michael* and the stories written after it. (pp. 39-40)

Lesley Hazleton, "Tales from Israel," in The New Republic *(reprinted by permission of* The New Republic; © *1981 The New Republic, Inc.), Vol. 184, No. 26, June 27, 1981, pp. 39-40.*

JUDITH CHERNAIK

Two qualities are immediately apparent on reading [the tales in *Where the Jackals Howl*]: the consummate, self-conscious craft of the writing, and the seriousness and truthfulness of the content. Kibbutz life provides a common background and inspiration—for apparently everyone on a kibbutz has a story. Two of the stories analyse a stern father's grief for a dead son. Others deal with sexual revenge—for the ideology of the kibbutz somehow fails to solve this most persistent of human problems.

Themes and images from one story recur in others: sunrise and sunset, the changing seasons, the extremes of climate . . . , the contours of a landscape rich in symbolic associations. The jackals of the title story, in particular, change shape and significance in each tale, as if in counterpoint to the human lives portrayed. On occasion this natural symbolism is made explicit, and becomes human and political: "It happens sometimes in the middle of the night that a plump house-dog hears the voice of his accursed brother. It is not from the dark fields that this voice comes; the dog's detested foe dwells in his own heart." In other stories the conflict between Jew and Arab is traced back to Cain and Abel, the tiller of the soil and the shepherd, one loved by God, the other rejected.

Most remarkable is the compassionate irony with which Oz treats all his characters, the maddened and the reasonable equally.

The political and moral debate about ends and means is argued endlessly but inconclusively. . . .

Oz is without doubt a voice for sanity, for the powers of imagination and love, and for understanding. He is also a writer of marvellous comic and lyric gifts, which somehow communicate themselves as naturally in English as in Hebrew. . . . Those who prefer realism in fiction may find that the final story, a retelling of the Biblical tale of Jephthah's daughter, suffers from an excessively self-conscious style and symbolism. But the stories on the whole show remarkable artistry and control and demonstrate the born story-teller's gift of creating characters who are at once inevitable and familiar, instantly recognizable and larger than life. The reader coming to Oz for the first time is likely to find his perception of Israel permanently altered and shaped by these tales.

Judith Chernaik, "The Story-Teller in the Kibbutz," in The Times Literary Supplement (© *Times Newspapers Ltd. (London) 1981; reproduced from* The Times Literary Supplement *by permission), No. 4095, September 25, 1981, p. 1092.*

DANIEL P. DENEAU

Although Oz has published two collections of novellas, *Where the Jackals Howl* is his only volume of short fiction . . . : seven of the eight stories were written in the early 1960's . . . , were published in 1965 . . . , and were revised in the 1970's. . . . In the long run, however, it makes little difference if the stories are revised apprentice work. Quality is quality, and *Where the Jackals Howl* should enhance Oz's reputation and widen his audience.

In one way six of the eight stories do speak of Oz's early preoccupation as a writer—life in the kibbutz, the type of life Oz himself has experienced since adolescence. For Oz the kibbutz does not appear to be a peaceful island: there are such menaces as jackals, nomads, storms, as well as lust and death within. And there is ambivalence: although Oz returns in several stories to the laughing, menacing jackals, which seem to be one symbol of "the accumulated menace outside," in the title story he describes, with sensitivity and perhaps compassion, a young jackal caught in a trap. In "**Nomad and Viper**" the thieving Bedouins provoke violence, but also, in a specific case . . . exert a romantic attraction which the author seems to respect. (pp. 82-3)

A mere enumeration may help to characterize the collection: *at times* straightforward realism, symbols, striking descriptions, fragmentary sentences, similes, effective repetition (sometimes Oz is praised for his lyrical prose), irony, fractured chronology, violent shifts or disjointed effects, and, perhaps most noteworthy of all, obliqueness or indeterminacy, to such a degree that some readers will be more mystified than pleased. For instance, in "**Where the Jackals Howl**" coherence-seekers will wonder about the interweaving of the story of the trapped jackal ("the child") and that of the seduced girl, seduced by a man who is equated to a furious stallion and who may be the girl's father; or in "**A Hollow Stone**" accounts of a storm-lashed Kibbutz are mixed with old Batya Pinski's history and current preoccupations, the publication of a collection of her dead husband's essays and her aquarium, filled with fish "both cold and alive," a "longed-for bliss." "**Before His Time**" begins with a detailed description of a dying bull and proceeds to glance at four members of a family whose lives hardly touch one another. In "**Strange Fire**" one is left wondering if a prospective mother-in-law, Lily Dannenberg, seduces her daughter's fiancé, to whose father Lily had been married briefly years before.

All of the stories are broken into numbered sections, the visual gaps suggesting the hermeneutic ones. Though each story deserves contemplation, **"Upon This Evil Earth,"** an imaginative expansion of the story of Jephthah . . . , appears to be the most compelling. Jephthah is a man who does not love words, who has eyes which look inward, who worships the "Lord of the wolves in the night in the desert," and who belongs only in the "desperate wasteland" between Israel and Ammon. One wonders if the predatory Jephthah—apparently a hero—should be linked to the predatory jackals and Bedouins with which the collection opens. . . . The stories are exciting, not moving. They are grim, but not depressing. (pp. 83-4)

Daniel P. Deneau, in a review of "Where the Jackals Howl and Other Stories," in Studies in Short Fiction *(copyright 1982 by Newberry College), Vol. 19, No. 1, Winter, 1982, pp. 82-4.*

ALLEN BELKIND

Amos Oz, a leading sabra writer of Israel's second generation, is less concerned than his elders with optimistically depicting Israel's Zionist destiny in an esthetic of socialist realism and more concerned with scrupulously capturing the existential angst of individuals of the kibbutz in a tone of tragic irony that sometimes approaches the absurd. . . .

The "jackals" motif, found everywhere [in *Where the Jackals Howl and Other Stories*], becomes a central symbol that sustains the intense climate of siege and danger. The kibbutz . . . represents Israel in miniature; the hungry jackals lurking outside the compound are the ever-threatening Arabs. Inside the kibbutz, human passions, symbolized by the *khamsin*—the fiercely hot desert wind—are usually on the verge of explosion in these tense dramas that occur there among the youth and the aging, driven by loneliness, their fantasies and their clashing ideas and temperaments. . . .

Oz's intense and poetic descriptions, which powerfully evoke the sense of Israel's physical and emotional climate, and his concern with the inner truths of the isolated individual remind one of Crane or Conrad, his irony and sensuality of Lawrence Durrell. Despite some tendency in his longer pieces toward a looseness of structure and some abrupt shifts in point of view between the individual and the collective, Oz is a writer of great gifts, worthy of international recognition.

Allen Belkind, in a review of "Where the Jackals Howl and Other Stories," in World Literature Today *(copyright 1982 by the University of Oklahoma Press), Vol. 56, No. 2, Spring, 1982, p. 400.*

NEHAMA ASCHKENASY

The stories [in *Where the Jackals Howl*] present a diversity of characters and human conflicts as well as a variety of locations; though most are set against the cohesive kibbutz community, we also get glimpses of the diabolic nights of the city, the bravado of the army camp, the menacing presence of the border, and even the stark charm of ancient Israel. However, these stories are unified by an overall pattern that juxtaposes an individual permeated by a sense of existential estrangement and subterranean chaos with a self-deceiving community col-

lectively intent upon putting up a facade of sanity and buoyancy in order to deny—or perhaps to exorcise—the demons from without and within.

The demons from without are the mad jackal, the furtive nomad, and the murderous enemy soldier—the foes from the animal as well as the human world—that surround the civilized, sedentary community, threatening to infect it with rabies, plunder it, and return it to primordial chaos.

Though the beast and the savage are fenced out, fought off, and kept at a safe distance, they find their allies in the heavily guarded, seemingly secure settlement. In **"Before His Time,"** they unleash dormant primitive and irrational forces in man's best friend, the dog, as well as in man himself. . . . (p. 58)

In another story, **"Nomad and Viper,"** the nomads bring out the savage in the young kibbutz members who hotheadedly suggest "making an excursion one night to teach the savage a lesson in a language they would really understand." And the girl Geula, believed to have a calming influence on the hottempered young men, responds to the savage rhythm with rapture: "In counterpoint came the singing of the nomads and their drums, a persistent heartbeat in the distance: One, one, two, One, one, two."

A recurrent stylistic structure in many stories is the shifting of the point of view from that of the collective "we" (or the "I" who speaks for the whole group and alternates between "I" and "we") to that of the alienated individual. Society's point of view usually provides the framework for the story, opening and closing it, and sometimes also intruding in the midst of the main plot. The collective voice is suspiciously optimistic, over-anxious to ascertain the normalcy and sanity of the community and the therapeutic effect of the collective body on its tormented member. But the voice of the individual is imbued with a bitter sense of entrapment, of existential boredom and nausea, coupled with a destructive surrender to the irrational and the antinomian.

The stories are deceptive in their narrative fidelity to true-to-life characters and locations. While they present the dilemma of the disaffected individual pitted against a cohesive society founded on a sense of shared destiny and concerted effort, the ultimate *raison d'être* of these stories is not that of social realism. True, we encounter characters in the grips of socio-psychological conflicts. . . . But these diversified conditions of *men* are masterfully converted by Oz into a vision of the condition of *man*. What we ultimately perceive is not only the kibbutz member (and by extension, the modern Israeli) trapped in a small, enclosed area, surrounded by enemies, but man, caught in what Camus has seen as the inherent absurdity of existence, namely, the fundamental incoherence of the human experience, and the sense of man's dereliction in an alien world.

The eight stories collected here are not of even quality. Two or three stand out as the most richly resonant as well as artistically controlled.

Of special interest is **"Nomad and Viper"** which presents a variation on the main motif by focusing on a feminine character, Geula, which gives an added dimension to the theme of the human predicament.

Geula's name (in Hebrew "redemption") provides a clue to this character's literary function, and directs us towards the three levels of meaning which exist in the story: the national, the sexual, and the existential.

Geula can be seen as a representative of the generation that realized the Zionist dream of secular redemption in the form of political independence. To this limited extent, Geula's constant urge to get out of the confining, artificial borders of the kibbutz, and her heightened awareness of the savage element that closes in on the kibbutz reflect the modern Israeli's claustrophobic sense of living in a constant state of siege. It also reveals the Israeli's mixed feelings in his assessment of the national endeavor as an imposition of the Western rational heritage or terrain populated by nomads and savages, whose primitive, barbaric presence constantly challenges the validity and judiciousness of the Zionist enterprise. (pp. 58-9)

Geula plays the role of the "other" in this story. But she is not the "other" in the sense that Simone de Beauvoir attributed to the term, that is, woman as the "other" vis-à-vis man. Geula's otherness, or sense of alienation, as a woman, is commuted by Oz into an image of the human otherness in the existential sense of man's alienation from the universe as well as from himself. Geula, considered the voice of reason and restraint in the kibbutz, surprises herself with her strong attraction to the savage presence and with her sudden, intense awareness of, and response to, the chaotic and irrational. She thus experiences what both Sartre and Camus saw as the essence of the existential "absurd," the unbridgeable gulf between rationality and experience.

While Geula's feminine predicament is converted into the image of the total human condition, Lily, the heroine of the story **"Strange Fire,"** is the traditional feminine temptress, a modern-day Lilith roaming the streets of Jerusalem at night on a mission of evil and destruction. Her "otherness" is that of the *Sitra Achra,* i.e. the "other side," the demonic and evil forces in man and in the universe.

"Before His Time" is a powerful tale, equal in its intensity to **"Nomad and Viper."** Again the themes of man's profound loneliness, his sense of entrapment, and the ultimate futility of human rational endeavor reverberate against the background of apparent social realism. (p. 59)

Oz's art proves that localism does not necessarily mean parochialism. The explosive and paradoxical reality of the kibbutz and modern Israel provides the necessary literary material in the writer's attempts to comprehend and epitomize not only the surface of this reality but the antinomian and the "other side" enfolded in it. Simultaneously, this realistic setting serves as an "objective correlative" in Oz's descent into the "heart of darkness" to capture and define the human condition. (p. 60)

Nehama Aschkenasy, "On Jackals, Nomads, and the Human Condition," in Midstream *(copyright © 1983 by The Theodor Herzl Foundation, Inc.), Vol. XXIX, No. 1, January, 1983, pp. 58-60.*

Robert B(rown) Parker

1932-

American novelist.

Parker's crime fiction places him as a prominent contemporary author within the hard-boiled tradition of Dashiell Hammett, Raymond Chandler, and Ross Macdonald. His best known works form a series consisting of nine novels, beginning with *The Godwulf Manuscript* (1973), and featuring Spenser, a tough but compassionate private-eye trained not only in espionage but also in gourmet cooking, physical fitness, and literature. One of Spenser's most endearing qualities is his sometimes self-depreciating but always witty sense of humor.

Parker wrote his dissertation on Hammett, Chandler, and Macdonald and although he knows the private eye tradition well, his success is largely based on the contemporary tone he maintains while remaining true to the conventions of the genre. Along with the standard element of suspense, Parker's emphasis lies in character development, through dialogue as much as through action, and the incorporation of social themes, most notably the distortion of the American dream.

Promised Land (1977), the fourth Spenser novel, was awarded the Edgar Allan Poe Award. Ironically, some critics feel this is one of his weaker works. For example, David Geherin, who acknowledges Parker's usual strength in characterization and dialogue, finds "an overemphasis on character analysis and an excessive talkiness that upsets the novelistic balance in *Promised Land*. . . ."

(See also *Contemporary Authors*, Vols. 49-52 and *Contemporary Authors New Revision Series*, Vol. 1.)

Photograph by Kathleen Krueger; courtesy of Delacorte Press

NEWGATE CALLENDAR

In the tradition of Hammett, Chandler and the other private-eye creators of the 1930's comes **"The Godwulf Manuscript"** by Robert B. Parker. . . . Parker's locale is Boston, and his private-eye—a tough, wise-cracking, unafraid, lonely, unexpectedly literate type—is in many respects the very exemplar of the species. He is called in to investigate the theft of a 14th-century illuminated manuscript from a college library. Along the way he runs into student activists, the mob, drugs, sex and the usual package. **"The Godwulf Manuscript"** is not notable for originality or ideas, but it is at least well written and does have a point of view about life. Its trouble is that it is simply too derivative to be anything more than lightweight.

Newgate Callendar, in a review of "The Godwulf Manuscript," in The New York Times Book Review *(© 1974 by The New York Times Company; reprinted by permission), January 13, 1974, p. 12.*

NEWGATE CALLENDAR

Parker must have learned a good deal from **"Godwulf"**; his new book is more deft, smoother and sharper in characterization. Where **"Godwulf"** read like a compilation of every private eye from Chandler on, **"God Save the Child"** has a great deal more personality and character.

Spenser still remains a smart aleck who shows his dislike for stupidity. He also is intelligent, educated, a gourmet cook and a mean man with his fists. In **"God Save the Child"** he is hired to find a missing 15-year-old boy; then the ransom notes start arriving. Spenser solves the case, of course, but along the way there are shrewd thrusts that animate the writing. The portrait of the mother is especially well done.

Newgate Callendar, in a review of "God Save the Child," in The New York Times Book Review *(© 1974 by The New York Times Company; reprinted by permission), December 15, 1974, p. 10.*

ROBIN WINKS

Robert Parker is perhaps the best of [the writers attempting to replace Chandler]. . . . [*Promised Land*] shows him gaining mastery over his material all of the time. The dialogue is good, without that cutesy-tough overtone one finds in so many imitators of Chandler, and while Spenser remains a bit self-romanticized, he is no more so than Marlowe and Archer. Anyone who complains about the lack of Chandlers ought to try [either *Mortal Stakes* or *Promised Land*]. . . .

Robin Winks, in a review of "Mortal Stakes," in The New Republic *(reprinted by permission of* The

New Republic; © *1977 The New Republic, Inc.),
Vol. 176, No. 12, March 19, 1977, p. 36.*

AGATE NESAULE KROUSE and MARGOT PETERS

Robert B. Parker has created Spenser, a Marlowe-like private eye who drinks a lot and makes tasty omelets, salad dressings, and women. In *The Godwulf Manuscript* (1973) he is inexplicably rude (Marlowe never is): to a university president who has been only courteous, he sneers, ''Is there something you'd like me to detect or are you just polishing up your elocution for next year's commencement?'' The detective is less interesting, however, than his antagonist, a small, weak, lecherous professor of medieval literature who early in the story is revealed to be also a radical, dope pusher, and murderer. This paragon is married to a huge, adoring woman who mothers him and eventually takes five bullets in the stomach so the little man can escape. He does. Spenser finds him cowering in the bathtub where he has wet himself in terror. Once under arrest, however, the medievalist revives and, assuming a lofty tone, lectures the police department on the brilliance of his criminal career. At this Boston university, administrators are phonies, professors cowardly murderers, and students (except the heroine) doped and mindless radicals. ''Down these mean streets a man must go who is not himself mean, who is neither tarnished nor afraid,'' said Raymond Chandler, Parker's model; but Spenser, despite a certain vitality, doesn't quite make the grade, perhaps because all imitations are only imitations, perhaps because a tough guy who bullies presidents, deans, professors, and students just isn't tough enough.

Agate Nesaule Krouse and Margot Peters, ''Murder in Academe'' (reprinted by permission of the authors), in Southwest Review, *Vol. 62, No. 4, Autumn, 1977, pp. 371-78.**

ROBIN WINKS

The Judas Goat is not [Robert Parker's] best book, but it is very good. Parker is one of those authors who . . . are always being compared with Chandler and Ross Macdonald . . . , and while the comparison is apt as a label for quality and tone, it no longer is very helpful, since Parker has established a voice of his own. *The Judas Goat* is tough, cynical, sexy in a realistic way, and just a mite sentimental, and it sends Parker's series detective, Spenser, off to London, Copenhagen, and Amsterdam to seek out (and as it happens, to destroy) a tiny band of terrorists who, in bombing a London restaurant, have maimed an American millionaire and killed his wife and daughters. Personal vengeance, stalking dogs, hounds of heaven, and yes judas goats are the subjects here, and it is all handled with taste and authenticity.

Robin Winks, in a review of ''The Judas Goat,'' in The New Republic *(reprinted by permission of* The New Republic; © *1978 The New Republic, Inc.), Vol. 179, No. 19, November 4, 1978, p. 54.*

H.R.F. KEATING

[A] literary strain has been present more or less in all [Robert Parker's] novels, even in *Mortal Stakes* which has a baseball setting (Parker is an avid sportsman). Spenser has been well called ''the thinking man's private eye'': it is easy to detect the presence not far over his shoulder of an author fully conversant with the whole tradition of the novelist as seer or even as therapist. There is a concern with human beings that rises at times to compassion and perhaps falls at other times to that commonish complaint among American novelists ''psychology showing through''.

But the seriousness that this indicates is always well compensated for by Parker's dialogue. Spenser is a wisecracking guy in the firm tradition of the Chandler shamus, and above and beyond this all the conversations in the books are splendidly swift and sharp. Parker likes to refer to the minutiae of current American life or to that store of trivial memories that any 40-year-old American has, and this gives his pages a liveliness and an up-to-dateness which is decidedly refreshing.

H.R.F. Keating, ''The Classic Private Eye,'' in The Times, *London (© Times Newspapers Limited 1978), November 4, 1978, p. 9.*

NEWGATE CALLENDAR

Robert B. Parker has written five books starring Spenser, the tough Boston operator, a one-man army. In his new book, **''Wilderness''** . . . , a different hero is introduced—a man named Aaron Newman, a writer, jogger, big and strong but saddled with doubts of self and wife.

Jogging along peacefully one morning, Newman sees a murder and can identify the killer, who turns out to be a psychopathic gangster. He tells the police what he knows, but when the gangster threatens his wife, Newman recants his evidence. But can he now live with himself? And how does his wife, who can be very bitchy, feel about it?

Thus, while there is plenty of action in **''Wilderness''**—indeed, nothing but action—the book ends up as a psychodrama in which a married couple is put through unusual stresses, understanding each other a great deal more when everything is over. The writing is as skillful as the previous Parker books have been. The author even makes credible the generally unbelievable situation in which normal citizens suddenly turn into tigers, taking on trained killers. Mr. Parker stacks the cards more evenly that most authors. The last part of the book takes place in the wilderness, with both sides stalking each other—and in the wilderness a city gangster is at a disadvantage.

Newgate Callendar, in a review of ''Wilderness,'' in The New York Times Book Review *(© 1979 by The New York Times Company; reprinted by permission), November 11, 1979, p. 22.*

DAVID GEHERIN

It should come as no surprise to a reader of *The Godwulf Manuscript* (1974) to discover striking similarities between it and the novels of Dashiell Hammett, Raymond Chandler, and Ross Macdonald, particularly when he remembers that Parker wrote his doctoral dissertation on the novels of those three writers. What is surprising, however, is the extent to which he has managed to stake out for himself an original claim to the territory already overrun by would-be successors to the three earlier masters of the hard-boiled detective novel. Parker manages the tricky task of evoking echoes of all three writers while at the same time creating a character and developing a style that are uniquely his.

The Godwulf Manuscript introduces Spenser, a thirty-seven-year-old Boston private detective. Physically fit, six-feet-one, one hundred and ninety-five pounds, an ex-heavyweight boxer who can bench press two hundred and fifty pounds ten times, Spenser is also an amateur sculptor and a gourmet cook who lavishes loving care on the preparation of food. . . . His vocabulary is sprinkled with literary allusions . . . and he displays a knowledge of such arcane subjects as pre-Shakespearean drama and the controversy over certain disputed words in the text of one of Hamlet's soliloquies. Moreover, the entire novel is narrated in a fresh, witty, and colorful style.

Comparisons with his predecessors—especially Sam Spade, Philip Marlowe and Lew Archer—are inevitable. Like Sam Spade, he is tough and often cynical. Like Philip Marlowe, he has a quick wit, an insolent tongue, and an observant eye for the pompous and absurd. Like Lew Archer, he frequently finds himself drawn into the personal lives of his clients. Like all three, especially Marlowe and Archer, he has a profound sympathy for life's victims and a particular fondness for the young. He has a romantic's belief in the possibility of a better world but a realist's awareness of the concrete problems of it as it is. He is a loner, preferring to follow his own private code of personal justice. (pp. 9-10)

Parker also follows the example of Chandler in choosing a name for his hero that evokes memories of a more romantic age: Chandler selected Marlowe, a name with echoes of Malory, author of *Le Morte d'Arthur*, a collection of tales about King Arthur and his knights; Parker, looking to the English Renaissance, selected Spenser after Edmund Spenser, author of *The Faerie Queen*, an English heroic poem which, among other things, contains knightly adventures as well as discussions of such issues as moral behavior and the principles of personal honor. (p. 11)

The plot [of *The Godwulf Manuscript*], though lacking the complexity of a Ross Macdonald story, moves briskly and provides enough development to keep the reader interested. There are no real surprises or sudden revelations; the solution of the case is the result of Spenser's detective work rather than luck, intuition, or convenient confessions. For the most part, each character and scene is well integrated into the plot, and Parker wastes little in the telling of the story. The characters are well defined, even the minor ones. . . . Parker's handling of individual scenes is outstanding, approaching Chandler at his best: [they show] Parker's skill in developing suspense, creating atmosphere, or adding a satiric edge to the action. Parker also gives his novel a gritty sense of realism, often simply by providing a list of details: the items in a refrigerator or medicine chest; the furnishings in a house; the variety of students walking across a campus. Such details give the novel a concrete sense of place, mood, and atmosphere.

But what stands out above all else is the character of Spenser. It is in this regard that *The Godwulf Manuscript* is such an accomplishment for a first novel, for Spenser springs fully developed into the reader's imagination. By contrast, Dashiell Hammett worked for several years to evolve the character of the Continental Op. . . . (pp. 12-13)

A close examination of the opening chapter of *The Godwulf Manuscript* illustrates Parker's skill in characterizing his hero. The first sentence of the novel, for example, establishes not only the setting for the action to follow but also reveals the narrator's attitude: "The office of the university president looked like the front parlor of a successful Victorian whorehouse." We learn immediately that the speaker has an eye for pretentious detail and an irreverent sense of humor. (p. 14)

The Godwulf Manuscript is not without its flaws. The resolution of the plot is too pat. The source of evil in the book turns out to be a crackpot whose misguided political idealism gets mixed up with a naïve and dangerous view of drugs as liberators of social consciousness. Parker fails to locate the evil in a larger context, neither placing it in a social frame, as Chandler does, nor in a familial one, as Macdonald does. Parker appears to be less interested in the *why* of crime than many of his predecessors were. Although most of the literary references and allusions are effective and appropriate, some, notably the many references to hell, don't work. Despite references to Dante's *Inferno,* Milton's *Paradise Lost,* and even a character modeled after Moloch, one of the fallen angels, there is no coherent attempt to relate the evil in the book to anything more significant than a demented character who gets himself involved with the mob.

Although the plot is well developed, some scenes are not effectively integrated into the novel. (p. 22)

Most of these flaws can be attributed to the inexperience of a first novelist. One does not wish to carp about them too much, for they are minor when compared to the successes of the book. . . . *The Godwulf Manuscript* is a remarkable first novel and a promising introduction to the series. (pp. 22-3)

In his second Spenser novel, *God Save the Child* (1974), Parker manages to avoid the problems of the follow-up performance, and takes a confident step forward in his development as a mystery writer. Having paid his debts to his celebrated predecessors in *The Godwulf Manuscript,* Parker moves out from under their shadow in his second novel. Of course, one cannot write a hard-boiled detective novel that is not indebted to the conventions of the genre and the influence of past masters. But Parker manages to avoid the obvious parallels he employed in *The Godwulf Manuscript.* Instead he concentrates on developing his material his own way. (pp. 23-4)

All of the qualities that distinguished *The Godwulf Manuscript* are here. . . . Furthermore, the rough edges and uncertainties of Parker's first novel have been eliminated. The plot, for example, is much more skillfully handled, more logically developed; the characters are more interesting; the excesses of Spenser's narrative have been reduced. All in all, in *God Save the Child* Parker exercises tighter control of his material than he did in his first novel. (p. 24)

One aspect of Spenser's character more fully developed in this novel is his private life, especially his relationship with women, or more accurately with one woman, Susan Silverman.

The wooing of Susan is handled with sensitivity and wit. (p. 25)

Such themes as the alienation of the young, the hostility between parent and child, the search for a substitute family structure, which were implied in *The Godwulf Manuscript,* are treated much more explicitly in *God Save the Child.* (p. 26)

In *The Godwulf Manuscript* the crime was traced ultimately to the aberration of a sick mind. In *God Save the Child,* Parker is much more careful to locate the root of the problem in a familial and a social context, and then to draw an interrelationship between the two. . . . [The] real crime in the novel is both simpler and more complex: the failure of the American family. (pp. 32-3)

What unifies the separate themes of the novel—the family tragedy, the corruption within the community, the sense of lost values—is Parker's emphasis on relationships: the flawed—between Kevin and his parents; the failed—between Marge and Roger Bartlett; the unethical—between Croft and his patients;

the corrupt—between Croft, Trask, and Harroway; the irresponsible—between Trask and the community of Smithfield. Set against this extensive catalogue of failures, however, are some positive and productive relationships: for example, the developing relationship between Susan and Spenser. . . . (pp. 38-9)

God Save the Child shows that Parker is . . . attempting to extend the dimensions of the detective novel. By combining the elements of the hard-boiled novel with his own interest in the psychology of his characters and their interrelationships, and with a critical attitude toward contemporary America and American values, Parker has written a mystery novel that resonates on several levels and suggests the direction in which his future Spenser novels will develop. . . .

Midway in his career, Raymond Chandler admitted that "the time comes when you have to choose between pace and depth of focus, between action and character, menace and wit. I now choose the second in each case." On the evidence of *Mortal Stakes* (1975), his third Spenser novel, Parker appears to have made the same choices, emphasizing as Chandler did vivid characterization, serious exploration of theme, graceful and witty writing. (p. 39)

In each of his three novels thus far, Parker has provided a wide range of experiences for his hero, each designed to reveal a different facet of his character. Unlike Lew Archer, who solves most of his cases using the same techniques of persistent questioning and infinite understanding, Spenser must extend himself in different ways, risk himself in a variety of demanding situations. . . . In *Mortal Stakes,* Parker shows Spenser's compassion through his defense of the Rabbs, but he also reveals Spenser's vulnerability, a quality that proclaims not his weakness but his humanness. (pp. 44-5)

In the final chapter of the novel, Spenser reviews with Susan the moral implications of his actions. Structurally, the scene is out of place, anticlimatic and unnecessary to the action which has been completed. Nevertheless it reminds us that a private eye like Spenser is a kind of existential hero who must create and constantly re-examine his code of behavior, which is based on such things as an awareness of his freedom, a realization of the need for self-imposed limits to that freedom, and an understanding of the nature of the world in which he exists. Spenser is particularly bothered by the realization that his and Rabb's code did not work. . . . Susan argues that he ought to outgrow all this "Hemingwayesque nonsense," but to Spenser what Hemingway said about the necessity for devising a code of behavior is anything but nonsense. The pervasive influence of Hemingway can be seen in all of Parker's writing; one can detect it in *Mortal Stakes* in the conception of Spenser's character and in the picture of the world that the novel presents. Spenser's actions in *Mortal Stakes* demonstrate that he shares Hemingway's perception that we live in a world characterized by disorder and uncertainty, but that it can be faced honorably and confidently with a coded pattern of behavior. (pp. 51-3)

Mortal Stakes is Parker's best novel. . . . It is Parker's most assured in its handling of material, it has interesting and believable characters and a strong sense of atmosphere. But above all it raises important questions about the role of the private eye, and it dramatizes such moral issues as the authenticity of personal behavior and the struggle to maintain ethical sensitivity in an imperfect and violent world. And it does all this without sacrificing the pace, suspense, and action of a good detective novel. In seeking to do his best as a private eye,

Spenser learns something about himself; in the process he grows from a believable and likable private eye into a convincing and vulnerable human being. . . .

Although each of Parker's first three Spenser novels was critically well received, it was his fourth, *Promised Land* (1976), that brought him widespread recognition. . . . Nevertheless, despite the acclaim it must be admitted that the novel is something of a disappointment, and its failures are in areas that, ironically, were responsible for the success of the first three novels. Parker's strength has never been in his plotting, and the shaky plot of *Promised Land* confirms this. His strangest features are characterization and dialogue, yet there is an overemphasis on character analysis and an excessive talkiness that upsets the novelistic balance in *Promised Land* and results in an often lifeless work that lacks the sparkle and vitality of the first three Spenser books. (p. 54)

Instead of acting like a defender of truth and justice, Spenser in *Promised Land* appears to be little more than a hired professional valued for his ability to perform a dirty job for people who are unable to save themselves from their own stupidity. (p. 57)

Spenser exchanges his knightly role as defender of the innocent for a new one, marriage counselor. (p. 59)

One cannot overlook the weaknesses in plot and the frequently inert quality of *Promised Land.* One reason for the latter problem is that, despite Spenser's appeal to Susan that "You really ought to watch what I do, and, pretty much, I think, you'll know what I am," more of his character is revealed through exposition, less through action, in this novel than in any of the others. (p. 68)

On the other hand, one should not underestimate Parker's success in incorporating personal drama, psychological insight, and social commentary into a serious exploration of contemporary American values. *Promised Land* echoes Fitzgerald's *The Great Gatsby* in its embodiment of a vision of America in the story of its characters and echoes Chandler's *The Long Goodbye* in its use of the detective novel for a serious examination of character, especially the character of the hero. And despite the problems with secondary characters, the main characters are vividly portrayed. Susan Silverman continues to grow as a character and as an influence on Spenser, and the introduction of Hawk adds a new dimension to the novel. Not only is he an interesting character in his own right, his role as foil to Spenser offers Parker a new way of defining his hero's character. (pp. 68-9)

Mortal Stakes demonstrated that Parker could successfully combine the elements of good mystery writing—plot, pacing, mystery, suspense—with such literary techinques as three-dimensional characterization, symbolism, and imagery to produce a serious and compelling exploration of theme. The failure of *Promised Land* to repeat that success proves how difficult it is to accomplish the task and illustrates all too clearly that once the delicate balance between theme and action is upset in a mystery novel, the work as a whole suffers. . . .

The Judas Goat (1978) is a novel with enough action, adventure, and suspense to suggest that Parker was aware of the flaws that weakened *Promised Land.* He sought to avoid them in his new novel by emphasizing what the earlier novel lacked—action—and by returning to those elements with which he had demonstrated his greatest skill—vivid characterization and witty dialogue. (p. 69)

[There are] some significant differences between *The Judas Goat* and the previous Spenser books. For one thing, the novel is, strictly speaking, not a mystery novel—there is nothing for Spenser to solve. . . . [The] focus is on suspense and adventure, not mystery. Also, Parker abandons his usual Boston setting for such colorful places as London, Amsterdam, Copenhagen, and Montreal. This not only gives him an opportunity to describe fresh locations, but more importantly it prohibits him from developing specifically American themes, as he did in *God Save the Child* and *Promised Land*. . . . Parker doesn't totally relinquish his interest in social issues, however, for *The Judas Goat* obviously makes a strong indictment against terrorism, especially against those radical groups which display so little concern for human life that they have no compunction about tossing a bomb into a crowded restaurant where innocent people are likely to be hurt or killed. However, this is not the kind of complex issue that demands elaborate development, since senseless killing of innocent victims is hardly a morally ambiguous matter. (pp. 70-1)

Parker also eliminates many of the symbolic layers that encumbered the action of some of his previous novels, especially *Promised Land,* and this, coupled with a determined shift in emphasis from mystery to action, achieves his goal of refocusing attention on Spenser. (p. 71)

The Judas Goat is an important novel for Parker not only because it shows his willingness to attempt new departures—placing Spenser in a foreign setting, for example; but also because in it he takes measures—more action, sharper characterizations, increased dosages of ironic humor—to correct the drift that marred *Promised Land*. The ironic humor, for example, prevents Spenser from taking himself too seriously (which he tended to do in *Promised Land*). . . . [Instances] of self-deprecating humor, coupled with Spenser's quick-witted jests with Hawk and typically good-natured sexual banter with Susan, give the novel a liveliness that was notably lacking in *Promised Land*. Moreover, the whole narrative style is as crisp and invigorating as anything Parker has written. He even makes those scenes where Spenser stands around waiting for something to happen interesting to read. (pp. 80-1)

[Spenser] has grown significantly, especially in the area of self-knowledge, thanks in part to the frequent confrontations between his conscience and his actions, but more importantly because of his ever-deepening relationship with Susan. Even when she is absent, as she is for much of *The Judas Goat,* her presence is felt. . . . Parker's handling of Spenser's relationship with Susan effectively disproves Chandler's assertion that the love story and the detective story cannot exist in the same book. Not only do they coexist in Parker's novels, the love story adds an element of tension by serving as a poignant reminder of the vast distance that separates the mean streets from the quiet ones.

With each novel Parker has exhibited growing independence from his predecessors, confidently developing his own themes, characters, and stylistic idiom. . . . However, despite his innovative efforts, he has remained faithful to the conventions of the genre, so effectively laid down by his predecessors. He has thus earned for himself the right to be designated *the* legitimate heir to the Hammett-Chandler-Macdonald tradition, which, thanks to the efforts of writers like Parker, shows no sign of diminishing. (pp. 81-2)

David Geherin, "Robert B. Parker," in his Sons of Sam Spade, The Private-Eye Novel in the 70s: Robert B. Parker, Roger L. Simon, Andrew Bergman *(copyright © 1980 by Frederick Ungar Publishing Co., Inc.),* Ungar, 1980, pp. 5-82.

ANATOLE BROYARD

In "Early Autumn," by Robert B. Parker, the private eye has come a long way from the dissolute days when he was a hell-raising, hard-drinking womanizer with a license to carry a gun. Spenser, Mr. Parker's detective, is a baby-sitter in the seventh novel of this popular series.

He salvages Paul, a 15-year-old boy whose divorced parents each want him only to spite the other. Paul is "thin, nasty, apathetic and withdrawn." In a surge of supererogation, Spenser takes him to Maine and starts him running, boxing, lifting weights, reading, talking, listening to music and building a house. As you can see, "Early Autumn" is a bildungsroman.

In spite of Spenser's baby-sitting, he's a pretty rough customer and "Early Autumn" mixes violence and compassion in a better-than-average way. The book has one small flaw and one not so small: Mr. Parker says jab when he means a straight left and Spenser and Susan wisecrack during their lovemaking.

Anatole Broyard, in a review of "Early Autumn," in The New York Times *(© 1981 by The New York Times Company; reprinted by permission), January 21, 1981, p. C20.*

PETER S. PRESCOTT

Last year in "Early Autumn," Spenser made a man of a 15-year-old boy vicitimized by his affectless parents. "Ceremony" seems an alternative version of that novel. This time the child with the destructive parents is a girl, a high-school dropout who volunteers for a life of prostitution, then finds herself a prisoner of it: finally, when freed by Spenser, she finds she has no other talent, no other aim in life. Spenser is faced with an interesting moral decision: what is best for this homeless child? Unpaid, saddled with a job he never wanted but now cannot let go, he's a modern paladin. "It's a way to live," he says. "Anything else is confusion." "How did you ever get to be so big without growing up?" Susan asks. It's lines like that, puncturing the private-eye ethic without leaving lasting damage, which make the Spenser novels so engaging.

The contrast between Spenser and Susan's loving sexiness and the calculated sexual exploitation of children works very nicely here. Another asset is Spenser's sidekick, an improbable, ever-loyal, brutally efficient black man named Hawk. Parker is treading on thin ice with him—his black man does the dirty work the white man really shouldn't do (in "Early Autumn" Hawk shot the mobster, who needed shooting, when Spenser couldn't)—but he slides over it with good humor. And in "Ceremony" he brings off with good taste a story about an appalling subject. (pp. 71-2)

Peter S. Prescott, "The New Stellar Sleuths: 'Ceremony'," in Newsweek *(copyright 1982, by Newsweek, Inc.; all rights reserved; reprinted by permission), Vol. XCIX, No. 23, June 7, 1982, pp. 71-2.*

Linda (Olenik) Pastan

1932-

American poet.

Since the publication of her first collection of poetry, *A Perfect Circle of Sun,* in 1971, Pastan has evidenced a gift for expressing the everyday events of human life in a compelling manner. The poet considers this "dailiness" to be the soul of her work. She writes of the complications of family relationships in *Aspects of Eve* (1975), the acceptance of loss in *The Five Stages of Grief* (1978), and the conflicts of desire and obligation in *Waiting for My Life* (1982).

Pastan has been praised for her clear, unpretentious writing. Such writing, critics feel, effectively persuades the reader to look closely at the commonplace and to see its wonder. Because of her spare style and domestic subject matter, however, Pastan's critics have also noted that, at times, her poems are saved from sentimentality only by their disarming, yet dignified innocence. She uses traditional topics such as love, aging, loss, loneliness, and the search for identity, and pairs them with established allusions from folktales, legends, and biblical stories.

(See also *Contemporary Authors,* Vols. 61-64 and *Dictionary of Literary Biography,* Vol. 5.)

THOMAS LASK

The individual poems in "**A Perfect Circle of Sun**" fit so nicely into the total work and complement one another so successfully that it is easy to believe that Linda Pastan had conceived a book rather than single poems. Her concerns are uniform: the ties of family that bind three generations, a received heritage that she would not willingly let slip, the love of man and woman, a commodity that remains a wonder to her. Her lyrics are short, clear and neatly bitten off at the end. No loose threads show and neither does the joinery.

"**Second Son,**" in spite of its fierce metaphors, is a tender tribute to the very young child. "**Notes From the Delivery Room**" takes a wry look at herself at a moment when she is supremely womanly and supremely vulnerable. In "**Skylight,**" a circumscribed view of the poet's surroundings is used as the light-attracting mirror of a telescope, to bring distances into small compasses. "**At the Jewish Museum**" is more than homage to her ancestors. It emphasizes the obligations the older generation imposed. . . .

She has an image-making power. Time and again the appropriate comparison comes to hand with ease when summoned. . . . If I have a complaint it is that the past is too contained, the poetry understated. I can sense the strength of her feelings, but she doesn't transmit it or, perhaps I should say, transmits it too easily.

Thomas Lask, "Voices from the Distaff Side," in The New York Times *(© 1972 by The New York Times Company; reprinted by permission), August 18, 1972, p. 29.**

JANET BLOOM

Linda Pastan has pursued her craft assiduously and her work will be favorably received by many who accept her inhibited tragic or pathetic attitude in which she fights for life by coddling herself and being deprived. Quite typically, in "**View**" [in *A Perfect Circle of Sun*] Pastan complains of a boy playing basketball under a tree she uses for poetic perceptions. Although the poem ends in a lively fashion . . . she basically wishes that her vision not be disturbed by life since she does not greet the disturbance with welcome or wonder, even if she does finally take it in. . . .

A Perfect Circle of Sun only invites the reader to look into it as into an easter egg with *mise en scène*—rather stark with no frosting—to admire the finesse and complexity of its small tableaux. The reader can only observe, cannot identify or participate, cannot be swept into a new angle or energy. Pastan's poems just go on being themselves in a hard shelled way. She does not often see or fight for life as sharing, exchanges, transfusions, but, as in "**Early Walk,**" sees it as eternal, if not hopeless, cold division. (p. 130)

There is virtue in Pastan's surefooted acceptance of life, as there is in her smooth technique—but at a cost. She never loses clarity and control; she miniaturizes and cuts off or pares down life, excluding its hazy, rough margins, confusions, and passions. She seems to have given up or in and serves up her poems as dull duck à l'orange neatly arranged under glass. (p. 131)

Yet Pastan has a toughness I like. My favorite poem in *A Perfect Circle of Sun* is **"Emily Dickinson"** because in it she goes straight out on a limb of admiration and doesn't have to break the limb or double back on it to some frozen balance or tepid impasse. . . . Pastan has an easy, strong, and direct rhythm; and a gift of observation . . . and sharp images. . . . I would like to see more of that boldness in Linda Pastan's work, and a reaching for a new air of expectation. . . . (pp. 131-32)

> *Janet Bloom, "A Plea for Proper Boldness," in* Parnassus: Poetry in Review *(copyright © Poetry in Review Foundation), Vol. 1, No. 1, Fall-Winter, 1972, pp. 130-34.**

CHOICE

The free verse [in the brief poems of *Aspects of Eve*] is in the objectivist vein, with short lines (sometimes one word) and little interest in stanzaic arrangement. . . . [Pastan] introspects on domestic concerns, but her ideas are [easy] to follow because of the precise figurative language. Although the verse is plain-spoken and direct, its disarming simplicity is not artless, for the poet conveys much with great economy of means. Her concise diction and carefully chosen imagery communicate with clarity and immediacy, suggesting William Carlos Williams at his sparest and least pretentious. There is nothing major here, nothing truly ambitious, but the individual poems express an unmistakable genuineness of feeling. Although the lack of intensity and passion is no doubt deliberate, the poems seem occasionally too casual, too mundane, to grasp and hold the imagination. (pp. 1447-48)

> *A review of "Aspects of Eve: Poems," in* Choice *(copyright © 1976 by American Library Association; reprinted by permission of the American Library Association), Vol. 12, No. 11, January, 1976, pp. 1447-48.*

PAUL RAMSEY

Linda Pastan's *Aspects of Eve* has dream images, essencing images, house and family and garden imagery, Old Testament imagery, classical imagery, usually in short narratives about coming to terms with her experience. The poems are sure of touch, rightly distanced. The terms are not small terms; she says important, clear words about some important subjects: death, endurance, kindness. Her poems go unexpected ways through several kinds of imagery and saying, and they work out as wholes, naturally, uncontrivedly. **"David"** and **"Algera"** are, in my judgment, the two best poems in the book; but my favorite is **"Folk Tale."** It's nice, among all the current goings-on, to have a poem for parents. (p. 539)

> *Paul Ramsey, "Image and Essence: Some American Poetry of 1975," in* The Sewanee Review *(reprinted by permission of the editor; © 1976 by The University of the South), Vol. LXXXIV, No. 3, Summer, 1976, pp. 533-41.**

KATHRYN RUBY

[*Aspects of Eve* is a] conventional and intense book. Despite frequent references to old myths—Greek, Biblical, and liter-

ary—these poems lose none of their relevance and power. The woman's voice is contemporary, whether as mother . . . or as a wife. . . . These poems about family life and parenthood are refreshing without being—I hate to say it—"sentimental." A personal book, without being private, *Aspects of Eve* bears reading and rereading. (p. 105)

> *Kathryn Ruby, "Chants, Parables, Sagas: New Books by Women Poets," in* Ms. *(© 1976 Ms. Magazine Corp.), Vol. V, No. 3, September, 1976, pp. 103-05.**

SAMUEL HAZO

For the poetry of Linda Pastan I have a continuing and solid—respect. Never baroque, never sentimental, never suffused with a militant feminism or any other transient *ism* that forces poetry to yield to ideology or sociology or worse. What is she then? Simply a competent poet. And not because of one or two good poems but because all her poems have a kind of uniform excellence. Now the earlier poems of *A Perfect Circle of Sun* and *Aspects of Eve* have a shelf companion in her new *The Five Stages of Grief*. Her language in this new book, as in its predecessors, is spare as gristle and just as hard and, if I'm not pushing the comparison too far, just as luminous. There is not a poem in the book that does not have the succinctness of final precision. . . . But succinctness is only half the story. The other and deeper half is vision. This is a woman with convictions; she is not satisfied to be mere litmus paper to the world. How can I describe this vision except to say that it is maturely Jewish in the humanistic sense in which Spinoza's vision is Jewish—an almost sophisticated mysticism leavened with wit and an awareness of the ironic. It is the very soul of the title poem as well as the poems like **"Self Portrait at 44"** and **"Because."** But the one that reveals it best is **"A Short History of Judaic Thought in the Twentieth Century."** . . . (pp. 537-38)

> *Samuel Hazo, "The Experience of the Idea," in* The Hudson Review *(copyright © 1978 by The Hudson Review, Inc.; reprinted by permission), Vol. XXXI, No. 3, Autumn, 1978, pp. 536-47.**

CHOICE

[Linda Pastan's *The five stages of grief: Poems*] bears resemblance to her previous works in its quality of imagery and consistency of tone. The imagery seems always familiar yet exactly correct, like an old myth restored in new words. These new words, the images and statements, then weave themselves into a voice that speaks, rails, sings of life, of its disappointments, inevitabilities, and possibilities. But this voice has the consistent tonal qualities a child remembers as being behind the stories heard read through the winter of sleepless nights. This consistency of tone unifies the whole volume as clearly as do the physical divisions, the five stages one goes through before the acceptance of grief—denial, anger, bargaining, depression, and finally acceptance. Even more important than the overall structure of the work is the fine structure of each poem. The poems are delicately crafted, like small carvings amazingly designed yet simple and totally precise in every detail. The content of the poems reflects intelligence, vitality, and a mind of forgiveness.

> *A review of "The Five Stages of Grief: Poems," in* Choice *(copyright © 1978 by American Library Association; reprinted by permission of the American*

Library Association), Vol. 15, No. 10, December, 1978, p. 1372.

PETER STITT

Linda Pastan is a master of the well-made poem. Her use of technique is so precise, so careful, that it seems she would be a perfect example to use in teaching young poets how to control their material. Her best poems are specimens, admirable for the telling way in which their point is made. She shows best, too, in single poems; her volumes tend not to have much cohesion—even when, as in *The Five Stages of Grief,* such cohesion is obviously an important goal for the volume. The book is arranged according to the five stages—denial, anger, bargaining, depression, acceptance—and the jacket tells us that the source of the original grief is coming to terms with our own death, our own life. The concept is vague, and its appearance in the poems is equally vague, perhaps all we could expect. There is another pattern present in the volume, one which seems in fact to undercut this one. In several poems, the speaker (obviously a woman) asks someone—husband, lover—not to abandon her. In the final poem, which is also the title poem, Pastan goes through all five stages of grief in response to the statement: "I lost you." Indeed, after acceptance is supposedly achieved, the poem ends with the speaker again plaintively uttering the same words: "I have lost you." In terms of theme, we seem to have gotten nowhere—in poem and book alike. (pp. 928-29)

Clarity and imagery are her strongest virtues; when she relies on these rather than on a flippant sense of humor, she can be counted on to produce outstanding work. (p. 930)

Peter Stitt, "Violence, Imagery, and Introspection," in The Georgia Review *(copyright, 1979, by the University of Georgia), Vol. XXXIII, No. 4, Winter, 1979, pp. 927-32.**

DESMOND GRAHAM

[Loneliness] provides the creative conflict out of which many of [Linda Pastan's] poems are made. After journal-like, imagistic beginnings, the colloquial style she develops through the four collections from which her *Selected Poems* . . . are taken, increasingly sets out to explore a double loneliness: that of a commitment to family relationships caught in a time-scale (children grow up etc.), and that of commitment to the isolated life of a poet. Her witty style and capacity to grow poems through extending and shifting metaphor widen the significances of these two areas, but her strength lies in her basic human understanding and her ability to find and time metaphors. (pp. 74-5)

Desmond Graham, in a review of "Selected Poems," in Stand *(copyright © by Stand), Vol. 22, No. 1 (1980), pp. 74-5.*

ALAN BROWNJOHN

Linda Pastan's *Selected Poems* are written almost entirely in a mode that lends itself to expressions of limitation and low spirits: short poems, short lines, mild sub-romantic diction. . . . Many of them teeter on the brink of sentimentality (and there is an obvious danger of sameness about the routine). Yet somehow they do draw away from it: a well-controlled, resolving image will often work successfully against the current pulling a poem down towards bathos. Now in her forties, she has only been writing during the 1970s, and it's encouraging to see that towards the end of this volume she is getting more strength and resonance into these modestly structured pieces.

Alan Brownjohn, in a review of "Selected Poems," in Encounter *(© 1980 by Encounter Ltd.), Vol. LIV, No. 4, April, 1980, p. 66.*

THE VIRGINIA QUARTERLY REVIEW

Linda Pastan's voice [in *Waiting for My Life*] grows in quiet maturity, as her poems continue to combine delicate irony of vision with grace and elegance of expression. Hers is a distinctive style, pure, clear, and precise, her images chosen with a sure sense of balance and proportion. The short lines and economy of language may give the impression of a slight poem, but this spareness corresponds to an aim for simplicity and integrity. (pp. 25-6)

A review of "Waiting for My Life," in The Virginia Quarterly Review *(copyright, 1982, by The Virginia Quarterly Review, The University of Virginia), Vol. 58, No. 1 (Winter, 1982), pp. 25-6.*

DAVE SMITH

"What do I mean by straight writing, I have been asked. I mean, in part, writing that is not mannered, overconscious, or at war with common sense," Marianne Moore wrote. Nothing could better describe the writing of Linda Pastan, which is everywhere accessible, clear, and straight. But it is a straightness that has some of Frost's walking stick to it. She is so in command of herself and of her abilities that you turn the pages of her fourth collection, *Waiting For My Life,* with almost the same expectations that you have when you fall asleep for the night, that tomorrow is entirely possible and probably more interesting than today. If Linda Pastan is like anybody now writing it is William Stafford; that steadiness, that willingness to be with everything in the world, to be just what one is, and to know it acutely.

Waiting For My Life begins with an epilogue and a prologue, in that order, which suggest that between the end and the beginning there is only one story. We imperfectly understand this story but we may not avert our faces, for if we do we are condemned to darkness and silence. This is the consequence of a fairy tale, a tale which is fabular but which must be impeccably true as it is local for the imagination. Pastan's poetry, like the good tale, legend, and dream, rides just above the bowing ice beneath which the black water waits. Death is less a direct threat in her than it is context, presence, the story within which all other stories fit and pulse. Artists, she says, "are only translators, uneasy/unequipped." The responsible translator must give us as much flesh as possible, not merely skeleton or dummy. Yet it is exactly the apprehended unknown we are always losing in our translations and I think this is why Pastan so frequently mentions secrets, codes, shadows, emblems, disguises; all those words which suggest the divided kingdom of tales. Often enough in her poems someone is saying we don't know what we want, only that we do *want.* This would constitute a pitiful vagueness in Pastan's book if it were not functional (and there are a few less than impressive, merely vague poems here); that is, the context of desire is slowly examined, given objects, brought to crisis, and to a degree resolved. A poet who knew less of her abilities and limits could not walk the lines that Linda Pastan does.

The tale of *Waiting For My Life* is that of a suburban woman and her "dailiness." . . . Emily Dickinson took her dailiness to the heights of metaphysical vision and, it may be, Dickinson is Pastan's ghost, though less perhaps in sound than in what to look at and how to show it. . . . Pastan's tale is, as I think Dickinson's was for the most part, the constant attempt to know how beauty accommodates itself to and survives the beast. Maybe that is all poetry's life ever is. If that is true it is because poetry, like the tale, will never go very far from the heart in crisis.

Perhaps the distinctive quality of *Waiting For My Life* is not the utter absence of bad writing, not the unfaltering professional excellence of the poet, and not even the lifting of suburban life to the tale's powerful recognition of what we are, we fearful and hopeful creatures. Rather it is the wry, wise depth of experience expressed with such scrupulous indifference to what everything *means* that we know this is the poetry of innocence; we know it is incapable of ignorance, deception, malevolence, or mendacity. Partly Pastan now writes what is called "autumnal" poetry; that which looks back on the harm's way that life is, and partly it is Pastan's ability to turn gnomic detail into understated symbols of how things flatly are. She shows us parents musing on the lives of grown children, on their own altered flesh, the weather, the slackened but not dead fevers of desire, those moments spent at windows in kitchens or gardens where we are astonished at the speed and movement that is all the not-us. And yet there is another distinction in this book, a sly presence not heretofore so evident in Pastan's poetry.

"Who is it accuses us of safety?" Linda Pastan asks in the middle section which she calls "**The War Between Desire and Dailiness.**" Her poem defends the sometimes domestic, sometimes introspective life this way: "We have chosen the dangerous life." Pastan would argue that the best defense is a good offense. A little like Hopkins rappelling the cliffs of the mind, Pastan now takes on those mountains of the suppressed life, fidelity and betrayal. They are, of course, metaphors for poetry, imagination, and knowledge. They ask Prufrock's questions about daring, presumption, change, and they have the real urgency of sexual passion. But this urgency is tempered by the recognition that love which is for some a salvation is for others betrayal and madness. Renewal and destruction, obligation and will, now sit at the heart of Pastan's writing like toad and prince. (pp. 40-1)

Linda Pastan has come to ask to what shall we be faithful, the aching thaw of desire or "echoes/from the buried chambers/ of the heart?" Dickinson spent a lifetime asking that question and her answer was to disappear into poems that refused any answer. Pastan says: "Let dailiness win." It sounds as if she has chosen safety but the line ends a poem with anything but conviction. In "**Returning,**" "**When the Moment Is Over,**" "**Eyes Only**" and others Pastan's sensuality gets the boy so much wanted. Who accuses her of safety? She does, down there in the heart's boneshop. *Waiting For My Life* is full of surprises that make it far from daily. It keeps a low heat, but it is radiant heat nonetheless. . . . (p. 41)

Dave Smith, "Some Recent American Poetry: Come All Ye Fair & Tender Ladies" (copyright © 1982 by World Poetry, Inc.; reprinted by permission of Dave Smith), in The American Poetry Review, *Vol. 11, No. 1, January-February, 1982, pp. 36-46.**

PUBLISHERS WEEKLY

Linda Pastan appeals to a broad audience, from the readers of serious poetry journals to the readers of women's magazines. Stark simplicity is her hallmark, and her values are conventional and family-oriented. Pastan's language is plain, her lines are short, her message is heartwarming. Within these small formats, she exhibits a fine technical skill and genuine inspiration. Many of her metaphors, which are never overly ingenious or forced, are chosen from the Bible and other classical sources. Pastan's work depicts continuity in the dailiness of life and the peaceable kingdom of domesticity. Drawn from four books that have appeared over a decade, [the poems in "**PM/AM: New and Selected Poems**"] are highly complementary. Many poems that seemed minor and fragmentary first time around are transformed by the unity of their context here. "**PM/AM**" merits a reexamination of Linda Pastan's place in contemporary poetry.

A review of "PM/AM: New and Selected Poems," in Publishers Weekly *(reprinted from the September 10, 1982 issue of* Publishers Weekly, *published by R.R. Bowker Company, a Xerox company; copyright © 1982 by Xerox Corporation), Vol. 222, No. 11, September 10, 1982, p. 73.*

HUGH SEIDMAN

"**PM/AM**" is a selection from Linda Pastan's four previous books, plus some newer poems. . . .

As her rather low-key title might imply, Miss Pastan is a chronicler of the quotidian, domestic world. . . .

Miss Pastan is clever at turning images and references to serve her purposes symbolically, though her poetry takes few overt risks of either form or subject and her main gesture is one of reiteration and confirmation rather than illumination of the sources and consequences of her obsessions and turmoils. (p. 33)

Besides family, . . . [some] poems invoke death, failed relationships, feminism and the role of the poet. . . . Her diction is uncomplicated and direct, with little overt manipulation for rhetorical effect or intellective complexity. . . .

At the end of "**Friday's Child,**" Miss Pastan [calls all words "epitaphs"]. . . . This may be true, but it is certainly just as true that words also imply energies of rebirth. It is this latter possibility of language that one often misses in her work, although one cannot deny that her vision has gained in depth over the years. Her last book has a stateliness and solidity of tone not reached in earlier ones, and there is evidence of more emotional opening out in some of her newest pieces. (p. 34)

Hugh Seidman, "Word Play," in The New York Times Book Review *(© 1983 by The New York Times Company; reprinted by permission), February 20, 1983, pp. 6, 33-4.**

Marge Piercy
1936-

American poet and novelist.

Piercy is a prominent and sometimes controversial author whose left-wing politics inform and shape her work. She has said that she became aware of social and political injustice at an early age. As her politics developed, Piercy's attitude and writing became more specifically feminist in focus.

Piercy has said that she doesn't "understand distinctions between private and social poetry"; the obliteration of that dichotomy—between "political" and "personal"—characterizes her fiction as well as her poetry. Her writing reflects a continual struggle to reconcile the disparity between an individual's attempt to realize his or her potential and the conditions of contemporary society working against such personal growth.

Although her novels are generally realistic reflections of contemporary society—for example, her recent *Braided Lives* (1983) explores the hardships encountered by a woman coming of age in the 1950s—Piercy has also experimented with science fiction. Her first attempt, *Dance the Eagle to Sleep* (1970), depicts a dystopia, drawing many parallels with the turmoil of the 1960s. *Woman on the Edge of Time* (1976) portrays a utopia set in the year 2137. In this novel Piercy restructures traditional institutions such as marriage, capitalism, and patriarchal power, offering an alternative equally beneficial to both men and women.

Piercy's voice, sometimes raw and angry, other times tender and warm, infuses her poems with a force so bold and immediate that it alienates some critics, while others praise her for her courageous and hearty energy. Her earlier volumes were marked by an outraged protest that has lightened with more recent works, notably *The Moon Is Always Female* (1980). In this volume her images draw on nature and commonplace objects to evoke not only anger, but also humor and a celebration of life.

(See also *CLC*, Vols. 3, 6, 14, 18 and *Contemporary Authors*, Vols. 21-24, rev. ed.)

JOHN LEONARD

Marge Piercy is full of exhortation. Her first novel ["**Going Down Fast**"]—about urban "renewal," the radical community, the tab-top non-calorific managerial class in Chicago—seizes you by the lapels (or the dashiki) and flings you into a bomb site. Her "fate" is man-made, a compound of power and venality; her method, a relentless exactitude, a Doris Lessing like accumulation of raw detail.

"**Going Down Fast**" refers both to buildings under the wrecker's ball and to the people living in those buildings, the permanently evicted. From multiple points of view Miss Piercy tells the interconnected stories of two young female teachers (Jewish, black), a blues singer, a welfare caseworker, an underground filmmaker. Their deceptions and accommodations

weave in and out of a political essay vividly describing how real estate promoters, social scientists and a university make war not for, but on, the poor.

Miss Piercy has previously published two books of poetry. Her gift attends her here, in evoking the awful grandeur of steel towns, the sexual magic of money, the claustrophobia of refuge, the desperation of the self-seeking and the self-deceived. That her characters should derive from their experience madness or death or radical commitment flows convincingly from the logic of the "fat" nation she examines.

Given our technology, Miss Piercy is saying, we no longer need a labor pool of the unskilled. Organized, such a labor pool (such Luddites, allied with ideologues) might inconvenience the mechanisms of consumption. We are, she says, prepared to rid ourselves of this inconvenience, while wearing our pieties like boutonnieres. I believe her, and her savage novel.

John Leonard, "Two Good Books, Two Different Realities," in The New York Times *(© 1969 by The New York Times Company; reprinted by permission), October 21, 1969, p. 45.**

MARTIN LEVIN

[Once inside Marge Piercy's "**Going Down Fast**"] you find a lively, vital montage of the protest establishment, Chicago style. The title implies a downbeat motif: a callously conceived university housing project slamming into a poor neighborhood thickly seeded with the intelligentsia. But before the walls come tumbling down, Miss Piercy exhibits some life styles that offer a low enough silhouette to survive urban demolition. . . .

Miss Piercy fills a rapidly shifting scene with well-defined characters, and attunes them to the swing of the wreckers' ball. . . . [She] gets beneath the skins of her dramatis personae, black and white. Some transient trappings notwithstanding, the motivation of Rowley and Anna is as durable as what moved Tristan and Isolde.

> *Martin Levin, in a review of "Going Down Fast,"*
> *in* The New York Times Book Review *(© 1969 by The New York Times Company; reprinted by permission), November 9, 1969, p. 70.*

ERICA JONG

Writers who serve two muses—the muse of poetry and the muse of prose—often find that their passionate and intense lyrical outbursts find their way into poems, while their longer speculations on society and the way people interact with each other psychologically and politically, grow into novels. This is the case with Marge Piercy, an immensely gifted poet and novelist whose range and versatility have made it hard for her talents to be adequately appreciated critically. (pp. 12, 14)

Though her novel, **"Small Changes,"** was rather too polemical for my taste, there is no denying that each of her novels has been breathtakingly ambitious and clearly the work of a major talent. I have followed her poems closely . . . and this new book, **"Living in the Open,"** is undoubtedly the best. The style is the same style Piercy had grown into by her first book: powerfully rhythmic free verse which uses vivid, often surreal images. . . . Piercy's is a poetry of statement as well as a poetry of image; often, in fact, the image *makes* the statement. . . . It is a poetry remarkably free of artifice for artifice's sake, free of posturing of any sort. It is direct, powerful and accessible without being unsubtle. . . . (p. 14)

> *Erica Jong, in a review of "Living In the Open," in* The New York Times Book Review *(© 1976 by The New York Times Company; reprinted by permission), September 12, 1976, pp. 12, 14, 16.*

JEAN ROSENBAUM

In her poems, Piercy strikes out at the attitudes, institutions, and structures which impede natural growth and development and thus destroy wholeness; she also celebrates the moments when life is consummate and joyful.

As a woman, Piercy is particularly concerned about women and their ability to participate with integrity in a fully-realized life. In a number of poems, she examines the female growing-up process in America; in each case, the young girl is shown to possess great potential strength and individuality which is slowly but surely diverted or covered over. (p. 194)

[As Piercy sees it, the] incredibly strong and vital woman inside the passive girl-child will eventually explode or bloom. The intense pressure demands resolution. The resolution is complex, however. Does the explosion preclude the bloom or does it cause it? What is destroyed by the grenade—the inner person or outward appearances and false, constricting assumptions?

What is necessary for the flower to bloom? Using the same image of the flower [found in **"The woman in the ordinary"**], the poem, **"The morning half-life blues,"** summarizes the situation by juxtaposing and contrasting the sterile, depersonalized, self-denigrating half-life endured by young working girls with the natural, productive lives for which they yearn. . . . In the poem, the world of metal and concrete assumes metaphorically the role of natural sustainer, but it cannot give real warmth or nourishment: The synthetic "fuzzy coats promised to be warm as fur," but they are not; the "grove of skyscrapers" should furnish a sheltering garden where individuals can cease being inanimate commodities, but here is no such garden. Piercy is not arguing for an isolated retreat from society but for a real community where "work is real" and life is not a half-life, where life can ripen into "sound fruit," not be frozen at its beginning.

If the fulfillment of healthy growth is the good to be striven for, then how can women—whose development is stunted at every stage by the culture in which they live, by the mothers and fathers and lovers and strangers with whom they interact, and by their own too passive acquiesence in the process—ever hope to achieve a mature strength, a unified wholeness? Piercy believes that first there must be a conscious experience of self-realization; a woman must become aware of herself as independent person. The woman must acknowledge that even though she has been formed in large part out of the pervading culture, she is still finally responsible for herself. She alone can initiate changing in her situation. The ability to do so, moreover, is already present in her, for she has great strength. . . . (pp. 195-97)

The birth of one's own world is an exultant event, but one which is often accompanied by pain. Part of the process of self-realization involves learning to be assertive, egotistical, convinced of one's own worth and independent strength. This is a positive, healthy development even though it may mean a slow and painful growth away from someone. . . . (p. 198)

The woman who has been her own magician, who knows and likes herself and accepts her inborn strength is magnificent to behold and deserving of praise. In her poem, **"Icon,"** Piercy describes such a woman: powerful, alert, unsubjugated, with mind and body interacting harmoniously. . . . (p. 199)

In addition to being whole within her self, a woman must interact with others, both women and men. She must resolutely retain her personal integrity while simultaneously searching out and sustaining the integrity of others. This task demands the ability to be open to experiencing other people, to be able to reach out and touch, to trust, to risk hurt. All of these things are made especially difficult by a culture in which competition and possession are primary values and values which extend to personal relationships. (p. 200)

If, in the past, women have been betrayed by other women, they have also been betrayed by the very men they have fought so hard to please, and the betrayal has been of the mind and spirit as well as the body. In a particularly painful and bitter poem, **"In the men's room(s),"** Piercy describes a woman who has believed that she will be accepted as men's equal if she ignores the typical bread and babies concerns of women and joins instead in the high-minded, abstract, intellectual pursuits of men. . . . Her recognition that men perceive an offering of "breasts and thighs" no matter what the woman's intent leads Piercy to reject "abstract nouns" as the absolute good. Traditionally, a male/female dichotomy has been assumed in which the male has been viewed primarily as an objective, rational, abstract theorizer, too busy with the important intellectual progress of the world to be bothered by daily problems. The female, on the other hand, has been viewed primarily as an emotional, subjective, grubby doer of ordinary tasks. Man equals mind equals significant mode of knowing and being; woman equals body equals lesser mode of knowing and being. What Piercy wants to do is to change the value assigned to these two modes; and, in addition, she wants to synthesize and unify the separate parts to form whole people: thinking, feeling men and women, confident in mind and body.

The idea sounds absurdly simple and almost self-evidently commonplace. Who would disagree? And yet, the difficulty of living the idea is made apparent in particular situations, in isolated experience of everyday life, and it is the difficulty of this struggle for completeness which underlies Piercy's poems of men and women together. (pp. 201-02)

> Jean Rosenbaum, "You Are Your Own Magician: A Vision of Integrity in the Poetry of Marge Piercy," in Modern Poetry Studies (copyright 1977, by Jerome Mazzaro), Vol. VIII, No. 3, Winter, 1977, pp. 193-205.

VICTOR CONTOSKI

Because of Marge Piercy's strong views on social reform, from the very beginning her work has almost automatically divided people into two groups: those opposed to wide-sweeping social reform, and those in favor of it. Nevertheless she finds herself in the rather ambiguous position of being recognized, even embraced, by both the Movement, loosely-bound groups dedicated to radical change in American life, and the Establishment. She writes about radical living styles, communes, war protests, and women's liberation; yet her books are published by such institutions as Pocket Books and Doubleday. The standard technique of propaganda, over-simplification, separates "them" from "us" in her work; yet once this distinction has been made, her best work, while retaining elements of propaganda, notes similarities between the two groups as well as differences. While it focuses on the social problems of America, it focuses also on her own personal problems, so that tension exists not only between "us" and "them," but between "us" and "me."

Not content to wait for happiness and prosperity in some other life, she is driven to find a social and personal happiness on this earth, and the driving force behind her poetry is a stubborn utopian vision. At the same time she remains aware—almost too aware—of the obstacles, social and personal, confronting her. In **"The Peaceable Kingdom"** (*Breaking Camp* . . .), she comments on the famous American painting by Edward Hicks wherein all animals live side by side in idyllic harmony. (pp. 205-06)

The poem contrasts Hicks's fantasy with the actual history of the United States. . . . This contrast between American dream and American reality motivates Marge Piercy's poetry. (pp. 206-07)

Her first book, *Breaking Camp* . . . , presents a rather strange mixture of styles. **"Last Scene in the First Act"** . . . , a clever, ironic meditation on a pair of lovers, shows the slick poetic technique of the academic poets of the 1950's. . . . In **"A Cold and Married War"** she complains of her lover's indifference: "His cock crowed / I know you not." There is even a sonnet.

But in spite of such superficial cleverness, a breathing person moves behind the poetry. We know her life, her concerns.

The first poem in the book, **"Visiting a Dead Man on a Summer Day"** . . . shows the poet in Graceland cemetery in Chicago where she has gone to visit the tomb of Louis Sullivan. She compares his grave with the Getty tomb and sees the contrast as symbolic of American life. (p. 207)

[This poem] has much in common with propaganda. Its subjects, the country, the past, the poor, are so vast that the poet cannot hope to develop completely her thoughts about them. Instead she relies on a common interpretation of history which she assumes she shares with the reader. The image of the poor housed in sewers and filing cabinets is a startling exaggeration which serves both poetry and propaganda. And the extreme imagery reinforces the basic divisions of the poem. On the one hand we have the heavy, the cold, the mechanical, and the closed-in darkness (mausoleum, iron, sewers, filing cabinets, and Chicago itself); on the other we have the light, the heat, and the organic (men, grass, meteor). Yet much of the impact of the poem comes from imagery that unexpectedly applies to both sides. People burn their body heat naturally, but they are also burned to death by mechanical means in Southeast Asia. And the state, which throughout the poem is associated with the cold and the mechanical, has a "vast rumbling gut" which digests its members—and we are shocked by the natural imagery in its unnatural context.

The basic imagery of **"Visiting a Dead Man on a Summer Day"**—even the title contains the basic contrast between cold and heat—is expanded throughout the rest of *Breaking Camp,* which itself progresses through summer and winter and ends with the approach of spring. **"S. Dead," "Hallow Eve with Spaces for Ghosts,"** and **"Landed Fish"** (which concerns the death of her Uncle Danny) are other poems which treat the relationship between the living and the dead. Body heat between lovers is reflected in the stars of the cosmos, and the image of the meteor, so seemingly casual in the last parts of **"Visiting a Dead Man"** and **"The Peaceable Kingdom"** underlies the entire book, indeed her entire utopian vision. Everything and everybody loses heat. People burn—literally in Vietnam, figuratively in love, and even mythologically when the sun god visits a sunbather and burns her to ashes. (pp. 208-09)

In contrast **"The Simplification"** . . . presents a capitalist, who like the poet, burns—but with coldness instead of heat. And his "burning" moves the business world. . . . Rooms *revolve* (beautiful word!) around him like planets around a sun, and suddenly we move from the specific to the general. The basic opposition of the two systems results not only from their differences in America in the 1960's but from their elemental opposition throughout the galaxies of our universe.

But, as the title **"The Simplification"** suggests, the poet is not content to rest with such broad division between the good and the bad. In **"The 184th Demonstration"** . . . she notes uneasily similarities between the two. (p. 209)

In the final poem of the book, **"Breaking Camp"** . . . spring begins, but it brings no corresponding regeneration to the human spirit. "Peace," the poet confesses, "was a winter hope." Civilization appears to be breaking up; an atomic holocaust threatens. . . . The poet and her lover, isolated from the rest of the world, follow their star, though significantly it is a *private* star, an inward light, "the north star of your magnetic conscience." The community seems to have vanished.

Hard Loving . . . bears a two line dedication: "from the Movement / to the Movement." The prefatory poem, **"Walking into Love"** . . ., which seems to continue the journey begun in the last poem of her previous book, sets a double focus.

> The eyes of others
> measure and condemn.
> The eyes of others are watches ticking no.
> My friend hates you.
> Between you I turn and turn
> holding my arm as if it were broken.

She seeks a personal and a social love, and both come hard. "Others" oppose the lovers. Even in her own group, one of her friends *hates* the lover (no half-way emotions in Piercy's circles). The poet is torn not only between society in general and her lover, but between him and a close friend; and this fragmentation of the radicals, the "we" of Piercy's elemental opposites, sets the tone of the book.

In the first of three sections, **"The Death of the Small Commune,"** she shows the difficulties of building a new society. **"Community"** . . . presents a demonstration in front of the Pentagon, "our Bastille," where generals "armed like Martians" seem to lack even the appearance of humans. Yet the next two poems show the defenseless poet threatened not by generals but by those around her. She no longer distinguishes between "them" and "us" but between "them" and "me." In **"Embryos"** . . . she is so frail that the very size of the physical world menaces her. . . . Then come poems concerning other members of the small commune, and the last three poems in the section deal with falling out of love, first with an individual, then with the community itself. (pp. 210-11)

Then she withdraws from the commune into a new personal relationship. Her social sense, always present, seems less imperative. When love comes, it is simple, intense, and physical. . . . Such love restores the poet. . . . (pp. 211-12)

Yet she cannot conceive an idealistic love that transcends the flesh. In **"Crabs"** . . . she looks at coitus from the point of view of the insects, a technique well suited to mocking romantic love. . . . The final lines of this apparently whimsical poem show the poet's bitterness. . . . The boundary between the real and the ideal remains. Indeed, the title *Hard Loving* seems like an understatement.

The poet then returns to a social context in the third section, **"Curse of the Earth Magician,"** striving to broaden her love so that she can share it with all her comrades. The symbol of the Pentagon returns. In spite of the failures in the first section, the poet here tries again to recapture at least part of the American dream, the Peaceable Kingdom. The man she loves serves not as a retreat into domesticity and the white suburbs but as a symbol of what society too can accomplish. Emboldened by her love, she speaks with a new certainty. A fatalistic Nordic philosophy runs through the section. . . . One must fight, though the battle and even the war might well be lost. Her fatalism, rage, and love make a haunting poetry, a poetry of propaganda such as we have not yet had in America. (p. 212)

The book ends with humanity at the point of making one of its most crucial choices. "Sisters and brothers in movement," she proclaims, "we carry in the wet cuneiform of proteins / the long history of working to be human." Mankind must either

"fail into ashes, / fail into metal and dry bones and paper, / or break through into a sea of shared abundance / where man shall join man / in salty joy, in flowing trust."

But in *To Be of Use* . . . we find a different kind of fragmentation of the "sisters and brothers" of the Movement. Here men are equated with the mechanical life-destroying forces in the universe, women with the natural life-enhancing ones. The first section of the book, **"A Just Anger,"** is composed of poems of outrage, an outrage directed, for the most part, against the male establishment that has condemned the poet and her sisters to secondary roles in life. Unfortunately most of the poems in this section fail as poetry because both oppressed and oppressors are utterly predictable. Yet if the level of poetry is somewhat below Piercy's usual standards because her rage is directed exclusively at "them," the poems are nevertheless important in that they present an aspect of the real world so far from the American dream that merely to describe it becomes a call for social reform.

The second section is more optimistic. The poet includes several love poems, although sex here is less a unification than a collision—sometimes an explosion. . . . In **"Doing It Differently"** she seeks new relationships between male and female, but social institutions intrude. The problem remains that personal equality cannot come without a corresponding change in institutions, which in turn cannot change without new personal relationships. (pp. 213-14)

The third section consists of eleven poems to woodcuts of tarot cards. Among the author's most ambitious work, they attempt nothing less than a remaking of some of the myths behind western culture. . . . [Her] emphasis on myth, as opposed to plain truth or lies, implies an emphasis on the non-rational, the subconscious, the archetypal, which hitherto have played but a small role in her work. (pp. 214-15)

The book ends with one of Marge Piercy's strangest poems, one which presents a mystic utopian vision of the future as a wondrous Child. But unlike her earlier glance at the Peaceable Kingdom, when she consciously reminded herself and the reader of the animals she had eaten, here is none of the rationality of the earlier experience. She who has always been so certain with words finds that she can describe her vision only in negative terms and questions. It blinds her, stuns her. (p. 215)

Marge Piercy's work as a whole shares much with propaganda: passionate commitment, power, and simplicity. Her poetry is emotional, righteous, and often clever, lacking, by and large, the subtle insights and revelations of wisdom, though it may be developing them. In her passion for a new order she sees motes everywhere, even in her own eyes, and casts them out with a vengeance—sometimes so violently she takes the eyes out with them. Much of her energy appears negative: she opposes more strongly than she supports; she hates more passionately than she loves. Yet in spite of these characteristics, or perhaps because of them, a vision of an ideal life, a Peaceable Kingdom, pervades her work, a vision that remains impressive precisely because she must work so hard to maintain it. (p. 216)

Victor Contoski, "Marge Piercy: A Vision of the Peaceable Kingdom," in Modern Poetry Studies *(copyright 1977, by Jerome Mazzaro), Vol. VIII, No. 3, Winter, 1977, pp. 205-16.*

JEROME MAZZARO

In Marge Piercy's *The Moon Is Always Female* . . . interests in epistemology are reduced to interests in female and male consciousness. For Piercy, poetry becomes a masking or "lateral sliding" continually threatened by a "woman inside" and a lover's demands. Love presumably is a mutual wanting wherein both parties fight each other for their fulfillments, each wrestling to open the other up (**"Arriving"**). Individual poems, however, are likely to stress only the woman's role and anguish. **"Excursions, incursions,"** for instance, describes a series of female/male encounters in which women are unwilling objects of sex fantasies, unwanted intruders into male domains, and betrayers of their mothers' dreams. Like its opposition of art and science, the poem is unsympathetic to male needs, programmatic, and conventional. Indeed, one gathers from these poems that, much as girls dress dolls, situations are continually adorned and readorned with apparel stamped not from Barbie patterns but from liberation cant. What Piercy wants ultimately is woman's choice—not only in goals and roles but also in childbearing. As a propagandist for these views, she may be excused for being polemical, two-dimensional, and sloganish, and the exaggerated oppositions and repetitions of the syntax may be seen as stemming more from oratorical technique than lyrical form. Her poetry is best when she is opposing either her lover (**"A battle of wills disguised," "Season of hard wind," "Apologies"**) or her mother (**"My mother's novel," "Crescent moon like a canoe"**), but one never senses that, as Stein claimed for poets, she has "ever felt anything in words." The poems are earned; the rhythms flat, more a result of workshops than of ear; and the words appear chosen for accuracy rather than joy. (pp. 457-58)

> Jerome Mazzaro, "At the Start of the Eighties," in The Hudson Review (copyright © 1980 by the Hudson Review, Inc.; reprinted by permission), Vol. XXXIII, No. 3, Autumn, 1980, pp. 455-68.*

ANNE STEVENSON

Marge Piercy is known in England mainly as a novelist. That the author of **Vida** and **Woman on the Edge of Time** is also a powerful, distinctively American poet may come as a surprise, even to her admirers. As might be expected, **The Moon is Always Female** reflects the uncompromising bias of the committed feminist, of which some of us by now are weary. But Marge Piercy's poems are so energetic and so intelligent that weariness is out of the question. This is, in fact, her sixth book of poems, and it is an excellent one. A tough, often humorous, sometimes angry view of herself emerges from the poems, yet they are free of embitterment. They lack that harsh edge of hysterical accusation—as if with a few nasty words one could instantly abolish half the human race—which spoils so many poems by women these days. Here, finally, is a feminist artist for whom one need rarely blush.

The Moon is Always Female is gratifyingly longer than most poetry volumes, and absorbing throughout. In effect, Ms Piercy is still a novelist in her poems; she has perfected an easy-flowing unrhymed line in which she says what she means with few frills. If you object to poems that tell you things, then you will not like this book. As for myself, I cannot resist delighting in such lines as "All / things have their uses / except morality / in the woods" (**"Indian pipe"**) or "I find it easy to admire in trees / what depresses me in people" (**"The doughty oaks"**). . . .

Apart from some endearing poems about her cats, Piercy's work scarcely qualifies as tender. Her love poems are fierce, even vulgar (possibly she *wants* to sound vulgar; vulgarity defeats gentility). Energy and exuberance render her extremely likable, however, even when she is howling—or preaching. . . .

It is possible, of course, to find all . . . [Piercy's] feminist rabble-rousing annoying. However good the advice, poetry may not be the best vehicle for it. Indeed, if Marge Piercy were *only* a rabble-rouser she would not be a poet. The fact is, she can be as subtle as anyone writing today. . . . All . . . [the poems here] are interesting, some are masterpieces. One called **"At the well"** borrows an aged witch from Celtic mythology and gives her a fight with an angel. The witch represents magic, if you like, or superstition; certainly fear of suffering and a longing for safety. The angel represents the trans-sexual spirit of existence itself: youth and age, pain and happiness, good and evil. In the course of the fight the witch thrusts the angel from her. "Get from me / wielder of the heart's mirages", she cries "I will follow you to no more graves." So the angel departs. The witch is left blind. Fortunately the moral is not drawn. The poem trembles with an ambiguity which is its power. **"At the well"** alone would convince me that Marge Piercy is one of America's major writers. . . .

[The] strength of Piercy's work is its outwardness, its frankness. Even if you do not agree with her, you have to meet Marge Piercy half way.

> Anne Stevenson, "The Heart's Mirages," in The Times Literary Supplement (© Times Newspapers Ltd. (London) 1981; reproduced from The Times Literary Supplement by permission), No. 4060, January 23, 1981, p. 81.

JUDSON JEROME

In my January column I promised I would return to the poetry of Marge Piercy. Now I'll tell you why. I had spent a rainy Sunday reading poetry—three volumes that day. The first two I read were by a member of the literary Establishment and were the kind of poetry I generally praise—for controlled metrical form, often with rhyme, understatement, wit, irony, rationality, a tone that is intellectual, genteel, delicately sensitive, precise. And I nodded half the day.

I was left with a throat dry with admiration. . . .

It happened that I had checked out the only available volume of Marge Piercy's poetry from our local library. I had recently read her latest novel, **Vida,** and was so excited by that book that I wanted to know her poetry better (which I had seen only occasionally, scattered in little magazines). After doing my duty with those other volumes that Sunday, I turned to Piercy. She relieved my parched throat.

The reason is simple. Her poetry is readable. Poem after poem made sense, was moving, engaging, amusing, entertaining, insightful. Each made a human connection. I felt as if I were being spoken to by a person who really wanted me to hear her and to know why it was important that I hear. (p. 56)

Readability, incidentally, has nothing much to do with difficulty. . . . Most of the poetry through the centuries has been difficult—but if it endured, it was also readable. The poetry of Marge Piercy is not simple. But, unlike much poetry published today, it was intended to be understood.

In addition to readability, it has gusto. As a critical term, *gusto* has fallen out of currency. . . . [Gusto] is not mere exuberance, but exuberance channeled by an insistence on accuracy. The exact hurrah. Or the exact bellow—for exuberance is not always expressed in celebration.

You get a little of the bellow and the hurrah in ["**What it costs**"], from Piercy's latest collection, *The Moon Is Always Female*. . . . Consider the possibilities, those hundreds of you who send me poems of disappointed love each year. You can whine about it—and most of you do. You can lash out at the lousy lover who had such bad judgment in leaving you—and many of you do that. Or you might, as this poem does, say: "This is *my* problem. I have to survive." (pp. 56, 58)

It is enthusiasm for life, so intent that it cannot afford sloppy responses, that generates Piercy's celebrations of love, of gardening and nature, of other strong people (especially strong women)—and her anger at the corporate system that indifferently poisons our lives, at our imperialistic wars, at male domination that feeds those evils, at small-mindedness and hypocritical self-seeking, at the leeches who attach themselves to her career as poet and novelist, at life-destroying forces everywhere. That gusto generates her powerful imagery, the energy of her clear, direct, no-nonsense sentences, and the throbbing rhythm of her lines.

Her poems are saved from propaganda simplicities by the recognition of difficulty. Her love poetry (usually to one person, usually to a man, but sometimes to a woman, and sometimes to groups in which she is linked by love) is more convincing than most because it almost always acknowledges the problems, both in herself and others, that interfere with simple joy. (p. 58)

One never senses complacency. Reading one of her more strident poems, "**For strong women**," I was amused to think of it in comparison with Kipling's "If." . . . Instructing his "Son" to be a man, Kipling describes a superhuman cool, a calm, cautious superiority. Piercy's ideal of strong women is one of passionate involvement, vulnerable, agonizing, torn by the inevitable "weakness" of craving love. (pp. 58-9)

Kipling, though, has one advantage over Piercy. No daughter, however encouraged by her mother (or father), is likely to memorize "**For strong women**," and so not even such scraps of this poem will be preserved as have been those scraps of "If" that remain in my mind after 30-odd years when the text is not at hand. (p. 59)

Memorability may not be an important goal for Marge Piercy. . . . But I think we have reached the point at which the label *poetry* has been stretched into meaninglessness. We may need new forms. (pp. 59, 61)

Meanwhile, we live with what we get—and if you want the rare experience of reading through a book of poetry with the pleasure and engagement you would have reading a book of good prose, try the work of Marge Piercy. . . . (p. 61)

Judson Jerome, "Grabbing the Gusto" (reprinted by permission of the author), in Writer's Digest, *Vol. 61, No. 7, July, 1981, pp. 56, 58-9, 61.*

KATHA POLLITT

The rise of feminism over the last 15 years has been accompanied by a proliferation of feminist novels—frankly didactic Bildungsromans whose subject is the education of a heroine, and of the reader, too, into the painful realities of woman's place. Some of these novels are complex and inventive. . . . Others are as pat as pamphlets. All, however, share a moral urgency, a zest for the role of tutor, that seem more characteristic of the 19th century than our own. . . .

Fifteen years is a long time, though—long enough, you'd think, for everyone not enrolled in a Total Woman seminar to have gotten the message. As I cracked open Marge Piercy's fat new novel ["**Braided Lives**"], which is about growing up female in the 50's, I must say I wondered if she could possibly have anything to say that has not already been said—and said and said—before. Does she? Well, yes and no.

If you remember—or fantasize—the 50's as an era of innocent pleasures and social harmony, think again. For Jill Stuart, our narrator, and her friends, the 50's mean McCarthyism, an intellectual climate of stodgy conservatism, sex without birth control, and a vicious, though covert, struggle for power between the sexes. Jill is impulsive, rebellious, smart, an outsider from the start, a half-Jewish tomboy who hangs out with the local toughs in her working-class Detroit neighborhood, writes poetry, and worries that her sex play with her girl friends means that she is "an L." A scholarship to college is her chance to escape the life of female drudgery that has already claimed her best friend, Callie, pregnant and married off to a garage mechanic by 16. Jill's parents think such a life is good enough for their daughter—the father out of indifference (he had wanted a son), the mother out of resentment at her own balked life that has come in middle age to border on lunacy.

At the University of Michigan at Ann Arbor, Jill discovers literature, politics and the rich female life of the dormitory. Her closest friend is her blonde, beautiful, boy-crazy cousin Donna, but there are others: sarcastic Julie; sad, hard-drinking Theo; Alberta Mann, the long-haired folk singer whose parents are Communists. Jill and her friends are the campus bohemians—they read Sartre, drink Chianti and scorn the "pink, plastic" girls who won't sleep with their boyfriends. Their hunger for experience, however, leads them smack up against the repressive sexual mores—and reality—of the day. One moment they are declaiming the need for total honesty with men and vowing that they will never end up possessive and dependent like their mothers. The next, they are worrying that they will do something "castrating" to their boyfriends, in whom they wouldn't dream of confiding their frequent pregnancy scares.

"Free love!" sneers Jill's mother, who sees men as powerful but stupid deities to be placated and deceived. And she is on to something. Jill's pretentious Existentialist-poet boyfriend Mike does dump Jill when her parents try to force him to marry her, just as Mrs. Stuart said he would. (p. 7)

Jill will recover from Mike's traumatic desertion and continue to look for a love that does not entail her subjection—with rich sinister Peter, with her townie thief, with warm intelligent Howie. We know from page one that Jill's quest is eventually successful—she will become the well-known poet and feminist activist who lives happily on Cape Cod with her lover and writes these memoirs. Not everyone fares so well. One friend will die of an illegal abortion. Another will become a civil-rights worker and be murdered by racists in the South. Julie will marry dopey Carl and subside into domesticity. Others, however, will blossom in the political ferment of the 60's: Alberta will become a feminist lawyer. The women's movement will rescue Theo from her madness. Stephanie will open a hippie boutique. As Jill says, "We were all a little crazy in the 50's, but we've been getting clearer and clearer ever since."

Hear, hear. It's always refreshing to have someone speak up for the 60's, and I'm sure I'm not the only veteran of those years who takes a certain pleasure in books that point out how bad the bad old days that preceded them really were. Much of Piercy's material will be familiar, even platitudinous, to readers of, say, "The Bell Jar," "The Women's Room" or even Ms. magazine. But the accent is placed in a new and bracing way.

Too many heroines of feminist novels are privileged, fragile innocents. A discouraging professor, a patronizing boyfriend, a pushy parent are enough to make them resign their ambitions and sleepwalk into obedient housekeeping for a husband the reader can see from the start is a creep. Piercy's women are fighters. Jill is as eager to explore sexuality as any young man; she listens to Mike and her professors disparage her poetry and keeps right on writing; she breaks laws. Donna also actively seeks sexual pleasure, and even when married persists, however furtively, in asserting her will. Even Jill's ignorant, witchy mother has her weapons, the old-fashioned female ones of hysteria and subterfuge.

Piercy burns with anger and conviction, and much of the time it's catching. We are as outraged as she by the doctors who refuse to fit Jill with a diaphragm because she is unmarried, by the abortions without anesthetic or follow-up care, by vital young women producing earnest, self-castigating Freudian analyses of their failure to "adjust."

I wish Piercy had been content to let a part stand for the whole. But as though afraid we will overlook some facet of female misery if she doesn't drum it into our heads, she methodically makes poor Jill & Company victims of every possible social cruelty and male treachery, usually more than once. Besides her two abortions and the rape, Donna is seduced as a teenager by her sister's husband, betrayed by a married man who tells her he's getting a divorce, addicted to tranquilizers by her psychiatrist and beaten by her husband, who also purposely makes the tiny hole in her diaphragm that results in the pregnancy that dooms her. . . . Even Jill, who is tougher than her friends, is sexually attacked by her boyfriend at age 14, forced to make love by Mike when she doesn't want to, sodomized against her will by Peter. And so on. All right, all right! I wanted to shout, I get the point!

Because Piercy is an intensely dramatic writer, none of this is, scene by scene, incredible. Cumulatively, though, it does wear one down. Were there *no* loving fathers in the 50's? *No* honorable boyfriends? *No* professors who encouraged their female students? There were times when I suspected that the author was unwilling to edit autobiographical material—"But Theo really *was* raped by her psychiatrist!"—and times when I thought she simply felt she owed it to women to recite the complete catalogue of female suffering. Whatever her reasons, they give "Braided Lives" a lurid predictability, like a kind of feminist National Enquirer, and a tone, too, of patronizing the reader.

While it never quite loses its energy and forward motion, "Braided Lives" is less compelling than Piercy's last novel, "Vida." . . . (pp. 7, 30)

That "Braided Lives" is as interesting as it is is a tribute to Piercy's strengths. She is blunt, she is heavy-handed—she's certainly no prose stylist—and yet by virtue of her sheer force of conviction, plus a flair for scene writing, she writes thought-provoking, persuasive novels, fiction that is both political and aimed at a popular audience but that is never just a polemic or just a potboiler. "Braided Lives" won't win any literary prizes, but it will make its readers pay more attention to the current attack on legal abortion, and make them more eager to defend the imperiled gains of the women's movement. For a novelist whose aim is didactic, that's no small compliment. (p. 3l)

Katha Pollitt, "A Complete Catalog of Female Suffering," in The New York Times Book Review (© *1982 by The New York Times Company; reprinted by permission), February 7, 1982, pp. 7, 30-1.*

RENEE GOLD

This is Marge Piercy's seventh novel, a fact that numerologists would have us believe augurs well for its success. A more substantial contribution to that success is the fact that *Braided Lives* is Piercy's best novel to date.

Those of us who have anticipated each of Piercy's offerings with increasing delight will not be disappointed; readers who are unfamiliar with Piercy's work but who enjoyed *The Bell Jar* or *The Women's Room* will need no further introduction to this novel. But the reader who has the most to gain in seeking out Piercy's work is the one to whom a blend of fiction and feminism seem anathema: *Braided Lives* offers a convincing and honest depiction of women's reality. . . .

Braided Lives has a great deal to do with finding one's own voice, a personal style in life as well as art. . . . Just as Piercy gave us an unerring vision of the radical underground of the 1970's in *Vida* and of the alternative lifestyles of the 1960's in *Small Changes,* this novel is a pointed and unsentimental look at a decade that both taught women their place and set the stage for a reversal of that education.

Braided Lives is, above all, a novel of conscience. Its vision is direct and unclouded by nostalgia or apology for the way we were. The women in *Braided Lives* are complex and conflicted: the unfolding of their stories compels us to see how society—embodied in the family, schools, the workplace, and marriage—marks each of us. Piercy may not offer the same compassion in her depiction of the novel's male characters, but the villain here is not one individual or even a particular group but rather a system (call it sexism, although the term is never used here) that oppresses all those who accept its rules.

Piercy does not yield to the temptation of making the past over in light of the present but provides, in brief passages, the compassionate and knowing voice of the present-day Donna who, at the age of forty-three, lives a life that is content and whole. Donna is a survivor, and she chooses to examine her own past out of a strong commitment to the present. . . .

The parallel voices of the young and middle-aged narrator remind us of how easily the hard-won advance of the women's movement—especially the availability of safe and legal abortion—may be jeopardized in a time of conservative reaction. Piercy does not flinch in her recital of a period that was both repressive to endure and painful to recall. But she also tells a story of personal courage and endurance, a statement about what some women and men have chosen to leave behind. That the journey back is honest and engaging is testament to Piercy's skill.

Renee Gold, in a review of "Braided Lives," in Wilson Library Bulletin (*copyright © 1982 by the H.*

W. Wilson Company), Vol. 56, No. 7, March, 1982, p. 548.

WENDY SCHWARTZ

For her seventh and most poetically written novel [*Braided Lives*], Marge Piercy has chosen a subject often tapped by women in their first books—growing up in the '50s without becoming conventional or going mad. . . .

Piercy gives up-to-date glimpses of her characters' lives in italicized passages, showing the beginning and the fruits of their political growth. She leaves the time in between, when ostensibly each went through great upheavals, to the reader's imagination. Piercy's previous works fill in the gap; she has made such changes her primary concern. Her power as a novelist, however, rests in her ability to present feminist radical politics in the context of a riveting story, and she hasn't really done that here.

The flash-forward biographical tidbits are tantalizing, for the events alluded to are fresher than those covered in more depth. They are, though, too sketchy to provide a satisfying picture of the characters "today." For example, after a horrifying account of Jill's self-induced abortion, Piercy offers in italics the information that she subsequently set up an illegal abortion service. A more complete and dramatic presentation of this later organizing effort would have had great power, and particular political relevance now.

But these pieces of the future elevate the predictable episodes of the '50s from the ghetto of personal experience to the foundations of the feminist realpolitik. Piercy has, shrewdly or unconsciously, used a revisionist process in choosing what to present; each scene obviously is a spark for later political development. Jill is taken through a series of unsatisfying and degrading relationships, but their importance becomes clear only when we are told, in italics, that she went through a period of rejecting men before finally accepting the love of a truly caring man.

In this novel, for the first time, Piercy presents her older characters in more than a perfunctory way, and uses her flash-forward technique, though to a lesser extent, to demonstrate growth in them as well. . . .

Because we don't witness the personal and political transformations of the characters, with all the doubts and backsliding entailed, the struggle to reach enlightenment seems deceptively easy, and life after revelation unrealistically sweet. But this makes *Braided Lives* the most positive of Piercy's works—the only one in which she holds out hope for personal fulfillment.

Wendy Schwartz, in a review of "Braided Lives" (reprinted by permission of The Village Voice *and the author; copyright © News Group Publications, Inc., 1982), in* The Village Voice, *Vol. XXVII, No. 13, March 30, 1982, p. 42.*

RON SCHREIBER

Shortly after I agreed to review Marge Piercy's latest collection of poems, *The Moon Is Always Female,* two poets warned me that this was a disappointing collection. Two other friends told me they had not yet read the book but they had heard it was not very good. Maybe it's true this time, I thought. The title, after all, did not seem promising, and all poets—especially prolific poets with great technical facility—do tend to repeat themselves.

I should have known better. . . .

The first two poems of "**The Lunar Cycle**" (the second section of the book) are alone worth the price of admission. The point is that when many magazines and publishers are printing poems and volumes of moderate technical proficiency and no energy at all, Piercy is continuing to write poems that matter to people's lives, men's lives as well as women's.

Some other things need to be said right off. There are three things that Piercy does technically as well as any American poet writing. She is the American master of the simile. In poem after poem similes continually startle a reader. . . . Secondly, she repeats phrases until they become litanies, but the phrases are colloquial, grounded in American speech. . . . Finally—and this is a more recent development—she has mastered long sentences that build, line after line, to a crescendo, and these she usually follows with short, simple sentences.

Yes, sometimes a simile seems contrived; it merely surprises. Like all prolific poets, Piercy sometimes does repeat herself, and a reader can say, "She has done that better elsewhere." Yes, some poems are relatively weak measured by the extremely high standards Piercy has set for herself. But Piercy writes with a learned intelligence. She simply knows more, in more detail, than most other poets know, and that knowledge may be the intimate experience of tides or the book knowledge of the behavior of dolphins. Both come alive in the poems. She is invariably passionate, even in quiet poems. And—what reviewers often forget because of the seriousness and political character of much of her work—she is a very funny poet. Auditors often laugh at Piercy's readings—not quiet, knowing chuckles, but roars full of gusto. An attentive reader of her books will do the same thing. . . .

Piercy also writes quiet, sure poems of precise observation—of her cats, for example, or a spider in the garden. She writes many love poems, some of them tender, some poems of anger and struggle. Often humor comes into fierce poems unexpectedly. Most readers will find themselves laughing, sometimes in the midst of intense seriousness—maybe a bitter laugh in the middle of an angry poem, but often a laugh full of relief and release. Humor, after all, is perspective; it keeps us going. . . .

"**The Lunar Cycle**" is an ambitious and, I think, successful sequence. There is a poem for each lunar month, and the poems range from "**The Right to Life**," which is primarily a public and political poem, to "**The great horned owl**," a poem about Piercy's own life and observations in late Cape Cod autumn, and "**The longest night**," based upon the poet's winter drive to Kansas City. Cumulatively, the poems reflect the various months of the lunar calendar, the year beginning with spring and ending with deep winter. They are variously private and public, among and within themselves. Piercy does not need to say that the personal and political are one; she illustrates the fact in poem after poem. So "**The Lunar Cycle**" is at once her personal year, the year of the seasons (especially on Cape Cod), and the year of public events. It is a feminist calendar and a far more comfortable one than that on which we base our dates. . . .

Then why the attacks? Why even the second-hand comments that a new book is not so good? I don't know the answers to those questions, but, given some of my sources, I doubt the answer is jealousy. Piercy, after all, continually offends. She is obstinately uppity. She is consistently radical in her politics, whatever the national trends. She names enemies. She is scholarly but thoroughly unacademic. And she is a highly intelligent (and emotional) woman writer who often aggressively flaunts her sexual nature. Any one of these characteristics is enough to make a particular reader want to cut her down. But, like the oak tree she writes about in her own yard, Piercy just keeps sprouting new leaves.

Ron Schreiber, in a review of "The Moon Is Always Female," in The American Book Review *(© 1982 by* The American Book Review*), Vol. 4, No. 3, March-April, 1982, p. 10.*

VICKIE LEONARD

The title, *Braided Lives,* is far too nice for this story of a young Jewish woman who leaves her working class home in Detroit and goes off to the University of Michigan in the 1950's. The title does not convey the dynamism and the brutality of the book. Piercy has ripped off the veneer of the "quiet 50's". With a driving determination, she wants to set the record straight that life for women, for Jews and the working class was difficult. A more apt title might have been "Blood on the Tracks" which would have prepared the reader for a "coming of age" novel that is unusual. . . .

If there are any readers who still swallow the phony "life is beautiful" mystique so carefully perpetated by President Reagan, Piercy is ready to shove their faces into the despair of downtown Detroit and the selfish brutality of Grosse Pointe. She even destroys any illusions about loyalty among friends.

Yet, unlike so many novelists that elegantly write that life stinks, Piercy argues that love, politics, food, sex, and friendship make life irresistible.

She is very present in this book since it's written in first person with present day comments from the narrator. It becomes almost impossible not to believe the book is autobiographical. . . .

Piercy doesn't want us to overlook any aspect of women's lives, even the details we would rather forget. Abortions, rapes, beatings—they're all packed into *Braided Lives.* Unlike *The Women's Room* which exposed sexism yet left the reader hanging, Piercy enthusiastically endorses politics as a solution. Make no mistake, though, this is not the book of a successful, self-satisfied writer who has found the answers. This is the book of a feminist who can honestly face the brutality in our lives and can still maintain a gluttonous appetite for life.

Two aspects of Piercy's writing which can't go unmentioned . . . are her views on lesbians and her portrayals of men. The main character in *Braided Lives* has her first sexual experiences with other girls. When this information gets out among her college friends, she never denies it or apologizes. She is very close to a woman in her dorm who is kicked out for a lesbian relationship. It is Jill who persists in learning the woman's address to write despite what eyebrows might be raised by this display of friendship. Jill is, though, only sexually involved with men as a college student.

In *Vida* and *Small Changes,* Piercy wrote dialogue between men and women which brought to life the men's subtle power plays. In *Braided Lives* Jill's first true love is the master of the artful tyrant. In the name of teaching her, he questions, un-

dercuts, and dismisses her every idea. My regret is that Michael is the only man who does this. Other men are selfish or demanding yet Piercy holds back showing how they operate. This is regrettable since nobody can write these scenes the way Piercy can. Plus, we women need to have explicit examples of how our everyday relationships with men can eat at our self-respect.

Braided Lives is Piercy's most explicitly feminist book since *Small Changes.* This time, though, every character is fully drawn. The book is good. Piercy is telling our stories as if they were her own.

Vickie Leonard, in a review of "Braided Lives," in Off Our Backs *(copyright © Off Our Backs* Inc. *1982), Vol. XII, No. 4, April, 1982, p. 23.*

PUBLISHERS WEEKLY

Marge Piercy has evolved through six books of poetry and seven novels . . . into the outstanding spokeswoman for the '60s generation. It is less her skill with language than her candor and her gutsiness that have earned her universal respect. Like George Sand, a political feminist of another era, Piercy embodies women's aspirations toward freedom and justice in their own lives and for the lives of others. Her selected poems ["**Circles on the Water**"] trace the integration of her public and personal roles into a single vision of the good—or perhaps useful—life. Her love poems, in particular, should be required reading for anyone contemplating a member of the opposite sex. In these parlous days of divorce between the sexes, we can think of no wiser teacher of the ways in which we can not only live together without bloodshed, but even overcome our pasts, our fears and our weaknesses, so we might finally come to love each other. (pp. 48-9)

A review of "Circles on the Water: Selected Poems," in Publishers Weekly *(reprinted from the April 9, 1982 issue of* Publishers Weekly, *published by R. R. Bowker Company, a Xerox company; copyright © 1982 by Xerox Corporation), Vol. 221, No. 15, April 9, 1982, pp. 48-9.*

SUZANNE JUHASZ

For over a decade Marge Piercy's has been the vehement and scrupulous voice of a political woman coming to terms with her times and herself. *Circles on the Water* is Piercy's selection of her poetry to date and contains poems from seven published volumes as well as seven new poems. Activist and feminist, Piercy has recorded the thoughtful but equally sensory experience of a woman with the difficult intent to both work and love. . . . Yet while her sentiments are consistently apt and accurate, their polemical nature, no matter how grounded in personal experience, all too often results in statements more like speeches than poetry. Her work is strong in images but slight in music, and her language has a flatness that is at odds with the fullness of her life.

Suzanne Juhasz, in a review of "Circles on the Water: Selected Poems," in Library Journal *(reprinted from* Library Journal, *July, 1982; published by R. R. Bowker Co. (a Xerox company); copyright © 1982 by Xerox Corporation), Vol. 107, No. 13, July, 1982, p. 1329.*

ROGER SCRUTON

Marge Piercy is an established author, and presumably has an established readership—though it is very difficult to gauge from *Braided Lives* what qualities of commitment and literary endurance are required in order to belong to it. The book is written in a chatty, cluttered style, too reminiscent of a woman's magazine to sustain the feminist ideology of the text; at the same time the succession of mundane episodes so lacks urgency that only a kept woman would have the time and curiosity to read with interest beyond the first twenty pages. . . .

At first we are treated to samples of [the protagonist's] poetry; later, poetry is exchanged for opinions. It is hard to say which is the more excruciatingly naïve. The author boldly assumes that one will have been so touched by her heroine's do-it-yourself abortion as to feel unquestioning sympathy for a woman's "right to choose", but this assumption is hardly consonant with the extreme crudeness with which the experience (like everything else) is described. . . .

Braided Lives, however, is a memorable book: it contains about the worst examples of English prose that I have come across in a published novel. The following sentence is not untypical: "I also find myself hard in love in a way I have to search far back in my life to match." The machine-gun fire of monosyllables, the desperate cliché ("deep in love") avoided only by an absurd figure of speech ("hard in love"), the obscurity of grammar and sentiment, the unfeeling casualness of tone, the loss of all simplicity and directness—such is characteristic of the entire idiom of the novel.

> *Roger Scruton, "Bodily Tracts," in* The Times Literary Supplement *(© Times Newspapers Ltd. (London) 1982; reproduced from* The Times Literary Supplement *by permission), No. 4138, July 23, 1982, p. 807.**

MARGARET ATWOOD

["**Circles on the Water**"] is gathered from 20 years of poetry and includes poems from seven books. Just cause for jubilation, since anyone who can survive 20 years of serious poetry writing in America right now deserves a medal of some sort. Also for retrospection: For those of Miss Piercy's age, this book will read like a cross section of their own archeology, for perhaps no other poet of this generation has more consistently identified herself with the political and social movements of her own times. (p. 10)

Miss Piercy has the double vision of the utopian: a view of human possibility—harmony between the sexes, among races and between humankind and nature—that makes the present state of affairs clearly unacceptable by comparison. The huge discrepancy between what is and what could be generates anger, and many of these are angry poems—which, for those who want poetry to be nothing but beautiful, will mean points off. Because her poetry is so deliberately "political"—which, for some, means anything not about ghosts and roses—how you feel about it will depend on how you feel about subjects such as male-female relations, abortion, war and poverty. Those who don't like these subjects will use adjectives like "shrill" to describe the poems. It's only during certain phases of American intellectual history that divisions are made between "poetry" and "politics," however; as Miss Piercy herself points out in her rather disarming introduction, the gap would not have been recognized by "Sophocles, Virgil, Catullus, Chau-

cer, Dryden, Wordsworth, Shelley, Arnold, Whitman, Blake, Goethe."

As Miss Piercy also points out, her poetry is both "personal"— that is, it has the recognizable speaking voice of an individual human being, not a voice issuing from behind a vatic ceremonial mask—and "public," meaning both that it addresses itself to public issues and that it is for a public. With some of these poems, one can almost hear not only the reading voice but the murmurs of response and the spontaneous applause at appropriate rhetorical moments. Taken as a whole—and I recommend you do so only slowly, as this is rich fare—this collection presents the spectacle of an agile and passionate mind rooted firmly in time and place and engaging itself with the central dilemmas of its situation. . . . Sometimes Miss Piercy's is a bewildered and lonely voice, albeit a voice that admits to such quailings. Her position has not been an easy or sheltered one. As she says, "a strong woman is a woman strongly afraid."

If poets could be divided into Prioresses and Wives of Bath, Miss Piercy would very definitely be a Wife of Bath. Low on fastidiousness and high on what Hazlitt called "gusto," earthy, bawdy, interested in the dailiness of life rather than in metaphysics, highly conscious of the power relationships between men and women but seeing herself by no means as a passive victim, she is ready to enter the fray with every weapon at her command. She is, in sum, a celebrant of the body in all its phases, including those that used to be thought of as vulgar. Surprisingly, her poetry is more humorous than her novels, although not all of it is what you'd call funny. The Wife of Bath was sometimes a savage ironist, and so is Miss Piercy. Neither has much interest in being ladylike. (pp. 10-11)

Essentially her poetry is a poetry of statement and story, and metaphor and simile are, characteristically, used by her as illustration rather than as structural principle. . . .

Miss Piercy's emotional range is great, and at her best she can make you laugh, cry, get angry; she can inspire you with social purpose and open doors through which you may walk into lived reality. . . . Miss Piercy's scale, even in her "nature" poems, which are more likely to be about zucchini and lettuces and compost heaps than tigers and loons, is human and encompasses all the grandeur and trivia that scale demands. The sublime and the infernal for her are situated in the here and now.

In a collection with so many high points, it's difficult to single out one or two. But for me Miss Piercy in top form . . . is to be found in "**Crescent moon like a canoe,**" a sad, courageous and moving poem that is not only about her own mother but about her own motives for poetry. This is poetry both wide open and fully controlled, flexible, tender, clear-sighted and compassionate, an act of forgiveness. Miss Piercy is finally a hopeful poet, but it's a hope that has been long and bitterly fought for. (p. 22)

> *Margaret Atwood, "Strong Woman," in* The New York Times Book Review *(© 1982 by The New York Times Company; reprinted by permission), August 8, 1982, pp. 10-11, 22.*

PUBLISHERS WEEKLY

Marge Piercy is a forceful, direct and widely read feminist poet. In ["**Stone, Paper, Knife**"], her ninth volume of verse, Piercy continues to write about the suffering of women, particularly at the hands of men, about love, sex, failed relation-ships, and living in the natural world. She voices the legitimate need for day care services, so that women with infants need not retreat from the world. . . . In many poems she strives for an understanding of love, calling it pleasure, work, studying, two rivers that flow together . . . and she bemoans the frequent cooling of passion after marriage. . . . And in **"What's that smell in the kitchen?"**—a poem for the subjugated women across America, full of hatred and hostility—she ventures that these women would really like to serve their husbands a dead rat, or grill them instead of a steak. These wry, tender, angry poems are accessible and at times moving, but often the point of view is predictable, the imagery redundant.

A review of "Stone, Paper, Knife," in Publishers Weekly *(reprinted from the January 7, 1983 issue of* Publishers Weekly, *published by R. R. Bowker Company, a Xerox company; copyright © 1983 by Xerox Corporation), Vol. 223, No. 1, January 7, 1983, p. 67.*

Harold Pinter

1930-

English dramatist, scriptwriter, short story writer, poet, director, and actor.

Pinter is widely regarded as one of the foremost living dramatists. His earliest plays, including *The Room* (1957) and *The Birthday Party* (1958), display certain theatrical techniques and themes which commentators have described as "Pinteresque." This term generally refers to dramatic scenarios that take place in a fixed setting and involve a few characters whose motivations are obscure, no less to themselves than to the audience, but whose actions plainly illustrate both the subtle and overt violence of human relationships and convey a well-controlled atmosphere of psychological unease. While the ambiguities and enigmas of these "comedies of menace" have been the focus of derogation as well as praise, Pinter's exacting and complex use of language in these works is a major factor in his presently high repute.

The Birthday Party was Pinter's first full-length drama and the first to be professionally produced. It had a short, unprofitable run and received severe abuse from critics, the most extreme of whom viewed the action of the play as obscurity bordering on nonsense. Two years later Pinter's next full-length drama, *The Caretaker* (1960), became as successful with audiences and reviewers as his first had been unsuccessful, seemingly a response to the greater realism and comic emphasis of the later work, but also as an indication that the "obscurities" of Pinter's writing were now being recognized as integral to his art. With the 1965 presentation of *The Homecoming*, often considered his most important work, Pinter was discussed as a major English-language dramatist. Since that time he has continued to produce a number of notable works for the stage, cinema, radio, and television, including film adaptations of John Fowles's *The French Lieutenant's Woman* (1981), Marcel Proust's *À la recherche du temps perdu* (1977), and his own drama *Betrayal* (1978).

Pinter's early plays were written during the era of the Angry-Young-Man generation of British authors, whose works were typified by a sense of disillusionment, working-class characters, and by bleakly mundane settings that led one critic to describe them as "kitchen sink" dramas. The 1950s were also the years when a number of works appeared, including Samuel Beckett's *Waiting for Godot* and Eugene Ionesco's *The Chairs*, that have been grouped under the epithet Theatre of the Absurd and share certain defining traits: philosophical nihilism, unconcern for realistic character psychology, and abandonment of the cause-and-effect type plots of naturalistic drama. While Pinter's works have much in common with these theatrical trends, critics emphasize that it is a combination of the two styles, whether deliberate or unpremeditated on the author's part, that distinguishes his plays.

Unrealistic characters who exchange realistic dialogue and dreamlike sequences acted out in naturalistic settings are identifying features of Pinter's early comedies of menace: *The Room, The Birthday Party, The Dumb Waiter* (1960), and several radio plays including *A Slight Ache* (1959) and *The Dwarfs* (1960). The exact nature of the menace is unspecified and arises from

the intrusion of one group of characters upon the enclosed security of another group, usually resulting in the upheaval or destruction of an isolated world within a room. The situation of Stanley, in *The Birthday Party*, is representative: he is a character with an indeterminate past life who becomes the sole renter at a seaside boardinghouse, where one day two men from an unidentified "organization" arrive, proceed to demoralize Stanley into a state of confused submission, and prepare to take him away for a "rest cure" at the end of the last act. Critics here observe the influence of Samuel Beckett and Franz Kafka, authors for whom Pinter has expressed high admiration. *The Hothouse*, first produced in 1980 but written around the time of *The Birthday Party*, has been described by Pinter as a "heavily satirical" play in which he was "trying to make a point, an explicit point." Despite the uncharacteristically explicit theme, this satirization of modern bureaucratic institutions and their dehumanizing effects has been appraised by critics as a worthy and representative example of Pinter's early work.

The Caretaker initiated Pinter's use of characters and backgrounds that are more recognizably realistic, in contrast to the absurdist atmosphere of his earlier plays. While the previous mood of menace is again present in this work, critics have found that Pinter now begins to examine its origins and workings more closely in the various gambits for dominance among the characters. According to its commentators, *The Caretaker* also introduces a number of themes developed in Pinter's later work, particularly those having to do with power, communication, personal identity, and the unreliability of memory and knowledge. Pinter's two subsequent full-length dramas, *The Homecoming* (1965) and *Old Times* (1970), are considered his most effective and artistic presentations of these concerns. The first play is often analyzed as a contest of manipulation in which the characters advance their positions as much by silence as by the multiple meanings of their speech; the second play, like much of Pinter's work, involves an intimate group of characters whose willingness to communicate with one another in the present is as questionable as the accuracy of their knowledge of the past.

In the more recent drama and film *Betrayal*, the truth about its characters is approached by reversing the chronological order—1977 to 1968—in which their actions are viewed, a stratagem that critics find apt, considering Pinter's concern with memory, but not one which brings this drama to the level of his earlier masterpieces. Among Pinter's current works are three short plays grouped under the title *Other Places*. The most highly praised of these is *A Kind of Alaska*, based on case histories of coma victims who have been restored to consciousness after spending years in an unconscious state. Examining, in the words of Martin Esslin, "time, reality, and the nature of the self," this work serves as the latest restatement, as well as extension, of "Pinteresque" subjects and the evolving styles in which they are treated.

(See also *CLC*, Vols. 1, 3, 6, 9, 11, 15; *Contemporary Authors*, Vols. 5-8, rev. ed.; and *Dictionary of Literary Biography*, Vol. 13.)

KATHERINE H. BURKMAN

Though Pinter is distinctly a poetic rather than a problem-solving playwright, he is by his own proud admission in large part a traditionalist. Despite his lack of certain kinds of explicit information about his characters and plot, in form Pinter is not as far from the well-made play of Ibsen as many of his fellow absurdists; he is fond of curtain lines and curtains, and he is ultimately concerned with the shape both of words and of his entire dramatic world. "For me everything has to do with shape, structure, and over-all unity," Pinter noted in an interview—a statement which does not contradict his assertion that his creative process is not conceptual, that he follows his characters whither they lead him.

The point is that Pinter's characters lead him continually to the very rhythmic structures which have informed great dramatic works since drama's origin in primitive ritual. (pp. 7-8)

Just as the primitive rites of ancient religions work their way into the structure of art, in drama as notably as in painting and sculpture, ritual becomes part of Pinter's dramatic world, in which it is used for the playwright's own tragi-comic purposes.

A reading of Pinter's plays in the light of the ritual rhythms which structure them involves an understanding of two distinct kinds of rituals which the playwright sets in counterpoint with each other. On the one hand, the plays abound in those daily habitual activities which have become formalized as ritual and have tended to become empty of meaning, an automatic way of coping with life. These automatic and meaningless activities contrast in the plays with echoes of sacred sacrificial rites which are loaded with meaning and force the characters into an aware-

ness of life from which their daily activities have helped to protect them. My contention is that beneath the daily secular rituals which Pinter weaves into the texture of his plays—"the taking of a toast and tea"—beat the rhythms of ancient fertility rites, which form a significant counterpoint to the surface rituals of the plays and which often lend the dramas their shape and structure. (p. 10)

[The] rituals of daily life are seen at one and the same time as comic and ineffectual, and as tragic and pathetic. Their emptiness is exposed with all the intellectuality of Ionesco's kind of irony, but the effort to sustain them is explored with all the sympathy of Beckett for his two *Godot* clowns, desperately improvising their routines in a void. (p. 12)

Pinter lends himself to ritual or mythical critical examination more than many of his contemporaries, partly because he focuses continually on the primitive qualities which lurk beneath the civilized veneer of modern life and erupt into that life, and partly because his determination to confront the mysterious, unsolvable regions of man's existence has led him into the realms of myth and ritual. The playwright disclaims any reading knowledge of anthropology, and his myth-making qualities are not the self-conscious ones of the poet Yeats. . . . He becomes rather the daytime dreamer who is drawn to the same ritual patterns which Northrop Frye suggests have drawn men through the centuries to deal in similar archetypal patterns with the mystery of our being. (pp. 14-15)

[Pinter], as he consciously or unconsciously traces basic ritual patterns in his dramatic world, is reaching back over the centuries to archaic rhythms which have always dominated drama at its best. He is also treating those rhythms in a highly individual, even unique, way and is moving at the same time in the mainstream of much in modern literature which has already gained the stature of the classic and which is pressingly and seriously relevant to our times. (p. 17)

Even though Pinter, contrary to Yeats, does not desire a "mysterious art," he has, nevertheless, achieved it. The mysterious and prophetic quality of his drama results, though, from an almost scientific attempt at dispassionate observation. When asked if he tried to make Barrett a sympathetic character in his film version of *The Servant*, Pinter did not consider such a task his concern. He said, "I am just concerned with what people are, with accuracy." (p. 131)

In dealing with his characters so accurately, Pinter has looked far beneath the surface of life, not only to the psychological depths of his characters' existence, but to their primitive archetypal nature. His characters and the actions of his plays remain mysterious, not because he withholds psychological explanation, but because he has sensed a deeper strand of reality than the particular psychology of a character. This other reality is of a ritual nature, the characters grouping to enact those ancient rites that imitate nature and insure and celebrate life's persistence and renewal.

Ritual functions in Pinter's dramatic world much as Jane Ellen Harrison suggests it functions in religion to keep the individual fenced-in soul open—"to other souls, other separate lives, and to the apprehension of other forms of life." The daily rituals that protect man from such openness and awareness are constantly undermined in Pinter's dramas by those sacrificial rites that impinge upon them and force contact. Goldberg and McCann disturb the breakfast rituals of *The Birthday Party* to conduct their own ritual party at which Stanley is sacrificed; and Petey can no longer hide behind his paper when the strips of it which

McCann has torn during the party fall out to remind him of Stanley's victimization. In *The Room* Rose can no longer hide behind her ritual breakfasts with her husband when Riley appears from the basement and involves her in his fate. . . . As much as his characters evade communication, Pinter involves them in an eventual confrontation. The structure is Aristotelian, the imitation of an action, and the impact of the characters upon one another, even in their silent exchanges, is as final and irrevocable as the impact of character on character in Greek tragedy. (pp. 132-33)

The struggle in the dramas is very often conceived of in Oedipal terms. Father-and-son competition is evident in Pinter's three major plays with the mother-wife the focus of the battle in *The Homecoming.* The sexual relationship is ritualized, however, so that the focus is not on neurotic relationships or Oedipus complexes so much as it is on the archetypal relationships of man and woman faced with the universal dilemma of Oedipal conflicts. Woman is often seen in these conflicts as mother, wife and whore—the over-possessive mother of *A Night Out,* for example, whom Albert identifies with a whore he picks up on the street. In *Tea Party* women are intiially divided as wife and secretary (whore), but by the end of the play the dying Disson sees them both as one and the same, whores catering to his usurping brother-in-law.

In *The Lover, The Collection,* and *The Homecoming*—plays that make a similar identification of the woman—Pinter is highly sympathetic with them. This sympathetic treatment seems to stem partly from a perception of the woman's ritual role in the transfer of power from dying god to the new god. Woman is not allowed the role of faithful wife if she is to preside at the ritual renewal of life and embrace and welcome the new god when he arrives. Ruth, the most complex of these divided women, is portrayed as the suffering victim of the power struggle that she loses and wins, the fertility goddess who says "yes" to life on whatever harsh terms it is offered.

The dramas move, then, beyond the particular psychological attributes of the battling characters to their archetypal roles in the ritual patterns in which they move. Pinter once remarked in an interview that a sameness of behavior "is rife in the world. As someone said 'we're all the same upside down.'" In a sense his dramatic world stresses that sameness as well as the patterns in which we all appear to move. (pp. 135-36)

Katherine H. Burkman, in her The Dramatic World of Harold Pinter: Its Basis in Ritual *(copyright © 1971 by the Ohio State University Press; all rights reserved), Ohio State University Press, 1971, 171 p.*

MARY JANE MILLER

A radio play which uses the qualities of sound and silence to the fullest extent cannot be translated into another medium without damage. If such plays use those attributes of radio which are unique—chiefly its intimacy, flexibility and ability to command not only absolute concentration but also active and continuous participation from the listener—then no visual treatment however fluid or evocative can avoid the problem of being too literal—of lessening both the sensual and the intellectual impact of the play. Successful radio dramatists invariably assume that their listeners possess active imaginations to add the completely personal dimension which makes a good radio play memorable to the audience.

To demonstrate that Harold Pinter's radio plays work in this way is, I think, to conclude that they are performed under ideal conditions only in the medium for which they were written—that is, on the radio.

As a playwright, Pinter possesses several easily identifiable characteristics. One is that he prefers to work with a small cast and a single setting. Most of the plays are set in rooms creating a claustrophobic effect. Whether created by sound or visually, the setting is invariably naturalistic in detail. Against this setting the characters act out inexplicable events. In radio, what information Pinter consents to give depends largely on cues like accent and idiom which reveal the speaker's class, geographical roots, and ethnic origin. Like many traditional playwrights, he also gives cues to interpretation through rhythm—the tell-tale repetitions, hesitations, incomplete sentences, phatic noises, and silences on which much of the subtext rests.

Pinter's predilection for claustrophobic atmosphere, naturalistic setting, and small casts is also ideal for radio. For a listener, it is easier to keep track of a few voices rather than a large number. Technically, one atmospheric location is easier to handle. Acting out Pinter's series of inexplicable situations in front of a naturalistic set creates uneasiness in an audience—a sense of threat. Radio can also work this way when naturalistic sound effects are the prelude and backdrop to surrealistic events. However, radio has an added advantage in that the naturalistic context can be faded out from the listener's consciousness and the world of the mind can take over.

The radio plays cover roughly the same range of themes dealt with in his stage plays. In *A Slight Ache,* as in *The Caretaker* and *The Homecoming,* a stranger attempts to break into a closed circle of people. Davies fails. The Matchseller and Ruth succeed. The triple nature of woman—wife, mother, whore—is one of the central themes in *A Night Out,* and *A Slight Ache* as well as *Landscape, The Homecoming,* and *The Lover.* The complex relations between victim and tormentor recur almost like an obsession in *The Dwarfs,* as well as *The Dumb Waiter, The Birthday Party* and *The Caretaker.* The unbreakable stranglehold of power exercised through blood ties, position, passivity or sexuality is another theme running through these plays.

The only theme unique to Pinter's radio work, as distinct from his stage work, also reflects the nature of the medium and that is the complete disintegration of a man's identity. This focus appears only in *The Dwarfs* where the radio convention of interior monologue, a form capable of fully evoking Len's hallucinations, is the core of the play. (pp. 403-04)

A Slight Ache contains many of the patterns evident in other early Pinter: an ambiguous, menacing intruder; an inexplicable struggle for power in which an apparently strong character, Edward, progressively weakens until he is replaced by another, the Matchseller; a whore/mother/wife figure who is middle-aged, sexually unsatisfied, who dreams of her youth and who transfers her allegiance from her husband to another man. Using these themes and characters, *A Slight Ache* looks back to *The Room* and *The Birthday Party* and forward to *The Caretaker* and even Ruth in *The Homecoming.* Flora's long soliloquy on her rape . . . also reminds one of Beth recalling her love affair in the dunes in *Landscape.* The same tone of passivity and of sensually savouring one's memories is common to both characters.

The symbolism in *A Slight Ache* is as concrete and explicit in meaning as the dumbwaiter, or Davies' papers in Sidcup. Edward's esoteric essays are obviously infertile and incomplete mental exercises symbolic of his sterile existence. His developing blindness is an old metaphor for waning prowess, mental and physical. The drawn-out death by scalding of the wasp trapped in the jam-pot works both as a piece of characterization (Edward's aggressive cruelty to an intruder), and as a paradigm of Edward's own destiny. The compulsively ordered and polished house and the lush, sunlit garden place the play in a firmly middle-class setting.

These motifs are worth noting as evidence of good playwriting, but they are of more interest to us as demonstrations of radio technique. References to the faculty of sight carry added emotional weight in radio, the blind medium. The opening sequence of the wasp works particularly well in sound since the noise of a wasp can be unbearably irritating. Pinter wakens the listener's senses through violent contrasts of glaring sunlight and heat and the deep shade of the scullery and the study which hide Edward. He chooses the most sensuous and musical names for his flowers: convolvulus, japonica, clematis, honeysuckle.

The Matchseller is also presented with the same highly charged physical detail. He smells. . . . He is a lump, a mouldering heap. . . . (p. 405)

And yet he changes before their eyes, from old to young, diseased to solid, nameless to named—all transformations which obviously occur in the minds of Edward and Flora but which may also be *happening* to the Matchseller. The radio version indicates that this process is actual with the lines: "You're getting up . . . you're moving . . . of your own volition . . . taking off your balaclava." followed by "You look younger." . . .

A Night Out belongs to a far more realistic tradition of playwriting. With the exception of Albert's abortive blow, the play does not particularly exploit the medium of sound—and yet the play's impact depends partly on the old-fashioned element of a surprise plot twist. We discover that Albert hasn't killed his mother after all and his brief moment of glory, already fading in the encounter with the prostitute is extinguished. For that part of the play to work, her appearance, alive and well, must come as a shock—and that is technically very difficult to achieve in the theatre, as a comparison of stage directions will show.

Act II, Scene iii of the stage version has this stage direction:

> *Albert lunges to the table, picks up the clock and violently raises it over his head. A stifled scream from the Mother.*

Obviously this is followed by a very swift blackout as he raises it. One second's mistiming on the part of the lighting-board operator and the climax of the play, the mother's appearance unharmed in the last scene, is lost. (p. 406)

A Night Out suffers comparatively little from a stage performance, given an intimate performing space and fluid staging conventions. It is a play that could comfortably join a television double bill with *The Collection* or *The Lover*. *A Slight Ache* suffers much more loss of immediate sensory and emotional impact and much of its prismatic puzzling complexity of point of view when it is staged. But the chief casualty of theatrical adaptation is *The Dwarfs*, Pinter's last and most interesting play for radio. (p. 407)

The Dwarfs is not like any of the other plays that Pinter wrote. In the first place, nothing happens—even at the minimal level of plot used in Pinter's other plays. Len simply exists with

Pete, with Mark, by himself, in his room or in the hospital. Nothing that Pete or Mark do or say seems to cause the changes in his head. One of Len's random remarks causes open conflict between Pete and Mark, but that is an ancillary event to the central development of the play, Len's descent into insanity. His progressive isolation is presented as a completely internal thing and it is never clear whether he cuts them off or they cut him off. It is true that in Pinter's stage plays Pinter often excludes decisive action from the stage action. We never know why Ben is ordered to kill Gus or whether Mick and Aston agree to kick Davies out of the flat, but we do see the results of these decisions in on-stage conflict. In *The Dwarfs* even that kind of action is abandoned. Len goes deeper into terror and emptiness without obvious external pressures of any kind.

The other characteristic of *The Dwarfs* which distinguishes it from Pinter's other work is that the dialogue presents a far more dense texture of symbolism and metaphor. (pp. 407-08)

[The original radio play of *The Dwarfs*] can be read or perceived simply as a successful invitation to participate in a period in one man's life when his sanity is dissolving. But there is no author's point-of-view toward this experience, no attitude imposed on the audience. The subjective nature of the medium permits the audience to perceive events through Len's senses, his memory and his hallucinations. As the layers of ambiguity open up, the listener makes of it what he can.

The fluidity and intimacy of radio requires imagination, concentration, and active, continuous interpretation from the listener. More important, because a radio play is, by nature of its sensory limitations, open-ended, the listener himself has active control over what he takes away. Because radio is not as compulsive a medium as television or the stage, the listener exercises extensive powers of consent to his own participation in the emotions and ideas of a radio play. When Pinter chose to write *Dwarfs* for radio he exploited these questions to create a more fascinating, many-sided protagonist, and to raise more complex and interesting questions about human consciousness than could ever be explored in the stage versions.

The *Dwarfs* is a classic of its kind—and its kind is radio. When it is transformed from print into performance, it should be heard, not seen—presented to an audience who listens. (p. 411)

> *Mary Jane Miller, "Pinter As a Radio Dramatist," in* Modern Drama *(copyright* Modern Drama, *University of Toronto), Vol. XVII, No. 4, December, 1974, pp. 403-12.*

RUSSELL DAVIES

Harold Pinter started off unluckily. He arrived on the London stage at a time when it was no longer fashionable for playwrights merely to exercise their gifts. They had to apply them, more or less explicitly, to social themes. . . .

Pinter has already done his best to lean obligingly in the direction of conventional naturalism and commitment by saying, "If you press me for a definition, I'd say that what goes on in my plays is realistic, but what I'm doing is not realism." It was wise of him not to claim that what he's doing is poetic: that sort of talk empties theaters. But it is clear that Pinter arrived at drama by way of poetry, and has remained faithful to an instinctive, organic method of composition, letting the voices do the talking and allowing what seems right to stand.

His knowledge of poetry, long before the plays appeared, was already very broad. It is said that two of the subjects in which his knowledge is encyclopaedic are the bus routes of London and the poetry of the Forties, including some of its very minor effusions. He himself wrote a great many poems at that time. . . . [Approximately] twenty poems have survived from the early and middle Fifties to form part of Pinter's collected *Poems and Prose*. Of these, rather more than a dozen are likely to do Dylan Thomas's reputation more good than Pinter's. The same vexatious mixture of exaltation and body-rot is on display here; and it is surprising to find Pinter, who has admitted to "a strong feeling about words which amounts to nothing less than nausea," still willing to contemplate these adolescent revivals, with their dangerously rich melanges of ripe old lexicographical rarities. . . .

Over the poem **"Chandeliers and Shadows"** is set an epigraph from *The Duchess of Malfi*—"I'le goe hunt the badger by owle-light: 'tis a deed of darknesse''—which further proclaims an affinity with Thomas's "Altarwise by owl-light" sequence (although with the mischievous side-effect of demonstrating Pinter's knowledge of where Thomas got his arresting "coin-age" from). If we consider the strong flavor of Swansea in these poems, it is perhaps surprising that Pinter's early dramatic efforts do not have even a tinge of Thomas's "play for voices" *Under Milk Wood* lingering on in them; but only in the long passage of double-headed browbeating by Goldberg and McCann in *The Birthday Party* is there a possible trace of the orchestrated First Voice/Second Voice patterns Thomas employed. Goldberg and McCann, in fact, are tiresomely contrapuntal; they weaken, in the end, the sense of threat. It may well have been overarranged dialogues such as this to which Pinter referred when he expressed dissatisfaction with *The Birthday Party*, on the grounds that there was "too much writing" in it.

The influence that had encouraged Dylan Thomas in his sing-song, paradoxically, taught Pinter his sinister restraint. This was Eliot. One of the first to notice that Pinter had so much Eliot in him was Kenneth Tynan. In fact, he pointed out "the source of the Pinter style" with great glee at the end of his ear-cropping review (after listening to *The Dumb Waiter*, so he says, with "half an ear"—such are the subtle ways of the semiconscious put-down). Tynan goes on to quote, from "Sweeney Agonistes," fragments of Sweeney and Swarts which, while not a dead ringer for Pinter, do vibrate with a sympathetic tinkle. Better, perhaps, would have been a patch of Doris and Dusty from the opening of Eliot's same "Aristophanic Melo-drama":

> *Doris:* You can have Pereira.
>
> *Dusty:*   What about Pereira?
>
> *Doris:* He's no gentleman, Pereira:
>   You can't trust him!
>
> *Dusty:*   Well, that's true. . . .
>
> *Doris:* No it wouldn't do to be too nice to
>   Pereira.

and so on. To note that the inconsequential jangliness of this has echoes in Pinter is only fair to Eliot; but it is hardly fair to pin the badge of Eliot on him without crediting him at the same time with having known what to do with this tradition when he got hold of it. *The Birthday Party* is very rich in post-Eliot experimentation, most of it, in effect, replacing the dis-

embodied ghostliness of Eliot's wan voices with a warm and rather repulsive collusion. The result is a kind of vaudeville crosstalk, crawling with innuendo, yet retaining some of Eliot's formal, bell-like antiphony. . . .

Commentators are still fond of remarking that Pinter characters "fail to communicate," but it's a hard charge to back up when so many of them take a positive delight in collaborating to limit the scope of conversation, reveling in the ambitionlessness of the topic, conspiring (like Stanley and Meg in their exchange about "succulent" fried bread) to exercise their techniques of insinuation. Eliot's objectification of emptiness becomes in Pinter, at times, a gloating celebration of it. (p. 22)

It is natural to hope to find, somewhere, a Pinter who actually lands on a meaning, fairly and squarely; and the most natural place to look is in the early prose pieces. Unfortunately, there are only three of these included in *Poems and Prose*. But in them is contained—to put it optimistically—what one most needs to know about Pinter's subject matter.

The simplest of the three to understand is a fragment called **"The Black and White,"** a monologue in what it is easy to think of, looking away from the text, as broad Cockney, but which on re-examination proves to signal its dialect origins only in the merest ellipses ("They only shut hour and a half"). The speaker is a vagrant woman who spends her time in London walking, or on buses, or looking at buses, or in the "Black and White," a cheap late-late café.

Monologues of this kind were not a rarity in the mid-Fifties: there were Revue actresses who specialized in them, and, indeed, Pinter's fragment later became a Revue sketch. But it has more than stage-pathos and Cockney "character." Or, rather, less—it has the sharp pain of neutrality. Its touch in such tiny matters as the preference for a definite over an indefinite article is very sure. When Pinter writes "They give you the slice of bread," and not "a slice," he cuts out from the phrase all social sense of the gesture. The dumb institutional act remains, frozen in habit. If it did not sound preachy, you could call Pinter, already, a virtuoso in the art of reproducing the authentic voice of the dispossessed.

He is certainly interested in that voice, and has gone on using it in many disguises. In *No Man's Land* it even became the feverish cultured purr of Gielgud. It is at its most famously garrulous in Davies, the tramp in *The Caretaker*, who, like the woman in **"The Black and White"** and many another Pinter character, "geographizes" the sprawl and collapse of his identity (his "papers" down in Sidcup; the loss of a shoe "just past Hendon" on the North Circular Road, etc.). (p. 23)

The motto for almost any Pinter character who talks long enough to begin hearing his own voice can be found in Beckett's *Malone Dies*: "I wonder if I am not talking yet again about myself. Shall I be incapable, to the end, of lying on any other subject?"

A few pages earlier in the same book, Malone can be heard considering his situation. "Present state. This room seems to be mine. I can find no other explanation to my being left in it. . . . Unless it be at the behest of one of the powers that be . . . I enquire no further in any case." This could hardly be closer in spirit to Pinter. It takes us right back to his remaining two early prose pieces: the two versions of the Kullus incident.

The first, dated 1949, is a gnomic sketch/poem (developed as *The Basement* later on) in which Kullus and his girl take over the narrator's room; this makes the narrator the outsider, and thus, in turn, the usurper. In *The Examination,* a narrative conducted in language not unlike that of a psychiatrist's report (though it is not clear what kind of "examination" is going on), the writer records how he formerly dictated the terms on which time shared with Kullus was passed, only to discover that Kullus—significantly expert in controlling silence—had begun to take over the "dominance." "For we were now in Kullus's room." (The date of this piece is 1954/1955. If not influenced by the French edition of 1950, Pinter must have been mightily encouraged to develop his theme when Beckett's 1955 translation of *Molloy* was published. It begins, "I am in my mother's room. It's I who live there now.")

If we really understood what Pinter had put of himself into the Kullus pieces—which really only tantalize with the impression they give of intense importance to their author—we would probably be happy to reunite the playwright with his ear and salute the pair of them. But then, if Pinter felt able to open Kullus up to that kind of inspection, he might well have no wish to write plays. As it is, practically everything he has written flows from the impulse first recorded in *Kullus.* Paranoia, class, desire to dominate and be dominated, sex (the pivotal role of women), the exchange of identities: these are not themes so much as mysterious stages in the process by which A Room becomes Someone's Room. (pp. 23-4)

[*Betrayal*] works up very little of the familiar atmosphere of puzzlement and dread. It takes a rather frigid, formal pleasure in working backward through time, starting its story of adultery amid the polite, uneasy epilogues of the affair in 1977, and tracing it all gradually back to its first hot, drunken moment of something-like-truth in 1968. "Nice sometimes to think back, isn't it?" is the punning clue; and though with Pinter, naturally enough, it isn't nice—the exchange of social and sexual hypocrisies has a morose and cynical edge, as of Feydeau farce taken apart and ground out in a sarcastically slow reverse gear—the play is comforting in the sense that its characters, and their guilt, are of a relatively familiar kind.

A publisher, a literary agent, a pretty wife who runs a gallery: far feebler talents than Pinter's have quarried such types for their deep-lying desire to sneer the world, and themselves, to extinction. *Betrayal* is by no means the least elegant of hatchet jobs on London's bookmen and their reputation-mongering (a memorable character in the play is a reputation called Casey, who never appears); but like its own stately, revolving stage set, it is unmistakably part of a world seen in terms of *La Ronde.* This is Pinter moving in "art circles," rather than getting trapped in his accustomed cube. And his new professional-class characters, so much more recognizable in their smugness than the old, are in the same degree more abstract too. It remains to be seen whether these figures are merely, in Eliot's words,

Tenants of the house,
Thoughts of a dry brain in a dry season.

and whether an instinctive life will burst in again on this upper story, reclaiming it for Pinter's old, insulting, implicating passions. (p. 24)

Russell Davies, "Pinter Land," in The New York Review of Books *(reprinted with permission from* The New York Review of Books; *copyright © 1979 Nyrev, Inc.), Vol. XXV, Nos. 21 & 22, January 25, 1979, pp. 22-4.*

RUDOLF STAMM

[Pinter's note in the 1980 text of *The Hothouse*] places *The Hothouse* between *The Birthday Party* and *The Caretaker*. What may appear surprising in this chronological arrangement is the relation between *The Birthday Party* and the lately produced play. Without the author's guidance spectators and readers would tend to consider *The Hothouse* as a preparatory exercise for *The Birthday Party*. It is a comparatively easy Pinter: his characteristic technique is used less economically and discreetly in it than in the other plays of the same period. One simple consequence of this appears in the length of the text. In the Methuen edition *The Hothouse* covers about 150 pages as against 30 for *The Room,* 40 for *The Dumb Waiter,* 80 for *The Caretaker* and 90 for *The Birthday Party.* It looks as if the play had not undergone the process of elimination and concentration that has led to the enigmatic compactness of the rest of his plays.

In spite of a number of loose ends there is a fairly complete and intelligible plot. The chief of what is a cross between a hospital, a mental home and a prison is gradually revealed to be a criminal, and the main members of his staff turn out to be not much better. After he has exasperated the so-called patients by a hypocritical Christmas address, composed of all the available platitudes and clichés, they break out of their cells and kill the whole staff with two exceptions, one of them the man who can carry the tale to the official in the Ministry and who seems to have engineered the whole catastrophe in order to become the successor of his liquidated chief. Thus a fairly well constructed crime story is neatly resolved in a concluding scene, and we are left with fewer questions to ponder than we have learnt to expect at the end of a Pinter play. Taking the author's hint we may read it as an experimental excursion into Ben Jonson's ferocious mode of satire and as a reaction to the reception of *The Birthday Party* by critics and audiences, many of whom had loudly complained of the young author's opacity.

We realize what the targets of his satire are right at the start of the performance. . . . The rules of the institution demand that the patients be deprived of their names and given numbers instead. The system does not seem to work too well since the chief himself is mixing up two numbers, one belonging to a patient that has died, the other to one who has given birth to a boy. . . . The whole system we encounter is depersonalized, rigid, resisting change, and it is strictly hierarchical. Roote is the top man, Gibbs is his inferior, Lush is Gibb's inferior, and far down on the ladder stands Lamb, the unfortunate novice on the staff. (pp. 291-92)

As the play proceeds we realize that hot passions are lurking under the frozen surface of the hierarchical system: rivalry, envy, hatred, and that almost the whole staff is hardly better than a pack of wolves ready to jump at each other's throats and eventually destroyed by the most cunning specimen, the enigmatic Gibbs. . . . [There] is little information concerning the so-called patients. Roote and Lush intermittently indulge in plenty of double-talk concerning the benefits enjoyed by them, but a number of hard facts come to light and give away the brutality of the institution. The death of number 6457 was caused by Roote if we can trust Gibbs's final report, and we can trust it once we have discovered that he knows much more about his superior's devious ways than Roote, in his desperate isolation, imagines. Roote is also the cause of the birth the report of which shocks him so deeply, and how the patients feel about it all appears in the final massacre of the staff, the account of which is received quite calmly by Lobb, the representative of the ministry, who seems aware—to use a phrase of T. S. Eliot's—that this sort of thing has occurred before, and invites Gibbs to take over.

Pinter's satire is aimed at the *libido dominandi;* he has constructed a model of a vicious circle of power; we witness the fall of the tyrannical top man and are left with the certainty that his successor will be worse and that the wheel will continue to turn without alteration. In a play of this type there is hardly any room for characterization in the traditional sense. We cannot trust what a figure says about himself or what other figures say about him. The information we get this way is mostly deceptions and lies. In his list of characters the author merely offers monosyllabic names and an age indication. In the case of Cutts the name is preceded by 'Miss'. Age and sex, like birth and death, are indubitable facts, for the rest we are referred to the behaviour of the figures and invited to draw our own conclusions. The main members of the gang show a remarkable family likeness. Their identity depends upon their place in the power game. Unless they have reached the top, they cringe to their superiors, whom they secretly hope to replace. In their dealings with inferiors they develop the very vices that disgust them in those they want to replace. Everybody is suspicious and ill at ease. Miss Cutts, the only female specimen, keeps harping on her femininity and is ready to sleep with all and sundry.

There is an extraordinary difference between seeing or reading this play for the first time and a second and third experience of it. The first viewing should be a treat for people who know their way about detective stories. But even they will not be able to catch all the clues to which we readily respond once we have seen the second act with its revelations and catastrophe. Then we have also gained an insight into the author's utterly pessimistic use of language. His figures cannot communicate through language. It is a weapon for them in their struggle for dominance, an instrument permitting them to disguise or hide their emotions and intentions. As a result of this the play moves on two different levels from beginning to end: the level of language, which is most deceptive when most florid, and the level below it, full of dark passions, plots, and secrets. In order to grasp what is going on down here we have got to listen and observe very carefully: an incoherence, a contradiction, a mere hesitation, a strange inflexion may be an important pointer. Pinter is following Freud where he turns lapses into the most revealing elements of speech.

An example of a telltale hesitation: in his account of how he worked his way up to his present position Roote mentions his predecessor: 'When my predecessor . . . retired . . . I was invited to take over his position.' When we come to the passage with a knowledge of the whole play, the three stops before and after 'retired' are full of sinister implications. His difficulty in finding the right word may hint that he had been responsible for his predecessor's death just as Gibbs will be responsible for Roote's death. The preceding sentence 'I didn't bribe anyone to get where I am', becomes overshadowed by a dark meaning, too, the negative statement calling for the positive complement 'but I had someone murdered to get where I am'. (pp. 293-94)

Together with the sometimes unaccountable pauses and the frequent staring of the interlocutors at one another the gestures unmask their deceitful language and help to create a sense of dubiety, of rottenness, and doom. In the second act the strains behind the correct relationship of Roote, Gibbs, and Lush lead to open outbreaks of hostility. The air is charged with violence.

Roote complains more than once that he feels hot, that the room is overheated, and once he adds ominously 'like a crematorium.'' . . . Lush appears over-fond of assuring him that the snow, which is the weather symbol of the first act, has now turned to slush. The playwright seems to enjoy having Lush harp on the slush outside. Whisky is another second act symbol. It is swallowed in increasing quantities, especially by Roote, who begins to act and talk wildly. He throws a whisky in Lush's face; he hits him in the stomach several times in an attempt to convince him that he himself as the chief is delegated, entrusted, appointed and authorized. He accuses Gibbs openly of an intention to murder him, and before the final outbreak we see knives in the hands of the antagonists. Roote's speeches grow more and more incoherent as he is getting drunk, but he has his moments of insight, and then his recurrent theme is a gnawing sense of doom.

Sporadically, the rapidly deteriorating situation is saved by a recourse to convention. After all it is Christmas, the day of the exchange of wishes for health and happiness, a day of toasts and gifts. The understaff have their raffle. Tubb, their representative, brings their best wishes and a Christmas cake to Roote, and even pretends that everybody, including the patients, is eager to hear his Christmas address. Roote is delighted to receive the gift of a beautiful cigar from Lush, of all people, but when he lights it and settles down to enjoy it, it explodes. Thus all the Christmas motifs, above all Roote's final address, turn farcical in this world of deception and violence. If Pinter has deprived it of any means of salvation, he has generously equipped it with technical devices. As we have seen they are very much in evidence in the interrogation-and-torture scene; Roote uses an intercom, which renders his human relations more difficult, and there is an amplifier, through which terrifying noises—a sigh, a keen, and a laugh—make themselves heard three times. All this machinery has an important function in creating the appropriate setting for Pinter's dehumanized society.

The play as a whole is planned and executed with the meticulous care which is a mark of Pinter's genius. The author of so many polysemantic plays decided to write a monosemantic one in this case, and he knew how to pursue his one aim relentlessly and successfully. This required a large-scale use of some of his favourite devices, a fact that annoyed him at a time when his passion for the achievement of the intensest effect through the most unobtrusive means was growing. He was well advised when he decided in 1979 that his outcry against an hierarchical, bureaucratic and inhuman organization of society, and against the abuse of language for the contrary of communication, should be no longer left unheard. The most poignant part of his satire concerns Lamb and the why and how he gets absorbed into the dismal system. Beside writing a powerful satire Pinter has succeeded in creating a modern hell, worthy of taking its place beside his purgatory ***The Birthday Party****.* (pp. 297-98)

Rudolf Stamm, '''The Hothouse': Harold Pinter's Tribute to Anger,'' in English Studies *(© 1981 by Swets & Zeitlinger B.V.) Vol. 62, No. 3, June, 1981, pp. 290-98.*

ENOCH BRATER

Pinter's characters in **Betrayal** are boring. Preoccupied with children, home, extramarital affairs, tablecloths, and happiness, they recite the lines that have been assigned to them as educated, pampered, polite, moderately cultivated, upper-mid-dle-class Londoners. Even their taste in modern literature is as unexceptional as it is predictable. Though they may occasionally feel obliged to read Yeats on Torcello or to take their summer holidays in the Lake District, what they really enjoy are the mundane little novels about ordinary people much like themselves in "the new Casey or Spinks." Here everything is ordered, fixed, and, above all, contained. Life does not pass these people by; it merely goes on for them. "Betrayal" is in this context a rather lofty word for such bourgeois and un-imaginative infidelities. For Pinter's people in this play only *think* there is depth to their passions: though their lives are not exactly meaningless, the fact is they are not especially interesting. What is there about this trio, then, that compels us to study in detail every move they make as we reconstruct their sad, sometimes comic, and always ironic chronicle of who-did-what-to-whom, when, where, and under-what-circum-stances? To answer these questions we must first take a hard look at some of the dramatic forms Pinter employs so skillfully in this work.

Pinter's drama has for a long time been far more compelling for narration rather than plot. How his story develops is more impressive than the story itself. In *Betrayal,* moreover, it is practically impossible to separate the two. Every critic, of course, will notice that this particular tale is told (almost) backwards. There are three prominent exceptions to this rule, signified in Scenes Two, Six, and Seven by the simple intrusion of the unexpected stage direction "Later." Let us review for a moment the sequence of the scenes in the order in which we see them performed. Scene One takes place in the Spring of 1977 in a London pub. Emma and Jerry are present. Scene Two takes place *later* that same spring in the study of Jerry's house. Robert and Jerry are present. Scene Three takes place in the Winter of 1975 at the flat Jerry and Emma have let at #31 Wessex Grove, Kilburn; in this scene, of course, only these two characters are present. Scene Four takes place in the Autumn of 1974 at Robert and Emma's house. This is the first time all three players are on stage at the same time. The scene begins with Robert and Jerry alone (the former summons his wife offstage, who replies, "I'll be down"), and will end with the highly charged emotional impact of Emma in her husband's arms after her lover has departed. . . . (pp. 503-04)

This is also the place where Pinter specifies an intermission is possible, literally pulling down the curtain on Emma's affair with her husband's "best man." Scene Five takes place in the Summer of 1973 in a hotel room in Venice. Only Robert and Emma are on stage, but Jerry insinuates himself as the crucial offstage presence in the shape of a critical letter which gets into the wrong hands at American Express. . . . (p. 504)

Scene Six takes place *later* the same summer back at the flat in Wessex Grove and features another duet for Emma and Jerry. For a moment we are back in Venice again: Emma has brought to the flat a tablecloth purchased there while on holiday. Scene Seven takes place *later* yet in the Summer of 1973 in an Italian restaurant in London where obligatory posters of Venezia make Emma the key offstage character. Robert and Jerry are on stage, along with the extra who takes the part of the waiter or "his son." . . . Paintings are difficult to see in the theater, but Pinter's waiter calls our attention to this one: "Venice, signore? Beautiful. A most beautiful place of Italy. You see that painting on the wall? Is Venice. . . . You know what is none of in Venice? . . . Traffico." . . . In Scene Eight we are back for the last time in Emma and Jerry's flat in the Summer of 1971

as the lovers meet again on stage. Scene Nine takes place in the Winter of 1968 in the bedroom of Robert and Emma's house. All three principals appear for the second time, but only in the following order: first Jerry is discovered alone, sitting in the shadows; Emma then comes in, is later joined by Robert; and the scene and play end after Robert leaves the room as Emma and Jerry *"stand still, looking at each other."* . . . Shades of T. S. Eliot: in my beginning is my end. In every scene Pinter has made highly efficient use of his offstage character: the "odd man out" is not really out at all. Two-character scenes are really three-character scenes, for the indirect action of each scene concerns the character who is not on stage at all.

The arrangement of scenes in *Betrayal* is, moreover, decep-tively simple. And it is far from being a gimmick. For the three forward movements in time, those that take place in Scenes Two, Six, and Seven, follow two crucial scenes of direct confrontation with "betrayal." In the opening scene of the play Emma betrays Jerry by implying that she has told her husband about their affair only the night before. This provides the dramatic necessity for the first forward movement, Jerry's confrontation with Robert. Jerry's mortification turns to indig-nation when he realizes that he has been betrayed not only once, but twice. Emma betrays him the night before when she deliberately misleads him, but Robert has betrayed him for four years by never letting on that he knew about their affair since the trip to Venice in 1973. . . . Scene Five, which stages the next major confrontation with betrayal, precedes the next two forward movements. Pinter uses the old device of a letter to make Robert aware of the fact that he has been betrayed. . . . The next two scenes move forward in time and show first Emma and Jerry in the flat (Scene Six), followed by Robert and Jerry in the Italian restaurant (Scene Seven). In the first of these two scenes we watch Emma avoid telling Jerry that Robert knows what has been going on. . . . The irony cuts deep when we next see Jerry telling Emma of his "terrible panic" when *her* letter from Venice was temporarily lost. . . . In the next scene Robert similarly avoids telling Jerry what he now knows for certain is an act of betrayal. . . . In *Betrayal,* therefore, it is the arrangement of the scenes that makes ironies accumulate and the drama as a whole possible. It is not so much *what we know* but *when we know it* that is responsible for the real tension that bristles so ferociously beneath the contained surface of this work. (pp. 504-06)

With its emphasis on visual statement, and especially in its concise arrangement of nine short scenes which move so un-inhibitedly back and forth in time, *Betrayal* shows more clearly than any previous Pinter play the profound effect his work in the movies has had on his dramatic technique. And although *Betrayal* reads at times like a filmscript, its real originality lies in the way it adapts certain cinematic strategies and makes them functional in terms of theater. *Betrayal* makes us con-cerned with the unities and disunities of time, with deception and self-deception, with the past in the present and the present in the past. In order to make these themes work on stage, the play must abandon realism's literal conformity to chronological time for the more representative patterning of temporality nor-mally associated with cinematography and film-editing. (p. 507)

In *Betrayal* Pinter has selected images for us by translating cinematic capabilities into what is for him a new theatrical idiom. His nine scenes of people talking allow the past to speak for itself. These may not be images for eternity, but they are without question concise momentary images of theatrical presentness. Pinter's characters are still "taking the mickey out of each other," to use Peter Hall's phrase, but his dramatic style now shows them doing it in a decidedly cinematic way. The facts of this betrayal may remain forever ambiguous, but the form in which it takes place on stage could not be more precise. Pinter has gone to the movies, but in a work like ***Betrayal*** he comes back, invigorated by his experience, to the theater. (pp. 512-13)

> *Enoch Brater, "Cinematic Fidelity and the Forms of Pinter's 'Betrayal'," in* Modern Drama *(copyright* Modern Drama, *University of Toronto), Vol. XXIV, No. 4, December, 1981, pp. 503-13.*

PETER J. CONRADI

In *The French Lieutenant's Woman,* itself a species of historical romance, albeit an ornately mannered and self-conscious one, [John] Fowles addresses the problem of repression and liberation as aspects both of the evolution of modern ethics, so that its major characters defy social convention, and also of the emancipation of the poetics of his chosen fictional form, so that the revelation and denunciation of the inauthenticities of his hero are accompanied by the attempt to expose the conventions and hypocrisies of the form. The 'liberation' of both novel-characters and readers is the apparent aim, albeit one that can never be achieved. The book may award us three endings: life, as Christopher Ricks pointed out, would give us an infinity. The particular three that we are given, moreover, are naturally not innocent. The narrative presence which is responsible for these manipulations, is in a real sense the book's true hero. Apart from disconcertingly materialising in the guise of a Wilkie-Collins-like villain to align itself with the characters it creates, it constantly interrupts the action to provide a knowing commentary on its own procedures, to document both the Victorian and the contemporary ages, and to act as umpire in a battle of the styles in which the two epochs—those of its subject-matter (1867) and composition(1967-8)—engage, awarding points to each but the game to neither. The garden into which we cannot return, it is made clear, is stylistic as much as socio-historical. (p. 42)

[The film made] from *The French Lieutenant's Woman* was, from the start, a different proposition. If the problems of adapting its 'stereoscopic vision' seemed even more vexed than those involved in transposing the earlier books, the news that Karel Reisz was directing and Pinter writing the screenplay must have raised expectations high. Besides being a playwright of great distinction Pinter is also a writer of screenplays of notable brilliance and economy. The necessary compression and elision involved in his writing a screenplay deriving from a novel—his screenplay of Robin Maughan's *The Servant* would be a case in point—often distils an aesthetic pleasure quite as powerful as the book afforded, or more so. The 'fidelity' of the transposition of a novel to the screen must result from the writer's skill at finding analogues in cinematic terms for the novel's qualities, and it is Pinter's strength that he is so unafraid of his own signature. Possibly for this reason so many of his screenplays incorporate a game. The deceptively quiet savagery of the cricket-match in ***The Go-Between,*** the ball-game in the stairwell of ***The Servant,*** the patrician scrimmage of ***Accident*** all come to mind. In ***The French Lieutenant's Woman*** he adds a game of Real Tennis (the old 'royal' tennis played on an indoor court) in which Charles and his lawyer Montague are seen playing. Usually the game encapsulates something of Pinter's vision of man as social animal involved in a feral contest

for mastery; the lexical play of the language-games of ordinary discourse are mirrored by the equally elaborately encoded games of sport, which, however, display openly—unlike ordinary language—their arbitrary yet tyrannical rules. In the case of the game of real tennis here, even the Victorian-at-play is shown as claustrophiliac, devoted, once more, to the culture of the small room. (pp. 48-9)

Pinter's script tackles the problem of finding equivalences in filmic terms for the self-reflexiveness, multiple endings, and all-pervasive tonal play of the narrative voice of the novel with characteristic nerve and originality. The solution, apparently suggested by the director Karel Reisz, was to set the love-story of Charles and Ernestina within another, the location romance of the actors presented as portraying them. The modern love-affair then acts as an acoustic chamber within which the Victorian affair can resonate, amplifying and ironising some of its meanings. It is a brilliant device. To those who object that the use of such location romances is itself a convention it might be returned that Fowles's interest in the novel, after all, was in exploring exactly such cultural stereotyping, and in the ways the culture of either period refuses easy individuality. (p. 49)

The epistemological drama acted out within the novel by the play of the authorial commentary inevitably disappears. What replaces it in the screenplay is the precise imbrication of the modern and Victorian love-stories. This, however, is significantly reduced in the film. Above all the device of the two stories permits a stunning and ingenious solution to the problem of the endings, as each story can pursue, separately but with increasingly ironic mirroring and doubling, and finally with increasing convergence, its own crisis. The last word of the film (though not, significantly, the last shot; and those who wish to protect their ignorance until seeing the film should cease reading here) is spoken by Mike, leaning out of the window of the Lake Windermere house where the story of Charles and Sarah has already ended, and during the unit party staged to celebrate the completion of filming. Anna has left and abandoned Mike just as Sarah had earlier abandoned Charles at Exeter, leaving only the wig in which she plays Sarah and the gunning of her car engine as she drives away. Mike, distraught, leans out of the window. The name that he shouts into the dark is Sarah's, not Anna's: the two stories have merged and become one; or to put it another way, the spatial metaphor by which it seems logical at the start to speak of the modern story 'enclosing' the Victorian one, as a space circumscribes a room, will no longer hold, for the boundary between 'inside' and 'outside' has teasingly disappeared.

That, at least, is how the screenplay reads, for such a moment has been ingeniously prepared for and worked towards in Pinter's crafting of the script. If this *coup* is somewhat lost on audiences in the cinema, or appears at best as a felicitous Freudian slip on Mike's part, then this must be because the film reworks the screenplay in such a way as to reduce substantially our readiness for it. Fowles may well be an apprentice of reticence, and Pinter is clearly a master, but the ambitious subtleties of his script have apparently not always survived the relentlessly demoticising urgencies of the medium itself. (pp. 50-3)

The film depends upon the useful convention—a quite false and artificial one surely, though perfectly plausible in its context—that a given film is likely to be shot in chronological sequence. Thus the action of *both* plots can then move from Lyme to Exeter, from Exeter to London, and finally to Lake Windermere, while the tensions between frustration and release, secrecy and revelation echo through and between each story-line. When Sarah disappears after her love-making with Charles at Endicott's hotel in Exeter, Anna disappears to a rendezvous with a French lover. Mike wants to pursue her to London as Charles wishes to pursue Sarah. A party at Mike's London home, staged by him so that he can see Anna, contains some notably Pinteresque moments. It introduces Mike's wife Sonia . . . about whom 'Mrs. Poulteney' . . . remarks 'So serene. Of course, she seems so serene, doesn't she, the wife?' That quizzical and comic focus on the repetition and defamil-iarisation of a word (serene) which charges and challenges and flattens it, and which both solicits and defeats the attempt at 'interpretation', is reminiscent of Pinter at his best. So is a later exchange about 'envy' between Sonia and Anna, where the equivocation of the signals being given out is rather dif-ferent. Each of these depends precisely on the gravitational pull we are invited to surmise that the unspoken/unsayable may have on the dialogue; on the power, that is, of a taboo, which renders the uttered phrases always shifty. The possibility of 'depth of meaning' always threatens paradoxically to impov-erish and empty what is expressed, making its indeterminacies bland. Such a semantically over-productive censorship, we note, is as much a feature of the 'modern' as of the 'Victorian' dialogue. (pp. 54-5)

For Fowles, in one fiction after another, the feudalising and the modernising of relations between the sexes are shown to be linked and the liaison between two kinds of fantasy—'lib-eration' and 'courtly love'—is perpetually re-solemnised. The film grants the Victorian love-story a happy ending, then con-trives to undercut this by suggesting through its setting—near the cradle of English literary Romanticism—and presenta-tion—deliberately aping a sugary genre painting—that we should perhaps be sceptical about taking this at face-value; and also by immediately cutting to the modern story which achieves its own closure at the unit party in the same house, staged to celebrate the completion of the film-within-the-film. A scene with 'Ernestina' doing a fan-dance in a Victorian corset to an enthusiastic audience, which is in the screenplay, is replaced in the film by a back-view of her, fists clenching, watching wistfully after Mike as he disappears into Anna's dressing-room—the same studio room in which Charles and Sarah at last re-met—hinting at a further modern love-triangle to reflect the Victorian one. The fan-dance might have given too much weight to the patronising assumption that we have, in very truth, now emancipated ourselves, even if Pinter himself is certainly too canny to have meant such a scene to be anything but ironic.

So the prosperous complications of Fowles' novel or Pinter's script do not always survive into the film. The effect that the film leaves you with is appropriately one of having been teased, but without a cunning or a circumspection which can fully satisfy. (pp. 55-6)

Peter J. Conradi, '''The French Lieutenant's Woman':
Novel, Screenplay, Film,'' in Critical Quarterly *(re-printed by permission of Manchester University Press),*
Vol. 24, No. 1, Spring, 1982, pp. 41-57.

ROBERT BRUSTEIN

The Hothouse is hardly the best written of Pinter's works or the most exquisitely engineered, but it has a kind of unbuttoned, careening energy I find impossible to resist, and it suggests a road he might have taken had he not chosen to perfect the art

of tergiversation. Most of Pinter's plays are not so much suggestive as evasive; his fondness for textual lacunae lays the burden of specificity on the actor. Since actors are hardly re-luctant to comply, Pinter's scenes tend to move down instead of forward, tantalizing us with their ciphers and hieroglyphs. It is not to denigrate this playwright's extraordinary crafts-manship to say there may be a lot less in his work than meets the eye. Pinter admits to being amused when commentators labor over the "meaning" of his works, continuing to insist (correctly, in my view) that they mean no more than they say. The trouble is that what they say has grown increasingly pre-cious, as if Pinter's closest pals these days were Bertie Wooster and Sebastian Flyte. His upper-class characters are so frozen and brittle that one wonders if he is satirizing their emotion-lessness or actually trying to celebrate their "cool."

As its title suggests, *The Hothouse*, mercifully, is hot. Com-pared with Pinter's other play of this period, *The Birthday Party,* which has not aged well, it is vivid, molten, on fire. The characters are unpressed, no matter how they try to arrange themselves; they are controllers, but out of control. The scene is a mental institution, where the keepers themselves are mad. The invisible patients are identified only by numbers; there are no doctors, only a combative staff of edgy, querulous, ambi-tious functionaries. Nobody recovers in this institution; the only action involves the power games of the administration. . . .

Pinter's typically clipped, terse, almost stacatto dialogue here is the agent of a strong emotional undercurrent which often breaks out into physical violence; and the play, for all its familiar Pinterian mystery and menace, also possesses a cogent farcical urgency that builds to a remorseless indictment of to-talitarian procedures. (p. 26)

The Hothouse shows us a Pinter moved more by a capacity for indignation than by a love of elegance—Pinter as redskin rather than paleface. This is a way of saying that it is animated by a boiling energy he hasn't shown in his work since *The Home-coming,* and a sense of personal engagement he perhaps has never shown. Resurrecting this work may suggest that, dis-satisfied with the wispy attenuations of his Mayfair period, he is preparing to turn volcanic once again. If so, I will look forward to his next play with a good deal more eagerness than I have awaited his works in the past. (p. 27)

Robert Brustein, "Pinter's New Play" (reprinted by permission of the author; © *1982 The New Republic, Inc.), in* The New Republic, *Vol. 186, No. 14, April 7, 1982, pp. 26-7.**

MARTIN ESSLIN

Which way is our leading dramatist going? Is Harold Pinter moving away from the extravagantly 'Pinteresque' situations and language of his earlier style—which he had revived with the re-discovery and exhumation of *The Hothouse*? or is he developing in the direction of a new, much more subtly search-ing exploration of his favourite themes of memory, the nature of the self and of reality; a direction in which he had embarked with *Betrayal*? . . .

[*Other Places*] gives an affirmative answer to *both* alternatives intimated by that question: two of the brief playlets in the triad are vintage Pinter, one, and by far the most interesting and fascinating delves ever more deeply into the new style and method.

[*Family Voices* is] essentially a radio play. It consists mainly of a montage of 'letters', letters that obviously have never been sent nor ever been received, between a young man—not yet 21, says the mother at one point—who has left home and has disappeared from his mother's ken, and the mother. The young man has found refuge in a house, in which he seems at first a lodger, later more like a member of the family. That house in inhabited by a number of people all called Withers who sport various titles, Lady Withers, the Hon Mrs Withers, etc. The young man is subjected to various types of sexual assault, hetero-as well as homosexual from these inmates. He enjoys his new home, yet at the end, when suddenly and unexpectedly the voice of his (perhaps dead?) father intrudes, he expresses a yearning to return home to his mother. There are echoes here of *The Birthday Party, The Homecoming* even of Pinter's earliest play *The Room*. But essentially this is a *radio* play and it is, I think, a mistake to stage it.

After all, the point of the piece is that it takes place within the young man's consciousness: *he* imagines the letters he might write to his mother, *he* imagines his mother's possible appeals to him, and in the end it is he who wonders whether his father might now be dead. By putting the son and the mother visibly in front of our eyes—however stylishly silhouetted against brilliantly lit screens—and by letting the father's voice come out of a black region between them, there is a clear indication that the mother and son are more real than the father; there is no more room to wonder whether the mother actually utters these sentiments, or whether they are merely within the son's imagination. (p. 20)

Victoria Station turns out to be, basically, another short radio play. The dialogue between a taxi controller and one of his drivers is conducted entirely through a radio intercom system. But here the fact that the controller is placed in a glass booth high above the stage, and the driver in a cab plunged in total darkness, but with headlights on and an area of light around his face, does at least not interfere with the essential message of the play. Which is that the driver has suddenly plunged out of the routine of his humdrum daily existence to the point that he has even forgotten what and where Victoria Station might be. He is standing by a dark park, perhaps at the Crystal Palace. But he is seeing the Crystal Palace in front of him, in spite of the fact that the Crystal Palace has, as the controller tells him, burned down ages ago, 'in the great fire of London'. The reason for the driver's change of consciousness is that he has fallen in love with his passenger, a beautiful girl now asleep on the backseat of his cab. In the end the controller, who, at the beginning compares himself to God, directing the world from above, realises the sterility of his confined position and announces his determination to come and join the driver.

This sketch is very funny; but also opens philosophical and metaphysical vistas: it contrasts our humdrum, realistic style of existence with a poetical one, the higher consciousness of someone who has fallen in love and lives the life of the imagination. But, in so short a piece, all this is merely hinted at. No doubt Pinter will explore it further in a more substantial form.

A Kind of Alaska touches similar concerns, but in a totally different style. . . . (pp. 20-1)

The play is very simple: a woman who fell into catatonia at the age of sixteen in the 1940s is waking up 29 years later at the age of 45. The doctor who is at her bedside tried to break the news of her predicament to her gradually; at the end she is confronted by her sister whom she knew as a schoolgirl and who has now become a middle-aged woman. Quite clearly: time, reality, the nature of the self are the themes that run underneath the realistic and soberly told account of this event. Pinter has here chosen a brilliant approach to all these profound problems. It is only gradually that Deborah, the patient, who at first thinks she has merely had a normal night's sleep, becomes aware that she has been imprisoned in a very narrow space; or in vast hall of mirrors; that she has been frozen in a kind of Alaska. . . .

A Kind of Alaska is a brilliant short play. This, it seems to me, is the direction that Harold Pinter will take to develop and surpass his already immense record of achievement. It is a minor masterpiece, foreshadowing, I hope, some major ones. (p. 21)

Martin Esslin, in a review of "Other Places" (© copyright Martin Esslin 1982; reprinted with permission), in Plays and Players, *No. 351, December, 1982, pp. 20-1.*

BERNARD F. DUKORE

Frequently Pinter's plays begin comically but turn to physical, psychological, or potential violence—sometimes, in varying sequences, to all three. Terror inheres in a statement in *The Room* that the onstage room, which is occupied, is to let. Although the play turns comic again, it ends on a note of physical violence.

In the early plays menace lurks outside, but it also has psychological roots. The titular room—in which the heroine lives, fearful of an outside force she does not specify—is dark. In *The Birthday Party* the sheltered young man fears visitors. In *The Dumb Waiter* outside forces menace a questioning killer. In *A Slight Ache* a psychologically disturbed man fears a man he invites inside. While menace may take the shape of particular characters, it is usually unspecified or unexplained—therefore, more ominous.

Partly because realistic explanations are absent, disturbing questions arise. One is unsure why characters visit others, why they commit inexplicable actions, why the others fear them. Frustrated reviewers or readers accuse Pinter of wilful obfuscation. Yet before he began to write plays, he had acted in conventional works with clear exposition and pat conclusions. The fact that his own, unconventional plays contain neither should alert one to the possibility that other dramatic aspects are more important, that Pinter's refusal to focus on answers to 'Who' and 'Why?' is a deliberate effort to focus on answers to 'What?' and 'How?' To put the matter another way, present activities, interrelationships, and stratagems are more dramatically important than past actions. His drama is not a matter of They have been, therefore they are; but rather, They do, therefore they are.

These early plays conform to the characteristics of the Theatre of the Absurd. . . . Their effective unsettling quality, with its fusion of realism and nonrealism, distinguishes Pinter's artistic signature from those of other writers of this genre. Because events and actions are unexplained, and apparently illogical or unmotivated, the world seems capricious or malevolent. One can rely upon nothing. What is apparently secure is not secure. A haven does not protect. A weapon vanishes without warning. Linguistic absurdity may suggest the absurdity of the human condition. Fear of a menace may suggest the universal trauma of man in the universe. (pp. 24-5)

The title *A Night Out* would seem to herald a departure from the interiors of Pinter's first five plays. With the benefit of hindsight, however, the departure probably derives from the medium for which he wrote the work, radio, which permits an easier flow through different locales than the stage does. When writing a play for the stage, in contrast to writing one for another theatrical medium . . . , Pinter usually thinks in terms of a clearly delineated space. The chief exceptions are the lyric *Silence*, whose dramaturgy is unique in the Pinter canon, and the multi-scenic *Betrayal*, whose structure may derive partly from his cinema experience. Furthermore the intrinsic quality of *A Night Out* suggests an emphasis not on the last word of the title but on the first two. Departure is temporary.

Nevertheless this play, like the two that follow [*The Caretaker* and *Night School*], is less enigmatic, mysterious, or unrealistic than Pinter's earlier work. (p. 46)

While the trio of plays . . . are to some extent enigmatic, their enigmas differ in kind from those of the earlier works. The nature of what is undefined is more specific and whatever mysterious qualities it may possess, the unreal is not among them. In short, these plays move toward greater realism. (p. 47)

In *The Room* and *The Birthday Party* characters who hope they have sanctuary try to defend themselves from intruders; in *A Night Out* a character tries to break out of his soul-stultifying haven. In contrast to all, a character in *The Caretaker* aims to find sanctuary. Unlike *The Room, The Birthday Party*, and *The Hothouse*, no unrealistic elements erupt in *The Caretaker;* yet, as in *The Hothouse*, electro-shock treatment in a mental institution figures prominently in it; and, as in *A Night Out*, its realistic mode is unbroken. (p. 48)

As in *The Collection*, infidelity is a subject of *The Homecoming*. As in *The Lover*, an unanticipated sexual arrangement concludes its action. As in *The Basement*, a woman's sexual allegiance shifts. As in *Tea Party*, a character who is unable to cope collapses. As in all these plays, but more savagely, characters in *The Homecoming* vie for positions of power, don protective masks, and both flippantly and abrasively mock each other.

To an all-male household—Max, a former butcher, his chauffeur brother Sam, and his sons Lenny and Joey, a pimp and a part-time boxer—the oldest son Teddy returns after six years in America, where he teaches philosophy, with his wife Ruth— a surprise to the family who did not know he had married or that he has three sons. At the end of the play the family proposes that Ruth stay, service them, and become a prostitute. After blurting out that Max's late wife Jessie committed adultery with his best friend, Sam collapses. Teddy leaves for America. Ruth remains. (p. 75)

The play disorients. A butcher cooks what one of his sons calls dog food. A young fighter is knocked down by his old father. A philosopher refuses to philosophise. A chauffeur is unable to drive. A pimp takes orders from his whore. The whore does not go all the way with a man. Words disorient, as when Lenny says of Teddy, 'And my goodness we are proud of him here, I can tell you. Doctor of Philosophy and all that . . . leaves quite an impression'. . . . The first phrase appropriate to an old woman not a young man, the triteness of the phrase that ends the first sentence, 'and all that' belitting the advanced

degree—these disorient, thereby conveying the impression that what is said is not what is meant.

During the opening dialogue Lenny reads the racing section of a newspaper while Max asks for scissors and a cigarette. Although Max wants them, what underlies his requests is a demand for acknowledgement and attention. Lenny's indifference to his reminiscences, questions, insults, and threats indicates that the exchange is commonplace. Usually Lenny says nothing, a suggestion of his superior status (indeed, if he were not dominant, Max would not behave as he does). When Lenny speaks, it is often to assert a prerogative or to silence Max. When he initiates a subject (horseracing), it is to re-establish his status by contradicting Max, and when Max continues on it, Lenny's only response is to request a change of subject. Lenny takes the mickey out of Max who understands what Lenny is doing. When Max loses his temper and threatens to hit Lenny with his walking stick, Lenny mocks him by talking in a childlike manner. Beneath and through the dialogue they struggle for power—demanding recognition of status and self. (pp. 75-6)

In their frequently vicious struggles for power, no character is clearly victorious. Does Teddy intend at the start to let the nature of his family take its course and claim Ruth? If so, or if not, he does not leave the London house unscarred. Is Ruth at the end in the position of Queen Bee? If so, she may for specified periods of time become a worker who supports the drones. (p. 84)

In most of Pinter's plays the past is unclear: Stanley's transgression (*The Birthday Party*), Aston's experience in the mental asylum (*The Caretaker*), adultery (*The Collection*), and so forth. More prominently than before, however, [*Landscape, Silence, Night*, and *Old Times*] focus on the past. Usually they are called memory plays.

Landscape has two characters, Beth and Duff, who live in the house of their former employer, apparently deceased. They reminisce. Her memories include the sea, the beach, and a man lying on a sand dune; his, a dog, a park, and a pub. Her memories are gentle and fragile; his, frequently vulgar and aggressive. They do not converse with each other.

Like a painting, *Landscape* contains no movement. The characters do not leave their chairs, which a kitchen table separates; and they are separated from their background, which is dim. Figuratively the stage picture is an immobile landscape. The vista is distant, in that the audience is unable to penetrate beneath the facades of the reminiscing characters. Despite the clarity of the figures in the foreground, the sketch is faint and shadowy.

What happens, what the audience perceives, is two characters, physically and emotionally separated from each other and their environment, dwelling on their memories. (pp. 85-6)

Two incompatible people, once loving, are isolated from each other, implicitly rejecting each other, uncommunicative in an unchanging landscape. The play's final line, spoken by Beth, is ambiguous. 'Oh my true love I said' . . . apparently tender, but invoking a past love and thereby rejecting the man presently near her, as his verbal rape had just demeaned her.

As in *Landscape*, the noncomic *Silence* situates each of its characters in a chair in a distinct area of the stage—visually symbolic of isolation. Unlike *Landscape*, a character occasionally moves to another character. What the three personae of *Silence* remember occurred when Rumsey was forty, Bates in his mid-thirties, and Ellen in her twenties—their ages as they appear on stage. (p. 87)

All three characters, having chosen solitary lives, remember the past when they were together. Silences often separate their mnemonic monologues that decreasingly dovetail each other, until after a long silence that concludes the play, memory seems to fade with the fading lights. Like *Landscape*, *Silence* is a verbal construct with minimal action and character interrelations—a recited piece, more poetic than dramatic.

Much shorter than either is *Night*, another memory play with no movement but, unlike the others, with a conventional story. Also unlike them, it is generally comic and unlike other Pinter plays has a celebratory conclusion. A married couple, both in their forties, have conflicting memories of their first stroll together. . . . 'Gentle' and 'sweet' are adjectives one does not usually apply to Pinter's plays, but both befit the lovely *Night*, wherein the past brings nostalgia, not dread. Pinter goes gently into *Night*.

These atypical works, however, seem to be experiments in craft and strengthenings of thematic concepts to be employed in a major work in which memory is prominent. Pinter's next play is that work, *Old Times*, written six years after *The Homecoming*, his last previous full-length play. (pp. 88-9)

In *Old Times*, Deeley and Kate, married, live on the seacoast. Anna, a former roommate of Kate's, visits them. The women reminisce. Later, Deeley and Anna say they met each other twenty years before. Their rivalry over Kate intensifies. Kate, asserting her dominant position, terminates their sparring. As terms like rivalry and sparring suggest, the stratagems, taunts, and power struggles that characterise plays like *The Collection* and *The Homecoming*, where the past is also important, are major factors in this play. (pp. 89-90)

Like *Landscape* and *Silence*, *Old Times* is a memory play, but unlike these plays, *Old Times* portrays, in terms of dramatic conflict, the past's influence on the present. Unlike *Night*, which also contains conflict, the resolution of *Old Times* is devastating—akin, in this respect, to that of the other full-length plays thus far analysed. (p. 98)

[In certain respects], Pinter's most recent plays recapitulate earlier themes and techniques. In other respects . . . , they move—sometimes provisionally, sometimes boldly—in new directions. With *Monologue* and *No Man's Land*, the familiar terrain is more obvious than the new; with *Betrayal*, the reverse. (p. 99)

Monologue is a monologue. Its meaning inheres in its title. In drama, a monologue refers to a solitary person speaking, but not to himself, as in a soliloquy, and it differs from dialogue. In *Monologue*, a solitary character talks, but not to himself. The title is also apt in that the play is about isolation, its speaker is alone from start to finish, and no dialogue or response is possible. Because Pinter employs the visual as well as the verbal, *Monologue* can be effective only when an audience sees the play, not simply hears it recited: the speaker talks to an empty chair. Whereas Eugene Ionesco uses many chairs, in his play *The Chairs*, to embody nothingness and to suggest the metaphysical void, Pinter in *Monologue* employs one empty chair to embody absence and to suggest the isolation and loneliness of the play's sole character. The stage picture—a man addressing an empty chair—is a concrete, theatrical metaphor of the subject.

The play's ambience is the subtle, tragicomic movement from friendship to loneliness, as the speaker increasingly reveals the depths of his affection for the man and love for the woman. In losing her, he also lost him, and he pleads for their friendship, offering to die for their children, if they have children. But an empty chair cannot respond. At the end of the play, he fully reveals his true isolation and loneliness. (pp. 99-100)

Although *No Man's Land* contains more than one character, its opening is almost a monologue by the garrulous Spooner, a down-at-heel, self-styled poet whom Hirst, a famous, prosperous writer, meets and brings home for a drink. Spooner attempts to ingratiate himself with his host and thereby to install himself in Hirst's home, replacing Foster and Briggs who are employed to protect Hirst from outside encroachment. Spooner's efforts fail. (p. 102)

No Man's Land may be the end of a phase in Pinter's writing, for it echoes many of his previous works. The ambience of menace recalls the early plays, and some of the menace is comic. Struggles for power between Spooner and Hirst's aides recall the works that focus on this theme, and as in those plays mockery is sometimes funny, sometimes threatening. (p. 104)

In *Betrayal* the backward movement, dramatic not narrative, is toward disillusion; the audience, having witnessed the end of the affair and its aftermath, understands how transitory are the lovers' feelings toward each other during the early time of the affair. The forward movement, more intermittent, is toward such revelations as how the husband deals with his friend after he has discovered his wife's infidelity with him. When the affair is about to begin, the audience has already seen how it ends. . . . [The] beginning that ends *Betrayal* is clear, and it fixes in art its retrieval of time lost.

The title is what the play is about, its pervading ambience, what happens in every scene. (pp. 107-08)

Despite the different dramaturgy of *Betrayal*, it uses familiar techniques and themes. Robert, for example, takes the piss out of Jerry, who is unaware of what lies beneath the surface. . . . Betrayal is also a theme of other plays by Pinter, including *The Collection* and *The Basement*. Furthermore, the last/chronologically first scene of *Betrayal* can be described in terms of the image Pinter employed for his first play: two people are alone in a room.

In such matters *Betrayal* recapitulates previous plays by Pinter. More important than similarities are major differences. In *Betrayal* Pinter provides what he refused to provide in earlier plays: verification. Also *Betrayal* is his only play in which the audience knows more than the characters do—excepting the first two scenes. *Betrayal* may be his most accessible play since it provides insight into his distinctive techniques. Because we know what happened or what the characters know before it happens or before they know it, we can perceive their manoeuvres as they evade, don masks, and mock each other. When Robert slyly taunts Jerry by asserting his own greater physical fitness, we understand (as Emma does and Jerry does not) his reference to his knowledge of her affair. When he refers to his folly as a publisher, we understand (as Jerry does not) his allusion to his folly as a trusting husband and friend. Because Pinter verifies actions and motivations, we can attend, without bafflement about the past, to the dramatic present.

Although Pinter has been writing plays for almost a quarter of a century, it seems likely from these recent works that his inventiveness is far from exhausted. To the contrary, he appears to be renewing himself, finding fresh areas and means to express his changing dramatic vision. Extending himself, he also maintains his footing on familiar terrain. His fresh starts are from fixed points, which provide solid technical bases for his dramatic departures. What the unmasked face of *Monologue,* the personal subject of *No Man's Land,* or the major dramaturgical departure of *Betrayal* may forecast is impossible to predict. One looks forward to the next Pinter play with the same eagerness one did ten or twenty years ago. A comparable statement can be made of few other contemporary dramatists. (pp. 114-15)

Bernard F. Dukore, in his Harold Pinter *(reprinted by permission of Grove Press, Inc.; copyright © 1982 by Bernard Dukore), Grove Press, 1982, 139 p.*

ROGER SCRUTON

Although Beckett and Pinter have less in common than meets the eye, nevertheless they share a fundamental premise: their characters are raw, vulnerable, dangerously exposed to one another. They speak words carefully, with painful consideration, as though every excess of communication puts their existence at risk. Words are swords to them, but also shields. The characters are ill at ease in company, but alert to language. Hence their utility for the modern theatre-goer, who lives, eats, drinks and breathes embarrassment, and who is never more embarrassed than by his recognition that he has no great message, and no private destiny, to convey.

Since his majestic attempt to "eff the ineffable" in the trilogy of novels, Beckett's literary career has involved a paring away, a steady elimination of all embellishments to his central theme. Although Beckett defines social sentiments, in social language, he has, in the end, only one character, and that character is a living ("if you call that living") contradiction: the self who struggles vainly to be the object of its own regard, the ghost which flits before every aspiration. To present this theme, Beckett originally required hallucinatory details, aborted stories, quarrelsome observations, narrated by subjects who fade first into each other, and then into the page. Beckett's subsequent minimalism is a stylistic achievement, an emancipation from redundancies.

Pinter's career has been in a way comparable. The new triptych of short tableaux, *Other Places* . . . , when seen in relation to *The Birthday Party,* or *The Caretaker,* represents a considerable economy and condensation. But Pinter's minimalism, while influenced by Beckett, is quite unrelated to the style or meaning of Beckett's recent playlets and pamphlets. It proceeds, not from the attempt to whittle down a single experience to its metaphysical pith, but rather from a constant venturing into new realms of experience, so that hesitation and silence take on increasingly masterful forms. Beckett's tone of voice is tetchy, disappointed, a kind of *gran rifiuto,* in the face of the perpetual elusiveness both of the "thou" and the "I." Pinter's voice has no such universal meaning. While it grows always from the impossible confrontation of human beings and their arbitrary desires, it varies minutely with the situation to which it is applied. Pinter's scenarios are carefully observed and ultra-realistic representations of English society. There has been a marked "upward mobility" over time; but even the most recent pieces remain wedded to actual situations, studied by an author whose ear for ordinary speech is preternaturally fine.

Family Voices (the first of the three tableaux) tells of a house in which characters from all periods of Pinter's career are assembled: a sluttish, good-for-nothing Mrs Withers; an old proletarian Mr Withers; another Mr Withers whose insane theatricality allows Pinter to recapture the setpiece style of the early plays; even a Lady Withers, whose title, however, proves baffling to the adolescent narrator. In this play, as in *Landscape,* there is no dialogue, only interlocking speech, as one character's voice flows into the silence vacated by the other's. A mother and a son write to each other letters which are never sent, or which, if sent, never arrive at their destination. To their lonely, reaching voices, a third is added, that of the man, husband of the one, father of the other, who has died since contact was lost. The situation deprives Pinter of the device with which he established his tone of voice, the familiar English repartee. The tense atmosphere of *The Caretaker* depends upon a to-ing and fro-ing of question and answer, from which the set speeches emerge as declarations of a longing comic in its ordinariness, and pathetic in its inability to elicit a response. *Family Voices* consists of questions which cannot be answered, and answers that wing off into the void in hopeless search for questions that would explain them. Were the mother and son actually to make contact, one feels, the intensity of their communication would be unbearable. But their non-communication is the source of a new comedy and pathos, as each slowly adjusts to the absence of the other.

The connection which is feared and longed for in *Family Voices* is granted in the sequel, *Victoria Station.* A cab-driver is contacted by his controller, who speaks from an office upstage, while the driver answers from the illuminated car below. . . . The controller, who obtains only bizarre, vacant-seeming responses, is at first exasperated, then angry, and then filled with loathing for this *274* who lies like a barrier across the stream of ordinary experience. But the loathing turns to need, and finally to a kind of tenderness; the driver likewise develops a need for the controller, imploring him not to seek the services of any rival. "Don't have anything to do with *135*", he cries. "He's not your man. He'll lead you into blind alleys by the dozen. They all will. Don't leave me. I'm your man. I'm the only one you can trust. . . ." And strangely, despite *274*'s inability to understand the simplest order, his words ring true.

The two characters are in the original Pinter mould: ordinary people suddenly thrown out of orbit by an arbitrary act of communication. But words, cast across the distance between the office and the cab, acquire unpredictable meanings. The characters become increasingly vulnerable with every verbal impact. By the time the scene fades it is clear that their lives have been irreversibly transformed. The controller leaves his office in search of the driver, like a man who turns his back on home and family for the sake of some catastrophic love.

A Kind of Alaska, the final tableau, continues the theme of distance. However, the distance is not of space but of time.

A victim of sleeping sickness (such as described by Oliver Sacks in *Awakenings*) is brought to life by an injection of L-Dopa, after 29 years of comatose inertia. The play describes her bewildered reaction, a child's soul in a middle-aged body, the fallen face of a ruined aunt, who listens to a voice, her own voice, describing birthdays, boy-friends, and parties. [The protagonist] conveys both the fear of the woman, and the forthright, virtuous cheekiness of the child, as they contend for possession of a body which has lain vacant for a generation. The woman, Deborah, is attended by a doctor, and by the doctor's wife, Deborah's younger sister. The effect of Deborah's illness is captured by the doctor's words: "Your sister was twelve when you were left for dead. When she was twenty

I married her. She is a widow. I have lived with you. . . ."
The words of the bystanders are succinct, hesitant, overcome,
while the sufferer herself rushes into speech, stumbles, retreats,
and then impetuously rushes again.

The scene is realistic, and uncompromisingly painful. It perfectly illustrates Pinter's boldness, and his appetite for new
material, in which he shows a scrupulous attention to an actual,
but uncanny, predicament. Beckett's Cartesian observer could
never sustain such concentrated interest. the Beckettian subject
lives only in the dark, the limedark of his ruminations. While
filled with compassion, it is a compassion inspired by failure,
itself born of metaphysical impossibility, to relate to the world
or to himself. (pp. 37-9)

The critics have been lavish in praise of *A Kind of Alaska.* But
surely, whatever its merits, it cannot really be described as
theatre. Deborah's unmanageable experience obliterates the
drama. In the face of it, the subsidiary characters become
gauche and frozen. None of the three can obtain a consistent
tone of voice; in the nature of the case, every voice is suspect.

When Davies, the caretaker, describes his shoes, saying, "You
see, they're gone, they're no good, the good's gone out of
them", the idiom leaps out at us, joining us to the cheerful
spirit of survival. In *Victoria Station,* the controller veneers his
sentiments with idiom, saving us again from sharing his perplexity. In *A Kind of Alaska,* however, everything is stark,
raw, absolute. The spectator, sensing the impossibility of response, suffers a growing discomfort. The Pinter voice no
longer operates. . . . There is no consolation, no idiom, no
normality. The spectator, outraged by sufferings which are
without resolution, withdraws his futile sympathy.

Oliver Sacks was deeply disturbed by the effects of the drug
L-Dopa. His description of the new miseries that were to confront his patients as they struggled, often in vain, to come to
terms with the imperfect consciousness which their illness had
left them, is heart-rending. It is hard to imagine a clearer
refutation of the myth upon which Beckett has relied in all his
writings—the myth of the transcendental spectator who lurks,
untouched and untouchable, within the arbitrary folds of human
flesh. Pinter has never given twopence for that myth. He rightly
perceives that a nothing would do as well as this transcendental
something about which nothing can be said. It is the writer's
responsibility to study words; human beings exist, not behind,
but within their utterance. Deborah is neither more nor less
than the words which come from her. The theatre of embarrassment perpetually forces us to discard the illusion that there
is an ego hiding behind our words. But this refutation of the
ego creates a need for its opposite, for community, for idiom,
for the consoling tone of voice which turns the individual into
a type, and disaster into comedy. (pp. 39-40)

Roger Scruton, "Pinter's Progress," in Encounter
*(© 1983 by Encounter Ltd.), Vol. LX, No. 1, Jan-
uary, 1983, pp. 37-40.*

Katherine Anne Porter

1890-1980

American short story writer, novelist, and critic.

Porter is widely acknowledged to be one of midcentury America's finest writers of short fiction. An excellent stylist, Porter endowed her work with precision of image and detail. Her perceptive psychological studies depend on a moment of illumination rather than action to express the truth of an experience. The novellas "Noon Wine" (1937) and "Pale Horse, Pale Rider" (1939) are usually lauded as her best work and considered almost perfect examples of the genre. However, it was her long-awaited novel, *Ship of Fools* (1962), which brought Porter wide readership and financial success.

The publication of *Ship of Fools* was a significant literary event since Porter's reputation had already been established as an expert in short fiction. Written over a twenty-year period when Porter was busy lecturing, traveling, and doing other writing, the novel describes an ill-assorted group of tourists traveling by ship from Vera Cruz to Bremerhaven in 1931. The novel has been seen as an allegory showing the moral malaise of the world drifting into World War II. While the initial reaction was enthusiastic for the most part, subsequent revaluations focussed on the shallowness of its stereotyped characterizations, the lack of plot development, and the falsity of its prophetic tone. Most commentators concluded that Porter's excellence in short fiction could not be sustained in a longer work.

Many of Porter's fictional themes and subjects are drawn from her life. Born into a poor Southern family and losing her mother and grandmother as a child, Porter determined to make something of herself and left the South for extensive sojourns in Mexico, Europe, and other parts of the United States. From her Mexican experience came such renowned stories as "María Conception" (1922), and "Hacienda" (1934). From her trips to Europe came an early short story about an American in Nazi Germany, "The Leaning Tower" (1944), and *Ship of Fools*. Her best work centers on her fictional counterpart, Miranda, a young girl growing up in the South. Miranda is the protagonist of "Pale Horse, Pale Rider," a sensitive love story touched by the tragedy of war. Other Miranda stories deal with the social and human initiation of a young girl growing up in a South coming to terms with its past. "Noon Wine" is also set in the South and perhaps best illustrates the overriding theme in Porter's work: that the basic humanity of people is often corrupted by outside forces. Many commentators feel that these stories reflect Porter's reconciliation with early memories and her unbreakable ties with the South.

(See also *CLC*, Vols. 1, 3, 7, 10, 13, 15; *Contemporary Authors*, Vols. 1-4, rev. ed., Vol. 101 [obituary]; *Contemporary Authors New Revision Series*, Vol. 1; *Something about the Author*, Vol. 23; *Dictionary of Literary Biography*, Vols. 4, 9; and *Dictionary of Literary Biography Yearbook: 1980*.)

EUDORA WELTY

Most good stories are about the interior of our lives, but Katherine Anne Porter's stories take place there; they show surface

only at her choosing. Her use of the physical world is enough to meet her needs and no more; she is not wasteful with anything. This artist, writing her stories with a power that stamps them to their last detail on the memory, does so to an extraordinary degree without sensory imagery.

I have the most common type of mind, the visual, and when first I began to read her stories it stood in the way of my trust in my own certainty of what was there that, for all my being bowled over by them, I couldn't see them happening. This was a very good thing for me. As her work has done in many other respects, it has shown me a thing or two about the eye of fiction, about fiction's visibility and invisibility, about its clarity, its radiance.

Heaven knows she can see. . . . There is, above all, **"Noon Wine"** to establish it forever that when she wants a story to be visible, it is. **"Noon Wine"** is visible all the way through, full of scenes charged with dramatic energy; everything is brought forth into movement, dialogue; the title itself is Mr. Helton's tune on the harmonica. **"Noon Wine"** is the most beautifully objective work she has done. And nothing has been sacrificed to its being so (or she wouldn't have done it); to the contrary. I find Mr. Hatch the scariest character she ever made, and he's just set down there in Texas, like a chair. There he stands, part of the everyday furniture of living. He's opaque, and he's the devil. Walking in at Mr. Thompson's gate—the same gate by which his tracked-down victim walked in first—he is that much more horrifying, almost too solid to the eyes to be countenanced. (So much for the visual mind.)

Katherine Anne Porter has not in general chosen to cast her stories in scenes. Her sense of human encounter is profound, is fundamental to her work, I believe, but she has not often allowed it the dramatic character it takes in **"Noon Wine."** We may not see the significant moment happen within the story's present; we may not watch it occur between the two characters it joins. Instead, a silent blow falls while one character is alone—the most alone in his life, perhaps. . . . Often the revelation that pierces a character's mind and heart and shows him his life or his death comes in a dream, in retrospect, in illness or in utter defeat, the moment of vanishing hope, the moment of dying. What Miss Porter makes us see are those subjective worlds of hallucination, obsession, fever, guilt. The presence of death hovering about Granny Weatherall she makes as real and brings as near as Granny's own familiar room that stands about her bed—realer, nearer, for we recognize not only death's presence but the character death has come in for Granny Weatherall.

The flash of revelation is revelation but is unshared. But how unsuspecting we are to imagine so for a moment—it *is* shared, and by ourselves, her readers, who must share it feeling the doubled anguish of knowing this fact, doubled still again when it is borne in upon us how close to life this is, to *our* lives. (pp. 30-2)

Katherine Anne Porter shows us that we do not have to see a story happen to know what is taking place. For all we are to know, she is not looking at it happen herself when she writes it; for her eyes are always looking through the gauze of the passing scene, not distracted by the immediate and transitory; her vision is reflective.

Her imagery is as likely as not to belong to a time other than the story's present, and beyond that it always differs from it in nature; it is *memory* imagery, coming into the story from memory's remove. It is a distilled, a re-formed imagery, for it is part of a language made to speak directly of premonition, warning, surmise, anger, despair. (p. 32)

Katherine Anne Porter's moral convictions have given her readers another way to see. Surely these convictions represent the fixed points about which her work has turned, and not only that but they govern her stories down to the smallest detail. Her work has formed a constellation, with its own North Star. (pp. 32-3)

In Katherine Anne Porter's stories the effect has surely been never to diminish life but always to intensify life in the part significant to her story. It is a darkening of the house as the curtain goes up on this stage of her own. . . .

Since her subject is what lies beneath the surface, her way—quite direct—is to penetrate, brush the stuff away. It is the writer like Chekhov whose way of working is indirect. He moved indeed toward the same heart and core but by building up some corresponding illusion of life. Writers of Chekhov's side of the family are themselves illusionists and have necessarily a certain fondness for, lenience toward, the whole shimmering fabric as such. Here we have the professional scientist, the good doctor, working with illusion and the born romantic artist—is she not?—working without it. Perhaps it is always the lyrical spirit that takes on instantaneous color, shape, pat-

tern of motion in work, while the meditative spirit must fly as quickly as possible out of the shell.

All the stories she has written are moral stories about love and the hate that is love's twin, love's impostor and enemy and death. Rejection, betrayal, desertion, theft roam the pages of her stories as they roam the world. (p. 33)

We hear in how many more stories than the one the litany of the little boy at the end of **"The Downward Path to Wisdom,"** his "comfortable, sleepy song": "I hate Papa, I hate Mama, I hate Grandma, I hate Uncle David, I hate Old Janet, I hate Marjory, I hate Papa, I hate Mama. . . ." It is like the long list of remembered losses in the story **"Theft"** made vocal, and we remember how that loser's decision to go on and let herself be robbed coincides with the rising "in her blood" of "a deep almost murderous anger." (p. 34)

I think it is the faces—the inner, secret faces—of her characters, in their self-delusion, their venom and pain, that their author herself is contemplating. . . .

If outrage is the emotion she has most strongly expressed, she is using outrage as her cool instrument. She uses it with precision to show what monstrosities of feeling come about not from the lack of the existence of love but from love's repudiation, betrayal. . . .

The anger that speaks everywhere in the stories would trouble the heart for their author whom we love except that her anger is pure, the reason for it evident and clear, and the effect exhilarating. She has made it the tool of her work; and what we do is rejoice in it. We are aware of the compassion that guides it, as well. Only compassion could have looked where she looks, could have seen and probed what she sees. Real compassion is perhaps always in the end unsparing; it must make itself a part of knowing. Self-pity does not exist here; these stories come out trenchant, bold, defying; they are tough as sanity, unrelinquished sanity, is tough.

Despair is here, as well described as if it were Mexico. It is a despair, however, that is robust and sane, open to negotiation by the light of day. Life seen as a savage ordeal has been investigated by a straightforward courage, unshaken nerve, a rescuing wit, and above all with the searching intelligence that is quite plainly not to be daunted. In the end the stories move us not to despair ourselves but to an emotion quite opposite because they are so seriously and clear-sightedly pointing out what they have been formed to show: that which is true under the skin, that which will remain a fact of the spirit. (pp. 34-5)

Seeing what is not there, putting trust in a false picture of life, has been one of the worst nightmares that assail her characters. . . . [We] watch the romantic and the anti-romantic pulling each other to pieces. Is the romantic ever scotched? I believe not. Even if there rises a new refrain, even if the most ecstatic words ever spoken turn out to be "I hate you," the battle is not over for good. That battle is in itself a romance.

Nothing is so naturally subject to false interpretation as the romantic, and in furnishing that interpretation the Old South can beat all the rest. Yet some romantic things happen also to be true. Miss Porter's stories are not so much a stand against the romantic as such, as a repudiation of the false. What alone can instruct the heart is the experience of living, experience which can be vile; but what can never do it any good, what harms it more than vileness, are those tales, those legends of more than any South, those universal false dreams, the hopes sentimental and ubiquitous, which are not on any account to be gone by. (pp. 35-6)

In my own belief, the suspense—so acute and so real—in Katherine Anne Porter's work never did depend for its life on disclosure of the happenings of the narrative (nothing is going to turn out very well) but in the writing of the story, which becomes one single long sustained moment for the reader. Its suspense is one with its meaning. It must arise, then, from the mind, heart, spirit by which it moves and breathes.

It is a current like a strand of quicksilver through the serenity of her prose. In fiction of any substance, serenity can only be an achievement of the work itself, for any sentence that is alive with meaning is speaking out of passion. Serenity never belonged to the *now* of writing; it belongs to the later *now* offered its readers. In Katherine Anne Porter's work the forces of passion and self-possession seem equal, holding each other in balance from one moment to the next. The suspense born of the writing abides there in its own character, using the story for its realm, a quiet and well-commanded suspense, but a genie. (p. 36)

Ask what time it is in her stories and you are certain to get the answer: the hour is fateful. It is not necessary to see the hands of the clock in her work. It is a time of racing urgency, and it is already too late. And then recall how many of her characters are surviving today only for the sake of tomorrow, are living on tomorrow's coming; think how we see them clearest in reference to tomorrow. . . . In **"Pale Horse, Pale Rider"** the older Miranda asks Adam, out of her suffering, "Why can we not save each other?" and the straight answer is that there is no time. The story ends with the unforgettable words "Now there would be time for everything" because tomorrow has turned into oblivion, the ultimate betrayer is death itself.

But time, one of the main actors in her stories—teacher, fake healer, conspirator in betrayal, ally of death—is also, within the complete control of Miss Porter, with his inimical powers made use of, one of the movers of her writing, a friend to her work. It occurred to me that what is *seeing* the story is the dispassionate eye of time. Her passionate mind has asked itself, schooled itself, to use Time's eye. (pp. 37-8)

There is in all Katherine Anne Porter's work the strongest sense of unity in all the parts; and if it is in any degree a sound guess that an important dramatic element in the story has another role, a working role, in the writing of the story, might this not be one source of a unity so deeply felt? Such a thing in the practice of an art is unsurprising. Who can separate a story from the story's writing?

And there is too, in all the stories, a sense of long, learning life, the life that is the story's own, beginning from a long way back, extending somewhere into the future. As we read, the initial spark is not being struck before our eyes; the fire we see has already purified its nature and burns steadied by purpose, unwavering in meaning. It is no longer impulse, it is a signal, a beacon.

To me, it is the image of the eye of time that remains the longest in the mind at her story's end. There is a judgment to be passed. A moral judgment has to be, in all reason, what she has been getting at. But in a still further act of judiciousness, I feel, she lets Time pass that judgment.

Above all, I feel that what we are responding to in Katherine Anne Porter's work is the intensity of its life, which is more powerful and more profound than even its cry for justice. (p. 38)

And how calm is the surface, the invisible surface of it all! In a style as invisible as the rhythm of a voice, and as much her own as her own voice, she tells her stories of horror and humiliation and in the doing fills her readers with a rising joy. The exemplary prose that is without waste or extravagance of self-indulgence or display, without any claim for its triumph, is full of pride. And her reader shares in that pride, as well he might: it is pride in the language, pride in using the language to search out human meanings, pride in the making of a good piece of work. A personal spell is about the stories, the something of her own that we refer to most often, perhaps, when we mention its beauty, and I think this comes from the *making* of the stories. (pp. 38-9)

It is the achieving of [the] crucial, . . . monumental moment in the work itself that we feel has mattered to Katherine Anne Porter. The reader who looks for the flawless result can find it, but looking for that alone he misses the true excitement, exhilaration, of reading, of re-reading. It is the achieving—in a constant present tense—of the work that shines in the mind when we think of her name; and in that achieving lies, it seems to me, the radiance of the work and our recognition of it as unmistakably her own.

And unmistakable is its source. Katherine Anne Porter's deep sense of fairness and justice, her ardent conviction that we need to give and to receive in loving kindness all the human warmth we can make—here is where her stories come from. (pp. 39-40)

Order and form no more spring out of order and form than they come riding in to us upon seashells through the spray. In fiction they have to be made out of their very antithesis, life. The art of making is the thing that has meaning, and I think beauty is likely to be something that has for a time lain under good, patient hands. Whether the finished work of art was easy or hard to make, whether it demanded a few hours or many years, concerns nobody but the maker, but the making itself has shaped that work for good and all. In Katherine Anne Porter's stories we feel their making as a bestowal of grace.

It is out of the response to her particular order and form that I believe I may have learned the simplest and surest reason for why I cannot see her stories in their every passing minute, and why it was never necessary or intended that a reader should. Katherine Anne Porter is writing stories of the spirit, and the time that fills those moments is eternity. (p. 40)

Eudora Welty, "Katherine Anne Porter: The Eye of the Story" (originally published as "The Eye of the Story," in The Yale Review, *Vol. LV, No. 2, Winter, 1966), in her* The Eye of the Story *(copyright © 1965 by Eudora Welty; reprinted by permission of Random House, Inc.), Random House, 1978, pp. 30-40.*

JANE FLANDERS

Katherine Anne Porter is seldom recognized as a feminist, and little known as a literary critic. She was both. . . . Porter exhibits in her work a well-trained critical intellect which frequently addressed itself, particularly during the early part of her career, to women's rights and women's concerns. Her book reviews from the 1920's provide ample evidence both of her critical abilities and of her commitment to the feminist cause. . . .

These early book reviews illustrate Porter's forthrightness, her liberal spirit, and her witty mastery of English. They trace the formation of her critical tastes and knowledge of her craft. . . . They warrant attention not because of the works discussed (most of which have long been buried in oblivion), but because they provide a new perspective on the author of **"Flowering Judas," "Old Mortality," "Pale Horse, Pale Rider," "Noon Wine,"** and *Ship of Fools.* (p. 44)

The subject of women's rights was so important to Katherine Anne Porter that it appears in a great number of her reviews, just as female characters and women's experience predominate in her fiction. Anyone interested in Porter's personal struggle for independence will find her comments on women and feminist issues very significant.

Critics often have overlooked the feminist orientation of Porter's work. William L. Nance has called her art "the art of rejection," a negative and subtly disapproving description of a quality of Porter's fiction and (by implication) her character which, positively phrased, can be called an affirmation of her independence and the rights of all women to self-realization in the face of centuries of oppression. Like countless other feminists of the twenties—like Virginia Woolf, for example, who had not yet published *A Room of One's Own* when Porter was expressing very similar opinions—Porter was manifestly committed to the cause of women's liberation. Moreover, as female authors have done since the seventeenth century, she expressed the commitment through devotion to her writing.

In content and form, Porter's essays and fiction demonstrate her faith in the written word as the signification of a woman's struggling sense of selfhood. They show her outrage and exasperation with conventional social patterns, especially male-dominated marriage and the creed of domesticity, sexual repression (which she saw as primarily crippling to women), and the pronouncements of self-appointed authorities of both sexes devoted to the status quo. She praises women who resist pressures to curb their nature, assert their opinions, defy parents, take lovers, educate themselves, and have the courage and self-awareness to give shape to their experience in writing. (pp. 44-5)

In sympathizing with . . . frustrated, maligned, unvalued, struggling, emotionally blocked, and intellectually undernourished women—as well as the rebels, bluestockings, and "viragos" who illustrate some other forms that liberation sometimes can take—Porter often seems to be speaking in a disguised way about herself, about her lone struggle to support herself without ceasing to follow her career as a writer. . . .

Even in reviews unrelated to women, her remarks consistently uphold a belief in human dignity: each individual's right to freedom, education, and self-expression. She hates narrowness, prejudice, humbug, self-serving moralism, pretentiousness, and dullness. She believes in the written words as a natural concomitant of self-knowledge and has repeatedly spoken of her own commitment to her art as the most valued goal of her life. With this as a background, it is inevitable that her views on the question of woman's essential nature, her proper sphere, and her fulfillment, should take a liberal form. And although Katherine Anne Porter is never a polemicist as a writer of fiction, her early reviews show the emergence of her feminist views in print and her preparation for the splendid portraits of women which fill her works. (p. 48)

Jane Flanders, "Katherine Anne Porter's Feminist Criticism: Book Reviews from the 1920's," in Frontiers: A Journal of Women Studies *(© copyright 1979, by the Frontiers Editorial Collective), Vol. IV, No. 2, Summer, 1979, pp. 44-8.*

ROBERT PENN WARREN

No exploration of Katherine Anne Porter's "personality" . . . can explain the success of her art: the scrupulous and expressive intricacy of structure, the combination of a precision of language, the revealing shock of precise observation and organic metaphor, a vital rhythmic felicity of style, and a significant penetration of a governing idea into the remotest details of a work. If, as V. S. Pritchett has put it, the writer of short stories is concerned with "one thing that implies many"—or much—then we have here a most impressive artist.

How did Katherine Anne Porter transmute life finally into art? In her journal of 1936, she herself provided a most succinct, simple, and precise answer to the question. All her experience, she writes, seems to be simply in memory, with continuity, marginal notes, constant revision and comparison of one thing with another. But now comes the last phase, that of ultimate transmutation: "Now and again, thousands of memories converge, harmonize, arrange themselves around a central idea in a coherent form, and I write a story."

The author here speaks as though each story were an isolated creation, called into being by the initial intuition of a theme. That, indeed, may have been her immediate perception of the process of composition. The work of any serious writer, however, is not a grab bag, but a struggle, conscious or unconscious, for a meaningful unity, a unity that can be recorded in terms of temperament or theme. In my view, the final importance of Katherine Anne Porter is not merely that she has written a number of fictions remarkable for both grace and strength, a number of fictions which have enlarged and deepened the nature of the story, both short and long, in our time, but that she has created an *oeuvre*—a body of work including fiction, essays, letters, and journals—that bears the stamp of a personality distinctive, delicately perceptive, keenly aware of the depth and darkness of human experience, delighted by the beauty of the world and the triumphs of human kindness and warmth, and thoroughly committed to a quest for meaning in the midst of the ironic complexities of man's lot.

Beyond generalizations, about her method of composition Katherine Anne Porter has given some more specific hints of the concerns underlying her work. In connection with the novel *Ship of Fools,* she once said all her literary life she had been obsessed with the attempt to "understand the logic of this majestic and terrible failure of the life of man in the Western World." This comment seems, at first glance, more cryptic than helpful, and may even evoke the suspicion that it springs from an unconscious need to establish the relation between the critically controversial novel and the earlier body of work seemingly so different. A review of her *oeuvre* reveals that, in spite of its sharp impression of immediacy, it is drenched in historical awareness.

Most obviously, we have the story of Miranda—a sharply defined person, but also a sort of alter ego of the author. In **"Old Mortality,"** Miranda, first as a child, then as a young woman with a broken marriage returning to a family funeral, grows into an awareness of the meaning of myth and time. (pp. 10-11)

Later, in **Pale Horse, Pale Rider,** we see Miranda again, she and her lover set against the hysteria of war, the lover dying, she herself dying into a new order of life—the life of the great ruthless machine of the modern world. We can regard **Pale Horse, Pale Rider** as a thematic prologue to **Ship of Fools,** in which we see all entrapped in their own complicity with this infernal machine.

This question is always present in the work of Katherine Anne Porter: What does our history—of the individual or in the mass—mean? World War II is only one episode in that long question, with the horror of Nazism only an anguishing footnote to a great process in which we are all involved. In the face of the great, pitiless, and dehumanizing mechanism of the modern world, what her work celebrates is the toughness and integrity of the individual. And the great virtue is to recognize complicity with evil in the self. (p. 11)

Robert Penn Warren, "The Genius of Katherine Anne Porter," in Saturday Review (© 1980 Saturday Review Magazine Co.; reprinted by permission), Vol. 7, No. 16, December, 1980, pp. 10-11.

DONALD E. STANFORD

Katherine Anne Porter, who died last September . . . , was best known to the public for her one and only novel, *Ship of Fools,* which, when published in 1962, immediately became a best seller. (p. 1)

Ship of Fools is a brilliant book. Porter herself was fond of it, and she pointed out to carping critics that it developed a major theme present in most of her work—the theme of the life of illusion, of self-deception. But it is not a great novel. The structure is loosely episodic and the crowded cast of characters is far too large. Porter apparently did not have the ability to construct a satisfactory plot of novel length that would bring into a significant relationship a few fully developed characters. *Ship of Fools* cannot stand comparison with the great Victorian novels nor with the major work of Henry James (whom, incidentally, Porter greatly admired). Her true genre was the short story and the novella (or long short story), and her accomplishments in those forms can stand any comparison. Porter once said, "I don't believe in style: The style is you," and she didn't like being called a stylist. Nevertheless, she may be, in fact, the greatest stylist in prose fiction in English of this century. There is of course the aforementioned Henry James, but a comparison, for example, of the opening pages of her **"Hacienda"** with the opening pages of *The Ambassadors* would be instructive to a young writer learning his craft. Sentence by sentence, paragraph by paragraph, Porter is better. Compared to her precise perceptions and carefully modulated rhythms, James's prose is somewhat slow-moving, ponderous, and diffuse. (pp. 1-2)

As time goes by, the accomplishments in American fiction, poetry, and criticism between the wars take on more and more significance. Katherine Anne Porter's stories, especially those written during this period, will be given an increasingly high position in our literary heritage. (p. 2)

Donald E. Stanford, "Katherine Anne Porter" (copyright, 1981, by Donald E. Stanford), in The Southern Review, Vol. 17, No. 1, January, 1981, pp. 1-2.

JAN NORDBY GRETLUND

[It] is a fact that K. A. Porter was as emotionally involved with the South as William Faulkner and Eudora Welty. Her love for her South is reflected in her writing. (p. 441)

Some critical comments demonstrate how fatal it can be to overlook K. A. Porter's emotional involvement with her native area. She created a myth from her family history, but she did not mistake the myth for reality. And she did not idealize or sentimentalize the past, yet she made it clear that there is no escape from it. The characters in her fiction see the past for what it is, so they may organize their lives in terms of the actual. And the past provides the standard by which they finally judge, and by which they are judged by the readers. Without knowledge of K. A. Porter's Southern background, it is easy to misjudge the perspective on the past in her fiction. It is only too easy to overestimate or underestimate the biographical elements. The Miranda figure seeks self-definition through her past and present. She rebels against the Old Order; but she is at once a part of the Old Order and apart from it, in the way K. A. Porter herself was. It would be a mistake, therefore, to see the Miranda stories as ending in "isolation and desolation," as claimed by George Hendrick [in his critical biography *Katherine Anne Porter*]. In a marginal comment, K. A. Porter has pointed out that she meant the stories to end "in an exhilaration of having faced one's destiny—[Miranda] wasn't frightened, wasn't sad, only resolved. A very positive state of being." As a consequence of the "isolation and desolation" interpretation of the stories, Cousin Eve's negative view of the past has been accepted as speaking more of the truth. "In what way?" asks K. A. Porter in another marginal comment, "Is a venomous view any more true than a romantic one? Is hatred more *true* than love?" Only a complete disregard for her love for the South makes the narrow negative interpretation possible.

A sound knowledge of K. A. Porter's biography could have prevented critics from obvious blunders. (pp. 442-43)

It is commonly held among critics that the closer K. A. Porter worked to the world of her youth, the more successful she was. When **"The Fig Tree,"** a long lost story, was published in 1960, both critics and readers were pleased. But she chose not to restrict herself to the Texas material. Her work does not, however, have to be *about* the South to reflect and embody the Southern experience. Could *Ship of Fools* have been written by anybody but a Southerner? As Louis D. Rubin, Jr., has put it [in his *The Curious Death of the Novel*]: "The way that Miss Porter looks at human beings, the things she thinks are important about them, the values by which she judges their conduct, are quite 'Southern,' even though none of the major characters are Southern" in the novel. In *Ship of Fools,* as in all her fiction, she faced the present and offered her commentary on it. The comments would have been different if her background had been different. Once she wrote, "Of the three dimensions of time, only the past is 'real' in the absolute sense that it has occurred, the future is only a concept, and the present is that fateful split second in which all action takes place." And what could be more "Southern"?

To K. A. Porter the Southern past was real and *not* a myth, for a part of Southern history is her own history. (pp. 443-44)

Jan Nordby Gretlund, "Katherine Anne Porter and the South: A Corrective," in The Mississippi Quarterly (copyright 1981 Mississippi State University), Vol. XXXIV, No. 4, Fall, 1981, pp. 435-44.

Muriel Rukeyser

1913-1980

American poet, biographer, translator, novelist, dramatist, scriptwriter, and author of children's books.

Although Rukeyser was for some time known mainly for the political nature of her poems, in recent years critics have begun to address the aesthetic qualities of her work. Her career, which began with the publication of *Theory of Flight*, winner of the Yale Series of Younger Poets Award in 1935, has been marked by a growing poetic refinement and the development of an intensely personal philosophy of life.

The thematic and stylistic changes that evolved over the course of Rukeyser's career dramatized her passionate, Whitman-esque quest for self-unification. What began as strictly political and impersonal grew into a subjective experience of the social, personal, and physical, as well as the political self.

(See also *CLC*, Vols. 6, 10, 15; *Contemporary Authors*, Vols. 5-8, rev. ed., Vols. 93-96 [obituary]; and *Something about the Author*, Vol. 22.)

HAROLD ROSENBERG

Miss Rukeyser's first book [*Theory of Flight*] is remarkable for its self-confidence and lack of hesitation. At twenty-one, she has already covered much of the technical ground of modern American verse, and has learned how to pick up everything she feels capable of consolidating into a poem. The result is a big book, in the quantitative sense; a book on an exceptionally even level of accomplishment; and her dexterity and energy in finding an approach to a great variety of contemporary material deserves respect. (pp. 107-08)

In her seventy-five close-packed pages appears a succession of city and country landscapes, narratives of a sentimental order, sensations, social sermons, self-revelations; conceived, most of them, from the vantage-point of American Marxist writing. In the main, her images are urban and her tonalities firm and impersonal, with occasional efforts towards the pure flash of modern surfaces.

Miss Rukeyser's verse, however, unlike that of the immediately preceding generation of modernists, does not emanate from the decorative or phenomenalistic fascination alone; it contains a moral will, a will to make itself useful as statement, and a will to warm itself against the major human situations of our day. Thus the subjective, rarely quieted in her, is redirected towards recurrent themes of class-oppression, death, the historical background, revolution. (p. 108)

It is to be expected that Miss Rukeyser's massive motives should contain many contradictions, since the tools of modern verse were by no means constructed for the ends for which she means to use them. These contradictions can be dissolved only through the operation of some dominant esthetic principle of selection and repudiation; it implies the rejection not only of words, lines, and poems, but also the rejection or transformation of whole approaches, whole subject-matters, whole

techniques—until the poet has stabilized the tradition of poetry about one technique which he has found appropriate to his revolutionary orientation. . . . [A] straining after beyond-meanings leads at times to downright bad taste, as in *The Strike* (an otherwise successful vignette). . . . (pp. 109-10)

The miners' strike . . . [has enough meaning in itself] without Miss Rukeyser's commentaries, if she can only get them to agitate on the page; to understand such subject-matter means to be able to dispense with the mystical-psychological overtones. . . .

Theory of Flight indicates conclusively that Miss Rukeyser has already overcome naiveté and awkwardness in the handling of her materials, and that, what is even more important, she knows the general angle from which to approach our world. She must now risk her technical acquisitions for the sake of a heightening of quality. (p. 110)

> *Harold Rosenberg, "Youth in Protest," in* Poetry *(© 1936 by The Modern Poetry Association; reprinted by permission of the Editor of* Poetry*), Vol. XLVIII, No. 2, May, 1936, pp. 107-10.*

LOUIS UNTERMEYER

If Muriel Rukeyser is—as I believe she is—the most inventive and challenging poet of the generation which has not yet reached thirty, it is because of her provocative language fully as much as because of her audacious ideas. The thoughts of youth are long, long thoughts, but it is the accent which insures poetry's surviving genius. . . .

Muriel Rukeyser, though only a few months more than twenty-six, has already had her disciples and her detractors. Her three volumes have disclosed an accumulating strength of purpose and an increasing originality of idiom. She first challenged attention with **"Theory of Flight."** . . . **"Theory of Flight"** pronounced a new symbolism as well as a new speech. The style was swift, abrupt, syncopated; it matched the speed of the strepitant post-war world, the crazy energy of murderous machines, the "intolerable contradiction" of flight. . . .

For her the images of war and industry are all too natural; for the city girl the early Mack truck pushing around the corner, tires hissing on the washed asphalt, is a more valid symbol of dawn than the ship of sunrise stranded on the eastern rims or the lark at heaven's gate. . . . It is significant that the tensity of feeling and the intensity of utterance pronounced in **"The Tunnel"** and **"The Structure of the Plane,"** followed a course at the Roosevelt School of the Air, and that the curiously choked, painfully mature **"Effort at Speech between Two People,"** one of the period's most moving love poems, was written when Muriel Rukeyser was still an undergraduate.

Even at this time the vocabulary was pointedly her own. The opening poem in **"Theory of Flight,"** one of the preparatory records mingling fragments of emotion and experience, constructed a person and a period. . . . The emotion, too powerful for its object, fumbled its way through the verse, but the language was certain of itself. . . .

[Her] second volume, **"U.S. 1,"** [is] an assimilation of influences and an effort at adult integration. Echoes could be recognized—chiefly reminders of Hart Crane and W. H. Auden—but her own voice came through with conviction if not always with clarity. . . . The main feature of her second volume is **"The Book of the Dead,"** a study of a place, a many angled portrait which is also a portent. Miss Rukeyser shows the West Virginia village riddled with silicosis, coughing to death, while the huge power plant (the reason for which it is dying) stands idle, empty, impotent. Twenty poems are used to illumine the picture from as many points of view. . . . (p. 11)

Inventiveness and daring are cumulatively evidenced in the rest of **"U.S. 1"**: in that nightmare parable of responsibility and irresponsible temperament, **"The Cruise,"** and the short poems in **"Night-Music."** Typical of her condensed diction—a suggestive shorthand—are the anguished **"The Child Asleep,"** the reminiscent and ironic **"More of a Corpse than a Woman,"** the half-dissonant, half-melodic **"The Drowning Young Man,"** and **"Boy with His Hair Cut Short."** This last, which could not possibly have been written in any but a period of disordered economics, illustrates Miss Rukeyser's method. The opening lines set the scene: the cheap rented room, the harsh electric light, the bleak depression, the boy out of work, the sister trying to make him more presentable, "erasing the failure of weeks with level fingers." (pp. 11-12)

For the craftsman, there is the deceptive prose statement varied by brusque image and casual rhyme; the alternation of abstractions and concrete objects; the overhanging sense of personal failure contrasted with the impersonal and brilliant sign, the always "successful" neon. But it does not take a craftsman to appreciate the quietly charged mood, the unresolved drama,

the articulate communication of small details and their huge implications.

Miss Rukeyser's intentness and originality progress further in her third volume, **"A Turning Wind."** Written between her twenty-third and twenty-fifth years, the book indicates continuing growth and complexity. Some critics identified the complexity with confusion; they complained of her "baffling style," the uncertainties of her "metaphysical soul-searching." A poet turned purist objected to her "indiscriminate scrambling of tenses and inexactness of pronominal references" as well as "the unrelieved bombardment of fragmentary phrases and half-sentences." . . .

There was something to be said for the reviewers too busy to wait for a poem to establish more than its tune. But there was little excuse for the impatience of those who know that poetry does not yield more than its surface music and outer meaning upon first reading. The complexities were obvious: the shifting tempi, the abrupt change of tense and action, the overcrowded lines, the hurtling emotion in runaway fever, the too swiftly juxtaposed images and allusive symbols. But the strength of her conviction and the power of its communication was equally obvious. Integrity is perceived even before it is understood; the meaning, sometimes muffled by her very rush of words, declares itself finally and fully. (p. 12)

[**"The Soul and Body of John Brown"**] is, perhaps, Miss Rukeyser's most important work up to date, for it embodies not only her credo and reveals her style at its richest, but it serves as a manifesto for her generation.

The motto of **"The Soul and Body of John Brown"** is from Joel: "Multitudes, multitudes in the valley of decision." It is a quotation which has a terrible choice of meanings, for the chapter from which it is taken is a prologue to the Day of Judgment—and it is our day which will be judged, judged by our own multitudes "in the valley of decision." The symbolism is emphasized with the entry of another Hebrew prophet, Ezekiel; for Ezekiel, thundering about the doom of nations, foretold the end of slavery and foreshadowed a spiritual resurrection. Joel . . . Ezekiel . . . John Brown . . . Miss Rukeyser synthesizes their apocalyptic visions, repudiates the self-willed doom of the appeasers and defeatists, faces the death-wish, and, feeling the line of the past, urges more freedom. She calls valiantly for reawakened life. (p. 13)

> *Louis Untermeyer, "The Language of Muriel Rukeyser," in* The Saturday Review of Literature *(© 1940, copyright renewed © 1967, Saturday Review Magazine Co.; reprinted by permission), Vol. XXII, No. 16, August 10, 1940, pp. 11-13.*

JOHN MALCOLM BRINNIN

In the poetry of Muriel Rukeyser, as represented in three volumes published between 1930 and 1939, it is possible to trace the history of a movement in American letters that was at the same time literary and political. Since her range is wide, and her methods pliable, she has expressed in these volumes the sentiments of many in her generation, and has suggested certain influences that reshaped and ultimately transformed them. (p. 554)

One of the most interesting phases of the transformation of the social poet in years of stress is the change in his use of language. In the case of Muriel Rukeyser, it moves from that of simple declarative exhortation, in the common phrases of the city man, to that of a gnarled, intellectual, almost private observation. In her earlier usage, images are apt to be simple and few; the whole approach is apt to be through the medium of urban speech. In the latter work, images become those of the psychologist, or of the surrealist, charged with meaning and prevalent everywhere. Parallel with this change is the increasing complication of symbols; the first are public, the last, even though they may represent universal issues, are privately conceived and privately endowed. In these changes may be found the central problem of the modern social poet. That is, how may he develop his talent in the full resources of the language and accumulated techniques, and yet speak clearly and persuasively to men about him. (p. 555)

Since the social poet is one to whom communication is the first and necessary virtue, his attempts to be strong and clear without seeming banal, and his attempts to use the complex resources of the English language in an original way, are twin problems that are as yet unresolved. Since the work of Muriel Rukeyser demonstrates both of these extremes, a careful examination of the shifts and expansions of her method and thought may lead to a meaningful resolution.

With the publication of her first volume, *Theory of Flight,* . . . American poetry found its first full-blown expression of the rebellious temper that prevailed on American campuses and among the younger intellectuals. Its success was immediate, and it took its place as the American equivalent of such work as that published by the new revolutionary group of English poets exemplified by Auden, Spender, and Lewis. . . . Miss Rukeyser was praised for the ruggedness of her technique, her experimentalism, and for the powerful utterance which, from a woman, seemed unique. (p. 556)

The first indication of a concern that becomes major in her succeeding work occurs in the poem, *Effort at Speech Between Two People.* Here, with overtones of Eliot and the personal frustrations of the twenties, is a suggestion that communication is ultimately impossible. (pp. 559-60)

This poem, in its isolation from the political temper of the rest of [*Theory of Flight*], seems unrepresentative. Its attitudes are adolescent, its sense of tragedy superficial and commonplace. However, in the light of Miss Rukeyser's later development, it assumes importance. It is the individualistic anchor in the first book which holds the author to her own emotions. When those emotions are forced to play upon the hazards of political action, a new conflict becomes manifest.

Soon after the personal acceptance of a place in the revolutionary movement, the author puts by the sheer expression of exhilaration in an attempt to realize an intellectual objectification of her position. One of the choices for this is the concept of flight in modern mechanical terms. . . . In this instance, all of history is seen as an attempt at human expansion in the terms of flight. And though the author knows that this attempt has produced no release from the human condition, she rejoices in the fact that it has produced an increasingly complex, and increasingly able, human community. . . . (pp. 560-61)

[In the first volume,] Miss Rukeyser manages, in a few passages, to incorporate into respectable poetry some of the more profound tenets of dialectical materialism. In this attempt, she succeeds in retaining a durable and clear language and, though her images are neither new nor particularly arresting, the quiet yet passionate expression of faith holds them together. They

are, consequently, not significant in themselves, but in unfamiliar juxtapositions. (p. 562)

In *The Lynchings of Jesus,* Muriel Rukeyser makes use, in poetic terms, of a tendency that was evident in the politics of the Popular Front movement of the early and middle years of the decade, i.e. the trick of rediscovering popular heroes as partisans of modern issues. The Marxist aspects of Lincoln's thought, for instance, or at least those aspects which could be shown as parallel to modern Marxist sentiments, were re-examined and publicized. Thus, in *Passage to Godhead,* Miss Rukeyser reinvokes the Christian legend. . . . The effect, though attained through methods that must remain suspect, is often rich both as drama and as poetry. Since any new interpretation of old mythology will have a local interest, that is part of the success here. . . . The strength of her partisanship assures a passionate viewpoint, while the new symbols, and the necessity for new imagery, test her poetic ingenuity.

Another strain in this book that, beginning unobtrusively, leads toward later complexity, is that suggested in the poem *Eccentric Motion.* This poem is similar to many of Auden's and of the English group of Oxford radicals who came to prominence in the early thirties. The language of the popular ballad, of the music-hall song, is used to make serious observation. There is a foreign ring here, quite alien to the body of Miss Rukeyser's work, yet one which persists through all of her books. . . . Perhaps more important than the suggestion of foreign influences, this poem shows that Miss Rukeyser retains, even in the days of her most outspoken commitment to a social program, a detached viewpoint: she is able to speak of herself and the society she abhors as "we." Thus, a completely minor poem suggests the whole turn of her latter work.

Theory of Flight makes a single impression: emotional, unhesitant affirmation. Though there are marginal suggestions of many new influences, none is realized in any distinctive poem. The poet's emphasis is clearly upon the thing said, and not the manner of expression. The volume is plethoric and sprawling, full of extravagances, yet rich and evocative. It would be only natural for the author of such a work to seek development in control.

In 1938, Muriel Rukeyser published her second book of poems, [*U.S. 1*], deriving its title from the federal highway that runs from Maine to Florida. This collection showed a stage in her development that was notable for tendencies toward objectification of those feelings that, in the earlier book, were expressed with emotional extravagance. This process was furthered by her use of a new form that had come into prominence in those years, a form that was neither straight fiction nor straight exposition but a dramatic presentation of facts that combined elements of both. This form went generally under the name of "reportage," and those who used it were concerned with aligning social data in the dramatic design of fiction. (pp. 563-65)

Interested in the new reportage, both through her reading and through her work with documentary films, Muriel Rukeyser set about to write a poetic account of the tragedy that was exposed in the deaths of thousands of miners in the state of West Virginia. . . . Miss Rukeyser went to West Virginia and used the methods of a reporter in speaking with many of the persons involved, learning at first hand the pitiful conditions in which they lived, examining company reports and stock quotations, speaking with owners and investigators alike.

The long title poem, *U.S. 1,* was the result. Though she managed to present in orderly fashion the findings of a good reporter, it is surprising to find, under the name of poetry, language as barren as statistics. Many of the poems in the sequence are barely distinguishable from routine newspaper commentary. Since there is no success anywhere in her attempt to crowd the facts of a committee report into the beat of poetry, the poem as a whole is a failure. It is too long, the language remote and unevocative, the arrangement of data completely lacking on dramatic contrasts. Unlike earlier instances where her dramatic sense brought life to an otherwise undistinguished poem, this work remains flat and prosaic.

U.S. 1 represents the most extreme limit of Miss Rukeyser's attempt to objectify and it is so successful, in the narrow sense, that all suggestions of the elevation of poetry have been objectified out of existence. In one or two passages, when the poet intrudes with extraneous commentary, there is a heightening of effect that only serves to point the weakness of a method so extreme. It is also significant in this regard to notice that, when the poet leaves the statistical approach to speak for herself, elements of poetry return momentarily, suggesting that, with balance, the method might not always end in failure. . . . (pp. 565-66)

In the middle section of this book, between the long reportage poem and the allegorical *Voyage,* occur a number of lyrics that rank with the finest examples of Miss Rukeyser's work. These have been achieved through a balance of subjective emotion and objective record. In *A Flashing Cliff,* for instance, Love, in its most abstract sense, becomes the source of human power, the revolutionary agent in all existence. . . . [This poem] shows the beginnings of a great concentration of language and ideas. Such fusion was not possible while the poet spoke in the single-mindedness of a political program. Opposites are not enjoined in slogans, since the words on a banner must be outspoken and immediately understandable. Yet, though the poet has come far from sloganizing, the new verse is built upon a use of language so complex, and a compression of ideas so intense, that it is unquestionably removed from the grasp of the lay reader, not even to mention the proletarian.

Here Miss Rukeyser comes to the crux of the problem of the social poet: whether to insist upon first premises, even though that means a static repetition of familiar ideology, or to exercise full imagination and the resources of language in an endeavor to contribute a new dimension to poetry, though that attempt, in its inevitable intellectual concentration, must deny the social audience.

In this middle stage, she makes no definite choice. There are poems compact and difficult to penetrate, but they are, nonetheless, exhilarating exercises in modern rhythms and textures. No matter how far afield she may go in the errors of obscurity her technique is never dull, most often brilliant. In a sense, the poet has fallen in love with language; a romance that was delayed by the demands of political conviction.

Among these complex poems are those wherein language is reduced to utter simplicity, wherein poetic excitement comes from the dramatic presentation of the idea, as in the tender *Boy With His Hair Cut Short.* . . . (pp. 567-68)

There are personal poems that are completely individual in expression, unique among her work in that they are removed, in almost every influence, from social relationships. These show a new symbolism that is almost always tenuous and psychological. Yet the power of her language, its oblique, beaten intensity, never fails to excite wonder. . . . (p. 568)

Though a new direction has been firmly established, there remain instances of hearkening back to the earlier role of prophetess. Though direct exhortation is almost gone, the convictions of the poet have remained strong. When she speaks out now, it is in her own voice as a sophisticated poet and not as a coiner of slogans. At the same time, speech that has a public significance is held in restriction by her use of special, intangible, almost private symbols. (p. 569)

[*U.S. 1*] accomplishes the separation of the poet from her comrades and from the radical vernacular, in the sense that only a part of her interest is centered upon the immediate conflict. The tragedy for the artist as a social consciousness lies in the fact that, as her powers as a poet expand in the terms of craft, she is isolated as an articulate leader among those who claim her allegiance. The partisan feels that it is much too early to examine the bases of modern consciousness, since the manifest battle is not won, and any deviation that means a slackening or diversion of effort from the immediate goal becomes inconsequential, if not reactionary. Thus, the poet is driven into a sense of loneliness out of all proportion. Her heart is in the same place, but the demands of her immense talent have not allowed her to remain static. A diversion of her art from her beliefs has taken place that is parallel to the diversion of art from life in America today. (pp. 569-70)

Because of the progressive development of early themes and devices of craft, it is possible to say that the books of Muriel Rukeyser are different not in kind, but in degree. *A Turning Wind,* the latest of her published works in poetry, reinforces that conviction. . . .

Instead of the barren objectification of social data that caused the failure of the poem *U.S. 1,* Miss Rukeyser has developed a strong and evocative set of symbols. (p. 570)

The hesitant, truncated passages of direct address that occurred here and there throughout [*U.S. 1*] give way to more forceful utterance. However it is obvious that the poet is no longer speaking to her first audience. Now she speaks almost exclusively to fellow artists, to those who, intellectual and sensitive, are in retreat. The poet, as one who has survived a general disillusion and bewilderment, is happy to reaffirm. (p. 571)

An earlier preoccupation with heroic character comes into evidence in the long last section of the book entitled *Lives.* In this sequence of biographical appreciations the poet celebrates individuals, only one of whom has been conspicuous for her devotion to the social good in explicit political terms. All of the others, in one degree or another, have been unsung heroes, quietly working in the arts and sciences with integrity and singularity of purpose. (pp. 571-72)

Though in *U.S. 1* there is a manifest separation of the artist from her whole function as a member of the human community, a reader feels that she is not completely conscious of this, that she is still somewhat bewildered at the change that has taken place. Dislocation of poetic sensitivity has, in these times, often led to semi-hysterical privacy, to the abortive use of imagery and symbolism from sources that are but half understood. Muriel Rukeyser barely misses this pitfall in parts of the second book, but if there has remained any doubt as to her powers of reintegration, they are dispelled upon reading the first poem in her most recent volume, the elegy, *Rotten Lake.* This poem established the poet anew; though she has given up public speech as a major premise, she is resolved within herself as never before. This resolution brings together not only craft and direction, but the inevitable disillusion of one who has seen the revolutionary temper of her contemporaries become dissipated and insignificant and who, herself, has been forced to reconcile grave doubts concerning the efficacy of certain policies. (pp. 572-73)

Muriel Rukeyser achieved her finest sequence of poems [in] the five elegies that begin the volume. These poems show an integration of method, a fibre of belief, a philosophical authority superior to all that has gone before. Their range includes all the strains that the poet has touched upon in earlier experimentation, so that, in the greatest expansion of her powers, she has achieved the closest fusion of them as well. Though she seems, at times, to have been caught like an innocent with visions and beliefs in a world of abject denial, almost always she is consciously reconstructing a faith that will match that of her adolescence.

The poet is returning, sadder but wiser. Denying much of experience, she finds strength in the simple faith of particular friends. Beyond that, she would attain the discipline of an unsentimental insight into the failing world in order to survive its terrors with dignity. She has come to terms with tragedy. (p. 573)

This is a resolution that seems likely to endure for Miss Rukeyser, since it contains both the core of her dedication and her escape. (p. 574)

> *John Malcolm Brinnin, "Muriel Rukeyser: The Social Poet and the Problem of Communication," in* Poetry *(© 1943 by The Modern Poetry Association; reprinted by permission of the Editor of* Poetry*), Vol. LXI, No. 4, January, 1943, pp. 554-75.*

OSCAR WILLIAMS

Muriel Rukeyser's latest book [*Beast in View*] is also her best, if for no other reason than that it contains her finest poem, **"Ajanta."** Here she has really achieved the height of a permanent poem, complete in its own logic and unity. Otherwise her book is a collection of forms which she has essayed to use in her assiduous search for techniques: lyric, sonnet, elegy, etc. These rhythmic shapes she uses much like planks being tested by the foot of an elephant about to cross a chasm. Miss Rukeyser's acumen over matters of choosing the right folklore, her fireworks of imagery, strain these forms without allowing them properly to shape a complete poem. Her general fault is an overabundance of material. In the midst of one poem she habitually begins another, and though practising a perpetual literary sleight-of-hand, sometimes manages to cover a hatrack of form with a mammoth smothering wool comforter of vocabulary. Yet certainly **"Ajanta"** is one of the important poems of the decade, and, in spite of my rather severe objections to Miss Rukeyser's lengthy discourse, this fourth book of hers is living, resonant with the activity of a poet at work. (p. 534)

> *Oscar Williams, "Ladies' Day," in* The New Republic *(© 1944 The New Republic, Inc.), Vol. III, No. 17, October 23, 1944, pp. 534-36.**

JAMES R. CALDWELL

I find it difficult to repress the opinion that in Muriel Rukeyser the age is finding one of its major voices. . . .

In a generation of artists all angry rejectors of this murderous world she rejects only arty rejection. In a time which declares . . . that the flux of experience is hopelessly intractable, and the only discoverable orders those self-contained in art or religion, she discovers an order intrinsic to both life and art. This is a radical integration, and while it appears in the warm and immediate apprehensions of a poet, it is responsible to the evidence of much modern knowledge and substantiated in excellent poetry. . . .

[Of the works **"The Life of Poetry," "Elegies,"** and **"Orpheus,"** one should read] **"The Life of Poetry"** first. It builds the frame of the theory and illumines the books of poetry. . . . It maps . . . the outlines of an esthetic into which are drawn, among others, the findings of Whitehead, Gibbs, Freud, and ultimately Hegel. Fundamental is the conviction of process as reality and of poetry as process, an emotional response, continuous with other forms of experience, "which accepts a world of process, a dynamic universe of time and growth relations." Basically related to poetry are the manifestations of dream and its involvements in wish and will, these taken socially as well as individually. The dialectical process is a third major key, seen not as a tight and easy rationale of class struggle but in a poetic vision of the eternal counterpoise and reconcilement of forces, and pervading the whole is the ideal for poetry and for life of full consciousness, free of inhibition, contempt, and neurotic coldness. . . .

Miss Rukeyser disowns little or nothing. With her poet's knack of seeing the symbolic meanings in events and the connections latent in them, and with various and deep reading she adduces and enriches from every quarter of contemporary life. . . .

The idea is, of course, far too big for the book, and strains at the bindings. The energies of her convictions in fact are hardly contained in the prose medium. Her exposition throbs toward the oracular and one has often to wait and let the reverberations subside.

The prose book throws much light on the two volumes of poetry and these upon one another. The dialectical theme of the seventh chapter of **"The Life"** emerges in the poetry of the **"Ninth Elegy,"** and both illustrate the **"Orpheus."** . . . Miss Rukeyser does not of course explain her poetry, but the prose makes visible a number of experiences in the process of translation from "life" to "art."

In the recreated myth of **"Orpheus,"** and in the moving lyrics of "outrage and possibility" which place the **"Elegies"** in the lineage of **"Piers,"** Whitman, and Melville there is that full, animate, and vivid power which gave distinction to her earlier books. All is firm, intense, and arresting. Yet I have a disturbing sense that in these recent poems Miss Rukeyser's motile, ringing energies are becoming over-agitated. Frenetic is too harsh a word, but her images and rhythms, like Shelley's, seem hurried and driven by a general passion behind and so external to all particular items of her experience.

> *James R. Caldwell, "Invigoration and a Brilliant Hope," in* The Saturday Review of Literature *(© 1950, copyright renewed © 1978, Saturday Review Magazine Co.; reprinted by permission), Vol. XXXIII, No. 10, March 11, 1950, p. 26.*

KENNETH REXROTH

The primary virtue of Muriel Rukeyser's poetry has always been a kind of mood, an instinctive organic awareness. Her work has a peasant quality, like the Dorset dialect poetry of William Barnes, the sense of the processes of life all interconnected and spreading illimitably away. Many of her poems have the same sonority as Barnes', a soft rumble and murmur of consonants, ''m'''s and ''l'''s and ''r'''s, with no sharp shifts of tonality in the vowels. . . .

Mood, flavor, they last longer than information. It is hard to realize that it is eight years since Miss Rukeyser's last book. Its impression lingers, definite and so easily recalled. Of all my generation she is the least violent, the most quietly assured. Ever since her long poems, **"Ajanta"** and **"Orpheus,"** she seems to have been working toward and around a kind of implicitly philosophical poetry, a species of unassuring, objectively presented but lucid and profound "wisdom literature." The meanings of like are not analyzed and explicated, they are responded to and embodied. Pre-eminently these poems are responses rather than reactions. . . .

"Body of Waking"—it is a very good title, because that is just what the poems are about, the organism, filled and complete, rising out of dream to continuously widening and deepening levels of realization. This book does not differ from the poet's others except for the years. It is the work of a more mature, a wiser woman.

At the beginning she was something of a child prodigy, but there is nothing at all prodigious about her work today. The promises are fulfilled, the facilities are all accomplishments now. There is no message, no rhetoric, there are no answers, and yet, there is the awareness of that which only knows all the answers—"body of waking."

Kenneth Rexroth, "Poetic Responses," in The New York Times Book Review *(© 1958 by The New York Times Company; reprinted by permission), October 19, 1958, p. 46.*

COLIN CAMPBELL

From Muriel Rukeyser's first volume of poems, **"Theory of Flight"** . . . , to her most recent, **"Waterlily Fire"** . . . , is a span of twenty-seven years and nine books, the years among the most crucial in the history of the American republic and the books among the most indicative in the history of contemporary American poetry. They animate each other, the years and the books, for the electric vitality of Miss Rukeyser's art stems partially from the tightness with which her poems are plugged into the socket of American experience, and they, in turn, offer the sort of interpretive comment upon that experience which demonstrates that poets do, after all, have something significant to tell us about ourselves.

But there is more to celebrate here than content. One reason why her works have maintained . . . a certain centrality and stability is that her techniques, her verbal strategies, are at once a statement and—this is important—a solution of the problem which may well decide whether poetry will thrive or perish in this pragmatic, acquisitive, machine-centered world of ours.

The problem, bluntly put, is that the bulk of the reading public cannot understand what modern poets are talking about. . . .

The mixing of comic and tragic moods, ellipsis, startling images, congested metaphors, learned allusions, all the standard puzzles of modern poetry can be amply illustrated on any page of Miss Rukeyser's book, and solved there also, solved by men and women able to unshackle their conception of what human

language can be made to do. In **"Waterlily Fire"** are emblemized all the dangers to the future of American poetry and all the hopes that a future is possible.

Colin Campbell, "American Poets: 'What Language Can Accomplish','" in The Christian Science Monitor *(reprinted by permission from* The Christian Science Monitor; *© 1962 The Christian Science Publishing Society; all rights reserved), October 25, 1962, p. 6.*

MAY SWENSON

Muriel Rukeyser has published a large body of work since her first collection, **Theory of Flight**, appeared when she was only twenty-one. It immediately marked her as an innovator, thoroughly American, Whitman-like in method and scope. Characteristic of her poetry, of which we now have a survey in **Waterlily Fire (Poems 1935-1962)**, is the big canvas, the broad stroke, love of primary color and primary emotion. Her method is the opposite of the designer's, her vision is never small, seldom introverted. Her consciousness of *others* around her, of being but one member of a great writhing body of humanity surging out of the past, filling the present, groping passionately toward the future, is a generating force in her work. She celebrates science as much as nature or the restless human heart. Lines from an early poem like **"The Gyroscope"** . . . are echoed in Part II **"The Island"** of her final poem in this collection. . . . Another main fulcrum of her work is psychological, even mystical (but it never departs from a physical, in fact, a sexual base), an exploration of being and becoming and then of re-becoming, growing out of her interest in Eastern philosophy as well as Western primitivism.

Waterlily Fire contains selections from eight former books, and a group of new poems all written in 1962. **U.S. 1** (1938) offers a sensuous and environment-conscious catalogue of Southern working people and their lives, reported with the instantaneous honesty of her camera eye; people are realized with the same all-embracing empathy to which we thrill in Whitman. **A Turning Wind** (1939) includes a group of life-sized portraits of her personal heroes and "saints": Gibbs, Ryder, Chapman, Ann Burlak, Ives. . . . There is a section of ten **Elegies** . . . "dedicated not to death but to war and love."

Beginning with **"Rotten Lake"** she reveals, in the interstices of apocalyptic scenes of world battle, her own soul-struggle . . . until, in the spilling of agonies, the created poems become a catharsis. . . . Although her proclivity is for the large spontaneous canvas, Miss Rukeyser is also master of the self-contained lyric, and it is good to have a choice of these, for instance from the volumes **Beast in View** (1944), **The Green Wave** (1947), and **Body of Waking** (1958). There are vivid poems that leave a single hypnotic impression on the mind, such as **"Eyes of Night Time," "Salamander," "Haying Before Storm."** Among the new poems, **"For a Mexican Painter"** is another such flawless lyric, wizardlike in its craft.

Miss Rukeyser's final section contains, as a crown piece, the striking **"Waterlily Fire"** in five parts, which is about the burning of Monet's *Waterlilies* in the Museum of Modern Art fire of 1958; it is also about the author's life on Manhattan Island, and (astonishingly) also about a nuclear war protest demonstration in City Hall Park in April, 1961. . . . There rises before us [in **"Waterlily Fire"**], without its being stated, a prophetic vision of what may be destroyed . . . and at the same time, what can be brought to birth, if men can be "touched, awakened . . . touched and turned one by one into flame'': a blossoming—of peace, love, art. (pp. 164-65)

May Swenson, "Poetry of Three Women," in The Nation (copyright 1963 The Nation magazine, The Nation Associates, Inc.), Vol. 196, No. 8, February 23, 1963, pp. 164-66.*

HELEN MERRELL LYND

Some reviewers may be disappointed that *The Orgy* does not provide the salaciousness its title suggests. Some may be embarrassed by an author who gives so much of herself in a book that is not labeled autobiography. More are bewildered by not knowing what label to put on it. It is not a novel, or a book about the Irish coast of Kerry, or a description of [the Fair,] an ancient ritual. . . .

The impossibility of putting this book into a customary classification is one reason for reading it. (p. 668)

A first reading of this book left me overwhelmed with its colors and shapes and sounds. I had been to a part of the world of whose location I was hardly aware on the map, and I had come to know it better than places many times revisited, because I had been there with a person of extraordinary perception and power of words to express it. . . .

With a second reading the people became more alive. A third reading brought the realization that they had been there from the beginning, but that I had been so absorbed in the immediate descriptions of the landscape and the Fair that I had not been fully aware of all that is implicit in them. Or of the symbolism of the Fair, and the weaving together of all the separate and contradictory parts of these three days. . . .

The finely experienced and imagined account of . . . three days on the Kerry coast presents in vivid imagery a profound philosophical problem, usually stated only abstractly: the nature of perception. . . .

Miss Rukeyser's allowing us to become aware of what associations she brought to Kerry and what those three days unfolded in her is what makes reading this book the unforgettable experience it is. For us, as for her, the Fair becomes a releasing and revealing event. (p. 670)

Some books enlarge the meaning of the words with which we try to describe them. *The Orgy* has, for me, enlarged the meaning of ''luminous.'' (p. 672)

Helen Merrell Lynd, "Three Days Off for Puck," in The American Scholar (copyright © 1965 by the United Chapters of Phi Beta Kappa; reprinted by permission of the publishers, the United Chapters of Phi Beta Kappa), Vol. 34, No. 4, Autumn, 1965, pp. 668, 670, 672.

RICHARD EBERHART

The poems of Muriel Rukeyser are primordial and torrential. They pour out excitements of a large emotional force, taking in a great deal of life and giving out profound realizations of the significance of being. She has a natural force which for decades has built up monuments in words of the strong grasp on life of a strong mind. . . .

Muriel Rukeyser for decades has consistently employed direct thrusts of strong emotion, a deep personal statement, in making

her poems. It is not ''confessional'' poetry as we understand it in Anne Sexton, but massive awareness of large phases of existence. She has a remarkable variety of styles within her major style. She is artful and can be experimental. She belongs to the Whitman school of large confrontations and outpourings rather than to any school of the rigidly constructed poem.

Her [poems in **"The Speed of Darkness"**] have splendors of passionate realization as had her earlier poems. (p. 24)

Her own voice comes through all these poems, real and unmistakable. It is an open poetry, open-ended. It is not systematic except in the inchoate system and thrust of the passions throwing off poems in a continuum of poetic realization. She is not dogmatic, not prideful, not despairing despite knowledge of much death and hatred in our time. . . . (pp. 24, 26)

There are many more poems on many subjects, short and long, which invite the reader to largeness of scope, tenderness, belief in life, honesty of perception, all the excellence of new work memorable and good. (p. 26)

Richard Eberhart, "Personal Statement," in The New York Times Book Review (© 1968 by The New York Times Company; reprinted by permission), June 23, 1968, pp. 24, 26.

LAURENCE LIEBERMAN

Muriel Rukeyser is a poet of dark music, weighty and high-minded. *The Speed of Darkness,* the title of her new book, is indicative of the oracular soothsaying quality of much of her writing—for me, a defeating tendency of her style which often nullifies any attentiveness to detail. Her mystical vision is so dominant in the mentality of some poems, the writing becomes inscrutable, as she packs her lines with excessive symbolism or metaphorical density.

Her firmest art is in the linear and straightforward delivery of her story-telling anecdotal poems, the longer biographical poems, and letter-poems to friends expressing an open declaration of personal faith. In all of these genres, her symbolism is balanced by clean, open statement. In **"Endless"** and **"Poem"** . . . , personal lyrics irradiating pathos from the recollection of harrowing life-moments, Miss Rukeyser achieves a naïve forthrightness—an artlessness—which, as in the most lastingly valuable personal letters (those of Keats, for example), derives a universal moral faith from plainspoken events authentically observed and recorded. In these poems, Miss Rukeyser is most nearly able to make her experience—her recollected terror and madness—our own. Her absorptively sympathetic portrait of the German artist, Käthe Kollwitz, one portion of a continuing sequence of biographical works (**"Lives"**) is the most arresting long poem in the new collection. Miss Rukeyser displays wisdom as self-critic in choosing to adapt so many recent poems from biographical and historical studies, since the task of accurately restoring a human lifetime in verse compels a precision in the enumeration of items of dailiness that offsets her frequent tendency to drift into cloudy abstraction. (pp. 232-33)

Laurence Lieberman, "Muriel Rukeyser" (originally published as "Critic of the Month, VII: A Confluence of Poets," in Poetry, Vol. CXIV, No. 1, April, 1969), in his Unassigned Frequencies: American Poetry in Review, 1964-77 (© 1969, 1977 by Laurence Lieberman; reprinted by permission of the author and the University of Illinois Press), University of Illinois Press, 1977, pp. 232-33.

VIRGINIA R. TERRIS

[In] the seventies, [we have come] to define Rukeyser as a poet far different from the one she has traditionally been assumed to be. The neglect her poetry has suffered has delayed recognition of her work as deeply rooted in the Whitman-Transcendental tradition.

Her belief in the unity of Being, her reliance on primary rather than on literary experience as the source of truth and the resultant emphasis on the self, the body and the senses, as well as the rhythmic forms and patterns that inevitably emerge from such beliefs, tie Rukeyser to her forebears in the nineteenth century. At the same time, through her highly personal contemporary voice, they project her into our era which, with its radical departures from traditional Transcendentalism, is yet a reaffirmation of it, with Rukeyser as one of its important figures.

Her desperate search for "identity"—in the Whitmanian sense—and for integration is evident beginning with her first volume. In *Theory of Flight* the self is alienated and apart from the technological society the poet attempts to confront and absorb. . . .

Also, the metaphor of silence, in relation to the self, one of the persistent themes in contemporary poetry, runs consistently through her work beginning with *Theory of Flight*. . . . In later books, particularly *Beast in View*, through an extraordinary break through, Rukeyser is to view silence as a positive attribute as well.

Still another phase of her poetic character constantly challenging the death imminent in alienation and its concomitant silence is the energy with which the poet attempts to oppose them, sometimes unconsciously and chaotically. . . . Energy is indeed a major quality of her poetry. Dams and dynamos, as well as the gyroscope of **"Theory of Flight,"** are manifestations of it. However, while the poet is proclaiming "all directions out," at the same time she fears disintegration, for as she proclaims "all directions out," in the same line she states that "all desires turn inward." The conflict between these contradictory forces is a theme even more deeply confounding for contemporary poetry than the threat of silence and alienation. And in Rukeyser's first book it manifests itself in this ambivalence. Or perhaps one can call it rather her attempt to balance opposing forces.

In *Theory of Flight* still another kind of energy anticipates her larger, more subtle themes having to do with the body. . . . (p. 10)

By the time Rukeyser writes *Ajanta,* she has shed the mechanical, impersonal metaphors for energy in her earlier volumes and become deeply personal. The self becomes the source of energy as the poet assumes her true "identity."

Already in her second book, *U.S. 1,* by its very structuring, Rukeyser is dividing poems of social content from those that approach experience in a personal way. There are qualifications as, for instance, in **"Night-Music,"** a section of personal poems that also have social content. But there is a vast difference between the reader's identification with Merl Blankenship in **"The Book of the Dead,"** the first section, and **"Boy with His Hair Cut Short"** of **"Night-Music."** The first poem, a terrifying statement of a man being done to death by the irresponsibility and greed of the owners of a silicate company, is written in journalistic style; we react to it with the same pity as we do to the horrors in the newspaper. (The author has felt constrained to document the material in the poem at the end of *U.S. 1.*) The second poem, in which a sister cuts her brother's hair so he can look for a job that will never turn up, has an immediacy that makes the experience happen to us as it is happening to him. Rukeyser is beginning to sift the public from the personal voice. She is beginning to touch experience with her bare hands.

A Turning Wind, her third book, marks a further flowering of Rukeyser's sensibilities as she moves from theorizing to experiencing and from the general imprecision and flatness of diction of her first two volumes to speech that is beginning to be animated by the experience it portrays. One feels the poetic tensions rising as the veil of abstractions begins to slip away. The poet is beginning to be able to face the world about her and within her and her relation to it more directly. You enter through her skin and through her mind.

In the four elegies which open the volume, the voice of the poet grapples with and triumphs over her internal contradictions of the first two books. She is successful to such a degree that she is able to distance them from her, evaluate them, and thus end their hold over her. . . . She moves into a larger, freer world.

"Ajanta," in Rukeyser's fourth book, *Beast in View,* marks the poet's first statement of this sense of achievement of integration with herself. . . . In this inner exploration, she is released from the bonds that have held her, her involvement with society. She recognizes at last that self-knowledge must precede all other kinds, that a sense of the reality of the self is the first reality without which there can be no others. . . . Never having been able to "suffer" before, she comes to "this cave where myth enters the heart again." With the opening of herself, the process of integration is able to begin.

And in this Jungian mode, of which Rukeyser is obviously aware, we find a compelling parallel in **"Ajanta"** with what she had been trying to achieve in her early "technological" approach.

Here, in **"Ajanta"** she discovers the positive use of silence, the silence that does not destroy life but renews it. (pp. 10-11)

By breaking through silence to speech, she has at last become familiar with her self as body. . . .

In *The Green Wave,* her fifth book, Rukeyser shifts from the mythic to the immediate world, her view of it deepened by her excursion into the cave. Closer to the self, she finds it to be more varied than the one she had known earlier and yet its many contradictions coexist with a minimum of distress through this acceptance of her self as the body. Rukeyser becomes more self-assured as she begins to rely more effectively on her personal voice. In *The Green Wave,* this increasing reliance is her major achievement.

In that same year of the publication of *The Green Wave,* Rukeyser published *Orpheus.* . . . Similar to the **"Ajanta"** in that both poems work within the mythic mode, *Orpheus* belongs to the Western, **"Ajanta"** to the Eastern, world. The locations themselves are a comment on the goals the poet is seeking, that of putting the world, her world, that of the poet and that of the bodily self, together. . . .

However, we find in her most recent volume [*Breaking Open*], in **"More Clues"** and in **"The Question,"** still gropings for her personal self as distinguished from her poetic self. It raises the question as to whether personal integration, which she is also striving for, is as important to her as poet as she would like it to be, and, even more to the point, whether the contradictory modes of living and thinking are not the fructifying modes of poetry. In short, it can be said that her emotional development as poet at this point seems to have circled back upon itself, but with a difference. Working with the same themes as she had earlier, her handling of them in her latest work has the assurance, directness and power of a poetic personality finally integrating and identifying with itself.

In *One Life,* a biography of Wendell Willkie, . . . the poems harken back to the social protest poems of the first two volumes. Much of the book is diary versified and weak because it departs from the source of strength Rukeyser has discovered in the intense, the personal, self. She accomplished nothing poetically in this volume, but lay fallow in preparation for a major development which was to come about soon in her work.

Having already recognized the self as poet, as the oracular instrument, Rukeyser is now able to focus singlemindedly on what she has only tentatively explored in earlier volumes. . . . Although Rukeyser is exploring many of the themes she had earlier explored—family tensions, social and technological issues and women exploited—she now moves into experiences that are hers uniquely. The sense of who she is, the ''I,'' spells itself out in **''After the Quarrel,'' ''Unborn Song''** and **''Pouring Milk Away.''** But it is not until you come to the end of *Body of Waking* that you discover poems with new joy, with new excitement in them. . . .

The painful ''silences'' of the early poems have been pushed aside for the many ''voices,'' the many ''songs.''

It is not until you read Rukeyser's *Speed of Darkness* that you realize the cause of the change of tone in the earlier volume. The poet, the vehicle of ''saying,'' had fused with the personal self and thus become exposed finally to the contradictions and irresolutions, the cruelties and crudities, of living, and so reached the culmination of its quest.

The revelation comes about not only through the fusion of the poet and the self, but also through the perceiving of the self through submersion in the Other. The self is learned through experiencing the Other, not as multitude but as intimate. . . .

Speed of Darkness is largely a book of love poems. In them, a new note of torment, of the pain of emotion, as she involves herself in love, echoes the pain the poet suffered years before when she was seeking the self. . . .

The title of Rukeyser's latest volume, *Breaking Open,* indicates that she feels she has succeeded in putting behind her the silences and alienations of the past. . . . *Breaking Open* contains some of Rukeyser's finest love poems. The eroticism of **''Looking At Each Other''** would be hard to surpass. She has reached at last, in the sexual mode, the selfhood she has been reaching for since her first venture. The unifying principle of her life she has discovered to be orgiastic, as in Whitman.

Yet paradoxically Rukeyser circles back to poems of social protest in her most recent book, many of which are notational, not very successful poems, except perhaps for the powerful **''Rational Man''** or the poem about the black woman who murdered her child.

Her most recent volume oscillates between the energy of the fully developed poems and the lassitude of many of the socially directed ones, so that the integration with the self and of the self with the world remains problematical, while her development as a poet has grown steadily in power, sensuosity and self-affirmation. We might consider her in many ways, in her strengths and in her weaknesses, a female counterpart of Walt Whitman.

We find, as we read Rukeyser's books in succession, that their affirmations and inconsistencies are peculiar to the Whitman-Transcendental tradition and form the resources which have supplied Rukeyser's poetry with its impulses, themes, images, tone and rhythms. Indeed, they form the very solid rock of her identity as poet. . . .

The Emersonian doctrine of correspondences begins to appear in *Theory of Flight*. . . . Later she views the concept in a political context in **''Correspondences''** [in *A Turning Wind*], explaining elsewhere that ''in time of the crises of the spirit . . . we begin to be aware of correspondences.'' . . .

The organic principle, springing from the belief in the oneness of all Being and underlying the aesthetic of Transcendentalism, spells itself out in supreme manner in *Leaves of Grass*. . . .

Yet conflicts that seem almost irreconcilable at all levels beset the Transcendentalist philosopher—those between the inner and the outer, between the light and the darkness, between the good and the evil, between the individual and society, between the citizen and the state. (p. 11)

The Transcendental interest in Oriental thought, evident in Emerson, Whitman and Thoreau, as well as in others of the group, points up further contradictions of the movement, which again reflect themselves in contradictory emotional attitudes, as in Rukeyser's work. . . . On the one hand, the contact with Oriental philosophy brought Thoreau, through its serenity, into a state of transcendence, as it did Rukeyser in **''Ajanta.''** On the other hand, the Whitman self may be rooted in the concept of ''unifying energy'' that he may have drawn from his reading of the *Bhagavid Gita*. Yet both concepts, though quite antithetic, are present in Rukeyser's poetry—**''Ajanta''** and *Orpheus*. . . .

But it is principally Melville and Whitman who elicit Rukeyser's attention in *The Life of Poetry* which serves to tie her most strongly to Transcendentalism. She is attracted to the two writers more than any other American literary figure, except possibly Hart Crane, because of their awareness of the conflicts both in the self and in the American culture. . . .

While Rukeyser's critical reasoning in *The Life of Poetry* is frequently difficult to follow, it is clear that Melville's struggle to recognize and surmount the contradictory aspects of nature and the self serve as his overriding attraction for her. In her most recent volume, *Breaking Open,* she is still involving herself in Melvilleian ideas, as in **''After Melville,''** and in Melvilleian analogies, as in **''In the Night the Night Sound Woke Us,''** in which we hear echoes of the nineteenth-century writer's ''The Berg: A Dream.''

However, although Rukeyser sees a common link between Melville and Whitman . . . Rukeyser turns more enthusiastically and more wholeheartedly to Whitman as guide and god. . . .

Rukeyser's own necessities and the directions American culture and literature have taken have elicited from the poet work uniquely her own, yet rooted in the permissions and instruments Whitman has allowed American poets since his day. . . .

Sharing the concept of Being as unified, they agree on certain details that, in general, other Transcendentalists minimize or ignore. For instance, both Whitman and Rukeyser recognize that death in any of its many guises must complement life if a sense of wholeness of existence is to be grasped. . . .

Both poets recognize the variety within the unity. For each, the self is the One but also the Many, all mankind is joined mystically and is thus one, and each human being partakes of the life of every other human being, living and dead and yet unborn, in all cultures and in all lands. The self of the poet is the mythic self. (p. 12)

Although many of Rukeyser's poems deal with the world beyond the American borders, they do so in the spirit of Whitman, who seeks to extend the borders of the spirit to the farthest reaches of the universe. Rukeyser's early admonition to ''FLY'' is merely a variant metaphor for the launching, the speeding, of the spider's filaments out of itself into the ''vacant, vast surrounding'' of the Whitman poem.

The acceptance, the fascination, of the immediate world of the senses allows the Transcendentalists not only to acknowledge the existence of science but to welcome its existence. . . . (pp. 12-13)

Believing that Western culture has set poetry and science in opposition to one another, Rukeyser sets forth her theoretical acceptance of science in *The Life of Poetry* where she points out the many parallels between the two—unity within themselves, symbolic language, selectivity, the use of the imagination in formulating concepts and in execution. Both, she believes, ultimately contribute to one another. . . .

[Rukeyser] joins Whitman in treating the physical body candidly, as in her most recent expressions of the self. . . .

[For] Rukeyser as for Whitman, both poets of ecstasy, truth is most fully revealed in metaphors of sexual intensity, in orgasm. (p. 13)

Rukeyser's poetic rhythms are closely allied to her feeling about the body and are expressive of the unity she seeks for in Being through sexual experience. . . . [The] poems for her become a physical thing, growing out of the bone and the muscle and the flesh, an extension of the organic theory of art adhered to by Emerson and other members of the Transcendental group. (pp. 13-14)

One significant extension of Rukeyser's sexuality has been in her interest in poetry about women. Although much remains to be settled in the political and economic realms of women's rights, it seems to me that the real accomplishment of the current feminist movement has been the achievement of sexual freedom for women. Women don't have to hide or compromise their physical natures any more but can honor their true feelings about sexuality. . . .

Rukeyser is, as she has called herself, a ''she-poet.'' There are no volumes of Rukeyser's poetry in which we are not aware that a woman is writing. Her writing has never accepted masculine pronouns by default. . . .

Not that Rukeyser's is a ''man-the-barricades'' kind of writing. The anguish comes out of her simply being a woman, with all its attendant crises, as in **''More of a Corpse Than a Woman.''** . . .

In much the same way as Dickinson moves around the subject of death, the ''Secret'' in the center, Rukeyser moves around the subject of women. . . . The significance of Rukeyser's growing concentration on the theme of women can be adduced from her absorption in the body and, as such, with the body of wholeness, creativity, birth and life, especially as it reveals itself in women. . . .

In her most recent volume she focuses on the Orphic metaphor solely on the woman experience. Disregarding the values she has attached to the legend earlier in **''In the Underworld''** . . . she infuses it with intensely personal feeling, identifying herself as woman not artist. Rooted in body experience, she spells out the shames, the agonies and the isolations of being woman. . . . As in *Orpheus,* where love of art causes the third finger to touch the lyre and thus initiate the rebirth process of the god, now love of a personal nature brings about the rebirth of a woman. . . . In *Breaking Open* she views women as scapegoats in the company of many other of society's scapegoats—children, artists, homosexuals, Germans, Jews, blacks, communists and so on, a further fusion of the woman thread with that of social protest, and similar to its fusion with the mythic. (p. 14)

Many would like to forget what she reminds us of, but hers is the voice of ''possibility and outrage,'' a phrase, the truths of which she had declared have their moments in the poetry of Melville and Whitman.

Rukeyser exists then chronologically, historically, thematically. Her poetry is in harmony with much that animates our own times. . . . Her canvas has encompassed a vast field—the self in its many guises, America and the world with all its beauty and ugliness, and even the limitless cosmos of metaphysical speculation. She has experimented with many modes of poetical expression, formal and informal. She is a poet of imposing dimensions. (p. 15)

Virginia R. Terris, ''Muriel Rukeyser: A Retrospective'' (copyright © 1974 by World Poetry, Inc.; reprinted by permission of Virginia R. Terris), in The American Poetry Review, *Vol. 3, No. 3, May-June, 1974, pp. 10-15.*

RACHEL BLAU DuPLESSIS

In poems about women, politics and war, and myth [Denise Levertov, Adrienne Rich, and Muriel Rukeyser] construct critiques of culture and ideology from a radical and often feminist point of view. The act of critique guides the central acts of perception in the poems. Their poems analyze women's assumptions and patterns of action, revealing the cultural norms that uphold traditional consciousness of women. The poets discuss the role of the individual in history, especially in the creation of social change. Their myths have an unusual dimension, for critique becomes the heart of the myth. Their myths are critical of prior mythic thought; they are historically specific rather than eternal; they replace archetypes by prototypes. The poets learned, from the critique of women's consciousness and from the discussion of the individual in history, to honor the experiences of individual and social change that belie cyclic interpretations of history and archetypal readings of their own lives. (pp. 280-81)

[Through] the flat, bold words of **''Despisals,''** Rukeyser has dramatized the power of the reader's assumptions. . . . For at first the reader is likely to be startled at the forbidden words and shocked that the poet did not exclude them. But because the theme of the poem is the rejection of all forms of shame and contempt, readers are taught that their normative expectations for the poem's tone and diction are a version of the repressive "despisals" the poem criticizes. (p. 283)

"**Käthe Kollwitz**" is one of Rukeyser's series of "**Lives**" telling the stories of humanistic, secular saints, investigating the qualities, character, and acts of selected women and men. In these poems Rukeyser documented the struggles and decisions of historical heroes, situating them on a human scale, at once accessible and inspiring to others. War is a living reality which Kollwitz must confront and transcend by an affirmation of life-giving values. Kollwitz's forging of her art is a model heroic act, since the "truth" of her art is transformative. (p. 288)

As a woman learns to "tell the truth" about her own life, giving voice to her voiceless feelings and groping toward the elucidation of repressed desperation, her full consciousness, born in this effort, will be able to serve others. In "**Käthe Kollwitz**" Rukeyser affirms the continuity between individual changes of consciousness and changes in the world. The difficulty . . . lies in learning to "tell the truth"; the transformation of the world, Rukeyser states, is a necessary result.

But this affirmation of continuity between psyche and its effects on history is, in another sense, exactly the problem. If a person told the truth about her life and about the life around her, would the world break open? How is it possible to move from individual awareness and transformation to the social change so acutely desired? In "**Breaking Open**" Rukeyser proposes a communion so intense that it "breaks open" the self to others, providing a new basis for community. Yet the affirmation at the end of this poem is mingled with a sense of failure. The difficulties may be attributable as much—or more—to the relative impasse of the left and the antiwar movement on this issue in the early 1970s as to a private lack of vision or perception on Rukeyser's part. This long poem is indeed a lyric document of its time.

The problem she sets in the poem is the "re-imagining" of a life sufficient to overcome the waste and destruction that is most acutely presented by the Vietnam War, so that her images and her acts will contribute to the realization of a new world and a new set of social relations. In prose meditations on the relationship between the outer and inner worlds, Rukeyser states that psyche and history are really versions of each other. . . . In order to reach history and the capacity to act in history, one must reach buried parts of personal life (our personal unconscious) which we hold in common with others (the collective unconscious). This recalls Rukeyser's argument in "**Despisals**" that our repressions, although laid down individually, in fact constitute a collective stratum that has immense repercussions for the social structure.

So, "breaking open" must simultaneously incorporate knowledge of our historical and our personal moments and must lead to a transformation of both—history through psyche and psyche through history. The poem sequence "**Searching/Not Searching**," in the same volume, can be read in conjunction with this search for transformation in "**Breaking Open**," for it illuminates the concern for the relationships of individual psychology and history. The phrase "inner greet," which appears in both poems . . . , describes those people with such self-knowledge and generosity of spirit that they create communion with others. In her argument, Rukeyser has put the emphasis on the level

and sacramental quality of the "inner greet" which must be attained to bring about social transformation.

She tests for this human capacity in several episodes, through her experiences as a prisoner, with the jury, in jail. She discovers in jail that some of the prisoners have already forged a community into which they welcome the poet. . . . The poem implicitly asks what allows some people to move beyond apparent social and structural impasses, such as prison, and enter, as prophets or avatars, the more human community that the poem foresees.

Rukeyser identifies the reasons in a section that begins "I do and I do," suggesting that the movement "to make the world"—a creative act, an act of affirmation and even of marriage—is the motivation for social change. But then, killing, torture, and repression are equally things people "do," and they may even feel satisfaction and righteousness in these acts. To this problem she suggests that by being in touch with the underlife of dream, desire, fantasy, and nonrational feeling, one can avoid becoming the "rational man" whose genocides and tortures she has catalogued in an earlier section. Postulating that the fullness of one's own inner life will prevent political horrors puts tremendous stress on the transformation of individuals. . . . The diction suggests that the experience is solid and verifiable, yet also absolute and unanalyzable. Hence the tone of the statement necessitates the "inner greet" of the reader, for others enter this affirmation only by an emotional commitment to celebration and communion. But the ending of the poem graphically presents, in unresolved form, a conflict between "yes" and "no"—two interpretations of what has been accomplished. One, which Rukeyser overtly holds, reaffirms that individual change on a dense enough scale has naturally brought about social change through the power of communion with others. The second interpretation cannot but see a defeat or impasse in these attempts, yet the defeat is not discussed. It appears alongside statements of transcendence. (pp. 288-90)

Explicitly antimythological, ["**The Poem as Mask**"] is an act of self-criticism, for it was written in direct opposition to an earlier mythic poem by Rukeyser called "**Orpheus**." The older poem, constructed like a court masque of English tradition, uses an organizing symbol of the power of music, centers on a static drama of transformation, and ends with a final song of unity. This is one of the few of her own poems which Rukeyser discusses in her critical work *The Life of Poetry*. Her section about the writing of "**Orpheus**" is the climax of that book. For the singer as sacred, the fragments of the human reunited as the divine, the transcendent experience of healing and power combined in the figure of Orpheus are motifs with great resonance for Rukeyser. But the poem, read now, is sluggish, wordy, held back from fullness. "**The Poem as Mask**" brings this earlier poem into question in a deliberate act of self-examination and self-criticism. (p. 293)

Rukeyser asks why she had censored her feelings, writing *him, god, myth* when she meant *me, human, my life*. She answers that as a woman, she was unable to affirm the concreteness and actuality of her life: a real loss of love, a real birth with actual dangers, the rescue of her newborn child and of herself. Thus her old use of the myth blunted her access to herself; the myth of Orpheus was a "mask" which now must be removed, not a "masque" of unity and joy. The old myth gave her feelings a shape, but it tampered with their authenticity. So she makes a vow at the end of the poem: "No more masks! No more mythologies!" But, while the vow is specifically and understandably antimythological, that refusal is an enabling act, and "for the first time" the myth is alive. . . . The new myth comes from the poet's orphic experiences of suffering, inspiration, and birth. In these final lines the "fragments" of the broken self are allowed to bring or to retain "their own music"; a polyphonic, multifaced composition contrasts with the linear, hierarchic melody sung out in the earlier **"Orpheus."** . . . Rukeyser finds the sources of real sacredness in the commonplace, in the biographical, and in the act of self-criticism itself, incorporating a changed attitude to her life and her work. **"The Poem as Mask"** is a myth of self-healing based on the process of critique. (pp. 293-94)

> *Rachel Blau DuPlessis, "The Critique of Consciousness and Myth in Levertov, Rich, and Rukeyser," in* Feminist Studies *(copyright © 1975 by Feminist Studies, Inc.), Vol. III, Fall, 1975 (and reprinted in* Shakespeare's Sisters: Feminist Essays on Women Poets, *edited by Sandra M. Gilbert and Susan Gubar, Indiana University Press, 1979, pp. 280-300).* *

KENNETH REXROTH

Muriel Rukeyser is the best poet of her exact generation. (p. xi)

It is curious to read [of] the attacks on Muriel Rukeyser by what were, in fact, political opponents, for her lack of "depth." Purely as a thinker, she is certainly more profound than anyone else in her generation. It's just that her thoughts were not their thoughts. She is one of the most important writers of the Left of her time, and now with the death of Neruda and the ever-increasing sterility of Louis Aragon, she ranks very high indeed. Unlike the other writers of the Left, she never paid much, if any, attention to the corkscrew twists of the party line. So the critics of the Left alternately embraced and damned her. . . . She does not have an ideology grafted into her head like these devices they attach to the brains of monkeys. She has a philosophy of life which comes out of her own flesh and bones. It is not a foreign body. . . . Muriel Rukeyser is a traditionalist. But when everybody was running about talking about one tradition or another but doing nothing about it, her tradition was not recognized or was despised. Muriel Rukeyser is not a poet of Marxism, but a poet who has written directly about the tragedies of the working class. She is a poet of liberty, civil liberty, woman's liberty, and all the other liberties that so many people think they themselves just invented in the last ten years. (pp. xi-xii)

Muriel Rukeyser believes in the community of love, not because she is convinced that it is going to win, but because it is true, it is the right way for human beings to live. She has been accused of "optimism," and this in a country where the Left thinks the revolution is just around the corner and the rest of the population continuously invents new euphemisms for graveyards. . . . In America you're either an optimist or a pessimist. Hardly anyone knows that "The world is a tragedy for those who feel, and a comedy for those who think." Muriel Rukeyser thinks and feels; and not only that, she seems to enjoy placing herself as an obstacle in the way of evil. Book after book has involved action—from personal investigation of the fate of miners doomed to die of silicosis in *U.S. 1,* to her fairly recent personal confrontation of a South Korean dictatorship in the case of a Catholic radical poet, Kim Chi-Ha, who had been condemned to death. (pp. xii-xiii)

What about Muriel's poetry? Her enemies have called it rhetorical, as though the **"Ode to the Confederate Dead"** was anything but rhetoric uncontaminated by intellect. She has a

sonority as deep as her deep laughter, and it is this sense of the power over language that distinguishes her from the women who preceded her in her tradition, Lola Ridge, Evelyn Scott, Beatrice Ravenel, or men like James Oppenheim, or Wallace Gould. . . .

Muriel Rukeyser does not embrace Zen, but she has more and more internalized her philosophy of life—but this in a special sense. It's one thing to be a suffragette, it's another thing to insist on being a woman, completely, in every sense of the word. (p. xiii)

"Ajanta" is purportedly a poem about the great painted caves in India, one of the high points of the world's art. When she wrote it, Muriel had never been to India, although, of course, she had seen the great portfolio of accurate reproductions. I have seen Ajanta, and I must say that the poem conveys, amongst other things, the feeling, the emotion, the very sensibility, of those long-gone Buddhist monks, that overwhelms you in the same way the poem does. **"Ajanta"** is an exploration with continuous discoveries of new meanings, of her own interior—in every sense. It is the interior of her mind as a human being, as a poet, and as a woman. It is the interior of her self as her own flesh. It is her womb. I am sure that she did not know, in those days, of the womb mandala of Tibetan and Japanese Shingon Buddhism, but in a sense that is what the poem is. We did not need Carl Jung to tell us that the mandalas of Buddhism and Hinduism are paradigms of the interior life, and that that life with its symbolic patterns is shared by all human beings to the extent that we all have the same physiology. After **"Ajanta,"** in fact, she wrote a poem of introspection into her own womb where, to use Buddhist symbolism, Maitreya was seated in Peace. It is in nine parts, one for each month of pregnancy, and it is unique in the literature of feminine poetry.

Like Walt Whitman, as the horizons darkened and the community of love seemed to grow more distant, Muriel has sought ever deeper into her self for its meaning. She is far from being a member of that most profitable fraternity—a disillusioned radical. The message now is not, if it ever was, "All power to the people!" . . . Power has fascinated Muriel since her first book, *Theory of Flight.* As is self-evident from her biography of Willard Gibbs, power has always meant to her not the power of Stalin or Mao that "comes out of the mouth of a gun." Power for her is the great dynamo within what used to be called the soul. Her later poems and her life have been devoted to research into the dynamics of that power, and as always, this has led her to actual physical confrontation with the mechanical power of despotism and exploitation. (pp. xiv-xv)

> *Kenneth Rexroth, in a foreword to* The Poetic Vision of Muriel Rukeyser *by Louise Kertesz (reprinted by permission of Louisiana State University Press; copyright © 1980 by Louisiana State University Press), Louisiana State University Press, 1980, pp. xi-xvi.*

JOHN TAGLIABUE

[The following poem, reprinted in its entirety, is a tribute to Muriel Rukeyser.]

It is difficult to see in this harsh light, in the glare of
   this machine place

with the ferocity of blandness, pollution, steel, trains
    and cars with tired people almost well adjusted to
    their lack of direction and their routine; Kafka is in
his grave; Camus lets out another call as he falls; the
    river is cold; the 385 dream songs are pieces of ice;
the Lewiston factories are making Marsden Hartley
    cumbersome and outraged again; once more he
    celebrates
the splash of the uplifted Atlantic wave and the terror
    and songs of Hart Crane; Homage to those shaken
    seers on Main Street; the cars
ride by, the energy crisis, the identity crisis, the failure
    of communication crisis; how can you forget the
    concentration camps

and all that went with them? but look at Muriel I say to
    my students, look at Muriel Rukeyser,
collect her large volume of poems, she has protected,
    with those activists we have overcome, the Song goes
    on;
her poems have collected our hope and power, to walk
    with her and them makes us see bold incorrigible
    indivisible Whitman ahead.

John Tagliabue, "'American Complicated with Integrity: Homage to Muriel'" (reprinted by permission of the author), in Harper's, *Vol. 262, No. 1571, April, 1981, p. 39.*

Jane (Vance) Rule

1931-

American-born Canadian novelist, short story writer, and essayist.

An avowed lesbian, Rule writes with clarity and insight about the struggles and triumphs peculiar to relationships among women. Her characters are typically outcasts, rejected by or rejecting contemporary society.

Although Rule was born and raised in the United States, she has lived in Canada for over twenty years. Her writing reflects many traditional Canadian themes, most notably the love of the landscape and the desire to escape the encroachment of modern technology. Her novel *The Young in One Another's Arms* (1977), for example, describes an assortment of young eccentrics who retreat from society in an attempt to construct an alternative mode of living. *Outlander* (1982), her recent collection of essays and short stories, follows a similar theme by portraying various aspects of life on the edge of contemporary culture.

Rule is also concerned with the relation of women to art. Her critical essays in *Lesbian Images* (1975) examine twelve women writers and how lesbianism has affected their lives and their work. The depth of her scope has led one critic to note that *Lesbian Images* "offers an expanded view of women in our culture."

(See also *Contemporary Authors*, Vols. 25-28, rev. ed.)

Photograph by Tee A Corinne; courtesy of Jane Rule

CHRISTOPHER SALVESEN

Reno, Nevada is the setting for a first novel which is a convincing example of its kind: *The Desert of the Heart* develops a moral situation until a decision is made which the reader feels has been fairly and interestingly worked for. Evelyn Hall, university teacher, unsuccessfully married for 16 years, has come for her divorce. She falls in love with a young girl who works in a casino. Gradually she realises her marriage has been a 'long detour' from her original nature. The conflict between what she knows to be natural and what she believes to be right is worked out on the equivocal stages of the Nevada desert and the gambling-club. . . . The setting is brilliantly used throughout: one of the central episodes, on a barren lake-shore bone-white with fossil snail-shells, recalls *Passage to India*. The pessimistic message of the caves ('Everything exists, nothing has value') seems here to be reversed; 'everything has value'—even sterility. But this, from the girl Ann, who lives for the moment, who identifies with the desert, comes perhaps to much the same. And her morality poses a question to Evelyn's more conventional liberal one. The sterile, beautiful landscape (and the pure, useless activity of gambling), can these really accommodate, let alone justify, their love? This is an intelligent novel, not afraid of ideas and not committed to them over-diagrammatically: there are some telling incidental scenes—the divorce hearing, a farcical wedding—and the two women talk with that unaffected graveness, peculiarly American, which can incorporate literary allusion and parlour-game psychology without strain.

Christopher Salvesen, "In the West Riding," in New Statesman (© 1964 The Statesman & Nation Publishing Co. Ltd.), Vol. LXVII, No. 1718, February 14, 1964, p. 260.*

THE TIMES LITERARY SUPPLEMENT

Miss Rule shows talent in setting [the scene of *The Desert of the Heart*], with its neon nights and torpid days in the huge desert, but becomes painfully sentientious in baring the tense and tawdry dramas of her sexual misfits. [The protagonists'] predicament is made real and even moving, but too much of what they think and say reads like a pastiche of the sentimental idealism one might expect from a romantic novelette about the first stirring of a more conventional kind of love.

A review of "The Desert of the Heart," in The Times Literary Supplement (© Times Newspapers Ltd. (London) 1964; reproduced from The Times Literary Supplement by permission), No. 3236, March 5, 1964, p. 201.

ANNE CONSTANCE PENTA

[*The Desert of the Heart,* a] startlingly explicit novel of lesbian love, is neither an apology nor an indictment. It is an objective portrayal of love between two women, love that progresses from the arousing of their first erotic instincts to their abandonment of conventional moral codes in a kind of desperate liberation.

Despite the uncanny physical resemblance that makes them look like mother and daughter, Ann Childs and Evelyn Hall are fifteen years and a whole society apart. Ann, a change-apron in a Reno gambling casino, moves with defiant gaiety in the garish chaos of Frank's club. Evelyn, a proper middle-aged college professor, comes to Reno to shed her husband, George. . . .

As Evelyn's looks are embodied in Ann, so is her identity as a mother figure. Relegated to a childless fate with George, she finds maternal compensation in her look-alike, Ann.

Ann, scarred by the childhood trauma of desertion by her nymphomaniac mother, sees in Evelyn the mother she yearned for but lost. This relationship, however, is ominously narcissistic. Meeting Evelyn is like seeing your double in a mirror, Ann remarks. "They say when you meet your double, you die."

Death here takes the form of the moral suicide of homosexuality. Although Evelyn has read somewhere that "all intelligent women are latent homosexuals," she is initially bewildered and offended by Ann's erotic power over her. . . . But social restraint gives way to compulsive lust and this insidious transition from lesbianism on the subconscious level to the overt act of homosexual love making is skillfully delineated by Miss Rule.

> Anne Constance Penta, in a review of "The Desert of the Heart," in Best Sellers (copyright 1965, by the University of Scranton), Vol. 25, No. 11, September 1, 1965, p. 222.

JODY HABERLAND

[*This Is Not for You,* a] sensitive yet almost documentary account of the college and early adult life of a woman, is unsettling because of its precarious balance between conscious emotional restraint and the force of a supreme desire to love. Kate, the protagonist, succumbs, through brief affairs, to her lesbianism, yet denies herself a relationship with her best friend Esther. By her sacrifice, whatever future fulfillment there might have been is lost. . . . The novel has substance and insight, and an intellectualism that at times may strike you as stilted or a bit contrived. Still, this slightly extraordinary account proves that love knows no limitations of person, place, or time—but that life is a corridor of doors and only one at a time may be opened and entered.

> Jody Haberland, in a review of "This Is Not for You," in Library Journal (reprinted from Library Journal, July 1970; published by R. R. Bowker Co. (a Xerox company); copyright © 1970 by Xerox Corporation), Vol. 95, No. 13, July, 1970, p. 2520.

BRUCE D. ALLEN

Amelia Larson is a crippled spinster dominated by the memory of her dead sister, whose painful diaries she is reading. She is uncertainly poised between past and present, like the old friends, relatives, and acquaintances who cluster around her. Embodiments of various generations, sexes, and life styles, they are people surprised by the intrusion of sexuality into their lives. . . . Yet loving proves their only escape from self-absorption. [Jane Rule] expertly renders façades that mask indecision, especially through dialogue. But [*Against the Season*] is too rigidly patterned: each character is a glaring thematic counterpart to some other one; every scene announces too loudly its structural function as some sort of "balance." The human element is there, but it is too obviously part of the design.

> Bruce D. Allen, in a review of "Against the Season" in Library Journal (reprinted from Library Journal, April 1, 1971; published by R. R. Bowker Co. (a Xerox company); copyright © 1971 by Xerox Corporation), Vol. 96, No. 7, April 1, 1971, p. 1291.

MICHELE M. LEBER

If lesbianism were accepted as just another way of loving—and if lesbian writers were not always taken in a sexual context—[*Lesbian Images*] would not be necessary, the author notes. A teacher, writer, feminist, and lesbian, Rule examines love between women in the work of 12 female authors (Radclyffe Hall, Gertrude Stein, Willa Cather, Vita Sackville-West, Ivy Compton-Burnett, Elizabeth Bowen, Colette, Violette Leduc, Margaret Anderson, Dorothy Baker, May Sarton, Maureen Duffy). Fluent and nonjudgmental, she considers to what extent the art of these women reflects their personal lives as well as their society. . . . This book should not be considered just a literary examination of one narrow facet of life; for beyond its insight into lesbianism, it offers an expanded view of women in our culture, and its value increases for that.

> Michele M. Leber, "An Expanded View of Women in Our Culture," in Library Journal (reprinted from Library Journal, June 15, 1975; published by R. R. Bowker Co. (a Xerox company); copyright © 1975 by Xerox Corporation), Vol. 100, No. 12, June 15, 1975, p. 1232.

ROBIN SKELTON

[*Lesbian Images*] is a sensible, witty, well-written book which provides us with new perspectives upon the lives and works of a number of women writers. . . . The biographical details, many of which are here given for the first time, are presented without sensationalism, and with a fine balance of sympathy and objectivity. The book's major weakness is the final chapter on "Recent Nonfiction," for here Ms Rule does not give herself enough space to deal with the complexity and fury of recent writings on lesbianism, and while her comments are, as always, shrewd, they appear occasionally to be less objective than those she makes in other chapters, and the book ends upon a somewhat hortatory note. It is, perhaps, more difficult for the nonpartisan reader to accept writing that is, in her own words, "extravagant, self-critical, self-mocking, self-aggrandizing" as being also "honest and terrible and awesome" than Ms Rule thinks. Such a reader may be inclined to feel that hysterical writing is bad writing, however significant sociologically and psychologically the presentation of that hysteria may be. This is a difficulty that faces any writer who tackles a subject in which aesthetic and sociological criteria become entangled with each other. On the whole, however, there is no doubt that this is an important book, and the most reasonable, balanced, and civilized contribution to the study of lesbianism in twentieth-century literature that we have yet had.

Robin Skelton, in a review of "Lesbian Images," in The Malahat Review *(© The Malahat Review, 1975), No. 36, October, 1975, p. 143.*

VICTORIA GLENDINNING

[*Lesbian Images*] begins with a brief history of Miss Rule's discovery of her own lesbianism, which is extremely interesting; she is generous, honest, and quite without bitterness or paranoia. This is the most valuable part of the book. She goes on to a whistle-stop history of attitudes to female inversion from Ancient Greece to the present day, paying particular attention to the position of the Christian churches; she also argues, persuasively, that most nineteenth and twentieth-century psychiatry is nothing but a translation of moral objections into medical terms.

The study of lesbianism in women writers which forms the main part of this book is unrewarding. There is little new that can be said in a few pages about Radclyffe Hall and Gertrude Stein, and the chapter on V. Sackville-West is drawn mainly from Nigel Nicolson's *Portrait of a Marriage*. Miss Rule searches the plots of novels by Margaret Anderson, Dorothy Baker, May Sarton and—jumping a few years—Maureen Duffy, finding varying degrees of caution, commitment, rebellion, resignation. . . . In her chapter on Elizabeth Bowen—who was an expert not so much on lesbianism as on the power one woman can have over another, a rather different thing—she misses that writer's most overtly lesbian character, and an exception to Miss Rule's grimly accurate statement that "Humour has been rare in fiction about lesbians": the fatal Theodora in *Friends and Relations*. . . .

Victoria Glendinning, "Women in Love," in The Times Literary Supplement *(© Times Newspapers Ltd. (London) 1976; reproduced from* The Times Literary Supplement *by permission), No. 3880, July 23, 1976, p. 904.*

BERTHA HARRIS

[*Lesbian Images*] intends to show what it means to be a lesbian who characterizes her reality in art; who shows "truth in the rich particular rather than in the lowest common denominator of a hundred case histories." These "images" of 12 novelists and literary personalities (13, when we count Jane Rule's own story) are, more than any other thing, a novelist's accomplishment—a skillful interweaving of plot and psychology, temperament and circumstance, life and work. And those who love Jane Rule's fiction . . . will find themselves once again keeping pleasureable company with the novelist who brought civilizing sense to the heartbreak-and-booze tradition in modern lesbian fiction. *Lesbian Images* is first and foremost a nonfictional development of one of Jane Rule's fictional concerns: to reveal the human symmetry of the lesbian; to dissipate the grotesque stereotypes. . . .

Unfortunately, the same qualities that generally give grace and strength to Jane Rule's prose and its content—discernment, good manners, compassion, tolerance—tend to resolve this collection of extraordinarily diverse women into a kind of sisterhood of lesbian sameness, as though each had been reborn as Jane Rule herself. . . .

There seems no other justification—other than the author's need for "heritage"—for linking Radclyffe Hall's preposterous images of martyrdom with the bisexual appetites of Colette; the onanistic fantasies of Leduc with the frail melodramas of Dorothy Baker; the dated Freudianism of Duffy with the asexual satire of Compton-Burnett. We are by now as familiar with the "male-identification" of Gertrude Stein and Radclyffe Hall as we are with the genius of the former and the stupidity of the latter. (p. 106)

Jane Rule's contribution is no news, as either traditional or feminist insight. Attempts to restore to us women whose lives and work have been distorted by "moral smugness, prejudice veiled in literary language, and embarrassed silence" are praiseworthy—and have been praised both in and out of the Women's Movement for several years. The central chapters of *Lesbian Images* make a point, however, that the author did not intend: sometimes the work of these women has been affected by lesbianism, but much more frequently it has been shaped by other factors, such as class, nationality, and blind loyalty to the patriarchal status quo.

Jane Rule describes lesbian "images"; but she has not defined lesbian literature or the sensibility that would lead us to evaluate it as a separate genre, with shared characteristics and feelings. Possibly because one does not exist. Neither heterosexuality nor lesbianism *alone* can create a cultural sensibility that in turn materializes as art. Difference—and literary genre—is first brought into being by shared metaphysical assumptions about the world and what we would like to happen in it. Jane Rule's images of lesbians are those of lesbians who share nothing in common but a desire to write. Both the known biographical facts and the vast dissimilarities in the emotional and material content of their works would not encourage us to presume an erotic conformity among them. Their writings, far from being the product of a purely lesbian imagination, are the reverse—part and parcel of the "heterosexual culture" whose domination Jane Rule so rightfully deplores.

Those lesbians who *are* attempting to make art informed by feminism rather than commanded by heterosexuality, who are imagining a present and a future tense in literature rather than inventing a "heritage," Jane Rule relegates to a few casual mentions in the back of the book. . . . [Rule] dismisses . . . all lesbian fiction with a feminist political bias. Art, she believes, is no fit place for politics.

Lesbian "images" become lesbian sensibility only when infused by what feminists understand as "consciousness." To realize consciousness as art is a long and arduous process, but one which every emerging civilization undergoes. When the zeal of the new lesbian-feminist writers seems less artistically satisfying than the conciliatory survival patterns of the old lesbian worlds, Jane Rule should remind herself of the remark she quotes from Stein's *Autobiography of Alice B. Toklas*: "When you make a thing, it is so complicated making it that it is bound to be ugly, but those that do it after you they don't have to worry about making it and they can make it pretty, and so everyone can like it when the others make it." *Lesbian Images* is a love affair with a "pretty" past. (pp. 106, 110)

Bertha Harris, "Rescued from Moral Smugness," in Ms. *(© 1976 Ms. Magazine Corp.), Vol. V, No. 3, September, 1976, pp. 106, 110.*

JOHN GLASSCO

Jane Rule's fifth novel [*The Young in One Another's Arms*] will probably be the first to find a wide audience, since it comes after the success of a timely work of non-fiction [*Lesbian Images*] and a gust of publicity. Two national magazines have already introduced to the whole country a woman who came across in her interviews as attractive, brilliant, courageous, enormously talented, industrious and—perhaps most appealingly of all—neglected. This combination adumbrates the way in which a large part of literary Canada likes to see itself, and Jane Rule thus appeared in these magazines as quintessentially Canadian. The image is even enhanced by the fact that she was born and bred in the United States.

I am one of those readers for whom the fifth novel is the first, one who admired *Lesbian Images* and looked forward to reading more Rule. I am disappointed, and my feelings go beyond the usual disappointment of finding that a writer has not written the book I expected. In this case, she has not even written either of the two books she seemed to promise in the early pages of the present novel. The first book she hasn't written is the story of that mysterious creature, the woman of 50; the second is the story of the flight of the American anti-war young to sanctuary in Canada. What she has written is the standard Canadian novel of retreat from urban evil to woodsy good, and in doing so has reached some surprising depths in sentimentality and tedium.

The setting is Vancouver, where Ruth Wheeler, one-armed as the result of an accident, lives with her mother-in-law (the name Ruth is no accident) and runs a boarding house for six lodgers. Five of them are the young who are frequently in one another's arms, and the sixth is a dim-witted shoe-clerk for whom Ruth feels responsible. But for whom does she not feel responsible? Ruth is a saint. . . .

The men of the house are the usual weaklings and misfits who make such an appeal to many women writers. . . .

With such a cast of characters much can happen, and much does—but with a strange effect of unreality since most of the action takes place off stage. These boarders exist in a climate of such cool permissiveness that attachments between them form and dissolve in a dreamy, meaningless manner; there is no emotion or interest generated by these changes and exchanges, reported but never explained. . . . (p. 3)

Indeed, much of the writing in this book does suggest the protracted case history of a multi-problem family as recorded by a social worker in the approved "non-judgmental" manner. For while Miss Rule contrives big scenes and raises big issues, she never fails to withdraw from them into flashbacks and ruminations. Under the busy crowded surface of the novel there lies an intractable passivity.

The second half of the book moves the group, now further altered by one death and the arrival of a newcomer, to an island community off Vancouver where they are to live communally and run a restaurant. In no time at all they are also delivering meals on wheels, operating a nursery school for neglected children, splitting firewood for the elderly, and in general behaving like a troop of badge-mad Boy Scouts. The sheer goodness of it all is difficult to take; it is also as unreal as everything else in the book, since these chores are performed without a single aching muscle, bead of sweat, or word of complaint. But by now it is clear that the novel's action has become little more than a self-indulgent reverie of the author's.

The book ends with all difficulties overcome. . . . The young are still in one another's arms, still safe and sheltered in the love of the rock-like Ruth.

It is hard to make goodness interesting, but the problem is not solved by making it sentimental. . . . *The Young in One Another's Arms* cannot, in the end, be regarded as anything but popular women's-magazine fiction. It is only fair to say that it makes no pretence of being anything else. (p. 4)

John Glassco, "Her Goodness, Our Grimace" (reprinted by permission of the Literary Estate of John Glassco), in Books in Canada, Vol. 6, No. 3, March, 1977, pp. 3-4.

SANDRA MARTIN

In her reader *Lesbian Images*, Jane Rule, herself a professed and practising lesbian, attempts to debunk the time-honoured theories that homosexuality is a sin and/or a sickness. For the most part she is successful, amassing a great deal of evidence to shore up her arguments about what lesbianism isn't. Unhappily she doesn't enlighten us much about what it is, claiming magisterially, "the reality of lesbian experience transcends all theories about it." (p. 87)

Rule argues that psychological theorists and practitioners who insist that lesbianism is a sickness are dangerous in that they often produce traumas in individuals who before suffered from nothing but a loving preference for their own sex. Lesbians, she complains, endure prejudices as ill-considered and unfounded as those traditionally heaped against left-handed people. The analogy is apt, for examples abound of the sorry repercussions of "correcting" a child's left-handedness. But what about the male and female homosexuals who genuinely believe they are sick and who want desperately to be cured? Won't they be tossed out along with the taboos?

Rule admits she is a polemicist. . . . Still, admitting her biases doesn't excuse her frequently sloppy logic or the strident tone with which she condemns anti-lesbian arguments.

Where is the merciless scrutiny that flayed such enemies as Father David Ford and Dr. David Reuben when Rule takes on current feminist literati? The chapter on recent non-fiction reads more like a progress report on the problems and strife within the women's movement than anything else, with Rule displaying an annoying reticence as though she were trying to placate all factions at once.

Certainly her own sense of separateness from lesbians who refuse or are unable to accept traditional roles of loyalty and commitment in their relationships is told much more effectively in fiction. In "My Country Wrong", one of the stories included in her collection *Theme for Diverse Instruments*, the narrator is on a Christmas trip from Canada to her native California. She looks up some old friends, including Lynn who takes her to a gay party. Lynn is obviously and desperately on the make, but it is the narrator who seems awkward, out of place, even faintly anachronistic in her "navy silk with a green silk coat." At one point the narrator, herself a lesbian, says, "I don't believe in fidelity though it is for me the only practical way to live." Like her narrator Rule seems slightly in awe of women who have abandoned (surpassed?) emotional bonds. (pp. 87-8)

[Rule explores] with candour and intelligence . . . the changing images of women as expressed through the lives and writings of more than a dozen widely read novelists. They range from women who wanted to be men . . . to women who were emotionally but not sexually engaged with other women . . . to women who recognized and tried to suppress the lesbian sides of their natures . . . to women proud to be women and lesbians. . . . Aside from any emotional responses we may have to the sufferings and uncertainties of these women, Rule's careful scholarship and sharp insights provide both a sturdy framework and a context for examining women's literature. To say *Lesbian Images* is timely is absurd; it is long past due.

Few of the stories in *Theme for Diverse Instruments* are about lesbianism per se, but they are all about women and loving relationships. Mainly Rule's women are stumbling through a maze of apprehensions, conditionings, and stereotypings as they grope towards a better understanding of themselves and others. It is a hard struggle and that's why so many of the characters seem alone and adrift, even sometimes alienated.

Rule begins by giving us a positive myth about women. The allegorical title story **"Theme for Diverse Instruments"** explores a matriarchical family where the women are prolific and dominant and the men by contrast infertile and ineffectual. (p. 88)

The myth established, we move on to the girl child. In **"My Father's House"** a little girl is playing with her elder brother and a friend. That is they are playing and she is joining in whenever they let her. In her isolation the little girl muses about a drawing in her colouring book and decides, "If she was going to be in the picture she'd have to draw herself in." "Drawing herself in" is precisely the problem facing women and the task that Rule has set herself in these stories. She succeeds admirably and yet I found this key story tainted by a slickness and a coyness. It seemed too pat, too simple. (pp. 88-9)

[In] **"Invention for Shelagh"**, Rule gives us herself. Ostensibly this is a series of journal entries—random notes for a letter to a close friend—but it becomes a clever and intimate collage. Rule weaves a delicate pattern amongst the abstract jottings that culminates in a self-portrait which depicts a woman who has confronted sex, career, money, identity, etc., and emerged as a loving, honest person. . . .

Lesbian Images and *Theme for Diverse Instruments* reinforce each other so completely that it is almost as though Rule consciously wrote one to complement the other. Together they make a marriage. (p. 89)

Sandra Martin, "The Age Old Dilemma" (reprinted by permission of the author), in Canadian Literature, *No. 72, Spring, 1977, pp. 87-9.*

EDITH MILTON

[*The Young in One Another's Arms*] is a rather dreadful piece of writing, about a one-armed woman about to be evicted from the Vancouver boarding house which she owns and which has been marked down by urban renewal. Presumably Rule intends Vancouver in particular, and the society of North American cities in general, to stand for what Yeats calls "no country for old men." But the machine-ruled, police-run world she describes hardly does well by birds in the trees or by the young, either. She sees the stereotypes of her boarding house, related as they are by weakness and by the bonds of affection rather than by legal ties and blood lines, as a new, ideal version of the human family, and she traces their sailing to Byzantium, their flight from demolition to Galiano Island. The multi-racial, cosmo-sexual, four-generation structure of the new family unit

is threatened from without by financial and political harassments, and from within, not surprisingly, by emotional cross-currents. But the greatest threat comes, probably, from the author, who works at the relationships among members of her circle with the earnest manipulations of a twelve-year-old trying to describe how it all was among the counselors at summer camp. She is utterly determined that it will all be good, and that they are all nice people, as they vault from bed to bed and from mood to mood, without her seeming to understand exactly why they do it, but only to know that, for purposes of plot, or summer camp, they do it. (pp. 261-62)

It is poignantly irritating to find Rule writing with the grave demeanor of someone sure of her own daring. She unfurls her vista of the free life and open sexuality to reveal a homey landscape halfway between Woolf in Bloomsbury and William Morris in Nowhere. Rule's trouble is that she is much too conscious of her didactic purpose; she builds her new society to serve as an example of how to eschew the flaws of ordinary family relationships. But then eschewing such flaws, something which can be done very nicely in the heads of adolescents packing mentally for a Better World, is not really a very convincing mode for personal survival, either in fact, or in fiction written for anyone over thirteen. (p. 262)

Edith Milton, in a review of "The Young in One Another's Arms," in The Yale Review (© 1977 by Yale University; reprinted by permission of the editors), *Vol. LXVII, No. 2, Winter, 1978, pp. 261-63.*

ANTHONY BRENNAN

The structure of [*The Young in One Another's Arms*] is untidy because it tracks erratically in pursuit of the disorganized lives of a large number of characters. It takes [the] orphans and exiles scarred by the callous brutality of a technological society a long time to realize that they might reconstitute themselves into a commune-type family unit. The "pigs" in the approved fashion of the 60's neatly help them to define the kind of society they do *not* want to belong to. Rule tries to hold the first half of the book together in a number of ways. Ruth recounts several childhood memories that are meant to illuminate matters but only confuse them in jerky, obtrusive transitions. What is missing from the book and what might have worked effectively are details of Ruth's relationship with her daughter. Rule gives us lots of evidence about the mistakes and contingent accidents that have littered Ruth's life. We are given a good grasp on how easily and unintentionally people victimize each other, how carelessly they have a disastrous agency in the lives of those they drift into alliance with. But about the daughter whose death shook Ruth most profoundly we learn virtually nothing. (p. 131)

[There] is in Rule a Forsterian tendency to formulate Ruth's wisdom into gnomic, thematic, portentous insights set out in italics for our better edification. The problem, however, is that Ruth seems to have grasped everything there is to learn about her situation when we are only half way through her story. The plot becomes more prominently complex and a number of the characters are sent into delaying arabesques while Ruth learns, through further losses, her lesson all over again. In the third quarter of the twentieth century we cannot be expected to sit still for magisterial assertions such as "only connect the passion and the prose" or "see life steady and see it whole." Jane Rule is more modest in her assessment of what is possible: "It's so hard to know what's right. . . . You do what you can, don't you? And you try to believe that you do. I tried to be responsible.'' . . . Emerging from strife-torn lives there is a young child to give us hope of renewal, but the tranquility achieved has little of the beaming confidence Forster could pour on Helen Schlegel's child rollicking in the hay.

Despite the carping footnote above there is a great deal to admire in this novel. Ruth's husband Hal and a black youth, Boy Wonder, are splendid portrayals. Mavis, newly aware of an ambiguity in her sexual feelings, grows steadily and impressively throughout the novel. In many details Rule conveys the way the careless arrangements of a large scale society can bruise the fragile young already maimed and disillusioned by the routine corruptions of a decaying democracy. . . . [These] people learn the skills of surviving and of loving and caring for others with all the vulnerability that that entails. We have to learn to live with loss and with the fact that our best intentions may hurt others. The genuine strength of Jane Rule's novel is that she can transmit the necessary pain involved in coming to terms with these discoveries and convince us of the courage required in facing up to our responsibilities to each other. . . . (p. 132)

> Anthony Brennan, "Survival Charters—Single Ticket or Group Fare" (copyright by Anthony Brennan; reprinted by permission of the author), in The Fiddlehead, No. 117, Spring, 1978, pp. 129-32.*

CARRIE MACMILLAN

Like Yeats' "Sailing to Byzantium", Jane Rule's *The Young In One Another's Arms* is concerned with the problem of aging, but whereas the poem proclaimed the possibility of transcending life and all its mortal limitations through the creation of lasting works of art, the novel takes the position that the old have a useful though not necessarily conventional role to perform in a world that is threatened increasingly by modern social, technological and political ills. In this world it is not age that is the issue, although the aged can provide experience and direction for the young, but rather it is one's attitude to one's fellow man and one's concern about finding alternatives to the prevailing malaise that are important. Rule takes the position that old and young must live life with all its multiple and variable qualities as best as circumstances allow, adapting and coping, even finding new patterns when necessary; in other words, the individual must make an art of life. (p. 153)

In addition to the universal question of mortality, Rule deals with some very contemporary issues in the novel, particularly that of modern progress. Like several other Canadian novels, *The Young In One Another's Arms* portrays the ills of technological society creeping into this country from the south. These ills are represented by a network of highways that weave menacingly through Ruth's life, past (revealed through memory) and present. There is, of course, the highway that destroys the Vancouver home, but there are also the highways Hal works on that destroy the British Columbia forests and ultimately him, the highway on which Ruth's daughter is killed while hitchhiking, and the highway that destroys the redwood valley of Ruth's youth in the American West and takes her father in a bulldozer accident. Ruth sees the highway as a destructive river that uproots people and casts them aside, leaving a debris of dead and wounded along its shore. She ran from the highway as a young girl, finding a substitute family in Clara and Hal, and she does so in middle age, as she joins the young on Galiano where the red of the arbutus reminds her of the redwoods of

her youth. Galiano is linked to the mainland not by a highway but by a ferry. (p. 154)

If the novel poses the problem of surviving in the modern world, it is also about the possibility of such survival, for ultimately it celebrates the ability of individuals to turn the negative into the positive and to survive. As in earlier Rule fiction this is effected through human relationships, and very unconventional ones at that. Ruth is an old-timer at the art of survival (her face bears signs of age far greater than is commensurate with her fifty-odd years; the others see her as a rock, something solid and dependable), and it is she who keeps the group together on Galiano. She learned early that one must search, adapt and compromise in order to achieve the things that are sustaining in this life: warmth, friendship and love. (pp. 154-55)

There are several fine qualities to this novel, one of the finest being Rule's style which is mature and sure, often lyrical and beautiful. The development of the character of Ruth Wheeler, largely internal, as she moves from near defeat to affirmation, is convincing and strong. One of Rule's real strengths is in her handling of human relationships, particularly female ones, an area being explored by many contemporary women writers. The mother-daughter bonds formed between Ruth and Clara and Ruth and Claire, the problematical lesbian relationship of Gladys and Mavis, and the four-generational relationships of Clara, Ruth, Gladys and Ruthie (Gladys' baby) suggest new possibilities in the subject matter of the novel. However, its strengths are also its weaknesses in that the men in the novel are often less convincing as characters than the women; in fact, there is a tendency (though not entirely pervasive) to present men as destroyers and women as builders, a disturbing generalization. Another weakness of the novel is the facile philosophy underlying it. Ruth and her "family" see the world in easy, dichotomous we-they terms, "we" epitomizing an oasis of love precariously surviving in the "they" world of insensitivity and destruction. Presumably the reader is supposed to sympathize with "we", yet in the end Rule does not convince us of why we should. Is love enough? Is escape to an island and communal living a satisfying solution to the social problems raised in the novel? Do not the members of the commune, when all is said and done, look as smug and self-congratulatory as Hal riding his grader? There is also the irony, never acknowledged by the commune, that it is supported by the very system it rejects. . . . However, the novel is worthy of attention for the qualities already mentioned, for its honest attempt to deal with issues and questions that are very much part of our time, and for its place in the development of an important contemporary writer, Jane Rule. (p. 155)

> Carrie Macmillan, "Sailing to Galiano," in Journal of Canadian Fiction (reprinted by permission from Journal of Canadian Fiction, 2050 Mackay St., Montreal, Quebec H3G 2J1, Canada), No. 24, 1979, pp. 153-55.

PUBLISHERS WEEKLY

["**Contract with the World**"] is a very fine novel, the third by the author of "**The Desert of the Heart**." It is an ambitious work focusing on the lives of eight friends, all in their early 30s, living in Vancouver. Most are artists, many are gay and the novel is, at heart, about both love and art and the politics of both. . . . [The characters's] lives keep shifting, turning, yet at some point all the characters make their "contract with the world," their commitment to life, to their own lives. At times the book is reminiscent of a Marge Piercy novel. It is big and complex and often remarkably insightful.

> *A review of "Contract with the World," in* Publishers Weekly *(reprinted from the August 1, 1980 issue of* Publishers Weekly, *published by R. R. Bowker Company, a Xerox company; copyright © 1980 by Xerox Corporation), Vol. 218, No. 5, August 1, 1980, p. 45.*

BARBARA AMIEL

Contemporary life is the subject matter . . . of **Contract With the World,** Jane Rule's new novel and her best writing to date. These characters, unlike the rather strident figures in her earlier work, have some real blood and spirit—if somewhat unlikely lives. There is Carlotta, the intense portrait painter whose high-C sensitivity leads her to forget eating. Carlotta has an affair with the husband of Alma, the voluptuous earth mother (and would-be writer) who discovers her bisexuality in the arms of Roxanne, the androgynous sound artist who beds Carlotta who is the friend of Pierre who commits suicide after his lover Allen gets caught in a raid involving underage boys. What Rule could have done with some humor in these situations is delicious to contemplate. But humor is a quality missing from her book. . . . All these people are in relentless torment. They are Artists facing some sort of existential crisis often tied up in their sexual identity.

Which makes one long for a contemporary Cervantes. *Don Quixote,* after all, was the story of a knight who went batty after overloading on the pop literature of his time, which was all about knights going off to rescue maidens from dragons. Cervantes' book was a takeoff, in part, on that cliché, with a mad Don Quixote out battling windmills. A current version would surely give us a brave artist battling the Canada Council for a grant to straighten out her sexual identity. By now these clichés of contemporary life that form the basis of Rule's novel— artists, homosexuals and women battling the world—need to be presented with the extraordinary freshness of Mavis Gallant and some new insight to make readers, who for the most part don't share such experiences, feel anything about them. It's not that Rule's embattled artists and sexually ambidextrous characters don't exist, but they are so much on the fringe of contemporary experience that one can't help wondering why they have become such a focal preoccupation of current literature. (pp. 56, 58)

> *Barbara Amiel, "Relentless Torment of Urban Souls," in* Maclean's Magazine *(© 1980 by* Maclean's Magazine; *reprinted by permission), Vol. 93, No. 39, September 29, 1980, pp. 56, 58.**

CATHERINE ROSS

Contract with the World, Jane Rule's fifth novel, begins where the education novel usually leaves off, with its characters newly launched into their various careers and relationships. It is tempting to think of the six main characters in this novel, like the six characters in Virginia Woolf's *The Waves,* as complementary parts of a composite human figure. They are all the same age. They are all, in one way or another, artists. And they are all intimately bound up in each other's lives as doubles, opposites, rivals, and lovers, both heterosexual and homosexual. The events of the novel, which extend over ten years and bring the characters to the age of thirty-five, involve them all in death and some at least in birth and rebirth.

The narrative of these ten years unfolds in a straightforward chronological way. But each of the book's six parts, as their titles indicate, puts a different character at the centre of that portion of the events that it narrates. . . . (p. 121)

[Characters] are brought into the novel with skill, in a manner resembling additions in a cumulative rhyme such as "The Farmer in the Dell." (p. 122)

Within the first thirty pages Jane Rule succeeds in establishing [her] agitated eccentrics as characters that the reader cares about. Each one is given a signature characteristic—Joseph, a one-note laugh of desperation; Allen, a self-mocking ironic tone; Alma, a deference to money and convention, and so on. Between them these friends represent a range of ethnic backgrounds . . . , a range of political parties . . . , and a range of conversational specialties (Carlotta specializes in suicide, Mike in Art, Pierre in homosexuality, etc.). As the narrator puts it, "All Joseph's friends seemed to wear attitudes like name tags, means of identity rather than principle."

The characters form symmetrical relationships of attraction and repulsion: *like* sometimes attracting, sometimes repelling *like.* . . . The polarities represented by the characters include the "ample-bodied" and the "frail-bodied," the crude and refined, violent and gentle, selfish and self-sacrificing, dependent and independent, and ordinary and bizarre.

In each section there is a crisis, usually of an exotic and sensational kind, which provides the energy for the regrouping of characters that occurs in the next section. . . . A lot happens in this book and happens at a brisk pace, both in the external action and in the inner lives of the characters: new pairings occur, attitudes change, and characters make exhilarating and alarming recognitions. . . . A lot for one novel to contain, but all is held successfully in place within a very firm design.

Within this elaborately worked out pattern, the author explores different styles of accommodation to the world and different ways of loving. Readers familiar with Jane Rule's other work will anticipate correctly that one concern will be lesbianism, the private dimensions of which are represented in the relation between Alma and Roxanne. The public and political context of homosexuality in Canada is also suggested by references to actual events such as the police raid on *The Body Politic* as well as to the fictional incident of violence in Surrey. When in the final scene the Surrey community attacks Carlotta's show, the book takes on the tone of the "angry mourner" that Jane Rule describes herself as being in **Lesbian Images.** . . . (pp. 122-23)

> *Catherine Ross, "Angry Mourner" (reprinted by permission of the author), in* Canadian Literature, *No. 89, Summer, 1981, pp. 121-23.*

JANET AALFS

[Jane Rule's] **Outlander** is a collection of stories and essays about the lives of lesbians. . . .

Outlander reflects the courage it takes to speak out of imposed silences—and in doing so, makes room for the stories that have not yet been told.

The strength of *Outlander*'s diversity lies in its portrayal of lesbians of different ages, class backgrounds, physical abilities—perspectives that are often overlooked. Its weakness is the absence of Third World lesbians. (p. 81)

Jane Rule's stories and essays inspire me to challenge my own view of the world, my place in it, and my relationships to others. The settings and characters she describes and brings alive with her words are ones that I am familiar with in some way—whether it is a certain look in the eye, tilt of the head, or recognizable personality. Those which I have not experienced directly become a part of me through her vivid use of words. These stories are about lesbians living on the edge—"Outlanders"—outside of society's rules, and yet never totally disengaged from the ways we have been affected by society's values. Without being idyllic or tragic, Jane Rule sustains a drama that expresses the day-to-day struggles of real people's lives.

"Home Movie" reads like a film in that it is so intensely visual, sensual, tactile. . . . This story shows the process of a woman learning to accept herself, her music, her feelings for women, and in that process, coming into her own. . . .

"The Day I Don't Remember" involves the never-ending feeling of being pulled to make our lives more acceptable, especially to our families of origin—and the contortions we go through to cover over who we really are when our identity and security are threatened. (p. 83)

"The Puppet Show" involves a threesome and a child. Lesbians with children have a whole set of problems to deal with that those of us who are childless can often not even imagine. . . .

What I appreciated most is how Rule seemed to understand the viewpoint of the child as well as the intricacies of the three women's relationships. (pp. 83-4)

"Outlander," the title story, is about life on the edge in an actual physical sense. In a harsh natural environment, you must be willing to accept help from people you might not otherwise be drawn to. Two women "companions" move to a farm in New Hampshire. They grow together in the struggle to weather harsh winter conditions and the various influxes of family members who have never been particularly sensitive to Ann, the main character, and her needs or desires. Ann is an alcoholic who has spent time at a sanatorium and is familiar with life on the "edge." With the help of Fran, whose role is originally a sort of nurse, Ann begins to understand her anger and where it comes from. As Fran has taken care of her, so Ann learns that she must finally care for Fran. . . . (p. 84)

My expectations of an author who is obviously committed to discovering the truth of our lives are high. Combining the story and essay form in one volume is consistent with Rule's dedication to presenting the characters she chooses as whole beings; dispensing with the separations of imagination and reason that we learn in American mass media culture at an early age. Rule's stories give us detail and in doing so break the silence of invisibility and denial that we as lesbians experience in the world. The essays create a larger framework for understanding the environment in which we live and that which we continue to create for ourselves. In combination, the vision is one of integrity and strength. (p. 85)

One of the dangers in speaking the truth is that we can become entrenched in feeling miserable about all that is wrong with the world and our lives. Jane Rule does not. She maintains a sense of humor, an irony that allows for transformation. In the midst of confusion, her characters keep fighting for dear life, often with laughter. (p. 86)

Rule does not romanticize our lives. . . . Because she does examine so many of the assumptions we are taught to make about what life is supposed to be like, I am struck by the absence of viewpoints other than mostly that of white America, despite a woman-identified cast. Still, *Outlander* paves the way for further exploration and discovery. Reading it inspired me to question myself and my perceptions. Rule's stories and essays give me a vision of hope for the future and growing older. . . . (p. 87)

Janet Aalfs, "Difficult but Not Impossible" (copyright © Fall 1982; reprinted by permission of the author), in Sinister Wisdom, *No. 21, Fall, 1982, pp. 81-7.*

Cynthia Propper Seton

1926-1982

American novelist and nonfiction writer.

Seton, who describes herself as a committed feminist, writes stylish, "serious" comedies about mature men and women and how the cultural changes that have occurred in America since the 1960s have affected their lives. Her female protagonists, often well-educated and formidably capable women who have spent most of their lives raising children, are portrayed as struggling to reconcile their pasts with what might have been and what is to come. Seton's male characters, usually stable professionals with traditional values, are also faced with the need to reexamine their lives and adjust their expectations. Typically, the well-established and familiar worlds of these men and women are disrupted by some dilemma, the resolution of which will have a significant impact on their lives.

Seton has won critical favor for her lively and finely crafted prose, ironic wit, and compassionate analyses of the well-intentioned lives of ordinary people. She is praised for her even-handed characterizations of men in works that clearly express an allegiance to women and a commitment to their liberation from traditional social alignments.

(See also *Contemporary Authors,* Vols. 5-8, rev. ed., Vol. 108 [obituary] and *Contemporary Authors New Revision Series,* Vol. 7.)

Courtesy of Paul Seton

PUBLISHERS WEEKLY

[The protagonist of *The Sea Change of Angela Lewes*] is fortyish, married to a professor at Smith, a mother, and a secret writer. Having had enough of her role of playing mother to her children and yielding wife to a boyish academic, Angela reassesses things. Part of her sea change comes from within, part from her not so sudden insights into her own family, the Porters, particularly the lives of her own mother and grandmother. . . . So Angela's own departure from her contented housewife's role has its roots in the past, her sea change becomes something of a family inheritance. What Mrs. Seton seems to be saying is that though men manage careers and families simultaneously, women can only cope with one at a time. The implications are curiously interesting, especially in an age of women's lib. Mrs. Seton's tale is intelligent, engaging, one that raises but doesn't solve some nagging questions.

A review of "The Sea Change of Angela Lewes," in Publishers Weekly *(reprinted from the June 21, 1971 issue of* Publishers Weekly, *published by R. R. Bowker Company, a Xerox company; copyright © 1971 by Xerox Corporation), Vol. 199, No. 25, June 21, 1971, p. 64.*

SUSAN E. BURKE

[In **"The Sea Change of Angela Lewes"**] Angela Porter Lewes' sea change is a personal, not a political, one. She is not, as the jacket copy implies (" . . . this novel is concerned with the question of equality between men and women") involved

in Womens' Lib heroics, though, unfortunately, toward the end of the book, the author feels an obligation to throw in a few very male chauvinistic statements for her heroine to do battle with; the triteness almost ruins the Angela she has been building.

Angela Lewes grew up in New England, oversized and plain, and married Charlie, a "boy-man," the handsome, always youthful type who finds an obedient and sheltered wife the most comfortable to live with. Angela easily complied with this need, because it coincided with her own. . . .

Eventually, simply through the secret act of writing (she's not an immediate success), she realizes that she has developed a self not dependent on her husband or her four children or her beloved father for its sustenance. She begins to feel her uniqueness and, instead of being self-deprecating, she becomes self-confident. Even her latent sexual powers are sparked by one of her husband's friends, whom she has loved for a long time, and by her agent, both gentle men who love her. Her sea change begins to finalize, to become Shakespearean, "into something rich and strange."

But Angela is not unique in her family: the other Porter women are no slouches at making themselves mistresses of their fates. Her grandmother, after dutifully raising her children and burying her husband, bolts to Europe at age fifty-nine, her native Czechoslovakia her destination, leaving only a don't-worry note for her children who never see her again. Her mother, shortly after Angela's wedding, has a nervous breakdown, goes to a psychiatrist, and turns her hobby of helping out at the ACLU into a law degree. Her friend and aunt, Jo, the maverick of the Porters, manages a deep love affair for twenty years with her sister Caroline's husband Bill, the most loved man in the book. Caroline herself, the least likable character, is a victim of her own rigidity and love of martyrdom, a walking cliche, but incredibly self-willed. It is her proclivity for child-bearing that Angela strove to imitate in her early years.

The Porter family with all its in-laws and outlaws does an uncommon amount of adapting, finding small exits from their conventional lives into satisfying existences. Perhaps for this reason the book evokes a sense of security and calm. Even the villains are harmless—Caroline is basically ignored, and Charlie is continually excused: "It wasn't his fault." Probably not. It's difficult to tell, though, because Charlie's personality is so negative that he seems more an intrusive presence than the pivotal character in Angela's life.

Mrs. Seton seems to have carried her characters around with her for years, now to set them down in outline form, as if they were solutions to geometry problems. She hesitates to let us do any figuring for ourselves, and even ends up explaining her own symbols. Perhaps she is too possessive of her people, and doesn't want to tempt our misinterpretation. Her affinity with Angela, for example, is striking: both went to Smith College, live in New England, are in their 40s, with handsome, not beautiful, features and very short hair (Angela cut hers while waiting for her lover in a hotel room), have four or five children, sold stories to the *Atlantic*, write about heroines and have similar maiden names (Propper and Porter). You wonder, and you mind, because it's hard to know what she means by doing that.

But this is Mrs. Seton's first novel. Maybe the next one (and hopefully there will be a second) will give us an answer.

Susan E. Burke, in a review of "The Sea Change of Angela Lewes," in Best Sellers *(copyright 1971, by the University of Scranton), Vol. 31, No. 11, September 1, 1971, p. 254.*

LUCY ROSENTHAL

[*The Half-Sisters*] does not have snappy one-liners but it does have an unflinching wit and seriousness and a sustained and subtle intelligence. And it has an idea—half-sisterhood—which may indeed be emblematic of the present state of relations among many women, whether blood sisters or not. Seton's prose takes some getting used to—she writes in what seems at first an almost fussy backhand slant—but it proves, after all, to serve her special and penetrating angle of vision on these two significantly intertwined lives. (p. 42)

Lucy Rosenthal, "Half-Sisterhood," in Ms. (© 1974 Ms. Magazine Corp.), Vol. II, No. 11, May, 1974, pp. 40-2.*

MARGARET ATWOOD

["**The Half-Sisters**"] is a snazzy, delightful novel, jaunty as a roadster and with something of its period flavor. It starts off in 1937 when its two 11-year-old heroines, energetic girls both, are spending August together as usual. They are related by marriage but not by blood—Erica's father has married Billie's mother—and are complementary rather than identical, Erica being plain, good and sensible, Billie stunning, bad and impulsive. . . .

Listening to Cynthia Propper Seton recount their ups and downs, their betrayals, dishonesties, loyalties and illuminations, is like listening to a witty, well-traveled, sophisticated and slightly eccentric rich aunt gossiping and passing judgments upon her acquaintances, a fascinating passtime when the aunt has the flair, style and pithiness of the author. Also you learn things. She reminds me a little of Mary Poppins—no nonsense, please—and also of Lord Chesterfield, as she delivers verbal fillips to her characters' egos with 18th century elegance and precision, then injects them with helpful epigrams. The setting, too, has its elegances: it's the kind of world in which people have large flats in New York and spend the summer yachting at Moriches, and the author, polite or innocently snobbish, assumes we all know all about it. This plebian didn't, but it's great fun to watch, especially since the point, as in tennis (Billie's game), is not the activity or the content but the polish. Seton does not waste our time.

The overview that emerges is a comic one, although muted by a sense of the great futilities lying beyond its perimeters. Life is a series of choices you didn't intend to make, can't see beyond and end up being trapped by, and one of the most important things you can learn (especially if female) is how to accommodate, how to compromise with grace. The "role models" (Erica would find this phrase intolerably sloppy) tend toward strong-willed women whose lives nevertheless don't quite work out, and men who are weak of chin or insensitive as stuffed rhinoceroses, though there are a few admirable exceptions. Womens Lib is not something these women go in for, but the daughters do. They thereby become, apparently, pains in the neck (Seton is hard on political simplistics of any kind). But good Erica does have her liberating moment: having spent all her life "taking orders," doing what she thinks she ought to do, she finally does something she wants to do. It happens to be sleeping with her husband's brother, and since **"The Half-Sisters"** is a comedy of a kind, she is not punished for it.

The jacket cover indicates that this is Seton's second novel. Having been so amused and informed by it—I was sorry when this quirky aunt got up to go, still keeping some of her secrets to herself—I wish I had read the first one.

Margaret Atwood, in a review of "The Half-Sisters," in The New York Times Book Review *(© 1974 by The New York Times Company; reprinted by permission), May 5, 1974, p. 7.*

PETER S. PRESCOTT

In *A Fine Romance* two American families converge in an eight-day package tour of Sicily. Kitty Winters has had six children and time to think about the women's movement. She has decided to stay with her husband, Gerard, but she makes quarrelsome demands, little stabs at his psyche that leave the poor insensitive man confused. Gerard never noticed the crisis in their marriage; he loves his wife but he doesn't listen to her. Her sniping leaves him lonely and frustrated. . . . Alexia Reed, eighteen years younger, reminds him of his erotic fantasies, but Gerard, for the time at least, is monogamous; touring the ruins of an ancient civilization he is mindful that it is from repression that civilizations are made.

From such ingredients a dull writer would have made a soap opera. Fortunately, Cynthia Seton is very clever. She writes about intelligent people who have read good books, are capable of good arguments and aware that they do not always say quite what they mean. Her adults are all, one way or another, walking wounded—Alexia has come to Sicily with her family to help her sister recover from a nervous breakdown—and think of themselves, at one time or another, as victims. Good novels about workable marriages are almost extinct today, but Seton's is one: it is witty, observant and precise—and, oddly for a story by a feminist, it offers more sympathy to the good, dull husband than to the resigned, uncomfortable wife. (pp. 108-09)

> Peter S. Prescott, "Connubial Blitz," in Newsweek *(copyright 1976, by Newsweek, Inc.; all rights reserved; reprinted by permission), Vol. LXXXVII, No. 20, May 17, 1976, pp. 108-09.*

PETER LaSALLE

[A Fine Romance] is a novel of manners in which much of the insight sparkles in delightfully intelligent conversation. All the characters discover a little more about themselves by the story's end, especially Dr. Winters and his wife. For the first time, they are seriously questioning the viability of a marriage that strikes others as ideal.

Though jacket copy should be the last source of a reviewer's information, a biographical note on the inside flap caught my attention: "Ms. Seton thinks of herself as a committed feminist who has, in this novel, lent two-thirds of her sympathy to the man." The statement does approximate the author's own stance, for this is very much a novel about women's rights—with mixed results. On the one hand, it is refreshing to have a novelist of such craft and intelligence face the feminist issue, which has produced a current boom in sloppily written, noisy fiction. (One need only think of Erica Jong's Fear of Flying and the truckload of imitations.) On the other hand, Seton's believable, quietly moving story lapses only when she forgets just how well she writes real dialogue and resorts to having her characters deliver stilted speeches. And these usually come from the likable Mrs. Winters on the subject of her rights as a woman. I have no argument with what Kitty Winters says; I simply object to the substitution of "message" for dialogue.

Seton's Italian setting, complete with archaeological sites and Mt. Etna for a climactic scene, suggests a carefully thought out symbolic pattern to echo the psychological metamorphoses going on. She also provides superb portraits of the Winters children, wide-eyed and lovably goofy, and, in the novelist aunt, offers intriguing thoughts on fiction writing in general. On the whole, a deft, handsome piece of work.

> Peter LaSalle, in a review of "A Fine Romance," *in* America *(reprinted with permission of America Press, Inc.; © 1976; all rights reserved), Vol. 134, No. 25, June 25, 1976, p. 571.*

THE NEW YORKER

[A Fine Romance is a] stylishly playful novel, set in Sicily, which never really frees itself sufficiently from its theroretical underpinnings (feminism, the pros and cons of monogamy) to

be fully engaging but which is nonetheless full of charm and wit. . . . None of the characters except Gerard Winters jells very much, but they all chatter amusingly and make a lot of mischief in the same places Odysseus did. The mood of the book falls somewhere between a Noël Coward musical and a lecture by Germaine Greer, and though it all adds up to very little it is consistently lively.

> A review of "A Fine Romance," *in* The New Yorker *(© 1976 by The New Yorker Magazine, Inc.), Vol. LII, No. 19, June 28, 1976, p. 90.*

LORE DICKSTEIN

Cynthia Propper Seton is all confidence, finesse and refinement. She is an experienced writer and an old pro at turning a neat, elegant phrase. "A Fine Romance" is her third novel and sixth book, but it is a disappointment. Fine points of morality—it is all right to have an affair, but not to break up a marriage—are a familiar strain in Seton's novels. In both previous novels, "The Sea Change of Angela Lewes" . . . and "The Half-Sisters" . . .—Seton's best book—married women in their late forties find themselves dissatisfied with the lives they have made for themselves: solid, 20-year-plus marriages, well-reared children, responsible, professional husbands. They inevitably turn to a new mode of living, usually involving a lover, a fledgling career, and/or women's liberation. It is the mid-life crisis given a feminist tint. Seton speaks for a generation whose voice is rarely heard in recent women's fiction; she belies the popular and mistaken notion that feminism belongs only to the young, who usually have little to lose.

But in "A Fine Romance," Seton focuses on a man—53-year-old Gerard Winters, M.D., an intelligent but rather boring fellow undergoing a "climacteric of the mind, not of the body." Winters, his wife Kitty, and four of their six children (fecundity runs rampant through Seton's novels) are on tour in Sicily, a trip they have taken to "relieve the very plotlessness of their lives." But the backdrop of a beautiful ancient civilization does little to enliven these dull, uninteresting characters. Kitty Winters, we are told, is a "new, primary, autonomous" woman of 47, but aside from reading Fernand Braudel's "The Mediterranean" on the tour bus—a rather heavy tome for sightseeing—she makes little impression. The conversations she and Gerard have with the other tour members—none of them memorable—are stuffy, hyperintellectual and boring.

The one light moment in the novel comes when moralistic Gerard, after 25 years of unadulterated monogamy, seduces another woman. Juxtaposed against the ironic but schmaltzy lyrics of Jerome Kern's "A Fine Romance," the steadfast, exasperatingly dependable Gerard deludes himself into thinking he is "a hot tomato." A hot tomato? He is more like a cabbage.

While Seton does not satirize Gerard, she denies him the compassionate insight she lavishes on the female protagonists of her previous novels. It is as if the author, in the words of one of her characters, "had always expected more from men [and] was often disappointed." If Gerard has failed Seton, perhaps she should go back to what evokes her best writing: the life crises of women. (pp. 18, 22)

> Lore Dickstein, in a review of "A Fine Romance," *in* The New York Times Book Review *(© 1976 by The New York Times Company; reprinted by permission), July 18, 1976, pp. 18, 22.*

SUSANNAH CLAPP

"One has to have a love affair", protests an acerbic lady novelist in *A Fine Romance:* "They're the only credible climax left." Her view is contested in Cynthia Propper Seton's own novel: first, by the lady novelist's languidly sardonic niece . . . , and, at the end, by the events of the novel itself. There is, of course, a love affair in *A Fine Romance,* but its consummation, though satisfactorily climactic for the participants, is not the novel's last word. The "inherent plotlessness" which Virginia Hume sees as dogging the lives of "civilized people" is allowed to continue: it is one of the acutenesses of this observant novel that being unsettled is represented neither as a condition which is necessarily superior (in lack of complacency) to being settled, nor as one which leads automatically to the solution of large questions about people's lives.

The flirtatious irony of its title (Fred Astaire's was "a fine romance, with no kisses") is present throughout, and serves the novel well. More than one romance (and more than one kind of romantic attitude) is featured, and for some time it is uncertain that any of them will come to anything. In fact, the expectations excited by the novel's cast and setting are both deflected and fulfilled. . . .

A Fine Romance is more argumentative than most novels, both in the amount of articulate discursiveness it allows its characters and in the degree of detachment with which these discourses are treated. Inevitably, there are moments in which opinions are produced with a completeness which suggests that a dialogue between tracts is about to take place. More interesting attitudes are suggested when a lot hangs in the air but little is deduced. The novel is good at supplying the things which couples won't or don't say to each other (Gerard "thought Kitty flattered herself she was a realist mainly by disliking Wordsworth"); it is unusually toughminded in refusing to succumb to the idea that people's thoughts are necessarily more truthful or accurate than their speeches; it is generous in its humour, and in its suggestion that people's accommodations are not quite the same as compromise.

Susannah Clapp, "Unsettling Accounts," in The Times Literary Supplement (© Times Newspapers Ltd. (London) 1977; reproduced from The Times Literary Supplement by permission), No. 3928, June 24, 1977, p. 751.

HELEN YGLESIAS

During the violent spring of 1968, Celia Dupont [protagonist of **"A Glorious Third"**], having reached the 45th year of her life, finds herself at that celebrated point at which all educated middle-class women arrive sooner or later. She is questioning the direction, the value and the meaning of her achievement. Mother of five daughters, wife of Philip, the editor of a liberal political weekly, Celia wants to go forth from the bastion of her ancestral mansion in the Bronx, where she has held happy dominion over family life, to make the last third of her life "a glorious third." . . .

But how to go about it? In the midst of student strikes and seizures, the war in Vietnam, assassinations, sexual revolution and the dozens of other upheavals of the late 1960's and early 70's, Celia embarks on a personal quest for knowledge. Her goal is to restock the pool of knowledge ideally shared by all educated people: "If by some miracle this country is restored, is regenerated—well, then, there I'll be, a national resource!"

Celia is speaking to a male friend (her husband's friend as well, naturally) who is an intellectual (naturally). He responds by pointing out that when Proust retreated to his room to write his great work, he did so "to prove that his life had been worthy of being lived," a concept that so moves Celia and her companion that the spiritual, intellectual and physical yearning converge, and (naturally) they "came into each other's arms."

Naturally would seem to be the wrong word. We are not only in the cool, ironic atmosphere of a comedy of manners, but in the realm of an elegant practitioner of the genre—in a place where nature and blood passions don't stand a chance. Celia and intellectual Peter never make it into bed, or even into a shared room on an idyllic European tour. Nature is finessed by Cynthia Propper Seton's highly polished style, by the fine edge of her wit and by an excessive use of literary allusion. (She not only invokes Proust but also George Eliot, T. S. Eliot, Jane Austen, Galsworthy, Joyce, Herzen, Yeats, Ruskin and others.) For Celia, who fell in love with her husband because he quoted Browning in his love letters and because he dared to like Chopin and Tchaikovsky at a moment when they "were definitely out," the sexual revolution is experienced as an opportunity "to be roused by a man's *mind*." Not consummation, but the avoidance of cliché is what they devoutly seek. Celia doesn't like to "follow the crowd," especially if "everybody has a lover." . . .

There is more to the novel than marital infidelity—consummated or not. With light, deft strokes, Mrs. Seton describes the strains of raising five daughters; the stresses of opinion-making on Philip as he wrestles with the political and familial problems of endorsing Hubert H. Humphrey for the 1968 elections; the humor in a husband-wife confrontation in which nothing meshes. And she pokes fun at the on-the-make young women liberationists.

But on its most sober level, **"A Glorious Third"** probes something deeply felt about relationships, apparently summed up for the author in the beautiful quote from E. M. Forster with which the book closes. Forster, who knows about passion, can dare the simplicity of his emotions when he observes: "Personal relationships seem to me to be the most real things on the surface of the earth. . . . We are more complicated, also richer than we knew and affection grows more difficult than it used to be, and also more glorious."

Apart from the weakness of ending a work of fiction with a quotation from another novelist, the sentiment Forster expresses seems inappropriate to the whole tone of the story. Mrs. Seton's loving scorn of her "humane" intellectuals invites no Forsterian response, but rather, at best, a lofty and amused affection. Despite all the author's skill, some readers will finish the book intensely irritated by the world of its essentially light-hearted, self-satisfied, comfortable creatures.

Helen Yglesias, "Personal Relations," in The New York Times Book Review (© 1979 by The New York Times Company; reprinted by permission), February 18, 1979, p. 14.

ABIGAIL McCARTHY

Cynthia Propper Seton is the kind of writer readers like to discover for themselves because she is a rare find. She is unique in her witty and compassionate view of the human comedy underlying the recurrent waves of contemporary movements. She is unique, also, in the deft, compressed, almost aphoristic style and the wry, sharp, funny, but always sympathetic tone with which she reveals it to us. . . .

Celia—wife and mother (of five daughters!), a woman "designed to be good," is 45 as ["**A Glorious Third**"] opens. . . .

Celia's world is that of the upper-middle-class liberals and intellectuals whose moral fervor fueled and funded the civil rights and peace movements. They exhort department store owners to use black models, make new and interesting friends at McCarthy fundraising rallies and spend Sundays at peace vigils in the Bronx. She and her editor husband Philip seem ideally suited to each other but "were now enduring a tension of considerable stress for them over the most intimate issue of them all: the choice of a Democratic presidential candidate." Actually Philip is also feeling the stress of middle-aged sexual yearnings focused on Lily, a young, vivid, and self centered feminist writer. . . .

[There is an] underlying seriousness with which [Seton] perceives our dilemmas and self-deceptions. Her Celia becomes a witness to the plight of those women who, aware of the need for struggle, are nevertheless reluctant to abandon the deepening of being and experience to be found in the family and the succession of the generations. Her placid plan for her personal future becomes complicated by the modern possibility of sexual adventure in mid-life. Her personal response will, perhaps, surprise readers.

It must be noted that, as a novel—a novel must, after all, tell a story—this book bogs down a bit in the second part. Perhaps it is because the setting and the characters seem a bit stock. Provence and the Riviera have provided a background for many idylls, middle-aged or otherwise. And the aging, unconventional free spirit (Celia's mother, Agnes) and her friends, the faithful and somewhat bitchy homosexual duo, are familiar figures. Celia and Peter Jacobs seem to fade in their company.

The reader's interest will quicken again aptly enough in the final third of the book. The freshness of the author's insight and irony plays like summer lightning around the final confrontation between Lily and Celia talking about lesbianism and abortion, thus rescuing the dialogue from the prevailing cant. And for this reader, at least, the final chapter, in which the succession of the generations is resumed, affirms—at least for the moment—Philip's conclusion that those of us alive today "are an aristocracy, an aristocracy of survivors."

> Abigail McCarthy, "A Woman Designed to Be Good," in Book World—The Washington Post (© 1979, The Washington Post), February 25, 1979, p. M3.

JOCELYN RILEY

"**A Glorious Third**" seems to have all the makings of a good novel, but somehow, the ingredients do not combine into a perfect whole; something is missing. Cynthia Propper Seton is a witty, perceptive, and intelligent observer of the social scene. Her characters are captured with small but telling details; her sense of comic timing makes for superb satire. The social criticism of "**A Glorious Third**" is exactly on target—pointed yet subtle, intellectual yet down-to-earth, sympathetic yet honest. Nowhere does she resort to the sentimentality or polemical exaggeration that undermine so many contemporary novels of mid-life crisis among the well-meaning, liberal, good-natured middle classes. Her women are no more ridiculous than her

men; her men no more ogres than her women. This absence of stereotyping by gender is a refreshing change.

Seton, in fact, seems to go back to an earlier era of good-natured social satire in novels. The tone of "**A Glorious Third**" has all the superficial gloss, wit, and charm of a novel by Henry James or Jane Austen. Celia Webb Dupont is married to Philip Dupont, who is the editor of an "old liberal weekly" magazine called "The State of the Union." The Duponts have raised five daughters in a big old family mansion in the Bronx, and have reached middle age. . . .

Lily Tucker is a young feminist who has just met the Duponts. . . . And then there is Peter Jacobs, a history professor who is also a recent acquaintance of the Duponts. . . .

Given these four main characters, the plot is fairly obvious: Philip falls —briefly—in love with Lily; Celia falls—briefly—in love with Peter. The Duponts extricate themselves and get back together, somewhat stronger for the experience. The novel even ends with the traditional comic ending: a wedding (of their daughter). Much intelligent social observation goes into fleshing out this time-worn plot.

But as one finishes "**A Glorious Third**," there is a feeling of hunger, akin to the feeling one has after eating nothing but candy for supper. *Bons mots*, like bonbons, are dessert, not the main meal. "**A Glorious Third**" shimmers and delights, but it does not finally satisfy. For all her insight and skill with words, Seton has failed to make her characters live for the reader.

> Jocelyn Riley, "Middle Muddle" (reprinted by permission of the author), in The Christian Science Monitor, April 18, 1979, p. 19.

SUSANNAH CLAPP

[*A Glorious Third*] is a novel in which there is a lot of kindness but little room for sentiment; although the main issues are resolved, most predictable dramas are deflected; confronted with dilemmas—about their ages and the age—characters attempt debate before lapsing into turmoil. People do a lot of talking in Mrs Seton's novels and though their words are not always weighty they are always weighed, both by the speakers and by a watchful narrative. This makes for some pernickety prose, in which nothing is allowed to exist without its attendant wryness; it also makes for some good jokes and for a generously inclusive argument. In demonstrating that the "vistas of vulnerability" opened by the self-conscious 1960s are not the only available avenues of sensitivity the novel puts a lot of people on the spot; it also finally lets them off the hook.

> Susannah Clapp, in a review of "A Glorious Third," in The Times Literary Supplement (© Times Newspapers Ltd. (London) 1979; reproduced from The Times Literary Supplement by permission), No. 4002, November 30, 1979, p. 76.

WILLIAM H. PRITCHARD

Over the past six years, Cynthia Seton has produced three deftly-written novels about men and women—and children—in very much the contemporary world of ideas and assumptions about marital fidelity, feminism, "finding" oneself, and all those other important and sometimes boring issues. But in *A Fine Romance* . . . , in *A Glorious Third* . . . , and now in *A*

Private Life, she refuses ever to be boring about them, since everything is invariably touched by her wit and made thereby lively, alive. The two earlier novels focussed on a husband, then a wife, confronted among other things by sexual temptation and meeting it in separate ways, though interestingly enough each time in Europe. Although Mrs. Seton is perfectly at home in writing about America, her characters have the leisure and the desire to go to Europe where they play out their not-so-passionate scene. The new novel focuses on a daughter, M.E.F. ("Fanny") Foote, who gets sent by a glossy magazine to do a piece on her aunt, the "private life" of the book's title, who abruptly left an academic career some years back and settled in southern France with her female friend, Lutécie. The magazine's editors smell a lesbian possibility and pay Fanny's way over there so she can get the goods on Aunt Carrie, emancipated before her time. But Fanny has other ideas, and anyway things are not at all what they may have seemed to be. (pp. 168-69)

[Seton's narrator] is very much concerned with ideas and with trying to see things as they are. Yet both these activities are impossible for her (though not always for her characters) unless they are seen ironically. So the book's opening paragraph takes us to the top of the Pompidou museum in Paris "through the maze of brisk businesslike rooms whose walls were filled with high-colored, rage-filled Berlin paintings—Grosz, Kokoschka, Köllwitz, Beckmann—Germans indicting Germans, very gratifying." It's those last two words which do the trick, alerting us that not to pay attention to nuance, but read for "story" rather, is to miss the whole tone and distinctive pleasure of the book. A strong, funny narrator is very much in evidence as she describes Fanny's parent's top floor Beacon Hill apartment, with a kitchen window through which a bit of the Charles can be seen: "It was a grand sight, the only view in the house. Fortunately both parents had a consuming interest in food and were in a position to look out of this window a lot." The bland expressions "were in a position to," the homely "a lot," pretend not to know what a good joke they're making. And a serious reflection about how in marriage two people are no longer intimidated by the outside world, ends up like this: "The endurance of a union becomes almost entirely an internal matter and depends upon the fierce sort of *will* Gordon Liddy has—says he has." Gordon Liddy's turning up here is fine enough, but the sly "says he has" makes it even better. Even near the end of the book, when Fanny discovers that her aunt's love affair was heterosexual after all and she feels both relieved, yet distressed that it mattered enough to make her feel relieved, we are given this comment: "Vaguely she hoped she would have risen above her smaller self, and in the meantime there was no need to bother." In the midst of so much satisfactory writing, it mattered less that (for me at least) the dénouement in Europe is less than inevitable, even somewhat diffuse in its presentation. This may have to do with the fact that, like Howells, Mrs. Seton looks on her own stories without solemnity, and is therefore wary of bringing things together in rousing good ways. Subtlety is the mode, and surprise is usually the result. She should be read. (p. 169)

William H. Pritchard, "Novel Discomforts and Delights," in The Hudson Review *(copyright © 1982 by The Hudson Review, Inc.; reprinted by permission), Vol. XXXV, No. 1, Spring, 1982, pp. 159-76.**

LORALEE MacPIKE

In the opening two paragraphs of [*A Private Life*], Seton demolishes Paris to the emotional level of a midwestern village after a Fourth of July celebration. This is but the first of a tour-de-force series of remarkable stylistic feats that will leave the sensitive reader laughing and gasping and seeing the world anew. Seton is at once dry and lush, as spare as a Vogue model yet as precise as a neurosurgeon. Her pithiness extends from style to structure as she weaves a story that keeps veering maddeningly away from what all the characters assume to be The Point and ends up more satisfactorily than either the reader or the characters themselves could have dreamed. And all this is less than 200 pages! . . .

By itself, this story would be charming but slight. Couched in Seton's inimitably delightful style, it is a real treat. No soapboxes. No raised fists. Just likeable women unraveling their unexpected lives. Now I must go back and read Seton's other novels; she is, as one critic has said, truly "a rare find."

Loralee MacPike, in a review of "A Private Life," in West Coast Review of Books *(copyright 1982 by Rapport Publishing Co., Inc.), Vol. 8, No. 3, May, 1982, p. 28.*

ALICE ADAMS

At moments when even the works of one's favorite Victorian novelists seem simply too long and too complex for a pleasant reread, and when one also lacks the stamina for some heavy unread classic—I have begun to face the fact I will never read "Don Quixote"—at those times there is a certain sort of novel for which a certain sort of addicted novel reader will yearn. We want, then, a fairly light but highly intelligent amusement: an early Mary McCarthy novel, say; a Muriel Spark; anything by Barbara Pym—and it is interesting that mostly women come to mind, as fulfillers of this particular need. . . .

Admirers of Cynthia Propper Seton undoubtedly find just those qualities of lightness and intelligence in her work, and with justification; her touch is light, and she is a highly intelligent writer.

"A Private Life" is Seton's eighth book, fifth novel, the other three being collections of essays. "A Fine Romance" is perhaps the best known of the other novels, and it contains a favorite Seton situation: a longstanding "good" marriage between two loyal and intelligent, well-intentioned people is suddenly confronted with an upsetting (usually sexual) and novel situation; in this case everything occurs during a trip to Sicily, when the couple in question have as traveling companions a group that includes a crafty woman writer, two beautiful young women, and an attractive, wily older man—a little more than someone for everyone. But sex, in fact, plays an unusually these days negative role in Seton's books; it is almost never the force behind anyone's changing his or her life, and is, generally, not one of the stronger marriage bonds. Which is, as I say, an unusual view, and one that some readers may find unsettling—or, worse, just slightly unconvincing.

"A Fine Romance" is a lighter, brighter book than either "The Half Sisters" or "A Glorious Third," which respectively precede and succeed it, although all of her novels could be called very good reads. She makes us almost believe in her longstanding, tried-and-true marriages, and almost wish that we knew such people. . . .

["A Private Life"] provides considerable entertainment of a fairly elevated nature. It is very nearly, as one of its characters puts her own yearning, "elegant, intellectual, sensual, but with a high moral tone.'' And this novel, along with Seton's other books, certainly approaches the excellence of those books mentioned earlier, by McCarthy, Spark or Pym. And if the comparison is somewhat unfair it should also be considered flattering; I intentionally set a high standard.

The differences, however, are instructive, I believe. What makes Spark's ''Memento Mori,'' to take an obvious example, a better book than any of those of Seton that I have so far read is a question, in my view, of illumination. One's ideas of life among the very old rich, English are enlarged by ''Memento Mori''; Spark, in her eccentric way, instructs—and with none of her characters is there the smallest question of credibility.

One does not gain new views, or larger ones of human life from the novels of Cynthia Seton—but very likely that is an unfair demand, from such light, bright and intelligent novels. It is simply one's wish, both greedy and critical, that a very good book, or books, should be even better.

Alice Adams, ''Seton's Light, Bright Touch Raises Comic Novel to High Level'' (reprinted by permission of the author), in Bookworld, Chicago Tribune, *May 9, 1982, p. 5 [revised by the author for this publication].*

JOAN SILBER

Cynthia Propper Seton calls her writing ''serious comedy''— a somewhat unlovely term for the genre once labeled civilized entertainment, bubbly in style but crusty in moral tone. Fanny Foote, the heroine of [*A Private Life*], is 26, mildly depressed, and working at a lowly clerical job at an imaginary feminist magazine whose editor, in a fit of brainstorming extravagance, decides to send her to France to write an article about her aunt. (Anyone familiar with the budgets of feminist magazines may find this implausible, but it's better just to let it pass). Fanny's Aunt Carrie runs a pension in the Provençal countryside which is famous for catering to arty and scholarly types; her partner in this enterprise is her friend Lutécie, and the editor compares them to Stein and Toklas—''a really viable homosexual model there.'' Or maybe not; part of Fanny's mission is to find out whether the pair is gay (no one knows) and to dig up whatever other gossip is handy.

There does seem to be some mystery surrounding the redoubtable Aunt Carrie. Everyone in the family has a different explanation about why she ran off to Europe 15 years before at age 34, abandoning a Boston academic career. (p. 46)

Fanny dashes off to France, where she is reunited with her aunt—a woman of good humor but strong character, who still makes everyone dress for dinner—and gets to meet the aging but ever-charismatic Lutécie, former opera star and grand hostess, who is worried about Carrie's new desire to go home. (pp. 46-7)

Fanny scraps the idea of writing an article which would violate her stalwart aunt's private life, and spends her time exploring the local churches with Titus Sidney, a knowledgeable and balding young man so initially unappealing that it is obvious he and Fanny are destined to fall in love. Anyway, there's nothing to write an article about. Carrie's straight as an arrow. . . .

Fanny's trip to France is meant to be the final step in her own growing up, solidifying her character through intensive exposure to medieval architecture and high-minded eccentrics— an antidote to all that transitory, trendy stuff back in New York. On returning, she quits her job and agrees (after a few complications) to marry Titus. They are both going to teach at a private school with unorthodox rules (no jeans, no semiotics) and intend to marry without first going to bed.

I must say that if I had known this was where the novel was heading, I wouldn't have enjoyed the journey quite so much. *A Private Life*'s blithely acerbic tone, seems (till the end) to be naturally evenhanded, unsparing of everybody. All sorts of details tickle the writer's satirical fancy, some of them irrelevant to the plot but too toothsome to resist. . . . Seton writes an artful, stylish, funny prose, wry and insightful; her moral, fortunately, comes at the end, where it can be disregarded. (p. 47)

Joan Silber, in a review of ''A Private Life'' (reprinted by permission of The Village Voice *and the author; copyright © News Group Publications, Inc., 1982), in* The Village Voice, *Vol. XXVII, No. 21, May 25, 1982, pp. 46-7.*

Arkadii (Natanovich) Strugatskii
1925-

Boris (Natanovich) Strugatskii
1933-

(Also transliterated as Arkady Strugatsky) Russian science fiction writer, editor, and translator.

(Also transliterated as Boris Strugatsky) Russian science fiction writer.

Combining the literary talents of Arkadii, who has worked as an editor and translator of Japanese and English literature, and the scientific expertise of Boris, an astronomer, astrophysicist, and computer mathematician, the Strugatskii brothers have produced high quality science fiction, popular both in their homeland and abroad. They began writing in the post-Stalin era when Ivan Efremov's *Andromeda* reinvigorated science fiction in Russia and when constraints on writers were gradually eased. Unlike Efremov, who emphasized technology and adventure, the Strugatskiis explore social themes and ethics, speculate on social evolution, and depict the degrading effects of bureaucracy. Even though their future worlds reveal the expansion of Communism, their less than optimistic projections of social evolution and their satirization of bureaucracy have led to censorship of some of their works. These works have remained in circulation through *samizdat*, an underground system for spreading dissident works.

431

The early works of the Strugatskiis are set in a "future history" framework, a device used by several Western science fiction writers. These stories are characterized by the conflict between utopian ideals and historical obstacles. In *Trudno byt' bogom; Ponedel'nik nachinaetsia v subbotu* (1966; *Hard to Be a God*), for example, a protagonist is sent to a planet steeped in war in order to intervene and effect social change but finds himself powerless to do so. The more primitive alien society is unwilling, perhaps unable, to accept new values. Typical of the Strugatskiis's work, *Hard to Be a God* presents an intricate dilemma for which there is no easy resolution. Later works are more satirical, being especially critical of the presumption that humans can control the universe.

The Strugatskiis's refusal to neatly resolve complex problems, unlike most science fiction writers, has helped them win international acclaim. Their tendency to leave the reader pondering the implications of their stories, their poignant observations of human aspirations and failings, and the humor that infuses their work have made them a popular writing partnership in contemporary science fiction.

(See also *Contemporary Authors*, Vol. 106.)

MARC SLONIM

The brothers Arkady and Boris Strugatski, popular Soviet science-fiction writers, are often compared to Ray Bradbury. Their first novel, **"The Country of Purple Clouds,"** which depicted a flight to Venus, was very popular in Russia in 1959 and was followed by other highly successful visions of the future and its technological complexities.

Lately, however, the brothers . . . seem to have taken a new tack. **"The Hellenic Secret"** (1966) and **"The Martians' Second Invasion"** (1967) were sharply criticized in the Soviet press as negative in outlook and politically ambiguous. These accusations probably led the Strugatskis to take refuge in the Siberian magazines Angara and Baikal; but the editors of these two periodicals were recently demoted for having published heretical works by the brothers, **"The Troika Fairy Tale"** and **"The Snail on the Slope."** The latter provoked the Moscow censors to such wrath that the offending issue of the magazine in which it appeared is unobtainable in libraries or bookstores.

"The Snail on the Slope" is a caricature of Soviet bureaucracy represented by a fantastic "Office of Forest Affairs," with departments of Scientific Security, Mechanical Penetration and Extermination and their numerous subsections that serve to conceal inefficiency and hypocrisy under the disguise of haste and bustle, useless paper work and idiotic orders. When an outsider, the idealistic scholar Perec, arrives to study the hidden forest, he finds the area neglected and laid waste. Drawn into the absurd machinery of the Office of Forest Affairs, Perec goes through a series of astounding adventures and learns the truth about the nightmarish institution. Pravda called this merciless satire "a libel on and defamation of Soviet reality." Refusing to take **"The Snail on the Slope"** as a simple fantasy, it stressed the political implications of the story's most grotesque and whimsical scenes.

> Marc Slonim, "Soviet Satire," in The New York Times Book Review (© 1970 by The New York Times Company; reprinted by permission), September 13, 1970, p. 71.

T. A. SHIPPEY

In several ways [*Hard To Be a God*] falls straight into an identifiable American [science fiction] sub-genre: the feudal planet on which agents of the advanced civilisation of Earth have the job of leading the natives anonymously to progress. Just like Poul Anderson or Lloyd Biggle or a dozen others, the Strugatskis make straight for a set of connected themes—the difficulty of changing belief-systems, the way in which innovations are misunderstood, the obstinate habit slaves have of understanding their masters better than their liberators, the danger that revolutions can turn out to be cyclic rather than spiral. Is this derivation, or parallel evolution? The question hardly matters, for in spite of the similarities of narrative convention the Russian novel remains wholly different both in tone and ideology from its American analogues.

Probably the main non-English feature is the implied theory of history. The protagonist Anton (or Don Rumata) in fact opposes his superiors of the Institute of Experimental History in wanting to become involved, to intervene in the processes of class-warfare and the decline of feudalism; but even he believes in the inevitability of those processes and wants only to speed them up. His situation, then, is that of an Orwell, unable to reconcile what he knows about the front line with what he is told back at base, and right at the end, indeed, he expresses a philosophy close to that of *Animal Farm*. But however sympathetic he is on a human level, we never really know whether Anton is right in his compassion or wrong in his weakness. At the end his involvement in the fighting, however anti-fascist it may be, is seen as a disgrace to his profession; and the stain on his fingers in the pastoral 'frame' may be strawberries, but looks like blood.

The genuineness of his dilemma is the strength of *Hard To Be a God*. There is no neat, technological finish as in its American counterparts. Instead the change has to be gained by blood; but the blood must be shed by natives, not outsiders. So the end is in a way depressing and in a way majestic, just like *Dr Zhivago*.

As we expect from Russian novels, also, the sweep of characterisation is astonishingly wide. And as we might *not* expect, the feudal scenes have a certain Gogol coarseness about them which could hardly be matched by the most inventive of Westerners. 'Water won't wash away your sins,' the peasants mutter cheerfully, 'so why, noble don, should I wash myself?' The forests are full of slave-raiding monks, the cities of bourgeois Sturmoviks with butcher's cleavers, the roads are crowded with fleeing 'bookworms', and everyone from king to beggar joins in worship of the mysterious Holy Mickey. Again, the rationalism of the genre seems to go down before something older and deeper. And yet, one must say, something closer to modern experience. In the centre of the palace revolution one is forced to think of Ekaterinburg; and Anton's private symbol for resistance to the laws of history is the skeleton he finds (or pretends to find) of a German soldier chained to his machine gun. Echoes like these involve the Strugatskis with their science fiction in a way that is hard for us to match.

> T. A. Shippey, "Beyond Belief," in New Statesman (© 1974 The Statesman & Nation Publishing Co. Ltd.), Vol. 87, No. 2235, January 18, 1974, p. 81.*

DARKO SUVIN

[The Strugatskii brothers] have created without doubt the most significant Soviet Science Fiction (further SF) after 1958. (p. 454)

The first phase of the Strugatskiis is—except for a few early stories—a "future history" system formally similar to the science-fictional model of Jules Verne's cycles or of newer U.S. writers such as Heinlein and Asimov. It is a not quite systematic series of novels and stories with interlocking characters and locations progressing from the end of the twentieth to the twenty-second century, realistically conveying life on a predominantly communist (classless) earth and human relations in explorations on and between the planets of the Solar system and some nearer stars. [Ivan] Efremov's monolithic leaders and huge exploits were here supplanted by young explorers and scientists finding romance in their everyday pioneering tasks. Retaining the utopian sense of absolute ethical involvement and personal honor, even the Strugatskiis' early protagonists—at times moody or vain, tired or capricious—were much more lifelike than the usual cardboard or marble figures in most Soviet SF. Together with the vividly depicted and variegated surroundings, the sure touch for detail and the adventure-packed action leading to some ethical choice, this immediately brought the young authors to the forefront of Soviet SF. But from good juvenile-adventure SF they quickly passed to a richer form in which the adventure level serves as vehicle for socio-philosophical exploration and understanding.

This first Strugatskii cycle is still fairly idyllic. Except for the occasional egotistic and capitalist survivals, conflicts take place—as they formulated it—"between the good and the better," i.e., within absolute and generally accepted ethics. Thus, the only fundamental conflict left is the epic adventure of man faced with and conquering nature as a "collective Robinson." . . . Yet at the end of the cycle—in *The Apprentices* and some stories such as *Wanderers and Travellers, The Puzzle of the Hind Foot,* and *The Rendez-Vous*—an element of open-ended doubt and of darkness enters into these somewhat aseptically bright horizons. Some protagonists die or retire, and some "come home" from cosmic jaunts to Earth and its problems. Though the future is still envisaged as a golden arrested moment of "noon," historical time with its puzzles, pain, and potentialities of regress begins to seep in as shadows of postmeridial experience lengthen. This adventure model is interlarded with quotations from neo-romantic poets such as R. L. Stevenson and Bagritskii. In the second phase, an adult exploration of a more complex and painful world concentrates, as one of its novels has it, on the "predatory things of our age"—a title appropriately enough taken from Russia's major poetic exploration of relationships in such a world by Voznesenskii.

The dialectics of innocence and experience, of utopian ethics and historical obstacles on the way to their enthronement provides henceforth the main tension and pathos of the Strugatskiis' opus. In their second phase they went about finding the proper form for such dialectics. The black horizon of a history where slavery and high technology go together appears in *An Attempted Escape,* though only as an exception (a backward planet) within the utopian universe of the first phase. In this work the Strugatskiis are still defensive about their new tack. Even stylistically, it is halfway between the careful realism of the extrapolative-utopian cycle and a new parable form, so that it reads as a first sketch for *It's Hard to be a God.* The protagonist—an escapee from Nazi concentration camps—and the paradoxical society are even less motivated than Mark Twain's Yankee in Camelot. Nonetheless, this story introduces the first full-fledged conflict of utopian innocence and twentieth-century experience using the highly effective device of a protagonist caught in a blind alley of history.

The first two masterpieces of the Strugatskiis are the long story *Far Rainbow* and the novel *It's Hard to be a God.* In both of them extrapolation gives way to a clearly focussed analogic or parabolic model of mature SF. In both, utopian ethics are put to the test of anti-utopian darkness, of an inhuman and apparently irresistible wave of destruction. (pp. 456-57)

It's Hard to be a God amounts to a *Bildungsroman* where the reader is the hero, learning together with the protagonist the nature of painful conflict between utopian human values—always the fixed Polar Star for the Strugatskiis—and the terrible empirical pressures of mass egotism, slavery to petty passions, and conformism. Under such pressures the great majority of people turn to religious fanaticism, mass murder or apathy. . . . Outside interference cannot liberate a people without introducing a new benevolent dictatorship: the Earthling "gods" are both ethically obliged and historically powerless to act. The true enemy is within each man: Slavery and Reason, narrow-minded class psychology and the axiological reality of a classless future, are still fighting it out, in a variant of Dostoevskii's Grand Inquisitor confrontation. The Strugatskiis' mature opus retains the utopian abhorrence of "the terrible ghosts of the past" and belief in the necessity of a humanized future, but it is also intensely aware of the defeats humanity has suffered since the heyday of utopianism in the early 1920's. Thus, from this time on their work takes its place with the insights of best SF—of Wells, London, and others—into the dangers of social devolution: it is a warning without pat answers, a bearing of witness, and "an angry pamphlet against tyranny, violence, indifference, against the philistinism which gives rise to dictatorships" (Revich). Even further, it is a significant rendering of tragic utopian activism, akin in many ways to the ethico-historiosophical (*geschichtsphilosophisch*) visions of the best Hemingway and of poets like Brecht (the protagonist's dilemma in this novel is not too dissimilar from that in *The Measures Taken*), Okudzhava, or Voznesenskii. It is no wonder this novel has become the most popular SF work in the USSR.

Predatory Things of Our Age returns to the anticipatory universe of the first cycle, with which it shares the protagonist, a Soviet cosmonaut turned UN Secret Service agent. His task is to flush out an evil new influence in the Country of the Fools, a wealthy, demilitarized capitalist state in a world dominated by socialism; this turns out to be addictive stimulation of pleasure centers, born of social demoralization and feeding into it. The story is a half-hearted try at a more precise Earthly localization of the concern with historical blind alleys, but its focus is blurred. The Country of the Fools is midway between an updated USA of Hemingway, Raymond Chandler, or gangster movies, and a folktale-like Never-never Land. Though vigorous and swift-paced, it is neither sufficiently concrete for precise sociopolitical criticism—as some Soviet critics were quick to point out—nor sufficiently generalized for a parabolic sociophilosophical model of a mass welfare state. *It's Hard to be a God* remains thus, in its clear and historically vivid yet sufficiently estranged localization, in its fusion of medieval and twenty to twenty-first century, public and private concerns (evident even in the epigraphs from Abelard and Hemingway), the supreme model of the Strugatskii's work until 1965.

Since explicit criticism of situations nearer home than its "thousand years and thousand parsecs from Earth" would have (among other sociological consequences) meant abandoning the SF genre and their readers, the Strugatskiis opted for the second possible way—a folktale-like parable form with increasingly satirical overtones. As different from their work so far, marked by growing precision and width of reference of a single model, their third phase is characterized by a variety of probings, formal manoeuverings and reading publics—from the juvenile to the most sophisticated one.

A sign of formal mastery, joined perhaps to a certain socio-logical bewilderment, can be seen in the changing Strugatskii protagonist. By this phase he has turned into the privileged point of view. As a rule he is, like Voltaire's Candide, a naive glance at the increasingly estranged and disharmonious world, but burdened by the additional twentieth-century problem of how to make sense of the events in a mass society with mo-nopolized information channels. This makes for anxiety, as in *The Snail on the Slope,* or activist response, as in *The Inhabited Island,* or a fusion of both, as in *The Tale of the Triumvirate.* In *The Second Martian Invasion,* however, the protagonist, ignorant as Candide, is also happy in his conformist ignorance. This Martian invasion does not need to use Wellsian heat-rays and gases to poison a nation but local traitors, economic cor-ruption, and misinformation. As befits the one-dimensional age, the calamity is muted, and thus more convincing and horrible. The whole story is a *tour-de-force* of identifying petty-bourgeois language and horizons, the almost unnoticeable nu-ances which lead down the slope of quislingism. It is "a gro-tesque which does not reside in the style but in the point of view" (Britikov). Stylistically, it is on a par with *It's Hard to be a God* and the first part of *Snail on the Slope* as the Stru-gatskiis' most homogeneous achievement. (pp. 458-59)

Perhaps a central place in their late work is due to the "Privalov cycle"—so far the novels *Monday Begins on Saturday* (1965) and *The Tale of the Triumvirate* (published only in the bi-monthly *Angara* for 1968). In an updated folktale garb, they embody the underlying atmosphere of this phase—a total in-vasion of human relationships by a lack of linear logic and sense. . . . *Monday Begins on Saturday* deals primarily with the use and charlatanic abuse of science. . . . The loose pic-aresque form—the "ideational adventures" of the candid pro-tagonist—can be used for hitting out at anything that fits the authors' bill. Thus one section, in which Privalov tests out a machine for travelling through "ideal times," is a spoof of SF from the utopias and *The Time Machine,* through technological anticipations and Soviet cosmic SF (with considerable self-parody), to western SF behind an "Iron Wall" dividing the Universe of Humanistic Imagination from the Universe of Fear-ing the Future where violent warfare with robots, aliens, vi-ruses, etc., reigns supreme.

The Tale of the Triumvirate (or *Troika*) is blacker, concentrating on a bureaucratic triumvirate—originally a commission for checking the plumbing system—that has usurped power in a country of unexplained social and natural phenomena, which it proceeds to "rationalize" by misusing or explaining them away. (pp. 460-61)

[The Strugatskiis'] last two novels seem to mark a pause in the highpowered experimenting and permanent renewal since *Far Rainbow. The Inhabited Island* is a reduction of the mature Strugatskii model to a "new maps of hell" adventure novel. It is still very good at that level, with the usual candid utopian protagonist on a closed world where high technology, espe-cially in new persuasion media, serves a military dictatorship. The environment and atmosphere, the development of the brisk plot and the hero passing through various strata of a people bereft of history, all betray the masterly touch. The insights into both Oligarchy and Underground politics, for example,

and into the fanaticism of the rank and file, are as convincing as anything in their opus: this was a well-used pause. However, their next and to date last published book, *Hotel "To the Lost Climber"* is a frank entertainment—a detective story with an SF twist (it turns out that all the puzzles are due to alien robots with strange powers). One can only hope that the hotel's name does not represent the Strugatskiis' decision—in the wake of the unpublished *Ugly Swans*—that no aesthetic or sociological space is at present left for avant garde socio-philosophical SF in the USSR.

The Strugatskiis' retreat from an ever-developing exploratory SF would be a considerable loss, for the space staked out by them is at the heart of Soviet SF. Their work was a permanent polemic—in their first phase against narrow technological-ad-venture SF of the Soviet 1950's, in the second against Efre-movian monolithism, in the third against linear progressiv-ism—and thus acted as an icebreaker clearing aesthetic navigation for the whole Soviet flotilla. More importantly, their three phases have built up the most coherent model in Soviet SF. From static utopian brightness it moved, through a return to the complex dynamics of history, to a final model where the static norm is felt as immorally anti-utopian. Concomitantly, the protagonist grew from a boy in a golden collective, through the pioneering subject of a painful cognitive education, to a solitary hero as final repository of utopian ethics who decides to fight back at inhumanity. The time horizons also evolved from extrapolated future, through a clash of past and future in analogic worlds, to a strongly estranged arrested time (e.g., blending a folktale past with futuristic science) where the future values find refuge in ethics as opposed to backward politics.

There are deficiencies in the Strugatskiis' vision. The junction of ethics with either politics or philosophy has remained un-clear; the localization of events has oscillated somewhat er-ratically, the sociophilosophical criticism has sometimes fitted only loosely into the science-fictional framework. Such limi-tations cannot be glossed over as they might grow in impor-tance, but they may to a great extent be due to the authors' wish to keep in contact with the readers. Nonetheless, half a dozen of the Strugatskii works approach major literature. Their final phase is a legitimate continuation of the Gogol' vein and of the great Soviet tradition of Il'f-Petrov or Olesha, at the borders of SF and satire as in Maiakovskii's late plays, Lem, or Kafka's *In the Penal Colony.* Further, the predatory bestiary into which people without cognitive ethics are transmuted, the strange countries and monsters becoming increasingly horrible as the authors and readers discover that the *de nobis fabula narratur*—all such aspects certify to their final source in the greatest SF paradigm, *Gulliver's Travels.* The Strugatskiis' work has some of Swift's fascination with language—a mim-icry of bureaucratese and academese, of philistine and fanatic jargon, irony and parody, colloquialisms and neologisms. Thus, they are polemic at the deepest literary level of work craft-manship and vision, making untenable what they termed the "fiery banalities" of the genre. Together with their less happy critical utterances, this hardly endeared them to its run-of-the-mill practitioners.

Perhaps most pertinent within the Russian tradition is the fact that the best of the final Strugatskii phase reads like an updating of Shchedrin's fables (e.g., *The Bear Governor*) and his chron-icle of Glupovo City and its rulers. However, the hero and ideal reader is no longer Shchedrin's *muzhik:* he is the con-temporary scientific and cultural intellectual bridging the "two cultures" gap, the reader of Voznesenskii and Voltaire, Wiener and Wells. Many Strugatskii passages read as a hymn to such young scientists who are also citizen-activists, inner-directed by and toward utopia. In **Monday Begins on Saturday,** for example, they are defined as having ''a different relationship with the world than normal people'' and believing that the sense of life resides in ''constant cognition of the unknown.'' The central source of the Strugatskiis' pathos is an ethics of cognition, sprung from a confluence of utopianism and modern philosophy of science. Such a horizon, of course, transcends Russian borders: it marks the Strugatskiis' rightful place in world SF. (pp. 461-63)

> *Darko Suvin, ''The Literary Opus of the Strugatskii Brothers,'' in* Canadian-American Slavic Studies/ Revue Canadienne-Américaine D'Etudes Slaves *(© copyright 1974 Charles Schlacks, Jr. and Arizona State University), Vol. 8, No. 3, Fall, 1974, pp. 454-63.*

URSULA K. Le GUIN

Roadside Picnic is a ''first contact'' story with a difference. Aliens have visited the earth and gone away again, leaving behind them several landing areas (now called The Zones) littered with their refuse. The picnickers have gone; the pack-rats, wary but curious, approach the crumpled bits of cellophane, the glittering fliptops from beercans, and try to carry them home to their holes . . .

Some of the mystifying and dangerous debris proves useful—eternal batteries which power automobiles—but the scientists never know if they are using the devices for their proper purpose, or employing (as it were) Geiger counters as hand-axes and electronic components as nose-rings. They cannot figure out the principles of the artifacts, the science behind them. An international Foundation sponsors research. A black market flourishes; ''stalkers'' enter the forbidden Zones and, at risk of various kinds of terrible and painful death, steal bits of Visitors' litter, bring the stuff out, and sell it, sometimes to the Foundation.

The implied picture of humanity is not flattering. In the traditional first contact story, communication is achieved by courageous and dedicated spacemen, and an exchange of knowledge, or a military triumph, or a big-business deal ensues. Here the aliens were utterly indifferent to us if they noticed our existence at all; there has been no communication, there can be no understanding; we are scarcely even savages or pack-rats—we are just garbage. And garbage pollutes, ferments. Corruption and crime attend the exploration of the Zones; disasters seem to pursue fugitives from them. A superintendent of the Institute thinks, ''My God, we won't be able to do a thing! We don't have the power to contain this blight. Not because we don't work well. . . . It's just that that's the way the world is. And that's the way man is in this world. If there had never been the Visitation, there would have been something else. Pigs always find mud.''

The book built on this dark foundation, is lively, racy, and likeable. It is set in North America—Canada, I assumed, I am not sure on what evidence—which may have some relevance to the economics of exploitation shown at work, but very little otherwise; the people are just ordinary people. But vivid, alive. The slimiest old stalker-profiteer has a revolting and endearing vitality. Human relations ring true. And there is courage and selflessness (though not symbolised by power, wealth, or a Star Fleet uniform) in the protagonist, Red, a stalker, a rough

and ordinary man. Humanity is not flattered, but it isn't cheapened. Most of the characters are tough people leading degrading or discouraging lives, but they are presented without sentimentality and without cynicism; the authors' touch is tender, aware of vulnerability.

Judging from **Hard to Be a God, The Final Circle of Paradise,** and this book, the Strugatsky brothers are immensely versatile writers; the traits common to all three books are rather subtle: a quality of good humor; of compassion; of emotional honesty. The ''premise'' of this one, the picnic-litter idea, could have lent itself to easy sarcasm, or to wishful thinking, or to sensationalism. There is irony, yearning, and adventure in the book, but it does not stick in any one vein; it is a novel. Complex in event, imaginative in detail, ethically and intellectually sophisticated, it is, in the last analysis, the story of a particular person, an individual destiny. Red is not an interchangeable part, as the protagonists of idea-stories are. It's his book. His salvation is at stake. The landscape has changed greatly, but see, there, that's Mt. Dostoyevsky, and there's the Tolstoy Range. . . .

The end, the very end, leaves me brooding. Is it a spiritual victory, or a raising of the irony to the next power? Perhaps both; for Red, epiphany and spiritual liberation; for humanity—what? ''HAPPINESS FOR EVERYBODY, FREE, AND NO ONE WILL GO AWAY UNSATISFIED''. . . . (pp. 157-58)

> *Ursula K. Le Guin, ''A New Book by the Strugatskys,'' in* Science-Fiction Studies *(copyright © 1977 by SFS Publications), Vol. 4, No. 12, July, 1977, pp. 157-59.*

ALGIS BUDRYS

The Strugatskys are among the most Westernized sources of Eastern European SF, and normally their work thus rings familiarly upon the ears of the American aficionado. But competitive pressure from Poland's Stanislaw Lem has apparently sent them back in search of their roots. The result in [the case of **Definitely Maybe**] is a story that combines the gloomy desperation of Yevgeny Zamyatin's seminal *We* with a Lem-like satirical strain expressed as slapstick humor.

The proposition is that the universe can sense attempted reversals of entropy—the grand thanatopsical running-down of all energy to the state of matter at Absolute Zero. The Strugatskys postulate that the universe wants it that way. Accordingly, whenever intelligent life begins making fundamental discoveries about how the universe works—discoveries which might have anti-entropic practical applications—the universe frustrates them. So far, so good, but by faking liquor orders at the grocery, sending nubile ''cousins'' to overwrought savants whose wives are on vacation, and causing mature trees to appear overnight in barren courtyards?

Zamyatin—a contemporary of H. G. Wells and, oddly enough, a spiritual father of Ayn Rand—finds his best Western reflection in George Orwell. What was passable in the early chaotic days of the 20th century in Russia, however, is not likely now. Nobody who lives there is going to publish a version of *1984* these days. Lem, a cantankerous and very self-aware personality, writes satires on human folly . . . carefully out of context. So it is perhaps inevitable that the Strugatskys' self-conscious universe is made frivolous rather than impressive, and that the principal satiric scenes feature drunken comic scientists declaiming at each other like dialecticians rather than like even broadly cartooned investigators of real things.

Definitely Maybe treats a grand theme slightly. Dedicated thought by the reader will, with patience, reveal the book that might have been written. The human struggle against total obliteration has inspired more than one work of genuine SF literature. The theme awaits proper satirical treatment because the human presumptuousness involved in any contention with infinity is, in truth, good for a gargantuan laugh, as readily as it is for a tear. Few, however, attempt that ambitious mode, preferring the clichéd up-and-at-'em treatment usually given it by conventional SFnists. A pity that circumstance—or something—frustrated the Strugatskys here.

Algis Budrys, *"Interstellar Chronicles,"* in Book World—The Washington Post *(© 1978, The Washington Post), September 3, 1978, p. E3.*

STANISLAW LEM

The Strugatskys and I both started with a tone of "happy futuristic optimism" and gradually arrived at a darker vision of things. . . . My pessimism (which, by the way, is far from absolute) originated with my despair in the lack of perfection to be found in human nature; the Strugatskys' on the other hand was a rather social type of despair. . . . [The Strugatskys] have tried very hard to turn their books into a kind of instrument of righteousness. I can even perceive a positive correlation between the very weakness of some of their titles and their stated intention of socially improving the "state of affairs" (*The Ugly Swans,* seen by them as an act of defiance and rehabilitation, attempts to present in a favourable manner the situation of the Jews in the Diaspora and is among their weakest novels). When the Strugatskys plan something, they do so within a narrower range than I am myself accustomed to, and appear to be more interested in emotional interactions than in providing a rational diagnosis; they function nearer to a pole of social criticism while I am more attracted to philosophical reflections. . . . Their books are generally more ethnocentric than mine, and this very ethnocentricity means that it must be difficult to understand them fully without having a personal knowledge of the social conditions in which their books were conceived (*Tale of the Troika* is, despite its farcical nature, far more realistic than a lot of readers might think, not having experienced certain local realities at first hand). It is precisely this aspect of the Strugatskys' output, which I would describe as using of sf for socio-political criticism, which must explain why they enjoy such a difficult reception outside Russia, as it too often implies a necessary knowledge of the things criticized therein. (pp. 48-9)

I am certainly not claiming that the above kind of criticism should not be practised in literature, but I don't think the Strugatskys' way is the right way to do it. If you are dealing in allegories and metaphors for a critical purpose, then it becomes necessary to achieve a comprehensive form of universality, just as in a scientific theory, capable of widespread application. (*Tale of the Troika* does not hit any specific targets of American life; on the other hand, *Memoirs Found in a Bathtub* does succeed in reaching targets in the American Establishment.) I would rather not take sides as to what is good and bad, but I feel that the Strugatskys have not managed to break out of the great socio-critical tradition of Russian literature, while I on the other hand have not allowed myself to surrender to the ethnocentricities of the traditions of Polish literature. . . . It

might appear something of a paradox that the Strugatskys, who put much more faith into the belief that literature could good-naturedly influence reality than I did, have experienced greater disappointment and have sunk into a deep form of misanthropy; a perfect example of this is their novel *Roadside Picnic.* Never in sf have I ever come across such an extreme example of contempt for humanity as in this book, where "visitors" treat humankind like parasites or noxious insects. I would also add that some of the Strugatskys' books (*Hard to be a God, Roadside Picnic*) are partly polemical answers to my own books (respectively *Eden* and *Solaris*). This could easily be documented by a direct comparison of the problems evoked in the novels. . . . I think this all simply describes the differences between the Strugatskys' attitudes and mine; however, I cannot state in a categorical manner that these differences explain why our books are received differently. (pp. 49-50)

Stanislaw Lem, *"The Profession of Science Fiction, XV: Answers to a Questionaire,"* translated by Maxim Jakubowski and Dolores Jakubowski, in Foundation *(copyright © 1979 by the Science Fiction Foundation), No. 15, January, 1979, pp. 41-50.*

GEORGE ZEBROWSKI

In the short time since its publication in English, *Roadside Picnic* has established itself as an important novel. . . . The hunting trips through this alien refuse area are fascinating. The effect of the unknown on the lives of the stalkers, scientists and townspeople is moving, often heartbreaking. What makes the story work are the human reactions and relationships, the sudden details that startle the reader but are part of the normal world of the story. The characters *accept* their world with all its changes, and so do we.

At one point a character speculates on the notion of reason as an explicit form of instinct, through which we approach and assimilate the unknown. It occurred to me as I was reading that the stalkers are much like science fiction writers, and that some bring back the genuine unknown, while others fake it, or bring back trivia. It's an adult, literate, mercilessly honest book—the kind of story that *Astounding* [Magazine] might have published if there had been no taboos on language and sex. The sense of human hurt is devastating.

Tale of the Troika, the companion novel in this bargain volume, is almost as good, but in a completely different vein. Not since Eric Frank Russell was at the height of his powers have I found so much laughter in a science fiction story. This one is extremely intricate, and probably impossible to get in one reading, unless you go very slowly. It's a combination of the Marx Brothers and screwy fairy tales and science fiction. There are many wonderful cameo appearances by strange creatures, aliens, bureaucrats, biological chimeras, etc. The settings are astonishingly implausible, yet treated with complete acceptance. I don't think I should try to describe this story. (p. 33)

Noon: 22nd Century is unlike any Strugatsky book I've seen to date. Its technique reminds me of Dos Passos, but on the scale of the solar system and beyond. One reads this book for the recurring characters, and for the gradual portrait of the future that emerges through the accretion of details, stories and settings. Many of the details are very winning, and I found quite a few of the short sequences very moving, the human beings quite appealing. The contrasts with our own times made me feel quaint. Inevitably, this kind of novel will not be to everyone's liking, but the authors have used the technique well, if not always successfully.

Definitely Maybe is an intriguing novel of confrontation with the unknown, along Lem-like lines. I think the book was grossly underrated by *F & SF*'s previous reviewer, [Algis Budrys, in the November, 1978 issue], as well as misunderstood. Since the book is now out in paper, and has been highly praised by countless others, I recommend that the . . . reader make up his or her own mind.

Prisoners of Power is a strong novel dealing with intervention in the affairs of a declining culture on another planet. We are reminded of *Hard to Be A God* by the same authors. Maxim's future world is unlike ours, but the planet he visits is more like our earth, giving us a double view—one from the past and one from the future.

The great virtues of *Prisoners of Power* lie in its treatment of the central problem: should a backward society be moved forward or left alone. We see this in the way that Maxim changes and hardens through his many adventures, and in the end we are also exhausted, changed. (p. 34)

> *George Zebrowski, in a review of "Roadside Picnic & Tale of the Troika," "Noon: 22nd Century," "Prisoners of Power," and "Definitely Maybe," in* The Magazine of Fantasy and Science Fiction *(© 1979 by Mercury Press, Inc.; reprinted from* The Magazine of Fantasy and Science Fiction*), Vol. 57, No. 1, July, 1979, pp. 33-5.*

C. R. PIKE

Since the late 1950s, [Arkady and Boris Strugatsky] have gradually fashioned a body of original and enlightened works of speculative literature. Remarkable in their perception of the conflicts between the individual and technology, between man and the universe which may or may not be his, the Strugatskys' stories and novels have achieved a unique status within Soviet literature and now deserve the attention of Western readers. . . .

[*Far Rainbow* is] satisfying as straightforward science fiction. Well-intentioned, but monomaniac scientists corrupt a tranquil planet with their "zero-T" experiments which finally release the lethal black Wave. The Strugatskys here quickly build a neat plot into a powerful Dostoevskyan climax of debate and choice, as to whether the children, the results of the scientists' experiments or the paintings and sculptures of the artists' colony are to fill the starship on its last departure from Rainbow.

The Second Invasion from Mars is an ironic, neo-Gogolian and anti-heroic revision of Wells. The weapons of the unseen aliens' now successful conquest are bribery and rumour. What they want is not "dead souls", but gastric juice, which they persuade the bovine masses to donate in exchange for money. The idea is amusing and the narrator a typically Russian busybody in the "skaz" tradition, but both the ideas and the humour are over-exposed in a story whose lines will be clear to most readers halfway through.

The Snail on the Slope, on the other hand, is a fantastic vision of extraordinary power, a difficult, demanding but rewarding work. Pepper is an outsider in the lunatic Directorate which is somehow responsible for the preservation *and* eradication of the Forest, Kandid a pilot now marooned in the forest with its strange, childlike inhabitants. Pepper's efforts to escape to the Forest immure him in the Directorate, while Kandid's attempted journey back to the Directorate results only in a new isolation.

The Strugatskys are not afraid to leave many questions unanswered. They write inscrutably of god-like "Maidens" reproduced by a lake, of zombie "deadlings", of lilac clouds which manufacture creatures in a Forest which is in a constant turmoil of vegetable or animal consumption and which seems to be the site of a war, or an enormous, but dislocated experiment, or both. Equally obscure, however, is the superficially rational work of the Directorate, with its unrevealed purposes, impenetrable Kafkaesque bureaucracy and meaningless directives. Both Pepper and Kandid are placed in situations of linguistic impasse: Pepper, as he attempts to understand the Directorate's opaque terminology, or the Director's simultaneously polyphonic speeches—Kandid, as he struggles to remember his native language against the stupefying jabber of the Forest people. Pepper ultimately succumbs to the discourse of the Directorate, whereas Kandid finally regains control of his thoughts and language, but they serve only to articulate to himself his alienation.

The Strugatskys warn of the dangerous complacency of our deficient understandings of the Other, as phenomena, people or societies. In the title epigraph and in the sub-text of the novel they compare man's journey, from unknowing to unknowing, to that of a snail mounting the slopes of Mount Fuji to its summit. Man and the snail are on a journey where the traveller's knowledge of the territory behind and around him is as precariously minimal and ambiguous as that of the ground beyond him. The journey is inevitable, its accomplishment will be the supreme triumph, one day the mountain will be revealed as a whole, "from above and from the side" as Kandid concludes, but until then there are no certainties. The sickeningly physical unreality of the Strugatskys' worlds, their apparently unresolvable mysteries and dangers, as well as the ready comparison of their parables to unquestionable revolution or dictatorship (although equally to the mindless passivity of democratic populations) obviously leave the Strugatskys open to attack within the Soviet Union. What is encouraging is that although they have been attacked, they have also been defended. They have stimulated an authentic debate on values and the approach of literature to individual and collective life, a debate in which the weight of both *Pravda* and *Izvestiia* has been felt. The English translators of the present works have obviously been faced with enormous problems, as a result of which there is sometimes a disparity in the English texts between fluent, graphic narrative and stumbling, literal dialogue, but this should not and does not mask the impressive edifice which the Strugatskys have created.

> *C. R. Pike, "Kandid Thoughts," in* The Times Literary Supplement *(© Times Newspapers Ltd. (London) 1980; reproduced from* The Times Literary Supplement *by permission), No. 4049, November 7, 1980, p. 1264.**

GERALD JONAS

[The stories of the Strugatsky brothers] present a curious blend of action and introspection. Their protagonists are often caught up in adventures not unlike those of pulp-fiction heroes, but the story line typically veers off in unpredictable directions, and the intellectual puzzles that animate the plots are rarely resolved. Their writing has an untidiness that is finally provocative; they open windows in the mind and then fail to close them all, so that, putting down one of their books, you feel a cold breeze still lifting the hairs on the back of your neck.

This sense of proximity to deeper mysteries is oddly underscored by reading the Strugatskys' fiction in translation. Unlike Stanislaw Lem, the Polish writer who works so brilliantly in the science-fiction mode, there is nothing "international" about the Strugatskys' sensibility. Precisely because they seem so rooted in their home culture—with references to dachas and central committees, and the assumption that the future of the human race will be determined by the vaguely benign forces of historical materialism—their accounts of encounters with alien life-forms take on added power for Western readers.

"Escape Attempt" consists of three short novels. In the title story two tourists from Earth who have nothing on their minds but a hunting holiday on a park-preserve planet are diverted to another planet where brutality among men is the order of the day. Barely human slaves and masters are locked in a clearly futile effort to understand and exploit a nonhuman technology whose artifacts are strewn across the landscape. The Earthmen's efforts to ameliorate the lot of the slaves only makes things worse. The moral of this oblique parable would seem to be that history is not as malleable as atomic forces and there is more to self-knowledge than a mastery of the genetic code.

In **"The Kid From Hell"** a subtler, better planned intervention in the affairs of a distant planet succeeds; a murderous war between two blood-thirsty societies is brought to an end. But the long-range impact of this intervention is called into question by the total lack of rapport between the leading intervener and a product of one of the warring societies who has been trained to do nothing but kill. In **"Space Mowgli"** an exploring party from Earth discovers on another planet that a human baby, the sole survivor of a wrecked space ship, has been raised to manhood by an indigenous life-form. But even this intermediary is unable to bridge the gulf between the human and the "other."

The creation of a truly convincing alien intelligence would seem by definition to be beyond the powers of the human mind. The Strugatskys wisely rely on indirection; they adumbrate the alien through a cumulative negation of human qualities. It may not be possible to transcend our personal and historical limitations in our search for meaning in the universe, but if we would try, we must begin by acknowledging the constraints—and that, in the end, is what the Strugatskys are saying. (pp. 13, 18)

> *Gerald Jonas, "Other Worlds than Earth," in* The New York Times Book Review *(© 1982 by The New York Times Company; reprinted by permission), December 19, 1982, pp. 13, 18.**

C(ecil) P(hillip) Taylor

1929-1981

Scottish dramatist and scriptwriter.

Taylor, a prolific author, for many years worked with and contributed plays to several theater groups in Scotland, helping to strengthen the Scottish theater while developing his style and craft. His use of local color, Scottish-Jewish socialist protagonists, and loose structure made his early plays seem exotic when staged outside Scotland. But by isolating and examining particulars of an individual or small group of people, Taylor hoped to reveal universal traits in humankind, a philosophy of drama that won modest success.

Taylor's early plays typically featured characters who thought of themselves as liberal, enlightened, and good. Taylor drew humor and drama from them as they·tried to adjust to events in their lives that conflicted with their liberal ideals. For these realistic social dramas Taylor created a character type that recurs in his plays, one who displays self-deception, often comic, while trapped in a conflict between ideals and the limitations of life.

With his two recently produced plays, *Good* (1982) and *Bring Me Sunshine, Bring Me Smiles* (1982), Taylor won wider recognition. *Good,* which is viewed as his triumph, examines how a good, intelligent, young German named Halder, could gradually succumb and find rationale for the evils of Nazism. *Good* has drawn both sharp praise and disapproval from critics, who have debated the merit of Taylor's presentation of Halder's subtle, unprovoked descent.

(See also *Contemporary Authors,* Vols. 25-28, rev. ed., Vol. 105 [obituary].)

Courtesy of Elizabeth A. Taylor

THE TIMES, LONDON

[*Happy Days Are Here Again*] asks to be taken on two levels: as an exciting exploration of guilt and as a piece of Marxist allegory. On neither does it succeed. If the suspense of the former had been more conscientiously maintained, the allegorical interpretation might have emerged more convincingly.

In form, the play strongly resembles Hugh Leonard's *The Poker Session.* A young prostitute, accidentally pregnant, having been despatched for an abortion, her Jewish uncle holds a party for the men responsible for her downfall. Himself apart, a lecherous cleric, a glib biology student, a wealthy capitalist, and a balding poet are all guilty parties. But the begetter of the child and the convenient scapegoat is a bovine electrical engineer. Accepting his major share of the guilt without question, he allows himself to be hanged by the remaining quintet. Their sense of release following the deed turns sour when they realise the moral consequence of their action.

On the realistic plane, the play is manifestly implausible. No man readily accepts execution as a means of expiating his sins. Unacceptable realistically, the same character cannot then be seriously regarded as the proletarian victim of a ruthless cap-

italist society. Mr. Taylor has made the mistake of building his allegory on an unsure foundation.

> *"Marxist Allegory Built on Unsure Foundation,"* in The Times, *London (© Times Newspapers Limited 1965), September 22, 1965,* p. 14.

THE TIMES, LONDON

[*Fable*] is a Marxist object lesson on a Christian theme. A newly converted lion and a polemical jackal discuss the pros and cons of slaying an antelope. Since the Bible teaches that the sins of the fathers are visited upon the third and fourth generations, the hungry lion feels free to stalk his prey. He promptly gets a spear in the chest and learns that while his grandchildren may pay for *his* sins he is squaring accounts run up by his forefathers. The play takes the form of a twee demonstration, and the moral is too over-simplified for its intellectual content to be taken seriously. It is fiendishly over-played and over-pointed, which only accentuates its slimness.

> *"Three Novelties in New Studio Theatre,"* in The Times, *London (© Times Newspapers Limited 1965), October 1, 1965, p. 15 A.*

THE TIMES, LONDON

Cecil P. Taylor, who ranks almost as the house dramatist of the Traverse Theatre Company, has won admiration as the comic laureate of Glasgow-Jewish Marxism; a limited field, but his own. [With *Who's Pinkus, Where's Chelm?* he] has now deserted it in favour of straight Jewish folklore with a resultant loss of wit, technique, and sense.

Chelm, in Jewish legend, is the town which God accidentally peopled entirely with fools—a smug community with no idea of how they compare with the world outside. Mr. Taylor's hero is one of its lowest citizens; an unemployed salesman who goes off to seek his fortune in the next town, but loses his way and finds himself back in Chelm. However, he has had a change of heart on the road and is, moreover, wearing a new suit; so the town that spurned him now puts all its business into his hands and makes him president of the synagogue.

The possibilities of this fable are ruined in the telling. Mr. Taylor gives it neither a fairy tale nor a socially realistic setting; all he provides is a standard stage Jewish framework (crafty Rabbi, garrulously possessive wife, &c.), which omits the all-important element of general idiocy: without this preparation, the turning point of the tale—where Pinkus and his home-town confront one another as if they had never met before—is impossible to swallow. And all that emerges from it is a restatement of Willie Loman's simple faith in *Death of a Salesman* that self-confidence and a good shoe-shine guarantee success.

Lacking wit, character, or invention, the writing does little more than register basic events. . . .

"Musical Hewn from Folk Tale," in The Times, London (© Times Newspapers Limited 1967), January 4, 1967, p. 6.

JOHN RUSSELL TAYLOR

[Though Cecil P. Taylor] has reversed the pattern of [John] Hopkins's and [Alan] Plater's careers by starting on the stage and taking up television, extensively though not exclusively, afterwards, in other respects he seems to belong very much in a group with them. Partly it is his journalistic background . . . , partly the genres in which he has worked—realistic social drama, musical documentary *à la* Plater. His most immediately distinctive contribution is his personal background, which is Glasgow-Jewish. But there is also his talent, which is variable, but at its best can produce drama which, in its own quiet way, stands comparison with the best the decade has had to offer.

He is at his best, I think, in *Bread and Butter* (1966), a slow-burning but finally very gripping piece. 'Gripping' sounds a curiously old-fashioned term of praise, but it is apt, for *Bread and Butter* gets full value from an element in general rather misprized by the newer dramatists (dedicated comedians apart): plot. There is, after all, something very comforting about a plot. However uninteresting we may find the characters and situations of a play initially, if we have perforce to spend a whole evening with them, it is practically inevitable that sooner or later we shall begin to feel at least a faint stirring of interest in how things will turn out, what will become of character A or B.

This is very much what happens in the course of *Bread and Butter*. Initially, the four characters who make up the cast seem uninteresting. The two men, Morris and Alec, are too broadly, simply what they are: Morris the perennial political enthusiast, haring off now after one political panacea, now after another, and Alec, the soft, silly listener to what other people say. Their women, Sharon and Miriam, are even more colourless and the background of working-class Jewish life in Glasgow between the wars, unfamiliar in the theatre, sounds much more attractively exotic than it is. Big events in the outside world come and go, but to Morris and Alec they impinge only as subjects for conversation, the groundwork on which Morris can embroider dizzying patterns of Marxist theory. The development is deceptively slow, the play almost static up to the half-way mark, which brings us to the end of the war, with Morris's fortunes on the down-grade and Alec's slightly on the up. The author's technique may seem limited and repetitive: in virtually every scene he uses to excess the old 'new drama' ploy of conversations continued at odds, with neither participant listening to the other—signifying, of course, failure to communicate or, as Pinter has it, fear of communication. Which is all very well in small doses, but continued obsessively in scene after scene can become extremely tiresome. However, by this time the plot has established its insidious hold: it has become quite interesting, in the most naïve, old-fashioned way, to know how things will all turn out for the two households.

And the second half not only answers this query, but does so far more tellingly than the question was posed in the first half. For by the end of the war, it transpires, Miriam, Alec's wife, who always did have her calculating side, has become warped about money to an extent which makes the mild, amiable Alec begin to question seriously whether, after twenty-odd years of married life, he really likes his wife at all—and decide that, all things considered, he doesn't. Not only do these two characters grow in stature and complexity, though, but so does Morris: his jealousy of Alec's quiet happiness, his dawning realization that one after another his all-purpose political solutions have let him down, his strange, contradictory relations with his wife, his family and his religion, all gradually fit together into a completely credible portrait of a rounded, inconsistent, coherent human being. Above all, the characters exist most intensely in relation to one another—particularly with Morris and Alec: the constancy of their relationship despite trials and vicissitudes, personal dramas within their respective households and changes in the world at large, is evoked with great delicacy and true, unsentimental feeling.

Nothing else Taylor has written is quite on this level of accomplishment, but none of his plays is altogether without distinction. *Allergy* (1966) is a one-acter about a Glasgow journalist torn between his Marxist principles and his hankering after private security—Morris and Alec rolled into one, as it were. His worries express themselves visibly in a disfiguring red rash which covers him when he arrives with a new girl-friend (for whom he has supposedly thrown over wife and job, though nothing is *definitely* decided yet) in a cottage in Ross occupied by a rather less complicated friend who grinds out a minority Marxist journal on his own hand-operated duplicating machine. The play is a very funny fantasia on the process of rationalization by which Christopher determines that he is actually allergic to adultery, and that really it is somehow more socialist to go back to his suburban life, away from germs and crude nature. The whole thing works beautifully in its own terms, and carries its meaning lightly, without demanding thoroughgoing 'interpretation'.

This is hardly true of *Happy Days are Here Again* (1965), which was interpreted by some as political allegory, by others as Theatre of the Absurd. Maybe it was neither, though fantasy it certainly was: the Jewish uncle of a prostitute now busy having an abortion gathers together five of her clients (a representatively various bunch including a poet, a capitalist, a cleric, a biology student and an electrical engineer) and leads them into a sort of inquest on the life of the absent tart. Symbolically (or absurdly, as the case may be) the engineer accepts the major share of the guilt, and lets the rest hang him; but then they have to deal with the moral consequences of their action. The effect was muddled and uncertain in tone; though originally written for the stage, the play worked much better in a shortened, rewritten form for radio. *Fable* (1965) is a one-act parable about a newly converted lion and a jackal discussing the morality of killing an antelope, which ends with the lion, doing what comes naturally to lions, being killed for his pains by a hunter, thereby paying for the sins of his ancestors as his descendants may pay for his. QED, but much too trite and obvious to work as drama.

An early play by Taylor, *Aa Went the Blaydon Races,* a lively costume piece about a Tyneside pitmen's strike of a century ago, fulfilled excellently its declared function of providing a piece of local pop theatre for the opening of the Flora Robson Theatre in Newcastle in 1962. A later venture into pop theatre, the musical *Who's Pinkus, Where's Chelm?* (1967) worked less well; a whimsical piece of Jewish folklore . . . , it takes place in a mythical village of fools from which Pinkus, the most foolish of them all, sets out to make his fortune in the next town, but loses his way and arrives back prepared for success with the single formula that it is not enough in life just to follow the dictates of your heart. All this plot (such as it is) is disposed of in the first act, and the second is occupied entirely with elaboration and repetition. The show sadly lacked wit, point, or even a good tune or two to give it an occasional lift. (pp. 186-90)

The television plays of his which achieved most notice . . . were *Thank U Very Much for the Family Circle* (1968), a realistic but scarcely riveting account of the family life of a shifty, opportunistic door-to-door salesman . . . , and his trilogy *Revolution* (1970), three half-hour plays linked by a common theme, in that each depicted a notable revolutionary—respectively Cromwell, Lenin and Castro—in a crucial period on the eve of his revolution. They were solid and respectable—Taylor has put together an interesting book, *Making a TV Play,* which details the whole history of the Cromwell episode—but lacked the clear individuality of Taylor's Glasgow-Jewish-Marxist pieces. It is not merely a matter of the exotic local colour, though no doubt that helps; it really does seem that Taylor's talent goes into overdrive when it draws on his fund of first-hand experience, but otherwise is all too liable to idle and hang back. (p. 190)

> *John Russell Taylor, "Three Social Realists: John Hopkins, Alan Plater, Cecil P. Taylor," in his* The Second Wave: British Drama for the Seventies *(reprinted by permission of Hill and Wang, a division of Farrar, Straus and Giroux, Inc.; in Canada by A D Peters & Co. Ltd; copyright © 1971 by John Russell Taylor), Hill and Wang, 1971, pp. 172-90.**

STEVE GRANT

Like Terence Rattigan's *Cause Célèbre,* C P Taylor's *Bandits* is based on a real murder case and attempts to reveal the moral background to the crime in a way which explains its cause and its effect. Taylor's chosen crime filled the front pages of the

northern editions in the mid-60's and inspired the Michael Caine movie, *Get Carter.* A petty but pushy crook is found dead on the beach outside Newcastle, one of 26 witnesses and participants in a case presided over by a super-cynical detective who cares more about the man cutting down trees outside his weekend caravan than the fate of just another 'bandit'.

Taylor's point of view is crystal clear: in the never-had-it-so-good era of the 60s we may have had the World Cup, Wilsonian government and the Beatles, but we also had Poulson, T Dan Smith and the Krays. While dreams were being spun, money was being made, in the dirty (and left-wing) book shops, the discos and in the clubs, of which the North East provided a bright glittering array filled with punters and pin-ball machines, easy fortunes and loose women. (p. 26)

The tale is indeed a bleak one: a pair of trigger-happy tearaways, a policeman with a doubting school teacher wife, a Tolstoy-spouting, philosophically cynical club tycoon, two sexually untuned lesbian school teachers, a few 'tarts', a recalcitrant fisherman peeved at finding the body, a babysitting schoolgirl high on sexual fear and fantasies, a Korean-serving Communist pitman and his part-time whore wife, one of whose 'clients' is the murdered villain. With a juke-box remorselessly bashing out oldy-goldies, the drug industry of 60s euphoria is exposed (though in a society where even the women are called 'man' drugs are unmentioned and unused): sex, power, money, politics—each one leaves the addict unsatisfied.

The strengths of Taylor's play lie not in the statement he makes about such a society, which is sadly familiar to most of us, but in the painstaking way in which he builds up his characterisations. Here is a writer genuinely concerned with coming to terms with the age of television drama and with audiences more used to it than to the experience of living theatre. Not only is the subject matter pertinently related to *Z Cars*, for instance, but the technique is distinctly televisual, cutting from one locale to another, to and fro in time, and from public *exchanges* to private monologue. Indeed, in using this method, Taylor also manages to contrast the interrogation of the detectives involved with the admissions and private deviations of the characters. . . . [Not] only does Taylor show the gap between lies and the truth, he also reveals that a good deal of sexual casualness is itself rooted in a deep sense of inner emptiness.

As well as two kinds of interrogation the piece climaxes with two 'trials': the 'real' one of evidence, and the confrontation between the crook and the man whose wife he is bedding. . . . [The character named Ray Purvis] is alone in his refusal to give up the search for some kind of moral imperative. His personal life is a mess, his war career has turned him to Communism and further sexual and political disenchantment. His conclusion is typically pessimistic, the world is like the dinosaur, extinction-bound, and though he has finally managed to terrify the victim . . . it is the club owners of this world who make the real profits. In that Purvis is finally duped. It is interesting that, on the night, both myself and many other critics seemed to be of the opinion that Purvis had killed the crook and that the arrested villain was *ironically* innocent. However, Taylor's stage directions (and this may be cheating) state simply: 'Three shots'. Indeed to make Purvis the real assassin distorts the meaning of the play, which deals strongly with the paralysis of the British socialist, faced as he is with no tradition of left-wing activism and no focus for *political* activity in his personal life. . . . If the critics have failed again then it must be argued that after a dense and often impenetrable

evening of facts, statements, cross-cuts and multiple characterisations, they can be forgiven for a lapse of this nature. (pp.
26-7)

Taylor's writing, though often quite brilliant in its attention to
detail, finally seems mannered when contrasted with exactly
the kind of drama it is trying so admirably to reflect—that of
television. What it does do, however, is show a seedy temple
in which sex and money are *the* twin pillars. (p. 27)

> *Steve Grant, in a review of "Bandits" (© copyright
> Steve Grant 1977; reprinted with permission), in* Plays
> and Players, *Vol. 25, No. 1, October, 1977, pp. 26-
> 7.*

GORDON GOW

The best thing about [the] sentimental comedy [*And a Nightingale Sang* . . .] by C P Taylor is the love affair it delineates
between Helen, a lame girl who has been almost reconciled to
the idea that love must pass her by, and Norman, a rather
simple but quietly emotional bloke who is sensitive to the fact
that Helen's nature has more beauty to it than one might glean
from the outward show. This somewhat fraught relationship is
sentimental, as I say, but it isn't sloppy. . . . [Even] when the
agony is piled on with the revelation that Norman has a wife
and child, the plucking of heartstrings is still carried out with
the most delicate finesse. . . .

Higher, however, than the eye of Hammerstein's elephant is
0the corn that grows elsewhere in the play. *And a Nightingale
Sang* . . . is a thick slice of life on the domestic front in
Newcastle-upon-Tyne during the years of the Second World
War. To my mind it would have been shrewder of Taylor to
throw the predicament of Helen and Norman into relief against
a mere background of other characters, but as things stand we
have five more figures cluttering the landscape quite prominently; and while I can see that they are intended to be lovable,
as the evening wore on I came very near to hating them.

The real trials of the piece are Helen's father, mother and
grandfather, all of them thoroughly credible and just as thoroughly dull. . . . The mother's role is most in need of pruning,
although her heavily established and ardent Roman Catholicism
pays off at length when it brings on a conflict of passing
amusement because father has joined the Communist Party.
Father has a saving grace as far as the play is concerned in
that every now and then he sits down at the piano and bashes
out, sometimes with a bit of singing thrown in, a smattering
of nostalgic tunes of the period which help, along with numerous carefully observed details such as the rarity of bananas
and the prevalence of spam sandwiches, to evoke the proper
feeling of period. But there is little to be said, if anything, in
grandfather's favour, and much to be regretted when he is
involved in some really awful jokes about the odours emanating
from a dead dog in a bag and a live cat in a basket.

The remaining two characters I thought a shade more tolerable,
Helen's younger sister Joyce . . . and her soldier husband Eric
. . . ; especially Joyce, a fairly selfish but utterly understandable minx of the era, . . . [who goes] into a panic when she
imagines herself pregnant (this is one of four false alarms in
the play—a serio-comic device that ought to be used more
sparingly) and fears that Eric, absent for the fighting, might
well suspect, and with cause, that he is not the father.

So it goes on, mercifully with enough mileage for Helen and
Norman who, by the end, have become completely endearing.

> *Gordon Gow, in a review of "And a Nightingale
> Sang . . ." (© copyright Gordon Gow 1979; re-
> printed with permission), in* Plays and Players, *Vol.
> 26, No. 11, August, 1979, p. 23.*

JOHN RUSSELL TAYLOR

[In *And a Nightingale Sang* . . .] at least C. P. Taylor is ser-
aphically free from any kind of message. Up to now he has
frequently seemed to be a talent in search of just the right
register: there has always been something likeable and warm
and ideosyncratically human about his plays, but also something a bit muddly and lacking in focus. *And a Nightingale
Sang* . . . has dispensed with the tentativeness: it strikes straight
into its central matter and scarcely puts a foot wrong after.
Mind you, it is not immediately apparent that it does so: at the
outset it seems to be just a loosely connected series of sketches
of life in Newcastle during the early days of the war and the
Blitz. It has a narrator, a plain, slightly crippled girl, . . . who
addresses us from stage in easily confiding tones, slipping
smoothly in and out of the action—a bit like *Forget-Me-Not-
Lane,* but less intricately organised. (p. 70)

[Before] we know it we are laughing. . . . But gradually things
emerge. The father plays his piano and sings his silly songs
and does a bit of light air-raid wardening; the mother babbles
about her only half understood religion; the younger daughter
vacillates for ever about whether she should marry her suitor
before he goes off to the war (what if he doesn't come back?
what, worse, if he does?); the grandfather shuffles from daughter to daughter and lodging to lodging, but always comes back
with his horrible cat in a basket. There are running jokes, and
tiny little notations of life which insensibly prepare us for a
realisation that these are not just comic stereotypes, they are
people who grow and change with time, more likeable and
more dislikeable and anyway more complex than we ever imagined. And in the midst of it all the crippled sister gradually
emerges as the central character. We follow the progress of
her unlikely affair with a visiting soldier, and guess at its
inevitable denouement. But nothing is forced, nothing is built
up to a degree of drama that the fragile structure cannot stand.
They live, and they survive. Everyone survives somehow. The
world does not end with a bang or a whimper; it just keeps on
keeping on. (pp. 70-1)

> *John Russell Taylor, in a review of "And a Night-
> ingale Sang . . . ," in* Drama *(reprinted by permis-
> sion of the British Theatre Association), No. 134,
> Autumn, 1979, pp. 70-1.*

ALLEN SADDLER

It is a long time, probably not within living memory, since the
farming community has had a reasonable representation in dramatic form. Dung slinging straw-in-the-hair folk groups have
become representative of country culture. In Taylor's play [*To
Be a Farmer's Boy*] the poetry of everyday speech comes to
life with vitality and force; dispelling forever (I hope) the
taciturn, crude and graceless yokel of popular legend. The main
character, a farmer eager for land, is cantankerous, crafty and
ruthless, even within his own family; but displays a love of
wild life, relishes the passing of the seasons, plays Bach on
the violin and reads avidly. These people are not saints or

sinners; not particularly bright or traditionally dim. Their black humour, apparent callousness and capacity for enjoying simple pleasures, their lust for land and pride in their isolation, arises naturally from their environment, and drew grunts of recognition from the audience.

Unfortunately, there are weaknesses in the play, which are entirely to do with the construction. Eleven short scenes, which dodge about in no particular chronological order, and a spare functional set, which, even for touring, lacks any warmth. Another fault is Taylor's method of using one character as a narrator, giving him all the best lines as asides. This fault is not so serious as in Taylor's *Not By Love Alone,* but still irritating. With the material at his disposal Taylor could have assembled a two-act play of three scenes each, following a logical time span, and it would have been a play of power and strength. I regret the chance thrown away. (p. 24)

> *Allen Saddler, in a review of "To Be a Farmer's Boy" (© copyright Allen Saddler 1980; reprinted with permission), in* Plays and Players, *Vol. 27, No. 6, March, 1980, pp. 24-5.*

BENEDICT NIGHTINGALE

What did the British theatre prematurely lose in Cecil Taylor last December?

Well, it may not be relevant to say so in a critical column; but it lost a very nice, very good man. . . .

He began his career in 1962 with *Aa Went te Blaydon Races,* a play he later admitted ingenuously expecting to provoke revolutionary incidents in the centre of Newcastle-on-Tyne. He was always a committed socialist, but one who increasingly came to annoy the ideologically straight and narrow, because he couldn't help seeing the flaws in the human material from which socialism would have to be built. His characters like to think of themselves as enlightened, progressive, or simply good. The drama, and usually the comedy, comes from their attempts to deflect, suppress or ignore whatever tends to contradict their illusions and undermine their self-esteem. *Good* itself is the extreme case. In it, a young intellectual actually ends up as one of the powers-that-be at Auschwitz, the victim of a moral erosion so subtle, so gradual, so invisible, that even then he seems only dimly aware of the hollowness of his self-professed humanity. And Taylor, always too observant, acute and (I suspect) self-knowing a writer to indulge in blacks and whites, tacitly presses the attack still further. How many of us, thrust into the same circumstances and subjected to the same pressures, can be absolutely confident of sustaining an integrity much flintier than this?

I'm inclined to think *Good* Taylor's best, most challenging play; but he wrote several that were more wryly witty and some that were wickedly funny. Myself, I have a special affection for his *Black and White Minstrels,* which was set in his native Glasgow and involved a self-consciously free-living and free-loving *ménage-à-quatre.* Its members were never at a loss for the latest radical catchphrase or snippet of psychiatric jargon— 'Why are you bored?' became 'Could you unravel this bored personality you're projecting?'—and yet their actions, which included the seduction and eviction of a black tenant, made it clear that their 'socialism' was mainly self-admiration, their 'liberalism' sexual greed. The play was mischievous, mocking, but by no means negative: a call to the left to purge itself of dishonesty rather than the cynical attempt to subvert radical

faith Taylor was sometimes accused of making. It would be well worth reviving, as would several of his other plays, notably *Allergy, Bread and Butter* and *Walter.*

> *Benedict Nightingale, "Good Man," in* New Statesman *(© 1982 The Statesman & Nation Publishing Co. Ltd.), Vol. 103, No. 2651, January 8, 1982, p. 23.**

BENEDICT NIGHTINGALE

Not long before his death last December, C. P. Taylor told the director of *Bring Me Sunshine* that he wanted to 'show working people exploring their own feelings, philosophies and relationships with the same concern and sensitivity that had usually been the province of plays of middle-class origin'. Insecurity and anxiety, marital ennui, parental unease, sexual envy, menopausal angst and other such commodities could afflict the families of unemployed Newcastle shipwrights as well as bank-managers from Eastbourne, Sittingbourne, or that well-known centre of genteel despair, Ayckbourn. That is what *Sunshine* points out, and points out with all Taylor's much-missed generosity of spirit and wry, forgiving humour, that tolerance of human failing which could (be it admitted) sometimes go too far. The play lacks the toughmindedness which *Good,* because of its theme, so amply displayed. Since none of the characters of *Sunshine* was going to end up wearing an SS uniform, burning books, or organising the 'humane' slaughter of the mentally crippled or racially uncongenial, Taylor could afford simply to enjoy the sight and sound of them being idiosyncratically, amusingly themselves; and enjoy it he evidently did, occasionally more than we can.

Yet even the more prolix episodes, such as an endless, enervating wrangle over the characters' convoluted sleeping arrangements, are observed with marvellous accuracy; and several of the better encounters don't seem prolix at all. The scene in which a feisty OAP disarms the protagonist's punk son and his tough-guy chum ('You've broken me Nazi dagger!') and proceeds to beat them up; a sexual invitation in a park, he nervous and awkward, she unbelieving, prickly, wincing affectedly at what doesn't really displease her; the coda to a booze-up, with the protagonist harangued, embraced and pledged undying friendship by a man he actually detests: all could be lifted from their contexts and used to illustrate a lecture on their author's quirky yet trenchant talent. Moreover, *Sunshine* offers a by no means unserious slant on a subject that continued to preoccupy Taylor, from *Allergy* to *Good.* What is the internal pathology and the external impact of those who mean well, or mean to mean well, or like to think of themselves as enlightened, progressive, or simply 'good'?

Ted, the podgy ex-shipwright, is the sort everybody likes and uses, whether as factotum, cook, or friendly ear. He is infinitely understanding, yet infinitely ineffective. He is so anxious to see other people's points of view that he hardly seems to have a view, or even an identity, of his own. His idea of quarrelling with his wife is to shout 'All right, then!' when she, maddened beyond endurance by his interminable niceness, yells, 'Can't we have a real disagreement, a real screaming-match?' He has cosy little chats with his son, which leave him half-convinced that the boy is right to throw away his job, take to drugs, commit the odd crime, and impregnate his girlfriend. And he watches helplessly while his wife gets emotionally entangled with an army sergeant, accusing himself of intolerance when their embryonic affair begins to bother him: 'I know it's nowt, but I don't *feel* it's nowt.' . . .

[Ted is] variously earnest, genial, flustered, glum and, by the end, as plausible as any character Taylor concocted. Here's an example, if much milder than Halder in *Good,* of the perils of being 'nice', of failing to say 'no' to those things to which 'no' must be said. Here's that split between mind and feeling, reason and instinct, which Taylor's work as a whole suggests he saw as a principal affliction of our times, as well as an unfailing source of comedy. And here, in this play as in *Bandits* and *Good,* he found a form for his characters' confusions and doubts, their mental and moral schizophrenia: fluid, flexible, capable of moving from meditation to interaction or description to dialogue at the touch of a button. *Good* . . . was his penultimate play; [*Bring Me Sunshine, Bring Me Smiles*], alas, was his last of all. Who can say what he might not have achieved had he lived?

Benedict Nightingale, "Nice One," in New Statesman (© 1982 The Statesman & Nation Publishing Co. Ltd.), Vol. 103, No. 2666, April 23, 1982, p. 30.*

ANTHONY MASTERS

Uneasy on occasion about C P Taylor's work, I can happily commend *Bring Me Sunshine* as a summing-up of his special perceptiveness and pity. Teddy, on whose cuddly middle-aged shoulders a whole Newcastle community sobs out its problems, is an inspired device for showing us the sorrows and misunderstandings of ordinary people's relationships—and Taylor's own affectionate frustration as he watches human folly and finds he must forgive it. Not many playwrights can send you out of the theatre a better person, but he was one of them.

Into Teddy's kitchen come the seekers for cocoa and sympathy, moaning that Teddy never understands but telling him just the same. His son Peter . . . gets his punk girlfriend Wendy pregnant, loses his supermarket job for playing custard pies with a strawberry gateau and eats a local mushroom so wild it sends him streaking up the road in his underpants. Wendy . . . can't decide whether to have his baby or stay as majorette in the kids' jazz band. Even Ted's own wife Carol . . . has an autumnal fling with a staff-sergeant who has ears like mug handles, and details to Ted every lovesick moment and every shared cup of coffee.

Such scenes leave Ted, and his author, between laughter and tears. Peter is ludicrously seduced in a strange bathroom by a girl so dirty he's tempted to make washing her neck part of the foreplay. Wendy wallops him and decides to marry him. How hopeless and how forgivable. And the better Ted knows people, the less he understands. Peter is in the thick of a knife fight one minute and a frightened child the next. So how can you judge, how can you condemn? . . .

Ted begins as a kind, shrewd, wryly funny man, so like the author in temperament and so physically unlike him. But the good listener, the agreeable man who always agrees, becomes as original a tragicomic character as Molière's Misanthrope or Hampton's Philanthropist. Has he got life where he wants it? Or has he ceased to feel, even to exist? Besieged by others' needs, does he know his own?

Thus an unpretentious comedy grows and grows; and, of course, Taylor's touch with Geordie speech and behaviour is sure. This

detail can distract, slow the action and actually trivialize it; but less so here than, for example, in the winsome *And A Nightingale Sang.* . . . (p. 32)

Anthony Masters, in a review of "Bring Me Sunshine" and "Good" (© copyright Anthony Masters 1982; reprinted with permission), in Plays and Players, No. 345, June, 1982, pp. 32-3.

PETER MORTIMER

[*Mortimer had been acquainted with Taylor as a publisher, theater critic, and friend. He saw nearly all of Taylor's seventy-odd plays performed in Scotland.*]

The British prefer their literary heroes to be dead, so it's not surprising that Taylor's true talents are only now being appreciated. . . .

One of the greatest tragedies about Taylor is that his death came at the moment of a major development in his work. . . . *Good,* with its subject matter of the well-intentioned young German slowly seduced by the Nazi machine . . . , marks a radical departure, a deadly serious play spiced throughout with an impish, almost daredevil humour.

Watching it, I remember similar sensations as when watching his study of small-time North-East crooks and the gambling world, *Bandits!;* that here was a kind of theatre not many people could write. (p. 16)

Fashion is a notorious servant in art. Many 'regional' dramatists go down to London and become parodies of themselves, or else use their working class roots to hammer home some well-battered political philosophy; the politics grabs more attention than the drama, and a lot of bosh is overpraised. This was one reason why Cecil was underappreciated: he rarely sat down with the intention of "saying" one set thing. He was alive, antennae wriggling all over the place.

His characters didn't merely represent points of view, or symbolise an aspect of modern civilisation (though obviously they often did that as well), they *lived.* They lived so much he couldn't resist making them turn to talk to the audience—one of his hallmarks. Even in mid-sentence he would at times freeze the action as a character turned to offer his confidentialities. And he did it with all the characters, not just an *Alfie*-type of monologue approach. This developed a great empathy between them and audience, and it worked especially well in . . . small intimate venues. . . .

Seeing the technique refined to such a degree makes it look easy, a dramatic short-cut even, but Taylor's secret was in dovetailing such confidences into the play itself, so we never had the impression of a character stopping to make a speech.

He was never what I call a fashionable hack, one of those moderately talented dramatists who happen to be saying the right things at the right time. Because he was more aware of the life forces, human motivations and absurdities, or at least considered them more important than set philosophies, critics weren't quite sure what to make of him. The plays managed *not* to be doom-laden, though they pinpointed all our most ridiculous foibles, inconsistencies, cruelties, and human weaknesses. When you stood back from them for perspective, you realised that in essence they were a *celebration* of humanity.

On the surface you could take some of Cecil's plays—the regional ones at least—and see a superior kind of *Coronation*

Street at work. I don't think he'd object to the description either, and I use 'superior' because in two hours on a live stage, he would manage to pack in as many issues, themes, and conflicts as would occupy a soap opera for 12 months. I remember one scene particularly from *Bring Me Sunshine,* where half a dozen characters gathered in the kitchen simultaneously, giving vent to their problems and crises. The author's tight control of the dialogue, and the way that, despite the verbal flack coming fast and furious from all quarters, the audience never loses track for a second symbolises the kind of technical achievement few contemporary playwrights could create. It is also, incidentally, one of the most hugely funny things I've seen for some time. . . .

Those who thought they knew what 'type' of playwright he was had to think again as he changed direction. *Happy Lies* with its dual setting of a working class Jarrow home, and a Madras slum pointed the way. *Good* took us further along the path, and at the time of his death, a play about Stalin was in the pipeline. We would, I'm sure, have seen a whole new dimension had he not died prematurely. . . .

When he died, many of us in the North-East weren't quite sure what to do, as if some guiding light had gone out. We never fully realised his inspiration until he was dead, then came the appreciation of him as a truly original writer and man who didn't use cheap tricks, wasn't publicity seeking, never worried where the spotlight was shining. Whatever he was doing, he cut through the fake, refused to allow distractions, and reached the essence.

I don't know anyone who did it better. (p. 17)

> Peter Mortimer, "C. P. Taylor: An Appreciation of His Work and Life," in Drama *(reprinted by permission of the British Theatre Association), No. 145, Autumn, 1982, pp. 16-17.*

FRANK RICH

When we first meet Halder . . . , the protagonist of C. P. Taylor's **"Good,"** he is a model of the urbane university professor. A novelist and literary critic, Halder is devoted to his wife and children, as well as to his one close friend, a Jewish psychiatrist named Maurice. But the place is Frankfurt, the year is 1933, and men can change without warning. It isn't too long before Halder has not only become a member of the Nazi party but has also played a direct role in SS book burnings and euthanasia "experiments" in the Jew-bashing Night of the Long Knives, and, finally, in Eichmann's genocide at Auschwitz.

Mr. Taylor's "play with music" . . . is an attempt to understand how all this could happen. The question raised is fascinating, because Halder is no cliché Nazi, no fire-breathing thug. He's more of an Albert Speer type, and yet, unlike Speer, he doesn't settle for practicing evil from a bureaucratic distance—Halder gets right into the bloody trenches of the Holocaust. Who wouldn't be eager to see how such a "good" man could turn totally rancid so fast?

The answer, however, never really comes. **"Good"** is an undeniably provocative work, and Mr. Taylor . . . has written it with an intelligent, light touch in a most imaginative form. But for all the author's efforts to break through our received ideas about the origins of Nazism and to avoid black and white moral imperatives, his play doesn't add anything to the generalities

of the past. Even if you give **"Good"** the full and sometimes laborious concentration it requires, you're likely to leave the theater feeling stimulated but unsatisfied.

The play's modus operandi is its cleverest aspect. The setting is an empty stage, with its bare-brick wall and gas pipes showing, and with stark police-interrogation lamps transversing the space from every angle. This arena is, one might say, the concentration camp of Halder's mind. **"Good"** unfolds inside its central character's psyche and, fittingly enough, has a stream-of-consciousness structure. All the supporting players remain on stage throughout, so that [Halder] can wander among them at will as he free-associates back and forth through time.

There are also five musicians afoot, who play yet another role in Halder's consciousness. As the protagonist explains at the start, he has been "bringing music into the traumatic moments" of his life since childhood. This mental music is his "anxiety neurosis"—a defense mechanism that allows him to drown out and escape thoughts he doesn't want to hear. It is also something of an artificial stage gimmick, particularly when the musical selections include such predictable choices as Weill and Wagner, but it is an amusing one that pays off in startling theatrical dividends at the play's very end.

Although some of the splintery scenes between the musical interludes are digressionary or repetitive, others are bristling. Once Mr. Taylor has converted Halder to villainy, he does a sharp job of showing how an intellectual might rationalize his corruption. To Halder, book burning can be "symbolic of a new and healthy" alternative to dusty university education. The Night of the Long Knives, if "looked at in perspective," is "basically a humanitarian action" because it encourages Jews to flee Germany. Ultimately, Halder can maintain that there is "no objective moral truth" and can resolve any qualms by declaring, "We probably are good, whatever that means."

The exchanges between Halder and Maurice, in which the men debate and contrast their respective dilemmas, are also vibrantly drawn—at least until we wonder why Halder doesn't help his beloved Jewish friend escape to Switzerland. Maurice—a man who is witty even in anger and panic, a Jew with unresolved feelings about his Jewishness—is easily the most complex character in **"Good."** (pp. 184-85)

But who is Halder? The vague reasons given for his conversion from liberal humanist to Nazi are the same old catch-all motivations: he opportunistically wishes to advance his career; he's self-centered; he lacks the strong sense of self-definition that a uniform might provide. Halder also has empty or troubled relationships with the various women in his life—relationships that are explored at excessive but unrewarding length. And, like all Nazis in works of this sort, from the Speer of "Inside the Third Reich" to the hero of the film "Mephisto," Halder has a special fondness for Goethe's "Faust."

This just isn't enough to go on. If that's what it takes to turn a decent, intelligent man into a full-fledged murderer, one might argue that the whole world was, and is, full of Nazis. And apparently that's exactly the real point Mr. Taylor wishes to make. In a note in the Playbill, he cites present-day "'crimes' of the West against the Third World" and says that he wrote his play in part to expiate his own culpability "in the Auschwitzes we are all perpetrating today." It's to make this debatable analogy—to suggest that we're all possibly "good Germans" like Halder—that Mr. Taylor has oversimplified and blurred the highly specific, sui generis genesis and nature of the Third Reich's own Auschwitzes in **"Good."** (p. 185)

Frank Rich, " 'Good', on Becoming a Nazi," in The New York Times *(© 1982 by The New York Times Company; reprinted by permission), October 14, 1982 (and reprinted in* New York Theatre Critics' Reviews, *Vol. XLIII, No. 13, October 18, 1982, pp. 184-85).*

JOHN SIMON

Concerning what may have been the late Cecil P. Taylor's best effort, **Bread and Butter,** the English critic Harold Hobson wrote that "if the play is about the sadness of time's destruction of our ideals," it is a very grave point that the two principal characters "never really had any ideals at all." In [*Good*] . . . the same problem obtains; this tale of how John Halder, a "good" German, gets sucked and suckered into the Nazi party fails right off the bat by not persuading us that we are dealing with a man of parts and ideals. . . .

Good makes no literal sense. No novelist-professors of literature became S.S. officers—the last thing the S.S. wanted or needed; indeed, writers of the elitist or rightist persuasion did not even make it, or want to make it, into the party on any level—*vide* George, Jünger, Benn, et al. In no case would the Nazis have picked such a marginal and irrelevant figure to confer prestige on their final solution: but if such prestige was the aim, why is Halder kept out of the limelight and not put to publicity use? Anyway, as written, the character of Halder could not have liquidated even the roaches in a small apartment, and could hardly have passed the physical examination required to get into the S.S.

And the play makes no literary sense, either. The relationship between Halder and the women in his life is insufficiently developed, and does not appear to be of the kind to drive a man of even middling intellect and character into monstrousness. Similarly, the friendship with Maurice is never properly established or dramatized, either in its strength or in its dissolution. And the blandishments or pressures of the Nazis are far too simplistic. Matters are further bogged down by Taylor's insistence on cocktail-party Brechtianizing. By way of an amiable alienation effect, we get an onstage band that continually butts in, various song turns by diverse cast members in German or English (with some songs wholly out of place and time), and steady scrambling of scenes, so that everything is interspersed with or superimposed on everything else. This effectively shoots down the few fledgling ideas *Good* may have, and sacrifices minimal communicativeness to Brecht and circuses. (p. 77)

[This] play that appears to address itself to a serious intellectual problem has almost nothing to say on the subject, and proceeds to disguise its nugacity by resorting to any number of modish—or, rather, outmoded—strategies. The result is neither intellectual nor honest non-intellectual theater but a flabby pseudointellectual rodomontade. (pp. 77-8)

John Simon, "All's Well That Ends 'Good'," in New York *Magazine (copyright © 1983 by News Group Publications, Inc.; reprinted with the permission of* New York *Magazine), Vol. 15, No. 42, October 25, 1982, pp. 77-8.*

BRENDAN GILL

["**Good**"] is superb theatre—a classic mingling of strong subject matter, entertaining presentation, and flawless acting. . . . [One] isn't likely to encounter a more satisfying experience on Broadway throughout the rest of the season. . . .

"**Good**" describes the rise of Hitlerism in the thirties as it affects the lives of two characteristic Germans, Halder and Maurice—the former a Christian, the latter a Jew. They are cultivated members of the upper middle class and are intimate friends. As the play begins, they agree that Hitler's attacks upon the Jews—still largely verbal in nature—are a temporary political aberration; once he has achieved sufficient power, he will abandon the attacks, for how is Germany to do without its Jews, who have provided so much of the country's artistic and scientific glory? Years pass, and Maurice is obliged to change his mind; he has become the victim of a formal program of anti-Semitism whose purpose is to exterminate him and all his kind. Halder, a much admired professor and novelist, can afford to continue his lifelong bent for accommodation. Hasn't he spent many years accommodating to a slatternly wife and a senile mother? Hasn't he manifested a discipline in regard to his career so rigid that his only weakness may be said to be his fondness for popular band music? He is convinced that he is an essentially good person, and that if he is ever confronted by authentic evil he will know how to deal with it.

The fact is, of course, that Halder's nominal goodness has little to do with virtue; it is a mere cosmetic niceness of manner and appearance, behind which he does whatever he pleases. When a pretty student falls in love with him, he abandons his wife for her, and not least willingly because the student keeps telling him how good he is. Like a man going down steps who believes himself to be climbing, Halder marches straight into Hitler's convenient embrace. The last scene is one to which every earlier moment of the play has unerringly aimed; it is a scene of such exceptional vividness that it deserves to be experienced at first hand, without any hints as to its nature. . . .

[Despite] its dark content, "**Good**" is often comic, and the playwright's art is such that we are able to laugh even at what we are appalled and frightened by. (p. 160)

Brendan Gill, "Steps Going Down" (© 1982 by Brendan Gill), in The New Yorker, *Vol. LVIII, No. 36, October 25, 1982, pp. 160-61.**

T. E. KALEM

History is a nightmare into which the antihero of *Good* sleepwalks. John Halder . . . is a decent enough human being. He is kind to his wife Helen . . . , though she is an execrably sloppy homemaker. Even if he has to cook the meal, he sees to it that his three children are properly fed. With his mother . . . , who is blind, senile and bitter, Halder is agonizingly solicitous. . . .

By vocation, Halder is a professor of German classics who also writes novels. He is the sort of man who is appalled by the fact that Goethe refused to send Beethoven money when the composer was in desperate need. . . . At *Good's* end, this decent, liberal-minded scholar has become Eichmann's right-hand man at Auschwitz.

How did it happen? Paradoxically, the late British playwright C. P. Taylor does not, initially, seem to be the best possible man to ask. He poses the question engrossingly, but most of the answers he provides seem either tantalizingly elusive or logically implausible. Halder is a congenital daydreamer. Not only the taste of reality but the feel of it eludes him. This fact is incorporated in the structure of the play by the presence on-stage of a six-man band. The musicians punctuate Halder's crises, conflicts and decisive indecision with marching songs, waltzes, jazz tunes and snatches of opera. These are the intravenous tranquilizers with which Halder suppresses the torment of truth. *Good* is a trip through the inner space of a troubled mind; just as others hear voices, Halder hears ironic and beguiling music. . . .

The bands play on, and Halder marches in lockstep. Only as he is greeted by the strains of Schubert's *March Militaire* from the camp's orchestra at the gates of Auschwitz does he realize that he has supped full of horrors. This time, and he shrieks it out, "The band was *Real!* The band was *Real!*" With this shattering climax, *Good* achieves a high pitch of luminous moral gravity. Venturing beyond easy and merely plausible answers about how a good man succumbs to evil forces, Playwright Taylor has etched the profile of an insidiously disarming process. That process was perhaps best described by Britain's belletrist of metaphysics, C. S. Lewis: "The safest road to Hell is the gradual one—the gentle slope, soft underfoot, without sudden turnings, without milestones, without signposts."

> *T. E. Kalem, "Gently Insidious Slope to Hell," in* Time *(copyright 1982 Time Inc.; all rights reserved; reprinted by permission from* Time*), Vol. 120, No. 17, October 25, 1982, p. 78.*

ROBERT BRUSTEIN

The difficulty with [*Good*] . . . is that it poses an all-too-familiar question and then completely fails to grapple with it.

The question is how generally ordinary and relatively decent people could have participated in or even tolerated Nazism, and I wonder if it needs to be asked again. Hannah Arendt first brought it up in her book on Eichmann; that perfectly normal family man, Rudolph Hess, who was also commandant of Auschwitz, provided some answers in his memoirs; Hochuth's

The Deputy carried the question to the stage and Styron's *Sophie's Choice* to the novel; it was even mentioned in *Bent*, Martin Sherman's play about homosexual prisoners in the concentration camp. Mr. Taylor writes as if we were totally innocent of any previous work on the subject, as if he had stumbled on it anew.

Taylor . . . wrote *Good,* he said, in response to a deeply felt trauma; but his characters react to atrocities with all the passion of people in lounge chairs discussing the test match scores. It may be that Taylor, an assimilated English Jew, was incapable of imagining absolute evil; or it may be that the language of the educated English upper classes is incapable of expressing outrage. I mean, how hateful can people be when they are identified as "Nahzis." Taylor, at all events, hasn't found much evil in these "Nahzis." Describing the origins of *Good,* he admits it was impossible for him to see "the Third Reich's war on the Jews . . . as simply criminal," especially when he equated these "anti-social activities" (his test match phrase for the Final Solution) with the "Peace Crimes of the West against the Third World—my part in the Auschwitzes we are all perpetrating today." The carelessness of the analogy, not to mention its imprecise language, staggers the mind, but it may explain why Taylor's treatment of the rise of Nazism is so surprisingly mild. (p. 24)

Taylor's design is clear but, to my mind, utterly muddleheaded. If we are all capable of participating in such atrocities, then nobody is to blame for them, because when everyone is potentially guilty, then no one is guilty. To force his point, Taylor is obliged to treat the most dreadful events in the most casual manner, but when you see people responding to "anti-social behavior" in a reasonable, bemused, and condescending fashion, then you soon realize you are not in Germany but England. . . . One leaves the theater comforted by the thought that, because of their detached national character, the English could never have produced Nazism; the question is whether this detachment is helping to understand it. (pp. 24-5)

> *Robert Brustein, "This 'Money-Got, Mechanic Age'" (reprinted by permission of the author; © 1982 The New Republic, Inc.), in* The New Republic, *Vol. 187, No. 19, November 15, 1982, pp. 23-5.**

Alice Walker

1944-

Black American novelist, short story writer, poet, and editor.

Walker is a highly regarded writer of powerfully expressive fiction. Her work consistently reflects her concern with racial, sexual, and political issues, particularly with the black woman's struggle for spiritual and political survival. Born into a large family of sharecroppers in the Deep South, Walker managed to obtain a college education in spite of poverty. Her political awareness, her Southern heritage, and her sense of the culture and history of her people form the thematic base of her material.

Walker's poetry, like her short stories, is praised for its honesty and depth of feeling but her literary reputation rests largely on her novels, especially the recently published *The Color Purple* (1982). Her most acclaimed work to date, this novel was awarded both the American Book Award and the Pulitzer Prize.

The Color Purple, **which is noted for its authentic use of black dialect, explores and expands upon concerns introduced in Walker's earlier works. Like her first novel,** *The Third Life of Grange Copeland* **(1970) and many of the short stories collected in** *You Can't Keep a Good Woman Down* **(1981),** *The Color Purple* **portrays the devastating effects of racial and sexual oppression. Walker, who has said that black women are the only people she respects "collectively and with no reservations," in this novel shows an intense empathy for the black woman who faces violent subjugation by black men, as well as white racists. Walker advocates "bonding" between black women as a defense against such oppression. Although grim in many respects, the overriding message of this novel is that "love redeems." While she spares no detail of the violence and painful hardships in the lives she portrays, Walker has a keen eye for the beauty and grace found in the most ordinary people or objects.**

(See also *CLC,* **Vols. 5, 6, 9, 19;** *Contemporary Authors,* **Vols. 37-40, rev. ed.;** *Contemporary Authors New Revision Series,* **Vol. 9; and** *Dictionary of Literary Biography,* **Vol. 6.)**

KATHA POLLITT

Like the Victorians, we consider certain subjects fit for fiction and others too hot to handle. Unlike the Victorians, however, we don't know we think that—we're too busy congratulating outselves on our sexual frankness to see that there might be other sorts of blindness and prudery. Nowhere is this more clearly demonstrated than in the contemporary short story. Anyone browsing among a recent year's worth of American magazines might reasonably conclude that short fiction is by definition a medium in which white middle-class writers express elegiac and seemly sentiments about such noncontroversial topics as divorce and the deaths of relatives and that when those same writers want to talk about what is *really* on their minds they turn to journalism—as have, many think, their readers.

For this reason I give Alice Walker . . . much credit for daring to engage in fictional terms (well, quasi-fictional terms, more on that later) some of the major racial-sexual-political issues of our time [in her recent collection **"You Can't Keep a Good Woman Down"**]. **"Advancing Luna—and Ida B. Wells"** examines the rape of a white civil rights worker by a black civil rights worker from the point of view of the black woman who is the victim's best friend. **"The Abortion"** dissects the complex effect on a black middle-class marriage of the wife's abortion. **"Coming Apart"** and **"Porn"** deal with male sadomasochistic sexual fantasies, as experienced by puzzled and insulted wives and girlfriends.

Its important, frankly political, semi-taboo subject matter should automatically make **"You Can't Keep a Good Woman Down"** fascinating to anyone, black or white, with his head not completely entrenched in the sand. Miss Walker has, moreover, at least one priceless literary gift: that of sounding absolutely authoritative: "And there was the smell of clean poverty . . . a sharp, *bitter* odor, almost acrid, as if the women washed themselves in chemicals." "She was attractive, but just barely and with effort. Had she been the slightest bit overweight, for instance, she would have . . . faded into the background where, even in a revolution, fat people seem destined to go." Then too, she has a watchful eye for . . . quirky, small details as the church pew, "straight and spare as Abe Lincoln lying down,'' lugged up from the rural South to decorate an East Village living room, or the ''overdressed'' Mai Tais in an Alaskan bar: ''in addition to the traditional umbrella, there were tiny snowshoes.''

These qualities give edge and sparkle to the more conventional stories, the ones in which Miss Walker has imagined herself into one version or other of the spunky, tough, irrepressible ''good woman'' of the title. I was not surprised, perhaps, but I was charmed by **''Nineteen Fifty-Five,''** in which we hear an old black blues singer (read Big Mama Thornton) contemplate the young white rock-and-roll singer (read Elvis Presley) who has risen to stardom by singing her song (read ''Hound Dog''). Equally vivid, and a little more unusual, is **''Fame,''** in which a crotchety, vain and brilliant old black writer receives an award—her 111th literary honor—from a collection of academic toadies she takes great pleasure in privately despising.

These comparatively modest stories, though, are outweighed by those that are at once more overtly political and more stylistically innovative. But as Miss Walker aims for more, she achieves less. These latter stories occupy a sort of middle ground between personal statement, political parable, conventional story and vaguely experimental fiction—and this is not a comfortable place for short stories to find themselves. As fiction, they must be about particular people, but as parable they must be about people as types. As personal statement, or as conventional fiction, they lead us to think we are hearing the voice of the author; the experimental techniques that Miss Walker employs subvert that assumption by calling our attention to the author as inventor and manipulator of every aspect of what we are reading.

Perhaps in order to cover over these conflicts, Miss Walker has relied heavily on the use of an elaborately detached, sardonic, flat-sounding prose style. But this tone is completely wrong for these stories: they are too partisan (the black woman is *always* the most sympathetic character). They are also too unfocused, too full of loose ends and unanswered questions and of characters that are half odd and interesting individuals and half political or narrative conveniences.

I never believed for a minute, for instance, that the black woman narrator was really the best friend of poor Luna, who allowed herself to be raped by a black man in Georgia rather than scream and possibly precipitate a lynching. A friend would have felt some human sympathy, along with however much political angst, or, if not, would have had to confront this lack. (p. 9)

Only the most coolly abstract and rigorously intellectual writer can bring off this sort of fictional-essayistic hybrid. Those who admired Miss Walker's previous work, in particular her fine novel **''Meridian,''** and her earlier volume of short stories, **''In Love and Trouble,''** will know that her strengths lie elsewhere. As a storyteller she is impassioned, sprawling, emotional, lushly evocative, steeped in place, in memory, in the compelling power of narrative itself. A lavishly gifted writer, in other words—but not of this sort of book. (p. 15)

Katha Pollitt, ''Stretching the Short Story,'' in The New York Times Book Review *(© 1981 by The New York Times Company; reprinted by permission), May 24, 1981, pp. 9, 15.*

CAROL RUMENS

[Alice Walker's *Meridian* and *You Can't Keep a Good Woman Down*] are difficult in that, to varying degrees, they presuppose

a certain special awareness on the part of their readers; they are also, at best, strong and passionately visionary pieces of prose with a quality of the epic poem. They are heirs to the dream of Martin Luther King, and are at the same time committed and coolly clearsighted concerning its progress. The feminism of . . . [Alice Walker] is the source of . . . [her] detachment; although the question of racial equality is primary, it is focussed through, and to some extent even diminished by, the often more urgently personal quest for sexual justice. . . . Her deepest concern is with individuals and how their relationships are affected by their confrontations with wider political and moral issues. The sexism inherent in historical racism and still beleaguering most attempts at honest radicalism is neatly teased out and laid bare.

Meridian is the most accessible of the books, and the most plural in its concerns. . . .

The narrative itself is solidly constructed and makes powerful use of symbols in a manner reminiscent of Toni Morrison.

The short stories . . . [in] *You Can't Keep a Good Woman Down* tend to be less subtly imagined. Often ruggedly open-ended in form, they suggest that Alice Walker is happier with a larger canvas. Some seem rather detached and essay-like. . . . In the best of them, as in *Meridian,* considerations of sexual and racial politics are resonant with universal moral overtones. There is the question posed by Luna, for example, a white sympathizer whose problem is ''whether in a black community surrounded by whites with a history of lynching blacks, she had a right to scream as Freddie Pye was raping her.'' Walker has a particular gift for capturing the pathos of sexual love; it is the subject of **''Laurel'',** a story of a black-white triangle in which colour, however, plays only a minimal part. . . . Walker's work should be admired . . . not because it represents a flowering of black or female consciousness, but because at best it brings to life the varied scents and colours of human experience.

Carol Rumens, ''Heirs to the Dream,'' in The Times Literary Supplement *(© Times Newspapers Ltd. (London) 1982; reproduced from* The Times Literary Supplement *by permission), No. 4133, June 18, 1982, p. 676.**

PETER S. PRESCOTT

Because I have an eerie feeling that any attempt I make to describe what happens in this story is likely to start the summer rush for the beaches, I want to say at once that **''The Color Purple''** is an American novel of permanent importance, that rare sort of book which (in Norman Mailer's felicitous phrase) amounts to ''a diversion in the fields of dread.'' Alice Walker excels at making difficulties for herself and then transcending them. To cite an example: her story begins at about the point that most Greek tragedies reserve for the climax, then becomes by immeasurably small steps a comedy which works its way toward acceptance, serenity and joy. To cite another: her narrative advances entirely by means of letters that are either never delivered or are delivered too late for a response, and most of these are written in a black English that Walker appears to have modified artfully for general consumption. (p. 67)

The letters begin with Celie addressing herself to God because she's ashamed to tell anyone else. Celie is black, ugly, not good at school work; she lives in rural Georgia in this century's second decade and is 14 when the man she takes to be her father begins to rape her. She bears this man two children, who are taken away; at his insistence, she marries a man who would rather have had her younger sister, Nettie. Others call Celie's husband Albert, but she cannot; unable to muster his name in her letters, she calls him "Mr.——." "You black, you pore, you ugly," Albert tells his wife, "you a woman . . . you nothing at all." Albert invites to their home his old mistress, a blues singer named Shug Avery, who arrives ill, with "the nasty woman disease." This event, which should break up any household, proves oddly restorative; a bond between Celie and Shug develops, almost to the exclusion of the useless Albert.

In time—the course of this novel covers more than 30 years—Celie discovers that the despicable Albert has been withholding letters written to her by Nettie, who has gone to West Africa as an apprentice missionary with the couple who adopted Celie's children. . . . Celie now writes to Nettie letters that her sister never receives. There is, in this parallel correspondence in which no letter ever hopes for an answer, something deeply moving: these sisters need each other desperately, but each must mature and survive without response from the other.

Love redeems, meanness kills—that is **"The Color Purple"**'s principal theme, the theme of most of the world's great fiction. Nevertheless—and this is why this black woman's novel will survive a white man's embrace—the redemptive love that is celebrated here is selective, even prickly. White folk figure rarely in its pages and never to their advantage, and black men are recovered only to the extent that they buckle down to housework and let women attend to business. For Walker, redemptive love requires female bonding. The bond liberates women from men, who are predators at worst, idle at best. (pp. 67-8)

In the traditional manner, Walker ends her comedy with a dance, or more precisely with a barbecue. "White people busy celebrating they independence from England July 4th," says Celie's stepson, "so most black folk don't have to work. Us can spend the day celebrating each other." In this novel, the celebration has been painfully earned. (p. 68)

Peter S. Prescott, "A Long Road to Liberation," in Newsweek *(copyright 1982, by Newsweek, Inc.; all rights reserved; reprinted by permission), Vol. XCIX, No. 25, June 21, 1982, pp. 67-8.*

MEL WATKINS

Without doubt, Alice Walker's latest novel is her most impressive. No mean accomplishment, since her previous books . . . have elicited almost unanimous praise for Miss Walker as a lavishly gifted writer. **"The Color Purple,"** while easily satisfying that claim, brings into sharper focus many of the diverse themes that threaded their way through her past work. . . .

Most prominent [of the book's major themes] is the estrangement and violence that mark the relationships between Miss Walker's black men and women. . . .

[Miss Walker has] dealt with [this] subject before. In her collection **"You Can't Keep a Good Woman Down,"** two stories (**"Porn"** and **"Coming Apart"**) assess the sexual disaffection among black couples. And the saintly heroine of the novel **"Meridian"** is deserted by a black lover who then marries a white civil-rights worker, whom he also later abandons. In **"Meridian,"** however, the friction between black men and women is merely one of several themes; in **"The Color Purple"** the role of male domination in the frustration of black women's struggle for independence is clearly the focus.

Miss Walker explores the estrangement of her men and women through a triangular love affair. It is Shug Avery who forces Albert to stop brutalizing Celie, and it is Shug with whom Celie first consummates a satisfying and reciprocally loving relationship. . . .

What makes Miss Walker's exploration so indelibly affecting is the choice of a narrative style that, without the intrusion of the author, forces intimate identification with [Celie]. . . . Most of the letters that comprise this epistolary novel are written by Celie, although correspondence from Nettie is included in the latter part of the book. Initially, some readers may be put off by Celie's knothole view of the world, particularly since her letters are written in dialect and from the perspective of a naïve, uneducated adolescent. . . .

As the novel progresses, however, and as Celie grows in experience, her observations become sharper and more informed; the letters take on authority and the dialect, once accepted, assumes a lyrical cadence of its own. . . .

The cumulative effect is a novel that is convincing because of the authenticity of its folk voice. And, refreshingly, it is not just the two narrator-correspondents who come vividly alive in this tale. A number of memorable female characters emerge. There is Shug Avery, whose pride, independence and appetite for living act as a catalyst for Celie and others, and Sofia, whose rebellious spirit leads her not only to desert her overbearing husband but also to challenge the social order of the racist community in which she lives.

If there is a weakness in this novel—besides the somewhat pallid portraits of the males—it is Netti's correspondence from Africa. While Netti's letters broaden and reinforce the theme of female oppression by describing customs of the Olinka tribe that parallel some found in the American South, they are often mere monologues on African history. Appearing, as they do, after Celie's intensely subjective voice has been established, they seem lackluster and intrusive.

These are only quibbles, however, about a striking and consummately well-written novel. Alice Walker's choice and effective handling of the epistolary style has enabled her to tell a poignant tale of women's struggle for equality and independence without either the emotional excess of her previous novel **"Meridian"** or the polemical excess of her short-story collection **"You Can't Keep a Good Woman Down."**

Mel Watkins, "Some Letters Went to God," in The New York Times Book Review *(© 1982 by The New York Times Company; reprinted by permission), July 25, 1982, p. 7.*

ROBERT TOWERS

There is nothing cool or throwaway in Alice Walker's attitude toward the materials of her fiction. The first book by this exceptionally productive novelist, poet, and short-story writer to come to my notice was *Meridian* (1976), an impassioned account of the spiritual progress of a young black woman, Meridian Hill, during the civil-rights struggle of the 1960s and its aftermath. . . . Though beset by serious structural problems and other lapses of craft, *Meridian* remains the most impressive fictional treatment of the "Movement" that I have yet read.

In *The Color Purple* Alice Walker moves backward in time, setting her story roughly (the chronology is kept vague) between 1916 and 1942—a period during which the post-Reconstruction settlement of black status remained almost unaltered in the Deep South. Drawing upon what must be maternal and grandmaternal accounts as well as upon her own memory and observation, Miss Walker, who is herself under forty, exposes us to a way of life that for the most part existed beyond or below the reach of fiction and that has hitherto been made available to us chiefly through tape-recorded reminiscences: the life of poor, rural Southern blacks as it was experienced by their womenfolk. (p. 35)

I cannot gauge the general accuracy of Miss Walker's account [of Celie's life] or the degree to which it may be colored by current male-female antagonisms within the black community. . . . I did note certain improbabilities: it seems unlikely that a woman of Celie's education would have applied the word "amazons" to a group of feisty sisters or that Celie, in the 1930s, would have found fulfillment in designing and making pants for women. In any case, *The Color Purple* has more serious faults than its possible feminist bias. Alice Walker still has a lot to learn about plotting and structuring what is clearly intended to be a realistic novel. The revelations involving the fate of Celie's lost babies and the identity of her real father seem crudely contrived—the stuff of melodrama or fairy tales.

The extended account of Nettie's experience in Africa, to which she has gone with a black missionary couple and their two adopted children, is meant to be a counterweight to Celie's story but it lacks authenticity—not because Miss Walker is ignorant of Africa . . . but because she has failed to endow Nettie with her own distinctive voice; the fact that Nettie is better educated than Celie—and a great reader—should not have drained her epistolary style of all personal flavor, leaving her essentially uncharacterized, a mere reporter of events. The failure to find an interesting idiom for a major figure like Nettie is especially damaging in an epistolary novel, which is at best a difficult genre for a twentieth-century writer, posing its own special problems of momentum and credibility.

Fortunately, inadequacies which might tell heavily against another novel seem relatively insignificant in view of the one great challenge which Alice Walker has triumphantly met: the conversion, in Celie's letters, of a subliterate dialect into a medium of remarkable expressiveness, color, and poignancy. I find it impossible to imagine Celie apart from her language; through it, not only a memorable and infinitely touching character but a whole submerged world is vividly called into being. Miss Walker knows how to avoid the excesses of literal transcription while remaining faithful to the spirit and rhythms of Black English. I can think of no other novelist who has so successfully tapped the poetic resources of the idiom. (p. 36)

Robert Towers, "Good Men Are Hard to Find," in The New York Review of Books *(reprinted with permission from* The New York Review of Books; *copyright © 1982 Nyrev, Inc.), Vol. XXIX, No. 13, August 12, 1982, pp. 35-6.**

DINITIA SMITH

As admirers of *The Third Life of Grange Copeland* and *Meridian* already know, to read an Alice Walker novel is to enter the country of surprise. It is to be admitted to the world of rural black women, a world long neglected by most whites, perhaps out of ignorance, perhaps out of willed indifference. The loss is ours, for the lives of these women are so extraordinary in their tragedy, their culture, their humor and their courage that we are immediately gripped by them. (p. 181)

No writer has made the intimate hurt of racism more palpable than Walker. In one of [*The Color Purple*'s] most rending scenes, Celie's step-daughter-in-law, Sofia, is sentenced to work as a maid in the white mayor's house for "sassing" the mayor's wife. In a fit of magnanimity, the mayor's wife offers to drive Sofia home to see her children, whom she hasn't laid eyes on in five years. The reunion lasts only fifteen minutes—then the mayor's wife insists that Sofia drive her home.

The Color Purple is about the struggle between redemption and revenge. And the chief agency of redemption, Walker is saying, is the strength of the relationships between women: their friendships, their love, their shared oppression. Even the white mayor's family is redeemed when his daughter cares for Sofia's sick daughter.

There is a note of tendentiousness here, though. The men in this book change *only* when their women join together and rebel—and then, the change is so complete as to be unrealistic. It was hard for me to believe that a person as violent, brooding and just plain nasty as Mr. ——— could ever become that sweet, quiet man smoking and chatting on the porch.

Walker's didacticism is especially evident in Nettie's letters from Africa, which make up a large portion of the book. (p. 182)

Walker's politics are not the problem—*of course* sexism and racism are terrible, *of course* women should band together to help each other. But the politics have to be incarnated in complex, contradictory characters—characters to whom the novelist grants the freedom to act, as it were, on their own.

I wish Walker had let herself be carried along more by her language, with all its vivid figures of speech, Biblical cadences, distinctive grammar and true-to-life starts and stops. The pithy, direct black folk idiom of *The Color Purple* is in the end its greatest strength, reminding us that if Walker is sometimes an ideologue, she is also a poet.

Despite its occasional preachiness, *The Color Purple* marks a major advance for Walker's art. At its best, and at least half the book is superb, it places her in the company of Faulkner, from whom she appears to have learned a great deal: the use of a shifting first-person narrator, for instance, and the presentation of a complex story from a naïve point of view, like that of 14-year-old Celie. Walker has not turned her back on the Southern fictional tradition. She has absorbed it and made it her own. By infusing the black experience into the Southern novel, she enriches both it and us. (pp. 182-83)

Dinitia Smith, "'Celie, You a Tree'," in The Nation *(copyright 1982* The Nation *magazine, The Nation Associates, Inc.), Vol. 235, No. 6, September 4, 1982, pp. 181-83.*

KLAUS ENSSLEN

The Third Life of Grange Copeland takes the adult life of its title character as the historical delimitation of its fictional action, roughly comprising three generations from the 1920's to the peak of the Civil Rights movement in the early 1960's (as marked by systematic black voters' registration, freedom marches and the first struggles for school integration). Half a century of family history is the narrative material used by the novel to dramatize essential changes in the conditions of black people in the rural South of the United States, beginning in total economic and psychological dependence and moving towards a certain measure of self-awareness as the ground for new self concepts and the social roles or life-plans based on them. Grange Copeland as a young man sets out, like millions of black men before him, with the socially propagated illusion that he will be able to provide a home and the necessary subsistence for himself and his attractive wife Margaret via his labor as a sharecropper in the heart of Georgia. Quite soon the efficient system of exploitation by manipulation of debt and wage cutting . . . begins to close its grip on Grange Copeland. He stops fighting the decay of dilapidated cabins unworthy of human habitation, he seeks escape from the total drain of physical energy and an overwhelming sense of helplessness in the arms of Josie, a prostitute he has known from before his marriage. He totally neglects his wife who after an initial phase of apathy begins to protest against this treatment by craving dissipation for herself, not disdaining even the white boss Shipley, and ends up giving birth to a second son obviously fathered by a white man, half-brother to her first child Brownfield (whose name graphically reflects the hopelessness of his parents). In spite of his basically unchanged affection for his wife, Grange, under the burden of his psychological humiliation and economic defeat goes through the inevitable escalation of violent quarreling and withdrawal and finally resorts to the classical escape of the black man denied any options for responsible action. Grange disappears, Margaret a few weeks later poisons herself and her younger child, leaving the 15-year-old Brownfield who under constant neglect has become so hard-boiled that he instinctively evades Shipley's effort to tie him to the soil and sets out on his own. (pp. 191-92)

Grange Copeland as the explicit central character of the novel dramatizes essential parts of the collective experience of his group. His answer to the total subjugation and discouragement on the economic level by an overpowering, cynical and hypocritical white world is an unshakable moral judgment—expressed at the beginning of the novel by Grange's avoiding to meet the eyes of his oppressor Shipley—a symbolic gesture of non-cooperation and masked contempt of long standing in Afro-American literature (frequently to be met with in the fugitive slave narratives of the 19th century). Grange's calm contempt for the white man's norms—interrupted only temporarily by his rebellious rage in the Harlem phase of his second life—contrasts sharply with Brownfield's attitude whose self-destructive hatred stamps him as a total victim of white domination. Grange and Brownfield are set up as contrasting figures embodying diametrically opposed options for the black man under white supremacy. Grange's flight from the sharecropper's condition is destructive towards his family, but not with regard to his own person: It turns self-aggression into the more constructive act of resistance against the norms of the South and initiates a learning process as prerequisite for a positive self-concept.

In New York Grange gets to know extensively the form of discrimination specific to the urban North, i.e. the exclusion of black people through ignoring them—Ellison's metaphor of invisibility is pointedly taken up by the text. . . . Grange . . . [finally returns] to the South where racial antagonism seems more honest to him in its personal virulence than in the impersonal undermining of self-esteem up North. His aloof retirement to his own land (even at the price of purposeful exploitation of a black woman) and his full dedication to [his youngest daughter] Ruth's education are signal acts of indi-

vidual independence from the dominant culture. It is true that Grange Copeland tends to view his social and moral separatism as a relic of past times, as soon as he is faced with the moral enthusiasm of black and white Civil Rights workers. But from the perspective of post-Civil Rights developments (both as seen in 1970 or in 1980) Grange's independent stance and tough scepticism as to possible changes in the minds of America's white citizens gains new relevance as part of the symbolic action of the novel.

At the same time, however, Grange Copeland as an heroic individual embodying the will to resist and to claim an autonomous base of living must raise serious problems with regard to representative group experience. Both his positive enhancement and its counterpart, Brownfield's negative demonization, result from a reduction of their fictional motivation to individual moral traits. Grange's unlimited ability for individual growth and accumulated insight, the same as Brownfield's progressive moral and practical disintegration, serve as contrasting foils to explicate individual worth or unworthiness. Brownfield in particular is a fictional character totally determined by his function as thematic contrast: The author moves him close to the stock figure of the gothic villain, when Brownfield finds pleasure in pouring poison into streams, or when he gloats (in an account to Josie) over the memory of how he deliberately exposed his last-born child to freeze to death while he himself enjoyed a particularly good night's sleep. Just as Brownfield's moral fiber seems unaffected by the collective suffering surrounding him, Grange's individual strength and improved self-image is largely unconnected to any collective culture or experience, neither deriving from them its sustenance nor flowing back into them as a reinvigorating force. Grange is always shown in terms of an individual consciousness struggling for self-assertion, never as part of a community of people with common aspirations. Yet he participates in group-specific networks—the rural and urban "tenderloin," i.e. amusement district, in his first and second life; the sale of moonshine whisky and cardplaying in his third life, used as a means of getting money towards a dowry for Ruth—collective areas of experience with a wealth of black folklore and the implications belonging to such cultural substrata. In contrast, however, to a view of cultural milieus as shaping and maintaining group cohesion which we get in texts like *The Autobiography of Malcolm X* (1965) or even in Wright's late novel written in exile *The Long Dream* (1958), Alice Walker's novel does not try to bring those factors to the fore of its fictional world. Similarly, when Grange is said to delve into the history of his people by reading all he can in New York, this remains clearly an ascription of an educationally or intellectually enlightening experience—it never gains the status of a revolutionizing reorientation from the survival strategy of a hustler to the collectively meaningful perspective of conscious dedication to a common goal. . . . (pp. 194-97)

Grange, among the characters on his semantic axis, is privileged in being the only one capable of accumulating wisdom and self-assurance—traits of his moral character he hopes to see brought to an as yet unheard of flowering in Ruth. The solidarity between Grange and Ruth (somewhat onesided and precarious, as it must appear) might be taken as at least partly overcoming the repression of black men and black women. Yet for its continuation it would depend on the dream of individual moral perfectibility in a restored or healed society—a dream that circumvents the central fact of sexuality in the relationship of black men and women. Thus the symbolic action of the novel can be said to release male-female solidarity as a model only on a plane of dream fantasy sharply removed from social options. When Grange experiences a kind of Rip-van-Winkle sensation in his confrontation with the vision of the Civil Rights workers—shown as resplendent apparitions of a new age and society—this motif makes explicit Grange's instinctive groping for a concrete utopia similar to the expectations of the Civil Rights era—the only context in which Ruth might be imagined as coming into her own, both as a person and a woman.

Such a vision (implied in Grange's individual attempt at autonomy, and made explicit in Civil Rights optimism) tends to exclude the majority of rural blacks in Grange's world who cannot afford personal intellectual and moral growth the way he does as the sum of a lifetime. With Mem, the mass of black people in the fictional world of *The Third Life of Grange Copeland* are kept prisoners in the anonymous culture of poverty, a community of stigmatized victims reinforcing their socially dictated dependence by holding back individual members via the classical crab-basket effect (group cohesion to prevent the escape of privileged individuals). These are the assumptions behind Brownfield's and Josie's patterns of action, and at some points in the text they become tangible in key situations (e.g. Josie and Mem not fighting their being pushed back into dependence). Grange, on the other hand, accumulates strength by escaping the conditions of his group rather than by an act of reinterpretation of a collective situation. This can be demonstrated in the way he puts to use inalienable parts of the cultural heritage of his group: In his angry Harlem phase Grange absorbs Uncle Remus folklore and collective history by reading, not via an oral tradition which would imply participation in rituals of collective memory and communicative reenactment. This group lore is then handed on to Ruth in a personal relationship excluding group participation—one could say in an ethically justified private space which while teaching a member of the young generation conclusions from the group experience, at the same time guarantees a splendid isolation of grandchild and grandfather. The 'lifting' of group lore to a morally purified realm is even more apparent in Grange's teaching Ruth to dance at home—the context of the black "tenderloin" as a communication subsystem of the group including its counter-white-protestant-ethic standards and sexual implications has been bowdlerized into a domesticated and respectable family realm and constellation. By extension, folk culture and experience through Grange's example is awarded an enlightening and constructive function only after being filtered by the reflected and consciously political appropriation of a militant individual consciousness—a function it apparently is not granted in its original context of group enactment.

The underlying point of reference for such a perspective is the axiomatic concept of an "inviolate sanctuary" of the individual soul, i.e. of an inherent worth or unworth of the individual and his moral substance. . . . The ignoring and underrating of group culture and community results in attributing collective insights into the norms of the white world, or the defensive code of the black group, to individual perception (mostly that of Grange as over-life-size impersonator of group experience). On the aphoristic level this comes through in Grange's aside "'Course the rumor is that they *is* people, but the funny part is why they don't act human'" (where Grange adopts the moral judgment and verbal stance of an unmistakably collective way of perception). With more fictional emphasis a reaction of racial group pride is attributed to Ruth at school: Shocked by a racist school book adorned with the murderous comments of a white fellow student, she challenges her teacher, gets an

evasive reaction and storms out of class cursing teacher, class and school system. This incident is presented as further proof for Ruth's moral courage and individual substance (she had already called her father a "son-a-bitch" when a small child), and she is shown as being completely alone in her class in mobilizing this sort of resistance, the rest of the students and the teacher remaining passive and subdued. Ruth's hatred in conjunction with her moral character automatically assumes moral worth and is seen as a token of strength—while Brownfield's hatred, lacking the required individual substance, is programmatically stigmatized by Grange and subsumed under his moral weakness. . . . (pp. 202-05)

Grange's violent end serves to complement the novel's central normative axis of individual moral worth: It springs from his manichean battle against the abject moral worthlessness of Brownfield, a demonic and destructive force which merely summons forth the additional support of the judicial system of the American South at the novel's end. Grange's main enemy, however, is the threat of thwarted moral growth, in himself as in others. While Brownfield uses white racism as an excuse for his individual moral decay, Grange has used it as crystallizing point for his moral rebirth—both processes, however, are seen in the context of the fictional world of *The Third Life* as options the individual is responsible for. Group cohesion, group culture or group knowledge remain at best at the periphery of this struggle for heroic self-realization or pathetic self-destruction—they are not seen as constituting factors in the individual's search for identity. (p. 206)

[In *The Third Life*] Alice Walker can be said to have attempted a kind of encompassing imaginative empathy with the world of the Southern black sharecropper giving due weight to the ubiquitous presence of physical and psychic violence and its burdening effect on the human capacity for self-expression. The deterioration of Mem's educated language under the onslaught of a brutal husband and situation is only the most explicit illustration of a perspective of hopelessness and its concomitant threat of inarticulateness, just as Grange's capacity for cumulative learning is meant to buttress Ruth's claim to more self-realization including self-articulation. (Compared to her Margaret remains inarticulate, Mem gains only a desperate spurt of self-expression, and Josie illustrates the attrition of a latent vague yearning for self-projection). But here again, whether for reasons of didactic emphasis or because of a more bitter vision of life resting on personal experience and temperament, Alice Walker chose to present a stark contrast in her novel between the general conditions of living of rural blacks as a collective group and the concrete utopia of an unusually privileged individual among them. While the author may claim that her first novel represents (as the gift of lonely exploration) "a radical vision of society or one's people that has not previously been taken into account," and is not necessarily fit "to second the masses' motions, whatever they are" [i.e. to encourage temporarily dominant aspirations of a given group], Alice Walker in *The Third Life* without doubt still falls short of what she has herself indicated as her over-all goal: "I am trying to arrive at that place where black music already is; to arrive at that unselfconscious sense of collective oneness; that naturalness, that (even when anguished) grace." In Alice Walker's eyes, only Zora Neale Hurston among her predecessors can be said to have captured this quality in the medium of narrative prose, being "so at ease with her blackness" that she could "capture the beauty of rural black expression" and saw "poetry" where others merely saw incorrect English. Of Hurston's major novel *Their Eyes Were Watching God* (1937)

Alice Walker said: "There is enough self-love in that one book—love of community, culture, traditions—to restore a world. Or create a new one."

Measured by this criterion, Walker's first novel only adumbrates the creation of a new world for black men and women on the basis of the destruction of an outlived, insupportable old world in which violence and hate dominated in external conditions as well as in the consciousness of black people. Stopping the self-destruction of black men and women and beginning a process of constructive self-renewal, on a personal as well as a family level, is the novel's thematic proposal. In Ruth's burgeoning expectations the tentatively reconstructed black family would of course call for complementation of the precarious partnership of grandfather and granddaughter by a new relationship of black men and women in general. How this new black family based on new black men and women might become reintegrated into the culture and community of the black group, remains elusive in Alice Walker's first novel. . . . The "sense of collective oneness" inherent in black music—and this must be said with due respect to the novel's creative achievement—is barely yet in sight, let alone within reach of attainment at the close of the symbolic action of *The Third Life of Grange Copeland.* (pp. 215-16)

> *Klaus Ensslen, "Collective Experience and Individual Responsibility: Alice Walker's 'The Third Life of Grange Copeland',"* in *The Afro-American Novel Since 1960,* edited by Peter Bruck and Wolfgang Karrer *(© 1982, B. R. Grüner Publishing Co.), Grüner, 1982, pp. 189-218.*

ELIZABETH BARTELME

In this arresting and touching novel [*The Color Purple*], Alice Walker creates a woman so believable, so lovable, that Celie, the downtrodden, semi-literate, rural black woman joins a select company of fictional women whom it is impossible to forget. (p. 93)

Alice Walker is, of course, a feminist and she understands well the circumstances that force a woman into an anti-man stance. Her gallery of women are living examples of man's inhumanity to women: Sophia, wife of Harpo, Albert's eldest son, who only wanting to be herself and not the fantasy woman Harpo thinks she ought to be, changes from a warm, happy woman to a bitter paranoic who only wants to get through her life without killing anyone. Mary Alice, "Squeak," who takes Sophia's place with Harpo when the latter is jailed for sassing the mayor's wife (white), and who allows her uncle, the warden to rape her in exchange for Sophia's freedom. Even Shug, the indomitable, has her share of suffering at men's hands. Only Nettie . . . seems to have escaped the general mayhem, and she is a curiously colorless character. Her letters, by comparison with Celie's, are pedantic, her nature prim. The other women leap out of the book, Nettie stays safely within its confines, as does her husband, Samuel.

But Alice Walker is too much of an artist to write a purely political novel, and so her feminist impulse does not prevent her from allowing her characters, women and men, to grow and change. The men in her story lead miserable lives, too, but like their women they begin to come to terms with what life doles out to them, and accept it. And the women turn from rage to acceptance as well. One of the best scenes in the book occurs as Mr. —— and Celie sit sewing on the front porch, old now and calm together, and talking about the lessons life has taught them. Albert tells her he has learned to wonder, to wonder about all the things that happen and "the more I wonder, he say, the more I love.

"And people start to love you back, I bet, I say.

"They do, he say, surprise. Harpo seem to love me. Sophia and the children . . ."

They go on sewing and talking and waiting for Shug to come home, and Celie says to herself, "If she come, I be happy. If she don't, I be content.

"And then I figure this the lesson I was supposed to learn."

And so bitterness leaches out into a hard-won wisdom, and the lively characters of Alice Walker's invention become human beings with a life of their own. She is a remarkable novelist, sometimes compared to Toni Morrison, but with a strong, individual voice and vision of her own, and a delicious humor that pervades the book and tempers the harshness of the lives of its people.

Opening with a dedication to the Spirit, the novel ends with a postscript: "I thank everybody in this book for coming. A. W., author and medium." This reader's thanks to the medium; may she call up hosts in the future. (pp. 93-4)

> *Elizabeth Bartelme, "Victory over Bitterness,"* in Commonweal *(copyright © 1983 Commonweal Publishing Co., Inc.; reprinted by permission of Commonweal Publishing Co., Inc.), Vol. CX, No. 3, February 11, 1983, pp. 93-4.*

Martin Walser

1927-

West German novelist, dramatist, essayist, and short story writer.

Although Walser has not achieved significant international recognition, in Germany his literary stature is considerable. In 1981 he received the Georg-Büchner prize—a prize awarded to authors who have made meaningful contributions to the contemporary culture of Germany.

Walser's early plays, notably *Eiche und Angora* (1962; *The Rabbit Race*), and novels show his concern with the post-World War II German society. He is highly critical of the German tendency to forget the past, and of the effect the postwar "economic miracle" is having on contemporary life.

His more recent works, including *Ein fliehendes pferd* (1978; *Runaway Horse*) and *Das Schwanenhaus* (1980; *The Swan Villa*), while still retaining critical commentary on German society, have expanded in thematic content to include Walser's growing preoccupation with the difficulty of differentiating between truth and fiction, memory and reality, and language and experience.

(See also *Contemporary Authors*, Vols. 57-60 and *Contemporary Authors New Revision Series*, Vol. 8.)

T. C. WORSLEY

German writer Martin Walser, takes a sharply satirical view of the mentality of his people [in his play **"The Rabbit Race"**].

The first half is a pretty broad swipe at the home-front Nazis as the war ends in 1945. Their chief anxiety is to find a formula by which they can save both their own town and their own skins from the advance of the Allies.

However, in the second half the town's simpleton emerges as the chief figure of the play. His Communism had earned him a spell in a concentration camp under the Nazis and there he had been both indoctrinated with the party philosophy, and unmanned in a medical experiment, for which he had volunteered.

Now that peace reigns in 1950 and the Nazis have returned to civilian life, this simpleton had become the town's pet. . . .

But the town pet suddenly becomes the town pest when, at a local ceremony celebrating the peaceful spirit of the new Germany, he makes the unpardonable gaffe of spouting Nazi philosophies and praising the Führer. He is hustled off hastily to the asylum.

It takes the psychiatrists 10 years to undoctrinate him. By the time he comes out it is 1960 and the wretched creature fails to fit in once again, for now it is he who is talking pacifism while the rest of his country is busy rearming. And it's the asylum again for him.

> *T. C. Worsley, "Satire on Germans Given at Edinburgh," in* The New York Times (© *1963 by The*

New York Times Company; reprinted by permission), August 23, 1963, p. 39.

CLIFFORD HANLEY

In *The Rabbit Race* Martin Walser has constructed a pageant of German hypocrisy during and after the Nazi era. (p. 231)

Mr. Walser . . . has something strong and genuine to say; he . . . might say it with more force in fewer words. It does occur to me that the heavy hammer-blows in which the Message is battered home may be a matter of national rhythm, and that this play, designed to rend the complacency of German audiences, might well have needed its grim ponderous pace in that context. But to a British audience—or any non-German audience—which takes so much of that particular Message for granted (we too are complacent in this) the lesson hardly needs so many verses. (p. 232)

> *Clifford Hanley, "Big Deals," in* The Spectator (© *1963 by* The Spectator; *reprinted by permission of* The Spectator), *Vol. 211, No. 7052, August 23, 1963, pp. 231-32.**

THE TIMES LITERARY SUPPLEMENT

In his earlier novels, short stories and plays Herr Martin Walser was preoccupied with social criticism, though the vehemence of that criticism sometimes suggested that his real quarrel was not so much with the west Germany of the *Wirtschaftswunder,* or indeed with any specific social and economic set-up, as with the depravity and conformism of anybody, anywhere, who was prepared to play the power game. His novels *Ehen in Philippsburg [Marriage in Philippsburg]* (1957) and *Halbzeit [Half Time]* (1960) were powerful and brilliant in parts, but they were less satisfactory as works of art than some of the short stories in his first book, *Ein Flugzeug über dem Haus* [1955].

In many respects Herr Walser's new novel [*Das Einhorn (The Unicorn)*] is even more ambitious than its two predecessors. The hero and narrator, Anselm Kristlein, has been taken over from *Halbzeit,* just as Beumann has been taken over from *Ehen in Philippsburg;* but the main emphasis has been shifted from social satire to a number of themes that are closer to Herr Walser's dominant concerns. . . .

The analysis of love, of different varieties of love, is only one of the themes that hold this book together. The unicorn of the title is symbolic not only of the erotically questing male, but also of the outsider—among other things. Kristlein's exploration of love is organically related to his social status and his ambitions as a writer. Since he is at once writing a book and presenting the raw material for the book, another principal theme is the discrepancy between truth and fiction, experience and memory. It is this discrepancy that defeats Kristlein, but gives Herr Walser ample scope for a critique both of love and of fiction. His sketches of the *Wirtschaftswunder* and its accompanying *Kulturwunder* are more devastating than ever in this larger context. . . . Though Herr Walser has found a distinct manner in this book, at once rich and vigorous, expressive and ironic, some of his verbalizing does tend to obscure the narrative line. . . .

Das Einhorn is by far the most successful of Herr Walser's major works to date, because all his remarkable gifts have been applied to a structure large and intricate enough to accommodate them. . . . Kristlein's final self-estrangement has to do with his failure to make the past and the present coalesce; and this failure suggests the need for a further development not only in his personal relations but also in the novel's analysis of love and, incidentally, of memory. Herr Walser has written a passionately truthful account of certain stages of love, but Kristlein's reticences about his married life mark its limits and its limitations.

> *"Varieties of Love," in* The Times Literary Supplement *(© Times Newspapers Ltd. (London) 1966; reproduced from* The Times Literary Supplement *by permission), No. 3367, September 8, 1966, p. 800.*

RUDOLF WALTER LEONHARDT

After the tightly constructed *Ehen in Philippsburg* and the amorphous, arbitrary *Halbzeit, Das Einhorn* comes as a happy combination of freedom and self-control. (p. 54)

Walser's "*Unicorn*" can be seen as a challenge to the Proustian attempt to regain the past through recollection: a dismal way to have again what was lost, Anselm Kristlein, the hero, muses in mockery of himself. Memory is the electricity of the brain, it is accidental, it is—nothing.

Anselm Kristlein, whom some readers will remember as the traveling salesman of "**Half-Time,**" is lying in bed and remembering. This is what the book is about. What happens then—and a great deal does happen—must always be referred back to Anselm Kristlein in bed: a bedtime story, if you like. . . .

The story originates from the commission by a Swiss lady publisher to aspiring-writer Kristlein to delineate precisely the act of love, and so rescue love from the clutches of the sexologists. His assignment is to depict love as it really is, without, however, losing its special quality. The lady believes in this special quality; Kristlein does not.

So Anselm begins—with his memories. . . . And although we learn a great deal about life in high society, about panel shows, about new impediments to writing the truth—love has not appeared. . . . (pp. 54-5)

Then an event occurs which shatters the comfortable, ironic pose of the intellectual, and so destroys his ability to record and analyze while remaining detached. Kristlein meets Orli. . . . Studies of sex procedure will not help here; neither will clinical observation. Nor will Orli be encompassed by irony, no matter how subtle. A new level of expressiveness is required and a troubling question is brought up: can the inadequacy of language in the face of reality be demonstrated without the suspicion arising that the fault is not in the narrator-demonstrator, but in the writer himself?

Walser's style, which is the result of the kind of storyteller he is, also creates difficulties. Walser's way of depicting a situation is to bombard it with words. Many of these words were obviously put down because one brought the next one to mind. Therefore, he is continually being advised to edit himself more strictly. . . .

I think that this is at least partly a misunderstanding. Walser would not be Walser if he let himself be prodded into the kind of spare writing characteristic of a Max Frisch novel. He is not mainly concerned with "hitting the mark" with words; he is more interested in the desire and torment that accompany both hitting and missing. (pp. 55-6)

Walser tries to use language that falls somewhere between the writing of Hermann Hesse and Henry Miller to tell about love. Obviously he is not going to succeed all the time.

But his Anselm Kristlein does not merely admit failure, he is in despair over it, and this seems a little exaggerated. He is really not doing as badly as all that. The climax of the story is only possible because the narrator cannot be content with the range of expression of his own language. . . .

"**The Unicorn**" is not the kind of book, as with Dickens or Balzac, that mirrors and exposes the society from which it comes. Reality here is both broader and narrower than this—as in the works of Sterne, Joyce and Proust. This book is about the reality of consciousness, of the pain that is in remembering and in forgetting, of the attempt to regain what is hopelessly lost. (p. 56)

> *Rudolf Walter Leonhardt, in a review of "Das Einhorn" (originally published under a different title in* Die Zeit, 1966), in Atlas, the Magazine of the World Press *(© 1967 copyright by The World Press Company), Vol. 13, No. 1, January, 1967, pp. 54-6.*

DONALD F. NELSON

Martin Walser is a curious example of a contemporary novelist who, despite more than a decade of prolific writing, has failed to gain appreciable recognition from Germany's literary critics. . . . There are two aspects of Walser's work that appear to disturb critics most: his apparent lack of concern for plot and for integration of detail into a unified whole, and his failure to present anything like a constructive alternative to the hypercritical and devastating picture he paints of postwar German society. With regard to the latter, it is true that Walser has not arrived at a synthesis of satire and the vision of a positive moral philosophy which has contributed in large measure to Heinrich Böll's success. But a criticism leveled at the lack of architecture in Walser's works which, from the point of view of traditional poetic theory, is their most vulnerable aspect, fails to do justice to the author, inasmuch as it overlooks the real literary merit of the work: the unity of style and subject. . . .

[Walser] shapes language into an apt idiom for his principal theme—the breakdown of social communication and the depersonalization of human behavior—and also for the undifferentiated character of the world he depicts. My focus is on the way language is used to express a particular quality of experience and perception. My observations are restricted to two prose works: *Die Ehen in Philippsburg* and *Halbzeit*. The breakdown of social communication, the depersonalization, leveling and stereotyping of human behavior, the increasing emphasis on the artifact—the most crucial aspects of our contemporary cultural crisis as Walser perceives it—are given symbolic representation in the details of his language use. (p. 204)

The breakdown of genuine communication in society involves a crisis of language. In his attitude toward language Walser is an adamant realist. . . . All of his attacks on contemporary language stem from the conviction that language has degenerated into a vast repertoire of formulas. . . . In short, language no longer corresponds to reality or to truth. This iconoclastic attitude toward conventional language occasionally finds expression bordering on nihilism. (p. 205)

In Walser's first novel, *Die Ehen in Philippsburg* (1957), the neophyte hero pays for his acceptance and integration into society by forfeiting both his individuality and his freedom. The protagonist, Hans Beumann, is in many ways a twentieth-century Parzival who succeeds in his struggle to be accepted by carefully observing and appropriating, through mimicry, the social behavior of the cocktail party set. . . . [The novel] is a satirical and scathing condemnation of postwar German society with its stereotyped language and behavior. Here the problems of communication and depersonalization are no longer treated on the abstract level of parabie, as in the early collection of stories, *Flugzeug über dem Haus* (1955); they are presented as symptoms of a cultural crisis. Now the problem is not primarily a lack of communication with a mute or apathetic environment reminiscent of Kafka, but rather that communication has become impersonal and stereotyped, devitalized by the ready-made phrase, just as human behavior has become depersonalized, undifferentiated, and stereotyped by mimicry and by set forms of gesture in social intercourse. A general social and cultural leveling is the result.

This depersonalization and leveling finds expression in certain recurrent linguistic traits: 1) the frequent use of an inanimate or impersonal subject in place of an animate or personal one; very often this takes the form of a *pars pro toto* in which a part of the body stands for the person; 2) the use of anaphoric or repetitive constructions; and 3) the preponderance of indirect discourse over direct discourse. The recurrence of these traits underscores the impersonality of communication and the depersonalization of the individual in a society that is distinctly

object-oriented, stressing the artifacts of its culture to the virtual exclusion of all human and personal values. (pp. 205-06)

It is not insignificant that indirect discourse or the absence of dialogue prevails over long tracts of Walser's prose. To cite one statistic: the entire novel consists roughly of 11,000 lines, of which only 450 or somewhat less than five percent are dialogue. This is all the more conspicuous in a novel in which social gatherings have such a large share in the plot. It is as though indirect discourse were the ironic insinuation that in an object-oriented society what people actually say is of no importance. In a world in which, in addition to the stereotyping of gesture and external appearance, speech has become largely standardized jargon and a genuine dialogue of mutual exchange and edification is virtually nonexistent, the functionality of direct discourse becomes restricted. When direct discourse does occur, it takes on the nature of a tiny island of dialogue surrounded by a vast ocean of impersonal and undifferentiated communication. Rather than exploiting dialogue as a means of revealing human inanities and foibles, Walser concentrates on externals, on physiognomy and gesture, which he analyzes with extreme and merciless precision. (p. 207)

[Mimicry] plays a central role in Walser's world. In the biological sense mimicry is the superficial resemblance which certain animals exhibit to other animals or to the natural objects of their environment, thereby securing concealment or protection. Applied to Walser's social world, mimicry means an expedient adjustment to the exigencies of the situation by wearing the prescribed face, by executing the prescribed gesture, and by saying the prescribed ready-made phrase. Mimicry is thus a most powerful force in causing a depersonalization and standardization of social communication and social behavior. In mimicry the individual simulates the form of his surroundings with the result that the world becomes undifferentiated in character. Hans Beumann, in his process of adaptation, develops into the adroit mimic and liar, deceiving his fiancée, Anne Volkmann, by pursuing extramural amorous adventures that brand him as a future adulterer. These acquired characteristics in a predominantly mimetic environment along with his forfeiture of individuality and freedom are the price he must pay for his ultimate acceptance into the social clique.

Halbzeit (1960) is the organic outgrowth of and sequel to *Die Ehen in Philippsburg,* both in plot and ideas. The hero, Anselm Kristlein, is an experienced and established Hans Beumann. He has become the inveterate mimic whose rise from traveling salesman to professional adman culminates in his becoming the "chosen one" to travel to New York, the Mecca of the admen. Here he is to learn the art of creating psychological obsolescence in commercial products for the purpose of creating new and artificial needs for the consumer. (pp. 210-11)

In *Halbzeit* the world of commercial advertising is the immense conditioning apparatus, manipulator, and leveler of human thought, language, and behavior. No other single force, Walser asserts, not even politics, has had such an impact on language as have business and public relations. This gigantic empire which holds such unprecedented sway over communication is the chief fashioner and dictator of the style of life in the postwar German society of the "economic miracle." Germany, Walser insinuates, has merely passed from the totalitarian dictatorship of National Socialism to the dictatorship of public relations philosophy and tactics. In fact, in *Halbzeit* many former high-ranking Nazis are participants in a huge advertising campaign aimed at brainwashing and conquering the consumer and making the incredible credible by adroit propaganda. The deep ramifications and unhappy consequences of this new style of life, its impact on communication and social behavior—this is what Walser strives to portray in his mammoth epic.

In *Halbzeit* the world unrolls before us like a perpetual series of television commercials and magazine ads. For a better appreciation of this technique we might imagine ourselves, for example, viewing television and witnessing on the screen nothing more than one commercial after another without interruption, or glancing through a magazine and finding nothing but advertisements on every page. Two things would become strikingly obvious to the critical observer: first, the disconnected, fragmentary, and stereotyped nature of the world depicted and of the communication taking place in it, and second, the exaggerated emphasis on the object. Television commercials and magazine advertisements tend generally to stress the object, the artifact. Parts of the body assume exaggerated importance. Camera close-ups focus attention on a particular part of the body: the hair, eyes, teeth, hands, and legs. The ironic paradox of the advertisement is that while it pretends to endow the object (human or artifact) with individuality and distinction, it actually makes a stereotype of it. The subject is depersonalized and transformed into an object. This is often the perspective from which Kristlein perceives the human objects in his environment. . . . (pp. 211-12)

So far-reaching and all-pervasive are the effects of commercialism as the dictator of the contemporary style of life that in *Halbzeit* all naturalness and genuineness of emotion and gesture have vanished. To a far more radical degree than Hans Beumann, Anselm Kristlein is dependent on mimicry in adapting himself to society and to life. Mimicry has become second nature to him, having evolved to the stage where it is the expression of the instinct for self-preservation. In one reference after another to a facial expression or to a mood Walser stresses their artificial and rehearsed character, usually by means of a verb which either denotes or implies artifice. . . . (pp. 212-13)

The competitiveness of the struggle for survival in the economic jungle is transferred to the social plane in the episode in which Walser depicts a grand social reception at the sumptuous villa of Herr Frantzke, the advertising magnate. Kristlein fully realizes that here amidst the pomp, luxury, and outward civility the Darwinian theory of natural selection and survival of the fittest is operative. (p. 213)

Walser is averse to all poetic embellishment in his description of the external world of inanimate objects. (p. 214)

In terms of language use and syntax, Walser's style is the correlate of the world he portrays: a world devoid of articulation, individuality, and substance. But it is not merely description which perpetually remains arrested in surface detail. In his intensive and burrowing psychological analysis Walser probes the very depths of a mimetic world in which truth is never on the surface of things, but is inward and concealed. (p. 215)

> *Donald F. Nelson, "The Depersonalized World of Martin Walser," in* The German Quarterly *(copyright © 1969 by the American Association of Teachers of German), Vol. XLII, No. 1, January, 1969, pp. 204-16.*

GERTRUD BAUER PICKAR

Walser's first novel, *Ehen in Philippsburg,* is often dismissed as the work of a novice and generally passed over in discussions of his other novels, *Halbzeit* and *Das Einhorn.* The reason for its exclusion is the apparent lack of similarity of this initial novel to his later works: it is narrated continually in the third person singular; there is no interplay of fictional levels which in subsequent novels is related to the use of the first person; the portrayal of character and plot lacks the complexity and ambiguity of the later works. Closer examination, however, reveals that features which are dominant in the other two novels are prefigured in *Philippsburg.* This work contains tentative indications of techniques which are to become characteristic of the following novels and incorporates devices which later reappear in variant forms.

This is true of the literary features related to narrative perspective to be discussed here: first, the use of fictional levels; second, the narration in first, second, and third person; third, the multiple personality, and fourth, the formularization of time. These features of Walser's three novels will be considered in this study, and an attempt will be made to evaluate the impact of their individual development upon the form and nature of the works.

Although *Philippsburg,* as noted above, lacks an interplay of fictional levels, it does exhibit narrative complexity. A changing perspective is created as each of the succeeding central figures becomes the focal point of the narrative. Parts one and four are told from Beumann's point of view, the second from Benrath's, the third from Alwin's. Each of these figures is observed, his exterior behavior is described, and his thoughts and feelings are revealed. However, despite the fact that the segments are narrated from the three different perspectives provided by the chief participants, continuity is maintained. The chronological sequence is preserved throughout and the stories of the different protagonists dovetail. Since no qualitative changes are induced by the shifting of focus, no discrepancies occur in the depiction of character and personality.

As in *Philippsburg,* the variation of narrative perspective in *Halbzeit* is related to the basic structure of the work. Here, however, it does not reflect a change in the lead person, as in the first novel, but stems rather from Anselm Kristlein's dual role. Anselm is both protagonist and ostensible narrator. His activities as protagonist provide the thematic content of the work. His account of the work's composition and his creative motivation is superimposed upon the narrative and furnishes the frame. Together they constitute a double perspective for viewing the events and experiences presented in the novel.

In the recollection of events of the past in *Halbzeit,* Anselm Kristlein as a fictional figure and Anselm as the presumptive narrator merge and function as one individual; in the presentation of the events of the fictional present, which comprises the narrative proper, the two Anselms often separate. This precipitates an alternation in narrative person and emphasizes the inherent duality of the novel's perspective.

The inclusion of Alissa's diary entries of the years preceding the opening of the novel provides a significant contrast to the detailed account of Anselm's day which it follows. It differs markedly in time span and in style and tone of formulation and places his day in a broadened context. More significantly, its depiction of the Anselm-Alissa relationship from her point of view echoes the multiperspective structural format of *Philippsburg.* The diary, however, offers the only variation of this kind in *Halbzeit,* and it marks the last appearance in Walser's novels of this device which was so extensively employed in his first one.

The use of hypothetical elements, on the other hand, has a quite different development. The often startling imagery which characterizes the presentation of Beumann's thoughts in *Philippsburg* prefigures the broader narrative breadth which the hypothetical is given in *Halbzeit.*

Anselm's flight of fancy, the frequent hypothetical incidents, and the projected scenes constitute a fictitious level, and one which is secondary to that of the main plot development. Besides providing stylistic variation, these products of the imagination, originating in the consciousness of the protagonist and revealed by the narrator, contrast with the fictional levels of the events of Anselm's life, related in the narrative. (pp. 48-9)

The complexity of the interdependence of these fictional planes is evident in the manifestations of the key relationship in *Halbzeit*—that of Anselm and Melitta. . . . There is an inherent difference between the Melitta of Anselm's experiences depicted in the novel and the Melitta of Anselm's memories and dreams who plays so large a role in the consciousness of the narrating Anselm. As the novel progresses, these discrepancies become increasingly apparent and lend narrative tension to the work. The inevitable confrontation between the two images of Melitta terminates this tension and precipitates the speedy resolution of the narrative threads.

Until the closing chapters of *Halbzeit,* the divergence in nature between the imaginary, or literary, realities created by the consciousness of the narrating Anselm and the events and incidents in which he is depicted as protagonist subliminally accompany the development of the novel. In *Einhorn,* such disparities have become basic to theme, material, and structure. This work is formulated upon the interplay of three fictional levels—constituted by the present, the remembered past, and the fictitious, the last of which encompasses both the fantasies and those writings supposedly authored by the character Anselm.

The period of time which the narrator spends in bed and which he presumably utilizes for the composition of his novel constitutes the present time of the work. This established temporal perspective is maintained throughout. It furnishes a basis from which to view and appraise the other events and time experiences and serves as an anchorage point from which the narrator retreats into the past. It provides both a contrast for his memories and fantasies and a justification for his discourses on the nature of memory. The past, presented as it is recalled by the narrator, its events recorded in chronological order, constitutes the second level. It is used both to illuminate the present and to contrast with Anselm's endeavors at reconstituting both past and present in his writings. These writings and the fantasies of the narrating ego insert the fictitious into the novel and comprise the third fictional level of the work. The three levels, however, do not remain static in their relationship to one another. . . . The depiction of an event as a conscious literary exercise of Anselm's disrupts the established pattern of narration and indicates a new development, one which is continued as the novel progresses.

What is overt in the case of the summer party is covert in the Orli-story which unfolds in the second half of the book. In this story, the experiences of Anselm the protagonist, his memories, and his fantasies as narrator are often indistinguishable from one another. The Orli-story is both contrasted and blended with the elements of the frame and its depiction of Anselm's self-imposed confinement and marriage. At one point, Anselm as narrator playfully concludes the Orli-episodes with the confrontation of Orli and Birga, his wife, and then reveals this as a fantasy. The Orli-story is concluded several chapters later, precipitating the conclusion of the work, just as the resolution of the Melitta-*Erlebnis* brought *Halbzeit* to its end. The fact that the period of time encompassed by the narrated past begins to approach that of the fictional present tends to sustain the fusion of fictional levels accomplished during the resolution of the Orli-episode. The delineation of these levels is never clearly reestablished. Their realities have become relativized and ambiguous and the entire work takes on a highly subjective coloration.

A similar tendency is evident in the treatment of the narrative person. In Walser's first novel the angle of perspective remains the same, although the point of reference changes; in *Halbzeit* and *Einhorn* the orientation remains that of Anselm, but the perspective is doubled. Thus the distinct segments of *Philippsburg,* each devoted to a lead figure and related consistently in the third person, have been replaced by a narrative in the first person singular which modulates into the third person.

The obvious basis for this structural feature rests in the dual role of Anselm Kristlein. As both the novel's protagonist and its ostensible narrator, he appears in both third and first person. His activities provide the thematic content of the novel, and his account of his creative endeavors and their motivation supplies its structural format. The alternation in narrative person is thus an integral element of the work. It is involved in the organizational basis for the novel and furnishes stylistic interest as well, occurring as it does at times even within a single sentence. . . . (pp. 50-2)

The casual shifting from first to third person and its association with the double function of Anselm are secondary features in *Halbzeit.* They become primary elements of *Einhorn* and contribute to the format of the work, supporting Anselm's roles as presumptive author and protagonist in the work and as fictional figure in the incorporated writings of Anselm and Melanie, his would-be publisher. Here, too, the trend toward increased fictionalization and toward a fusing of previously defined areas is evident. . . . As the novel proceeds, the distinction in the use of person becomes blurred and is occasionally suspended. Switches in person are frequent. The first person slips into the third, the third into the first. (pp. 52-3)

Though the basis for the change in person is provided by the identification of the narrator with the novel's protagonist, its use within the novel is closely allied to that of the multiple personality, a structural and thematic feature which is recurrent in Walser's works and discussed in his theoretical writings as well. . . .

The multiple personality first enters into the novel series tentatively through the imagery of *Philippsburg.* Hans Beumann speaks of setting up a translator within himself to express his opinions in socially acceptable forms . . . ; he describes himself as having ten orchestras within his head which he, as sole conductor, must bring into harmony. . . .

In *Halbzeit* the feature of the multipersonality is further expanded. Anselm as narrator frequently records his inner conversations with himself. He even provides one specific aspect of his personality with independent name and character and introduces this figment of his imagination into the story of Galileo Cleverlein. Anselm uses him to rationalize his behavior and invests him with more "realistic" or calculating thinking—

or as Anselm prefers to view it, with more scientific vocabulary. Their relationship is clearly delineated in their verbal exchanges and furnishes a number of humorous interludes. (p. 53)

The multiple personality assumes major proportions in *Einhorn*. It is related both thematically to the various roles of Anselm and stylistically to the changing perspective. Its existential basis in Walser's view of the complexity of personality is revealed in numerous discussions and in imagery and phrases. (p. 54)

The development [of the multiple personality] . . . is internally related to the use of person and contributes to the progression in narrative complexity which marks the novels. Its effect supports their increasing subjectivity, a tendency also evident in the treatment of time.

Though the time span of the three works varies but little—all the novels cover less than a year—a clearly recognizable progression in the use of narrated time begins with *Ehen in Philippsburg*. A straightforward narrative in chronological sequence, it exhibits the least complex presentation of the time experience. The changes in perspective do not interfere with the chronology maintained throughout the entire novel as a single and continuous unit. . . . The only interruptions in the narrative flow are the excursuses into Klaff's writings and diary—a technique which Walser explores and exploits at length in *Halbzeit* and *Einhorn*.

In *Halbzeit*, the narration opens with Anselm's awakening and closes with his falling asleep. His release from the hospital at the outset and again at the end of the novel reenforces the previously evoked suggestion of the natural demarcation of birth and death. The events of the months, so encompassed, which are portrayed in the work, are presented in chronological sequence, as in *Philippsburg*. However, the progression of time is strikingly irregular. It is slowed into a depiction of the stream of consciousness and contains gaps, such as the weeks spent in America. Additional material drawn from beyond the temporal bounds of the narrative span is included. . . . The frame frequently intrudes into the narration, interrupting the temporal representation of the narrative. . . . The time flow is also suspended by flights of fancy and slowed down for detailed presentation of supplementary material. . . . However, neither these digressions nor the numerous hypothetical incidents and projected scenes or conversations interfere with the continuity of the story nor affect the impression of a chronological presentation.

In the last novel, time is no longer construed as a gentle flow in which the present slips into the past and the future into the present in an uninterrupted continuum, as it was portrayed in *Philippsburg* and to a lesser extent in *Halbzeit*. The three months of *Einhorn* assume a static nature; the incidents of the novel are not primarily spaced in time, nor developed or contrasted in a chronology, but are separated and related by the fictional level they present. Although there is a chronology within each of these levels in *Einhorn*, the interaction between them is so extensive that the chronology loses its significance. The interplay of the time strata implicit in these levels—the immediate present of the narrator's confinement to bed, the past as he recalls it, and the extratemporal events of his imagination and writings—becomes secondary. As a consequence, time loses its dominance as a structural feature and becomes an aspect of the novel's conceptual scheme. It has been internalized.

In a sense, the development evident in each of the narrative aspects discussed above is one of internalization. The structural aspects of the novels have become increasingly complex, perhaps also increasingly artificial, or at least increasingly focused upon the literary aspects of the work rather than upon textual ones. Time, figures, and events have been internalized by the literary work, relativized by their depiction and reconstruction, and subjectivized by the personalized narration. (pp. 54-6)

At the conclusion of *Einhorn*, the narrator's consciousness of the world, of events, persons, and emotions has replaced those events or persons as the substance of the novel. The novel is concerned with the narrator's view of the world he presents. Its events and figures become mixed and ultimately fused with his own formulations. . . .

Most appropriately Walser's latest narrative work . . . is entitled *Fiction*. Although it is not the anticipated novel which was to conclude the Kristlein series, it does develop the tendency toward the abstract and emphasizes the fictional and even fictitious basis of a literary work. (p. 56)

> *Gertrud Bauer Pickar, "Narrative Perspective in the Novels of Martin Walser" (originally a paper presented at the Irvine MLA German 5 Conference in April, 1970), in* The German Quarterly *(copyright © 1971 by the American Association of Teachers of German), Vol. XLIV, No. 1, January, 1971, pp. 48-57.*

DIETHER H. HAENICKE

Martin Walser's . . . novels mirror German society of the fifties and early sixties. *Marriage in Philippsburg* (1957) is a conventionally narrated novel depicting the social climb of a young man into the "high society" of a small German city. *Half Time* (1960) and *The Unicorn* (1966) are more cutting in their critique of the conditions in prosperous postwar Germany. In style essentially more complicated, they show Walser's obvious effort to pattern his hero, at least to some extent, after himself. Both novels have the same protagonist, Anselm Kristlein, who in *Half Time,* thanks to his gift of articulation, reaches the position of public relations manager for a large concern and obtains entry into the upper echelon of society. Here Walser especially attacks verbal clichés, as well as the hollowness of the roles most people play. In *Unicorn* Kristlein has become a writer commissioned by a woman publisher to write a work of non-fiction on love. Walser's critique of social conditions continues in this novel and focuses, in the form of a parody, on the bureaucratic aspects of literary life. He describes the futile attempt to write a factual book about love. Walser's novels tend to be structurally somewhat weak; his great literary talent is to be found in the realm of detailed description. (p. 393)

> *Diether H. Haenicke, "Literature Since 1933," in* The Challenge of German Literature, *edited by Horst S. Daemmrich and Diether H. Haenicke (reprinted by permission of the Wayne State University Press; © 1971 by Wayne State University Press), Wayne State University Press, 1971, pp. 350-404.**

THE TIMES LITERARY SUPPLEMENT

Josef Georg Gallistl [the protagonist of *Die Gallistl'sche Krankheit*] will doubtless attain a certain fame as the literary representation of the runner doomed to bring up the tail in the West German rat-race. His account of his "disease" is a triumph for Martin Walser's gifts as a humorist: a very amusing, rather sad book about the competitiveness that has run wild in West German society since 1945, and the opposing urge to transcend it and get together, which has had all too little opportunity of expressing itself in the conditions of the Federal Republic.

G. is the seventh and least member of a group of friends living in Wiesbaden. His professional character remains uncertain to the last; but the others are an architect (A.), a bank manager (B.), a chemist (C.), a writer (D.), a cor anglais-player (E.), and a television executive (F.). They are bound to each other by sturdy mutual dislike, and by the need of each to assure himself of his social identity. Their pecking order follows the alphabet, so that G. is full of envy and hatred of the others, as impotent to impress or please them as he is to hold down a job, or get his writing published in the world at large.

Weighed down by the completeness of his failure, G. begins to withdraw, and in doing so observes that a baulked craving for success bedevils the lives of A., B., C., D., E. and F. no less than his own. "Gallistl's disease", he finds, is endemic. For a while he refuses to have any further truck with society, shuts himself up in his room, and, like Kafka's salesman-insect, is fed by benevolent relatives and friends who place portions of food for him on the windowsill.

Up to this point *Die Gallistl'sche Krankheit* has a personally felt, immediate quality. The final section, which describes the disease's cure, is perhaps inevitably less compelling. . . .

It is doubtful whether G. is really converted to communism. In fact we are left with the impression that Gallistl turns to the communists primarily because they are there, because he likes them, and because he has had to break with his other friends in any case. Martin Walser has painted his portrait with a pragmatic honesty that allows both his humour and his humanity to flourish.

"*G and Co*," in The Times Literary Supplement (© Times Newspapers Ltd. (London) 1972; reproduced from The Times Literary Supplement by permission), No. 3661, April 28, 1972, p. 465.

THE TIMES LITERARY SUPPLEMENT

Der Sturz is the third novel in a trilogy centred on the figure of Anselm Kristlein. It is full of allusions to the earlier *Halbzeit* and to a lesser extent, *Das Einhorn;* and both characters and events are very like those of the previous novels. The big difference is that *Der Sturz* is pervaded by a strong odour of decay and putrefaction. . . .

In many respects, this novel is complementary to *Halbzeit*. There, Kristlein was a climber struggling to reach the pinnacle of fashionable society, here he is seen slithering down the same social slope he had previously ascended. The important thing is to know whether, as Walser claims, Kristlein's fate can be blamed on the social conditions prevailing in the Federal Republic. German reviewers of *Der Sturz* have varied between accepting Walser's own thesis and claiming that the root of Kristlein's problems is not social but purely individual. . . .

These reservations need not, however, invalidate *Der Sturz* as a book about the fortunes of the individual in West German society. The two themes Walser identifies, the burden of having to earn money and the total dependence of the employee, are valid ones. The book is most successful in its juxtaposition of the fate of the employee, who waits, usually in vain, for some

kind of recognition from those above him, and the life of the successful, who are compensated at every turn by a sense of freedom and well-being.

Walser's skills as a writer have seldom been in dispute, and *Der Sturz* is marvellously resourceful and varied in style. What is more controversial is the subject-matter of his novels. Seen as a whole, this trilogy probably has no equal as a portrayal of the society created by postwar prosperity in West Germany. What is peculiar to Walser's work is that, unlike Günter Grass or Heinrich Böll, he describes this society largely in terms of the present, with little reference to the Nazi past. One may dispute his interpretation of the Federal Republic as a society where the dominating factors of the free market economy and the social forces it unleashes lead the individual into a permanent Darwinian struggle for survival, but the world he creates is unmistakably that of modern Germany.

"*Rotting Away*," in The Times Literary Supplement (© Times Newspapers Ltd. (London) 1973; reproduced from The Times Literary Supplement by permission), No. 3735, October 5, 1973, p. 1156.

G. B. PICKAR

The dramas and radio plays of Martin Walser range in nature from the epic *Eiche und Angora* to the conversational *Zimmerschlacht*. . . . Though they differ in the degree of political commitment and social criticism they embody and display striking diversity in subject, format and mood, they frequently share a common feature: the use of symbols as a structural element. In each case, the symbols are thoroughly integrated into the thematic framework of the drama and provide a supporting structure for its presentation.

Key images are frequently indicated by the title, as Walser's drama *Eiche und Angora* illustrates. In this drama, the words 'Eiche' and 'Angora' refer to concrete elements in the work with specific and important roles and reflect two of the themes fundamental to the drama's conceptual design. . . .

In his choice of the oak ['Eiche'], Walser employs accepted connotations to facilitate the understanding of thematic content and to project his drama's message, and the characters themselves indicate an awareness of the traditional role of the oak as the embodiment of the Germanic. (p. 186)

The idea of racism anticipated in the references to oak and forest is more fully presented in references to the Angora rabbits, the second element of the title. Unlike the oak, the validity and the ramifications of the Angora rabbits as a symbol are dependent upon their employment within the drama and are gradually developed within that work. Bred and raised as a superior breed, the Angoras represent racial superiority and racial purity and, by inference, inject this subject repeatedly into the conversations. . . .

There is intentional irony in the concern for race with which Walser imbues Alois for Alois himself, quite unknowingly, has been the victim of the racial policies of the Nazis. (p. 187)

The connotative use of the Angora rabbits, however, is not limited to this aspect. They represent the foreign, the exotic, the non-Germanic as well as the racially pure, providing thus a double counterpart to the Germanic oak. Depending upon the need or mood of the moment, Alois's rabbits serve both as model and as scapegoat, just as he, too, is exploited or rejected. . . . [In the scene where Alois hangs the pelts of his slain rabbit on the oak tree], which for all intents and purposes concludes the drama, Teutonic oak and Angora rabbit are visually joined as objects. Yet the gap between them has been neither bridged nor narrowed. The images, so thoroughly integrated into the thematic texture of the play and so essential to its structure, remain as clear evidence of the unresolved problems they project.

Der Schwarze Schwan, a sequel to *Eiche und Angora* and the second work in Walser's intended trilogy on the recent history of Germany, similarly revolves around a key image expressed in the title. Originating with the answer which a SS officer gave the boy Rudi when he asked what the initials stood for, *Schwarzer Schwan* symbolizes the problem which ultimately drives Rudi to suicide. The swan, symbol for narcissistic reflection, is black, just as Rudi's image of himself is darkened by his fear of his own potential for evil. This association, and the identity problem which it precipitates, is the central theme of the drama. (pp. 187-88)

The entire work is composed around the ramifications of the symbol black. Its associations with the questions of guilt, evil, and death unite the drama's themes and motifs; its uses join past, present, and future into a single consciousness; its identification with the swan provides the thematic orientation for the work.

In a similar conscious manner, Walser constructed *Zimmerschlacht* around the dual implication of the title, the war of the sexes staged within the bounds of the drawing room and the two encounters with the mouse which Trude, the wife, imbues with all the characteristics of a battle.

The episodes with the mouse exemplify the basic problem— the marital struggle—and illuminate it, revealing the irreconcilable differences in the natures of the two individuals involved. (p. 189)

Just as in *Der Schwarze Schwan,* colour is employed in *Zimmerschlacht* to support the thematic development of the work and provide a structural bond. Red, as the colour of blood, of battle, and of passion, connects the marital struggle and its basis in Felix's inadequacies as a man, with the incidents involving the mouse. . . .

Walser's other dramatic work of marital conflict, *Ein grenzenloser Nachmittag,* is constructed around a ping-pong game. As the 'Hörspiel' opens, a couple is playing ping-pong and the game is continued during the radio play. The thuds of the ball being hit resound behind the conversation, setting the mood and providing the pattern for the verbal exchange. The game is not only discussed by the couple, Eduard and Gisa, but also constitutes a concrete representation of their existence. (p. 190)

In these works, symbols act as bonding agents for the component parts and contribute to the unified development of character, plot, and situation. They are linked to the dominant themes of each work and integrated into their development, serving both to emphasize and promote the inherent thematic intent. Since they are developed in each work in a fashion unique to it, the plays and 'Hörspiele' appear consciously constructed around essential symbols which are repeated or redefined, contributing a distinctive quality to Walser's dramatic writing. (p. 191)

G. B. Pickar, "Symbols As Structural Elements in the Dramatic Works of Martin Walser," in Modern Languages, *Vol. LIV, No. 4, December, 1973, pp. 186-91.*

STUART PARKES

The dramatist who has possibly been most aware of the legacy of Brecht is Martin Walser—at least in his early plays. Parallel with these plays, he evolved a theory of the theatre, which was a clear response to Brecht. Whilst respecting Brecht's achievement, he no longer considered Brecht's methods as suitable for portraying the changed social and political situation, pointing out, for instance, that *Mother Courage* would probably not offend most armaments manufacturers. Walser formulated what he called 'Realismus X', a realism that would avoid Brechtian parables without just being a reproduction of external reality. A mixture of symbolism and realism would reveal what lay hidden beneath the surface of reality. After *Der Abstecher* [*The Detour*], which tends towards the theatre of the absurd, Walser sought to apply his theories in what he called a German chronicle, of which, however, only two of the three planned parts were completed.

The first play *Eiche und Angora* (*The Rabbit Race* . . .) seeks to compare different reactions to the changes in German society that took place between 1945 and 1960. . . . It is through these events that Walser seeks to show the development of German society, in particular the continuing power of the bourgeoisie. He is also at pains to show that character is largely a product of circumstance, that adaptability is a prime human quality. The Nazi is no longer a daemonic figure but, in many ways, similar to the majority of other people. This is the originality of Walser's conception, different as it is from those of Zuckmayer and Hochhuth. Unfortunately the play suffers a little from repetitiveness and from an uncomfortable mixture of tragic and comic elements, particularly in the presentation of the permanent victim of social change, Alois, through whom Walser seeks to show the passivity of the German working class.

The second play in the planned trilogy *Der Schwarze Schwan* (*The Black Swan* . . .) extends Walser's view of Nazism. If the Nazi is often little different from the rest, it follows that not being involved in Nazi crimes may often be more a matter of circumstance than of character. This is what plagues Rudi Goothein, a boy too young to have been involved with Nazism, especially when he learns of his father's crimes. As he tries to confront his father with the past, he cannot escape the question of what he would have done in the same circumstances. Since the play also specifically questions society's attitude to the whole Nazi past, in particular its refusal to accept any responsibility, it is a most uncomfortable work. It is only regrettable that the *Hamlet*-like plot—Rudi finally commits suicide—rather disintegrates before the end of the play.

Walser's most interesting attempts to write a new kind of socially relevant play cannot, therefore, be judged as entirely successful. More recently he has formulated a new idea of the theatre, plays which should concentrate not on plot but on revealing individual consciousness. After *Die Zimmerschlacht* (*Home Front* . . .), often compared with *Who's Afraid of Virginia Woolf?*, whose private theme appears a reaction against the political nature of the previous plays, he attempted this in *Ein Kinderspiel* (*Child's Play* . . .). The play shows a brother and sister seeking to come to terms with the influence of their capitalist father. Their success gives the play a political element; it reflects Walser's enthusiasm for the student rebellion of the late sixties. It is too soon to say, though, whether he has found a new outlet for his considerable talents. (pp. 137-38)

Stuart Parkes, "West German Drama Since the War," in The German Theatre: A Symposium, *edited by*

Ronald Hayman (© Oswald Wolff (Publishers) Ltd.
1975), Wolff, 1975, pp. 129-50.*

ULF ZIMMERMANN

The case of Franz Horn and the chronically clenched teeth that
are its symptom result, as Walser demonstrates in this bestselling novel [*Jenseits der Liebe*], from a compounding of pressures: the pressure to succeed in the economic-miracle society
(familiar from his **Kristlein trilogy**) and the psychological pressures—the sense of self-doubt, inferiority and guilt—of failing
within that society.

Horn, an average man of forty-four, has spent seventeen years
working, suppressing everything else for the success of a den-
ture company. But recently his usefulness to the firm has begun
to decline. . . . Yet even as he now willfully neglects his
business obligations, he acquiesces—with almost malicious
relish—in his society's values and thus convinces himself of
his monstrous worthlessness.

Kafka connoisseur that he is, Walser has Horn reach this conviction via truly Kafkaesque casuistry. Moreover, from the very
beginning—strikingly like Gregor Samsa's awakening, with
Franz Horn waking up to find his teeth clenched beyond his
control—to Horn's final view of himself as monstrous, the
novel appears a contemporary "Metamorphosis." But Horn's
fate may be worse: he seems condemned to live on, isolated
and superfluous, beyond love. Perhaps such literary similarities
are all too predominant, given too the dental motif shared with
Grass's *Local Anaesthetic*. And perhaps the dehumanizing effects, the artificialities of this society and the impotence of its
individual member are all too familiar as well. Yet Walser's
own style, his penetrating empathy and engaging wit make it
a fresh demonstration as convincing as it is enjoyable.

Ulf Zimmermann, in a review of "Jenseits der Liebe,"
in World Literature Today *(copyright 1977 by the*
University of Oklahoma Press), Vol. 51, No. 2, Spring,
1977, p. 271.

GERALD A. FETZ

Martin Walser, like many in his generation of German writers,
concerned himself in his early works primarily with the problem of confronting and attempting to come to terms with the
immediate German past. By confronting his readers with that
unpleasant and unfortunate past, he attempted to cure the sudden case of amnesia which was an all too common reaction
among Germans to that past. In all of his subsequent works as
well one finds Walser to be a writer with a keen sense for
society's—particularly West Germany's—illusions, problems,
weaknesses and injustices. His main characters are rarely granted
a great deal of sympathy, and he is especially critical of those
who abuse power and of those who are either so blind or so
subservient that such abuse becomes not only possible, but
virtually inevitable. Walser is a writer who is committed to
progressive social change, but, unlike Brecht, for example, he
is a writer with no specific program to bring about such changes.
That fact lends a note of pessimism, even resignation, to Walser's works, but it also, perhaps, is what makes him a realist.

Walser's eighth and latest play, *Das Sauspiel* (which, when
literally but inadequately translated, is *The Swinegame*), was
written five years after his seventh play, *Ein Kinderspiel*. The
time between these two plays is significant since *Das Sauspiel*

displays a distinct shift in style, a new theme (it is the first
historical play by Walser to deal with the not-so-recent past),
and a development in political thinking which leads Walser
toward a more definite political stance than in his previous
works. (p. 249)

Walser was originally asked by the city of Nuremberg to write
a play to commemorate the 450th anniversary of the Reformation's success there, but when it became clear that the play
would be critical of the city's proud "humanistic tradition,"
the request was withdrawn. Walser, however, was intrigued
with what he found during his research and completed the play.
(p. 250)

Walser's *Sauspiel* is . . . firmly based on a considerable amount
of historical research, necessary because Walser wants to make
substantive, accurate statements about history, about revolution, and about the Reformation in Nuremberg. . . . *Das Sauspiel* is not, however, a documentary play in the tradition of
Peter Weiss, Rolf Hochhuth, or Heinar Kipphardt, but much
of the historical material in the play—songs, statistics, statements by individual characters—is taken directly from primary
sources, and the essential events, actions and character portrayals, if not every minute detail in the play, are historically
verifiable.

Das Sauspiel carries the subtitle *Szenen aus dem 16, Jahrhun-
dert* (Scenes from the 16th Century) and it is just that: a series
of twenty-three loosely connected scenes, including both prologue and epilogue, in which dramatic development, when it
exists at all, is subordinate to the sovereignty of the individual
scenes. The indebtedness to Brecht is found not only in the
open, *epic* structure, which includes several songs, but also in
the fact that it is clearly a *Lehrstück* (Learning Play). (pp. 250-
51)

Das Sauspiel is an intriguing history play, bold and provocative.
It is also stageworthy drama, colorful, witty, musical, and, at
times, comical. And although it differs in style, choice of theme
and in overall execution from other contemporary German history plays, *Das Sauspiel* can be viewed as representative in
many ways of this revitalized dramatic genre. (p. 260)

Gerald A. Fetz, "Martin Walser's 'Sauspiel' and the
Contemporary German History Play," in Comparative Drama *(© copyright 1978, by the Editors of*
Comparative Drama*), Vol. 12, No. 3, Fall, 1978,*
pp. 249-65.

K. S. PARKES

Martin Walser has often been accused by his detractors of
writing novels without form and plays without plot. It is therefore surprising that he should now for the first time write a
novella [*Ein fliehendes Pferd*], the genre which, as all students
of German literature know, demands a single narrative marked
by an extraordinary incident. The extraordinary incident is that
the staid middle-aged schoolmaster Helmut Halm causes his
old school and university friend Klaus Buch to fall from his
yacht and apparently drown during a sailing trip on Lake Constance. . . .

The story . . . contrasts two attitudes to middle age. Yet both
men, like the horse of the title, are seeking to escape. Helmut
is clearly afraid of the demands of life, while Klaus's youth-
fulness is only a fasçade that covers up a deep insecurity. . . .

There is none of Walser's sometimes strident criticism of West German society in this work. At the same time, the events do reflect the pressures of life in what he sees as an over-competitive society.

> *K. S. Parkes, "Competition Corner," in* The Times Literary Supplement *(© Times Newspapers Ltd. (London) 1978; reproduced from* The Times Literary Supplement *by permission), No. 3994, October 20, 1978, p. 1236.*

ULF ZIMMERMANN

The fleeing horse, the Boccaccian falcon of Walser's *Novelle*, is the expressive image for the frantic blind rush of escape in which the . . . two main characters [of *Ein fliehendes Pferd*] are caught up. Middle-aged when they meet again, the school acquaintances Helmut Halm and Klaus Buch have spent the years seeking to elude the constricting forces of contemporary society, though in entirely opposite ways. Halm has withdrawn into himself, building a fortress of fat, as he sees it, from within which he can anticipate the perfect inertia of death. Buch meanwhile has entered a high-speed race for life in his hyperactive pursuit of health and youth.

More or less enviously, each man admires the other's seeming success—Buch Halm's apparent calm intellectual acceptance of life, and Halm Buch's energetic physical engagement in it. It is at this point of opposition that one of the many elements of parody comes to bring the *Novelle* to its traditional turning point. Just as Halm has been very taken with Buch's young (second) wife, his own wife has of course become somewhat infatuated with Buch. But unlike Goethe's, these elective affinities do not come to reaction—precisely because of Halm's awareness of them. . . .

[The] book ends essentially where it began—with a repetition of its first sentence.

So things stay the same: the society which forces the individual to live only on the run, and the individual who can find no alternative routes in that society. By showing this so pointedly in these two individual cases, Walser's book seems all the more insistent on the necessity of social change.

> *Ulf Zimmermann, in a review of "Ein fliehendes Pferd," in* World Literature Today *(copyright 1979 by the University of Oklahoma Press), Vol. 53, No. 2, Spring, 1979, p. 281.*

NOEL L. THOMAS

Perhaps all writers of German fiction should be compelled to write *Novellen*. Or perhaps only after a period of apprenticeship in the *Novelle* should German authors be allowed a sortie into the realm of the novel. Martin Walser seems to have got the procedure the wrong way round. After almost twenty years in the wilderness of the novel Martin Walser has at long last produced a *Novelle* of almost classical dimensions [*Ein fliehendes Pferd*]. . . .

In the novel *Das Einhorn* . . . the unicorn runs away with the author, though in accordance with tradition it does find refuge in a number of ladies; in *Ein fliehendes Pferd* the author (or at least one of the characters) captures the horse. *Das Einhorn* is a tremendous imaginative extravaganza and the reader is enormously impressed and fascinated by the author's fertile inven-

tiveness and linguistic élan. Yet the gulf between reality and fantasy is on occasions so great that the reader sometimes finds himself wandering, stunned, in a no-man's land, bereft of orientation. The characters to whom the narrator, Anselm Kristlein, introduces us are characters around whom he weaves a web of amorous adventure, though they do exist, in terms of the novel, on the fringe of his fantasy or they are characters, such as Orli, who are merely creatures of his fertile exuberance. The narrative does not rivet the attention of the reader. All is subordinate to the dictatorship of the imagination. *Die Gallistl'sche Krankheit* . . . is referred to by its author as a novel, yet has the length of a *Novelle* and is much easier to encompass. However, the main character and narrator is more alienated from society, more isolated and more readily inclined to plunge into the abyss of subjectivity than Anselm. Hence those characters who do occur in the novel are more phantom-like than Anselm's companions. Nor does a plot provide any compensation for a surfeit of subjectivity, though a voice does appear, calls Gallistl back from the brink and reintegrates the fragments of his atomised soul. *Die Gallistl'sche Krankheit* is a smaller 'baggy monster' than *Das Einhorn*, if one may use Henry James' definition of the novel.

Ein fliehendes Pferd is a pluralistic society: plot, characters, imagery, imagination, and 'philosophy' are all perfectly healthy institutions, complement and constrain each other and hence prevent the dictatorship of the imagination or of subjectivity. Furthermore there is a constitution as provided by the framework of the *Novelle* and Walser faithfully adheres to the conventions of the establishment. (p. 168)

As a story it grips the attention of the reader and the narrative is presented in a concentrated form, which avoids repetition and irrelevant detail. Those who wish to indulge in the game of hide and seek which is referred to in academic terms as defining the *Novelle* will find all the elements they require: the 'unerhörte Begebenheit', the concise narrative technique, the symbolism and its accompanying ramifications, and the 'Wendepunkt' are all there for those who seek. Furthermore the book is exceptionally stimulating from both the psychological and the social point of view. . . . It may be safely assumed that Walser wishes to say something meaningful about the social—and political—reality of West Germany and that he seeks to ascribe a representative significance to the confrontation between the two men. At no point in the *Novelle*, however, is the political scene within the Federal Republic mentioned nor are any political principles expounded. Yet in *Ein fliehendes Pferd* Martin Walser shows the interplay between psychological and sociological factors and makes indirect inferences about the political environment which affects the psychological and social context. . . . *Ein fliehendes Pferd* may be offered for consumption as one author's particular representation of the West German situation, a representation which, expressed in terms of the individual, is gripping, subtle, open-ended, stimulating and humorous. (p. 171)

> *Noel L. Thomas, "Martin Walser Rides Again: 'Ein fliehendes Pferd'," in* Modern Languages, *Vol. LX, No. 3, September, 1979, pp. 168-71.*

C. D. INNES

Like Dürrenmatt, Walser took Brecht's parables as his starting point, but instead of analysing social structures in general terms to convince an audience of the need for political action (Brecht) or to challenge them to imagine a more rational world (Dürrenmatt), his aim is to create a state of self-awareness through recognition. Reality is defined by perception, not by objective fact, and in his novels details of everyday life are presented through the protagonists' vision, existing only as components of a stream of consciousness. This worm's eye or key-hole perspective, accumulating minutae to portray the mentality of a representative figure—ironically named Kristlein, petty Christ, in *Half Time (Halbzeit)* and *The Unicorn (Das Einhorn)* —is not possible on the stage, and in his plays Walser replaces it with an openly symbolic world. In *Rabbit Race* this is deliberately crude. The oak around which the action takes place stands for typically Prussian virtues. Inhabited by crows and a solitary nightingale (the castrasted Alois), Germany is a Choral Society. The ground defended in 1945 is an area of historic graves. These are all clichés from the popular imagination, and the extreme naturalism of the setting parodies the fake idyllicism of German *Gemütlichkeit*—real trees and bushes on a hillock, which in the original Berlin production was built on a revolve and turned to show different vistas as the characters moved through the wood in obvious imitation of Reinhardt's classic *trompe l'oeil* staging of *A Midsummer Night's Dream*. . . . Every time the word 'nature' was mentioned the twittering of birds was heard, and the whole play was presented as a folk-song, culminating in set-pieces like the artificial sweetness in a castrato rendition of 'Über allen Gipfeln ist Ruh'. These popular images are contrasted throughout with the characters' actions to reveal their emptiness. Instead of imitating the symbolic qualities of the oak in the confusion of the final stages of the war, the Nazi officials allow Alois, whom they have just condemned to death for treason, to tie them up around it so that they can save themselves by claiming to be prisoners of the Allies if the SS arrive, or of the SS if the Allies win. The German *Götterdämmerung* is reduced to a shabby farce; the German audience's imaginary world is discredited. (p. 126)

In *The Black Swan* Walser's techniques are less open to misunderstanding. Instead of the structural contrasts of *Rabbit Race,* where the attitudes of the 1960s are juxtaposed with those of 1945 and 1950, the same characters being shown reversing their principles twice—a double negative implying that the German present is no different to the fascism which officially no longer exists—in this play the past is seen indirectly by its distorting effect on personalities. Again the setting is metaphoric, but here the symbolism is an expression of the characters' neuroses, and the atmosphere evoked by descriptions of the oppressive air like wet clothes, spiders' webs or soot, is a psychological one. . . . The protagonist, a youth who bears the same name as his father, Rudi Goothein, once a doctor in a concentration camp, is obsessed by guilt feelings for his father's crimes. In a reverse transference he claims responsibility for these atrocities, committed before he was born, is taken for treatment to one of his father's former colleagues, Liberé, who now runs a psychiatric clinic, and finally commits suicide under a tree pruned in the seven-branched shape of a Jewish candelabra. The play is based on *Hamlet*, and it is never clear whether Rudi is actually deluded or simulating madness to force the older generation to assume responsibility for their past, which is the psychiatrist's diagnosis. . . . (pp. 128-29)

On the surface *The Black Swan* appears a psychological case-history; but there is no exploration of personal motives, Rudi's identification with his father is left unexplained, and the actions of the characters are determined by symbolic relationships rather than being expressions of their personalities. Walser intends his figures to be representative as well as individualised—hence

their ironic names, Goothein being literally 'good death', while Liberé, a false name for a false freedom, is really called Leibnitz, which is intended to indicate that fascism had its roots in acceptable philosophers and must thus be seen as part of the mainstream of German development, not an abberation.

Similarly while the plot concerns an individual's suicide, the structure is a paradigm of all the possible reactions to guilt. Rudi takes on himself the guilt that his father refuses to face. Liberé acknowledges his responsibility to himself but leads a life of pretence to avoid the consequences of his past, while his daughter Irm, the Ophelia-figure to Rudi's Hamlet, demonstrates the extreme psychological effects of adaptability. She has persuaded herself to believe the lie that they were in India during the war, only to find that her escapism still contains the elements of concentration camps. Her imagination has simply transposed the chimneys of Auschwitz into Indian burning ghats, and her fascination with these self-imposed 'memories' of Suttee symbolises her retreat from reality. At times the two levels fail to merge, as in the suggestion that Irm's state results from being raped by her teacher as a child. Quite apart from being too obvious a political reference, this lacks conviction, having apparently left no discernible traces in her personality or attitude to sex. But the intention of this double vision is clearly to challenge the audience's self-awareness, a game of truth which is perhaps too overtly spelt out: the present can only be meaningful if the past is acknowledged and if one is conscious of one's own potentialities. (pp. 129-30)

Walser developed his theory of a new form of theatrical realism while writing these plays. . . . Rejecting 'newspaper realism' and 'discussion theatre' as superficial, he defined theatre as 'the place where society's consciousness is presented for analysis, noting and testing its developments'. In Walser's special use of the term, realism *('Realismus X')* is an internal revelation of something unperceived. Anything accepted has already become a cliché, a substitute for perception which disguises the true relationship of people to their social environment. Established intellectual viewpoints and the stylistic forms that express them being automatically 'idealistic,' falsifying experience, drama must be anti-ideological, continually dealing with new concepts of reality. . . . Walser's focus, then, is on the spectator's state of awareness rather than external events, and the structure of his drama is intended to affect this state, not to reflect preconceived notions about 'reality'.

The practical implications of this can be seen in *Rabbit Race* and *The Black Swan*. Both are deliberately artificial in style, 'imaginary fables' designed to express contemporary consciousness by contrasting the present with memory of the immediate past, an exaggeratedly unpleasant picture that the spectator 'gradually recognises . . . as far more relevant to him than he had suspected. A topical spark has detonated.' This immediacy is also present in the details of the fable. Since the subject of these plays is modes of vision, their conditioning and manipulation, any distancing in the form of a Brechtian emigration to a fantasy world would only confuse. Being subjective, perspectives that alter with the personal experience of different spectators, the material of this type of drama cannot be represented directly in the fate of a conventional protagonist, and the model form that Walser has developed is in many ways an adequate stylistic solution. It both provides a structure, unrelated to plot or naturalistic considerations, which catches states of consciousness at the only point they become visible, in transition, and allows the use of symbolic characters, which show these states of consciousness in all their major variations.

At the same time the necessity for the audience to identify with the symbols limits the relevance of this type of drama. Dürrenmatt's Güllen stands for all the western world, Walser's oak has a specifically German reference. His approach, when he outlines it in general terms, seems to have a wide validity . . . but as examples of this approach his plays are narrow in scope, and the themes are non-transferable, while a technique that actually succeeds in discomposing its spectators . . . is hardly designed to attract a wide public. So it is unfortunate, but unsurprising, that Walser's plays are almost unknown outside and, however respected, seldom performed inside Germany. (pp. 130-32)

C. D. Innes, "Models," in his Modern German Drama: A Study in Form *(© Cambridge University Press 1979), Cambridge University Press, 1979, pp. 101-32.**

ULF ZIMMERMANN

"Seelenarbeit" is the self-help the doctor prescribes for Xaver Zürn's stomach pains, which for lack of physical causes he must diagnose as psychosomatic. For Zürn's symptoms, much like Franz Horn's "lockjaw" in *Jenseits der Liebe* . . . , result from the pressures of conforming his self to the role precast for him by those Fates of the modern world, socioeconomic forces. . . .

Though he has retained only the buildings of the old family farm, leaving his brother the land, Zürn is at bottom still a farmer, unhappy with any ties but those to the land. Yet now he finds himself perennially moving about, chauffeuring a rich industrialist and Mozart fanatic around the European economic community. (p. 97)

The ending, like much of the story, has something of the air of resignation, that proverbially quiet desperation, so palpably fixed in that earlier case of the world's ineluctable role-casting power, Max Frisch's *Stiller*. Yet just as there, in *Seelenarbeit* too, that air is made less oppressive by a generous admixture of wrily humorous elements: along with the comically laconic side of Zürn's portrait, there are numerous satiric cameos such as those of his two daughters, who complement one another in their "hip" extremes. And though the whole may seem less sharply critical than some earlier Walser, his sparklingly fresh and crisply ironic style remains at its bracing best. (p. 98)

Ulf Zimmermann in a review of "Seelenarbeit," in World Literature Today *(copyright 1980 by the University of Oklahoma Press), Vol. 54, No. 1, Winter, 1980, pp. 97-8.*

G. P. BUTLER

Runaway Horse ends as it began: in answer to Sabina's question "What really happened . . .?", Helmut starts to tell the tale we have just read. It is told very cleverly, a far richer, subtler, wittier story than any brief synopsis can hope to show. Its appeal derives not only from Walser's singular ability to state and suggest what people think and feel, not only from the memorably elusive character of "HH" and his particular predicament suddenly one summer, but also from the sadness it engenders. To be afforded "no enlightenment" makes a nice change; to be left to reflect on why the Halms and the Buchs have become who they are, and on what lies ahead of them, makes for melancholy—unless you can disown them altogether.

G. P. Butler, "The Secrets of H H," in The Times Literary Supplement *(© Times Newspapers Ltd. (London) 1980; reproduced from* The Times Literary Supplement *by permission), No. 4035, July 25, 1980, p. 836.*

JOHN NEVES

Gone are the days when Martin Walser had fundamental doubts about West German society, and gingerly explored the claims of communism to offer a better life for the common man. So much is clear from his latest novel [*Das Schwanenhaus*], a humorous account of the professional and family tribulations of a reasonably well-to-do estate agent. In spite of the fact that his tribulations include the pregnancy of one of his unmarried daughters and an unnerving capacity for running up large debts, the sense of social stability and bourgeois good-living is such that the atmosphere of the book is a kind of late twentieth-century Biedermeier.

It is once again the story of a man barely able to cope with the demands of either his job or of his family, floundering through life, dependent on the indulgence of colleagues and the support of his wife. But in this case the hero's inadequacy is scarcely painful, and is accompanied by many material compensations. In fact he is not really the failure who played the central role in Walser's earlier novels, the failure who was at the same time a rebel against materialism and the *leistungsprinzip*, but an easy-going fellow who knows how to appreciate his niche in life.

As a result *Das Schwanenhaus* has much less to say that is of relevance to the human condition in general. It lacks the poignancy of humorous writing in which there is an underlying theme of tragedy. Readers of Walser's earlier novels will remember Gallistl's despair at being eternally the last in the pecking order of his friends in *Die Gallistl'sche Krankheit,* and Franz Horn's sense of permanent inferiority as a salesman in *Jenseits der Liebe,* as being both very funny and very sad, and at the same time indicative of something rotten in the social order. . . .

Das Schwanenhaus reflects the more cautious and socially less concerned atmosphere of the late 1970s. . . .

[The protagonist, Dr. Gottlieb Zürn,] has no problems. But he is still worried by the fact that real success eludes him. Real success would be embodied in getting the Schwanenhaus commission. The Schwanenhaus is a country house in *jugendstil* worth about 2,000,000 marks, the sole agency for which would boost both his status in the estate agents' fraternity and his finances. Needless to say, he fails to get the commission, partly because at one point, in the manner of Walserian heroes, he is seized by a combination of fright and irrational rebellion against the exigencies of his way of life, and refuses to keep an appointment with the owner of the Schwanenhaus. . . .

In fact Zürn, in spite of his yearning for success, has difficulty in coping with life at all. There is no question of his offering any leadership to his family. . . . Such security as he enjoys, both in his private and his professional life, he owes to his wife. Nevertheless it is adequate to keep his head above water. He is never in danger of going under. And that is the weakness of *Das Schwanenhaus*. It is at heart an idyll, an idyll of bumbling incompetence perhaps, but nevertheless redolent with inner and outer contentment. And that is why it is not as amusing or thought-provoking as some of its predecessors.

John Neves, "Bumbling towards Content," in The Times Literary Supplement (© Times Newspapers Ltd. (London) 1980; reproduced from The Times Literary Supplement by permission), No. 4044, October 3, 1980, p. 1108.

INGE JUDD

For several decades, German novelist Walser has formed his dark notions of contemporary German society into novels of quiet sarcasm. . . . [*The Swan Villa*] satirizes a group of real estate brokers in Southern Germany. The beautiful natural surroundings, the wealth, the worldly opportunities of all protagonists stand in contrast to a progressive deterioration of environment and soul. . . . In spite of a colorful story line and much emoting, none of the characters ever amounts to more than an array of desperate attitudes and uncoordinated hunches. The reader becomes informed and remains untouched.

Inge Judd, in a review of "The Swan Villa," in Library Journal (reprinted from Library Journal, October 1, 1982; published by R. R. Bowker Co. (a Xerox company); copyright © 1982 by Xerox Corporation), Vol. 107, No. 17, October 1, 1982, p. 1897.

ERNST PAWEL

Gottlieb Zürn, the hero of this brief but brilliant novel ["**The Swan Villa**"], is a product of the German economic miracle, a lawyer who switched to real estate and rode the postwar boom to moderate affluence. Having done his bit to help develop the once grassy slopes of Lake Constance into high-rise condominiums, now in midlife he feels depressingly underdeveloped himself, obsolete and disposable, a banal character trapped in a banal dilemma. All Martin Walser does, in limpid prose and with the sure touch of a compassionate surgeon, is to bare the man's heart and trace the pathways of his pain. But in the process he evokes a life in our time, distinct from any other and yet subject to the same laws of supply and excessive demand that govern the lives of the multinational middle class throughout today's global village. . . .

Mr. Walser, though awarded the Group 47 Prize in 1955, proved wayward and disconcerting from the start. For one thing, he had no ties to the nostalgic radicalism of the 20's that still infected so many of his contemporaries. For another, he came to literature via Kafka, on whom he wrote a first-rate dissertation in 1951 after completing his studies in history and German literature. The Kafka influence is all too obvious in his early stories, but it may have helped to inspire the uncompromising clarity and attention to detail with which he later began to probe the nexus between private agony and public nightmare. He was among the first to look beyond the "undigested past" of the Nazi era and at present-day Germany—a postindustrial society more closely linked in spirit to the New World than to the ruins and memories of the Old. (p. 11)

One of Mr. Walser's major achievements is that he faced the reality of the present before other writers did, and struggled to articulate it in his fiction.

His first attempts to tackle social themes inspired some witty, literate but essentially conventional satire. "**Marriage in Phillipsburg**," his first novel, . . . depicts the greed, stupidity and moral imbecility of the *Wirtschaftswunderkinder*—the parasitical profiteers of the economic miracle—with a cold if rather trendy indignation. But in the works that followed—"**Halftime**," "**The Unicorn**" and "**Runaway Horse**"—Mr. Walser moved beyond these limited perspectives toward a far more integrated vision. His protagonists, middlemen all, whether selling soap, real estate, high-powered prose or their own brains, are committed to the Sisyphean task of stimulating progress by creating ever more insatiable demands for ever more superfluous products. At the same time they are profoundly vulnerable human beings with cruel flashes of self-awareness who far transcend their symbolic role.

Striking a proper balance between these parallel visions of society and of the individual trapped in it, keeping both in equally sharp focus while tracing the intricate relationship between them, takes sophistication and literary skills of the highest order. In "**The Swan Villa**," . . . Mr. Walser has come closer than ever to meeting the challenge. (pp. 11, 19)

[His language is] as starkly functional as his subject. . . .

This book has grace, style and wisdom. It should be read. (p. 19)

Ernst Pawel, "The Empty Success of Herr Zürn," in The New York Times Book Review (© 1982 by The New York Times Company; reprinted by permission), October 10, 1982, pp. 11, 19.

MARION GLASTONBURY

Martin Walser's protagonist [in *The Swan Villa*] is an estate agent, and the eponymous Swan Villa an exquisite property on the shores of Lake Constance, admired in childhood and now up for sale. Which of the rival dealers will be favoured with an exclusive listing? Gottlieb is haunted by the beauty of the frescoes and stained glass, by the prospect of the commission, by the memory of his bankrupt parents, by the urge to impress clients, patrons and competitors, and by the wish to see his four wayward daughters safely provided for. . . .

Harassed by conflicting impulses, he envies his wife's calm consistency of purpose and resents her with an intensity that is the obverse of gratitude, a measure of his own dependence on her. As Gottlieb hangs upon the outcome of business strategy and market forces, alternating between ambition and self-abasement, a solid picture of a society in crisis emerges from the turmoil of his thoughts. *The Swan Villa* embodies with rare percipience and topicality a complex living relationship between love and money.

Marion Glastonbury, "Charmed Circle," in New Statesman (© 1983 The Statesman & Nation Publishing Co. Ltd.), Vol. 105, No. 2712, March 11, 1983, p. 27.*

Evelyn (Arthur St. John) Waugh

1903-1966

English novelist, short story writer, travel writer, essayist, critic, biographer, journalist, and poet.

Evelyn Waugh has been called one of the greatest prose stylists of the twentieth century for his novels of social satire on the failures of modern society. Although probably best known for *Brideshead Revisited* (1945), and most highly praised for *A Handful of Dust* (1934), Waugh also produced a substantial body of influential writing in other genres.

Waugh came from a literary family which included his father, editor-publisher Arthur; his brother, novelist Alec; and later, two of his own children, writers Auberon and Harriet. As an indifferent student at Oxford, Waugh became involved in the fast-paced, fashionably decadent world of the "Bright Young Things" (the rich young "flappers" of Britain). He eventually satirized his experiences at Oxford in *Vile Bodies* (1930). That book followed *Decline and Fall* (1928), an attack on the corrupt modern world which victimizes the innocents who live in it. *Decline and Fall* exemplifies Waugh's steadfast reaction against institutions which were fraudulent or abused power. This early work, the chief characteristic of which was farce, introduced some of his important themes, one of them being a desire to return to a past that he considered morally superior to the present.

Many of Waugh's ideas concerning betrayal and morality seemed to be the result of the dissolution of his first marriage. Another important influence on his writing was his conversion from Anglicanism to Catholicism in his search for stability and refuge from the secular world he found so distasteful. Among his so-called "Catholic novels," was his greatest commercial success, *Brideshead Revisited*, a novel about moral decay, religious conviction, nostalgia, and the British aristocracy. Much of the significance of *Brideshead* has been credited to Waugh's new direction in his writing, particularly in the more optimistic religious overtones. Although some critics praised the novel as his greatest success, others condemn it for its ponderous and sentimental writing. Some point out that the plot does not meld well with the theology and that the religious message is lost. The lushness and the romanticism which attracted many readers led others to complain that it conflicted with the satire. *Brideshead* served as a turning point in yet another matter besides religion—it allowed Waugh to show his skill as a stylist and as a deft manipulator of characterization, rather than simply a clever satirist. Two others of his Catholic books are *Edmund Campion* (1935) and *Helena* (1950), factual and fictional biographies, respectively, of a martyr and a saint.

A Handful of Dust (1934), Waugh's statement on soulless contemporary society, is also a caution about the pitfalls of over-idealizing the past. The book is considered by many critics to be the best of his early work, and perhaps his writing as a whole. It is his first use of a theme which recurs throughout his subsequent work: the plight of the genteel Christian (read aristocratic Catholic) man as the inevitable victim of the corrupt present. His characters believe in the Myth of Decline and, in order to escape this era's decadence, they seek mean-

Photograph by Mark Gerson

ing, beauty, and "rightness" in the past, a Golden Age which actually exists only in their minds. This preoccupation results, however, in the same neglect of responsibility, the same selfishness and insensitivity to immediate crises that these people condemn in others. Many critics believe that Waugh's characterizations become rounder and his satire more subtle in *A Handful of Dust*. Still others, however, see it as a satisfying continuation of the farcical treatment and the two-dimensional portrayals of the earlier works.

After his divorce, Waugh traveled constantly, often as a correspondent. During this period he produced fiction, reviews, articles, a biography, and a number of outstanding travel books. Among the latter are *Labels* (1930), *Remote People* (1931), *Ninety-Two Days* (1934), and *Waugh in Abyssinia* (1936). In them, he sheds the "London Waugh" and allows himself to be charming, tolerant, and sympathetic. Even in these, however, he comments in a humorous vein on the eccentricities he finds throughout the world. His travels in Africa also served as material for two novels: *Black Mischief* (1932), a look at the failure of imposing European standards upon African nations, and *Scoop* (1938), a satire on journalism.

Waugh also served in the Royal Marines during World War II and the experiences of those years appear in a number of his books. *Put Out More Flags* (1942) looks at the unreality of the early months of the war, the bungling bureaucracy of the military establishment in organizing the war effort, and the lives which would be destroyed by the catastrophe. It is often considered an introduction to the three novels which constitute the *Sword of Honour* trilogy: *Men at Arms* (1952), *Officers and Gentlemen* (1955), and *Unconditional Surrender* (1961). These books, published as one volume in 1965, comprise his final long work. The trilogy is yet another which has been hailed as containing his best and most compassionate writing. It features his first real hero, Guy Crouchback, and traces Guy's romantic idealism at the beginning of the war through his bleak pessimism at its conclusion. A decent man seeking decency in the world, Guy decides that only personal good works can provide spiritual comfort and communion amid a secular wasteland. An underlying theme in the trilogy is Waugh's own disillusionment with England's betrayal of its traditional standards of honor and integrity as a result of the war.

In addition to fiction and travel, Waugh was a prodigious letter writer. *The Letters of Evelyn Waugh* (1980) have recently been published—approximately 800 out of some 4,500 which were available—and the result has produced a picture of a compassionate, loyal, humane person. This contrasts sharply with the image presented in his *Diaries* (1976) of a misanthropic snob with an exaggerated disregard for the rest of humanity. Waugh began a projected three volume autobiography, but only one volume, *A Little Learning* (1964), was ever published. Two other pieces of his writing, however, are also regarded as autobiographical: *Work Suspended* (1942), an unfinished book which reflects Waugh's increasing feelings of alienation at the time and which portrays an artist who is isolated from contemporary society; and, *The Ordeal of Gilbert Pinfold* (1957), the story of a middle-aged writer who experiences a nervous breakdown, paralleling a time in Waugh's own life. Two other recently published works are *A Little Order* (1977), the only collection of some of his journalism, and a fragment of a "prequel" to *Brideshead*, "Charles Ryder's Schooldays" (1945), published together with eleven other stories which had a limited printing in 1936 under the title *Mr. Loveday's Little Outing and Other Sad Stories*. One of these, "By Special Request," is an alternate ending to *A Handful of Dust*.

Waugh's importance to modern English literature owes much to his style and craftsmanship. Earlier works were characterized by clever phrasing and broadly humorous plots, but in later works, he translated his observations into complex ironic structures, unifying content with form. Waugh also managed, for the most part, to maintain a balance between involvement and detachment toward his characters. Some critics contend that Waugh's books are timeless because their worlds transcend current history. Others, however, believe that his books will not endure because of his nostalgic preoccupations, the rigidity of his opinions and outlook, and the restricted range of his intellectual and political focus. The assessments of his writing skills are, nevertheless, virtually uniform in their recognition of his comic inventiveness, his highly individualistic style, his devotion to clarity and precision, and his ability to entertain.

(See also *CLC*, Vols. 1, 3, 8, 13, 19; *Contemporary Authors*, Vols. 85-88, Vols. 25-28, rev. ed. [obituary]; and *Dictionary of Literary Biography*, Vol. 15.)

EDMUND WILSON

The new novel by Evelyn Waugh—*Brideshead Revisited*—has been a bitter blow to this critic. I have admired and praised Mr. Waugh [see excerpt in *CLC*, Vol. 13], and when I began reading *Brideshead Revisited,* I was excited at finding that he had broken away from the comic vein for which he is famous and expanded into a new dimension. The new story—with its subtitle, *The Sacred and Profane Memories of Captain Charles Ryder*—is a "serious" novel, in the conventional sense, and the opening is invested with a poetry and staged with a dramatic effectiveness which seem to promise much. An English officer, bored with the Army, finds himself stationed near a great country house which has been turned into soldiers' quarters. It is a place that he once used to visit—his life, indeed, has been deeply involved with the Catholic family who lived there. The story reverts to 1923, at the time when Charles Ryder was at Oxford and first met the younger son of the Marchmains, who became his most intimate friend. This early section is all quite brilliant, partly in the manner of the Waugh we know, partly with a new kind of glamor that is closer to Scott Fitzgerald and Compton Mackenzie. It is the period that these older writers celebrated, but seen now from the bleak shrivelled forties, so that everything—the freedom, the fun, the varied intoxications of youth—has taken on a remoteness and pathos. The introduction of the hero to the Catholic family and the gradual revelation of their queerness, their differences from Protestant England, is brought off with accomplished art, and through almost the whole of the first half of the book, the habitual reader of Waugh is likely to tell himself that his favorite has been fledged as a first-rank straight novelist.

But this enthusiasm is to be cruelly disappointed. What happens when Evelyn Waugh abandons his comic convention—as fundamental to his previous work as that of any Restoration dramatist—turns out to be more or less disastrous. The writer, in this more normal world, no longer knows his way: his deficiency in common sense here ceases to be an asset and gets him into some embarrassing situations, and his creative imagination, accustomed in his satirical fiction to work partly in two-dimensional caricature but now called upon for passions and motives, produces mere romantic fantasy. The hero is to have an affair with the married elder daughter of the house, and this is conducted on a plane of banality—the woman is quite unreal—reminiscent of the full-dress adulteries of the period in the early nineteen-hundreds when Galsworthy and other writers were making people throb and weep over such fiction as *The Dark Flower*. And as the author's taste thus fails him, his excellent style goes to seed. The writing—which, in the early chapters, is of Evelyn Waugh's best: felicitous, unobtrusive, exact—here runs to such dispiriting clichés as "Still the clouds gathered and did not break" and "So the year wore on and the secret of the engagement spread from Julia's confidantes and so, like ripples on the water, in ever widening circles." The stock characters—the worldly nobleman, the good old nurse—which have always been a feature of Waugh's fiction and which are all right in a harlequinade, here simply become implausible and tiresome. The last scenes are extravagantly absurd, with an absurdity that would be worthy of Waugh at his best if it were not—painful to say—meant quite seriously. The worldly Lord Marchmain, when he left his wife, repudiated his Catholic faith, and on his deathbed he sends the priest packing, but when the old man has sunk lower, the priest is recalled. The family all kneel, and Charles, who is present, kneels, too. Stoutly though he has defended his Protestantism, his resistance breaks down today. He prays that this time the dying man will not reject the final sacrament, and lo, Lord Marchmain makes the sign of the cross! The peer, as he has drifted toward death, has been soliloquizing at eloquent length: "We were knights then, barons since Agincourt, the larger honors came with the Georges," etc., etc., and the reader has an uncomfortable feeling that what has caused Mr. Waugh's hero to plump on his knees is not, perhaps, the sign of the cross but the prestige, in the person of Lord Marchmain, of one of the oldest families in England.

For Waugh's snobbery, hitherto held in check by his satirical point of view, has here emerged shameless and rampant. His admiration for the qualities of the older British families, as contrasted with modern upstarts, had its value in his earlier novels, where the standards of morals and taste are kept in the background and merely implied. But here the upstarts are rather crudely overdone and the aristocrats become terribly trashy, and his cult of the high nobility is allowed to become so rapturous and solemn that it finally gives the impression of being the only real religion in the book.

Yet the novel is a Catholic tract. The Marchmain family, in their various fashions, all yield, ultimately, to the promptings of their faith and bear witness to its enduring virtue; the skeptical hero, long hostile and mocking, eventually becomes converted; the old chapel is opened up and put at the disposition of the troops, and a "surprising lot use it, too." Now, this critic may perhaps be insensible to some value the book will have for other readers, since he is unsympathetic by conviction with the point of view of the Catholic convert, but he finds it impossible to feel that the author has conveyed in all this any actual religious experience. In the earlier novels of Waugh there was always a very important element of perverse, unregenerate self-will that, giving rise to confusion and impudence, was a great asset for a comic writer. In his new book, this theme is sounded explicitly, with an unaccustomed portentousness and rhetoric, at an early point in the story, when he speaks of "the hot spring of anarchy" that "rose from deep furnaces where was no solid earth, and burst into the sunlight—a rainbow in its cooling vapors with a power the rocks could not repress," and of course it is this hot spring of anarchy, this reckless, unredeemed humanity, that is supposed to be cooled and controlled by the discipline of the Catholic faith. But, once he has come to see this force as sin, Evelyn Waugh seems to be rather afraid of it: he does not allow it really to raise its head—boldly, outrageously, hilariously or horribly—as he has in his other books, and the result is that we feel something lacking. We have come to count on this Serpent; we are not used to seeing it handled so gingerly; and, at the same time, the religion that is invoked to subdue it seems more like an exorcistic rite than a force of regeneration. (pp. 298-301)

The comic parts of *Brideshead Revisited* are as funny as anything that the author has done, and the Catholic characters are sometimes good, when they are being observed as social types and get the same kind of relentless treatment as the characters in his satirical books. I do not mean to suggest, however, that Mr. Waugh should revert to his earlier vein. He has been steadily broadening his art, and when he next tries a serious novel, he may have learned how to avoid bathos.

In the meantime, I predict that *Brideshead Revisited* will prove to be the most successful, the only extremely successful, book that Evelyn Waugh has written, and that it will soon be up in the best-seller list somewhere between *The Black Rose* and *The Manatee*. (p. 302)

Edmund Wilson, "Splendors and Miseries of Evelyn Waugh" (1946), in his Classics and Commercials: A Literary Chronicle of the Forties (reprinted by permission of Farrar, Straus and Giroux, Inc.; copyright 1950 by Edmund Wilson; copyright renewed © 1978 by Elena Wilson), Farrar, Straus and Giroux, 1950, pp. 298-305.

STEVEN MARCUS

It is almost certain that Evelyn Waugh is the finest entertainer alive. It is certain that both Waugh and the kind of book he writes are supremely distasteful to many of the most serious people. . . . Waugh has been variously characterized as nasty, hateful, snobbish, trivial, reactionary, vindictive, fawning, immature, pompous, and rude, ascriptions which are substantially true yet somehow beside the point. The general repugnance of the contemporary intellectual for the literature of entertainment is, I think, related to his dislike of Waugh. . . . Our culture has to an unprecedented degree succeeded in dividing our entertainment from our elevation. . . . [We] are quick to mistrust any piece of writing which does not seem immediately to challenge profound assumptions or elicit the most delicate moral choices. Our less ponderous relations to literature have suffered an attrition, and it is possible that a certain kind of literature— the kind I assume Waugh to represent—is losing the capacity to express anything significant. (pp. 88-9)

[But] Waugh is essentially a comedian, and his early novels are celebrations of Mayfair, not satires of it. Nothing is more patent than that he loved . . . all the raffish, bored, useless, picaresque characters who fill the pages of his earliest novels. These novels, and *Black Mischief, A Handful of Dust* and *Scoop,* are successful because of the purity of their comic vision— they are elaborated spoofs. Remarking the absurdity and waste of a particular social life, they omit its real consequences. The worst fate that overtakes anyone in them (besides, of course, being bored) is being eaten by cannibals, or reading Dickens aloud to a madman—grisly consummations, but merely grisly. Although Waugh understood that the assumptions his "bright young things" lived by were preposterous, he was honest enough not to deny that, with certain qualifications, their standards were sympathetic to his own. They were thundering snobs, xenophobes, opportunists, ignoramuses, and thoroughly cultivated ladies and gentlemen. Like Waugh they were more outspoken than an American can easily imagine, and like Waugh they accepted with an abandoned equanimity their misfortune in being three hundred years too late. In his early novels Waugh was able to sustain a tone of bemused mournfulness over a society bent on smashing itself to pieces, while at the same time depicting the feckless innocence of both those who were most active in the smashing and those most hurt by it. The matrix of his comedy is this conjunction of the most abrupt and violent events with the most innocent villains.

Waugh's initial vein was a shallow one, though, and sometime in the late thirties it began to run thin; Basil Seal, who had once blithely survived a meal made of his sweetheart's flesh, could not survive his own self-pity, and Waugh's repining over the evanescence of his generation soured his appetite for comedy. He wrote a couple of slim, adequate satires, *The Loved One* and *Scott-King's Modern Europe,* and he wrote two pretentious novels about his religion, *Brideshead Revisited* and *Helena,* his most conspicuous failures. They failed because Waugh's snobbery and growing biliousness could not accommodate themselves to humane, religious impulses; indeed, they overrode his Christianity and made it seem just slightly disreputable. . . . Even Catholicism, most hierarchic of religious dispensations, is too democratic for Waugh, whose admiration of "blood" and class will always compromise his obligations to the poor in heart and spirit and pocketbook. The unpleasant atmosphere of *Brideshead Revisited* was directly a result of the far-reaching disagreement between Waugh and his religion.

In the last few years, however, Waugh has found himself again, and has just published the second part of a novel in two volumes, *Men at Arms* and *Officers and Gentlemen.* These volumes belong with his finest comedy, and they show a surprising maturity, for in them Waugh has been able to poke fun even at his Catholicism. But their excellence derives principally from his having found something that again exhilarates him: the Army. Waugh fell in love with the Army in much the same way, and for the same reasons, that he fell in love with Mayfair twenty years ago. The Army, Waugh finds, is more interesting in its distinctions of position and privilege (and in its ability to harbor the pretenders to them) than a society which has been "democratized"; it is the final repository of the remnants of class and tradition, of unlimited pride in inheritance, of true values, and of honor. It is also very funny. Through its ranks move some of the phoniest, most brazen picaroons in English literature, and in its infinite, inefficient reaches lurk the grotesques, fossils, and fantasts of all good burlesque. (pp. 90-3)

The qualities that make them interesting and worthy are not organic to their structure or their moral implication, but are there in the things that exist before the reader's eye, in the events arranged and acted out.

These outward, superficial virtues can be sustained only by a professional writer, and the remarkable attractiveness of Waugh and his fellow entertainers, Graham Greene, Henry Green, and Joyce Cary, is inseparable from the unobtrusive rectitude, the professional style, of all their writing. What we feel in them is a kind of superb efficiency in expending their talents. They seem most of the time to have been able to calculate just what they can do, and they do it with the strictest economy of effort. By fully exploiting their comparatively modest talents they rise above their rank and demand comparison with America's more serious writers, writers of demonstrably finer intelligence and fuller seriousness than these entertainers but less gifted in their capacity for articulating the intelligence they have to communicate. (pp. 97-8)

> *Steven Marcus, "Evelyn Waugh and the Art of Entertainment" (originally published in* Partisan Review, *Vol. XXII, No. 3, 1956; copyright © 1956 by Steven Marcus; reprinted by permission of Random House, Inc.), in his* Representations: Essays on Literature and Society, *Random House, 1975, pp. 88-101.*

JULIAN JEBB (Interview with EVELYN WAUGH)

INTERVIEWER: E. M. Forster has spoken of "flat characters and round characters"; if you recognize this distinction, would you agree that you created no "round" characters until *A Handful of Dust?*

WAUGH: All fictional characters are flat. A writer can give an illusion of depth by giving an apparently stereoscopic view of a character—seeing him from two vantage points; all a writer can do is give more or less information about a character, not information of a different order.

INTERVIEWER: Then do you make no radical distinction between characters as differently conceived as Mr. Pendergast and Sebastian Flyte?

WAUGH: Yes, I do. There are the protagonists and there are characters who are furniture. One gives only one aspect of the furniture. Sebastian Flyte was a protagonist.

INTERVIEWER: Would you say, then, that Charles Ryder was the character about whom you gave most information?

WAUGH: No, Guy Crouchback. [*A little restlessly*] But look, I think that your questions are dealing too much with the creation of character and not enough with the technique of writing. I regard writing not as investigation of character, but as an exercise in the use of language, and with this I am obsessed. I have no technical psychological interest. It is drama, speech, and events that interest me.

INTERVIEWER: Does this mean that you continually refine and experiment?

WAUGH: Experiment? God forbid! Look at the results of experiment in the case of a writer like Joyce. He started off writing very well, then you can watch him going mad with vanity. He ends up a lunatic.

INTERVIEWER: I gather from what you said earlier that you don't find the act of writing difficult.

WAUGH: I don't find it easy. You see, there are always words going round in my head; some people think in pictures, some in ideas. I think entirely in words. By the time I come to stick my pen in my inkpot these words have reached a stage of order which is fairly presentable.

INTERVIEWER: Perhaps that explains why Gilbert Pinfold was haunted by voices—by disembodied words.

WAUGH: Yes, that's true—the word made manifest.

INTERVIEWER: Can you say something about the direct influences on your style? Were any of the nineteenth-century writers an influence on you? Samuel Butler, for example?

WAUGH: They were the basis of my education, and as such of course I was affected by reading them. P. G. Wodehouse affected my style directly. Then there was a little book by E. M. Forster called *Pharos and Pharillon*—sketches of the history of Alexandria. I think that Hemingway made real discoveries about the use of language in his first novel, *The Sun Also Rises.* I admired the way he made drunk people talk.

INTERVIEWER: What about Ronald Firbank?

WAUGH: I enjoyed him very much when I was young. I can't read him now.

INTERVIEWER: Why?

WAUGH: I think there would be something wrong with an elderly man who could enjoy Firbank. (pp. 110-11)

INTERVIEWER: It is evident that you reverence the authority of established institutions—the Catholic Church and the army. Would you agree that on one level both *Brideshead Revisited* and the army trilogy were celebrations of this reverence?

WAUGH: No, certainly not. I reverence the Catholic Church because it is true, not because it is established or an institution. *Men at Arms* was a kind of uncelebration, a history of Guy Crouchback's disillusion with the army. Guy has old-fashioned ideas of honor and illusions of chivalry; we see these being used up and destroyed by his encounters with the realities of army life.

INTERVIEWER: Would you say that there was any direct moral to the army trilogy?

WAUGH: Yes, I imply that there is a moral purpose, a chance of salvation, in every human life. Do you know the old Protestant hymn which goes: "Once to every man and nation/ Comes the moment to decide"? Guy is offered this chance by making himself responsible for the upbringing of Trimmer's child, to see that he is not brought up by his dissolute mother. He is essentially an unselfish character.

INTERVIEWER: Can you say something about the conception of the trilogy. Did you carry out a plan which you had made at the start?

WAUGH: It changed a lot in the writing. Originally I had intended the second volume, **Officers and Gentlemen,** to be two volumes. Then I decided to lump them together and finish it off. There's a very bad transitional passage on board the troop ship. The third volume really arose from the fact that Ludovic needed explaining. As it turned out, each volume had a common form because there was an irrelevant ludricous figure in each to make the running.

INTERVIEWER: Even if, as you say, the whole conception of the trilogy was not clearly worked out before you started to write, were there not some things which you saw from the beginning?

WAUGH: Yes, both the sword in the Italian church and the sword of Stalingrad were, as you put it, there from the beginning.

INTERVIEWER: Can you say something about the germination of **Brideshead Revisited?**

WAUGH: It is very much a child of its time. Had it not been written when it was, at a very bad time in the war when there was nothing to eat, it would have been a different book. The fact that it is rich in evocative description—in gluttonous writing—is a direct result of the privations and austerity of the times.

INTERVIEWER: Have you found any professional criticism of your work illuminating or helpful? Edmund Wilson, for example?

WAUGH: Is he an American?

INTERVIEWER: Yes.

WAUGH: I don't think what they have to say is of much interest, do you? (pp. 112-13)

INTERVIEWER: Do you think it just to describe you as a reactionary?

WAUGH: An artist must be a reactionary. He has to stand out against the tenor of the age and not go flopping along; he must offer some little opposition. Even the great Victorian artists were all anti-Victorian, despite the pressures to conform.

INTERVIEWER: But what about Dickens? Although he preached social reform he also sought a public image.

WAUGH: Oh, that's quite different. He liked adulation and he liked showing off. But he was still deeply antagonistic to Victorianism.

INTERVIEWER: Is there any particular historical period, other than this one, in which you would like to have lived?

WAUGH: The seventeenth century. I think it was the time of the greatest drama and romance. I think I might have been happy in the thirteenth century, too.

INTERVIEWER: Despite the great variety of the characters you have created in your novels, it is very noticeable that you have never given a sympathetic or even a full-scale portrait of a working-class character. Is there any reason for this?

WAUGH: I don't know them, and I'm not interested in them. No writer before the middle of the nineteenth century wrote about the working classes other than as grotesques or as pastoral decorations. Then when they were given the vote certain writers started to suck up to them.

INTERVIEWER: What about Pistol . . . or much later, Moll Flanders and—

WAUGH: Ah, the criminal classes. That's rather different. They have always had a certain fascination.

INTERVIEWER: May I ask you what you are writing at the moment?

WAUGH: An autobiography.

INTERVIEWER: Will it be conventional in form?

WAUGH: Extremely.

INTERVIEWER: Are there any books which you would like to have written and have found impossible?

WAUGH: I have done all I could. I have done my best. (pp. 113-14)

> *Julian Jebb, in an interview with Evelyn Waugh in April, 1962 (originally published in* Paris Review, *Vol. 8, No. 30, Summer-Fall, 1963), in* Writers at Work: The "Paris Review" Interviews, third series, *edited by George Plimpton (copyright © 1967 by The Paris Review, Inc.; reprinted by permission of Viking Penguin Inc.), The Viking Press, 1967, pp. 103-14.*

JAMES F. CARENS

Brideshead Revisited, less a satire than a romance, marks the first accomplishment of the second stage of Evelyn Waugh's career. Though something of the old, hard brilliance remains, there is a new tone of lush nostalgia in this work, the first of Waugh's novels in which his Roman Catholicism is pervasive. Indeed, excepting **Helena,** it is Waugh's only novel to date in which a religious theme has been dominant; although Guy Crouchback is a Catholic and Roman Catholicism figures constantly in **Men at Arms, Officers and Gentlemen,** and **Unconditional Surrender,** the essential theme of these three volumes is the total collapse of civilized values which is the concomitant of war. In effect, in **Brideshead Revisited** Evelyn Waugh turned from the nihilistic rejection of his early satires to an affirmative commitment; to satisfy the other impulse of the artist-rebel, as Albert Camus has described him, Waugh affirmed a vision which he believed gave unity to life. **Brideshead Revisited** was his "attempt to trace the divine purpose in a pagan world."

Reviewing *Brideshead,* Edmund Wilson [see excerpt above], who had most highly praised the earlier satires, concluded that in this more normal world the novelist "no longer knows his way"; he found the novel to be "disastrous." By contrast, a reviewer for the *Catholic World* judged *Brideshead* "a work of art." (p. 98)

A novel which has provoked such diverse views deserves consideration. It may be an imperfect work; it can scarcely be a vapid one. Since the apologetic nature of the work is an issue, we should, before analyzing the effects of the subordination of satire to romance, determine whether Evelyn Waugh's vision has given life a form it does not have.

In honesty to the novel, we must note at once that if by "apology" we mean a systematic and reasoned defense of a theological system, then *Brideshead* is not an apology for anything. It is not a preachy book. To be sure, the Catholicism of the Flytes is sometimes discussed. But, if we turn to the longest discussion of a theological nature in the novel, one provoked by Bridey's insistence that his dying father must receive Extreme Unction, we find not didacticism but, instead, satire. The course of the conversation proves that most of the family are confused about the issue. (pp. 99-100)

Over this entire scene Waugh has cast his satirical irony; the scene exists for novelistic rather than dogmatic reasons, since it prepares for an important event in the action (Lord Marchmain's conversion), satirizes the varied and confused nature of religious faith among these people, and indicates a significant stage in the development of Ryder's character. Waugh must surely be absolved of apologetic didacticism.

Similarly, if by "apologetic novel" we mean one that crudely or even subtly simplifies experience and glosses over certain of life's complexities so as to flatter a fixed system of belief, then again *Brideshead* cannot be classified as such a work. . . . Indeed, the author gives us no reason to believe that he is making a case for his Catholics qua Catholics, for the lives of the Marchmains and of Charles Ryder are not pretty ones, and their Catholicism is no easy consolation. Only Cordelia, the younger daughter, finds an honest contentment in faith. Her elder brother's religion is narrow adherence to system (which Waugh ridicules); and her mother's is resignation to suffering. The others—Lord Marchmain, Sebastian, Julia, and Ryder—know no rest.

Only if we choose to equate apologetics with the presentation of Catholics and Catholicism, through a "Catholic" vision of life, may we argue that the novel is an apology. (pp. 100-01)

If we grant that *Brideshead* is no mere work of apology, if we grant that its purpose is pre-eminently aesthetic rather than didactic, and if, as surely we must, we grant a writer the choice of a Catholic view of life, how do we account for the fact that *Brideshead* does not fulfill the promise of its brilliant satirical opening? I believe that Sean O'Faolain is illuminating on this point when he suggests that "the theme . . . is universally valid; the treatment is not." Perhaps an exploration of Waugh's "treatment," which depends upon the relation between his satire and his values, will pinpoint the reason for the failure.

Brideshead Revisited is elaborately architectonic, as are other later Waugh novels. Subtitled *The Sacred and Profane Memories of Captain Charles Ryder,* the novel begins in the profane modern world and ends in the sacristy of the chapel at Brideshead. In the prologue and the epilogue, which represent the present, we find the novel's most sustained satire. As the bitterly ironic prologue opens, Charles Ryder, a captain in the British Army during World War II, is shifted from one army camp to a second locale. Arriving at night, he does not discover until morning that his new headquarters are the baroque country seat of the Flytes. This discovery moves Charles in Book I to memories of his undergraduate days and of his warm friendship with Sebastian; and in Book II, wherein Sebastian, Lord Marchmain, and Julia are all drawn back to their faith by the urgency of God's will, to memories of his love affair with Lady Julia. Book I takes place in the middle twenties and Book II in the late thirties; the intervening years are sketched in so that continuity, in the chronological sense at least, is not impaired. In the epilogue, surrounded by the "sudden frost" of the modern age, Ryder enters the chapel at Brideshead, where he is revivified by the sight of a "small red light," the sacristy lamp, signifying to him the redemptive survival of faith in a pagan world. The prologue and the epilogue are something more than a mechanical use of the frame technique; they are not merely a device for setting off the memories, but a means of expressing Waugh's emotional attitude toward the past and his satirical view of the present.

Waugh's satirical-ironic projection of a sordid present against the rich traditions of the past is strikingly effective. The landscape of the prologue, bringing into relief the traditional values which Waugh associates with Brideshead, has symbolic force. (pp. 102-03)

For all these depressing satirical contrasts of the prologue and epilogue, however, and for all the pleasing parallels of several returns to faith, which we find in the body of the novel, the structure of *Brideshead* is not a success. A brief examination of the organization of the two major divisions may provide an explanation of this failure. Book I, composed of eight chapters, contains 201 pages; Book II, having five chapters, occupies 116 pages. So the first book of *Brideshead* is well over half again as long as the second book, . . . Is it possible that *Brideshead* has what Henry James called a "misplaced middle," that having extended himself in sentimentally recreating the glories of a vanished past and particularly of youth, Waugh then scanted what ought really to be the center of the novel, the religious conflict engendered by the love of Julia and Ryder? Perhaps Waugh himself answered this question when he revised *Brideshead* (1960), and divided the original two books into three, apparently in an attempt to emphasize Julia's role and to subordinate the Sebastian-Oxford part to the whole.

More disturbing even than the structural flaw of *Brideshead* is the novelist's tendency so to romanticize experience that his tone degenerates into sentimentality. Nowhere is this tendency more pronounced than in the Julia-Ryder love affair, a relationship which provokes one purple passage after another. (pp. 105-06)

The consequences of the subordination of satire to sentiment are particularly evident in the point of view—that of the first-person narrator, Charles Ryder—from which Waugh has chosen to present the novel. This fictional device, whatever its merits, has also its dangers. Not only has the first-person narrator contributed to the structural defect, but his presence has nearly banished from the novel the objective, ironic, satirical detachment which had hitherto distinguished Waugh's art. In *Brideshead,* Waugh is totally committed to his hero's, and his own, strengths—a love of the past, a sense of beauty, a moral awareness of the sterility of much contemporary life. But Waugh is also committed to Ryder's weaknesses—snobbery, smugness, narrowness of sympathy, and superficial idealizations. (pp. 106-07)

The terrible weaknesses of the Marchmain family are fully developed, but so many excuses are made for them (which is not done for the nonupper-class, minor characters, nearly all of whom are satirized), so extravagant are Ryder's claims for them, so romanticized is their class position, so much nostalgia is lavished on the life they were able to lead before the war, so many indications are given of their exclusive right to consideration, so much of Ryder's smugness and self-satisfaction permeates the whole, that the novel seems to accept Brideshead and everything it entails totally and at the expense of all other beings.

But the last words on **Brideshead** really belong to Evelyn Waugh. In the preface to the revised edition—itself a comment on the original—Waugh left no doubt at all as to his dissatisfaction with this work, which had damaged his reputation at the same time that it brought fame. He frankly admitted that its "rhetorical and ornamental language" had become "distasteful" to him. Indeed, in the very act of offering the revised novel to a new generation of readers, as "a souvenir of the Second War rather than of the twenties or of the thirties with which it ostensibly deals," he seemed to be unconvinced that he had greatly improved it. And, it must be said, the revised novel is not a success. Although Waugh did curb some of the excesses of the original, he did not obliterate its grosser qualities. (pp. 109-10)

> *James F. Carens, in his* The Satiric Art of Evelyn Waugh *(copyright © 1966 by the University of Washington Press), University of Washington Press, 1966, 195 p.*

MICHAEL HOWARD

Evelyn Waugh was forty-one when the war—his war—ended in 1945. It is an age when most successful professional men have achieved their first senior position and look forward to a further twenty five years of increasing power, responsibility, and probably happiness. Many if not most creative artists, having passed through initial stages of imitativeness and experiment, have found their distinctive style and go on productively enriching it until the end of their lives. Not so Evelyn Waugh. "My life ceased with the war", he wrote nine years later. Alas, it did not. He lived on for another twenty years to die at the comparatively early age of sixty-three: twenty years of accidie spent seeking relief from rural loneliness and boredom in drunkenness and worse boredom in London; toppling over occasionally into clinical insanity; dependent for his writing, on introspection and memory; rejecting the world as totally as if he had entered a monastery, but without finding any alternative discipline and peace.

This melancholy picture of Evelyn Waugh is perhaps overdrawn in the collection [*The Letters of Evelyn Waugh*], for out of 600 pages two thirds are taken up by his easily recoverable correspondence of the post-war years. . . . This was the period in his life when Waugh, cut off for long periods from his scattered friends and at his wits' end to know how to pass his time, found most relief in letter-writing. Nor should one set too much store by letters written in hours of loneliness and despair. . . . Uprooted from the metropolitan culture that he despised but on which he remained so dependent, he found no alternative pleasures in the country. . . . He hated what he could see of the world and he hated himself. And though he

was a totally committed Roman Catholic, he found no consolation in his religion. It simply presented him with a set of bleak, incontrovertible facts from which no personal comfort whatever could be drawn.

It is tempting to generalize from Evelyn Waugh about his generation and about the state of England as a whole. Up to a point it is justifiable to do so—so long as we start by recognizing his unique qualities. Of these the most important were ruthlessness and intensity. Both are to be seen in the glaring eyes of the young man drawn and painted by Henry Lamb as well as those of the portly old buffer in loud tweeds photographed in later life. Both are also to been seen in his prose, from which (except in the disastrous first version of **Brideshead Revisited**) every inessential word had been pruned. . . . He did nothing by halves and had no time for those who did. He made no effort to understand politics. . . . The whole teeming energy of the United States he totally rejected; in his eyes Americans were either boors or bores. He appears to have had no interest in music of any kind. In the arts he despised virtually everything which had been produced in his lifetime. As for literature, he prided himself on being out of touch with everything that had happened since the war. . . . But without curiosity there can be no new experience; and without new experience a creative artist, unless he has the genius to create new worlds every day out of familiar experience, rapidly declines into sterility.

All this was something that Evelyn Waugh quite deliberately brought on himself. He created his *persona* with dedicated care, as he admitted in **The Ordeal of Gilbert Pinfold**. "The part for which he cast himself", he wrote there, "was a combination of eccentric don and testy colonel, and he acted it strenuously, before his children at Lychpole and his cronies in London, until it came to dominate his whole personality. . . . He offered the world a front of pomposity mitigated by indiscretion, that was as hard, bright and antiquarian as a cuirass."

These letters, on the whole, show how consistently and effectively he played that part, but there are some that show a deeper humanity. His love letters to his second wife during their courtship are as tender and moving as any in the English language. He wrote to his children with wisdom and affection; and his letters to a few old friends—notably Lady Mary Lygon—sparkled as entertainingly through the 1950s as they had in that infinitely remote decade, the 1930s. But these letters to his close friends are in many respects the saddest of all. He told his son Auberon that he had made all his friends at Oxford or in the Army, but that was not strictly true; many of them came from the Metroland period between the two. Certainly he made no new friends after the war, and his correspondence with his contemporaries chronicles with melancholy but typical ruthlessness the aging and disintegration of the Bright Young People he did so much to make famous, their decline into drunkenness, disease, senility, and all too frequently suicide. . . .

But it was in this cage of parrots that Evelyn Waugh had chosen to pass his life, from Oxford onwards. As with so many of his brilliant and unhappy generation, his time at university was not, as it is with most young people, an adolescent preliminary to a life of ever deepening maturity and enjoyment. Rather it was an experience of total self-fulfilment to be prolonged if possible throughout life. The party had to go on. Nothing must change. Affectations acquired during those years hardened into dogmas. Friends clung together for mutual comfort in a rapidly changing world to which they refused to adjust. Though rejecting the *mores* of their parents, they looked back with nostalgia on an age which had vanished while they were still children, and spent their lives trying to escape from the bleak realities of the new one. They had neither certainties inherited from the past nor hopes for a happier future. They only had one another.

This was the world of Evelyn Waugh, and he had no illusions about it, or about himself. That merciless eye illuminated all it saw with a brilliant and lurid light. Beyond that all was darkness, and soon everything would be darkness. By his own standards he was guilty of two of the deadliest of sins: accidie and despair. .

Even by his own lights Evelyn Waugh was not an attractive figure, but he was an honest and honourable one. The implacable God he worshipped had given him the gift of Faith in abundance, but little Hope, and even less Charity. Rather more of the latter might not have made him a better writer, but it would surely have made him a happier man.

> *Michael Howard, "In the Parrot-Cage," in* The Times Literary Supplement (© *Times Newspapers Ltd. (London) 1980; reproduced from* The Times Literary Supplement *by permission), No. 4046, October 17, 1980, p. 1164.*

PAUL FUSSELL

One of the saddest of recent literary sights has been the stacks of unwanted copies of Evelyn Waugh's **"Diaries"** . . . visible all over town. While the works of, say, Harold Robbins have moved briskly, Waugh's have languished, sad casualties of the apparent American war against wit. It's as if Waugh were too clever, as well as too hard, for us. A pity, because Waugh is much needed as an antidote to the current solemnity, earnestness, literal-mindedness and verbal sloppiness. . . .

Waugh is indispensable today, for one thing, because he is that rarity, a writer who cares about language. He knows that writing is an affair of words rather than soul, impulse, "sincerity" or an instinct for the significant. If the words aren't there, nothing happens. And in our atmosphere where verbal accuracy and elegance and wit seem almost to have disappeared, Waugh is one of the heroes, perhaps one of the saints, of verbal culture. He is extraordinarily sensitive to idiom and its social and ethical implications, and in these letters he reveals himself to be, like Jonathan Swift, a master parodist of styles. He can do the novelist Henry Green by deploying "like" as a conspicuously illiterate conjunction. He can return to the idiom of nursery and schoolroom by using endless repeated "so's" as connectives between narrative moments. He can send up would-be colorful travel writing and would-be portentous military reporting. He is adept at Cockney rhyming-slang and at adolescent-in-group slang (a sinking ship is "sinkers," sleeping-draughts "sleepers," congratulations "gratters"). . . .

[In the correspondence included in **"The Letters of Evelyn Waugh"** he] is pained to have to inform Louis Auchincloss that he misuses "mutual" and to remind Nancy Mitford that "nobody" and "each" are singular. When Graham Greene sends him his novel, "The End of the Affair," in 1951, Waugh writes back that he greatly admired it but that Greene has written "cornice" when he meant "buttress." (Greene kissed the rod and made the change in the next printing.) As a devoted friend he informs Harold Acton that he has committed the vulgar error of mistaking the meaning of "inverse ratio," and he pronounces himself "shocked" to find the gossip columnist and member of Parliament Tom Driberg "falling into the pop-ular misuse of 'expertise.'" . . . Waugh is sensitive to every pert or pretentious or fraudulent or cowardly usage.

All this may sound as if these letters reveal their author as a terrible prig. "I am by nature a bully and a scold," he admits. "I am a bigot and a philistine." Indeed, there are some terribly embarrassing Catholic doctrinal letters to Clarissa Churchill abusing her brutally for her apostasy in marrying a divorced man, Anthony Eden. But there's another side. Waugh is vulnerable and tender. He addresses his wife as "My darling love child," and, laying aside his elaborately constructed role of the outrageous Catholic Tory, says to her again, "Darling Laura, I love you. Thank you for loving me."

His handicap was an excessively developed sense of honor. This provided the dynamics of idealism and disappointment in his trilogy **"Sword of Honor"** and led to some preposterous behavior as an officer during the war, when he stuffily insisted that everyone in the Royal Marines and the Army act in accordance with their professed ideals of heroism and self-abnegation. . . . Waugh cared about these things, and it is the ethical intensity, excessive and rigorous as it sometimes grows, that makes these letters so instructive. He sees everything in moral terms, and his comedy is possible only because of his never-resting moral imagination. (p. 3)

His firm sense of what is morally right supports his conviction of an author's obligation to write meticulously well. Nancy Mitford is the recipient of most of his strong views here. "It is the difference (one of the 1000 differences) between a real writer & a journalist," he tells her, "that she cares to go on improving after the reviews are out & her friends have read it & there is nothing whatever to be gained by the extra work." Thomas Merton also receives some much-needed advice, which he's let himself in for by sending "The Waters of Siloe" to Waugh for praise. "You tend to be diffuse," Waugh tells him, "saying the same thing more than once. I noticed this in 'The Seven Storey Mountain' and the fault persists. It is pattern-bombing instead of precision-bombing. . . . It is not art. . . ." . . . Once writing is understood as an art and a craft rather than a mystery, one's obligation to do it well is clear. (pp. 3, 36)

These letters, running from Waugh's 11th year to the year he died, at 63, bring him entirely alive, even more than the admirable **"Diaries."** . . .

Reviewing this book in England, Reyner Heppenstall has concluded that "Waugh clearly never had anything to teach us, except that a man may act like a fool and yet remain a master of English prose narrative, perhaps the finest in this century." But Waugh actually has a lot to teach us, especially if we aspire to write. In these letters one serious recurring theme is the writer's obligation to write well by revising. . . . In addition to reminding writers of the hell that awaits them if they send out sloppy work, Waugh teaches another valuable lesson, and one we greatly need: namely, the usefulness of the comic vision in transforming anger and violence into verbal art and verbal play. (p. 37)

> *Paul Fussell, "A Hero of Verbal Culture," in* The New York Times Book Review (© *1980 by The New York Times Company; reprinted by permission), November 2, 1980, pp. 3, 36-7.*

V. S. PRITCHETT

About Evelyn Waugh as a novelist: It is certain that he was a master in the hardheaded and militant tradition of English social comedy, of which both wit and the fantasies of malice are the graces, even the cement. He appeared as the immediate successor of the Saki of "The Unbearable Bassington," of Max Beerbohm, of the hilarious fairy tales of Wodehouse and the romantic flightiness of Firbank. Their comfort had been savaged by the 1914 war, and Waugh's line was the comedy of outrage. (Our own sour "black" comedy was yet to come.) But as a man—what was he? Like his father before him, as we can guess from the son's brief autobiography, "A Little Learning," and from a large selection of his . . . [correspondence in **"The Letters of Evelyn Waugh,"**] Waugh was a born actor and impersonator, with a bent for exaggeration and caricature and a delight in the inadmissible. . . .

Waugh's many selves and persistent impersonations are candidly and divertingly projected in his letters. He has the naturalness of the best letter writers. . . . His spell as a letter writer lies in his gift for changing his tone to beguile or tease most of his correspondents. He knows that a good letter must have some of the inconsequence of talk. (p. 109)

In his talking style, he has Bryon's art of slipping into one-line asides. Olivia Plunket-Greene—an early flame of his schoolmastering days—is in 1948 "stark mad. She broke her arm writing a letter." About Heralds: "All Heralds stammer." Randolph Churchill is three times as fat as before. Since the Budget, all the members of White's are yelling that they are ruined, except the really rich, who now sit apart smoking their pipes, because they turned themselves into registered companies in Costa Rica. (p. 110)

The last letter in this volume, written ten days before his death, was to Lady Mosley. . . . As the letter proceeds, he slips in one of those news flashes of gossip which the best letter writers know will make their correspondents laugh: "John Sutro had hallucinations of poverty and was cured by electric shock." . . .

One understands why these letters are so enjoyable: it is because Waugh treats society as a Wonderland in which he plays the part of a rude, libellous, yet domestic Alice. (p. 114)

> *V. S. Pritchett, "A Form of Conversation" (© 1980 by V. S. Pritchett), in* The New Yorker, *Vol. LVI, No. 44, December 22, 1980, pp. 109-10, 112, 114.*

JAMES TRAUB

Evelyn Waugh belongs in the select company of Swift and Twain and a very few others in English literature's Pantheon of Haters. Newspaper editors apparently kept Waugh's corrosive juices flowing by assigning the ever-hard-up author such topics as "Why Glorify Youth?". . . . and, as a dyspeptic young man, he reciprocated by writing, for example, of the English girl, "how one longs to give you a marron glacé, a light kiss and put you under the chair, with the puppies and kittens who are your true associates." But this is mere bull-in-the-china shop iconoclasm. Age and piety only made Waugh more ferocious, as in his jeremiad against Stephen Spender: "to see him fumbling with our rich and delicate language is to experience all the horror of seeing a Sèvres vase in the hands of a chimpanzee."

This is the Waugh most of us know. But this fine selection of his journalism [*A Little Order*], most of it dashed off for a quick buck, shows him, if anything, a finer appreciator than derogator. His paeans to late Victorian furniture, architecture and design show a profound familiarity with the subjects and rap-

turous attachments to the objects. Better still are his brief reviews in praise of neglected authors, including P. G. Wodehouse, Max Beerbohm, Henry Green, Ronald Firbank and Angus Wilson. Here Waugh proves himself too dedicated a craftsman to let prejudice stand in the way of judgment. Though he predictably discards D. H. Lawrence, "who wrote squalidly," he speaks of Hemingway as "a master"—"lucid and individual and euphonious."

Though written over a period of 40 years, these 55 articles show a fixity of taste and outlook almost unheard of in journalism. Waugh ever delighted in extending generally repugnant ideas to their most unpleasant conclusion, and these essays continually find him playing Swiss Guard to a demoralized aristocracy. In an introduction to a suitably reactionary book by one T. A. McInerny, he even advocates a society based on four estates—monarchy, aristocracy, "industry and scholarship," and manual labor. Have any of our contemporary conservatives the courage of such medieval convictions?

> *James Traub, in a review of "A Little Order," in* The New York Times Book Review *(© 1981 by The New York Times Company; reprinted by permission), January 25, 1981, p. 14.*

CHARLES CHAMPLIN

The principal item of interest in this collection of Evelyn Waugh short stories [**"Charles Ryder's Schooldays and Other Stories"**] most of them first published in 1936, is the title piece, a lately discovered prequel—as they do say these days—to **"Brideshead Revisited."**

Written in 1945, it gives us a glimpse of the novel's narrator, the rather recessive Charles Ryder, as a fifth former of 15 or 16 at Spierpoint, his public school (not one of the great public schools, being less than a century old).

Dreadful place, invented, it seems clear, out of Waugh's unpleasant memories of his own school days at Lancing. . . .

Waugh always wielded a stiletto pen, and his account of the school, the mean traditional tyrannies of upperclassmen over lowerclassmen, the pettifogging life, the posturing, and the cliques and the collective loneliness, is of the regimen that was meant to build character. Waugh seems to demonstrate that it achieved the opposite, burring off spontaneity and individuality to achieve a sheen of mannered snobbery.

Ryder is already the incipient artist, an observant loner who has had a schoolboy crush on one of the masters who went off to war (the year is 1919). He is making a stab at passive resistance to the conformities of school life, but looks nothing like a leader who will one day march from the playing fields to triumph at Waterloo. What is clear is that he'll be an instant disciple for Sebastian at Oxford a couple of years hence.

The other item of particular amusement is **"By Special Request,"** an alternate ending to **"A Handful of Dust,"** which for many of us is the best and sharpest of Waugh's early comic novels, a satire on the golden youth and fast times of the post-World War I period.

The novel's ending—protagonist Tony, beyond hope of rescue, condemned to reread Dickens aloud endlessly to a mad jungle chieftain—is horrifying and blackly comical in equal measures.

In the story, which concluded the serialized version, Tony never goes near the Brazilian jungle but takes a long cruise and returns to an ending satiric and sardonic in its own way, nastier because closer to reality and also predicting a long future.

"Incident in Azania" is a Saki-like story of colonials at play, using some of the characters Waugh invented for another of his splendidly malicious early comic novels, **"Black Mischief,"** which foreshadowed the difficulties of African colonies going independent.

The other stories, unavailable as a group for years, are amusing now mostly as period pieces, and as fresh reminders (to readers new or old) that Waugh early found a unique voice, sly, waspish, economical, disdainful both of snobs and common folk but by no means entirely misanthropic, as grew clearer with his own passing years.

Above all, Waugh was a prose stylist for whom a boring sentence was the most mortal of sins. His **"Excursion in Reality"** finds a well-reviewed but broke young novelist (whose morning mail includes several overdue bills and "six pages of closely reasoned abuse from a lunatic asylum in the North of England") hired to do a screenplay that will make a good yarn out of "Hamlet."

Several story conferences later it has become "The White Lady of Dunsinane," to get some kilts into the action. No difficulty discerning here the eye and the intelligence that would later compose **"The Loved One."**

> Charles Champlin, *"A Novel Narrator Years Before 'Brideshead',"* in Los Angeles Times Book Review *(copyright, 1982, Los Angeles Times; reprinted by permission), October 3, 1982, p. 3.*

PAUL FUSSELL

Nobody would argue that vintage Waugh lurks in any of his short stories or that we meet there anything like the magisterial wit of *A Handful of Dust, Ninety-Two Days,* or *The Ordeal of Gilbert Pinfold.* Short forms tempt Waugh toward his melodramatic, schoolboy-rag side—he needs more room to develop nuance and the appearance of sympathy with his characters. Still, [*Charles Ryder's Schooldays and Other Stories*] is a worthwhile collection of short pieces if not a startling one, eleven of the twelve stories having first appeared in book form as far back as 1936. . . .

Twelve stories for $12.95, plus tax. It works out to about $1.13 per story, certainly moderate as reading matter goes today. . . . But even Waugh's most frantic admirers would have to admit that some of these stories are worth less than $1.13. **"Cruise"** (**"Letters from a Young Lady of Leisure"**), with its repeated tag-line "Goodness how sad," I'd rate at about 35 cents. On the other hand, some of these stories are worth more than $1.13. **"Mr. Loveday's Little Outing,** despite the crudity of the irony, is a valuable ($2.75?) enactment of the theme that the violent and irrational are often housed quite comfortably within the benign and the reasonable. **"Excursion in Reality,"** a satire on the philistine stupidities of filmmaking, probably seemed funnier in 1932 than now, but it's still worth about $2.00. **"Bella Fleace Gave a Party"** is right up there too, almost unbearably wrenching with its intermingling of wit and pathos. **"Winner Takes All,"** about a meddling mother's arranging things so that her elder son triumphs in all ways over her

younger, thus paying homage to the sacred tradition of British primogeniture snobbery, is another valuable bit of irony. . . .

Another valuable piece of goods is the Saki-like **"On Guard,"** largely about Millicent Blade's boyish nose, the feature all suitors fall for, but less because it's hers and cute than because it's like the noses of the younger boys they used to love at school. . . . This story is a brilliant and thoroughly honest depiction of an important truth—that when a public-school Englishman loves and marries a woman, he's likely to do so because she reminds him of some kid he used to love at school. It's like Charles Ryder's "thing" about Sebastian Flyte. No wonder so much elegiac nostalgia attaches to the British understanding of "schooldays."

And what about the title story? . . . As comparison with Waugh's autobiography *A Little Learning* suggests, the fiction here is too close to an autobiographical transcript of actuality; it's full of attractive texture but weak in action, plot, and significance. But although not worth $1.13, it has some interest because it's another one of Waugh's stabs at his lifelong theme, in which the worthy junior (younger brother, or junior officer) is shafted by the convention that elders or seniors, no matter how undeserving, get the goodies. (p. 38)

These stories are a handy reminder that Waugh's reputation as a social snob may need reconsidering, no matter how badly such a second look might unsettle uncritical celebrators of *Brideshead Revisited.* If in that overripe fantasy, manufactured in the grim 1940s, he seems at pains to register his worshipful intimacy with the aristocracy, in these stories of the 1930s he exhibits for the unearned-income set an intellectual and moral disdain hard to distinguish from that of a contemporary Marxist-Leninist. If he'd conceived Sebastian Flyte in 1935, he'd have had little trouble discerning from the start the selfishness, cruelty, and fatuity behind those expensive good looks. In **"Mr. Loveday's Little Outing,"** the person who gets the apparently harmless Mr. Loveday released from the lunatic asylum (whereupon he immediately strangles a girl) is Angela, a representative of the upper orders. There's no reason in the logic of the story why she should be an aristocrat. Waugh makes her one solely to suggest the dangerous susceptibility of that class to willful, sentimental, silly impulses, which superior station provides the freedom to gratify. In the alternative ending to *A Handful of Dust*—included in this book as if it were a short story—Tony and Brenda Last, ruined by money, go on as before, she adulterously in the country, he adulterously in a new London flat. In **"Cruise"** the young lady "of leisure" writing home from her costly pleasure trip is characterized not just as a social ninny but as a rich and therefore dangerous illiterate unable to read, spell, or punctuate. No one comes to Bella Fleace's elaborate party because she's forgotten to mail the invitations, and she's forgotten to mail them because she's a scatter-brained aristocrat, yes-womaned on all sides, who doesn't notice that her senility has reduced her now to equality with any other forgetful old lady. Despite their sometimes dubious success as art, these stories do convey the valuable news that if Waugh ended as something like a snob, he didn't at all begin that way. (pp. 38-9)

> Paul Fussell, *"The Genesis of a Snob,"* in The New Republic *(reprinted by permission of* The New Republic; © *1982 The New Republic, Inc.), Vol. 187, No. 3542, December 6, 1982, pp. 38-9.*

Edmund White III

1940-

American novelist, dramatist, and nonfiction writer.

With his first novel, *Forgetting Elena* (1973), White established a reputation as a new novelist of great promise. His elegant, self-conscious prose has been compared with that of Marcel Proust and Oscar Wilde, as have his decidedly homosexual viewpoint and sensibility. Like the work of F. Scott Fitzgerald, White's fiction frequently focuses on what he sees as the sad and shallow lives of the idle rich. *Nocturnes for the King of Naples* (1978), White's second novel, is comprised of a series of brooding monologues by a young man who has lost his lover. Critics point out that in spite of its close focus on homosexuality, this work has a wide appeal. Such critics feel that the novel's stylistic virtues and ambitious intellectual aims make it interesting to a diverse group of readers. *A Boy's Own Story* (1982), White's recent novel, has received generally positive reviews. It is a *bildungsroman* told through the point of view of an alienated and precocious narrator similar to J. D. Salinger's Holden Caulfield.

White's nonfictional work includes *States of Desire* (1980), a sociological study of gay communities and gay lifestyles in the United States. Most critics praise this book as one of the few accurate and intelligent studies on the subject. Some point out, however, that because White focuses, as he does in his fiction, on upper-middle class members of the gay community, his study is not conclusive.

(See also *Contemporary Authors*, Vols. 45-48.)

WILLIAM R. EVANS

Holden Caulfield was right, America is full of phonies. More of them infest the literary jungle than any other part of our society. When a writer wants to tell a trivial story he has to do it in style. Sometimes his style is original. More often it is copied from a fashionable giant, say Joyce or Kafka. Rafts and rafts of phony novels by unknown writers come floating down the literary waters. (p. 96)

Edmund White's **"Forgetting Elena"** is a typical pastiche. Interesting at first, it dawdles off into gibberish and pseudo-sophistication. Before it ends, however, there is a blaze of stylish glory. Undoubtedly the best writing is in the last chapter. Read the beginning and the end of **"Forgetting Elena"** and you will have sampled the best it has to offer. Concerned with pretentious conversation, it tries to make Fire Island seem like a fascinating place. Replete with sex, it pulls out all the in stops of today's writing. Tomorrow it will be forgotten, piled on a heap of discarded novels. . . . This is a simple novel told in a complex way. If you like solving cross word puzzles you might enjoy White's book. If you are looking for something worthwhile to read, skip it. (pp. 96, 99)

> *William R. Evans, in a review of "Forgetting Elena,"* in Best Sellers *(copyright 1973, by the University of Scranton), Vol. 33, No. 4, May 15, 1973, pp. 96, 99.*

SIMON KARLINSKY

[*Forgetting Elena*] utilizes a marvelously fresh and inventive narrative device right from the very beginning: an amnesiac young man gradually realizes that he is caught in a cross fire of several contending coteries who battle for dominance in a closely knit little social group on a summer resort island. The narrator-hero is eager to please his hosts and to do the socially accepted thing, but he has no idea of his own status within the group and he has forgotten the code for distinguishing the desirable from the reprehensible in that particular milieu.

The somewhat fantastic island on which the action is set is easily identifiable as New York's own Fire Island, with its highly stylized rites, charades and inbred snobberies. . . . But what might at first seem to be merely a witty parody of a particular subculture's foibles and vagaries actually turns out to be something far more serious and profound. In a sequence of three stunning chapters (Chapters II-IV) the hero is made to tote loads of pine needles in a wheelbarrow, not knowing whether this is a rare honor or a humiliating punishment; he joins what he thinks are two fellow outcasts for a stroll on the beach, only to realize that this has made him a member of the most fashionable and sought-after ingroup on the island; and a mysterious woman explains to him the mechanisms for achieving social ascendancy. These chapters present us with nothing less than a semiology of snobbery, its complete sign system. White's analysis of the drives and pressures common to *all* groupings, cliques and coteries which are based on the presumption of the members' superiority to the rest of mankind is as revealing and thorough as the one performed by Roland Barthes on the ways in which fashion works in his ground-breaking *Système de la mode*. (pp. 23-4)

As Edmund White gradually unravels for us the emotional disguises his islanders resort to in order to throw a cloak of elegance over the starkness of their basic drives, he is as attentive to significant social minutiae as Jane Austen was in *Emma*, as surrealistically inventive in contrasting his characters' social masks and their true selves as Gogol was in "Madman's Diary" and "The Nose," and as geometrically precise in his disposition of dissimilar characters, landscapes, objects and emotions as Robbe-Grillet was in *Jealousy*. These varied predecessors come to mind while reading this or that portion of *Forgetting Elena,* but actually the novel owes little to any of them. Under its surface guise of a mocking, light-hearted comedy of manners, decked out in a style of almost balletic buoyancy, *Forgetting Elena* is an astounding piece of writing—profound, totally convincing and memorable. (p. 24)

Simon Karlinsky, "America, Texas and Fire Island," in The Nation *(copyright 1974 The Nation magazine, The Nation Associates, Inc.), Vol. 218, No. 1, January 5, 1974, pp. 23-4.**

J. D. McCLATCHY

In [*Nocturnes for the King of Naples*], White resumes his exploration of the textuality of experience, but moves from ritual to romance.

As its pretext, the novel evokes and is addressed to a lost, and therefore ideal, lover—presumably an older man who rescued the narrator, was later betrayed by him and died. In one sense, then, it is the Psyche's reminiscence of Eros, and its chapters are the narrator's meditations on the echoes of an original erotic transcendence in his subsequent affairs and ménages, which comprise the world of experience fallen from a mysterious grace. As a narrative ploy, White's sensuous scholium has the emotional power and melo-dramatic advantages of Proust's brooding over the captive and vanished Albertine. But White's quest is at once as intimate as and more extensive than Proust's, since his conjured and elusive god—the fallible god that love's religion creates—is only invoked as *you*. . . . (p. 97)

"You," the second person, the Other within us and abroad. Episodes of the novel's "amorous history" are purposely juxtaposed with literally homesick, fantastic memories of the narrator's parents, a romantic suicide and a sexual pasha. As the perspective shifts from that of love's victim to that of love's child, one realizes the scope of White's quest and its repertory of images. Insofar as this child is father of the narrator, the novel's eerie nostalgia identifies the lost redemptive *you* not only with versions of the Other but with stages of the self's own past. Or, perhaps it would be more accurate to say, that the interfacing family romance becomes our clue that the novel's indulgent memories are its dialogue of self and soul.

If that suggests that *Nocturnes* can be read as a long, perplexed invocation of the artist's muse, there is a further sense in which it can be devised as a cunning apostrophe to the reader himself, the *you*-as-audience implicit in any fiction's calculation and appeal. And we are meant to be wooed not only by the plot's haunting refrains but by White's baroque style itself. His text has a mind of its own; conceits, introduced to define and or-

nament an immediate detail, generate independent lives of their own and wander on until one senses how cleverly their images are latent or overt readings of the tale itself. White writes a heady, luxuriant prose, which he plies with a poet's prodigal finesse and a moralist's canny precision. Nabokov's example may be held up to this book, even against it, but White is a superior stylist of both erotic theology and plangent contrition. And his special gift is his ability to empty out our stale expectations from genres . . . and types . . . and to reimagine them in a wholly intriguing and convincing manner. The astonishing stylistic virtuosity of *Nocturnes* may distract an absorbed but careless reader from White's power to create compelling contemporary myths. But it is that power that dominates his moving portrait of refracted feeling. This book more than fulfills the terms of "promising novelist" that *Forgetting Elena* prompted. White must now be reckoned an important one, and reckoned with as a crucial figure among those attempting to transform the novel from transcript to text. *Nocturnes* is a brilliant, provocative, and commanding achievement. (p. 98)

J. D. McClatchy, "Baroque Inventions," in Shenandoah *(copyright 1978 by Washington and Lee University; reprinted from* Shenandoah: The Washington and Lee University Review *with the permission of the Editor), Vol. XXX, No. 1, Fall, 1978, pp. 97-8.*

JOHN YOHALEM

The impressionistic novel is getting a new lease on life from Edmund White, whose dreamy **"Forgetting Elena"** had a success of esteem some years back, and who in his second novel has abandoned such concessions to the reader as linear story-telling.

"Nocturnes" is a series of apostrophes to a nameless, evidently famous dead lover, a man who awakened the much younger, also nameless narrator not to sexuality . . . but to the possibilities of sexual friendship. Though he well remembers why he found it stifling and why he fled, it was an experience that the narrator feels he did not justly appreciate and that he has long and passionately—and fruitlessly—sought to replace on his own terms.

The matter is not quite a catalogue . . . but a series of self-consciously artful vignettes from a life passed between Bohemian and cafe societes, in Italy and Spain, on a decaying American estate, on the New York piers. Hapless and abominable Dad and hysterical Mom lurk in the background, but up front and center are rich and amorous young women, poor and callow but beautiful young men, a couple of dogs who get the best press and—in the full splendor of the spotlight—the narrator: a boy and his prose.

It is exquisite prose, gooey and fantastic as Italian pastry, mounds of it, piled on prodigally. Elegant plays on words abound and must be sifted out. Mr. White can't seem to help himself—everything inspires him to metaphor: "Jagged traces of temples emerging out of the ground in the way wisdom teeth erupt through the gums"; "He paces around me with the tact and forbearance of a god who knows that by answering a mortal's prayer and appearing before him, the gift may blind the devotee or strike him dumb and will certainly unsuit him to the rest of his ordinary days"; "My father is one of those gloomy statues who guard the entrances of churches but when he bends down . . . he changes from portal knight to gaudy day, a ring on every finger and his bald dome shiny and veined."

But where Proust, for a possible comparison, piled phrase upon phrase, hoping by the addition of each to hone an interpretation finer, to gather sensations more completely, to delineate more precisely the exact quality of each experience, Mr. White . . . is more in love with the sound of his own verbiage. He devises wordy confections because they may themselves be beautiful, not to add to the perfect accounting of his experience. He seems to be hugging himself through words and his talent; and, to do him justice, his passion often seems to be requited. But this is narcissistic prose, and "Nocturnes" is a narcissistic novel—which is not to deny the rareness of its beauty, only the breadth of its appeal.

External constraint imposed on creativity, in such ways as form or even censorship, can itself be an inspiration. The artist is challenged to surmount restrictions and turn them to his own account—as older composers explored the accepted tonalities and forms, implying new possibilities, straining at but obeying the conventions. . . . In "Forgetting Elena," for whatever reasons of popular taste or censorship in the marketplace, Mr. White disguised his own sexuality, and that incognito seemed to give his art a nervous, mysterious charm, a bewildering but wonderful evasion of certainty—and it was also, perhaps, responsible for the creation of a most appealing heroine.

None of the characters in "Nocturnes"—the garrulous, melancholy erotic faun who tells it, the aristocratic ghost to whom it is recounted, or the endless procession of cunningly realized but unsympathetic eccentrics who people the recollections—is as attractive as either Elena or the hypersensitive amnesiac who tells her story. Thus, Mr. White's layered, plateresque prose, appropriate to the predicament and the creature of "Elena," seems more self-indulgent and excessive here.

This is not to condemn Mr. White for a step that must have seemed, in the present climate, admirable and, indeed, necessary. . . . "Nocturnes" is a set of delicious, affected prose poems by a writer of great talent and high art. If he has not been so successful a novelist the second time out as the first, he has all the materials of success and may soon order them more perfectly.

John Yohalem, "Apostrophes to a Dead Lover," in The New York Times Book Review *(© 1978 by The New York Times Company; reprinted by permission), December 10, 1978, p. 12.*

RICHARD GOLDSTEIN

White is the co-author of **The Joy of Gay Sex,** perhaps the drolest example of that most persistent genre, the how-to-feel-good-about-being-dirty Baedeker, and **States of Desire** is a kind of **Joy of Gay Society**—middle-class society, to be precise. In its demure way, this is as didactic a treatise on homosexual experience as has ever been written. You will not read about rejection in this book—certainly not rejection by the author, who reserves contempt . . . for those souls who have allowed religion or personal trauma to interfere with sexual expressiveness.

There is only one state of desire in this book: hospitality. Everyone gets laid and the worst disaster is shallowness; no one ends up in the colostomy ward. Everyone is as "out" as anyone could hope to be, and the direction of oppression is always from the outside in. No one questions the potential for gratification in gay society, and the author offers an anthropologist's tacit consent to all its institutions, except perhaps bitchiness. There are demurrers in this book, a reluctance to

endorse certain practices the author suspects are unhealthy per se—pederasty, s&m, the elevation of impulse into dogma. But the nature of his uncertainty may be social rather than essential. The desire to be omnisentient is a form of decorum Edmund White cannot quite forgo.

Nowhere in **States of Desire** is there any sense of how different gay life is for a working-class homosexual, for a lesbian, or for a black. Some attempt is made to represent minority experience within the gay community—some acknowledgement of racism is offered, and *faute de mieux,* an intriguing account of Amerindian attitudes in the Southwest. There is a brief tap on the knuckles somewhere between Cincinnati and Washington, D.C., for the role gay people play in gentrification, and the author offers the tried-and-true apology for inattentiveness to women's issues. . . .

White's first novel, **Forgetting Elena,** comes much closer to an amused critique of gay culture than anything in this book. It is tautly executed sci-fi, set in a kingdom that could only be Fire Island, and radiant with the enigma of sexual discovery. But **States of Desire** is journalism, a form of public discourse, and therefore obligated to the ego, as a humanist like White must think fiction is obligated to the id. Could an overactive sense of social responsiblity have hampered his art, much as (we are told by some) an undue sensitivity produces the desire to experience pain as arousal?

One may argue with White's observations, but one must welcome them, so deftly do they slide past the sphincter of skepticism. This lubricated prose, tasteless, odorless, capable of heating up with friction, and easily soluble in the shower or douche, is the nicest thing about **States of Desire.** The author's persona, as open and appreciative as the ever-young men of San Francisco he describes, is a particularly attractive bonus to his intelligence. If the bookstore is the ultimate gay bar, **States of Desire** is a hot number for all it connotes without egregiousness. No screaming here, no leather, no luxe; just the serviceable allure of a man who knows how to make the object of his desire relax.

States of Desire is acute, if not conclusive, writing from the finest stylist working in candidly gay prose. The "ethnic" sensibility, as formative for White as Jewish values are for Philip Roth, distills but does not devour his individuality. The book can be read, much as Christopher Isherwood's *Berlin Stories,* for its fidelity to history, to experience, to craft. (p. 41)

Richard Goldstein, "Modus Eroticus" (reprinted by permission of The Village Voice *and the author; copyright © News Group Publications, Inc., 1980), in* The Village Voice, *Vol. XXV, No. 4, January 28, 1980, pp. 41-2.*

PAUL COWAN

If there were a truth-in-packaging law for books, Edmund White's "States of Desire" would violate it. For he subtitles his book "Travels in Gay America" but rarely mentions lesbians, or settled homosexual couples, or homosexuals who are as interested in their work as in sex, or those who help one another kick drugs and booze rather than abuse them. Instead, he devotes most of his 336 pages to a journey through promiscuous, all-male America—a desolate place to live.

Using a conventional picaresque structure, Mr. White wanders from city to city, but he does not display the kind of literary gifts that would allow him to create a memorable account of the voyage. Travel writers have a special job: to escort their less venturesome readers through unfamiliar physical or psychological terrain. (p. 12)

However, Mr. White . . . is an inadequate guide. Though his book is partly autobiographical, he never tries to help readers who don't share his sexual preference to understand his assumptions or the assumptions of the people he describes. Indeed, the men he meets rarely seem to interest him, except as potential sexual conquests.

He does nonetheless talk to homosexuals who want to discuss serious problems: he encounters homosexual Mormons in Utah who long to return to their strict, puritanical faith; homosexual Cubans in Miami who are outcasts from their own community and from the Anglo-dominated gay-rights movement; a black man in Atlanta who loves being a parent; a businessman in Portland who is trying to force himself to become heterosexual. But Mr. White never explores their feelings to the point where his characters become real or his own half-hidden commitments and doubts begin to surface. That's probably one reason why his journey doesn't seem to furnish him with any lasting personal discoveries. Ironically, he is self-revealing throughout much of the book without displaying much self-knowledge.

Though he seems to like the promiscuous America he portrays, he never makes it seem even remotely attractive to an outsider. He does, however, make it seem a singularly unhealthy place. At a Fire Island party, for example, men mix Tuinals and Scotch, or Quaaludes and vodka, then use angel dust, cocaine and a drug called MDA to subdue their anxieties and intensify their desire. From Boston to Portland, Mr. White describes night lives filled with similar concoctions. (pp. 12-13)

His America is an atomized country, with few children or parents, with little sense of the past or future. Transient places—bars and baths—are the most important locales. Random sex is an exalted activity. . . .

In that environment, a man must be forever young and attractive. . . . Most people in **"States of Desire"** share a dread of getting old. . . .

In this journey through the baths, the bars, the streets full of preening young men, the narcotized one-night stands that are the signposts of nearly every city he visits, Mr. White shares what seems to me his characters' tragic self-delusion. According to Mr. White's description—though not in his rather muddled, complacent assertions—they seem to live in a modern-day inferno, where they despise their own aging flesh, where they inflict ceaseless physical and psychological harm on themselves and one another, all in the name of human happiness. That, to me, is a region close to emotional darkness. . . .

[Mr. White] might have prompted me to see the world he portrays in a somewhat more sympathetic light, and, not incidentally, he might have written a fine, revealing book instead of an aimless, shapeless narrative that sometimes borders on pornography—if only he had enough simple human curiosity, enough skill as an interviewer, enough command of structure and language to show us how he and the people he encountered arrived at the psychological land they occupy now. (p. 13)

> *Paul Cowan, "The Pursuit of Happiness," in The New York Times Book Review (© 1980 by The New York Times Company; reprinted by permission), February 3, 1980, pp. 12-13.*

PUBLISHERS WEEKLY

White's shimmering style in this memoir of a homosexual childhood makes every sentence a pleasure to read, and then once that initial savoring is past, we can linger with his on-target observations and candid retrospection. **"A Boy's Own Story"** is by no means limited to a homosexual audience—it touches universal bases with smashing success. The narrator recalls his days as a precocious, intellectual boy, the only son in a broken home. . . . Enchanted by books, dreaming of entering elegant worlds where he'll be appreciated, the boy is drawn to exotic characters . . . while dying to be accepted by his own peer group. White's revelation of the boy's self-conscious, devious efforts at being liked is wonderfully etched with a fine point—and the humor of terror recollected in tranquility.

> *A review of "A Boy's Own Story," in* Publishers Weekly *(reprinted from the August 6, 1982 issue of* Publishers Weekly, *published by R. R. Bowker Company, a Xerox company; copyright © 1982 by Xerox Corporation), Vol. 222, No. 6, August 6, 1982, p. 57.*

J[AMIE] B[AYLIS]

Edmund White's four previous books split neatly into two general categories—novels highly acclaimed for their polished prose . . . and nonfiction books on gay society. . . . *A Boy's Own Story* is a poignant combination of the two genres, a first-person novel . . . about a boy growing up homosexual in the 1950s, and written with the flourish of a master stylist. (pp. 75-6)

The story winds fluently through events of the narrator's youth. The boy is cursed with a maddening family. . . . The boy contends with a succession of friends, fantasies, bohemians, camp counselors, and schoolmasters, and a self-absorbed psychoanalyst.

This is a sympathetic evocation of a youth's faltering realization but ultimate acceptance of his homosexuality. . . . While the boy's emerging sexuality dominates the story, White has succeeded in demonstrating that this, however disquieting, is only one of the throes of his coming of age. It is an endearing portrait of a child's longing to be charming, popular, powerful, and loved, and of his struggles with adults, whom he discovers to be frequently inept and hypocritical—all the more engaging because it is told with such sensitivity and elegance. (p. 76)

> *J[amie] B[aylis], in a review of "A Boy's Own Story," in* Harper's *(copyright © 1982 by* Harper's Magazine; *all rights reserved; reprinted from the October, 1982 issue by special permission), Vol. 265, No. 1589, October, 1982, pp. 75-6.*

CATHERINE R. STIMPSON

Edmund White has crossed "The Catcher in the Rye" with "De Profundis," J. D. Salinger with Oscar Wilde, to create an extraordinary novel. It is a clear and sinister pool in which goldfish and piranhas both swim.

In **"A Boy's Own Story,"** a nameless narrator looks back at his youth with irony, affection and sorrow. What he sees is a child as alienated, self-conscious and perceptive as any protagonist in the whole catalogue of 20th-century *Bildungsromane*. His parents are divorced. His older sister torments him. Because his eccentric father is rich, the boy has material comforts. Because his mother is flighty, his access to both parents is erratic. . . .

This partially deprived child of privilege flees into books and fantasy, which, because they have the order and logic of art, can console him for disorder of life. In them he is majestic, powerful and saved.

A romantic, the boy loves and desires men. . . . His dreams have elements of eros, elegance and power. In them a glamorous older man may sweep him away; or he, a harsh and desirable young aristocrat, will spurn such a figure.

Indeed, the subject of "A Boy's Own Story" is less a particular boy than the bodies and souls of American men: the teachers and masters; the lovers, brothers, hustlers and friends; the flawed fathers who would be kings to sons who should be princes. Mr. White writes, with shimmering sensuousness, of the male body—of the play of muscle, of light on skin, of the curl of hair.

In this novel, the boy is growing up in the 1950's. He loathes homosexuality. It taints touch, turns scent to stench. At best it is a stage that young girls of perfect femininity will help him through. The boy wants to be popular, not a sissy. The narrator says, "I see now that what I wanted was to be loved by men and to love them back but not to be a homosexual." . . .

Like so many American novels about coming to maturity, "A Boy's Own Story" asserts that growing up is a descent into painful knowledge, indecency and repression.

Shadowing "A Boy's Own Story" are ghosts of legendary figures other than Holden Caulfield or Oscar Wilde: Orpheus, Adonis, Don Juan, Rimbaud, Verlaine, Hemingway, the Beats. The boy rummages through myth and art for models of manhood, love and sex. . . . Tradition, incapable of giving the boy real support, is merely titillating. Revising tradition, Mr. White honors the beauty and warns us against the guilt, against the mutilation of male love and homosexual desire.

In "Forgetting Elena" Mr. White mourned the loss of a figure who was at once muse, sister and female lover, in "Nocturnes for the King of Naples" a father and a male lover. In "A Boy's Own Story" he laments the loss of innocence and boyhood. This book is as artful as his two earlier novels but more explicit and grounded in detail, far less fanciful and elusive. . . .

"A Boy's Own Story" has a compelling exactitude. Balancing the banal and the savage, the funny and the lovely, [White] achieves a wonderfully poised fiction.

> *Catherine R. Stimpson, "The Bodies and Souls of American Men," in* The New York Times Book Review *(© 1982 by The New York Times Company; reprinted by permission), October 10, 1982, p. 15.*

ALAN HOLLINGHURST

A Boy's Own Story is on the face of it a book about growing up; behind its title lies the salubrious little-manly world of the *Boy's Own Paper,* with its emphasis on adventure, instruction and initiative; further off stand Mark Twain, Richard Jefferies, H. O. Sturgis, even Forrest Reid. Edmund White's primary irony is to make his the story of a homosexual boy; the time-scheme is jigged around so that there is some brisk buggery in the first chapter, and the sexual latencies of the Edwardian literature of boyhood are rendered emphatically overt. This is,

in fact, a mere showing of the hand: there is next to no sexual description in the rest of the book, for its real subject is not sex but sensibility. The preliminary cornholing with Kevin in *A Boy's Own Story* is an exception in an early life which is all unfocused longing, reiterative fantasy . . . and vain speculation.

Many of White's observations are piercingly acute, his ruminations subtle and irresistible. His settings—schools, summerhouses, medium-sized towns—are poignantly caught. He evokes the extreme singleness and the baroque imaginative convolutions of adolescence with absolute conviction. He describes with precision the years of vacuous joshing, the defensive inarticulacy of boys, and how this particular boy reads into such inarticulacy a belief in passions which are not only unspoken but prove not to exist. He focuses a welcome degree of attention on the significance of art and classical music for youngsters, worlds in which the articulation of fantasy scenarios is miraculously achieved. But this precision and art are often rendered by preciosity and artiness.

From the start we recognize a tendency to elaborate metaphor: "The night, intent seamstress, fed the fabric of water under the needle of our hull"; "the waves dragon scales writhing under a sainted knight's halo"; when he evokes "the *fell* of shame" the intensely self-conscious usage must be an echo of Hopkins. Nineties feyness is one ingredient in a manner that shows a disconcerting instability. Time and again a dense but effective paragraph is whipped up to an ecstasy of metaphorical contrivance. When we read of fish as "dripping, squirming ore being extracted from the lake's mines" we hear the tones of a school prize essay, the metaphor being pursued to the full extent of its failure. But then, "the terrible, decaying Camembert of my heart"; "the torso flowering out of the humble calyx of his jeans"; "the windblown hair intricate as Velázquez's rendering of lace"; "a dog's stale turd leeched of everything except its palest quintessence" are turns of speech which, supposedly drawing us into keener insight, succeed only in distancing us in mirth, embarrassment or incredulity. A recurrent image of the unrecognized latency of the boy is that of princes, or kings, in disguise; but when we read "I was basalt with indignation" we are hearing the forced and yet strangely complacent diction of queens. People whom White evokes "tangled up in the tulle of thought" are indulging in something closely akin to the drag-ball of his language.

As the novel's concern is with sensibility so its success, and its convincingness as invented autobiography, will depend on the sensibility with which it is rendered. This remains critically uncertain. Is White merely writing in as fine a fashion as he can; or is he intentionally challenging some assumed norm of decorous heterosexual writing by creating a style that is overblown, self-advertising, narcissistic, the livery of a specifically homosexual literary position? The caressing artifice with which the boy is treated by the man he has become locks them in a strange bond of vanity, but it is impossible to assess how consciously and how ironically this quality is established and admitted by Edmund White.

> *Alan Hollinghurst, "A Prince of Self-Approval," in* The Times Literary Supplement *(© Times Newspapers Ltd. (London) 1983; reproduced from* The Times Literary Supplement *by permission), No. 4194, August 19, 1983, p. 875.*

Appendix

THE EXCERPTS IN CLC, VOLUME 27, WERE REPRINTED FROM THE FOLLOWING PERIODICALS:

America
The American Book Review
American Film
The American Poetry Review
The American Scholar
Arizona Quarterly
The Atlantic Monthly
Atlas, the Magazine of the World Press
Best Sellers
Book Week—The Sunday Herald Tribune
Book World—Chicago Tribune
Book World—The Washington Post
Booklist
Books Abroad
Books and Bookmen
Books in Canada
Bookworld, *Chicago Tribune*
Boston Review
The Boston University Journal
The Bulletin of the New York C. S. Lewis
  Society
Canadian-American Slavic Studies/Revue
  Canadienne-Americaine D'Etudes Slaves
The Canadian Forum
Canadian Literature
Chicago Tribune
Choice
The Christian Century
The Christian Science Monitor
The Chronicle Review
CLA Journal
Commentary
Commonweal
Comparative Drama
Comparative Literature

Critical Quarterly
Drama
Encounter
English Studies
L'Esprit Créateur
Essays in Criticism
Feminist Studies
fiction international
The Fiddlehead
Foundation
Frontiers: A Journal of Women Studies
The Georgia Review
German Life & Letters
The German Quarterly
The Guardian Weekly
Harper's
The Hudson Review
The Illustrated London News
The Iowa Review
Journal of Black Studies
Journal of Canadian Fiction
Journal of Popular Culture
The Kenyon Review
Kirkus Reviews
Library Journal
The Listener
London Magazine
London Review of Books
The London Times
Los Angeles Times Book Review
Maclean's Magazine
The Magazine of Fantasy and Science
  Fiction
The Malahat Review
The Massachusetts Review

Midstream
The Mississippi Quarterly
MLN
Modern Drama
Modern Languages
Modern Poetry Studies
Ms.
The Nation
The National Observer
National Review
New Boston Review
The New Leader
The New Republic
New Society
New Statesman
The New Statesman & Nation
New York Herald Tribune
New York Herald Tribune Book Review
New York Herald Tribune Books
New York Herald Tribune Weekly Book
  Review
New York *Magazine*
The New York Review of Books
The New York Times
The New York Times Book Review
The New Yorker
Newsweek
Novel: A Forum on Fiction
The Observer
Odyssey Review
Off Our Backs
Parnassus: Poetry in Review
Partisan Review
Philological Quarterly
Plays and Players

Ploughshares
Poetry
Prairie Schooner
Publishers Weekly
Quill and Quire
Saturday Night
Saturday Review
The Saturday Review, *New York*
The Saturday Review of Literature
Scandinavian Studies
School Library Journal
Science Fiction & Fantasy Book Review
Science Fiction Studies
The Sewanee Review
Shenandoah

Sinister Wisdom
The Southern Review
Southwest Review
The Spectator
Stand
Studies in Short Fiction
Theater
Theology Today
Time
The Times Educational Supplement
The Times Literary Supplement
The Times, *London*
Twentieth Century Literature
University of Toronto Quarterly
The Village Voice

The Virginia Quarterly Review
The Wall Street Journal
Wascana Review
West Coast Review of Books
Western American Literature
Western Humanities Review
Wilson Library Bulletin
World Literature Today
Writer's Digest
The Yale Review

THE EXCERPTS IN CLC, VOLUME 27, WERE REPRINTED FROM THE FOLLOWING BOOKS:

Bargen, Doris G. The Fiction of Stanley Elkin. *Lang, 1979.*

Bilik, Dorothy Seidman. Immigrant-Survivors: Post-Holocaust Consciousness in Recent Jewish Fiction. *Wesleyan University Press, 1981.*

Bly, Robert. Introduction to Late Arrival on Earth: Selected Poems of Gunnar Ekelöf, *by Gunnar Ekelöf. Translated by Robert Bly and Christina Paulston. Rapp & Carroll, 1967.*

Brench, A. C. The Novelist's Inheritance in French Africa: Writers from Senegal to Cameroon. *Oxford University Press, 1967.*

Brown, Terence. Northern Voices: Poets from Ulster. *Rowman and Littlefield, 1975.*

Burke, John Gordon, ed. Regional Perspectives: An Examination of America's Literary Heritage. *American Library Association, 1973.*

Burkman, Katherine H. The Dramatic World of Harold Pinter: Its Basis in Ritual. *Ohio University Press, 1971.*

Carens, James F. The Satiric Art of Evelyn Waugh. *University of Washington Press, 1966.*

Clurman, Harold. The Naked Image: Observations on the Modern Theatre. *Macmillan, 1966.*

Conard, Robert C. Heinrich Böll. *Twayne, 1981.*

Daemmrich, Horst S., and Haenicke, Diether H., eds. The Challenge of German Literature. *Wayne State University Press, 1971.*

Dathorne, O. R. Introduction to King Lazarus: A Novel, *by Mongo Beti. Macmillan/Collier, 1971.*

Dukore, Bernard F. Harold Pinter. *Grove Press, 1982.*

Geherin, David. Sons of Sam Spade, The Private-Eye Novel in the 70s: Robert B. Parker, Roger L. Simon, Andrew Bergman. *Ungar, 1980.*

Geherin, David. John D. MacDonald. *Ungar, 1982.*

Gilbert, Sandra M., and Gubar, Susan, eds. Shakespeare's Sisters: Feminist Essays on Women Poets. *Indiana University Press, 1979.*

Greiner, Donald J. Comic Terror: The Novels of John Hawkes. *Memphis State University Press, 1978.*

Hayman, Ronald, ed. The German Theatre: A Symposium. *Wolff, 1975.*

Hershinow, Sheldon J. Bernard Malamud. *Ungar, 1980.*

Innes, C. D. Modern German Drama: A Study in Form. *Cambridge University Press, 1979.*

Jarrell, Randall. Kipling, Auden & Co.: Essays and Reviews, 1935-1964. *Farrar, Straus and Giroux, 1980.*

Kernan, Alvin B. The Imaginary Library: An Essay on Literature and Society. *Princeton University Press, 1982.*

Lieberman, Laurence. Unassigned Frequencies: American Poetry in Review, 1964-77. *University of Illinois Press, 1977.*

Lindblad, Ishrat. Pamela Hansford Johnson. *Twayne, 1982.*

Lindskogg, Kathryn Ann. The Lion of Judah in Never-Never Land: The Theology of C. S. Lewis Expressed in His Fantasies for Children. *Eerdmans, 1974.*

Lippit, Noriko Mizuta. Reality and Fiction in Modern Japanese Literature. *M. E. Sharpe, 1980.*

Marcus, Steven. Representations: Essays on Literature and Society. *Random House, 1975.*

McMurray, George R. Gabriel García Márquez. *Ungar, 1977.*

Mellard, James M. The Exploded Form: The Modernist Novel in America. *University of Illinois Press, 1980.*

Miyoshi, Masao. Accomplices of Silence: The Modern Japanese Novel. *University of California Press, 1974.*

Murdoch, Brian, and Read, Malcolm. Siegfried Lenz. *Wolff, 1978.*

Nadeau, Robert. Readings from the New Book on Nature: Physics and Metaphysics in the Modern Novel. *University of Massachusetts Press, 1961.*

Nathan, Leonard, and Larson, James. Introduction to Songs of Something Else: Selected Poems of Gunnar Ekelöf, *by Gunnar Ekelöf. Translated by Leonard Nathan and James Larson. Princeton University Press, 1982.*

O'Donnell, Patrick. John Hawkes. *Twayne, 1982.*

Palmer, Eustace. The Growth of the African Novel. *Heinemann, 1979.*

Petersen, Gwenn Boardman. The Moon in the Water: Understanding Tanizaki, Kawabata, and Mishima. *University Press of Hawaii, 1979.*

Plimpton, George, ed. Writers at Work: The "Paris Reviews" Interviews, third series. *The Viking Press, 1967.*

Rexroth, Kenneth. Foreword to The Poetic Vision of Muriel Rukeyser, *by Louise Kertesz. Louisiana State University Press, 1980.*

Ross, Joan, and Freed, Donald. The Existentialism of Alberto Moravia. *Southern Illinois University Press, 1972.*

Ross, Nancy Wilson. Introduction to The Temple of the Golden Pavilion, *by Yukio Mishima. Translated by Ivan Morris. Alfred A. Knopf, Inc., 1959.*

Rukeyser, Muriel. Foreword to Selected Poems of Gunnar Ekelöf, *by Gunnar Ekelöf. Translated by Muriel Rukeyser and Leif Sjöberg. Twayne, 1967.*

Santore, Anthony C., and Pocalyko, Michael, eds. A John Hawkes Symposium: Design and Debris. *New Directions, 1977.*

Simon, John. Uneasy Stages, A Chronicle of the New York Theatre, 1963-1973. *Random House, 1975.*

Sjöberg, Leif. A Reader's Guide to Gunnar Ekelöf's "A Mölna Elegy." *Twayne, 1973.*

Smith, Larry. Lawrence Ferlinghetti: Poet-at-Large. *Southern Illinois Press, 1983.*

Soyinka, Wole. Myth, Literature and the African World. *Cambridge University Press, 1976.*

Taylor, John Russell. Anger and After: A Guide to the New British Drama. *Methuen & Co Ltd, 1962.*

Taylor, John Russell. The Second Wave: British Drama for the Seventies. *Hill and Wang, 1971.*

Tolkien, J.R.R. The Letters of J.R.R. Tolkien. *Edited by Humphrey Carpenter and Christopher Tolkien. Allen and Unwin, 1981, Houghton Mifflin, 1981.*

Walsh, Chad. The Literary Legacy of C. S. Lewis. *Harcourt Brace Jovanovich, 1979.*

Welty, Eudora. The Eye of the Story. *Random House, 1978.*

Wilson, Edmund. Classics and Commercials: A Literary Chronicle of the Forties. *Farrar, Straus and Giroux, 1950.*

Yamanouchi, Hisaaki. The Search for Authenticity in Modern Japanese Literature. *Cambridge University Press, 1978.*

Cumulative Index to Authors

This index lists all author entries in the Gale Literary Criticism Series and includes cross-references to other Gale sources. References in the index are identified as follows:

AITN: *Authors in the News*, Volumes 1-2
CA: *Contemporary Authors* (original series), Volumes 1-109
CANR: *Contemporary Authors New Revision Series*, Volumes 1-11
CAP: *Contemporary Authors Permanent Series*, Volumes 1-2
CA-R: *Contemporary Authors* (revised editions), Volumes 1-44
CLC: *Contemporary Literary Criticism*, Volumes 1-27
CLR: *Children's Literature Review*, Volumes 1-6
DLB: *Dictionary of Literary Biography*, Volumes 1-23
DLB-DS: *Dictionary of Literary Biography Documentary Series*, Volumes 1-3
DLB-Y: *Dictionary of Literary Biography Yearbook*, Volumes 1980-1982
NCLC: *Nineteenth-Century Literature Criticism*, Volumes 1-5
SATA: *Something about the Author*, Volumes 1-30
TCLC: *Twentieth-Century Literary Criticism*, Volumes 1-12
YABC: *Yesterday's Authors of Books for Children*, Volumes 1-2

Author Index

Cheever, Susan 1943- ....CLC 18
See also CA 103
See also DLB-Y 82

Chekhov, Anton (Pavlovich)
1860-1904................TCLC 3, 10
See also CA 104

Chernyshevsky, Nikolay Gavrilovich
1828-1889..................NCLC 1

Chesnutt, Charles Waddell
1858-1932..................TCLC 5
See also CA 106
See also DLB 12

Chesterton, G(ilbert) K(eith)
1874-1936................TCLC 1, 6
See also CA 104
See also SATA 27
See also DLB 10, 19

Ch'ien Chung-shu 1910-..........CLC 22

Child, Philip 1898-1978 ....CLC 19
See also CAP 1
See also CA 13-14

Childress, Alice 1920-........ CLC 12, 15
See also CANR 3
See also CA 45-48
See also SATA 7
See also DLB 7

Chitty, (Sir) Thomas Willes 1926-
See Hinde, Thomas
See also CA 5-8R

Chomette, René 1898-1981
See Clair, René
See also obituary CA 103

Chopin, Kate (O'Flaherty)
1851-1904..................TCLC 5
See also CA 104
See also DLB 12

Christie, Agatha (Mary Clarissa)
1890-1976............CLC 1, 6, 8, 12
See also CANR 10
See also CA 17-20R
See also obituary CA 61-64
See also DLB 13
See also AITN 1, 2

Christie, (Ann) Philippa 1920-
See Pearce, (Ann) Philippa
See also CANR 4

Ciardi, John (Anthony) 1916-......CLC 10
See also CANR 5
See also CA 5-8R
See also SATA 1
See also DLB 5

Cimino, Michael 1943?- ....CLC 16
See also CA 105

Clair, René 1898-1981 ....CLC 20
See also Chomette, René

Clark, Eleanor 1913-..........CLC 5, 19
See also CA 9-12R
See also DLB 6

Clark, Mavis Thorpe 1912?-.......CLC 12
See also CANR 8
See also CA 57-60
See also SATA 8

Clarke, Arthur C(harles)
1917-...............CLC 1, 4, 13, 18
See also CANR 2
See also CA 1-4R
See also SATA 13

Clarke, Austin 1896-1974........ CLC 6, 9
See also CAP 2
See also CA 29-32
See also obituary CA 49-52
See also DLB 10, 20

Clarke, Austin C(hesterfield)
1934-......................CLC 8
See also CA 25-28R

Clarke, Shirley 1925- ....CLC 16

Claudel, Paul (Louis Charles Marie)
1868-1955...............TCLC 2, 10
See also CA 104

Clavell, James (duMaresq)
1924-.................. CLC 6, 25
See also CA 25-28R

Cleese, John 1939-
See Monty Python

Clemens, Samuel Langhorne 1835-1910
See Twain, Mark
See also CA 104
See also YABC 2
See also DLB 11, 12, 23

Cliff, Jimmy 1948-................CLC 21

Clifton, Lucille 1936- ....CLC 19
See also CLR 5
See also CANR 2
See also CA 49-52
See also SATA 20
See also DLB 5

Clutha, Janet Paterson Frame 1924-
See Frame (Clutha), Janet (Paterson)
See also CANR 2
See also CA 1-4R

Coburn, D(onald) L(ee) 1938-......CLC 10
See also CA 89-92

Cocteau, Jean (Maurice Eugene Clement)
1889-1963...........CLC 1, 8, 15, 16
See also CAP 2
See also CA 25-28

Coetzee, J(ohn) M. 1940-..........CLC 23
See also CA 77-80

Cohen, Arthur A(llen) 1928- ....CLC 7
See also CANR 1
See also CA 1-4R

Cohen, Leonard (Norman)
1934-........................CLC 3
See also CA 21-24R

Cohen, Matt 1942-................CLC 19
See also CA 61-64

Colette (Sidonie-Gabrielle)
1873-1954.................TCLC 1, 5
See also CA 104

Collins, Hunt 1926-
See Hunter, Evan

Collins, (William) Wilkie
1824-1889..................NCLC 1
See also DLB 18

Colman, George 1909-1981
See Glassco, John

Colvin, James 1939-
See Moorcock, Michael

Colwin, Laurie 1945- .... CLC 5, 13, 23
See also CA 89-92
See also DLB-Y 80

Comfort, Alex(ander) 1920-........CLC 7
See also CANR 1
See also CA 1-4R

Compton-Burnett, Ivy
1892-1969...........CLC 1, 3, 10, 15
See also CANR 4
See also CA 1-4R
See also obituary CA 25-28R

Condon, Richard (Thomas)
1915-.................CLC 4, 6, 8, 10
See also CANR 2
See also CA 1-4R

Connell, Evan S(helby), Jr.
1924-..................... CLC 4, 6
See also CANR 2
See also CA 1-4R
See also DLB 2
See also DLB-Y 81

Connelly, Marc(us Cook)
1890-1980.....................CLC 7
See also CA 85-88
See also obituary CA 103
See also obituary SATA 25
See also DLB 7
See also DLB-Y 80

Conrad, Joseph 1857-1924......TCLC 1, 6
See also CA 104
See also SATA 27
See also DLB 10

Cook, Robin 1940-................CLC 14
See also CA 108

Cooke, John Esten 1830-1886.....NCLC 5
See also DLB 3

Cooper, James Fenimore
1789-1851................. NCLC 1
See also SATA 19
See also DLB 3

Coover, Robert (Lowell)
1932-................... CLC 3, 7, 15
See also CANR 3
See also CA 45-48
See also DLB 2
See also DLB-Y 81

Copeland, Stewart (Armstrong) 1952-
See The Police

Coppard, A(lfred) E(dgar)
1878-1957................. TCLC 5
See also YABC 1

Coppola, Francis Ford 1939-.......CLC 16
See also CA 77-80

Corcoran, Barbara 1911-..........CLC 17
See also CANR 11
See also CA 21-24R
See also SATA 3

Corman, Cid 1924-................CLC 9
See also Corman, Sidney
See also DLB 5

Corman, Sidney 1924-
See Corman, Cid
See also CA 85-88

Cormier, Robert (Edmund)
1925-........................CLC 12
See also CANR 5
See also CA 1-4R
See also SATA 10

Cornwell, David (John Moore) 1931-
See le Carré, John
See also CA 5-8R

Author Index

Author Index

Author Index

Author Index

Author Index

Author Index

Cumulative Index to Critics

Aalfs, Janet
Jane Rule **27**:422

Aaron, Daniel
Thornton Wilder **15**:575

Aaron, Jonathan
Tadeusz Rózewicz **23**:363

Aaron, Jules
Jack Heifner **11**:264

Abbey, Edward
Robert M. Pirsig **6**:421

Abbott, John Lawrence
Isaac Bashevis Singer **9**:487
Sylvia Townsend Warner **7**:512

Abeel, Erica
Pamela Hansford Johnson **7**:185

Abel, Elizabeth
Jean Rhys **14**:448

Abel, Lionel
Samuel Beckett **2**:45
Jack Gelber **6**:196
Jean Genet **2**:157
Yoram Kaniuk **19**:238

Abernethy, Peter L.
Thomas Pynchon **3**:410

Abicht, Ludo
Jan de Hartog **19**:133

Ableman, Paul
Brian Aldiss **14**:14
Beryl Bainbridge **22**:45
Jurek Becker **19**:36
William S. Burroughs **22**:85
J. M. Coetzee **23**:125
Len Deighton **22**:116

William Golding **17**:179
Mary Gordon **13**:250
Mervyn Jones **10**:295
Michael Moorcock **27**:351
Piers Paul Read **25**:377
Mary Renault **17**:402
Anatoli Rybakov **23**:373
Andrew Sinclair **14**:489
Scott Sommer **25**:424
D. M. Thomas **22**:419
Gore Vidal **22**:438

Abley, Mark
Margaret Atwood **25**:65
Harry Crews **23**:136
William Mitchell **25**:327
Agnès Varda **16**:560

Abraham, Willie E.
William Melvin Kelley **22**:249

Abrahams, Cecil A.
Bessie Head **25**:236

Abrahams, William
Elizabeth Bowen **6**:95
Hortense Calisher **2**:97
Herbert Gold **4**:193
Joyce Carol Oates **2**:315
Harold Pinter **9**:418
V. S. Pritchett **5**:352

Abrahamson, Dick
Sue Ellen Bridgers **26**:92
John Knowles **26**:265
Norma Fox Mazer **26**:294

Abrams, M. H.
M. H. Abrams **24**:18
Northrop Frye **24**:209

Abramson, Doris E.
Alice Childress **12**:105

Abramson, Jane
Peter Dickinson **12**:172
Christie Harris **12**:268
Rosemary Wells **12**:638

Acheson, James
William Golding **17**:177

Acken, Edgar L.
Ernest K. Gann **23**:163

Ackerman, Diane
John Berryman **25**:97

Ackroyd, Peter
Brian Aldiss **5**:16
Martin Amis **4**:19
Miguel Ángel Asturias **8**:27
Louis Auchincloss **6**:15
W. H. Auden **9**:56
Beryl Bainbridge **8**:36
James Baldwin **5**:43
John Barth **5**:51
Donald Barthelme **3**:44
Samuel Beckett **4**:52
John Berryman **3**:72
Richard Brautigan **5**:72
Charles Bukowski **5**:80
Anthony Burgess **5**:87
William S. Burroughs **5**:92
Italo Calvino **5**:100; **8**:132
Richard Condon **6**:115
Roald Dahl **6**:122
Ed Dorn **10**:155
Margaret Drabble **8**:183
Douglas Dunn **6**:148
Bruce Jay Friedman **5**:127
John Gardner **7**:116
Günter Grass **4**:207
MacDonald Harris **9**:261
Joseph Heller **5**:179

Mark Helprin **10**:261
Russell C. Hoban **7**:160
Elizabeth Jane Howard **7**:164
B. S. Johnson **6**:264
Pamela Hansford Johnson **7**:184
G. Josipovici **6**:270
Thomas Keneally **10**:298
Jack Kerouac **5**:215
Francis King **8**:321
Jerzy Kosinski **10**:308
Doris Lessing **6**:300
Alison Lurie **4**:305
Thomas McGuane **7**:212
Stanley Middleton **7**:220
Michael Moorcock **5**:294;
  27:350
Penelope Mortimer **5**:298
Iris Murdoch **4**:368
Vladimir Nabokov **6**:358
V. S. Naipaul **7**:252
Joyce Carol Oates **6**:368
Tillie Olsen **13**:432
Grace Paley **6**:393
Frederik Pohl **18**:411
Davi Pownall **10**:418, 419
J. B. Priestley **9**:441
V. S. Pritchett **5**:352
Thomas Pynchon **3**:419
Frederic Raphael **14**:437
Simon Raven **14**:442
Peter Redgrove **6**:446
Keith Roberts **14**:463
Judith Rossner **9**:458
May Sarton **4**:472
David Slavitt **5**:392
Wole Soyinka **5**:398
David Storey **4**:529
Paul Theroux **5**:428
Thomas Tryon **11**:548

Critic Index

Critic Index

Critic Index

Critic Index

Critic Index

Critic Index

Critic Index

Critic Index

Critic Index

Critic Index

Critic Index

Critic Index

Critic Index

Critic Index

Critic Index

Critic Index

Critic Index

CUMULATIVE INDEX TO CRITICS

CONTEMPORARY LITERARY CRITICISM, Vol. 27

Critic Index

Critic Index

Critic Index

Critic Index

Critic Index

Critic Index

Critic Index

Critic Index

Critic Index

Critic Index

Critic Index

Critic Index

Critic Index

Critic Index

Critic Index

Critic Index

Critic Index

Critic Index

Critic Index